PROCEEDINGS

OF THE

1997 INTERNATIONAL CONFERENCE

ON

PARALLEL PROCESSING

PROCEEDINGS

OF THE

1997 INTERNATIONAL CONFERENCE

ON

PARALLEL PROCESSING

August 11–15, 1997

Editor: Hank Dietz, Purdue University

Co-Editor: Rudolf Eigenmann, Purdue University–*Software*

Co-Editor: Jose A.B. Fortes, Purdue University–*Architecture, Networking & Telecommunications*

Co-Editor: Susanne Hambrusch, Purdue University–*Algorithms & Applications*

Sponsored by
International Association for Computers and Communications
The Ohio State University

IEEE
COMPUTER
SOCIETY

Los Alamitos, California

Washington　　•　　Brussels　　•　　Tokyo

IEEE Computer Society Order Number PR08108
ISBN 0-8186-8108-X
ISBN 0-8186-8110-1 (microfiche)
IEEE Catalog Number 97TB100162
ISSN 0190-3918

Additional copies may be ordered from:

IEEE Computer Society	IEEE Service Center	IEEE Computer Society	IEEE Computer Society
Customer Service Center	445 Hoes Lane	13, Avenue de l'Aquilon	Ooshima Building
10662 Los Vaqueros Circle	P.O. Box 1331	B-1200 Brussels	2-19-1 Minami-Aoyama
P.O. Box 3014	Piscataway, NJ 08855-1331	BELGIUM	Minato-ku, Tokyo 107
Los Alamitos, CA 90720-1314	Tel: + 1-908-981-1393	Tel: + 32-2-770-2198	JAPAN
Tel: + 1-714-821-8380	Fax: + 1-908-981-9667	Fax: + 32-2-770-8505	Tel: + 81-3-3408-3118
Fax: + 1-714-821-4641	mis.custserv@computer.org	euro.ofc@computer.org	Fax: + 81-3-3408-3553
E-mail: cs.books@computer.org			tokyo.ofc@computer.org

Editorial production by Penny Storms

Cover art production by Alex Torres

Printed in the United States of America by Technical Communication Services

Table of Contents

Keynote Address
  Speaker: Thomas Sterling, NASA/JPL Cal Tech

Session 1A: Parallel Algorithms

Session 1B: Network Modeling

Session 1C: Compilers I - Data Layout And Access

PREFACE

In its 26th year, the International Conference on Parallel Processing was again fortunate to receive submissions of many excellent research papers, which we were intent on evaluating in the most rigorous way possible. Every paper submitted was fully peer reviewed, with an average of over three reviews collected for each paper. Using a WWW-based server to collect the reviews, we were able to create summary evaluations including quantitative rankings. These served as guides to help the program committee focus its attention, and also were used to ensure consistent and fair handling of papers. Through this careful review process, the efforts of the program committee and referees yielded the following acceptance figures:

	Submitted	Accepted Regular		Accepted Concise		Accepted Regular or Concise	
Algorithms	50	8	(16.0%)	11	(22.0%)	19	(38.0%)
Architecture	87	18	(20.7%)	13	(14.9%)	31	(35.6%)
Software	61	11	(18.0%)	13	(21.3%)	24	(39.3%)
Total	198	37	(18.7%)	37	(18.7%)	74	(37.4%)

We believe that the selected papers truly represent the finest work in this field... a field that is much different from what it was just a few years ago.

This field is simultaneously shriveling and blossoming. Parallel processing has received a lot of "bad press" over the past few years. Many of the companies that we came to know as the leaders in parallel processing have disappeared, been absorbed, or changed direction. Despite this, nearly every modern computer is now a parallel machine! Yes, the parallelism is generally modest, a superscalar unit here and a small shared memory multiprocessor there; however, VLSI technology and market pressures make increasing use of parallelism a requirement.

Consider what happened in the early days of the automobile industry. There were vehicles powered by various types of engines, steering tillers as often as steering wheels, etc. — and then there came a time when most car companies died and simultaneously the notion of a car became somewhat accepted and standardized. It was not the death of the industry, but the start of its full impact on and integration into society. Automotive research had to focus on integrating all aspects of the system to make things work, and work for "real" use, but there was more need for research to guide the field than there ever had been before.

As the International Conference on Parallel Processing begins its second quarter century, I see our field at the edge of a comparable golden era, bringing parallel processing into everyone's life. In this proceedings, in the conference activities, and in the minds and laboratories of the participants, we are drawing the plans for the "Model T" of parallel processing.

The tutorials (chaired by Dhabaleswar Panda), keynote address (by Thomas Sterling), panels (organized by H. J. Siegel, Matt O'Keefe, David Padua, and myself), and workshop (chaired by Matt O'Keefe), all help to bring this new challenge into focus. I thank these people, and also Mike Liu, who, as General Chair, has managed the financial and other arrangements for the conference. Nicky Danaher's help in processing hardcopy submissions and Penny Storms' coordination of the IEEE Computer Society Press publication of the proceedings were also invaluable. Perhaps most of all, however, the entire field owes thanks to Tse-yun Feng. Tse may now be taking a lesser role in running the conference, but his 25+ years of dedicated effort not only built this conference, but effectively defined the field.

— Hank Dietz, Program Chair
Purdue University, School of ECE

Program Committee
Chair: Hank Dietz, Purdue University, School of ECE

Algorithms & Applications
Co-Chair: Susanne Hambrusch, Purdue University, Department of CS

Gianfranco Bilardi	University di Padova, Italy & University of Illinois, Chicago
Janice Cuny	University of Oregon
Sajal Das	University of North Texas
Frank Dehne	Carleton University
Ian Glendinning	VCPC, Austria
Ananth Grama	Purdue University
John Reif	Duke University
Eric Schwabe	Northwestern University
Benjamin Wah	University of Illinois

Architecture, Networking, & Telecommunications
Co-Chair: Jose A. B. Fortes, Purdue University, School of ECE

Jean-Loup Baer	University of Washington
Prith Banerjee	Northwestern University
Laxmi N. Bhuyan	Texas A&M University
Chita R. Das	Penn State University
Jose Duato	U. Politecnica de Valencia, Spain
Jean-Luc Gaudiot	University of S. California
Allan D. Knies	Intel
Rami Melhem	University of Pittsburgh
Lionel M. Ni	Michigan State University
C. Raghavendra	Washington State University
U. Ramachandran	Georgia Tech
Josep Torrellas	University of Illinois
M. Valero	U. Politecnica de Cataluna, Spain

Software
Co-Chair: Rudolf Eigenmann, Purdue University, School of ECE

Helmar Burkhart	University of Basel, Switzerland
Siddharta Chatterjee	University of North Carolina
Michael Gerndt	KFA Juelich, Germany
Mary Hall	Caltech
Hironori Kasahara	Waseda University, Japan
Zhiyuan Li	University of Minnesota
Calvin Lin	University of Texas
Kathryn McKinley	University of Massachusetts
Sam Midkiff	IBM T.J. Watson Research Center
Jagannathan Ramanujam	Louisiana State University
Martin Rinard	University of California, Santa Barbara
P. Sadayappan	Ohio State University
Satoshi Sekiguchi	Electrotechnical Labs, Japan
Henk Sips	University of Delft, The Netherlands
Peyi Tang	University of S. Queensland, Australia
Hans Zima	University of Vienna, Austria

Referees (Peer Reviewers)

Seth Abraham
George Adams
Nidhi Agrawal
Kento Aida
Albert Alexandrov
James Allen
Donald Alpert
Mostafa Ammar
Craig Anderson
James Anderson
Jennifer Anderson
Fred Annexstein
Alfred Arnold
Anish Arora
Andrea C. Arpaci-Dusseau
Eduard Ayguade
Jean-Loup Baer
Nader Bagherzadeh
Prith Banerjee
Mohammad Banikazemi
Sujoy Basu
Kenneth E. Batcher
Ramon Beivide
Stefan G. Berg
Emery Berger
Fausto Bernardini
Rudolf Berrendorf
Sergei Bezrukov
Amiya Bhattacharya
Sourav Bhattacharya
Laxmi Bhuyan
Ricardo Bianchini
Gianfranco Bilardi
Barbara Birchler
Rupak Biswas
Taisuke Boku
Raj Boppana
Rajesh Bordawekar
Bella Bose
Jeffrey Bradford
Thomas Brandes
Peter Brezany
Helmar Burkhart
Wayne Burleson
Stuart Campbell
Calin Cascaval
Luis Diaz de Cerio
Dhruva R. Chakrabarti
Suresh Chalasani
Steve Chapin
Sid Chatterjee
Chung-Ta Cheng
Sung-Eun Choi

Janice Cuny
Donglai Dai
Chita Das
Sajal Das
Frank Dehne
Jason Ding
Max Domeika
Jose Duato
Michel Dubois
S. Dutta
Harald Ehold
Rudolph Eigenmann
Takahashi Eiichi
Nils Ellmenreich
Dick Epema
Rickard Faith
Niandong Fang
Afonso Ferreira
Renato Figueiredo
Eric Fleury
Jose A. B. Fortes
Manoj Franklin
Jean-Luc Gaudiot
Steven Geffner
Ashish Gehani
Arjan J.C. van Gemund
Michael Gerndt
Arif Ghafoor
Milind Girkar
Ian Glendinning
Beverly Gocal
Stephen Goddard
Ken Goldman
Antonio Gonzalez
Eugene Gorbatov
Ananth Grama
Ronald Greenberg
John A. Gunnels
Manish Gupta
Sandeep K. S. Gupta
Mary Hall
Vivek Halwan
Susanne Hambrusch
Per Hammarlund
Ching-Chih Jason Han
Eui-Hong Han
Evan Harris
Luddy Harrison
Gerhard Hejc
Kieran T. Herley
Stephen Alan Herrod
James Hicks
Helmut Hlavacs

C.T. Howard Ho
Raymond Hoare
Mike Hoerhammer
Hiroki Honda
Vincent Hummel
Costin Iancu
Maximilian Ibel
Baback Izadi
Rohit Jain
Stephen Jenks
Hong Jiang
Xiangmin Jiao
Guohua Jin
Chris Joerg
Pramod G. Joisha
Scott Jordan
Boleslaw K.Szymanski
Munenori Kai
Nirav Kapadia
George Karypis
Hironori Kasahara
Stefanos Kaxiras
Wayne Kelly
Ram Kesavan
Christoph W. Kessler
Dongsoo Kim
Geunmo Kim
SunEuy Kim
Sunil Kim
Chung-Ta King
Peter Klausler
Allan D Knies
Pavlos Konas
Leonidas Kontothanassis
David M. Koppelman
Gabriele Kotsis
David Koufaty
Ulrich Kremer
Dilip Krishnaswamy
Vijay Kumar
Ding-Ming Kwai
Winam Kwon
Shahram Latifi
Hyuk-Jae Lee
Jaejin Lee
S-Y Lee
Chien-Wei Li
Keqin Li
Yao Li
Zhiyuan Li
Wei-Kuo Liao
Calvin Lin
H.X. Lin

Wen-Yen Lin
Kevin Liu
Jack Lo
Virginia Lo
Fabrizio Lombardi
Pedro Lopez
Jens Mache
Yoshitaka Maekawa
Syed M. Mahmud
M.P. Malumbres
D. Manivannan
Philippe J. Marchand
Maria-Cristina Marinescu
Jose F. Martinez
Xavier Martorell
Kathryn McKinley
Phil McKinley
Eduard Mehofer
Piyush Mehrotra
Rami Melhem
Sam Midkiff
Jose Miguel
Zina Ben Miled
P. Mohapatra
Ajay Mohindra
Sungdo Moon
Jose E. Moreira
Daniel Mosse
Brian Murphy
Matt W. Mutka
Halima El Naga
Walid Najjar
Hidemoto Nakada
David Nassimi
Robert N. Newshutz
Thu D. Nguyen
Lionel Ni
Rishiyur S. Nikhil
Natawut Nupairoj
Lars Nyland
Wataru Ogata
Sven M. Paas
David Padua
Yunheung Paek
Scott Pakin
Yi Pan
Dhabaleswar K. Panda
Christos Papadopoulos
Behrooz Parhami
Keshab K. Parhi
Fabrizio Petrini
Jim Pierce
Andrea Pietracaprina
Viktor K. Prasanna

Gerald Pretot
Geppino Pucci
Chunming Qiao
Wenjian Qiao
Xiaohan Qin
Donna Quammen
C. S. Raghavendra
Kishore Ramachandran
Srikanth Ramamurthy
J. Ramanujam
N. Ranganathan
Sanjay Ranka
John Reif
Martin Rinard
Ed Rothberg
Kathleen Ruchti-Crowley
Radu Rugina
Shefali Sanghani
Vivek Sarin
Dan Scales
Wolfgang Schreiner
Eric Schwabe
Chandra Sekharan
Satoshi Sekiguchi
Amit Sengupta
Gautam Shah
Hemal Shah
Yi Shang
Weisong Shi
Chulho Shin
Behrooz Shirazi
H. Shrikumar
Ness B. Shroff
Bart Sinclair
Robert Sinclair
Vineet Singh
Mukesh Singhal
Henk Sips
Ramesh Sitaraman
Anand Sivasubramaniam
Stephen Skedzielewski
Jonas Skeppstedt
Arun K. Somani
Hyojeong Song
Pradip Srimani
Cliff Stein
James M. Stichnoth
Jaspal Subhlok
Zheng Sun
Yoshio Tanaka
Peiyi Tang
Kwon Tcheun
Rajeev Thakur
Ioannis G. Tollis

Josep Torrellas
Pedro Trancoso
Gonazlo Travieso
Chau-Wen Tseng
Hung-Yu Tseng
Shambhu Upadhyaya
Aniruddha Vaidya
Nitin H. Vaidya
Mateo Valero
Miguel Valero
A. Venkatachar
Xavier Verians
Benjamin Wah
Lei Wang
Tao Wang
Yi-Min Wang
Jerrell Watts
David Wong
Wayne Wong
Jie Wu
Jingling Xue
Sudhakar Yalamanchili
Liuxi Yang
Mingyao Yang
Tao Yang
Ted C. Yang
Tse-Yu Yeh
Pen-Chung Yew
Byung S. Yoo
Akimasa Yoshida
H. Y. Youn
Xin Yuan
Rumi Zahir
Ellen Zegura
Ye Zhang
Hans Zima
Taieb Znati

Keynote Address

Thomas Sterling
NASA / JPL Cal Tech

Session 1A

Parallel Algorithms

Optimal Sorting Algorithms on Incomplete Meshes
with Arbitrary Fault Patterns

Chi-Hsiang Yeh and Behrooz Parhami
Department of Electrical and Computer Engineering
University of California,   Santa Barbara, CA 93106-9560, USA

Abstract

In this paper, we propose simple and efficient algorithms for sorting on incomplete meshes. No hardware redundancy is required and no assumption is made about the availability of a complete submesh. The proposed robust sorting algorithms are very efficient when only a few processors are faulty and degrade gracefully as the number of faults increases. In particular, we show that 1-1 sorting (1 key per healthy processor) in row-major or snakelike row-major order can be performed in $3n + o(n)$ communication and comparison steps on an $n \times n$ incomplete mesh that has an arbitrary pattern of $o(\sqrt{n})$ faulty processors. This is the fastest algorithm reported thus far for sorting in row-major and snakelike row-major orders on faulty meshes and the time complexity is quite close to its lower bound.

1 Introduction

A *d*-dimensional mesh consists of $n_1 n_2 \cdots n_d$ processors of degree $2d$ arranged in an $n_1 \times n_2 \times n_3 \times \cdots \times n_d$ grid. When wraparound links are used for all dimensions, a *d*-dimensional torus results. Because of their scalability, compact layout, constant node-degree, desirable algorithmic properties, and many other advantages, meshes and tori have become popular topologies for the interconnection of parallel processors.

Sorting is one of the most important and useful building blocks in the development of parallel applications. Various algorithms have been developed for sorting on mesh-connected computers [4, 5, 6, 8, 9]. These algorithms usually assume that a fault-free mesh is available. For computing on incomplete meshes, Cole, Maggs, and Sitaraman [1] have shown that an $n \times n$ mesh can be emulated with constant slowdown on an $n \times n$ mesh that has $n^{1-\varepsilon}$ faulty processors for any fixed $\varepsilon > 0$. In [2], Kaklamanis et. al. showed that almost every $n \times n$ *p*-faulty mesh and any mesh with at most $n/3$ faults can sort n^2 packets in $O(n)$ time.

These results are of great theoretical importance but the algorithms are quite complicated and the leading constants for the running times are large. In [7], an elegant but suboptimal robust sorting algorithm based on shearsort has been proposed. However, the robust shearsort can only be executed on meshes with bypass capacity over faulty processors [7].

In this paper, we propose efficient algorithms for sorting on incomplete meshes. No hardware redundancy or bypass capability is required and no assumption is made about the availability of a complete submesh. The proposed algorithms can be executed at high speed in the presence of a small number of faults and degrade gracefully as the number of faults increases. They may even work on meshes whose rows and columns are all incomplete and meshes without any complete submesh. In particular, we show that sorting in row-major or snakelike row-major order can be performed in $3n + o(n)$ communication and comparison steps (excluding precalculation time) on an $n \times n$ bidirectional mesh that has an arbitrary pattern of $o(\sqrt{n})$ faults, assuming that each healthy processor has one of the keys to be sorted. These are the best results reported thus far for sorting on incomplete meshes under the assumed fault conditions and ranking orders. The techniques and results given in this paper can be easily extended to higher dimensional meshes and tori as well as to a variety of other fault-tolerant algorithms, such as semigroup and prefix computation, selection, permutation, fast Fourier transform, and matrix multiplication.

The remainder of the paper is organized as follows. In Section 2, we introduce the basic scheme and several techniques for efficient sorting on incomplete meshes. We also develop simple and efficient algorithms for sorting on a subset of healthy processors which we call a virtual submesh. In Section 3, we derive efficient subroutines for redistributing data from/to all healthy processors to/from virtual submeshes. We then develop a robust sorting algorithm and analyze its complexity for several fault assumptions. In Section 4 we conclude the paper.

2 Sorting on a subset of healthy processors

In this section, we introduce a simple and efficient scheme based on virtual submeshes for solving various problems on incomplete meshes without hardware redundancy. We then develop several techniques for performing sorting on virtual submeshes with negligible overhead compared with fault-free meshes.

2.1 Virtual submeshes (VSMs)

The basic scheme for the proposed robust sorting algorithms is to redistribute the data on the original mesh to a subset of the healthy processors, which we call a virtual submesh, and then use the virtual submesh to emulate algorithms on the corresponding mesh. In this subsection, we describe the simplest version of virtual submeshes.

We first select a $p_1 \times p_2$ submesh within the original incomplete mesh. The selected submesh is called a *boundary mesh (BM)*. A row (or column) within the boundary mesh that has no faulty processor is called a *complete BM-row* (or a *complete BM-column*, respectively). The $m_1 m_2$ processors at the intersections of the m_1 complete BM-rows and the m_2 complete BM-columns within the boundary mesh form the virtual submesh (VSM). A row (or column) within the boundary mesh with at least one faulty processor is called an *incomplete BM-row* (or an *incomplete BM-column*, respectively). Note that a complete BM-row (or BM-column) may be part of an incomplete row (or column) of the entire mesh. Two examples for simple VSMs are illustrated in Figs. 1 and 2a. Fig. 1 shows a virtual submesh within an $n_1 \times n_2 = 6 \times 7$ incomplete mesh with 6 faulty processors. The shaded circles represent the $m_1 \times m_2 = 3 \times 4$ VSM within the $p_1 \times p_2 = 5 \times 6$ boundary mesh. The numbers in circles represent the logical processor addresses in the VSM. In Fig. 2a, the entire 6×7 mesh is selected as the boundary mesh and the 4×5 VSM is comprised of the 20 shaded nodes.

Let M be the total number of items to be sorted and a be the *load factor*, the maximum number of items per processor, in the VSM. Then we have load factor $a = \left\lceil \frac{M}{m_1 m_2} \right\rceil$ when the data are spread approximately evenly on the VSM. When there is only one item to be sorted per healthy processor and the number of faults is not large, we can have $a = 2$. The load factor for the VSM in Fig. 1 is 3 and the one for the VSM in Fig. 2a is 2, assuming one key per healthy processor.

The proposed basic scheme for performing robust sorting involves 3 stages, as described below. We assume that a preprocessing stage has identified a virtual submesh to be used (perhaps at reconfiguration time).

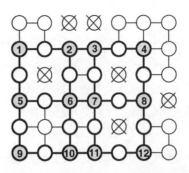

Figure 1. A 3-by-4 VSM represented by shaded circles. The intersections of rows 2–6 and columns 1–6 form the 5-by-6 boundary mesh.

<u>**Virtual-Submesh Emulation:**</u>

- <u>Stage 1</u>: The data items to be sorted are redistributed evenly to the processors on the VSM such that a processor has at most a items. On the VSM, a processor that has fewer than a items pads its list with ∞ as its "dummy element(s)".

- <u>Stage 2</u>: The VSM emulates a-a sorting on an $m_1 \times m_2$ mesh.

- <u>Stage 3</u>: The sorted data items are redistributed back to healthy processors of the original $n_1 \times n_2$ incomplete mesh with proper ordering.

Since processors of the VSM belong to complete BM-rows and complete BM-columns, a naive method to implement Stage 2 is to directly emulate a transmission over the N (or E, W, S) link of a processor by sending the data item over a path consisting of all the N links between the processor and its *virtual N (or E, W, S) neighbor* in the VSM. When the boundary mesh is complete (that is, no faulty processor exists within it), no degradation is caused by Stage 2 using the naive method.

Let f_{BM} be the total number of faulty processors in the boundary mesh. By using the previous naive method, sorting on the $m_1 \times m_2$ VSM requires $O((a + f_{BM})(m_1 + m_2))$ time in the worst case by emulating an optimal sorting algorithm. In the following subsections, we will develop several techniques to significantly reduce the slowdown factor.

2.2 Compaction/expansion (C/E) techniques

In this subsection, we present a useful technique, which we call the *compaction/expansion (C/E) technique*, that can significantly reduce the time required for sorting on a VSM.

5

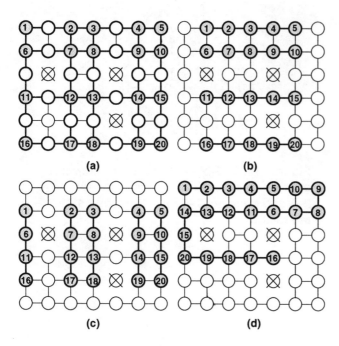

Figure 2. A 4-by-5 VSM (a) and its compacted rows (b), columns (c), and snake (d).

Sorting on each row of the VSM based on the C/E technique involves 4 phases:

C/E-Row Sort (CERS):

- Phase 1 (precalculation): Each complete BM-row performs semigroup and prefix computation to determine the total number t of incomplete BM-columns within the boundary mesh and, for each processor the number l of incomplete BM-columns to its left.

- Phase 2 (compaction): The items in each processor of the VSM are shifted to the left by $l - \lceil t/2 \rceil$ positions if $l - \lceil t/2 \rceil > 0$ and the items are shifted to the right by $\lceil t/2 \rceil - l$ positions if $l - \lceil t/2 \rceil < 0$.

- Phase 3: A row sort is peformed within each of the m_2-node linear arrays (compacted rows).

- Phase 4 (expansion): The sorted items in each of the m_2-node compacted rows are shifted back to processors of the VSM; this is the inverse of Phase 2.

Phase 1 can be done in $O(p_2)$ time using algorithms for semigroup and prefix computation on a fault-free p_2-node linear array. This precalculation phase only needs to be executed once after a new processor or link failure. Phases 2

and 4 can each be done in $a \lceil t/2 \rceil$ time. The integer t is usually small and we have $t < p_2$ and $t \le f_{BM}$, where f_{BM} is the total number of faults within the boundary mesh. Clearly, Phase 3 can be done in $O(am_2)$ time using odd-even transposition sort, neighborhood sort, or their modified versions.

Compared with sorting on an m_2-node linear array, Phases 1,2 and 4 are the overhead for performing row sort on the VSM. Since Phase 1 is a precalculation phase and only needs to be executed once, Phases 2 and 4 constitute the *effective overhead*. Compared with the naive method which in the worst case has $O(f_{BM}p_2)$ effective overhead, that of CERS is significantly reduced to $O(af_{BM})$. As a case in point, the naive method that does not use the C/E technique has overhead $\Theta(m_2)$ even when there is only one faulty processor within the boundary mesh; while algorithm CERS has overhead $2a$ when there are one or two faulty processors within the boundary submesh. Column sort can be executed in a manner similar to the row sort algorithm CERS. Figure 2 provides an example for sorting on a VSM based on the C/E technique. The shaded circles in Fig. 2a represent a 4×5 VSM within a 6×7 mesh with 3 faulty processors. The shaded circles in Fig. 2b represent the positions of data items for performing row sort based on the C/E technique upon completion of Phase 2 of algorithm CERS. The processors that hold the data elements from a row of the VSM are collectively called a *compacted row*. The number i in a circle represents the position for the data item that was initially held by processor i of the VSM. The shaded circles in Fig. 2c represent the positions of data items for performing column sort based on the C/E technique. The processors that hold the data elements from a column of the VSM form a *compacted column*.

Sorting $2m_2$ elements on an m_2-node bidirectional linear array requires m_2 communication steps and $2m_2$ comparison steps by directly emulating odd-even transposition sort on a $2m_2$-node linear array [4, 6]. As a result, algorithm CERS can be performed using $m_2 + o(m_2)$ communication steps and $2m_2$ comparison steps (excluding precalculation time) when $a = 2$ and $f_{BM} = o(m_2)$. Clearly, when $f_{BM} = o(m_2)$, the slowdown factor for row sort on the VSM is $1 + o(1)$ for any fault pattern.

2.3 A simple sorting algorithm on VSMs

By using the C/E technique, sorting on a VSM can be easily done by emulating shearsort on meshes. More precisely, we can sort on the VSM by performing row sort in Phases $1, 3, 5, ..., 2\log_2 m_1 - 1$ and column sort in Phases $2, 4, 6, ..., 2\log_2 m_1$, using algorithm CERS and the column-sort version of algorithm CERS. Since each pair of steps can be done in $O(a(m_1 + m_2 + t))$ time, sorting on an $m_1 \times m_2$ VSM can be done in $O(a(m_1 + m_2 + t)\log m_1)$ time.

Similarly, if we emulate Revsort [9] using the C/E technique, sorting on VSMs can be performed in $O(a(m_1 + m_2 + t) \log \log m_1)$ time. The resultant overhead is negligible when $f_{BM} = o(\min(m_1, m_2))$ (that is, the overhead is only $o(a(m_1 + m_2) \log m_1)$ compared with shearsort and only $o(a(m_1 + m_2) \log \log m_1)$ compared with Revsort on an $m_1 \times m_2$ complete mesh).

2.4 Odd-even transposition on the snakelike path

Although sorting based on emulating shearsort is simple, the required time is suboptimal. To obtain optimal sorting algorithms on VSMs, we have to emulate optimal sorting algorithms on meshes. These algorithms need to perform odd-even transposition sort on the overall snakelike path and may result in significant degradation using the naive method described in Subsection 2.1. In this subsection, we present a more complicated compaction/expansion process for odd-even transposition on the overall snakelike path of a VSM.

Similar to the CERS algorithm, the items to be sorted will be "compacted" onto part of the snakelike path consisting of all the m_1 complete subrows and the processors bridging two complete subrows if they are not physically contiguous. For simplicity, we consider sending the items to the first $m_1 m_2$ processors of the snake. Performing k steps of odd-even transposition along the overall snake of the VSM based on the compaction/expansion process involves 4 phases:

C/E-Snake Odd-Even Transposition (CEST):

- Phase 1: (precalculation) Prefix computation is performed along the snakelike path of the VSM to determine, for each processor, the number u of processors before it that do not have any item to be sorted.

- Phase 2: (compaction) The items in each processor are sent to the processor u positions before it.

- Phase 3: k odd-even transposition steps are performed along the $m_1 m_2$-node subsnake (compacted snake).

- Phase 4: (expansion) The sorted items in the $m_1 m_2$-node compacted snake are sent back to processors belonging to the VSM; this is the inverse of Phase 2.

Figure 2d shows a *compacted snake* of a VSM, which is comprised of the processors that hold the data elements from the entire snake of the VSM. The numbers in circles represent the original positions of the data items in the VSM.

Phase 1 can be performed using a variant of parallel prefix computation on a mesh by ignoring the processors on incomplete BM-rows except for those on the rightmost (or a middle) complete BM-column. Note that the prefix values of processors in a BM-row is computed either from left

to right or from right to left according the direction of the snake. This precalculation phase requires $O(p_1 + p_2)$ time. If we have the results of the precalculation phases for both algorithm CERS and its column-sort version available, the prefix values for Phase 1 can be determined directly by the numbers of incomplete BM-rows and BM-columns and the position of a processor in $O(1)$ time.

If we implement Phase 2 by shifting the items along the snake, the time required can be as large as $\Theta(f_{BM} m_1)$ in the worst case. One way to implement Phase 2 in considerably shorter time is to first send each item to the complete BM-row to which it belongs or the immediately following complete BM-row if the new position of the item is not on a complete BM-row. Then we route data items on each complete BM-row and the vertical segment before it, until the addresses of processors originally holding the items are in ascending order and each processor (except for the last u processors along the snakelike path) has a items. Upon completion, all the items to be sorted along the snake of the VSM are redistributed to a subsnake of length $m_1 m_2$ within the snakelike path of the boundary mesh. Phase 2 can thus be performed in $O(f_{BM})$ (for routing on BM-columns) $+ \max(p_2, ap_2/2) + O(f_{BM})$ (for routing on BM-rows and vertical segments) $= \max(p_2, ap_2/2) + O(f_{BM})$ steps.

Thus, Phase 2 and its inverse phase, Phase 4, can each be done in $p_2 + o(p_2)$ time when $a = 2$ and $f_{BM} = o(p_2)$. Phase 3 clearly requires $O(k)$ time.

Based on these C/E techniques, various optimal algorithms for sorting on VSMs can be obtained by simply emulating optimal sorting algorithms (e.g., several recursive sorting algorithms and the (modified) Schnorr/Schamir sorting algorithm [5, 6, 9]).

2.5 General VSMs

In some cases, VSMs of the type used thus far may become quite small with a relatively small number of faulty processors, leading to a large load factor a, and thus a significant slowdown, in emulating mesh algorithms. In such cases, we can use *pairwise complete rows* and *pairwise complete columns* to simulate complete rows and columns, respectively. We briefly introduce the techniques as follows.

Pairwise complete columns are defined as two adjacent columns that contain at least one path from the top row to the bottom row. Pairwise complete rows are defined analogously. We can then define a more general version of VSMs by selecting a processor from each of the intersections of these (pairwise) complete rows and columns. An example is shown in Fig. 3. Detection of a pairwise complete column can be easily done as follows. By sending two signals originating from the left and right columns in the column pair, up to two paths are obtained if the signals do not switch column

7

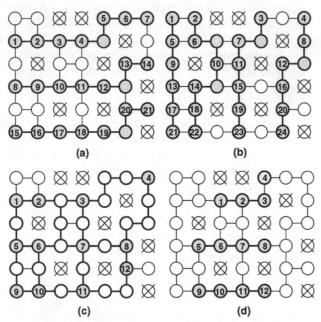

Figure 3. Pairwise complete rows/columns. (a) Pairwise complete rows. (b) Pairwise complete columns. (c) A resultant 3-by-4 VSM. (d) Compacted rows of the VSM.

unless a faulty processor or link is encountered. At least one of the two constructed paths is guaranteed to have the shortest length among all possible paths within the two columns. To emulate a complete column on a pairwise complete column, we can use the C/E technique on the constructed path in a manner similar to algorithm CERS. Figure 3d provides an example where each row of a VSM is compacted to speed up row sort.

This technique can be easily generalized to utilize all (reasonably short) nonoverlapping paths from the top BM-row to the bottom BM-row and nonoverlapping paths from the leftmost BM-column to the rightmost BM-column to obtain a larger VSM at the intersection of these paths. The top/bottom row and the leftmost/rightmost column of a boundary mesh can also be paths that are not straight. The analysis for algorithms on the simplest version of VSMs can be extended to the general version of VSMs by substituting p_1, p_2, and t with $p_{1,max}$, $p_{2,max}$, and t_G, respectively, where $p_{1,max}$ and $p_{2,max}$ are the maximum lengths of column paths and row paths, respectively, within the generalized boundary mesh, and $t_G = \max(p_{1,max} - m_1, p_{2,max} - m_2)$. When $p_{1,max} = \Theta(m_1)$ and $p_{2,max} = \Theta(m_2)$, optimal sorting algorithms for the VSM can be obtained by simply emulating optimal sorting algorithms on meshes using C/E techniques.

3 Robust sorting on incomplete meshes

In this section, we derive fast algorithms to perform 1-1 sorting on an $n \times n$ incomplete mesh that has $f = o(\sqrt{n})$ faulty processors, where each healthy and connected processor holds one of the keys to be sorted.

3.1 Mapping an incomplete mesh onto a VSM

In this subsection, we describe how to select a proper VSM and map the incomplete mesh onto it.

We use the entire incomplete mesh as the boundary mesh. We select $m_1 = n - o(n)$ complete rows and the middle $m_2 = n/2 + o(n)$ complete columns, such that $m_1 \times m_2 \geq (n^2 - f)/2$. We also require that the selected complete rows be separated by no more than $f + 1$ hops if some complete rows are not selected. Then the intersections of the selected m_1 rows and m_2 columns form a desired VSM. Since there are no more than $o(\sqrt{n})$ faulty processors, the existence of such VSMs is guaranteed. Obviously, the number of items per processor is $a = 2$ for 1-1 sorting on such incomplete meshes. For simplicity of algorithm description, we assume that $\sqrt{n}$ is an integer. We call each of the n $\sqrt{n}$-by-$\sqrt{n}$ submeshes of the incomplete mesh a *block*, and a $\sqrt{n}$-node complete row (or column) within a block a *complete block-row* (or *complete block-column*). A block is crossed by at least $\sqrt{n} - f$ complete block-columns and complete block-rows.

To sort the items in row-major order, we first perform a prefix computation in row-major order to determine the number of healthy processors that precede each of the healthy processors. Then the ith healthy processor is mapped onto the $\lceil i/2 \rceil^{th}$ processor in the VSM in snakelike row-major order. Figure 4 illustrates such a mapping for a 6×7 mesh with 3 faulty processors (as shown in Fig. 4a) onto a 4×5 VSM (Fig. 4d). To sort the items in snakelike row-major order, blockwise order, or other orderings, we perform a prefix computation in the respective order, and map each healthy processor onto the VSM in snakelike row-major order.

3.2 Data redistribution

In this subsection, we introduce an efficient algorithm for performing *data redistribution*, which moves data from healthy processors, each having one data item, to the corresponding processors in the VSM. We then analyze its performance and show that it is optimal for row-major and snakelike row-major mapping orders.

The algorithm DR for data redistribution is comprised of 4 phases:

Data Redistribution (DR):

- Phase 1: In each block, all data items are routed to a nearby complete block-row.

- Phase 2: In each block, all data items are spread approximately evenly along the block-row onto processors at the intersections of complete columns and complete block-rows.

- Phase 3: Each data item is sent along the complete column to which it currently belongs to the complete row to which the data item will belong in the VSM.

- Phase 4: Each data item is sent along the complete row to which it currently belongs to the desired position in the VSM.

Phase 1 can be done by first routing any data item to one of the complete block columns/rows that surround the item, and then routing it along the complete block-columns to a nearby complete block-row within its block. The desired location for each data item at the end of Phase 2 can be determined by performing prefix computation in each complete block-row, which is a precalculation step and requires only $O(\sqrt{n})$ time. If a processor in a complete column has a constant number of data items at the end of the initial step for Phase 1, it can skip the latter step and Phase 2 without increasing the leading constant of the running time. Figure 4 provides an example for moving data from a 6×7 incomplete mesh with 3 faulty processors (Fig. 4a) to a 4×5 VSM (Fig. 4d) using algorithm DR. In Fig. 4b, the original incomplete mesh is partitioned into 6 blocks. The number i in a circle represents the current position for the data item that was held by processor i of the original incomplete mesh upon completion of Phase 2. Note that processors belong to complete columns have skipped the second step of Phase 1 and Phase 2. Figure 4c shows the intermediate positions for data items upon completion of Phase 3.

Lemma 3.1 *Data redistribution from an $n \times n$ incomplete mesh with $o(\sqrt{n})$ faulty processors in row-major or snakelike row-major orders onto an appropriate VSM in snakelike row-major order (as described in Subsection 3.1) can be performed in $3n/4 + o(n)$ steps.*

Proof: Since complete block rows/columns are separated by no more than $o(\sqrt{n})$ hops, at most $o(n)$ data items are surrounded by nearby complete block-columns and complete block-rows. Therefore, the first step of Phase 1 of algorithm DR can be executed in $o(n)$ time, and at the end of this step, no more than $o(n)$ data items will be located between 2 nearest intersection nodes of complete block rows and columns along a column. Since the distance between two complete block-rows is $o(\sqrt{n})$, the second step of Phase

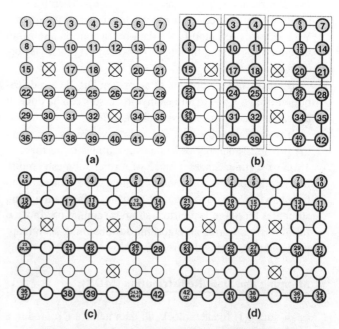

Figure 4. Data redistribution from the incomplete mesh to a VSM using algorithm DR. (a) The 39 data elements. (b) Positions after Phase 2. (c) Positions after Phase 3. (d) The final positions.

1 requires $o(\sqrt{n}) + o(n) = o(n)$ time. Since no more than $o(n)$ data items will be routed along a complete block-row during Phase 2 and the length of a block-row is $\sqrt{n}$, Phase 2 requires no more than $o(n)$ time. Upon completion of Phase 2, there are $\sqrt{n} + o(\sqrt{n})$ data items in every complete block-column. Since an item only needs to be routed for no more than $o(n)$ hops during Phase 3, this phase requires $o(n)$ time. The maximum distance for a data item to be routed during Phase 4 is $3n/4 + o(n)$. For row-major and snakelike row-major orders, a $\sqrt{n}$-node complete block-row will holds no more than $2\sqrt{n}$ items at the end of Phase 3 since it is impossible for data items from three different rows to be mapped onto the same row of the VSM for either of the orders. This property is sufficient to show that the maximum number of items that can cross a processor in one direction during Phase 4 is no more than $3n/4 + o(n)$. The worst possible case occurs at a processor X in the $\frac{5n}{8}$-th column of the incomplete mesh (i.e., the $(\frac{3n}{8} \pm o(n))$-th column in the VSM), when the healthy processors at the intersections of two nearby rows and columns $5n/8 + 1, 5n/8 + 2, \ldots, n$ are mapped to processors that are to the left of processor X in the VSM. As a result, Phase 4 can be performed in $3n/4 + o(n)$ time for row-major and snakelike row-major orders. $\square$

Note that for some ranking orders (e.g., blockwise order), the maximum number of items that will cross a processor in one direction during Phase 4 is $n + o(n)$. Therefore, algorithm DR requires $n + o(n)$ time for such ranking orders. We can, however, modify the data-redistribution algorithm to reduce its running time to $3n/4 + o(n)$ for blockwise ordering.

By reversing the process of algorithm DR, data redistribution from a VSM to all healthy processors can be done in the same time for respective ranking order.

If we use algorithm DR and its inverse process based on the previous mapping orders as subroutines to perform 1-1 robust sorting, Stages 1 and 3 of virtual-submesh emulation require $3n/2 + o(n)$ communication steps. The required time can be reduced to $n + o(n)$ by using different mapping strategies for Stage 1 of virtual-submesh emulation. In what follows, we describe an algorithm for obtaining such mapping and performing data redistribution.

Mapping and Data Redistribution (MDR):

- Phase 1: In each block, all data items are routed to a nearby complete block-column.

- Phase 2: In each block, all data items are spread approximately evenly along the block-column onto processors at the intersections of complete rows and complete block-columns.

- Phase 3: Each data item is sent along the complete row to which it currently belongs until each processor of the middle $n/2 + o(n)$ complete columns has 2 items (except for the leftmost or rightmost ones).

- Phase 4: An appropriate VSM has to include all the processors that currently have at least one item. If a processor in the VSM has fewer than 2 items, it is padded with dummy values ∞.

Lemma 3.2 *Data redistribution from an $n \times n$ incomplete mesh with $o(\sqrt{n})$ faulty processors onto an $(n - o(n)) \times (n/2 + o(n))$ VSM can be optimally executed in $n/4 + o(n)$ steps.*

Proof: From algorithm MDR, it can be seen that the row number of the new position in the VSM for a data item is at most $o(\sqrt{n})$ from the row number of its original position, and the column number of the new position in the VSM for a data item is at most $n/4 + o(n)$ from that of its original position. Moreover, data elements can be concentrated at the middle $n/2 + o(n)$ complete columns in a pipelined manner so that no more than $n/4 + o(n)$ data elements need to be sent across a link. The required time is clearly $n/4 + o(n)$ for algorithm MDR. $\square$

3.3 A $3n$-step robust sorting algorithm

In this subsection, we show that 1-1 sorting can be performed in $3n + o(n)$ communication and comparison steps on an $n \times n$ incomplete mesh that has an arbitrary patterns of $o(\sqrt{n})$ faults.

For simplicity of algorithm description, we choose m_1 and m_2 to be the sixth powers of integers. (There exist $o(n^{1/6})$ possible integers for both m_1 and m_2.) The boundary mesh for the VSM is partitioned into $(m_1 m_2)^{1/6}$ blocks, which we call *VSM blocks*. More precisely, each VSM block contains exactly $(m_1 m_2)^{5/6}$ processors of the original VSM arranged as an $m_1^{5/6}$-by-$m_2^{5/6}$ small virtual submesh, but may have more than $m_1^{5/6} m_2^{5/6}$ processors in it. A "column of VSM blocks" is called a *vertical VSM slice*.

The proposed robust sorting algorithm first redistributes the data items to the VSM, then emulates the Schnorr/Schamir sorting algorithm [5, 9] modified for 2-2 sorting using larger blocks on the VSM, and finally redistributes sorted data back to healthy processors.

The robust sorting algorithm is composed of 10 phases:

Robust Sorting (RS):

- Phase 0: Redistribute data items from each of the healthy processors in the incomplete mesh to an appropriate VSM using algorithm MDR.

- Phase 1: Sort each VSM block.

- Phase 2: Perform an $m_2^{1/6}$-way unshuffle of the VSM-columns. (That is, permute the columns such that the $m_2^{5/6}$ columns in each VSM block are distributed evenly among the $m_2^{1/6}$ vertical VSM slices.)

- Phase 3: Sort each VSM block into snakelike row-major order.

- Phase 4: Sort each column of the VSM in linear order using the C/E technique. (That is, sort the $2m_1$ data items in each VSM-column as an $m_1 \times 2$ mesh in row-major order.)

- Phase 5: Collectively sort VSM blocks 1 and 2, VSM blocks 3 and 4, VSM blocks 5 and 6,..., of each vertical VSM slice into snakelike row-major order.

- Phase 6: Collectively sort VSM blocks 2 and 3, VSM blocks 4 and 5, VSM blocks 6 and 7,..., of each vertical VSM slice into snakelike row-major order

- Phase 7: Sort each row of the VSM in linear order according to the direction of the overall snake using algorithm CERS.

- **Phase 8:** Perform $2\sqrt{m_1}$ odd-even transposition steps on the overall snake of the VSM (without using the C/E technique).

- **Phase 9:** Redistribute each of the data items from the VSM in snakelike row-major order to the appropriate healthy processor in the incomplete mesh in row-major order for row-major sorting (or in snakelike row-major order for snakelike row-major sorting) using the inverse process of algorithm DR.

Theorem 3.3 1-1 *sorting (1 key per healthy and connected processor) in row-major or snakelike row-major order on an $n \times n$ bidirectional mesh that has an artibrary pattern of $o(\sqrt{n})$ faulty processors can be performed in $3n + o(n)$ communication and comparison steps (excluding precalculation time).*

Proof: The correctness of algorithm RS can be proved using 0-1 principle [3] and the proof is similar to those given in [5, pp. 148–151] and [9]. From Lemmas 3.1 and 3.2, Phases 0 and 9 can be performed in $n/4 + o(n)$ and $3n/4 + o(n)$ communication steps, respectively. To perform 2-2 sorting on all VSM blocks for Phases 1 and 3 of algorithm RS (or VSM block pairs for Phases 5 and 6) in parallel, each VSM block (or VSM block pair, respectively) is sorted by emulating shearsort on it. These phases require $O(n^{5/6} \log n)$ time as shown in Subsection 2.3. Phase 2 requires $n/2 + o(n)$ communication steps since the width of the VSM is $n/2 + o(n)$ hops and no more than $n/2 + o(n)$ items will cross a link in the same direction during this phase. From the analysis given in Subsection 2.2, we know that Phase 4 requires $m_1 + o(n) = n \pm o(n)$ communication steps and $2m_1 = 2n - o(n)$ comparison steps while Phase 7 requires $m_2 + o(n) = n/2 + o(n)$ communication steps and $n + o(n)$ comparison steps (without precalculation time). Since two neighboring processors of the VSM are separated by no more than $f + 1 = o(\sqrt{n})$ hops, Phase 8 requires at most $o(n)$ communication steps and $O(\sqrt{n})$ comparison steps by directly performing the odd-even transposition steps (that is, by using the naive method mentioned at the end of Subsection 2.1). $\square$

When data are input/output to/from VSMs directly, sorting can be performed in $2.5n + o(n)$ communication steps and $3n + o(n)$ comparison steps on an $n \times n$ VSM within an incomplete mesh that has an arbitrary pattern of $o(\sqrt{n})$ faults. This result can be easily generalized to incomplete meshes with $o(n)$ faults by using larger VSM blocks. The running time has the same leading constant as the best known algorithms for 1-1 sorting on an $n \times n$ fault-free mesh [4, 6].

We can generalize algorithm RS for incomplete meshes with larger f by using larger blocks for Phases 0 and 9 (i.e.,

algorithms MDR and DR). The time required for sorting on an $n \times n$ incomplete mesh with f faults is $O(n + f^2)$, where $f < (1 - \varepsilon)n$ for any fixed $\varepsilon > 0$. The extra $O(f^2)$ communication steps are required by algorithms DR and MDR for worst-case fault patterns.

4   Conclusion

In this paper, we have proposed efficient robust algorithms for sorting on incomplete meshes. The proposed algorithms are efficient when the number of faults is not large and degrade gracefully as the number of faults increases. In particular, we showed that sorting on an $n \times n$ incomplete mesh that has $o(\sqrt{n})$ faulty processors can be performed in $3n + o(n)$ communication and comparison steps. This is the fastest algorithm reported thus far for sorting on an incomplete mesh in row-major and snakelike row-major orders. These techniques can also be applied to a variety of other important problems to obtain robust algorithms with negligible overheads. Details of these results will be reported in the future.

References

[1] Cole, R., B. Maggs, and R. Sitaraman, "Multi-scale self-simulation: a technique for reconfiguring arrays with faults," *ACM Symp. Theory of Computing*, 1993, pp. 561-572.

[2] Kaklamanis, C., A.R., Karlin, F.T. Leighton, V. Milenkovic, P. Eaghavan, S. Rao, C. Thomborson, and A. Tsantilas, "Asymptotically tight bounds for computing with faulty arrays of processors," *Proc. Symp. Foundations of Computer Science*, vol. 1, 1990, pp. 285-296.

[3] Knuth, D.E., *The Art of Computer Programming*, vol. 3, *Sorting and Searching*, Reading, Mass., Addison-Wesley, 1973.

[4] Kunde, M. "Concentrated regular data streams on grids: sorting and routing near to the bisection bound," *Proc. Symp. on Foundations of Computer Science*, 1991, pp. 141-150.

[5] Leighton, F.T., *Introduction to Parallel Algorithms and Architectures: Arrays, Trees, Hypercubes*, Morgan-Kaufman, San Mateo, CA, 1992.

[6] Nigam, M. and S. Sahni, "Sorting n^2 numbers on $n \times n$ meshes," *IEEE Trans. Parallel Distrib. Sys.*, vol. 6, no. 12, Dec. 1995, pp. 1221-1225.

[7] Parhami B. and C.-Y. Hung, "Robust shearsort on incomplete bypass meshes," *Proc. Int'l Parallel Processing Symp.*, 1995, pp 304-311.

[8] Park, A. and K. Balasubramanian, "Reducing communication costs for sorting on mesh-connected and linearly connected parallel computers," *J. Parallel Distrib. Comput.*, vol. 9, no. 3, Jul. 1990 pp. 318-322.

[9] Schnorr, C.P. and Shamir, A., "An optimal sorting algorithm for mesh connected computers," *Proc. Symp. Theory of Computing*, 1986, pp. 255-263.

Broadcast-Efficient Sorting in the Presence of Few Channels *

Koji Nakano[†] Stephan Olariu[‡] James L. Schwing[‡]

Abstract

We present simple and broadcast-efficient ranking and sorting algorithms on the broadcast communication model (BCM, for short) with few communication channels. At the heart of our algorithms is a new and elegant sampling and bucketing scheme whose main feature is that the resulting buckets are well balanced, making costly rebalancing unnecessary. The resulting ranking algorithm uses only $2\frac{n}{k} + o(\frac{n}{k})$ broadcast rounds, while $3\frac{n}{k} + o(\frac{n}{k})$ broadcast rounds are needed for sorting on a k-channel, n-processor BCM whenever $k \leq \sqrt{\frac{n}{\log n}}$. These bounds are fairly tight, when compared with the trivial lower bound of $\frac{n}{k}$ broadcast rounds necessary to permute n items using k communication channels.

Keywords: broadcast communication model, wireless computing, mobile computing

1 Introduction

Recently, the widespread proliferation of wireless networks, personal communication systems (PCS), and mobile computing, has motivated researchers to study the broadcast communication model (BCM, for short) consisting of a number of processing hosts that communicate via a cluster of dedicated channels. The model specifically excludes processor-to-processor links, making the channels the only way the hosts may communicate. Due to the absence of processor-to-processor links the BCM approximates quite accurately a wireless environment; moreover, the addition of new hosts and the removal of those wishing to disconnect is far less complicated than in the case of classic interconnection networks [2, 3].

Computational problems solved on the BCM model include computing the extrema [5], sorting and selection [3, 7, 9], and graph theoretical problems [2, 10]. Specifically, Levitan [5] and Levitan and Foster [6] have shown that if broadcast conflicts are resolved in constant time, then in a single-channel, n-processor BCM the maximum and minimum of n items can be computed in $O(\log n)$ time. They have also shown that on the same platform the task of sorting n items takes

O(n) time, while the task of computing a minimum spanning tree of an n-vertex graph takes $O(n \log n)$ time. Later, Dechter and Kleinrock [3] have addressed the problem of sorting n items in a single-channel p-processor ($p \leq n$) BCM. They have shown that if broadcast conflicts can be resolved in constant time, then the n items can be sorted in $O(\frac{n}{p} \log \frac{n}{p} + n)$ time. More recently, Marberg and Gafni [7] have shown that on a k-channel, p-processor, conflict-free BCM a sequence of n items stored $\frac{n}{p}$ per processor can be sorted in $O(\frac{n}{k} + n_{max})$ time, where $k \leq p \leq n$, $k^2(k-1) \leq n$ and n_{max} is the largest number of items ever stored by a processor during the course of the algorithm. Yang *et al.* [11] have improved on the results of Marberg and Gafni [7] and Dechter and Kleinrock [3] by showing that the running time can be reduced to $O(\frac{n}{p} \log \frac{n}{p} + \frac{n}{k} \log^2 k)$. Nakano [8] presented a sorting algorithm based on the well known columnsort. His algorithm requires $O(\frac{n}{k})$ broadcast rounds. This algorithm is asymptotically optimal, however, has s large constant factor. $O(\frac{n}{k} + \frac{n \log n}{p})$ time for local computations.

We propose a new and elegant sampling and bucketing scheme that yields a fast and simple ranking and sorting algorithm in the BCM model. The resulting algorithm features a very small number constant. In case $k \leq \sqrt{\frac{n}{\log n}}$, our ranking algorithm needs $2\frac{n}{k} + o(\frac{n}{k})$ broadcast rounds; at the same time, $3\frac{n}{k} + o(\frac{n}{k})$ broadcast rounds are needed for sorting n items on a conflict-free k-channel, n-processor BCM.

2 The BCM

The Broadcast Communication Model (BCM) involves p processors PE(1), PE(2), ..., PE(p) all having access to, and communicating via, k ($k \geq 1$) communication channels CC(1), CC(2), ..., CC(k), as illustrated in Figure 1. We shall refer to a p-processor, k-channel BCM as BCM(p, k). In unit time, a processor can perform an arithmetic or boolean operation, broadcast data on one of the channels or read the message being broadcast on one of the channels (these two channels may or may not be the same). All the operations described above involve handling at most O($\log n$) bits of information. In one time unit several processors can read from the same channel but

---

*Work supported by NASA grant NCC1-99, by NSF grant CCR-9522093, by ONR grant N00014-97-1-0526, and a grant from the Hori Information Science Promotion Foundation.

[†]Dept. of Electrical and Computer Engineering, Nagoya Institute of Technology, Showa-ku, Nagoya 466, JAPAN

[‡]Department of Computer Science, Old Dominion University, Norfolk, Virginia 23529, USA

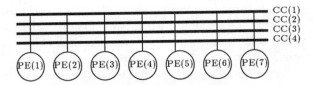

Figure 1: *Illustrating the BCM(7,4)*

at most one processor can broadcast to a channel.

As in [2, 10, 11] we assume a synchronous platform: all the processors execute the same instruction in lock-step. Each processor is assumed to know its own identity within the machine and to have a local memory consisting of $O(\frac{n}{p})$ registers, where n is the size of an arbitrary input. Each register is assumed to be able to store an item represented in at most $O(\log n)$ bits. In accord with other researchers [2, 3, 5, 7, 8, 9, 10], we assume ideal channel communications. Although inexact, recent experiments seem to indicate that this is a reasonable working hypothesis [4].

3 Basics

We begin by illustrating a simple data movement that allows to route n items stored one item per processor to n different destinations in $\frac{n}{k}$ broadcast rounds on a BCM(n, k). Let $d : \{1, \ldots, n\} \to \{1, \ldots, n\}$ be a one-to-one map. The task of *permutation routing* on the BCM(n, k) involves routing for all i, $(1 \leq i \leq n)$, the item $a(i)$ stored by processor PE(i) to processor PE($d(i)$). It is important to note that although processor PE($d(i)$) expects to receive an item, it does not know where this item originates. Permutation routing can be performed in an optimal number of broadcast rounds on the BCM(n, k).

Lemma 3.1 *The task of permutation routing can be performed on the BCM(n, k) in $\frac{n}{k}$ broadcast rounds.*

Proof. For every i, $(1 \leq i \leq n)$ consider the map $d(i) \to [round(d(i)), channel(d(i))]$ that associates with $d(i)$ the ordered pair $[round(d(i)), channel(d(i))]$ such that

- $round(d(i)) = \left\lceil \frac{d(i)}{k} \right\rceil$, and

- $channel(d(i)) = (d(i) - 1) \bmod k + 1$.

Clearly, this map is a bijection. Moreover, for every i, both processors PE(i) and PE($d(i)$) compute the ordered pair $[round(d(i)), channel(d(i))]$. Processor PE($d(i)$) reads channel $channel(d(i))$ in the $round(d(i))$-th broadcast round. It is on this channel that processor PE(i) broadcasts the message intended for PE($d(i)$). Thus, the task can be completed in $\left\lceil \frac{n}{k} \right\rceil$ broadcast rounds which is best possible. □

Assume that n data items have been pretiled onto a BCM($n, 1$), also called the *single-channel* BCM, with

processors PE(1), PE(2), ..., PE(n) such that processor PE(i) stores item $a(i)$, $(1 \leq i \leq n)$. The *rank* of an item is one larger than the number of items smaller than it. The *ranking* problem is to compute the rank of every item. Taking turns, from $PE(1)$ to $PE(n)$, the processors broadcast the item they hold on the channel. All the other processors read the value being broadcast and update a local counter. For every processor $PE(i)$, $(1 \leq i \leq n)$, this counter records the number of data items that are smaller than a_i. It is clear that after n broadcast rounds every processor can compute the rank of the item it holds.

Lemma 3.2 *The task of ranking n items stored one per processor in a BCM($n, 1$) can be performed in n broadcast rounds.*

Further, by additional permutation routing, we have

Lemma 3.3 *The task of sorting n items stored one per processor in a BCM($n, 1$) can be performed in $2n$ broadcast rounds.*

By a similar algorithm to Lemma 3.2, we have

Lemma 3.4 *The task of computing the prefix-sums (also the sum) of n integers stored one per processor in a BCM($n, 1$) can be performed in n broadcast rounds.*

Our ranking and sorting algorithm relies, in part, on the following results.

Lemma 3.5 *[8] The tasks of ranking and sorting n items stored one per processor in a BCM(n, k) can be performed in $O(\frac{n}{k})$ broadcast rounds if and $k \leq n^{1-\epsilon}$ for every fixed $\epsilon > 0$.*

4 The Sampling Scheme

The *sampling scheme*, illustrated in Figure 2, partitions the n items $A = \{a(1), a(2), \ldots, a(n)\}$ into k, $(1 \leq k \leq \sqrt{n})$, buckets $B(1), B(2), \ldots, B(k)$ such that

- $B(1) < B(2) < \ldots < B(k)$, that is, for every i, $(1 \leq i \leq k - 1)$, all the items in bucket $B(i)$ are smaller than those in bucket $B(i+1)$, and

- no $B(i)$ contains more than $\frac{n}{k} + O(\sqrt{n})$ items.

Suppose that A consists of k sorted sequences $A(1), A(2), \ldots, A(k)$, each of size $\frac{n}{k}$ and write $A(i) : a(i, 1) < a(i, 2) < \cdots < a(i, \frac{n}{k})\}$ Assume, further, that each subset $A(i)$ is partitioned into $\sqrt{n}$ groups $A(i, 1), A(i, 2), \ldots, A(i, \sqrt{n})$, each of size $\frac{\sqrt{n}}{k}$, such that for each $j \leq \sqrt{n}$, $A(i, j) = \{a(i, (j-1)\frac{\sqrt{n}}{k} + 1), a(i, (j-1)\frac{\sqrt{n}}{k} + 2), \ldots, a(i, j\frac{\sqrt{n}}{k})\}$. Clearly, A is partitioned into $k\sqrt{n}$ groups. Let Sample(A) be a set of $k\sqrt{n}$ items consisting of the smallest item in each $A(i, j)$. Let $s(1) < s(2) < \cdots < s(k\sqrt{n})$ be items in Sample(A) enumerated in non-decreasing order. We further partition Sample(A) into k subsets $S(1), S(2), \ldots, S(k)$ each of size $\sqrt{n}$, such that $S(i) = \{s((i-1)\sqrt{n}+1), s((i-1)\sqrt{n}+2), \ldots, s(i\sqrt{n})\}$. Let Pivot($A$)$= \{v(1) < v(2) < \cdots < v(k)\}$ be the set of smallest item $v(i) = s((i-1)\sqrt{n}+1)$ in each $S(i)$. Pivot(A) induces a natural partition of A into k buckets $B(1), B(2), \ldots B(k)$ such that, for all $1 \leq j < k$, $B(j) = \{a \in A \mid v(j) \leq a < v(j+1)\}$ and such that $B(k) = \{a \in A \mid v(j) \leq a\}$. What is less obvious, however, is that the resulting buckets are well balanced in the following sense:

Lemma 4.1 $B(1) < B(2) < \ldots < B(k)$, and no $B(i)$, $(1 \leq i \leq k)$, contains more than $\frac{n}{k} + O(\sqrt{n})$ items.

Proof. The first part of the claim follows immediately from the construction of the buckets. To prove the second part, let us estimate the number of items in $A(i) \cap B(j)$. If $A(i) \cap S(j)$ contain q items, then $A(i) \cap B(j)$ contains fewer than $(q+1)\frac{\sqrt{n}}{k}$ items. Since $S(j) = \cup_{1 \leq i \leq k}(A(i) \cap S(j))$ has $\sqrt{n}$ items, $B(j) = \cup_{1 \leq i \leq k}A(i) \cap B(j)$ has at most $(\sqrt{n}+k) \cdot \frac{\sqrt{n}}{k} = \frac{n}{k} + \sqrt{n}$ items. $\square$

5 The proposed algorithms

Throughout this section we assume that the input is a collection of n items $a(1), a(2), \ldots, a(n)$ stored one item per processor on a BCM(n, k) in such a way that for every i, $(1 \leq i \leq n)$, processor PE(i) stores, initially, item $a(i)$. Our ranking algorithm follows.

Step 1 Using its index i, each processor identifies the group $A(i)$ to which its own item $a(i)$ belongs. Assign channel CC(i) to group $A(i)$ and compute the rank of each item within each group $A(i)$. By Lemma 3.2 this task can be completed in $\frac{n}{k}$ broadcast rounds.

Step 2 Using the rank computed in Step 1, each processor determines whether its own item is in Sample(A); recall that an item belongs to Sample(A) if and only if its rank modulo $\frac{\sqrt{n}}{k}$ is 1. With this information available, route the items in Sample(A) to the first $k\sqrt{n}$ processors PE(1), PE(2), $\ldots$, PE($k\sqrt{n}$). This latter task can be performed in $\sqrt{n}$ broadcast rounds by using the algorithm of Lemma 3.1.

Step 3 Sort Sample(A) using the algorithm of Lemma 3.5. Since Sample(A) contains at most $k\sqrt{n}$ items and k channels are available, this task can be performed in $O(\sqrt{n})$ broadcast rounds. At this moment, each PE(i), $1 \leq i \leq k\sqrt{n}$, stores an item $s(i)$.

Step 4 Using its index, each processor PE(i), ($1 \leq i \leq k\sqrt{n}$), determines whether the item $s(i)$ from Sample(A) it stores belongs to Pivot(A).

Step 5 Each processor determines the identity of the bucket $B(1), B(2), \ldots, B(k)$ to which its own item belongs. The detail of this step will be explained later.

With a careful implementation, the task specific to this step can be performed in $\log k$ broadcast rounds.

Step 6 Each processor determines the rank of its own item within $A(i) \cap B(j)$, where the item is both in $A(i)$ and in $B(j)$. As it turns out, this step can be performed in $k \log \frac{n}{k} + k$ broadcast rounds.

Step 7 Each processor determines the rank of its own item within $B(j)$, where the item is in $B(j)$. As will be seen later, when implementation details will be discussed, the task specific to this step can be performed in at most $\frac{n}{k} + O(\sqrt{n})$ broadcast rounds.

Step 8 Compute the rank of each $B(j)$ (i.e. the correct rank of the minimum item in $B(j)$ over all items in A). To do this, broadcast the rank of minimum item in $A(i) \cap B(j)$ to CC(j) for every j. By adding up the rank broadcast and subtracting $k - 1$ from the result, one can obtain the rank of $B(j)$. Now, computing the rank of each input item amounts to adding this rank, as an offset, to the rank of each item within $B(i)$ and by subtracting one from the result. This step needs k broadcast rounds.

The remainder of this section presents the implementation details of Steps 5, 6, and 7.

Details of Step 5 Assign each channel CC(i) ($1 \leq i \leq k$) to $v(i)$. Then, $v(i)$ is broadcasted through channel CC(i) in every $\log k$ broadcast rounds. During these $\log k$ rounds, each processor identifies to which bucket its own item belongs by the binary search technique as follows: first, every processor receive the median $v(\frac{k}{2})$ and check if its item is smaller than it. If small, then receive $v(\frac{k}{4})$ and check its item is smaller than it, otherwise receive $v(\frac{3k}{4})$ and check in the same way. Continuing similarly, each processor can identify the bucket its item belongs to in $\log k$ rounds.

Details of Step 6 Assign each channel CC(i) ($1 \leq i \leq k$) to $A(i)$. For each i and j, find the minimum item in $A(i) \in B(j)$ by the binary search as follows: First, broadcast the index of the bucket having the median $a(i, \frac{n}{2k})$ of $A(i)$ to CC(i). If this index is larger than j, then broadcast the index of the bucket having $a(i, \frac{3n}{4k})$ and check it is larger than j, otherwise broadcast the index of the bucket having $a(i, \frac{n}{4k})$ and check in the same way. Continuing similarly, we can find the minimum item $A(i) \cap B(j)$. This needs $\log \frac{n}{k}$ broadcast rounds. Further, since this is executed for all j ($1 \leq j \leq k$), the minimum item in every $A(i) \cap B(j)$ can be determined in $k \log \frac{n}{k}$ broadcast rounds. After that, the rank of each minimum items in $A(i) \cap B(j)$ is broadcasted and processors that has items in $A(i) \cap B(j)$ receives it. By comparing the rank of the minimum item and its own item, the rank of the item within $A(i) \cap B(j)$ can be determined. This needs k broadcast rounds. Totally, Step 6 can be done

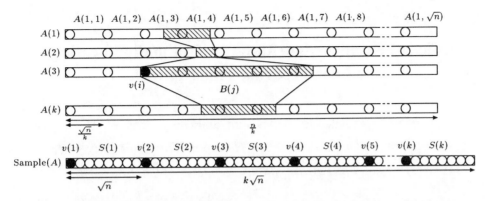

Figure 2: *Illustrating our sampling scheme*

in $k \log \frac{n}{k} + k$ broadcast rounds.

Details of Step 7 Assign each channel $CC(j)$ to $B(j)$, to compute the rank of item within each bucket $B(j)$ by the algorithm for Lemma 3.2. To apply the algorithm, broadcast items in $A(1) \cap B(j)$ to $CC(j)$. Since each processor knows the rank of its own item within $A(1) \cap B(j)$, items in $A(1) \cap B(j)$ can be broadcasted one by one. from the minimum item. We can identify whether all items in $A(1) \cap B(j)$ have been already broadcasted, because no item is broadcasted (null broadcast) just after the maximum item in $A(1) \cap B(j)$ is broadcast. After this null broadcast, the same procedure is executed for $A(2) \cap B(j)$, ..., $A(k) \cap B(j)$. Since the all items in $B(j)$ have been broadcast through $CC(j)$, the rank of item within $B(j)$ can be computed by the technique used in Lemma 3.2. This task takes at most $\frac{n}{k} + O(\sqrt{n})$ broadcasts. We have the following important result.

Theorem 5.1 *The task of ranking a collection of n items stored one per processor in a $BCM(n,k)$ can be performed in $2\frac{n}{k} + k \log \frac{n}{k} + O(\sqrt{n})$ broadcast rounds, whenever $k \leq \sqrt{n}$.*

Corollary 5.2 *The task of sorting of n items can be performed in $3\frac{n}{k} + k \log \frac{n}{k} + O(\sqrt{n})$ broadcast rounds on the $BCM(n,k)$, whenever $k \leq \sqrt{n}$.*

Thus, if $k = o(\sqrt{\frac{n}{\log n}})$, the ranking can be done in $2\frac{n}{k} + o(\frac{n}{k})$ broadcast rounds, while sorting takes $3\frac{n}{k} + o(\frac{n}{k})$ broadcast rounds.

References

[1] J. I. Capetanakis, Tree algorithms for packet broadcast channels, *IEEE Transactions on Information Theory*, IT-25, (1979), 505–515.

[2] G.-H. Chen and W.-W. Liang, Conflict-free broadcasting algorithms for graph traversals and their applications, *Parallel Computing*, 18, (1992), 439–448.

[3] R. Dechter and L. Kleinrock, Broadcast communication and distributed algorithms, *IEEE Transactions on Computers*, C-35, (1986), 210–219.

[4] V. K. Garg and J. E. Wilkes, *Wireless and Personal Communication Systems*, Prentice-Hall, Englewood Cliffs, NJ, 1996.

[5] S. Levitan, Algorithms for broadcast protocol multiprocessors, *Proc. 3rd International Conference on Distributed Computing Systems*, 1982, 666–671.

[6] S. Levitan and C. C. Foster, Finding and extremum in a network, *Proc. International Symposium on Computer Architecture*, Austin, Texas, 1982, 321–325.

[7] J. M. Marberg and E. Gafni, Sorting and selection in multi-channel broadcast networks, *Proc. International Conference on Parallel Processing*, St-Charles, Illinois, August 1985, 846–850.

[8] K. Nakano, Optimal sorting algorithms on bus-connected processor arrays, *IEICE Transactions Fundamentals*, E-76A, 11, (1994), 2008–2015.

[9] K. V. S. Ramarao, Distributed sorting on local area networks, *IEEE Transactions on Computers*, C-37, (1988), 239–243.

[10] C. B. Yang, R. C. T. Lee, and W.-T. Chen, Parallel graph algorithms based upon broadcast communications, *IEEE Transactions on Computers* C-39, (1990), 1468–1472.

[11] C. B. Yang, R. C. T. Lee, and W.-T. Chen, Conflict-free sorting algorithms under single and multi-channel broadcast communication models, *Proc. ICCI'91*, LNCS 497, Springer-Verlag, 1991, 350–359.

Efficient Parallel Algorithms for Optimally Locating a k-Leaf Tree in a Tree Network

Shan-Chyun Ku, Wei-Kuan Shih, and Biing-Feng Wang

Department of Computer Science, National Tsing Hua University

Hsinchu, Taiwan 30043, Republic of China

Abstract

In this paper, an efficient parallel algorithm is proposed for finding a k-tree core of a tree network. The proposed algorithm performs on the EREW PRAM in $O(\log n \log^* n)$ time using $O(n)$ work.

1. Introduction

Recently, in [6], Peng *et al.* studied the problem of finding a *k-tree core* of a tree network. A k-tree core of a tree network is a minimum distancesum subtree with exactly k leaves. Efficient algorithms for finding a k-tree core of a tree network have an application in the placement of the k copies of a data object in the tree network [6]. Two algorithms for finding a k-tree core of a tree network were proposed in [6]. One performs in $O(kn)$ time and the other performs in $O(n\log n)$ time, where n is the number of vertices in the tree network. Both Peng *et al.*'s algorithms perform in a step-by-step refining manner. Thus, it is hard to parallelize their algorithms.

In this paper, an efficient parallel algorithm is proposed for finding a k-tree core of a tree network. The proposed algorithm performs on the EREW PRAM in $O(\log n \log^* n)$ time using $O(n)$ work (time-processor product). Besides being efficient on the EREW PRAM, in the sequential case, our algorithm for finding a k-tree core of a tree network is more efficient than the two algorithms previously proposed in [6].

2. Notation and preliminary results

Let T denote the tree network under consideration. Let V and E denote the vertex set and the edge set of T respectively. Let $n=|V|$. The n vertices in V are labeled with 1, 2, ..., and n respectively. Denote *label*(v) as the label of a vertex $v \in V$. The tree network is undirected. Each edge $e \in E$ has an arbitrary positive length $w(e)$. A leaf of T is a vertex with degree one. Let m be the number of leaves of T. For any two vertices u and v in V,

the distance of u and v, denote by $d(u, v)$, is the length of the unique path connecting u and v. The distance from a vertex to a subtree is defined as the shortest distance from the vertex to any vertex in the subtree. We denote $d(v, X)$ as the distance from a vertex v to a subtree X of T.

The distancesum of a subtree X of T, denoted by $Sum(X)$, is the total distance from X to the vertices of T. That is, $Sum(X)=\sum_{v\in V} d(v, X)$. A k-tree core of T is a minimum distancesum subtree of T with exactly k leaves. Clearly, as a consequence of the minimum distancesum criterion, a leaf of a k-tree core shall be a leaf of T.

The Euler-tour technique and tree contraction are two of the major parallel techniques used in this paper. These two techniques are well-known and thus are not described in this paper. Readers not familiar to them may refer to [4] for a clear description. We assume that the data structure representing T is adjacent lists, to which Euler-tour technique and tree contraction can be applied efficiently.

The following results are needed for the algorithm we shall propose in the next section. All the results are derived from the two techniques mentioned above.

Lemma 1 [4]: An undirected tree can be oriented into a rooted tree with a specified root in $O(\log n)$ time using $O(n)$ work on the EREW PRAM.

Lemma 2 [4]: For each vertex v in a rooted tree, the depth of v (the distance from the root to v), the height of T_v, and the number of vertices contained in T_v can be computed in $O(\log n)$ time using $O(n)$ work on the EREW PRAM, where T_v is the subtree rooted at v.

Lemma 3 [5]: A 2-tree core of a tree can be determined in $O(\log n)$ time using $O(n)$ work on the EREW PRAM.

3. Finding a k-tree core

In this section, we propose an efficient parallel algorithm on the EREW PRAM for finding a k-tree core of T.

*   This research is supported by the National Science Council of the Republic of China under grant NCS-84-2221-E-007-002.

Let r be an endpoint of a 2-tree core of T. In this section, we assume that T is rooted at r. For each vertex v in T, denote $p(v)$, $depth(v)$, T_v, and $size(v)$ as the parent of v, the depth of v, the subtree rooted at v, and the number of vertices contained in the subtree rooted at v, respectively.

Let $P_{v,l}$ be the path from a vertex v to a leaf l of T_v. The *distance saving* of this path is defined as
$$Save(P_{v,l})=Sum(v)-Sum(P_{v,l}).$$
Let the path $P_{v,l}$ be given as $(u_1, u_2, ..., u_t)$, where $u_1=v$ and $u_t=l$. It is not difficult to verify that $Save(P_{u_i,l})$

$= Save(P_{u_{i+1},l}) + w((u_i,u_{i+1})) \times size(u_{i+1})$ for $1 \le i \le t-1$. Thus, the value of $Save(P_{v,l})$ can be computed as

$\sum_{1 \le i \le t-1} w((u_i,u_{i+1})) \times size(u_{i+1})$.   Let $MaxSave(v)=$

$\max\limits_{l \text{ is a leaf of } T_v} \{Save(P_{v,l})\}$. Clearly, we have $MaxSave(v)=$

$\max\limits_{u \text{ is a child of } v} \{w((v,u)) + MaxSave(u)\}$.

Let v be a vertex of T. Let l_1 and l_2 be two leaves of the subtree T_v. We say that l_1 *beats* l_2 at the vertex v iff either (1) $Save(P_{v,l_1}) > Save(P_{v,l_2})$ or (2) $Save(P_{v,l_1})$

$= Save(P_{v,l_2})$ and $label(l_1)>label(l_2)$. We say that a leaf l of T_v *dominates* T_v iff no leaf in T_v beats l at v. Denote $DomiLeaf(v)$ as the leaf dominating T_v. Note that by definition, $Save(P_{v,DomiLeaf(v)})=MaxSave(v)$. Also note that if $DomiLeaf(v)=DomiLeaf(p(v))$, we have $MaxSave(p(v))=w((p(v),v)) \times size(v)+MaxSave(v)$.

Let l be a leaf in T and the path $P_{r,l}$ be given as $(u_1, u_2, ..., u_t)$, where $u_1=r$ and $u_t=l$. Clearly, there exists a vertex u_q, $1 \le q \le t$, such that the subtrees T_{u_q}, $T_{u_{q+1}}$, ..., and T_{u_t} are dominated by l but the other subtrees T_{u_1}, T_{u_2}, ..., and $T_{u_{q-1}}$ are not. Denote $DomiEnd(l)$ as the vertex u_q. The *dominated path* of l, denoted by $DomiPath(l)$, is the path from $DomiEnd(l)$ to l. Clearly, for any two leaves l_1 and l_2 in T, $DomiPath(l_1) \cap DomiPath(l_2)=\emptyset$.

As an illustrative example, let us consider the tree network depicted in Figure 1. In the figure, each edge of the tree network has a length 1 and the vertex u_1 is the root, which is an endpoint of a 2-tree core of the network. For each vertex u_i in the network, the values of $size(u_i)$, $MaxSave(u_i)$, $DomiLeaf(u_i)$, and $DomiEnd(u_i)$

are listed in Table 1. The dominated paths of the leaves of the network are depicted in Figure 2.

We define the *importance* of a leaf l of T to be
$$R(l)=\begin{cases} Save(P_{x,l}) & \text{if } l \text{ dominates } T, \\ w((p(x),x)) \times size(x) + Save(P_{x,l}) & \text{otherwise,} \end{cases}$$
where $x=DomiEnd(l)$. Note that if l dominates T, $DomiEnd(l)=r$. We say that a leaf l_1 is *more important than* another leaf l_2 iff either (1) $R(l_1)>R(l_2)$ or (2) $R(l_1)=R(l_2)$ and $label(l_1)>label(l_2)$. The *rank* of a leaf l in T, denoted by $rank(l)$, is the number of leaves in T that are more important than or as important as l. In other words, $rank(l)=i$ iff l is the i-th most important leaf in T. Throughout this section, we denote a_i as the leaf with rank i in T, $1 \le i \le m-1$. Clearly, a_1 is the leaf dominates T and thus $DomiEnd(a_1)=r$.

Consider the tree network in Figure 1 again. For each leaf u_i in the network, we list the values of $R(u_i)$ and $rank(u_i)$ in Table 2.

Clearly, have the following lemma.

Lemma 4: If a leaf l_1 beats another leaf l_2 at some vertex, we have $R(l_1) \ge R(l_2)$ and $rank(l_1)<rank(l_2)$.

Let $G_1=DomiPath(a_1)$. And, for $i=2, 3, .., $ and $m-1$, let G_i be the sub-graph obtained from G_{i-1} by adding the path $DomiPath(a_i)$ and the edge $(p(DomiEnd(a_i)), DomiEnd(a_i))$. That is, $G_i=G_{i-1} \cup DomiPath(a_i) \cup \{(p(DomiEnd(a_i)), DomiEnd(a_i))\}$.

Lemma 5: The vertex $p(DomiEnd(a_i))$ is contained in G_{i-1}, $2 \le i \le m-1$.

Proof: Let $x=DomiEnd(a_i)$. By definition, the subtree $T_{p(x)}$ is not dominated by a_i. Let y be the leaf that dominates $T_{p(x)}$. Since y beats a_i at $p(x)$, by lemma 4, we have $rank(y)<i$. Thus, the path $DomiPath(y)$ is included in G_{i-1}. Since $p(x)$ is a vertex on $DomiPath(y)$, it is contained in G_{i-1}. The lemma holds.   Q.E.D.

From lemma 5, we can easily conclude that G_i is a subtree of T with $i+1$ endpoints (including the root r). The two subtrees G_{i-1} and G_i differ only in the path from $p(DomiEnd(a_i))$ to a_i. Thus, we have $Sum(G_i)=$

$Sum(G_{i-1})- Save(P_{p(DomiEnd(a_i)),a_i}) =Sum(G_{i-1})-R(a_i)$.

We have the following lemma.

Lemma 6: G_i is a subtree of T with $i+1$ endpoints, where $1 \le i \le m-1$.   And, $Sum(G_i)=Sum(G_{i-1})-R(a_i)=Sum(r)-$

$\sum_{1 \le j \le i} R(a_j)$, where $Sum(r)=\sum_{v \in V} depth(v)$.

Since a_1 dominates T, among all paths from r to

the leaves, P_{r,a_1} is the one with the maximum distance saving. Since r is an endpoint of a 2-tree core of T, we obtain the following lemma.

Lemma 7 [5]: The subtree G_1 is a 2-tree core of T.

Peng *et al.* showed that k-tree cores have the following interesting "nesting" property.

Lemma 8 [6]: Every $(k-1)$-tree core is contained in a k-tree core.

Theorem 1: G_{k-1} is a k-tree core of T, $2\leq k\leq m$.

Proof: Using lemmas 6~8, this theorem can be proved by induction on k. Because of limitations of pages, the details are omitted. An interested reader may consult [7] for the details.   Q.E.D.

Now, we are ready to propose our algorithm for finding a k-tree core of T. The algorithm is as follows.

ALGORITHM k-Tree_Core$(T(V, E))$
Step 1: Identify an endpoint r of a 2-tree core of T. And then, orient T into a rooted tree with root r.
Step 2: For each vertex v in T, compute $size(v)$ and $depth(v)$.
Step 3: For each vertex v in T, compute $MaxSave(v)$ and $DomiLeaf(v)$.
Step 4: /* For each leaf l in T, determine $R(l)$. */
  4.1: For each internal vertex v in T, broadcast $DomiLeaf(v)$ to its children.
  4.2: For each vertex v in T, if $v=r$, set $R(l)=MaxSave(v)$; otherwise, if $v\neq r$ and $DomiLeaf(v)\neq DomiLeaf(p(v))$, set $R(l)=w((p(v), v))+MaxSave(v)$, where $l=DomiLeaf(v)$.
Step 5: Find the leaf x in T with $rank(x)=k-1$.
Step 6: /* Compute G_{k-1}, which is a k-tree core of T. */
  6.1: For each leaf l in T, if $l=x$ or l is more important than x, assign a number 1 to l; otherwise assign a number 0 to l.
  6.2: For each vertex v in T, compute $A(v)$ as the largest number contained in the leaves of T_v. (Note that after sub-step 6.2, $A(v)=1$ iff v is contained in G_{k-1}.)
  6.3: Obtain G_{k-1} from T as follows: for each vertex v, if $A(v)=0$ remove v and the edge $(v, p(v))$.

Step 7: Compute $Sum(G_{k-1})$ as $\sum_{v\in V} depth(v) - \sum_{l\text{ is a leaf in }G_{k-1}} R(l)$.

The correctness of the above algorithm is ensured by lemma 6 and theorem 1. The parallel running time of the algorithm is discussed as follows.

By lemmas 1, 2, and 3, steps 1 and 2 take $O(\log n)$ time using $O(n)$ work. Since $MaxSave(v)=$

$$\max_{u\text{ is a child of }v} \{w((v,u))+MaxSave(u)\},$$ the computation of $MaxSave(v)$'s is similar to that of $height(v)$'s, where $height(v)$ denotes the height of the subtree T_v. Thus, using tree contraction, $MaxSave(v)$'s can be computed in $O(\log n)$ time using $O(n)$ work. Clearly, during the computation of $MaxSave(v)$'s, we can maintain some information to produce the values of $DomiLeaf(v)$'s. Therefore, step 3 can be done in $O(\log n)$ time using $O(n)$ work. It was showed by Cole and Vishkin [3] that the prefix computation of a linked list can be computed in $O(\log n)$ time using $O(n)$ work on the EREW PRAM. For each vertex v, the children of v are stored in the adjacent list of v. Thus, with the help of Cole and Vishkin's prefix computation algorithm, the broadcasting performed in sub-step 4.1 can be done in $O(\log n)$ time using $O(n)$ work. After the broadcasting, each vertex $v\neq r$ has the values of $DomiLeaf(v)$ and $DomiLeaf(p(v))$. Thus, sub-step 4.2 can be performed in $O(1)$ time using $O(n)$ work. Step 5 is the most critical step. We will discuss its running time later. Clearly, sub-steps 6.1 and 6.3 can be done in $O(\log n)$ time using $O(n)$ work. By tree contraction, sub-step 6.2 can be easily done in $O(\log n)$ time using $O(n)$ work. Clearly, step 7 can be done in $O(\log n)$ time using $O(n)$ work. Therefore, except step 5, all steps in algorithm k-Tree_Core can be implemented in $O(\log n)$ time using a total of $O(n)$ work. We have the following theorem.

Theorem 2: If the $(k-1)$-th element of a set of $m-1$ elements can be found in $O(I)$ time using $O(W)$ work on the EREW PRAM, a k-tree core of a tree network can be computed in $O(I+\log n)$ time using $O(W+n)$ work on the EREW PRAM, where m is the number of leaves in the tree network.

It was showed by Cole [2] that the $(k-1)$-th element of a set of $m-1$ elements can be determined in $O(\log m\log^* m)$ time using $O(m)$ work on the EREW PRAM. Since $m\leq n$, we have the following corollary.

Corollary 1: A k-tree core of a tree network can be computed in $O(\log n\log^* n)$ time using $O(n)$ work on the EREW PRAM.

Since the maximum (minimum) of m numbers can be easily computed in $O(\log m)$ time using $O(m)$ work on the EREW PRAM, we have the following corollary.

Corollary 2: If k (or $m-k$) is a constant, a k-tree core of a tree network can be computed in $O(\log n)$ time using $O(n)$ work on the EREW PRAM, where m is the number of leaves of the tree network.

Using Cole's parallel merge sort [1], we can obtain the following corollary.

Corollary 3: A *k*-tree core of a tree network can be computed in $O(\log n)$ time using $O(n+m\log m)$ work on the EREW PRAM, where m is the number of leaves of the tree network.

Note that if $m=O(n/\log n)$, the work in corollary 3 is linear.

4. Concluding remarks

A *k-tree center* of a tree network is a subtree with exactly *k* leaves that minimizes the distance from the farthest vertex to the subtree. Using the same idea of this paper, it has been shown in [7] that a *k*-tree center of a tree network can be computed in $O(\log n\log^* n)$ time using $O(n)$ work on the EREW PRAM.

In this paper, no constraint is placed on the size of the *k*-tree core. In [8], the problem of finding a *k*-tree core with a specified diameter *l* of a tree network has been studied. Efficient algorithms for finding *k*-tree core with a specified diameter have applications in distributed database systems. Two sequential algorithms have been proposed in [8]; one performs in, $O(n^2)$ time, and the other performs in $O(lkn+ln\log n)$ time. Both the algorithms are extensions of the *k*-tree core algorithm proposed in this paper.

References

[1] R. Cole, "Parallel merge sort," *SIAM Journal on Computing*, vol. 17, no. 4, pp. 770-785, 1988.

[2] R. Cole, "An optimally efficient selection algorithm," *Information Processing Letters*, vol. 26, no. 6, pp.295-299, 1988.

[3] R. Cole and U. Vishkin, "Approximate parallel scheduling, Part I: The basic technique with applications to optimal parallel list ranking in logarithmic time," *SIAM Journal on Computing*, vol. 17, no. 1, pp. 128-142, 1988.

[4] J. Jaja, *An Introduction to Parallel Algorithms*, Addison Wesley, 1992.

[5] S. Peng and W.-T. Lo, "A simple optimal parallel algorithm for a core of a tree," *Journal of Parallel and Distributed Computing*, vol. 20, pp. 388-392, 1994.

[6] A. Peng, A. B. Stephens, and Y. Yesha, "Algorithms for a core and k-tree core of a tree," *Journal of Algorithms*, vol. 15, pp. 143-159, 1993.

[7] B.-F. Wang, "Finding a *k*-tree core and a *k*-tree center of a tree network in parallel," manuscript.

[8] B.-F. Wang, W.-K. Shih, and S. Peng, "Efficient algorithms for finding a *k*-tree core of a specified diameter in a tree network," in preparation.

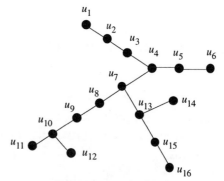

Figure 1. A tree network.

u_i	u_1	u_2	u_3	u_4	u_5	u_6
$size(u_i)$	16	15	14	13	2	1
$MaxSave(u_i)$	65	50	36	23	1	0
$DomiLeaf(u_i)$	u_{11}	u_{11}	u_{11}	u_{11}	u_6	u_6
$DomiEnd(u_i)$	--	--	--	--	--	u_5

u_i	u_7	u_8	u_9	u_{10}	u_{11}
$size(u_i)$	10	5	4	3	1
$MaxSave(u_i)$	13	8	4	1	0
$DomiLeaf(u_i)$	u_{11}	u_{11}	u_{11}	u_{11}	u_{11}
$DomiEnd(u_i)$	--	--	--	--	u_1

u_i	u_{12}	u_{13}	u_{14}	u_{15}	u_{16}
$size(u_i)$	1	4	1	2	1
$MaxSave(u_i)$	0	3	0	1	0
$DomiLeaf(u_i)$	u_{12}	u_{16}	u_{14}	u_{16}	u_{16}
$DomiEnd(u_i)$	u_{12}	--	u_{14}	--	u_{13}

Table 1. $size(u_i)$, $MaxSave(u_i)$, $DomiLeaf(u_i)$, and $DomiEnd(u_i)$.

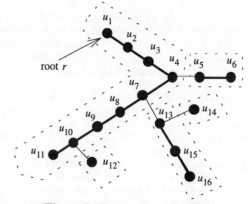

Figure 2. The dominated paths.

u_i	u_6	u_{11}	u_{12}	u_{14}	u_{16}
$R(u_i)$	3	65	1	1	7
$Rank(u_i)$	3	1	5	4	2

Table 2. $R(u_i)$ and $Rank(u_i)$.

Efficient Parallel Algorithms on Distance-Hereditary Graphs (Extended Abstract)

Sun-yuan Hsieh *
Dept. of Computer Science & Info. Eng.
National Taiwan University, Taiwan
e-mail: d3506013@csie.ntu.edu.tw

Chin-Wen Ho
Dept. of Computer Science & Info. Eng.
National Central University, Taiwan
e-mail: hocw@csie.ncu.edu.tw

Tsan-sheng Hsu †
Institute of Information Science
Academia Sinica, Taiwan
e-mail: tshsu@iis.sinica.edu.tw

Ming-Tat Ko
Institute of Information Science
Academia Sinica, Taiwan
e-mail: mtko@iis.sinica.edu.tw

Gen-Huey Chen
Dept. of Computer Science & Info. Eng.
National Taiwan University, Taiwan
e-mail: ghchen@csie.ntu.edu.tw

Abstract

In this paper, we present efficient parallel algorithms for finding a minimum weighted connected dominating set, a minimum weighted Steiner tree for a distance-hereditary graph which take $O(\log n)$ time using $O(n+m)$ processors on a CRCW PRAM, where n and m are the number of vertices and edges of a given graph, respectively. We also find a maximum weighted clique of a distance-hereditary graph in $O(\log^2 n)$ time using $O(n+m)$ processors on a CREW PRAM.

1 Introduction

A graph is *distance-hereditary* if every two vertices have the same distance in every connected induced subgraph containing both (where the *distance* between two vertices is the length of a shortest path connecting them). Properties and optimization problems in distance-hereditary graphs have been extensively studied during the past two decades [2, 7, 8, 9, 11].

A *dominating* set D of a graph $G = (V, E)$ is defined as $D \subseteq V$ such that every vertex in $V \setminus D$ is either in D or is adjacent to some vertex in D. A dominating set D is *connected* if the subgraph induced by D is connected. For a given graph G and a set $K \subseteq V$ (of *terminal vertices*), a *Steiner tree* is a tree which spans all vertices of K. The *connected dominating set problem CD* (respectively, *Steiner tree problem ST*) asks for a minimum cardinality connected dominating set (respectively, Steiner tree). In this paper, we consider the following weighted version of the CD and ST on distance-hereditary graphs. Let $w(v)$ be a non-negative weight associated with each vertex v in

*Supported in part by Institute of Information Science, Academia Sinica, Teipei, Taiwan.

† Supported in part by NSC Grant 86-2213-E-001-012.

G. We want to find a connected dominating set D (respectively, Steiner tree T) such that $\sum_{v \in D} w(v)$ (respectively, $\sum_{v \in T} w(v)$) equals the smallest possible value. We show that the above problems can be solved in $O(\log n)$ time using $O(n + m)$ processors on a CRCW PRAM, where n and m are the number of vertices and edges of a given graph, respectively.

A graph C is a *clique* if there is an edge between every pair of vertices. We say that C is a *clique of G* if C is an induced clique of G. If each vertex is assigned a non-negative weight, a *maximum weighted clique* is a clique of G with the maximum total weight. In this paper, we also compute a maximum weighted clique of a distance-hereditary graph in $O(\log^2 n)$ time using $O(n + m)$ processors on a CREW PRAM.

2 Preliminaries

This paper considers finite, simple loopless, undirected and connected graphs $G = (V, E)$, where V and E are the vertex and edge set of G, respectively. Let $n = |V|$ and $m = |E|$. The *distance* $d_G(x, y)$ or $d(x, y)$ between two vertices x and y in G is the length of a shortest x-y path in G. Let v be a vertex of G. We denote the *neighborhood* of v, consisting of all vertices adjacent to v, by $N(v)$, and the *closed neighborhood* of v, the set $N(v) \cup \{v\}$, by $N[v]$. Let S be a subset of V. We denote $N(S)$ the *open neighborhood of S*, that is the set of vertices in G, exclusive of S, which are adjacent to any vertex in S. We also denote $N[S] = N(S) \cup S$. The *subgraph induced by S*, denoted by $\langle S \rangle$, consists of the vertices of S and edges (x, y) with $x, y \in S$ and $(x, y) \in E$.

The *hanging* of a connected graph $G = (V, E)$ at a vertex $u \in V$, denoted as h_u, is the collection of sets $L_0(u)$, $L_1(u),..., L_t(u)$ (or simply $L_0, L_1,..., L_t$ when no ambiguity arises), where $t = \max_{v \in V} d_G(u,v)$ and $L_i(u) = \{v \in V : d_G(u,v) = i\}$ for $0 \le i \le t$. For any vertex $v \in L_i$ and vertex set $S \subseteq L_i$, $1 \le i \le t$, let $N'(v) = N(v) \cap L_{i-1}$ and let $N'(S) = N(S) \cap L_{i-1}$. Any two vertices $x, y \in L_i$ ($1 \le i \le t-1$) are said to be *tied* if x and y have a common neighbor in L_{i+1}. A *homogeneous set* of a graph G is a set A of vertices such that every vertex in $V(G) - A$ is adjacent to either all or none of the vertices of A.

A graph is a *cograph* (also a P_4-free graph) [5] if it is either a vertex, the complement of a cograph, or the union of two cographs (where by union of two graphs $G_1 = (V_1, E_1)$ and $G_2 = (V_2, E_2)$ we mean the graph $G = (V_1 \cup V_2, E_1 \cup E_2)$). A cograph G has a parse tree representation called *cotree*, denoted by T_G, with (a) the leaves of T_G are the vertices of G; (b) the internal nodes of T_G are labelled 0 or 1; (c) 0 nodes and 1 nodes alternate along every path staring from the root; (d) two vertices x and y of the cograph are adjacent if and only if the least common ancestor of x and y in T_G is a 1 node. In the following, we introduce properties of distance-hereditary graphs.

Proposition 2.1 *[8] Suppose $h_u = (L_0, L_1, ..., L_t)$ is the hanging at u of a connected distance-hereditary graph. If $x, y \in L_i$ ($1 \le i \le t$) are in the same component of $<L_i>$, or x and y are tied, then $N'(x) = N'(y)$.*

Fact 1 *A hanging of a connected distance-hereditary graph can be computed in $O(\log n)$ time using $O(n + m)$ processors on a CRCW PRAM.*

Proof: An implementation is described as follows. (a) We first find an arbitrary spanning tree S for G in $O(\log n)$ time using $O((m + n)\alpha(m,n)/\log n)$ processors on a CRCW PRAM, where α is the inverse Ackermann function [4], and then transform it into a rooted tree with the root u in $O(\log n)$ time using $O(n)$ processors on an EREW PRAM [10]. (b) For each vertex $v (\ne u)$, we associate it with a number $num(v)$ which is the distance from v to u in S (the computation of distances for those non-root vertices can be done in $O(\log n)$ time using $O(n/\log n)$ processors on an EREW PRAM [10]). (c) For each vertex x, let $(x,y) \in E(T)$ if $num(y)$ is the smallest value in $\{num(z)| z \in N(x)\}$. This can be done in $O(\log n)$ time using $O(n + m)$ processors on an EREW PRAM by the sorting algorithm described in [3]. It can be verified that $T = (V, E(T))$ is a quasi-breadth-first-search tree which is a hanging at u. It has been shown that a quasi-breadth-first-search tree is also a breadth first search tree on a distance-hereditary graph [6]. Note that L_i is the set of vertices $x \in T$, such that the unique path from x to u is of length exactly i. **Q.E.D**

Proposition 2.2 *[2] Suppose $h_u = (L_0, L_1, ..., L_t)$ is a hanging of a connected distance-hereditary graph at u. For any two vertices $x, y \in L_i$, $i \ge 1$, $N'(x)$ and $N'(y)$ are either disjoint, or one of the two sets is contained in the other.*

We call a family of subsets *arboreal* if any two elements of the family are either disjoint or comparable (by set inclusion). For example, $\{\{1,2,3\}, \{1,2\}, \{4\}\}$ is an arboreal family of subsets of $\{1,2,3,4\}$. Given an arboreal family of distinct subsets, denoted by $S_1, S_2, ..., S_r$, we can define a partial order $\preceq$ between S_i's by $S_p \preceq S_q \Leftrightarrow S_p \subseteq S_q$,

where $1 \le p, q \le r$. An element S_p is said to be *minimal* in the given family if $S_p \not\supseteq S_q$, for all $q \ne p$ and $1 \le q \le r$.

In [8], Hammer and Maffray defines an equivalence relation $\equiv_i$ between vertices of L_i by $x \equiv_i y$ means x and y are in the same connected component of L_i or x and y are tied. Let $\equiv_a$ be defined on $V(G)$ by $x \equiv_a y$ means $x \equiv_i y$ for some i. They make explicit the structural aspects of distance-hereditary graphs by deriving the following characteristics.

Proposition 2.3 *[8] Let u be a vertex of a connected distance-hereditary graph G and let h_u be the hanging at u of G. Let $R_1, R_2, ..., R_r$ be the equivalence classes of the relation $\equiv_a$. Then, (a) the graph obtained from G by shrinking each R_j into one vertex is a tree rooted at u (for convenience, we call such a tree an equivalence-tree T_{h_u}.); (b) each R_j induces a P_4-free subgraph; (c) for each j, the family $\{N'(R_k) : N'(R_k) \subseteq R_j\}$ is an arboreal family of homogeneous subsets of R_j.*

3 Minimum Weighted Steiner Tree

This section deals with the weighted Steiner tree problem on a distance-hereditary graph with the terminal vertex set K. Given a hanging h_u, where u is an arbitrary vertex of K, let T_{h_u} be the equivalence-tree defined in Proposition 2.3. Note that each node ω in T_{h_u} represents an equivalence class, denoted by R_ω. For each node ν in a rooted tree T, let $T(\nu)$ be the subtree rooted at ν. We present our algorithm below.

Algorithm WCD
Input: A distance-hereditary graph $G = (V, E)$ and a set $K \subset V$ composed of terminal vertices.
Output: A minimum weighted Steiner tree T on K.
Step 1. Let u be an arbitrary vertex in the target set K and let $U = K$. Determine a hanging h_u and construct the equivalence-tree T_{h_u}.
Step 2. For each node ω in T_{h_u}, if all of the following conditions (a) $\bigcup_{\chi \in V(T_{h_u}(\omega))}\{R_\chi \cap K\} \ne \emptyset$, (b) $N'(R_\omega)$ contains no vertex in K, and (c) $N'(R_\omega)$ contains no proper subset $N'(R_\nu)$, such that the node ν in T_{h_u} satisfies that $\bigcup_{\chi \in V(T_{h_u}(\nu))}\{R_\chi \cap K\} \ne \emptyset$; hold, then select a minimum weighted vertex $y \in N'(R_\omega)$ and add it to U.
Step 3. Find a spanning tree T for $<U>$, which is the desired output.

Theorem 3.1 *Algorithm WCD generates a minimum weighted Steiner tree for the distance-hereditary graph in $O(\log n)$ time using $O(n + m)$ processors on a CRCW PRAM.*

Proof: For each vertex $w (\ne u) \in K$, it can be verified that there is a path, connecting w and u, in $<U>$ after Step 2. Thus $<U>$ is a connection of K. We then show that $<U>$ has the minimum weight. Observe that for each node ω in T_{h_u} satisfying conditions (a), (b) and (c) in step 2 of algorithm WCD, a minimum weighted connection of K must contain a vertex of $N'(R_\omega)$. Since the algorithm selects a vertex with the minimum weight from ω, the weight of U is clearly minimum. After executing Step 3, the algorithm finds an arbitrary spanning tree T for $<U>$. By definition, T is a minimum weighted Steiner tree.

We now analyse the time-processor complexities. In Step 1, the implementation of a hanging is described in Fact 1. We note that the computation of T_{h_u} can be done by finding the equivalence classes with respect to h_u. It takes $O(\log n)$ time using $O(n + m)$ processors on a CRCW PRAM. In step 2, associate each vertex v with $tag(v)$ such that $tag(v) = 1$ for $v \in K$ and $tag(v) = 0$ otherwise. Using the above information, the Euler-tour technique [10] can be applied to check the condition (a) which takes $O(\log n)$ time with $O(n/\log n)$ processors on an EREW PRAM. Condition (b) can be checked in $O(\log n)$ time using $O(n/\log n)$ processors on an EREW PRAM by slightly modifying optimal parallel prefix-sum computation [10]. A method to check condition (c) can be done similar to the implementation of the algorithm in Section 3 for finding a connected dominating set. In Step 3, finding a spanning tree can be done in $O(\log n)$ time using $O((m+n)\alpha(m,n)/\log n)$ processors on a CRCW PRAM [4]. **Q.E.D.**

4 Maximum weighted Clique

It is easy to see that any clique of a distance-hereditary graph G belongs to $L_i \cup L_{i+1}$ for some $0 \le i \le t - 1$. Let R denote an equivalence class of G with respect to h_u.

Observation 1 *A maximum weighted clique of a distance-hereditary graph is a maximum weighted clique of some* $< R \cup N'(R) >$.

We call $< R \cup N'(R) >$ a *candidate subgraph of a maximum weighted clique*. For abbreviation, we also call it is a candidate subgraph. Since there are at most n equivalence classes for G, we have the following observation.

Observation 2 *There are $O(n)$ candidate subgraphs for a distance-hereditary graph.*

For two graphs G_1 and G_2, the *join* of G_1 and G_2, denoted by $G_1 \oplus G_2$, is the graph consists of $G_1 \cup G_2$ and all edges joining $V(G_1)$ and $V(G_2)$ [12]. From structure characteristics of G, every candidate subgraph $< R \cup N'(R) > = < R > \oplus < N'(R) >$. If C_1 and C_2 are maximum weighted cliques of R and $N'(R)$ respectively, then $C_1 \oplus C_2$ is a maximum weighted clique of $< R \cup N'(R) >$. By Observation 2 and 1, a maximum weighted clique of G is a clique with the maximum weight among $O(n)$ candidate subgraphs.

It is assured by Proposition 2.3 that $< R >$ and $< N'(R) >$ are cographs. In [1], Abrahamson, et. al. present an algorithm to find a maximum weighted clique of a cograph G: Given a cotree T of G a maximum weighted clique can be found by applying the tree contraction technique to T which takes $O(\log n)$ time using $O(n/\log n)$ processors on an EREW PRAM. Hence, if cotrees T_1 and T_2 for $< R >$ and $< N'(R) >$ are given, a maximum weighted clique of the candidate subgraph $< R \cup N'(R) >$ can be computed by applying the algorithm in [1] to T_1 and T_2. But it is necessary to construct cotrees for each R and $N'(R)$, the above algorithm takes a large number of processors to achieve the desired computation. Here we provide a different way (described latter) which requires fewer processors than the above one.

For any node ν in a tree T, let $leaf(\nu)$ be the leaves of $T(\nu)$ (recall that $T(\nu)$ is the subtree of T rooted at

ν). Let $\mathcal{S}_R = \{S|$ there is an equivalence class R' with $N'(R') = S$ and $S \subseteq R\}$. By the algorithm in [1], given a cotree T all maximum weighted cliques of cographs induced by $leaf(\nu)$, where ν is an internal node of T, can be found simultaneously in $O(\log n)$ time using $O(n/\log n)$ processors on an EREW PRAM (see [1] for details). Based on this result, we concentrate our effort to construct a special cotree T_R for $< R >$ such that for each $S \in \mathcal{S}_R$ there exists a node ν in T_R with $leaf(\nu) = S$ and $T_R(\nu)$ is a cotree of $< S >$. For convenience, we call T_R a *canonical cotree*.

Lemma 4.1 *If a canonical cotree of $< R >$ is given, all maximum weighted cliques of $< S >$, where $S \in \mathcal{S}_R$, can be computed in $O(\log |R|)$ time using $O(|R|/\log |R|)$ processors on an EREW PRAM.*

In the following, we show how to construct the canonical cotree for $< R >$. By Proposition 2.3, $\mathcal{S}_R$ is the arboreal family of homogeneous subsets of R. Let $\mathcal{S}'_R = \mathcal{S}_R \cup \{R\}$. According to the partial order $\preceq$ defined in Section 2, we first construct an auxiliary tree structure A_R as follows. We create $|\mathcal{S}'|$ nodes where each node represents an element (a set) in $\mathcal{S}'_R$. Let S_ν denote the set represented by the node ν in A_R, and $par(\nu)$ (respectively, $child(\nu)$) be the parent (respectively, children) of ν. For any two created nodes α and β, there is a directed edge from α to β if $S_\alpha \preceq S_\beta$ and no other S_γ satisfies $S_\alpha \preceq S_\gamma \preceq S_\beta$.

Lemma 4.2 *The auxiliary tree structure A_R can be constructed in $O(\log p)$ time using $O(p + q)$ processors on an EREW PRAM, where $p = |R|$ and $q = |E(< R >)|$.*

Proof: Suppose $R = \{v_1, v_2, ..., v_p\}$ and $\mathcal{S}_R = \{S_1, S_2, ..., S_r\}$. Let $S_i = N'(R_i)$ where R_i is an equivalence class. For ease of description, we assume the vertices are represented by their indices. So $R = \{1, 2, ..., p\}$. We construct A_R as follows. Let u be any vertex of R_i and $S_i = \{t_1, t_2, ..., t_k\}$, where $t_i \in \{1, 2, ..., p\}$. Note that $N'(u) = S_i$. We assign $|S_i|$ processors to the edges $(u, t_1), (u, t_2),..., (u, t_k)$ for creating tuples $(t_1, i), (t_2, i),..., (t_k, i)$. Thus there are totally $\sum_{i=1}^{r} |S_i|$ created tuples that are stored in an array B.

We first sort those tuples according to their first indices. Then B is divided into p blocks (recall that $|R| = p$) $B_1, B_2, ..., B_p$, where B_i records those tuples $(i, a)'s$ for all a such that $i \in S_a$. We then sort the tuples in each B_i according to the cardinalities of those sets indicated by second indices. Suppose $(i, a_1), (i, a_2), ..., (i, a_k)$ are the sorted elements in B_i and let α_i be the created node representing S_{a_i}. Set $par(\alpha_i) = \alpha_{i+1}$, $1 \le i \le k - 1$ and let $par(\alpha_k)$ be the node representing R.

After executing the above algorithm, A_R can be constructed. The correctness follows directly from the property that if $S_p \preceq S_q$ then: (i) $|S_p| < |S_q|$ and (ii) $x \in S_p$ implies $x \in S_q$. Using the sorting algorithm described in [3], the implementation can be done in $O(\log p)$ time using $O(p + q)$ processors on an EREW PRAM. **Q.E.D**

Lemma 4.3 *A canonical cotree T_R can be generated in $O(\log^2 p)$ time using $O(p + q)$ processors on a CREW PRAM, where $p = |R|$ and $q = |E(< R >)|$.*

Proof: Given the auxiliarly tree structure A_R, we generate a tree T_R in the following way. Let us consider the cograph $< S_\nu >$ for each node $\nu \in A_R$. We first shrink each $< S_\chi >$ in $< S_\nu >$, where $\chi \in child(\nu)$, into a vertex s_χ called *shrinked vertex*. Since S_χ is a homogeneous set of $< S_\nu >$, the resulting graph, denoted by H, is still a cograph. Applying the algorithm in [6] to H, a cotree T_H can be constructed for H in $O(\log^2 p)$ time using $O(p+q)$ processors on a CREW PRAM. Note that each shrinked vertex is a leaf in T_H. There are totally $|\mathcal{S}'_R|$ constructed cotrees. For each leaf of the generated cotrees, if it is a shrinked vertex s_χ, we replace it with the "corresponding" cotree T_χ. It takes a constant time using $O(p)$ processors.

We now show that T_R is the canonical cotree of $< R >$. Clearly, T_R has the following properties: (1) the leaves of T_R are all vertices of R, (2) each internal nodes are either 0 node or 1 node, and (3) if two vertices x and y of $< R >$ are adjacent, the least common ancestor of x and y in T_R is a 1 node (this property can be verified from the fact that $\mathcal{S}_R$ is a family of homogeneous sets of R). Moreover, from the construction of T_R, for each $S \in \mathcal{S}_R$ there exists a node ν in T_R such that $leaf(\nu) = S$. Hence T_R is a canonical cotree of $< R >$. **Q.E.D**

Remark: Note T_R is not the standard form of the cotree since it violates the definition (c) (refer to Section 2.1) that 0 nodes and 1 nodes alternate along every path staring from the root. For an internal node ν of a cotree with children $\mu_1, \mu_2,..., \mu_k$, let $G(\nu)$ be the cograph induced by $leaf(\nu)$ and G_{μ_i} be the cograph induced by $leaf(\mu_i)$. From the definition (d), if ν is a 1 (respectively, 0) node, $G(\nu) = G(\mu_1) \oplus G(\mu_2) \oplus \cdots \oplus G(\mu_k)$ (respectively, $G(\nu) = G(\mu_1) \cup G(\mu_2) \cup \cdots \cup G(\mu_k)$). According to the above observation, the definition (c) can be relaxed (note that this kind of cotree representation is no longer unique).

Theorem 4.4 *The maximum weighted clique problem for distance-hereditary graphs can be solved in $O(\log^2 n)$ time using $O(n+m)$ processors on a CREW PRAM.*

Proof: It takes $O(\log n)$ time using $O(n+m)$ CRCW processors to determine a hanging and compute the equivalence classes by Fact 1 and Lemma 5.2. By Observation 2, we have $O(n)$ candidate subgraphs, i.e., $O(n)$ candidate cliques. According to Lemma 4.3, we compute canonical cotrees for those equivalence classes of G in $O(\log n^2)$ time using $O(n+m)$ processors on a CREW PRAM. By applying the algorithm in [1] to canonical cotrees, $O(n)$ candidate cliques can be found in $O(\log n)$ time using $O(n/\log n)$ processors on an EREW PRAM. Thus we can find the one with the largest totall weight in $O(\log n)$ time using $O(n/\log n)$ processors [10]. **Q.E.D**

5 Minimum Weighted Connected Dominating Set

Given a hanging h_u, let $R_1, R_2,..., R_r$ be those equivalence classes of the relation $\equiv_{l+1}$ (see Proposition 2.3). Let $\mathcal{S} = \{S \subset L_l|$ there exists an R_i with $N'(R_i) = S\}$. For convenience, we call $\mathcal{S}$ the *upper-neighborhood system* of L_{l+1}. By Proposition 2.3, $\mathcal{S}$ is arboreal. So the partial order $\prec$ described in Section 2 can be defined on $\mathcal{S}$. Let $\mathcal{U} = \{\overline{S} \in \mathcal{S}|$ there exists no $S' \in \mathcal{S}, S \not\supseteq S'\}$, i.e., $\mathcal{U}$

is the set composed of those minimal elements of $\preceq$. We call $\mathcal{U}$ the *minimal upper-neighboorhoods* of L_{l+1}. For each $S \in \mathcal{U}$, we select a vertex $x_s \in S$ with the minimum weight. Let $D_l = \{x_s| S \in \mathcal{U}\}$.

Lemma 5.1 *[11] Suppose $G = (V, E)$ is a connected distance-hereditary graph with a non-negative weight function w on vertices. Let u be a vertex of minimum weight and $h_u = (L_0, L_1, ..., L_t)$ be the hanging at u. Then, one of the following three sets of vertices is a minimum weighted connected dominating set of G: (1) $\cup_{l=1}^{t-1} D_l$; (2) $\cup_{l=1}^{t-1} D_l \cup \{u\}$; (3) some vertex of G.*

Lemma 5.2 *Given a hanging h_u, D_l, for all $1 \leq l \leq t-1$, can be computed in $O(\log n)$ time using $O(n+m)$ processors on a CRCW PRAM.*

Proof: We first compute the auxilary tree structure A_R for each $R \subseteq L_l$ (see Lemma 4.2). Let $leaf(A_R)$ denote the leaves of A_R. So $\mathcal{U} = \{S|S \in leaf(A_R), R \subseteq L_l\}$ (recall that $\mathcal{U}$ is the minimal upper-neighborhood of L_{l+1}). Clearly, D_l can be determined from $\mathcal{U}$. **Q.E.D.**

Theorem 5.3 *A minimum weighted connected dominating set for distance-hereditary graphs can be found in $O(\log n)$ time using $O(n+m)$ processors on a CRCW PRAM.*

References

[1] K. Abrahamson, N. Dadoun, D. G. Kirkpatrick, and T. Przytycka, "A simple parallel tree contraction algorithm," *Journal of Algorithms*, vol. 10, no. 2, pp. 287-302, 1989.

[2] H. J. Bandelt and H. M. Mulder, "Distance-hereditary graphs," *Journal of Combinatorial Theory Series B*, vol. 14, no. 1, pp. 182-208, 1986.

[3] R. Cole, "Parallel merge sort," *SIAM Journal on Computing*, vol. 17, no. 4, pp. 770-785, 1988.

[4] R. Cole and R. Thurimella, "Approximate parallel scheduling, II: application to optimal parallel graph algorithms in logrithmic time," *Information and Computation*, vol. 92, no. 1, pp. 1-47, 1991.

[5] D. G. Corneil, H. Lerchs, and L. S. Burlingham, "Complement reducible graphs," *Discrete Applied Mathematics*, vol. 3, pp. 163-174, 1981.

[6] E. Dahlhaus, "Efficient parallel recognition algorithms of cographs and distance-hereditary graphs," *Discrete Applied Mathematics*, vol. 57, pp. 29-44, 1995.

[7] A. D'atri and M. Moscarini, "Distance-hereditary graphs, steiner trees, and connected domination," *SIAM Journal on Computing*, vol. 17, no. 3, pp. 521-538, 1988.

[8] P. L. Hammer and F. Maffray, "Complete separable graphs," *Discrete Applied Mathematices*, vol. 27, pp. 85-99, 1990.

[9] E. Howorka, "A characterization of distance-hereditary graphs," *Quarterly Journal of Mathematics Oxford Series 2*, vol. 28, pp. 417-420, 1977.

[10] J. Ja'Ja', *An Introduction to Parallel Algorithms*, Addison Wesley, 1992.

[11] Hong-Gwa Yeh and Gerard J. Chang, "Weighted connected domination and Steiner trees in distance-hereditary graphs," manuscripts, 1994.

[12] A. A. Zykov, On some properties of linear complexes. *Mathematics Sbornik*, vol. 24, pp. 163-188, 1949.

Session 1B

Network Modeling

_____

Multidimensional Network Performance with Unidirectional Links

James R. Anderson and Seth Abraham
School of Electrical and Computer Engineering
Purdue University
West Lafayette, Indiana 47907
{jranders, abraham}@ecn.purdue.edu

Abstract

A stochastic analysis of multidimensional networks with unidirectional links between nodes is presented, which is more accurate than previous models and valid for the hypercube. The results are reconciled with those of previous researchers who have reported conflicting conclusions. In addition to the classic constraints of constant link width, pin-out, and bisection width, a new constraint, constant maximum throughput, is introduced. This constraint dramatizes the performance and cost trade-offs between different network topologies.

1. Introduction

Among the many interconnection networks that can be used to connect the processors in a parallel computer, the family of multidimensional networks has received a great deal of attention, due to the large number of commercial parallel computer systems in which they are used. Examples of these networks, sometimes called k-ary n-cubes, include the 2 dimensional mesh and the binary hypercube. Several researchers have compared the performance of these machines; however it is not immediately clear how to reconcile their results with each other. This paper undertakes a study of multidimensional networks with unidirectional links and explains why previous results appear to be at odds. It also introduces an improved analysis that yields a simple closed form solution that is more accurate than previous studies.

A good summary of current interconnect strategies for parallel computers appears in the 1996 ICPP workshop [1]. A one dimensional mesh with radix k is the familiar ring. In two dimensions, there are k^2 nodes, and each node belongs to two rings, one in each dimension. In general, an n dimensional mesh with radix k has $N=k^n$

nodes. These networks can be routed using dimension order routing, in which a message is routed along the ring in the highest dimension until its destination address matches the current node address in that dimension. For the hypercube, the routing is equivalent to the familiar "bit correction" algorithm [11].

One of the earliest comparisons of multidimensional networks examines static network measures such as node degree, network diameter, and average routing distance [13]. Dally was the first to quantify the implementation costs of different multidimensional networks and compare their performance under a constant cost constraint [6]. He chose to equate costs by holding the network bisection width constant. (Network bisection width is related to the VLSI area required for laying out the network [12].) His work uses unidirectional networks, and concludes that low dimensional networks provide the most cost effective interconnection.

Abraham and Padmanabhan [3] observed that wiring constraints may not always be applicable, since many wiring schemes are not bounded by VLSI-like constraints. They introduced a pin-out constraint and applied a more sophisticated analysis. Their analysis applies to bidirectional networks and also confirms Dally's result that low dimensional structures are best when the constant bisection width constraint is used. However, when a constant pin-out constraint is considered, higher dimensional networks provide better performance. The analysis does not consider wiring delays that might inflict an additional penalty on higher dimensional networks.

Agarwal [4] also used a pin-out constraint (which he terms constant node size). He analyzed networks under constant bisection, constant pin-out, and constant link width. (The latter reduces to unconstrained analysis.) He obtains results similar to Dally's, although he favors networks of higher dimensionality than Dally. However, his analysis in the presence of message contention contains approximations that in some cases underestimate and in

26

other cases overestimate performance. In a comparison study, such approximations have potential pitfalls. We will discuss Agarwal's analysis in more detail later.

Scott and Goodman [10] consider the effects of pipelining the messages on the communication links. This technique reduces the effects of long wire delays and decouples throughput and latency issues. They also examine the time required for switching a message compared to the time required to transmit the message over the link. The majority of their analytical analysis is for a non-contention model, although they do provide extensive network simulations for contention situations.

In view of the variety of conclusions that have been reached about multidimensional networks, a more accurate analysis is needed. In section 2, we begin our analysis by developing a simple closed form expression for queue waiting time. When our analysis departs from Agarwal's, we explain what approximations have been removed. Section 3 examines the maximum traffic load handled by a network before the links saturate and explains why the hypercube must be handled slightly differently. Section 4 presents equations for the latency of the system when message length exceeds the width of network links and messages must be broken into flits. When we select appropriate parameters, our performance expression matches the extensive simulations of [10]. Section 5 presents performance results under the constant pin-out and bisection width constraints for various network topologies. A new constraint, constant maximum throughput, is also introduced, which dramatizes the difference between network topologies and clearly illustrates the performance and cost trade-offs between high and low dimensional networks. Section 6 concludes the work.

2. Unidirectional queue waiting time

Our derivation of the average waiting time for a message received at the queue of an output link is based on the analysis of Kruskal and Snir [9] for buffered indirect networks. Similar to the model used by Kruskal and Snir, our model assumes an infinite buffer at each output link and a uniform traffic distribution. Infinite queues are a well known approximation for finite length queues, since, typically, a queue length of 2 or 4 is sufficiently large to approximate infinity [7]. Also, we assume the output queues can accept messages from multiple input links during a single cycle. In addition, a multiple-accepting PE scheme is assumed, in which multiple messages (up to the number of input links) may be accepted by the PE in a single cycle [2].

The average waiting time, w, of a message packet in an output queue can be found from the expectation, $E[A]$, and variance, $V[A]$, of the arrival process A. As in [9],

$$w = \frac{V[A]}{2E[A](1 - E[A])} - \frac{1}{2}. \qquad (2.1)$$

In the following sections, we will derive $E[A]$ and $V[A]$ using the conditional routing probabilities of the switch and the probability that a message is generated by a PE during a clock cycle. Within any switch of the network, a message can be routed from the PE to itself or any of the n output links, or it can be routed from any of the n input links to the PE or any output link of equal or lower dimension.

To model a network with uniform traffic distribution, assume that every node in the network sends a single message to every other node in the network, including itself. Thus, the PE at each node transmits and receives k^n messages. From this assumption the number of messages routed through a single switch can be derived.

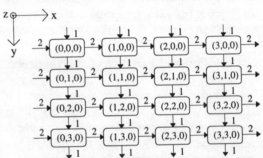

Fig. 2.1. Bottom layer (z=0) of k=4, n=3 network.

Consider the example shown in Figure 2.1, which shows the bottom layer of a three dimensional network with end-around connections. Each node is identified with three coordinates that describe its position in the network. The numbers next to the links are the input/output link numbers of the nodes. Recall that dimension order routing means the messages are routed from highest dimension to lowest dimension. For example, if the PE at node (2,1,0) sends a message to the PE at (0,2,1), the message will travel the following path: (2,1,0) → (3,1,0) → (0,1,0) → (0,2,0) → (0,2,1).

We choose the switch at node (0,0,0) to be analyzed (any node can be chosen since the network is symmetrical). Clearly, the number of messages routed from the PE to itself within any node is one. Now, consider the messages routed from the PE at node (0,0,0) to each of the output links. These are the messages that are generated at node (0,0,0) and sent to another node in the network. In general, the number of messages routed from the PE to output link j, $0 \le j < n$, is $k^j(k-1)$. Conditional routing probabilities can be derived by dividing the number of messages routed from source to destination by the total number of messages routed from the source. Since the total number of messages from the PE is k^n, we have,

$$P_{pe,pe} = k^{-n} \quad (2.2)$$

$$P_{pe,j} = k^{j-n}(k-1) \quad (2.3)$$

The subscripts in the above equations refer to the source and destination within the switch. For example $P_{pe,j}$ is the probability that a message sent from the PE is routed to output link j. The other conditional routing probabilities can be derived in a similar manner (details are available in [5]), and are given by,

$$P_{i,pe} = 2k^{-i-1} \quad (2.4)$$

$$P_{i,j} = \begin{cases} (k-2)/k, & \text{if } i = j \\ 2k^{j-i-1}(k-1), & \text{if } i > j \end{cases} \quad (2.5)$$

The subscript i is the input link number, where $0 \le i < n$. Of course, $P_{i,j} = 0$ if $i < j$, since a message arriving at an input link routes to an output link of equal or lower dimension.

2.1. Expectation and variance of arrival process

We now derive the expectation and variance of the arrival process. Two key observations are that the arrival of messages on the links of the network is a series of independent Bernoulli trials and that the different network links are independent of one another.

Define the message arrival probabilities as shown in Figure 2.2, where m_g is the probability a message is generated at the PE of the switch.

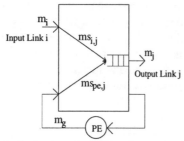

Fig. 2.2. Arrival probabilities for a single node.

The probability of a message arriving on one of the internal switch links that feed the output queue of an output link depends on both the probability that a message arrives at one of the message sources (an input link or the PE) and the probability that the message is routed to the queue of an output link. Specifically, $ms_{i,j} = P_{i,j} m_i$ and

$ms_{pe,j} = P_{pe,j} m_g$. Now, if A_j is the arrival process at the queue of output link j, $E[A_j]$ is given by,

$$E[A_j] = ms_{pe,j} + \sum_{i=j}^{n-1} ms_{i,j} = P_{pe,j} m_g + \sum_{i=j}^{n-1} P_{i,j} m_i \quad (2.6)$$

By the conservation of messages, $E[A_j]$ must also be the same as the expected number of departures from output link j. Since output link j is the same as input link j of the adjacent node, $E[A_j] = m_j$. The above recurrence can be solved to find $m_j = m_g(k-1)/2$. Since this does not depend on j, we drop the subscript for m.

To derive the variance of the arrival process, we recall that for a Bernoulli trial of probability p, the variance is $p(1-p)$. In addition, for independent random variables, the variance of the sum of the random variables is the sum of the variance of each random variable. Thus,

$$V[A_j] = P_{pe,j} m_g \left(1 - P_{pe,j} m_g\right) + \sum_{i=j}^{n-1} P_{i,j} m \left(1 - P_{i,j} m\right)$$

$$= m_g \left(\frac{k-1}{2}\right) - \frac{m_g^2}{4k} \frac{(k-1)^2}{(k+1)} \left[8k^{2(j-n)+1} + k^2 - 3k + 4\right] \quad (2.7)$$

Although the expectation of the arrival process is the same for each output queue, the variance of the arrival process is different for different output queues within the switch. It is interesting to note that the highest-dimension output queue ($n-1$) has the lowest variance, while the lowest-dimension output queue (0) has the highest variance. Intuitively this is expected, since a lower-dimension output link can receive messages from more input links than a higher-dimension output link. The difference between the variance at the highest-dimension output link and the lowest-dimension output link decreases as the radix, k, increases.

2.2. Average waiting time

Now that the expectation and variance of the arrival process at output queue j have been determined, we can use (2.1) to determine the average waiting time of a message in the output queue, w_j. In following sections we will analyze the expected latency for a message routed from randomly chosen source and destination nodes. The crux of the analysis will be based on the average queue waiting time incurred by a message at each of the nodes through which it passes. Since source and destination nodes for a message are chosen using a uniform random distribution, a message passing through a particular node is equally likely to incur a delay at any of the n output queues. Thus, the queue waiting time for a particular node can be averaged across the n output queues to obtain

28

the average time that a message will spend in the output queue of a node. After dropping negligible terms,

$$\overline{w} = \frac{2m_g\left[k^3 - k^2 - k + 1 - \dfrac{2k}{n}\right]}{k(k+1)^2\left(2 - m_g(k-1)\right)}.$$ (2.8)

Thus, we have a relatively simple closed form equation with which to model the output queue delay as the network configuration changes.

2.3. Comparison to previous model

As mentioned in section 1, the only closed form analytical model that exists for the average queue waiting time in a direct-connected network using dimension order routing, other than the model presented in this paper, is the model proposed by Agarwal in [4]. Agarwal's model uses the same expectation of the arrival process as our model, but estimates the variance by assuming that a message can arrive at an output queue from an input link of the same dimension or the next-highest dimension (in terms of Agarwal's switch definition, it is the next-lowest dimension). Using this assumption, an intuitive argument is used to derive the variance of the arrival process. However, the assumption leads to inaccuracies in the average queue waiting time.

In the case of low-dimensional networks, such as $n=2$, Agarwal's assumption leads to an over-estimation of the wait, because there are only two output queues and both are assumed to receive messages from two input links. However, the highest-dimension output queue can only receive messages from an input link of the same dimension. Thus, Agarwal's model over-estimates the variance of the highest-dimension output queue, causing the average waiting time to be significantly over-estimated. For example, when $n=2$, $k=8$, and the traffic load is 75% of maximum, Agarwal's model predicts a queue waiting time that is 60% greater than that predicted by our model.

In the case of high-dimensional networks, such as $n=6$, the four lowest-dimension output queues receive messages from more than two input links. As a result, Agarwal's assumption causes an under-estimation of the variance at these four output queues, which results in an under-estimation of the average waiting time. For example, when $n=6$, $k=4$, and the traffic load is 75% of maximum, Agarwal's model predicts a queue waiting time that is 11% lower than that predicted by our model.

Also, Agarwal's model is not valid for the unidirectional hypercube case ($k=2$), as it predicts a negative queue waiting time. However, the hypercube is an impor-

tant alternative to consider when designing a network, and our model is valid for the hypercube structure.

3. Network saturation

A network saturates when the average waiting time for a message in the output queue of a node approaches infinity. The average waiting time approaches infinity when m approaches unity, or the term $(2-m_g(k-1))$ approaches zero. Thus, the message generation rate at which the network saturates is given by, $m_{g,sat}=2/(k-1)$. As a result, we find that $m_{g,sat}$ only depends on the network radix and is independent of network dimension. Consequently, the choice of network radix determines the maximum offered load that a network can satisfy.

When $k=2$ (hypercube) and m_g is at a maximum of unity (the maximum is unity because it is a probability), the network links are only 50% utilized ($m=0.5$). In order to fully utilize the network links, more than one message must be introduced into the network during each network cycle. Due to space limitations, the analysis of this situation cannot be presented. Details are available in [5].

We first redefine m_g to be a message generation *rate*. With this definition, it can be shown that the equation for average queue waiting time must be corrected by adding,

$$\overline{w_{cf}} = \frac{4\left(m_g - 1\right)\left(1 - 4^{-n}\right)}{3n \cdot m_g\left(2 - m_g\right)}.$$ (3.1)

This corrective factor is only necessary for the hypercube network when $1 < m_g \leq 2$.

It can also be shown that $m_{g,sat}=2/(k-1)=2$ for the hypercube. Thus, the hypercube network saturates at a message generation rate of 2. All other networks with greater radix (considering only even radices) saturate at message generation rates of unity or less. Thus, the hypercube saturation point is much higher than that of other network configurations, which allows the hypercube to move much more data during each clock cycle than networks with a higher radix.

4. Message latency

Under basic message switching, an output buffer fully receives a message before transmitting the message to the next node. Using the results for average queue waiting time derived in section 2, the average latency for a message to be transmitted between two nodes in a message switching network can be derived. Our derivation relies heavily on the results presented by Abraham and Padmanabhan for virtual cut-through switching [3].

For an n-dimensional unidirectional network with end-around connections, a message must take an average of $(k-1)/2$ hops in each of the n dimensions. Thus, the average number of hops is given by, $h=n(k-1)/2$.

If the length of a message is L bits and each network link is W bits wide, and if $L>W$, the message must be split into t_m flits, where $t_m=\lceil L/W \rceil$. When we consider messages of more than one flit, the saturation point of the network must be scaled, such that $m_{g,sat}=2/[(k-1)t_m]$.

At a switch, the header must be decoded before the message can be switched to the appropriate output queue. Since the destination address of the message is sufficient for dimension order routing, the message header need only be $\log_2 N$ bits long. Thus, the number of flits in the header is $t_h=\lceil (\log_2 N)/W \rceil$.

Virtual cut-through, described in [8], occurs if the output link is free and the message is allowed to bypass the entire output buffer (full cut-through) or any portion of the output buffer (partial cut-through). Wormhole routing, which is also commonly used in message switching, is a special case of an unbuffered virtual cut-through system in which blocked messages are held in place rather than being dropped [6].

For a unidirectional network, the probability of zero arrivals at output queue j, called $a_{0,j}$, and the probability of only one arrival at output queue j, called $a_{1,j}$, is,

$$a_{0,j} = \left(1-P_{pe,j}m_g\right)\prod_{i=j}^{n-1}\left(1-P_{i,j}m\right)$$

(4.1)

$$a_{1,j} = a_{0,j}\left[\frac{P_{pe,j}m_g}{1-P_{pe,j}m_g}+\sum_{i=j}^{n-1}\frac{P_{i,j}m}{1-P_{i,j}m}\right]$$

(4.2)

In the case of the hypercube, when $1<m_g\le 2$, these equations must be adjusted slightly (details available in [5]).

Using the analysis in [3], the cycles that are saved by using virtual cut-through switching can be written,

$$cut_j = \frac{t_m m}{1-a_{0,j}}\left[1-m\left(a_{0,j}+a_{1,j}\right)\right]+\frac{(t_m+1)m}{2a_{0,j}}\left(1-m\cdot a_{0,j}\right)$$

(4.3)

Similar to the method we used to find the average queue waiting time for a message flit at a particular node, the cut cycles saved at a particular node can be averaged across the n output queues to obtain the average cut cycles that a message saves at the output queue of a node.

Using the average queue waiting time from section 2, the average time a message packet spends in the output queue and server is shown in [9] to be one cycle longer than the waiting time. Applying the previous results, the average message latency in a unidirectional network with dimension order routing and virtual cut-through is,

$$T = \left[\left(\overline{w}+1\right)h+1\right]t_m +(h+1)t_h -\overline{cut}\cdot h$$

(4.4)

Note that since we are dealing with flits rather than whole messages, we must substitute $t_m\cdot m_g$ in place of m_g in the average queue waiting time given by (2.8).

Equation (4.4) assumes that a single clock cycle is required to transfer a message flit across the switch-to-switch links and also to move the flit across the switch from input buffer to output buffer. However, for networks of different dimensionality, clock cycle times may be different, since as dimensionality increases, both switch size and wire length between nodes increases. In order to compare networks of different dimensionality, we must normalize the clock cycle times.

In a synchronous network, the clock cycle time is physically limited to either the time it requires to transmit a message flit from one node across the switch-to-switch links to the next node (wire delay), or the time to move a flit across the switch from input buffer to output buffer (switch delay).

Switch size (number of input and output links) increases linearly with an increase in network dimension, and switch delay may increase with switch size due to the additional logic complexity. However, we assume that the increase in delay due to additional logic for a reasonable range of dimensions is not significant, and the switch delay is constant for different network dimensions.

Wire delay is proportional to the wire length, which is dependent on the layout and configuration of the network. As network dimensionality increases, the length of the longest wire in the network also increases. Define scaling factor, wf, as the factor by which the clock cycle time grows as the longest wire (or maximum wire delay) grows with increased network dimensionality. Also, let S be the ratio of switch delay to wire delay in a three dimensional network. Using the same scaling factor used in [10] for nonpipelined-channel networks, the wire factor for a three-dimensional implementation is given by,

$$wf = \begin{cases} 1+N^{1/3}/(k\cdot S) \text{ , if } k>2 \\ 1+N^{1/3}/(4\cdot S) \text{ , if } k=2 \end{cases}$$

(4.5)

To allow networks of different dimensions to be equitably compared, the latency found using (4.4) must be multiplied by the wire factor of (4.5) to normalize the clock cycle times of different networks. If the switch delay dominates and $S\gg 1$, then $wf\approx 1$ and dimensionality has little effect on the wire factor. However, if the wire delay determines the physical limit on the clock cycle time, the wire factor penalizes higher dimension networks for the increased wire length that is required for three dimensional implementation.

5. Performance comparisons

As mentioned in the introduction, the three constraints that have been commonly identified in the literature are constant link width, constant pin-out, and constant bisection width. Each constraint is motivated by a different design concern that may arise as a network is implemented.

The constant link width constraint means that the link width, W, between nodes is held constant as the dimension and radix of the network is changed. Constant pin-out means that the number of input and output wires at a node is held constant as dimension and radix of the network is changed [3][4]. This constraint is motivated by a limitation that may exist on the number of pins from a chip or board used in the network. For unidirectional networks, each node has n input and n output links. Thus, pin-out is related to network dimension and link width by the equation, $pins=2 \cdot n \cdot W$. Constant bisection width means that the network is divided into two halves at the point which the largest number of wires crosses the bisection plane [6]. The constraint is a way of holding wiring complexity fixed. For a unidirectional network with end-around connections, the number of wires crossing the bisection is $bis=2 \cdot W \cdot k^{n-1}$.

In addition to these three classic constraints, we introduce a new constraint, constant maximum throughput. The maximum throughput of a network is directly dependent on the maximum rate at which the processing element at each node can release messages into the network before the network saturates and the average message latency approaches infinity. Thus, under the maximum throughput constraint, $m_{g,sat}$ is held constant while the network dimensionality is changed. This constraint allows the performance of networks of different dimensionality to be compared when all network configurations saturate at the same message generation rate. In each of the other three constraints, the saturation point, or maximum throughput, of each network configuration is different, obscuring the true relative performance capabilities of different dimension networks.

Using different constraints, the performance of five different configurations of a unidirectional network of 4096 nodes is examined in the following sections. The average message latency for virtual cut-through switching, given by (4.4), (multiplied by the wire factor) is shown as the message generation rate is increased. The performance of the networks is presented with $S=1$, representing the situation in which wire delay is equivalent to switch delay in a three dimensional network but becomes dominant as network dimensionality is increased.

Under all constraints, the message length is taken to be 268 bits (256 data bits and 12 address bits).

Message length can impact the relative performance of different network configurations in some situations. However, due to space limitations, we limit our analysis to a practical message length (268 bits). Also, we do not present results for the constant link width constraint.

5.1. Constant pin-out constraint

Table 5.1 lists the five configurations for a 4096-node unidirectional network under a constant pin-out constraint of $pins=192$. Figure 5.1 shows the average message latency for the systems in Table 5.1, with each curve in the figure labeled with the network dimension.

Table 5.1. Network configurations for Fig. 5.1.

n	k	W	$pins$	bis	$m_{g,sat}$
2	64	48	192	6144	0.0053
3	16	32	192	16384	0.0148
4	8	24	192	24576	0.0238
6	4	16	192	32768	0.0392
12	2	8	192	32768	0.0588

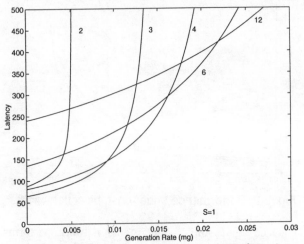

Fig. 5.1. Performance under constant pin-out.

The 3 dimensional network has the lowest latency for low values of m_g, although the 2 and 4 dimensional networks offer comparable performance. However, as the message generation rate increases, the 6 and 12 dimensional networks quickly provide better performance as the networks of higher radix (lower dimension) saturate. Thus, as the traffic load increases, low dimensional networks saturate while higher dimensional networks can still accommodate the traffic.

Scott and Goodman [10] conducted simulations of the same set of systems described in Table 5.1 for non-pipelined networks. They also found that 3 dimensional networks perform best under light traffic loads. Their results are qualitatively very similar to those of Figure 5.1.

5.2. Constant bisection width constraint

Table 5.2 shows the same set of networks under a constant bisection width constraint of bis=16384. Figure 5.2 shows the average message latency as the message generation rate is increased for each of the networks.

Table 5.2. Network configurations for Fig. 5.2.

n	k	W	$pins$	bis	$m_{g,sat}$
2	64	128	512	16384	0.0106
3	16	32	192	16384	0.0148
4	8	16	128	16384	0.0168
6	4	8	96	16384	0.0196
12	2	4	96	16384	0.0299

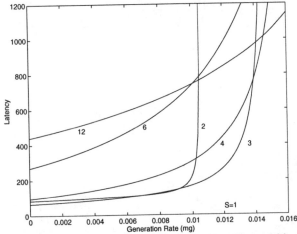

Fig. 5.2. Performance under cnst. bisection width.

Once again, the 3 dimensional network performs best until it reaches saturation, at which point the hypercube (n=12) offers better performance. Also, the results shown in Figure 5.2 are qualitatively the same as the simulation results under constant bisection width in [10] for nonpipelined networks. In addition, the 3 dimensional network was also found in [10], via simulation, to be superior for low traffic loads.

The superior performance of the 3 dimensional network for both constraints can be explained by our use of the wire factor, in the calculation of average message latency. Recall that the wire factor assumes the network is implemented in three physical dimensions. Our result of superior 3 dimensional performance is consistent with

Dally's conclusion that the dimensionality of a network should be the same as the number of physical dimensions used to implement the network [6].

However, Dally did not take into account message contention as the traffic load in a network increases, and his conclusion is only valid if the message generation rate is low enough for the effects of message contention to be negligible. Our analytical results and the simulation results of [10] both show that the 3 dimensional network only offers superior performance at relatively low traffic levels. In order to compare the performance of networks of different dimension on a more equitable basis, we must apply the constant maximum throughput constraint, which assures that all network configurations are able to service the same traffic loads before saturating.

5.3. Constant maximum throughput constraint

Table 5.3 shows the five configurations of a 4096-node network under a constant maximum throughput constraint of $m_{g,sat} \cong 0.015$ ($m_{g,sat}$ is directly proportional to maximum throughput). Thus, each curve in Figure 5.3 has the same asymptotic saturation point. Due to the ceiling operation involved in the calculation of t_m, the value of $m_{g,sat}$ can only be approximately set to 0.015 for different network configurations.

The curves in Figure 5.3 represent the performance of different network dimensions when the minimum link width is chosen such that the different configurations can handle the same range of traffic loads. The 3 dimensional network is once again superior at lower traffic levels, confirming Dally's conclusion when contention is not a factor. In striking contrast to the results using other constraints, for the constant maximum throughput constraint, the lowest dimensional network (n=2) offers the best performance at high traffic levels. However, in order to achieve the same saturation point for all network configurations, a tremendous amount of hardware must be used for the low dimensional network compared to the high dimensional network. For example, moving from a 12 dimensional configuration to a 2 dimensional configuration requires an increase in link widths by a factor of 67, an increase in pins by a factor of 11, and an increase in bisection width by a factor of 2.

The hypercube (n=12) has latencies of at least ten times that of the 2 dimensional network (at low m_g). In addition, the lower-dimensional networks offer a "flatter" performance curve, which means message latencies do not experience a significant increase until the traffic load is close to saturation. However, increasing the hypercube link width to W=4 brings the performance much closer to that of the lower dimensional networks.

The constant maximum throughput constraint provides a network designer with a more effective method for choosing a network configuration. With knowledge of the maximum and typical traffic load offered to the network, a designer can use performance curves similar to those of Figure 5.3 to quickly determine the network configurations which meet the required performance level. Then, based on the link width, pin-out, and bisection width, the most cost-effective network implementation given the current technology can be determined.

Table 5.3. Network configurations for Fig. 5.3.

n	k	W	$pins$	bis	$m_{g,sat}$
2	64	134	536	17152	0.0159
3	16	30	180	15360	0.0148
4	8	14	112	14336	0.0143
6	4	6	72	12288	0.0148
12	2	2	48	8192	0.0149

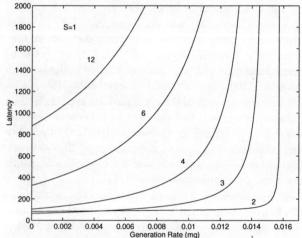

Fig. 5.3. Performance under cnst. max throughput.

6. Conclusion

We have presented a more accurate closed form expression for average queue waiting time in a multidimensional mesh. Our analysis does not rely on the approximations present in the analysis of [4], is valid for the hypercube network, and is inherently contention-based. In addition, the results of our analysis qualitatively match the simulation results presented in [10].

We demonstrated that performance is highly dependent on offered load. To emphasize this point, we introduced the constant maximum throughput constraint, which compares networks on the basis of an equal ability to handle a range of traffic load. This constraint is fundamentally different than previous constraints, which are

based on some characterization of hardware implementation costs. Results under the new constraint clearly show that a low dimensional network, while offering the lowest message latency, must be significantly more expensive than a comparable high dimensional network and in some cases may be impractical to implement. A parallel system designer must carefully consider not only implementation issues, such as switch and wiring complexity, but also the maximum and typical traffic load that will be offered to the network before selecting a suitable network topology.

References

[1] S. Abraham, C. Stunkel, W. Hsu, P. Yew, and L. Ni, "Interconnection networks," in *Proceedings of the 1996 ICPP Workshop on Challenges for Parallel Processing*, Bloomingdale, IL, Aug. 1996, pp. 44-83.

[2] S. Abraham and K. Padmanabhan, "Performance of the direct binary *n*-cube network for multiprocessors," *IEEE Trans. Comput.*, vol. 38, no. 7, pp. 1000-1011, July 1989.

[3] S. Abraham and K. Padmanabhan, "Performance of multicomputer networks under pin-out constraints," *J. Parallel and Distributed Computing*, vol. 12, pp. 237-248, July 1991.

[4] A. Agarwal, "Limits on interconnection network performance," *IEEE Trans. Parallel and Distributed Systems*, vol. 2, no. 4, pp. 398-412, Oct. 1991.

[5] J. Anderson, "Multidimensional Network Performance," MS Thesis, Purdue University, West Lafayette, IN, 1997.

[6] W.J. Dally, "Performance analysis of *k*-ary *n*-cube interconnection networks," *IEEE Trans. Comput.*, vol. 36, no. 5, pp. 775-785, June 1990.

[7] D. Dias and J. Jump, "Packet switching interconnection networks for modular systems," *Computer*, vol. 14, no. 12, pp. 43-53, Dec. 1981.

[8] P. Kermani and L. Kleinrock, "Virtual cut-through: A new computer communication switching technique," *Computer Networks*, vol. 3, pp. 267-286, 1979.

[9] C.P. Kruskal and M. Snir, "The performance of multistage interconnection networks for multiprocessors," *IEEE Trans. Comput.*, vol. C-32, no. 12, pp. 1091-1098, Dec. 1983.

[10] S.L. Scott and J.R. Goodman, "The impact of pipelined channels on *k*-ary *n*-cube networks," *IEEE Trans. Parallel and Distributed Systems*, vol. 5, no. 1, pp. 2-16, Jan. 1994.

[11] H. Sullivan and T. R. Bashkow, "A large scale, homogeneous, fully distributed parallel machine, I," in *International Symposium on Computer Architecture*, 1977, pp. 105-117.

[12] C.D. Thompson, "Area-time complexity for VLSI," in *Annual Symposium on Theory of Computing*, May 1979, pp. 81-88.

[13] L.D. Wittie, "Communication structures for large networks of microcomputers," *IEEE Trans. Comput.*, vol. C-30, no. 4, pp. 264-273, Apr. 1981.

Network Performance under Physical Constraints

Fabrizio Petrini and Marco Vanneschi
Dipartimento di Informatica, Università di Pisa
Corso Italia 40, 56125 Pisa, Italy
tel +39 50 887228, fax +39 50 887226
e-mail: {petrini,vannesch}@di.unipi.it

Abstract

The performance of an interconnection network in a massively parallel architecture is subject to physical constraints whose impact needs to be re-evaluated from time to time. Fat-trees,and low dimensional cubes have raised a great interest in the scientific community in the last few years and are emerging standards in the design of interconnection networks for massively parallel computers.

In this paper we compare the communication performance of these two classes of interconnection networks using a detailed simulation model. The comparison is made using a set of synthetic benchmarks, taking into account physical constraints, as pin and bandwidth limitations, and the router complexity. In our experiments we consider two networks with 256 nodes, a 16-ary 2-cube and 4-ary 4-tree.

1 Introduction

Fat-trees and low-dimensional cubes are emerging standards in the design of interconnection networks for parallel machines.

Fat-trees have been adopted by many research prototypes and commercial machines [1]. The data network of the Connection Machine CM-5 uses two distinct fat-trees [2] and is composed of routing chips that have either two or four parent connections. The Data Diffusion Machine (DDM) is a virtual shared memory architecture that implements a hierarchical COMA cache coherence protocol in the internal switches of a fat-tree [3]. The communication chip Elite is the basic building block of the Meiko CS-2 network [4]. This network takes the form of a quaternary fat-tree. Its design is based on a multistage network and has the property that the overall communication bandwidth remains constant at each level. Other references to fat-trees include [5] [6]. Unfortunately, not much is known on the communication performance of the fat-trees. Most of the literature deals with the CM-5 and focuses on raw network performance [7] [8] [9].

Thanks to their simplicity and expandability, low-dimensional cubes have been adopted as interconnection networks by many massively parallel machines. In the Stanford Dash there are two distinct cubes that support the cache coherence mechanisms [10]: one is dedicated to the requests and the other to the replies, in order to avoid deadlocks caused by the coherency protocols. Other important academic prototypes that use low-dimensional cubes are Alewife [11] and the J-machine [12]. This list also includes many of the most popular commercial machines. The Cray T3D [13] and T3E [14] use a three-dimensional cube [13] and the topology of both the Intel Delta and Paragon is a bi-dimensional cube [15].

A fair comparison of the communication performance of these machines is not an easy task because they all have different technological characteristics. On the other hand, theoretical models of the interconnection network often prove overly simplistic and are not able to capture important performance aspects [16] [17].

In this paper we try to face this problem with a detailed simulation model using a set of synthetic benchmarks representative of shared memory computation and common parallel algorithms. Our experiments are conducted on a quaternary fat-tree and a bi-dimensional cube, whose communication performance is properly equalized taking into account physical limitations as the router complexity, wire delay and density [18]. This paper is an attempt to compare apples with apples: with our simulation model we try to eliminate all implementation dependent details and to compare the essential features of the two interconnection networks.

The remainder of this paper is organized as follows. Sections 2 and 3 overview the two families of interconnection networks, the k-ary n-trees and the k-ary n-cubes. Section 4 describes the relevant details of the simulation model and Section 5 presents the methodology that we use to normalize the physical characteristics of the two interconnection networks in order to make a fair comparison. Sections 6 and 7 introduce the main characteristics of the experimental results and the

34

traffic patterns used as benchmarks. The performance of a quaternary fat-tree and a bi-dimensional cube, both with 256 nodes, are displayed separately in Sections 8 and 9 and compared in Section 10. An overview of the experimental results and some concluding remarks are given in Section 11.

2 k-ary n-trees

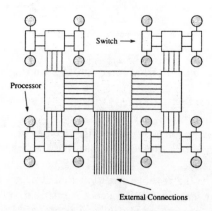

Figure 1: The structure of a fat-tree. Processors are located at the leaves, while internal nodes contain switches. At the root there are some external connections available to recursively build a bigger network or to interface it to the external world.

The fat-tree is an indirect interconnection network based on a complete binary tree. Unlike traditional trees in computer science, fat-trees resemble real trees, because they get thicker near the root. A set of processors is located at the leaves of the fat-tree and each edge of the underlying tree corresponds to a bi-directional channel between parent and child.

The arity of the internal switches of the fat-tree increases as we go closer to the root: this makes the physical implementation of these switches unfeasible. For this reason some alternative constructions have been proposed that use building blocks with fixed-arity [19]. These solutions trade connectivity with simplicity: incoming messages at a given switch in a "full" fat-tree may have more choices in the routing decision than in a corresponding network with fixed-arity switches.

k-ary n-trees [20] are a particular subclass of the fat-trees and borrow from the k-ary n-butterflies [21] the topology of the internal switches. A k-ary n-tree has k^n leaf nodes and n levels of k^{n-1} switches. Each switch has $2k$ links. A 4-ary 2-tree is shown in Figure 2

Minimal adaptive routing between a pair nodes on a k-ary n-tree can be easily accomplished sending the packet to one of the common roots or *nearest common*

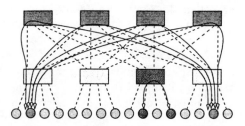

Figure 2: A 4-ary 2-tree. A packet can follow any minimal path passing through a nearest common ancestor of source and destination.

ancestors (NCA) of source and destination and from there to the destination. That is, each packet experiences two phases, an *ascending* adaptive phase to get to one of the NCA, followed by a *descending* deterministic phase. The performance of a wormhole network can be enhanced mapping two or more virtual channels on each physical channel [22]. In our experiments we will examine three variants of the adaptive algorithm, with one, two and four virtual channels. They simply pick the less loaded link in the ascending and descending phases, that is the link that has the maximum number of free virtual channels (a fair choice is made when more links are in a similar state).

3 k-ary n-cubes

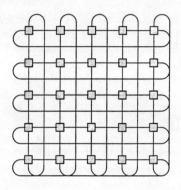

Figure 3: A 5-ary 2-cube.

A k-ary n-cube is characterized by its dimension n and radix k, and has a total of k^n nodes. The k^n nodes are organized in an n-dimensional grid, with k nodes in each dimension and wrap-around connections. The binary hypercube is a special case of k-ary n-cube with $k = 2$. Also, the two-dimensional torus is another special case with $n = 2$. Figure 3 shows an example of k-ary n-cube.

Routing algorithms on the k-ary n-cubes are deadlock-prone and require sophisticated strategies for deadlock-avoidance. In this paper we compare two algorithms, each offering a different degree of adaptivity: *deterministic* [23] and minimal adaptive based on *Duato*'s methodology [24] [25].

The deterministic algorithm is a dimension order routing based on a static channel dependency graph. Packets are sent to their destination along a unique minimal path. The potential deadlocks caused by the wrap-around connections are avoided doubling the number of virtual channels and creating two distinct virtual networks. Packets enter the first virtual network and switch to the second virtual network upon crossing a wrap-around connection. Our version of the deterministic algorithm uses four virtual channels for each physical link (two channels for each virtual network).

Rather than using a static channel dependency graph, Duato's methodology only requires the absence of cyclic dependencies on a connected channel subset. In our adaptive algorithm, based on this methodology, we associate four virtual channels to each link: on two of these channels, called *adaptive* channels, packets can be routed along any minimal path between source and destination. In the remaining two channels, called *deterministic* or *escape* channels, packets are routed deterministically when the adaptive choice is limited by network contention [26]. An interesting characteristic of this algorithm is that, once in the escape channels, packets can re-enter the adaptive channels, that is the channel allocation policy is non monotonic. A central point of this algorithm is the interface between the processor and the router. We assume that packets can enter the network passing through a single injection or memory channel placed between the processor and the router. This limitation, known as *source throttling*, makes the network throughput stable when the network operates above saturation [27] [28].

4 Relevant details of the network model

This section presents a router model and a simulation environment, that are used in the following sections to analyze the performance of the k-ary n-trees and the k-ary n-cubes under various traffic loads and flow control strategies. This model is evaluated in the SMART (Simulator of Massive ARchitectures and Topologies) environment [29].

Figure 4 outlines the internal structure of a routing switch. We can distinguish the external channels or links, the input and the output buffers or lanes that implement the buffer space of the virtual channels and an internal crossbar. The switch has bidirectional channels and each channel on the single direction is logically

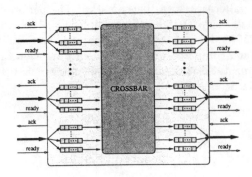

Figure 4: The internal structure of a routing switch.

composed of three interfaces: a *data path* that transmits messages on a flit level, the *ready* lines that flag the presence of a flit on the data path and specify the virtual channel where the flit is to be stored and the *ack* lines in the reverse direction that send an acknowledgment every time buffer space is released in the input lanes. The processing nodes have a compatible interface with the same number of virtual channels.

A flit is moved from an output lane to the corresponding input lane in a neighboring node in T_{link} cycles, when there is at least a free buffer position. Each output lane has associated a counter that is initialized with the total number of buffers in the input lane, it is decremented after sending a flit and it is incremented upon receiving and acknowledgment. When multiple lanes are enabled, an arbiter picks one of them according to a fair policy.

When a header flit reaches the top of an input lane, the routing algorithm tries to establish a path in the crossbar with a suitable output lane, that is neither full nor bound to another input lane. This path will remain in action till the transmission of the tail flit of the packet. Our model allows the routing of a single header every $T_{routing}$ cycles.

Although a physical link services in each direction at most one virtual channel every T_{link} cycles, multiple virtual channels can be active at the input and output ports of the crossbar. The internal flit propagation takes $T_{crossbar}$ cycles. Every time a flit is moved from an input lane to the corresponding output lane, a feedback is sent back to the neighboring switch or node to update the counter of free positions.

Each node generates packets of 64 bytes and the destinations are distributed uniformly or according a static communication pattern, as explained in more detail in the following sections. The simulator collects performance data only after 2000 cycles, to allow the network to reach steady state and each simulation is halted after 20000 cycles.

5 Performance Normalization

In this study we would like to compare networks with the same number of processing nodes and routing chips. If we consider a k-ary n-tree with parameters (k_1, n_1) and a k-ary n-cube with parameters (k_2, n_2), we require that $k_1^{n_1} = k_2^{n_2}$ (same number of processors) and $n_1 k_1^{n_1-1} = k_2^{n_2}$ (same number of routing chips). These equations imply $k_1 = n_1$, and the total number of processing nodes $N = k_1^{k_1}$. A 4-ary 4-tree and a 16-ary 2-cube satisfy these conditions, so we will consider these two networks in the experimental evaluation.

A fair comparison of interconnection networks should also take into account physical constraints as the pin count, wire delay, bisection width [18] and the router complexity [30]. In our experiments we normalize the communication performance by setting the flit and the data path size on the fat-tree at two bytes and at four bytes on the cube. If we consider a 4-ary 4-tree and a 16-ary 2-cube, this normalization can be interpreted in the following ways.

Technological constraints limit the number of pins on a given chip. In a quaternary fat-tree, the arity of the routing switches is eight, while the arity of the routing chip in a bi-dimensional cube is four, if we do not consider the connection with the local processing node. By doubling the data paths on the cube we have the same pin count on both routing chips.

Both k-ary n-trees and k-ary n-cubes have $n*k^n$ links. The quaternary fat-tree has got twice as many links as a bi-dimensional cube and our normalization equalizes the overall (peak) communication bandwidth.

There is another important consideration: with this normalization the two networks have the same theoretical upper bound under uniform traffic. For the k-ary n-cubes this upper bound corresponds to twice the bisection bandwidth[1]. k-ary n-trees are not bisection-bandwidth limited and the upper bound is simply the unidirectional bandwidth of the links connecting the processing nodes to the network switches.

Other important parameters are the router complexity and the wire delays. Adaptive algorithms have more degrees of freedom but require larger crossbars and more complex arbitration. So these advantages are often offset by increased clock cycles. Chien in [30] has proposed a cost model to make fair comparisons between routing algorithms. It can be applied to evaluate the router

delays of the deterministic and the minimal adaptive algorithms for the cubes and the adaptive algorithms for the fat-trees outlined in Section 2

This model has gained consideration in several performance studies [31] [32]. It assumes a 0.8 micron CMOS gate array technology for the implementation of the routing chip. The three delays $T_{routing}$, $T_{crossbar}$ and T_{link} are computed as follows.

Routing a message involves address decoding, routing decision and header selection. According to [30] the routing decision has a delay that grows logarithmically with the number of alternatives, or degree of freedom, offered by the routing algorithm. Denoting by F the degree of freedom, the model estimates the routing delay in

$$T_{routing} = 4.7 + 1.2 \log F \ ns. \qquad (1)$$

The time required to transfer a flit from an input channel to the corresponding output channel is the sum of the delay involved in the internal flow control unit, the delay of the crossbar and the set-up time of the output channel latch. The crossbar delay grows logarithmically with the number of ports P. Therefore the crossbar time is

$$T_{crossbar} = 3.4 + 0.6 \log P \ ns. \qquad (2)$$

The time required to transmit a flit across a physical link includes the wire delay and the time required to latch it at destination. Low-dimensional cubes as the two-dimensional ones can be easily embedded in the three-dimensional space with constant length wires. If virtual channels are used, the virtual channel controller has a delay logarithmic in the number of virtual channels V. The delay of links with short wires is estimated by the model in

$$T_{link}^s = 5.14 + 0.6 \log V \ ns. \qquad (3)$$

In our experiments the deterministic algorithm uses four virtual channels as the minimal adaptive algorithm based on Duato's methodology, in which there are two adaptive and two escape channels on each link. Both input and output buffers can contain four flits. Thus the algorithms map four virtual channels on each physical channel ($V = 4$) and the internal crossbar has four inputs from each link plus an injection channel from the local node ($P = 17$). The only difference is the routing delay which is influenced by the degree of adaptivity. In the deterministic routing we have only two virtual channels available in a single direction ($F = 2$). With the adaptive algorithm the number increases to six ($F = 6$), four adaptive channels in two directions plus two deterministic channels.

---

[1]The network capacity can be determined by considering that 50% of the uniform random traffic crosses the bisection of the network. Thus if a cube has bisection bandwidth B, each of the N nodes can inject $2B/N$ traffic at the maximum load.

	$T_{routing}$	$T_{crossbar}$	T_{link}^s	T_{clock}
Det.	5.9	5.85	6.34	6.34
Duato	7.8	5.85	6.34	7.8

Table 1: Delays of the two routing algorithms for the cube, expressed in nanoseconds

	$T_{routing}$	$T_{crossbar}$	T_{link}^m	T_{clock}
1 vc	8.06	5.2	9.64	9.64
2 vc	9.26	5.8	10.24	10.24
4 vc	10.46	6.4	10.84	10.84

Table 2: Delays of the three variants of the adaptive algorithm for the fat-tree, expressed in nanoseconds

We can now apply this model to find the clock cycles induced by the three routing algorithms. These results are summarized in Table 1. In the deterministic algorithm the limiting factor is the link delay, while the routing delay is the bottleneck of the minimal adaptive algorithm. In both cases the clock cycle is set to the maximum of the three delays.

When we embed a quaternary fat-tree with 256 nodes in the three-dimensional space some wires are inevitably longer than others. The delay of links with medium length wires [32] can be estimated by the model in

$$T_{link}^m = 9.64 + 0.6 \log V \ ns. \tag{4}$$

In our experiments we will consider three variants of the adaptive algorithm, with one, two and four virtual channels. As in the cubes, the input and output buffers can contain up to four flits. The values of P and F can be directly computed from the number of virtual channels. The degree of freedom F of a packet in the ascending phase is $(2k - 1) * V$, because it can take any of the ascending or descending links and the crossbar size P is $2k * V$. Table 2 reports the delays of the three flow control strategies. From these results we can see that 4-ary 4-trees with one and two virtual channels are wire limited and there is no impact of the virtual channels on the clock cycle. With four virtual channels the gap between routing and the link delays is narrow. With more virtual channels the routing complexity becomes the limiting factor.

In our experiments the delays $T_{routing}$ $T_{crossbar}$ and T_{link} are equalized to a single clock cycle, which is set to maximum of the three delays, the link delay. ·

6 Experimental Results

The performance of an interconnection network under dynamic load is usually assessed by two quantitative parameters, the *accepted bandwidth* or *throughput* and the *latency*.

Accepted bandwidth is defined as the sustained data delivery rate given some offered bandwidth at the network input. Two important characteristics are the saturation point and the sustained rate after saturation. Saturation is defined as the minimum offered bandwidth where the accepted bandwidth is lower than the global packet creation rate at the source nodes. It is worth noting that, before saturation, offered and accepted bandwidth are the same. The behavior above saturation is important because the network and/or the routing algorithm can become unstable, with a consequent performance degradation. We usually expect the accepted bandwidth to remain stable after saturation, both in the presence of bursty applications that require peak performance for a short period of time and applications that operate after saturation in normal conditions, e.g. when executing a global permutation pattern.

The *network* latency is the average delay spent by a packet in the network, from the insertion of the header flit in the injection lane till the reception of the tail flit at the destination. It does not include the source queuing delay. The *end-to-end* latency rises to infinity above saturation and is impossible to gain any information in this case. For this reason, the network latency is often preferred to analyze the network performance.

The first sets of experimental results of each traffic pattern are presented according to the Chaos Normal Form[2] (CNF). The CNF uses two graphs, one to display the accepted bandwidth and the other to display the network latency. In both graphs the x-axis corresponds to the offered bandwidth normalized with the maximum bandwidth that can be accepted under uniform traffic.

In the final comparison we use absolute measurements units because we compare routing algorithms that involve different implementations and, consequently, different clock cycles.

7 Message Generation

In our model each node generates packets according to the following traffic patterns. To describe these patterns, let each node of the k-ary n-cube or k-ary n-tree $p_0, p_1, \ldots, p_{n-1}$ also be labelled with a number in base k resulting from the concatenation of the p_i. The binary representation of $p_0 p_1 \ldots p_{n-1}$ is $a_0 a_1 \ldots a_{(n \log_2 k)-1}$[3].

---

[2]See http://www.cs.washington.edu/research/projects/lis/ chaos/www/presentation.html for more details on the presentation of simulation results of network routing studies.

[3]We will assume that k is a power of two and n is even.

Also, let $\overline{0} = 1$ and $\overline{1} = 0$.

Uniform traffic. Destinations are chosen at random with equal probability between the processing nodes.

Complement traffic. Each node sends only to the destination given by $\overline{a_0 a_1 \ldots a_{(n \log_2 k)-1}}$.

Bit reversal. Each node sends only to the destination given by $a_{(n \log_2 k)-1} a_{(n \log_2 k)-2} \cdots a_0$.

Transpose. Each node sends only to the destination given by

$a_{(\frac{n}{2} \log_2 k)} a_{(\frac{n}{2} \log_2 k)+1} \cdots a_{(n \log_2 k)-1} a_0 a_1 \cdots a_{(\frac{n}{2} \log_2 k)-1}$.

These traffic patterns illustrate different features. The uniform one is a standard benchmark used in network routing studies. This generation pattern can be considered representative of well-balanced shared memory computations. In the complement traffic all the packets cross the bisection of the network. Bit reversal and transpose, are important because they occur in practical computations [21].

8 Fat-Tree

Under uniform traffic the adaptive routing algorithm saturates at 36% of the capacity with 1 virtual channel, 55% with 2 virtual channels and 72% with 4 virtual channels, as shown in Figure 5 a). In all cases the post saturation behavior is stable, with a constant throughput for any offered bandwidth.

These results confirm the importance of the flow control strategy. Wormhole routed fat-trees with a single virtual channel do not achieve good throughput, due to blocking problems. When a packet is stopped at an intermediate switch on the descending phase [4], all the links on the path from the node/switch where the tail flit is stored to the current switch are blocked. Other packets could profitably use these links. In fact, with 4 virtual channels doubles the accepted bandwidth, reaching a considerable 72%. This comes at a price. The condivision of the links between two or more packets slightly increases the network latency for moderate loads.

The CNF of the complement traffic shows an interesting behavior. As can be seen in Figure 5 c), the saturation point is around 95% of the capacity for all flow control strategies. This permutation pattern doesn't create any congestion in the descending phase. The use of more than a virtual channel is counterproductive in terms of network latency (Figure 5 d): this is mainly due to the link multiplexing, that increases the tail latency. At steady state, there are as many packets in progress as the number of virtual channels in each link. The network latency with 1 virtual channel remains stable until the offered load is 70% of the capacity and experiences a minor increase of the head latency after this point.

---

[4] The adaptive routing algorithm used in the experiments can have conflicts on the descending phase only.

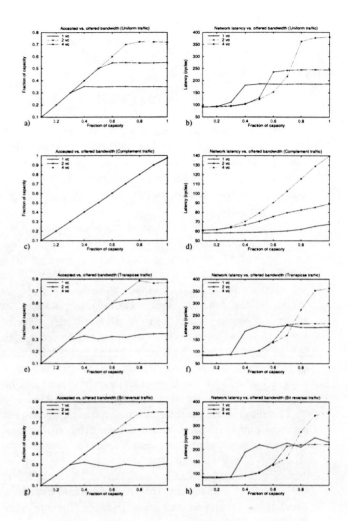

Figure 5: Communication performance of a 4-ary 4-tree with adaptive routing and one, two and four virtual channels.

With 2 virtual channels the head latency has a similar behavior, while the tail latency converges to the upper bound after 70% of the capacity. The complement traffic belongs to a wide class of permutations that map a k-ary n-tree into itself. These permutations do not generate any congestion on the descending phase and are called *congestion-free* [33].

Bit reversal and transpose permutations have a similar distribution of the destinations in terms of distance. It can be easily noted, looking at the numerical representation shown in section 7, that in both cases there are $k^{n/2}$ nodes at distance 0 (that is source and destination are on the same node) and $(k-1)k^{n/2+i-1}$ nodes at distance $n + 2i$, $i \in \{1, \ldots, n/2\}$. The average distance d_m

is given by

$$d_m = \frac{k-1}{k^{n/2}} \sum_{i=1}^{n/2} (n+2i)k^i. \qquad (5)$$

For a 4-ary 4-tree $d_m = 7.125$, which is very close to the network diameter. The performance results of these communication patterns are very similar. From the CNF of the transpose shown in Figure 5 e) we can see that the saturation points are at 33%, 60% and 78% of the capacity with 1, 2 and 4 virtual channels. An analogous behavior for the bit reversal can be seen in Figure 5 g).

8.1 Discussion

The congestion-free communication patterns are an important characteristic of the k-ary n-trees. They can be routed reaching optimal performance with a simple routing algorithm and flow control strategy. They are analogous to local communication in direct topologies, as the k-ary n-cubes. The results obtained on the complement traffic generalize to the whole class of congestion-free patterns and are expected to scale with the number of nodes with an accepted bandwidth that approximates the network capacity. Message latency is only influenced by the flow control overhead and can be deterministically estimated with tight upper bounds.

The remaining communication patterns, uniform, bit reversal and transpose, generate congestion in the descending phase and are very sensitive to the flow control strategy. They all saturates at about $35-40\%$ of the capacity with 1 virtual channel, $55-60\%$ with 2 virtual channels and around 75% with 4 virtual channels. From these results we can argue that the expected performance of different permutation patterns is mainly influenced by the flow control strategy. Also, in all these cases, switching from 1 to 4 virtual channels doubles the accepted bandwidth.

9 The Cube

We can now compare the performance of the deterministic and the minimal adaptive algorithm. In Figure 6 a) we can see that the adaptive algorithm saturates at 80% of the capacity while the deterministic stops at 60%. The network latency is low for both algorithms: before saturation is stable at about 70 cycles and packets spend on the average 150 and 130 cycles in the network at saturation, respectively the deterministic and the adaptive algorithm.

In the complement traffic all packets are reflected across the logical center of the network. Each packet traverses the network bisection, halving the theoretical upper bound. Looking at Figure 6 c), we can see that the throughput of the deterministic algorithm is very close to optimality at 47% of the capacity, while the minimal

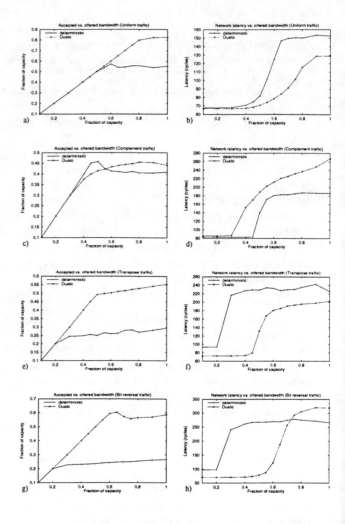

Figure 6: Communication performance of a 16-ary 2-cube with deterministic and minimal adaptive routing.

adaptive algorithm experiences an early saturation at 35% of the capacity. This phenomenon has been observed in [34] too. The complement is unusual since dimension order routing helps prevent conflicts. This behavior is confirmed in Figure 6 d), where we can see a wide gap between the network latencies at medium loads.

In the transpose traffic the destination of each packet is a reflection of the source along the diagonal. This causes a continuous area of congestion along this diagonal and on the opposite corners of the logically flattened torus. The adaptive algorithm provides better performance in this case with 50% of the capacity, more than twice than the deterministic one.

Unlike the previous traffic patterns, bit reversal has

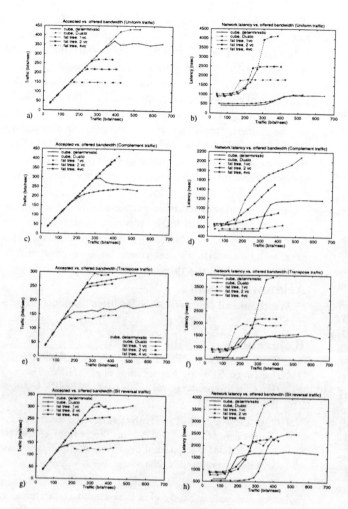

Figure 7: Normalized communication performance of a 16-ary 2-cube and a 4-ary 4-tree.

In Figure 7 a) we can see that the bi-dimensional cube outperforms the quaternary fat-tree under uniform traffic. The Duato's algorithm has the highest saturation throughput, about 440 bits/nsec and is followed by the deterministic algorithm with 350 bits/nsec. The minimal adaptive algorithm has a performance advantage over the deterministic one even when the router complexity is taken into account. It is surprising, at least at first glance, to see that the best throughput of the fat-tree is only 280 bits/nsec and is achieved with four virtual channels. The version with one virtual channel stops at 150 bits/nsec, at about one third of the best throughput on the cube. In the cube the latency of both algorithms before saturation is stable at about half μsec and the network latency in a saturated network is only one μsec. In the fat-tree we pay the penalties of the narrow data paths, the longer wires and the router complexity. The first factor increases the tail latency, because worms of the same size require more flits. The other two factors increase the multiplicative factor represented by the clock cycle. As a result, the network latency on the fat-tree is much higher and reaches 4 μsec at saturation when we use four virtual channels. The network latency under normal traffic conditions is about one μsec, twice the latency on the cube.

The complement traffic is a very particular permutation pattern for both topologies. On the one hand it is a difficult pattern for the cube, because it stresses the topological limitation of the bisection bandwidth. On the other hand, it generates no form of contention on the fat-tree. The saturation points on the fat-trees are all around 400 bits/nsec while the best result on the cube is provided by the deterministic algorithm with 280 bits/nsec. The network latencies on the cube are around 0.5 and 0.7 μsec before saturation, respectively with the deterministic and the adaptive algorithm. When we use more than a virtual channel on the fat-tree we must pay the routing overhead and the network latency with four virtual channels reaches 1.5 μsec when the network is close to saturation.

For the transpose and bit reversal traffics we can distinguish two classes of algorithms. The first class includes the adaptive algorithm on the cube and the versions with two and four virtual channels on the fat-tree. The saturation points of these algorithms are grouped in a short interval between 250 and 300 bits/nsec. In the second class there are the deterministic algorithm of the cube and the adaptive algorithm of the fat-tree with a single virtual channel, whose saturation points are between 100 and 150 bits/nsec. We also must note the low average latency of the adaptive algorithm based on Duato's methodology, only half μsec. In the presence

no easy geometric interpretation. There are 16 nodes that have a palindrome bit string and do not inject any packet into the network. They generate some underloaded areas that are located along or near the two main diagonals according to a symmetric layout. As in the previous case, the adaptive algorithm provides better performance both in terms of throughput and network latency. The saturation points are 60% and 20% of the capacity.

10 The Two Networks Compared

We are now ready compare the two interconnection networks using the cost model introduced in Section 5. The raw data already shown in Sections 8 and 9 are filtered to take into account the router complexity and the wire delay.

of non uniform traffic it pays to have adaptive routing on the cube and more virtual channels on the fat-trees.

11 Conclusion

In this paper we have analyzed two popular interconnection networks, a bi-dimensional cube and a quaternary fat-tree. We have compared the communication performance of these interconnection networks using a detailed simulation model, taking into account important parameters as the bisection width, the router complexity and the wire delay. In the experimental evaluation we have considered a 4-ary 4-tree and a 16-ary 2-cube, two networks with same number of processing nodes and routers, whose communication performance has been properly normalized. From the body of experimental results we have gathered so far we can draw some considerations.

The first important result is that the bi-dimensional cube outperforms the quaternary fat-tree under uniform traffic, both in terms of network throughput and latency. The highest saturation throughput is reached by the adaptive algorithm based on Duato's methodology with 440 bits/nsec and the deterministic algorithm with 350 bits/nsec, while the best throughput on the fat-tree is 280 bits/nsec with 4 virtual channels. The network latency on the cube is only 0.5 μsec below saturation, about half the latency on the fat-tree. This is mainly due to the pin count limitation, that allows larger data paths on the cube and the wire delay, that increases significantly the clock cycle.

The fat-tree provides a slightly better throughput in the presence of non-uniform traffic patterns. The complement is a difficult pattern for the cube because it stresses the topological limitation of the bisection bandwidth: in this case the best saturation points are 400 bits/nsec for the fat-tree and around 250 bits/nsec for the cube. With the transpose and bit reversal traffics the throughput with two and four virtual channels on the fat-tree is tantamount to the adaptive algorithm on the cube. On the other hand the cube provides lower latency with all the communication patterns.

An important characteristic of the fat-tree is that its communication performance is not sensitive to the permutation pattern, because the bisection bandwidth it is not a topological limitation in this network. So we have a predictable performance. In the cube the performance depends on how the communication patterns relate to the bisection bandwidth. This problem is alleviated by the adaptive algorithm. It is also worth noting that the adaptive algorithm maintains a performance advantage over the deterministic one even when we consider the router complexity.

The performance of the fat-tree is mainly sensitive to

the flow control strategy in use: for all traffic patterns but the complement one, the saturation point with one virtual channel is 150 bits/nsec, between 200 and 250 bits/nsec with two and around 300 bits/nsec with four virtual channels. The network latency in a non saturated network is nearly the same for all the three variants, about a μsec. Virtual channels have a modest impact on the router complexity of the fat-tree, whose limiting factor is the wire delay. When we use four virtual channels the routing delay is equalized with the wire delay, so we expect a diminishing return with more virtual channels.

As the performance of interconnection networks becomes increasingly limited by physical constraints as the wire delay, we expect that low-dimensional cubes will increase the gap with the fat-trees, because they can be easily mapped on the three-dimensional space.

Acknowledgments

We thank all the reviewers for their insightful comments.

References

[1] C. E. Leiserson, "Fat-Trees: Universal Networks for Hardware Efficient Supercomputing," *IEEE Transactions on Computers*, vol. C-34, pp. 892–901, October 1985.

[2] C. E. Leiserson *et al.*, "The Network Architecture of the Connection Machine CM-5," in *Proceedings of the 4th Annual ACM Symposium on Parallel Algorithms and Architectures*, pp. 272–285, June 1992.

[3] H. L. Muller, P. W. A. Stallard, and D. H. D. Warren, "An Evaluation Study of a Link-Based Data Diffusion Machine," in *Proceedings of the 8th International Parallel Processing Symposium, IPPS'94*, (Cancun, Mexico), pp. 115–128, April 1994.

[4] Meiko World Incorporated, *Computing Surface 2 reference manuals*, preliminary ed., 1993.

[5] S. Haridi and E. Hagersten, "The Cache Coherence Protocol of the Data Diffusion Machine," in *PARLE'89, Parallel Architectures and Languages Europe*, vol. I, pp. 1–18, June 1989.

[6] Kendall Square Research, *Technical Summary*, 1th ed., 1991.

[7] T. T. Kwan, B. K. Tatty, and D. A. Reed, "Communication and Computation performance of the CM-5," in *Supercomputing'93*, pp. 192–201, November 1993.

[8] M. Lin, R. Tsang, D. H. C. Du, A. E. Klietz, and S. Saroff, "Performance Evaluation of the CM-5 Interconnection Network," Tech. Rep. AHPCRC Preprint 92-111, University of Minnesota AHPCRC, October 1992.

[9] A. Martin and D. Bader, "Performance of the CM-5 ENEE 646." unpublished, January 1994.

[10] D. Lenoski, J. Laudon, *et al.*, "The Stanford DASH Multiprocessor," *IEEE Computer*, pp. 63–79, March 1992.

[11] A. Agarwal, B. H. Lim, D. Kranz, and J. Kubiatowicz, "APRIL: A Processor Architecture for Multiprocessing," in *Proceedings of the 17th Annual International Symposium on Computer Architecture*, pp. 104–114, May 1990.

[12] R. Suaya and G. Birtwistle, eds., *VLSI and Parallel Computation*, ch. Network and Processor Architecture for Message-Driven Computers. Morgan Kaufmann Publishers, 1990.

[13] Cray Research Inc., *Cray T3D System Architecture Overview*, 1th ed., September 1993.

[14] S. L. Scott and G. M. Thorson, "The Cray T3E Network: Adaptive Routing in a High Performance 3D Torus," in *HOT Interconnects IV*, (Stanford University), August 1996.

[15] K. Hwang, *Advanced Computer Architecture: Parallelism, Scalability, Programmability*. McGraw-Hill, Inc., 1993.

[16] Z. G. Mou, "Comparison of Multiprocessor Networks with the Same Cost," in *International Conference on Parallel and Distributed Processing Techniques and Applications (PDPTA'96)*, vol. I, (Sunnyvale, CA), pp. 539–548, August 1996.

[17] D. C. Burger and D. A. Wood, "Accuracy vs. Performance in Parallel Simulation of Interconnection Networks," in *International Symposium on Parallel Processing*, April 1995.

[18] A. Agarwal, "Limits on Interconnection Network Performance," *IEEE Transactions on Parallel and Distributed Systems*, vol. 2, pp. 398–412, October 1991.

[19] C. E. Leiserson and B. M. Maggs, "Communication-Efficient Parallel Algorithms for Distributed Random Access Machines," *Algorithmica*, vol. 3, pp. 53–77, 1988.

[20] F. Petrini and M. Vanneschi, "*k*-ary *n*-trees: High Performance Networks for Massively Parallel Architectures," in *Proceedings of the 11th International Parallel Processing Symposium, IPPS'97*, (Geneva, Switzerland), pp. 87–93, April 1997.

[21] F. T. Leighton, *Introduction to Parallel Algorithms and Architectures: Arrays, Trees, Hypercubes*. San Mateo, CA, USA: Morgan Kaufmann Publishers, 1992.

[22] W. J. Dally, "Virtual Channel Flow Control," *IEEE Transactions on Parallel and Distributed Systems*, vol. 3, pp. 194–205, March 1992.

[23] W. J. Dally and C. L. Seitz, "Deadlock-Free Message Routing in Multiprocessor Interconnection Networks," *IEEE Transactions on Computers*, vol. C-36, pp. 547–553, May 1987.

[24] J. Duato, "A New Theory of Deadlock-Free Adaptive Routing in Wormhole Networks," *IEEE Transactions on Parallel and Distributed Systems*, vol. 4, pp. 1320–1331, December 1993.

[25] J. Duato, "A Necessary and Sufficient Condition for Deadlock-Free Adaptive Routing in Wormhole Networks," *IEEE Transactions on Parallel and Distributed Systems*, vol. 6, pp. 1055–1067, October 1995.

[26] J. Duato, "A Necessary and Sufficient Condition for Deadlock-Free Adaptive Routing in Wormhole Networks," in *International Conference on Parallel Processing*, vol. I - Architecture, pp. I–142–I–149, 1994.

[27] W. J. Dally and H. Aoki, "Deadlock-Free Adaptive Routing in Multicomputer Networks Using Virtual Channels," *IEEE Transactions on Parallel and Distributed Systems*, vol. 4, pp. 466–475, April 1993.

[28] F. Petrini and M. Vanneschi, "Minimal Adaptive Routing with Limited Injection on Toroidal *k*-ary *n*-cubes," in *Supercomputing 96*, (Pittsburgh, PA), November 1996.

[29] F. Petrini and M. Vanneschi, "SMART: a Simulator of Massive ARchitectures and Topologies," in *International Conference on Parallel and Distributed Systems Euro-PDS'97*, (Barcelona, Spain), June 1997.

[30] A. A. Chien, "A Cost and Speed Model for *k*-ary *n*-cube Wormhole Routers," in *Hot Inteconnects '93*, (Palo Alto, California), August 1993.

[31] J. Duato and P. López, "Performance Evaluation of Adaptive Routing Algorithms for *k*-ary *n*-cubes," in *First International Workshop, PCRCW'94* (K. Bolding and L. Snyder, eds.), vol. 853 of *LNCS*, (Seattle, Washington, USA), pp. 45–59, May 1994.

[32] J. Duato and M. P. Malumbres, "Optimal Topology for Distributed Shared-Memory Multiprocessors: Hypercubes Again?," in *Second International Euro-Par Conference, Volume I*, no. 1123 in LNCS, (Lyon, France), pp. 205–212, August 1996.

[33] S. Heller, "Congestion-Free Routing on the CM-5 Data Router," in *First International Workshop, PCRCW'94* (K. Bolding and L. Snyder, eds.), vol. 853 of *LNCS*, (Seattle, Washington, USA), pp. 176–184, May 1994.

[34] M. L. Fulgham and L. Snyder, "A Comparison of Input and Output Driven Routers," in *Second International Euro-Par Conference, Volume I*, no. 1123 in LNCS, (Lyon, France), pp. 195–204, August 1996.

[35] D. R. Helman, D. A. Bader, and J. Jájá, "Parallel Algorithms for Personalized Communication and Sorting with an Experimental Study," in *Proceedings of the 8th Annual ACM Symposium on Parallel Algorithms and Architectures*, (Padova, Italy), June 1996.

An Improved Analytical Model for Wormhole Routed Networks with Application to Butterfly Fat-Trees

Ronald I. Greenberg
Mathematical and Computer Sciences
Loyola University
6525 North Sheridan Road
Chicago, IL 60626
rig@math.luc.edu

Lee Guan
Electrical Engineering
University of Maryland
College Park, MD 20742
leeguan@eng.umd.edu

Abstract

A performance model for wormhole routed interconnection networks is presented and applied to the butterfly fat-tree network. Experimental results agree very closely over a wide range of load rate. Novel aspects of the model, leading to accurate and simple performance predictions, include (1) use of multiple-server queues, and (2) a general method of correcting queuing results based on Poisson arrivals to apply to wormhole routing. These ideas can also be applied to other networks.

keywords: interconnection network, wormhole routing, latency, throughput, butterfly fat-tree

1 Introduction

Many recent multicomputers have adopted *wormhole* [3] routing techniques to reduce the communication latency for fine-grained parallel programs. Several performance models have been presented for wormhole routing. Dally [2] focused on k-ary n-cube networks, and the other works have been primarily geared towards improving accuracy or simplicity of some aspects of the prior models. In particular, Draper and Ghosh [4] present a simple model that is particularly accurate for binary hypercubes. The common feature of these models is the use of results from queuing theory in an iterative fashion working backwards from message destination to message source.

None of the prior works, however, lead directly to a suitable model for the network of particular interest in this paper, the butterfly fat-tree. Fat-trees constitute an interesting class of networks due to their area-universality properties (e.g., [5, 6, 9]) and their influence on the design of actual parallel computers [1, 10].

There are several ways that modeling the butterfly fat-tree differs from modeling k-ary n-cubes. First, the butterfly fat-tree is not node-symmetric, so it does not suffice to analyze the traffic situation at a single node. Still, the butterfly fat-tree has a very regular

structure, and deadlock never results when messages are routed over shortest paths. Deadlock avoidance schemes for k-ary n-cubes produce some complication in the sense that they create asymmetry among different links in the network, but they actually lead to a major simplification by fixing a specific path for any message with a given source and destination. In the butterfly fat-tree, messages often have a choice among two outgoing links from a node, necessitating the use of multiple-server queuing models.

In this paper, we first present an improved general model for analyzing wormhole routed networks in Section 2. In Section 3, we apply the model to the butterfly fat-tree network and compare to simulation results. Concluding remarks are included in Section 4.

2 A Wormhole Routing Model

This section presents a general approach to analyzing the performance of wormhole routed interconnection networks. The measures we seek to compute are average latency and throughput.

The model presented in this section is based on the following assumptions, common to other analyses: (1) Arrivals at each source node are Poissonian, and destinations are uniformly random. (2) Worms have a fixed length longer than the diameter of the network. (3) Contentions at incoming links to a node are resolved according to First-Come First-Served (FCFS) scheduling. (4) Messages arriving at destinations are immediately consumed at the rate of one flit per time step, i.e., no blocking is encountered at destinations.

2.1 Average Latency

An interconnection network consists of processing elements (PE) and routing elements (RE). In direct networks(e.g., k-ary n cubes) a node consists of both a PE and an RE. In indirect networks (e.g., tree-based networks where processors are placed at leaves) processing elements and routing elements are separate

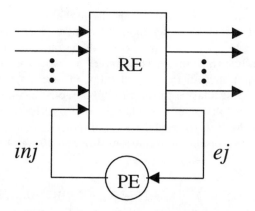

Figure 1: A general routing model. A network consists of processing elements (PE) and routing elements (RE). A PE is attached to an RE through an injecting channel and an ejecting channel.

nodes. Figure 1 shows a general routing model that can be used to represent both direct and indirect networks. a PE is always attached to an RE through an injecting channel and an ejecting channel. An RE, however, may or may not have a PE attached to it.

When a message is generated at a processing node j, it encounters the following latencies: 1) A waiting time $W_{inj,j}$ for the injecting channel. This waiting time doesn't depend on the routing scheme (store-and-forward or wormhole), and can be determined as long as the behavior of message arrival rates and the service time for the injecting channel are known. Under the Poisson arrival assumption the waiting time can be resolved using the M/G/1 model. 2) A service time $x_{inj,j}$ at the injecting channel. This is the time from the moment the first flit of the message is accepted by the injecting channel to the moment the last flit of the message has left the injecting channel. In wormhole routing, the flits of a message spread over many links on the message's path. When the head flit is blocked, the other flits of the worm are blocked in place. Under the long-worm assumption, the service time at the injecting channel includes the waiting times due to blocking at all subsequent channels. 3) An additional time to traverse the rest of the channels on the message's path. Under the assumptions that the length of the worm is longer than the diameter of the network and that there is no blocking at the destination, when the tail of the message has left the injecting channel, the head of the message must have arrived at the destination; the rest of the message will be received one flit per clock step. Therefore, it will take another $D-1$ clock steps for the entire message to be received at the destination, where D is the length of the path.

From the above analysis we can write the the latency L_j for the message injected at node j as

$$L_j = W_{inj,j} + x_{inj,j} + D - 1 \ . \tag{1}$$

Averaging over all processing nodes (and the probability distribution of message generation), the average latency $\overline{L}$ for the entire network is then

$$\overline{L} = \frac{1}{N} \sum_j \overline{L}_j = \frac{1}{N} \sum_j \left(\overline{W}_{inj,j} + \overline{x}_{inj,j} \right) + \overline{D} - 1 \ , \tag{2}$$

where N if the number of processing nodes in the network and $\overline{D}$ is the average message distance.

The service time at the injecting channel $x_{inj,j}$ depends on the service time of the subsequent channels. More precisely, the service time of a channel is the sum of the waiting time and the service time encountered at the channel immediately following it. Service times are resolved in the reverse order of the channels traversed, from the last channel (ejecting channel) backwards to the injecting channel.

2.2 Waiting Times and Service Times

At any RE, messages from an incoming channel i may be routed to outgoing channels denoted by $j = 0$, 1, etc. The service time for the incoming channel depends on the service times and waiting times at all possible outgoing channels. Denote the probability that a message from incoming channel i is routed to outgoing channel j by $R_{i|j}$, the service time for incoming channel i can then be expressed as

$$x_i^{in} = \sum_j (x_j + w_{i|j}) \cdot R_{i|j} \ , \tag{3}$$

where x_j is the service time for the outgoing channel j and $w_{i|j}$ is the waiting time for outgoing channel j of messages from incoming channel i. The above equation states that the service time at a channel depends on the service time of the subsequent channel and the waiting time for the subsequent channel.

The mean waiting times $w_{i|j}$ is caused by contention for the outgoing channel j. When a message is blocked, it must wait for the message that is holding the outgoing channel to be fully serviced. (A worm in service can not be preempted since only the head flit contains routing information.) This motivates us to take advantage of well-known queuing models that have been employed to analyze store-and-forward routing.

When an outgoing channel is treated as single server, results from the M/G/1 model [8] can be used:

$$\overline{W}_{M/G/1} = \frac{\rho \overline{x}(1 + C_b^2)}{2(1 - \rho)} \ , \tag{4}$$

where $\rho = \lambda \overline{x}$ is the server utilization, λ is the rate of message arrivals destined for the outgoing channel, $\overline{x}$

45

is the mean service time, and $C_b^2 = \frac{\sigma_b^2}{\bar{x}^2}$, where σ_b^2 is the variance of service time distribution. In light of arguments of Draper and Ghosh [4, p. 206], we adopt the following approximation:

$$C_b^2 = \frac{(\bar{x} - s/f)^2}{\bar{x}^2} \, , \qquad (5)$$

where s and f are the length of the message and the flit width respectively, so that s/f is the length of the message in flits.

Substituting for ρ and C_b^2 in Equation 4, we have

$$\overline{W}_{M/G/1} = \frac{\lambda \bar{x}^2}{2(1 - \lambda \bar{x})} \cdot \left[1 + \frac{(\bar{x} - s/f)^2}{\bar{x}^2} \right] \, . \qquad (6)$$

In certain situations, multiple outgoing links from a switch must be treated as one multi-server channel. This is usually due to the existence of redundant paths to increase bandwidth. Multiple-server systems with general service time distributions (M/G/m queues) are more complicated than M/G/1 queues, but we make use of an approximation of Hokstad [7] that leads to:

$$\overline{W}_{M/G/2} = \frac{\lambda^2 \bar{x}^3}{2(4 - \lambda^2 \bar{x}^2)}(1 + C_b^2) \, . \qquad (7)$$

We again use Equation 5 to approximate C_b^2, yielding:

$$\overline{W}_{M/G/2} = \frac{\lambda^2 \bar{x}^3}{2(4 - \lambda^2 \bar{x}^2)} \cdot \left[1 + \frac{(\bar{x} - s/f)^2}{\bar{x}^2} \right] \, . \qquad (8)$$

But the M/G/m model assumes independent arrivals at the inputs of a switch, all of which may block one another, which is not accurate for wormhole routing. Once an input link is occupied by a worm, there can be no more arrivals on that link until the first worm is fully serviced. Thus, once a worm arrives on a link, it only needs to wait for worms from other incoming links. Therefore, to use the M/G/m waiting time result, we multiply by a blocking probability $P_{i|j}$:

$$w_{i|j} = P_{i|j} W_j \, , \qquad (9)$$

where $P_{i|j}$ should reflect the probability that m messages deemed to be in service by the M/G/m model actually emanate from m distinct incoming links other than link i. A simple approximation is

$$P_{i|j} = 1 - m \frac{\lambda_i^{\text{in}}}{\lambda_j} R_{i|j} \, , \qquad (10)$$

where λ_i^{in} is the total message rate on incoming channel i, λ_j is the total message rate on outgoing channel j, and the number of servers, m, is less than the number of incoming links. When $m = 1$, the expression is

exact, i.e., $P_{i|j}$ is 1 minus the probability that an arbitrary message destined for output j is from input i. For larger m, we approximately account for the probability that any of the servers holds a message from input i; if all the arrival rates on incoming links are modest relative to the rate on outgoing channel j, the probabilities of multiple arrivals from the same input in the M/G/m model are small enough to safely ignore.

By combining Equations 3, 9 and 10 we obtain the service time for messages on incoming channel i:

$$x_i^{\text{in}} = \sum_j \left[x_j + (1 - m \frac{\lambda_i^{\text{in}}}{\lambda_j} R_{i|j}) W_j \right] R_{i|j} \, . \qquad (11)$$

Equation 11 is used together with Equations 6 and 8 to iteratively resolve the service times for all channels. Average latency is then determined from Equation 2.

2.3 Throughput

Throughput is another important metric of network performance. Through the above analysis, waiting times at each link on a route can be obtained, from which we can determine the service time at the source. To find the throughput, the source service time is set equal to the reciprocal of the source arrival rate [2]. At this operating point messages are being offered as fast as the network can deliver them; the network saturates and can accept no more traffic.

3 Analysis of Butterfly Fat-trees

Section 2 presented a general performance model for wormhole routed networks. We now apply the general model to the butterfly fat-tree. We start with a brief description of the network. We then determine the message rates, service time and waiting time to each channel. Latency and throughput are then resolved and compared with results from empirical simulations.

3.1 The Butterfly Fat-Tree

We use the butterfly fat-tree with N processors as shown in Figure 2. Each node is labeled by a pair of indices (l, a), where l represents the level of the node in the network and a represents the address of the node in that level. The level of a node is its distance from the leaves. At the lowest level ($l = 0$) are the N processors with addresses 0 to $N-1$. Each switch $S(l, a)$ has six ports: $parent_0$, $parent_1$, $child_0$, $child_1$, $child_2$ and $child_3$. The processors are connected to $N/4$ switches at the 1st level such that processor $P(0, a)$ is connected to the $child_{a \bmod 4}$ of switch $S(1, \lfloor a/4 \rfloor)$. At the l-th level (for $l = 1$ to $\log_4 N$) there are $N/2^{l+1}$ switches. The connections of a switch are determined by the switch's address as follows: $parent_0$ of $S(l, a)$ is connected to $child_i$ of $S(l + 1, \lfloor \frac{a}{2^{l+1}} \rfloor \cdot 2^l + a \bmod 2^l)$, and $parent_1$ of $S(l, a)$ is connected to $child_i$ of $S(l + 1, \lfloor \frac{a}{2^{l+1}} \rfloor \cdot 2^l + (a + 2^{l-1}) \bmod 2^l)$, where $i = \lfloor \frac{a \bmod 2^{l+1}}{2^{l-1}} \rfloor$.

46

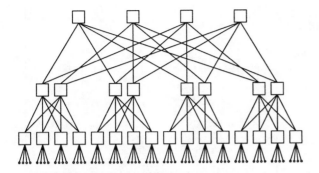

Figure 2: Butterfly Fat-Tree With 64 Processors

There is more than one shortest path between a pair of leaves in the butterfly fat-tree. More precisely, a message can take any of the two up links from a switch, if the destination is not in the subtree rooted at the switch. (There is no redundancy for down links.) When a worm needs to go up, it selects an up-link randomly, if that link is blocked, it tries the other, and if both are blocked, it waits.

3.2 Message Arrival Rates

To obtain the message arrival rates to each link, we assume the mean departure rate of a node is equal to the mean arrival rate provided that the network is not saturated [4]. Note that in a butterfly fat-tree, links that are at the same level and run in the same direction (up or down) are symmetrical, hence there is no need to distinguish among them. We can label the links and their arrival rates by a pair of indices $\langle i, j \rangle$ where i is the starting level of the link and j is the ending level of the link in the network, $0 \leq i, j \leq n$ with $n = \log_4 N$.

Assume each processor injects messages into the network at a rate of λ_0. Under steady state conditions, we have $\lambda_{0,1} = \lambda_{1,0} = \lambda_0$ for links between the processors ($l = 0$) and the first level switches ($l = 1$).

Now consider links between switches between level l and $l + 1$ ($1 \leq l < n$). Since there are $N = 4^n$ processors in the system, a message may have $4^n - 1$ destinations, of which $4^l - 1$ can be reached without going up from level l. Then, the probability that a message goes up from level l, denoted $P_l^{\uparrow}$, is

$$P_l^{\uparrow} = \frac{4^n - 4^l}{4^n - 1} , \qquad (12)$$

and the probability that a message goes down is

$$P_l^{\downarrow} = 1 - P_l^{\uparrow} . \qquad (13)$$

$P_l^{\downarrow}$ is used later when computing service times.

The total message rates going up from level l to level $l + 1$ is $P_l^{\uparrow} 4^n \lambda_0$. There are $\frac{4^n}{2^l}$ links between level l and $l+1$. The message rate to each channel going from level

l to level $l + 1$ is $\lambda_{l,l+1} = P_l^{\uparrow} 4^n \lambda_0 / (4^n / 2^l) = \lambda_0 P_l^{\uparrow} 2^l$. The message rate going downward from level $l + 1$ to level l equals that going up from level l to level $l + 1$ due to symmetry. In summary, we have

$$\lambda_{l,l+1} = \lambda_0 \frac{4^n - 4^l}{4^n - 1} 2^l \qquad (14)$$

$$\lambda_{l+1,l} = \lambda_{l,l+1} . \qquad (15)$$

3.3 Waiting and Service Times

Since a message is received by the destination processor one flit at a clock as soon as the head flit has reached the destination, the service time for links from a level 1 switch to a processor is deterministic, i.e, the length of a worm:

$$x_{1,0} = s/f . \qquad (16)$$

The mean waiting time $\overline{W}_{1,0}$ is determined using Equation 6, i.e.,

$$\overline{W}_{1,0} = \overline{W}_{M/G/1}(\lambda_{1,0}, x_{1,0}) . \qquad (17)$$

For any other down-going channels from level $l + 1$ to level l ($1 \leq l < n$), there are 4 possible outgoing channels (the 4 children), each with the same probability ($1/4$). The mean service time $\overline{x}_{l+1,l}$ is determined using Equation 11:

$$\overline{x}_{l+1,l} = \overline{x}_{l,l-1} + \left(1 - \frac{1}{4} \frac{\lambda_{l+1,l}}{\lambda_{l,l-1}}\right) \overline{W}_{l,l-1} . \qquad (18)$$

The mean waiting time $\overline{W}_{l+1,l}$ is determined using $\overline{x}_{l+1,l}$:

$$\overline{W}_{l+1,l} = \overline{W}_{M/G/1}(\lambda_{l+1,l}, \overline{x}_{l+1,l}) . \qquad (19)$$

Now consider up-going channels, starting with channel $\langle n - 1, n \rangle$. There are only 3 possible outgoing channels (siblings) after traversing channel $\langle n - 1, n \rangle$, each with the same probability ($1/3$). Therefore

$$\overline{x}_{n-1,n} = \overline{x}_{n,n-1} + \left(1 - \frac{\lambda_{n-1,n}}{\lambda_{n,n-1}} \frac{1}{3}\right) \overline{W}_{n,n-1}$$

$$= \overline{x}_{n,n-1} + \frac{2}{3} \overline{W}_{n,n-1} . \qquad (20)$$

The mean waiting time $\overline{W}_{n-1,n}$ is determined using the two-server model (Equation 8), i.e.,

$$\overline{W}_{n-1,n} = \overline{W}_{M/G/2}(\lambda_{n-1,n}, \overline{x}_{n-1,n}) . \qquad (21)$$

For any other up-going channels from level $l - 1$ to level l ($1 \leq l < n - 1$), a message may go upward from level l with probability $P_l^{\uparrow}$ or go downward with probability $P_l^\downarrow$. In the case that the message goes upward, there are two redundant up-going channels that are treated as one two-server channel. In the case that the message goes downward, there are three possible outgoing channels (siblings), each with the same probability (1/3). Therefore the mean service time is

$$\overline{x}_{l-1,l} = \left[\overline{x}_{l,l+1} + \left(1 - \frac{\lambda_{l-1,l}}{\lambda_{l,l+1}} P_l^\uparrow\right) \overline{W}_{l,l+1}\right] P_l^\uparrow$$
$$+ \left[\overline{x}_{l,l-1} + \left(1 - \frac{P_l^\downarrow}{3}\right) \overline{W}_{l,l-1}\right] P_l^\downarrow \quad (22)$$

The mean waiting time $\overline{W}_{l-1,l}$ is determined using the two-server model (Equation 8)

$$\overline{W}_{l-1,l} = \overline{W}_{M/G/2}(\lambda_{l-1,l}, \overline{x}_{l-1,l}) , \quad (23)$$

except for $l = 1$. Channel $\langle 0, 1 \rangle$ is from processor to first level switch with no redundant channel; therefore, the single server model should be applied, i.e.,

$$\overline{W}_{0,1} = \overline{W}_{M/G/1}(\lambda_{0,1}, \overline{x}_{0,1}) , \quad (24)$$

3.4 Average Latency

Now we can use Equation 2 to compute the average latency. For the butterfly fat-tree, $x_{inj,j} = x_{0,1}$ and $W_{inj,j} = W_{0,1}$. Since all processors are equivalent due to symmetry, averaging over injecting channels is unnecessary. Therefore the latency is determined as

$$\overline{L} = \overline{W}_{0,1} + \overline{x}_{0,1} + (\overline{D} - 1). \quad (25)$$

3.5 Throughput

Maximum throughput is computed by setting the source service time to the reciprocal of the source arrival rate, i.e.,

$$\overline{x}_{0,1} = \frac{1}{\lambda_0} . \quad (26)$$

Source service time $\overline{x}_{0,1}$ increases as arrival rate increases, while $\frac{1}{\lambda_0}$ is a monotonically decreasing function of λ_0. Graphically, if $\overline{x}_{0,1}$ and $\frac{1}{\lambda_0}$ are plotted against arrival rate, the maximum throughput is the arrival rate at the intersection of the two curves. In practice we let source arrival rate increase (starting at a small value) until the above equation is satisfied.

3.6 Experimental Validation

The performance model for the butterfly fat-tree was validated through comparisons with simulations. Fixed length messages are used for the simulation. Latencies from the model and simulation were compared for networks with up to 1024 processing nodes. Messages of 16, 32 and 64 flits in length are studied. Figure 3 shows the result of the comparisons for average latencies with 1024 processors. The model produced accurate predictions on latency and throughput for all cases under study.

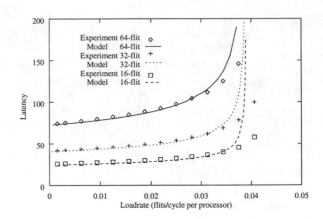

Figure 3: Comparisons of latency and throughput between model and simulation for 1024-processor

4 Conclusion

We have presented a general performance model for wormhole routed networks and applied it to the fat-tree network. Included in the process was the use of two-server queuing models, and the framework can be extended for networks that require queuing models with more than two servers

Average latency and maximum throughput for the butterfly fat-tree network were analyzed using the the model presented and validated through comparison with simulation results. The model was simple but produced very accurate predictions of performance.

References

[1] J. Beecroft et al. Meiko CS-2 interconnect Elan-Elite design. *Parallel Computing*, 20:1627–1638, Nov. 1994.

[2] W. J. Dally. Performance analysis of k-ary n-cube interconnection networks. *IEEE Trans. Computers*, 39(6):775–785, June 1990.

[3] W. J. Dally and C. L. Seitz. Deadlock-free message routing in multiprocessor interconnection networks. *IEEE Trans. Computers*, C-36(5):547–553, May 1987.

[4] J. T. Draper and J. Ghosh. A comprehensive analytical model for wormhole routing in multicomputer systems. *J. Par. Dist. Comp.*, 23:202–214, 1994.

[5] R. I. Greenberg and C. E. Leiserson. Randomized routing on fat-trees. In S. Micali, editor, *Randomness and Computation*. Volume 5 of *Advances in Computing Research*, pages 345–374. JAI Press, 1989.

[6] R. I. Greenberg and H.-C. Oh. Universal wormhole routing. *IEEE Tr. Par. Dist. Sys.*, 8(3):254–262, 1997.

[7] P. Hokstad. Approximations for the M/G/m queue. *Operations Research*, 26(3):510–523, 1978.

[8] L. Kleinrock. *Queueing Systems*, vol. I. J. Wiley, 1975.

[9] F. T. Leighton et al. Randomized routing and sorting on fixed-connection networks. *J. Alg*, 17(1):157–205.

[10] C. E. Leiserson et al. The network architecture of the connection machine CM-5. In *Proc. 4th ACM Symp. Parallel Alg. and Arch.*, pages 272–285, 1992.

Performance and Implementation Aspects of Higher Order Head-of-Line Blocking Switch Boxes

Michael Jurczyk[*]
School of Electrical and Computer Engineering
Purdue University
1285 Electrical Engineering Building
West Lafayette, IN 47907-1285, USA
jurczyk@ecn.purdue.edu

Abstract

Nonuniform traffic can degrade the overall performance of multistage interconnection networks substantially. This performance degradation was traced back to higher order head-of-line blocking (higher order HOL-blocking) effects within the network in the literature. This paper further elaborates on higher order HOL-blocking networks, on their performance under nonuniform traffic patterns, and on methods on how to efficiently implement switch boxes to construct higher order HOL-blocking networks. An analytical upper bound of the achievable network bandwidth under nonuniform traffic patterns is derived and compared to simulation results. Furthermore, it is discussed how central memory buffered switch boxes can be efficiently changed into higher order HOL-blocking switch boxes through only minor changes in the switch box control path. With those switch boxes, high network performance under nonuniform traffic patterns can be achieved with regular hardware effort.

1. Introduction

In many multiprocessor systems, multistage interconnection networks (MINs) are used to interconnect the processing elements (PEs) (i.e., processor/memory pairs), or to connect the processors with memory modules [8]. Blocking MINs consist of stages of switch boxes and provide a unique path between any source and destination pair, and different source/destination paths might share common links and/or switch boxes [8]. In this paper, one class of MINs, the multistage cube networks, are considered, which are representatives of a family of topologies that includes the omega, baseline, and butterfly networks [8].

Nonuniform traffic patterns, such as hot-spot traffic, can cause congestion within the MIN and thereby degrade

---

*The author is now with the CECS-department at the University of Missouri at Columbia.

the overall performance of the MIN substantially. Under a hot-spot traffic pattern, all processors send data to the same destination [5]. If the traffic rate to that hot destination exceeds a certain threshold, a saturation tree of full switch buffers can build up from the last network stage to the first one. The network is overloaded and even data not destined for the hot-spot is delayed substantially.

Several concepts to alleviate saturation tree effects on network performance have been proposed. These concepts can be divided into three main classes: combining [5], flow control techniques [6], and enhanced switch box designs [2]. Combining techniques result in high hardware overhead and might fail under certain traffic scenarios. Flow control techniques often result in decreased performance under uniform traffic. Enhanced switch box designs can alleviate saturation tree effects, while requiring less hardware, as compared to combining techniques. In this paper we focus our attention on the performance and implementation aspects of a specific enhanced switch box architecture, the higher order HOL-blocking switches [3].

In the next section, the network topology and the traffic models used in this paper are defined. After reviewing higher order HOL-blocking in Section 3, an analytical upper bound of the achievable bandwidth of HOL-blocking networks under nonuniform traffic patterns is derived and compared to simulation results in Section 4. Finally, implementation aspects of higher order HOL-blocking switch boxes are discussed in Section 5.

2. Network and traffic models

The network model assumed in this paper is a synchronous, multi-buffered store-and-forward packet switching **multistage cube network** [8], that connects $N=2^n$ inputs with N outputs. The network is constructed from $s = \log_B N$ stages of BxB switch boxes. The stages are numbered from s-1 (stage next to the sources) to 0 (stage next to the destinations). Stage j consists of N/B switch boxes; two consecutive stages are connected via N network links. A multistage cube network with $N=8$ and $B=2$ is shown in

Figure 1. At most one packet is transferred over any network link in each network cycle (including the network inputs and outputs) and a PE discards a packet that cannot be injected into the network as a result of full buffers in the first network stage. A backpressure mechanism is assumed so that no packets are lost within the network.

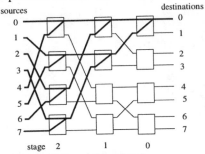

Figure 1: An 8x8 multistage cube network

For **uniform traffic**, each processor generates λ fixed-sized data packets per cycle ($0 \leq \lambda \leq 1$) under a Bernoulli process to be sent through the network; λ is the network load. The destinations of these packets are uniformly distributed.

In many multiprocessing applications, nonuniform traffic patterns are applied to the interconnection network which can result in significant network contention. To study the performance of higher order HOL-blocking in networks under such traffics, the hot-spot traffic was chosen, which is known to produce large contention in multistage cube networks [5]. **Hot-spot traffic** is characterized by a nonuniform distribution of memory accesses, where one memory (the **hot-spot**) is accessed more often than others. In this traffic model, each processor generates a Bernoulli load of λ packets per cycle. A fraction h of those packets ($0 \leq h \leq 1$) is routed to the hot-spot, while the other packets are sent to uniformly distributed destinations. The hot-spot traffic is characterized by the hot-spot message rate λ_h at the hot network output which is determined by (see [5]):

$$\lambda_h = \lambda * (hN + 1 - h). \quad (1)$$

A destination can process at most one packet in each network cycle. Thus, as long as $\lambda_h \leq 1$, the network is not overloaded. Under this condition, the asymptotical maximum traffic rate per PE λ_0 at which the network is not overloaded yet can be calculated to:

$$\lambda_0 = \frac{1}{hN + 1 - h} \cdot \quad (2)$$

If the traffic rate λ exceeds λ_0 in a network with backpressure, a **saturation tree**, i.e., the tree formed by all hot network links and filled buffers, builds up inside the network from the hot network output port to all network input ports [5]. The bold lines in Figure 1 show the saturation tree resulting from a hot-spot at network output 0.

3. Higher order head-of-line blocking

If switch boxes are connected to form a network, additional HOL-blocking effects might occur even in switch boxes free of conventional HOL-blocking (like in output buffered switch boxes). These additional HOL-blocking effects were first studied in [3] and were termed *higher order HOL-blocking* (HOL_k-*blocking*). It was shown that the switch box buffer sharing of different paths through a multistage network influences the blocking behavior and therefore the performance of that network under nonuniform traffic patterns. In order that this paper be self-contained, the definitions of HOL_k-blocking and of the HOL-blocking order H of a network are repeated in the following [3]:

Definition 1: Let PS_1 be the set of path segments of length k ($k>0$) that begin at an arbitrary input link of stage j and end at input link l_1 of stage j-k (k-$1 \leq j < s, 0 \leq l_1 < N$) in a multistage cube network. Let PS_2 be the set of path segments of length k that begin at any input link of stage j and end at input link $l_2 \neq l_1$ of stage j-k. A network exhibits **HOL_k-blocking** behavior if any path segments $p_1 \in PS_1$ and $p_2 \in PS_2$ share buffers.

If a network is HOL_k-blocking for a certain $k=k_0$, path segments $p_1 \in PS_1$ and $p_2 \in PS_2$ of length k_0 will share buffers. If the path segments are extended to a length $k > k_0$, they will still share those buffers. Thus, if a network is HOL_k-blocking for $k=k_0$, it will also be HOL_k-blocking for any $k > k_0$. Based upon this characteristic, a network HOL-blocking order H can be defined:

Definition 2: The **HOL-blocking order H** ($0 \leq H < s+1$) of a network is equal to the minimum k for which the network is HOL_k-blocking. These networks are termed **HOL_H networks**.

In [3], it was also discussed how networks and switch boxes can be classified using the HOL_k-blocking characteristic. It was shown that, in order to obtain an HOL_H network, BxB output buffered switch boxes with $N_{ob} = B^{H-2}$ parallel output buffers per output port have to be used in that network. Thus, for example, a 2x2 HOL_4 switch box needs $N_{ob} = B^{H-2} = 4$ parallel output buffers at each switch box output port. In Figure 2, examples of HOL_1, HOL_2, HOL_3, and HOL_4 switch boxes are depicted.

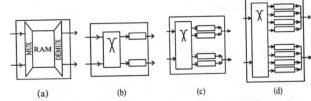

(a)　　　(b)　　　(c)　　　(d)

Figure 2: 2x2 (a) HOL_1, (b) HOL_2, (c) HOL_3, and (d) HOL_4 switch boxes

It should be noted that central memory buffered switch boxes have a blocking order of $H=1$, while conventional output buffered switches have the order $H=2$.

4. Performance of HOL_k-blocking networks

An upper bound of the bandwidth of HOL_H networks under nonuniform traffic patterns is now derived. Nonuniform traffic patterns are assumed in which saturation trees start at output links of stage $s\text{-}R$ ($0 < R \le s$) and reach all network inputs. R equals the depth of the saturation tree. Let λ_0 be the maximum network load for which a saturation tree will not build up within a network under steady-state nonuniform traffic. For network loads higher than λ_0, a saturation tree will build up from output links of stage $s\text{-}R$ ($0 < R \le s$), and will reach all network inputs. Assume an idealized network in which, under uniform traffic, serious congestion will not occur, e.g., through the use of infinite length switch buffers. This assumption results in an upper bound bandwidth. Then, Theorem 1 holds:

Theorem 1: The upper bound BW_{up} of the bandwidth of an HOL_H multistage cube network under nonuniform traffic in a steady state is determined by:

$$BW_{up} =$$

$$\begin{cases} \lambda & , \lambda \le \lambda_0 \quad (3a) \\ \lambda_0 + \left(1 - \dfrac{1}{B^{H-1}}\right) \times (1-h) \times (\lambda - \lambda_0) & , \lambda > \lambda_0, \\ & 1 \le H \le R+1 \quad (3b) \\ \lambda_0 + \left(1 - \dfrac{1}{B^{R}}\right) \times (1-h) \times (\lambda - \lambda_0) & , \lambda > \lambda_0, \\ & H > R+1 \quad (3c) \end{cases}$$

Proof of 3a): For network loads less than λ_0, a saturation tree that reaches all network inputs does not exist within the network yet. The hot packets have only a negligible influence on the cold packets so that the network bandwidth under this hot-spot traffic is only slightly less than the bandwidth under uniform traffic. Thus, $BW_{up} = \lambda$. $\square$

Proof of 3b): For network loads higher than λ_0, a saturation tree exists up to the network inputs in steady state and will block and fill the switch box buffers within the tree. Due to Definitions 1 and 2, paths from input links of stage $s\text{-}1$ to different input links of stage $s\text{-}H$ in HOL_H networks do not share any buffers, but paths from input links of stage $s\text{-}1$ to different input links of stage $s\text{-}H\text{-}1$ share buffers. Now assume that $H \le R+1$. In this case, the length of the paths that do not share any buffers is less than or equal to the length of the saturation tree. The saturation tree of full buffers within an HOL_H network will then block only those packets traveling from an input link of stage $s\text{-}1$ to a hot input link of stage $s\text{-}H$ (see Definition 1). Because of the multistage cube network topology, the probability P_{HL} that a packet with a uniformly distributed destination address is destined for a particular hot input link of stage $s\text{-}H$ in a multistage cube network equals:

$$P_{HL} = \frac{1}{B^{s-1-(s-H)}} = \frac{1}{B^{H-1}} \quad . \quad (4)$$

The probability P_{HP} that a packet travels on a hot path from the network input up to an input link of stage $s\text{-}H$ is $P_{HP} = h + (1-h) * P_{HL}$ and the probability P_{NHP} that a packet does not travel on a hot path up to stage $s\text{-}H$ is

$$P_{NHP} = (1 - P_{HP}) = (1-h) \times \left(1 - \frac{1}{B^{H-1}}\right). \quad (5)$$

Then, the network load can be split into nonhot and hot

parts:

$$\lambda = \underbrace{P_{NHP} \times \lambda}_{\text{nonhot part}} + \underbrace{(1 - P_{NHP}) \times \lambda}_{\text{hot part}} \quad . \quad (6)$$

Now consider a network load higher than λ_0. Then, $\lambda = \Delta + \lambda_0$, with $\Delta > 0$, and

$$\lambda = \underbrace{P_{NHP} \times \lambda}_{\text{nonhot part}} + \underbrace{(1 - P_{NHP}) \times \Delta + (1 - P_{NHP}) \times \lambda_0}_{\text{hot part}} \quad (7)$$

Because the saturation tree reaches all network inputs, only the $(1-P_{NHP})*\lambda_0$ part of the hot network load, which causes the saturation tree to build up, will be accepted into the network; the $(1-P_{NHP})*\Delta$ part will be discarded by each PE. The nonhot part of the network load is not influenced by the saturation tree and, as a result of the idealized network assumption, will be fully accepted by the network. Thus the upper bound bandwidth of an HOL_H network ($H \le R+1$) under nonuniform traffic equals:

$$BW_{up} = P_{NHP} \times \lambda + (1 - P_{NHP}) \times \lambda_0 \quad . \quad (8)$$

Substituting P_{NHP} in Equation (8) with the term in Equation (5) will generate Equation (3b). $\square$

Proof of 3c): $H > R+1$. In this case, the length of the paths in an HOL_H network that do not share buffers is larger than the depth of the saturation tree. Thus, a variation of H will not affect the saturation tree effects within the network so that, in this case, the network bandwidth is independent of H and is determined by the saturation tree length R. These networks therefore have a bandwidth behavior equal to HOL_{R+1} networks, so that the bandwidth is determined by Equation 3(b) with $H = R+1$. $\square$

In Figure 3, the resulting network bandwidth as a function of the network load of a 1024x1024 multistage cube network is depicted for 2x2 switches with a total buffer capacity C of 32 packets per switch under hot-spot traffic with $h=0.01$ (Figure 3a) and $h=0.1$ (Figure 3b). Also, the analytical upper bound bandwidths using Equations (2) and (3) ($R=s$ for hot-spot traffic) are shown. The performance of an output buffered network under uniform traffic is depicted as well to judge the obtainable performance increase of higher HOL-blocking orders. All simulation results shown were obtained through the use of a parallel network simulator [4] running on a MasPar MP-1 SIMD computer.

Equation (5) resembles closely the simulated network bandwidth of HOL_H networks under nonuniform traffic patterns for a wide range of traffic loads (this is also true for other hot-spot loads, network and switch sizes). The analytical results deviate from the simulation results at high loads only, because at those loads, the assumption made in the derivation of Equation (3) (serious congestion will not occur under uniform traffic) no longer holds. The increase of the HOL-blocking order H results in a higher maximum network bandwidth under hot-spot traffic. Also, switches with an HOL-blocking order larger than two will outperform central memory buffered switches (with $H=1$) and output buffered switches (with $H=2$) under nonuniform traffic patterns. These results are also valid for other non-

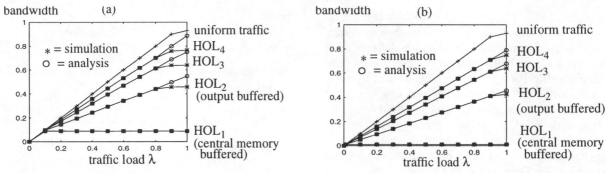

Figure 3: Bandwidth vs. load of a 1024x1024 network comprised of 2x2 switch boxes with buffer space of C=32 packets under hot-spot traffic with (a) h=0.01 and (b) h=0.1

uniform traffic patterns under which saturation trees exist within the network (e.g., under a wide variety of permutation traffic patterns).

Thus, to obtain high performance data communication in a parallel processing system even under nonuniform traffic patterns, a network with the highest achievable HOL-blocking order should be used. The next section will discuss how an HOL-blocking order of up to 5 can be achieved with regular hardware effort.

5. Implementation issues

Consider, for example, a 2x2 HOL_4 switch box with output buffers. Compared to a conventional output buffered switch box (Figure 2b) that needs a 2x2 internal crossbar, the HOL_4 switch needs an internal 2x8 crossbar (see Figure 2d). In general, a BxB HOL_H switch box needs a BxB^{H-1} crossbar if that switch is implemented with conventional output buffers. This results in a high hardware requirement in the data path of a switch box because of the high number of cross points within the crossbar and because of the high wiring needs. Thus, it is not feasible to construct higher order HOL-blocking switch boxes in output buffer technology. Instead, higher order HOL-blocking switch boxes can be constructed without any changes in the data path when the central memory buffering technology is used. This will be shown in the following.

First, the hardware implementation of a conventional central memory buffered switch box will be discussed. To simplify the discussion, a 2x2 switch box (see Figure 2a) is assumed (the discussion is valid for larger switch boxes as well). A packet arriving at one of the switch box input ports will be stored in one of the central memory cells (as long as there is space available). The control path will select a memory address in which the packet will be buffered. When a packet is read out of the memory, the control path has to keep track of the switch output port to which that specific packet is destined. One way to implement this is to use three FIFO address queues in the control path of a 2x2 switch box, as depicted in Figure 4 [1]. In one queue, the *empty queue buffer* (**EQB**), the addresses of all empty central memory cells are stored. Furthermore, there are two FIFO *output queue buffers* (OQB$_0$ and OQB$_1$). In OQB$_0$,

the addresses of those central memory cells are stored in which packets reside that are destined to switch box output port 0, while the addresses of memory cells that contain packets destined to switch output port 1 are stored in OQB$_1$. Once a packet is dequeued from the memory, its central memory address is transferred from its corresponding OQB back to the EQB. There exist several ways to implement the FIFO output queue buffers (OQBs). One efficient way is through the use of shift registers as read and write pointers into the memory array of the buffer [7]. This is depicted in Figure 5. An OQB consists of a memory array with C cells. Instead of using an address decoder to select one of the memory cells, C bit long and one bit wide shift registers are used. A '1' circulates through each shift register that selects one specific memory cell. Each time after an address is written into the buffer, the write shift register is shifted once. Each time after an address is read from the buffer, the read shift register is shifted once.

Now consider a 2x2 HOL_4 switch box that uses central memory buffering. Instead of having eight individual output buffers (four per output port), the central memory buffer has to be divided into eight virtual queues. This can be done by dividing each OQB into 4 subqueues of length $C/8$ each, as shown in Figure 6. Thus, each write and read pointer consists of four individual sub-pointers. Some additional logic has to be introduced at the outputs of the shift register to ensure that only one of the sub-shift registers will select a memory cell at any time. Because at most one packet can leave a switch box port during any network cycle, but multiple output queues are present at each output port, an arbitration logic has to select one of those multiple parallel queues during each network cycle (see Figure 6).

Thus, in general, to convert a conventional central memory buffered BxB switch box into a BxB HOL_H switch box, the read and write pointers of each of the B OQBs in the control path of the switch have to be split into B^{H-2} sub-pointers of length C/B^{H-1} bits each and a queue selection logic has to be added to each of the B read pointers. Extra logic is needed in the control path but this hardware overhead is compensated by the fact that each OQB is shortened from its original length of C to a length of C/B. Thus, a central memory switch can be converted into an HOL_H switch box with very little hardware overhead. The only limiting

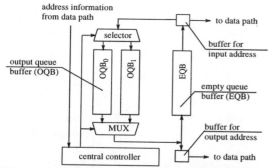

Figure 4: Control path of a 2x2 central memory buffered switch box

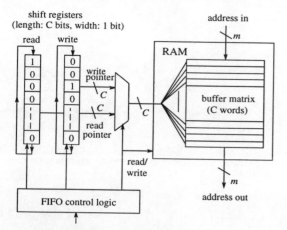

Figure 5: Block diagram of an FIFO OQB

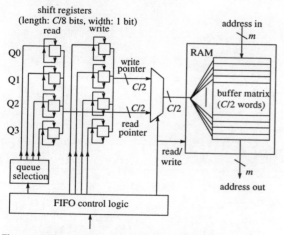

Figure 6: Block diagram of an HOL_4-FIFO OQB

factor of converting a central memory switch into an HOL_H switch is the size of the central memory needed. In [3] it was shown that in order to achieve optimal performance under uniform traffic, each parallel output queue in an HOL_H switch box should have a minimum capacity of $D_{min} > 1$ packets. Because a BxB HOL_H switch box consists of B^{H-1} individual output queues, the central memory of that switch should have a minimum capacity of $Z_{min} = D_{min} * B^{H-1}$ packets. For example, assuming $D_{min} = 4$ and a justifiable central memory size of 64 packets per switch box, 2x2 switches can be implemented with an HOL-

blocking order of up to $H=5$ that results in a high network performance under nonuniform traffic patterns, as was shown in Section 4.

6. Summary

In this paper, an analytical study of the performance of higher order HOL-blocking networks under nonuniform traffic patterns was conducted. An upper bound of the achievable network bandwidth was proposed and compared to simulation results of HOL_H-networks under hot-spot traffic patterns. The analysis predicts the bandwidth very closely for a wide range of network loads. It was observed that higher order HOL-blocking networks provide a higher bandwidth under nonuniform traffic patterns, compared to lower order HOL-blocking networks of the same topology. It was also shown, that central memory buffered switch boxes can be efficiently changed into higher order HOL-blocking switch boxes through only minor changes in the switch box control path. The achievable HOL-blocking order depends solely on the size of the central memory within each switch box. With a regular central memory size of 64 packets, HOL-blocking orders of up to $H=5$ can be achieved that results in a substantial performance increase of networks under nonuniform traffic patterns.

References

[1] T. R. Banniza, G. Eilenberger, B. Pauwels, and Y. Therasse, "Design and technology aspects of VLSI's for ATM switches," *IEEE Journal on Selected Areas in Communications*, Vol. 9, No. 8, October 1991, pp. 1255-1264.

[2] M. Jurczyk and T. Schwederski, "Switch box architecture for saturation tree effect minimization in multistage interconnection networks," *1995 International Conference on Parallel Processing*, August 1995, pp. I/41-I/45.

[3] M. Jurczyk and T. Schwederski, "Phenomenon of higher order head-of-line blocking in multistage interconnection networks under nonuniform traffic patterns," *IEICE Transactions on Information and Systems*, Vol. E79-D, No. 8, August 1996, pp. 1124-1129.

[4] M. Jurczyk, T. Schwederski, H. J. Siegel, S. Abraham, and R. Born, "Strategies for the implementation of interconnection network simulators on parallel computers," *International Journal in Computer Systems*, to appear, 1997.

[5] G. F. Pfister and V. A. Norton, "'Hot spot' contention and combining in multistage interconnection networks," *IEEE Transactions on Computers*, Vol. C-34, No. 10, October 1985, pp. 933-938.

[6] S. L. Scott and G. S. Sohi, "The use of feedback in multiprocessors and its application to tree saturation control," *IEEE Transactions on Parallel and Distributed Systems*, Vol. 1, No. 4, October 1990, pp. 385-398.

[7] A. Schwarz, *Study and implementation of the control path of a central memory buffered switch box*, Master's Thesis, IND, University of Stuttgart, Germany, 1992.

[8] H. J. Siegel, *Interconnection Networks for Large-Scale Parallel Processing: Theory and Case Studies, Second Edition*, McGraw-Hill, New York, NY, 1990.

Session 1C

Compilers I
Data Layout and Access

Data Distribution Analysis and Optimization for Pointer-Based Distributed Programs[*]

Jenq Kuen Lee   Dan Ho   Y. C. Chuang
Department of Computer Science
National Tsing-Hua University
Hsinchu, Taiwan

Abstract

A critical question remains open if the compiler can understand the distribution pattern of pointer-based distributed objects built by application programmers, and perform optimization as effectively as the HPF compiler does with distributed arrays. In this paper, we address this challenging issue. In our work, we first present a parallel programming model which allows application programmers to build pointer-based distributed objects at application levels. Next, we propose a distribution analysis algorithm which can automatically summarize the distribution pattern of pointer-based distributed objects built by application programmers. Our work, to our best knowledge, is the first work to attempt to address this open issue. Our distribution analysis framework employs Feautrier's parametric integer programming as the basic solver, and can always obtain precise distribution information from the class of programs written in our parallel programming model with static control. Experimental results done on a 16-node IBM SP-2 machine show that the compiler with the help of distribution analysis algorithm can significantly improve the performance of pointer-based distributed programs.

1 Introduction

With the support of distributed pointers and abstract object types in parallel C/C++ systems such as DINO[19], Split-C[4], Olden[5], and parallel C++[14, 3] environments, application programmers now can build user-level pointer-based distributed structures such as distributed linked list, graph, tree, mesh, and many other application-level structures. For example, programmers or library designers can build a distributed tree with a global name space on distributed memory architectures by constructing a subtree with SPMD computation by each processor (SPMD is a parallel computation model that every processor executes the same program, but different set of data), and then link the subtrees together via distributed pointers. After the construction of the structures, the distributed tree can then be manipulated as though the shared memory and global name space are available. However, just as in the compilation process of HPF language, the compiler needs the data distribution information of the builtin distributed arrays to generate efficient communication codes in emulating the global name space on distributed memory architectures, it remains an open question how the distributed information of user-defined linked distributed structures can be passed to compilers for optimizations.

In this paper, we are interested in answering the above question from the viewpoints of fundamental compiler technology, — "Can the compiler be intelligent enough to automatically understand the distribution pattern of pointer-based distributed objects built by application programmers, and perform optimization as effectively as HPF does with distributed arrays?". In our work, we first present a parallel programming model which allows application programmers to build pointer-based distributed objects at application levels. Next, we propose a distribution analysis algorithm which can automatically summarize the distribution pattern of pointer-based distributed objects built by application programmers. Our work, to our best knowledge, is the first work to attempt to address this open issue. Previously, the research work of pointer analysis[2, 9, 10, 17], have mainly focused on gathering the aliases information of pointer programs on flat shared memory parallel machines, and do not provide the distribution information needed for compiler optimization on distributed memory parallel architectures. Our distribution analysis framework employs Feautrier's parametric integer programming[15, 16] as the basic solver, and can always obtain "precise" distribution information from the class of programs written in our parallel programming model. We say the information is precise, because at any given program continuation point, we can always identify the exact memory instance which a pointer is pointing to, or the exact memory instance which a field of a memory instance is pointing to. Traditionally, in scalar data flow equations[1] and alias analysis[17], conservative estimation will return a set of memory instances which a pointer may be pointing to, while in our case, we will always return a unique one.

The summary information of the distribution informa-

---
[*]This work was supported in part by NSC of Taiwan under grant No. NSC85-2213-E-007-050 and NSC85-2221-E-007-031. The correspondence author's e-mail address is jklee@cs.nthu.edu.tw.

tion of the programs we gather from our analysis algorithm is called "raw distribution information" in this paper. The raw distribution information we gather is always precise, and can be converted into different "cooked" data distribution pattern for different compiler optimization purposes. For example, we can try to infer the raw distribution patterns into a form of cooked patterns to see along a pointer direction (such as "next"), if it is distributed by "Block" (which has each processor get a consecutive block of elements), "Cyclic"(which is a round-robin rotation), "Collapse"(which mean no distribution), or "Block-Cyclic" (which is a round-robin rotation, but each time each processor takes a small block number of elements), as simiarly in the distribution information in HPF. In our experiments, we have successfully gathered the cooked information, "Block", "Cyclic", "Block-Cyclic", and "Collapse" for linked list, mesh, range trees[20, 9], etc. For other optimization purposes such as affinity analysis[5], one might be interested in calculating the probability of a pointer (says "next") pointing to a remote reference.

Our distribution analysis algorithm is currently being incorporated into an experimental parallel C++ environment[13, 14] at IBM SP-2 machines to experiment with unstructured and irregular scientific applications with pointer structures. Preliminary experimental results done at 16-node IBM SP-2 show that the compiler with the help of our distribution analysis algorithm can significantly improve the performance of pointer-based distributed programs.

The remainder of the paper is organized as follows. Section 2 describes our parallel programming model which allows programmers to build their own distributed data structures with SPMD computation. Section 3 presents our data distribution analysis framework which can obtain distribution patterns of the program written in our model. Finally, Section 4 concludes the paper with the discussion on experimental results, solver frameworks, and related work.

2 Parallel Program Model

2.1 The Source Language

In this section, we describe the programming model we provide for users to construct distributed data structures. In the model, the construction of distributed data structures is done in SPMD mode, and after the construction programmers can use it as a shared structure. Here, we can draw an analogy between our model and HPF model. In HPF, we have "extrinsic" functions. In the extrinsic mode, a program is executed in SPMD model, and the program is back to run with shared memory semantics once it gets back from extrinsic mode to the normal mode. The extrinsic mode is used to link with library routines. In our model, programmers or library designers can build a distributed tree with a global name space on distributed memory architectures by constructing a subtree

with SPMD computation by each processor (SPMD is a parallel computation model that every processor executes the same program, but different set of data), and then link the subtrees together via distributed pointers. The work done above can be considered in an extrinsic mode. After the construction of the structures, the distributed tree can then be manipulated by users in the normal mode to have shared-memory semantics and global name space.

To build distributed structures in our model, programmers first need to specify the dimension of the processor array, and then three steps are used to construct the distributed data structures. The three step sequence is described below. First, programmers write SPMD programs to construct locally linked data structures. Then, a barrier synchronization is performed after the SPMD parallel step. This is shown as the step 1 in the parallel C++ code below.

```
class object {
    distributed  object *next;
    data    a;
    object();
};
object::object(){
 distributed object *q, *p, *r;
 distributed object *tail, *PointerArray[#P];
 /* Step 0:Specify how processor id is named */
 SetProcDim(OneDim);
 /*Step 1:SPMD Construct Locally Linked Structures*/
 r= NULL; tail =NULL;
 for (i=0; i<N/#P; i++)  {
     q = malloc(sizeof(object));
     if (i==0) tail = q;
     q->next =r;
     r = q;
 }
 barrier();
 /* Step 2: Broadcast */
 broadcast (r,PointerArray);
 /* Step 3: chain up */
 chain_up(tail,PointerArray[(pid+1)mod #P],''next'');
}
```

In the second step, a broadcast operation is performed. The broadcast operation is done as follows. Each processor running in SPMD mode provides a pointer pointing to the local linked data structure. The information is then broadcast to all the processor. Each processor then receives a vector of pointer, the value of which comes from the contribution of each processor. After the broadcast operation is done, the kth element of the gathered array coming from processor k.

In the third phase of the program, a chain_up operator is provided so that the program can chain a local pointer with the pointer broadcasted in the previous section. The pointer (such as "next" or "previous") can be specified in the chain_up operator. If two fields are specified, the first one is used as the forward pointer, and the second is used as the backward pointer. The chain_up operator in the above example, will chain PointerArray[(pid+1) mod #p] into the "next" field of pointer tail. That is

$$tail-> next = PointerArray[(pid+1)mod\#p]$$

The three steps above can be repeated arbitrary times. In addition, any one of the step can be omitted by programmers. Broadcast and chain_up are used here as communication primitives in SPMD mode while without compiler support. The model is used as a reference to demonstrate our automatic distribution analysis algorithm.

2.2 Restrictions

We restrict our parallel programming model to be with static control. The concept of the program with static control is first introduced by Feautrier[16]. In the programs, a set of unknown integer variables are allowed. The set of integer variables, which are only defined only once in the program, and whose value depends only on the outside world, are called structure parameters. The programs are with the domain of loop nests where the loops bounds, conditional expressions in the branch, and array indices are all affine functions of the set of structure parameters.

We allow pointer expression in the program which is not seen in Feautrier[16]. However, we do not allow recursive programs[7]. The distributed data structures built by users have to be done by loops instead of recursive programs. As we are interested in demonstrating the essential idea of the existence of a sound solution to the problem, we choose a slightly restricted, but well-documented subset of the programs. We think our work provides a sound theoretic basis for the open issue – "Can the compiler be intelligent enough to automatically understand the distribution pattern of pointer-based distributed objects built by application programmers?". It can not only be used as an important basis for possible future improvements toward full solutions, but also be directly used for a specification language, where a slightly restricted program is acceptable.

3 Distribution Analysis Algorithm

3.1 Notations

In this section, we give the basic notations needed for our distribution analysis algorithm. Figure 1 gives a summary of the variables and notations used. We give the detailed descriptions for the key definitions below. First, to summarize the distribution information of distributed linked structures, we need to give a naming scheme[2], to name the heap allocated objects (by new or malloc). Without loss of generality, throughout this paper, we will only summarize the distribution information of heap allocated objects. Our naming scheme is based on the processor number, loop index, and statement number as follows.

Definition 1 To distinguish different instances of locations created by a dynamical allocation statment in a loop, we use an absolute occurrence number. The location created by loop index $(i_1, i_2, \cdots, i_n)$, processor number, $(p_1, p_2, \cdots, p_k)$, and in the statement number $< s' >$ has the absolute occurrence number $((p_1, p_2, \cdots, p_k), (i_1, i_2, \cdots, i_n), s')$. This instance is denoted as $m_{((p_1, p_2, \cdots, p_k), (i_1, i_2, \cdots, i_n), s')}$.

Consider the following code:

Code Fragment 1
```
        l= NULL;
        for (i=0; i<M; i++)  {
S1:         q = malloc(sizeof(object));
S2:         q ->next = l;
S3:         l = q;
        }
L1: /* End of Loop */
```

The memory instance allocated at statement S1 is denoted as $m_{p,i,S1}$, where p is the processor number, i is the loop index, and $S1$ is the statement number. Totally, instances $m_{p,i,S1}, 0 \le p < \#P, 0 \le i < (M-1)$, are created in the code above, as the program is executed in SPMD mode, and each processor will execute the code above.

Our goal of this paper is to find a distribution summary for user-defined distributed structures. The summary graph to represent the result of our summary is defined as follows.

Definition 2 A Summary Distribution Graph (SDG) is defined as

$$\delta(((p_1, \cdots, p_k), (i_1, \cdots, i_n), s), field, continuation)$$

$$= \begin{cases} m_{(p_1^1, \cdots, p_k^1), (i_1^1, \cdots, i_n^1), s_1} & | \quad \gamma_1 \\ m_{(p_1^2, \cdots, p_k^2), (i_1^2, \cdots, i_n^2), s_2} & | \quad \gamma_2 \\ \cdots \\ m_{(p_1^m, \cdots, p_k^m), (i_1^m, \cdots, i_n^m), s_m} & | \quad \gamma_m \end{cases}$$

where $(p_1, ..., p_k)$ is the processor number, $(i_1, ..., i_n)$ is the loop index, s is the statement number, k is the number of the dimension of the processor array, n is the depth of the nested loops, γ_i represents a set of integer intervals defined based on the constraints related to $(p_1, p_2, ..., p_k)$ and $(i_1, ..., i_n)$, and continuation is the program continuation defined in Figure 1.

For example, in the *Code Fragment 1*, we will have the summary graph as follows.

58

$$\begin{array}{lll}
m_i & \in MemInst & = ProcSet \times LoopIndexSet \times StmtNo \\
L & \in Continuation & = StmtNo \times IterSet + StmtNo \\
\delta & \in SummaryGraph & = (ProcSet \times LoopIndexSet \times StmtNo) \times FieldName \times Continuation \rightarrow MemInst \\
\tau & \in MemInstForExp & = Expression \times IterSet \times StmtNo \rightarrow MemInst \\
Q & \in Aliases & = PointerVar \times IterSet \times StmtNo \rightarrow MemInst \\
q & \in PointerVar & \text{pointer} \\
s_i & \in StmtNo & = Z^+ \\
p_i & \in ProcSet & = Z^+ \\
b, u & \in IterSet & = ProcSet \times LoopIndexSet \\
\alpha, \beta & \in Expression & \text{expression of the program} \\
next & \in FieldName & \text{a field name of a structure} \\
\#P & \in ProcessorNum & = N \\
I & \in LoopIndexSet & = Z^+
\end{array}$$

Figure 1: Variable Notations

$$\delta((p, i, S1), next, L1)$$

$$= \left\{ \begin{array}{ll} NULL & \mid \quad i = 0, 0 \leq p < \#P - 1 \\ m_{p,i-1,S1} & \mid \quad 0 < i < M, 0 \leq p < \#P - 1 \end{array} \right.$$

To use the notation in Definition 2, we have γ_1 as $(i = 0, 0 \leq p < \#P - 1)$ and γ_2 as $(0 < i < M, 0 \leq p < \#P - 1)$. δ states that the content of the "next" of memory instance $m_{p,i,S1}$ at a given program continuation point, $L1$, is $NULL$ if $(i = 0, 0 \leq p < \#P - 1)$, and $m_{p,i-1,S1}$ if $0 < i < M, 0 \leq p < \#P - 1$. We will show how the summary graph can be gotten in the next sub-sections.

Next, in order to calculate the summary graph, we need two auxiliary functions. The first auxiliary function, Q, is to calculate the alias information (the memory instance) for a pointer variable at a given continuation point. The function is defined as follows.

Definition 3 Given a pointer variable q, and a program continuation point (s, b), the alias function, Q, returns the alias of q at the program continuation point (s, b). The alias function, Q is defined as

$$Q(q, b, s) = \left\{ \begin{array}{ll} m_{u_1} & \mid \quad \gamma_1 \\ m_{u_2} & \mid \quad \gamma_2 \\ \cdots & \\ m_{u_k} & \mid \quad \gamma_k, \end{array} \right.$$

where γ_i represents a set of integer intervals as similarly in Definition 2, m_{u_i} represents a memory instance, q is a pointer variable in the program, b is the iteration index, and s is the statement number.

In the definition above, b represents iteration index. As shown in Figure 1, b belongs to $IterSet$ which is equivalent to $ProcSet \times LoopIndexSet$. We again use the example in *Code Fragment 1* to show the functionality of the function, Q. Suppose we want to find out the aliases of q at statement S3 with iteration number b (let b be euqal to (p, i)).

Then we have
$$Q(q, b, S3)$$
$$= Q(q, (p, i), S3) = m_{p,i,S1}, 0 \leq i < M - 1, 0 \leq p < \#P.$$

Again, we will show how the alias function can be calculated in the next sub-sections. In addition, suppose we want to find out the aliases of l at statement S2 in *Code Fragment 1*. We then have
$$Q(l, b, S2) = Q(l, (p, i), S2)$$

$$= \left\{ \begin{array}{ll} NULL & \mid \quad i = 0, 0 \leq p < \#P \\ m_{p,i-1,S1} & \mid \quad 0 < i < M - 1, \\ & \quad 0 \leq p < \#P. \end{array} \right. \quad (1)$$

The second auxiliary function is a function, τ, to find the memory instance for a given program expression at a given program continuation point. It's defined below.

Definition 4 An auxiliary function, τ, is defined as

$$\tau(e, b, s) = \left\{ \begin{array}{ll} m_{u_1} & \mid \quad \gamma_1 \\ m_{u_2} & \mid \quad \gamma_2 \\ \cdots & \\ m_{u_k} & \mid \quad \gamma_k \end{array} \right.$$

where γ_i represents a set of integer intervals, and e is an expression in the program, b is the iteration index, m_{u_i} is a memory instance, and s is the statement number.

The auxiliary function, τ, above is similar to the function Q except for that it's more general to report the memory instance for any pointer expression (such as q->next). Finally, we need to define the notation to represent the program precedence order.

Definition 5 Let s_1, s_2 be the statement numbers, and b_1, b_2 be the iteration index. Then we define $(b_1, s_1) \prec (b_2, s_2)$ if (b_1, s_1) is executed before (b_2, s_2) in the program execution order.

3.2 Solutions of Data Distribution Analysis

In this section, we will give the equations to calculate the functions δ, Q, and τ. The result of the function, δ, directly represents the summary of the distributed information of programs. The summary information, δ, in our framework is called "raw distribution information". The raw distribution information we gather is always precise, and can be converted into a variety of "cooked" data distribution patterns, later, for different compiler optimization purposes. Our proposed framework is modelled closely based on the methodologies used in array data flow analysis[6, 15, 16, 18], which are originally used to find the data dependence among array elements. We introduce additional processor concept, pointer and aliases formula, and distribution information into the equations which greatly expand array data flow analysis framework to be able to summarize distribution pattern for pointer-based distributed structures. We give the formula below to calculate δ, Q, and τ, respectively.

The Calculation of Aliases Identity

First, we show how to calculate the alias function, Q. Suppose we have the code fragment below.

Code Fragment 2

```
      for (i=0; i <M ; i++)
      {
s_1 :        q = β_1
             . . .
s_3 :        q = β_2
             . . .
s_a :          = q . . . /* Use of q */
             . . .
s_k :        q = β_k
      }
```

Suppose q is a pointer variable, and $s_1, s_2, ..., s_k$ are the only statements with writes to the variable q. Then, the aliases of q at statement s_a with iteration number b can be calculated from the write sequence of $s_1, s_2, ..., s_k$.

Let $R_{s_i,s_a}(q, b)$ represents the set of writes produced at statement s_i to potentially become the alias of q at statement s_a with iteration b. Then we have

$$R_{s_i,s_a}(q,b) = \{(u, \tau(\beta_i, u, s_i)) | (s_i, u) \prec (s_a, b), u \in IterSet_{s_i}\}.$$

The formula above lists all the legal iteration indexes, u ($u \in Iterset_{s_i}$) such that (s_i, u) precedes (s_a, b), while the alias is $\tau(\beta_i, u, s_i)$. Each element in $R_{s_i,s_a}(q, b)$ is a potential alias to q at iteration b, but only the one with the lexicographic maximum (the last write) of the set is the real alias of q at iteration b. Let T_{s_i,s_a} represent the set with the last write. Then we have

$$T_{s_i,s_a}(q,b) = Max_{\prec} R_{s_i,s_a}(q,b).$$

$Max_{\prec} R_{s_i,s_a}(q, b)$ is defined as follows.

$$Max_{\prec} R_{s_i,s_a}(q,b) \equiv$$
$$\{(u, \tau(\beta_i, u, s_i)) | (u, \tau(\beta_i, u, s_i)) \in R_{s_i,s_a}(q,b) \text{ and }$$
$$\forall(u', \tau(\beta_i, s_i, u')) \in R'_{s_i,s_a}(q,b) \Rightarrow (s_i, u') \prec (s_i, u)\}$$

Note that if the set is empty, that means q is $\perp$ or defined at a previous continuation point. Here, since we have statements, $s_1, ..., s_k$, we need to summarize all the statements. Therefore, we have

$$Q'_{s_a}(q,b) = Max_{\prec}\{R_{s_i,s_a}(q,b), i = 1, ..., k\}$$

Finally, we only need to pick up the second field of each element of Q' to form the set of aliases.

$$Q(q,b,s_a) = \{j | (u, j) \in Q'_{s_a}(q,b)\}$$

Auxiliary Function: τ

Next, we give the equations for the auxiliary function, τ, which finds the memory instance for a given program expression, α, at statement s_i with iteration index b. We have

$$\tau(\alpha, b, s_i) = \begin{cases} m_{b,s_i} & if \quad \alpha \text{ is malloc} \\ Q(q,b,s_i) & if \quad \alpha \text{ is } q \\ NULL & if \quad \alpha \text{ is NULL} \\ \delta(Q(q,b,s_i), next, (s_i, b)) & if \quad \alpha \text{ is } q \rightarrow next. \end{cases}$$

The main algorithm we need for this paper is for the calculation of the summary graph at the end of a given for-loop. The summary graph information at the end of the allocation subroutine (such as constructor) is the final result we need for our optimization. However, as we can see in the calculation of the auxiliary function, τ, we might need the summary graph information at arbitrary continuation point of a given program. Therefore, we give our formula below to be used at an arbitrary continuation point of a given program.

Summarized Graph Calculation at Arbitrary Continuation Point

Suppose we have the following code fragment.

Code Fragment 3

```
      for (i=0; i <M ; i++)
      {
s :        ... = malloc(...)
           . . .
s_1 :      q_1 -> next = α_1
           . . .
s_a :      ... =.../*To calculate the summary graph here*/
s_2 :      q_2 -> next = α_2
           . . .
s_k :      q_k -> next = α_k
      }
```

Assume $s_1, s_2, ..., s_k$ are the only statements which have the writes to the "next" field of objects in the program. As we want to summarize the memory instances with the "next" field, we are only interested in the write to the "next" field. Therefore, we only need to consider statements $s_1, s_2, ..., s_k$. To calculate

δ, without loss of generality, we can first try to find out the set of iterations and instances at statment s_i writing to the "next" field of memory instance $m_{b,s}$ preceding the the continuation point (t, s_a), where t is the iteration index. Let M_{s_i,s_a} be the set. Then we have

$$M_{s_i,s_a}(b, next, t) = \{(u, \tau(\alpha_i, u, s_i))|$$
$$(s_i, u) \prec (s_a, t), Q(q_i, u, s_i) = m_{b,s}, u \in IterSet_{s_i}\}.$$

At statement s_i, there could be several writes to the memory instance $m_{b,s}$, and we are only interested in the one with the lexicographic maximum (the last write). Let K_{s_i,s_a} be the set of the last write. Then we have

$$K_{s_i,s_a}(b, next, t) = Max_{\prec} M_{s_i,s_a}(b, next, t).$$

where $Max_{\prec} M_{s_i,s_a}(b, next, t)$ is defined as follows.

$$Max_{\prec} M_{s_i,s_a}(b, next, t) \equiv \{(u, \tau(\alpha_i, u, s_i))|(u, \tau(\alpha_i, u, s_i))$$
$$\in M_{s_i,s_a}(b, next, t) \; and \; \forall(u^{'}, \tau(\alpha_i, u^{'}, s_i))$$
$$\in M_{s_i,s_a}(b, next, t) \Rightarrow (s_i, u^{'}) \prec (s_i, u)\}$$

But since we have statements, $s_1, ..., s_k$, we need to summarize all the statements. Therefore, we have

$$\delta^{'}(b, next, (t, s_a)) = Max_{\prec}\{K_{s_i,s_a}(b, next, t), i = 1, ..., k\}.$$

The summary graph only needs the second tuple of the above information, so we have

$$\delta(b, next, (t, s_a)) = \{j|(u, j) \in \delta^{'}(b, next, (t, s_a))\}.$$

3.3 Examples

In the following, we give two examples to demonstrate how our framework works. The systematic solver to solve the problem will be given in the next sub-section by using parametric integer programming.

Our first example is a program to build a one dimensional linked list as follows.

Code Fragment 4
```
UserObject::UserObject(){
    distributed UserObject *q, *r;
    distributed UserObject *tail, *Pointer[#P];
L0: r=NULL, tail =NULL;
L1: for (i=0; i < (N/#P)-1; i++) {
S1:     q = malloc(sizeof(UserObject));
S2:     if (i==0) tail = q;
S3:     q->next = r;
S4:     r = q;
    }
L2: /* Barrier */
L3: broadcast (r, Pointer);
L4: chain_up(tail,Pointer[(pid+1)mod #P],''next'');
L5:}
```

We need to first calculate the summary graph at the program point "L2". In addition, the only write to the "next" field of the objects is in statement S3, so we have

$$\delta(b, next, L2) = Max_{\prec} M_{S3}(b, next, L2). \quad (2)$$

We then calculate M_{S3}.
$$M_{S3}(b, next, L2)$$
$$= \{(u, \tau(r, u, S3))|Q(q, u, S3) = m_{b,s_1}, u \in IterSet_{S3}\} \quad (3)$$

Next, we calculate $Q(q, u, S3)$. After a series of calculations according to the formula in Section 3.2, we have

$$Q(q, u, S3) = m_{u,S1}. \quad (4)$$

We then calculate $\tau(r, u, S3)$ as follows.

$$\tau(r, u, S3) = Q(r, u, S3)$$

Next, we have
$$Q(r, (pid, i), S3)$$
$$= \begin{cases} NULL & | \quad i = 0 \\ Q(q, (pid, i-1), S4) & | \quad 0 < i < (N/\#P)\&\& \\ & \quad (0 \le pid \le (\#P - 1)) \end{cases} \quad (5)$$

Combining equations 2, 3, 4, and 5, we get
$$\delta((pid, i, S1), next, L3)$$
$$= \begin{cases} m_{pid,i-1,S1} & | \quad 0 < i < (N/\#P)\&\& \\ & \quad (0 \le pid \le (\#P - 1)) \\ NULL & | \quad i = 0 \end{cases} \quad (6)$$

Next, we need to do the broadcast and chain-up operations, and we need to know where r and $tail$ are pointing to.

$$Q(r, pid, L2) = Q(q, pid, L2) = m_{pid, N/\#P-1}$$

$$Q(tail, pid, L2) = m_{pid,0}$$

The chain-up operation basically does the following

$$M_{(pid,0,S1)}- > next = m_{(pid+1)mod\#P, N\#P-1, S1} \quad (7)$$

Combining results at (6) and (7), we have the summary information as follows.
$$\delta((pid, i, S1), "next", L5) =$$

$$\begin{cases} m_{pid,i-1,S1} & | \quad 0 < i < N/\#P - 1, \\ & \quad 0 \le pid \le (\#P - 1) \\ m_{(pid+1)mod\#P, N/\#P-1, S1} & | \quad 0 \le pid \le (\#P - 1), \\ & \quad i = 0 \end{cases} \quad (8)$$

The distribution information we get from (8) is a precise information, and is a "raw" information. The raw distribution information can then be converted into different "cooked" data distribution patterns depending on the purpose of compiler optimizations. In this example, we can further infer that the distribution along the "next" direction is by "Block" distribution.

Next, we will look at our second example to build a two dimensional range tree[20][9]. Figure 2 illustrates an example of the construction of a distributed range tree. An interesting multi-dimensional tree structure which is a binary tree of binary tree, and the leave node is again linked together. The source program of the construction of the distributed range tree in

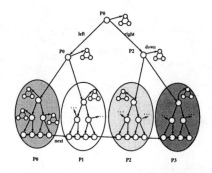

Figure 2: Two Dimensional Range Tree

SPMD mode is listed in Appendix. We first calculate the summary information at program point L1. It summarizes the lower part of the subtree at each processor.

$\delta((p, i, j, S1), left, L1)$

$$= \begin{cases} m_{p, i+1, 2*j, S1} & \mid & 0 \le i < (N-1) \&\& \\ & & 0 \le j < 2^i \\ NULL & \mid & i = N-1, 0 \le j < 2^i \end{cases} \quad (9)$$

$\delta((p, i, j, S1), right, L1)$

$$= \begin{cases} m_{p, i+1, 2*j+1, S1} & \mid & 0 \le i < (N-1) \&\& \\ & & 0 \le j < 2^i \\ NULL & \mid & i = N-1, 0 \le j < 2^i \end{cases} \quad (10)$$

Next, we will try to summarize the information at program point L2. It summarize the "next" information in the leave nodes. We have

$\delta((p, N-1, j, S1), next, L2)$

$$= \begin{cases} m_{p, N-1, j+1, S1} & \mid & 0 \le j < (2^{N-1}) - 1 \\ m_{p+1, N-1, 0, S1} & \mid & 0 \le p < \#P - 1, j = 2^{N-1} \\ NULL & \mid & p = \#P - 1, j = 2^{N-1}. \end{cases} \quad (11)$$

Next, we summarize the information at program point L3. It constructs the upper tree of the distributed tree. We have

$\delta((p, stride, S2), left, L3)$

$$= \begin{cases} m_{p, 0, 0, S1} & \mid & stride = 1, \\ & & (p \, mod(stride * 2)) = 0 \\ m_{p, stride/2, S2}, & \mid & 1 < stride < \#P, \\ & & (p \, mod \, (stride * 2)) = 0 \end{cases} \quad (12)$$

$\delta((p, stride, S2), right, L3)$

$$= \begin{cases} m_{p+stride, 0, 0, S1} & \mid & stride = 1, \\ & & (p \, mod \, (stride * 2)) = 0 \\ m_{p+stride, stride/2, S2} & \mid & 1 < stride < \#P, \\ & & (p \, mod \, (stride * 2)) = 0. \end{cases}$$
$$(13)$$

Similarly, we can summarize the subtree in the "down" direction. In addition, because the summary information in (9), (10), (11), (12), and (13) do not over-write each other, so the final summary information is the add up of those information. If they over-write each other, we need to again calculate the set of the last write elements. The distribution information we get above is a precise, but a "raw" information. We

can further conclude that along the "next" direction, the distribution is by block. In addition, if we will follow the "left" pointer, it will never cross processor boundaries to reach remote references, and similarly, it will not cross the processor boundary in the "down" direction.

4 Discussion and Related Work

Our equations developed in Section 3.2 can be solved through a sequence of applications of parametric integer programming. The parametric integer programming[15] is originally developed for array data flow analysis. It's basically a form of integer programming, but allowing unknow variables in the equation so that you will get a parametric solution for the unknown variables in your program. The call-graph can be solved by applying parametric integer programming to the leaf nodes first, and then apply them into the upper level of the tree one by one. Due to space limitations, we leave the details in a full version of this paper in http://falcon.cs.nthu.edu.tw/~jklee/. Our distribution analysis algorithm is currently being incorporated into an experimental parallel C++ environment[13, 14] at IBM SP-2 machines. Preliminary experimental results done at 16-node IBM SP-2 (code translation partly by hand codes) show that the compiler with the help of our distribution analysis algorithm can significantly improve the performance of pointer-based distributed programs. We also leave the detailed experimental results in the full version of our paper in our home page due to space limitations.

Previously, the research work of pointer analysis [17, 9, 10, 2] have mainly focused on gathering the aliases information of pointer programs on flat shared memory parallel machines, and do not provide the distribution information needed for compiler optimization on distributed memory parallel architectures. The work done in [7, 11] can infer the shape of the data structures to be a tree, linked list, or a graph, but still do not provide the processor concept and distribution information for distributed memory architectures. It will be interesting to see if Harrison's work can be used as a basis to further extend our work towards recursive programs due to more extensible naming schemes for heap objects.

References

[1] A. Aho, R. Sethi, J. Ullman. *Compilers Principles, Techniques, and Tools*, Addison-Wesley, 1985.

[2] Francois Bodin. *Data Structure Analysis in C Programs*, Technical Reports, IRISA, 1991.

[3] Bodin, F., Beckman, P., Gannon, D., Narayana, S., and Yang, S. Distributed pC++: Basic Ideas for an Object Parallel Language, *Scientific Programming*, 2(3), Fall 1993.

[4] D. Culler, A. Dusseau, S. Goldstein, A. Krishnamurthy, S. Lummetta, T. von Eicken, and K. Yelick. *Parallel Programming in Split-C*, In Proceedings of Supercomputing '93, pp. 262-273, 1993.

[5] M. C. Carlisle, A. Rogers. *Software Caching and Computation Migration in Olden*, Proceedings of ACM SIGPLAN Conference on Principles and Practice of Parallel Programming, pp. 29-39, July 1995.

[6] J. F. Collard, P. Feautrier. *Fuzzy Array DataFlow Analysis*, Proceedings of ACM SIGPLAN Conference on Principles and Practice of Parallel Programming, pp. 92-101, July 1995.

[7] William Harrison. *The Interprocedural Analysis and Automatic Parallelization of Scheme Programs*, Lisp and Symbolic Computation, 2:3/4, pp. 179-396, 1989.

[8] Gwan-Hwan Hwang, Jenq Kuen Lee, and Dz-Ching Ju. An Array Operation Synthesis Scheme to Optimize Fortran 90 Programs, Proceedings of ACM SIGPLAN Conference on Principles and Practice of Parallel Programming, pp. 112-122, July 1995.

[9] L. Hendren, J. Hummel, A. Nicolau. *Abstractions for Recursive Pointer Data Structures: Improving the Analysis and Transformation of Imperative Programs*, Proceedings of ACM SIGPLAN PLDI, 1992.

[10] J. Hummel, L. Hendren, A. Nicolau. *A General Data Dependence Test for Dynamic, Pointer-Based Data Structures*, Proceedings of ACM SIGPLAN PLDI, 1994.

[11] R. Ghiya and L. Hendren. *Is it a Tree, a DAG or Cyclic Graph? A Shape Analysis for Heap-Directed Pointers in C*, Proceedings of ACM POPL, 1996.

[12] Koelbel, C., Loveman, D., Schreiber R., Steele, G., and Zosel, M. *The High Performance Fortran Handbook*, MIT-press, Cambridge, 1994.

[13] Jenq Kuen Lee, In-Kuen Tsaur, San-Yih Hwang. *Parallel Array Object I/O Support on Distributed Environments*, Journal of Parallel and Distributed Computing, 40, 227-241, 1997.

[14] Jenq Kuen Lee and D. Gannon. *Object-Oriented Parallel Programming: Experiments and Results*, Proceedings of Supercomputing '91, New Mexico, November, 1991.

[15] Paul Feautrier. *Parametric Integer Programming*, RAIRO Recherche Operationnelle, 22:243-268, Sep. 1988.

[16] Paul Feautrier. *Dataflow Analysis of Array and Scalar References*, International Journal of Parallel Programming, 20(1):23-52, Feb. 1991.

[17] W. Landi, B. Ryder, S. Zhang. *Interprocedural Modification Side Effect Analysis with Pointer Aliasing*, Proceedings of ACM SIGPLAN Conference on Programming Language Design and Implementation, pp. 56-68, 1993.

[18] Dror E. Maydan, Saman P. Amarasinghe, and Monica S. Lam. *Array Data-FLow Analysis and Its Use in Array Privatization*, Proceedings of Principles of Programming Language, 1993.

[19] M. Rosing, . Schnabel, R. Weaver. *Scientific Programming Languages for Distributed Memory Multiprocessors: Paradigms and Research Issues*, Languages, Compilers, and Runtime Environments for Distributed Memory Machines, editors, Joel Saltz, P. Mehrotra, North Holland, 1992.

[20] Hanan Samet. *The Design and Analysis of Spatial Data Structures*, Addison-Wesley, 1990.

Appendix

A Multi-Dimensional Range Tree.

```
    /* Build the local subtree */
    for (i=0; i<N; i= 2*i) {
    /* To build one level subtree */
    for (j=0; j <= 2**i; j++)
      {
S1:     next_nodes[j]= new node;
        if (i!= (N-1) next_nodes[j]->down =Alloc_2ndDimTree();
        if ((i==0)&&(j==0)) root = next_nodes[0];
        else {
          if (j % 2) cur_nodes[j/2]->left=next_nodes[j];
          else       cur_nodes[j/2]->right=next_nodes[j];
        }
      }
    /* House-keeping before going into next level */
    for (k=1; k<2*i; k++)
        cur_nodes[k]= next_nodes[k];
    }
L1: /* Chain-Up the next pointer in the leave nodes */
    for (i=1; i< 2^N-1;i++)
        cur_nodes[i]->next=cur_nodes[i+1];
    broadcast(ProcArray, cur_nodes[0]);
    chain_up(cur_nodes[2^n],ProcArray[pid+1],''next'');
L2: /* Link up the local subtree between each processor */
    for (stride=1; stride<=#P, stride= stride*2)
      {
        broadcast(ProcArray,root);
        if ((pid % stride)==0)   {
S2:       root1= new node;
          root1->down =Alloc_2ndDimTree();
          root1->left =root;
          chain_up(root1,ProcArray[pid+stride], ''right'');
          root=root1;
        }
      }
L3:  /* END of Program */
    }
Alloc_2ndDimTree() {
    node *root,rrot1,cur_nodes[MAXSIZE],next_nodes[MAXSIZE];
    for (i=0; i<N; i= 2*i)   {
    /* To build one level subtree */
    for (j=0; j <= 2**i; j++)
      {
S3:     next_nodes[j]= new node;
        if ((i==0)&&(j==0)) root = next_nodes[0];
        else {
          if (j % 2) cur_nodes[j/2]->left=next_nodes[j];
          else       cur_nodes[j/2]->right=next_nodes[j];
        }
      }
    /* House-keeping before going into next level */
    for (k=1; k<2*i; k++)
        cur_nodes[k]= next_nodes[k];
    }
    /* Chain-Up the next pointer in the leave nodes */
    for (i=1; i< 2**N-1;i++)
      cur_nodes[i]->next=cur_nodes[i+1];
    return(root);
}
```

Automatic Partitioning of Data and Computations on Scalable Shared Memory Multiprocessors

Sudarsan Tandri
IBM Canada Ltd.
Toronto, Ontario, Canada, M3C 1V7
tandri@vnet.ibm.com

Tarek S. Abdelrahman
Dept. of Electrical and Computer Engineering
The University of Toronto
Toronto, Ontario, Canada, M5S 3G4
tsa@eecg.toronto.edu

Abstract—*This paper describes an algorithm for deriving data and computation partitions on scalable shared memory multiprocessors. The algorithm establishes affinity relationships between where computations are performed and where data is located based on array accesses in the program. The algorithm then uses these affinity relationships to determine both static and dynamic partitions for arrays and parallel loops. Experimental results from a prototype implementation of the algorithm demonstrate that it is computationally efficient and that it improves the parallel performance of standard benchmarks. The results also show the necessity of taking shared memory effects (memory contention, cache locality, false-sharing and synchronization) into account—partitions derived to minimize only interprocessor communications do not necessarily result in the best performance.*

1 Introduction

Scalable Shared Memory Multiprocessors (SSMMs) are becoming increasingly used as platforms for high-performance scientific computing because they both scale to large numbers of processors and support the familiar shared memory abstraction. Scalability is achieved by physically distributing shared memory among the processors. However, this fragmentation of memory results in *non-uniform* access latencies—the latency for accessing the local portion of shared memory is less than the latency for accessing non-local or remote portions. Consequently, careful placement of data in shared memory is essential for scaling performance. Examples of SSMMs include the Stanford Flash [10], the University of Toronto Hector [16] and NUMAchine [17], the KSR1 [13], the HP/Convex Exemplar [3], and the SGI Origin 2000 [7].

Automatic parallelization of scientific applications on shared memory multiprocessors has been mainly concerned with the detection of parallelism and the scheduling of parallel-loop iterations [2]. Hence, it is not surprising that on SSMMs issues related to data placement have been ignored by compilers and delegated to the operating system. Page placement policies, such as "first-hit" and "round-robin" place pages in the physically-distributed shared memory as these pages are initially accessed [11, 16]. Unfortunately, operating system policies are oblivious to application data access patterns and manage data at too coarse of a granularity. It is too often the case that such policies fail to enhance memory locality, cause contention and hot-spots, and lead to poor performance [11].

Data partitioning is an approach used by compilers for distributed memory multiprocessors, such as High-Performance Fortran (HPF) [9], to map array data onto separate address spaces. Although such partitioning of arrays is not necessary on SSMMs because of the presence of a single coherent address space, data partitioning can be used to enhance memory locality—the compiler can place an array partition in the physical memory of the processor that uses it the most. Furthermore, data partitioning can eliminate false sharing, reduce memory contention and enhance cache locality across loop nests [15]. However, the task of selecting good data partitions requires the programmer to understand both the target machine architecture and data access patterns in the program. Consequently, porting programs to different machines and tuning them for performance becomes a tedious and laborious process [8]. It is desirable to automatically derive data and computation partitions by the compiler.

In this paper, we describe and experimentally evaluate an algorithm (called CDP) for automatically partitioning data and computations on SSMMs. Automatic data and computation partitioning has been an active area of research in recent years [1, 5, 8]. However, this research targeted distributed memory multiprocessors and derived partitions that reduce interprocessor communications. The algorithm we describe in this paper takes into account shared memory effects, including memory contention, cache locality, false-sharing and synchronization, in deriving partitions. Experimental results on 3 multiprocessors show that the parallel performance of standard benchmarks using our derived data and computation partitions compares favorably to the parallel performance of the benchmarks using operating system policies. Parallel execution time is reduced on average by factors of 2.15 on the Hector multiprocessor, 1.91 on the Convex Exemplar, and 2.04 on the KSR1. The results also demonstrate the importance of taking shared memory effects into account, and the computational efficiency of our approach.

The remainder of this paper is organized as follows. Section 2 gives a brief background on data and computation partitioning. Section 3 describes the CDP algorithm. Section 4 presents experimental results. Section 5 reviews related work. Finally, Section 6 gives concluding remarks.

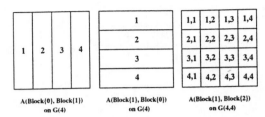

Figure 1: Examples of data partitions

Below each part of the figure:
A(Block{0}, Block{1}) on G(4)   A(Block{1}, Block{0}) on G(4)   A(Block{1}, Block{2}) on G(4,4)

2 Background

Data partitioning divides an array into regular partitions and assigns each partition to a processor. It is specified using a processor geometry, a distribution attribute for each array dimension and a mapping between the dimensions of the array and the dimensions of the processor geometry.

The processor geometry is a n-dimensional cartesian grid of virtual processors $G(P_1, P_2, \cdots, P_n)$, where P_i is the number of processors in the ith dimension of G, and $P_1 \times P_2 \times \cdots \times P_n = P$ is the total number of processors.

An array dimension is partitioned or distributed by assigning it a distribution attribute. The Block attribute slices an array dimension into blocks of contiguous elements and assigns each block to one processor. The Cyclic attribute partitions an array dimension by distributing the array elements in this dimension to processors in a round-robin fashion. The BlockCyclic attribute specifies that b contiguous array elements in a dimension are assigned to the same processor followed by the next b elements to the next processor in a round-robin fashion; b is the block size of the BlockCyclic distribution. The * attribute is used to indicate that an array dimension is not partitioned.

The mapping between the distributed dimensions of an array and the dimensions of the processor geometry defines how the array is partitioned. A one-to-one mapping is used to assign a processor geometry dimension to each distributed dimension of an array [9]. In this paper, such mapping is denoted by appending the dimension of the processor geometry to the distribution attribute. For example, Block{1} indicates that an array dimension is mapped onto dimension 1 of the processor geometry. A mapping of an array dimension to the non-existent dimension 0 of the processor geometry is also used to indicate that this dimension is not partitioned, and is hence equivalent to *. Thus, Block{0} implies that a dimension is not partitioned, even though it is assigned a distribution attribute. Figure 1 shows some common data partitions.

The partitioning of an array is *static* if it is fixed throughout the execution of the program. However, in some programs it is beneficial to have an array partitioned differently in different parts of the program. In these cases, the partitioning is referred to as *dynamic*. Dynamic partitioning requires the remapping the array elements, and hence, incurs run-time overhead.

Computation partitioning is specified in a similar manner. A distribution attribute specifies the partitioning of a parallel loop and a mapping to geometry dimensions specifies the assignment of loop iterations to processors.

3 The CDP Algorithm

3.1 Overview

The goal of the CDP algorithm is to derive partitions for arrays and loops such that overall execution time is minimized. *Affinity* is said to exist between a parallel loop and an array dimension because of a reference to the array, if the parallel loop iterator appears in the subscript expression of the array dimension. Non-local memory accesses can be avoided for such a reference by partitioning the parallel loop and the array dimension using the same distribution attribute *and* by mapping both the array dimension and the parallel loop to the same dimension of the processor geometry. In general, however, there can be multiple references to the same array in multiple loop nests. When conflicting selections of the distribution attribute and/or the mapping to processor geometry dimensions arise, a *partitioning conflict* is said to exist.

When there are no partitioning conflicts for an array, it is possible to derive a unique static data partition that minimizes non-local memory accesses to the array in all loop nests. However, when there are partitioning conflicts, there exists more than one possible partition for the array. The possible partitions must be evaluated to determine one(s) that result in minimal execution time.

Consider the example shown in Figure 2. It consists of two loop nests L1 and L2, each having three loops. All loops in both loop nests are parallel. The subscript expressions in the first, second and third dimensions of all references to B in both loop nests are functions of the parallel loop iterators i, j and k respectively. Non-local memory access can be minimized if each array dimension and the corresponding parallel loop are partitioned and mapped similarly. Hence, there are no partitioning conflicts for this array. In contrast, the second dimension of array A is accessed in L1 using the parallel loop iterator j and in L2 using the parallel loop iterator k. If the partitionings of loops j in L1 and k in L2 are not the same, then a partitioning conflict exists for the second dimension of A. The second dimension of A may be partitioned similar to the j loop in L1 or to the k loop in L2, with or without dynamic partitioning. In general, the number of possible partitions in a program with partitioning conflicts is exponential and examining all possible partitions is NP-hard [8]. The CDP algorithm uses the affinity relationships and a cost model to prune the space of possible partitions.

The CDP algorithm consists of 3 phases. In the first phase, affinity relationships between array dimensions and parallel loops are captured using a graph representation. Distribution attributes and a mapping to dimensions of the processor geometry are derived for the array dimensions and parallel loops using these affinity relationships. In the second phase of the algorithm, arrays with partitioning conflicts are re-examined to determine partitions that minimize overall execution time. It is in this phase that machine specific information, such as the cost of cache, local, and remote memory accesses, the penalty for contention, and the overhead of synchronization, are considered. In the last

```
L1: forall k = 2 to N-1
      forall j = k to N
        forall i = 1 to N
          A(i,j) = B(i,j,k-1)+ B(i,j,k)
                    +B(i,j,k+1)+A(i,j)
        end for
      end for
    end for

L2: forall k = 1 to N
      forall j = 2 to N-1
        forall i = 2 to N-1
          C(i,j,N-k+1) = A(i-1,k)
                          -A(i+1,k)+B(i,j,k)
        end for
      end for
    end for
```

Figure 2: The running example.

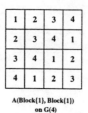

A(Block{1}, Block{1})
on G(4)

Figure 3: An example of new data partitions.

phase of the CDP algorithm, a mapping of the virtual processors of the processor geometry to physical processors is determined.

3.2 New Data Partitions

In this section we introduce a new set of distribution attributes. These attributes, when combined with non-one-to-one mappings of array dimensions to processor geometry dimensions, result in data partitions not previously feasible on distributed memory multiprocessors, but are possible to support on SSMMs because of the presence of a shared address space. The benefits of the new partitions will be seen in Section 3.3.

We define six new distribution attributes. The RBlock, RCyclic and RBlockCyclic are the "reverse" of the regular Block, Cyclic and BlockCyclic distribution attributes, respectively. The assignment of the array partitions to processors in the case of reverse attributes is done in a decreasing order starting with processor P instead of an increasing order starting with processor 1, as in regular attributes [9]. In addition, we synthesize regular and reverse attributes to obtain the *compound* attributes: BlockRBlock, CyclicRCyclic and BlockCyclicRBlockCyclic. In these attributes, elements in an array dimension are divided into two halves. Elements in the first half are partitioned using regular attributes while elements in the second half are partitioned using corresponding reverse attributes.

The mapping between array dimensions and processor geometry dimensions is also relaxed to allow an array dimension to be associated with more than one dimension of the processor geometry and to similarly allow more than one array dimension to be associated with the same dimension of the processor geometry. For example, the (Block{1}, Block{1}) partitioning of the 2-dimensional array A shown in Figure 3 results in both array dimensions being partitioned and mapped onto a 1-

dimensional processor geometry. The array is sliced into blocks of contiguous elements along both its dimensions. The resultant blocks are then assigned to processors such that a processor is not assigned two blocks in the same row or column. That is, a block (i, j) maps to processor $((i-1)+(j-1)) \bmod P + 1$ in the linear array of P processors. This partitioning of the array is called a *latin square* and is useful in alleviating contention [15]. This partitioning is computationally expensive on distributed memory multiprocessors because of the complexity of finding the owner of each element of the array.

3.3 Data-Computation Affinity

The purpose of this phase of the algorithm is to establish affinity between arrays and parallel loops in the program and to derive static partitions for arrays with no partitioning conflicts.

3.3.1 Processor Geometry Dimensionality

The initial step of the CDP algorithm is to determine the dimensionality of the processor geometry. The processor geometry is determined by the number of array dimensions that contain parallel loop iterators, since it is those dimensions that potentially get distributed. It is desired to select a small geometry dimensionality while maintaining parallelism to reduce array fragmentation in shared memory.

A *parallelism matrix* $M = [m_{ij}]$ is built for an array. It has a row for each loop nest in the program and a column for each dimension of the array. An entry m_{ij} is set to 1 if the subscript expression in dimension j of a reference to the array in loop nest L_i contains one or more parallel loop iterators; otherwise, m_{ij} is set to 0. The OR_Mask is defined as the result of ORing the matrix elements along the columns, i.e. along the dimensions of the array. The AND_Mask is the result of ANDing the elements along the columns. The *visible parallelism* is defined as the sum of elements in a row of the parallelism matrix. Hence, the OR_Mask indicates which dimensions of the array are accessed by a parallel loop iterator in one or more loop nests. Similarly, the AND_Mask indicates which dimensions of the array are accessed by a parallel loop iterator in *every* loop nest in the program. Finally, the visible parallelism indicates the maximum number of array dimensions that can be distributed in a loop nest.

In order to determine the smallest number of array dimensions that can be distributed, each array is considered individually. If the OR_Mask of the array is 0, then none

	A_1	A_2	Visible Parallelism
L1	1	1	2
L2	1	1	2
OR_Mask	1	1	
AND_Mask	1	1	

Figure 4: The parallelism matrix for array A of the running example.

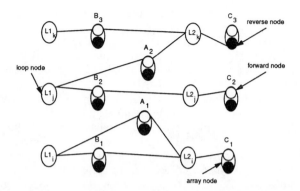

Figure 5: The ALAG for the running example.

of the dimensions of the array will be distributed. If the AND_Mask is not 0, then the number of non-zero elements in the mask is used as the dimensionality of the processor geometry for the array. However, it is possible for the OR_Mask to be non-zero, and for the AND_Mask to be 0, indicating that a dimension of the array is accessed by a parallel loop iterator in some, but not all, loop nests in the program. In this case, the dimensionality of the processor geometry for the array in a loop nest is determined by the visible parallelism in the loop nest; it is the one determined most often (i.e., statistical mode) for the array across the loop nests.

The dimensionality of the processor geometry for the entire program is chosen as the statistical mode of the dimensionalities for the arrays in the program.

The dimensions of each array that can potentially be distributed are determined using the AND_Mask and OR_Mask. If the number of 1's in the AND_Mask of an array is greater than or equal to dimensionality of the processor geometry, then the array dimensions indicated by 1 in the AND_Mask are chosen, and the array can potentially be partitioned only along these dimensions. However, if the number of 1's in the AND_Mask is less than the dimensionality of processor geometry, then all array dimensions indicated by 1 in the OR_Mask of the parallelism matrix are chosen since any of these dimensions can be distributed. Arrays in which both the AND_Mask and the OR_Mask are 0 are not distributed and are replicated to avoid contention.

The parallelism matrix for array A in the running example (Figure 2) is shown in Figure 4, where A_1 and A_2 correspond to the first and the second dimensions of A respectively. A 2-dimensional processor geometry is chosen for A based on the AND_Mask. A 3-dimensional processor geometry is chosen for B and C. Hence, a 3-dimensional geometry is chosen for the program. Both dimensions A_1 and A_2 are distributed based on the AND_Mask. All the three dimensions of B and C are also distributed based on their respective AND_Masks.

3.3.2 The ALAG

A graph, called the *Array-Loop Affinity Graph (ALAG)*, is constructed to capture affinity relationships between arrays and computations. The ALAG is an undirected bipartite graph (V, E), where each vertex or node $v \epsilon V$ corresponds to either a parallel loop or an array dimension, and each edge $e \epsilon E$ connects a loop node to an array dimension node. There is a loop node for each parallel loop in the program. Similarly, there is an array dimension node for each array dimension that can potentially be distributed.

An array dimension node has two subnodes, a *forward* subnode and a *reverse* subnode. There is an edge between a loop node l_i and the forward subnode of an array if there is a reference to the array in which a subscript expression has a positive coefficient of the iterator i. Similarly, there is an edge between a loop node l_i and the reverse subnode of an array if there is a reference to the array in which a subscript expression has a negative coefficient of the iterator i. Two references to an array, one with positive and the other with negative coefficients of a parallel loop iterator result in two edges from the loop node to the array dimension node; one to the forward subnode and one to the reverse subnode.

Figure 5 shows the ALAG for the running example. The nodes labeled $L1_k$, $L1_j$, $L1_i$, $L2_k$, $L2_j$, and $L2_i$ correspond to the parallel loops in the program. Nodes labeled A_1, A_2, B_1, B_2, B_3, C_1, C_2, and C_3 correspond to the distributed dimensions of arrays A, B and C respectively. An edge connects the forward node of A_1 because of the references to A in L1. In contrast, an edge connects the reverse node of C_3 to loop node $L2_k$ because of the negative coefficient of j in the reference $C(i, j, N - k + 1)$ in loop L2.

3.3.3 Initial Distribution Attributes

Loop nodes are assigned initial distribution attributes to balance the load of the corresponding parallel loop. Load imbalance occurs when the computations inside a parallel loop increase or decrease with the iteration number of the loop, or with the iteration number of a loop that encloses the parallel loop. Traditionally, the Cyclic distribution attribute is used to balance the load. The CyclicRCyclic distribution attribute better balances workloads, but introduces additional overhead [14]. Hence, we opt to use CyclicRCyclic only for the outermost parallel loop, and use Cyclic for inner parallel loops. Loop nodes are assigned a ∗ attribute when their corresponding parallel loops are load balanced.

Array dimension nodes are assigned distribution attributes to enhance access locality for corresponding array references. An array that is referenced only once in a loop nest for which each subscript expression is a function of a single loop iterator does not pose any requirements with respect to the selection of a distribution attribute. Hence, array nodes introduced because of only such references are assigned the ∗ distribution attribute.

However, if an array is referenced in an iteration of a parallel loop more than once, all elements accessed by the iteration must be co-located to enhance locality. For example, if $X(a*i)$ and $X(a*i+c)$ are two references to an array X in an iteration of a parallel loop i, then both data elements accessed must be assigned to the same processor. This is done by assigning the corresponding array dimension nodes the Block attribute.

When an array subscript expression is a function of multiple loop iterators, the relative nesting of parallel and sequential loops determines the distribution attribute of the array dimension node. Consider an array X that is referenced as $X(a*i+b*j)$ in a loop nest where i (outer) and j (inner) are loop iterators. If the j loop is parallel and the i loop is sequential, small segments of the array X are accessed by the iteration space of the j loop and the outer sequential loop i controls a sweep through the entire array. Hence, the array dimension node is assigned a BlockCyclic distribution attribute, with the block size equal to b, the coefficient of the parallel loop iterator in the array subscript expression. In contrast, when the i loop is parallel and j is sequential, large chunks of the array are accessed by each processor. In this case, the array dimension node is assigned a Block distribution attribute. If both i and j loops are parallel, the array dimension node is also assigned a Block distribution attribute to favor outer loop parallelism.

Initial distribution attributes are assigned to the forward and reverse subnodes of an array dimension separately. Since an array can be referenced in multiple loop nests, conflicting initial attributes of an array dimension node can result. In such cases, the BlockCyclic attribute is used.

In the running example, loop node $L1_k$ is assigned CyclicRCyclic attribute to balance the load. In contrast, loop node $L1_j$ is assigned Cyclic attribute to balance the load. All other loop nodes are assigned a ∗ distribution attribute because load balancing is not an issue. The forward subnode of array dimension nodes B_3 and A_1 are assigned a Block distribution attribute. All other array dimension nodes are assigned a ∗ distribution attribute.

3.3.4 Final Distribution Attributes

The initial distribution attributes do not ensure that parallel loops and array dimensions whose subscript expressions are functions of the parallel iterators are partitioned similarly. Hence, in this step of the algorithm, connected nodes in the ALAG are made to have the same distribution attribute. We refer to such a condition as *consensus*.

When the distribution attributes of two connected nodes in the ALAG are not the same, a *conflict* is said to exist. This conflict is resolved using the conflict resolution graph shown in Figure 6. The resolution of two distribu-

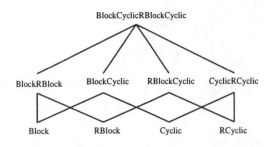

Figure 6: Conflict resolution graph.

tion attributes is the least common ancestor in the conflict resolution graph. For example, the attributes Cyclic and Block resolve to BlockCyclic. The BlockCyclic attribute allows both locality of access to be maintained through the selection of an appropriate block size, and allows load to be balanced by distributing the blocks Cyclicly. A node in the conflict resolution graph can be its own least common ancestor. A distribution attribute in conflict with the ∗ attribute resolves to the attribute itself.

For each array dimension node, the distribution attributes of the forward and reverse subnodes are first made consistent by having the distribution attribute of the forward subnode be the reverse of the reverse subnode. An iterative process is then used to reach consensus. In each iteration, the distribution attribute of a forward node is compared to that of each node directly connected to it. A conflict is resolved as described above. Since all distribution attributes have one common ancestor, the process is guaranteed to terminate.

In the running example, the distribution attribute of B_3 is forced to be BlockCyclicRBlockCyclic(BCRBC) resolving its distribution attribute Block and the CyclicRCyclic distribution attribute of loop node $L1_k$ connected to it. When consensus is reached, nodes $L1_k$, $L1_j$, $L2_k$, $L2_j$, A_2, B_3, B_2, C_3 and C_2, are partitioned using the BCRBC distribution attribute. Nodes $L1_i$, $L2_i$, A_1, B_1 and C_1 are partitioned using the Block distribution attribute.

3.3.5 Processor Geometry Dimension Assignment

Parallel loops and distributed array dimensions must be assigned processor geometry dimensions to complete the partitioning of computations and data. The goal of this assignment is to ensure that elements of arrays required by an iteration of a parallel loop are assigned to same processor that executes the iteration. In other words, it is desired to have connected nodes in the ALAG map onto the same processor geometry dimension.

Processor geometry dimensions are first assigned to loops and distributed array dimensions in loop nests in which the number of parallel loops is equal to the dimensionality of the processor geometry. It is in these loop nests that all parallel loops must indeed execute in parallel. The first such loop nest in the program is considered first. Parallel loops are assigned geometry dimensions from outermost to innermost, assigning the highest geometry dimension to the outermost loop and the lowest dimension to the innermost loop. The assignment of dimensions to loops is then *propagated* to array dimensions using the ALAG. The geometry dimension assigned to a loop node is also assigned to all array nodes connected to the loop node. An array dimension node may be assigned more than one dimension of the processor geometry based on the number of loop nodes connected to it.

The next loop nest in which the number of parallel loops is equal to the geometry dimensionality is considered. Parallel loops whose corresponding loop nodes in the ALAG are connected to array dimension nodes that have already been assigned a geometry dimension are assigned the same geometry dimension. Parallel loops that are not assigned geometry dimensions in this way are assigned a dimension as described for the first loop nest from outermost to innermost, but only geometry dimensions that have not been assigned to a loop node in the current loop nest are considered. The dimension assignment to each loop node is then propagated to all the array dimension nodes connected to it, and the process is repeated for the remaining loop nests in which the number of parallel loops is equal to the geometry dimensionality.

In loop nests in which the number of parallel loops is not equal to the geometry dimensionality, either some parallel loops will not be assigned a geometry dimension and hence will execute sequentially, or some of the geometry dimensions will go unused. Such loop nests are also considered one at a time. First, geometry dimensions are assigned to parallel loops by propagating geometry dimensions from array nodes to loop nodes and by assigning available geometry dimensions to parallel loops that remain without a geometry dimension outermost loop to innermost loop in a loop nest. If the number of parallel loops in a loop nest is greater than the geometry dimensionality, then some loops will not be assigned a geometry dimension. However, if the number of parallel loops is less than the geometry dimensionality, some of the geometry dimensions will not be utilized.

Figure 7 shows the processor geometry assignment for the running example. Loop nodes $L1_k$, $L1_j$ and $L1_i$ are assigned geometry dimensions 3, 2 and 1 respectively. These assignments are propagated to array dimension nodes A_2, B_1, B_2, and B_3. Loop nodes $L2_k$, $L2_j$ and $L2_i$ are assigned dimensions 3, 2 and 1 respectively based on the assignments of B_3, B_2 and B_1. Consequently, the array dimension nodes C_3, C_2 and C_1 also are assigned geometry dimensions 3, 2 and 1 respectively. Because A_2 is connected to both $L1_j$ and $L2_k$, it gets the geometry assignment of both these loop nodes 2, 3. For arrays B and C no partitioning conflicts exist and static partitions are determined. However there is a partitioning conflict for A and all possible data partitions must be evaluated to determine if dynamic partitioning is necessary.

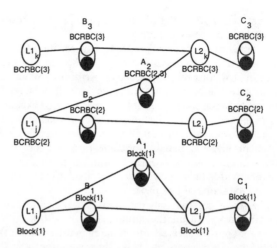

Figure 7: Processor geometry assignment for running example.

3.4 Dynamic Array Partitions

The partitions derived so far by the algorithm establish affinity between data accessed and computations through static array partitions. For arrays for which a one-to-one mapping between the distributed dimensions of the arrays and the dimensions of the processor geometry, static partitions make accesses to the arrays local across all loop nests in the program. However, for arrays for which a one-to-one mapping is not used, remote memory accesses result in some or all of the loop nests. The geometry dimension assignment was made for such arrays to satisfy multiple locality requirements in the different loop nests. Since a parallel loop is partitioned along only a single dimension of the processor geometry, partitioning an array dimension along multiple dimensions of the geometry results in non-local accesses. Similarly, partitioning multiple dimensions of the array along a single dimension of the processor geometry also results in non-local accesses. Hence, the partitioning of these arrays in the loop nests in which they are referenced is re-evaluated to determine if dynamic partitioning may result in better program performance.

The assignment of geometry dimensions to array dimension is explored in selecting appropriate data partitions. The permutations of the geometry dimensions (including dimension 0 or no partitioning) for each dimension of an array is the set of possible data partitions for the array in the program. In the running example, the 2-dimensional array is partitioned on a 3-dimensional processor geometry using A(Block{1}, BCRBC{2, 3}), and its partitioning should be re-evaluated. The set of possible data partitions are: A(Block{0}, BCRBC{0}) which replicates the array completely; A(Block{1}, BCRBC{0}), A(Block{0}, BCRBC{2}), A(Block{0}, BCRBC{3}), and A(Block{0}, BCRBC{2, 3}) which partially replicate the array; A(Block{1}, BCRBC{2}) which results in local accesses to the array in the first loop nest, but not the second; A(Block{1}, BCRBC{3}) which results in local accesses to the array in the second loop nest, but not the first; and A(Block{1}, BCRBC{2,3}) which results in non-local accesses in both loops.

In order to select an appropriate data partition for any array, the time to access the array in each loop nest must be estimated for each of the above partitions. When the partitions differ across loop nests, the array must be repartitioned between loop nests, or loop nests must be executed in a pipelined fashion. Machine-specific information, such as cache, local, and remote memory accesses latencies, cost of synchronization, penalty for contention, and cost of redistribution are used to estimate the time for array accesses. Cost estimation heuristic used are described in [14], and are beyond the scope of this paper.

The set of possible data partitions is searched to determine the data partitions that minimize the overall execution time. A depth-first search with pruning is used to limit the size of the search space and make the search practical.

3.5 Processor Geometry Mapping

The final step of the CDP algorithm is to determine the number of processors in each dimension of the processor geometry, and to map its virtual processors to physical processors.

Factors of the number of processors P are used to generate possible processor geometries. For example, when $P = 8$, possible 2-dimensional processor geometries are $(1, 8)$, $(2, 4)$, $(4, 2)$ and $(8, 1)$. The costs of cache, local and remote memory accesses for loop nests are determined given the data and computation partitions for each geometry and the one with the minimal cost is selected. The heuristics used to calculate the costs of local and remote memory accesses and the number of cache misses are beyond the scope of this paper and are discussed in [14].

The physical processors are viewed as a linear array and virtual processor $(p_1, p_2, \cdots, p_n)$ is assigned to the physical processor numbered $\sum_{i=1}^{n} p_i \prod_{j=1}^{i-1} P_j$. Thus, for a 2-dimensional processor geometry, this mapping implies a column-major order assignment of virtual processors to physical processors. This mapping allows inner loops to execute on adjacent physical processors, which typically improves performance because on SSMMs remote memory access latency to close-by processors is lower.

4 Experimental Results

We implemented our algorithm in a prototype compiler called *Jasmine*, which is being developed at the University of Toronto. The compiler has four major phases: parallelism detection, cache locality enhancement, memory locality enhancement and code generation. We use the Polaris compiler [2] from the University of Illinois for parallelism detection. The algorithm described in this paper constitutes the memory locality enhancement phase.

The compiler was used to automatically determine data and computation partitions for applications and to generate parallel code. The resulting parallel code was executed on 3 multiprocessor platforms to measure performance;

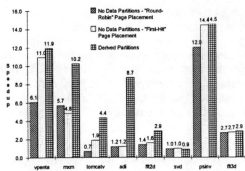

Figure 8: Performance on a 16-processor Hector.

Hector [16], an HP/Convex Exemplar SPP1000 [3] and a KSR1 [13].

We present three sets of results in this section. The first set shows that the overall performance of the applications is improved by placing array data in memory using the partitions derived by our compiler, as opposed to relying on operating system policies. The second set shows that partitions derived by our compiler taking into account shared memory effects in addition to interprocessor communications lead to better performance than partitions derived taking only interprocessor communications into account. The last set of results shows the computational efficiency of our framework and that it compares favorably to that of other approaches.

4.1 Overall Performance

We applied our compiler prototype to the 8 benchmark applications summarized in Table 1. The data partitions derived by the compiler for the main arrays in each application on each of the 3 multiprocessor platforms are shown in Table 2. The processor geometry is a linear array unless otherwise indicated.

The speedup (with respect to sequential execution) of the parallel applications with and without the use of our data and computation partitions on the Hector multiprocessor is shown in Figure 8. The performance of the applications without data partitions refers to their performance using supported operating system page placement policies and partitioning the outermost parallel loop in each loop nest. In the case of Hector, two policies are supported, "first-hit" and "round robin" [16]. The performance of the applications with data partitions is better on average by a factor of 2.15 compared to their performance with page placement policies, which validates our approach to data placement.

The speedup of the applications on the HP/Convex Exemplar with and without data partitions shown in Figure 9. The Exemplar only supports the "round-robin" page placement policy [3]. Similar to Hector, the performance of the applications on the Exemplar is better on average by a factor of 1.91 using our algorithm compared to relying on the page placement policy.

The speedup of the applications on the KSR1 is shown in Figure 10 (fft2d and fft3d were not executed on the

Table 1: Application characteristics.

Application	Lines of Code	No. of Proc- -edures	No. of parallel loop nests	No. of Arrays	Array dimensi- -onality	Brief Summary
vpenta	126	2	7	9	2/3	inverts three pentadiagonal matrices
mxm	50	2	2	3	2	matrix multiplication
tomcatv	195	1	9	7	2	mesh generation program
ADI	35	1	5	3	2	stencil computation
fft2d	250	2	11	4	1/2	2-D fast fourier butterfly computation
svd	319	1	16	5	1/2	decomposes a 2-D array
psinv	20	1	1	2	3	computes 3-D potential field
fft3d	70	2	3	2	3/1	3-D fast fourier butterfly computation

Table 2: Derived data partitions.

Application	Hector (16 Processors)	Convex (30 Processors)	KSR1 (16 Processors)
vpenta	F(*,Block{1},*)	F(*,Block{1},*)	F(*,Block{1},*)
mxm	A(*,*)	A(*,*)	A(*,*)
	C(*,Block{1})	C(*,Block{1})	C(*,Block{1})
tomcatv	RX(Block{1},*)	RX(Block{1},*)	RX(Block{1},*)
ADI	X(Block{1},Block{1})	X(*,Block{1}) /Pipelining	X(*,Block{1}) /X(Block{1},*)
fft2d	X(*,Block{1}) /X(Block{1},*)	X(*,Block{1}) /X(Block{1},*)	X(*,Block{1}) /X(Block{1},*)
svd	U(BCRBC{1},BCRBC{1})	U(BCRBC{1},BCRBC{1})	U(BCRBC{0},BCRBC{1})
psinv	U(*,Block{1},Block{2})	U(*,Block{1},Block{2})	U(*,Block{1},Block{2})
proc. geom.	(16, 1)	(6, 5)	(8, 2)
fft3d	Z(*,Block{1},Block{2})	Z(*,Block{1},Block{2})	Z(*,Block{1},Block{2})
proc. geom.	(1, 16)	(1, 30)	(1, 16)

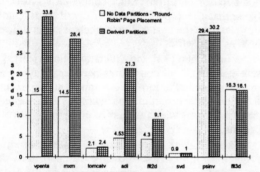

Figure 9: Performance on a 30-processor HP/Convex.

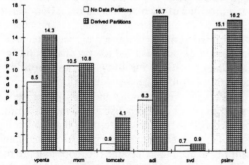

Figure 10: Performance on a 16-processor KSR1.

KSR1 multiprocessor due to native compiler limitations).

Since the KSR1 is a COMA multiprocessor, the performance of the applications without data partitions refers to their performance with the underlying hardware which copies and replicates data on demand. Again, the performance of the applications with our derived partitions is better on average by a factor of 2.04.

4.2 Impact of Shared Memory Effects

In this section we show the impact of shared memory effects. That is, we show that data and computation partitions derived by our compiler taking into account cache locality, false sharing, contention and synchronization in addition to interprocessor communications outperform partitions derived for distributed memory multiprocessors taking only interprocessor communications into account. We use one application due to space limitations, and refer the reader to [14] for more results.

The psinv kernel is used to show the impact of cache locality. The kernel performs a nearest-neighbor computation using two 3-dimensional arrays inside a triply nested loop nest. All three loops in the nest are parallel. With 16 processors, both arrays would be partitioned on distributed memory multiprocessors using (*,Block{1},Block{2}) and a (4,4) 2-dimensional processor geometry in order to minimize interprocessor communications. Using our algorithm, the arrays are also partitioned using (*,Block{1},Block{2}), but using a (8,2) processor geometry with the outermost parallel loop

71

mapped to the 2nd dimension of the geometry and the next inner loop mapped to the 1st dimension. The innermost loop is executed sequentially to avoid false sharing.

The execution time of `psinv` on the KSR1 is shown in Figure 11 for possible processor geometries and for three array sizes. The curves are normalized with respect to the (16,1) geometry. When the size of the arrays is small (64x64x64), execution time is minimized by the (4,4) geometry. However, when the size of the arrays is larger execution time is minimized using the (8,2) geometry.

The impact of processor geometry on performance is due to cache locality, as can be deduced from Figures 12 and 13. Figure 12 shows the average measured number of cache lines accessed from remote memory modules (i.e., interprocessor communications), normalized with respect to the (16,1) geometry. The number of remote memory accesses is minimal when the processor geometry is (4,4) for all data sizes, which validates its choice for distributed memory multiprocessors. Figure 13 shows the average measured number of cache misses from a processor cache, again normalized with respect to the (16,1) geometry. When the data size is small (64x64x64), the data used by a processor mostly fits into the 256-Kbyte processor cache and the misses from the cache in this case reflect remote memory accesses. Hence, the best performance is attained using the (4,4) geometry, which minimizes remote accesses.

However, when the arrays are larger, the cache capacity is no longer sufficient to hold all array data across successive iterations of the outer parallel loop, and the number of cache misses increases. When the number of processors assigned to the inner parallel loop increases (1st geometry dimension), less inner loop iterations are assigned to a processor, and the size of data accessed those iterations decreases. The size of data accessed across iterations of the outer parallel loop on a processor decreases, and hence, the number of misses from the cache decreases. The (4,4) geometry minimizes the amount of remote memory access, but the (16,1) geometry minimizes the amount of cache misses. The CDP algorithm considers both factors and strikes a balance with the (8,2) geometry to result in best overall performance.

4.3 Computational Efficiency

Table 3 gives the time taken by the prototype compiler to derive data and computation partitions for each application on a Sun SPARCstation 10. It also shows the number of array and loop nodes in the ALAG, the number of array and loop nodes re-evaluated for dynamic partitioning, the total size of possible partitions and the number of partitions actually examined, and the number of processor geometry choices considered. In half of the benchmarks static data partitions are derived directly from the ALAG. The pruned search is successful in limiting the number of partitions examined when partitioning conflicts exist.

The computational efficiency of our algorithm is favorable compared to that of other approaches (see Section 5). For example, in cases where partitions are ob-

Table 3: Measurements from the Jasmine compiler.

Application	No. of Array/ Loop nodes	No. of Arrays/ Loops re-eval.	Possible/ Examined Part.	No. of Processor Geometry Choices	Total Compile Time (mS)
vpenta	9/9	–/–	–/–	1	31
mxm	3/4	–/–	–/–	1	5
tomcatv	7/11	–/–	–/–	1	14
ADI	6/5	3/5	$3*4^5/116$	1	280
fft2d	4/11	1/9	$4^9/1591$	1	5184
svd	5/16	1/13	$4^{13}/240$	1	1993
psinv	4/3	–/–	–/–	5	197
fft3d	3/6	1/3	$16^3/16$	5	697

tained directly from the ALAG our algorithm is more efficient than solving 0–1 integer programming problems of sizes 2595×338, 170×59, 1940×354, and 15×1 for `vpenta`, `mxm`, `tomcatv` and `psinv` respectively, using Bixby's approach.

5 Related Work

Automatic approaches for deriving data and computation partitions have focused primarily on distributed memory multiprocessors. These approaches first derive data partitions that minimize some metric of performance, then use the *owner-computes* rule [6] to determine corresponding computation partitions. Since communications is the main factor that affects performance on distributed memory multiprocessors, the cost of interprocessor communications is used as the metric.

Li and Chen [12] and Gupta and Banerjee [5], represent the alignment constraints between array dimensions in a program in the form of a component alignment graph, then apply graph-partitioning heuristics to derive only static array partitions which minimize interprocessor communications.

Bixby et al. [8] formulate a 0–1 integer programming problem to represent all possible data partitions and their associated costs. Their approach relies on the assumption that good partitions for the program can be obtained by dividing the program into phases or segments and analyzing data partitions of each segment alone. Data partitions are allowed to change across segments. The cost of a data partition is determined using a static performance estimator. Garcia et al. [4] also use 0–1 integer programming to derive static data partitions for arrays, but use profiling to more accurately estimate the costs of partitions.

Anderson, Amarasinghe and Lam [1] present an algebraic framework for both distributed memory multiprocessors and SSMMs. They determine data and computation partitions that minimize interprocessor communications. Profiling is used to determine the loops that are most commonly executed. A static data partition is then derived for these loops, hence reducing the cost of array repartitioning. Transformations are then applied to reduce false sharing

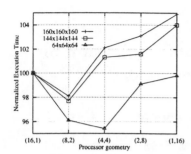 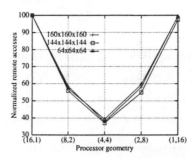 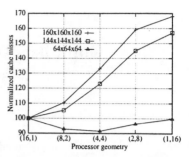

Figure 11: Execution time of `psinv`.   Figure 12: Remote accesses in `psinv`.   Figure 13: Cache misses in `psinv`.

and synchronization. The effect of memory contention is ignored.

In contrast, the algorithm presented in this paper targets SSMMs and takes all shared memory affects into consideration. The partitions are obtained without the run-time profiling. Our algorithm derives dynamic partitions using an efficient pruned search.

6 Conclusion

Data partitioning is proposed as a mechanism for data placement on SSMMs. Determining good partitions can be difficult for programmers. In addition, cache locality, contention, synchronization and false sharing must be considered in the selection of partitions on SSMMs. This paper described an algorithm to automatically derive data and computation partitions for a program taking into account such factors. Experimental results show that the use of the data and computation partitions derived by our algorithm improve the performance of the standard benchmark applications over the use of operating system policies for page placement. Experimental results also demonstrate the importance of taking shared memory effects into consideration; data and computation partitions that are derived to only minimize interprocessor communications do not necessarily lead to the best performance.

References

[1] J. Anderson, S. Amarasinghe, and M. Lam. Data and computation transformations for multiprocessors. In *Proc. of PPoPP*, 1995.

[2] W. Blume et al. Polaris: Improving the effectiveness of parallelizing compilers. In *Languages and Compilers for Parallel Computing*, pages 141–154, 1994.

[3] Convex Computer Corporation. *Convex Exemplar System Overview*. Richardson, TX, USA, 1994.

[4] J. Garcia, E. Ayguade, and J. Labarta. A novel approach towards automatic data distribution. In *Proc. of the Workshop on Automatic Data Layout and Performance Prediction*, 1995.

[5] M. Gupta and P. Banerjee. Automatic Data Partitioning on Distributed Memory Multiprocessors. *IEEE Trans. on Parallel and Distributed Systems*, 3(2):179–193, 1992.

[6] S. Hiranandani, K. Kennedy, and C. Tseng. Compiling Fortran D . *CACM*, 35(8):66–79, 1992.

[7] Silicon Graphics Inc. *The SGI Origin 20000*. Mountain View, CA, 1996.

[8] K. Kennedy and U. Kremer. Automatic data layout for High Performance Fortran. In *Proc. of Supercomputing*, 1995.

[9] C. Koelbel et al. *The High Performance Fortran Handbook*. The MIT Press, Cambridge, MA, 1994.

[10] J. Kuskin et al. The Stanford FLASH Multiprocessor. In *Proc. of ISCA*, pages 302–313, 1994.

[11] R. LaRowe Jr., J. Wilkes, and C. Ellis. Exploiting Operating System Support for Dynamic Page Placement on a NUMA Shared Memory Multiprocessor. In *Proc. of PPoPP*, pages 122–132, 1991.

[12] J. Li and M. Chen. Compiling Communication-Efficient Programs for Massively Parallel Machines. *Journal of Parallel and Distributed Computing*, 2(3):361–376, 1991.

[13] Kendall Square Research. *KSR1 Principles of Operation*. Waltham, MA, 1991.

[14] S. Tandri. *Automatic Data and Computation Partitioning on Scalable Shared Memory Multiprocessors (in preperation)*. PhD thesis, Department of Computer Science, University of Toronto, 1997.

[15] S. Tandri and T. Abdelrahman. Computation and data partitioning on scalable shared memory multiprocessors. In *Proc. of PDPTA*, 1995.

[16] Z. Vranesic et al. The Hector Multiprocessor. *IEEE Computer*, 24(1):72–79, 1991.

[17] Z. Vranesic et al. The NUMAchine Multiprocessor. Technical Report CSRI-324, Computer Systems Research Institute, University of Toronto, 1995.

Compiler Techniques for Effective Communication on Distributed-Memory Multiprocessors

Angeles G. Navarro   Yunheung Paek[†]   Emilio L. Zapata   David Padua[†]

Dept of Computer Architecture, Univ. of Málaga, Spain
{angeles,ezapata}@ac.uma.es

† Dept. of Computer Science, Univ. of Illinois at Urbana-Champaign
{y-paek,padua}@cs.uiuc.edu

Abstract

The Polaris restructurer transforms conventional Fortran programs into parallel form for various types of multiprocessor systems. This paper presents the results of a study on strategies to improve the effectiveness of Polaris' techniques for distributed-memory multiprocessors. Our study, which is based on the hand analysis of MDG and TRFD from the Perfect Benchmarks and TOMCATV and SWIM from SPEC benchmarks, identified three techniques that are important for improving communication optimization. Their application produces almost perfect speedups for the four programs on the Cray T3D.

1 Introduction

The problem of compiling for distributed memory multiprocessors has been studied extensively in recent years [2, 4, 5]. One of the many projects on this subject centers around *Polaris* [1], a parallelizing compiler which automatically transforms sequential Fortran 77 programs into parallel form without programmer intervention. Unlike most other approaches, the techniques currently implemented in Polaris pay little attention to data distribution across processors. In fact, Polaris applies a simple data distribution strategy which block-distributes all shared data objects in the parallel programs regardless of their access patterns. The lack of data distribution strategies is compensated by the use of advanced techniques for privatization and communication optimization and for work distribution [3]. These techniques have proven quite effective on a collection of codes from the Perfect and SPEC Benchmarks when the target machine is the Cray T3D.

Despite these good results, there is still much room for improvement. This paper presents the results of a study on additional techniques needed to improve the effectiveness of Polaris for distributed-memory mul-

tiprocessors. Our study, which is based on the hand analysis of the four programs, TOMCATV and SWIM from SPEC benchmarks and MDG and TRFD from the Perfect Benchmarks, identifies three new techniques important to improving Polaris' effectiveness.

2 Automatic Parallelization

When generating code for distributed-memory machines with a global address space, Polaris applies five passes: a *parallelism detection* stage, a *work partitioning* stage, a *data privatization* stage, a *data distribution* stage, and a *data localization* stage. A more detailed description can be found in [3].

Starting with a conventional Fortran77 program, Polaris generates a parallel version for a global address space machine. The target code has a Single Program Multiple Data (SPMD) form. Barriers and locks are used to control explicitly the flow of execution of processors in the SPMD code. Program variables are declared explicitly as either private or shared. Shared arrays can be distributed by BLOCK and CYCLIC directives. PUT/GET operations are used to allow the processors asynchronous access to any data object in the system.

In the first phase of the transformation procedure, Polaris detects parallelism from the input program [1]. In the second phase, Polaris tries to distribute parallel work evenly while ignoring data distributions. In the third phase, Polaris analyzes the data regions that each individual processor will access and identifies the private data. In the fourth phase, Polaris declares all non-privatized arrays as shared and BLOCK-distributed across the target machine. Then, in the fifth phase, Polaris inserts PUT/GET operations (polaris_put and polaris_get routines) to localize the non-local accesses to these shared arrays by following the *shared data copying scheme* [3]. In this scheme, shared memory is used as a repository of values for private memory.

3 Additional Optimization Techniques

As mentioned in Section 1, we have found that the techniques enumerated in Section 2 produce good speedups on the Cray T3D for the collection of programs we have evaluated. In fact, a previous study [3] showed that data privatization substantially increases the probability that the processors fetch their data from local memory, thus reducing the overall communication overhead. Furthermore, data privatization presents additional benefits in the T3D by providing more chances for processors to use data caches for their computations. The reason is that, in this machine, shared data are not cached even when they reside in local memory.

Through the hand analysis reported in [6], we identified some additional optimizations that are needed to further improve performance. Strategies to reduce the number of PUT/GET operations, which are based on the cross-loop access region analysis, are discussed in Section 3.1. A second optimization is to improve data locality by distributing arrays according to the data access pattern in a program. In Section 3.2, we discuss one data access pattern commonly encountered in an important class of scientific applications; we also present an automatic data distribution technique that minimizes the communication costs and memory requirements for these applications.

3.1 Communication Overhead

Because the communication optimization algorithm currently implemented in Polaris is relatively simple, the communication overhead is sometimes unnecessarily large and scalability is hindered. In the next two subsections we analyze where this overhead arises and propose additional techniques based on access region analysis to reduce the overhead.

3.1.1 Placing Communication Operations

In the shared data copying scheme, it is crucial to avoid consuming an excessive amount of space for private data. Also, it is important to minimize communication overhead by reducing the calls to polaris_put/get primitives. In this scheme, the copy-level is a loop nest level at which the elements of the shared array are copied by using these primitives. There is an obvious trade-off between time and space when choosing the copy-level. Currently, Polaris usually chooses the innermost copy-level since this copy-level allows us to exploit the data pipelining technique if the implementation of the polaris_put/get routines is non-blocking.

In real cases, we have found that it is often better to perform copy operations at outer copy levels. Therefore, the strategy we propose here is to use access region analysis to gather the elements of each shared array accessed at all inner levels of nesting, and to perform copy operations at the outermost loop level possible. Although this strategy may consume more space for private data, there are several advantages to copying at the outermost levels: the amount of private memory needed for each processor decreases with the number of processors; the memory required to allocate private data can be managed using dynamic allocations functions; and, saving space is less important than optimizing time in general cases.

3.1.2 Redundant PUT/GET Elimination

The parallel programs generated by Polaris contain many redundant PUT/GETs due to the lack of a cross-loop analysis for the shared data copying scheme. The scheme currently implemented in Polaris generates polaris_put/get calls for each individual loop nest. The elimination improved the execution times and scalability of studied programs, as we will discuss with real programs in Section 4. In order to eliminate redundant PUT/GETs, we need to extend the access region analysis to a set of consecutive loops. Based on the cross-loop access region analysis, we try to determine the *upwards-exposed regions* and *downwards-exposed regions* for the shared arrays in the set of loops.

3.2 HALO Access Pattern

Data distribution is an important issue in the code generation for distributed memory multiprocessors. As discussed in Section 2, the current Polaris data distribution strategy is *access-pattern-insensitive* in that it simply chooses BLOCK distribution regardless of the data access patterns in a program. For very regular programs, however, previous work suggests that other data distribution policies improve performance. These strategies could be implemented in the data distribution stage in the Polaris transformation procedure to complement data privatization and localization techniques in Polaris.

In our studies, we focused on the regular data access pattern in a loop where all the subscript expressions for the array of interest are of the form: $X(I \pm K)$, where I is the loop index and K is an arbitrary constant. We call this type of access pattern the *HALO access pattern*. The HALO access pattern is similar to a new data distribution pattern, called SHADOW region, which is included in one of the approved extensions of the new specification of High Performance Fortran.

We have found that the current strategy of Polaris causes excessive communication for arrays with that kind of access pattern. These communications cannot be eliminated by the techniques presented in Section 3.1. The proposed algorithm identifies when an array X has the HALO access pattern and is given a new distribution type HALO to denote this access pattern. The other arrays will still have the BLOCK distribution.

Whether the distribution type is HALO or BLOCK, both types of arrays are declared as shared and are block-distributed with the directive BLOCK in the data distribution stage. However, in the data localization stage, we allocate arrays with the HALO distribution to private memory of processors additional private space, called the *halo area* and the *frontier area*. To define the halo area and the frontier area, we refer to the example in Figure 1, which shows the HALO data distribution for array X.

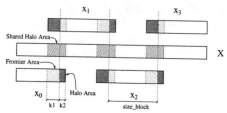

Figure 1: Halo Area and Frontier Area for array X with four processors

In the parallel code, for the array X with HALO distribution, we can hoist the PUT/GET operations out of the loop where X is accessed to copy the initial input and the final result for the loop computation. In addition, we now need extra operations, *create halo* and *update halo*, which are described as follows:

Create halo performs a polaris_get operation to copy the initial value to the halo area of processors from the portion of the shared array corresponding to the halo area, called the *shared halo area*. This create halo operation involves the communication between neighboring processors.

Update halo deals with the intermediate results generated during the loop execution. The changes in the frontier area of processors during the current iteration t of the loop must be copied to the halo area of their neighboring processors before starting the next iteration $t + 1$. This operation involves two steps: first, all the frontier areas of the processors are written back to the corresponding shared halo area simultaneously; then, the processors update their halo area by copying the corresponding shared halo area.

The halo area and shared halo area can be generalized for multidimensional data arrays, where Polaris must build a halo area and a shared halo area for each dimension, and manage each as we have explained for one-dimensional arrays.

4 Case Studies

All the results presented in this section are based on experiments on the T3D, one of the commercial distributed-memory machines that Polaris targets. The T3D is a scalable machine with special hardware and software features to support a global address space efficiently.

The programs we have studied were parallelized automatically first with Polaris and manually later. The automatic versions were obtained from the transformation procedure described in Section 2. The speedups and efficiencies shown here have been calculated versus the sequential execution time. Based on the performance analysis of the automatic versions, we developed the optimization techniques discussed in Section 3, and applied the techniques to generate the manual versions.

Figure 2 shows the speedup comparisons from 1 to 64 processors, using the automatic and manual versions of TOMCATV, TRFD, SWIM, and MDG.

4.1 TOMCATV

The computational kernel of TOMCATV is the MAIN_do140 loop. This loop is a multiply-nested serial loop with several inner loops parallelized by Polaris. Polaris generates PUT/GET calls around the inner parallel loops. Cross-loop analysis revealed that there are redundant copy operations in this automatic version. We, therefore, manually applied the techniques discussed in section 3.1.2. We detected that two important arrays used in the MAIN_do140 loop have the HALO access pattern. Therefore, we applied the technique described in Section 3.2 to further reduce the communication overhead. If we consider only the loop MAIN_do140, we get superior efficiency of 98% for 32 processors and 95% for 64 processors. As shown in Figure 2 the manual version improves the speedups by approximately a factor of two.

4.2 TRFD

TRFD is another good example of the importance of access-pattern-sensitive data distribution strategies. Polaris does not exploit locality of data on loop iterations due to its lack of a more complete data distribution stage. We identified array X as the most important array in TRFD. By using access pattern information, the columns of X can be privatized. Also, we found that the shared data copying scheme chooses a fourth level of the nested loops as a copy-level for the array X to generate PUT/GETs. By hoisting the PUT/GET operations out of the innermost loop nests, the manual version tried to minimize the communication overhead resulting from the copying operations. Using all of these tactics we can achieve a speedup of 30 on 32 processors and 55 on 64 processors for the whole program. These results show, as other researchers have indicated, the importance of the access-pattern-sensitive data distribution strategies to complement the data privatization and localization techniques in Polaris.

4.3 SWIM

SWIM contains an outermost serial loop that calls four subroutines. All these subroutines have the same loop nest structure and the same access pattern to data arrays. The major loop nests in SWIM are all doubly-nested and Polaris parallelizes all these loops, thus generating PUT/GETs for each loop nest. Similar to TOMCATV, the major overhead of SWIM in the automatic version of Polaris comes from redundant PUT/GET operations between consecutive loops that access the same data region. We found that these redundant operations could be eliminated by cross-loop analysis. Also, in SWIM, most arrays are found to have the HALO area patterns. Based on all these analyses of this program, we manually transformed the original SWIM to a parallel form for the T3D and we achieved a linear speedup for the whole program and a global efficiency of 98% for 32 processors and 96% for 64 processors.

4.4 MDG

In MDG we achieved superlinear speedups (on fewer than 16 processors), or almost the linear speedups. As can be seen in Figure 2, we were unable to develop a manual version based on conventional data distribution techniques that outperformed the automatic version. One reason is that MDG has irregular data access patterns and a single static distribution cannot be determined to satisfy all the data access patterns in the program. Also, there are frequent requirements for reduction operations which requires expensive global communication. As a result, we conclude that, in codes that need frequent global data sharing or that contain irregular data access patterns, the shared data copying scheme can be a better solution than more elaborate data distribution algorithms. In Figure 2, the manual version shows slightly better scalability in the speedup curves on more than 32 processors. This is made possible by the techniques

for reduction of communication overhead discussed in Section 3.1.

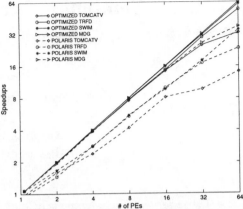

Figure 2: Performance comparison

5 Summary and Conclusions

In this paper, we analyzed several optimization issues for Polaris and outlined some new techniques to overcome limitations of the original techniques in Polaris. To measure the impact of these new techniques, we applied them manually in some benchmarks. We reached efficiencies of 98% for SWIM, 99% for computational kernel of TOMCATV (i.e., scorning the reading file), 93% for TRFD, and 84% for MDG for 32 processors on the T3D. Through our study, we concluded that if a few simple data distribution and communication techniques are combined with the compiling techniques in Polaris, it is possible to automatically generate the parallel code for the distributed memory multiprocessors and to obtain good parallel performance.

References

[1] W. Blume, R. Doallo, R. Eigenmann, J. Grout, J. Hoeflinger, T. Lawrence, J. Lee, D. Padua, Y. Paek, W. Pottenger, L. Rauchwerger, P. Tu, "Parallel Programming with Polaris", IEEE Computer, pp. 78-82, Dec. 1996

[2] S. Hiranandani, K.Kennedy, and C. Tseng. Compiler Optimizations for FORTRAN D on MIMD Distributed-Memory Machines. *Proc. of Supercomputing'91*, 1991.

[3] Y. Paek, D. Padua, "Compiling for Scalable Multiprocessors with Polaris", *To appear in Parallel Processing Letters*, World Scientific Publishing, UK, 1997

[4] B. Chapman, P. Mehrota, H. Moritsch, H. Zima, Dynamic Data Distributions in Vienna Fortran, *Supercomputing '93 Proceedings*, 1993

[5] J. Li and M. Chen. Compiling Communication-Efficient Programs for Massively Parallel Machines. *Journal of Parallel and Dsitributed Computing*, 2(3):361-376, 1991.

[6] A. G. Navarro, Y. Paek, E.L. Zapata, D. Padua, "Performance Analysis for Polaris on Distributed Memory Multiprocessors", 3rd Workshop on Automatic Data Layout and Performance Prediction, Barcelona, Spain, Jan. 1997.

Combining Loop Fusion with Prefetching on Shared-memory Multiprocessors*

Naraig Manjikian
Department of Electrical and Computer Engineering
University of Toronto
Toronto, Ontario, Canada M5S 3G4
email: nmanjiki@eecg.toronto.edu

Abstract—*The performance of programs consisting of parallel loops on shared-memory multiprocessors is limited by long memory latencies as processor speeds increase more rapidly than memory speeds. Two complementary techniques for addressing memory latency and improving performance are: (a) cache locality enhancement for latency reduction and (b) data prefetching for latency tolerance. This paper studies the benefit of combining loop fusion for locality enhancement with prefetching. Experimental results are reported for multiprocessors with support for prefetching. For a complete application on an SGI Power Challenge R10000, combining loop fusion with prefetching improves parallel speedup by 46%.*

```
do i=1,N
   b[i] = 2 * a[i]
end do                        do i=1,N
                                 b[i] = 2 * a[i]
do i=1,N                         c[i] = a[i] + 1
   c[i] = a[i] + 1            end do
end do
   (a) Original loops            (b) Fused loop
```

Figure 1: Example of loop fusion

1 Introduction

Shared-memory multiprocessors based on high-speed commodity microprocessors are used increasingly to address a variety of computational challenges [5]. Despite the prevalence of multiprocessors, performance remains limited by long memory access latencies, particularly for contemporary high-speed microprocessors [8]. This problem persists even with caches that are designed to reduce the average memory access latency.

There are two complementary techniques for addressing latency. *Cache locality enhancement* reduces latency by reordering computation, especially in nested loops, to increase the probability of reusing data from the cache [1]. *Data prefetching* tolerates latency by initiating memory requests in advance of data usage; latency is hidden by overlapping it with computation. Prefetching is especially effective for loops with regular data access patterns [4, 7].

This paper studies the benefit of combining loop fusion for cache locality enhancement with prefetching on shared-memory multiprocessors. We have previously developed a fusion technique called the *shift-and-peel* transformation [6] that enhances locality while preserving parallelism. Other researchers have studied prefetching alone on shared-memory multiprocessors [4, 7]. This paper provides experimental results to characterize the combination of techniques on contemporary multiprocessors.

2 Loop Fusion and Prefetching

Caches reduce effective memory latency by exploiting data reuse, provided that data remains cached between uses. In hardware, increasing cache size and associativity reduces the occurrence of misses that diminish cache locality [8].

Software cache locality enhancement for nested loops relies instead on transformations that reorder loop iterations to increase the likelihood of retaining reused data in the cache; some examples are unimodular transformations, tiling, and loop fusion [1]. All loop transformations require dependence analysis to detect iteration ordering constraints that must be preserved for correctness.

Loop fusion exploits data reuse across sequences of loop nests. Fusion combines the bodies of adjacent loops into a single loop body, as shown in Figure 1, provided that there are no fusion-preventing dependences. For multiprocessors, the resulting loop should be parallelizable (i.e., no serializing dependences). We have previously developed a technique called the *shift-and-peel* transformation [6] that overcomes both fusion-preventing dependences and serial-

*This research was funded by NSERC (Canada) and ITRC (Ontario). The author was supported by a V. L. Henderson Research Fellowship. The SGI Power Challenge and HP/Convex SPP1000/SPP1600 were provided by the University of Michigan Center for Parallel Computing.

78

do i=1,N
    s = s + a[i]
end do

(a) Original loop

```
do i=1,N-2,2
    prefetch(a[i+2])
    s = s + a[i]
    s = s + a[i+1]
end do
do i=N-1,N
    s = s + a[i]
end do
```

(b) Prefetching with cache line size of 2

Figure 2: Example of prefetching

Table 1: Codes used in experiments

Name	Lines of code	Fused loop sequences	Longest sequence
Jacobi	12	1	2
LL18	24	1	3
filter	247	1	10
hydro2d	4292	3	10

Table 2: Number of arrays referenced and written

Name	Original		Fused	
	ref.	written	ref.	written
Jacobi	4	2	2	2
LL18	16	6	9	6
filter	33	14	8	6

```
do t=1,T
  do j=2,N-1
    do i=2,N-1
      b[i,j]=(a[i+1,j]+a[i-1,j]+a[i,j+1]+a[i,j-1]) / 4
    end do
  end do
  do j=2,N-1
    do i=2,N-1
      a[i,j]=b[i,j]
    end do
  end do
end do
```

Figure 3: Jacobi kernel

izing dependences to fuse sequences of parallel loop nests. Experiments have shown the benefit of this technique for applications on shared-memory multiprocessors.

In contrast, data prefetching hides latency by overlapping memory accesses with computation. Prefetch requests are issued in advance of data usage, either automatically by hardware or explicitly by software. Hardware techniques range from sequential prefetching of adjacent cache lines to adaptive stride-detection techniques [4]. Software-controlled prefetching relies on prefetch instructions that must be inserted and scheduled in executable code to instruct hardware to issue prefetch requests. For nested loops, this task can be automated within a compiler; Figure 2 illustrates loop unrolling and loop splitting [7] to schedule prefetches for successive cache lines.

3 Experimental Evaluation

The experimental evaluation described in this section studies the combination of fusion and prefetching on shared-memory multiprocessors. Experiments were conducted on an SGI Power Challenge multiprocessor consisting of MIPS R10000 microprocessors [11]. Each R10000 runs at 196 MHz, and has a 1-Mbyte external cache, and 32-Kbyte internal caches for instructions and data. The R10000 supports software-controlled prefetching. The native compiler automatically inserts prefetch instructions into the executable code, and also provides a flag to disable this feature.

Experiments were also conducted on HP/Convex Exemplar SPP1000 and SPP1600 multiprocessors [3]. The SPP1000 uses 100-MHz HP PA7100 microprocessors with 1-Mbyte data caches that do not support prefetching. The SPP1600 uses 120-MHz HP PA7200 microprocessors with hardware prefetching of adjacent cache lines [2]. The PA7200 also has one more integer unit than the PA7100.

3.1 Codes Used in Experiments

Table 1 describes the codes used in the experiments. Jacobi is a PDE solver, and LL18 is from the Liver-more Loops benchmark. The hydro2d application is from the SPEC95 benchmark, and filter is a subroutine from hydro2d. The shift-and-peel transformation [6] is required for legal fusion and subsequent parallelization; fusion is limited to parallel outermost loops. The transformation is automated in a prototype source-to-source compiler implementation [6]. The transformed source code is then processed by the native compiler for each multiprocessor.

The loop nests of interest access similarly-sized arrays. As a result, the expected number of memory accesses is directly proportional to the number of arrays referenced and written in the original and fused loops. Table 2 provides this information for the kernels. These figures are later used to determine the expected number of cache misses and writebacks. To explain Table 2, consider the Jacobi kernel in Figure 3. Arrays a,b are referenced in both pairs of inner i,j loops for a total of 4 array references to memory. Both arrays are also written. Fusing the inner j loops should reduce the number of referenced arrays to 2 (still with 2 writes). Similar reasoning applies for LL18 and filter. The reduction in the number of written arrays after fusion of filter arises because the same arrays are modified in different loop nests in the original code, but modifications should be written back only once to memory after fusion.

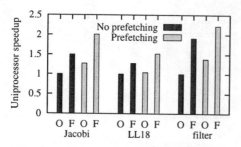

Figure 4: Power Challenge speedups (O=orig.,F=fused)

Table 3: Expected and measured number of cache misses

Name	Original		Fused	
	expected	measured	expected	measured
Jacobi	40000	39659	20000	19770
LL18	160000	163314	90000	89728
filter	132660	125132	32160	34811

Table 4: Expected and measured number of writebacks

Name	Original		Fused	
	expected	measured	expected	measured
Jacobi	20000	19308	20000	19129
LL18	60000	58376	60000	57407
filter	56280	55252	24120	25183

3.2 Uniprocessor Speedups for Kernels

The first results are for the three kernels on the SGI Power Challenge where prefetching can be disabled. Uniprocessor speedups are shown in Figure 4. For each kernel, speedups are determined relative to the execution time without loop fusion or prefetching. The array sizes are $400x400$ for Jacobi and LL18, and $402x160$ for filter; the 1-Mbyte cache capacity is exceeded in all cases. Combining loop fusion with prefetching results in the best performance; fusion results in fewer memory accesses and prefetching hides part of the remaining latency.

Table 3 compares the expected and measured number of cache misses (including prefetches). The expected number is determined from the number of arrays referenced in Table 2 and the array size. The measured number is obtained with the *perfex* tool that uses dedicated counters in the R10000 microprocessor [13]. The figures in Table 3 reflect misses in the *secondary* cache. The results for all three kernels are in close agreement.

To explain the derivation of the expected number of cache misses, consider the Jacobi kernel. Without fusion, 4 arrays are referenced (see Table 2). The array size is $400x400$, array elements are 8 bytes, and the cache line size is 128 bytes. Hence, each execution of the original loops should incur approximately $(4x400x400x8)/128 = 40000$ cache misses. With fusion, only 2 arrays should be referenced, resulting in approxi-

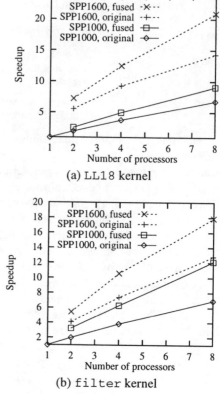

(a) LL18 kernel

(b) filter kernel

Figure 5: Multiprocessor speedups on SPP1000/SPP1600

mately 20000 cache misses.

Table 4 compares the expected and measured number of writebacks. The calculation of the expected number of writebacks is performed in a similar manner as above using the number of written arrays in Table 2. Once again, the results are in close agreement.

3.3 Multiprocessor Speedups for Kernels

Multiprocessor kernel speedups obtained on the SPP1000 and SPP1600 are presented in this section (multiprocessor results could not be obtained on the Power Challenge because of limited access). Figure 5 shows the speedup for LL18 and filter (Jacobi speedups are similar, but omitted for brevity). *All speedups are relative to the execution time without fusion on one processor of the SPP1000 with no prefetching.* Hence, higher speedups indicate better absolute performance (i.e., reduced execution time). A direct performance comparison of the different microprocessors is necessary because prefetching on the SPP1600 is hardware-initiated and cannot be disabled; speedups without prefetching can only be obtained on the SPP1000. Fusion and parallelization require the shift-and-peel transformation. Array sizes are $1024x1024$ for LL18 and $1602x640$ for filter. Figure 5 indicates that combining fusion with hardware prefetching (available only on

80

Table 5: Cache misses for parallel execution

Name	P	Original		Fused	
		expect.	meas.	expect.	meas.
LL18	2	2097152	2106030	1179648	1192240
	4	1048576	1052390	589824	596249
	8	524288	525588	294912	298289
filter	2	4229280	4122660	1025280	1298850
	4	2114640	2059990	512640	653192
	8	1057320	996078	256320	330362

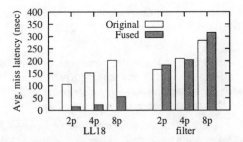

Figure 6: Average cache miss latency on SPP1600

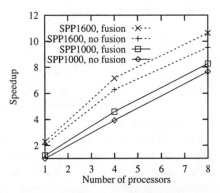

Figure 7: `hydro2d` on SPP1000/SPP1600

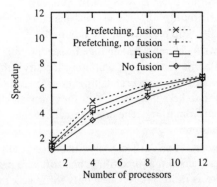

Figure 8: `hydro2d` on Power Challenge

the SPP1600) provides the best performance.

Table 5 compares the expected and measured number of cache misses (including prefetches) on one processor of the SPP1600. The expected number *per processor* is derived from Table 2, and the measured number per processor is obtained with the SPP1600 hardware performance monitor. The results are in close agreement. The larger difference for `filter` arises from the implementation of the shift-and-peel transformation [6], which divides the loop computation into a fused portion, and a small set of peeled iterations. With more processors, fewer misses are incurred for the fused portion, but the misses for the peeled iterations remain the same, and the `filter` kernel has more peeled iterations than the other kernels. Nonetheless, fusion substantially reduces the number of misses in all cases.

The average *observed* cache miss latency on one processor of the SPP1600 was also measured. The results for `LL18` and `filter` are shown in Figure 6. In all cases, the average latency increases as more processors are used because of the increased load on the memory system. Figure 6 shows that fusion for `LL18` dramatically improves the effectiveness of latency hiding with prefetching. On the other hand, `filter` does not show the same behavior because it performs fewer arithmetic operations in each loop body.

3.4 Complete Application Speedups

This section describes results for the `hydro2d` application from which `filter` was extracted. The `hydro2d` application also contains two other sequences of three loop nests that are fused. The array size is 802x320 for these experiments. Figure 7 shows parallel speedups for the `hydro2d`

application on the SPP1000 and SPP1600. All speedups are with respect to the execution time without fusion on one processor *of the SPP1000* with no prefetching. Once again, a comparison of different microprocessors is needed because prefetching on the SPP1600 cannot be disabled. The combination of loop fusion with hardware prefetching provides the best performance.

Figure 8 shows the parallel speedups for the `hydro2d` application on the SGI Power Challenge. All speedups are with respect to the execution time without fusion or prefetching on one processor. The combination of techniques provides the best performance. For example, at 4 processors, prefetching alone improves speedup by only 18%, whereas fusion alone improves speedup by 29%. The combination of fusion and prefetching at 4 processors improves speedup by 46% over execution using neither technique, and by 23% over prefetching alone.

Figure 8 also shows the effect of using more processors with a fixed problem size. The data size per processor decreases, with greater likelihood of retaining all data in the aggregate cache capacity. Hence, the need for locality enhancement and prefetching diminishes. This trend is evident in Figure 8, where at 12 processors, there is little difference in parallel performance among the alternatives.

4 Related Work

Porterfield [9] provides simulated cache hit ratios for 12 loop-based programs when prefetching data one iteration before its use. Hit ratios increase from 70%-90% to over 98% for 10 of the programs. Although Porterfield discusses transformations for locality enhancement, no results are reported in combination with prefetching.

Wolf [12] discusses locality enhancement within loop nests using unimodular transformations and tiling. Performance results for 8 programs and 7 kernels are obtained with an experimental compiler implementation. There is no significant benefit for the 8 programs; the cache captures reuse within loops. However, tiling improved performance for matrix multiplication and Gaussian elimination kernels. No results with prefetching are reported.

Mowry [7] reports simulated speedup for software-controlled prefetching. Combining locality enhancement within loop nests with prefetching provided additional benefits for two kernels. One kernel for Gaussian elimination benefited from tiling. The other kernel benefited from loop permutation.

Saavedra et al. [10] present simulation results for unimodular transformations, tiling, and software prefetching. Cache miss ratios are reported only for matrix multiplication. They conclude that prefetching alone performs better than prefetching with tiling because tiling introduces additional cache misses due to cache conflicts. They do not report speedups, nor do they consider other applications.

In summary, previous work has primarily addressed individual loop nests when combining locality enhancement with prefetching. In contrast, this paper considers fusion of multiple loops, which is then combined with prefetching.

5 Conclusion

The performance of high-speed microprocessors used in contemporary shared-memory multiprocessors is limited by memory latency. To improve performance, latency must be reduced or tolerated. This paper has studied the complementary benefits of combining loop fusion for cache locality enhancement with prefetching on shared-memory multiprocessors. Experimental results have been provided for kernels and a complete application. The measured performance improvements confirm the complementary benefit of combining techniques; results for the complete application on an SGI Power Challenge indicate that parallel speedup improves by 46%.

References

[1] David F. Bacon, Susan L. Graham, and Oliver J. Sharp. Compiler transformations for high-performance computing. *ACM Computing Surveys*, 26:345–420, December 1994.

[2] Kenneth K. Chan, Cyrus C. Hay, John R. Keller, Gordon R. Kurpanek, Francis X. Schumacher, and Jason Zheng. Design of the HP PA 7200 CPU. *Hewlett-Packard Journal*, 47(1), February 1996. Available at http://www.hp.com/hpj/journal.html.

[3] Convex Computer Corporation. *Convex Exemplar System Overview*. Document No. 080-002293-000, Richardson, TX, 1994.

[4] Fredrik Dahlgren and Per Stenström. Evaluation of hardware-based stride and sequential prefetching in shared-memory multiprocessors. *IEEE Transactions on Parallel and Distributed Systems*, 7(4):385–398, April 1996.

[5] Daniel Lenoski and Wolf-Dietrich Weber. *Scalable Shared-memory Multiprocessing*. Morgan Kaufmann, San Francisco, 1995.

[6] Naraig Manjikian and Tarek S. Abdelrahman. Fusion of loops for parallelism and locality. *IEEE Transactions on Parallel and Distributed Systems*, 8(2):193–209, February 1997.

[7] Todd C. Mowry. *Tolerating Latency Through Software-Controlled Data Prefetching*. PhD thesis, Department of Electrical Engineering, Stanford University, March 1994.

[8] David A. Patterson and John L. Hennessy. *Computer Architecture: A Quantitative Approach*. Morgan Kaufmann, San Mateo, CA, second edition, 1996.

[9] Allan K. Porterfield. *Software Methods for Improvement of Cache Performance on Supercomputer Applications*. PhD thesis, Department of Computer Science, Rice University, April 1989.

[10] Rafael H. Saavedra, Weihau Mao, Daeyeon Park, Jacqueline Chame, and Sungdo Moon. The combined effectiveness of unimodular transformations, tiling, and software prefetching. In *Proceedings of the 10th International Parallel Processing Symposium*, pages 39–45, Honolulu, HI, April 1996.

[11] Silicon Graphics, Inc. *POWER CHALLENGE: Technical Report*. Mountain View, CA., 1996. Available at http://www.sgi.com/Products/software/PDF/pwr-chlg/.

[12] Michael E. Wolf. *Improving Locality and Parallelism in Nested Loops*. PhD thesis, Department of Computer Science, Stanford University, August 1992.

[13] Marco Zagha, Brond Larson, Steve Turner, and Marty Itzkowitz. Performance analysis using the MIPS R10000 performance counters. In *Proceedings of Supercomputing'96*, Pittsburgh, PA, November 1996. Available at http://www.supercomp.org/sc96/proceedings/.

Session 2A

Embeddings and Routings

Efficient Multicast Algorithms in All-Port Wormhole-Routed Hypercubes

Vivek Halwan and Füsun Özgüner
Department of Electrical Engineering
The Ohio State University
Columbus, OH 43210
{vhalwan,ozguner}@ee.eng.ohio-state.edu

Abstract

This paper presents several recursive heuristic methods for multicasting in all-port dimension-ordered wormhole-routed hypercubes. The methods described are stepwise contention-free and are primarily designed to reduce the number of communication steps. Experiments show that the number of steps can be significantly reduced compared to depth contention-free solutions previously described. These methods are also shown to be source-controlled depth contention-free and can be considered a generalization of the broadcast method described in [1], which is the most efficient method known.

1 Introduction

This paper investigates the multicast (or one-to-many) communication pattern in all-port dimension-ordered wormhole-routed hypercubes, which involves the delivery of the same message from a source node to an arbitrary number of destinations. Multicast is an important communication pattern found in a variety of applications, such as, data replication, signal processing, and network simulation. *Wormhole routing* [2] is becoming the trend in the design of the future generation of parallel machines. The *hypercube* is an attractive topology due to several of its desirable properties, such as, symmetry, high connectivity, fault tolerance and embedding of other common topologies, such as, meshes, rings and trees.

Several multicast solutions have been described in the literature [3, 4, 5]. The authors in [6] also describe a series of heuristic multicast algorithms for all-port hypercubes. These existing algorithms are based on the UCAST algorithm [4] for the one-port model. The UCAST algorithm is time-optimal (i.e., it requires the minimum number of steps) for the one-port model and it is also depth contention-free, which avoids the potential for contention even if the communication steps are not fully synchronized. The all-port

methods based on the UCAST algorithm, however, are depth contention-free and take some advantage of the all-port capability, but they are not time-optimal. These algorithms become particularly inefficient when the multicast involves a large number of nodes in the hypercube. This occurs primarily because, by restricting to the class of depth contention-free solutions, the algorithms do not efficiently take advantage of the all-port capability. For example, considering the broadcast (one-to-all) pattern in particular, the performance of these all-port methods is only equivalent to the UCAST algorithm for the one-port model. The authors in [1], on the other hand, describe a broadcast algorithm that is optimal, within a multiplicative constant, for the all-port model.

In this paper, we take a similar approach to the broadcast algorithm in [1], in which the cube is recursively partitioned in a way that balances the load among the nodes involved in the communication process. We describe multicast algorithms that are stepwise contention-free and that can substantially reduce the number of communication steps compared to [6], even though they are not always depth contention-free. In addition to avoiding contention within every step, we show that these algorithms are also guaranteed to be depth contention-free, provided that each source node synchronizes its own set of outgoing messages, independently from the messages from other sources. We refer to these algorithms, with this weaker form of depth contention, as *source-controlled depth contention-free*. Similarly, solutions for other collective operations have been reported in the literature [7, 8], which take advantage of reducing the number of communication steps even though they are not depth contention-free.

The rest of this paper is organized as follows. Section 2 describes the basic notation, terminology and some key theorems used throughout this paper. Section 3 presents a general multicast algorithm and several methods based on this general approach. These methods are analyzed in Section 4 and their performance is evaluated in Section 5. Finally, concluding remarks are given in Section 6.

2 Preliminaries

Throughout this paper, each node in an n-dimensional hypercube (Q_n) is represented by a unique n-bit binary address $(b_{n-1}b_{n-2}...b_i...b_0)$. We use d_i to refer to the ith dimension in the cube. A k-dimensional subcube in a Q_n is represented by a unique n-tuple $(c_{n-1}c_{n-2}...c_i...c_0)$, where $c_i \in \{0, 1, X\}$, with exactly k coordinates with value "X". We refer to a k-cube ($k \leq n$) as a k-dimensional subcube of an n-dimensional hypercube. We assume the deterministic dimension-ordered routing and, without loss of generality, that the descending dimension order is used.

Definition 1 - *Reachable Sets.* Given a source node $S = (s_{n-1}, s_{n-2}, ..., s_i...s_0)$ in a Q_n, the *reachable set from S along d_i*, $R_i^n(S)$, $i \in \{0, 1, ..., n-1\}$, is the set of nodes in the subcube $(s_{n-1}s_{n-2}...s_{n-i} \ \overline{s_i}X^i)$. In addition, we also define $R_n^n(S)$ as the unary set that includes only the source node S. Figure 1, for instance, shows all the reachable sets $R_i^4(0000)$, for $i = \{0, 1, 2, 3, 4\}$.

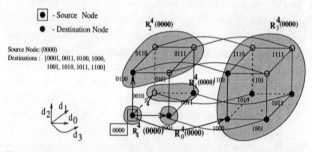

Figure 1: Reachable sets from the source node (0000) for a multicast with eight destinations in a Q_4.

Theorem 1 - *The reachable sets $R_i^n(S)$, $i \in \{0, 1, ..., n\}$, for any given source S, are disjoint and include all the nodes in Q_n, i.e., they form a partition of the set of the nodes in Q_n.*

Proof: The proof is given in two steps:

i - The reachable sets are disjoint. Assume, by contradiction, that a node $\beta = (b_{n-1}b_{n-2} \ ... \ b_i \ ... \ b_0) \in Q_n$ is in both $R_j^n(S)$ and $R_k^n(S)$, for an arbitrary j and k, $j > k$. Since, $\beta \in R_j^n(S)$, $b_j = \overline{s_j}$. However, since $\beta \in R_k^n(S)$ also, and $b_i = s_i$, $\forall i \mid i \in \{n-1, n-2, ..., j, ..., k+1\}$, then $b_j = s_j$, which is a contradiction. Thus, the reachable sets are disjoint.

ii - The reachable sets include all the nodes in Q_n. By definition, $S \in R_n^n$. Consider an arbitrary node $\beta = (b_{n-1}b_{n-2} \ ... \ b_i \ ... \ b_0) \in Q_n$, $\beta \neq S$. Let b_k be the first bit, from left to right, that differs from the corresponding bit in the source address $(s_{n-1}s_{n-2}...s_i...s_0)$; clearly, $\beta \in R_k^n(S)$. $\qquad \square$

Theorem 2 - *Considering a descending dimension-ordered routing, paths of messages sent along different ports from a common source are node-disjoint.*

Proof: With a descending dimension-ordered routing, a message from a source node $(s_{n-1}s_{n-2} \ ... \ s_i \ ... \ s_0)$ sent along d_i can only reach the nodes with address $(s_{n-1}s_{n-2} \ ... \ s_{i+1} \ \overline{s_i}X^i)$, which correspond to all the nodes in the set $R_i^n(S)$. By Theorem 1, the reachable sets are disjoint. Paths of messages sent along different ports are, therefore, node-disjoint. $\qquad \square$

From Theorem 2 it is apparent that a source node can send messages along different ports simultaneously, and reach an arbitrary destination node in each of the reachable sets of the cube, without facing contention. This property can be used for multicasting in all-port hypercubes. Consider, for example, the multicast problem in Figure 1, where the source node is (0000) and there are eight destinations; the source node is also included in the destination set. The destination nodes can be grouped according to the reachable sets relative to the source:

$G_0 = \{0001\} \subset R_0^4$
$G_1 = \{0011\} \subset R_1^4$
$G_2 = \{0100\} \subset R_2^4$
$G_3 = \{1000, 1001, 1010, 1011, 1100\} \subset R_3^4$
$G_4 = \{0000\} \subset R_4^4$

The source can select one receiving node in each of the sets above. Due to wormhole routing, however, the receivers do not need to be adjacent to the source, since a message can bypass the intermediate nodes towards the destination. After the first communication step, five nodes will have the message. The cube can then be subdivided into five disjoint subcubes, each with only one informed node, and the process can then be repeated with each of these informed nodes as a source node within its subcube. This approach is conceptually similar to the one presented in [6] for the multicast operation. In their work, however, the need for avoiding any potential for depth contention often keeps the algorithms from selecting the receiving nodes and from partitioning the cubes efficiently, which results in more communication steps than needed. With the W-sort algorithm [6] for example, after the first communication step, all the nodes in the set $\{0000, 0001, 0011, 0100, 1000\}$ have the message, as illustrated in Figure 2(a). The cube partitioning tree presents the informed nodes and the corresponding subcubes assigned in each step. Notice that node (1000) is assigned the entire half-cube (1XXX) and is the only active source in the second communication step, which is inefficient. The W-sort algorithm requires a total of three steps, as illustrated by the multicast tree in Figure 2(a).

In this paper, as opposed to [6], we focus on minimizing the number of communication steps while keeping the process contention-free within each step, even though it may potentially not be depth contention-free. This can be accomplished by selecting the receiving nodes in each reachable set and by partitioning the cubes in a way that balances the size of the subcubes after each step. Figure 2(b) illustrates a different solution for the same multicast problem; in this case, due to a more adequate selection of receivers and partition of the cube, more nodes get involved in the second step of the multicast operation, which then requires only two steps to complete. This is similar in concept to the divide-and-conquer approach presented in [1] for broadcast. The multicast problem, however, is more complex, since, both the number and the location of the destination nodes is arbitrary. This requires more general methods for selecting the receivers and for subdividing the cube in each communication step. These methods are presented in the following section.

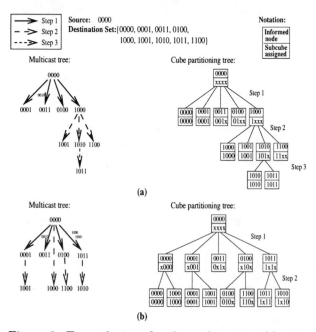

(a)

(b)

Figure 2: Two solutions for the multicast problem in Figure 1. (a) The W-sort algorithm [6]. (b) A solution that requires fewer communication steps.

3 Multicast Algorithms
3.1 A General Algorithm

The phases of a general recursive multicast algorithm are formalized in Figure 3. The inputs to the algorithm are the *cube* and the *dest_node_set*. In the first communication step, the algorithm is executed only by the initial source, the parameter *cube* is the entire hypercube (X^n), and *dest_node_set* is the complete destination set. The algorithm is then executed by all the informed nodes using the assigned subcube as the parameter *cube*. The *dest_node_set* is the subset of the destination nodes contained in this subcube. The algorithm assumes that the source node is also in the destination set; therefore, it is only executed if there is more than one node in the destination set. The phases of the algorithm are described below:

```
all_port_multicast( cube, dest_node_set ) {

     if( |dest_node_set| > 1) {
P1 -   dest_in_reach_set = find_nodes_in_reach_sets(dest_node_set);
P2 -   recv_set  = select_recvs_in_reach_sets(dest_in_reach_set);
P3 -   subcube_list  = partition_cube(recv_set);
P4 -   dest_nodes_in_subcube = find_dest_nodes_in_each_cube(subcube_list, dest_node_set);
P5 -   send(msg, recv_set);
P6 -   all_port_multicast( subcube_list(0), dest_nodes_in_subcube(0));
     }
}
```

Figure 3: Description of a general multicast algorithm.

P1- The nodes in the *dest_node_set* are grouped according to the reachable sets relative to the source.

P2- One destination node in each group is selected as a receiver. Notice that the source node is always selected, as it is in the destination set and is the only node in the set $R_k^k(Source)$. These nodes form the *recv_set* and correspond to the informed nodes in the following communication step.

P3- Based on the elements in the *recv_set*, the cube is partitioned into subcubes, with the criteria that one receiver appears in each subcube containing destination nodes still to be reached. This forms the list *subcube_list*; *subcube_list(0)* corresponds to the subcube assigned to the current source. The partitioning method also attempts to balance the size of the subcubes, in order to minimize the size of the largest resulting subcube.

P4- The destination nodes in the current cube are grouped according to the partition blocks in the *subcube_list*. This forms the *dest_nodes_in_cube* list.

P5- The message is output to each node in the *recv_set*. This message contains the actual data, appended with the *subcube_list* and the *dest_nodes_in_cube* information.

P6- If there are destination nodes to be reached in the subcube assigned to the current source (*sub-cube_list(0)*), i.e., if $|dest\_nodes\_in\_cube(0)| > 1$, the Phases P1-P5 are repeated using this destination subset and the subcube *subcube_list(0)*.

In the worst case, n steps will be needed to complete the multicast operation in an n-dimensional hypercube. The efficiency of this algorithm depends on the method used for selecting the receivers (Phase P2) and on how efficiently the cube is partitioned (Phase P3). These phases are related and an compatible match is needed to efficiently perform the operation. The heuristics utilized in this paper attempt to balance the size of the subcubes in the partition. This is motivated by the recursive nature of the general algorithm. Considering a random distribution of the destination nodes, if the cube is split into equally sized subcubes, the size of the largest subcube is minimized and the destination set is subdivided in an approximately even fashion, so that the multicast problem is optimally reduced for the following step of the operation. It is also important to keep the computational complexity of these methods low. Notice, however, that this algorithm allows for a parallel execution on all informed nodes, which is an advantage. In addition, in certain cases, if the same set of destinations needs to be reached repeatedly, it may be acceptable to use more complex methods to schedule the communication steps. Several heuristic methods, with different levels of complexity, are presented in the following subsections.

3.2 The Cube Partitioning Based (CPB) Method

This heuristic method concentrates on deriving an efficient partition of the cubes from a given set of receivers. During Phase P2, one destination node is selected, at random, from each reachable set (Figure 4(a)). With this set of receivers, Phase P3 is executed according to Figure 4(b). The partitioning phase is recursive, and partitions the cube along one dimension in each phase. This phase attempts to minimize the size of the largest resulting subcube by assigning an approximately equal number of receivers to each side of the cube during a split. Before describing the cube partitioning phase, it is appropriate to define the following terms:

Definition 2 - *One-(Zero-) count k-tuples.* Given a set G of nodes in a k-cube, the *one-count* of G, $N(G)$, is the k-tuple $(n_{k-1}, n_{k-2}, ..., n_i, ..., n_0)$, where, n_i is the number of nodes in G with the ith bit equal to "1". The *zero-count* of G, $Z(G) = (z_{k-1}, z_{k-2}, ..., z_i, ..., z_0)$, is defined similarly. For example, in the 5-node set

$G = \{0001, 0100, 0101, 1011, 1101\}$, $N(G) = (2, 3, 1, 4)$ and $Z(G) = (3, 2, 4, 1)$.

Definition 3 - *Even-split dimension.* Given a set G of nodes in a k-cube, the *even-split-dimension* of G, $e(G)$, is the dimension d_i along which $|n_i - z_i|$ is minimal. For $G = \{0001, 0100, 0101, 1011, 1101\}$, for example, $e(G) \in \{2, 3\}$, and $|n_e - z_e| = 1$.

Definition 4 - *One-(Zero-) bound subset, One-(Zero-) bound subcube.* Given a set G of nodes in a k-cube, the *one-(zero-) bound subset* along d_i, G_i^1 (G_i^0), is the set of all the nodes in G with the ith coordinate equal to "1"("0"). For $G = \{0001, 0100, 0101, 1011, 1101\}$ and $i = 2$, for example, $G_2^1 = \{0100, 0101, 1101\}$ and $G_2^0 = \{0001, 1011\}$. Correspondingly, given a cube $C = (c_{k-1}c_{k-2}...c_i...c_0)$, we define the $(k-1)$-cubes $C_i^1 = (c_{k-1}c_{k-2}...c_{i+1}1c_{i-1}...c_0)$ and $C_i^0 = (c_{k-1}c_{k-2}...c_{i+1}0c_{i-1}...c_0)$ as the *one-bound* and *zero-bound* subcubes along d_i, respectively.

In Phase P3, the first dimension selected for splitting a k-cube is the even-split dimension of the set of receivers (*recv_set*). After this split, the process is repeated for each of the $(k-1)$-cubes (the zero-bound and the one-bound subcubes). In this case, the even-split dimension is computed considering only the corresponding subset (the zero-bound or the one-bound subset) of the *recv_set*. This process is repeated until only one receiver is left in each subset.

A multicast tree resulting from the CPB method, applied to the problem in Figure 1, is shown in Figure 5(c). This multicast takes two communication steps, and the execution of the algorithm by the source (0000) during the first communication step is illustrated in Figures 5(a) and 5(b). One node is selected from each set, at random, and this forms the *recv_set* {0000, 0001, 0011, 0100, 1011}. The cube is partitioned using the even-split dimensions (Figure 5(a)). The leaves of the tree represent the receivers in the first step of the multicast tree and the corresponding subcubes assigned to them for the second communication step. The table in Figure 5(b) contains the information that is appended to the multicast message in the first communication step.

3.3 The Receiver Selection Based (RSB) Method

The RSB method, unlike the CPB method above, uses a predefined order of dimensions for splitting the cube (Phase P3). Phase P2 is based on a heuristic method that attempts to select the receiving nodes to minimize the size of the largest subcube when the predefined partitioning sequence is applied. This can be best achieved if, in each step, there is an equal

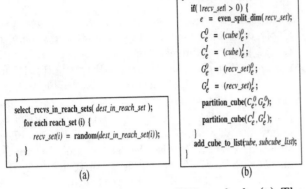

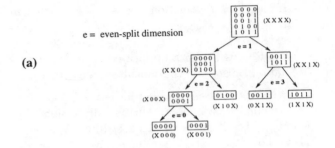

(a)

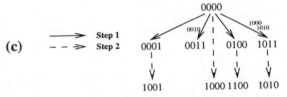

(b)

Figure 4: Description of the CPB method. (a) The receivers are selected at random in Phase P2. (b) The cube partitioning Phase P3 uses the even-split dimensions.

Figure 5: Example of the CPB method for the multicast problem in Figure 1. (a) Phase P3, during the first communication step. (b) The resulting receivers, subcubes and the destination subsets. (c) The final multicast tree with height two.

number of receivers in the two subcubes.

The fixed sequence of dimensions used for partitioning a k-cube is $(0, 1, ..., k-1)$. This is because, on the average, due to the descending dimension-ordered routing, it is more likely to find an even-split dimension along the lower dimensions of the k-cube. This becomes clear by observing that the $(k+1)$ potential receivers from a source node $(b_{k-1}b_{k-2}...b_i...b_0)$ are $(\overline{b_{k-1}}X^{k-1})$, $(b_{k-1}\overline{b_{k-2}}X^{k-2})$, ..., $(b_{k-1}b_{k-2}...\overline{b_i}X^i)$, $(b_{k-1}b_{k-2}...\overline{b_0})$ and $(b_{k-1}b_{k-2}, ..., b_0)$, where $X \in \{0, 1\}$ represents the address bits that need to be determined by the receiver selection method. If we consider dimension d_{k-1}, for example, notice that there is only one receiver node in the $(\overline{b_{k-1}})$-bound subcube, while the other k remaining potential receivers are in the (b_{k-1})-bound subcube. Therefore, (d_{k-1}) is not likely to be an even-split dimension. On the other hand, as we move along to the lower dimensions, it becomes more likely to find an even-split dimension by choosing the receiver addresses accordingly. The same argument is valid in a recursive mode, i.e., once we partition the cube along d_0, for example, d_1 is then the most likely choice for an even-split dimension in each of the (b_0)-bound and the $(\overline{b_0})$-bound $(k-1)$-cubes.

The RSB method is formally presented in Figure 6. In the receiver selection phase, initially, the nodes that are the only destination nodes in a reachable set are assigned as receivers, since there is no choice for selection in this case. Next, one receiver node is selected from each of the remaining reachable sets in sequence. The algorithm updates a partial set of the nodes already assigned as receivers, the *partial_recv_set*, after each new receiver is selected. The selection method

also keeps the *zero-count* and the *one-count* of the *partial_recv_set*. The destination nodes in the reachable set being considered form a *candidate_set* and the routine that selects one node among the candidates works as follows. According to the sequence used for splitting, the first dimension along which the cube is split is d_0. Thus, in the selection process, if $z_0(partial\_recv\_set) > n_0(partial\_recv\_set)$, it is preferred, for an even split to occur along d_0, to consider only the candidates with a "1" in the address bit 0. In this case, unless there are no nodes with this property, only the nodes with address bit 0 equal to "1" are kept as candidates. Similarly, the *zero-count* and the *one-count* are updated considering only the nodes in the *partial_recv_set* with a "1" in address bit 0. A reverse procedure would be adopted if $z_0(partial\_recv\_set) < n_0(partial\_recv\_set)$. The process above is then repeated considering the subsequent dimensions in the sequence $(0, 1, ..., k-1)$, one at a time, until only one node is left in the *candidate_set*. This is repeated for each reachable set. Once all the receivers are selected, the cube is partitioned using the dimension sequence $(0, 1, ..., k-1)$.

An illustrative example, for the multicast problem in Figure 1, is shown in Figure 7. Figure 7(c)

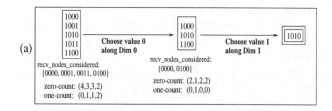

```
select_recvs_in_reach_sets(dest_in_reach_set) {

  partial_recv_set = φ ;
  for each reachable_set(i){
    if( |dest_in_reach_set(i)| =1 )
      add_node_to_partial_recv_set(dest_in_reach_set(i)(0));
  }

  for each reachable_set(i) such that |dest_in_reach_set(i)| > 1 {
    Z = zero_count(partial_recv_set);
    N = one_count(partial_recv_set);
    candidate_set = dest_in_reach_set(i);
    recv_nodes_considered = partial_recv_set;

    j = -1;
    do {
      j = j + 1;
      if( Z(j) > N(j) ) {
        if(|one_subset(dest_in_reach_set(i), j)| > 0){
          candidate_set = one_subset(candidate_set, j);
          recv_nodes_considered = one_subset(recv_nodes_considered, j);
        } else {
          recv_nodes_considered = zero_subset(recv_nodes_considered, j);
        }
      } else {
        if( |zero_subset(dest_in_reach_set(i), j)| > 0) {
          candidate_set = zero_subset( candidate_set, j);
          recv_nodes_considered = zero_subset(recv_nodes_considered, j );
        } else {
          recv_nodes_considered = one_subset(recv_nodes_considered, j);
        }
      }
      Z = zero_count(recv_nodes_considered);
      N = one_count(recv_nodes_considered);
    } until(|candidate_set | = 1);
    add_node_to_partial_recv_set( candidate_set(0), partial_recv_set );
  }

  recv_set = partial_recv_set;
}
```

```
e = -1;

partition_cube(recv_set) {
  e = e + 1;
  if( |recv_set| > 0) {
    C_e^0 = (cube)_e^0;
    C_e^1 = (cube)_e^1;
    G_e^0 = (recv_set)_e^0;
    G_e^1 = (recv_set)_e^1;
    partition_cube(C_e^0, G_e^0);
    partition_cube(C_e^1, G_e^1);
  }
  add_cube_to_list(cube, subcube_list);
}
```

(a)   (b)

Figure 6: Description of the RSB method. (a) The receiver selection Phase P2. (b) The cube partitioning Phase P3, which uses a fixed dimension sequence.

shows the multicast tree with height two, resulting from this method. Figure 7(a) and (b) show the result of the RSB method executed by the source (0000) in the first communication step. In summary, initially, the *partial_recv_set* is the set {0000, 0001, 0011, 0100}, which contains the only destination nodes in their corresponding reachable sets. For the reachable set R_3^4, the selection algorithm is applied, and it results in the selection of the node (1010). With the complete *recv_set*, the cube is then partitioned using the fixed dimension sequence.

3.4 The Random Selection Fixed Partition (RSFP) Method

The RSFP method is a combination of the CPB and the RSB methods, but it is computationally more efficient. It relies on the property that an even-split dimension is more likely to be found along the lower dimensions of the cube. Thus, this method uses the fixed dimension sequence $(0, 1, ..., k-1)$ for splitting a k-cube. It differs from the RSB method by selecting

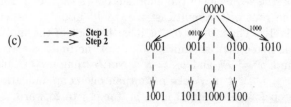

(b)

Receivers	Cubes	Destination Subsets
0000	(X 0 0 0)	0000, 1000
0001	(X X 0 1)	0001, 1001
0011	(X X 1 1)	0011, 1011
0100	(X 1 0 0)	0100, 1100
1010	(X X 1 0)	1010

Figure 7: Example of the RSB method for the problem in Figure 1. (a) Phase P2 in Step 1. (b) The resulting receivers, subcubes and the destination subsets. (c) The final multicast tree with height two.

the receiving nodes at random. The complexity of these three methods is analyzed in the next section and their performance is compared in Section 5.

4 Analysis

4.1 Contention issues

It is important to maintain that the messages involved in a multicast operation contention-free. Theorem 3 below shows that the general algorithm described in Figure 3 is stepwise contention-free.

Theorem 3 - *The general algorithm is stepwise contention-free.*

Proof: During a communication step, the paths of messages sent from a common source are node-disjoint, by Theorem 2, since the receivers are in disjoint reachable sets. The paths of messages sent from different sources are also node-disjoint, since they are in disjoint partitions of the cube. Thus, clearly, all communication steps are contention-free. □

Theorem 3 guarantees that there is no contention if the communication steps are synchronized. In addition, if we assume that a source node waits for all of its outgoing messages to reach the destinations before starting the next communication step, and also that none of these destinations starts to forward the message until this occurs, then the algorithm is guaranteed to be depth contention-free. We denote algorithms with this property as *source-controlled depth contention-free.*

Theorem 4 - *The general algorithm is source-controlled depth contention-free.*

Proof: It needs to be shown that no contention is possible between any pair of messages in the multicast tree. Consider two arbitrary messages, $(\alpha : I^\alpha \to D^\alpha)$ and $(\beta : I^\beta \to D^\beta)$, scheduled, respectively, for the communication steps i and j; I^α and I^β are the informed nodes that generate α and β, respectively, and D^α and D^β are their destinations. Let $P^\alpha = (p_1^\alpha, p_2^\alpha, ..., p_l^\alpha, ..., p_u^\alpha)$ and $P^\beta = (p_1^\beta, p_2^\beta, ..., p_l^\beta, ..., p_v^\beta)$, be the sequence of the informed nodes that lead from the root of the multicast tree to I^α and I^β, respectively. Thus, $p_1^\alpha = p_1^\beta$, as it is the root of the multicast tree, i.e., the initial source of the multicast (S), and $p_u^\alpha = I^\alpha$ and $p_v^\beta = I^\beta$. Notice that $u \leq i$, and $v \leq j$, as it may take more than one communication step for an informed node p_l^α (or p_l^β) to forward the message to the following node p_{l+1}^α (or p_{l+1}^β). Let k be the leftmost index for which P^α and P^β diverge, i.e., $p_l^\alpha = p_l^\beta$, $1 \leq l \leq k$, and $p_{k+1}^\alpha \neq p_{k+1}^\beta$ (if p_{k+1}^α and p_{k+1}^β exist). Assuming, without loss of generality, that $u \leq v$, three cases are possible:

(1) $u = v = k$ (Figure 8(a)). In this case, $I^\alpha = I^\beta$ and neither α nor β can start until the message is received by this common source. In this case, if,
- $i = j$, α and β are *concurrent* but they are sent along node-disjoint reachable sets.
- $i \neq j$, α and β are *not concurrent*, since the transfer is source-controlled.

(2) $v > u = k$ (Figure 8(b)). In this case, $I^\alpha = p_k^\alpha = p_k^\beta$, and I^β only receives the message sometime after this node. Neither α nor β can start until $I^\alpha = p_k^\beta$ receives the message. Let $(\gamma : p_k^\beta \to p_{k+1}^\beta)$ be the next message along P^β; γ precedes β. Two cases are possible:
- α and γ are *scheduled concurrently* by the common source. α and β, which are sent along node-disjoint reachable sets, reach the destinations D^α and $D^\gamma = p_{k+1}^\beta$; from the source-controlled assumption, p_{k+1}^β only forwards the message after α reaches D^α; therefore α and β are not concurrent.
- α and γ are *not scheduled concurrently* by the common source. In this case, if α is sent before γ, α and β are not concurrent as β can only be generated after γ. If γ is sent first, then α and β are in disjoint partitions of the cube.

(3) $v > k$, $u > k$ (Figure 8(c)). Neither α nor β can start until $p_k^\alpha = p_k^\beta$ receives the message. Consider $(\theta : p_k^\alpha \to p_{k+1}^\alpha)$ and $(\gamma : p_k^\beta \to p_{k+1}^\beta)$, which precede α and β, respectively. Two cases are possible:
- θ and γ are *scheduled concurrently* by $p_k^\alpha = p_k^\beta$. By the source-controlled assumption, θ and γ are received by p_{k+1}^α and p_{k+1}^α before any of these nodes forwards the message. Since p_{k+1}^α and p_{k+1}^β each has a disjoint subcube assigned, α and β will not contend for a common channel.
- θ and γ are *not scheduled concurrently* by $p_k^\alpha = p_k^\beta$. In this case also, α and β follow disjoint paths, since they will be sent along disjoint partitions of the cube. $\square$

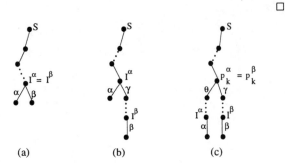

Figure 8: Illustration of the three cases used in the proof of Theorem 4.

Theorem 4 guarantees that no contention exists even if messages originating from different source nodes are not synchronized. Due to the overhead involved in synchronizing, the communication steps may be left completely unsynchronized, which, in the worst case, may only result in a partial contention among a few messages.

4.2 Complexity of the algorithms

Phases P1–P4 determine the complexity of the general algorithm in Figure 3. Considering d destination nodes in a k-cube, Phases P1 (grouping the d nodes in reachable sets) and P4 (grouping the d nodes in terms of the partitions of the cube) can each be completed in $O(dk)$ time. Phases P2 and P3 depend on the method used to select the receivers and to partition the cube.

Up to $(k + 1)$ nodes may be selected as receivers in one communication step, corresponding to one in each reachable set. In Phase P2, the CPB and the RSFP methods randomly select the receivers, which can be accomplished in $O(k)$ time. The RSB method uses the algorithm in Figure 6(a). Considering the external *for loop*, the internal *do-until loop* and the operation performed within a loop, this algorithm can be completed in $O(k^3)$ time.

In Phase P3 the RSB and the RSFP methods use a fixed partitioning sequence, which can be done in $O(k^2)$ time. The CPB method computes the even-split dimension before every split, which can be completed in $O(k^2)$ time. As this may have to be performed up to k times, the CPB method needs $O(k^3)$ time.

Thus, with the CPB and RSB methods, each iteration of the recursive algorithm can be completed in $O(dk + k^3)$ time. Using the RSFP method, each iteration requires $O(dk + k^2)$ time.

5 Experimental Results

The multicast methods described in Section 3 were experimentally evaluated and the results are presented here. In the experiments, the size of the destination set was varied, and the experiments were repeated 100 times with the nodes selected at random in each case. The algorithms were compared in terms of the average number of steps needed to complete the multicast operation.

For a multicast pattern involving d destination nodes in an n-cube, a theoretical lower bound for the number of communication steps is $\lceil log_{n+1}(d+1) \rceil$ [1]. The graph in Figure 9 compares the performance of the three heuristic multicast methods in Section 3 on a 10-cube, with the W-sort algorithm [6] and the lower bound. All three methods outperform the W-sort method, especially when the number of destinations is large. In general, among the three methods described here, the more complex methods perform better. It is observed that, for the one-to-all pattern, the RSB method performs as well as the broadcast method in [1], which is an optimal solution (within a multiplicative constant of the lower bound for broadcasting). This is a direct consequence of the fact that the RSB method essentially turns into the optimal solution when the destination set is the entire set of the nodes in the cube. Thus, the RSB method can actually be seen as a generalization of this optimal broadcast method.

6 Conclusions

In this paper, a recursive approach for multicasting in all-port dimension-ordered wormhole-routed hypercubes is introduced, which can be viewed as a generalization of a method presented earlier in [1] for the broadcast pattern. Several methods based on this approach are described, with different levels of computational complexity. These methods are shown to be stepwise contention-free and source-controlled depth contention-free. Comparisons with an earlier method [6] shows a significant reduction in the number of communication steps.

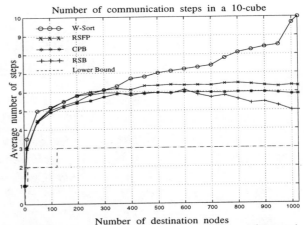

Figure 9: Average number of steps for a multicast in a 10-cube.

References

[1] C.-T. Ho and M. Kao, "Optimal broadcast in all-port wormhole-routed hypercubes," *IEEE Transactions on Parallel and Distributed Systems*, vol. 6, no. 2, pp. 200–204, 1995.

[2] L. Ni and P. McKinley, "A survey of wormhole routing techniques in direct networks," *IEEE Computer*, no. 2, pp. 62–76, 1993.

[3] R. Boppana, S. Chalasani and C. Raghavendra, "On multicast wormhole routing in multicomputer networks," *Proceedings of the IEEE Symposium on Parallel and Distributed Processing*, pp. 722-729, 1994.

[4] X. Lin and L. Ni, "Multicast communication in multicomputer networks," *IEEE Transactions on Parallel and Distributed Systems*, vol. 4, no. 10, pp. 1105–1117, 1993.

[5] P. McKinley, A. Esfahanian and L. Ni, "Unicast-based multicast communication in wormhole-routed networks," *IEEE Transactions on Parallel and Distributed Systems*, vol. 5, no. 12, pp. 1252–1265, 1994.

[6] D. Robinson, D. Judd, P. McKinley and B. Cheng, "Efficient multicast in all-port wormhole-routed hypercubes," *Proceedings of Supercomputing*, pp. 792- 801, 1993.

[7] Y. Tsai and P. McKinley, "A broadcast algorithm for all-port wormhole-routed torus networks," *IEEE Transactions on Parallel and Distributed Systems*, vol. 7, no. 8, pp. 876–885, 1996.

[8] Y. Tseng and S. Gupta, "All-to-all personalized communication in a wormhole-routed torus," *IEEE Transactions on Parallel and Distributed Systems*, vol. 7, no. 5, pp. 498–505, 1996.

A Class of Fixed-Degree Cayley-Graph Interconnection Networks Derived by Pruning *k*-ary *n*-cubes

Ding-Ming Kwai and Behrooz Parhami

Department of Electrical and Computer Engineering
University of California
Santa Barbara, CA 93106-9560, USA

Abstract

We introduce a pruning scheme to reduce the node degree of k-ary n-cube from 2n to 4. The links corresponding to n − 2 of the n dimensions are removed from each node. One of the remaining dimensions is common to all nodes and the other is selected periodically from the remaining n − 1 dimensions. Despite the removal of a large number of links from the k-ary n-cube, this incomplete version still preserves many of its desirable topological properties. In this paper, we show that this incomplete k-ary n-cube belongs to the class of Cayley graphs, and hence, is node-symmetric. It is 4-connected with diameter close to that of the k-ary n-cube.

1. Introduction

Direct networks whose nodes possess a fixed number of neighbors, or degree, can be derived by removing links from a highly connected one. Such a "pruning" scheme is meant to reduce the node degree to a small(er) constant. In the reduced network, nodes are clustered into groups or partitioned into hierarchical levels; each node is provided with a subset of the original connections and each group collectively has the same communication capability as a node in the original network.

For example, the cube-connected cycles (CCC) [10] and periodically regular chordal (PRC) ring [9], in which links of various dimensions and lengths are distributed to a group of nodes, can be viewed as having been derived from pruning richer networks [5]. Networks obtained by pruning richer basis networks, such as hypercubes or circulants, inherit advantages from the original networks, and:

- Achieve logarithmic diameter with an optimally chosen group size.
- Simulate the original network easily and efficiently.
- Have simpler, as well as more regular, VLSI layout.

Whereas pruning leads to reduced node degree, cross-product networks [11] work in the opposite direction in that they increase the node degree to accommodate more connections. The *k*-ary *n*-cube, typically used in direct networks that span multiple dimensions, is simply the cross product of *n* *k*-node rings. Pruned versions of 3D torus have been shown to be quite effective [2], [8]. In this paper, we apply the pruning method to the more general *k*-ary *n*-cube and derive some of its properties.

Our presentation is organized as follows. In Section 2, we describe the structure and basic topological properties of the incomplete *k*-ary *n*-cube. Section 3 shows that a modified form of the incomplete *k*-ary *n*-cube, in which one dimension is allowed to be different, includes CCC as a special case. Motivated by the fact that CCC is a Cayley graph, we prove in Section 4 that the incomplete *k*-ary *n*-cube also belongs to the class of Cayley graphs. Section 5 contains our conclusions.

2. Structure and Basic properties

Consider a *k*-ary 3-cube, where *k* is an even number. The k^3 nodes may be thought of as being positioned in an array consisting of *k* rows, *k* columns, and *k* layers, and connected by dimension X, Y, and Z links, respectively. In the pruned *k*-ary 3-cube, the dimension X and Y links are removed alternately from every other layer. Each node (x, y, z) is connected to two neighbors $(x, y, z \pm 1)$. The other two neighbors of (x, y, z) are $(x \pm 1, y, z)$ if z is even or $(x, y \pm 1, z)$ if z is odd. Here it will be understood that all node indices are calculated modulo *k*.

Because dimensions X and Y can be permuted without changing the connectivity, this leads to a node-transitive graph of degree 4. As an example, Fig. 1 shows a pruned *k*-ary 3-cube with $k = 4$.

A *k*-ary *n*-cube, where $n > 3$, may be similarly pruned to constant degree of 4 by following the above scheme. In such a network, each node $(a_0, a_1, \ldots, a_{n-1})$, denoted as an *n*-digit radix-*k* vector, is connected to four neighbors

$(a_0, a_1, \ldots, a_{n-1} \pm 1)$ and $(a_0, \ldots, a_i \pm 1, \ldots, a_{n-1})$ if a_{n-1} mod $(n-1) = i$. In order to assure that an equal number of dimensional links are provided, we require k to be a multiple of $n - 1$. Hence every $n - 1$ nodes around the k-node ring in dimension $n - 1$ possess a complete set of the dimensional links.

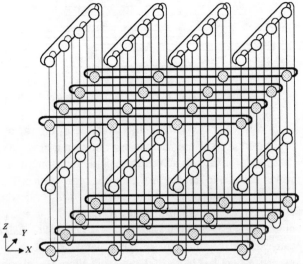

Fig. 1. Incomplete 4-ary 3-cube by alternately removing X and Y links.

Theorem 1 follows directly from the definition of the incomplete k-ary n-cube and from the observation that node-disjoint rings can be found either along dimension $n - 1$ or collectively along dimensions 0 through $n - 2$.

Theorem 1: An incomplete k-ary n-cube contains k^{n-1} disjoint rings of k nodes.

Given two nodes $A = (a_0, a_1, \ldots, a_{n-1})$ and $B = (b_0, b_1, \ldots, b_{n-1})$, the *Lee* distance [3] between them is defined as $\sum_{i=0}^{n-1} |\Delta d_i|$ where $|\Delta d_i| = \min\{|b_i - a_i|, k - |a_i - b_i|\}$. Each offset $|\Delta d_i|$ is the minimum number of routing steps along dimension i in moving from A to B. In the complete k-ary n-cube, the Lee distance is also the length of the shortest path. Since the route can be either forward or backward along dimension i, to indicate the direction we denote

$$\Delta d_i = \begin{cases} |\Delta d_i| & \text{if } b_i - a_i \ (\text{mod } k) \le a_i - b_i \ (\text{mod } k) \\ -|\Delta d_i| & \text{otherwise} \end{cases}$$

Theorem 2 states that the diameter of the incomplete k-ary n-cube is equal to or only slightly larger than that of its unpruned counterpart.

Theorem 2: The diameter of the incomplete k-ary n-cube is

$$D = \begin{cases} (n-1)\lfloor k/2 \rfloor + \max\{2n - 4, \lfloor k/2 \rfloor\} & \text{if } k \ge 2(n-1) \\ (n-1)\lfloor k/2 \rfloor + \max\{n - 3 + \lfloor k/2 \rfloor, k\} & \text{if } k = n - 1 \end{cases}$$

Proof: Without loss of generality, we can select node $(0, 0, \ldots, 0)$ as the source and route to a node with offsets $(\Delta d_0, \Delta d_1, \ldots, \Delta d_{n-1})$. Consider the increase in the maximum routing distance relative to that of the k-ary n-cube. In order to gain access to the dimensions whose links have been removed from nodes, extra steps may have to be taken along dimension $n - 1$.

From $(0, 0, \ldots, 0)$, dimension 0 and $n - 1$ links are directly accessible and can be taken, if needed, as in the complete k-ary n-cube. As we take the required $|\Delta d_{n-1}|$ hops along dimension $n - 1$, links for the other $n - 2$ dimensions become accessible. Thus if $|\Delta d_{n-1}| \ge n - 2$, we encounter links for all possible dimensions. Consequently, the missing links do not contribute any extra hop to the length of the shortest path. We will not consider this case in the remainder of the proof.

If $|\Delta d_{n-1}| < n - 2$, then additional hops are needed to gain access to the links other than those encountered along dimension $n - 1$. Because of this, routing along dimension $n - 1$ in the direction dictated by the sign of Δd_{n-1} may not be the best choice.

Case 1: Route normally along dimension $n - 1$. In this case, $|\Delta d_{n-1}|$ of the $n - 2$ dimensions are accessible. We take $2(n - 2 - |\Delta d_{n-1}|)$ extra hops for the remaining $n - 2 - |\Delta d_{n-1}|$ dimensions, going "beyond" the destination and returning. The total routing distance in this case is $\sum_{i=0}^{n-2} |\Delta d_i| + 2n - 4 - |\Delta d_{n-1}|$.

Case 2: Route in reverse along dimension $n - 1$. In this case, we will visit $k - |\Delta d_{n-1}|$ nodes; the number of extra hops is $k - 2|\Delta d_{n-1}|$. If $k - |\Delta d_{n-1}| \ge n - 2$, then nothing more is needed and the total routing distance becomes $\sum_{i=0}^{n-2} |\Delta d_i| + k - |\Delta d_{n-1}|$. On the other hand, if $k - |\Delta d_{n-1}| < n - 2$, then as argued above for Case 1, we need $2(n - 2 - k + |\Delta d_{n-1}|)$ extra hops, making the total routing distance $\sum_{i=0}^{n-2} |\Delta d_i| + 2n - 4 - k + |\Delta d_{n-1}|$.

To continue the proof, it is more convenient to handle the special case $k = n - 1$ separately. Recall that k is a multiple of $n - 1$. For $k \ge 2(n - 1)$, we have $k - |\Delta d_{n-1}| > n - 2$; Case 2 has a larger distance than Case 1. The routing distance of the latter is maximized for $|\Delta d_{n-1}| = 0$, leading to the diameter of $(n - 1)\lfloor k/2 \rfloor + \max(\lfloor k/2 \rfloor, 2n - 4)$. This proves the first part of the equation.

For $k = n - 1$, we have $k - |\Delta d_{n-1}| \ge n - 2$ if $|\Delta d_{n-1}| \le 1$. Since $n \ge 3$, Case 2 is better, leading to the maximum $(n - 1)\lfloor k/2 \rfloor + k$. The remaining case of $|\Delta d_{n-1}| \ge 2$ makes the routing distance $\sum_{i=0}^{n-2} |\Delta d_i| + 2n - 4 - |\Delta d_{n-1}|$ based on Case 1 and $\sum_{i=0}^{n-2} |\Delta d_i| + 2n - 4 - k + |\Delta d_{n-1}|$ based on Case 2. The smaller of the two is maximized when they are equal, leading to the maximum $(n - 1)\lfloor k/2 \rfloor + n - 3 + \lfloor k/2 \rfloor$. This proves the second part of the equation. $\square$

The diameter of the incomplete k-ary n-cube is at most $k - 2$ larger than that of its unpruned counterpart. This worst case occurs when $k = n - 1$ and $n \geq 7$, as we rewrite it in the following form and solve for the maximum.

$$D = \begin{cases} n\lfloor k/2 \rfloor + \max\{2n - 4 - \lfloor k/2 \rfloor, 0\} & \text{if } k \geq 2(n - 1) \\ n\lfloor k/2 \rfloor + \max\{n - 3, \lceil k/2 \rceil\} & \text{if } k = n - 1 \end{cases}$$

In the case where $k \geq 4n - 4$, the diameter is the same as that of the k-ary n-cube, i.e., $D = n\lfloor k/2 \rfloor$.

Bisection width of a network is the minimum number of links that must be removed in order to divide the network into two equal halves. This measure relates to communication capacity on the one hand and also sets a lower bound on wire length for a given diameter. The bisection width of the incomplete k-ary n-cube can be obtained as $2k^{n-1}/(n - 1)$ by considering, for example, the number of links cut by a hyper-plane near $a_0 = k/2$. For such a division, the only links that would be removed are in dimension 0. Note that the bisection width is a factor of $n - 1$ lower than that of complete k-ary n-cube.

3. Generalization to Cube-Connected Cycles

In this section, we apply our pruning scheme to a generalized incomplete k-ary n-cube which can give rise to n-cube connected cycles (n-CCC).

One way to generalize the incomplete k-ary n-cube is to allow dimension $n - 1$ to be longer than k, the size of all other dimensions. Let us assume that dimension $n - 1$ has l nodes and $l > k$. Now, k can be any positive integer but l is restricted to be a multiple of $n - 1$. The diameter can be correspondingly modified to

$$D = \begin{cases} (n - 1)\lfloor k/2 \rfloor + \max\{2n - 4, \lfloor l/2 \rfloor\} & \text{if } l \geq 2(n - 1) \\ (n - 1)\lfloor k/2 \rfloor + \max\{n - 3 + \lfloor l/2 \rfloor, l\} & \text{if } l = n - 1 \end{cases}$$

The n-CCC can be derived from pruning an $(n + 1)$-D torus with $2 \times \ldots \times 2 \times n$ nodes, i.e., $k = 2$ and $l = n$ (see Fig. 2 for an example). Substituting 2 for k and $n + 1$ for n into the above equation leads to the diameter $D = n + \max\{n + \lfloor n/2 \rfloor - 2, n\}$, as given in [7]. This expression deserves some attention. Several textbooks mistakenly regard $2n$ as the diameter which is true only for $n \leq 5$. Based on the proof of Theorem 2, we briefly describe the derivation as follows.

To route through the first n dimensions, each taking one step, one can choose decreasing or increasing dimension order. In either case, the path does not need to return to the starting dimension (e.g., from dimension 0 back to dimension $n - 1$), if the offset $|\Delta d_n|$ between source and destination is non-zero. The number of steps via the

dimension n links is at most $n - 1$. For $\Delta d_n = 0$, clearly up to n steps may be required.

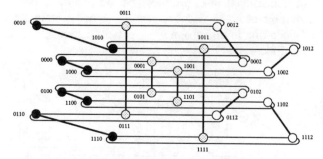

Fig. 2. An incomplete $2 \times 2 \times 2 \times 3$ 4D torus view of 3-CCC.

If $\Delta d_n = \lfloor n/2 \rfloor$ ($-\lfloor n/2 \rfloor$), the worst case for $\Delta d_n \neq 0$, routing in decreasing (increasing) dimension order takes $\lfloor n/2 \rfloor - 1$ forward (backward) steps along dimension n, which is equal to, or one less than, the other choice. This, however, cannot constitute the longest path if $n = 3$ when no step is taken along dimension n. Hence, for $n \geq 4$, the diameter is $n + n - 1 + \lfloor n/2 \rfloor - 1 = 2n + \lfloor n/2 \rfloor - 2$. We can express the diameter in the general form $D = n + \max\{n + \lfloor n/2 \rfloor - 2, n\}$ and note that there are at most three nodes diametrically opposite to $(a_0, \ldots, a_{n-1}, a_n)$:

$$\begin{cases} (a_0 + 1, \ldots, a_{n-1} + 1, a_n) & \text{if } n = 3 \\ (a_0 + 1, \ldots, a_{n-1} + 1, a_n), & \\ \quad (a_0 + 1, \ldots, a_{n-1} + 1, a_n \pm \lfloor n/2 \rfloor) & \text{if } n = 4, 5 \\ (a_0 + 1, \ldots, a_{n-1} + 1, a_n \pm \lfloor n/2 \rfloor) & \text{if } n \geq 6 \end{cases}$$

4. Node Symmetry based on Cayley graphs

The k-ary n-cube, including its special case of hypercube or binary n-cube, is known to belong to the class of Cayley graphs of cyclic groups. As a result, the networks are node-transitive. The incomplete k-ary n-cube and its generalized version share the same property. Our proof method is similar to that used for proving that the n-CCC is a Cayley graph [4].

Let $*$ be an associative binary operator and Ω be some subset (generator set) from a finite group Γ such that

1) The identity $\iota \notin \Omega$;
2) If $\omega \in \Omega$, then its inverse $\omega^{-1} \in \Omega$.

A Cayley graph [1] can be defined as a digraph whose node x is connected to node $x * \omega$ ($x, x * \omega \in \Gamma$) if and only if $\omega \in \Omega$. The size $|\Omega|$ of the generator set Ω determines the node degree of a Cayley graph. We refer the reader to [6] for a detailed discussion on the symmetry properties of Cayley graphs.

Theorem 3: The incomplete k-ary n-cube and its generalized version with dimension $n-1$ being longer, are Cayley graphs.

Proof: To facilitate our manipulation, we express the node address as $(\hat{a}, b)$, where $\hat{a} = [a_0, a_1, \dots, a_{n-2}]^T$ is an $(n-1)$-vector and $b = a_{n-1}$. Define the operator $*$ as

$$(\hat{a}, b) * (\hat{v}, \omega) = (\hat{a} + \Phi^b \cdot \hat{v}, \ b + \omega)$$

where $(\hat{v}, \omega) \in \Omega$ and Φ is an $(n-1) \times (n-1)$ matrix

$$\Phi = \begin{bmatrix} 0 & 0 & 0 & \cdots & 0 & 1 \\ 1 & 0 & 0 & \cdots & 0 & 0 \\ 0 & 1 & 0 & \cdots & 0 & 0 \\ \vdots & \vdots & \vdots & & \vdots & \vdots \\ 0 & 0 & 0 & \cdots & 1 & 0 \end{bmatrix}$$

The first addition is component-wise modulo k and the second addition is modulo l. Also, note that Φ has a periodic property: $\Phi^i = \Phi^{i + f(n-1)}$, where $0 \le i \le n-2$. It is easy to derive the identity $\iota = ([0, 0, \dots, 0]^T, 0)$. The proof is complete by selecting $\Omega = \{([0, 0, \dots, 0]^T, 1),$ $([0, 0, \dots, 0]^T, k-1), ([1, 0, \dots, 0]^T, 0), ([k-1, 0, \dots, 0]^T, 0)\}$. The generator set Ω is closed under inverse, making all links bidirectional. Hence, the operator $*$ connects $([a_0, \dots, a_{n-2}]^T, a_{n-1})$ to $([a_0, \dots, a_{n-2}]^T, a_{n-1} \pm 1)$ and $([a_0, \dots, a_i \pm 1, \dots, a_{n-2}]^T, a_{n-1})$ if $a_{n-1} \bmod (n-1) = i$. This is exactly the definition for the incomplete k-ary n-cube given in Section 2. □

For the incomplete k-ary n-cube, a stronger conclusion may be drawn, in addition to the node transitivity inherent from the Cayley graphs. Observe that each link is in a cycle of length k. A mapping of the link to any other link is also in a cycle of length k, implying that the incomplete k-ary n-cube is also edge-transitive. One important consequence of edge transitivity is that the connectivity (or the number of parallel paths between any two nodes) is the largest possible, i.e., equal to the node degree [6]. Such parallel paths provide a means of selecting alternate routes, and thus, increase the fault tolerance capability.

5. Conclusion

We have applied a pruning scheme to the k-ary n-cube to reduce its node degree from $2n$ to 4. We showed that by removing links from the k-ary n-cube in a periodic fashion, many of its desirable properties can be preserved. The pruned network remains in the class of Cayley graphs, with diameter close to that of the original network.

In a way, this indicates that the k-ary n-cube itself is quite resilient since it allows the removal of a large number of its links while maintaining these properties. A complementary conclusion is that such a highly connected topology is not necessary to obtain these properties. Given the same node complexity and capacity, we can use a smaller node degree and expand the channel width to achieve lower communication latency.

Our pruning scheme can be easily extended to higher-degree incomplete k-ary n-cubes. For instance, to prune to node degree of six (rather than four), we can maintain two common dimensions and periodically assign one of the remaining $n-2$ dimensions to nodes. Although such a scheme in general does not significantly improve the network diameter, and only slightly increases the bisection width, it does facilitate the embedding of 2D and 3D meshes into the resulting networks.

References

[1] S. B. Akers and B. Krishnamurthy, "A Group-Theoretic Model for Symmetric Interconnection Networks," *IEEE Trans. Computers*, vol. 38, pp. 555–566, Apr. 1989.

[2] R. Alverson, D. Callahan, D. Cummings, B. Koblenz, A. Porterfield, and B. Smith, "The Tera Computer System," *Proc. Int'l Conf. Supercomputing*, Amsterdam, Netherlands, June 1990. pp. 1–6.

[3] B. Bose, B. Broeg, Y. Kwon, and Y. Ashir, "Lee Distance and Topological Properties of k-ary n-cubes," *IEEE Trans. Computers*, vol. 44, pp. 1021–1030, Aug. 1995.

[4] G. E. Carlson, J. Cruthirds, H. Secton and C. Wright, "Interconnection Networks Based on Generalization of Cube-Connected Cycles," *IEEE Trans. Computers*, vol. C-34, pp. 769–772, Aug. 1985.

[5] D.-M. Kwai and B. Parhami, "A Generalization of Hypercubic Networks Based on Their Chordal Ring Structures," *Parallel Processing Letters*, vol. 6, pp. 469–477, 1996.

[6] S. Lakshmivarahan, J.-S. Jwo, and S. K. Dhall, "Symmetry in Interconnection Networks Based on Cayley Graphs of Permutation Group: A Survey," *Parallel Computing*, vol. 19, pp. 361–401, 1993.

[7] D. S. Meliksetian and C. Y. R. Chen, "Optimal Routing Algorithm and the Diameter of the Cube-Connected Cycles," *IEEE Trans. Parallel and Distributed Systems*, vol. 4, pp. 1172–1178, Oct. 1993.

[8] J. Nguyen, J. Pezaris, G. Pratt, and S. Ward, "Three-Dimensional Network Topologies," *Proc. Int'l Workshop Parallel Computer Routing and Communication*, Seattle, WA, May 1994, pp. 101–115.

[9] B. Parhami, "Periodically Regular Chordal Ring Networks for Massively Parallel Architectures," *Proc. Symp. Frontiers of Massively Parallel Computation*, McLean, VA, Feb. 1995, pp. 315–322.

[10] F. P. Preparata and J. Vuillemin, "The Cube-Connected Cycles: A Versatile Network for Parallel Computation," *Communications of the ACM*, vol. 24, pp. 300–309, May 1981.

[11] A. Youssef, "Design and Analysis of Product Networks," *Proc. Symp. Frontiers of Massively Parallel Computation*, McLean, VA, Feb. 1995, pp. 521–528.

Embedding of Binomial Trees in Hypercubes with Link Faults

Jie Wu, Eduardo B. Fernandez, and Yingqiu Luo
Department of Computer Science and Engineering
Florida Atlantic University
Boca Raton, FL 33431

Abstract

We study the embedding of binomial trees with variable roots in n-dimensional hypercubes (n-cubes) with faulty links. A simple embedding algorithm is first proposed that can embed an n-level binomial tree in an n-cube with up to $n-1$ faulty links in $\log(n-1)$ steps. We then extend the result to show that spanning binomial trees exist in a connected n-cube with up to $\lceil \frac{3(n-1)}{2} \rceil - 1$ faulty links. Our results reveal the fault tolerance property of hypercubes and they can be used to predict the performance of broadcasting and reduction operations, where the binomial tree structure is commonly used.

1 Introduction

The *binomial tree* [5] is one of the most frequently used spanning tree structures for parallel applications in various systems, especially in hypercube systems. Lo et al. [4] have identified the binomial tree as an ideal computation structure for parallel divide-and-conquer algorithms. Hsu [3] showed the use of the binomial tree in prefix computation. The binomial tree structure also has been widely used in performing data accumulation (also called reduction) and data broadcasting.

As the number of processors in a computer system increases, the probability of processor failure also increases. In a spanning binomial tree of a hypercube, if any link used to connect two nodes becomes faulty, the tree will be disconnected. This might jeopardize applications that use this tree. The challenge is to identify a spanning binomial tree that connects all the nodes in the system using only healthy links.

The above problem resembles an embedding problem that deals with mapping a host graph (the binomial tree) into a target graph (the hypercube). There are two types of embedding problems [2]: *specified root embedding* and *variable root embedding*. In the specified root embedding problem the root of the binomial tree must be mapped to a specified node in the hypercube, while in the variable root embedding problem the root of the binomial tree can be mapped to any node in the hypercube.

Algorithms for embedding binary trees into healthy hypercubes have been developed by Wu [6] and Bhatt and Ipson [1]. Clearly, algorithms for embedding binomial trees into a specified root of hypercubes with faulty links might not exist even when there is only one faulty link. This is because any faulty links that are adjacent to the root node will destroy all the possible binomial trees originated from that root node. Among variable root embedding algorithms, Chan [2] studied embedding binary trees into hypercubes with faulty nodes, but relatively little work has been done on embedding of binomial trees in faulty hypercubes. Wu [7] proposed an embedding of incomplete spanning binomial trees into hypercubes with faulty nodes.

In this paper, we focus on finding spanning binomial trees in faulty hypercubes with faulty links only. First, a simple embedding algorithm is given that can tolerate $n-1$ faulty links in an n-cube. We then determine a lower bound on the degree of fault tolerance in hypercubes with faulty links. The bound is $\lceil \frac{3(n-1)}{2} \rceil - 1$ in a connected n-cube. We also provide a embedding scheme based on two simple construction schemes, *extending scheme* and *connecting scheme* (proposed in this paper), to identify spanning binomial trees in the given n-cube. Due to the space limitation, all the proofs of the theorems are omitted, they can be found in [8].

2 Preliminaries

The n-dimensional hypercube (n-cube), Q_n, is a graph having 2^n nodes labeled from 0 to $2^n - 1$. Two nodes are joined by an edge if their addresses, as binary integers, differ in exactly one bit. More specifically, every node a has a bit sequence $a_n a_{n-1} \cdots a_d \cdots a_1$ and a_d is called the d-th bit (also called the d-th dimension) of the address. Let node

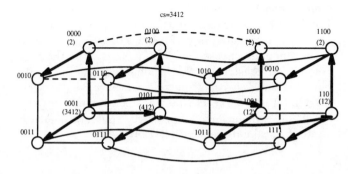

Figure 1: A Q_4 with three faulty links

a^d be the neighbor of node a along dimension d. Every m-dimensional subcube Q_m (m-subcube, or simply m-cube) has a unique address $q_n q_{n-1} \cdots q_d \cdots q_1$ with $q_d \in \{0,1,*\}$, where exactly m bits take the value $*$, a don't-care symbol representing either 0 or 1. For example, $10**$ denotes a 2-cube with four nodes: $1000, 1001, 1011, 1010$. Sequence $a_n a_{n-1} \cdots a_{d+1} - a_{d-1} \cdots a_1$ represents a dimension d link connecting two nodes that differ in the d-th bit. Figure 1 shows a Q_4 with three faulty links -000, $0-10$, and $111-$.

A partition of Q_n along the d-th dimension generates two $(n-1)$-cubes, denoted by $Q_{n-1}^{(d)}$ and $Q_{n-1}^{'(d)}$. In our later discussion, we will omit d in both cubes if it does not cause confusion.

The *spanning binomial tree* is a special spanning tree in a hypercube. A 0-level binomial tree (B_0) has one node. An n-level (B_n) is constructed out of two $(n-1)$-level binomial trees by adding one edge between the roots of the two trees and by making either root the new root. A B_n can also be constructed from $B_{n-1}, B_{n-2}, ..., B_1, B_0$ by using a node s (the root node) to connect the root nodes of these trees. To embed a spanning binomial tree in an n-cube, each B_i should be a spanning binomial tree of an i-cube. More specifically, $B_{n-1}, B_{n-2}, ..., B_1, B_0$ are spanning binomial trees in subcubes $Q_{n-1}', Q_{n-2}', ..., Q_1', Q_0'$, respectively, where these subcubes constitute a partition of Q_n (excluding the root node s). The above partition can be generated using the following procedure: Q_n is split into two $(n-1)$-cubes, $Q_{n-1}(s \in Q_{n-1})$ and $Q_{n-1}'(s \notin Q_{n-1}')$, along the d_1-th dimension. Q_{n-1} is further divided into two $(n-2)$-cubes along the d_2-th dimension. This process continues until Q_1 is divided into two 0-cubes, Q_0' and $Q_0 = s$, along the d_n-th dimension. The dimension sequence $d_1 d_2 ... d_n$ that determines the partition is called the *splitting sequence* (ss) associated with the node s performing the partition. The above process is also called a *splitting*

process. The set $\{Q_{n-1}', Q_{n-2}', ..., Q_0', Q_0 = s\}$ is a partition of Q_n. The splitting sequence is also called *coordinate sequence* (cs) which determines a spanning binomial tree. Each node in the cube has its own coordinate sequence (which can be the same cs). The coordinate sequence at a node with respect to a specific root node is a subsequence of the associated cs and this subsequence includes only the dimensions of the largest subcube Q_{n-i}' in which the node is a root node of the spanning binomial tree of Q_{n-i}'. Basically, the coordinate sequence decides how the subcube should be partitioned. In Figure 1, each node has the same $cs = 3412$, the coordinate sequence of each node with respect to the root node 0001 is listed under the node address.

There are two basic constructing schemes for a binomial tree. The *extending scheme* is normally used if there is a fault-free dimension, otherwise the *connecting scheme* is applied.

- **Extending Scheme**: If Q_n can be divided into two $(n-1)$-cubes Q_{n-1} and Q_{n-1}' along a fault-free dimension d, we can construct an $(n-1)$-level binomial tree B_{n-1} in one of these two subcubes, say Q_{n-1}. By extending along dimension d, we can construct an n-level binomial tree B_n from B_{n-1}. The root node remains unchanged and all the leaf nodes in B_{n-1} are connected to the corresponding nodes in Q_{n-1}'. That is, each connection is a link along dimension d.

- **Connecting Scheme**: Suppose Q_n is divided into two $(n-1)$-cubes Q_{n-1} and Q_{n-1}'. with two $(n-1)$-level binomial trees B_{n-1} and B_{n-1}' in Q_{n-1} and Q_{n-1}', respectively, and their roots are connected by a healthy link in dimension d (this dimension may or may not be fault-free). We can construct an n-level binomial tree B_n by randomly choosing one of two roots as the new root of B_n and connecting roots of B_{n-1} and B_{n-1}' by that healthy link in dimension d.

Note that in the extending scheme, cs is the reverse of the splitting sequence, while the splitting sequence derived by recursively applying the connecting scheme is cs. Figure 1 shows a spanning binomial tree with root node 0001. This spanning tree can be interpreted in different ways: (1) It is constructed using the extending scheme by expanding a spanning binomial tree in $**0*$ (with root 0001) to include $**1*$. (2) The tree is generated by combining two spanning binomial trees in $*0**$ (with root 0001) and $*1**$ (with root 0101) through the connecting scheme, i.e., by connecting roots 0001 and 0101 with 0001 being the new root.

3 Embedding in n-cubes with up to $n-1$ Faulty Links

In an n-cube only $2^n - 1$ out of $n \cdot 2^{n-1}$ links are used for embedding an n-level binomial tree. This provides many ways of selecting a spanning binomial tree in n-cubes even in the presence of faulty links.

Theorem 1: *An n-level binomial tree can be embedded using at most $\log(n-1)$ subcube splits in an n-cube Q_n in the presence of up to $n-1$ faulty links.*

The extending scheme can be used to construct a spanning binomial tree in an n-cube with up to $n-1$ faults. The coordinate sequence of a potential root node a will be a randomly-selected splitting sequence of one of the fault-free subcubes that contains node a concatenating the reverse of a splitting sequence, where the splitting sequence defines the order of dimensions along which the n-cube is split into small cubes until the subcube that contains node a is fault-free.

procedure BT(f_k, Q_k, rss) return (a root and its cs)
/* f_k is the set of faulty links in Q_k */
/* rss is the reverse of a ss before reaching Q_k */
if Q_k is fault-free **then**
  { randomly choose a node in Q_k as the root;
    select ss as a permutation of dimensions in Q_k;
    $cs := ss \parallel rss$ /* cs at the root node */   }
else
  { $Q_k = Q_{k-1} + Q'_{k-1}$ along a fault-free dimension d;
    $f_k = f_{k-1} + f'_{k-1}$, where $f_{k-1} \in Q_{k-1}$, $f'_{k-1} \in Q'_{k-1}$;
    $rss = d \parallel rss$; /* insert d to the front of rss */
    if $|f_{k-1}| \le |f'_{k-1}|$
    then $\mathbf{BT}(f_{k-1}, Q_{k-1}, rss)$
    else $\mathbf{BT}(f'_{k-1}, Q'_{k-1}, rss)$ }

The root and its cs for a binomial tree can be located by a call $\mathrm{BT}(f, Q_n, \phi)$, where f is the fault set in the target cube Q_n and ϕ is the empty set. Note that BT generates only one root node and a global cs (in the sense that each node in the cube has the same cs). The BT algorithm can be easily extended to a general one, where each node in a fault-free Q_k can be a root node and selects different splitting sequences of dimensions in Q_k, and then the reverse splitting sequence is attached to obtain different cs's for different root nodes. The time complexity of BT is $\Theta(n)$

We use the example in Figure 1 to explain how the BT algorithm works. As dimension 2 is fault-free, we split Q_4 into $**0*$ and $**1*$, and each node will carry a reverse splitting sequence 2. Because $**0*$ contains fewer faults than $**1*$, the BT algorithm chooses $**0*$ for further splitting. Both dimensions 1 and 3 are fault free in $**0*$ and we assume that

dimension 1 is chosen. Thus $**0*$ is split into $**00$ and $**01$. The reverse splitting sequence of each node in $**0*$ is updated into 12. As $**01$ is fault-free, we can randomly choose a node, say 0001, to be the root node and construct a 2-level binomial tree in $**01$ by randomly choosing splitting sequence 34. We then extend it into a 4-level binomial tree by combining the splitting sequence and the reverse splitting sequence into a coordinate sequence $3412 = 34\|12$.

4 Embedding in Connected n-cubes with up to $\lceil \frac{3(n-1)}{2} \rceil - 1$ Faulty Links

When the number of faulty links is more than n, a spanning binomial tree may not exist if there is an isolated node. Even for a connected n-cube, if a splitting dimension is not carefully selected, the subcubes can be disconnected. Therefore it is rather complex to construct an n-level binomial tree in a connected n-cube when the faulty links are more than n. The following results show that by carefully choosing root nodes and the coordinate sequence at each node, we can still find spanning binomial trees in n-cubes in the presence of up to $\lceil \frac{3(n-1)}{2} \rceil - 1$ faulty links.

Theorem 2: *Given $n \ge 4$ and $\delta = |f| - n \ge 0$, there exist at least $2^{n-\delta} - 2^{\delta+1} - 2^\delta$ nodes that can be chosen as the root of an n-level binomial tree in a connected n-cube Q_n with $|f|$ link faults, where $n \le |f| < \lceil \frac{3(n-1)}{2} \rceil$.*

Theorem 3: *Given $n \ge 4$, there exist n-level binomial trees in a connected n-cube Q_n in the presence of up to $\lceil \frac{3(n-1)}{2} \rceil - 1$ faulty links.*

In order to obtain the correct coordinate sequence for each node (instead of one global cs as in BT), we consider separately the splittings along fault-free dimensions and the ones along faulty dimensions. In BT1 we use ss_h to record the splitting on fault-free dimensions and ss_f to record the splitting on faulty dimensions. In ss_h, a new splitting dimension is inserted as the first element of the sequence, while in ss_f it is appended as the last element of the sequence. The final splitting sequence cs is obtained by concatenating ss_f and ss_h, i.e., $cs = ss_f \| ss_h$.

procedure BT1$(f_k, Q_k, ss_f\text{'s and } ss_h\text{'s in } Q_k)$
return$(root_{Q_k})$
/* f is the set of faulty links in Q_k */
/* ss_h's and ss_f's are ss's before partitioning Q_k */
if $|f_k| < \frac{3(k-1)}{2}$ **then**
{ **if** there exist fault-free dimensions **then**
  { $Q_k = Q_{k-1} + Q'_{k-1}$ along fault-free dimension d;
    $f_k = f_{k-1} + f'_{k-1}$, where $f_{k-1} \in Q_{k-1}$, $f'_{k-1} \in Q'_{k-1}$;

$ss_h = d \| ss_h$ }
else
{ $Q_k = Q_{k-1} + Q'_{k-1}$ along a dimension d' such
that each subcube has at least one link fault
or dimension d' has at least two link faults ;
assume $f_{k-1} \in Q_{k-1}$ and $f'_{k-1} \in Q'_{k-1}$;
$ss_f = ss_f \| d'$ /* ss_f is for each node except for
the ones with an adjacent faulty link along d' */ }
if Q_{k-1} is fault-free then
{ $root_{Q_k}$ = all the nodes in Q_{k-1};
ss_h= a splitting sequence of $Q_{k-1} \| ss_h$
/* nodes in Q_k may have different ss_h's
using different splitting sequences */ }
else
$root_{Q_{k-1}}$ =**BT1**$(f_{k-1}, Q_{k-1}, ss_f$'s and ss_h's in $Q_{k-1})$;
if Q'_{k-1} is fault-free then
{ $root_{Q_k}$ = all the nodes in Q'_{k-1};
ss_h= a splitting sequence of $Q'_{k-1} \| ss_h$}
else
$root_{Q'_{k-1}}$ =**BT1**$(f'_{k-1}, Q'_{k-1}, ss_f$'s and ss_h's in $Q'_{k-1})$;
if there exist fault-free dimensions then
$root_{Q_k} = root_{Q_{k-1}} \cup root_{Q'_{k-1}}$
else
$root_{Q_k} = \{ a,b | (a,b)$ is a healthy link, where
$a \in root_{Q_{k-1}}$ and $b \in root_{Q'_{k-1}} \}$ }
else $root_{Q_k} = \phi$

The coordinate sequence cs of each root node is included in the return messages $root_{Q_k}$ through a call
BT1$(f, Q_n, ss_f$'s $= \phi$ and ss_f's $= \phi)$. For fault-free
dimensions, we use the extending scheme to calculate
ss_h and root nodes. For faulty dimensions, we use the
connecting scheme to calculate ss_f and root nodes.
The time complexity of BT1 is $\Theta(n^3)$. Once a specific node is chosen as the root of the binomial tree,
we need to calculate coordinate sequences for all the
nodes with respect to this root node. The following
procedure CS (coordinate sequence calculation) produces a coordinate sequence of each node which is a
subsequence of the associated cs. At each node, it
basically deletes some dimensions from the associated
cs which have already been used during the splitting
process.

Procedure CS(r_k, Q_k) /* r_k is the root of Q_k */
if $k \geq 1$ then
{ choose the first element d of cs associated with r_k,
which has not been chosen; delete d from all cs's
in Q_k, except the one associated with r_k;
split Q_k into Q_{k-1} and Q'_{k-1} along dimension d;
CS(r_k, Q_{k-1});
CS(r_k^d, Q'_{k-1}) }

5 Conclusion

We have determined a lower bound on the number
of link faults that can be tolerated to ensure the existence of spanning binomial trees in a connected hyper-
cube. Our bound is $\lceil \frac{3(n-1)}{2} \rceil - 1$ faults in a connected
n-cube. Note that the actual bound can be higher.
However, with more faults included the probability
of generating a connected hypercube will be reduced,
making the assumption of the bound unrealistically
restrictive. Therefore, a better bound can be only of
theoretically interest. Two embedding schemes have
been proposed based on the number of faulty links in
the given n-cube.

References

[1] S. N. Bhatt and I. C. F. Ipsen. How to embed trees
in hypercubes. Yale University Res. Rep. RR-443,
Dec. 1985.

[2] M. Y. Chan, F. Y. L. Chin, and C. K. Poon. Optimal simulation of full binary trees on faulty hypercubes. Technical Report, Dept. of Computer
Science, University of Hong Kong, 1991.

[3] W. J. Hsu, C. V. Page, and J. S. Liu. Computing prefixes on a large family of interconnection
topologies. *Proc. of the 1992 International Conference on Parallel Processing.* Aug. 1992, III, 153-
159.

[4] V. M. Lo, S. Rajopadhye, S. Gupta, D. Keldsen,
M. A. Mohamed, and J. Telle. Mapping divide-
and-conquer algorithms to parallel architectures.
*Proc. of the 1990 International Conference on Par-
allel Processing.* Aug. 1990, III, 128-135.

[5] H. Sullivan, T. Bashkow, and D. Klappholz. A
large scale, homogeneous, fully distributed parallel
machine. *Proc. of the 4th Annual Symposium on
Computer Architecture.* March 1977, 105-124.

[6] A. Y. Wu. Embedding of tree networks into hypercubes. *Journal of Parallel and Distributed Computing.* 2, (3), August 1993, 238-249.

[7] J. Wu. Tight bounds on the number of l-nodes in
a faulty hypercube. *Parallel Processing Letters.* 5,
(2), 1995, 321-328.

[8] J. Wu, E. B. Fernandez, and Y. Luo. Embedding of
binomial trees in hypercube multiprocessors with
link faults. Tech. Rep. TR-CSE-96-60, Florida Atlantic University, 1996.

An Optimal Multiple Bus Network for Fan-in Algorithms

Hettihe P. Dharmasena

Ramachandran Vaidyanathan*

Department of Electrical & Computer Engineering
Louisiana State University, Baton Rouge, LA 70803-5901
{evdhar,vaidy}@ee.lsu.edu

Abstract

We consider a class of algorithms called Fan-in algorithms, with numerous applications in problems involving semigroup operations. We present a multiple bus network (MBN) that runs any Fan-in algorithm in optimal number of steps. The degree and loading of this MBN are each 3. We prove that the product of the degree and loading of any MBN that runs a Fan-in algorithm in optimal time is at least 9. This establishes the proposed MBN to be optimal.

Keywords: *interconnection networks, multiple bus networks, Fan-in algorithms, parallel algorithms, lower bounds*

1 Introduction

In this paper we consider a class of networks called Multiple Bus Networks (MBNs). An MBN consists of a set of processors that communicate through a set of buses. MBNs have several advantages [4] over point-to-point networks (such as the mesh, hypercube, etc.). They also capture features of other models such as the *Passive Optical Star* (*POS*) [2]. Buses have also been used in a variety of ways to enhance the mesh topology [4, 5] and in reconfigurable systems [7].

In this paper we propose an MBN suited for running "Fan-in Algorithms" (also called "binary tree algorithms" [6]), with applications in a large number of problems involving semigroup operations. Vaidyanathan and Padmanabhan [9] have proposed an MBN that runs Fan-in algorithms in optimal number of steps. This MBN has a non-constant loading (maximum number of processors that may be connected to a bus), however, which makes it difficult to implement. Although considerable work on semigroup operations has been reported for enhanced meshes (see [5] for additional references), they are for most part restricted by architectural features that only allow polynomial time solutions. Moreover, these architectures use one bus per row or column of the mesh; as a result, the loading of these architectures is polynomial in the number of processors. Two notable exceptions [3, 8] are based on hierarchical buses that result in MBNs

with non-constant degree (maximum number of buses a processor may be connected to).

The MBN proposed in this paper runs Fan-in algorithms in optimal (logarithmic) time. Moreover, its degree and loading are each 3, regardless of the problem size. We prove that for any MBN that runs a Fan-in algorithm in optimal time, its loading is at least 3 and that reducing its degree to 2 results in a non-constant loading. This implies that the product of the degree and loading of any MBN that runs a Fan-in algorithm in optimal time is at least 9 and establishes the proposed MBN to be optimal.

As mentioned above, "Fan-in MBNs" have several applications. They can also be used to replace the "row and column buses" of enhanced meshes to obtain a bus-based counterpart of the mesh-of-trees [4, 6] that can be used as a general purpose computing platform.

In the next section we present some preliminary ideas. In Section 3, we describe the proposed MBN and prove it optimal in Section 4. Finally in Section 5 we summarize our results and make some concluding remarks.

2 Preliminaries

A $P \times B$ *Multiple Bus Network* (*MBN*) has P processors and B buses. Each processor is connected to a subset of the set of buses. The processors are assumed to work synchronously (SIMD model). Two processors may communicate in one unit of time, provided they are connected to a common bus. However, only one pair of processors may use a bus at any given point in time.

The maximum number of buses to which a processor may be connected is called the *degree* of the MBN. The maximum number of processors connected to any given bus is called the *loading* of the MBN. The degree and loading are important parameters that determine the cost and implementability of the MBN. The degree of an MBN is indicative of the number of input/output ports needed per processor. A large loading can introduce a significant delay or attenuation of the signal traversing a bus. Figure 1 shows a 16×8 MBN whose degree and loading are each 3.

For any associative binary operation $\circ$, a *Fan-in algorithm*, *Fan-in(n)*, accepts 2^n inputs $i_0, i_1, \cdots, i_{2^n-1}$ (for some integer $n \geq 1$) at the leaves of a complete binary tree (called the *Fan-in tree* and denoted by $\mathcal{F}(n)$)

*Supported in part by the National Science Foundation under Grant No. CCR-9503882 and the Louisiana Board of Regents through the Louisiana Education Quality Support Fund under contract number LEQSF(1994-96)-RD-A-07.

and produces one output, $i_0 \circ i_1 \circ \cdots \circ i_{2^n-1}$, at the root of $\mathcal{F}(n)$. The algorithm proceeds level by level from the leaves to the root, applying the operation $\circ$ at each internal node to the partial results at its children. Figure 2 shows $\mathcal{F}(4)$.

To run $Fan\text{-}in(n)$ on a network with 2^n processors, each node of $\mathcal{F}(n)$ is mapped to a processor of the network. In Figure 2, the numbers within circles denote processors.

To run $Fan\text{-}in(n)$ on a $2^n \times B$ MBN, each node of $\mathcal{F}(n)$ is mapped to a processor and each *non-trivial edge* (whose end points are mapped to distinct processors) of $\mathcal{F}(n)$ is mapped to a bus of the MBN. In fact, $\mathcal{F}(n)$ (with nodes and non-trivial edges appropriately labeled) completely specifies a $2^n \times B$ MBN and the method used to run $Fan\text{-}in(n)$ on it. Figure 2 shows $\mathcal{F}(4)$ corresponding to the MBN in Figure 1.

In running a Fan-in algorithm on an MBN, we assume that in one "step" a processor can read from or write on each bus it is connected to and perform an internal operation using operands from its local memory or input ports. The following restrictions apply, however: (i) Each value sent or received by a processor uses a different bus, and (ii) the pair of processors sending and receiving a value must be connected to a common bus.

In this paper, we will only consider the problem of running $Fan\text{-}in(n)$ on a $2^n \times 2^{n-1}$ MBN; it can be shown that there is no loss of generality in this assumption.

3 The Proposed MBN

In this section we propose a $2^n \times 2^{n-1}$ MBN, $M(n)$, that runs $Fan\text{-}in(n)$ optimally in n steps, for any integer $n \geq 1$. The degree and loading of $M(n)$ are each 3. For $n = 1$, each of the two processors of $M(1)$ is connected to the only bus; clearly this is the only possibility and is therefore optimal. For the remaining discussion, we assume that $n \geq 2$.

Let the processors and buses of $M(n)$ be indexed $0, 1, \cdots, 2^n - 1$ and $0, 1, \cdots, 2^{n-1} - 1$, respectively. Figure 1 shows $M(4)$. It is straightforward to generalize this structure for any $n > 1$. It is easy to see that for $0 \leq i < 2^{n-1}$, processor $2i$ is connected only to bus i, and processor $2i + 1$ is connected only to buses i, $2i$ and $2i + 1$ (if they exist). Similarly for $0 \leq i < 2^{n-1}$, bus i is connected only to processors $2i$, $2i + 1$ and $\left(2 \left\lfloor \frac{i}{2} \right\rfloor + 1\right)$. Thus the degree and loading of $M(n)$ are each 3.

Figure 2, with nodes and non-trivial edges labeled with processor and bus indices, respectively, shows how $M(4)$ runs $Fan\text{-}in(4)$. In running $Fan\text{-}in(n)$ on $M(n)$, each processor initially holds an input. In the first step processor $2i + 1$ receives an input from processor $2i$ (via bus i) and performs the operation $\circ$. In step s (where $2 \leq s \leq n$), processor $2i + 1$ (where $0 \leq i < 2^{n-s}$) sends a partial result to processor $\left(2 \left\lfloor \frac{i}{2} \right\rfloor + 1\right)$, receives partial results from processors $4i + 1$ and $4i + 3$, and applies the operation $\circ$ on the partial results received. At the end of step n, processor 1 hold the result of $Fan\text{-}in(n)$.

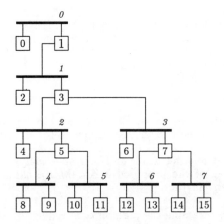

Figure 1: $M(4)$

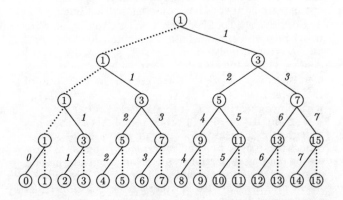

Figure 2: Running $Fan\text{-}in(4)$ on $M(4)$

Theorem 1 *For any $n \geq 1$, the $2^n \times 2^{n-1}$ MBN, $M(n)$, runs $Fan\text{-}in(n)$ optimally in n step. Moreover, the degree and loading of $M(n)$ are each 3.* ∎

4 Optimality of $M(n)$

A $2^n \times 2^{n-1}$ MBN will be said to be *optimal for Fan-in algorithms*, iff it runs $Fan\text{-}in(n)$ optimally in n steps and the product of its degree and loading is the least possible. In this section we first show that for $n > 1$ any MBN running $Fan\text{-}in(n)$ has a degree of at least 2 and a loading of at least 3. Next we prove that if the MBN runs $Fan\text{-}in(n)$ in n steps and if its degree is 2, then its loading is $\Omega(\sqrt{n})$. Therefore for large n, the product of the degree and loading of any MBN that runs $Fan\text{-}in(n)$ in n steps is at least 9. This establishes that the MBN, $M(n)$, is optimal for Fan-in algorithms.

An MBN is said to be *connected* iff there is a path between any pair of processors.

Lemma 2 *For $n > m \geq 1$, any connected $2^n \times 2^m$ MBN has a degree of at least 2 and a loading of at least $2^{n-m} + 1$.*

Proof: If the degree is 1 and if the MBN has connections to each of its $2^m \geq 2$ buses, then the MBN cannot be connected. Since at least one processor is connected to ≥ 2 buses, the number of connections in the MBN is $\geq 2^n + 1$, so the loading is $\geq \lceil \frac{2^n+1}{2^m} \rceil = 2^{n-m} + 1$. $\blacksquare$

Any MBN running a Fan-in algorithm has to be connected. If the Fan-in algorithm is to run in optimal time, then $m = n - 1$ and the lower bounds on the degree and loading are 2 and 3, respectively. Thus, the loading of the proposed MBN, $M(n)$, cannot be reduced any further.

We now examine the possibility of reducing the degree of the MBN to 2. The MBN proposed in [9] runs Fan-in algorithms in optimal time and has a degree of 2; its loading is non-constant, however. We now prove that a degree 2 MBN that runs Fan-in algorithms in optimal time, always has non-constant loading.

Consider a $2^n \times 2^{n-1}$ MBN, $X(n)$, that runs $Fan\text{-}in(n)$ in n steps and whose degree and loading are 2 and L, respectively. For any $1 \leq s \leq n$, let $X_s(n)$ denote a $2^n \times 2^{n-1}$ MBN, that includes only those connections of $X(n)$ that are used in at least one of the steps $1, 2, \cdots, s$. Let $X_0(n)$ be a $2^n \times 2^{n-1}$ MBN with no connections. Clearly, $X_n(n) = X(n)$.

For any $0 \leq s \leq n$, a processor of $X_s(n)$ that has a degree of 2 is said to be a *full processor of step s*; otherwise, it is a *non-full processor of step s*. A processor holding a partial result or an input at the end of step s (or at the beginning of step $s + 1$), is called a *result processor of step s*; otherwise, it is a *non-result processor of step s*.

Clearly, all 2^n processors are non-full, result processors of step 0; i.e., at the start of the algorithm.

Lemma 3 *For any $1 < s \leq n$, if p is a non-full, result processor of step s, then p is a non-full, result processor of steps $1, 2, \cdots, s$.*

Proof: If p holds a result at the end of step s, but not at the end of step $s - 1$, then it must have obtained two partial results during step s. This requires p to have two connections and be a full processor of step s. $\blacksquare$

Corollary 4 *For any $L \leq s \leq n$, each result processor of step s is a full processor of step s.*

Proof: Let p be a non-full, result processor of steps s; i.e., of steps $1, 2, \cdots, s$, by Lemma 3. It is sufficient to now prove that $s < L$. Let p receive a partial result for step t (where $1 \leq t \leq s$) from processor p_t, via the only bus b (say) that p is connected to. Therefore, bus b is connected to processors in the set $\{p\} \bigcup \{p_t : 1 \leq t \leq s\}$.

Consider processor p_t that sends a partial result to p during step t. If p_t is a result processor of step t, then it must receive 2 partial results from processors different from p (in addition to sending a partial result to p). This is not possible as one of the (at most 2) buses that p_t is connected to is used by p. Since

this bus (bus b) is used by p during steps $1, 2, \cdots, s$, processor p_t cannot be a result processor of steps $t, t + 1, \cdots, s$. Therefore, $p_t \notin \{p_x : t < x \leq s\}$ and so $\{p\} \bigcup \{p_t : 1 \leq t \leq s\}$ has $s + 1$ processors, all of which are connected to bus b. Since the loading of $X(n)$ is L, $s + 1 \leq L$, or $s < L$. $\blacksquare$

Let $\langle p, b \rangle$ denote a connection between processor p and bus b. In our analysis, we will consider only those connections $\langle p, b \rangle$ for which p is a full processor, that participates in some step $s \geq L$. Since a lower bound on the loading is sought, some connections can be ignored.

To account for the connections considered, we now associate each connection with a processor. For each processor p and step $s \geq L$, define a set $\Gamma_s(p)$ of connections. Each connection in $\Gamma_s(p)$ is said to be *owned by processor p in step s*. (We will show later that if $p_1 \neq p_2$, then $\Gamma_s(p_1)$ and $\Gamma_s(p_2)$ are disjoint.) We now define $\Gamma_s(p)$.

1. If p is a result processor of step L, then it is also a full processor of step L (by Corollary 4). Let p be connected to buses b_1 and b_2. For each such p, define $\Gamma_L(p) = \{\langle p, b_1 \rangle, \langle p, b_2 \rangle\}$. If p is not a result processor of step L, then define $\Gamma_L(p)$ to be empty.

2. For $s > L$, let p be a result processor of step s that receives partial result(s) from (not necessarily distinct) processor(s) p' and p'' via bus(es) b' and b'', respectively. Define $\Gamma_s(p)$, $\Gamma_s(p')$ and $\Gamma_s(p'')$ as follows.

$$\begin{aligned} \Gamma_s(p) &= \Gamma_{s-1}(p) \bigcup \{\langle p_1, b' \rangle, \langle p_2, b'' \rangle\} \\ \Gamma_s(p') &= \Gamma_{s-1}(p') - \{\langle p_1, b' \rangle\} \\ \Gamma_s(p'') &= \Gamma_{s-1}(p'') - \{\langle p_2, b'' \rangle\} \end{aligned}$$

where $\langle p_1, b' \rangle \in \Gamma_{s-1}(p')$ and $\langle p_2, b'' \rangle \in \Gamma_{s-1}(p'')$; since we are interested primarily in the cardinality, $|\Gamma_s(p)|$, of $\Gamma_s(p)$, $\langle p_1, b' \rangle$ (resp., $\langle p_2, b'' \rangle$) can be any element of $\Gamma_{s-1}(p')$ (resp., $\Gamma_{s-1}(p'')$). We note that if p receives only one value in step s, then $p' = p''$, $b' = b''$ and $p_1 = p_2$.

In summary, for each partial result received by processor p from processor p', via bus b, processor p' transfers ownership of a connection on bus b to processor p. If processor p does not send or receive any partial result in step s, then $\Gamma_s(p) = \Gamma_{s-1}(p)$.

Lemma 5 *For any $s \geq L$,*
(i) If $p_1 \neq p_2$, then $\Gamma_s(p_1)$ and $\Gamma_s(p_2)$ are disjoint.
(ii) If $\langle p', b \rangle \in \Gamma_s(p)$, then p is connected to b.
(iii) If p is a result processor of step s, then $\Gamma_s(p)$ has a connection of the form $\langle p', b \rangle$, for each bus b to which p is connected.

Proof: Observe that in part 2 of the definition of $\Gamma_s(p)$, the sets $\Gamma_s(p)$ and $(\Gamma_s(p'), \Gamma_s(p''))$ are disjoint, and the connections added to $\Gamma_s(p)$ are $\langle p_1, b' \rangle$ and $\langle p_2, b'' \rangle$, where b' and b'' are buses to which p is connected. These observations, coupled with the fact that Lemma 5 holds for step L completes the proof. $\blacksquare$

Remarks: If the sets $\Gamma_s(p)$ are used to count the number of connections in $X(n)$, then part (i) of Lemma 5 ensures that no connection is counted more than once. However, some connections may not be counted at all; this does not affect the result as a lower bound on the loading is sought. Part (ii) is used later in Theorem 8. Part (iii) ensures that the transfer of ownership in part 2 of the definition of $\Gamma_s(p)$ is always possible.

Lemma 6 *For any step $s \geq L$, if p is a result processor of α of steps $L, L+1, \cdots, s$, then $|\Gamma_s(p)| \geq \alpha$.*
Proof: Omitted for brevity. ∎

For any step $s \geq L$, a bus b of $X(n)$ is said to be *active in step s* iff it is connected to at least one result processor of step s. If a bus is used to carry a partial result in step s, then it must be active in step s. However, a bus that is active in step s need not be used in step s. In the following lemma, we prove that the pool of buses that could be active at a step shrinks with each step, thereby forcing a few buses to have a large number of connections.

Lemma 7 *For any step $s > L$, bus b is active in step s, then it is also active in step $s-1$.*
Proof: Let b not be active in step $s-1$. Suppose at step s, processor p connected to b becomes a result processor of step s, thereby making b active in step s. If p is a result processor of step $s-1$, then it must be a full processor of step $s-1$ (by Corollary 4) that is connected to b in step $s-1$. This is not possible as b is assumed not to be active in step $s-1$.

Therefore p cannot be a result processor of step $s-1$ and must receive two partial results one of which is via bus b. Let p receive these partial results from processors p' and p'', both of which are full, result processors at step $s-1$. Moreover, one of them must be connected to b in step $s-1$, which again contradicts the assumption that b is not active in step $s-1$. ∎

We are now in a position to prove the main result of this section.

Theorem 8 *For any $n \geq 2$, if a $2^n \times 2^{n-1}$ MBN with degree and loading of 2 and L, respectively, runs Fan-in(n) in n steps, then $n \leq L^2 + 2L - 1$.*
Proof: From Lemma 7, there is bus, b, that is active in steps $L, L+1, \cdots, n$. Let b be connected to $\ell \leq L$ processors, $p_1, p_2, \cdots, p_\ell$, all of which are full processors of step n. For $1 \leq i \leq \ell$, let the two buses to which processor p_i is connected be b and b_i. Also let processor p_i be a result processor α_i times from step L to step n.

From Lemma 5(ii), each element of $\Gamma_n(p_i)$ is a connection to either b or b_i. Since the loading of the MBN is L, $\displaystyle\sum_{i=1}^{\ell} |\Gamma_n(p_i)| \leq \ell + \ell L \leq L^2 + L$. From Lemma 6 we also have $\displaystyle\sum_{i=1}^{\ell} |\Gamma_n(p_i)| \geq \sum_{i=1}^{\ell} \alpha_i$. Since b is an active bus of steps $L, L+1, \cdots, n$, $\displaystyle\sum_{i=1}^{\ell} \alpha_i \geq n - L + 1$.

Thus, $\displaystyle n - L + 1 \leq \sum_{i=1}^{\ell} \alpha_i \leq \sum_{i=1}^{\ell} |\Gamma_n(p_i)| \leq L^2 + L,$ which implies that $n \leq L^2 + 2L - 1$. ∎

Theorem 8 establishes $M(n)$ to be optimal.

5 Concluding Remarks

In this paper we have presented a $2^n \times 2^{n-1}$ MBN, $M(n)$, that runs *Fan-in(n)* optimally in n steps. This MBN has a constant degree and loading of 3 each. We proved that this degree-loading product of 9 for $M(n)$ is the lowest possible for any MBN that runs Fan-in algorithms optimally.

Vaidyanathan and Padmanabhan [9] have proposed an MBN with degree 2 and loading $O(n)$. The problem of bridging the gap between this upper bound and the lower bound of $\Omega(\sqrt{n})$ is open.

References

[1] A. Ali and R. Vaidyanathan, "Exact Bounds on Running ASCEND/DESCEND and FAN-IN Algorithms on Synchronous Multiple Bus Networks," *IEEE Trans. Parallel & Distrib. Sys.*, **7**, 1996, pp. 783–790.

[2] P. Berthomè, Th. Duboux, T. Hagerup, I. Newman, and A. Schuster, "Self-Simulation for the Passive Optical Star Model," *Proc. European Symp. on Algorithms*, 1995, pp. 369–380.

[3] D. A. Carlson, "Solving Linear Recurrence Systems on Mesh Connected Computers with Multiple Global Buses," *J. Parallel & Distrib. Comput.*, **8**, 1990, pp. 89–95.

[4] O. M. Dighe, R. Vaidyanathan and S. Q. Zheng, "The Bus-Connected Ringed Tree: A Versatile Interconnection Network," *J. Parallel & Distrib. Comput.*, **33**, 1996, pp. 189–196.

[5] S. Fujita and M. Yamashitar, "Fast Gossiping on Mesh-Bus Computers," *IEEE Trans. Comput.*, **45**, 1996, pp. 1326–1330.

[6] F. T. Leighton, *Introduction to Parallel Algorithms and Architectures: Arrays · Trees · Hypercubes*, Morgan Kaufmann Publishers, San Mateo, CA, 1992.

[7] K. Nakano, "A Bibliography of Published Papers on Dynamically Reconfigurable Architectures," *Parallel Proc. Letters*, **5**, 1995, pp. 111–124.

[8] C. S. Raghavendra, "HMESH: A VLSI Architecture for Parallel Processing," *Proc. Conf. on Algs. & Hardware for Parallel Proc.*, 1986, pp. 76–83.

[9] R. Vaidyanathan and A. Padmanabhan, "Bus-Based Networks for Fan-in and Uniform Hypercube Algorithms," *Parallel Comput.*, **21**, 1995, pp. 1807–1821.

Session 2B

Parallelism Management

Multiscalar Execution along a Single Flow of Control

Krishna K. Sundararaman
Intel Corporation
1900 Prairie City Road
Folsom
CA 95630, USA
ksundara@pcocd2.intel.com

Manoj Franklin
Dept. of Electrical and Computer Engineering
Clemson University
221 Riggs Hall
Clemson, SC 29634-0915, USA
mfrankl@blessing.ces.clemson.edu

Abstract

The multiscalar processing model extracts instruction level parallelism from ordinary programs by splitting the program into smaller, possibly dependent, tasks, and parallelly executing multiple tasks using multiple execution units. Past work had advocated pursuing multiple flows of control in the multiscalar processor. We first illustrate the problems involved in pursuing multiple flows of control. We then discuss a methodology to obtain good performance from multiple tasks extracted from a single line of control. We also present the results of simulation studies that verify the potential of this method. These results, obtained with a set of SPEC92 benchmarks, show better issue rates when a single line of control is pursued in the multiscalar processor. The primary reason for this improvement is the ability to have better load balancing among the execution units.

1 Introduction

Recent advances in VLSI technology have enabled millions of transistors to be placed in a single chip. Current processors incorporate about 15 million transistors in a chip, and technology projections predict this number to reach about 100 million by A.D. 2000 [7]. One way these resources are being used is for incorporating performance-enhancing hardware features, targeted towards exploiting different kinds of parallelism. A processor of this kind that has good potential for exploiting instruction-level parallelism (ILP) is the *multiscalar processor* [4] [5] [14]. It exploits ILP by parallelly executing multiple blocks of code (called *tasks*) in multiple, decentralized execution units that are connected together using a ring-type network. A major tenet of the multiscalar processing paradigm is its ability to parallelly execute tasks that have control dependences as well as data dependences between them.

The primary goal of this research is to investigate the potential of following a single line of control in the multiscalar processor. Why study single line of control, at a time when multiple flows of control (MFC) is being touted to replace it soon [2] [8] [13]? First, branch prediction accuracies have improved significantly in recent years, thanks to 2-level prediction schemes [15], correlation-based prediction schemes [11], and hybrid prediction schemes [1]. These prediction schemes have prediction accuracies averaging over 95% for non-numeric programs, pushing the average distance between mispredictions to 100+ instructions. Second, the debilitating effect of hard-to-predict (short) branches can be overcome to a large extent by using predicated execution [9]. Third, today it is possible to execute branches out-of-order [10] while pursuing a single flow of control. Lastly, run-time scheduling is a lot easier on the hardware when a single flow of control is pursued. There is a significant amount of complexity involved in supporting multiple flows of control, as evidenced by the descriptions given in [2] [4]. Consequently, it becomes important to evaluate the effectiveness of following a single line of control in the multiscalar processor.

The rest of this paper is organized as follows. Section 2 provides background information on the multiscalar processor. Section 3 provides a fresh look at pursuing speculative execution along multiple flows of control, and details the hurdles involved in implementing multiple flows of control in the multiscalar processor. Section 4 describes a methodology for executing multiple threads from a single flow of control (SFC) in the multiscalar processor. Section 5 presents the performance results of SFC-based multiscalar execution and MFC-based multiscalar execution, obtained through detailed simulation studies. These results show that pursuing a single line of control within tasks provides better performance in the multiscalar processor. Section 6 presents the conclusions.

2 Background

2.1 Multiscalar Processor

The multiscalar processor [4] [5] [14] employs a new execution model for extracting large quantities of ILP from ordinary programs. Figure 1 gives the block diagram of a multiscalar processor. It consists of multiple execution units (EUs) that are connected by a unidirectional ring-type network. This provision, along with hardware head (H) and tail (T) pointers, imposes a sequential order among the units, the head pointer indicating the oldest active EU.

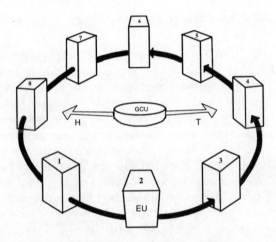

Figure 1: Block Diagram of an 8-Unit
Multiscalar Processor

A program executes on the multiscalar processor as follows. Each cycle, if the tail EU is idle, the global control unit (GCU) predicts the next task in the dynamic instruction stream, and invokes it on the tail EU; a task is a subgraph of the control flow graph (CFG) of the executed program. After invocation, the tail pointer is advanced, and the invocation process continues at the new tail in the next cycle. Thus, the GCU steps through the CFG, distributing tasks (speculatively) to the multiscalar's EUs. The tasks being executed in parallel can have both control dependences and data dependences between them. Each active EU executes the instructions in its task, maintaining the appearance of sequential semantics within the tasks and between the tasks. When the head EU completes its task, the instructions in its task are committed, and the head pointer is advanced, causing that EU to become idle. When a task misprediction is detected, all EUs between the incorrect speculation point and the tail are discarded in what is known as a *squash*. The tail pointer is adjusted to point to the EU at the incorrect speculation point, and the invocation process resumes along the correct path.

The parallel EUs support a single, conventional set of logical registers as well as a conventionally addressed memory system. Register results are dynamically routed among the EUs with the help of a unidirectional ring-like network. Memory references may be executed out of order, speculatively, without knowledge of preceding loads or stores. Memory address hazards are resolved dynamically, many in parallel, with a hardware address resolution mechanism [6].

2.2 Example

Figure 2 ahows a CFG consisting of three basic blocks A, B, and C, with block B *control-dependent* on the conditional branch in A, and block C *control-independent* of the branch. Two multiscalar tasks, T0 and T1, have been formed; the first task contains a diamond-shaped control structure, and the second task is control-independent of the first task. At run-

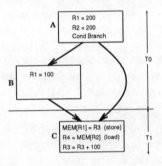

Figure 2: Example Control Flow Graph and Code

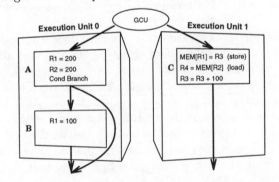

Figure 3: Multiscalar Execution of Example Code

time, the multiscalar processor executes multiple dynamic tasks in the EUs, as shown in Figure 3, effectively establishing a large dynamic window of tasks. Notice that no prediction is done at the "internal" branch point of task T0 in establishing the overall dynamic window of tasks, and this can potentially provide higher prediction accuracies at the task level.

3 Multiple Flows of Control

A typical program encompasses many alternative paths, out of which only one is taken when the program is executed with a specific set of inputs. In the early days, a processor would strictly follow this *single flow of control* (SFC); when a conditional branch is encountered, it would wait until the branch is resolved. With the introduction of speculative execution, the methodology of pursuing an SFC took a slightly different turn. The most likely path was speculated by predicting the outcome of conditional branches, and this path was pursued, with provisions to recover and pursue the correct path when a prediction was found to be incorrect. Today's processors typically do out-of-order execution within the speculated path, without giving any considerations to the control dependences within the path [13]. Notice that it is possible to use multiple sequencers to fetch different portions of the speculated path, once the path is determined by means of a predictor. For instance, once the predictor has predicted the conditional branch in basic block A to be fall-through (i.e., the predictor has decided the path ABC), then three separate sequencers can be used to fetch the instructions belonging to blocks A, B, and C, and it would still amount to speculative execution along an SFC.

When speculating along an SFC, recovery from a misprediction involves squashing all of the subsequent instructions, including those that are not control-dependent on the mispredicted branch (which would be fetched and executed again). For instance, when a misprediction for the branch in block A is detected, block C has to be squashed too, although it has to be fetched and executed again in the alternate path, AC. Recent papers have advocated following *multiple flows of control (MFC)* to avoid this inefficiency [2] [8]. Processors that follow MFC have knowledge about the control dependences within the code that it is currently executing, and use that knowledge to selectively squash only the portion of code that is control dependent on the mispredicted branch.

In the execution depicted in Figure 3, the multiscalar processor is pursuing MFC because it is executing in parallel two control-independent tasks. The first task encompasses two alternate flows of control. Irrespective of which one of these is taken at run-time, the task executed in EU 1 is the same, namely T1. If the conditional branch in task T0 is found to be mispredicted, no squashing is done in EU 1 and subsequent EUs. It is this aspect of multiscalar processor—executing MFC—that we investigate in this paper.

3.1 Parallelism Limits

Previous studies [8] had found that without doing *speculative execution within multiple flows of control*, the amount of parallelism available with multiple flows of control is quite limited. That is, when a control sequencer encounters a conditional branch, it must predict the branch outcome and proceed, instead of waiting for the branch to be resolved[1]. Although the upper limit of theoretically exploitable parallelism was found to be high when both speculation and multiple flows of control were pursued, a major assumption had been used in that study concerning potential data dependences from control-dependent portions of code to control-independent portions of code. We shall illustrate this with our example CFG.

In this CFG, although the store instruction MEM[R1] = R3 in block C is control-independent of the outcome of the branch in block A, the store address is dependent on the branch's outcome. Assume that the branch was incorrectly predicted to be *fall-through*, and that both R1 = 100 and MEM[R1] = R3 were executed before detecting this misprediction. When the misprediction is detected, the store instruction has to be re-executed (because of the change in R1) even though it is control-independent of the mispredicted branch, and the studies in [8] do not include such re-executions. Similarly, if the branch is incorrectly predicted to be *taken*, the store has to be re-executed when this midprediction is detected owing to the store address' data dependence on the R1 = 100 instruction that is newly introduced into the execution path. If the effect of such re-executions is considered, the difference in parallelism limits between speculative execution along an SFC and speculative execution along MFC is likely to shrink.

Furthermore, the studies in [8] had obtained average branch prediction accuracies of about 90% for non-numeric benchmarks. After that study was done in 1992, branch prediction accuracies have improved substantially. Today, a variety of high-accuracy branch prediction schemes, such as 2-level predictors [15], correlation-based predictors [11], and hybrid predictors [1] yield more than 95% branch prediction accuracy for non-numeric programs. Another blow to the imposition of branches was the advent of predicated execution [9], which can be effectively used to eliminate (short) hard-to-predict branches. As branch prediction accuracies increase, the benefits of MFC nat-

---

[1] It is certainly possible to pursue both outcomes of the branch simultaneously; however, that would lead to exponential growth in hardware requirements if many predicted-but-unresolved branches are present in the instruction window.

urally tend to decrease. Finally, the studies in [8] had assumed that SFC-based processors need to execute branches in sequential order. This is overly restrictive, considering that today's SFC-based processors execute branches out-of-order (e.g. MIPS R10000).

3.2 Implementation Hurdles

We saw that speculative execution along MFC offers a performance advantage only when there are mispredictions in which subsequent portions of the hardware window contain code that is both control-independent of the mispredicted branch and data-independent of both the squashed code and the newly introduced code. Next, let us look at some of the implementation issues involved in allowing the hardware to pursue speculative execution along multiple flows of control.

The first implementation hurdle relates to determining data dependence violations at times of recovery from mispredictions. Data dependence violations occurring through memory are naturally more difficult to determine than those occurring through registers. Consider again the example code of Figure 2. Assume that the conditional branch of task T0 was mispredicted to be taken, and that both the store and the load instructions of task T1 have been already executed (to address 200). After recovering from the misprediction, the `R1 = 100` instruction is newly introduced into the instruction window. It is obvious that the store instruction has to be re-executed (because its address changes due to the change in R1's value). What is not so obvious is that the load instruction should also be re-executed because there was a data dependence between the store and the load in the incorrectly speculated path (in which the store address and load address are same), whereas there is no data dependence between them in the new path (in which their addresses are different). Thus, the memory dependence checking hardware has to re-check for memory dependences when a store instruction is re-executed, squashed, or introduced into the middle of the instruction window.

The second hurdle relates to implementing *selective re-execution* of instructions whose data dependences have been violated due to squashing of code or introduction of new code. For example, the store instruction and load instruction in the above example have to be selectively re-executed, whereas the `R3 = R3 + 100` instruction need not be re-executed. The importance of selective re-execution cannot be overemphasized here; if all of the instructions after a mispredicted branch are squashed whenever a data

dependence is violated, then the benefit obtained by pursuing MFC will inevitably be lost.

The third implementation hurdle relates to bringing in additional code into an EU at times of recovery from incorrect speculation. For instance, when recovery is carried out in the previous example code, an additional instruction has to be brought into EU 0. One option to do this is to leave space in the EU for the longer path whenever a control speculation is made; however, that could result in underutilization of the EU's instruction window structure.

3.3 Performance Hurdles

Let us next look at the performance hurdles involved in pursuing MFC. First of all, our recent experiments with state-of-the-art branch predictors show only a factor of 2 improvement in available parallelism for MFC over SFC even when an infinite size instruction window is used. With instruction windows of size less than 100, there is only modest difference in available parallelism. Secondly, the additional available parallelism may not easily translate to performance in multiscalar processors! The main reason for this is the difficulty in providing *load balancing* among the EUs while pursuing MFC. In multiscalar execution, because tasks must be committed in order, cycles may be lost if tasks are not (roughly) of the same size in terms of dynamic instructions. Consider the scenario depicted in Figure 4, where a big task has been assigned to EU 0, and a small task has been assigned to EU 1. Even though EU 1 is able to complete its

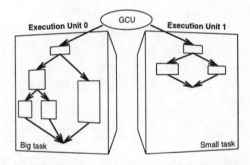

Figure 4: Illustrating Load Balancing's Importance in Multiscalar Processors

small task quickly, it has to wait for the big task in EU 0 to be completed and committed, before committing its task. Lastly, the increased hardware complexity of implementing MFC could lead to increased cycle time. It is difficult to quantify this increase without doing a detailed hardware implementation, which is beyond the scope of this paper.

4 SFC-Based Execution

The existence of the hurdles detailed above prompted us to investigate the potential of pursuing a single line of control in the multiscalar processor. A simple way to do this is to predict the outcome of each conditional branch. However, if predictions are done at the branch level, at the rate of one prediction per clock cycle, then the multiscalar processor cannot advance more than a basic block at a time. Therefore, we use higher-level predictors like the one proposed in [3]. The basic idea is to form tree-like tasks, containing multiple paths, from the dynamic CFG so that a single path can be predicted from the tree, and pursued.

4.1 Tree-Like Tasks

Figure 5 shows the generic structure of a tree-like task of depth 3. Each depth consists of one or more straightline blocks of code. All blocks except the

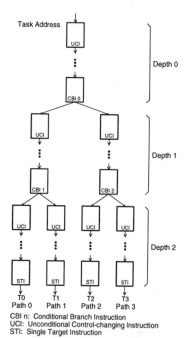

Figure 5: Generic Structure of a Tree-like Task that Encompasses 4 Tree-Paths

last one at each depth are terminated by an unconditional control-changing instruction (UCI), such as a procedure call or an unconditional branch. The last blocks of depths 0 and 1 are terminated by conditional branch instructions (CBI), whereas the last blocks of depth 2 are terminated only by single-target instructions (STI), such as unconditional branches, procedure calls, and non-control-changing instructions. Such a

definition allows up to 4 paths (called *tree-paths*) to be encompassed in a task, and up to 2 conditional branches and any number of single-target control-changing instructions in each tree-path. Thus, a tree-path may have a call to a function, and also a return from the function back to the calling place, thereby inlining the function automatically. The task has 4 targets {T0, T1, T2, T3}, one corresponding to each tree-path. The 4 tree-paths are encoded {0, 1, 2, 3}.

Each tree-path is a snapshot, or portion of the trace, of a possible dynamic instruction sequence. The length of a tree-path is restricted by two factors— by the maximum number of instructions it is allowed to have and by the maximum number of conditional branches it is allowed to have. The former limit is chosen to provide some sort of *load balancing* among the multiple EUs in the multiscalar processor, *i.e.*, to have tree-paths of roughly the same length. The latter limit is chosen so that the task predictor needs to do only an 1-out-of-4 prediction while selecting a tree-path through a task, which can be done with good accuracy [3]. A tree-path is specified by its starting address and a 2-bit number that encodes the outcomes for the 2 conditional branches (if any) encompassed within the tree-path. The tree-paths could be built up as the program executes, or could be generated by a post-compilation phase of the compiler.

With tree-like tasks, multiscalar execution proceeds as follows. The GCU has the address of the next task to be allocated to the tail EU. It makes an 1-out-of-4 prediction to select one of the four tree-paths contained in the task, and conveys the task address and the selected tree-path number to the EU. Once the GCU selects a path through a task, the next task is automatically decided because the start address of the next task is an attribute of the selected tree-path.

An incorrect tree-path prediction will be detected when the appropriate conditional branch in the tree-path is executed. When a misprediction is detected, recovery actions are taken by squashing the tasks in the subsequent EUs. In addition, the tree-path containing the incorrect prediction is also squashed, and the correct tree-path is invoked in the same EU. If no run-time scheduling is done within EUs, then the part of this tree-path before the incorrect branch need not be squashed, because it will be common to the old (incorrect) path as well as the new (correct) tree-path.

4.2 Icache Organization

Next, let us consider the issue of storing tree-like tasks in the first level (L1) local icaches present in each

EU. Although a conventional cache organization, with some added information about the control changes in a task, will suffice for storing the instructions of a task, this may not be the best approach for storing tree-like tasks. We propose to use an alternative organization, similar in spirit to the trace cache proposed in [12]. In this organization, instructions of a tree-path are stored together in the icache in their dynamic trace order, and not in their compiled order. The cost of this approach is potential redundancy among the icache lines due to multiple tree-paths having same instructions.

4.3 Advantages

Perhaps the biggest advantage of pursuing a single flow of control in the multiscalar processor is *hardware simplicity*; none of the implementation complexities listed in section 3.2 are present. A consequence of following SFC-based execution is that run-time reordering of instructions within a task (if deemed necessary) becomes easier to do in hardware. Another advantage of SFC-based execution is the ease of doing *load balancing* among the EUs. In SFC-based execution, because the length of a tree-path is not dependent on run-time behavior, the length is known at tree-path formation time, which makes it easy to form tree-paths that are roughly of the same size.

Another aspect unique to the multiscalar style of execution is that if the "internal" branches in a task are predicted locally by an EU, then the prediction accuracies are likely to be poor, because each EU has only partial history information about each branch. Thus, the speculative path followed within a task by an EU when following MFC is likely to be less accurate than the path followed by an EU that takes its cues from a GCU that makes more accurate tree-path predictions at the global level, using complete history.

5 Experiments and Results

5.1 Experimental Framework

Our simulator uses the MIPS-I instruction set. Benchmark programs are compiled to MIPS-I executables using the MIPS compiler. A task decider program takes the MIPS-I executables, and decides the tasks. The executable and the task information are then fed to a multiscalar simulator. The simulator models all aspects of the multiscalar architecture accurately and in detail and gives the exact time to execute the benchmark program on a real multiscalar processor. The simulator accepts executable images of programs

(along with task information), and simulates their execution; it is not trace driven. The simulator also incorporates a mini-operating system to handle the system calls made by the simulated program. The code executed during the system calls are not taken into account in the performance results. Each of the benchmarks is simulated for 100 million instructions.

For benchmarks, we used a set of programs from the SPEC92 benchmark suite. For measuring performance, we use *useful instruction completion rate (UICR)* as the metric. Notice that nops and squashed instructions are not counted while calculating UICR.

There are many parameters that can be varied while conducting the simulation studies. We fixed the following parameters so that they do not distract us from the tradeoffs under investigation.

- Each tree-path is restricted to 16 instructions.

- The number of execution units is fixed at 8.

- Dynamic scheduling is performed in each EU, and up to 4 instructions per cycle are executed from each active EU.

- Each execution unit has a 4Kwords local icache, with a miss latency of **4 cycles**.

- 100% hit ratio is assumed for the global icache.

- The common, L1 dcache is 64Kbytes, direct-mapped, and has an access latency of **2 cycles**.

5.2 MFC Scheme Simulated

For comparison purposes, we also simulated the traditional multiscalar processor that pursues speculative execution along MFC. In this scheme, the task decider forms tasks by identifying from the CFG subgraphs that are control-independent of each other. However, many a times, such tasks have too much variance in size. In order to reduce this variance, we prune the number of instructions in a task to a particular value (32 in our experiments). When a task is pruned, it will most likely have multiple, control-dependent, target PC values. Because the instructions in a task form a subgraph of the CFG, and may not be from a contiguous portion of the compiled code, there is a plethora of ways the task decider can do the pruning. To give the best treatment to the MFC case, up to 4 possible tasks are formed for each possible task start address. Each of these tasks is restricted to 32 instructions, but may have arbitrary number of conditional branches and flows of control within it.

If the latest task allocated by the GCU to an EU has multiple targets, then the GCU makes a prediction to determine the most likely successor target. Another dynamic predictor within the GCU selects one out of the 4 tasks starting at that target address, and assigns it to the tail EU. Within each EU, further speculation is done to select the most likely path through the task that is currently allocated to it. The branch predictions within each task are carried out by means of a global, 3-bit saturating counter-based predictor. Notice that a pattern-based (2-level) predictor does not work well for intra-task predictions, because the intra-task predictions in the multiscalar processor are not done as per the program's sequential execution order.

Let us explain how the implementation issues mentioned in section 3.2 are addressed in this simulation study. When an intra-task branch prediction is found to be incorrect, local recovery actions are taken, which might involve squashing some instructions and fetching new instructions. Notice, however, that control-independent instructions in the same EU or subsequent EUs are not squashed when a data dependence is found to have been violated. Instead, the affected instructions are re-executed when their correct operands become available. Store instructions that are on a locally speculated path are not executed until all conditional branches before it (in that task) are resolved. This avoids the need to remove an executed store from an incorrect path or the need to re-execute a store, thereby avoiding the associated memory data dependence checking problem. Lastly, the hardware scheduler in each EU is made bigger to accommodate the bigger task sizes that are encountered in MFC-based execution because of the presence of instructions from alternate flows of control.

5.3 Experimental Results

5.3.1 Instruction Completion Rate

Figure 6 presents the UICR obtained for an 8-unit multiscalar processor. Each benchmark has 2 bar charts; the lighter shade corresponds to MFC-based execution, and the darker shade corresponds to SFC-based execution. It can be seen that SFC-based execution using tree-like tasks has performed better than the MFC case, as expected. The main reason for this improvement is better load balancing among the EUs.

5.3.2 Average Task Size

Table 1 presents the average task sizes obtained for MFC-based execution and SFC-based execution. For

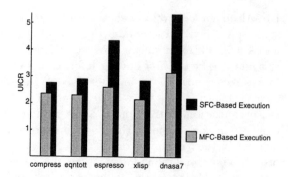

Figure 6: Useful Instruction Issue Rate with 8 EUs

Benchmark	Average Task Size		SFC-Based Execution
	MFC-based Execution		
	Overall Size	Useful Size	
compress	12.68	9.61	10.57
eqntott	26.33	7.94	7.79
espresso	20.16	8.37	9.69
xlisp	14.20	7.44	8.35
dnasa7	26.05	25.07	15.65

Table 1: Overall Task Size and Useful Task Size

MFC-based execution, two sets of task sizes are presented. The overall task size denotes the size of a multiscalar task, whereas the useful task size denotes the average number of instructions that are actually committed from a task. These values are different because multiple flows of control are embedded in a task. For SFC-based execution, the overall task size and the useful task size are the same. We can see from the table that there is a substantial difference between the overall task size and the useful task size for MFC-based execution, necessitating bigger instruction window in the EUs. Quite often, many of these useless instructions are fetched and executed (because of poorer local branch prediction accuracies (c.f. Table 2)), only to be discarded later. Note that it takes additional cycles to fetch and execute the useless instructions.

5.3.3 Average Task Prediction Accuracy

Table 2 presents the prediction accuracies that we obtained. The second and third columns present the task prediction accuracy (TPA) and the local branch prediction accuracy (BPA), respectively, for MFC-based execution. The last column gives the task prediction accuracy for SFC-based execution. From the table, it can be seen that the task prediction accuracies obtained with SFC-based execution are somewhat comparable to those obtained with MFC-based execution. We can also see that the intra-task branch prediction accuracies for MFC-based execution are not very high.

| Benchmark | Prediction Accuracies | | |
| | MFC-based Exec. | | SFC-Based Exec. |
	TPA	BPA	TPA
compress	83.21%	89.63%	84.88%
eqntott	95.64%	94.31%	91.85%
espresso	95.93%	95.06%	93.83%
xlisp	92.49%	90.48%	94.68%
dnasa7	99.06%	98.28%	99.45%

Table 2: Prediction Accuracies

6   Summary and Conclusions

Pursuing multiple flows of control, as we know it today, has benefits only when it is difficult to obtain high branch prediction accuracies and if there are not many data dependences from the control-dependent portions of a mispredicted branch to nearby control-independent portions of code. Implementing speculative execution along multiple flows of control in the hardware raises several implementation complexities. As branch prediction accuracies continue to improve, and get closer to 100%, the benefits accrued by pursuing multiple flows of control begin to fade.

This paper investigated the potential of executing multiple tasks from a single line of control (SFC-based execution) in the multiscalar processor. A simulation study of SFC-based multiscalar execution showed better instruction completion rates. Based on these results, we believe that with the continuing increases in branch prediction accuracies, SFC-based execution is more advantageous for the multiscalar processor.

Acknowledgements

This research was supported by the US National Science Foundation (NSF) under Research Initiation Award grant CCR 9410706.

References

[1] P-Y. Chang, E. Hao, and Y. N. Patt, "Alternative Implementations of Hybrid Branch Predictors," *Proc. 28th International Symposium on Microarchitecture*, 1995.

[2] P. Dubey, K. O'Brien, K. M. O'Brien, and C. Barton, "Single-Program Speculative Multithreading (SPSM) Architecture: Compiler-assisted Fine-Grained Multithreading," *Proc. International Conference on Parallel Architecture and Compilation Techniques (PACT '95)*, 1995.

[3] S. Dutta and M. Franklin, "Control Flow Prediction with Tree-like Subgraphs for Superscalar Processors," *Proc. 28th International Symposium on Microarchitecture*, pp. 258-263, 1995.

[4] M. Franklin, "The Multiscalar Architecture," *Ph.D. Thesis, Technical Report 1196*, Computer Sciences Department, University of Wisconsin-Madison, 1993.

[5] M. Franklin and G. S. Sohi, "The Expandable Split Window Paradigm for Exploiting Fine-Grain Parallelism," *Proc. 19th Annual International Symposium on Computer Architecture*, pp. 58-67, 1992.

[6] M. Franklin and G. S. Sohi, "ARB: A Hardware Mechanism for Dynamic Reordering of Memory Operations," *IEEE Transactions on Computers*, vol. 45, no. 5, pp. 552-571, May 1996.

[7] P. P. Gelsinger, P. A. Gargini, G. H. Parker, and A. Y. C. Yu, "Microprocessors circa 2000," *IEEE Spectrum*, vol. 26, no. 10, pp. 43-47, October 1989.

[8] M. S. Lam and R. P. Wilson, "Limits of Control Flow on Parallelism," *Proc. 19th Annual International Symposium on Computer Architecture*, pp. 46-57, 1992.

[9] S. A. Mahlke, *et al*, "Characterizing the Impact of Predicated Execution on Branch Prediction," *Proc. 27th International Symposium on Microarchitecture*, pp. 217-227, 1994.

[10] MIPS Technologies, Inc. *R10000 Microprocessor User's Manual*, Version 1.1, January 1996.

[11] S-T. Pan, K. So, and J. T. Rahmeh, "Improving the Accuracy of Dynamic Branch Prediction Using Branch Correlation," *Proc. Fifth International Conference on Architectural Support for Programming Languages and Operating Systems (ASPLOS-V)*, pp. 76-84, 1992.

[12] E. Rotenberg, S. Bennett, and J. E. Smith, "Trace Cache: a Low Latency Approach to High Bandwidth Instruction Fetching," *Proc. 29th International Symposium on Microarchitecture (MICRO-29)*, pp. 24-34, 1996.

[13] J. E. Smith and G. S. Sohi, "The Microarchitecture of Superscalar Processors," *Proc. IEEE*, pp. 1609-1624, December 1995.

[14] G. S. Sohi, S. E. Breach, and T. N. Vijaykumar, "Multiscalar Processors," *Proc. 22nd International Symposium on Computer Architecture*, pp. 414-425, 1995.

[15] T-Y. Yeh and Y. N. Patt, "Alternative Implementations of Two-Level Adaptive Branch Prediction," *Proc. 19th Annual International Symposium on Computer Architecture*, pp. 124-134, 1992.

Efficient Processor Allocation Scheme for Multi Dimensional Interconnection Networks

Hyunseung Choo, Hee Yong Youn, Gyung-Leen Park, and Behrooz Shirazi
Department of Computer Science and Engineering
The University of Texas at Arlington
Arlington, TX 76019-0015
choo@cse.uta.edu

Abstract – *The task scheduling policy and the processor allocation scheme affect the system performance significantly. In this paper, we propose an efficient processor allocation scheme for 3D mesh interconnection network with a simple FIFO scheduling policy. Complexity analysis shows that the allocation and deallocation of the scheme are $O(\text{LWH}^2)$ and $O(\text{LH})$, respectively, which are better than earlier schemes. Comprehensive computer simulation shows that the average allocation time of the proposed scheme is improved up to about 25% comparing to the best earlier 3D approach.*

1 Introduction

With advances in VLSI technologies, inter-processor communication networks, and routing algorithms, multicomputers have become practical solutions for large applications. Various architectures have been proposed for connecting the nodes in the multicomputers. Typical examples are hypercube [1,2], two dimensional (2D) mesh [3,4], three dimensional (3D) mesh [5], and 3D torus multicomputer systems [6]. Many processor allocation schemes for hypercube and 2D mesh have been presented [7-9], while there are not many schemes for 3D mesh and torus due to its recent release. Qiao and Ni [10] have proposed an allocation scheme for 3D torus using free list based on best-fit approach. This scheme focused mainly on processor utilization and solved the problem of internal fragmentation of the allocation method in Cray T3D. Youn et al. [11] have presented an allocation scheme using scan search. The scheme is based on first-fit approach and significantly decreases the average allocation time compared to [10].

We propose a processor allocation scheme for 3D mesh based systems. Since earlier studies [7,11] reveal that best-fit approach does not necessarily outperform first-fit one, we employ the first-fit strategy to minimize the allocation time. This scheme is developed especially for the interconnection network of Intel TeraFLOP supercomputer and also can be extended for 3D torus multicomputers [12]. The 9,216 Pentium Pro processors of the system are organized into a $38 \times 32 \times 2$ mesh, where each node contains more than one processor. The allocation

time complexity of the proposed scheme is smaller than the earlier one as shown in section 3.

The rest of the paper is organized as follows. The proposed scheme is presented in section 2. In section 3, the proposed scheme is evaluated and compared with the existing schemes. Finally, we conclude the paper.

2 Proposed Allocation Scheme

A three-dimensional (3D) mesh, $3DM\ (L, W, H)$, is an $L \times W \times H$ cubic grid of LWH nodes. Each node in $3DM$ is represented by a coordinate (x, y, z) $(1 \leq x \leq L,$ $1 \leq y \leq W,\ 1 \leq z \leq H)$, and each edge corresponds to a direct communication link. We assume that the length, width, and height indices increase from left to right, front to rear, and bottom to top beginning from 1.

The *identity* of a submesh $S(l, w, h)$ in $3DM$ with length l, width w, and height h consists of two 3D coordinates $((x, y, z), (x', y', z'))$, where (x, y, z) and (x', y', z') are called the *base* and *end* of S, respectively. The left-front-bottom node of the submesh is the *base* and the right-rear-top node is the *end* of S. The *size* of the submesh S is defined as the number of nodes in the submesh, i.e. $l \times w \times h$. A *busy submesh* is a 3D submesh in which all the nodes are currently allocated to a task and thus busy. A *free submesh* is an available 3D submesh for the allocation.

2.1 Data Structures

We employ novel data structures that are different to the list of busy submeshes of other schemes. The busy submesh list is usually implemented as a linked list. They maintain purely essential information for identifying busy and free submeshes effectively.

Let a busy (free) segment be a neighboring busy (free) nodes in an x-dimensional row of the 3D mesh. In this scheme, we collect busy segments of the front and rear faces of each and every 3D busy submesh. Assume that $B(l, w, h) = ((x, y, z), (x', y', z'))$ represents a busy submesh. The busy segments of the front and rear faces of B for recognizing the 3D busy region are stored in two 2D data structures called $FRONT$ and $REAR$. They are initialized to NILs at the beginning.

114

Rows (y, z), $(y, z + 1)$, ..., (y, z') of the $FRONT$ contain front face busy segments $[x, x']$, and also rows (y', z), $(y', z + 1)$, ..., (y', z') of the $REAR$ have rear face busy segments $[x, x']$. Therefore, $FRONT_{y,z}$, ..., $FRONT_{y,z'}$ and $REAR_{y',z}$, ..., $REAR_{y',z'}$ contain a busy segment $[x, x']$. $FRONT$ and $REAR$ list busy segments of each row. Each of them is called *busy segment list* (BSL). No two busy segments overlap in the BSL because a submesh can be allocated to a single task due to none time-sharing property. Adjacent segments are merged into a longer segment. A busy segment can be splitted due to deallocation.

In figure 1, there are four busy submeshes–$B_1(3, 2, 2)$ $= ((1,1,1), (3,2,2))$, $B_2(1, 2, 2) = ((4,1,1), (4,2,2))$, $B_3(1, 4, 2) = ((1,1,3), (1,4,4))$, and $B_4(2, 4, 2) = ((2,1,3), (3,4,4))$–in $3DM(4, 4, 4)$. After allocating B_1 and B_2, BSLs $FRONT_{1,1}$, $FRONT_{1,2}$, $REAR_{2,1}$, and $REAR_{2,2}$ all have $[1,4]$. In other words, busy segments $[1,3]$ from the B_1 and $[4,4]$ from the B_2 are merged to $[1,4]$. Similarly, after allocating B_3 and B_4, BSLs $FRONT_{1,3}$, $FRONT_{1,4}$, $REAR_{4,3}$, and $REAR_{4,4}$ all have $[1,3]$. All other $FRONT$ and $REAR$ BSLs remain NIL.

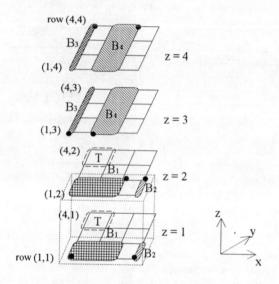

row (4,4)

B_3 B_4

(1,4) $z = 4$

(4,3)

B_3 B_4

(1,3) $z = 3$

(4,2)

T

B_1

(1,2) $z = 2$

B_2

(4,1)

T

B_1

row (1,1) $z = 1$

B_2

Figure 1. B_1, B_2, B_3, B_4, and $T(2, 2, 2)$ in $3DM(4, 4, 4)$.

We operate a 3D window–$3DW(L, t\_wd, t\_ht)$–starting from $(1, 1, 1)$ for a newly scheduled task $T(t\_ln, t\_wd, t\_ht)$. Nodes that are inside the current window are considered each time. If the current window does not have a free submesh of size $t\_ln \times t\_wd \times t\_ht$, it moves to the increasing indices of y-coordinate first, and then to z-coordinate. Another novel data structure–Window information list (WIL)–keeps the information on $FRONT$ BSLs found in $3DW$ and the number of overlapped segments called multiplicity factor. Initially, the multiplicity factor is 0. Hence, WIL is a list of elements whose element–$([a, b], m)$–consists of a segment $[a, b]$ and its multiplicity factor m, i.e. $[a, b]$ is the resulting segment of intersections of m busy segments referred to $FRONT$ in 3DW. INITIALIZE_WIL() initializes WIL to $([1, L], 0)$.

Segments in WIL indicate busy or free consecutive neighboring nodes with their multiplicity factors for those designated rows in $3DW$, while each BSL of $FRONT$ and $REAR$ includes the consecutive busy nodes of the row allocated to task(s)–busy segments only. No representation for free segments is necessary.

WIL_SEARCH(t_ln) finds the first free segment of length at least t_ln of which multiplicity factor is 0 in WIL by linear search. It returns the x-coordinate of the base of the free segment detected. If none of the required size is detected in WIL, -1 is returned. INSERT_TO_WIL($FRONT_{i,j}$) inserts busy segment(s) of the BSL $FRONT_{i,j}$ to WIL by increasing the multiplicity factor(s) of the range of the segment(s). This operation may split and/or merge the existing WIL elements depending on the multiplicity factors and adjacency. DELETE_FROM_WIL($REAR_{i,j}$) deletes busy segment(s) of the BSL $REAR_{i,j}$ from WIL by decreasing the multiplicity factor(s) of the range of segment(s). Splitting and/or merging the existing WIL elements may also occur as in INSERT_TO_WIL(). All those three procedures discussed above are bounded by $O(L)$ in the worst case.

2.2   Window Sliding

Given the busy submesh $B(l, w, h)$ in 3DM, we have h busy segments for the front (rear) face of the busy submesh in $FRONT$ ($REAR$). Assume any layer where B resides, say z. Busy nodes of B in layer z reside between rows y and y', and between columns x and x' of length l. The two busy segments $[x, x']$ of B in layer z are prepared one in $FRONT_{y,z}$ to notify WIL the lower limit of the submesh in the layer and the other in $REAR_{y',z}$ for the upper limit in terms of y-coordinate. WIL collects all busy segments for the lower limits of busy submeshes from $FRONT$ BSLs of designated rows in 3DW.

WIL collects $t\_wd \times t\_ht$ $FRONT$ BSLs of the 3DW for the task $T(t\_ln, t\_wd, t\_ht)$ by the INSERT_TO_WIL(). WIL_SEARCH(t_ln) is executed to detect a free segment of size at least t_ln in WIL for the allocation of T. If positive, we allocate it to T. Otherwise, we slide 3DW one unit along the increasing indices of y-coordinate by deleting BSLs $REAR_{1,1}$, $REAR_{1,2}$, ..., $REAR_{1,t\_ht}$ of current window from WIL and inserting BSLs $FRONT_{t\_wd+1,1}$, $FRONT_{t\_wd+1,2}$, ..., $FRONT_{t\_wd+1,t\_ht}$ to maintain the size of $t\_wd \times t\_ht$ 3D window. It has the effect of sliding $3DW$ from $((1, \underline{1}, 1), (L, \underline{t\_wd}, t\_ht))$ to $((1, \underline{2}, 1), (L, \underline{t\_wd + 1}, t\_ht))$. The deletion implies that some busy segments–used to be in the region of the previous window, but no longer in the new window–should be out of the new window. The insertion means that some busy segments which are newly involved in the new window should be inside of it. If the $3DW$ slides the entire area of the same layers and no free submesh for the allocation is found, we slide the window one level up along the z-dimension, and restart the same process again including the new layer from the smallest y-coordinate position. From now on, we call our scheme as *window sliding* (WS) scheme.

115

1. If (number of free processors $< L \times W \times H$), go to **Step 5**.

2. INITIALIZE_WIL();
   for $j = 1$ to t_wd do
       for $k = 1$ to t_ht do
           INSERT_TO_WIL($FRONT_{j,k}$);
   SAVED_WIL = WIL;
   $k_1 = 1$; $k_2 = t\_ht$;

3. **While** ($base\_found \leq 0$ and $k_2 \leq H$) **do**

3.1   if ($k_1 > 1$)
           WIL = SAVED_WIL;
           for $j = 1$ to t_wd do
               DELETE_FROM_WIL($FRONT_{j,k_1-1}$);
               INSERT_TO_WIL($FRONT_{j,k_2}$);
           SAVED_WIL = WIL;

3.2 $j_1 = 1$; $j_2 = t\_wd + 1$; $changed$ = FALSE;

3.3 $base\_found$ = WIL_SEARCH(t_ln);

3.4   while ($base\_found \leq 0$ and $j_2 \leq W$) do

3.5   for $k = k_1$ to k_2 do
               if (HEAD($REAR_{j_1,k}$) $\neq$ NIL)
                   $changed$ = TRUE;
                   DELETE_FROM_WIL($REAR_{j_1,k}$);
               if (HEAD($FRONT_{j_2,k}$) $\neq$ NIL)
                   $changed$ = TRUE;
                   INSERT_TO_WIL($FRONT_{j_2,k}$);

3.6 $j_1 = j_1 + 1$; $j_2 = j_2 + 1$;

3.7   if ($changed$ == TRUE)
               $base\_found$ = WIL_SEARCH(t_ln);
               $changed$ = FALSE;

3.8   if ($base\_found \leq 0$) $k_1 = k_1 + 1$; $k_2 = k_2 + 1$;

4. If ($base\_found > 0$)
       Allocate the free submesh whose base is (x, y, z) to T, where $x = base\_found$, $y = j_1$, and $z = k_1$. Add busy segments of front and rear faces of T to $FRONT$ and $REAR$, respectively.
       Stop.

5. Wait until deallocation occurs.

Figure 2. The procedure for the processor allocation.

In figure 1, with $T(2,2,2)$, the first 3D window of rows (1,1), (1,2), (2,1), and (2,2) constructs WIL: ([1,4],1) by inserting BSLs $FRONT_{1,1}$, $_{1,2}$, $_{2,1}$, and $_{2,2}$ to WIL. It does not have any free segment of length at least two, and thus we slide $3DW$ one unit along y-dimension and reconstruct WIL by deleting BSLs $REAR_{1,1}$ and $_{1,2}$ from WIL, and inserting $FRONT_{3,1}$ and $_{3,2}$ to WIL. Hence, the second 3D window includes the rows (2,1), (2,2), (3,1), and (3,2). Here, $REAR_{1,1}$, $_{1,2}$, $FRONT_{3,1}$, and $_{3,2}$ are all empty lists. Therefore, no change is necessary in WIL. We slide the window again to find a base for T. Deleting BSLs $REAR_{2,1}$ and $_{2,2}$ from WIL and inserting $FRONT_{4,1}$ and $_{4,2}$ from WIL change the WIL to ([1,4],0). We find free submesh to accommodate T with base (1,3,1) and end (2,4,2).

We focus on the main part of processor allocation and deallocation algorithms for the simplicity. Initially, the $base\_found$ flag is set to -1 (base not found yet.) Figure 2 shows the processor allocation procedure.

3   Performance Evaluation

We discuss about the comparison of time complexities and computer simulation results. In [10], if a deallocation occurs, the whole free list has to be recalculated completely. Therefore, it takes $O(L^4 W^4 H^4)$ in the worst case. The deallocation time of [11] is $O(LWH)$ because it involves the searching and deleting a submesh from the busy list of length $O(LWH)$. The proposed scheme requires only $O(LH)$ because the height of the deallocated submesh is bounded by $O(H)$ while removing the busy segments from $FRONT$ and $REAR$ takes $O(L)$.

We analyze the time complexity of the allocation algorithm of our scheme. Step 3.5 for reconstructing WIL due to the window sliding along the y-dimension of the same layer takes the largest time, and it thus decides the time complexity of our scheme. The height of the window is bounded by $O(H)$ and deleting and adding BSLs to WIL take $O(L)$ each. We repeat WIL construction whenever the window slides, while the window sliding is limited to $O(WH)$ times. Therefore, the time complexity of step 3.5 is $O(LWH^2)$, which dominates the allocation time of our scheme. The time complexity of allocation and deallocation of ours and earlier schemes are summarized in table I. It also compares the memory space requirement.

TABLE I. TIME COMPLEXITY FOR PROCESSOR ALLOCATION AND DEALLOCATION.

	Allocation	Deallocation	Memory
[10]	$O(L^4 W^4 H^4)$	$O(L^4 W^4 H^4)$	$O(L^3 W^3 H^3)$
[11]	$O(LW^2 H^2)$	$O(LWH)$	$O(LWH)$
WS	$O(LWH^2)$	$O(LH)$	$O(LWH)$

The environment of the event-driven simulation is same as others. Since, the simulation results for different mesh sizes follow a similar trend, we report the simulation results for only the $38 \times 32 \times 2$ mesh system of Intel TeraFLOP supercomputer. The simulator was developed on Sun Ultra SPARC system running Sun OS 5.5.

Task service time and inter-arrival time are assumed to have the exponential distribution with the means of MSVT (mean task service time) and MIAT (mean task inter-arrival time), respectively. The length l, width w, and height h of incoming tasks are assumed to follow decreasing, exponential, and uniform distributions. For the decreasing distribution, the range of 1 through L is divided into four intervals and the probability that a side length of an incoming task falls into one of the intervals decreases as the values in the interval increase. The probabilities that the meshlength falls into the range $[1, L/8]$ is 0.4, $[L/8 + 1, L/4]$ is 0.2, $[L/4 + 1, L/2]$ is 0.2, and finally $[L/2 + 1, L]$ is 0.2. The similar method is applied to the meshwidth and meshheight. The distribution of l, w, and h within each interval is uniform. Essentially, a decreasing distribution on l, w, and h represents a system with more tasks requesting relatively small submeshes. For the exponential distribution, the mean size for each dimension is selected as the half of meshlength, meshwidth, and meshheight, respectively. Those values exceeding the legal range were discarded. The lengths, widths, and heights of the tasks are generated separately based on the above distributions.

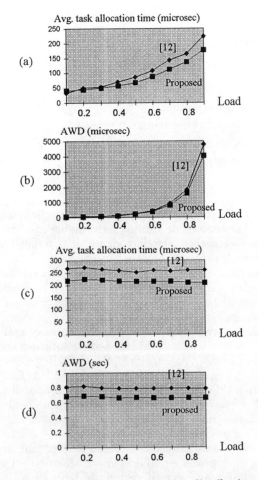

Figure 3. Comparisons in various distributions.

Figure 3(d) compares the AWD of the two schemes in exponential distribution. The waiting delay shows significantly better performance for the entire range of load.

4 Conclusion

We have proposed an efficient allocation scheme for 3D mesh-connected multicomputers which has complete recognition capability. The scheme was investigated assuming Intel TeraFLOP supercomputer as the target architecture. Comparison of time complexity with two recently proposed allocation schemes reveals the simplicity of the scheme. Comprehensive computer simulation shows that the average allocation time of the proposed scheme is improved up to about 25% than the best earlier 3D approach. This is achieved by employing an efficient search mechanism based on 3D window sliding, and manipulating novel data structures called *FRONT/REAR* and Window Information List.

References

[1] NCUBE Corp., *NCUBE/ten: An Overview*, Beaverton, OR, Nov. 1985.

[2] C. L. Seitz, "The cosmic cube," Commun. ACM, vol. 28, no. 1, pp. 22-23, Jan. 1985.

[3] Intel Corporation, *Paragon XP/S Product Overview*, 1991.

[4] Intel Corporation, *A Touchstone DELTA System Description*, 1991.

[5] T.G. Mattson, D. Scott, and S. Wheat, "A TeraFLOP Supercomputer in 1996: the ASCI TFLOP System," Int'l Parallel Processing Symposium, April, 1996.

[6] R. E. Kessler and J. L. Schwarzmeier, "CRAY T3D: A new dimension for Cray research," in Proc. COMPCON, pp. 176-182, Feb. 1993.

[7] S.M. Yoo and H.Y. Youn, "An efficient task allocation scheme for two-dimensional mesh connected systems," Int'l Conf. on Dist. Comp. Systems, pp. 501-508, May 1995.

[8] C. Morgenstern and P. Fouque, "Efficient submesh allocation using interval sets," Proc. Hawaii Int'l Conf. on System Sciences, pp.II-493-501, Jan. 1994.

[9] T. Lin, W-K. Huang, F. Lombardi, and L.N. Bhuyan, "A submesh allocation scheme for mesh-connected multiprocessor systems," Int'l Conf. on Parallel Processing, pp. II-159-163, Aug. 1995.

[10] W. Qiao and L. M. Ni, "Efficient processor allocation for 3D tori," IEEE Int'l Parallel Processing Symp., pp. 466-471, April 1995.

[11] H.Y. Youn, H. Choo, S.M. Yoo, and B. Shirazi, "Dynamic task scheduling and allocation for 3D torus multicomputer systems," Int'l Conf. on Parallel Processing, III-199-206, Aug. 1996.

[12] H. Choo, H.Y. Youn, and S.M. Yoo, "An efficient submesh allocation scheme for 3D torus multicomputer systems," Int'l Symp. on Parallel Algorithms/Architecture Synthesis, pp. 83-90, Mar. 1997.

In order to study the performance of the schemes under different load, we define *load* as $(n \times MSVT)/(N \times MIAT)$. Here, n is the average size of the requested submesh in terms of the number of processors, and N is the total number of processors in the system. In the simulation, we fix MSVT to be 10 time units and adjust MIAT according to the desired load. The performance measures employed are the *average task allocation time* which is the actual time a task at the head of the waiting queue takes to be allocated, and the *average waiting delay* (AWD) which is the actual time a task spent in the system before processor allocation. It is measured by the individual task delay. The AWD is the time period between the time when the task arrives in the system and the time when processors are allocated to the task. Processor utilization is not our concern to compare among first-fit based schemes.

Figure 3(a) plots the average allocation time of our scheme and 3D mesh version of [11] scheme for decreasingly distributed task length, width, and height. Figure 3(b) compares the AWD of the two schemes under different workload from 0.1 to 0.9 in decreasing distribution. Under the relatively high input load, the waiting delay shows noticeably better performance. Figure 3(c) plots the average allocation time for exponential distribution.

An Integrated Processor Management Scheme for the Mesh-Connected Multicomputer Systems *

Chung-yen Chang and Prasant Mohapatra
Department of Electrical and Computer Engineering
Iowa State University, Ames, Iowa 50010
E-mail: prasant@iastate.edu

Abstract

The performance of a multicomputer system depends on the processor management strategy. Processor management deals with processor allocation and job scheduling. Most of the processor allocation and job scheduling schemes proposed in the literature incur high implementation complexity and are therefore impractical to be integrated. In this paper, we propose an integrated processor management scheme that includes a bypass-queue *scheduling policy and a* fixed-orientation *allocation algorithm. Both policies have very low complexities and are hence suitable to be integrated. Both policies improve the system performance considerably when applied in isolation. The integrated scheme provides even better performance.*

1 Introduction

Several processor allocation algorithms have been proposed for the mesh-connected systems in the literature [1]–[3]. These algorithms allocate a job to a set of contiguous processing nodes to minimize the distance of communication paths and to avoid the interprocess interference. Contiguous allocation leads to several fragmented groups of processors that cannot be used for the new tasks. Fragmentation is the main factor that limits the performance of multicomputer systems. Non-contiguous allocation algorithms [4] have been proposed to eliminate the fragmentation problem. Because of the unpredictable communication latency caused by non-contiguous allocations, they may not be suitable for a variety of application environments.

Job scheduling is concerned with the sequencing of jobs for allocation. The high complexities of the several allocation algorithms restrict the use of any complicated scheduling policy. The ordinary first-come-first-serve (FCFS) discipline severely restricts the performance of a multicomputer system. In the FCFS scheduling, a waiting job will block all the following jobs from being serviced even if there are idle processors in the system. Scheduling schemes proposed in [5, 6] avoid the idling of processors by rearranging

the order of jobs to be executed. These scheduling schemes have shown promising performance improvement. However, they introduce significant overhead to the already complex allocation process.

Most of the allocation and scheduling schemes that demonstrate higher performance incur high time and implementation complexity. The integration of such allocation and scheduling schemes is thus impractical. In this paper, we propose an integrated processor management policy which considers both allocation and scheduling issues. An efficient job scheduling policy based on a *bypass-queue* (BQ) is proposed. A *fixed-orientation* (FO) allocation scheme is also proposed to be used in combination with the bypass-queue policy. Both schemes have low complexity and are therefore suitable for integration.

Extensive simulations are conducted to evaluate the proposed processor management schemes. The BQ scheduling and FO allocation are both shown to provide good performance for multicomputer systems when applied alone. It is further shown that the integrated processor management scheme performs better than using a single approach.

The rest of this paper is organized as follows. The detailed discussions about the proposed processor management schemes are in Section 2. The simulation results and the comparison with other policies are presented in Section 3. The last section concludes this study.

2 The Proposed Schemes

To combine the advantages of both processor allocation and job scheduling, an integrated processor management policy is proposed. The integrated policy consists of a job scheduling policy based on the *bypass-queue* (BQ) technique, and a *fixed-orientation* (FO) allocation algorithm.

2.1 Bypass-Queue (BQ) Scheduling

It is observed that the fragmentation problem is worsen by the blockade situation incurred while using the FCFS discipline. Many processors can be left idle even when there are jobs waiting for executions. By executing the jobs in a carefully arranged order, the blocking effect of the FCFS queue can be diminished as reported in [5, 6]. However, these schemes require

*This research was supported in part by the National Science Foundation through the grants CCR-9634547, MIP-9628801, and CDA-9617375.

multiple queues and have high implementation complexity.

A bypass queue is a variation of the FCFS queue without the blocking problem. Jobs in a bypass-queue are checked for allocation in the order of their arrival as is done in the FCFS queue. A job is allowed to bypass the unallocated jobs if it can be allocated. The process continues until all the jobs in the queue have been checked or an executing job departs from the system. In case of a departure, the entries in the queue are checked for allocation starting from the head of the queue. To ensure that every job can obtain the service after a reasonable waiting time, a threshold time is set for the system. The threshold time is the maximum time a job allows other jobs to bypass it before getting allocated. If any of the jobs waits longer than the threshold time, the bypassing is disabled and the jobs are served in a strict FCFS manner. Because of the threshold time, a job only has to wait for the release of the occupied nodes by other jobs if it has waited longer than the threshold time and is at the head of the queue. The jobs bypassing the blocked ones help better utilize the system.

2.2 Fixed-Orientation (FO) Allocation

The feasibility of non-contiguous allocation algorithms depends on the trade-offs between communication latency and queuing delay. In this paper, we consider only the contiguous allocation scheme. Among the contiguous algorithms, the schemes proposed in [2, 3] perform better because they allocate jobs in an alternative orientation when the requested submeshes cannot be found in one orientation. However, checking alternative orientations increases the complexity of the algorithm.

We propose a fixed-orientation algorithm for the mesh systems. Instead of checking alternative orientations to allocate a job, we allocate all rectangular submesh requests in the same orientation. The orientation for allocation is chosen according to the orientation of the system. If a job requests a submesh with different orientation than the chosen orientation, it is rotated before allocation.

The FO allocation has two advantages over the other algorithms. First, the allocation time is smaller compared to algorithms which check for alternative orientations. Because all jobs are allocated in a fixed orientation, our algorithm only needs to check for the available submesh in one orientation. Second, the fixed-orientation allocation has less fragmentation. Consider the example shown in Figure 1 with jobs arriving in the labeled order. If the allocator only checks the submesh in the requested orientation, job 4 ends up being blocked as shown. By forcing all the jobs to be allocated in the same orientation, all 4 jobs can be accommodated. There is still fragmentation due to the dynamic departure of the jobs. However, the simulation results in Section 3 indicate that the few fragmentation associated with fixed-orientation algorithm has insignificant impact on its performance.

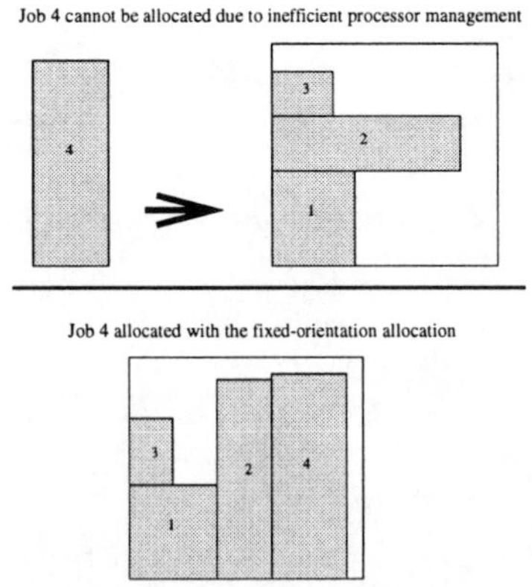

Figure 1: Reducing Virtual Fragmentation with the Fixed-Orientation Allocation.

2.3 Implementation of the Integrated Scheme

To take advantage of both processor allocation and job scheduling, the proposed BQ scheduling and FO allocation are used in combination as an integrated processor management scheme. A flag _rotated is associated with every job in the system. It is set upon the arrival of a job by comparing the orientation of the request and the orientation used for allocation. If this flag is set, address translation of the processors as discussed in [2] is required upon the allocation of this job. A linked list is used to implement the bypass-queue. All the waiting jobs are appended to the end of the list for allocation. The information contained in the linked list include the size, submission time, and the flag _rotated of the waiting jobs. Variable th_time is the threshold time set for the bypass-queue scheduling while _submission represents the submission time of the job at the head of the queue.

The integrated scheme consists of two main processes, job arrival and job departure, and is listed in Figure 2. The complexity for the FO allocation is equal to the first-fit and best-fit algorithm. It is more efficient than the algorithms [2, 3] that check alternative orientations for allocation. The manipulation of the bypass-queue does not introduce any significant overhead to the FCFS system. It does increase the number of allocation attempts because of the bypassing. Therefore, it is even more important to use an allocation algorithm with a low complexity such as the FO algorithm. The value of threshold time affects the performance of the integrated scheme. A system administrator can determine the threshold time based on individual system's need.

3 Performance Evaluation

Extensive simulations are conducted to evaluate the proposed schemes using a (32×32) mesh. Job arrivals are assumed as a Poisson process. Service time for a job is assumed to be exponentially distributed. The

Job Arrival:

Step 1 Check the orientation of the incoming job. Change the orientation and set _rotated if necessary.

Step 2 If queue is not empty, append the incoming job to the tail of the queue. Goto step 4.

Step 3 If queue is empty, check for allocation of the incoming job. If job is successfully allocated, assign processors to it and perform the required address translation when _rotated is set. Otherwise, put the job at the head of the queue.

Step 4 Wait for next arrival or departure.

Job Departure

Step 1 If queue is empty, goto step 4, else set _submission to the submission time of the first job in the queue. Choose the first job in queue as the candidate for allocation.

Step 2 If candidate is allocable, assign nodes to the candidate with proper address translation (if required) and remove it from the queue. If the last job in the queue has been checked, goto step 4.

Step 3 If (current_time − _submission < th_time), set the next job in queue as candidate. Set _submission to the submission time of the first job in the queue and goto step 2.

Step 4 Wait for next arrival or departure.

Figure 2: The Proposed Scheme.

arrival rate is calculated from the *traffic ratio* which is defined as $\frac{arrival\ rate}{service\ rate}$. A high traffic ratio represents a system under high load. The mean service time of a job is assumed to be 5 time units. We assume two different distributions for the submesh requests. The uniform distribution assumes the side-lengths of a job range from 1 to 32 with equal probabilities. We also assumed a truncated normal distribution for the side-lengths of a job in which the mean is set to 16.5 and the variance is 6.6. Any value outside the interval of [1,32] is truncated. The performance measures are derived by averaging the results obtained through the completion of 10,000 jobs.

3.1 Bypass-Queue Scheduling

Figure 3 shows the effect of using the bypass-queue with different threshold time using the first-fit and adaptive-scan allocation algorithms. The average turnaround time of jobs is efficiently reduced by the BQ scheduling for both allocation schemes. The operational range of the system is also increased. With the FCFS queue, the system gets saturated quickly for traffic above 1.5. With the bypass-queue, the system has a higher saturating point. Only the results for uniform job size distribution is shown. The normal job size distribution exhibits similar behavior.

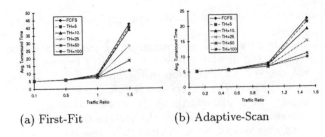

(a) First-Fit (b) Adaptive-Scan

Figure 3: Effect of the Bypass-Queue Scheduling.

3.2 Fixed-Orientation Allocation

The FO scheme is compared with the first-fit and adaptive-scan allocations. Figure 4 illustrate the comparisons with the uniform job size distribution and the normal job size distribution, respectively. The FO scheme outperforms the first-fit algorithm as expected because of the reduced fragmentation. It provides shorter turnaround time than the first-fit algorithm for all traffic ratios. The average turnaround time is reduced by as much as 42% from the first-fit algorithm at traffic ratio of 1.5 in Figure 4(a).

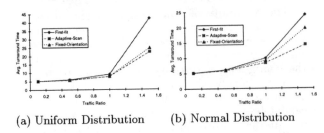

(a) Uniform Distribution (b) Normal Distribution

Figure 4: Effect of Different Allocation Algorithms.

The adaptive-scan does have less fragmentation than the FO scheme because of the alternative orientations of jobs it utilizes. However, the nearly identical performance of the FO allocation indicates that this difference is insignificant. By properly arranging the allocation of jobs, the FO scheme avoids fragmenting the system in most cases. The adaptive-scan gains its slightly better performance at the price of a higher computational complexity. Under low traffic, the FO and the adaptive-scan performs equally well with negligible difference. At higher traffic ratio, the adaptive-scan starts to perform slightly better than the fixed-orientation scheme. This is because in a heavily loaded system, jobs arrive and depart more frequently and more serious fragmentation is observed. The adaptive-scan solves the fragmentation by checking alternative orientation for submesh allocation and therefore takes more time to perform. In our simulations, the adaptive-scan takes 20% to 30% more time to complete the allocation process. The fixed-orientation allocation is feasible to be used in an integrated processor management policy because of its low computation demand.

3.3 The Integrated Policy

The integrated processor management scheme is simulated and the results are in Figure 5. The lines labeled *AS* is the average turnaround time obtained for the adaptive-scan algorithm using FCFS queue. It is included for comparison because the adaptive-scan scheme has the best submesh recognition ability. The integrated scheme delivers better performance than the adaptive-scan with a small threshold time. Increasing the threshold time further reduces the average turnaround time of jobs. Both the BQ scheduling and the FO allocation contribute to this performance improvement. Because of the less fragmentation of the FO allocation, more jobs can bypass other jobs in the queue and get executed.

Larger jobs have the tendency to be passed by other jobs with the BQ scheduling. Therefore, we compare the variance of the average turnaround time in Figure 6. Contrary to our expectation, the variance does not increase when the threshold time increases. The variance is actually reduced when larger threshold is used. This is attributed to the fact that a larger threshold time reduces the turnaround time so efficiently that most of the jobs can be served within a short period of time and thus results in a small variance. A low variance for the turnaround time is a good property for the system because most of the jobs can be expected to finish within a certain range of the average.

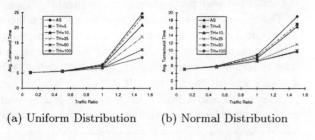

(a) Uniform Distribution   (b) Normal Distribution

Figure 5: The Integrated Processor Management Policy.

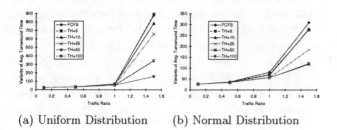

(a) Uniform Distribution   (b) Normal Distribution

Figure 6: Variance of the Avg. Turnaround Time.

4 Concluding Remarks

Processor allocation and job scheduling are both efficient ways of improving the performance of multicomputer systems. It is therefore desirable to integrate processor allocation and job scheduling to take advantage of both the approaches. The high complexities associated with existing processor allocation algorithms and job scheduling strategies makes the integration of the two approaches impractical. In this paper, we propose a bypass-queue scheduling policy and a fixed-orientation allocation algorithm. Both schemes have very low computational complexity and are therefore suitable for integration.

Simulation results indicate that the bypass-queue scheduling and the fixed-orientation allocation both provide good system performance when applied in isolation. Integrating these two schemes improves the system performance further. The ease of implementation and the performance make the proposed integrated processor management scheme highly attractive.

References

[1] Y. H. Zhu, *"Efficient Processor Allocation Strategies for Mesh-Connected Parallel Computers,"* Journal of Parallel and Distributed Computing, 16, pp. 328-337, 1992.

[2] J. Ding and L. N. Bhuyan, *"An Adaptive Submesh Allocation Strategy for Two-Dimensional Mesh Connected Systems,"* Proc. of Int. Conf on Parallel Processing, Vol. II, pp. 193-200, Aug. 1993.

[3] D. D. Sharma and D. K. Pradhan, *"A Fast and Efficient Strategy for Submesh Allocation in Mesh-Connected Parallel Computers,"* Proc. of the 5th IEEE Symp. on Parallel and Distributed Processing, pp. 682-693, Dec. 1993.

[4] W. Liu, V. Lo, K. Windisch, and B. Nitzberg, *Non-continuous Processor Allocation Algorithms for Distributed Memory Multicomputers,"* Proc. of the 1994 Int. Conf. on Supercomputing, pp. 227-236, 1994.

[5] D. Das Sharma and D. K. Pradhan, *"Job Scheduling in Mesh Multicomputers,"* Proc. Int. Conf. on Parallel Processing, vol. II, pp. 251-258, 1994.

[6] D. Min and M. W. Mutka, *"Efficient Job Scheduling in a Mesh Multicomputer Without Discrimination Against Large Jobs,"* Proc. of the IEEE Symposium on Parallel and Distributed Processing pp. 52-59, October, 1995.

Quantitative Analysis on Caching Effect of I-Structure Data in Frame-Based Multithreaded Processing

Hyong-Shik Kim   Soonhoi Ha   Chu Shik Jhon

Department of Computer Engineering
Seoul National University
Seoul 151-742, KOREA

E-mail: {hskim,sha,csjhon}@comp.snu.ac.kr

Abstract

Since long latency due to remote memory access could be tolerated by rapidly switching to another thread in multithreaded processing, caching I-structure data is expected to have less beneficial effect on the performance than caching ordinary data. In this paper, we show that caching I-structure data could improve the overall performance in spite of latency tolerating property of multithreading. Our quantitative analysis reveals that the most important caching effect of I-structure data in frame-based multithreading is the enhancement of frame parallelism. It reduces the idle time due to latency by lowering latency sensitivity and at the same time decreases the thread processing time by exploiting more processors.

1. Introduction

Multithreading allows a processor to tolerate long unpredictable latency by rapidly switching to a ready-to-run(shortly ready) thread. A frame-based multithreaded model is evolved from dataflow computation model by enlarging the granularity of scheduling unit. In frame-based multithreaded model, an activation frame(shortly frame) is allocated when invoking a code block, which corresponds to a function or a loop body. Each frame maintains local variables of the code block as well as the execution state, which are called *context*.

A code block in frame-based multithreading breaks down into self-scheduling threads. When a thread is completed, another ready thread which shares the frame is scheduled without any context switch. Such a sequence of threads is called a *quantum*. In case there are no more threads waiting to be executed in the code block, the context switch occurs.

In addition to frames, there is another kind of memory called a global heap memory(shortly heap) which is shared by all code blocks. I-structure[1] is commonly used for the heap because of its simple synchronization primitives and its non-strictness property, which allows access to an individual element before the entire structure is constructed.

It is generally believed that the locality of reference in a program can be exploited using cache memories(shortly caches), which reduce memory latency and thus improve the overall performance. However it is not clear that the same kind of benefit is applicable to I-structure memory,[1] because a request for I-structure memory access which incurs long unpredictable latency needs not be resolved immediately after being issued. Instead, its response is made to be served by another thread in order to tolerate the latency involved in I-structure memory access.

Kavi *et al.*[2] suggested instruction, data(operand), and I-structure cache memories for ETS(Explicit Token Store) model. Culler *et al.*[3] introduced I-structure caches for TAM(Threaded Abstract Machine) implemented on CM-5. Both showed that caching I-structure data could improve the execution time. However, they did not analyze the underlying reasons of such performance improvement.

This paper evaluates quantitatively the caching effect of I-structure data in detail. According to our experimental results, I-structure caches could improve the performance in spite of latency tolerating property of multithreading. With a simple analytic model, we will investigate whether such performance improvement is made possible just by shortening average latency, or whether there is another factor by which I-structure caches decrease the execution time.

2. I-Structure Caches

Our I-structure cache keeps only the values of I-structure elements excluding the deferred lists for simpler organization and operation. Consequently, the state of an element is either full or empty, and all the deferred elements are regarded as empty in I-structure caches.

Four basic I-structure operations are structure allocation, deallocation, fetch of an element, and store, which are represented as `ialloc`, `ifree`, `ifetch`, and `istore` respectively in this paper.

As for `ialloc` operations, I-structure caches are not in-

---

[1]Hereafter we call a heap which saves I-structure data as *I-structure memory*.

volved. The requests are directly delivered to the I-structure memory, where actual allocation is performed. To minimize the heavy overhead of coherence management,[2] all `ifree`'s are accumulated until the system runs low on storage, and then they are serviced by flushing all caches without the investigation upon the individual blocks.

When an `ifetch` operation turns out to be a hit by an I-structure cache, a response message which carries the value is generated and immediately fed back without any remote latency.[3] When the value is not found in the cache, a request message is generated and sent to the I-structure memory. A response message for `ifetch` does not carry just an element but a whole cache block.

An `istore` operation first updates the appropriate cache block if it exists. In case of a cache miss, a new cache block is not allocated, thus not affecting I-structure cache. Concurrently with the update, a message is sent to the I-structure memory as a write-through cache does, because there may be an associated deferred list waiting to be resolved.

3. Experiments

Simulation is performed with our own instruction level event-driven simulator which augmented the SPIM simulator[4]. The simulator handles system calls for multithreading and supports facilities for message transmission between processors.

The target system is composed of eight processors which are connected through a network in which all packets are transmitted in a constant delay and without contention. The execution times are measured assuming that every R2000 instruction takes a unit time and system calls require the predefined execution times.

We use four benchmark programs: MMT, paraffins, speech, and DTW.[4] Since they are all represented in TL0 language[5], they are first translated into R2000 instructions and system calls such as `ifetch` and `istore` by our own TL0-to-R2000 compiler.

Figure 1 analyzes hit ratios for various cache sizes. All experiments are performed with the communication delay of 100 unit times, and the cache size and the cache block size are assumed to be 64K bytes and 4 elements respectively. Larger cache improves the hit ratio for all benchmark programs as far as the size does not exceed 64K bytes. Although the locality of reference is not expected to be remarkable for I-structure data, the hit ratios are high espe-

---

[2]Since the *single assignment rule* guarantees that any I-structure element is not modified once defined during its lifetime, the coherence problem on caching I-structure data occurs only when a whole structure is deallocated.

[3]Of course, the thread which will be activated by that message could pick up the value for itself, which may lead to better performance. However, a response message is generated, as if a miss, to guarantee the transparent processing regardless whether I-structure data are cached or not.

[4]They are a part of multithread programs provided by U. C. Berkeley, and can be found at `ftp://ftp.cs.berkeley.edu/pub/TAM/`.

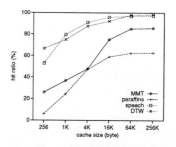

Figure 1. Hit ratio analysis

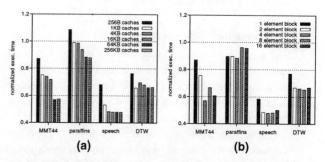

(a)   **(b)**

Figure 2. Experimental results (a) on cache size (b) on cache block size

cially for speech and DTW. The hit ratios of paraffins are generally much lower than those of others. The detailed investigation explains that it is due to its little spatial locality.

Figure 2 shows the cache effect on the overall performance in terms of the normalized execution time that is the ratio of the execution time with caches to the execution time without caches. Figure 2(a), where cache block size is assumed to be 4 elements, reveals there is good performance improvement found even with small caches. As for speech, the execution time decreases to about a half when the I-structure data are cached. The reduction of the execution time for paraffins is not remarkable. The cache size of 256 bytes even degrades the performance due to cache miss penalty. Since workloads are distributed frame by frame at run-time, larger caches may make the performance worse transiently in some cases. Figure 2(b), where the cache size is set to 64K bytes, confirms that bigger block size does not guarantee better performance due to the increased miss penalty. In our experiments, 4 element block brings the balanced performance.

4. Quantitative Analysis

In this section, we build a simple analytic execution time model in order to evaluate caching effects of I-structure data in detail. The suggested execution time model helps us estimate how much each parameter such as average latency, quantum size and the degree of parallelism affects total execution time. In order to validate the model, we compare the reduced fraction of total execution time estimated by the model and that measured by experiment.

Table 1. Notation

symbol	meaning
l	average latency
q	average quantum length measured in time units
n_a	average number of active frames in a system
n_r	average number of ready frames (including active frames) in a system
n_m	number of message packets
s	latency sensitivity

4.1. Execution time model

The basic assumption upon which the model is based is that the reduced amount of total execution time by incorporating I-structure caches is the sum of the reduced amount of partial execution times which may be calculated independently. As a first step towards modeling the execution time, therefore, we divide the total execution time into a variant part affected by caching and the other invariant part. Idle time due to latency (T_l), overall thread processing time which includes the idle time due to lack of work (T_w), frame switching time (T_s), and message packetizing/unpacketizing time (T_m) belong to the variant part, while system call overhead to support threaded processing except frame switching time (T_f) is included in the invariant part. The total execution time is represented as the sum of five partial execution times as $T = T_l + T_w + T_s + T_m + T_f$.

Table 1 explains the meaning of the symbols which will be used throughout the rest of the papers. *Latency sensitivity*, s, is introduced in order to anticipate the fraction of latencies which could eventually degrade the performance without being tolerated. As s approaches 1, latencies are not tolerated that much, thus increasing the execution time.

Given the partial execution times without caches and the program parameter values, the reduced amount of each partial execution time is calculated as follows.[5]

$$\Delta \widetilde{T_l} = T_l \cdot \frac{s - s'}{s} \qquad (1)$$

$$\Delta \widetilde{T_w} = T_w \cdot \frac{n_a' - n_a}{n_a'} \qquad (2)$$

$$\Delta \widetilde{T_s} = T_s \cdot \frac{q' - q}{q'} \qquad (3)$$

$$\Delta \widetilde{T_m} = T_m \cdot \frac{n_m - n_m'}{n_m} \qquad (4)$$

The symbols with ′ are the parameter values with I-structure cache.

4.2. Latency sensitivity

According to the analytical performance models of multithreaded processors which were suggested by Agarwal[6]

and Saavedra-Barrera *et al.*[7] respectively, a multithreaded processor gains the saturated efficiency, if the time the processor spends servicing the other threads to tolerate a latency-incurring request exceeds the time to process the request. Saavedra-Barrera *et al.* formalize the condition as

$$(N - 1)(R + C) > L, \qquad (5)$$

where N is the number of threads in the processor, and R, C, and L represent average interval between the requests, switching time between threads, and average latency respectively.

However, Saavedra-Barrera's model could not be applied directly to our frame-based multithreaded system. First, context switch does not always occur even when a latency-incurring request is met since there may be runnable threads to be scheduled within the same quantum. If there are n_a active frames and n_r ready frames, consequently, the alternative works to tolerate the latency is assumed approximately as $\frac{n_r}{n_a}$, not $\frac{n_r - n_a}{n_a}$, runnable frames. That is different from Saavedra-Barrera's model, where only $N - 1$ threads except the current one are regarded as alternative. Second, a context switch does not occur on every request, but on every quantum switch. R in (5), therefore, is replaced by the quantum length, q. Replacing L in (5) by average latency, l, the inequality is rewritten as

$$\frac{n_r}{n_a} \cdot (q + C) > l, \qquad (6)$$

where the left-hand expression means the time servicing alternative frames for each active processor, and the right-hand one is the time required to process the individual request by the processor. If we assume C in inequality (6) is negligible compared with q,[6] the inequality is simplified to

$$\frac{n_r}{n_a} \cdot \frac{q}{l} > 1. \qquad (7)$$

If inequality (7) does not hold, the fraction of tolerable latencies is simply the amount of the left-hand expression. Even when the inequality holds, however, there would be still intolerable latency, because n_r, n_a, q, and l are all taken as averages over the whole range of execution time. Even worse, the latency incurred by a processor could not be tolerated at all, if the processor is not active any more after the current quantum is completed.

Now we define s, the latency sensitivity of a frame-based multithreaded system, as

$$s = 1 - \frac{n_a}{n} \cdot \min(\frac{n_r}{n_a} \cdot \frac{q}{l}, \ k), \qquad (8)$$

where n is the number of processors, k is the maximum fraction of latencies which could be tolerated.[7]

---

[5]Due to the space limitation, we omit all the intermediate expressions.

[6]Note that quantum length, q, is much longer than average interval between requests, R in (5).

[7]k is 1, of course, for an ideal multithreaded system.

Table 2. Quantitative Analysis

	MMT	paraffins	speech	DTW
s	0.876	0.814	0.956	0.914
s'	0.365	0.692	0.153	0.255
$\Delta \widetilde{T} / T$	0.507	0.120	0.561	0.461
$\Delta \widetilde{T}_l / T$	0.349	0.087	0.257	0.262
$\Delta \widetilde{T}_w / T$	0.157	0.037	0.282	0.152
$\Delta \widetilde{T}_s / T$	0.006	0.001	0.023	0.048
$\Delta \widetilde{T}_m / T$	-0.005	-0.003	-0.001	-0.001
$\Delta T / T$	0.431	0.115	0.520	0.337

$\min(\frac{n_r}{n_a} \cdot \frac{q}{l}, k)$ means the maximum fraction of the latencies tolerated by n_a active processors, and thus $\frac{n_a}{n} \cdot \min(\frac{n_r}{n_a} \cdot \frac{q}{l}, k)$ is for the whole system composed of n processors since any latency could not be tolerated at inactive processors. In the following analysis, n is 8, which is the number of processors in the previous experiments, and k is assumed to be 0.95.

4.3. Analysis

Table 2 shows the reduced fractions of partial execution times $(\frac{\Delta \widetilde{T}}{T})$,[8] which are estimated with the model. The measured fraction of total execution time $(\frac{\Delta T}{T})$ is given at the bottom for the purpose of comparison with the estimated value. The first two rows reveal how much the latency sensitivity is affected by caching I-structure data. For all benchmark programs, the latency sensitivities are lowered in a certain degree and the system becomes saturated with the frames, when I-structure caches are adopted.

The caching effects on the execution time are found fourfold. T_l is certainly reduced by avoiding latencies with caches. T_w is decreased by making more processors active. It is believed that prompt responses by cache hits seem to exploit frame parallelism rapidly by activating frames which would still wait otherwise. T_s is shortened by enlarging the quantum size. However, T_m is rather increased because additional messages are needed to deliver the cache blocks although message traffic between processors is actually reduced.

For all the programs, the performance improvement is mostly from $\frac{\Delta \widetilde{T}_l}{T}$ and $\frac{\Delta \widetilde{T}_w}{T}$, which are due to the lowered latency sensitivities and the enhanced frame parallelism respectively. Note that the latency sensitivity is not affected only by the reduction of average latency. The number of active frames also has a great effect on latency sensitivity as shown in the equation (8).

Therefore, both $\Delta \widetilde{T}_l$ and $\Delta \widetilde{T}_w$ are commonly affected by the number of active frames, n_a. As n_a increases, so does $\Delta \widetilde{T}_w$. $\Delta \widetilde{T}_l$ also depends on n_a, because latency sensitivity

---

[8] The symbol capped with $\tilde{}$ indicates that the value is estimated by the model.

is limited only by n_a for the saturated system. The fact that the number of active frames affects both $\Delta \widetilde{T}_w$ and $\Delta \widetilde{T}_l$ explains the overestimation of $\frac{\Delta \widetilde{T}}{T}$ over $\frac{\Delta T}{T}$.

In summary, the most important caching effect of I-structure data in frame-based multithreading is proved to be the enhancement of frame parallelism measured by the number of active frames, which reduces the idle time due to latency by lowering latency sensitivity and at the same time decreases the thread processing time by exploiting more processors.

5. Concluding Remarks

In this paper, we showed that caching I-structure data could improve the overall performance, although multithreading inherently tolerates the latency incurred by I-structure memory access. According to our quantitative analysis, caching I-structure data decreases latency sensitivity as well as average latency. The latency sensitivity, not the average latency, has a great effect on reducing the idle time due to latency. It is also observed that the I-structure caches enhance frame parallelism by making prompt responses rapidly and thus activating frames which would still wait otherwise. The enhanced parallelism certainly decreases the thread processing time by exploiting more processors. The enhancement of frame parallelism, therefore, is regarded as the most important caching effect of I-structure data in frame-based multithreading, because the lowered latency sensitivity is also affected by the frame parallelism.

References

[1] Arvind, R. S. Nikhil, and K. K. Pingali. I-Structures: Data Structures for Parallel Computing. *ACM Transactions on Programming Languages and Systems*, 11(4):598–632, Oct. 1989.

[2] K. Kavi, A. Hurson, E. Abraham, and P. Shanmugam. Design of Cache Memories for Multi-Threaded Dataflow Architecture. In *Proceedings of the 22th Annual International Symposium on Computer Architecture*, pages 253–264, June 1995.

[3] D. Culler, S. Goldstein, K. Schauser, and T. Eicken. Empirical Study of a Dataflow Language on the CM-5. In L. Bic, G. Gao, and J.-L. Gaudiot, editors, *Advanced Topics in Dataflow Computing and Multithreading*, pages 187–210. IEEE Computer Science Press, 1995.

[4] J. Larus. SPIM S20: A MIPS R2000 Simualtor. Technical Report No. 966, University of Wisconsin, Department of Computer Science, Sept. 1990.

[5] S. C. Goldstein. The Implementation of a Threaded Abstract Machine. Master's thesis, University of California at Bekerley, Computer Science Division, May 1994.

[6] A. Agarwal. Performance Tradeoffs in Multithreaded Processors. VLSI Memo 89-566, M.I.T., Oct. 1989.

[7] R. H. Saavedra-Barrera, D. E. Culler, and T. von Eicken. Analysis of Multithreaded Architectures for Parallel Computing. In *Proceedings of the 2nd Annual ACM Symposium on Parallel Algorithms and Architectures*, pages 169–178, July 1990.

Session 2C

IO and Data Structures in Distributed Systems

Improving the Performance of Out-of-Core Computations[*]

M. Kandemir[†] J. Ramanujam[‡] A. Choudhary[§]

Abstract

The difficulty of handling out-of-core data limits the potential of parallel machines and high-end supercomputers. Since writing an efficient out-of-core version of a program is a difficult task and since virtual memory systems do not perform well on scientific computations, we believe that there is a clear need for compiler-directed explicit I/O approach for out-of-core computations. In this paper, we present a compiler algorithm to optimize locality of disk accesses in out-of-core codes by choosing a good combination of file layouts on disks and loop transformations. The transformations change the access order of array data. Experimental results obtained on IBM SP-2 and Intel Paragon provide encouraging evidence that our approach is successful at optimizing programs which depend on disk-resident data in distributed-memory machines.

1 Introduction

It is now widely acknowledged that due to increasing gap between speeds of high performance processors and memory subsystems, compiler optimizations aimed at improving the locality characteristics of programs are extremely important. Since the overall system performance is limited by the speed of the slowest unit, I/O subsystems of supercomputers constitute a bottleneck for applications that access huge amounts of data. A computation which operates on disk-resident arrays are called *out-of-core*, and an optimizing compiler for out-of-core computations is termed as *out-of-core compiler*. In contrast a computation which operates on data sets in memory is called *in-core*. Traditionally, in scientific computations, I/O is handled in two different ways: virtual memory (VM) and explicit file I/O. Although VM ensures correctness for programs whose data sizes far exceed the size of available memory, it has been observed that the performance of scientific applications that rely on VM is generally poor due to frequent paging in and out of data [5]. Our experiments confirm these results as for example shown in Figure 1 for the nest given in Figure 4:A. Figure 1 shows the performance improvement obtained by explicit I/O against VM on the Intel Paragon. Since the Intel Paragon has 32 MBytes node memory, three arrays each of which contains $1K \times 1K$ elements of size 8 bytes represent the largest amount of data per node in our input set that can fit into memory. (Note that all sizes of data sets in this paper are given on a per-node basis). So, as expected, for cases with 512×512 and $1K \times 1K$ arrays, VM performs better. But starting from $2K \times 2K$ arrays explicit I/O outperforms the VM and the performance improvement is highly significant. In the optimized approach, even for 512×512 and $1K \times 1K$ arrays, explicit

[*]Supported by NSF Young Investigator Award CCR-9357840 and by CCR-9509143. J. Ramanujam is supported in part by an NSF Young Investigator Award CCR-9457768 by CCR-9210422.

[†]CIS Dept., Syracuse University, Syracuse, NY 13244.

[‡]ECE Dept., Louisiana State University, Baton Rouge, LA 70803.

[§]Corresponding Author, ECE Dept., Northwestern University, Evanston, IL 60208-3118, e-mail: choudhar@ece.nwu.edu

I/O has been performed. This and similar experiments convince us that the VM is not a viable alternative for out-of-core computations.

Explicit file I/O, however, has it own problems. The task of programming I/O is tedious and error-prone. The low-level I/O decisions made by programmers also severely affect the portability of applications [11]. We show in this paper that a compiler approach based on explicit I/O can be very successful provided careful attention is paid to the layout of data in files. Note that the term layout is used to describe layout of data in files, e.g., column-major or row-major storage, and *does not* denote partitioning or decomposition of data among processor memories.

Since, due to high I/O startup costs, accessing data on disk is usually orders of magnitude slower than accessing data in memory, it is essential to reduce the number as well as the volume of the disk accesses. In this paper, we make the following contributions. First, we present a compiler algorithm based on explicit file I/O to reduce the time spent in disk I/O on distributed-memory message-passing machines. Our algorithm automatically transforms a given loop nest to exploit locality on disks, assigns appropriate disk layouts for out-of-core arrays, and partitions the available node memory across the out-of-core arrays, all in a unified framework. Secondly, we present performance results for several kernels on an IBM SP-2 and on an Intel Paragon. These results provide enough evidence that our algorithm can be very useful for compilation of out-of-core codes in distributed-memory machines. Thirdly, we discuss the impact of the algorithm on multiprogramming, and comment on the interaction between our algorithm and cache optimization techniques [8].

2 Compiling Out-of-Core Codes

In order to translate out-of-core programs, the compiler has to take into account the data distribution on disks, the number of disks used for storing data etc. The compilation of an out-of-core loop nest consists of two phases. In the first phase, called *in-core phase*, the out-of-core arrays in the source HPF program are partitioned according to the distribution information and bounds for local out-of-core arrays are computed. The second phase, called *out-of-core phase*, involves adding appropriate statements to perform I/O and communication. The local out-of-core arrays are first tiled according to the node memory available in each processor and the resulting tiles are analyzed for communication. The loops are then modified to insert necessary I/O calls. We identify three major issues to be exploited in order to generate efficient code for out-of-core computations: access pattern, storage layouts on disk, and memory allocation. The access pattern is generally a function of distribution directives and control constructs such as loops, conditional statements etc. Since in scientific computations most of the execution time is spent in loop nests, we will consider loops as the sole factor determining the access pattern along with the data distribution directives. On the other hand, the storage layout for an h-dimensional array can be in one of the $h!$ forms, each of which corresponds to layout of data on disk linearly by a nested traversal of the axes in

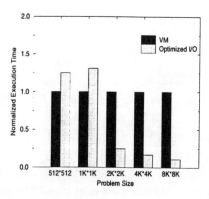

Figure 1: Optimized I/O vs. Virtual Memory (VM) on Intel Paragon.

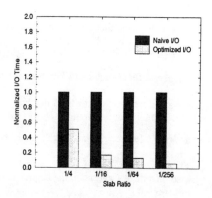

Figure 2: Optimized I/O vs. Unoptimized (naive) I/O on IBM SP-2.

some predetermined order. The innermost axis is called *the fastest changing dimension*; for example, for row-major storage layout of a two-dimensional array the second axis is the fastest changing dimension. And lastly, since node memory is a limited resource, it should be divided optimally among competing out-of-core arrays such that the total I/O time is minimized. A compiler for out-of-core codes should optimize the access pattern, storage layout and memory allocation together in order to exploit the locality as much as possible. In this paper, we offer an automatic method by which an optimizing compiler can achieve this goal.

Tiling (also known as blocking) is a technique to improve the locality and is a combination of strip-mining and loop permutation [17, 18]. It can be used to automatically create blocked versions of programs, and when it is applied it replaces the original loop with two new loops: a tiling loop and an element loop. The compilation methodology for in-core data-parallel programs can be naively extended for out-of-core computations as follows: after the node program is determined, the loops are tiled and appropriate I/O calls are inserted between tiling loops. If no optimization is performed, *data tiles* with sides of equal length in each dimension are fetched from disk, and the available memory is decomposed as evenly as possible across the arrays involved. We believe that the code produced by this naive method may not perform well due to the following reasons.

1. In this method, the order of tiling loops is the same as that of the original loops. As will be shown later, for many nests encountered in practice that order of tiling loops may not be the best to exploit the data locality on disks.

2. Assuming a fixed disk layout such as row-major or column-major may not be a good idea. In out-of-core computations, fixed layout strategy can lead to poor results on secondary storage. Since most of the known approaches like [7] and [17] are based on the fixed layout strategy, we believe their effect on optimizing I/O is limited.

3. When more than one array is involved in computation, during memory allocation it might be better to favor (by allocating more memory) the frequently accessed arrays over the others.

Our solution involves deriving the best loop transformation and disk layouts, and allocating the available node memory optimally.

2.1 Motivation for Optimized I/O

In order to illustrate the performance improvement that can be obtained by compiler optimizations over the naive explicit I/O approach described before, we consider the nest shown in Figure 4:A, assuming that arrays A, B and C are $n \times n$ out-of-core arrays. In this example, using HPF-like distribution directives, we assume that array A is distributed in row-block, the array B is distributed in column-block across the processors, and the array C is replicated. Also, with out-of-core computations, the compiler directives apply to data on disks. In the naive translation, after obtaining the node program, the compiler tiles all four loops and inserts I/O statements between tiling loops. A sketch of the resulting code is given in Figure 4:B, assuming n is an exact multiple of S, the tile size; and p is the number of processors. In the translated code the loops u, v, w and y are called *tiling loops* and the computation inside the tiling loops is performed on data tiles (sub-matrices) rather than individual array elements. In other words, there are four more loops called *element loops* (not shown for sake of clarity) that iterate over the individual array elements of data tiles of A, B and C. It should be emphasized that a reference such as $A[u, v]$ denotes a data tile of size $S \times S$ from file coordinates (u, v) as upper-left corner to $(u + S - 1, v + S - 1)$ as lower-right corner. A reference like $A[u, 1 : n]$, on the other hand, denotes a data tile of size $S \times n$ from $(u, 1)$ to $(u + S - 1, n)$, i.e. a block of S consecutive rows of the out-of-core matrix A.

With Figure 4:B, during the execution, square tiles of size $S \times S$ (shown as shaded blocks in Figure 4:D) are read from disks. Note that this tile allocation scheme implies the memory constraint $3S^2 \leq M$ where M is the size of the node memory. However, by applying our approach which is described in the following sections, the compiler generates the code in Figure 4:C directly from the code in Figure 4:A. It decides on a row-major disk layout for A and C and a column-major disk layout with B; the optimized code shown in Figure 4:C is obtained after appropriate transformation of the tiling loops. The tiles of size $S \times n$ are allocated for A and C, and a tile of size $n \times S$ is allocated for B as shown in Figure 4:G, resulting in the memory constraint $3nS \leq M$. Since, for some dimensions, the tile size is equal to n (the array size), the tiling loops w and y disappear.

We ran the naive and optimized versions of this example nest on a single node of IBM SP-2 with $4K \times 4K$ double arrays, varying the amount of available node memory. Figure 2 shows the I/O times normalized with respect to the naive (unoptimized) version. It should be noted that the performance improvement is significant especially with the small values of *slab ratio* (SR), the ratio of

Step 1 Initialize $i = 1$. Set data tile size for each dimension of each array to S.

Step 2 Set $\vec{\ell_i}^C.Q = (0, 0, ..., 0, 1)$ and $\vec{\ell_k}^C.Q = (\delta, \delta, ..., \delta, 0)$ for each $k \neq i$, where δ denotes *dont-care*.

Step 3 Set the disk layout for C such that i^{th} index position will be the fastest changing position.

Step 4 For each array reference A on the RHS that has $\vec{\ell_l}^A = \vec{\ell_i}^C$ for some l, try to set the disk layout for A such that the lth dimension will be the fastest changing dimension.

Step 5 Choose an array reference A for which the equality in **Step 4** does not hold. Initialize $j = 1$.

Step 6 Set $\vec{\ell_j}^A.Q = (0, 0, ..., 1, 0)$ and $\vec{\ell_k}^A.Q = (\delta, \delta, ..., \delta, 0, 0)$ for each $k \neq j$. If this step is consistent with the previous steps go to **Step 7**, otherwise increment j and go to the beginning of this step. If there exist inconsistencies for all j values, then initialize $j = 1$, and set $\vec{\ell_j}^A.Q = (0, 0, ..., 1, 0, 0)$ and $\vec{\ell_k}^A.Q = (\delta, \delta, ..., \delta, 0, 0, 0)$ for each $k \neq j$, and repeat **Step 6** and so on. If no T^{-1} is found then fill the remaining entries arbitrarily observing the *dependences* and *non-singularity*.

Step 7 Repeat **Step 6** for all reference matrices of a particular A (Of course, all reference matrices for a particular A should have the same distribution).

Step 8 Repeat **Step 6** for all distinct array references.

Step 9 Record the obtained transformation matrix. Also record, for each array, the loop index position which appears in the fastest changing position for that array.

Step 10 Increment i and go to **Step 2** (try a different layout for the LHS array C).

Step 11 Compare all the recorded transformation matrices and their associated layouts, and choose the best alternative (see the explanation in Section 4).

Step 12 Divide the arrays into groups according to the selected disk layouts of the associated files. For each array, if a loop index appears in the fastest changing array dimension, and does not appear in any other dimension of any reference in that group, increase the tile size in that dimension to full array size for that reference.

Step 13 Re-evaluate the memory constraint to set the value of S.

Figure 3: Algorithm for optimizing locality in out-of-core computations.

available node memory size to total size of out-of-core arrays. Note that a smaller slab ratio indicates less available node memory. We believe that the Figures 1 and 2 indicate the need for compiler-directed optimized explicit I/O approach for out-of-core computations.

After briefly reviewing the loop transformation theory in Section 3, in Section 4 we present our optimization algorithm which contains the steps necessary to obtain the I/O optimized node programs from global name space programs. In Section 5, we present our experimental results. In Section 6, we show how our technique can be extended to handle the global I/O optimization problem and finally we conclude the paper in Section 7.

3 Review of Loop Transformations

We focus on loops where both array subscripts and loop bounds are affine functions of enclosing loop indices. A reference to an array X is represented by $X(\mathcal{L}\vec{I} + \vec{b})$ where $\mathcal{L}$ is a linear transformation matrix called *array reference matrix*, $\vec{b}$ is offset vector and $\vec{I}$ is a column vector representing the loop indices $i_1, i_2,...,i_n$ starting from the outermost loop. Linear mappings between iteration spaces of loop nests can be modeled by nonsingular matrices [7]. Since the transformation matrices for general array references obtained by our approach are not necessarily unimodular, we need a general non-singular transformation scheme rather than a simpler unimodular transformation framework. If $\vec{I}$ is the original iteration vector,

after applying linear transformation T, the new iteration vector is $\vec{J} = T\vec{I}$. Similarly if $\vec{d}$ is the distance/direction vector, on applying T, $T\vec{d}$ is the new distance/direction vector. A transformation is *legal* if and only if $T\vec{d}$ is lexicographically positive for every $\vec{d}$ [18]. On the other hand, since $\mathcal{L}\vec{I} = \mathcal{L}T^{-1}\vec{J}$, it is clear that $\mathcal{L}T^{-1}$ is the new array reference matrix after the transformation. We denote T^{-1} by Q. An important characteristic of our approach is that using the array reference matrices, the entries of Q are derived systematically. For the rest of the paper, the reference matrix for array X will be denoted by $\mathcal{L}^X$ whereas the ith row of the reference matrix for array X will be denoted by $\vec{\ell_i}^X$. Unless otherwise stated, the word *loop* in this paper refers to *tiling loop*; and the element loops and communication statements will not be shown for sake of clarity.

4 Disk Locality Algorithm

Let $i_1, i_2,...,i_n$ be loop indices of the original nest, and $j_1, j_2,...,j_n$ be the loop indices of the transformed nest, starting from outermost position. An explanation of our algorithm for a single statement follows. (The modifications necessary for multiple LHSs and multiple nests are discussed in Section 6)

- Our transformation matrix should be such that the LHS array of the transformed loop should have the innermost index as the only element in one of the array dimensions and that in-

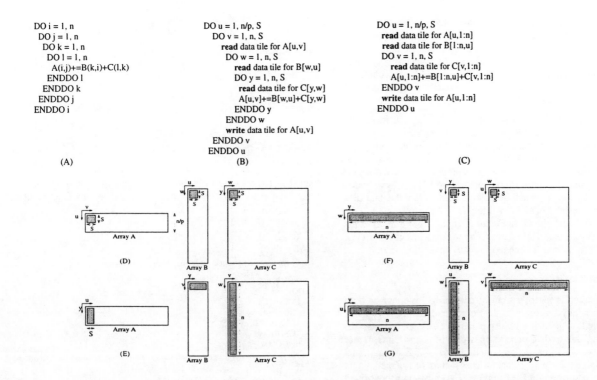

```
DO i = 1, n
  DO j = 1, n
    DO k = 1, n
      DO l = 1, n
        A(i,j)+=B(k,i)+C(l,k)
      ENDDO l
    ENDDO k
  ENDDO j
ENDDO i
```

(A)

```
DO u = 1, n/p, S
  DO v = 1, n, S
    read data tile for A[u,v]
    DO w = 1, n, S
      read data tile for B[w,u]
      DO y = 1, n, S
        read data tile for C[y,w]
        A[u,v]+=B[w,u]+C[y,w]
      ENDDO y
    ENDDO w
    write data tile for A[u,v]
  ENDDO v
ENDDO u
```

(B)

```
DO u = 1, n/p, S
  read data tile for A[u,1:n]
  read data tile for B[1:n,u]
  DO v = 1, n, S
    read data tile for C[v,1:n]
    A[u,1:n]+=B[1:n,u]+C[v,1:n]
  ENDDO v
  write data tile for A[u,1:n]
ENDDO u
```

(C)

Figure 4: (A) An out-of-core loop nest. (B) Straightforward translation. (C) I/O optimized translation. (D)-(G) Different Tile Allocations.

dex should not appear in any other dimension for this array. In other words, after the transformation, the LHS array C should be of the form $C(*, *, ..., j_n, ..., *, *)$ where j_n (the new innermost loop index) is in the rth dimension and $*$ indicates a term independent of j_n. This means that the rth row of the transformed reference matrix for C is $(0, 0, ..., 0, 1)$ and all entries of the last column, except the one in r^{th} row, are zero. After that process the LHS array can be stored on disk such that the rth dimension will be the fastest changing dimension. This exploits the spatial locality on disk, for this reference.

- Then the algorithm works on one reference from the RHS at a time. If a row s in the data reference matrix is identical to r^{th} row of the original reference matrix of the LHS array, then this RHS array is considered to be stored on disk such that the sth dimension will be the fastest changing dimension.[1]

- If the condition above does not hold for a RHS array A, in that case the algorithm attempts to transform the reference to $A(*, *, ..., \mathcal{F}(j_{n-1}), ..., *, *)$ where $\mathcal{F}(j_{n-1})$ is an affine function of j_{n-1} and other indices except j_n, and $*$ indicates a term independent of both j_{n-1} and j_n. This helps to exploit the spatial locality at the second innermost loop. If no such transformation is possible, the j_{n-2} is tried and so on. If all loop indices are tried unsuccessfully, then the remaining entries of Q are determined considering the data dependences and non-singularity. A modified version of the completion algorithms presented by Li [7] can be used for this purpose.

---
[1] Note that having such a row s does not guarantee that the array will be stored on the disk such that the sth dimension will be the fastest changing dimension.

- After a transformation and corresponding disk layouts are found, the next alternative layout for the LHS is considered and so on. Among all feasible solutions, the best one is chosen. Although several approaches can be taken to select the best alternative, we found the following scheme both accurate and practical: Each loop in the nest is numbered with its level (depth), the outermost loop getting the number 1. Then, for each reference in the nest, the level number of the loop whose index sits in the fastest changing dimension for this reference is recorded. The number for all references in the nest are summed up, and the alternative with the maximum sum is chosen. As an example, if, for a two-deep nest with three references, an alternative exploits the locality for the first reference in the outer loop, and for the other references in the inner loop, the sum for this alternative is $1+2+2 = 5$.

- After choosing the best alternative, the following memory allocation scheme is applied: First, data tile size for each dimension of each array is set to S, a parameter whose value depends on the size of the available memory. For example, if a loop nest contains a one-dimensional array, two two-dimensional arrays and a three-dimensional array, the algorithm first allocates a tile of size S for the one-dimensional array, a tile of size $S \times S$ for each of the two-dimensional arrays, and a tile of size $S \times S \times S$ for the three-dimensional array. This allocation scheme implies the memory constraint $S^3 + 2S^2 + S \leq M$ where M is the size of the node memory. After that, the arrays are divided into groups according to disk layouts of the associated files (i.e. the arrays with the same disk layout are placed in the same group). The algorithm then handles the groups one by one. If a loop index appears in the fastest changing array dimension of the group, and does not appear in any other dimension of any reference in that group, the compiler increases the tile size in that dimension to full (local) array size for that reference. The memory constraint should be adjusted accordingly. Note that any inconsistency between the groups (due to a common loop index) should be resolved by not changing the original (initial) tile sizes.

The following points should be noted. First, the transformation matrix obtained by the above approach should be non-singular and must preserve the data dependence relations. Second, our algorithm considers all possible storage layouts, of which the row-major and column-major layouts are only two alternatives. Third, it should be noted that the algorithm first optimizes the LHS array as much as possible. This is important because of the fact that the data tiles for this array are both read and written.

The algorithm is shown in Figure 3. In the algorithm, C is the array reference on the LHS whereas A represents an array reference from RHS. The symbol $\times$ denotes the *don't care* condition.

4.1 Constraints

During the compilation of an out-of-core program either or both the following may be true: (a) the compiler does not have complete knowledge about the access pattern or storage layouts; (b) the compiler, due to data dependences or other constraints, is not able to change the access pattern or storage layout. Each unknown or unmodifiable information about access pattern or storage layouts constitutes a constraint for the compiler. The constraints mentioned can originate from different factors. For example, data dependence relations may render all but one (tiling) loop order illegal. The practical significance of this is that the compiler cannot change the loop order, but it can customize the disk layouts to optimize the locality. In another case, the storage layout of a specific array might not be set to a desired form, because the array has already been created on disk and changing the layout on disk would be too expensive.

We now focus on the problem of optimizing locality when some or all array layouts are fixed, as this case frequently occurs in practice. We note that each fixed layout requires that the innermost loop index should be in the appropriate array index position (dimension), depending on disk layout of the array. For example, suppose that the disk layout for a h-dimensional array is such that the dimension k_1 is the fastest changing dimension, the dimension k_2 is the second fastest changing dimension, k_3 is the third etc. The algorithm should first try to place the new innermost loop index j_n only to the $k_1{}^{th}$ dimension of this array. If this is not possible, then it should try to place j_n only to the $k_2{}^{th}$ dimension and so on. If all dimensions up to and including k_h are tried unsuccessfully, then j_{n-1} should be tried for the $k_1{}^{th}$ dimension and so on. As we will show later, this modified algorithm with the constrained layouts is very important for global I/O optimization.

4.2 Example

This section presents an example to show the working of the algorithm. Due to space concerns, we do not show the steps or the parts of the steps which lead to unsuccessful trials.

Consider the example shown in Figure 4:A. Figure 4:B presents a naive out-of-core translation for it. The tile allocations for this naive version are illustrated in Figure 4:D. The array reference matrices are as follows:

$$L^A = \begin{bmatrix} 1 & 0 & 0 & 0 \\ 0 & 1 & 0 & 0 \end{bmatrix}, L^B = \begin{bmatrix} 0 & 0 & 1 & 0 \\ 1 & 0 & 0 & 0 \end{bmatrix} \text{ and } L^C =$$

$$\begin{bmatrix} 0 & 0 & 0 & 1 \\ 0 & 0 & 1 & 0 \end{bmatrix}.$$ The algorithm works as follows:

$$L^A.Q = \begin{bmatrix} 0 & 0 & 0 & 1 \\ \delta & \delta & \delta & 0 \end{bmatrix}.$$ Therefore $q_{11} = q_{12} = q_{13} = q_{24} = 0$ and $q_{14} = 1$.

$$L^B.Q = \begin{bmatrix} \delta & \delta & \delta & 0 \\ 0 & 0 & 0 & 1 \end{bmatrix}.$$ Therefore $q_{34} = 0$.

$$L^C.Q = \begin{bmatrix} \delta & \delta & 1 & 0 \\ \delta & \delta & 0 & 0 \end{bmatrix}.$$ Therefore $q_{33} = q_{44} = 0$ and

$q_{43} = 1$. At this point $T^{-1} = Q = \begin{bmatrix} 0 & 0 & 0 & 1 \\ q_{21} & q_{22} & q_{23} & 0 \\ q_{31} & q_{32} & 0 & 0 \\ q_{41} & q_{42} & 1 & 0 \end{bmatrix}.$ We

set the unknowns to the following values: $q_{22} = q_{23} = q_{31} = q_{41} = q_{42} = 0$ and $q_{21} = q_{32} = 1$, and obtain $T^{-1} = Q = \begin{bmatrix} 0 & 0 & 0 & 1 \\ 1 & 0 & 0 & 0 \\ 0 & 1 & 0 & 0 \\ 0 & 0 & 1 & 0 \end{bmatrix}.$

The resulting code is as follows.

```
DO u = 1, n/p, S
  DO v = 1, n, S
    DO w = 1, n, n
      DO y = 1, n/p, n/p
        A[y,u]+=B[v,y]+C[w,v]
      ENDDO y
    ENDDO w
  ENDDO v
ENDDO u
```

Arrays A and C are column-major whereas the array B is row-major. By using our memory allocation scheme explained earlier, a tile of size $n/p \times S$ is allocated for A, of size $n \times S$ for C, and of size $S \times n/p$ for B. The final memory constraint is $2nS/p + nS \leq M$. Tile allocations are shown in Figure 4:E.

Next the algorithm considers the other alternative layout (row-major) for A.

$$L^A.Q = \begin{bmatrix} \delta & \delta & \delta & 0 \\ 0 & 0 & 0 & 1 \end{bmatrix}.$$ Therefore $q_{14} = q_{21} = q_{22} = q_{23} = 0$ and $q_{24} = 1$.

$$L^B.Q = \begin{bmatrix} \delta & \delta & 1 & 0 \\ \delta & \delta & 0 & 0 \end{bmatrix}.$$ Therefore $q_{13} = q_{34} = 0$ and $q_{33} = 1$.

$$L^C.Q = \begin{bmatrix} \delta & \delta & 0 & 0 \\ \delta & \delta & 1 & 0 \end{bmatrix}.$$ Therefore $q_{43} = q_{44} = 0$. At

this point $T^{-1} = Q = \begin{bmatrix} q_{11} & q_{12} & 0 & 0 \\ 0 & 0 & 0 & 1 \\ q_{31} & q_{32} & 1 & 0 \\ q_{41} & q_{42} & 0 & 0 \end{bmatrix}.$ By setting $q_{12} =$

$q_{31} = q_{32} = q_{41} = 0$ and $q_{11} = q_{42} = 1$, $T^{-1} = Q = \begin{bmatrix} 1 & 0 & 0 & 0 \\ 0 & 0 & 0 & 1 \\ 0 & 0 & 1 & 0 \\ 0 & 1 & 0 & 0 \end{bmatrix}.$

The resulting code is as follows.

```
DO u = 1, n/p, S
  DO v = 1, n, S
    DO w = 1, n ,n
      DO y = 1, n, n
        A[u,y]+=B[w,u]+C[v,w]
      ENDDO y
    ENDDO w
  ENDDO v
ENDDO u
```

Arrays A and C are row-major whereas the array B is column-major. Tiles of size $S \times n$ are allocated for A and C, and a tile of size $n \times S$ is allocated for B. The final memory constraint is $3 \times n \times S \leq M$. Tile allocations are shown in Figure 4:G. Notice that since tile sizes are equal to array sizes for some array dimensions, the loops w and y disappear and the optimized code given earlier in Figure 4:C is obtained. Also note that although we could have chosen one of these two alternatives as the best alternative by using our criterion based on loop levels as explained earlier, we have presented here the tile allocations for both the alternatives for illustrative purposes.

We now revisit example shown in Figure 4, this time assuming fixed row-major disk layouts for all arrays. Due to lack of space, we do not show the formulation; but after our constraint-based algorithm is run, the tiles of size $S \times S$ are allocated for B and C, and a tile of size $S \times n$ is allocated for A. The final memory constraint is $nS + 2S^2 \leq M$. Tile allocations for this constrained version are shown in Figure 4:F. Note that the two array references in this constrained version are not optimized due to fixed layout requirement. This is the main reason that the locality optimizations adopted by out-of-core compilers should take into account both disk layouts and loop transformations.

4.3 Analytical Approach

In this subsection, using an analytical model, we evaluate the effectiveness of the algorithm presented in this paper at reducing the number of I/O calls. In order to get a clear formulation, we assume that at most n elements can be accessed in a single I/O call, where n being the array size in one dimension and the loop upper bound. Let C_f, t_f and M be the startup cost[2] for a file read (write), cost of reading (writing) an element from (into) file, and size of available memory respectively. If we assume that I/O cost of reading (writing) l consecutive array elements from (into) file can be approximated by $C_f + l \times t_f$, then the total I/O cost of the naive out-of-core translation shown in Figure 4:B (*excluding write costs*) is

$$T_{overall} = \underbrace{\frac{n^2 C_f}{S} + n^2 t_f}_{T_A} + \underbrace{\frac{n^3 C_f}{S^2} + \frac{n^3 t_f}{S}}_{T_B} + \underbrace{\frac{n^4 C_f}{S^3} + \frac{n^4 t_f}{S^2}}_{T_C}$$

under the memory constraint $3S^2 \leq M$. The T_A, T_B and T_C represent the I/O costs for the arrays A, B and C respectively. The overall I/O cost of the I/O optimized version (Figure 4:C), on the other hand, is

$$T_{overall} = \underbrace{nC_f + n^2 t_f}_{T_A} + \underbrace{nC_f + n^2 t_f}_{T_B} + \underbrace{\frac{n^2 C_f}{S} + \frac{n^3 t_f}{S}}_{T_C}$$

under the memory constraint $3nS \leq M$. The overall I/O costs for the versions with fixed layouts are computed similarly. These formulae clearly show that, for reasonable values of M, our algorithm is very effective at reducing the number as well as the volume of disk accesses. We computed the number of I/O calls for different input sizes for the example in Figure 4. Figures 5:A and B illustrate the curves representing the number of I/O calls (coefficient of C_f) for $2K \times 2K$ and $4K \times 4K$ double arrays respectively on logarithmic scales. We consider four different versions: unoptimized (naive) version (Ori), optimized version assuming fixed column-major layout for all arrays (Col), optimized version assuming fixed

row-major layout for all arrays (Row), and the version that is optimized by our approach (Opt). It should be emphasized that the curves for the optimized versions are overestimates, because of the fact that we assume at most n elements can be read in a single I/O call. The effectiveness of our approach at reducing the number of I/O calls is clearly reflected on these curves. For example, for $4K \times 4K$ double arrays with a memory size of 10^3 elements, the number of I/O calls required for Ori, Col, Row and Opt versions are approximately 5×10^5, 2×10^5, 1.5×10^5 and 1.5×10^4 respectively.

4.4 Other Levels of Memory Hierarchy

Our algorithm is applicable to optimize the data traffic on memory-cache hierarchy as well. It is interesting to note that for some nests, the optimized loop order is the same for both caches and main memories. As an example, under column-major layouts for all arrays, for matrix-multiplication, our algorithm obtains a nest which is the same nest obtained by [7] and [8] for cache memories. The other optimized nest obtained by our algorithm for the matrix-multiplication is the same nest used in [6], for fixed row-major layouts. Since, even if the disk layouts are fixed, our approach considers all possible loop transformations; in the worst case it replicates the results based on the loop transformations alone to optimize the locality, if the temporal locality is not taken into account.

During the experiments it was observed that the I/O time constitutes at most 41% of the total execution time for our experimental suite. That is, in order to obtain the best performance in out-of-core computations both tiling loops and element loops should be optimized. After the disk layouts and the tiling loops are optimized by the algorithm presented in this paper, the element loops can be optimized by using the methods offered by McKinley *et al.* [8], Li [7] or Wolf and Lam [17].

5 Experimental Results

The experiments were performed by hand using PASSION [16], a run-time library for parallel I/O. PASSION routines can be called from C and Fortran, and different out-of-core arrays can be associated with different disk layouts. All the reported times are in seconds. The experiments were performed for different values of *slab ratio* (SR), the ratio of available node memory to the size of out-of-core local arrays combined. Notice that the SR is both an abstract variable and a good indicator of the behavior of the out-of-core programs under different memory constraints. Table 1 shows the I/O times of four different versions (Ori, Col, Row and Opt as explained above) of the example shown in Figure 4 on single nodes of IBM SP-2 and Intel Paragon. Figure 6 presents the normalized I/O times of these four versions with $4K \times 4K$ (128 MByte) double arrays on varying number of processors on SP-2. Figure 7 gives the speedups for Ori (original, unoptimized) and Opt versions.

We also applied our optimizations to a number of common kernels. The experiments were conducted on *four* nodes of SP-2 with $4K \times 4K$ two-dimensional and $4K$ one-dimensional double arrays, and the results are shown in Figure 8 as normalized I/O times. Figure 8:(A) gives the performance improvement obtained on a matrix-transpose loop that contains the statement $B(i,j) = A(j,i)$. Our algorithm assigns column-major layout for array A and row-major layout for array B. It then allocates a tile of size nS to A, and a tile of size Sn to B. The performance improvement on the innermost statement of the iterative-solver is given in Figure 8:(B). For this example, our heuristic associates column-major layout for all arrays. Figure 8:(C) shows the results of our optimizations on

---

[2] Startup cost can be thought as sum of the average values for seek time and rotational latency. Although the authors understand that a fixed startup cost is not very realistic; it is not clear, in their opinion, how a varying startup cost can be incorporated in a compilation framework.

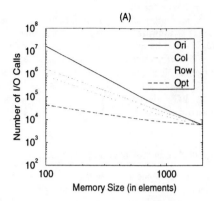
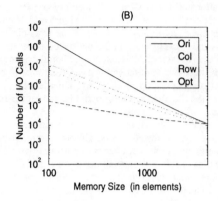

Figure 5: (A) Number of I/O calls for the example shown in Figure 4 for $2K \times 2K$ double arrays. (B) Number of I/O calls for the example shown in Figure 4 for $4K \times 4K$ double arrays.

Table 1: I/O times (in seconds) for the example shown in Figure 4 on SP-2 and Paragon.

| | IBM SP-2 | | | | | | | | Intel Paragon | | | | | | | |
| | $2K \times 2K$ arrays | | | | $4K \times 4K$ arrays | | | | $2K \times 2K$ arrays | | | | $4K \times 4K$ arrays | | | |
SR	Ori	Col	Row	Opt	Ori	Col	Row	Opt	Ori	Col	Row	Opt	Ori	Col	Row	Opt
1/4	152	138	131	77	363	311	281	199	1159	1050	988	208	5172	4431	4001	1273
1/16	623	577	524	105	1441	1108	1074	441	2320	2141	1951	252	7360	5668	5412	1344
1/64	4224	3111	2462	563	8384	6449	5912	1422	19201	14141	11760	576	28864	22002	20257	2304
1/256	25087	21627	19298	1566	48880	35759	30055	4584	99583	83848	76245	3028	192512	141370	117270	8193

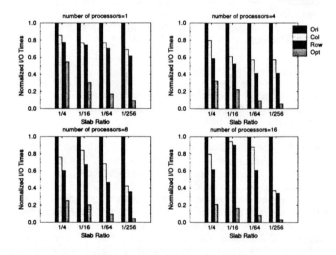

Figure 6: Normalized I/O times for our example with $4K \times 4K$ (128 MByte) double arrays on SP-2.

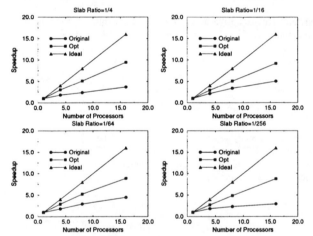

Figure 7: Speedups for unoptimized and optimized versions of our example with $4K \times 4K$ double arrays on SP-2.

matrix-smoothening (four-point relaxation) nest. Our algorithm associates row-major layout for all arrays. Finally Figure 8:(D) illustrate the performance improvement on matrix-vector multiplication (Y=AX). It is interesting to note that in this example all layout combinations are equally good as far as the I/O cost is concerned. Going with column-major layout for all arrays, our compiler allocates a data tile of size nS for A, a tile of size n for Y, and a tile of size S for X. From these results we conclude the following:

1. For all examples the Opt (I/O optimized) version performs much better than the Ori (naive) version. The reason for this result is that in the Opt version, array accesses are optimized as much as possible. For example as shown in Figure 4:G, by using the I/O optimization technique presented in this paper all three array accesses are optimized.

2. When the slab ratio is decreased, the effectiveness of our approach (Opt) increases (see Figure 6). As the amount of node memory is reduced, the Ori performs many number of small I/O requests, and that in turn degrades the performance significantly. The Opt version, on the other hand, continues with the optimized I/O no matter how small the node memory is.

3. As shown in Figure 7, the Opt version also scales better than the Ori (original, unoptimized) for all slab ratios.

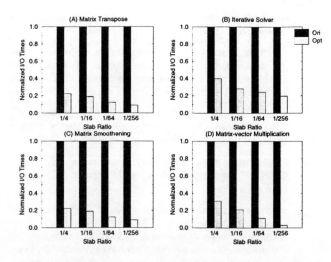

Figure 8: Normalized I/O times for different nests. (A) Matrix transpose. (B) Iterative solver. (C) Matrix smoothening. (D) Matrix-vector multiplication.

4. When the slab ratio is very small, the optimized versions with fixed layouts for all files also perform much better than the Ori (see Figure 6).

5. Experiments on two different platforms (Paragon and SP-2) with varying compile-time/run-time parameters such as available node memory, array sizes, number of processors etc., demonstrate that our algorithm is quite robust.

6   Global I/O Optimization

In this section, we show how our algorithm can be extended to work on multiple nests. Notice that a single loop nest with multiple LHSs (i.e. multiple statements) can be handled in a similar manner if we think the nest as distributed [18] over the individual statements.

Since a number of arrays can be accessed by a number of nests and these nests may require different layouts for a specific out-of-core array, the algorithm should find a layout for that array that satisfies the majority of the nests. In the following we present sketch of a simple heuristic. Our approach is based on the concept of *most costly nest*, the nest which takes the most I/O time. The programmer can use *compiler directives* to give hints about this nest, or we can use a metric such as multiplication of the number of loops and the number of arrays referenced in the nest. The nest which has the largest resulting value can be marked as the most costly nest. Then the algorithm proceeds as follows. First, the most costly nest is fully optimized by using the algorithm presented in this paper. After this step, disk layouts for some of the arrays will be determined. Then each of the remaining nests can be optimized using the approach presented for the constrained layout case in Section 4.1. After each nest is optimized, new layout constraints will be obtained, and these will be propagated for optimization of the next nest.

Figure 9 shows an algorithm for global I/O optimization. The functions Unconstrained() and Constrained() implement the algorithms for the unconstrained and constrained layout cases respectively. constraints refers to a set that holds the array layout constraints and updated after each nest is processed. Before the main loop, estimated cost of each nest i is computed using a metric and the nests are sorted according to non-increasing values of Cost(i) into Nest_List (e.g. Nest_List(1) is more costly than Nest_List(2) etc.). Then the most

```
for (each loop nest i) compute Cost(i);
endfor;
sort nests according to non-increasing values
   of Cost(i) into Nest_List;
Unconstrained(Nest_List(1),&new_constraints);
constraints = new_constraints;
while (there is a nest in the Nest_List)
   Current_Nest = next nest in the Nest_List;
   Constrained(Current_Nest,constraints,
               &new_constraints);
   constraints = constraints ∪ new_constraints;
endwhile;
```

Figure 9: A global I/O optimization algorithm

costly nest Nest_List(1) is optimized using Unconstrained() whereas the others are optimized inside the while loop using Constrained(). Notice that besides returning new_constraints both Unconstrained() and Constrained() also compute the loop transformation for each nest (not shown for clarity).

We note that the global I/O optimization problem is very similar to the problem of determining the appropriate data decomposition across the processors for multiple nests [9]. We are currently investigating whether or not the techniques developed for the data decomposition problem can be applied for the disk layout optimization for multiple nests.

7   Related Work

Iteration space tiling has been used for optimizing the cache locality in several papers [7, 17]. McKinley *et al.* [8] proposes an optimization technique consisting of loop permutation, loop fusion and loop distribution. They do decide individual file layouts but assume a column-major storage for all arrays. The assumption of a fixed layout strategy prevents some array references getting optimized as shown earlier in this paper, and that in turn may cause a substantial performance loss. But as indicated earlier, after our approach is applied, we strongly recommend the use of an in-core locality optimization technique for data tiles in memory.

In [3], a unified approach to locality optimization which employs both control and data transformations is presented for in-core problems in distributed shared-memory machines. This model can be adapted to out-of-core computations as well. But we believe our approach is better than that of [3] because of the following reasons: (1) The approach given in [3] depends on a *stride vector* whose value should be guessed by the compiler beforehand; our approach does not have such a requirement; (2) Our approach is more accurate, as it does not restrict the search space of possible loop transformations whereas the approach in [3] does; (and) (3) Our extension to multiple nests (global optimization) is also simpler than the one offered by [3] for global optimization, because we use the same algorithm for each nest. In the future, we intend to implement the algorithm in [3], enhance it by a suitable memory allocation scheme for out-of-core computations and compare it with our approach on different programs.

Another compiler-directed optimization, prefetching, is used by [10] for caches and by [11] for main memories. We believe that the compiler-directed prefetch is complimentary to our work in the sense that once the I/O time is reduced by our optimization, the remaining I/O time can be hidden by prefetching.

There has been a few papers on out-of-core compilation. The approaches can be divided into two groups: The first group considers optimizing the performance of virtual memory (VM). The most notable work is from Abu-Sufah *et al.* [1], which deals with optimizations to enhance the locality properties of programs in a VM environment. Among the program transformations used are loop fusion, loop distribution and tiling (page indexing). In principle, our disk layout determination scheme can be applied for optimizing the performance of the VM as well (by changing tile sizes to take the page size into account). But we believe that the impact of the I/O optimizations based on VM will be limited compared to those based on explicit file I/O due to the following reasons.

1. The fixed page sizes present a problem. Even if the computation requires a small portion of a data tile, a full page containing the data is brought into memory. Or, conversely, even if there is enough bandwidth for fetching a number of pages, the VMs generally bring one or two pages after every page fault, wasting the bandwidth.

2. The performance of the VM depends mostly on the page replacement policy of the operating system, which in turn, is out of control of the compiler. In particular, even if a chunk of data will not be used any more, the replacement policy can keep that chunk in memory for a long time [11].

In [4], the functionality of a ViC*, a compiler-like preprocessor for out-of-core C* is described. Several compiler methods for out-of-core HPF programs are presented in [15] and [2]. In [12], compiler techniques to choreograph I/O for applications based on high-level programmer annotations are investigated. The techniques in [15] and [12] are specifically designed for parallel machines whereas our approach can also be used on uniprocessors. To our knowledge, non of the previous work on out-of-core computations considers the compiler-directed disk layout transformations.

8 Summary and Conclusions

The difficulty of efficiently handling out-of-core data limits the performance of supercomputers as well as the enormous potential of parallel machines. Since coding out-of-core version of a problem might be a very onerous task and virtual memory does not perform well in scientific programs, we believe that there is a need for compiler-directed explicit I/O approach for parallel architectures. Unfortunately, fixed layout strategies adopted by current popular compilers prevent the potential spatial locality on disks from being exploited.

In this paper we presented a compiler algorithm to optimize the locality on disks by changing the access pattern and disk layouts. Our technique can easily be employed as a part of an out-of-core compilation framework like [4], [12] or [15]. An important characteristic of the approach is that it also optimizes the nests with arrays whose layouts are constrained. We show that this is important for global I/O optimization as well. An area of future work is integrating this technique with the techniques designed to eliminate I/O costs originating from communication requirements of out-of-core parallel programs [2]. We also intend to employ the algorithm presented in this paper in in-core compilers, and investigate its effectiveness at determining memory layouts and in improving cache performance.

References

[1] W. Abu-Sufah. On the Performance Enhancement of Paging Systems Through Program Analysis and Transformations, *IEEE Transactions on Computers*, C-30(5):341–355, 1981.

[2] R. Bordawekar, A. Choudhary and J. Ramanujam. Compilation and Communication Strategies for Out-of-core programs on Distributed Memory Machines. In *Journal of Parallel and Distributed Computing*, 38(2):277-288, Nov. 1996.

[3] M. Cierniak and W. Li. Unifying Data and Control Transformations for Distributed Shared Memory Machines. Technical Report 542, Dept. of Computer Science, University of Rochester, NY, Nov. 1994.

[4] T. H. Cormen and A. Colvin. ViC*: A Preprocessor for Virtual-Memory C*. Dartmouth College Computer Science Technical Report PCS-TR94-243, Nov. 1994.

[5] J. del Rosario and A. Choudhary. High Performance I/O for Parallel Computers: Problems and Prospects. *IEEE Computer*, Mar. 1994.

[6] M. S. Lam, E. Rothberg and M. E. Wolf. The Cache Performance and Optimizations of Blocked Algorithms. In *Proc. Fourth International Conference on Architectural Support for Programming Languages and Operating Systems*, Apr. 1991.

[7] W. Li. Compiling for NUMA Parallel Machines, Ph.D. Thesis, Cornell University, Ithaca, NY, 1993.

[8] K. McKinley, S. Carr, and C.W. Tseng. Improving Data Locality with Loop Transformations. *ACM Transactions on Programming Languages and Systems*, 1996.

[9] U. Kremer. Automatic Data Layout for Distributed Memory Machines. Ph.D. thesis, Technical Report CRPC-TR95559-S, Center for Research on Parallel Computation, Oct. 1995.

[10] T. C. Mowry, M. S. Lam and A. Gupta. Design and Evaluation of a Compiler Algorithm for Prefetching. In *Proc. Fifth International Conference on Architectural Support for Programming Languages and Operating Systems*, Oct. 1992.

[11] T. C. Mowry, A. K. Demke and O. Krieger. Automatic Compiler-Inserted I/O Prefetching for Out-of-Core Applications. *Proc. Second Symposium on Operating Systems Design and Implementations*, Seattle, WA, Oct. 1996.

[12] M. Paleczny, K. Kennedy and C. Koelbel. Compiler Support for Out-of-Core Arrays on Parallel Machines. CRPC Technical Report 94509-S, Rice University, Houston, TX, Dec. 1994.

[13] J. Ramanujam. Non-unimodular transformations of nested loops. In *Proc. Supercomputing 92*, pp. 214–223.

[14] J. Ramanujam and A. Narayan. Automatic data mapping and program transformations. In *Proc. Workshop on Automatic Data Layout & Performance Prediction*, Apr. 1995.

[15] R. Thakur, R. Bordawekar and A. Choudhary. Compiler and Run-time Support for Out-of-Core HPF Programs. In *Proc. 1994 ACM International Conference on Supercomputing*, pp. 382–391, Manchester, UK, Jul. 1994.

[16] R. Thakur, A. Choudhary, R. Bordawekar, S. More and K. Sivaramkrishna. PASSIONate Approach to High-Performance Parallel I/O, In *IEEE Computer*, Jun. 1996.

[17] M. Wolf and M. Lam. A Data Locality Optimizing Algorithm. In *Proc. ACM SIGPLAN 91 Conf. Programming Language Design and Implementation*, pp. 30–44, Jun. 1991.

[18] M. Wolfe. High Performance Compilers for Parallel Computing. Addison-Wesley, 1996.

A Framework for Parallel Tree-Based Scientific Simulations

Pangfeng Liu

Department of Computer Science
National Chung Cheng University
Chia-yi, Taiwan 62107

Jan-Jan Wu

Institute of Information Science
Academia Sinica
Taipei, Taiwan 11529

Abstract

Abstract

This paper describes an implementation of a platform-independent parallel C++ N-body framework that can support various scientific simulations that involve tree structures, such as astrophysics, semiconductor device simulation, molecular dynamics, plasma physics, and fluid mechanics. Within the framework the users will be able to concentrate on the computation kernels that differentiate different N-body problems, and let the framework take care of the tedious and error-prone details that are common among N-body applications. This framework was developed based on the techniques we learned from previous CM-5 C implementations, which have been rigorously justified both experimentally and mathematically. This gives us confidence that our framework will allow fast prototyping of different N-body applications, to run on different parallel platforms, and to deliver good performance as well.

1 Introduction

1.1 *N*-body problem and tree codes

Computational methods to track the motions of bodies which interact with one another have been the subject of extensive research for centuries. So-called "*N*-body" methods have been applied to problems in astrophysics, semiconductor device simulation, molecular dynamics, plasma physics, and fluid mechanics.

The problem can be simply stated as follows. Given the initial states of N bodies, compute their interactions according to the underlining physic laws, usually described by a partial differential equation, and derive their final states at time T. The common and simplest approach is to iterate over a sequence of small time steps. Within each time step the change of state on a single body can be directly computed by summing the effects induced by each of the other $N-1$ bodies. While this method is conceptually simple, vectorizes well, and is the algorithm of choice for small prob-

lems, its $O(N^2)$ arithmetic complexity rules it out for large-scale simulations involving millions of particles.

Beginning with Appel [1] and Barnes and Hut [2], there has been a flurry of interest in faster algorithms. Greengard and Rokhlin [5] developed the fast multipole method with $O(N)$ arithmetic complexity under uniform particle distribution. Sundaram [15] subsequently extended this method to allow different bodies to be updated at different rates. Thus far, however, because of the complexity and overheads in the fully adaptive three dimensional multipole method, the algorithm of Barnes and Hut continues to enjoy application in astrophysical simulations. Parallel implementations of Barnes-Hut's algorithms are described in [12, 13, 14, 16, 17], and parallel fast multipole implementations include [6, 7, 11, 13].

All these N-body algorithms explore the idea that the effect of a cluster of particles at a distant point can be approximated by a small number of initial terms of an appropriate power-series. The Barnes-Hut algorithm uses a single-term, center-of-mass approximation. To apply the approximation effectively, these so called "tree codes" organize the bodies into a hierarchy tree in which a particle can easily find the appropriate clusters for approximation purpose. We will describe this tree structure in details later in the discussion of Barnes and Hut's algorithm, which our implementation is based upon.

1.2 *N*-body framework

Most of the N-body tree codes use similar tree structures and exhibit similar computation patterns. There are two levels of similarity. First, a fluid mechanics code and a molecular dynamics code may differ only in the interaction rules. The tree structures are basically the same except for the data stored in tree nodes and the implementation-dependent tree representation. Secondly, different N-body tree algorithms may use the same data structure. For example, fast multipole method and Barnes-Hut's algorithm use the same oct-tree structure – they differ only in how they manipulate the trees. Therefore, a general N-body framework helps in developing tree codes for different N-body domains, and in implementing different N-body algorithms as well.

Unfortunately, all the previous N-body implementations did not consider reusability and portability – they do not separate the generic data structure from the application-dependent computation kernel, and they are built for one N-body problem on one particular machine. Therefore, it will take considerable efforts to convert an astrophysics simulation code running on one machine into a fluid dynamic code running on another, even though many aspects of the codes are similar. One must reorganize the code to salvage any reusable parts manually, and piece together these fragments to form a new program which the new computation kernel will hopefully fit into. This "cut-and-paste" human intervention is time consuming and error-prone.

In addition, parallel machines are notoriously difficult to program. One must "think in parallel" to write programs that not only compute the results correctly, but also schedule all the processors properly to avoid racing, even deadlock conditions. As a result, parallel programming often involves many intricate and error-prone details. Therefore, users should reuse existing working codes whenever possible. In the context of N-body computation, we should abstract out the common ingredients of tree codes so that they can be reused in different N-body problems.

The goal of this project is to develop a general N-body framework that eases the difficult task of writing efficient parallel N-body codes. The framework was developed based on our previous CM-5 implementations [3, 4, 10], in which we developed sound techniques that have been carefully studied both experimentally [9] and mathematically [8]. We expect that these proven techniques will guide us towards the ultimate goal of writing efficient parallel N-body programs with ease.

The remainder of this paper is organized as follows. Section 2 explains the Barnes and Hut's algorithm. Section 3 briefly describes our previous parallel N-body astrophysics code implemented on Connection Machine CM-5 using Barnes and Hut's algorithm, Section 4 describes the class hierarchy in our C++ N-body framework, and Section 6 concludes.

2   The Barnes-Hut algorithm

We will focus on the Barnes-Hut algorithm as an example of N-body tree code. The Barnes-Hut algorithm proceeds by first computing an oct-tree partition of the three-dimensional box (region of space)

enclosing the set of particles. The partition is computed recursively by dividing the original box into eight octants of equal volume until each undivided box contains exactly one particle[1]. An example of such a recursive partition in two dimensions and the corresponding BH-tree are shown in Figure 1. Note that each internal node of the BH-tree represents a cluster. Once the BH-tree has been built, the mass and the location of the centers-of-mass of the internal nodes are computed in one phase up the tree, starting at the leaves.

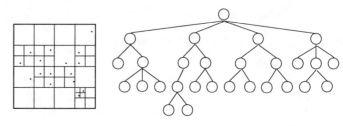

Figure 1: BH tree decomposition

To compute accelerations, we loop over the set of particles observing the following rules. Each particle starts at the root of the BH-tree, and traverses down the tree trying to find clusters that it can apply center-of-mass approximation. If the distance between the particle and the cluster is far enough, with respect to the radius of the cluster, then the acceleration due to that cluster is approximated by a single interaction between the particle and a point mass located at the center-of-mass of the cluster. Otherwise the particle visits each of the children of the cluster. Formally, if the distance between a particle and a cluster is more than RADIUS(cluster)$/\theta$, then we will approximate the effect of that cluster as a point mass. We can adjust the value of θ to balance the approximation error and the execution time. Note that nodes visited in the traversal form a sub-tree of the entire BH-tree and different particles will, in general, traverse different sub-trees. The leaves of the subtree traversed by a particle will be called *essential data* for the particle because it needs these nodes for interaction computation.

Once the accelerations on all the particles are known, the new positions and velocities can be computed. The entire process, starting with the construction of the BH-tree, is now repeated for the desired number of time steps.

---

[1]In practice it is more efficient to truncate each branch when the number of particles in its subtree decreases below a certain fixed bound

3 Parallel Implementation

In the following subsections, we point out the differences between our parallel implementations [3, 4, 9, 10] and the generic sequential Barnes-Hut algorithm.

3.1 Data partitioning

The default strategy that we use to distribute bodies among processors is *orthogonal recursive bisection* (ORB). The space bounding all the bodies is recursively partitioned into as many boxes as there are processors, and all bodies within a box are assigned to one processor. Each separator divides the workload within the region equally. The ORB decomposition can be represented by a binary tree, which is stored in every processor. The ORB tree is used as a map which locates points in space to processors.

We chose ORB decomposition for several reasons. First, it provides a simple way to decompose space among processors, and a way to quickly map points in space to processors. Secondly, ORB preserves data locality reasonably well and permits simple load-balancing. Thus, while it is expensive to recompute the ORB at each time step [13], the cost of incremental load-balancing is negligible from our experience [9].

3.2 Building the BH-tree in parallel

We chose to construct a representation of a distributed global BH-tree because we wanted to investigate abstractions that allow the programmer to use a global data structure without having to worry about the details of distributed-memory implementation. For this reason we separated the construction of the tree from the details of later stages of the algorithm. This has proven to be extremely helpful in our framework implementation.

We construct the BH tree as follows. Each processor first builds a local BH-tree for the bodies within its domain. At the end of this stage, the local trees will not, in general, be structurally coherent. The next step is to make the local trees structurally coherent with the global BH-tree by adjusting the levels of all leaves which are split by ORB bisectors. A similar process was developed independently in [13].

Once level-adjustment is complete, each processor computes the centers-of-mass on its local tree without any communication. Next, each processor sends its contribution to an internal node to the owner of the node, defined as the processor whose domain contains the center of the internal node. Once the transmitted data have been combined by the receiving processors, the construction of the global BH-tree is complete.

3.3 Collecting essential data

Once the global BH-tree has been constructed it is possible to start calculating accelerations. The naive strategy of traversing the tree, and transmitting data-on-demand, has several drawbacks: (1) it involves two-way communication, (2) the messages are fine-grain so that either the communication overhead is prohibitive or the programming complexity goes up, and (3) processors can spend substantial time requesting data for BH-nodes that do not exist.

It is significantly easier and faster for a processor to first collect all the essential data for its local particles, then compute the interactions the same way as in the sequential Barnes-Hut method since all the essential data are now available. In other words, the owner of a data must determine where its data might be essential, and send the data there. Formally, for every BH-node α, the owner of α computes an annular region called *influence ring* for α such that those particles α is essential to must reside within α's influence ring. Those particles that are not within the influence ring are either too close to u to apply center-of-mass approximation, or far away enough to use u's parent's information. With the ORB map it is straightforward to locate the destination processors to which α might be essential. Once all processors have received and inserted the essential data into the local trees, all the essential data are available.

3.4 Communication

The communication phases can all be abstracted as an "all-to-some" problem, in which each processor sends a set of personalized messages to dynamically determined destination processors. Therefore, the communication pattern is irregular and dynamically changing.

We used a randomized protocol to solve the all-to-some communication problem. The protocol alternates sends with receives to avoid exhausting communication channels reserved for messages that are sent but not yet received, and randomly permutes the destination so that any processor will not be flooded by incoming messages at any given time. In an earlier paper [8] we developed the atomic message model to investigate message passing efficiency. Consistent with the theory, we find that sending messages in random order worked best.

Figure 2 gives a high-level description of the parallel implementation structure. Note that the local trees are built only at the start of the first time step.

4 N-body Framework

We divide the C++ *N*-body framework into three layers: *generic tree layer*, *Barnes-Hut tree layer*, and *application layer*. Each latter layer is built on top of the former layer. The *generic tree layer* supports

```
Build local BH trees.

For every time step do:
    1. Construct the BH-tree representation
        (a) Adjust node levels
        (b) Compute partial node values on local trees
        (c) Combine partial node values at owning processors
    2. Owners send essential data
    3. Calculate accelerations
    4. Update velocities and positions of bodies
    5. Update local BH-trees incrementally
    6. If the workload is not balanced update the ORB
       incrementally
```

Figure 2: Outline of code structure

simple tree construction and manipulation methods. System programmers can build special libraries using classes in the *generic tree layer*. For example, we have built a *Barnes-Hut Tree layer* using the *generic tree layer* (Sec 4.2). The application programmer can write application programs using classes in the *Barnes-Hut tree layer*, or any other special library developed from the *generic tree layer*. We will demonstrate these usage by writing a gravitational *N*-body code (Sec 4.3). Figure 3 illustrates the class hierarchy in these three layers.

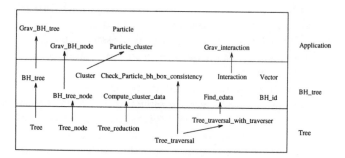

Figure 3: The class hierarchy in *generic tree*, *Barnes-hut tree*, and *application* layers.

4.1 Generic tree layer

The *generic tree layer* is the foundation of our framework from which complex tree structures can be derived. The class Tree serves as a container class in which every tree node has a pointer to a data of the given data type. The desired data type is given as a template parameter, along with the maximum number of children one tree node can have.

We define basic tree manipulation methods in the generic tree layer, including inserting a new child from a leaf, deleting an existing leaf, performing tree reduction and traversal. We keep the interface simple by restricting all the deletion/insertion to the leaves and

let the Tree class user take care of more sophisticated and specific tree structure updating.

```
template <class Data, const int n_children>
class Tree_node {
protected:
    Data *data;
    Tree_node *children[n_children];
};
template <class Data, class Tree_node, class Tree,
          const int n_children>
class Tree_reduction {
public:
    virtual void init(Data*) = 0;
    virtual void combine(Data *parent, Data* child) = 0;
    void reduction(Tree* tree);
};
template <class Data, class Tree_node, class Tree,
          const int n_children, class Node_id>
class Tree_traversal {
public:
    virtual bool process(Data*) = 0;
    void traverse(Tree *tree);
};
template <class Data, class Tree_node, class Tree,
          class Traverser>
class Tree_traversal_with_traverser :
public Tree_traversal<Data,Tree_node,Tree,N_CHILD,BH_id>
{
protected:
    Traverser *traverser;        // who is traversing?
};
```

Figure 4: Generic tree and reduction/traversal classes.

We have also implemented two tree operations – *reduction* and *traversal*, as special classes. Objects instantiated from the reduction class compute the data of a tree node according to the data of its children, e.g. computing the center of mass in Barnes-Hut's algorithm. Objects instantiated from the traversal class walk over the tree nodes and perform a user-defined operation (denoted as *per node function*) on each tree node (Figure 4). We implement these two tree operations as separate classes instead of methods in the Tree class mainly because they require their own data (not shown in Figure 4 for clarity) to function. For example, both operations maintain their current locations in the tree for easy access to tree nodes. In addition, we implement the class Tree_traversal_with_traverser, a traversing class in which we have to specify who is traversing the tree, as a subclass of Tree_traversal. For example, a particle will use Tree_traversal_with_traverser to collect its essentail data because we need the position of the particle to determine the distance, and we need only Tree_traversal to reset the tree node data.

We implemented the tree reduction/traversal operations in an application-independent manner. Both operations are implemented as class templates so that users can supply tree and tree node types for customized tree reduction/traversal operations. For tree reduction, users are required to provide two functions: `init(Data*)` and `combine(Data *parent, Data* child)`, which tell `reduction` class how to initialize and combine the data in tree nodes, respectively. The class `Data` is the data type stored in each node of the tree on which the reduction operation is to be performed. For tree traversal, users are required to provide the per node function `bool process(Data*)` that is to be performed on every tree node. The boolean return value indicates whether the traversal should continue further down the tree. By separating the application code from the tree reduction/traversal classes, these operations become application independent.

4.2 Barnes-Hut tree

On top of *generic tree* layer we build a layer called `BH_tree`. This layer supports tree operations required in most of the N-body tree algorithms – it supports tree operations common to both BH algorithm and fast multipole method, and all the special operations used in the Barnes-Hut method.

By extending the `Tree` class, each tree node in `BH_tree` contains a data cluster, and the data cluster of each leaf node contains a list of bodies[2]. The types of the particle and cluster are given by the user of the `BH_tree` class as template parameters `AppCluster` and `AppBody`. This abstraction captures the structure of a BH tree without any application specific details.

```
template<class AppBody>
class Cluster {
protected: Link_list<AppBody*> body_list;
public:  void add(AppBody* b);
};
template<class AppCluster, class AppBody>
class BH_tree : public Tree<AppCluster, N_CHILD> {
 public:
  void insert_body(AppBody*);
  void remove_body(AppBody*, Tree_node<AppCluster, N_CHILD>*);
};
template<class AppCluster, class AppBody, class Tree_node,
       class Tree, const int n_children>
class Compute_cluster_data: public
       Tree_reduction<AppCluster, Tree_node, Tree, n_children>{
public:
  void init(AppCluster* cluster) {
    cluster->reset_data();
    if (cluster->get_type() == Leaf)
      for (every body in cluster's body_list)
        cluster->add_body(body); }
  void combine(AppCluster* parent, AppCluster* child)
    {parent->add_cluster(child);}
};
```

Figure 5: BH tree layer classes.

The `BH_tree` class also supports several operations: computing cluster data, finding essential data, computing interaction, and checking particle and BH box for consistency. Most of these methods can be reused in implementing the fast multipole method.

---

[2]Recall that each leaf may have more than one particle.

Cluster data computation is implemented as a tree reduction (Figure 5). `init(AppCluster* cluster)` resets the data in the cluster and if the cluster is a leaf, it combines the data of the bodies from the body list into the data of the cluster. The other function `combine(AppCluster* parent, AppCluster* child)` adds children's data to parent's. By defining the actual computation as a method of the cluster, the reduction class is independent of the way how the data are combined in the application.

The essential data finding class `Find_edata` inherits `Tree_traversal_with_traverser` with two additional lists for essential clusters and bodies (Figure 6). The *traverser* is the particle that collects essential data. The per node function `process(AppCluster*)` inserts the clusters that can be approximated into `essential_clusters` list, and adds the bodies from leaf clusters that cannot be approximated into `essential_bodies` list. The traversal continues only when traverser cannot apply approximation on an internal cluster.

```
template<class AppCluster, class AppBody, class Tree_node,
       class Tree>
class Find_edata: public Tree_traversal_with_traverser
               <AppCluster,Tree_node,Tree,AppBody> {
  Link_list<AppBody*> essential_bodies;
  Link_list<AppCluster*> essential_clusters;
public:
  bool process(AppCluster* c) {
    if (c->is_edata_for(traverser)) {
      essential_clusters.insert(c); return(0);
    } else if (c->get_type() == Leaf) {
      for (every body in c's body list)
        if (body != traverser)
          essential_bodies.insert(body);
      return(0);
    } return(1);  }
};
template<class AppBody, class AppCluster, class Result>
class Interaction {
  AppBody *subject;
  Link_list<AppBody*>* body_list;
  Link_list<AppCluster*>* cluster_list;
  Result result;
public:
  void compute() {
    result.reset();
    for (every body in body_list)
      result += body_body_interaction(subject, body);
    for (every cluster cluster_list)
      result += body_cluster_interaction(subject,cluster);}
  virtual Result body_body_interaction(AppBody*,AppBody*)=0;
  virtual Result body_cluster_interaction(AppBody*,
                               AppCluster*)=0;
};
```

Figure 6: Class for finding essential data and interaction computation.

After collecting the essential clusters and bodies, a body can start computing the interactions. We implemented the interaction computation in an application-independent manner. The computation class `Interaction` (Figure 6) goes through the essential data list[3] and calls for functions to compute body-to-body and body-to-cluster interactions defined by the user of `Interaction`.

After bodies are moved to their new positions, they may not be in their original BH boxes. Therefore, the tree structure must be modified so that it becomes consistent with the new particle positions again. We implemented this as a tree traversal class `Check_particle_bh_box_consistency`, which collects bodies that wandered off their BH boxes, followed be a series of insertion/deletion tree operations. This function is universally useful for all tree code because the dynamic tree structure is expensive to rebuild, and relatively cheap to patch up.

4.3 Application Layer

The gravitational N-body application is built upon the `BH_tree` layer. First we construct a class `Particle` for bodies that attract one another by gravity, then we build the cluster type `Particle_cluster` from `Particle` (Figure 7). Next, in the `Particle_cluster` class we define the methods for computing/combining center of mass and the methods for testing essential data.

```
class Particle {
protected:
  Real mass;
  Vector position;
  Vector velocity;
};
class Particle_cluster: public Cluster<Particle> {
protected:
  Center_of_mass center_of_mass;
public:
  void reset_data();   // center of mass computation
  void add_body(Particle *p);
  void add_cluster(Particle_cluster* child);
  bool is_edata_for(Particle*);   // find essential data
};
class Grav_interaction:
public Interaction<Particle, Particle_cluster, Vector> {
public:
  Vector body_body_interaction(Particle*, Particle*);
  Vector body_cluster_interact(Particle*,Particle_cluster*);
};
typedef Tree_node<Particle_cluster, N_CHILD> Grav_BH_node;
typedef BH_tree<Particle_cluster, Particle> Grav_BH_tree;
```

Figure 7: Classes for a gravitational N-body application.

Then, in class `Grav_interaction`, which is derived from the class template `Interaction`, we define methods to compute gravitational interactions. We specify the gravitation interaction rules in the definition of `body_body_interaction` and `body_cluster_interaction`.

Finally, we define the BH-tree type `Grav_BH_tree` and tree node type `Grav_BH_node`. These two data

---

[3]Lists obtained from the class `Find_Edata`.

types serve as template parameters to instantiate BH-tree related operations, like `Compute_cluster_data`, `Find_edata`, and `Check_particle_bh_box_consistency`.

4.4 Parallel implementation

Using only the class libraries provided in the three layers described in previous subsections, we could model N-body simulations on uniprocessors. For parallel execution of programs, we require additional abstractions for parallelism.

In our current implementation, we assume SPMD (single program multiple data) model for parallel computation. Under this model, we would require abstractions for data mapping and interprocessor communication. We have designed two groups of classes for this purpose – `Mapper` classes that are responsible for defining the geometry of the tree structure, and `Communicator` classes that provide all-to-some communications that are common in N-body simulations.

Mapper classes

The `Mapper` classes define the geometry of data structures (e.g. BH trees in N-body simulations). Over the course of a simulation, `Mapper` objects are created during the construction of data structure objects (e.g. BH tree objects). When created, a `Mapper` object invokes the data partitioning function specified by the user or performs default behavior when no partitioning strategy is specified, it then gathers and caches geometry information from the partitioning function. In later stage of a simulation, the `Mappers` mediate object operations that require interprocessor communication.

In our previous parallel C implementation, we constructed a ORB partitioner and two associated geometry resolution functions: `data_to_processor` (that translates a data coordinate to a processor domain) and `dataset_to_processors` (that translates a rectangular box, which contains multiple data, to a set of processor domains). In addition, we defined a simple data structure `MappingTable` to store the ORB map. These data and methods have been integrated into the `Mapper` classes in our parallel framework. As part of this research effort, we are also extending the `Mapper` class to incorporate a number of commonly used partitioning strategies and user-defined mapping methods.

```
template <class Data, class DataSet, class ProcessorDomain,
          class MappingTable>
class Mapper {
protected:
  MappingTable table;
public:
  virtual ProcessorDomain data_to_processor(Data*)=0;
  virtual Link_list<ProcessorDomain>
          dataset_to_processors(DataSet*)=0;
};
```

Communicator classes

The `Communicator` classes support general purpose all-to-some communications for N-body tree codes. A `Communicator` class defines two functions: `extract` (that, when given a data pointer, constructs an outgoing data) and `process` (that processes each incoming data). When a `communicator` is constructed, it goes over the list of data pointers, calls `extract` to build outgoing data, packs many outgoing data into actual messages, sends/receives all the messages according to the communication protocol, and finally unpacks messages and calls `process` to perform appropriate actions.

```
template <class Data, class DataPacket>
class Communicator {
protected:
  Link_list<Data*> *data_list[MAX_NUM_PROCESSORS];
  DataPacket send_buffer[MAX_BUFFER_SIZE];
  DataPacket receive_buffer[MAX_BUFFER_SIZE];
public:
  void communication_protocol();
  virtual DataPacket extract(Data*)=0;
  virtual process(DataPacket*)=0;
};
```

The technique we developed for `communicator` has proven to be both efficient and general enough to support all-to-some communication in N-body tree codes. For instance, the essential data gathering was implemented as a tree traversal followed by a communicator phase. The tree traversal goes over the BH nodes, computes the proper destination set where the tree node might be essential, and appends its address to a pointer list to that destination. Each destination processor will have a separate pointer list that contains the addresses of those tree nodes that might be essential to the destination's local particles. The `extract` routine assures that only essential parts of a tree node are transmitted. The `process` routine inserts incoming data into the local tree. All the message packing/unpacking/transmission are handled by `communicator`.

5 Experimental Results

We demonstrate the flexibility of our library by writing a gravitational N-body code on a network of workstations. It took us only a few days to write all the necessary data structures and control logics for the gravitational simulation, since we inherited most of the tree and cluster structures from the BH tree layer. All we had to write are those segments specific to the gravitational simulation, including body-to-body and body-to-cluster interactions, the rules to combine center-of-mass, and data structures for particles and particle clusters.

N	sequential time	parallel time	speed up
8000	14.39	5.84	2.46
16000	20.40	6.28	3.25
24000	33.05	9.80	3.37
32000	45.91	13.25	3.46
40000	60.07	17.5	3.43
48000	73.82	21.03	3.50
56000	90.23	26.17	3.44
64000	103.59	29.17	3.55

Table 1: Timing comparison between the parallel C++ code using the framework and a sequential C implementation.

We conducted the experiments on four Ultra Sparc workstations connected by a fast ethernet network, located at Academia Sinica, Taiwan. The communication library functions were implemented in MPI version 1.0.4. To get a fair speedup number we compare our parallel execution time with the timing from a highly optimized sequential C code written by Barnes and Hut. Both the sequential and the parallel code use exactly the same Barnes-Hut algorithm. The input configuration is a set of uniformly distributed particles in three dimension. Table 1 summarizes the timing results from both codes.

Our parallel code developed from the tree framework has overhead from both the communication and extra function calls inevitable in object-oriented style of programming. However, the timing data shows a reasonably good speedup, even if compared with a highly optimized sequential C code. As the problem size increases, the speedup reaches a steady 3.5 with four processors. We plan to conduct more experiments on larger number of processors to evaluate the effects of communication on the simulation efficiency.

The major overhead in the C++ version is in the essential data collection process. Our implementation collects all the essential data and put them in a linked list, then compute the interactions one element at a time from the list. We chose this method mainly to separate the data collection process from the computation. However, we pay the overhead of allocating linked list element through expensive dynamic memory allocation. We will improve the efficiency by a customized dynamic memory management mechanism in which we will have better control over the allocation/deallocation process. Another approach would be to compute the interaction on-the-fly while traversing the tree. Both methods will be implemented and included into the final version of the library.

6 Conclusion

In this paper, we have presented the implementation of our framework for parallel and distributed N-body simulations. We start from the generic tree class and proceed to increasingly complex tree structures. By separating abstractions of data structures from computation details, our N-body framework is applicable to other tree-based scientific simulations as well.

Our experience with developing fast methods for gravitational simulations on the Connection Machine CM-5, and preliminary experience with vortex dynamics applications give us confidence that such a framework will be invaluable to applications scientists and engineers. For computer scientists, such a framework will also allow design effort and heavy-duty optimization to be expended exactly where it is most needed, without restricting the generality or portability of related code.

We have implemented a gravitational N-body code using the class libraries provided in this framework. As expected, using the framework greatly shortened the development time of this code. The performance of this code is competitive to its C implementation as well. To further evaluate our framework, we plan to implement a number of application programs, including a molecular dynamics code, a vortex simulation code, and the 3-d fast multipole method, using the class libraries we have developed.

Acknowledgments

This research is supported in part by National Science Council of Taiwan under grant 86-2213-E-001-010, the Institute for Mathematics and its Applications with funds provided by the National Science Foundation of USA, and a special start-up grant from National Chung Cheng University of Taiwan.

References

[1] A.W. Appel. An efficient program for many-body simulation. *SIAM Journal on Scientific and Statistical Computing*, 6, 1985.

[2] J. Barnes and P. Hut. A hierarchical $O(N \log N)$ force-calculation algorithm. *Nature*, 324, 1986.

[3] S. Bhatt, P. Liu, V. Fernadez, and N. Zabusky. Tree codes for vortex dynamics. In *International Parallel Processing Symposium*, 1995.

[4] V. Fernadez, N. Zabusky, S. Bhatt, P. Liu, and A. Gerasoulis. Filament surgery and temporal grid adaptivity extensions to a parallel tree code for simulation and diagnostics in 3d vortex dynamics. In *Second International Workshop in Vortex Flow*, 1995.

[5] L. Greengard and V. Rokhlin. A fast algorithm for particle simulations. *Journal of Computational Physics*, 73, 1987.

[6] L. Johnsson and Y. Hu. personal communication. 1993.

[7] J. F. Leathrum Jr. and J. Board Jr. The parallel fast multipole algorithm in three dimensions. *manuscript*, 1992.

[8] P. Liu, W. Aiello, and S. Bhatt. An atomic model for message passing. In *5th Annual ACM Symposium on Parallel Algorithms and Architecture*, 1993.

[9] P. Liu and S. Bhatt. Experiences with parallel n-body simulation. In *6th Annual ACM Symposium on Parallel Algorithms and Architecture*, 1994.

[10] P. Liu and S. Bhatt. A framework for parallel n-body simulations. In *Third International Conference on Computational Physics*, 1995.

[11] L. Nyland, J. Prins, and J. Reif. A data-parallel implementation of the adaptive fast multipole algorithm. In *DAGS/PC Symposium*, 1993.

[12] J. Salmon. *Parallel Hierarchical N-body Methods*. PhD thesis, Caltech, 1990.

[13] J. Singh. *Parallel Hierarchical N-body Methods and their Implications for Multiprocessors*. PhD thesis, Stanford University, 1993.

[14] J. Singh, C. Holt, T. Totsuka, A. Gupta, and J. Hennessy. Load balancing and data locality in hierarchical N-body methods. Technical Report CSL-TR-92-505, Stanford University, 1992.

[15] S. Sundaram. *Fast Algorithms for N-body Simulations*. PhD thesis, Cornell University, 1993.

[16] M. Warren and J. Salmon. Astrophysical N-body simulations using hierarchical tree data structures. In *Proceedings of Supercomputing*, 1992.

[17] M. Warren and J. Salmon. A parallel hashed oct-tree N-body algorithm. In *Proceedings of Supercomputing*, 1993.

Fault-Tolerant Parallel Applications Using Queues and Actions

J.Smith and S.Shrivastava
Department of Computing Science,
The University of Newcastle upon Tyne,
Newcastle upon Tyne,
NE1 7RU UK
{jim.smith, santosh.shrivastava}@newcastle.ac.uk

Abstract

There are many techniques supporting execution of large computations over a network of workstations (NOW) but data intensive computations are usually run on high performance parallel machines. A NOW comprising individual user's machines typically has a low performance interconnect and suffers arbitrary changes of availability. Exploiting such resources to execute data intensive computations is difficult, but even in a more constrained environment there is an unfulfilled need for fault-tolerance. The structuring approach presented fulfills this need. Performance exceeding 100 Mflop/s is demonstrated for large fault-tolerant out of core examples of matrix multiplication and Cholesky factorisation using five 133 MHz Pentium compute machines.

1 Introduction

The attraction of exploiting a readily available NOW to perform parallel computations is widely acknowledged. It is also recognised that a NOW typically has disadvantages compared to a tightly coupled multiprocessor, including a lower performance interconnect and a greater need for fault-tolerance. Experiments have been performed to statically partition data intensive computations over a NOW, e.g. [6].

The most well known approach to fault-tolerance in parallel computations is transparent checkpointing; either consistent, e.g. [19, 21, 27] or log based e.g. [26, 13, 31]. A transparent mechanism may be unlikely to take advantage of computation structure and minimise the amount of data saved. A non transparent checkpointing scheme for a statically partitioned computation [25] maintains a parity copy of distributed partitions of computation state in memory on a spare machine arguing that for data intensive computations the loss of transparency allows significant optimisation.

CALYPSO [5] implements a language which allows an application to be structured out of parallel loops possibly separated by serial code. The compiler converts a parallel loop to a collection of thread segments, each corresponding to an iteration of the loop. These are distributed between a potentially varying collection of slaves. A slave accesses shared data by page faulting but at the end of a thread segment computes a set of diffs for each page and sends this back to the server. It is possible to generalise the approach to employ multiple memory servers [11], but as in the previous approach computation state is contained within virtual memory.

If there is only a modest number of machines available to perform a large data intensive computation it is usual to control I/O through the use of out of core techniques. The approach described here locates computation state in a shared object repository which may be distributed over multiple machines and employs techniques adapted from queued transaction processing to support a somewhat similar computation structure to that of CALYPSO but manipulating disk based state.

1.1 A Fault-Tolerant Bag of Tasks

If a computation may be partitioned into a collection of tasks which can each be performed by a separate process, then a single process may be assigned to control distribution of these tasks to a collection of slave or worker processes distributed on separate machines. In a simple implementation the master binds to a known port and serves requests from the slaves. Any number of slaves may be started up, possibly by the master, and each issues requests to the same port on the same machine. A slave executes a loop in which it performs the currently assigned task then returns results to the master and is assigned a new task. The master is responsible for combining results and may also perform file I/O on behalf of the slaves. In Linda, where the term "bag of tasks" appears to originate [8], a similar structure takes a more decoupled form. The master places tasks in the shared tuplespace and then waits for results to be placed into tuplespace by the slaves.

Example applications are ray tracing [20], seismic computations [1, 17] and materials science [30]. The data manipulated is easily managed by a single disk with all I/O being performed by the master process.

If the computation is long running it is desirable to be able to tolerate likely failures such as a machine crash. If it is assumed that a crash can be diagnosed through a message timeout then slave failure can be detected by installing an extra process on each machine and periodically sending a probe message to each slave. If a slave fails, the master has a record of the task last assigned to that slave and may therefore re-assign it to another slave.

If the master fails, the slaves continue but then may have to keep retrying to send results until the master is restored. It may also be assumed that the crashes of concern will cause loss of data in volatile memory but not that on disk storage. Then if there is only a single master, it is possible to avoid loss of work completed already at the time the master fails if the master writes results to disk as they arrive.

Using a reliable multicast mechanism it is possible to tolerate a number of failures by replicating the master, e.g. [10].

Fault-tolerant implementations of a bag of tasks type structure have been reported in the context of Linda e.g. [3, 18]. However existing systems make no provision for manipulating distributed disk based state consistently.

1.2 I/O

While RAID technology [9] can be employed to increase bandwidth to disk storage on a single machine, it is ultimately necessary to seek further bandwidth increases through distributing data over multiple nodes.

It is then possible to take advantage of the structure of a computation and its state to make important savings both in individual accesses and through coordinating distributed I/O [12]. Application fault-tolerance still requires a further mechanism, such as checkpointing. Largely, the work is confined to the realm of parallel machines. Systems aimed at workstation clusters include PIOUS [22] and VIP-FS [16]. PIOUS employs a transaction mechanism to ensure sequential consistency but neither system of itself ensures that an application can tolerate machine failures.

A NOW comprising individual user's machines may be susceptible to any user deciding independently to reboot his machine and furthermore, the machines may be of varied type. It may be that data intensive computations are suited more to a separate cluster of machines with a higher specification interconnect and may therefore be under common administration. However it is argued that individual machine failures can still occur and that the ability to stop any individual machine is of benefit not just to the system administrator but also in the course of sharing a restricted resource. The work described here demonstrates

how data intensive applications can be structured so as to tolerate any number of machine failures without rolling back other machines.

A difficulty arises in attempting to extend the simple bag of tasks structure described earlier, in that it is no longer possible for the master to perform all I/O. While the master can remain responsible for task distribution, the slaves now perform I/O via separate servers on the machines hosting shared state. It is then necessary to ensure consistency between state distributed between different machines and the notification made to the master. It is suggested that a convenient model for building fault-tolerant parallel applications which overcomes this problem can be derived from queued transaction processing [15].

2 Using Queues and Actions

Atomic actions operating on persistent state provide a convenient framework for introducing fault-tolerance [15]. An early design study [4] considered the use of atomic actions as a mechanism to support fault-tolerant parallel programming over a NOW, though using a static partitioning.

Atomic actions have the well known properties of:

serialisability, in that an execution consisting of multiple concurrent atomic actions which access shared state appears to execute according to some serial ordering of the atomic actions,

failure atomicity, in that all effects of a computation contained within an atomic action are undone on failure of that action,

permanence of effect, such that once a state update is committed, it is not lost, barring catastrophic failure.

A convenient model is for this state to be encapsulated in the instance variables of persistent objects and accessed through member functions. Within these functions the programmer places lock requests, e.g. read or write to suit the semantics of the operation, and typically surrounds the code within the function by an atomic action, starting with *begin* and ending with *commit* or *abort*. Operations thus enclosed which can include calls on other atomic objects are then perceived as a single atomic operation. The infrastructure manages the required access from and/or to disk based state. Such objects may be distributed on separate machines, e.g. for performance, and replicated to increase availability.

At the application level, the following enhancements add fault-tolerance to a bag of tasks application.

1. The slave begins an atomic action before fetching a task from the bag, and commits the action after writing the corresponding result. If the slave fails the action aborts, all work pertaining to the current task is

recovered and the task itself becomes available again in the bag.

2. The shared objects are replicated on at least $k + 1$ machines, so that the failure of up to k of these machines may be tolerated.

3. A special object contains a description of the computation and data objects and the computation's completion status. This object may be queried at any time to determine the status of the computation and may be replicated for availability. It is a convenient interface for a process to be started on an arbitrary machine to join in an ongoing computation.

2.1 Atomicity

In database terms, the slave is coordinator for the atomic action and the machines hosting shared objects are participants. The coordinator has responsibility for ensuring consistency between distributed state which is updated during the course of an atomic action. Through the well known *two phase commit protocol* [15] the coordinator can ensure that all distributed state is correctly updated eventually regardless of intervening participant failures. In this work however it is important to be able to tolerate failure of the coordinator, i.e. slave. In a simple database system tolerance to coordinator failure can be achieved through the coordinator writing locally a persistent record called an *intentions list* which details the updates to be committed. In the event of coordinator failure it is then possible to ensure that eventual commit is consistent with notification to a human operator, but such failure can lead to "blocking" such that the database items locked during that transaction remain unavailable until the failed coordinator is restored. The general problem of tolerating coordinator failure without the need for such blocking is addressed by non-blocking commit protocols [2]. Here however the application characteristics can be exploited so as to minimise the cost of tolerating coordinator failure without blocking. In the bag of tasks structure the user is concerned only with the outcome of the overall computation, not individual actions. A simple solution then is to always abort any incomplete work in the event of a slave failure and let an alternative slave redo the corresponding task.

The correctness requirement is that each task description must remain in the bag until corresponding work is completed. Assuming each task entails computing from read only parameters, a unique output and then writing it, idempotency is guaranteed. Correctness may be ensured by careful ordering of updates during commit processing. In the applications reported here it is sufficient to commit objects in the reverse of the order in which they were touched within the action. The RPC subsystem is responsible for detecting orphan processes and terminating them

cleanly [23]. Overall, failure atomicity is weakened in a controlled way to take advantage of the semantics of operations performed within the action.

2.2 Implementing a Bag of Tasks

A convenient structure with which to implement the bag is a recoverable queue, similar to that described in [7], which may be regarded as a possible implementation of a semiqueue [32]. If an element is dequeued within a transaction, then it is write-locked immediately, but only actually dequeued at the time the transaction commits. Since only the single element is locked, concurrent dequeues are supported. The *dequeue* operation returns a status which allows the caller to distinguish between the situation where the queue is empty and that where entries remain but are all locked by other users.

2.3 Computation Structuring

A simple computation can be implemented using a single bag of tasks. However, some computations cannot be decomposed into a single set of independent tasks. It is then possible to divide up a computation into a number of parallel steps, in the style of CALYPSO. However, while in CALYPSO a sequential code segment is executed by the master, it is possible instead to represent such a section of code by a bag containing only a single task. Such structuring is considered elsewhere [28].

In some situations it may be preferable to allow tasks to depend on the results generated by other tasks in the same bag. It is then necessary to employ some synchronising mechanism such that a task can be blocked until some prior task has completed and produced output. In a correct execution, a static ordering of tasks may be used to ensure that a needed block will at least be in the process of being computed when a slave computing a dependent block attempts to access it, such that conventional read and write locks are adequate. However, where any slave may fail at any time it is quite possible for a slave to attempt to access a block which is not ready and yet not actually being generated by another slave.

A simple mechanism is to employ a flag which indicates whether a corresponding task result has been written or not. Concurrent access to the flag is controlled through locks obtained within the scope of an action. The ordering criteria described above is sufficient to ensure that the flag is consistent with the task result.

In any parallel application, deadlock may arise due to faulty implementation. However if individual process failures are tolerated then any process effectively waiting for completion of such a failed task will block. The queue is ordered so that the first slave to seek work following a failure will take the aborted job. However, if all slaves apart from the failed one are blocked, the application stalls.

Rather than including some form of deadlock detection, a simple expedient adopted here is to ensure that slaves do not wait indefinitely. Instead a slave waits only for some application specific interval for any object flag, before aborting its current task and returning to seek work from the queue. To avoid a waiting slave abandoning partially completed work, this interval should be larger than any period which the slave might genuinely have to wait for, essentially greater than the duration of any task in this application.

3 Experiment

Two applications are implemented using the Arjuna tool kit [24], an object-oriented programming system that implements in C++ the object and action model described in section 2. The applications are dense matrix multiplication and dense Cholesky factorisation. In each case matrices are composed of blocks, for locality [14], and a task defined as the computation of a single block of the result.

In the case of matrix multiplication, a task entails a block dot product of a row of blocks in the first and column of blocks in the second operand matrices. For Cholesky factorisation the blocked left looking algorithm for "pool of tasks" is copied directly from [14, §6.3.8]. Delaying access to a block of the result matrix till the block is ready is achieved transparently within the distributed matrix object by means of an array of synchronisation flags described in section 2.3

Fuller description of the application structure together with details of performance modelling and measurements over a network of HP9000 machines connected by Ethernet is described in [29]. Here the applications have been ported to a network of Viglen genie PCI P5/133 machines having 32 Mbytes main memory and 256 Kbytes secondary cache and running Linux version 2.0.23. Two of the machines have a pair each of MAXTOR 540SL disks connected via fast SCSI 2 controllers. The object store is distributed between the four MAXTOR disks and the two local disks on each object store node are managed as a RAID-0 pair through the *md* [33] software. Interconnection is via EN155p–MF ATM Adaptors from Efficient Networks to a ForeRunner ASX–200WG ATM switch from Fore systems. The performance of the fault-tolerant parallel implementations using five slaves in this configuration is summarised below.

Application	MM ($9K^2$)		CF ($15K^2$)	
Task size (elements)	600^2	750^2	600^2	750^2
Tasks	225	144	325	210
Time (seconds)	13179	12611	11521	10922
Performance (Mflop/s)	111	116	98	103
Recovery (seconds)	146	219	89	130

In the event of slave failure and immediate resumption, or replacement by a spare, the failure free execution time is increased by a recovery time due to the loss of aborted work. The effect on overall runtime may be mitigated to some extent if the total number of tasks is not a multiple of the number of slaves. However in the worst case where in a failure free execution all slaves would finish at nearly the same time, the actual recovery time is the cost of between zero and one task executions, the *average recovery* shown above being half of the maximum.

Space restrictions here preclude detailed performance analysis, but a fuller treatment of such issues is given in [28, 29]. The performance of the low level matrix multiplication primitive is measured at 27 Mflop/s. In the experiment, the computation rate peaks at 25 Mflop/s per slave so there is clearly potential for supporting a greater number of slaves. In an alternative experiment, connection is via fast ethernet hub supporting a measured transfer rate of 4.6 Mbyte/s and object store located on a single IBM Pegasus disk supporting measured transfer rate of 2.8 Mbytes/s. In this configuration, multiplication of two 3000^2 matrices achieved an overall I/O rate of 1.7 Mbytes/s compared to a maximum expected of 1.74 Mbyte/s. However at a runtime of 386 s the need for fault-tolerance is probably not overwhelming. In the examples shown in the table above, there is significant benefit available from fault-tolerance, yet the impact on performance is not great.

4 Summary

As the size of a computation increases it may outrun disk provision at a single machine either in volume or bandwidth. The system described here is attractive because a shared object store need not be centralised at a single machine, but can instead be distributed over a number of machines. Previous work demonstrated feasibility but now a port to exploit the performance of the recently acquired ATM network demonstrates the the non-dependence of the toolkit on special hardware or software facilities. Further, the performance in the newer configuration demonstrates significant performance benefit through parallelism and fault-tolerance. The conclusion suggested is that using a shared object repository with queues and actions for application structuring as demonstrated seems to offer a low cost way of effectively exploiting modest hardware resources to perform large scale data intensive computations.

Acknowledgements

The work reported here has been supported in part by research and studentship grants from the UK Ministry of Defence, Engineering and Physical Sciences Research Council (Grant Number GR/H81078) and ESPRIT project

BROADCAST (Basic Research Project Number 6360). The support of M. Little, G. Parrington and S. Wheater with implementation issues relevant to this work is gratefully acknowledged.

References

[1] G. S. Almasi and A. Gottlieb. *Highly Parallel Computing.* Benjamin/Cummings, 2nd edition, 1994. ISBN 0-8053-0443-6.

[2] O. Babaoglu and S. Toueg. Understanding non blocking commit. Technical Report UBLCS-93-2, University of Bologna, Department of Mathematics, Feb. 1993.

[3] D. E. Bakken. *Supporting Fault-Tolerant Parallel Programming in Linda.* PhD thesis, University of Arizona, Aug. 1994.

[4] H. E. Bal. Fault tolerant parallel programming in Argus. *Concurrency: Practice and Experience*, 4(1):37–55, Feb. 1992.

[5] A. Baratloo, P. Dasgupta, and Z. M. Kedem. CALYPSO: A novel software system for fault-tolerant parallel processing on distributed platforms. In *4th International Symposium on High Performance Distributed Computing.* IEEE, Aug. 1995.

[6] A. Benzoni and M. L. Sales. Concurrent matrix factorizations on workstation networks. In A. E. Fincham and B. Ford, editors, *Parallel Computation*, pages 273–284. Clarendon Press, 1991.

[7] P. A. Bernstein, M. Hsu, and B. Mann. Implementing recoverable requests using queues. *ACM SIGMOD*, pages 112–122, 1990.

[8] N. Carriero and D. Gelernter. *How To Write Parallel Programs: A First Course.* MIT Press, 1991. ISBN 0-262-03171-X.

[9] P. M. Chen, E. K. Lee, G. A. Gibson, R. H. Katz, and D. A. Patterson. RAID: high-performance, reliable secondary storage. *ACM Computing Surveys*, 26(2):145–185, June 1994.

[10] T. Clark and K. P. Birman. Using the ISIS resource manager for distributed, fault-tolerant computing. Technical Report 92-1289, Cornell University Computer Science Department, June 1992.

[11] P. Dasgupta, Z. M. Kedem, and M. O. Rabin. Parallel processing on networks of workstations: A fault-tolerant, high performance approach. In *15th International Conference on Distributed Computing Systems*, Vancouver, BC, Canada, May 1995. IEEE.

[12] J. M. del Rosario and A. Choudhary. High performance I/O for parallel computers: Problems and prospects. *IEEE Computer*, pages 59–68, Mar. 1994.

[13] E. N. Elnozahy and W. Zwaenepoel. Manetho: Transparent rollback-recovery with low overhead, limited rollback and fast output. *IEEE Transactions on Computers*, May 1992.

[14] G. H. Golub and C. F. V. Loan. *Matrix Computations.* John Hopkins University Press, second edition, 1989. ISBN 0-8018-3772-3.

[15] J. Gray and A. Reuter. *Transaction Processing: Concepts and Techniques.* Morgan Kauffman, 1993.

[16] M. Harry, J. M. del Rosario, and A. Choudhary. VIP-FS: A virtual, parallel file system for high performance parallel and distributed computing. In *the Ninth International Parallel Processing Symposium*, pages 159–164, April 1995.

[17] P. Hoogerbrugge and R. Mirchandaney. Experiences with networked parallel computing. *Concurrency: Practice and Experience*, 7(1), Feb. 1995.

[18] K. Jeong. *Fault-Tolerant Parallel Processing Combining Linda, Checkpointing, and Transactions.* PhD thesis, New York University, Jan. 1996.

[19] M. F. Kaashoek, R. Michiels, H. E. Bal, and A. S. Tanenbaum. Transparent fault-tolerance in parallel Orca programs. In *Proceedings of the Symposium on Experiences with Distributed and Multiprocessor Systems III*, pages 297–312, Newport Beach, CA, Mar. 1992.

[20] C. Kolb. *rayshade.* ftp://ftp.cs.yale.edu, May 1990. version 3.0.

[21] J. Leon, A. L. Fisher, and P. Steenkiste. Fail-safe PVM: A portable package for distributed programming with transparent recovery. Technical Report CMU-CS-93-124, School of Computer Science, Carnegie Mellon University, Pittsburgh, PA 15213, Feb. 1993.

[22] S. Moyer and V. S. Sunderam. Parallel I/O as a parallel application. *International Journal of Supercomputer Applications*, 9(2):95–107, Summer 1995.

[23] F. Panzieri and S. K. Shrivastava. Rajdoot: A remote procedure call mechanism supporting orphan detection and killing. *IEEE Transactions on Software Engineering*, 14(1):30–37, Jan. 1988.

[24] G. D. Parrington, S. K. Shrivastava, S. M. Wheater, and M. C. Little. The design and implementation of Arjuna. *USENIX Computing Systems Journal*, 8(3):225–308, summer 1995.

[25] J. S. Plank, Y. Kim, and J. J. Dongarra. Algorithm-based diskless checkpointing for fault tolerant matrix operations. In *25th International Symposium on Fault-Tolerant Computing*, June 1995.

[26] M. L. Powell and D. L. Presotto. Publishing: a reliable broadcast communication mechanism. In *9th ACM Symposium on Operating System Principles*, pages 100–109, 1983.

[27] J. Pruyne and M. Livny. Managing checkpoints for parallel programs. In *Workshop on Job Scheduling Strategies for Parallel Processing, International Parallel Processing Symposium*, 1996.

[28] J. Smith. *Fault Tolerant Parallel Applications Using a Network Of Workstations.* PhD thesis, University of Newcastle upon Tyne, 1996. Forthcoming.

[29] J. A. Smith and S. Shrivastava. Performance of data and compute intensive programs over a network of workstations. *Theoretical Computer Science*, 1997. To appear in special issue for Euro-Par'96 papers.

[30] V. S. Sunderam, G. A. Geist, J. J. Dongarra, and R. J. Manchek. The PVM concurrent computing system: Evolution, experiences, and trends. *Parallel Computing Vol. 20(4)*, pages 531–546, 1993.

[31] G. Suri, B. Janssens, and W. K. Fuchs. Reduced overhead logging for rollback recovery in distributed shared memory. In *25th International Symposium on Fault-Tolerant Computing*, Pasadena, California, June 1995. IEEE.

[32] W. Weihl and B. Liskov. Implementation of resilient, atomic data types. *ACM Trans. Prog. Lang. Syst.*, 7(2):244–269, Apr. 1985.

[33] M. Zyngier. *md.* ftp://sweet-smoke.ufr-info-p7.ibp.fr in directory /pub/Linux/, Apr. 1996. version 0.35.

Message Encoding Techniques For Efficient Array Redistribution[1]

Yeh-Ching Chung[2] and Ching-Hsien Hsu

Department of Information Engineering
Feng Chia University, Taichung, Taiwan 407, ROC
Tel : 886-4-4517250 x2706
Fax : 886-4-4515517
Email : ychung, chhsu@pine.iecs.fcu.edu.tw

Abstract- In this paper, we present message encoding techniques to improve the performance of BLOCK-CYCLIC(kr) to BLOCK-CYCLIC(r) (and vice versa) array redistribution algorithms. The message encoding techniques are machine independent and could be used with different algorithms. By incorporating the techniques in array redistribution algorithms, one can reduce the computation overheads and improve the overall performance of array redistribution algorithms. To evaluate the performance of the techniques, we have implemented the message encoding techniques into some array redistribution algorithms on an IBM SP2 parallel machine. The experimental results show that the execution time of array redistribution algorithms with the message encoding techniques is 3% to 22% faster than those without the message encoding techniques.

Keywords: array redistribution, distributed memory multicomputers, message encoding.

1. Introduction

Array redistribution, in general, can be performed in two phases, the send phase and the receive phase. In the send phase, a processor P_i has to determine all the data sets that will be sent to destination processors, pack those data sets, and send those packed data sets to their destination processors. In the receive phase, a processor P_i has to determine all the data sets that will be received from source processors, receive those data sets, and unpack data elements in those data sets to their corresponding local array positions. This means that each processor P_i should compute the following four sets.

- Destination Processor Set (DPS[P_i]) : the set of processors to which P_i has to send data.
- Send Data Sets ($\bigcup_{P_j \in DPS[P_i]}$ SDS[P_i, P_j]) : the sets of array elements that processor P_i has to send to

its destination processors, where SDS[P_i, P_j] denotes the set of array elements that processor P_i has to send to its destination processor P_j.

- Source Processor Set (SPS[P_j]) : the set of processors from which P_j has to receive data.
- Receive Data Sets ($\bigcup_{P_i \in SPS[P_j]}$ RDS[P_j, P_i]) : the

sets of array elements that P_j has to receive from its source processors, where RDS[P_j, P_i] denotes the set of array elements that processor P_j has to receive from its source processor P_i.

Since array redistribution is performed at run-time, there is a performance trade-off between the efficiency of a new data decomposition for a subsequent phase of an algorithm and the cost of redistributing data among processors. Thus efficient methods for performing array redistribution are of great importance for the development of distributed memory compilers. In this paper, we present the *message encoding techniques* to improve the performance of array redistribution algorithms. For the message encoding techniques, in the send phase, a source processor encodes the unpacking information into messages that will be sent to its destination processors. In the receive phase, for a destination processor, according to the encoded unpacking information, one can perform unpacking process without calculating the RDS.

The paper is organized as follows. In Section 2, a brief survey of related work will be presented. In Section 3, the message encoding techniques for array redistribution will be described in details. The encoding and unpacking algorithms used by the message encoding techniques for array redistribution will be given in Section 4. The performance evaluation will be presented in Section 5

2. Related Work

Gupta *et al.* [2] derived closed form expressions

---

[1] The work of this paper was partially supported by NSC of R.O.C. under contract NSC-86-2213-E035-023.
[2] The correspondence addressee.

to efficiently determine the send/receive processor/data sets. Similar approaches was also presented in [1,6,9,12]. Thakur *et al.* [10, 11] presented algorithms for run-time array redistribution in HPF programs. In [8], Ramaswamy *et al.* used a mathematical representation, PITFALLS, for regular data redistribution. Similar approach in finding the intersections between LHS and RHS of array statements was also presented in [3].

Kaushik *et al.* [5] proposed a multi-phase redistribution approach for array redistribution. In [14], portion of array elements were redistributed in sequence in order to overlap the communication and computation. In [15], a spiral mapping technique was proposed to reduce communication conflicts when performing a redistribution. Kalns and Ni [4] proposed a processor mapping technique to minimizes the amount of data exchange for redistribution. In [7], a generalized circulant matrix formalism was proposed to reduce the communication overheads redistribution. Walker *et al.* [13] used the standardized message passing interface, MPI, to express the redistribution operations.

3. Message Encoding Techniques

In general, the BLOCK-CYCLIC(s) to BLOCK-CYCLIC(t) redistribution can be classified into three types,

- s is divisible by t, i.e. BLOCK-CYCLIC($s=kr$) to BLOCK-CYCLIC($t=r$) redistribution,
- t is divisible by s, i.e. BLOCK-CYCLIC($s=r$) to BLOCK-CYCLIC($t=kr$) redistribution,
- s is not divisible by t and t is not divisible by s.

To simplify the presentation, we use $kr{\rightarrow}r$, $r{\rightarrow}kr$, and $s{\rightarrow}t$ to represent the first, the second, and the third types of redistribution, respectively, for the rest of the paper.

Definition 1: Given a BLOCK-CYCLIC(s) to BLOCK-CYCLIC(t) redistribution, BLOCK-CYCLIC(s), BLOCK-CYCLIC(t), s, and t are called the *source distribution*, the *destination distribution*, the *source distribution factor*, and the *destination distribution factor* of the redistribution , respectively.

Definition 2: Given an $s{\rightarrow}t$ redistribution on $A[1:N]$ over M processors, the *source (destination) local array* of processor P_i (P_j), denoted by $SLA_i[0:N/M-1]$ ($DLA_j[0:N/M-1]$), is defined as the set of array elements that are distributed to processor P_i (P_j) in the source (destination) distribution, where $0 \le i, j \le M-1$.

Definition 3: Given an $s{\rightarrow}t$ redistribution on $A[1:N]$ over M processors, the *source (destination) processor* of an array element in $A[1:N]$ or $DLA_j[0:N/M-1]$ ($SLA_i[0:N/M-1]$) is defined as the processor that owns the array element in the source (destination) distribution, where $0 \le i, j \le M-1$.

Definition 4: Given an $s{\rightarrow}t$ redistribution on $A[1:N]$ over M processors, we define $SG : SLA_i[m] \rightarrow A[k]$ is a function that converts a source local array element $SLA_i[m]$ of P_i to its corresponding global array element $A[k]$ and $DG : DLA_j[n] \rightarrow A[l]$ is a function that converts a destination local array element $DLA_j[n]$ of P_j to its corresponding global array element $A[l]$, where $1 \le k, l \le N$ and $0 \le m, n \le N/M-1$.

Definition 5: Given an $s{\rightarrow}t$ redistribution on $A[1:N]$ over M processors, a *global complete cycle* (*GCC*) of $A[1:N]$ is defined as M times the least common multiple of s and t, i.e., $GCC=M{\times}lcm(s,t)$. We define $A[1:GCC]$ as the first global complete cycle of $A[1:N]$, $A[GCC+1:2{\times}GCC]$ as the second global complete cycle of $A[1:N]$, and so on.

Definition 6: Given an $s{\rightarrow}t$ redistribution, a *local complete cycle* (*LCC*) of a local array $SLA_i[0:N/M-1]$ (or $DLA_j[0:N/M-1]$) is defined as the least common multiple of s and t, i.e., $LCC = lcm(s, t)$. We define $SLA_i[0:LCC-1]$ ($DLA_j[0:LCC-1]$) as the first local complete cycle of $SLA_i[0:N/M-1]$ ($DLA_j[0:N/M-1]$), $SLA_i[LCC:2{\times}LCC-1]$ ($DLA_j[LCC:2{\times}LCC-1]$) as the second local complete cycle of of $SLA_i[0:N/M-1]$ ($DLA_j[0:N/M-1]$), and so on.

3.1 The Message Encoding Technique for $kr{\rightarrow}r$ Redistribution

Due to the page limitation, we omit the proof of lemmas presented in this paper.

Lemma 1: Given an $s{\rightarrow}t$ redistribution on $A[1:N]$ over M processors, $SLA_i[m]$, $SLA_i[m+LCC]$, $SLA_i[m+2{\times}LCC]$, ..., and $SLA_i[m+N/M{\times}LCC]$ have the same destination processor, where $0 \le i \le M-1$ and $0 \le m \le LCC-1$. ∎

Lemma 2: Given a $kr{\rightarrow}r$ redistribution on $A[1:N]$ over M processors, for a source processor P_i and array elements in $SLA_i[x{\times}LCC:(x+1){\times}LCC-1]$, if the destination processor of $SG(SLA_i[a_0])$, $SG(SLA_i[a_1])$, ..., $SG(SLA_i[a_{\gamma-1}])$ is P_j, then $SG(SLA_i[a_0])$, $SG(SLA_i[a_1])$, ..., $SG(SLA_i[a_{\gamma-1}])$ are in the consecutive local array positions of $DLA_j[0:N/M-1]$, where $0 \le x \le N/GCC-1$ and $x{\times}LCC \le a_0 < a_1 < a_2 < ... < a_{\gamma-1} < (x+1){\times}LCC$. ∎

Lemma 3: Given a $kr{\rightarrow}r$ redistribution on $A[1:N]$ over M processors, for a source processor P_i, if $SLA_i[a]$ and $SLA_i[b]$ are the first element in $SLA_i[x{\times}LCC: (x+1) \times LCC -1]$ and $SLA_i[(x+1) \times LCC: (x+2) \times LCC -1]$, respectively, with the same destination processor P_j and $SG(SLA_i[a]) = DG(DLA_j[\alpha])$, then $SG(SLA_i[b]) = DG(DLA_j[\alpha + kr])$, where $0 \le x \le N / GCC-2$ and $0 \le \alpha \le N / M - 1$. ∎

Given a $kr{\rightarrow}r$ redistribution on $A[1:N]$ over M processors, for a source processor P_i, we assume that there are γ array elements in $SLA_i[0:LCC-1]$ whose destination processor is P_j. In the receive phase, if the first array element of the message will be unpacked to $DLA_j[\alpha]$, according to Lemmas 1, 2, and 3, the first γ array elements of the message will be unpacked to $DLA_j[\alpha:\alpha+\gamma-1]$, the second γ array elements of the message will be unpacked to $DLA_j[\alpha+kr:\alpha+kr+\gamma-1]$, the third γ array elements of the message will be unpacked to $DLA_j[\alpha+2kr:\alpha+2kr+\gamma-1]$, and so on. Therefore, if we know the values of α and γ in the send phase and encode the values of α and γ as the first and the second elements of a message, respectively, then we can perform the unpacking process without computing the receive data sets in the receive phase.

Given a $kr{\to}r$ redistribution on $A[1:N]$ over M processors, for a source processor P_i, the values of α and γ can be computed by the following equations:

$$\alpha = \begin{cases} \lfloor rank(P_i) \times k / M \rfloor \times r & \text{if } rank(P_i) \geq mod(rank(P_i) \times k, M) \\ (\lfloor rank(P_i) \times k / M \rfloor + 1) \times r & \text{otherwise} \end{cases} \quad (1)$$

$$\gamma = \begin{cases} (\lfloor k/M \rfloor + 1) \times r & \text{if } mod(rank(P_i) + M - \\ & mod(rank(P_i) \times k, M), M) < mod(k, M) \\ \lfloor k/M \rfloor \times r & \text{otherwise} \end{cases} \quad (2)$$

where $rank(P_i)$ and $rank(P_j)$ are the ranks of processors P_i and P_j, respectively.

3.2 The Message Encoding Technique for $r{\to}kr$ Redistribution

<u>Lemma 4</u>: Given a $r{\to}kr$ redistribution on $A[1:N]$ over M processors, for a source processor P_i and array elements in $SLA_i[x{\times}LCC:(x+1){\times}LCC-1]$, if the destination processor of $SG(SLA_i[a_0])$, $SG(SLA_i[a_1])$, ..., $SG(SLA_i[a_{\gamma-1}])$ is P_j, and $SG(SLA_i[a_0]) = DG(DLA_j[\alpha])$, then $SG(SLA_i[a_r]) = DG(DLA_j[\alpha + Mr])$, $SG(SLA_i[a_{2r}]) = DG(DLA_j[\alpha + 2Mr])$, ..., and $SG(SLA_i[a_{\gamma-r}]) = DG(DLA_j[\alpha + (\gamma/r-1) \times Mr])$, where $0 \leq \alpha \leq N / M-1$, $0 \leq x \leq N/GCC-1$ and $x{\times}LCC \leq a_0 < a_1 < a_2 < ... < a_{\gamma-1} < (x+1){\times}LCC$. ∎

Given an $r{\to}kr$ redistribution on $A[1:N]$ over M processors, for a source processor P_i, we assume that there are γ array elements in $SLA_i[0:LCC-1]$ whose destination processor is P_j. In the receive phase, if the first array element of the message will be unpacked to $DLA_j[\beta]$, according to Lemmas 1, and 4, the first γ array elements of the message will be unpacked to $DLA_j[\beta:\beta+r-1]$, $DLA_j[\beta + Mr : \beta + Mr + r - 1]$, $DLA_j[\beta + 2Mr : \beta + 2Mr + r - 1]$, ..., and $DLA_j[\beta+(\gamma/r-1){\times}Mr:\beta+(\gamma/r-1){\times}Mr+r-1]$; the second γ array elements of the message will be unpacked to $DLA_j[\beta + kr : \beta + kr + r - 1]$, $DLA_j[\beta + kr + Mr : \beta + kr + Mr + r - 1]$, $DLA_j[\beta + kr + 2Mr : \beta + kr + 2Mr + r - 1]$, ..., and $DLA_j[\beta + kr + (\gamma/r-1) \times Mr:\beta+kr+(\gamma/r-1){\times}Mr+r-1]$, and so on. Therefore, if we know the values of β and γ β, then we can perform the unpacking process without computing the RDS in the receive phase.

Given an $r{\to}kr$ redistribution on $A[1:N]$ over M processors, for a source processor P_i, the value of γ can be computed by Equation 2. The value of β can be computed by the following equation,

$$\beta = mod(rank(P_i) + M - mod(rank(P_j) \times k, M), M) \times r \quad (3)$$

4. Incorporate Message Encoding Techniques with Array Redistribution Algorithms

To incorporate the message encoding techniques with the $kr{\to}r$ and $r{\to}kr$ redistribution algorithms, we need the following four algorithms.

Algorithm kr_to_r_encoding(k, r, M)
1.   For each destination processor P_j in DPS[P_i] do
2.   { calculate α and γ using Equations 1 and 2, respectively;
3. $send\_mes_j[0] = \alpha$;
4. $send\_mes_j[1] = \gamma$; }
end_of_kr_to_r_encoding

Algorithm kr_to_r_unpacking(k, r, M, N)
1. P_j receives a message $recv\_mes_i$ from source processor P_i
2. $\alpha = rcev\_mes_i[0]$; $\gamma = recv\_mes_i[1]$;
3. $length_i = 2$; $cycle = N / (M \times kr)$; $count = 0$; $index = \alpha - kr$;
4.   **while** ($count < cycle$)
5.   { $index += kr$;
6.   **for** ($x = 0$; $x < \gamma$; $x{+}{+}$)
7. $DLA_j[index+x]$ $= recv\_mes_i[length_i{+}{+}]$;
8. $count{+}{+}$; }
end_of_kr_to_r_unpacking

Algorithm r_to_kr_encoding(k, r, M)
1.   For each destination processor P_j in DPS[P_i] do
2.   { calculate β and γ using Equations 3 and 2, respectively;
3. $send\_mes_j[0] = \beta$;
4. $send\_mes_j[1] = \gamma$ }
end_of_r_to_kr_encoding

Algorithm r_to_kr_unpacking(k, r, M, N)
1. P_j receives a message in $recv\_mes_i$ from source processor P_i
2. $\beta = recv\_mes_i[0]$; $\gamma = recv\_mes_i[1]$;
3. $length_i = 2$; $cycle = N / (M \times kr)$;
4. $count = 0$; $index = \beta - kr$;
5. $local\_index = 0$;
6.   **while** ($count < cycle$)
7.   { $index += kr$;
8. $local\_index = index - M \times r$;
9.   **for** ($x = 0$; $x < \gamma / r$; $x{+}{+}$)
10.   { $local\_index += M \times r$;
11.   **for**($y = 0$; $y < r$; $y{+}{+}$)
12. $local\_array(local\_index+y)$ $= recv\_mes_i(length_i{+}{+})$; }
13. $count {+}{+}$; }
end_of_r_to_kr_unpacking

---

5. Performance Evaluation and Experimental Results

To evaluate the performance of the proposed

message encoding techniques, we have implemented the message encoding techniques into algorithms presented in [10, 11] for $kr \to r$ and $r \to kr$ redistribution on a 16-nodes SP2. We called algorithms with and without the message encoding techniques MET_REDIS and REDIS, respectively.

Table 1 gives the execution time and the percentages of the performance improvement of MET_REDIS over REDIS. The execution time of redistribution in the synchronous communication model is about 15% to 22% faster than that of REDIS. In the asynchronous model, the execution time of redistribution is about 3% to 7% faster than that of REDIS. We have noted that the improvement percentage of the synchronous model is greater than that of the asynchronous model. This is because that the computation and communication can be overlapped in the asynchronous model, but can not be overlapped in the synchronous model. For the cases of $k = 10, 20, 50$, and BLOCK to CYCLIC (and vice-versa) redistribution, we have similar results (Due to the page limitation, we did not show the results here).

6. Conclusions

In this paper, based on $kr \to r$ and $r \to kr$ redistribution, we have developed the message encoding techniques. The message encoding techniques are machine independent and could be used with different array redistribution algorithms. By incorporating the techniques in array redistribution algorithms, one can reduce the computational overheads. The experimental results show that the execution time of array redistribution algorithms with the message encoding techniques is 3% to 22% faster than those without the message encoding techniques.

References

[1] S. Chatterjee, J. R. Gilbert, F. J. E. Long, R. Schreiber, and S.-H. Teng, "Generating Local Address and Communication Sets for Data Parallel Programs," *JPDC*, Vol. 26, pp. 72-84, 1995.

[2] S. K. S. Gupta, S. D. Kaushik, C.-H. Huang, and P. Sadayappan, "On Compiling Array Expressions for Efficient Execution on Distributed-Memory Machines," *JPDC*, Vol. 32, pp. 155-172, 1996.

[3] S. Hiranandani, K. Kennedy, J. Mellor-Crammey, and A. Sethi," Compilation technique for block-cyclic distribution," In *Proc. ACM Intl. Conf. on Supercomputing*, pp. 392-403, July 1994.

[4] E. T. Kalns, and L. M. Ni, "Processor Mapping Technique Toward Efficient Data Redistribution, " *IEEE TPDS*, vol. 6, no. 12 , December 1995.

[5] S. D. Kaushik, C. H. Huang, J. Ramanujam, and P. Sadayappan, "Multiphase array redistribution: Modeling and evaluation," In *Proc. of IPPS*, pp. 441-445, 1995.

[6] K. Kennedy, N. Nedeljkovic, and A. Sethi, "Efficient address generation for block-cyclic distribution," In *Proc. of Intl. Conf. on Supercomputing*, Barcelona, pp. 180-184, July 1995.

[7] Y.-W. Lim, Prashanth B. Bhat, and Viktor, K. Prasanna, "Efficient Algorithms for Block-Cyclic Redistribution of Arrays," *Proceedings of the Eighth IEEE Symposium on Parallel and Distributed Processing*, pp. 74-83, 1996.

[8] S. Ramaswamy, B. Simons, and P. Banerjee, "Optimization for efficient array Redistribution on Distributed Memory Multicomputers," *JPDC*, Vol. 38, pp. 217-228, 1996.

[9] J. M. Stichnoth, D. O'Hallaron, and T. R. Gross," Generating communication for array statements: design, implementation, and evaluation," *JPDC*, Vol. 21, pp. 150-159, 1994.

[10] R. Thakur, A. Choudhary, and G. Fox, "Runtime array redistribution in HPF programs, " *Proc. 1994 Scalable High Performance Computing Conf.* , pp. 309-316, May 1994.

[11] Rajeev. Thakur, Alok. Choudhary, and J. Ramanujam, "Efficient Algorithms for Array Redistribution, " *IEEE TPDS*, vol. 7, no. 6 , JUNE 1996.

[12] A. Thirumalai and J. Ramanujam, "HPF array statements: Communication generation and optimization," *3th workshop on Languages, Compilers and Run-time system for Scalable Computers*, Troy. NY, May 1995.

[13] David W. Walker, Steve W. Otto, "Redistribution of BLOCK-CYCLIC Data Distributions Using MPI," Technical Report ORNL/TM-12999, Computer Science and Mathematics Division, Oak Ridge National Laboratory, 1995.

[14] A. Wakatani and M. Wolfe, "A New Approach to Array Redistribution: Strip Mining Redistribution," In *Proc. of Parallel Architectures and Languages Europe*, July 1994.

[15] A. Wakatani and M. Wolfe, "Optimization of array redistribution for distributed memory multicomputer, " In *Parallel Computing(submitted)*, 1994.

Table 1 : The percentages of the performance improvement of MET_REDIS over REDIS.

BLOCK-CYCLIC(4) to BLOCK-CYCLIC(2)				BLOCK-CYCLIC(2) to BLOCK-CYCLIC(4)			
(Synchronous)				(Synchronous)			
SIZE	REDIS	MET REDIS	Improvement	SIZE	REDIS	MET REDIS	Improvement
64	0.7	0.597	14.7%	64	0.456	0.405	7.6%
640	0.811	0.627	22.7%	640	0.572	0.523	8.6%
6400	2.056	1.76	14.4%	6400	2.165	2.031	6.2%
(Asynchronous)				(Asynchronous)			
64	0.52	0.506	2.7%	64	0.424	0.395	6.8%
640	0.635	0.613	3.5%	640	0.455	0.431	5.3%
6400	1.816	1.694	6.7%	6400	2.087	1.957	6.2%

Time unit : ms

Panel 1

Wide-Spread Acceptance of General-Purpose Large-Scale Parallel Machines: Fact, Future, or Fantasy?

Moderator and Organizer:
H.J. Siegel, Purdue University

Panelists:
H.J. Siegel, Purdue University
B.H. Alper, Cambridge Parallel Processing
V. Kumar, University of Minnesota
R. Linderman, Rome Laboratory
D. Marinescu, Purdue University
J.D. McCalpin, Silicon Graphics, Inc.
M. Wolfe, The Portland Group, Inc.

Session 3A

Scheduling I - Algorithms

A Parametrized Branch-and-Bound Strategy for Scheduling Precedence-Constrained Tasks on a Multiprocessor System

Jan Jonsson *

Department of Computer Engineering
Chalmers University of Technology
S-412 96 Göteborg, Sweden

janjo@ce.chalmers.se

Kang G. Shin

Real-Time Computing Laboratory
Dept. of Elec. Engr. and Computer Science
University of Michigan, Ann Arbor, MI 48109

kgshin@eecs.umich.edu

Abstract

In this paper we experimentally evaluate the performance of a parametrized branch-and-bound (B&B) algorithm for scheduling real-time tasks on a multiprocessor system. The objective of the B&B algorithm is to minimize the maximum task lateness in the system. We show that a last-in-first-out (LIFO) vertex selection rule clearly outperforms the commonly used least-lower-bound (LLB) rule for the scheduling problem. We also present a new adaptive lower-bound cost function that greatly improves the performance of the B&B algorithm when parallelism in the application cannot be fully exploited on the multiprocessor architecture. Finally, we evaluate a set of heuristic strategies, one of which generates near-optimal results with performance guarantees and another of which generates approximate results without performance guarantees.

1 Introduction

Since its introduction in the field of artificial intelligence, the branch-and-bound (B&B) strategy has been successfully used for finding optimal or near-optimal solutions to the problem of scheduling tasks on multiprocessor architectures. Recent work includes B&B strategies for task scheduling on distributed real-time systems [1], digital signal processing systems [2], and fault-tolerant systems [3]. The B&B strategy is an efficient method for searching the solution space of a scheduling problem. The solution space is often represented by a search tree where each vertex in the tree represents either a complete or a partial solution to the problem. With the aid of intelligent rules for selecting vertices to explore/expand and pruning (deleting) vertices that do not lead to an optimal solution, the complexity of the search can be drastically reduced as compared to that of an exhaustive implicit enumerative search. However, because the inherent exponential complexity of the B&B strategy cannot be completely eliminated, its applicability is in general restricted to small systems. When the application char-

acteristics and/or the processing architecture are known and can be exploited very efficiently, however, the B&B strategy can perform well even for large systems [4, 5].

In this paper, we show how the B&B strategy can be used for non-preemptive scheduling of precedence-constrained tasks on a multiprocessor system subject to individual task deadlines. In particular, we show how a B&B algorithm can be applied to minimize the maximum *task lateness*, that is, the difference between a task's completion time and its deadline. For hard real-time systems where all tasks must be scheduled to meet their deadlines, the maximum task lateness indicates the scalability of the scheduled system workload. To evaluate the various aspects of the B&B strategy, we adopt a parametrized notation introduced by Kohler and Steiglitz [6].

Because the addressed scheduling problem is usually NP-complete [7], many heuristic approaches have been proposed to solve the problem in an efficient manner. For independent tasks on one processor, efficient B&B algorithms were proposed by Baker and Su [8], and McMahon and Florian [9]. A generalization of these algorithms was proposed by Lageweg *et al.* [10] for the case of precedence-constrained tasks. Optimal polynomial-time algorithms for precedence-constrained tasks on one processor have been proposed for the case when all release times are equal [11], as well as for preemptive scheduling [12]. For the multiprocessor case, on the other hand, only a few B&B algorithms have been reported in literature, addressing the problem of optimizing the schedules for deadline-constrained tasks. Peng and Shin [1] proposed an algorithm to minimize the *system hazard* (maximum normalized task response time), and Hou and Shin [4] proposed an algorithm to maximize the *probability of no dynamic failure* (all tasks meet their deadlines in the presence of component failures). The algorithms in [1, 4] both utilize a version of the optimal polynomial-time algorithm in [12] to minimize their performance measures. Recently, Abdelzaher and Shin [5] presented an algorithm for improving an initial solution where the assignment of tasks to processors is fixed and known beforehand.

The following features distinguish our B&B approach

---

*This work was done while the author was at the Real-Time Computing Laboratory, Department of Electrical Engineering and Computer Science, University of Michigan, Ann Arbor. He was supported in part by a grant from the Volvo Research Foundation.

from others. First, we consider all possible permutations of scheduling tasks on a set of processors subject to a given set of precedence constraints. This is in contrast to the methods proposed in [1, 4] where the order of tasks is irrelevant as long as the precedence constraints are taken into account. Whenever this latter characteristic of the scheduling operation applies, all redundant vertices can be pruned from the search tree. Second, we allow related tasks to be assigned to different processors. This allows us to efficiently exploit the inherent parallelism in the application and hence increase the likelihood of meeting task deadlines. This flexibility in task distribution is not offered by task assignment techniques like those in [1, 5]. Third, by using non-preemptive run-time scheduling and hence allowing preemptions to occur only at task boundaries, we can easily include the cost of hardware context switches and still find the optimal solution. The presence of a non-negligible context switch overhead makes it very hard to find feasible schedules if unconstrained preemption is allowed.

The main contributions of this paper are as follows.

C1. We show that a last-in-first-out (LIFO) vertex selection rule outperforms the least-lower-bound (LLB) rule by at least an order of magnitude for the addressed problem. This is an interesting result since it shows that the LLB rule, the "default" rule in many B&B strategies, is not necessarily the best for all multiprocessor scheduling problems.

C2. We propose an efficient lower-bound function for the B&B algorithm under realistic assumptions on processor contention during scheduling. An experimental evaluation shows that our lower-bound function outperforms other techniques by almost an order of magnitude when task parallelism cannot be fully exploited on the system. Because the B&B strategy is computationally tractable only for systems with a relatively small number of processors, the quality of the proposed lower-bound function is all the more important.

C3. We present techniques that can significantly reduce the number of searched vertices at the price of either near-optimal results with performance guarantees or approximate results without performance guarantees. In particular, we find that by scheduling tasks in a fixed depth-first order, good approximate results can be attained at a very low computational cost.

The rest of the paper is organized as follows: Section 2 describes the assumed system and states the problem. Section 3 discusses the parametrized B&B algorithm. Section 4 describes the experimental setup. Section 5 presents the experimental evaluation. Section 6 discusses complementary results, and Section 7 summarizes the results in this paper.

2 System Models

2.1 The multiprocessor system

The multiprocessor system consists of a set $\mathcal{P} = \{p_q : 1 \leq q \leq m\}$ of identical processors. The processors communicate using an interconnection network. We assume that the interconnection network is an arbitrary topology that could include dedicated as well as shared links. The communication between two tasks residing on the same processor is done via accessing shared memory and its cost is assumed to be negligible. The communication cost associated with a message between two tasks on different processors is expressed as the product of the message length and the "nominal communication delay." The nominal delay is the worst-case communication delay that reflects the scheduling strategy used by the underlying interconnection network. We assume that the system is so designed that communication in the network can take place concurrently with processor computation.

2.2 The task system

We consider a real-time application that consists of a set $\mathcal{T} = \{\tau_i : 1 \leq i \leq n\}$ of tasks. Each task $\tau_i \in \mathcal{T}$ is characterized by a 4-tuple $\langle c_i, \phi_i, d_i, T_i \rangle$. The worst-case execution time c_i includes various architectural overheads such as the cost for cache memory misses, pipeline hazards and context switches. We also assume that the cost for packetizing and depacketizing messages are constant and included in the worst-case execution time of communicating tasks. The phasing ϕ_i is the earliest time at which the first invocation of the task will occur, measured relative to some fixed origin of time. The relative deadline d_i is the time within which the task must complete its execution, once it has been invoked. The period T_i is the time interval between two consecutive invocations of τ_i.

Let τ_i^k denote the kth invocation of the task, $k \in \mathbf{Z}^+$. The dynamic behavior of τ_i^k is then characterized by the pair (a_i^k, D_i^k), where the absolute arrival time $a_i^k = \phi_i + T_i(k-1)$ is the earliest time at which τ_i^k is allowed to start its execution, and the absolute deadline $D_i^k = a_i^k + d_i$ is the time by which τ_i^k must complete its execution.

Precedence constraints between tasks in a task set $\mathcal{T}$ are represented by an irreflexive partial order $\prec$ over $\mathcal{T}$. If task τ_j cannot begin its execution until task τ_i has completed its execution, we write $\tau_i \prec \tau_j$. In this case τ_i is said to be a *predecessor* of τ_j, and, conversely, τ_j a *successor* of τ_i. In addition, whenever $\tau_i \prec \tau_j$ and the condition $\neg(\exists \tau_k : (\tau_i \prec \tau_k) \wedge (\tau_k \prec \tau_j))$ holds, we write $\tau_i \prec\!\!\cdot\, \tau_j$. In this case, τ_i is said to be a *direct predecessor* of task τ_j and τ_j a *direct successor* to τ_i. A task which has no predecessors is called an *input task*, and a task which has no successors is called an *output task*.

The activities associated with message transfer from task τ_i to task τ_j are handled by a *communication channel* $\chi_{i,j}$ characterized by the tuple $\langle m_{i,j}, a_{i,j}, d_{i,j} \rangle$, where $m_{i,j}$ denotes the maximum message size, $a_{i,j}$ the message arrival time, and $d_{i,j}$ the relative deadline of the message. The real communication cost for sending a message depends on the communication scheduling strategy employed in the system and cannot be determined until the tasks have been assigned to processors.

159

The computational and communication demands of a task set, and intertask precedence constraints, are represented by a directed acyclic task graph $\mathcal{G} = (\mathcal{N}, \mathcal{A})$. $\mathcal{N}$ is a set of nodes representing the tasks in the set $\mathcal{T}$. $\mathcal{A}$ is a set of directed arcs representing the precedence constraints between the tasks in $\mathcal{T}$, that is, if $\tau_i \prec \tau_j$ then $(\tau_i, \tau_j) \in \mathcal{A}$. Each node in $\mathcal{N}$ is annotated with a non-negative weight representing the computational demand of the corresponding task. For those arcs in $\mathcal{A}$ that represent communication channels, a non-negative weight is used for representing the message size.

A time-driven non-preemptive multiprocessor schedule for a task set $\mathcal{T}$ and a multiprocessor architecture $\mathcal{P}$ is the mapping of each task $\tau_i \in \mathcal{T}$ to a *start time* s_i and a processor $p_i \in \mathcal{P}$. The task is then scheduled to run without preemption on processor p_i in the time interval $[s_i, f_i]$, with its *finish time* being $f_i = s_i + c_i$. The time interval $[a_i, D_i]$, denoted by w_i, is called the *execution window* of τ_i. For periodic tasks, the static task parameters are assumed to satisfy $d_i \leq T_i$, that is, the execution windows of two invocations of the same task don't overlap in time. Furthermore, the execution time c_i cannot exceed the length $|w_i|$ of any execution window.

The schedule is said to be *valid* if (i) the conditions $s_i \geq a_i$ and $f_i \leq D_i$ are satisfied for each task τ_i, and (ii) all precedence constraints defined by the partial order $\prec$ over $\mathcal{T}$ are met. A task set is said to be *feasible* if there exists a valid schedule for the task set. We say that a task set is *schedulable* by a scheduling algorithm $\mathcal{S}$ if it produces a valid schedule for the task set.

2.3 Problem statement

For the system described in the previous sections, we want to find a schedule for a given set of tasks — a one-to-one mapping from each task to its assigned processor and start/stop times — such that the maximum task lateness $L_{max} = \max\{f_i - D_i : \tau_i \in \mathcal{T}\}$ is minimized. As a secondary performance measure we want to minimize the number of vertices searched, indicating the computational complexity of the B&B algorithm.

3 B&B Algorithm

The search for a solution to the multiprocessor scheduling problem is performed with the aid of a *search tree* that represents the solution space of the problem, that is, all possible permutations of task–to–processor assignments and schedule orderings. Each vertex in the search tree represents one specific task–to–processor assignment and schedule ordering, and one or many vertices represent the optimal solution whenever one exists. The *root vertex* of the search tree represents an empty schedule and each of its descendant vertices (children) represents the scheduling of one specific task on one specific processor. The children of each of these child vertices represents the scheduling of yet another task on one processor.

A *goal vertex* in the search tree represents a complete solution where all tasks have been scheduled on the processors. An "acceptable" complete solution is also called a *feasible* solution. An *intermediate vertex* represents a partially-complete schedule. The *level* of a vertex is the number of tasks that have been assigned to any processor in the current schedule. The *cost* of a vertex is the quality of the schedule represented by the vertex; in this paper, it is the maximum task lateness for the schedule represented by the vertex.

When no precedence constraints exist between tasks, the number of goal vertices in a search tree is $n!m^n$ for a multiprocessor system with n tasks and m processors. If precedence constraints exist, the number of goal vertices can be greatly reduced. If the maximum number of child vertices of a vertex is k, then the number of goal vertices in the search tree is at most $k^n m^n$. Because of the exponentially growing number of vertices in the search tree, vertices are normally not generated until the B&B algorithm needs to explore them. Whenever a new vertex is generated and it could lead to an optimal solution, it will be referred to as an *active vertex*. The order in which the vertices in the search tree will be explored is governed by a set of rules that are often heuristic. As will be demonstrated later, the choice of rules dictates the performance of the B&B algorithm. The power of the B&B strategy lies in alternating branching and bounding operations on the set of active vertices. Branching refers to the process of generating the child vertices of an active vertex, while bounding refers to the process of evaluating the cost of new child vertices.

To describe our B&B algorithm, we will use the parametrized notation introduced by Kohler and Steiglitz [6]. A B&B algorithm for solving a permutation problem such as the multiprocessor scheduling problem can then be characterized by a 9-tuple $\langle B, S, E, F, D, L, U, BR, RB \rangle$, where B is the vertex branching rule, S the vertex selection rule, E the vertex elimination rule, F the characteristic function, D the vertex domination rule, L the lower-bound cost function, U the upper-bound solution cost, BR an inaccuracy limit for the cost of a feasible solution, and RB are upper bounds on the time and space resources that are available for solving the problem.

F is used for eliminating partial solutions that will not lead to a valid complete solution. D is used for comparing partial solutions and eliminating "inferior" partial solutions. While F and D have been shown to be very efficient in reducing the complexity of B&B algorithms, we have chosen not to use them, in order to preserve our results as general as possible. As has been successfully demonstrated in [1, 2, 4], the effects of F and D are most powerful when they are designed with a specific processor scheduling strategy in mind.

BR is an indicator on how far the cost for a feasible solution is allowed to deviate from that of the optimal solution. This limit is useful when near-optimal results with performance guarantees [13, pp. 121-151] are desired. When

```
Algorithm BRANCH-AND-BOUND:

1.  initialize active set AS with root vertex;
2.  set best vertex v_u to root vertex;
3.  while { AS ≠ ∅ } loop
4.     select a vertex v_b in AS according to vertex
          selection rule S;
5.     if { stop condition for S } then
          break loop;
6.     generate a set DB of child vertices to vertex v_b
          according to vertex branching rule B;
7.     calculate the cost L(v) for each vertex v in DB
          using the lower-bound function L;
8.     eliminate vertices in DB and AS according to
          vertex elimination rule E;
9.     move all remaining vertices in DB to AS;
10. end loop;
```

Figure 1: The branch-and-bound algorithm.

performance guarantees are desired, the cost L_{opt} for the optimal solution and the cost L_{acc} for a feasible solution are related as given by the relation $|L_{opt}| \leq |L_{acc}| \leq (1 + BR)|L_{opt}|$. This means that when the inaccuracy limit $BR = 0\%$, the only feasible solution is the optimal one.

The resource bound RB can be viewed as a triple $\langle$TIMELIMIT, MAXSZAS, MAXSZDB$\rangle$, where TIME-LIMIT is the maximum allowable time to find a solution, MAXSZAS is the maximum allowable size of the set of active vertices, and MAXSZDB is the maximum allowable number of child vertices of any vertex. Should the time limit be exceeded, the algorithm either fails or terminates with the best solution found so far. Should any of the storage bounds be exceeded, the algorithm must dispose of one or more of the active intermediate solutions, thereby running the risk of missing the optimal solution.

In [6] it is proven that (i) one cannot lose by eliminating those newly-generated vertices that exceed an upper-bound solution cost, and that (ii) one cannot lose by using a better solution as the initial upper bound. Similar results have been reported for the well-known A* algorithm [14].

3.1 Algorithm

Figure 1 shows a pseudo-code form of the parametrized B&B algorithm. The algorithm takes a task graph as the input and produces an annotated task graph containing information about task start and finish times for the best schedule. In this algorithm, an *active set AS* is used to hold all the active vertices.

The algorithm in Figure 1 differs slightly from the one proposed in [6] in that goal vertices are never inserted into the set of active vertices. Instead, a goal vertex either becomes the new best vertex if its cost is lower than the cost of the currently best vertex, or it will be pruned. Using this strategy, many unnecessary insertions into the active set are avoided. The different steps of the algorithm are described below in detail.

Initialize active set (Step $1-2$): In this step the root vertex is created and initialized with an empty schedule. The cost of the root vertex is set according to the upper-bound cost U. The root vertex is then inserted into the active set AS and a variable v_u (best vertex) is set to the root vertex.

Select a vertex to explore (Step 4): A branch vertex v_b is selected among the active vertices according to the vertex selection rule S.

Generate child vertices (Step 6): A set DB of child vertices is generated according to the vertex branching rule B.

Calculate child vertex costs (Step 7): A lower bound on the cost of each vertex in DB is calculated using a lower-bound function L. Each vertex's set of tasks is scheduled on their processors and the overhead introduced by tasks not yet scheduled is estimated.

Eliminate vertices (Step 8): The vertices in DB and AS are now inspected as to whether they are capable of guiding the search to a feasible or optimal solution. The vertex elimination rule E determines which vertices to keep and which ones to prune.

Move remaining child vertices (Step 9): Move the child vertices in DB after the vertex elimination step applied to AS.

Repeat until no vertices remain (Step 3, 5 and 10): The main loop in the algorithm is repeated until no vertices are left in AS or until the stop condition for the vertex selection rule is satisfied. Unless the best vertex v_u is the root vertex, in which case the algorithm has failed to find a solution, v_u will be the optimal solution.

3.2 Vertex selection rule S

From the set AS of currently-active vertices, the vertex rule S selects the next candidate vertex to be explored by the B&B algorithm.

The following three vertex selection rules are commonly used in literature:

- The Least-Lower-Bound (LLB) rule, S_{LLB}, selects the vertex $v \in AS$ that has the least lower-bound cost $L(v)$. The stop condition for S_{LLB} is reached when the lower-bound cost of the selected vertex is equal to, or higher than, the current upper-bound cost $L(v_u)$.

- The First-In-First-Out (FIFO) rule, S_{FIFO}, selects the vertex $v \in AS$ that was generated first. The stop condition for S_{FIFO} is reached when AS is empty.

- The Last-In-First-Out (LIFO) rule, S_{LIFO}, selects the vertex $v \in AS$ that was generated last. The stop condition for S_{LIFO} is reached when AS is empty.

The FIFO strategy is very inefficient for multiprocessor scheduling because its objective is to search for a solution at the lowest possible vertex level. For a multiprocessor scheduling problem where all goal vertices are at the same level, the FIFO strategy will generate all intermediate vertices before finding any complete solution. Since this is a very ineffective strategy, we will not discuss or analyze S_{FIFO} any further, but instead focus on S_{LLB} and S_{LIFO}.

3.3 Vertex branching rule B

The vertex branching rule is instrumental in guiding the traversal of the search tree, based mainly on task precedence constraints. For each vertex in the search tree, there is a set of *ready* tasks; a task is said to be ready when all of its predecessors have been scheduled. One important factor to take into account at this stage is the *commutativity* of the underlying processor scheduling operation. A processor scheduling operation is said to be *commutative* if the order in which tasks are scheduled on the processors doesn't matter to the final scheduling result. Whenever commutativity applies, it is possible to identify those vertices that will yield the same scheduling result regardless of the order in which they are explored. All but one of these vertices can then be pruned before the algorithm is applied, which will significantly reduce the complexity of the algorithm. An example of a commutative processor scheduling operation is the one proposed by Baker *et al.* [12]. This operation has been successfully used in the B&B algorithm proposed in [1, 4]. It should be noted, however, that commutativity only applies for the B&B algorithms in [1, 4] under the assumption that the ideal preemptive scheduling strategy in [12] is used and that interprocessor communication scheduling is also commutative. For a non-preemptive scheduling strategy, the single-processor scheduling problem would be NP-complete [13], thereby effectively prohibiting the use of such strategies as those used in [1, 4].

Specifically, we will evaluate the following vertex branching rules.

- The Depth-First (DF) rule, B_{DF}, selects the task to use for generation of a child vertex from the head of a list sorted according to a depth-first traversal of the task graph.
- The Breadth-First-One-Task (BF1) rule, B_{BF1}, selects the task to use for generation of a child vertex from the head of a list sorted according to the level of a task. The level of a task is calculated in the same manner as in [4].
- The Breadth-First-All-Tasks (BFn) rule, B_{BFn}, selects all available tasks to use for generation of child vertices.

Both DF and BF1 are unable to guarantee an optimal solution unless processor and communication scheduling operations are commutative, whereas BFn guarantees to find an optimal solution if any.

3.4 Upper-bound solution cost U

An upper-bound solution cost is used to initialize the root vertex. The more accurate the upper-bound cost is, the faster the B&B algorithm will get because more vertices can be pruned at each step.

3.5 Lower-bound cost function L

A lower-bound cost function is used for the bounding operation where "pessimistic" estimates on the maximum task lateness are calculated for newly-generated vertices. So, it

---

```
Algorithm U/DBAS:
1.  set v̂_u to the goal vertex in DB with the lowest cost;
2.  if { v̂_u exists and L(v̂_u) < L(v_u) } then
3.      remove v̂_u from DB;
4.      set v_u := v̂_u
5.  end if;
6.  prune each vertex v in DB/AS for which L(v) ≥ L(v_u);
```

Figure 2: The vertex elimination rule $E_{U/DBAS}$.

---

is important to estimate the lateness for those tasks not yet scheduled. The lower bound $\hat{L}$ on the maximum task lateness for the task set $\mathcal{T}$ is defined as

$$\hat{L} = \max\{\hat{f}_i - D_i : \tau_i \in \mathcal{T}\}$$

where $\hat{f}_i$ is the estimated finish time of task τ_i.

We will evaluate two lower-bound cost functions. The first function, L_{LB0}, is similar to the one used in [4]. Starting with the output tasks, task τ_i's estimated finish time $\hat{f}_i$ is defined recursively as:

$$\hat{f}_i := \begin{cases} f_i \\ \max(\{\hat{f}_i\} \cup \{\max\{\hat{f}_j, a_i\} + c_i : \tau_j \prec \tau_i\}) \end{cases}$$

The first case in this equation applies when τ_i has been assigned to and scheduled on a processor; otherwise, the second case applies.

The second lower-bound function, L_{LB1}, is similar to L_{LB0} but also takes processor contention into account. Starting with the output tasks, task τ_i's estimated finish time is defined recursively as:

$$\hat{f}_i := \begin{cases} f_i \\ \max(\{\hat{f}_i\} \cup \{\max\{\hat{f}_j, a_i, \ell_{min}\} + c_i : \tau_j \prec \tau_i\}) \end{cases}$$

Here, ℓ_{min} is the earliest time at which a new task can be scheduled on any processor.

3.6 Vertex elimination rule E

The vertex elimination rule is applied after calculating a lower-bound cost for all newly-generated vertices. Its main use is in the elimination of vertices in DB and/or AS that will not lead to a feasible solution.

We will evaluate one such rule, called the Upper-Bound-Cost-to-DB-and-AS (U/DBAS) rule, $E_{U/DBAS}$. This rule compares the cost of every vertex in DB and AS with the cost of the current upper-bound cost of vertex v_u and removes all those vertices with equal or higher costs. A pseudo-code form of the algorithm for this rule is shown in Figure 2.

4 Experimental Setup

The experimental platform used consists of a shared-bus homogeneous multiprocessor system whose size ranges from 2 to 4 processors. The shared bus is time-multiplexed in such a way that the communication cost between two processors is one time unit per transmitted data item.

4.1 Workload

In the experiments[1], a set of task graphs were generated using a random task graph generator. Each task graph contains between 12 and 16 tasks. Task execution times were chosen randomly according to a uniform distribution with mean execution time of 20 time units. Task execution times are allowed to deviate by at most ±99% from the mean execution time. An end-to-end deadline was chosen for each input–output task pair in the generated graph in such a way that the overall laxity ratio of the end-to-end deadline to the accumulated task graph workload corresponds to 1.5. The precedence constraints in the task graph were also randomly generated. The number of successors/predecessors to each task was chosen at random to be in the range of 1 to 3, and the depth of the task graph was chosen to be between 8 and 12 levels. The number of data items in each message passed between a pair of tasks was chosen in such a way that the communication–to–computation cost ratio (CCR) (of the average message communication cost to the average task execution time) is 1.0.

4.2 Deadline assignment

To assign arrival times and deadlines to each task in $\mathcal{T}$, we used the deadline assignment technique proposed in [16]. Each series of direct successors between an input–output task pair is assigned *slices*, non-overlapping execution windows, of the task pair's end-to-end deadline. The slicing technique is suitable for distributing end-to-end deadlines in real-time systems, because it allows individual tasks to be scheduled independently of each other, thereby allowing for different scheduling strategies on different processors.

4.3 Task scheduling

We used a task scheduling strategy that assumes a non-preemptive time-driven processor run-time model. A new task is scheduled on a processor at the earliest possible start time, while taking into account possible interprocessor communication costs and arrival time constraints of the task, but later than all tasks that have previously been scheduled on the processor. This scheduling strategy exhibits a time complexity that is quadratic in the number of tasks in the system. Unfortunately, the simplicity of the scheduling operation implies that it is not commutative.

4.4 Upper-bound estimation

An initial upper-bound cost U for the B&B algorithm was derived by applying a polynomial-time Earliest-Deadline-First (EDF) algorithm. For each scheduling step, the EDF algorithm selected one task from all schedulable tasks. The task with the closest absolute deadline was selected, and then scheduled on the processor that yielded the earliest start time. The set of schedulable tasks was then updated.

---

[1]All modeling and simulation experiments were performed within FEAST [15], a framework for evaluation of allocation and scheduling techniques for distributed hard real-time systems.

5 Experimental Evaluation

In this section we evaluate the performance of the B&B strategy presented in Section 3. Unless specifically noted, the following B&B parameter choices were used: $BR = 0\%$, TIMELIMIT = 4 hours, MAXSZAS = ∞, and MAXSZDB = ∞. The observed performance indices were (i) the number of searched vertices and (ii) the maximum task lateness. In Figure 3, the plots for the number of searched vertices and the maximum task lateness are located in the upper and lower part in the figure, respectively. As a reference, we have also included in all plots the results obtained for the greedy EDF algorithm in Section 4.4.

In all the plots presented, every reported value is an average of the observed performance data, taken over the set of simulation runs, one for each parameter combination. The number of simulation runs were chosen in such a way that a 90% (95%) confidence level could be achieved for a maximum error within 10% (0.5%) of the average values reported for the number of generated active vertices (maximum task lateness). Simulations that exceeded the time limit as defined by TIMELIMIT were removed from the evaluation. These simulations were found to constitute less than 1% of all simulation runs for each reported value and the confidence levels presented above have been calculated without including the removed simulations.

5.1 Effect of vertex selection rule

Figure 3(a) illustrates how the performance of the B&B algorithm is affected by different choices of vertex selection rule S. Each plot shows the performance of the algorithm when vertex selection was made according to the S_{LLB} and S_{LIFO} rule, respectively.

As can be seen in the upper plot, S_{LIFO} outperforms S_{LLB} by more than an order of magnitude for all system sizes. This is a totally unsuspected result since S_{LLB} has been predominantly used in almost all B&B scheduling algorithms for real-time scheduling. For instance, when scheduling for minimized makespan (schedule length), a good lower-bound cost for an "early" vertex (at a low level in the search tree) is an indicator for a good complete solution. This correlation between the cost of an early vertex and a goal vertex is not necessarily provided when scheduling to minimize task lateness.

The performance of S_{LIFO} differs from that of the greedy EDF algorithm by a little more than an order of magnitude for a small system, and up to two orders of magnitude for a larger system. As can be seen in the lower plot, however, the B&B algorithm yields 5% better (more negative) task lateness for a small system and approximately 3% better task lateness for larger systems.

5.2 Effect of lower-bound function

Figure 3(b) illustrates how the performance of the B&B algorithm is affected by different choices of lower-bound function L. Each plot shows the performance of the algorithm when the lower-bound cost was calculated according

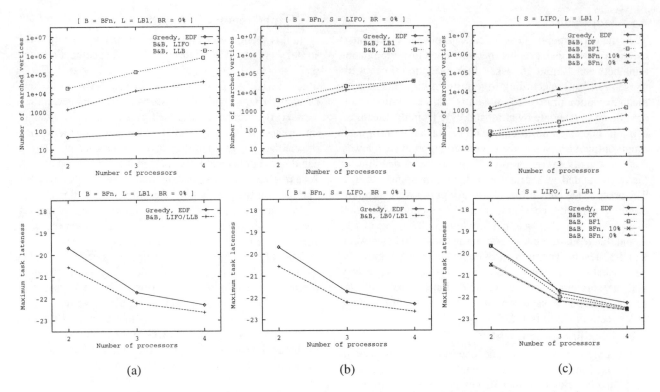

Figure 3: Performance as a function of: (a) vertex selection rule; (b) lower-bound function; (c) approximation strategy.

to L_{LB0} and L_{LB1}, respectively.

As can be seen in the upper plot, L_{LB1} outperforms L_{LB0} by approximately half an order of magnitude for a small system. As the system size increases, however, the performance of the two functions converge, since for larger systems the application parallelism can be exploited better and the adaptive characteristics of L_{LB1} become less significant.

5.3 Effect of approximation strategy

Figure 3(c) illustrates how the performance of the B&B algorithm is affected by different choices of approximation method. Each plot shows the performance of the algorithm when the lower-bound cost was calculated according to L_{LB1}. Results for the approximate vertex branching rules B_{DF} and B_{BF1} are shown, as are two versions of the branching rule B_{BFn}: one near-optimal with $BR = 10\%$, and one optimal with $BR = 0\%$. Also included in the plots are the results obtained for the optimal B&B algorithm with $S = S_{LIFO}$.

As can be seen in the upper plot, the approximate vertex branching rules outperform near-optimal ones by a little more than an order of magnitude. Among the approximate vertex branching rules, B_{DF} yields a small but significant performance gain over B_{BF1}, but this advantage comes at the price of worse (less negative) task lateness as can be seen in the lower plot. It is worth noting that, for a small system, the task lateness for B_{DF} is worse than that for the greedy EDF algorithm. This can be attributed to the fact that if the application parallelism exceeds the available process-

ing parallelism, a depth-first traversal will schedule some input tasks much later than a breadth-first traversal would do. As input tasks are delayed, their successor tasks will be delayed, hence increasing the potential for worsening task lateness. As the system size increases, more parallelism can be exploited in the system and the task lateness of both approximative vertex branching rules converge to that of the optimal. Also apparent in the plots is that the performance gain attained for B_{BFn} with performance guarantees is at best 100% as compared to an optimal version, while the maximum task lateness is kept very close to the optimal one.

6 Discussion

Due to space limit, we have omitted the results of some complementary experiments. We will briefly summarize these results here. We have evaluated the B&B strategy for task graphs with varying degrees of parallelism. Using the same basic experimental setup in Section 4, we found that when the parallelism in the task graph increases, a lower-bound cost function that takes processor contention into account will give even better performance for the B&B algorithm. We have also evaluated the B&B strategy for different values on the communication–to–computation cost ratio (CCR). Here, we found that lower CCR gives better B&B algorithm performance. This is because the cost estimates derived by lower-bound cost functions will be more accurate, thus making the B&B algorithm converge faster.

We have also investigated the impact of an upper-bound

solution cost on the performance of the B&B algorithm. We found that by using a greedy algorithm to derive approximate initial upper-bound costs, the performance of the B&B algorithm was improved by more than 200% as compared to an approach where the initial upper-bound cost was set to a positive value.

Finally, we remark on the practicality of the B&B strategy. In our simulations, the size of the simulated system had to be restricted because of limitations in the hardware simulation milieu. All simulations were made using a SPARCstation-4 machine with 64 Megabyte primary memory, running the SunOS 5.5 operating system. For some simulations, such large amounts of active nodes had to be maintained in virtual memory that machine performance was degraded significantly because of system thrashing, that is, constant shuffling of virtual memory pages to and from the machine's hard disk swap area. This behavior was particularly apparent during those simulations that employed the LLB vertex selection rule because of its quite random (with respect to virtual memory location) access pattern among the active vertices. For those simulations that employed the LIFO vertex selection rule, system thrashing did not occur since the access pattern for this rule matches very well the page replacement strategy used by the SunOS operating system, that is, LRU. This, of course, is another reason for choosing the LIFO rule over the LLB rule.

7 Conclusions

In this paper we have evaluated how effective the B&B strategy can be in finding optimal multiprocessor schedules of precedence-constrained tasks. In particular, we found that if intelligent rules for vertex selection, branching and elimination are used in the B&B algorithm, the problem of minimizing the maximum task lateness can be solved within reasonable time for moderate-size systems. For larger system sizes where machine and time limitations become a major concern, approximate versions of the B&B algorithm are viable alternatives to faster but less accurate greedy algorithms.

References

[1] D.-T. Peng and K. G. Shin, "Static Allocation of Periodic Tasks with Precedence Constraints in Distributed Real-Time Systems," *Proc. of the IEEE Int'l Conf. on Distributed Computing Systems*, New Port Beach, California, June 1989, pp. 190–198.

[2] K. Konstantinides, R. T. Kaneshiro, and J. R. Tani, "Task Allocation and Scheduling Models for Multiprocessor Digital Signal Processing," *IEEE Trans. on Acoustics, Speech, and Signal Processing*, vol. 38, no. 12, pp. 2151–2161, Dec. 1990.

[3] S. M. Shatz, J.-P. Wang, and M. Goto, "Task Allocation for Maximizing Reliability of Distributed Systems," *IEEE Trans. on Computers*, vol. 41, no. 9, pp. 1156–1168, Sept. 1992.

[4] C.-J. Hou and K. G. Shin, "Replication and Allocation of Task Modules in Distributed Real-Time Systems," *Proc. of the IEEE Int'l Symposium on Fault-Tolerant Computing*, Austin, Texas, June 15–17, 1994, pp. 26–35.

[5] T. F. Abdelzaher and K. G. Shin, "Optimal Combined Task and Message Scheduling in Distributed Real-Time Systems," *Proc. of the IEEE Real-Time Systems Symposium*, Pisa, Italy, Dec. 5–7, 1995, pp. 162–171.

[6] W. H. Kohler and K. Steiglitz, "Enumerative and Iterative Computational Approaches," *Computer and Job-Shop Scheduling Theory*, E. G. Coffman, Jr, Ed., chapter 6, pp. 229–287. Wiley, New York, 1976.

[7] P. Brucker, M. R. Garey, and D. S. Johnson, "Scheduling Equal-Length Tasks under Treelike Precedence Constraints to Minimize Maximum Lateness," *Mathematics of Operations Research*, vol. 2, no. 3, pp. 275–284, Aug. 1977.

[8] K. R. Baker and Z.-S. Su, "Sequencing with Due-Dates and Early Start Times to Minimize Maximum Tardiness," *Naval Research Logistics Quarterly*, vol. 21, no. 1, pp. 171–176, Mar. 1974.

[9] G. McMahon and M. Florian, "On Scheduling with Ready Times and Due Dates to Minimize Maximum Lateness," *Operations Research*, vol. 23, no. 3, pp. 475–482, May/June 1975.

[10] B. J. Lageweg, J. K. Lenstra, and A. H. G. Rinnooy Kan, "Minimizing Maximum Lateness on One Machine: Computational Experience and Some Applications," *Statistica Neederlandica*, vol. 30, no. 1, pp. 25–41, 1976.

[11] E. L. Lawler, "Optimal Sequencing of a Single Machine Subject to Precedence Constraints," *Management Science*, vol. 19, no. 5, pp. 544–546, Jan. 1973.

[12] K. R. Baker, E. L. Lawler, J. K. Lenstra, and A. H. G. Rinnooy Kan, "Preemptive Scheduling of a Single Machine to Minimize Maximum Cost Subject to Release Dates and Precedence Constraints," *Operations Research*, vol. 31, no. 2, pp. 381–386, Mar./Apr. 1983.

[13] M. R. Garey and D. S. Johnson, *Computers and Intractability: A Guide to the Theory of NP-Completeness*, Freeman, New York, 1979.

[14] P. E. Hart, N. J. Nilsson, and B. Raphael, "A Formal Basis for the Heuristic Determination of Minimum Cost Paths," *IEEE Trans. on Systems Science and Cybernetics*, vol. 4, no. 2, pp. 100–107, July 1968.

[15] J. Jonsson and J. Vasell, "Evaluation and Comparison of Task Allocation and Scheduling Methods for Distributed Real-Time Systems," *Proc. of the IEEE Workshop on Real-Time Applications*, Montreal, Canada, Oct. 21–25, 1996, pp. 226–229.

[16] J. Jonsson and K. G. Shin, "Deadline Assignment in Distributed Hard Real-Time Systems with Relaxed Locality Constraints," *Proc. of the IEEE Int'l Conf. on Distributed Computing Systems*, Baltimore, Maryland, May 27–30, 1997, pp. 432–440.

Real-Time Job Scheduling in Hypercube Systems[†]

O-Hoon Kwon*, Jong Kim*, SungJe Hong*, and Sunggu Lee**

*Dept. of Computer Science and Engineering
**Dept. of Electronic and Electrical Engineering
Pohang University of Science and Technology
San 31 Hyoja Dong, Pohang 790-784, KOREA
E-mail : jkim@postech.ac.kr

Abstract

In this paper, we present the problem of scheduling real-time jobs in a hypercube system and propose a scheduling algorithm. The goals of the proposed scheduling algorithm are to determine whether all jobs can complete their processing before their fixed deadlines in a hypercube system and to find such a schedule. Each job is associated with a computation time, a deadline, and a dimensional requirement. Determining a schedule such that all jobs meet before their respective fixed deadlines in a hypercube system when preemption is not allowed is an NP-complete problem. Hence, we present a heuristic scheduling algorithm for scheduling non-preemptable real-time jobs in a hypercube system. Finally, we evaluate the proposed algorithm using simulation.

Keywords – deadline, feasible schedule, hypercube, real-time scheduling, subcube.

1 Introduction

In recent years, the hypercube structure has received much attention as a parallel architecture because of its scalability, regularity, recursiveness, and rich topology that includes or matches the structure of many interesting problems. Most of all, since a hypercube can be partitioned into subcubes, it is appropriate for the multiprogramming environment in which many programs are executed on different subcubes at the same time. A *job* is a program executed in parallel on a set of processors. Each job is composed of several *tasks* executed on a processor. As usual, all jobs are assumed to be independent, but tasks in a job may be dependent.

Managing computing resources in a hypercube system consists of two steps. First, a job must be chosen from among those waiting for execution (*job scheduling*). Next, a particular free subcube within the hypercube must be allocated to that job (*processor allocation*). Many processor allocation algorithms have been proposed for hypercube systems. They include the Buddy scheme, Modified Buddy, MSS, Gray Code,

Free List, etc. [6]. On the other hand, job scheduling has been largely neglected. Recently, Krueger *et al.* [5] showed that job scheduling has far greater impact on performance than processor allocation. They found that choosing a suitable scheduling algorithm is far more important than finding an optimal processor allocation algorithm.

When a job has a deadline (known as real-time job), the problems of processor allocation and job scheduling become more complex. That is, the resource manager must not only specify an ordering of jobs to meet the deadline of each job, but must also determine the specific processor to be used. Zhu and Ahuja [1] have studied the problem of real-time job scheduling in a hypercube system. In their research, they assumed that preemption is not allowed and all jobs in the job set have the same deadline. Even though the same deadline assumption is very strong and unpractical for real-time applications, the job scheduling problem in such a hypercube system is proven as NP-Complete [1]. If each job has its own deadline, the problem is exacerbated.

In this paper, we consider the problem of scheduling hard real-time jobs in a hypercube system. Our research efforts are focused on the development of a suitable heuristic algorithm which can be efficiently implemented. We consider a scheduling algorithm in a dynamic environment in which the algorithm has complete knowledge of currently active jobs, but new jobs, not known to the algorithm when it is scheduling the current set, may arrive. When a new real-time job enters the hypercube system, the schedulability of it for the current job set including the new job and jobs in the ready queue is tested. If the current job set with a newly arrived job is schedulable, the new job is put into the ready queue. Otherwise, it is informed that the new job cannot be executed in this system. We propose a heuristic real-time scheduling algorithm for a hypercube system which supports the allocation of a subcube for each job. We also evaluate the proposed algorithm using simulation.

The remainder of the paper is organized as follows. In Section 2, we describe the system model and defines formally the problem discussed in this paper. Section 3 presents the proposed algorithm and an example of the algorithm. Section 4 analyzes the algorithm via

---

† This research was supported in part by STEPI under contract.

simulation studies. Finally, in Section 5, we summarize this paper and give our concluding remarks.

2 System Model and Problem Definition

Given a set $J = \{J_i : 1 \leq i \leq n\}$ of n independent hard real-time jobs to be run on an m-cube, a job J_i is characterized by the following three parameters: C_i (its computation time), D_i (its deadline), and R_i (its dimensional requirement).

The above characterization means that a job J_i requires an R_i-dimensional subcube during C_i units of time and J_i must finish executing before the deadline D_i. From the above characteristics, we can obtain another important characteristic, the laxity. The laxity (L_i) of a job J_i is the time obtained by subtracting its computation time (C_i) from its deadline (D_i). We assume all jobs are hard real-time, aperiodic, independent, nonpreemptable, and ready to start execution at the time of invocation of the scheduling algorithm. We also assume that the resources requested by a job are used throughout the job's execution time.

Based on the above system model, we will define formally the problem studied in this paper.

The *real-time job scheduling (RTJS) problem* in hypercube systems is to determine whether each job in a job set J can complete its execution before its deadline in a hypercube system and to provide such a schedule if it exists. The real-time job scheduling problem in a hypercube system can be formally stated as follows:

Real-Time Job Scheduling(RTJS) in a hypercube system
Instance : an m-dimensional hypercube and a list of jobs $J = \{J_1, J_2, \cdots, J_n\}$, where $J_i = (C_i, D_i, R_i)$, $1 \leq i \leq n$ (C_i : computation time, D_i : deadline, R_i : subcube dimension)
Problem : determine whether every job in J can complete its execution before its deadline and find such a schedule if it exists.

If addresses of processors in a k-dimensional subcube are between $[h \cdot 2^k, (h+1) \cdot 2^k - 1]$, the subcube is called k-dimensional *basic subcube*. If all requested subcubes are *basic subcubes*, this job scheduling problem is equivalent to a variant of the *two dimensional bin packing* problem [4].

3 Real-time Job Scheduling Algorithm

In this section, we first present a heuristic scheduling algorithm and then give an example of the algorithm in operation.

3.1 Overview of the proposed scheduling algorithm

The proposed scheduling algorithm consists of *job scheduling* and *processor allocation*. For processor allocation, we use the BL (Bottom-Left) [2] scheme which is similar to the simple Buddy scheme. This is because the choice of processor allocation scheme does not result in a big difference in the performance of the proposed scheduling algorithm. For job scheduling, we use a heuristic search algorithm. The heuristic search algorithm is based on the classical idea that scheduling is a search problem. The search space has a tree structure. Any intermediate vertex of the search tree represents a partial schedule. Each leaf or terminal vertex represents a complete schedule. The heuristic search algorithm tries to determine a feasible schedule for a subset of jobs and then increases the size of the subset by including one more job at a time until all jobs are scheduled or the algorithm fails to find a feasible schedule.

The algorithm works as follows : It starts at the root of the search tree, which is an empty schedule, and extends the schedule (with one more job) by moving to one of the vertices at the next level in the search tree until a feasible schedule is derived. When moving to one of the vertices at the next level, we select the job with the smallest laxity among the remaining jobs. When extending the partial schedule at each level of search tree, the algorithm determines whether it is *strongly-feasible* or not. A partial schedule is said to be *strongly-feasible* if *all* the schedules obtained by extending it with any one of the remaining jobs are also feasible [3].

It may happen that a partial feasible schedule is found not to be *strongly-feasible* when the current partial schedule is extended by another job, say J. Then, it is appropriate to stop the search since none of the future extensions involving the job J will meet its deadline. However, it is possible to backtrack and to continue the search even after finding a non-strongly-feasible schedule. Backtracking is done by discarding the current partial schedule, returning to the previous partial schedule, and extending it by choosing a different job. In our algorithm, we limit the number of backtracks to a certain number so that the algorithm finishes within a polynomial time. Note that the algorithm may fail to find a feasible complete schedule by limiting the number of backtracks. From the following theorem, we know that the complexity of strong feasibility test is $O(m)$ without regard to the number of jobs.

Theorem 1: (Strong Feasibility Test in a Hypercube System) When extending the partial schedule at each step of the algorithm in order to determine whether it is *strongly-feasible* or not, at most $m + 1$ jobs of the remaining jobs in an m-cube are sufficient to test for strong feasibility.

The proof for this theorem is omitted due to lack of space. The interested reader can obtain the proof from [8].

3.2 Data Structures

The proposed scheduling algorithm uses the following three data structures. Note that the system is an m-dimensional hypercube system.

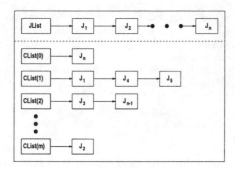

Figure 1: Data structures used by the scheduling algorithm

- $JList$: A list of jobs already determined as schedulable. Jobs in the $JList$ are linked in increasing order of laxity.

- $CList$: $CList$ consists of $m + 1$ independent lists, marked as $CList(k)$, $0 \le k \le m$, in Figure 1. $CList(k)$ is a list of jobs requesting a k-dimensional subcube and waiting for scheduling. Jobs in the $CList$ are linked in increasing order of laxity.

- $ProcT$: A rectangle of size $p \times q$, where p is 2^m and q is the latest deadline among the jobs to be scheduled. Any allocated job J_i is represented as a box in $ProcT$ that indicates what subcube to be used from what time to what time.

3.3   Scheduling algorithm

The inputs of the proposed algorithm are a new job J_{new}, $JList$ and $CList$, and the output of that is $ProcT$. We assume that there are $n - 1$ jobs in $JList$ and a new job J_{new} arrives. The $n - 1$ jobs in $JList$ are already determined to be schedulable. The scheduling algorithm tries to find a feasible schedule for n jobs including the new job J_{new}. The new job J_{new} is entered into $JList$ and $CList$ is also updated to reflect all n jobs. Let k be the number of allowed backtracks. The proposed scheduling algorithm is as follows:

Strong-Feasible-Scheduling
$(J_{new}, JList, n, CList, m, ProcT, k)$

Insert J_{new} into $JList$;
for (job = 0; job < n; job++)
    for (backtrack=0; backtrack<k; backtrack++)
        Select the first job (J_{min}) in $JLIST$;
        if (Test-Strong-Feasibility
                $(J_{min}, ProcT, CList, m)$==TRUE)
            Remove J_{min} from $JList$ and $CList$;
            BL $(J_{min}, ProcT, m)$;
            escape from for-loop;
        endif;
    endfor;
    if (backtrack == k)

---

        remove J_{new} from $JList$;
        return(UNFEASIBLE);
    endif;
endfor;
return(FEASIBLE);

Test-Strong-Feasibility$(J_{min}, ProcT, CList, m)$

for (dim=0; dim<m; dim++)
    if $CList(dim)$ is empty, skip this step;
    else
        Select the first job(J_f) in $CList(dim)$;
        BL($J_f, ProcT, m$);
        if J_f is not located within D_f,
            return(FALSE);
    endif;
endfor;
return(TRUE);

The procedure BL in the algorithm represents the Bottom-Left processor allocation scheme [2].

The time complexity of the proposed algorithm is as follows. There are two nested loops in the procedure **Strong-Feasible-Scheduling**. The loop body runs within $O(m)$ since at most one job from each dimension is selected for the strong feasibility test. Therefore the overall time complexity of the proposed algorithm is $O(nmk)$ where n and k represent the number of jobs and the number of backtracks, respectively.

4   Simulation

In this section, we evaluate the performance of the proposed algorithm by simulation. What we are interested in is the percentage of job sets for which a feasible schedule is found by the algorithm from all job sets that have at least one feasible schedule. Our simulation process consists of two steps. First, assuming that the number of jobs is n and the dimension of hypercube is m, we generate a fixed number of schedulable job sets which have at least one feasible schedule. Next, we count the number of job sets for which the algorithm finds a feasible schedule among the generated schedulable job sets.

4.1   Simulation Method

We generate jobs according to a very tight schedule without leaving any spare time units on the 2^m processors.

The job set generator is used only for the purpose of generating a set of jobs with a feasible schedule. The generated job set is then used as an input to the scheduling algorithm, i.e., the scheduling algorithm has no knowledge of the schedule itself but is only given the jobs and their requirements. The detail description for the job set generation have been omitted due to lack of space. The interested reader can obtain it from [8].

In the job set generator, we used a fixed value of 1 as the minimum computation time and 10 as the maximum computation time.

The performance metric used is the *success ratio* (SR) defined in the following manner [7]: Assume that N job sets are generated according to certain distributions, where each job set is guaranteed to have at least one feasible schedule. Let N_f be the total number of job sets for which a scheduling algorithm finds a feasible schedule. Then, the success ratio (SR) of the algorithm is given as $SR = \frac{N_f}{N}$.

4.2 Results and Analysis

We evaluated the heuristic scheduling algorithm using simulation. We examined the effect of and the number of backtracks on the success ratio(SR).

Table 1: The effect of the number of backtracks on the success ratio

#Bac trac kings	Success Ratio(SR)					
	3 cube	4 cube	5 cube	6 cube	7 cube	8 cube
0	0.75	0.91	0.95	0.98	0.98	0.99
1	0.85	0.95	0.97	0.99	0.99	1.00
2	0.85	0.95	0.98	0.99	0.99	1.00
3	0.85	0.95	0.98	0.99	0.99	1.00
4	0.85	0.95	0.98	0.99	0.99	1.00
5	0.85	0.95	0.98	0.99	0.99	1.00
6	0.85	0.95	0.98	0.99	0.99	1.00

To examine the effect of the number of backtracks on the success ratio (SR), we varied the number of backtracks from 0 to 6 and the size of the hypercube from 3 to 8 while the number of jobs is set to 20. We also generated 100 job sets for this experiment. Table 1 shows the effect of the number of backtracks on the success ratio (SR). From Table 1, we can see that the success ratio (SR) becomes the maximum at a certain number, and then there is no difference if the number of backtracks is larger than that number. We can see that the number of backtracks required is dependent on the hypercube size. However, the number of backtracks which results in the maximum SR is fixed for each size and very small.

Overall, we can conclude that the proposed algorithm guarantees success ratio (SR) of more than 95% in most useful cases with hypercube dimension > 3.

5 Conclusion

In this paper, we described the problem of scheduling hard real-time jobs in a hypercube system. Since the real-time job scheduling problem in a hypercube system is an NP-complete problem, we proposed a heuristic scheduling algorithm. The proposed algorithm finds a feasible schedule by extending a partial schedule by including one additional job which guarantees a strong feasibility. In case that there is no more jobs that guarantees a strongly feasible schedule, the current partial feasible schedule is canceled and returns to the previous partial feasible schedule — this is known as *backtracking*. The time complexity of the proposed algorithm is $O(nmk)$ where n represents the number of jobs, m represents the dimension of hypercube, and k represents the number of allowed backtracks. The performance of the proposed algorithm is evaluated by simulation. The simulation results show that the algorithm shows the best performance when the number of backtracks is set to a certain fixed number and there is no difference in the performance if the number of backtracks is set to larger than that number. In most useful cases (with hypercube dimension > 3), the proposed algorithm shows a success ratio (SR) exceeding 95%. This means that, for any job set having a feasible schedule, the probability that the proposed algorithm will find no feasible schedule is at most 5%.

References

[1] Yahui Zhu and Mohan Ahuja, "On job scheduling on a hypercube," *IEEE Trans. on Parallel and Distributed Systems*, pp. 62–69, January 1993.

[2] B. S. Baker, E. G. Jr. Coffman, and R. L. Rivest, "Orthogonal packings in two dimensions," *SIAM Journal on Computing*, Vol.9, pp. 846–855, 1980.

[3] Krithi Ramamritham, John A. Stankovic, and Perng-Fei Shiah, "O(n) scheduling algorithms for real-time multiprocessor systems," *Proceedings of the International Conference on Parallel Processing*, pp. 143–152, 1989

[4] E. G. Jr. Coffman, M. R. Garey, D. S. Johnson, and R. E. Tarjan, "Performance bounds for level-oriented two-dimensional packing algorithms," *SIAM Journal on Computing*, Vol.9, pp. 808–826, 1980.

[5] P. Krueger, T.-H. Lai, and V.A. Radiya, "Job scheduling is more important than processor allocation for hypercube computers," *IEEE Trans. on Parallel and Distributed Systems*, pp. 488–497, May 1994.

[6] J. Kim, C. R. Das, and W. Lin, "A top-down processor allocation scheme for hypercube computers," *IEEE Trans. on Parallel and Distributed Systems*, pp. 20-30, January 1991.

[7] Fuxing Wang, Krithi Ramamritham, and John A. Stankovic, "Bounds on the performance of heuristic algorithms for multiprocessor scheduling of hard real-time tasks," *Proceedings of the Real-Time Systems Symposium*, pp. 136–145, 1992.

[8] O. Kwon, J. Kim, S. Hong, and S. Lee, "Real-time job scheduling in hypercube systems," Technical Report CS-HPC-97-001, Pohang University of Science and Technology, 1997.

Hindsight Helps: Deterministic Task Scheduling with Backtracking

Yueh-O Wang   Nancy M. Amato*   D. K. Friesen

Department of Computer Science

Texas A&M University

College Station, Texas 77843-3112

{yuehow,amato,friesen}@cs.tamu.edu

Abstract

This paper considers the problem of scheduling a set of precedence-related tasks on a nonpreemptive homogeneous message-passing multiprocessor system in order to minimize the makespan, *that is, the completion time of the last task relative to start time of the first task. We propose a family of scheduling algorithms, called* IPR *for immediate predecessor rescheduling, which utilize one level of backtracking. We also develop a unifying framework to facilitate the comparison between our results and the various models and algorithms that have been previously studied. We show, both theoretically and experimentally, that the* IPR *algorithms outperform previous algorithms in terms of both time complexity and the makespans of the resulting schedules. Moreover, our simulation results indicate that the relative advantage of the* IPR *algorithms increases as the communication constraint is relaxed.*

1 Introduction

This paper considers the problem of scheduling a set of precedence-related tasks on a nonpreemptive homogeneous message-passing multiprocessor system in order to minimize the *makespan*, that is, the completion time of the last task relative to start time of the first task. This problem is NP-complete, and few polynomial time scheduling algorithms are known even if strong restrictions are placed on the problem. For example, Rayward-Smith [12] showed that the problem of optimally scheduling a set of tasks whose precedence relation forms a directed acyclic graph (DAG) on $m > 1$ processors is NP-complete even when all tasks have unit time execution cost and unit time communication delays. Moreover, if we assume that communication delays are zero, then the scheduling problem is NP-complete even if the execution cost of each task is either one or two time units. If we further assume that all tasks have identical execution costs, then polynomial time algorithms are known if either there are only two processors in the system, or the precedence relation of the tasks forms a tree [9].

Nevertheless, the complexity of the scheduling problem varies according to the constraints we place on the following factors: (i) the relative magnitudes of the execution costs and the communication delays (costs), (ii) the structure of the precedence graph, and (iii) the number of processors in the system. Due to the difficulty of efficiently obtaining optimal schedules, recent research has emphasized *heuristic* approaches which produce near-optimal solutions in polynomial time. Another strategy is to *restrict* the problem so that an optimal makespan for the restricted problem can be found in polynomial time. Both restriction and heuristic approaches are studied in this research.

1.1 Preliminaries

In this work we consider a system with an arbitrary number of nonpreemptive homogeneous processors that communicate via message passing. The precedence relationships between tasks are known before-hand, as are the execution costs and communication delays. If two tasks are scheduled on different processors, the communication delay between them is independent of the processors on which they are scheduled. The system is assumed to be collision-free, so that no messages are lost and all messages are sent in a finite amount of time. The system is contention-free, that is, the channel processors are independent of the task processors, and all processors may be executing tasks at the same time that communication is taking place.

In the task scheduling problem we are given a set $T = \{1, 2, \ldots, n\}$ of n tasks, each with a processing time u_i. The tasks in T can be arranged in a directed acyclic graph, called a *precedence graph* (DAGPG), in which each edge represents a temporal relationship between two tasks. Task j is an *immediate predecessor* of task i if the edge (j, i) is present in the DAGPG; such an edge implies that the execution of task i cannot be initiated until after task j has completed execution and its communication to task i. Each edge (j, i) has a weight c_{ji} representing the communication delay from task j to task i. The graph is called an *in-forest* precedence graph (IFPG) if each node has at most one out-going edge; a connected IFPG is called an *in-tree* precedence graph (ITPG).

1.2 A unifying framework for task scheduling

It is sometimes difficult to make meaningful comparisons between task scheduling algorithms since they are often described and analyzed with respect to different (restricted) versions of the problem. Versions of the task scheduling problem, henceforth referred to as *models*, may vary according to the constraints placed on the structure of the precedence graph, the number of processors available, and the (relative) magnitudes of the computation cost and the communication delay. Accordingly, we suggest representing a model by three parameters $M(G, P, C)$, where G denotes the structure of the precedence graph, P denotes the number of processors available, and C denotes the constraints placed on the communication delay. The models considered by most previous work, and in this paper, can be categorized within this framework by selecting appropriate values for the parameters. (See Table 1.)

The most general, NP-complete version of the problem is represented by model $M(G0, P0, C0)$. If C is more restricted than Cd_1 and less restricted than Cd_2, we say $Cd_1 < C < Cd_2$; similarly for G and P. For example, $C0 < C1 < C2 < C3 < C4$. The natural extension of

*Supported in part by the NSF under CAREER Grant CCR-9624315 and Grant CDA-9529442 and by NATO under Grant CRG 961243.

170

Table 1: **Representative Parameters for** $M(G, P, C)$

G — Structure of Precedence Graph	
$G0$	DAGPG (directed acyclic graph)
$G1$	ITPG (in-tree)
P — Number of Processors Available	
$P0$	*insufficient* (limited or bounded)
$P1$	*sufficient* (as many as needed or unbounded)
C — Communication Constraints	
$C0$	arbitrary (not constrained)
$C1$	comm. delay less than exec. cost of sender ($c_{ij} \leq u_i$)
$C2$	coarse-grain ($\max_j\{c_{ji}\} \leq \min_j\{u_j\}$, $\max_j\{c_{ij}\} \leq \min_j\{u_j\}$)
$C3$	comm. delay less than exec. cost of smallest task
$C4$	unit execution cost and unit communication delay

this ordering to models enables us to draw meaningful comparisons between them. For example, $M(G0, P0, C0) < M(G1, P1, C1) < M(G1, P1, C2)$. Note however, that comparisons between parameters are not necessarily meaningful, that is, this framework defines a partial order for the various models that have been studied.

1.3 Previous work

The problem of scheduling a set of n tasks with precedence relationships on a nonpreemptive multiprocessor system with $m > 1$ identical processors has been studied by many researchers. Most previous work can be classified as either list scheduling algorithms [12, 5, 6, 17, 1, 10, 2] or cluster scheduling algorithms [3, 4, 7, 8, 9, 11, 13, 15, 16]. Due to space constraints, we do not describe the various approaches here; details can be found in [14]. Using the $M(G, P, C)$ framework, Table 2 gives a summary of the previous work most relevant to our research, where $OPT(I)$ denotes the makespan of the optimal schedule.

1.4 Our results

In this work, we study possible optimal algorithms and heuristic solutions for models which have $G \in \{G0, G1\}$, $P \in \{P0, P1\}$, and $C0 \leq C \leq C2$. Most previous work has been on more restricted models with $C \geq C2$, that is, models with more restrictive communication requirements. We propose a family of algorithms called IPR, for *immediate predecessor rescheduling*. We analyze the running time and prove worst-case bounds on the makespans of the resulting schedules for the models $M(G1, P1, C)$, $M(G1, P0, C)$, and $M(G0, P1, C)$, where $C1 \leq C \leq C2$. For these models, we show that IPR finds schedules with smaller makespans than previous algorithms while maintaining the same or only slightly larger running times.[1] We also present simulation results for the models $M(G1, P1, C0)$ and $M(G1, P1, C1)$, and compare the resulting makespans with those obtained by some previously proposed scheduling algorithms. In our experiments, IPR consistently obtained smaller makespans than all of the previous algorithms with which we compared it. A summary of our results is contained in Table 3, where $OPT(I)$ denotes the makespan of the optimal schedule. The diagram shows the relationships between the models; an arrow from a to b indicates a is more restricted than b.

2 The IPR algorithms

In addition to the makespan of the schedule produced, the time required to compute the schedule is also a critical concern. Most of the algorithms mentioned above do not apply any backtracking or look ahead scheme since that would

---

[1]Details omitted here due to space constraints can be found in [14].

complicate the algorithm and increase the time complexity. In this paper we propose a set of scheduling algorithms which utilize one level of backtracking. These algorithms obtain improved schedules without significantly increasing the scheduling time (see Table 3). We call these algorithms IPR, for *immediate predecessor rescheduling*.

A study of previous scheduling algorithms shows that optimal makespans cannot be obtained when the communication constraint is less restrictive unless multiple predecessors of a task are allowed to be scheduled on the same processor. A naive approach which considers scheduling all possible combinations of predecessors on a single processor would have unacceptable time complexity. IPR balances the conflicting requirements of minimizing both the makespan and the scheduling time by considering only the immediate predecessors of a task. It has a running time of $O(n \log n)$. The description of IPR given below is general and applies to any model $M(G1, P1, C)$. However, how close the makespan obtained is guaranteed to be to optimal depends on the communication constraint C.

algorithm: IPR

1. schedule each leaf of the IFPG on a different processor

2. while (there exists an unscheduled task)

    (a) $i \leftarrow$ an unscheduled task with scheduled predecessors

    (b) $\theta \leftarrow \{t_1, t_2, \ldots, t_{e_i}\}$, task i's immediate predecessors, sorted in nonincreasing order of $f_{t_j} + c_{t_j i}$

    (c) find $U \subseteq \theta$ and processor p_U on which to schedule task i and U that minimizes the start time of task i

The only non-trivial step is 2(c). Using the facts stated below, we can devise a scheme for it that runs in $O(e_i + \log e_i)$ time. Let the set θ be defined as in Step 2(b).

Fact 1: If task i's start time cannot be reduced by scheduling some $t_r, r \in \theta$, on the same processor as task i, then task i's start time cannot be reduced by scheduling any $t_j, j > r$, on the same processor as task i.

Fact 2: For those predecessors which are to be scheduled on the same processor as task i, the best order to schedule them is according to their start times.

These facts can be exploited to compute the subset $U \subseteq \theta$ and the processor p_U as follows. By Fact 1, we can consider the tasks in θ in order and the rescheduling process can be terminated as soon as it is determined that the start time of task i cannot be improved. Moreover, the best solution will be obtained when U consists of a consecutive set of the immediate predecessors $\{t_1, t_2, \ldots, t_k\}$, for some $k \leq e_i$, and, by Fact 2, these tasks should be scheduled in order of their start times. Finally, whenever a new predecessor t_j is considered for inclusion in the set U, it is simple to verify that the only processors that need to be considered for scheduling $U \cup \{t_j, \text{task } i\}$ are the processor on which t_j is currently scheduled and the processor p_U selected for $U \cup \{\text{task } i\}$ (which is initially the processor on which t_1 was scheduled). The correctness of this approach follows directly from Facts 1-2. Using an appropriate data structure, it can be implemented in $O(e_i + \log e_i)$ time. Details can be found in [14].

The running time of IPR is dictated by the time spent in Steps 2(b) and 2(c) of the while loop. Recall that e_i is

Table 2: Summary of Most Relevant Previous Work

Algorithm	Model	Time	Makespan
ETF [6]	$M(G0,P0,C.0)$	$O(n^2m)$	$(2 - \frac{1}{m})OPT(I) + C_l$
JLP [1]	$M(G1,P1,C3)$	$O(n)$	$OPT(I)$
JLP/D [1]	$M(G0,P1,C3)$	$O(n^2)$	$OPT(I)$
T [10]	$M(G1,P1,C2)$	$O(n)$	$OPT(I)$
T_{DUP} [10]	$M(G0,P1,C2)$	$O(n^2)$	$OPT(I)$
DSC [16]	$M(G1,P1,C2)$	$O((e+n)\log n)$	$OPT(I)$

Table 3: Summary of the IPR Algorithms

Algorithm	Model	Time	Makespan
IPR	$M(G1,P1,C2)$	$O(n \log n)$	$OPT(I)$
	$M(G1,P1,C1)$	$O(n \log n)$	$\frac{6}{5}OPT(I)$
IPR/S	$M(G1,P1,C2)$	$O(n)$	$OPT(I)$
	$M(G1,P1,C1)$	$O(n)$	$\frac{6}{5}OPT(I)$
IPR/D	$M(G0,P1,C2)$	$O(n^2 \log n)$	$OPT(I)$
	$M(G0,P1,C1)$	$O(n^2 \log n)$	$\frac{6}{5}OPT(I)$
IPR/LP	$M(G1,P0,C2)$	$O(n^2)$	$\frac{3}{2}OPT(I)$
	$M(G1,P0,C1)$	$O(n^2)$	$\frac{9}{5}OPT(I)$

Relationships Between Models

$M(G0,P0,C0)$ — ETF — Least Restricted

$M(G0,P1,C1)$ — IPR/D

$M(G1,P1,C1)$ — IPR(IPR/S)

$M(G1,P0,C1)$ — IPR/LP

$M(G0,P1,C2)$ — IPR/D, T_{Dup}

$M(G1,P1,C2)$ — IPR(IPR/S), T, DSC

$M(G1,P0,C2)$ — IPR/LP

$M(G0,P1,C3)$ — JLP/D

$M(G1,P1,C3)$ — JLP — Most Restricted

Table 4: Simulation Results

Algorithms	Model $M(G1,P1,C0)$			Model $M(G1,P1,C1)$		
	better	worse	same	better	worse	same
IPR vs JLP	396	0	104	51	0	449
IPR vs DSC	396	0	104	51	0	449
IPR vs MCCP	447	6	47	344	1	155
IPR vs DCP	440	3	57	359	0	141
JLP vs DSC	0	0	500	0	0	500
JLP vs MCCP	403	43	54	336	3	161
JLP vs DCP	339	86	75	339	3	158
DSC vs MCCP	403	43	54	336	3	161
DSC vs DCP	339	86	75	339	3	158

the number of immediate predecessors of task i, the task being considered in the current iteration. The sorting required in Step 2(b) takes $O(e_i \log e_i)$ time for each iteration, or $O(n \log n)$ time overall since $\sum_i e_i = O(n)$. As mentioned above, Step 2(c) takes $O(e_i + \log e_i)$ time per iteration, or $O(n)$ time overall. Thus, the running time of IPR is dominated by the sorting in Step 2(b) and is $O(n \log n)$.

It can be shown that for $M(G1, P1, C)$, IPR constructs schedules with optimal makespans when $C \geq C2$, and when $C1 \leq C < C2$, it constructs schedules that are at most $\frac{6}{5}OPT(I)$, that is, makespans at most $\frac{6}{5}$ the length of the optimal makespan [14].

2.1 Other versions of the IPR algorithm

We have designed and analyzed several variations of the basic IPR algorithm discussed above (see Table 3).

One version, called IPR/S for *simple* IPR, is a modification of IPR that avoids the sorting in Step 2(b) and reduces the running time to $O(n)$. It has essentially the same worst-case makespan bounds as IPR; the only exception is when the IFPG has height less than three.

If task duplication is allowed, a modification of IPR, called IPR-DAG/D, can schedule DAGPGs; the basic idea is that a task is duplicated if more than one of its successors would be scheduled on the same processor as that task. The running time of IPR-DAG/D is $O(n^2 \log n)$ and it provides the same performance guarantees as IPR.

If the number of processors is limited ($P0$), then IPR can be used as a subroutine in an algorithm we call IPR/LP which runs in time $O(n^2)$ and achieves a worst-case performance bound of $\frac{9}{5}OPT(I)$ if $C1 \leq C \leq C2$.

3 Experimental comparison

Viewed in our model framework, it is clear from the theoretical results presented in Tables 2 and 3 that the IPR algorithms are superior to previous methods for models with communication constraints in the range $C1 \leq C < C2$. We

now examine IPR's behavior using simulation and compare its performance to some previous algorithms. None of the other algorithms have been theoretically analyzed for models with $C < C2$. The simulation was performed for two models — $M(G1, P1, C0)$ and $M(G1, P1, C1)$.

The algorithms we selected to compare with IPR were JLP [1], DSC [16], DCP [8], and MCCP [16]. We chose DSC and JLP as representatives of the cluster and list scheduling algorithms, respectively. DSC was selected since it is the only cluster scheduling algorithm that has been both theoretically and experimentally analyzed. JLP was selected since it can easily be compared with DSC and because the other list scheduling algorithms achieve either the same, or only slightly improved, makespans. In addition, we chose the cluster scheduling algorithm MCCP since it can optimally schedule worst-cases for JLP, DSC, and IPR.

All algorithms were coded in C++ and run on a Unix system. We generated 500 test cases for each model. The number of tasks in each test case was randomly generated in the range [1, 500], and the execution costs and communication delays were randomly generated in the range [1, 100]. The communication constraint $C1$ was enforced by setting the communication delay to be the remainder after dividing by the sender's execution cost.

The results for each model are given in Table 4, and graphically in Figures 1 and 2 for models $M(G1, P1, C0)$ and $M(G1, P1, C1)$, respectively. In the graphs, the test cases are partitioned into 10 groups according to the number of tasks; group 0 for test cases with 1-50 tasks, group 1 for test cases with 51-100 tasks, etc. The average makespan for each group is shown in the graph. Our simulations show that IPR achieves the smallest makespans among the algorithms studied. The next best algorithms are JLP and DSC, followed by DCP and then MCCP.

Thus, our simulation results reinforce the theoretical analysis and moreover, indicate that the relative advantage of IPR increases when the communication constraint is unrestricted ($C0$).

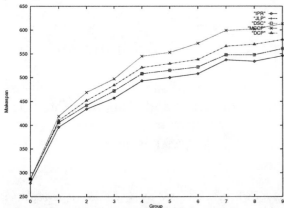

Figure 1: Scheduling algorithm comparison for $M(G1, P1, C0)$.

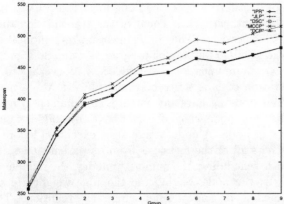

Figure 2: Scheduling algorithm comparison for $M(G1, P1, C1)$.

4 Conclusion

This paper introduces the IPR family of scheduling algorithms which utilize one level of backtracking. To facilitate the comparison between the various models and algorithms that have been studied we proposed the $M(G, P, C)$ model framework. We have seen, both theoretically and experimentally, that the IPR algorithms outperform previous algorithms in terms of both time complexity and the makespan of the resulting schedules. Our results indicate that the relative advantage of the IPR algorithms increases as the communication constraint is relaxed; most previous algorithms have been proposed and analyzed for models with more restricted communication constraints.

The improved makespans obtained by the IPR algorithms result from the use of backtracking. Indeed, without backtracking, schedules with acceptable makespans can only be guaranteed in a more restricted model, such as those with much smaller communication delays. However, backtracking potentially increases the scheduling time significantly, which is not desirable since it would waste resources making the decision. The IPR algorithms balance these conflicting requirements by using only one level of backtracking.

References

[1] F. Anger, J. Hwang, and Y. Chow. Scheduling with sufficient loosely coupled processors. *J. of Parallel and Dist. Comp.*, 9:87–92, 1990.

[2] S. Darbha and D. P. Agrawal. SDBS: A task duplication based optimal scheduling algorithm. In *Proc. of Scalable High Performance Computing Conference*, pages 756–763, May 1994.

[3] H. El-Rewini and T. G. Lewis. Scheduling parallel program tasks onto arbitary target machines. *J. of Parallel and Distributed Computing*, 9(2):138–153, June 1990.

[4] A. Gerasoulis and T. Yang. A comparison of clustering heuristics for scheduling directed acyclic graphs on multiprocessors. *J. of Parallel and Distributed Computing*, 16:276–291, 1992.

[5] R. L. Graham. Bounds on multiprocessing timing anomalies. *SIAM J. Appl. Math.*, 17:416–429, 1969.

[6] J. Hwang, Y. Chow, F. Angers, and C. Lee. Scheduling precedence graphs in systems with interprocessor communication times. *SIAM J. Comput.*, 18(2):244–257, April 1989.

[7] A. A. Khan, C. L. McCreary, and M. S. Jones. A comparison of multiprocessor scheduling heuristics. In *Proc. of the 1994 International Conference on Parallel Processing*, volume 2, pages 243–250, August 1994.

[8] Y.-K. Kwok and Ishfaq Ahmad. A static scheduling algorithm using dynamic critical path for assigning parallel algorithms onto multiprocessors. In *Proc. of the 1994 International Conference on Parallel Processing*, volume 2, pages 155–159, August 1994.

[9] T. G. Lewis and H. El-Rewini. Parallax: A tool for parallel program scheduling. *IEEE Parallel and Distributed Technology*, pages 62–72, May 1993.

[10] D. R. Lopez. *Models and Algorithms for Task Allocation in a Parallel Environment*. PhD thesis, Computer Science Department, Texas A&M University, 1992.

[11] C. McCreary and H. Gill. Automatic determination of grain size for efficient parallel processing. *Communication of the ACM*, 32(9):1073–1078, September 1989.

[12] V. J. Rayward-Smith. UET scheduling with interprocessor communications delays. Technical Report SYS-C86-06, School of Information Systems, University of East Anglia, Norwich, NR4 7TJ, 1986.

[13] V. Sarkar. *Partitioning and Scheduling Parallel Programs for Multiprocessors*. MIT Press, Massachusetts, 1989.

[14] Y. Wang, N. M. Amato, and D. K. Friesen. Hindsight helps: A backtracking scheme for scheduling concurrent tasks. Technical Report 97005, Department of Computer Science, Texas A&M University, May 1997.

[15] M. Wu and D. D. Gajski. Hypertool:a programming aid for message-passing systems. *IEEE Trans. on Parallel and Distributed Systems*, 1(3):330–343, July 1990.

[16] T. Yang and A. Gerasoulis. A fast static scheduling algorithm for dags on an unbounded number of processors. In *Proc. of Supercomputing'91*, pages 633–642, 1991.

[17] C. Yen, S. S. Tseng, and C.-T. Yang. Scheduling of precedence constrained tasks on multiprocessor systems. In *Proc. IEEE First International Conference on Algorithms and Architectures for Parallel Processing*, pages 379–382, April 1995.

Local Search for DAG Scheduling and Task Assignment

Min-You Wu and Wei Shu
Department of Computer Science
State University of New York at Buffalo
wu,shu@cs.buffalo.edu

Jun Gu*
Dept. of Electrical and Computer Engineering
University of Calgary
gu@enel.ucalgary.ca

Abstract

Scheduling DAGs to multiprocessors is one of the key issues in high-performance computing. Local search can be used to effectively improve the quality of a scheduling algorithm. In this paper, based on topological ordering, we present a fast local search algorithm which can improve the quality of DAG scheduling algorithms. This low complexity algorithm can effectively reduce the length of a given schedule.

1 Introduction

Scheduling computations onto processors is one of the crucial components of a parallel processing environment. In this paper, we consider static scheduling algorithms that schedule an edge-weighted directed acyclic graph (DAG) to a set of homogeneous processors to minimize the completion time. Since the static scheduling problem is NP-complete in its general forms [2], there has been considerable research effort in this area resulting in many heuristic algorithms [28, 1, 29, 21]. In this paper, instead of suggesting a new scheduling algorithm, we present an algorithm that can improve the scheduling quality of the existing scheduling algorithms by using a fast local search technique. This algorithm, called *TASK* (Topological Assignment and Scheduling Kernel), systematically minimizes a given schedule in a *topological order*. In each move, the dynamic cost (i.e., *tlevel*) of a node is used to quickly determine the search direction. It can effectively reduce the length of a given schedule.

2 DAG Scheduling

A directed acyclic graph (DAG) consists of a set of nodes $\{n_1, n_2, ..., n_n\}$ connected by a set of edges,

each of which is denoted by $e_{i,j}$. Each node represents a task, and the weight of node n_i, $w(n_i)$, is the execution time of the task. Each edge represents a message transferred from one node to another node, and its weight, $w(e_{i,j})$, is equal to the transmission time of the message. The communication-to-computation ratio (CCR) of a parallel program is defined as its average communication cost divided by its average computation cost on a given system. In a DAG, a node which does not have any parent is called an entry node whereas a node which does not have any child is called an exit node. A node cannot start execution before it gathers all of the messages from its parent nodes. In static scheduling, the number of nodes, the number of edges, the node weight, and the edge weight are assumed to be known before program execution. The edge weight among two nodes assigned to the same processing element (PE) is assumed to be zero.

The objective in static scheduling is to assign nodes of a DAG to PEs such that the schedule length or makespan is minimized without violating the precedence constraints. Many algorithms can be employed in static scheduling including MCP [28], DSC [29], DLS [21], etc. Although these algorithms produce relatively good schedules, they are usually not optimal. Sometimes, the generated schedule is far from optimal. In this paper, we propose a fast local search algorithm, *TASK* (Topological Assignment and Scheduling Kernel), to improve the quality of schedules generated by an initial scheduling algorithm.

3 Local Search for Scheduling and Task Assignment

Local search was one of the early techniques for combinatorial optimization. The principle of local search is to refine a given initial solution point in the solution space by searching through the neighborhood of the solution point. There have been two major periods for the development of local search. Early greedy local search method was able to solve small uncon-

---

*Presently on leave at: Dept. of Computer Science, Hong Kong Univ. of Science and Technology, Kowloon, Hong Kong, gu@cs.ust.hk

strained path-finding problems such as TSP [14, 19]. During the middle and late eighties, more powerful techniques for randomized local search were developed. These include conflict minimization, random variable selection, and pre-, partial, and stochastic variable selection [3, 5, 6, 22, 23, 25, 24, 26]. These randomized local search algorithm can handle large size constraint satisfaction problem (CSP) and constrained optimization problems efficiently.

The n-queen problem is a benchmark for constraint satisfaction problem. Analytical solutions for the n-queen problem exist but they cannot solve general search problems and have no use in practice. In practice a search algorithm is used. The satisfiability (SAT) problem is a binary CSP problem. The scheduling and task assignment problems are well-known as CSP/satisfiability problems. SAT model formulates scheduling and task assignment problems precisely. CSP model expressively characterizes scheduling and task assignment operations.

There were several significant local search solutions to the scheduling and task assignment problems. The *SAT1* algorithm was the first local search algorithm developed for the satisfiability problem during the later eighties [3, 4, 5, 7]. These local search solutions to the SAT problem were applied to solve several large-scale industrial scheduling and task assignment problems.

N-queen problem was a model for the early study of local search algorithms for scheduling and task assignment. During the later eighties, IBM and NASA were working on a number of important scheduling and task assignment projects. The underlying structure of the n-queen problem, represented by a complete constraint graph, gives a relational model with fully specified constraints among the multiple objects [3]. Variations on the dimension, the objects' relative positions, and the weights on the constraints led to a **hyper-queen** problem model which consists of several simple and basic models:

- **n–queen** problem: the *base* model. N queens are indistinguishable and the constraints among queens are specified by the binary values (i.e., 1 or 0).

- **w–queen** problem: the *weighted* n-queen model. N queens are distinguishable (each is associated with a cost) and the constraints among queens are specified by some weights.

- **3d–queen** problem: queens are to be placed in a 3-dimensional ($l \times m \times n$) rectangular cuboid.

A special case, **nm–queen**, is to place queens on an n by m rectangle.

- **q+–queen** problem: more than one queens are allowed to be placed on the same row or the same column.

Based on the n-queen, the *hyper*-queen problem can model the objects/tasks, the performance criteria, the timing, spatial, and resource constraints for a wide range of scheduling and task assignment problems. This made the n-queen problem a general model for many industrial scheduling and task assignment problems. By a remarkable coincidence, the models of several difficult scheduling projects at that time were either the n-queen or the *hyper*-queen problems [12, 27]. All of them required efficient solutions to the n-queen or *hyper*-queen problems.

Many practical applications based on *hyper*-queen models have been developed [8, 26]. These include task scheduling (static or dynamic), real-time system, task assignment, computer resource management, VLSI circuit design, air traffic control, communication system design, and so on. Scheduling problems modeled by various queen models have specific performance criteria and are known to be NP-hard. When scheduling computational tasks onto multiprocessors, for example, one can use a *hyper*-queen model where there are $q+$ weighted queens to be placed on a t by p rectangle. Let t denote the execution time, p the number of processors, q_i the execution time of the ith task, and c_{ij} the communication time from the ith task to the jth task, the goal is to place the *task queens* onto the t by p table and minimize the longest execution path, following the given topological constraints.

Following local conflict minimization [3], a $QS1$ algorithm was developed during late 1987 and was implemented during early 1988. It was the first local search algorithm developed for the n-queen problem [3, 22, 23]. Three improved local search algorithms for the n-queen problem were developed during 1988 to 1990 [16, 13]. $QS2$ is a near linear-time local search algorithm with an efficient random variable selection strategy [24]. $QS3$ is a near linear-time local search algorithm with efficient pre- and random variable selection and assignment [24]. $QS4$ is a linear time local search algorithm with efficient partial and random variable selection and assignment techniques [25, 26]. Compared to the first local search algorithm [3], partial and random variable selection/assignment heuristics have significantly improved search efficiency by orders of magnitude. $QS4$, for example, was able to solve 3,000,000 queens in a few seconds.

Since the early development of local search solutions for scheduling and task assignment applications during the late eighties, more than one hundred industrial companies worldwide have developed these scheduling software systems for various applications. Three years after releasing the $QS1$ algorithm, in 1990, Minton *et al.* independently reported a similar local search algorithm for the n-queen problem [15]. A major difference between Minton's algorithms and Sosic and Gu's algorithms is that Minton's first algorithm was a one dimensional local search without using random heuristics.

Recently local search solutions have been introduced for DAG scheduling and task assignment [8, 26, 9, 10, 11]. A typical randomized local search algorithm for DAG scheduling was implemented in a recent Applied Optimization course project and found to be efficient [11, 17] (also in Figure 1 and [18]). In this algorithm, a node is randomly picked from the blocking node list, where a blocking node is defined as a node that has the potential to block critical path nodes. Then the node is moved to a randomly selected PE. If the schedule length is reduced, the move is accepted. Otherwise, the node is moved back to its original PE. Each move, successful or not, takes $O(e)$ time to compute the schedule length, where e is the number of edges in the graph. To reduce its complexity, a constant $Max\_iteration$ is defined to limit the number of steps so that only $Max\_iteration$ nodes are inspected. The time taken for the algorithm is proportional to $e \times Max\_iteration$. Moreover, randomly selected nodes and PEs may not be able to significantly reduce the length of a given schedule. Even if the $Max\_iteration$ is equal to the number of nodes, leading to a complexity of $O(en)$, the random search algorithm still cannot provide a satisfied performance.

---

construct the blocking node list
searchstep = 0
do {
     pick node n_i randomly from blocking node list
     pick a PE P randomly
     move n_i to PE P
     if schedule length does not improve
          move n_i back to its original PE
     } while (searchstep++ < MAXSTEP)

Figure 1: **RAND:** a randomized local search algorithm for DAG scheduling.

4 Local Search with Topological Ordering for Scheduling

We propose a fast local search algorithm utilizing topological ordering for DAG scheduling. The algorithm is called *TASK* (Topological Assignment and Scheduling Kernel). In this algorithm, the nodes in the DAG are inspected in a *topological order*. In this order, it is not required to visit every edge to determine whether the schedule length is reduced. Time spent on each move can be drastically reduced so that inspecting every node in a large graph becomes feasible. Also, in this order, we can compact the given schedule systematically.

For a given graph, in order to describe the *TASK* algorithm succinctly, several terms are defined as follows:

- $tlevel(n_i)$, the largest sum of communication and computation costs at the top level of node n_i, i.e., *from an entry node to n_i*, excluding its own weight $w(n_i)$.

- $blevel(n_i)$, the largest sum of communication and computation costs at the bottom level of node n_i, i.e., *from n_i to an exit node*.

- The critical path, CP, is the longest path in a DAG. The length of the critical path of a DAG is

$$L_{\mathrm{CP}} = \max_{n_i \in V}\{L(n_i)\},$$

where $L(n_i) = tlevel(n_i) + blevel(n_i)$ and V is the node set of the graph.

If the given graph has been previously scheduled, more terms are defined:

- Node n_i has been scheduled on $PE\ pe(n_i)$.

- Let $p(n_i)$ be the *predecessor node* that has been scheduled immediately before node n_i on PE $pe(n_i)$. If node n_i is the first node scheduled on the PE, $p(n_i)$ is *null*.

- Let $s(n_i)$ be the *successor node* that has been scheduled immediately after node n_i on PE $pe(n_i)$. If node n_i is the last node scheduled on the PE, $s(n_i)$ is *null*.

One of characteristics of the *TASK* algorithm is its independence of the algorithm that was used to generate the initial schedule. As long as the initial schedule is correct and every node n_i has available $pe(n_i)$, $p(n_i)$, and $s(n_i)$ nodes, application of *TASK* guarantees that the new schedule of the graph is better than or equal to the initial one. The *TASK* algorithm is shown in Figure 2.

procedure TASK (*DAG_Schedule*)
begin
/* initialization */
Construct a scheduled DAG;
for node $i := 0$ to $n - 1$ **do**
  $L(n_i) := tlevel(n_i) + blevel(n_i)$;
$L_{CP} := \max_{0 \le i < n} L(n_i)$, the longest path in DAG;

/* search */
while there are nodes in *DAG* to be scheduled **do**
begin
  $i :=$ pick_a_node_with_Max_$L(n_i)$;
  for each PE k
    obtain $L^k(n_i)$ by moving n_i to PE k;
  $t :=$ pick_a_PE_with_Min_L^k;
  if $t == pe(n_i)$ **then** /* if no improvement */
    let node n_i stay at PE $pe(n_i)$;
  else begin /* if there are improvements */
    move node n_i from PE $pe(n_i)$ to PE t;
    modify_pseudo_edges_in_DAG;
    propagate_tlevel_of_n_i_to_its_children;
  end;
  mark n_i as being scheduled;
end;
end;

Figure 2: **TASK:** Topological Assignment and Scheduling Kernel, a local search algorithm based on topological ordering for fast scheduling.

The input of the algorithm is a given DAG schedule generated by any heuristic DAG scheduling algorithm. In the first initialization step, a *scheduled DAG* is constructed, which contains scheduling and execution order information. To enforce the execution order in each *PE*, some *pseudo edges* (with zero weights) are inserted to incorporate the initial schedule into the graph. The *for* loop in the initialization computes the value of *blevel* of each node in the scheduled DAG and initializes *tlevel* for entry nodes. Every edges are marked *unvisited*. The variable $next_k$ points to the next node that has not been inspected in PE k. Initially, none of nodes is inspected so $next_k$ points to the first node in PE k.

In the *while* loop, a ready node n_i with the maximum value $L(n_i) = tlevel(n_i) + blevel(n_i)$ is selected for inspection. Ties are broken by $tlevel(n_i)$. A node is ready when all of its parents have been inspected. In this way, the nodes are inspected in a topological order. Although other topological orders, such as *blevel*, *tlevel*, or *CPN-dominate* can be used, L has been shown to be a good indicator to determine the

node order of inspection [29].

To inspect node n_i, in the *for* loop, the value $L(n_i) = tlevel(n_i) + blevel(n_i)$ is re-calculated for each PE. To conduct the recalculation at *PE* k, node n_i is pretended to be inserted right in front of $next_k$. Here, $tlevel(n_i)$ can be varied if any of its parent nodes was scheduled to either *PE* k or *PE* $pe(n_i)$. Similarly, $blevel(n_i)$ can be varied if any of its child nodes was initially scheduled to either *PE* k or *PE* $pe(n_i)$. Because the *tlevels* of its parent nodes are available and the *blevels* of its child nodes are unchanged, the value of $L(n_i)$ in every PE can be easily computed. The values indicate the degree of improvement by local search. With the new $L(n_i)$'s recalculated for every *PE*, node n_i is then moved to the PE that allows the minimum value of $L(n_i)$. If node n_i has been moved to PE t, the corresponding pseudo edges are to be modified. The *tlevel* of n_i is propagated to its children so that when a node becomes ready, its *tlevel* can be computed. This process continues until every node is inspected.

The time complexity of the *TASK* algorithm is $O(e + np)$, where e is the number of edges, n is the number of nodes, and p is the number of PEs.

In the following, we use an example to illustrate the operation of the *TASK* algorithm.

Example. Assume the DAG shown in Figure 3 has been scheduled to three PEs by a DAG scheduling algorithm. The schedule is shown in Figure 4(a), in

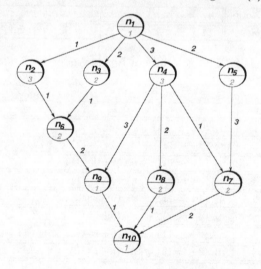

Figure 3: A DAG for Example 1.

which three pseudo (dashed) edges have been added to construct a scheduled DAG, one from node n_6 to node n_8, one from node n_3 to node n_9, and one from node n_4 to node n_5 (not shown in Figure 4(a)). The schedule length is 14. The *blevel* of each node is computed as shown in Table 1. Tables 2 and 3 trace the

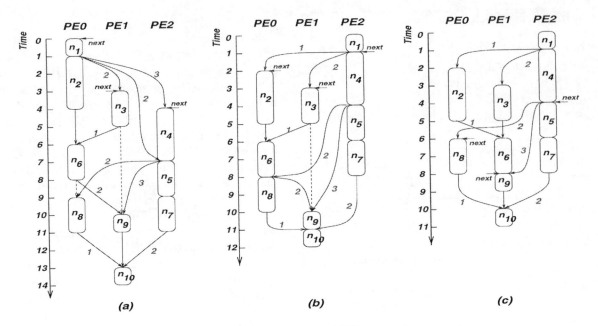

Figure 4: An example of *TASK*'s operations.

tlevel + blevel = L values for each step. In Table 2, "√" indicates the node with the largest *L* value and is to be inspected in the current step. In Table 3, "*" indicates the original PE and "√" the PE where the node is moved to.

Table 1: The Initial *blevel* Values

Node	n_1	n_2	n_3	n_4	n_5	n_6	n_7	n_8	n_9	n_{10}
blevel	14	9	9	10	7	6	5	4	2	1

Table 2: The *L* Values of Ready Nodes for Node Selection

Iter.	
1	n_1 (0+14=14) √
2	n_2 (2+9=11), n_3 (3+9=12) √, n_4 (1+10=11)
3	n_2 (2+9=11), n_4 (1+10=11) √
4	n_2 (2+9=11) √, n_5 (4+7=11)
5	n_5 (4+7=11), n_6 (6+6=12) √
6	n_5 (4+7=11) √, n_8 (6+4=10), n_9 (8+2=10)
7	n_7 (6+5=11) √, n_8 (6+4=10), n_9 (8+2=10)
8	n_8 (6+4=10) √, n_9 (8+2=10)
9	n_9 (8+2=10) √
10	n_{10} (10+1=11) √

First, there is only one ready node, n_1, which is a CP node. Its *L* value on PE 0 is $L^0(n_1) = 0 + 14 = 14$. Then the *L* values on other PEs are computed: $L^1(n_1) = 0 + 14 = 14$, $L^2(n_1) = 0 + 12 = 12$, as shown in Table 3. Thus, node n_1 is moved from PE 0 to PE 2, as shown in Figure 4(b). The L_{CP} of the DAG is

Table 3: The *L* Values for PE Selection

Iter.	Node	PE 0	PE 1	PE 2
1	n_1	0+14=14*	0+14=14	0+12=12 √
2	n_3	3+11=14	3+9=12*	1+12=13
3	n_4	4+12=16	5+9=14	1+10=11*
4	n_2	2+9=11*	5+10=15	4+10 =14
5	n_6	6+6 =12*	6+4=10√	6+9=15
6	n_5	5+10 =15	8+10 =18	4+7 =11*
7	n_7	9+6 =15	9+4 =13	6+5=11*
8	n_8	6+4 =10*	8+4=12	8+4 =12
9	n_9	10+3=13	8+2=10*	8+4=12
10	n_{10}	10+1=11	10+1=11*	10+1=11

reduced to 12. In iterations 2, 3, and 4, moving nodes n_3, n_4, and n_2 do not reduce any *L* value. In iteration 5, node n_6 is moved from PE 0 to PE 1 as the *L* value is reduced from 12 to 11, as shown in Figure 4(c). In the rest five iterations, nodes n_5, n_7, n_8, n_9 and n_{10} do not move.

5 Performance study

The *TASK* algorithm is faster than other existing scheduling algorithms. It can effectively reduce the scheduling length generated by other existing scheduling algorithms by 20% to 30%.

Table 4 compares the complexities of some important scheduling algorithms. The *TASK* algorithm has the lowest complexity, where n is the number of nodes, e the number of edges, p the number of PEs, and s the *MAXSTEP* in the random search algorithm.

Table 4: Complexities of Scheduling Algorithms

MCP [28]	$n^2 \log n$
DSC [29]	$(e+n)\log n$
DLS [21]	pn^3
$RAND$ [18]	se
$TASK$	$e + pn$

In this section, we present the performance results of the $TASK$ algorithm and compare the $TASK$ algorithm to the random local search algorithm. We performed experiments using synthetic DAGs as well as real workload generated from the Gaussian elimination program.

We use the same random graph generator in [18]. The synthetic DAGs are randomly generated graphs consisting of thousands of nodes. The sizes of the random DAGs were varied from 1000 to 4000 with an increment of 1000. The weights on the nodes and edges were generated randomly so that the average value of CCR corresponded to 0.1, 1, or 10.

We evaluate performance of these algorithms in two aspects: the schedule length generated by the algorithm and the running time of the algorithm.

Table 5 shows the comparison of the random local search algorithm, $RAND$, and the $TASK$ algorithm on 4 PEs. Performance data are the average over ten graphs. $MAXSTEP$ is set to be 64 according to [18]. The comparison is conducted for different sizes and different CCRs. The CPN-Dominate algorithm [18] generates the initial schedules. The value in the column "Initial" is the length of the initial schedule; that in the column "$+RAND$" is after the random local search algorithm conducted on the initial schedule; and that in the column "$+TASK$" is after the $TASK$ algorithm conducted on the initial schedule. The columns "%" following "$+RAND$" and "$+TASK$" are the percentage of improvement of the initial schedule. The running times (in seconds) of the random local search algorithm and the $TASK$ algorithm are also shown in the table, as well as their ratio. As it can be seen from the tables $TASK$ is much more effective and faster than random local search. Increasing the value of $MAXSTEP$ in the random local search algorithm can improve its performance. However, even if the $MAXSTEP$ is equal to the number of nodes, the random search algorithm does not perform as well as the $TASK$ algorithm. The search order is important. The order with the L value is superior than the random search order. Furthermore, if $MAXSTEP$ is equal to the number of nodes, the random search algorithm is extremely slow because the running time is proportional to $MAXSTEP$.

6 Conclusion

Local search is a powerful method for solving NP-hard optimization problems. It can be applied to improve the quality of existing scheduling and task assignment algorithms. An important issue in local search is to find a good indicator for the most promising search direction. The value of $tlevel + blevel$ is selected in the $TASK$ algorithm. It has shown a satisfactory performance. $TASK$ is a low-complexity high-performance local search algorithm for static DAG scheduling. It can quickly reduce the length of a given schedule generated by other scheduling algorithms.

Acknowledgments

This research was partially supported by NSF Grants CCR-9505300 and CCR-9625784, NSERC Research Grant OGP0046423, NSERC Strategic Grant MEF0045793, and NSERC Strategic Grant STR0167029.

References

[1] H. El-Rewini and T.G. Lewis. Scheduling parallel program tasks onto arbitrary target machines. *Journal of Parallel and Distributed Computing*, Jun. 1990.

[2] M.R. Garey and D.S. Johnson. *Computers and Intractability: A Guide to the Theory of NP-Completeness.* W.H. Freeman, 1979.

[3] J. Gu. Parallel algorithms and architectures for very fast search. Technical Report UUCS-TR-88-005, 1988.

[4] J. Gu. How to solve Very Large-Scale Satisfiability problems. Technical Report UUCS-TR-88-032. 1988, and UCECE-TR-90-002, 1990.

[5] J. Gu. Efficient local search for very large-scale satisfiability problem. *SIGART Bulletin*, 3(1):8–12, Jan. 1992, ACM Press.

[6] J. Gu. Local search for satisfiability (SAT) problem. *IEEE Trans. on Systems, Man, and Cybernetics*, 23(4):1108–1129, Jul. 1993, and 24(4):709, Apr. 1994.

[7] J. Gu and Q.P. Gu. Average time complexities of several local search algorithms for the satisfiability problem. Technical Report UCECE-TR-91-004, 1991. In *Lecture Notes in Computer Science*, Vol. 834, pp. 146-154, 1994.

[8] J. Gu. *Optimization Algorithms for the Satisfiability (SAT) Problem. In* Advances in Optimization and Approximation., pages 72–154, 1994.

Table 5: Comparison for Synthetic DAGs (4 PEs)

# of nodes	CCR	Schedule length					Running time (s)		
		Initial	+RAND	%	+TASK	%	RAND	TASK	ratio
1000	0.1	2536	2536	0.0	2531	0.2	16.4	0.76	21.6
	1	2818	2813	0.2	2669	5.3	5.43	0.25	21.7
	10	5095	5083	0.2	4462	12.4	9.13	0.43	21.2
2000	0.1	5011	5011	0.0	4994	0.3	41.8	1.91	21.9
	1	5506	5498	0.1	5226	5.1	18.4	0.82	22.4
	10	11002	10980	0.2	8873	13.4	21.7	1.02	21.3
3000	0.1	7728	7728	0.0	7582	1.4	28.1	1.27	22.1
	1	7707	7698	0.1	7475	2.1	81.2	3.57	22.7
	10	15619	15586	0.2	11953	15.6	38.7	1.76	22.0
4000	0.1	10088	10087	0.01	9937	1.0	57.3	2.54	22.6
	1	10665	10648	0.2	10145	4.1	88.2	3.90	22.6
	10	21436	21419	0.1	17390	12.5	55.5	2.58	21.5

[9] J. Gu, M.Y. Wu, and W. Shu. Fast local search algorithms for DAG scheduling and task assignment. Private communications, Summer 1995.

[10] J. Gu. Local search for large-scale scheduling and task assignment problems. Lectures in COMP 680: Applied Optimization, HKUST, Fall 1995.

[11] J. Gu, B. Du, and Y.K. Kwok. Design efficient local search algorithms for DAG scheduling. COMP680 Applied Optimization Course Project Meeting, HKUST, Fall 1995.

[12] M.D. Johnston. Scheduling with neural networks — the case of the Hubble Space Telescope. In *NASA Memo*, 1989.

[13] W. Lewis Johnson. Letter from the editor. *SIGART Bulletin*, 2(2):1, April 1991, ACM Press.

[14] S. Lin. Computer solutions of the traveling salesman problem. *Bell Sys. Tech. Journal*, 44(10):2245–2269, Dec. 1965.

[15] S. Minton, M.D. Johnston, A.B. Philips, and P. Laird. A heuristic repair method for constraint satisfaction and scheduling problems. *Artificial Intelligence*, 58:161–205, 1992.

[16] V. Kumar. Algorithms for constraint satisfaction problems. *The AI Magazine*, 13(1):32–44, 1992.

[17] Y.K. Kwok. A linear time DAG scheduling algorithm using local search. COMP680 Applied Optimization Course Project, Dec. 14, 1995.

[18] Y.K. Kwok, I. Ahmad, and J. Gu. FAST: A low-complexity algorithm for efficient scheduling of DAGs on parallel processors. In *Proc. of Int'l Conference on Parallel Processing*, pp. (II) 150 — 157, 1996.

[19] C.H. Papadimitriou and K. Steiglitz. *Combinatorial Optimization: Algorithms and Complexity*. Prentice Hall, Englewood Cliffs, 1982.

[20] R. Puri and J. Gu. An efficient algorithm for computer microword length minimization. *IEEE Transactions on CAD*, 12(10):1449–1457, Oct. 1993.

[21] G.C. Sih and E.A. Lee. A compile-time scheduling heuristic for interconnection-constrained heterogeneous processor architectures. *IEEE Trans. on PDS*, 4(2):175–187, Feb. 1993.

[22] R. Sosič and J. Gu. How to search for million queens. Technical Report UUCS-TR-88-008, Feb. 1988.

[23] R. Sosič and J. Gu. A polynomial time algorithm for the n-queens problem. *SIGART Bulletin*, 1(3):7–11, Oct. 1990, ACM Press.

[24] R. Sosič and J. Gu. Fast search algorithms for the n-queens problem. *IEEE Trans. on Systems, Man, and Cybernetics*, SMC-21(6):1572–1576, Nov./Dec. 1991.

[25] R. Sosič and J. Gu. 3,000,000 queens in less than one minute. *SIGART Bulletin*, 2(2):22–24, Apr. 1991.

[26] R. Sosič and J. Gu. Efficient local search with conflict minimization. *IEEE Trans. on Knowledge and Data Engineering*, 6(5):661–668, Oct. 1994.

[27] H.S. Stone and J.M. Stone. Efficient search techniques – an empirical study of the n-queens problem. *IBM J. Res. Develop.*, 31(4):464–474, July 1987.

[28] M.Y. Wu and D.D. Gajski. Hypertool: A programming aid for message-passing systems. *IEEE Trans. PDS*, 1(3):330–343, July 1990.

[29] T. Yang and A. Gerasoulis. DSC: Scheduling parallel tasks on an unbounded number of processors. *IEEE Trans. on PDS*, 5(9):951–967, Sept. 1994.

Software-Based Deadlock Recovery Technique for True Fully Adaptive Routing in Wormhole Networks *

J. M. Martínez, P. López, J. Duato

Facultad de Informática
Universidad Politécnica de Valencia
Camino de Vera s/n
46071 - Valencia, SPAIN
E-mail: {jmmr,plopez,jduato}@gap.upv.es

T. M. Pinkston

SMART Interconnects Group
EE-Systems Dept.
University of Southern California
Los Angeles, CA 90089-2562
E-mail: tpink@charity.usc.edu

Abstract

Networks using wormhole switching have traditionally relied upon deadlock avoidance strategies for the design of deadlock-free routing algorithms. More recently, deadlock recovery strategies have begun to gain acceptance. In particular, progressive deadlock recovery techniques are very attractive because they allocate a few dedicated resources to quickly deliver deadlocked packets, instead of killing them. Deadlock recovery is based on the assumption that deadlocks are rare. Very recently, the frequency of deadlock occurrence was measured [21, 18], showing that deadlocks are highly unlikely when enough routing freedom is provided. However, deadlocks are more prone when the network is close to or beyond saturation. Additionally, some performance degradation has been observed at saturation. Similar performance degradation behavior at saturation was also observed in networks using deadlock avoidance strategies [9].

In this paper we take a different approach to handle deadlocks and performance degradation. We propose the use of an injection limitation mechanism that prevents performance degradation near the saturation point and reduces the probability of deadlock to negligible values even when fully adaptive routing is used. We also propose an improved deadlock detection mechanism that only uses local information, detects all the deadlocks, and considerably reduces the probability of false deadlock detection over previous proposals. In the rare case when impending deadlock is detected, our proposed recovery technique absorbs the deadlocked message at the current node and later re-injects it for continued routing towards its destination. Performance evaluation results show that our new approach to deadlock handling is more efficient than previously proposed techniques.

Keywords Wormhole switching, adaptive routing, deadlock recovery, deadlock detection, virtual channels.

*This work was supported by the Spanish CICYT under Grant TIC94–0510–C02–01 and an NSF Career Award, grant ECS-9624251.

1 Introduction

Wormhole switching [8] has become the most widely used switching technique for multicomputers and distributed shared-memory multiprocessors, and it is also being used for networks of workstations [5]. The use of virtual channels can increase network throughput considerably by dynamically sharing the physical bandwidth among several messages [7]. However, it has been shown that virtual channels are expensive, increasing node delay considerably [6]. Therefore, the number of virtual channels per physical channel should be kept small.

An alternative approach to increase throughput consists of using adaptive routing [13]. However, deadlocks must be handled efficiently. A deadlock occurs in an interconnection network when no message is able to advance toward its destination because the network buffers are full. A simple and effective approach to handle deadlocks consists of restricting routing so that there are no cyclic dependencies between channels [8]. A more efficient approach consists of allowing the existence of cyclic dependencies between channels while providing some escape paths to avoid deadlock, therefore increasing routing flexibility [9, 11]. However, such deadlock avoidance techniques require dedicated resources to provide those escape paths. Usually, those dedicated resources are virtual channels, thus preventing the use of all the virtual channels for fully adaptive routing. Deadlock recovery strategies overcome this constraint, but the cost associated with existing deadlock recovery strategies can be higher than necessary, especially with regressive techniques which kill and later re-inject deadlocked messages at the original source node [19, 14]. Progressive deadlock recovery strategies, like *Disha* [2, 3], are more efficient as only a few dedicated resources are allocated to quickly deliver deadlocked packets, instead of killing them. One central buffer per node is enough to route deadlocked messages to their destination by preempting network bandwidth from non-deadlocked packets only when impending deadlock is detected.

Progressive deadlock recovery techniques usually achieve a higher performance than deadlock avoidance techniques because they require less dedicated resources to handle deadlocks [3]. However, both techniques may produce severe performance degradation when the network is close to saturation. Performance degradation at the saturation point was studied in [9, 15] and, more recently, in [21, 18]. In [9], this situation was described as occurring when messages block cyclically faster than they are drained using the escape path. Although this can be mitigated by adding several virtual channels per physical channel, this solution is expensive and is overkill for most networks. In [21, 18], the frequency of deadlock occurrence on k-ary n-cubes using a true fully adaptive minimal routing algorithm with deadlock recovery was measured. It was shown that deadlocks rarely occur when sufficient routing freedom is provided, but they are more likely to occur when the network is close to or beyond saturation. Although this suggests that deadlock recovery techniques are viable, they suffer similar performance degradation at network saturation due to the phenomenon described in [9]. In fact, performance degradation at saturation can be more pronounced in Disha-based recovery techniques than in deadlock avoidance-based techniques since less resources (and, therefore, less bandwidth) are provided to drain cyclically blocked messages [4]. Thus, regardless of the technique used to handle deadlocks, performance degradation should be addressed. Draining cyclically blocked messages may require more bandwidth than is provided by existing deadlock recovery and deadlock avoidance techniques.

In this paper, a different approach is taken to handle both deadlocks and performance degradation. We propose the use of the injection limitation mechanism proposed in [15] to prevent performance degradation near the saturation point. It consists of limiting message injection when the network is heavily loaded. As a by-product, the probability of deadlock is reduced to negligible levels even when fully adaptive routing is used with only a few virtual channels. We also propose an improved deadlock detection mechanism that uses only local information to more accurately detect deadlocks and considerably reduce false deadlock detection over previous proposals [14, 2]. In the rare cases when deadlocks are suspected, we propose a new software-based progressive recovery technique that absorbs (as opposed to killing) the deadlocked message at the current node and later re-injects it from the current node for continued routing towards its destination. This technique has some points in common with the software-based fault-tolerant routing mechanism proposed in [20]. Indeed, both techniques can be combined for increased performance and reliability. Thus, our new progressive deadlock recovery technique incorporates simple mechanisms that minimize performance degradation at saturation as well as the occurrence of deadlocks, improves deadlock detection and simplifies the recovery procedure. The main contributions of this paper are a software-based progressive deadlock recovery technique that requires no buffers to handle deadlocks (although it requires some buffer space in the local node), an improved deadlock detection mechanism, and a detailed study of the behavior of those mechanisms.

Section 2 gives background on deadlock avoidance and recovery techniques, highlighting the motivation for this work. Section 3 describes the message injection limitation mechanism used to reduce deadlock probability and performance degradation. Section 4 presents our improved deadlock detection mechanism that more accurately differentiates between false deadlock (congestion) and true deadlocks. Section 5 presents our simpler yet efficient software-based deadlock recovery strategy that benefits from the other mechanisms proposed in this paper. Section 6 gives the performance results of true fully adaptive routing with our proposed deadlock recovery mechanisms compared against previously proposed adaptive routing algorithms using other deadlock avoidance techniques. Finally, some conclusions are drawn in Section 7.

2 Background

As presented in [4], the theory of deadlock avoidance proposed in [9] can be easily extended to support progressive deadlock recovery. Indeed, both deadlock handling techniques are very similar from a theoretical point of view. Both of them allow fully adaptive routing on some set of resources while providing dedicated resources to escape from deadlock. The theories proposed in [9, 4] provide a static view of the network, allowing one to formally prove that escape resources are enough to avoid or recover from any deadlocked configuration: if several messages block cyclically waiting for resources held by other messages, these theories guarantee that some resources will become available sooner or later and that all the messages will be able to proceed. However, from a more practical point of view, guaranteeing that escape resources will become available sooner or later may not yield the highest performance.

Consider a network using unrestricted fully adaptive wormhole routing over virtual channel resources. The routing flexibility provided by this algorithm produces cyclic dependencies between channels in most topologies. When the network is heavily loaded (close to or beyond the saturation point), messages block cyclically very quickly. If escape resources are not able to drain messages from those cycles fast enough, messages will have to wait for a long time. As a consequence, those blocked messages will occupy channel bandwidth and, thus, decrease network throughput considerably. Additionally, the latency of those messages will also increase considerably. This behavior was first described in [9]. The important point here is that at least one of the following must occur to mitigate this behavior: either escape resources must provide enough bandwidth to drain messages blocking cyclically (regardless of whether deadlock avoidance or recovery is used) or a mechanism(s) must prevent the build-up of cyclically blocked messages that would subsequently need to be drained.

Deadlock avoidance and progressive deadlock recovery techniques mainly differ in the way they supply escape paths and in when those paths are used. Consider first how escape paths are supplied. Deadlock avoidance techniques have traditionally relied upon virtual channels to supply escape paths [9, 11]. Progressive deadlock recovery techniques like Disha [2, 3, 4] use a flit-sized central buffer to supply the escape paths and route over these buffers by preempting network bandwidth from nondeadlocked packets so as to quickly resolve impending deadlock. In both cases, escape paths are implemented as additional dedicated resources in the router (although Disha-based recovery requires less router resources and, therefore, achieves higher performance before network saturation). Consider next the issue of when escape paths are used. Deadlock avoidance techniques typically allow the immediate use of escape resources when a message is blocked (although it is possible to limit their use by using time-outs [10]). Deadlock recovery techniques, however, generally limit the use of escape resources allowing only those messages suspected of being involved in deadlock to use them; otherwise, the limited bandwidth offered by recovery resources would quickly saturate. Existing deadlock detection mechanisms use only crude time-out information on blocked messages and do not use other relevant information such as physical channel activity. This makes the mechanism susceptible to mistaking congestion for deadlocks, particularly when messages are blocked for long periods of time waiting for resources occupied by long messages which are not blocked.

We believe a simple injection limitation mechanism can keep the network below its saturation point to prevent the build-up of cyclically blocked messages that could lead to deadlock formation and/or performance degradation. We also believe that deadlock detection can be made more accurate to keep recovery resources from becoming saturated with nondeadlocked messages by associating the time-out mechanism with physical channel inactivity instead of just message blocking. These fine-tuning mechanisms minimize the probability of packets recovering from suspected deadlocks to such infinitesimal levels that allow the router to be simplified by not requiring any edge or central buffers to supply escape/recovery paths. We believe that the buffer space already provided at each node can be utilized as a low-cost solution to this even more highly improbable case. Simulation results confirm our belief that highest possible performance without degradation can be achieved.

3 Message Injection Limitation

In this section, we briefly describe the message injection limitation proposed in [15]. As we mentioned above, there is some performance degradation when the network reaches saturation. The problem can be stated as follows: Latency increases with network traffic until a certain point (saturation point) is reached, at which time the latency value increases considerably while throughput (accepted traffic) tails off. In other words, accepted traffic noticeably decreases when the saturation point is reached.

Performance degradation within the network occurs when routing algorithms allow cyclic dependencies between channels. When traffic becomes high, messages block cyclically faster than they are drained by the escape paths, thus increasing latency and decreasing throughput. Provided that there are some escape resources to drain messages blocking cyclically, deadlock cannot occur, but messages wait for a long time in the network. One solution to this problem is to increase routing freedom by adding more virtual channels [9, 21, 18]; then messages will have less probability of being involved in cyclic dependencies. However, an excessive number of virtual channels could lead to a reduced clock frequency [6].

Another solution is to control network traffic to ensure that it is always under the performance degradation point. But traffic is often global in nature. Thus, it is not feasible to easily measure it at each node. As an approximation, traffic can be estimated locally by counting the number of busy virtual output channels at each node [15]. We have found that the average number of busy virtual output channels at each router monotonically increases with network load. Hence, we can establish that there is a useful correlation between the number of busy virtual channels and the network tending to saturation. This allows us to approximate global traffic rate by simply monitoring the number of busy virtual output channels local to a router. We use this in implementing our injection limitation mechanism to avert network saturation.

When the number of busy virtual output channels surpasses a threshold value, the router prevents the injection of new messages, keeping them at the source node. If we properly select the threshold value, there is a high probability that the network will never reach saturation and performance degradation can be mitigated. A simple implementation of this mechanism requires only a register which holds the threshold value, a comparator, and a counter associated with each router, which are not in the critical path. The counter is incremented each time a successful route is established (another output virtual channel becomes occupied) and is decremented when the tail of a message leaves the router. Of course, this mechanism will increase the delay of those messages that are not injected into the network at once, but the average message delay can actually be less than that obtained by the same adaptive algorithm without the injection limitation mechanism because of the degradation mentioned above. Results show that performance degradation as measured by the tailing-off of throughput is eliminated completely [15]. Moreover, the increment in message latency produced by the injection limitation is negligible for the whole range of network traffic. In [16] we present an in-depth discussion of this and other message injection limitation mechanisms.

4 Improved Deadlock Detection Mechanism

Previously proposed deadlock detection mechanisms are based on measuring the inactivity time of blocked messages [2, 14]. In this section, we describe a more accurate deadlock detection mechanism that better distinguishes between messages blocked due to network congestion and messages blocked due to likely impending deadlock.

A deadlock detection mechanism should have two important features. First, it should be simple; it should not add needless complexity to the network that could reduce performance and/or increase cost. Second, it should be implemented as a distributed mechanism, working only with local information available at each router.

Instead of measuring the time a message is blocked, the proposed mechanism measures the time that channels requested by messages are inactive due to the current messages occupying them remaining blocked. Transmission activity is monitored in all the virtual output channels that can be used by a given blocked message. A message is only presumed to be deadlocked if all the alternative virtual output channels that are requested by that message contain blocked messages. It should be noted that when the routing algorithm uses all the virtual channels in each physical channel in the same way, it is only necessary to monitor activity in the physical channels. This is the case for true fully adaptive routing.

This mechanism can be implemented as follows. A counter is associated with each output physical channel. This counter is incremented every clock cycle and is reset when a flit is transmitted across the physical channel. Thus, the counter contains the number of cycles that this channel is inactive. Note that this counter also indicates the number of cycles since the last flit transmission across any of the virtual channels in that physical channel. This time is continuously compared with a given threshold. If it is greater than this threshold, a one-bit flag (inactivity flag) is set indicating that the physical output channel is inactive. The flag is reset when a flit is transmitted across the physical channel.

The routing control unit is assigned to message headers in a round-robin fashion. Blocked headers are also routed in order to determine whether some of the output channels requested by them became free. Every time a message is routed, if all the feasible virtual output channels are busy, then the inactivity flags associated with the corresponding physical output channels are checked. If all of these flags are set, then there is no activity through any of the feasible physical output channels, and the message is presumed to be involved in a deadlock.

It is important to note that the counters and inactivity flags are associated with physical output channels, instead of virtual channels. This is only correct if the routing algorithm can use all the virtual channels of a given physical channel in the same way as with true fully adaptive routing. This considerably simplifies the implementation.

In order to implement the mechanism, the only required hardware is a counter, a comparator and a single bit latch associated with each physical output channel. If we want a programmable threshold, then another register is needed. However, in order to simplify the comparison between the counter and threshold value, it is recommendable to select a power of two for the threshold value. In this case, a single output bit of the counters is enough to indicate that the threshold has been reached. No comparators and registers are needed. In addition, the router must be modified to check the inactivity flags every time an unsuccessful routing is made.

Finally, it should be noted that the mechanism will detect all possible deadlocks, but also some false deadlocks depending on the threshold used. Thus, the mechanism must be properly tuned, choosing the appropriate threshold.

5 Software-Based Deadlock Recovery

Wormhole networks have traditionally relied upon deadlock avoidance for the design of deadlock-free routing strategies [17]. Thus, routing algorithms usually have some constraints in order to avoid deadlocks. Recently, the frequency of deadlock occurrence in k-ary n-cube networks using wormhole switching was measured emperically [21, 18]. From this study, we know that deadlocks are very rare, especially when two or more virtual channels are used with true fully adaptive routing. Moreover, the message injection limitation mechanism described in Section 3 can be used to further reduce the probability of reaching deadlocked configurations.

Let us assume that true fully adaptive minimal routing is used. This routing algorithm imposes no restrictions on the use of virtual and physical channels, except that paths should be minimal. Also, let us assume that message injection is limited by using the mechanism proposed in Section 3. The mechanism described in Section 4 is used for deadlock detection. Although deadlock detection is highly improbable, it could still be detected. So, a recovery mechanism is required.

It is easy to see that in a deadlocked configuration, at least one of the messages involved in it will have its header at the head of an input buffer, waiting for an output channel. Also, the proposed deadlock detection mechanism only presumes that a message is deadlocked if its header is being routed (it is at the head of an input buffer). Thus, all we have to do in order to recover from deadlock is to remove that message from the network by ejecting it at the current node. This can be easily accomplished by the router when it detects a possibly deadlocked message. The router selects the internal memory channel at the current node for this message, as if this node were its destination. A control bit is required to distinguish between normal and deadlocked messages.

Finally, removed messages must be re-injected into the network at a later time. This is also easy to accomplish.

If the software messaging layer detects reception of a message whose destination is not the current node, it must inject the message again into the network. The true message destination can be found in the message header.

The proposed mechanism is a low-cost progressive deadlock recovery technique. Instead of killing deadlocked messages [14, 19], it absorbs them at the current node, allowing them to make progress at a later time. The main advantage of this technique is its simplicity. The proposed recovery mechanism does not even require dedicated buffers in the router to recover from deadlock. It is enough to have some buffer space in the local node. Moreover, programmable network interfaces based on powerful processsors and large buffer memory are emerging as a viable host for communication operations [5], being the future host for message handlers without involving the processor. These network interfaces meet the buffer requirements of software-based deadlock recovery. By keeping the deadlock recovery operations in the interface, we gain some efficiencies, since messages do not have to traverse the I/O bus and the memory hierarchy of the local node. Therefore, this mechanism provides improvement over Disha by requiring a simpler router design. However, the software-based recovery mechanism assumes that a processor is associated with every node, and this is not true for all networks. In those cases, Disha should be preferred. On the other hand, the described mechanism is a software solution which is always slower than a hardware one. However, taking into account that deadlocks are not frequent, the proposed mechanism will not be used frequently. It may even happen that deadlocks are never detected, provided that the other mechanisms proposed in this paper are properly tuned. Additionally, routing can be done without any restrictions, increasing overall performance. Thus, the mechanism proposed in this paper makes the common case fast.

It must be noted that the proposed recovery strategy does not increase performance over Disha [2, 3], but it eliminates the requirement of using buffers (edge or central) for deadlock recovery. In addition, this mechanism provides more routing flexibility because it allows unrestricted use of non-minimal paths. However, Disha only allows non-minimal paths to normal messages; routing of deadlocked messages requires minimal paths. This property is interesting for the implementation of fault-tolerant routing. Moreover, the software-based deadlock recovery mechanism proposed in this paper can be easily combined with the software-based fault-tolerant routing strategy proposed in [20]. As this deadlock recovery technique imposes no routing restrictions, non-minimal routing could be used in the presence of faults, thus improving fault tolerance and performance with respect to [20]. Fault tolerant routing is beyond the scope of this paper and is the subject of future research.

6 Performance Evaluation

In this section, we evaluate by simulation the behavior of true fully adaptive routing algorithms using the deadlock recovery strategy proposed in this paper.

The evaluation methodology used is based on the one proposed in [9]. The most important performance measures are latency (time required to transmit a message) and throughput (maximum traffic accepted by the network). Traffic is the flit reception rate. Latency is measured in cycles. Traffic is measured in flits per node per cycle.

Taking into account the sizes of current multicomputers and the studies about the optimal number of dimensions [1], we have evaluated the performance of the new algorithms on a 8-ary 3-cube network (512 nodes).

6.1 Network Model

Our simulator models the network at the flit level. Each node of the network consists of a processor, its local memory and a router. The router contains a routing control unit, a switch, and several physical channels. The processor is connected to its router by four independent channels.

The routing control unit computes the output channel for a message as a function of its destination node, the current node and the output channel status. The routing algorithm can use any minimal path to forward a message toward its destination. In addition, several virtual channels per physical channel can be used. In other words, all virtual channels in all the feasible directions can be used. This algorithm is referred to as True Fully Adaptive Routing algorithm (TFAR). The routing control unit can process only one message header at a time. It is assigned to waiting messages in a demand-slotted round-robin fashion (including those messages generated in the local processor). When a message gets the routing control unit but it cannot be routed because all the alternative output channels are busy, it must wait in the input buffer until its next turn. The deadlock recovery strategy proposed in Section 5 is used, together with the deadlock detection mechanism described in Section 4.

The internal router switch is a crossbar. Thus, it allows multiple messages to traverse it simultaneously without interference. It is configured by the routing control unit each time a successful routing is made.

Physical channels can be split into several virtual channels. Virtual channels are assigned to the physical link using a demand-slotted round-robin arbitration scheme. Each virtual channel has an associated buffer with capacity for four flits.

6.2 Message Generation

Message traffic and message length depend on the applications. For each simulation run, message generation rate is assumed to be constant and the same for all the nodes. Once the network has reached a steady state, the flit generation rate is equal to the flit reception rate (traffic). We evaluate the full range of traffic, from low load to saturation. Message destination is randomly chosen among all the nodes. Short messages (16 flits), long messages (64 flits) and bimodal message lengths (60% of 16-flit messages and 40% of 64-flit messages) are considered.

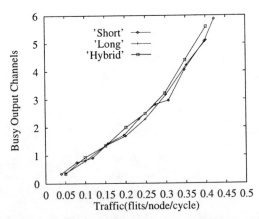

Figure 1: Busy output channels versus traffic for a 512-node 3-D torus with a true fully adaptive routing algorithm with 2 virtual channels per physical channel.

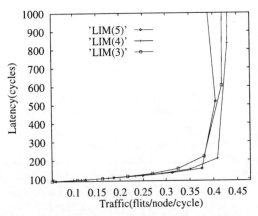

Figure 2: Average message latency versus traffic for a 512-node 3-D torus with a true fully adaptive routing algorithm with 2 virtual channels per physical channel.

6.3   Adjusting Message Injection Limitation

In this section, we select the appropriate threshold for the message injection limitation mechanism described in Section 3.

As an example, Figure 1 shows the average number of busy virtual output channels versus traffic for the TFAR routing algorithm with 2 virtual channels per physical channel. The number of busy virtual output channels when the network is close to saturation is almost the same for all the message lengths analyzed. In particular, there are almost 6 busy channels on average. The plot for the TFAR algorithm with 3 virtual channels per physical channel (not shown) has a similar shape. In this case, there are 9 busy virtual output channels when the network is saturated. The optimal value for the injection limitation threshold should be close to these values. In Figure 2 we can see the performance of the TFAR algorithm with 2 virtual channels per physical channel with several injection limitation thresholds. Taking into account that the results do not depend on message length, for the sake of shortness, the results are only shown for one message length. In order to remove the performance degradation of the routing algorithm, message injection must be avoided if the number of busy output channels exceeds 4 virtual channels. For the TFAR routing algorithm with 3 virtual channels per physical channel, message injection must be avoided if the number of busy output channels exceeds 8 virtual channels. These values of busy virtual output channels were used as thresholds for the message injection limitation mechanism in the simulation results presented in Sections 6.4 and 6.5.

6.4   Frequency of Deadlock Detection

In this section we tune the deadlock detection mechanism proposed in Section 4. Tables 1 and 2 show the number of messages detected as possibly deadlocked for different values of the threshold for the TFAR routing algorithm with 2 virtual channels per physical channel, measured in

Threshold	64 cycles		32 cycles		16 cycles	
Traffic	NDM	Tout	NDM	Tout	NDM	Tout
0.30	0	0	0	2	0	11
0.35	0	1	0	4	0	15
0.40	0	2	2	11	2	30
0.44	0	13	4	43	11	107

Table 1: Number of messages detected as possibly deadlocked for the new detection mechanism (NDM) and previously proposed mechanism based on time-outs (Tout). True fully adaptive routing algorithm with 2 virtual channels per physical channel is used with 16-flit messages.

clock cycles. A message is included in the count if it has been detected as possibly deadlocked using the indicated threshold in any of the checkpoints. The tables show the values for the new detection mechanism proposed in this paper (NDM) and previously proposed mechanisms based on time-outs (Tout). However, no message deadlocked during the simulations, since all messages arrived at their destinations. The statistics have been gathered periodically during the simulations. The simulations have been run for a number of cycles high enough to deliver 100,000 messages. As we can see in Table 1, the routing algorithm with 2 virtual channels per physical channel and short messages requires a threshold not lower than 64 cycles in order to avoid false deadlock detections using the NDM. From Table 2, if messages are long, the threshold must be 4 times higher ($\geq$ 256 cycles), matching the relationship between lengths for long and short messages. Similar thresholds are required when 3 virtual channels per physical channel are used in the true fully adaptive routing algorithm.

Therefore, the optimal value for the threshold depends on message length. The only simple solution consists of

Threshold	256 cycles		128 cycles		64 cycles	
Traffic	NDM	Tout	NDM	Tout	NDM	Tout
0.23	0	0	0	1	0	4
0.29	0	0	0	1	0	6
0.35	0	0	0	2	0	10
0.41	0	4	0	10	2	32
0.43	0	13	3	40	9	96

Table 2: Number of messages detected as possibly dead-locked for the new detection mechanism (NDM) and previously proposed mechanism based on time-outs (Tout). True fully adaptive routing algorithm with 2 virtual channels per physical channel is used with 64-flit messages.

splitting messages into fixed length packets. However, the proposed mechanism considerably reduces the number of false deadlock detections over crude time-outs. Moreover, no deadlocks are detected even when the network reaches the saturation point, provided that the threshold is properly tuned. This is not the case for detection mechanisms based on crude time-outs. These mechanisms detect a much higher number of false deadlocks for the same time-out value. Additionally, the number of detected deadlocks increases very quickly when the network approaches saturation. Hence, the proposed deadlock detection mechanism considerably improves over previously proposed ones.

We are currently evaluating the influence of message destination distribution on the deadlock detection mechanism. Also, we are trying to improve this mechanism to make it less dependent on message length.

6.5 Performance Comparison

In this section we compare the performance of true fully adaptive routing and the proposed progressive deadlock recovery mechanism with previously proposed fully adaptive routing algorithms using deadlock avoidance [12]. Note that preemptive progressive deadlock recovery techniques (like Disha [3]) achieve the same performance as the proposed recovery mechanism, assuming that both of them use the same injection limitation and deadlock detection mechanisms and that the additional router complexity required in Disha does not impact clock frequency.

In particular, the TFAR routing algorithm for a k-ary n-cube with 2 and 3 virtual channels per physical channel with the message injection limitation mechanism described in Section 3 and the deadlock recovery mechanism proposed in Section 5 is compared against the deterministic routing algorithm (Det) proposed in [8] and the fully adaptive routing algorithm (FAR) proposed in [12]. The deterministic algorithm uses two virtual channels per physical channel, while the fully adaptive one uses three virtual channels per physical channel. For message ejection and re-injection at intermediate nodes, we assumed a delay of

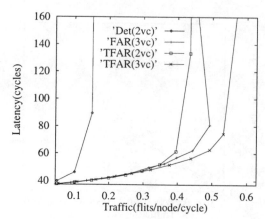

Figure 3: Average message latency versus traffic for a 512-node 3-D torus using different routing algorithms (Deterministic, Fully Adaptive Routing (FAR), and True Fully Adaptive Routing (TFAR). Short messages are assumed.

200 cycles. The threshold for deadlock detection was four times the size of the longest message.

Taking into account that the results for the three message lengths considered have the same shape, for the sake of shortness, we will only show the results for short messages in Figure 3. The TFAR routing algorithm achieves a throughput three times higher than the deterministic algorithm, with the same number of virtual channels. The fully adaptive routing algorithm with 3 virtual channels achieves only a slightly higher throughput than the true fully adaptive routing algorithm with only two virtual channels. The best results are achieved by the true fully adaptive routing algorithm with 3 virtual channels per physical channel, which achieves about a 15% more throughput than the fully adaptive one and lower latency than any other routing algorithm for the full range of traffic. No deadlocks were detected during the simulations. In addition, the true fully adaptive routing algorithm has no performance degradation at saturation. These results show the effectiveness of the proposed mechanisms for message injection limitation and deadlock detection, therefore enabling the use of simple software-based deadlock recovery mechanisms.

7 Conclusions

In this paper, we proposed a set of mechanisms that minimize the hardware requirements to handle deadlocks. In particular, we proposed an injection limitation mechanism that reduces the probability of deadlock to negligible values, and eliminates performance degradation at the saturation point. This mechanism only requires measuring the number of busy output channels at each node. We also proposed an improved deadlock detection mechanism that considerably reduces the probability of false deadlock detection. It is based on monitoring flit advancement across the channels requested by blocked messages. Both mechanisms are tunable through simulation. The combination of these two mechanisms is so effective that no deadlocks were detected during the simulations, even when using a true fully adaptive routing algorithm. Hence, these mechanisms enable the use of simple and inexpensive techniques for deadlock recovery. Thus, we proposed a software-based progressive deadlock recovery mechanism that requires no buffers to recover from deadlocks. It is based on the absorption of messages detected as being deadlocked at the current node and their re-injection into the network. Although the absorption of messages incurs a high latency, false deadlock detection has been reduced to negligible values, making software-based deadlock recovery feasible. In addition, this deadlock recovery mechanism can be easily combined with the software-based fault-tolerant routing strategy proposed in [20].

The proposed mechanisms were combined with a true fully adaptive routing algorithm for the 3D-torus that can route messages following any minimal path. Any number of virtual channels per physical channel can be used. This routing algorithm was evaluated and compared with other well-known routing algorithms (deterministic [8] and fully adaptive with a deadlock avoidance mechanism [12]). The results show that the true fully adaptive routing algorithm achieves a reduction in message latency for the full range of traffic while increasing throughput for both short (16-flit) and long (64-flit) messages.

In conclusion, we proposed a set of mechanisms to handle deadlocks that require a very small amount of hardware, eliminate performance degradation at saturation point, reduce the frequency of deadlock to negligible values, and considerably reduce the probability of false deadlock detection. To the best of our knowledge, this is the first feasible deadlock handling technique for wormhole networks that requires no dedicated buffer resources to handle deadlocks.

References

[1] A. Agarwal, "Limits on interconnection network performance", *IEEE Trans. on Parallel and Distributed Systems*, vol. 2, no. 4, pp. 398–412, Oct. 1991.

[2] Anjan K. V. and T. M. Pinkston, "DISHA: A deadlock recovery scheme for fully adaptive routing," in *Proc. of the 9th Int. Parallel Processing Symposium*, April 1995.

[3] Anjan K. V. and T. M. Pinkston, An efficient fully adaptive deadlock recovery scheme: DISHA," in *Proc. of the 22nd Int. Symposium on Computer Architecture*, June 1995.

[4] Anjan K. V., T. M. Pinkston and J. Duato, "Generalized theory for deadlock-free adaptive routing and its application to Disha Concurrent," in *Proc. of the 10th Int. Parallel Processing Symposium*, April 1996.

[5] N. J. Boden, D. Cohen, R. E. Felderman, A. E. Kulawik, C. L. Seitz, J. Seizovic and W. Su, "Myrinet - A gigabit per second local area network," *IEEE Micro*, pp. 29–36, February 1995.

[6] A. A. Chien, "A cost and speed model for k-ary n-cube wormhole routers," in *Proc. of Hot Interconnects'93*, August 1993.

[7] W. J. Dally, "Virtual-channel flow control," *IEEE Trans. on Parallel and Distributed Systems*, vol. 3, no. 2, pp. 194–205, March 1992.

[8] W. J. Dally and C. L. Seitz, "Deadlock-free message routing in multiprocessor interconnection networks," *IEEE Trans. on Computers*, vol. C–36, no. 5, pp. 547–553, May 1987.

[9] J. Duato, "A new theory of deadlock-free adaptive routing in wormhole networks," *IEEE Trans. on Parallel and Distributed Systems*, vol. 4, no. 12, pp. 1320–1331, December 1993.

[10] J. Duato, "Improving the efficiency of virtual channels with time-dependent selection functions," *Future Generation Computer Systems*, no. 10, pp. 45–58, 1994.

[11] J. Duato, "A necessary and sufficient condition for deadlock-free adaptive routing in wormhole networks," *IEEE Trans. on Parallel and Distributed Systems*, vol. 6, no. 10, pp. 1055–1067, October 1995.

[12] J. Duato and P. López, "Performance evaluation of adaptive routing algorithms for k-ary n-cubes," in *Proc. of the Workshop on Parallel Computer Routing and Communication*, May 1994.

[13] P. T. Gaughan and S. Yalamanchili, "Adaptive routing protocols for hypercube interconnection networks," *IEEE Computer*, vol. 26, no. 5, pp. 12–23, May 1993.

[14] J. H. Kim, Z. Liu and A. A. Chien, "Compressionless routing: A framework for adaptive and fault-tolerant routing," in *Proc. of the 21st Int. Symposium on Computer Architecture*, April 1994.

[15] P. López and J. Duato, "Deadlock-free adaptive routing algorithms for the 3-D torus: Limitations and solutions," in *Proc. of Parallel Architectures and Languages Europe 93*, June 1993.

[16] P. López, J.M. Martínez, J. Duato and F. Petrini, "On the reduction of deadlock frequency by limiting message injection in wormhole networks," in *Proc. of the Workshop on Parallel Computer Routing and Communication*, June 1997.

[17] L. M. Ni and P. K. McKinley, "A survey of wormhole routing techniques in direct networks," *IEEE Computer*, vol. 26, no. 2, pp. 62–76, February 1993.

[18] T.M. Pinkston and S. Warnakulasuriya, "On deadlocks in interconnection networks", in *Proc of the 24th Int. Symposium on Computer Architecture*, June 1997.

[19] D. S. Reeves, E. F. Gehringer and A. Chandiramani, "Adaptive routing and deadlock recovery: A simulation study," in *Proc. of the 4th Conference on Hypercube, Concurrent Computers & Applications*, March 1989.

[20] Y. Suh, B.V. Dao, J. Duato and S. Yalamanchili, "Software based fault-tolerant oblivious routing in pipelined networks," in *Proc. of the 1995 Int. Conference on Parallel Processing*, August 1995.

[21] S. Warnakulasuriya and T.M. Pinkston, "Characterization of deadlocks in interconnection networks," in *Proc. of the 11th Int. Parallel Processing Symposium*, April 1997.

Turn Grouping for Efficient Barrier Synchronization in Wormhole Mesh Networks*

Kuo-Pao Fan   Chung-Ta King

Department of Computer Science
National Tsing Hua University
Hsinchu, Taiwan 300, R.O.C.
`king@cs.nthu.edu.tw`

Abstract

Barrier is an important synchronization operation. On scalable parallel computers, it is often implemented as a collective communication with a reduction operation followed by a distribution operation. In this paper, we introduce a systematic way of generating efficient algorithms to perform barrier synchronization in mesh networks. The scheme works with any base routing algorithm derivable from the turn model [1]. Our scheme extends the *turn grouping* method proposed in [9] with two new algorithms, *Tail_to_Central* and *Central_to_Tail*, for scheduling the message transmission in the reduction and distribution phase respectively. Simulation results show that our approach can take advantage of the adaptivity of the turn-model based routing algorithms and outperform methods proposed previously.

Keywords: Barrier synchronization, interconnection network, adaptive routing, messaging passing, turn model

1 Introduction

A barrier is a synchronization operation in which all participating processors must arrive at the synchronization point before any of them is allowed to proceed further [2, 6]. On scalable parallel computers, barrier synchronization is often implemented as a collective communication. There are two phases in the collective communication. In the *reduction* phase, all member nodes engage in a reduction operation by sending and/or receiving synchronization messages. The *central node* eventually receives the reduced message and decides that all member nodes have arrived at the barrier. Next comes the *distribution* phase, in which the central node multicasts a synchronization message to inform all the members to proceed.

Due to its importance, hardware, software, or hybrid approaches to supporting barrier synchronization have been proposed [2, 3, 4, 5]. Among the schemes, the one using *multidestination messaging* [7, 8] has attracted a lot of attention [5]. The basic concept of multidestination messaging is to carry multiple destination addresses in a message so that a single message can be sent to multiple destinations. At each intermediate destination node, the router replicates the message, sends one copy to the local processor and forwards the other to the next destination. To implement barrier synchronization, the scheme proposed in [5], for example, uses two different types of multidestination worms, *gather* and *broadcasting*, in the reduction and distribution phase respectively. The destination traversing order specified in the message header must conform to the base routing algorithm [8].

Unfortunately, the scheme proposed in [5] only works for dimension-ordered routing algorithms. For other base routing algorithms, such as those derived from the turn model [1], this scheme cannot take full advantage of their adaptivity. Furthermore, this scheme implicitly assumes that nodes perform the operations in lock steps. In other words all the nodes involved in a particular step of the synchronization will complete the send or receive of the synchronization message at the same time. This assumption is impractical for scalable parallel computers.

In this paper, we discuss how a general methodology, called *turn grouping*, can be used to develop barrier synchronization algorithms on wormhole mesh networks. The methodology works with any routing algorithms based on the turn model [1]. The turn model was chosen for our study because it is a very general model for designing wormhole-based adaptive routing algorithms. Our method can take full advantage of the adaptivity of such routing algorithms to efficiently support barrier synchronization with reduced

---
*This work was supported in part by National Science Council under grants NSC-86-2213-E-007-043 and NCHC-86-08-024.

latency. In addition, nodes involved in a barrier can execute asynchronously during each phase of a barrier.

The turn grouping methodology was first proposed in [9] to support multicast, which is a general form of the distribution operation. To apply the methodology to implement barrier synchronization, we need to do the extra work of developing a reduction phase which also conforms to the base routing algorithm. Furthermore, since the algorithm proposed in [9] did not consider the adaptivity of the base routing algorithm, we need to address this issue too.

Among the various techniques discussed in [9], only the grouping method is adopted here to partition the member nodes of a barrier synchronization into disjoint groups. Two new algorithms *Tail_to_Central* and *Central_to_Tail* are proposed in this paper to arrange the steps to perform the reduction and distribution phase based on the disjoint groups. Experimental results show that our method outperforms that in [5] by taking advantage of the adaptivity of the base routing algorithm.

The rest of the paper is organized as follows. In Section 2, we describe the system model and give an overview of the turn grouping method. Extension of the turn grouping method to support barrier synchronization is given in Section 3. In Section 4, we present some architectural supports required for a barrier synchronization and the complete barrier synchronization algorithm based on the turn grouping method. Performance of the proposed schemes will be discussed in Section 5. Finally, we conclude this paper in Section 6.

2 Preliminaries

2.1 System Model

In this paper, we consider a model of the scalable parallel computers, in which an ensemble of processing nodes are interconnected through an n-dimensional mesh network. Figure 1(a) shows the node architecture of the model system. Each node includes a processor, a local memory, and a network router.

The router is responsible for sending messages to or receiving messages from neighboring nodes through the external channels. In an n-dimensional mesh, each node has at most $2n$ neighbors. Thus, there are $2n$ external input channels and $2n$ external output channels. In the following discussion, the notation $+IN_p$ ($+OUT_p$) denotes the external input (output) channel which is connected from the positive direction in dimension p.

The processor and the router are connected through the internal channels. The processor sends messages to the

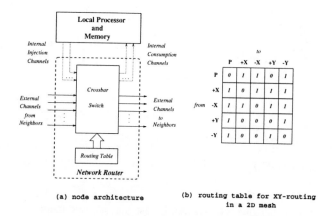

(a) node architecture   (b) routing table for XY-routing in a 2D mesh

Figure 1: A model of scalable parallel computers

router via the *internal injection channels* and receives messages via the *internal consumption channels*. The crossbar switch within the router connects the input channels to the output channels according to the routing table. The routing table specifies the possible output channels that an incoming message from an input channel can be routed. An example of the routing table is shown in Figure 1(b), which specifies the *XY-routing* algorithm for a 2D mesh network.

In this paper, we assume that the routing algorithm specified in the routing table is minimal and deadlock-free and conforms to the turn model. We also assume that the router supports wormhole-based multidestination message passing. Finally, to make sure that the multidestination messaging is deadlock-free, the number of the internal consumption channels is assumed to be large enough [8]. On the other hand, only one internal injection channel will be sufficient for our purpose.

2.2 Overview of Turn Grouping

A very important step in multidestination messaging is to partition the destination nodes into disjoint groups [5, 7, 8]. Each group can be reached by one multidestination message. If the base routing algorithm conforms to the turn model, then the turn grouping method proposed in [9] can be used for partition. The turn grouping method is reviewed briefly below.

Given a base routing algorithm conforming to the turn model, the routing table in the routers specifies the possible turns that a message may be routed. If a message entering through an input channel p can be forwarded to an output channel q, then p and q are said to form an *allowable turn*; otherwise, they form a *prohibited turn*. According to the possible 0-degree and 90-degree prohibited turns, we can examine the *pturn-dependence* relationship

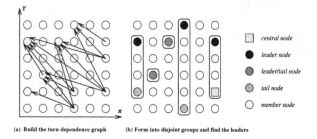

(a) Build the turn dependence graph   (b) Form into disjoint groups and find the leaders

	central node
	leader node
	leader/tail node
	tail node
	member node

Figure 2: An example illustrating the turn grouping method

between the member nodes of a barrier synchronization. Given two nodes X=$(x_1,x_2,...,x_n)$ and Y=$(y_1,y_2,...,y_n)$ in an n-dimensional mesh and a 0-degree prohibited turn PT=$(+IN_p,-OUT_p)$ in dimension p, we say that X is *pturn-dependent* on Y with respect to PT if $x_p < y_p$ and $x_i = y_i$, where $1 \le i \le n$ and $i \ne p$. Similarly, for a 90-degree prohibited turn PT=$(+IN_p,+OUT_q)$ between dimension p and dimension q, we say that X is *pturn-dependent* on Y with respect to PT if $x_p < y_p$ and $x_q > y_q$.

From the pturn-dependence relationship between the member nodes, the *pturn-dependence graph* of a given barrier synchronization can be built. Consider the example shown in Figure 2, in which there are ten member nodes, $\{(0,1), (0,4), (1,2), (2,4), (3,0), (3,1), (3,5), (5,1), (5,3), (5,4)\}$, engaged in a barrier synchronization on a 6×6 2D mesh network. Suppose the base routing algorithm is the *west-first* algorithm [1], then the corresponding pturn-dependence graph is shown in Figure 2(a). We only depict the edges corresponding to the *south-east* prohibited turn [1] so that the graph is readable.

To partition the member nodes into disjoint groups, a graph coloring algorithm is then applied to the pturn-dependence graph. After coloring, member nodes with the same color are partitioned into the same group. The groups are disjoint. In this example five groups are generated as shown in Figure 2(b).

For each group, members in the group can be reached with a multidestination message. Thus, it is necessary to find a *valid multidestination route* among the members so that their sequence in the header of the multidestination message can be determined. A sequence of the destinations are linked by a valid multidestination route with respect to the base routing algorithm if all the turns along the route are allowable. The first (last) node in the route is called the *leader* (*tail*) node.

In [9], a valid multidestination route is determined by arranging the members according to their coordinates. One

node with the largest or the smallest coordinate is chosen to be the *leader* node. The remaining nodes are then linked according to their distances to each other. In Figure 2(b), the leaders are chosen to be the node with the largest x and y coordinates. Note that within each group, the sequence from the tail node to the leader node is also linked by a valid multidestination route.

3 Extension to Barrier Synchronization

In this section, we discuss the issues involved in applying turn grouping to support barrier synchronization. Given a barrier synchronization with an arbitrary number of member nodes, turn grouping can be used to partition the members into disjoint groups. The member nodes in each group is linked by a valid multidestination route conforming to the base routing algorithm. Among the groups, the tail node of the group with the smallest coloring number will be designated as the *central node* of the whole barrier synchronization.

Based on the disjoint groups, the barrier synchronization can be implemented in four steps. In step 1, the leader node of each group sends a reduction message through every member in the group to the tail node. In step 2, the reduction from the tail nodes of all the groups to the central node is performed. In step 3, the central node multicasts a message to the tail nodes to inform them of the end of the barrier. Finally in step 4, each tail node forwards the message to other members in the same group. Steps 1 and 4 can be done easily following the valid multidestination route and its reverse route, respectively. In the following, two greedy algorithms, *Tail_to_Central* and *Central_to_Tail*, will be introduced to perform steps 2 and 3.

3.1 Algorithm Tail_to_Central

The algorithm to schedule the steps for the reduction from the tail nodes to the central node is shown in Figure 3. The algorithm requires *no-of-rphase* phases and each phase will invoke a startup delay. Member nodes involved at each phase is recorded in *RMEMBER[barrier-id,phase,tail]*, where $1 \le phase \le no\text{-}of\text{-}rphase$. Note that the tail node with the smallest coloring number is the central node.

According to the algorithm, the reduction starts from the tail node t_1, which has the largest coloring number. Steps (3)–(6) try to find a valid multidestination route to link as many tail nodes as possible. If all the tail nodes are covered, then step (6) also checks whether the central node can be appended to the resultant multidestination route. If so, then only one phase is needed to perform the whole reduction. Otherwise, two phases are needed. However, if not all the tail nodes are covered after steps (3)–(6), then step (7) is performed to start another phase. The process is repeated starting from the last tail node reached in the previous phase.

In the following, we use the example in Figure 2 to explain the algorithm. We have the set of tail nodes $T = \{(0,1), (1,2), (2,4), (3,0), (5,1)\}$. The central node is $(5,1)$. Figure 4(a) shows the route to reduce from all the tail nodes to the central node, which is obtained from Algorithm *Tail_to_Central*. In this example, only one valid multidestination route is needed to link from the tail node $(0,1)$ to all other tail nodes and the central node. Thus, only one phase is needed.

3.2 Algorithm Central_to_Tail

The Algorithm *Central_to_Tail* schedules the steps to multicast the distribution message from the central node to the tail node of each group. The complete algorithm is shown in Figure 5. Again, it will need *no-of-dphase* phases to do the distribution and the member nodes involved in each phase is denoted *DMEMBER[barrier-id,phase,tail]*.

Step (2) tries to find a valid multidestination route from the central node to the tail node with the largest coloring number, which covers as many other tail nodes as possible. If all the tail nodes are covered, then only one phase is needed. Otherwise, another phase is required. In steps (4) and (5), each tail node which has been linked by a valid multidestination route tries to link other uncovered tail nodes. These steps will be repeated until all the tail nodes are linked.

In Figure 4(b), we use the same example to illustrate the algorithm. Only one phase is needed for the central node to link to all the tail nodes. Figure 6 shows the complete steps to perform the example barrier synchronization based on the west-first routing algorithm. The barrier synchronization procedure and the required architectural supports are described in the next section.

4 Barrier Synchronization Based on Turn Grouping

4.1 Architectural Supports

Our barrier synchronization requires three types of synchronization messages, *reduction worm*, *distribution worm*, and *merge worm*, to accomplish. The formats of these worms are shown in Figure 7(a). The three multidestination worms are different from the normal multicast/broadcast message. First, the message length of these worms is usu-

---

Algorithm Tail_to_Central

Input:
    the set of m tail nodes of a barrier synchronization b, and the set of k prohibited turns $PT = \{PT_1, PT_2, ..., PT_k\}$

Output:
    the number of phases: *no-of-rphase*, and *RMEMBER[b, phase,tail]*, where $1 \leq phase \leq$ *no-of-rphase*

(1) Sort the m tail nodes into a decreasing order $T = \{t_1, t_2, ..., t_{m-1}, t_m\}$ according to their coloring number. The node t_m is the central node.

(2) Let *no-of-rphase* = 1, RMEMBER[*b,no-of-rphase,t_1*]=$\emptyset$, $i = 2$, $TF[1]$ = SET, and $TF[2..m-1]$ = NOTSET, *count*=1, *turnaround* = FALSE.

(3) If $i > m - 1$, then goto (6).

(4) If $TF[i]$ = NOTSET, then goto (5); otherwise let i++ and goto(3).

(5) Check whether *RMEMBER[b,no-of-rphase,tail]* + $\{t_i\}$ can be linked by a valid multidestination route. If so, *RMEMBER[b,no-of-rphase,tail]* = *RMEMBER[b,no-of-rphase,tail]* + $\{t_i\}$, $TF[i]$ = SET, *count*++, and *turnaround* = TRUE. Let i++, and goto (4).

(6) If *count* $\neq m - 1$, then goto (7); otherwise check whether *RMEMBER[b,no-of-rphase,tail]* + $\{t_m\}$ can be linked by a valid multidestination route. If so, *RMEMBER[b,no-of-rphase,tail]* = *RMEMBER[b,no-of-rphase,tail]* + $\{t_m\}$. Otherwise, let t_x be the last node in *RMEMBER[b,no-of-rphase,tail]*, *no-of-rphase* ++, and *RMEMBER[b,no-of-rphase, t_x]* = $\{t_m\}$. Exit.

(7) If *turnaround* = TRUE, then let *turnaround* = FALSE, $i = 2$, and goto (4). Otherwise, let t_x be the last node in RMEMBER[*b,no-of-rphase,tail*], *no-of-rphase*++, RMEMBER[*b,no-of-rphase*,tail(t_x)] = $\emptyset$, $i = 2$, and goto (4).

Figure 3: The algorithm to determine the routes to reduce from the tail nodes to the central node

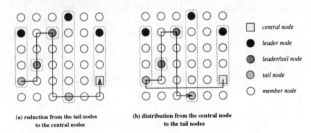

(a) reduction from the tail nodes to the central nodes

(b) distribution from the central node to the tail nodes

□ central node
● leader node
◐ leader/tail node
◉ tail node
○ member node

Figure 4: The routes for reduction and distribution in the example barrier synchronization using the west-first routing algorithm

Algorithm Central_to_Tail

Input:

the set of m tail nodes of the barrier synchronization b, and the set of k prohibited turns $PT = \{PT_1, PT_2, ..., PT_k\}$

Output:

the number of phases to perform distribution: *no-of-dphase*,
DMEMBER[b,phase,tail], where $1 \leq phase \leq$ *no-of-dphase*

(1) Sort the tail nodes into an increasing order $T = \{t_1, t_2, ..., t_m\}$ according to their coloring number. Now, t_1 is the central node. Let *TF*[1..m] = NOT-SET, *no-of-dphase* = 1.

(2) Let *TF*[1] = SET, *count* = 1, and *DMEMBER[b,no-of-dpahse,t_1]* = ∅. Find a valid multidestination route from the the central node t_1 to the tail node t_m and cover as many other tail nodes as possible. If t_i can be added, then let *TF*[i] = SET, *count* ++, and *DMEMBER[b,no-of-dphase,t_1]* = *DMEMBER[b,no-of-dphase,t_1]* + $\{t_i\}$. Let *TF*[m] = SET, *count*++, and *DMEMBER[b,no-of-dphase,t_1]* = *DMEMBER[b,no-of-dphase,t_1]* + $\{t_m\}$.

(3) Check whether any uncovered node among $t_{m-1},...,t_2$ can still be appended to *DMEMBER[b,no-of-dphase,t_1]*. If *count* = m, then EXIT; otherwise, let *no-of-dphase* ++ and goto (4).

(4) For every t_x, where x starts from m down to 1, if TF[x] = SET, then let $i = m - 1$, and do the following steps. When all the nodes are done, then goto (5).

    (4.1) If $i \geq 1$, then check whether *TF*[i] = NOTSET. If so, then goto (4.2); otherwise, $i--$ and goto (4.1). However if $i < 1$, then check whether *count* = m. If yes, then EXIT; otherwise, goto (4.3).

    (4.2) Check whether *DMEMBER[b,no-of-dphase,t_x]* + $\{t_i\}$ can be linked by a valid multidestination route. If so, *DMEMBER[b,no-of-dphase,t_x]* = *DMEMBER[b,no-of-dphase,t_x]* + $\{t_i\}$, *TEMP*[i] = SET, *count*++, *turnaround* = TRUE, $i--$, and goto (4.1). Otherwise, $i--$, and goto (4.1).

    (4.3) If *turnaround* = TRUE, then $i = m - 1$, *turnaround* = FALSE, and goto (4.2).

(5) If *count* < m, then let *no-of-dphase*++, TF=TF + *TEMP*, $i = m - 1$, and goto(4).

Figure 5: The algorithm to determine the routes to distribute from the central node to the tail nodes

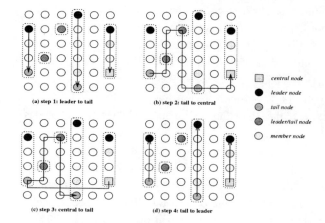

(a) step 1: leader to tail   (b) step 2: tail to central

(c) step 3: central to tail   (d) step 4: tail to leader

▫ *central node*
● *leader node*
◓ *tail node*
◑ *leader/tail node*
○ *member node*

Figure 6: The steps to perform the example barrier synchronization

ally very short since no data flits need be included. Also a barrier synchronization identification number should be specified in the message header. Note that when a multi-destination multicast/broadcast message passes through the router of each intermediate destination node, its data flits must be duplicated into the processor. However, there is no need to do data duplication for these three worms in each intermediate destination.

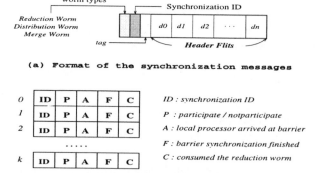

(a) Format of the synchronization messages

	ID	P	A	F	C	
0	ID	P	A	F	C	ID : synchronization ID
1	ID	P	A	F	C	P : participate / notparticipate
2	ID	P	A	F	C	A : local processor arrived at barrier
.....						F : barrier synchronization finished
k	ID	P	A	F	C	C : consumed the reduction worm

(b) Synchronization table

Figure 7: Architectural supports for barrier synchronizations using turn grouping

To support barrier synchronization, each processor/router interface should maintain a *synchronization table* as shown in Figure 7(b). There are k buffers in the table for supporting k concurrent barrier synchronizations. Each buffer contains five components, ID, P, A, F, and C. The field ID is used to identify the barrier synchronization. Each barrier synchronization has a unique identification number. The bit P is used to indicate whether the local processor involves in the corresponding barrier synchronization. The bit A indicates whether the processor has arrived at the barrier. It is set by the processor. The bit C is set when the router consumes a reduction worm. It is used to support asynchronous execution between processors. The F bit indicates whether the barrier synchronization is finished. This bit will be set by the router at the reception of a distribution message. When that happens the router also resets the A and C bits and informs the processor to proceed.

The reduction worm is initiated by the leader node at the reduction phase. When the reduction worm reaches each destination node, it will first match the *synchronization id* specified in the header with the synchronization table. Then, it checks whether bits P and A in that entry are set. If so, then the reduction worm proceeds to the next destination node; otherwise, it is blocked at that router until bit A is set. When the message arrives at the last node specified in the header, the message is consumed by that node and bit C in the synchronization table of that router is set. The bit C will be used by the merge worm.

When the router of a tail node consumes a reduction worm, it will check whether it needs to initiate a merge worm. This depends on the results generated by Algorithm *Tail_to_Central*. When a merge worm passes through the router of a tail node, it looks up the synchronization table to match the synchronization number and check whether the C bit is set. If so, then it traverses to the next tail node; otherwise, it is blocked at that router until C is set. When the merge worm reaches the central node, all the member nodes have already arrived at the barrier and the reduction phase is finished.

The distribution worm is used in the distribution phase. From Algorithm *Central_to_Tail* we can decide which member node should initiate a distribution worm and the associated header information. When the distribution worm arrives at each destination, it will first match the synchronization number in the synchronization table and then set the corresponding bit F to 1. At the same time, A and C are reset to 0. When F is set, the router will inform the local processor to proceed.

4.2 The Barrier Synchronization Procedure

The complete barrier synchronization procedure is shown in Figure 8. The procedure is executed by every member node participating in the barrier synchronization. Step (1) runs the algorithms to obtain the schedule to implement the barrier synchronization. In parallel iterative computations, if the member nodes of a barrier synchronization are fixed, then this step only needs to be executed

once and the schedule can be used throughout the computation. Step (3) performs the reduction phase and steps (4)–(5) perform the distribution phase. The synchronization table is updated in each iteration in step (6).

4.3 An Illustrative Example

In this subsection, we illustrate the barrier synchronization procedure with the example barrier synchronization based on *north-last* routing algorithm. In the north-last routing algorithm, the two prohibited turns are *south-east* and *south-west* [1]. Figure 9(a) shows the edges in the pturn-dependence graph of the example multicast corresponding to the south-east prohibited turn. Graph coloring results in six groups as shown in Figure 9(b). By choosing the leader in each group as the node with the smallest x and the largest y coordinates, the resultant leader set is $L = \{(3,5),(0,4),(5,4),(1,2),(3,1),(1,1)\}$ and the tail set is $T = \{(3,5),(2,4),(5,3),(1,2),(5,1),(3,0)\}$. The central node is $(3,0)$.

In Figure 9(c), if a group has more than one member node, then the leader node initiates a reduction worm to visit every other member node in the group. This reduction worm is consumed by the tail node of the group. After this step, the tail node with the largest coloring number, node $(3,5)$, initiates a merge worm to visit all the other tail nodes and finally reach the central node as shown in Figure 9(d). Now, all the member nodes have finished the reduction phase of the barrier synchronization. In Figure 9(e), the central node initiates the distribution worm to the tail nodes. This process requires two steps. After each tail node has received the distribution worm, it sends a distribution worm to other member nodes in the same group as shown in Figure 9(f).

5 Performance Study

In this section, we evaluate the performance of the proposed barrier synchronization procedure. The experiments were conducted by varying the number of destination nodes. The destination nodes were generated randomly. The performance metric used in the evaluation is the total latency of a barrier synchronization. The latency is the interval from the time when the leader node performs the reduction phase until the time when all the member nodes receive the distribution message. For simplicity, we assume that all the leader nodes perform the reduction at the same time. In each experiment, we performed the simulation 100 times to obtain the average latency. We will only consider 2D mesh networks in the evaluation. Due to space limitation, only results for networks with 32×32 nodes are shown. Other

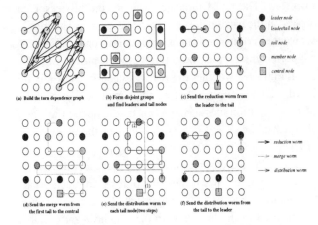

Figure 9: The steps to perform the example barrier synchronization using the north-last routing algorithm

Barrier Synchronization Procedure

Input:

the set of member nodes of a barrier synchronization b, and the set of k prohibited turns $PT = \{PT_1, PT_2, ..., PT_k\}$

(1) Run the turn grouping algorithm to determine the grouping of the member nodes. If *my_id* belongs to a tail node, then run Algorithm *Tail_to_Central* to obtain the routes to perform the reduction from the tail nodes to the central node. If *my_id* is the central node or a tail node, then run Algorithm *Central_to_Tail* to arrange the routes to perform the distribution from the central node to the tail nodes.

(2) Let table[b,P] = 1 and table[b,A] = 1.

(3) If *my_id* is a leader node of group i, then initiate a reduction worm to the other nodes in this group and goto (4). If *my_id* is a tail node or the central node, then perform the following steps.

    (a) Wait for a reduction worm. When it is received, let table[b,C]= 1 and rph = 1.

    (b) If $RMEMBER[b,rph,my\_id] \neq \emptyset$, then initiate a merge worm to reach the other nodes in this set.

    (c) Let rph++. If $rph \leq no\text{-}of\text{-}rphase$, then goto (b); otherwise goto (4).

(4) If *my_id* is the central node or a tail node, then perform the following steps. Otherwise, goto (6).

    (a) Let dph = 1.

    (b) If $DMEMBER[b,dph,my\_id] \neq \emptyset$, then initiate a distribution worm to reach the other nodes in this set.

    (c) Let dph++. If $dph \leq no\text{-}of\text{-}dphase$, then goto (b); otherwise goto (5).

(5) For the central node and each tail node, check whether table[b,F] = 1 or not. If so, then initiate a distribution worm to the other nodes in the same group.

(6) Wait until table[b,F] = 1. If so, let table[b,A] = 0, table[b,C] = 0, table[b,F] = 0, and EXIT.

Figure 8: The procedure to perform the barrier synchronization

simulation results can be found in [10].

In the following discussion, the barrier synchronization using the west-first, north-last, negative-first, and XY-routing as the base routing algorithm are denoted *turn-west*, *turn-north*, *turn-nega*, and *turn-xy* respectively. The method proposed in [5] is denoted *mw*. The parameters used in experiments are as follows: The network size was 32×32. The message startup delay (t_s) was 1 *msec* or 10 *msec*. The link propagation delay (t_p) was taken to be 5 *nsec*. The delay inside the router (t_{node}) for handling multidestination messages was assumed to be 40 *nsec*.

The simulation results are shown in Figure 10. From this figure, we can see that when the number of member nodes is large, turn-west has the lowest latency, followed by turn-north, turn-nega, mw, and turn-xy. This is because in this case, the total traversing distances do not vary much. The total number of startup delays is the dominating factor of the whole barrier synchronization latency.

When the number of member nodes is small and the startup delay is 10 *msec*, as shown in Figure 10(b), we find that turn-west still has the lowest latency. In this case the startup delay is large and again dominates the latency. The traversing distance becomes less of a factor. But when the startup delay is 1 *msec* as shown in Figure 10(a), we find that turn-west has a very high latency. The reason is that the time spent on traversing the member nodes is large, which cannot be neglected with a small startup delay.

A special case in Figure 10 is when the number of member nodes equals the network size. This case is also called the *complete set barrier synchronization*. Turn-nega now has the highest latency and other algorithms are the same. This is because the negative-first routing algorithm groups the member nodes along the diagonal of the 2D mesh and thus the number of member nodes in different groups is different. The largest group contains $2N$ member nodes in an $N \times N$ mesh network. Therefore, the traversing latency will be larger. This phenomenon is more obvious when the startup delay is small. In a complete set barrier synchronization, all the algorithms require the same number of startup delays.

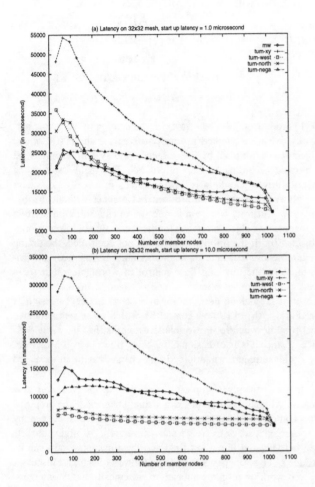

Figure 10: A comparison of the barrier synchronization latencies with (a) $t_s = 1.0\ msec$, (b) $t_s = 10.0\ msec$.

6 Conclusions

On scalable parallel computers, barrier synchronization is usually implemented as a collective communication. In this paper, we introduce a systematic way of generating efficient algorithms to perform barrier synchronization in mesh networks. The proposed barrier synchronization algorithms are based on multidestination messaging and work with any base routing algorithm that is derivable from the turn model. Performance evaluation shows that when the number of nodes participating in a barrier synchronization is large, our method can achieve a lower synchronization latency than the method proposed in [5]. One key factor is because our method takes into account of the adaptivity of the base routing algorithms. In the future, we will study the support of collective communications in switch-based irregular networks [11] by extending the turn grouping method.

References

[1] C. J. Glass and L. M. Ni, "The Turn Model for Adaptive Routing," *Proceedings of the International Symposium on Computer Architecture*, pages 278-297, 1992.

[2] H. Xu, P. K. McKinley, and L. M. Ni, "Efficient Implementation of Barrier Syncronization in Wormhole-routed Hypercube Multicomputer," *Journal of Parallel and Distributed Computing*, 16:172-184, 1992.

[3] S. S. Shang and K. Hwang, "Distributed Hardwired Barrier Synchronization for Scalable Multiprocessor Clusters," in *IEEE Trans. on Parallel and Distributed System*, June, 1995.

[4] C. J. Beckmann and C. D. Polychronopoulos, "Fast Barrier Synchronization Hardware," in *Proceeedings of Supercomputing*, pp. 180–189, Nov. 1991.

[5] D. K. Panda, "Fast Barrier Synchronization in Wormhole K-ary N-cube Networks with Multidestination Worms," *Journal of Future generation Computer Systems(FGCS)*, Nov. 1995.

[6] P. K. Mckinley, Y. J. Tsai and D. F. Robinson, "A survey of Collective Communication in Wormhole-Routed Massively Parallel Computers," *Technical Report, MSU-CPS-94-35*, Dept. of Computer Science, Michigan State University, 1994.

[7] X. Lin and L. M. Ni, "Deadlock-free Multicast Wormhole Routing in Multicomputer Networks," *Proceedings of the International Symposium on Computer Architecture*, pages 116-124, 1991.

[8] D. K. Panda, S. Singal, and R. Kesavan, "Multidestination Message Passing in Wormhole k-ary n-cube Networks with Base Routing Conformed Paths," *Technical Report, OSU-CISRC-12-95-TR54*, Dep. of Computer Science, Ohio-state University.

[9] K. P. Fan and C. T. King, "Turn Grouping for Supporting Efficient Multicast in Wormhole Mesh Networks," in *Proceeedings of the Sixth Symposium on the Frontiers of Massively Parallel Computing(Frontiers'96)*, Oct. 1996.

[10] K. P. Fan and C. T. King, "Turn Grouping for Efficient Barrier Synchronization in Wormhole Mesh Networks," *Technical Report*, Dept. of Computer Science, National Tsing Hua University, Taiwan.

[11] W. Qiao and L. M. Ni, "Adaptive Routing in Irregular Networks Using Cut-Through Switches," in *Proceedings of the International Conference on Parallel Processing*, Chicago,IL, Aug 1996.

Throttle and Preempt: A New Flow Control for Real-Time Communications in Wormhole Networks

Hyojeong Song
Dept. of CS, CAIR
KAIST
Taejon 305-701
Korea
hjsong@camars.kaist.ac.kr

Boseob Kwon
Switching Technology Division
ETRI
Taejon 305-350
Korea

Hyunsoo Yoon
Dept. of CS, CAIR
KAIST
Taejon 305-701
Korea
hyoon@camars.kaist.ac.kr

Abstract

In this paper, we study wormhole routed networks and their suitability for real-time traffic in a priority-driven paradigm. A traditional blocking flow control in wormhole routing may lead to a priority inversion in the sense that high priority packets are blocked by low priority packets for unlimited time. This uncontrolled priority inversion causes the frequent deadline missing. This paper therefore proposes a new flow control called throttle and preempt *flow control, where high priority packets can preempt network resources held by low priority packets, if necessary. As a result, this flow control does not cause priority inversion. Our simulations show that the throttle and preempt flow control dramatically reduces deadline miss ratio without extra virtual channels. It is also observed that the throttle and preempt flow control offers shorter delay for non-real-time traffic than existing real-time flow control does.*

1 Introduction

Over the last decades, many efforts have been made to improve the network performance of multicomputers. Currently, wormhole routing, designed for low latency and high throughput at a low cost, is widely accepted for most multicomputers[9]. Also, real-time applications are vigorously emerging to exploit increased power of multicomputers, such as multimedia service, automated manufacturing and industrial process control, etc.[1], [8], [11], [12].

In wormhole routing, a packet is divided into a number of small *flits*(flow control digits). The header flit of a packet governs the route and remaining flits follow it in a pipelined fashion. If the header flit encounters a channel already in use, the header flit and all remaining flits are blocked by the nature of *blocking flow control* in wormhole routing. To reduce blocking effect which involves network performance degradation, Dally introduced virtual channel concept in [4] : multiple virtual channels, each of which is realized with its own flit buffer and control, can share one physical channel, with a reduction in blocking. However, virtual channels are also arbitrated by blocking flow control, so the blocking effect still exists. Also, the cost of many virtual channel systems is expensive.

In order to support real-time communication in wormhole networks, we have adopted a priority-driven paradigm[10], where objects are prioritized by their urgency and system resources are arbitrated according to their priorities. The main issue of the priority-driven paradigm is how resources in a real-time system are allocated to objects in a prioritized manner without *priority inversion*. Priority inversion is referred to as a situation where a higher priority object must wait for the processing of lower priority objects[10]. If the priority inversion is not controlled, the timing requirement of real-time applications cannot be satisfied[12]. Unfortunately, the blocking flow control in wormhole routing can lead to uncontrolled priority inversion. Hence, even at low network load, blocking flow control may cause frequent missing of deadlines. Also, Li's flow control[8], which is the representative real-time flow control in wormhole networks, has the same deficiency, since it is an extension of blocking flow control. Moreover, Li's scheme requires multiple virtual channels with an increased cost.

In this paper, we propose a new *throttle and preempt* flow control without the need of extra virtual channels. The proposed flow control enables an urgent packet to preempt a channel held by a non-urgent packet, to avoid priority inversion. So, urgent packets can be delivered in a short time and deadline miss ratio can be reduced. This paper is organized as follows. Section 2 discusses related work on resource allocation strategies in multicomputers, and a new flow control is proposed in Section 3. Simulation model and results are presented in Section 4, and Section 5 summarizes this paper.

2 Related Work

In this section, we briefly mention previous channel allocation strategies for wormhole networks, and then for store-and-forward networks.

When multiple header flits contend for the same channel in a wormhole network, FCFS and Round-Robin arbitration policy have been used by most multicomputers such as Intel Paragon[6] and Cray T3D[3]. The FCFS policy assigns the channel to the header flit with the earliest arrival time at a router, while the Round-Robin policy assigns the channel to the header flit in a round-robin basis.

The first work to exploit the timing property of a packet is found in [8]. In [8], for a wormhole network with the same number of virtual channels as the number of priority levels, a packet can request only a virtual channel(s) which is(are) numbered lower than or equal to its priority. For example, for a network with 4 virtual channels numbered 0, ..., 3 and priority levels of 0(lowest), ..., 3(highest), a packet with priority 1 can request only for virtual channel 0 or 1. By reserving more virtual channels for high priority packets, this scheme intends to reduce blocking probability of high priority packets. However, we can easily imagine priority inversion. Suppose each of the virtual channel numbered $k(0 \leq k \leq 3)$ has been assigned for the packet with priority k, respectively. If a new packet with priority 3 arrives and requests one of the virtual channels, it must be blocked, even though lower priorities packets hold virtual channels. Further, this scheme requires as many virtual channels as priority levels, which leads to a complex router[4].

Balakrishnan[1] proposed the PPCS-RT(Preemptive Pipelined Circuit Switching for Real-Time messages) mechanism in a pipelined circuit switching(PCS) which is a variant of wormhole routing. In PCS[5], a packet is transmitted during the data delivery phase along the path which is set up in the path establishment phase. Unlike original PCS, PPCS-RT allows the channel preemption during the path establishment phase, and reduces the priority inversion. But, the priority inversion remains unsettled in the data delivery phase.

Toda[12] studied real-time communications in store-and-forward multicomputers. In [12], priority inheritance scheme is proposed, where a blocked packet forwards its high priority to blocking packets to resolve priority inversion. However, in wormhole routing, flits of a packet exist over several nodes at the same time by the nature of a pipelined transmission. Hence, priority inheritance is not suitable for a wormhole network because it takes a long time to forward the high priority to the header flits of blocking packets.

Rexford[11] proposed a new router architecture with the capability of both wormhole routing and store-and-forward switching. For the store-and-forwarded real-time traffic, it requires the path establishment phase before transmission, and makes an intermediate router schedule packets by their priorities during the data delivery phase. If it is applied to wormhole networks without the path establishment phase, each wormhole router just schedules packets by their priority, which also causes a priority inversion. That is, once a free channel is assigned to a low priority packet, a high priority packet to arrive sometimes later must wait for the low priority packet.

In this paper, to avoid priority inversion, we propose a new flow control for wormhole networks without the need of extra virtual channels.

3 Throttle and Preempt Flow Control

In wormhole networks, priority inversion occurs, when a high priority packet requests the channel held by a low priority packet. However, if a high priority packet preempts the channel, advances to the next node, and makes its own route there as in Figure 1, the priority inversion can be avoided.

The proposed throttle and preempt flow control consists of two fundamental policies : *throttle* policy always reserves room in

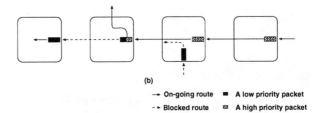

Figure 1: A high priority packet preempts the channel held by a low priority packet, advances to the next node, and makes its own route there.

network resources for high priority packet to preempt, and *preempt* policy enables high priority packets to actually preempt network resources. The proposed flow control can be adopted on any deadlock-free wormhole routing with arbitrary topologies under the following assumptions :

1. there are MAX_PRI(≥ 1) priority levels in a system where priority level of 0 is the lowest and priority level of MAX_PRI - 1 is the highest,

2. each network node is input-buffered,

3. the size of input buffer is MAX_PRI or more than. The reason for this assumption is explained in Section 3.1,

4. without preemption, an input buffer cannot contain flits belonging to different packets, and

5. the number of virtual channels per physical channel can be one or more.

3.1 Throttle Policy

Suppose, as shown in Figure 2, when input buffer *ib* of node 2 is full with flits of packet P_q with low priority q, packet P_p with high priority p arrives at node 3 and requests channel *oc*. Even though the priority of packet P_p is higher than that of packet P_q, packet P_p cannot preempt channel *oc* from packet P_q, because input buffer *ib* is full.

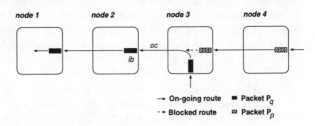

Figure 2: Without throttle policy, a high priority packet P_p can not preempt channel *oc*.

Our throttle policy has distinct treatment for packets with different priorities : a high threshold for a high priority packet, and a low threshold for a low priority packet. In detail, packet P_q is allowed to move to an input buffer, only if the buffer has room to receive more than MAX_PRI $- q - 1$ flits. Therefore, when packet P_p requests the channel held by packet P_q, it can always preempt it, since there is room in the input buffer for at least $p - q(> 0)$ flits. This throttle policy enforces the size of an input buffer as MAX_PRI flits or more than, in order that even packets with the lowest priority could come into an input buffer(Assumption 3 above). Figure 3 illustrates that, for the input buffer of four flits and MAX_PRI of four, packet P_i with priority $i(0 \leq i \leq 3)$ can use the input buffer only up to $i + 1$ flits.

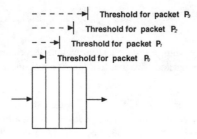

Figure 3: Example of throttle policy

3.2 Preempt policy

Preempt policy lets a high priority packet actually preempt the network resources from a low priority packet. This preemption occurs over two adjacent nodes at a time, i.e., for the output channel at the previous node and for the associated input buffer at the next node. We explain the preemption over two nodes sequentially, first output channel preemption and then input buffer preemption.

Output Channel Preemption   Output channel oc held by packet P_q with priority q is preempted by packet P_p with priority p, if following conditions hold :

- the header flit of packet P_p arrives,
- there is no free output channel for packet P_p,
- packet P_p desires the channel oc,
- priority q is lower than priority p, i.e., $q < p$.

The procedure of channel preemption is shown in Figure 4. Figures 4(a) shows that packet P_p enters node 3 and packet P_q is occupying output channel oc. Then, packet P_p interrupts packet P_q and moves forward through output channel oc, as shown in Figure 4(b). Remaining part of the packet P_q is blocked during the interruption, and its transmission is resumed, after the tail flit of packet P_p has left channel oc and its associated input buffer ib, as shown in Figure 4(c). Multiple preemptions may occur when another packet P_n with priority $n(> p)$ comes to node 3 and requests channel oc. Then, channel oc is again preempted by packet P_n, and packet P_p is blocked, too. After packet P_n has completely left channel oc and input buffer ib, the transmission of P_p is resumed. Also, after the complete departure of packet P_p, packet P_q can be resumed.

For the realization of the above procedures, a new architectural support is required : *preemption stack* for each output channel. The preemption stack is a set of registers to record which input buffers hold preempted packets, in the ascending order of their priorities. That is, the top register of the preemption stack points to the input buffer, which holds the packet with the highest priority among preempted ones. On preemption, for the newly interrupted packet P_{top}, its input buffer's identifier is pushed onto the top of the preemption stack, because P_{top} has higher priority than any

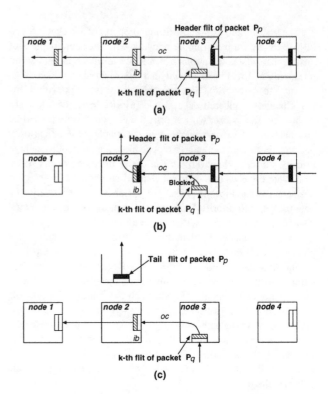

Figure 4: Example of preempt policy

other packets already preempted. When the output channel and its associated input buffer get free, and if there is no arrival of a higher priority packet than packet P_{top}, a request is granted from input buffer to hold P_{top}, and the top entry of the stack is popped off. The preemption stack takes its name from its stack operation. The number of registers of the stack is bounded by MAX_PRI $-$ 1, which is the maximum number of preemptions for each output channel.

Input Buffer Preemption   After preempting output channel oc, packet P_p preempts input buffer ib which is already held by packet P_q, as shown in Figure 4(b). On arrival of the header flit of packet P_p at a non-free buffer ib, input buffer ib is taken over for packet P_p. From this time, input buffer ib is fed with flits of packet P_p, and sends out these flits. Only after the tail flit of packet P_p has departed from input buffer ib, packet P_q can be again fed into, as shown in Figure 4(c). During the interruption of packet P_q at node 2 and node 3, the downstream nodes continue to move forward the precedent flits of packet P_q. After all precedent flits pass through, reserved channels for packet P_q will be idle at the downstream nodes, before its resumption. Such an idle on timing, called bubble[2], is inevitably inserted into the middle of packet P_q. However, we expect that the bubble has a negligible effect on the real-time performance, because, by our preempt policy, urgent packets with high priority can also preempt the idle channels. The negligible effect will be shown in Section 4.

For the realization of above procedures, we need new architectural supports : *history stack* and *LPFO(Last Packet First Out) buffer*. Recall that the header flit makes a routing decision and trailing data flits follow it in wormhole routing. Hence, in generic wormhole routing, a register is needed to keep the routing decision for each input buffer. However, for throttle and preempt flow control, before the tail flit of a packet passes though an input buffer, it may be preempted by another one. So, we additionally need a set of registers to store several routing decisions for each input buffer, and it is called history stack. This makes preempted packets be resumed correctly along its old route. It is obvious that the history stack operates in a stack manner and the number of its registers is also MAX_PRI − 1, as the preemption stack.

As mentioned above, we need a new buffer called LPFO buffer. This buffer makes flits of the last arrived packet be sent first. Hence, flits of a high priority packet can bypass those of a low priority packet(s). After transmitting the tail flit of the last packet, the LPFO buffer resumes the transmission of the previous packet.

3.3 Fundamental Properties

Theorem 1 *Priority Inversion Freedom:*
With the throttle and preempt flow control, a header flit F_h can advance to the next node at the next time, except when desired output channels are being used by packets with higher or equal priorities.

Proof. Let the *outgoing channel set*, $OC(h)$, be defined as the set of permissible output channels for the header flit F_h, by a routing algorithm. If there exist any free channels in $OC(h)$, the header flit F_h can advance to the next node at the next time, by the routing algorithm. Even when there are no free channels, if there is a channel in $OC(h)$, called oc_{victim}, held by a lower priority packet, the preempt policy makes the header flit F_h immediately acquire channel oc_{victim} and its associated input buffer, which has a room for at least one flit by throttle policy. ∎

The throttle and preempt flow control enforces usage of network resources as priority-based. Predictable ordered usage according to priorities is essential for real-time performance[1]. Theorem 1 directly leads to the following corollary.

Corollary 1 *With the throttle and preempt flow control, the packet of priority $q+1$ can be delivered without any blocking, even if the entire network has been saturated with packets with priority q or lower, and no node is removing any low priority packets.*

Proof. By theorem 1, the packet with priority $q+1$ can always advance to the next node immediately, because there exist only lower priority packets in the network. That is, the packet with priority $q+1$ is delivered from its source to its destination without any blocking. ∎

Even in real-time systems, it is common that real-time packets and non-real-time packets may exist at the same time. For an industrial process control system, usually the volume of real-time packets for control is small, while the volume of non-real-time data packets is large. In this case, the real-time flow control is desirable whose performance is not strongly affected by non-real-time traffic, to make a robust system. Corollary 1 refers to such a behavior of throttle and preempt flow control.

4 Experimental Evaluation

To evaluate the performance of our throttle and preempt flow control(TP), we compare it with other two flow control poli-

cies: the Li's flow control(LI)[8] and conventional FCFS flow control(FCFS)[3],[6].

4.1 Simulation model

Network Model To limit the search space, we have fixed some important parameters : packet length of 32 flits, mesh size of 16×16, and buffer size of 16 flits. Entire simulations are conducted for a dimension-order routing[9], because of its simplicity. Our simulations vary the the number of virtual channels(vc) from one to eight where, for conventional FCFS flow control[3],[6], physical channel bandwidth is shared in a round-robin basis among multiple virtual channels. For the Li's flow control and the throttle and preempt flow control, the usage of the physical channel is enforced by priority-based arbitration.

Traffic Model It is considered that non-real-time traffic as well as real-time traffic may exist simultaneously in realistic systems. Hence, we conducted simulations with the fraction α of real-time traffic(0.5 in our study) and the fraction $(1 - \alpha)$ of background non-real-time traffic, also called best-effort traffic[7]. For the best-effort traffic, each node generates packets for random destinations, in a way that the distribution of their inter arrival time is geometric with same mean.

Based on linear bounded arrival process[11], we assume that there are M real-time connections $C_1, C_2, ..., C_M$ (we fix M as five times the number of network nodes), whose source and destination nodes are randomly placed in a network. Each connection $C_i (1 \leq i \leq M)$ generates one packets every I_i cycles. By the given network load ρ, and the fraction α, we can derive the mean of I_i over all $C_i (1 \leq i \leq M)$, called I_{mean}. We make each I_i uniformly distributed from $[\frac{1}{2} \times I_{mean}, \frac{3}{2} \times I_{mean}]$. Whenever each real-time packet is generated at its source node, laxity before deadline is randomly chosen from $k \times$ Expect_lat, for $k = 1, 2, 3, ...,$ MAX_PRI-1, where MAX_PRI fixed as eight in our study, and Expect_lat is the expected transmission time from its source to destination without any blocking. Priority of each packet is decided by the least laxity first priority mapping[10], where packets with the least laxity get the highest priority of MAX_PRI-1.

Results We evaluate real-time performance in terms of miss ratio, or the portion of real-time packets to violate their deadlines, while measuring best-effort traffic in terms of its average latency. For LI which was originally studied only with vc=MAX_PRI, we make the adjacent priority levels appropriately merged for the case of $vc <$MAX_PRI.

In Figure 5, shown are the miss ratios of the three flow control schemes, where FCFS with vc=1 marks the highest. The miss ratios of LI get decreased with larger vc, though, they are sharply increased after the network load of 0.3. However, TP's miss ratios slowly increase even with vc=1 after network load 0.3. Because LI partially solves priority inversion, high priority packets may be blocked by low priority packets, which leads to a high miss ratio especially for a high network load. On the other hand, with TP to totally avoid priority inversion, high priority packets can make it independent of low priority packets, which results in a low miss ratio. From these results, we can also assert that the performance degradation due to the bubble effect is not significant, as mentioned in the previous section.

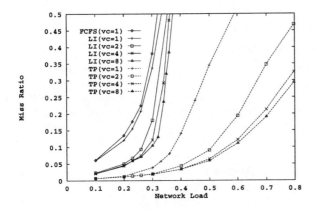

Figure 5: Miss ratios versus network load(ρ)

We measure the performance of best-effort traffic for TP and LI when real-time performance is sufficiently satisfied for each scheme. Figure 6 shows the average latency for best-effort traffic for $vc=4$ and $vc=8$, where TP always has lower latency than LI. This is due to the unique nature of wormhole networks, by which the number of virtual channel affects the performance more severely than the size of a buffer[4]. Notice that LI limits the best-effort packets in the usage of virtual channels, while TP prohibits the best-effort packets from excess use of input buffers.

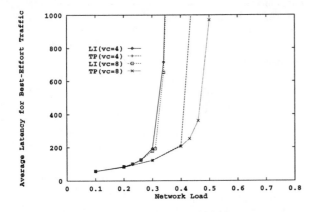

Figure 6: Average latency of best-effort traffic versus network load(ρ)

5 Conclusion

Meeting message deadline constraints in communication networks has been an important issue for many multicomputer applications. In this paper, we have addressed this issue in a priority-driven paradigm for the multicomputers with wormhole routing.

We have found that blocking flow control in wormhole routing cannot be applied to the priority-driven paradigm. Because it can lead to uncontrolled priority inversion, deadline miss ratio may be increased unpredictably. In this paper, we proposed a new flow control, *throttle and preempt flow control*, for resolving the priority inversion problem. The proposed flow control prohibits low priority packets from using input buffers beyond their allowed limit, so that high priority packets can always preempt the low priority packets to use the channels, if necessary. Hence, the throttle and preempt flow control does not cause priority inversion.

Simulation results showed that the conventional FCFS flow control does not satisfy the timing property of real-time applications. Also, it has been observed that the proposed flow control outperforms the existing real-time flow control of Li under various conditions with real-time traffic and best-effort traffic.

Acknowledgments

The authors are grateful for the discussion with Dr. Lillykutty Jacob, Dr. Jai-Hoon Chung, and Dr. Byungho Kim. Their help has made this paper more complete.

References

[1] S. Balakrishnan and F. Ozguner, "A Priority-Based Flow Control Mechanism to Support Real-Time Traffic in Pipelined Direct Networks," in *Proc. of the ICPP*, 1996

[2] C. M. Chiang and et al., "Multicast in Extra-Stage Multistage Interconnection Networks," in *Proc. of the Sixth IEEE Symposium on Parallel and Distributed Processing*, 1994.

[3] Cray Research Inc., *Cray T3D System Architecture Overview*, 1993.

[4] W. J. Dally, "Virtual Channel Flow Control," *IEEE Tr. on PDS*, vol. 3, no. 2, pp. 194–205, 1992.

[5] P. T. Gaughan and S. Yalamanchili, "A Family of Fault-Tolerant Routing Protocols for Dircet Multiprocessir Network," *IEEE Tr. on PDS*, vol. 6, no. 5, pp. 482–497, 1995.

[6] Intel, *Paragon XP/S Product Overview*, 1991.

[7] J. H. Kim and A. A. Chien, "Rotating Combined Queuing(RCQ): Bandwidth and Latency Guarantees in Low-cost, High-performance Networks," in *ISCA '23 Proc.*, pp. 226–236, 1996.

[8] J. P. Li and M. W. Mutka, "Priority Based Real-Time Communication for Large Scale Wormhole Networks," in *Proc. of the IPPS*, 1994.

[9] L. M. Ni and P. K. McKinley, "A Survey of Wormhole Routing Techniques in Direct Networks," *IEEE Computer*, vol. 26, no. 2, pp. 62–76, 1993.

[10] R. Rajkumar, ed., *Synchronization in Real-time Systems: A Priority Inheritance Approach*. Kluwer Academic Publishers, 1991.

[11] J. Rexford, J. Hall, and K. G. Shin, "A Router Architecture for Real-time Point-to-point Networks," in *ISCA '23 Proc.*, pp. 237–246, 1996.

[12] K. Toda, K. Nishida, E. Takahashi, S. Sakai, and T. S. a nd Y. Yamaguchi, "A Priority Forwarding Scheme for Real-time Multistage Interconnection Networks and Its Evaluation," *IEICE Tr. on Fundamentals*, vol. E00-X, no. 2, 1995.

Tree-Based Multicasting on Wormhole Routed Multistage Interconnection Networks*

Vara Varavithya and Prasant Mohapatra
Department of Electrical and Computer Engineering
Iowa State University, Ames, IA 50011
E-mail: {vara,prasant}@iastate.edu

Abstract

In this paper, we propose a tree-based multicasting algorithm for Multistage Interconnection Networks. We first analyze the necessary conditions for deadlocks in MINs. Based on these observations, an asynchronous tree-based multicasting algorithm is developed in which deadlocks are prevented by serializing the initiations of branching operations that have potential for creating deadlocks. The serialization is done using a technique based on grouping of the switching elements. The preliminary simulation results are encouraging as it lowers the latency by almost a factor of 4 when compared with the software multicasting approach proposed earlier.

1 Introduction

Multistage Interconnection Networks (MINs) have been extensively studied and adopted as an interconnection fabric for multiprocessor systems. Multiprocessor systems increase their computing speed by performing several computations concurrently. These activities often require coordination and synchronization between processing elements through interprocessor communication which can be either one to one (unicast) or within a group of processors (collective). Most contemporary systems use wormhole routing for interprocessor communication.

An important communication primitive in collective operations is the multicast communication. Multicast communication is concerned with sending a single message from a source node to a set of destination nodes. The software-based approach has a higher latency as it incurs several communication steps [1]. To enhance the multicast performance, the multicast operations need to be supported at the hardware level. The multistage interconnection networks inherit the tree structure which can be effectively used to efficiently support multicast communication. In tree-based multicasting, a multihead message is sent out of the switch and the multiple headers are forwarded either synchronously or asynchronously. The tree-based multicasting scheme proposed by Chiang and Ni [2] requires the multicast headers in different branches to be forwarded synchronously. In asynchronous tree-based

multicasting, multiple headers are allowed to be forwarded independent of each other. The asynchronous approach is preferred because of the ease of implementation. However, it is more prone to deadlocks. One approach to implement the asynchronous multicasting is through the use of buffers at each switch to prevent deadlocks [3, 4].

In this paper, we first analyze necessary conditions for deadlocks in the tree-based multicasting operations. Based on the study of deadlock problems, an asynchronous tree-based multicasting (ATBM) scheme is proposed for multicasting in MINs using the wormhole switching technique. To prevent deadlocks, the switches are grouped based on the layered networks and multiple tree operations are serialized within the groups. The proposed scheme is different from the previously proposed asynchronous [3] schemes in the sense that the multicast communication can be completed in a single start-up step and only small buffers are required for each input channels. The simulation results show that our approach performs significantly better than the software multicasting scheme while incurring low hardware overheads compared to the previously proposed multicasting schemes.

This paper is organized as follows. Preliminaries are presented in Section 2. The deadlock issues and the proposed algorithm are discussed in Section 3. Performance evaluations are given in Section 4. The concluding remarks are listed in Section 5.

2 Preliminaries

In this paper, we consider unidirectional MINs. The processor's communication channels are connected to the input ports of the MIN. The output ports of the MIN are connected (wrapped around) to the input ports of the processors. A MIN using $b \times b$ switches with S stages and R rows has $N = b^S$ processing nodes. A switch at row i and stage j is labeled as (i, j) where $[i \in (0, 1, \ldots, R-1)]$ and $[j \in (0, 1, \ldots, S-1)]$. In this paper, we consider the *baseline* networks as the basis of our discussions. However, other classes of MINs can also employ the same technique developed in our work.

To support the tree-based multicast operations, a replication mechanism is required. The degree of replication can vary between 2 and b (broadcast at the

*This research was supported in part by the National Science Foundation under the grants MIP-9628801, CCR-9634547, and CDA-9617375.

switch). The flit can be copied to the multiple output ports simultaneously or in sequence. The replicated flits can be forwarded either independently or synchronously.

The network throughput and communication latency are usually considered as the performance metrics of MINs. Throughput is the number of the packets delivered per unit time. In multicast communication, the multicast latency refers to the time between the message initiation and the reception of entire message at all the destinations.

3 Asynchronous Tree-Based Multicasting (ATBM) Algorithm

3.1 Deadlock Issues

Deadlocks in tree-based multicasting generally involve multiple multicast messages that perform the tree operations at the same stage. Consider the switch level deadlock configuration shown in Figure 1 (a). Message A from the upper port of switch 2 acquires the lower buffer of switch 3 and requests for the lower port of switch 4. Message B from the lower port of switch 2 holds the lower buffer of switch 4 and requests for the lower port of the switch 3. Both messages perform the switch broadcast operation at the same switch. Since both messages request the buffers that are held by the other, a deadlock cycle is formed. A variety of priority schemes are proposed in [2] to resolve this scenario.

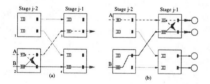

Figure 1: Switch level deadlock configurations.

If the switches in the last stage have the capability to process more than one incoming message concurrently, the throughput is increased. The number of incoming messages that the processor can concurrently absorb is usually dependent on the number of consumption channels. If the number of consumption channels is equal to the number of input ports, the messages that arrive the last stage will eventually be consumed. Figure 1 (b) shows a possible deadlock configuration developed from the tree operation at the last stage. This problem can be solved using multiple (b) consumption channels.

To illustrate the general concept behind the formation of deadlock cycles, the abstract deadlock configurations are shown in Figure 2. In Figure 2 (a), two messages perform a switch broadcast operation at the stage zero. These two messages request the same buffers at stage three. Deadlock occurs when messages acquire common buffers in one branch and

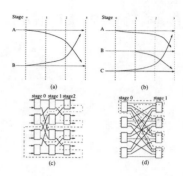

Figure 2: Abstraction of multicast deadlocks and network partitioning in MINs.

request the common buffers in the other branch. Figure 2 (b) show a possible deadlock that involves more than two messages.

A MIN using $b \times b$ switches can be viewed as a set of b overlapped networks. For example, we can partition the buffers and channels of a MIN using 2×2 switches into two separate sets, as shown in Figure 2 (c). These two separate sets have no buffers or channels in common. Similarly, the 16 nodes with 4×4 switches can be partitioned into four separate sets of buffers and channels as shown in Figure 2 (d).

Lemma 1: A buffer deadlock cycle can be formed by the multicast messages only when they belong to the same overlapped network.

Proof: Messages generated from different overlapped networks will not request for the same buffers. Therefore, the deadlock configuration needs to involve at least two messages in the same overlapped network. It is also important to note that deadlocks involving consumption channels can be formed.

Lemma 2: The deadlock configuration must involve at least two multicast messages that perform tree operations at the same stage.

Proof: When a switch broadcast operation is performed at the jth stage switch, the upper branch message may use switches only in $\frac{N}{b^j}$ rows in the later stages (baseline network). If messages A and B perform broadcast operations only at j^{th} and $(j+1)^{th}$ stages, respectively, A can request the same buffer(s) in B's path. However, message B will not request the same buffers in the other branch of the message A. Therefore, *two multicast messages performing broadcast operations in different stages cannot create deadlock.*

3.2 The Proposed Algorithm

We propose a method that modifies the routing operations to prevent deadlocks in the asynchronous tree-based multicasting operation in MINs. On the basis of the necessary conditions for deadlock discussed in Section 3.1, we can form groups of switches at every stage such that only the multicast messages using the switches in the same group have a potential to create deadlock configurations. Two multicast messages within the group may request the same buffers at any stage. From Lemmas 1 and 2, we can conclude that deadlocks are possible only when there are multiple tree operations in the same overlapped network at the same stage. From these observations we are motivated toward an asynchronous tree-based multicasting scheme that serializes the tree operations at every stage within a group of switches thus disallowing concurrent tree operation in a group at the same stage. Using this serialization technique, the deadlock cycles are prevented.

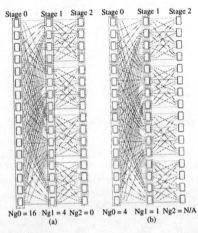

Figure 3: Switch grouping of the 64 nodes in a baseline network.

We divide the switch grouping methods into two cases: one for single consumption channel, and the other for b consumption channels. For the single consumption channel model, each switch constitutes a group at the last stage since multiple multicast messages at the last stage can only request the same consumption channels at the same switch. The tree operations that are initiated in the same switch (at the last stage for this case) can create the deadlock. Therefore, they are serialized to prevent the cyclic dependency. The last stage switches in the b consumption channels model do not have to be grouped since once the message reaches the input port, it will be eventually consumed by the processor. In the stage $S-2$, there are b switches in a group in the single consumption channel model. The number of switches in the group N_{gj} at stage ($j \in [0, 1, ..., j, ..., S-2]$) for the single consumption channel model is given by, $N_{gj} = b^{(S-1)-j}$ and for the b consumption channels model, $N_{gj} = b^{(S-2)-j}$. For the baseline networks, the (i, j) switch belongs to group $[k, j]$, i.e., the switch belong to group k at stage j. The group label $[k, j]$ can be calculated using the equation, $k = \lfloor \frac{i}{N_{gj}} \rfloor$.

The grouping example for the single consumption channel model is shown in Figure 3 (a) for 64 nodes using 4×4 switches baseline network. The dashed lines

Routing Algorithm(message_header)
1. If (unicast_message)
      forward a flit to the output port specified
      in the routing_tag;
2. If (multicast_message)
      perform routing calculation;
      If (tree operation)
           wait to obtain the token;
           hold the token;
           replicate and forward the header flit;
           Release the token after the header flits
           arrive at the destination(s);
      else
           forward the header flit to the output ports;

Figure 4: The ATBM routing algorithm.

represent the switches in the same group at each stage of the baseline network. Figure 3 (b) shows the grouping for b consumption channels model. It is important to note that the number of switches in the group at each stage for b consumption channels model is significantly less than the single consumption therefore it allows more concurrent tree operations.

Additional hardware is required for serializing the tree operations in the switches of the same group. A control line can be implemented at each stage that interconnects the switches of a group. The token can be passed from one switch to another through the control lines in a round robin fashion within a group. When a switch is ready to do a multicast operation, it waits until it gets the token. The switch holds the token while multicasting a message and releases it after the header of message arrives at the destination. As the number of stages in MINs is usually small, the waiting time for the token will be within limits and multiple multicast messages can proceed if there is no blocking. This hardware modification is simpler and faster than the feedback mechanism required in synchronous multicasting [2] which requires the permutation of the whole multicast tree. The formal description of the algorithm is given in Figure 4.

4 Performance Evaluation

A flit-level wormhole routed network simulator is developed to evaluate the performance of ATBM algorithm. We design the experiments to evaluate the performance of the 2×2 and 4×4 switch-based baseline MINs networks. MINs of 16, 32, 64, and 256 nodes are considered in our study. The multicast header is assumed to fit in one flit using bit string encoding scheme [5]. The simulation parameters are set to the current trend of the technology.

To simulate a realistic environment, we generate a mixture of unicast and multicast traffic. The number of multicast destinations in a multicast operation

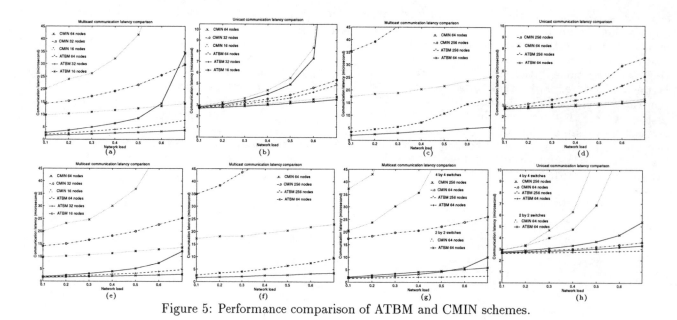

Figure 5: Performance comparison of ATBM and CMIN schemes.

is assumed to have an average of $\frac{N}{2}$ with a standard deviation of $\frac{N}{4}$. The size of unicast and multicast messages are fixed to 128 flits and 64 flits, respectively.

We compare the ATBM scheme with the CMIN algorithm [1] to show the performance improvement from supporting the multicast at the hardware level. The CMIN algorithm is the binomial unicast-based multicast algorithm which requires $\lceil \log_2(d+1) \rceil$ communication steps to complete the multicast operation to d destinations. The multicast tree structure is constructed such that the blocking is minimized.

Figure 5 (a) shows the multicast communication latency for baseline networks using 2×2 switches. The single consumption channel model is assumed. The mixture of the traffic is set to 20% multicast traffic with 80% unicast traffic. The ATBM algorithm has less multicast latency by a factor of four compared to the software multicast scheme. Figure 5 (b) shows the comparison of unicast latency. Both unicast and multicast latencies of the ATBM algorithm are lower than the respective latencies of the CMIN algorithm. At heavy load, the multicast operations tend to be blocked at the early stage. Therefore, they do not congest the network.

The simulation results for baseline MINs using 4×4 switches are shown in Figure 5 (c) and (d). Similar trends can be observed for both multicast and unicast latency. As discussed in Section 4, the b consumption channel model can enhance the performance of the ATBM scheme. Figure 5 (e) and (f) show the multicast latency under the b consumption channel model with a little performance improvement for the ATBM scheme compared to the one port model results. The proportion of multicast and unicast traffic is set to 50% for the simulation results in Figure 5 (h) and (g). The ATBM scheme gives even better performance for high ratio of multicast traffic.

5 Conclusions

We have examined the deadlock problems associated with asynchronous wormhole switching – based multicasting in MINs. The proposed tree-based approach avoids deadlock by serializing the messages that are prone to deadlocks. The deadlock prone messages are identified using a grouping technique. The grouping is based on the topological interconnection of the switches. The proposed technique uses less hardware while providing the same or better performance than previously proposed hardware multicasting scheme for MINs.

References

[1] C. Chiang and L. M. Ni, "Efficient software multicast in wormhole-routed unidirectional multistage networks," *Proc. Symp. of Parallel and Distributed Processing*, pp. 106–113, 1995.

[2] C. Chiang and L. M. Ni, "Deadlock-free multihead wormhole routing," *Proc. 1st High Performance Computing-Asia*, 1995.

[3] R. Sivaram, D. K. Panda, and C. B. Stunkel, "Fast broadcast and multicast on wormhole multistage networks using multiport encoding," *Proc. 8th Symp. on Parallel and Distributed Processing*, pp. 36–45, Oct. 1996.

[4] M. Malumbres, J. Duato, and J. Torrellas, "An efficient implementation of tree-based multicast routing for distributed shared-memory multiprocessors," *Proc. 8th Symp. on Parallel and Distributed Processing*, pp. 186–189, Oct. 1996.

[5] C. Chiang and L. M. Ni, "Multi-address encoding for multicast," *Parallel Computer Routing and Communication Workshop*, pp. 146–160, May 1994.

Session 3C

Consistency and Communication

The Affinity Entry Consistency Protocol *

Cristiana B. Seidel[†‡], R. Bianchini[†], and Claudio L. Amorim[†]

[†]COPPE Systems Engineering   [‡]Dept. of Systems Engineering
Federal Univ. of Rio de Janeiro (UFRJ)   State Univ. of Rio de Janeiro (UERJ)

`{seidel,ricardo,amorim}@cos.ufrj.br`

Abstract

In this paper we propose a novel software-only distributed shared-memory system (SW-DSM), the Affinity Entry Consistency (AEC) protocol. The protocol is based on Entry Consistency but, unlike previous approaches, does not require the explicit association of shared data to synchronization variables, uses the page as its coherence unit, and generates the set of modifications (in the form of diffs) made to shared pages eagerly. The AEC protocol hides the overhead of generating and applying diffs behind synchronization delays, and uses a novel technique, Lock Acquirer Prediction (LAP), to tolerate the overhead of transferring diffs through the network. LAP attempts to predict the next acquirer of a lock at the time of the release, so that the acquirer can be updated even before requesting ownership of the lock.

Using execution-driven simulation of real applications, we show that LAP performs very well under AEC; LAP predictions are within the 80-97% range of accuracy. Our results also show that LAP improves performance by 7-28% for our applications. In addition, we find that most of the diff creation overhead in the AEC protocol can usually be overlapped with synchronization latencies. A comparison against simulated TreadMarks shows that AEC outperforms TreadMarks by as much as 47%. We conclude that LAP is a useful technique for improving the performance of update-based SW-DSMs, while AEC is an efficient implementation of the Entry Consistency model.

1 Introduction

Software-only distributed shared-memory systems (SW-DSMs) provide programmers with a shared-memory abstraction on top of message-passing hardware. These systems provide a low-cost alternative to shared-memory computing, since they can be built with standard workstations and operating systems. However, several applications running on SW-DSMs suffer high communication and coherence-induced overheads that limit performance.

SW-DSMs based on relaxed consistency models can reduce these overheads by delaying and/or restricting communication and coherence transactions as much as possible. The Munin system

[5], for instance, delays the creation and transfer of diffs (encoded modifications to shared pages) until lock release operations, so that messages can be coalesced and the negative impact of false sharing alleviated. TreadMarks [2] delays the coherence transactions even further, until the next lock acquire operation. The Midway [3] system also delays communication and coherence operations until a lock acquire transaction, but restricts these operations to the data that are associated with the lock.

Although effective at improving the performance of SW-DSMs, these protocols still involve a substantial amount of overhead: In Munin, updates are propagated to *all* processors sharing data modified within critical sections; on a page fault in TreadMarks, the faulting processor has to wait for diffs to be computed, received, and applied to the page before proceeding with its computation; in Midway, the processor acquiring a lock can only resume execution after the data associated with the lock become consistent locally.

Our work is based on the observation that all of these sources of overhead can be alleviated by dynamically predicting the lock acquisition order, and generating diffs away from the critical path of the processors that need them. In this paper we propose a novel SW-DSM, the Affinity Entry Consistency (AEC) protocol. The protocol hides the overhead of generating and applying diffs behind three types of synchronization delays: coherence processing at lock and barrier managers, waiting for a lock to become available, or waiting for all processors to reach a barrier.

In addition, the AEC protocol uses a novel technique, Lock Acquirer Prediction (LAP), for tolerating the overhead of transferring diffs through the network in Single Program Multiple Data (SPMD) applications. LAP attempts to predict the next acquirer of a lock at the time of the release, so that the acquirer can be updated even before requesting ownership of the lock. When the lock releaser makes a correct prediction, the protocol overlaps the communication and coherence overheads on the releaser with useful computation on the acquirer. In case of an incorrect prediction, the overlapped updates are wasted and the overhead of bringing data to the lock acquirer is exposed. When successful, LAP can also reduce the synchronization overhead in the presence of lock contention, since it effectively reduces the duration of critical sections and therefore the amount of time locks are held. LAP may be applied in other update-based SW-DSMs. In release-consistent systems such as Munin, LAP can be used to restrict the update traffic, while in systems like Midway, it can be used to overlap communication and computation.

*This research was supported by Brazilian FINEP/MCT, CNPq, and CAPES.

As in protocols based on Entry Consistency and its descendant Scope Consistency [9], in AEC a processor entering a critical section only receives the data associated with the section. In addition, the AEC protocol attempts to predict the lock acquisition order using LAP, hides coherence-related overheads, uses the page as its coherence unit, automatically associates data in a critical section with the lock that delimits it, and rarely requires program modifications to execute correctly.

Using execution-driven simulation of real applications, we show that LAP performs very well under AEC; LAP predictions are within the 80-97% range of accuracy. Our results also show that LAP reduces the amount of time devoted to memory access faults by as much as 62%. Overall, LAP improves performance by 7-28% for our applications. In addition, we find that most of the diff creation overhead in the AEC protocol can usually be overlapped with synchronization latencies. A comparison against simulated TreadMarks shows that AEC outperforms TreadMarks by as much as 47%. Most of this performance improvement is a result of lower data access and synchronization overheads. We conclude that LAP is a useful technique for improving the performance of update-based SW-DSMs, while AEC is an efficient implementation of the Entry Consistency model.

The remainder of this paper is organized as follows. The next section describes the three basic prediction techniques that comprise the LAP technique. Section 3 describes the AEC protocol in detail. Section 4 presents our methodology, application workload, and an overview of TreadMarks. In section 5 we present the results of our evaluation of LAP and AEC. We relate our work to previous contributions in section 6. Finally, in section 7, we present our conclusions and proposals for future improvements to AEC.

2 Predicting the Lock Acquisition Order

Our Lock Acquirer Prediction (LAP) technique attempts to predict the next acquirer of a lock based on three lower-level techniques: *waiting queue*, *virtual queue*, and *lock transfer affinity*. The next subsection describes these techniques in detail. Subsection 2.2 describes how these low-level techniques are combined to produce our LAP strategy.

2.1 Low-Level Techniques

Our first and simplest low-level technique, waiting queue, relies on the fact that the FIFO queue of processors waiting for access to a certain lock is a perfect description of the lock's acquisition order. So, if there is contention for a lock, the first processor on the FIFO queue will be the next acquirer of the lock.

However, a waiting queue for a lock might not exist at the time of the lock release, if there is only light competition for the lock. Thus, the idea behind our virtual queue technique is to create the waiting queue in advance of the processors actually requesting acquisition of the lock. We implement this strategy by inserting the transfer of *lock acquire notices* to the lock manager in the source code of applications. A virtual waiting queue is then created with

the notices sent by the processors that intend to grab the lock in the near future. The next acquirer of the lock will likely be among the first few processors in the virtual queue.

Note that the burden of implementing virtual queues need not be placed on the programmer; a compiler can easily insert lock acquire notices in the applications. In this study we insert the notices manually to demonstrate that they are useful and therefore to motivate their implementation in a compiler.

The previous strategies may fail to produce a potential next lock acquirer, so we also define the lock transfer affinity technique. This technique is based on the fact that, for some SPMD applications, the next acquirer of a lock L_k released by processor P_i is frequently part of a small set of processors. Our lock transfer affinity technique uses the past history of lock ownership transfers to compute a set of potential next acquirers of the lock.

More specifically, we define the affinity $A_{ij}(k)$ of processor P_i for processor P_j, with respect to lock L_k, as the number of previous ownership transfers of L_k from P_i to P_j. In addition, we define the *affinity set $S_i(k)$* of processor P_i with respect to lock L_k as the set of processors P_j with affinity $A_{ij}(k)$ 60% greater than the average affinity P_i has for other processors.[1]

2.2 The Lock Acquirer Prediction Technique

The LAP strategy combines the low-level techniques just described to compute the *update set* $U_i(k)$ that potentially contains the processor P_j, the next acquirer of lock L_k released by processor P_i. The size z of the update set is determined in advance by the user. The algorithm used to combine the techniques and compute $U_i(k)$ proceeds as follows:

1. If the waiting queue is not empty then $U_i(k)$ = the processor at the head of the queue; End.

2. Include the processors in $S_i(k)$ in $U_i(k)$;

3. If $U_i(k)$ is not complete (i.e. the number of processors in $U_i(k)$ is smaller than z), then include processors from the intersection of the virtual queue and the set of processors such that $A_{ij}(k) > 0$;

4. If $U_i(k)$ is still not complete, then insert processors from the virtual queue first and then the processors with $A_{ij} > 0$; End.

3 The AEC Protocol

In this section we describe our AEC protocol, which illustrates how an Entry Consistency-based protocol can take advantage of the LAP technique, while hiding the overhead of generating diffs behind synchronization delays.

3.1 Overview

The basic idea of AEC is to have a lock releaser send all modifications ever made inside the critical section protected by the lock

---

[1] Our threshold of 60% is admittedly arbitrary; we plan a study of the effect of varying this threshold for the near future.

to the processors in the update set (as determined by the lock's manager). These modifications are described by diffs, but diffs for the same page are merged into a single diff. The acquirer attempts to hide the overhead of applying these diffs and generating diffs for any pages modified outside of critical sections behind the synchronization overhead. Unfortunately, at the lock release point, the generation of diffs of the pages modified inside a critical section cannot be overlapped, in order to prevent the next lock acquirer from seeing potentially stale data.

Shared data modified outside of critical sections pose an interesting problem in this scheme, since the affinity concept does not apply to barriers. For this reason, shared data protected by barriers receive a different treatment than data protected by locks in AEC; barrier-protected data are kept coherent via invalidates. More specifically, diffs of barrier-protected data are generated eagerly, at the time of a lock acquire or a barrier arrival, and propagated to other processors only on access faults.

Thus, AEC attempts to hide the overhead of generating and applying diffs behind three types of delays:

- coherence processing at the lock and barrier managers;

- waiting for a lock to become available; or

- waiting for all processors to reach a barrier when there is load imbalance.

Figures 1 and 2 present a summary of the protocol actions involved in AEC, as a result of lock and barrier operations and on access faults to shared data. The next few subsections detail these actions.

3.2 Locks

On a lock acquire operation, the acquiring processor sends a message to the lock manager requesting ownership of the lock. Right after sending the request to the manager, the processor starts applying any diffs it has already received for being in the update set of a previous lock owner. Diffs are only applied to pages that are currently valid at the acquiring processor, so that only the pages that are likely to be used are updated; other diffs are saved for application at the time of an access fault to the corresponding page. The diffs are applied until they are exhausted or the manager's reply is received and the processor finds out who the last lock owner was. If all these diffs are applied before the receipt of the manager's reply, the acquiring processor starts generating the diffs corresponding to the shared data it modified outside of critical sections. Diffs are created until there are no more modified pages or the manager's reply is received. The twins used to generate these diffs are saved and all modified pages are write-protected. At this point, if the manager's reply has already arrived, the acquiring processor continues applying the diffs received, but only if the processor that sent them is indeed the last owner of the lock.

Upon receipt of the lock ownership request, the manager computes the new update set of the acquiring processor. In case the lock is currently taken by some other processor, the manager simply enqueues the id of the requesting processor at the end of a waiting queue for the lock. In case the lock is currently available, the manager replies to the acquiring processor's request with its new update set, the id of the last releaser, and a message informing whether the acquiring processor is in the update set of the last releaser. If the acquiring processor is not in the update set, the reply from the manager also includes a list of pages to invalidate.

Obviously, the lock acquire operation becomes much simpler when the last releaser of a lock is the acquiring processor itself, since there is no need to apply diffs, invalidate pages, or deal with a separate last owner.

On a lock release operation, the releasing processor generates diffs corresponding to modifications made inside the critical section it is about to leave, merges them with diffs received from the last owner of the lock, and sends the resulting diffs to its update set. After that, the releaser sends a message to the lock manager with a list of all pages represented in the merged diffs. This message also indicates that the releaser is giving up the ownership of the lock. Finally, the releasing processor unprotects all pages that had been modified outside the critical section and that were not modified inside it. Any diffs for these pages can be thrown away and their associated twins reutilized.

Note that the messages with the merged diffs must contain a lock acquire counter, so that the processors receiving different sets of diffs for the same lock can determine the most up-to-date one. This capability is important in the following scenario: suppose processor p holding a lock incorrectly guesses that processor q will be the next acquirer of the lock. Later, the actual next acquirer r correctly guesses q to be the next acquirer. Since processor q will receive two sets of merged diffs, in no particular order, it must be able to discard the outdated set.

3.3 Barriers

On a global synchronization event such as a barrier, each processor has to receive information on modifications performed inside and outside of critical sections. Our protocol implements barriers by dividing program execution into *steps*; a new step begins each time the processors depart from the barrier. Every processor has a step counter.

On the arrival at a barrier, each processor sends three lists to the barrier manager describing the step: a list of all lock variables it owned, a list of all pages accessed in the critical sections corresponding to these locks; and a list of all pages modified outside of critical sections. After these lists are sent to the barrier manager, the local processor starts to create the diffs corresponding to modifications made outside of critical sections. In effect, processors overlap the diff generation with barrier waiting time. However, in order to avoid generating diffs for pages that no other processor shares, a diff is only created for a page that was accessed by other processors in the previous barrier step and for which the local processor has received at least one request.

After the manager has received the messages from all processors, it determines, for each processor p, the set of processors to which p must send its diffs (corresponding to modifications made within critical sections) and/or notices that pages have been written outside of critical sections, the so-called *write notices*. A processor q is a candidate to receive diffs or write notices only if it has a valid copy of the page. A processor p sends a diff to processor q if p was the last owner of the lock under which the page was modi-

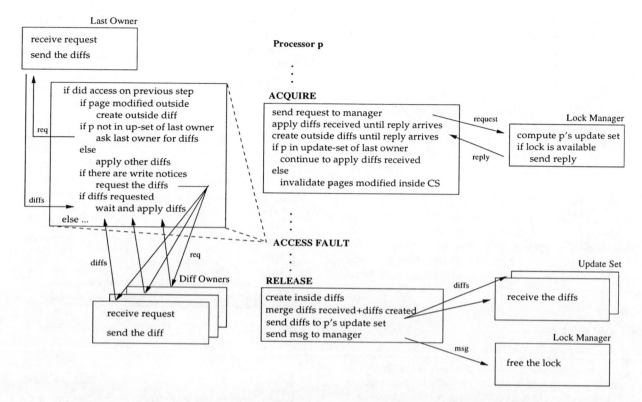

Figure 1: Actions Involved in Lock Operations and Access Faults Inside Critical Sections.

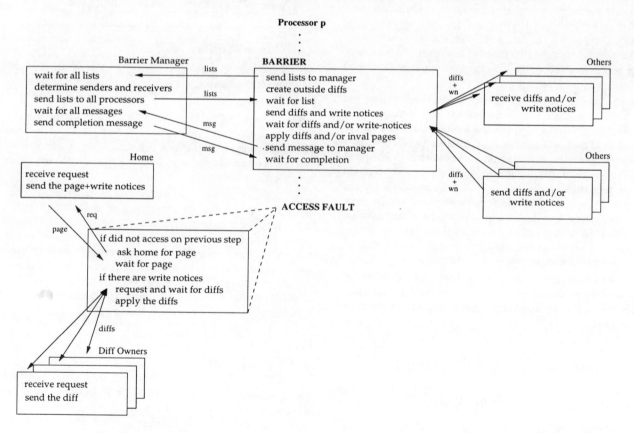

Figure 2: Actions Involved in Barrier Operations and Access Faults Outside Critical Sections.

fied. A processor p sends a write notice about a page to processor q if p modified the page outside of a critical section. In effect, this strategy avoids sending messages to processors that have not used the page, or that have already seen a write notice for it.

Since processors without valid copies of a page receive neither diffs nor write notices for it, they will need help at the time of an access fault to the page. The barrier manager, at the end of each step, chooses one of the processors with a valid copy of the page on arrival at the barrier to be the page's *home processor*; the processor that will help other processors reconstruct the page on access faults to it. The id of the home processor for each page is sent to all processors along with the set of processors they must communicate with.

After receiving these messages from the manager, the processors exchange diffs and write notices as specified by the manager. All diffs received are applied, while write notices cause the invalidation of the corresponding pages. After having completed these actions, processors communicate again with the manager, which can then determine the successful completion of the barrier event.

3.4 Access Faults

At the time of an access fault, the faulting processor must decide when it accessed the page last. If the processor did not access the page on the previous barrier step, it is not able to reconstruct the page independently, and must ask the page's current home node for help. In case the home node has a valid copy of the page, it sends it to the faulting processor. Otherwise, it sends the page and the write notices to be used by the requesting processor in bringing its copy of the page up-to-date. If the processor accessed the page on the previous step, the fault occurred as a result of one or more write notices received. In this case, the processor does not need to fetch a new copy of the page.

With a copy of the page in memory, the faulting processor can now collect the diffs it needs to validate the page. If the processor took the access fault while in a critical section and it was not in the update set of the last releaser, it asks the last releaser for the diffs it needs and applies them. If the faulting processor was in the update set of the releaser, it must apply any diff it previously received for the page but was unable to apply as it did not have a copy of the page at the time. Write faults inside of critical sections must be treated carefully, since the same page may have been modified outside of the critical section also. If a diff has not been created for the page before entering the critical section, the diff must be created and the corresponding twin eliminated.

For both inside and outside faults, if there are write notices (received during a barrier event in the past) for the page faulted on, the processor must then collect the necessary diffs according to the write notices.

4 Methodology and Workload

4.1 Multiprocessor Simulation

Our simulator consists of two parts: a front end, Mint [13], that simulates the execution of the processors and their registers, and

Constant Name	Default Value
Number of procs	16
TLB size	128 entries
TLB fill service time	100 cycles
All interrupts	4000 cycles
Page size	4K bytes
Total cache	256K bytes
Write buffer size	4 entries
Cache line size	32 bytes
Memory setup time	cycles
Memory access time	2.25 cycles/word
I/O bus setup time	12 cycles
I/O bus access time	3 cycles/word
Network path width	16 bits (bidir)
Messaging overhead	400 cycles
Switch latency	4 cycles
Wire latency	2 cycles
List processing	6 cycles/element
Page twinning	5 cycles/word + mem accesses
Diff appl/creation	7 cycles/word + mem accesses

Table 1: Defaults for System Params. 1 cycle = 10 ns.

Appls	# locks	# acq events	# barrier events
IS	1	80	21
Raytrace	18	3111	1
Water-ns	518	28128	33
FFT	1	16	7
Ocean	4	3328	900
Water-sp	6	533	33

Table 2: Synchronization events in our applications.

a back end that simulates the SW-DSM protocol and the memory system in great detail. The front end calls the back end on every shared data reference. The back end decides which computation processors block waiting for memory (or other events) and which continue execution.

We simulate a network of workstations with 16 nodes in detail. Each node consists of a computation processor, a write buffer, a first-level direct-mapped data cache (all instructions and private data accesses are assumed to take 1 cycle), local memory, an I/O bus, and a mesh network router (using wormhole routing). Network contention effects are modeled both at the source and destination of messages. Memory and I/O bus contention are fully-modeled. Table 1 summarizes the default parameters used in our simulations. All times are given in 10-ns processor cycles.

4.2 Workload

Our applications follow the SPMD model. Five of them come from the Splash-2 suite [14], while IS comes from Rice University. The applications exhibit widely different synchronization characteristics, as can be observed in table 2.

Appl	var #	# of lock events	% of total lock events	success rate			
				LAP	waitQ	waitQ+affinity	waitQ+virtualQ
IS	0	80	100.0%	92.0%	87.0%	92.0%	-
Raytrace	1	2049	65.9%	96.0%	96.0%	96.0%	-
	2-17	1046	33.6%	87.0%	3.4%	87.0%	-
Water-ns	4-515	27696	98.4%	80.4%	0.0%	66.0%	49.6%
FFT	0	16	100.0%	87.0%	87.0%	87.0%	-
Ocean	0	3200	96.2%	89.0%	78.0%	89.0%	-
Water-sp	0	240	47.2%	97.0%	95.0%	97.0%	-

Table 3: LAP Success Rates for $z = 2$.

IS uses bucket sort to rank an unsorted sequence of keys. In the first phase of the algorithm, each processor ranks its set of keys and updates a shared array with the rankings computed. In the second phase, each processor accesses the shared array to determine the final rankings of its keys. IS sorts 64K keys. The only lock in IS protects the shared array.

Raytrace renders a three-dimensional scene (*teapot*) using ray tracing. A ray is traced through each pixel in the image plane. The image plane is partitioned among processors in contiguous blocks of pixel groups, and distributed task queues (one per processor) are used with task stealing for load balancing. There is one lock to protect each task queue and one lock for memory management; the lock to assign an id to each ray has been eliminated, since id's are not really used.

Water-nsquared evaluates forces and potentials that occur over time in a system of water molecules. Water-nsquared uses an $\mathcal{O}(n^2)$ algorithm to compute these forces and potentials. The algorithm is run for 5 steps and the input size used is 512 molecules. Some locks accumulate global values but the majority of locks are used to update molecule forces. There is one lock for each water molecule.

FFT performs a complex 1-D FFT that is optimized to reduce interprocessor communication. The data set consists of 1M data points to be transformed, and another group of 1M points called roots of units. Each of these groups of points is organized as a 256 × 256 matrix. Locks are only used for initializing process ids.

Ocean studies large-scale ocean movements based on eddy and boundary currents. The input size we use is a 258 × 258 grid. Locks are used to identify processors and when processors compute local sums.

Water-spatial solves the same problem as Water-nsquared, but with an $\mathcal{O}(n \log n)$ algorithm. The algorithm is also run for 5 steps with 512 molecules. Locks are used for accessing only global values rather one lock per molecule.

Like under Scope Consistency, parallel applications might need slight modifications under AEC in two situations: a) when data are written within a critical section and are subsequently accessed without acquiring the corresponding lock; and b) when data are written outside of critical sections and must be visible before the next barrier. However, none of the applications in this study required modifications.

4.3 TreadMarks

In section 5 we compare the performance of our protocol against the one of TreadMarks. We chose to compare against TreadMarks instead of Midway, since, just like AEC, TreadMarks does not require the explicit association between shared data and synchronization variables. TreadMarks implements a lazy release consistency protocol in which the propagation of the modifications made to a shared page (diffs) is deferred until a processor suffers an access miss on the page. TreadMarks divides the program execution in intervals and computes a vector timestamp for each interval so that, on an acquire operation, it can determine the set of invalidations (write notices) the acquiring processor needs to receive. This vector describes a partial order between intervals of different processors. More details about TreadMarks can be found in [2].

5 Evaluating LAP and AEC

In this section we evaluate the performance of the LAP technique, the overlapping of diff generation and application with synchronization, and the AEC protocol.

5.1 Evaluating the LAP Technique

The lock managers in AEC compute update sets and maintain the waiting and virtual queues, and the affinity matrix A_{ij}. We evaluated LAP under AEC with the size z of the update set $U_i(k)$ varying from 1 to 3. Due to space limitations, however, we only present results for $z = 2$.

For each lock variable L_k, the lock manager computes the LAP success rate $H(k)$ as follows:

$$H(k) = \frac{no. \; times \; acquirer \; P_j \; was \; in \; U_i(k) \; of \; releaser \; P_i}{no. \; acquires \; executed \; on \; lock \; L_k}$$

In Table 3, we evaluate the contribution of each low-level prediction technique to the overall LAP success rate for the applications in our suite. The table shows, for each application and lock variable, the number of lock acquire events the variable is responsible for, the percentage of this number of events with respect to the total number of lock acquires, and the LAP success rates for each of its low-level techniques. The column labeled LAP presents $H(k)$, which combines the waiting queue, virtual

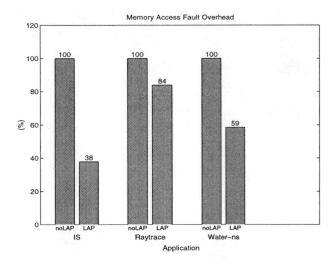

Figure 3: Access Fault Overheads Under AEC without LAP (noLAP) and AEC (LAP).

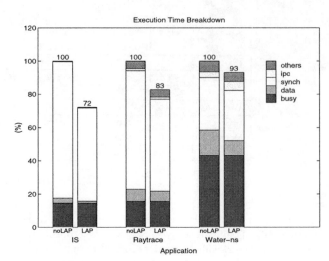

Figure 4: Running Time Under AEC without LAP (noLAP) and AEC (LAP).

queue, and affinity techniques; column waitQ presents the success rate of the waiting queue technique when applied in isolation; column waitQ+affinity presents the success rate of the combination of the affinity and waiting queue techniques; column waitQ+virtualQ presents the success rate of the combination of the waiting and virtual queue techniques[2].

Note that, due to the large number of lock variables in some of our applications, our table only presents data for variables with a reasonably high percentage of events. In addition, the table groups the variables that are logically related in the applications. A group's success rate is computed as the average success rate of the group variables weighted by the number of events of each variable. In Raytrace, all variables that protect the different task queues are put in a single group (var2-17). Water-nsquared, variables 4-515 protect the water molecules' structure.

As can be seen in the table, the LAP success rate is high, varying between 80% and 97% for the more important lock variables in our applications. For IS, one of the lock variables of Raytrace, FFT, Water-spatial, and Ocean, the waiting queue is the most effective technique. The virtual queue technique has a significant impact on the LAP success rate of Water-nsquared. The lock transfer affinity technique is effective for most lock variables of Raytrace, Water-nsquared, and Ocean.

In order to investigate the robustness of our results, we experimented with values of z in the range 1-3 and found that, increasing z from 1 to 2, increases the LAP success rate significantly. However, further increasing z to 3 improves the accuracy of LAP by very little; no more than 10%. Since a larger update set means that more data must be transferred through the network, $z = 2$ seems to be the best size.

In addition, we compared the LAP results taken from our simulated AEC to similar simulation-based implementations of the technique in TreadMarks and in a locally-developed release-

consistent SW-DSM. Our results show that the LAP success rate does not vary significantly for applications with a large number of synchronization events per lock variable, even though the timing and ordering of these events (and therefore the outcome of the low-level techniques that comprise LAP) do change under the the the different DSMs. Comparing LAP under AEC and TreadMarks, for instance, we find that success rates do not vary by more than 10% for our lock-intensive applications. This result demonstrates the robustness of the LAP technique.

5.2 Evaluating LAP Under AEC

Since we apply LAP in our implementation of AEC to reduce the number of times processors are required to fetch remote diffs, it should have a direct effect on the overhead of memory access faults as observed by each processor. Thus, in figure 3, we evaluate the effectiveness of LAP under AEC, in terms of the overhead of access faults under AEC without LAP (left bar) and AEC (right bar) on a simulated 16-processor system. In AEC without LAP the data modified inside of a critical section are not eagerly transferred from releasers to acquirers of the corresponding lock. Instead, these transfers are done lazily at access faults.

In figure 3 we only plot data for the applications for which most of the synchronization overhead comes from lock operations. The bars in the figures are normalized with respect to the AEC without LAP results. The figure shows that LAP reduces the overhead of access faults by as much as 62% for IS. The smallest improvement, 16%, is achieved for Raytrace, since in this application almost 80% of the access fault overhead comes from cold-start access faults and twin generation latencies. LAP does not address these two types of overhead.

Whether improvements in access fault overhead significantly influence the overall execution time depends on the relative importance of this type of overhead and on the (indirect) effect of these improvements on other types of overheads. More specifically, a reduction in access fault overhead inside a critical section

---

[2] Virtual queues were only implemented when the success rate of the waiting queue technique was not high enough (less than 85%) and when the variable had a significant number of lock acquire events.

significantly influences the lock waiting time when the application suffers from heavy lock contention.

In figure 4 we plot the simulated execution time of the same applications under AEC without LAP (left) and AEC (right) running on 16 processors. The bars in the figures show execution time broken down into busy time (busy), memory access fault overhead (data), synchronization time (synch), IPC overhead (ipc), and other overheads (others). The latter category is comprised by TLB miss latency, write buffer stall time, interrupt time, and the most significant of them, cache miss latency. The busy time represents the amount of useful work performed by the processor. Data fetch latency is a combination of coherence processing time and network latencies involved in fetching data as a result of page faults. Synchronization time represents the delays involved in waiting at barriers and lock acquires/releases. IPC overhead accounts for the time spent servicing requests coming from remote processors.

A running time comparison between AEC and AEC without LAP shows that the LAP improvements in fault overheads for IS and Raytrace have a significant effect on overall performance; LAP improves the performance of IS by 28% and the performance of Raytrace by 17%. The main reason for these results is that these applications exhibit heavy lock contention (as seen in table 3), and thus any improvement in fault overhead entails a similar reduction in lock synchronization latency. For instance, in IS the 62% reduction in access fault overhead induces a 42% reduction in the length of the critical section, which in turn produces a 37% improvement in lock synchronization overhead.

In addition, IS barriers are more efficient in the presence of LAP, again as a side-effect of the shorter critical sections entailed by the technique. In this application the barrier event occurs right after the highly-contended critical section, which serializes the execution of all processors. Thus, any extra cycles spent in the section contribute to greater waiting times at the barrier. More specifically, AEC without LAP entails 9 M more cycles in critical section time per processor than AEC. These extra cycles and the 66 M extra cycles spent waiting to acquire the lock under AEC without LAP account for the difference in barrier performance between the two versions of our protocol.

The running time improvement achieved by LAP on Water-nsquared comes solely from a reduction in the access fault overhead, as this application exhibits virtually no lock contention.

5.3 Evaluating the Benefits of Hiding Diff-Related Overheads

The overlapping of diff generation and application with synchronization overheads is also an important technique in the AEC protocol. A barrier event usually provides a good opportunity for overlapping as a result of load imbalance, while a lock acquire operation can significantly hide overheads when the acquiring processor is blocked as a result of lock contention. Lock release operations do not allow for overlapping overheads.

Table 4 presents data on the size of diffs and the extent to which our protocol is able to hide their generation cost. The leftmost column of the table lists our applications, while the other

Appl	Size	Merged Size	Merged	Create	Hidden
IS	6140	6102	94%	5M	1.7%
Raytrace	351	83	22%	23M	85.6%
Water-ns	2332	104	34%	116M	74.6%
FFT	5280	6	0.02%	15M	99.9%
Ocean	2964	11	0.06%	107M	99.3%
Water-sp	727	15	6%	12M	96.9%

Table 4: Diff statistics in AEC.

columns present the average size of diffs in bytes (Size), the average size of the diffs resulting from merges at lock release points (Merged Size), the percentage of diffs that are merged (Merged), the overall cost (in cycles) per processor of generating diffs (Create), and the percentage of this cost that is hidden by AEC (Hidden).

The table shows that diffs are generally large in our applications, except for Raytrace and Water-spatial. For these applications, processors are only responsible for relatively small chunks of data in each page, such as a small number of water molecules in Water-spatial. The merged diffs are almost always very short; the exception here is IS in which processors write the whole shared array inside critical sections. Merged diffs only represent a non-negligible percentage of the total number of diffs in the three applications where the synchronization overhead is dominated by lock operations: IS, Raytrace, and Water-nsquared. The time it takes to generate diffs may represent a large percentage of the overall running time of applications. The results in the table show that a significant percentage of the diff creation cost is hidden in all applications except IS. The reason for this result is that in IS the vast majority of diffs are created at lock release points, where diff creation cannot be overlapped with other overheads.

AEC also allows for hiding the overhead of applying diffs in applications with lock synchronization. However, only Water-nsquared benefits from this characteristic of AEC, as the protocol hides 13% of the program's diff application cost.

5.4 Comparing AEC vs. TreadMarks

In this section we compare the performance of AEC against that of TreadMarks. We compare performance against TreadMarks instead of Midway, since, differently from Midway, both AEC and TreadMarks do not require the explicit association between shared data and synchronization variables. In figures 5 and 6, we plot the simulated execution time of each of our applications under TreadMarks (left) and AEC (right) running on 16 processors. The bars in the figures are broken down into the same categories as in figure 4. These figures show that our protocol outperforms TreadMarks for all but one application. The performance differences in favor of AEC range from 4% for Ocean to 47% for Raytrace. AEC and TreadMarks perform virtually the same for Water-nsquared.

Most of the improvement achieved by AEC comes from great reductions in synchronization and access fault times. Regarding the data access time improvement, there are two reasons why AEC leads to lower overhead than TreadMarks: a) the most important

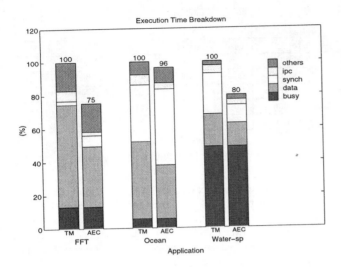

Figure 5: Execution Times Under TM and AEC.

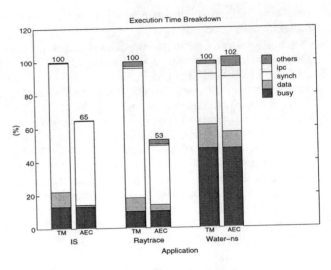

Figure 6: Execution Times Under TM and AEC.

one is that in TreadMarks diff creation is part of the critical path of both the generator and requester of the diff (thus, the diff creation overhead shows up under both `data` and `ipc` times in Tread-Marks); and b) when LAP can correctly predict lock acquisition order, the lock acquirer does not take page faults within the critical section and thus need not fetch diffs from other processors.

For FFT, Ocean, Water-spatial, and Water-nsquared, the differences in access fault times are mostly a result of performing diff creation away from the critical path of processors. For IS, Raytrace, and to some extent Water-nsquared, these differences come from LAP's elimination of most page faults within the applications' critical sections.

The synchronization overhead of IS, Raytrace, and Water-spatial is much greater under TreadMarks than under AEC. IS, Raytrace, and Water-spatial exhibit more efficient lock synchronization under AEC again as a result of shorter critical sections and heavy lock contention. In addition, barriers are more efficient under AEC for IS and Water-spatial, again as a side-effect of the shorter critical sections entailed by LAP and the program structure with a barrier following a highly-contended critical section.

Synchronization overheads are not always smaller under AEC however, as seen in the Water-nsquared, FFT, and Ocean results. For all these applications the barrier performance is degraded under AEC, while the lock performance is roughly the same under the two protocols. For applications such as Water-nsquared, LAP generates load imbalance in the initial phases of computation, as the technique requires a certain number of lock transfers before it can predict them correctly. The problem is that during these phases some processors predict transfers correctly and others do not. The resulting load imbalance hurts the performance of barriers.

For FFT and Ocean, the performance of barriers is worse under AEC for a different reason. In these applications, AEC generates a large number of diffs during most barrier events, increasing the utilization of the local memory buses, which in turn degrades AEC's messaging performance. This is a serious problem for AEC, given that it requires more messages than TreadMarks at barrier events.

6 Related Work

Current SW-DSMs rely on relaxed memory consistency models that require the virtual shared memory to be consistent only at special synchronization events. In Release Consistency (RC) [7], operations on shared data are only guaranteed to be seen by all processors at lock release operations. Lazy Release Consistency (LRC) [10] further relaxes RC by delaying coherence actions until the next lock acquire operation. Entry consistency (EC) [3] proposes an even more relaxed model of memory consistency that explores the relationship between synchronization objects that protect critical sections and the shared data accessed within the sections. Like LRC, EC delays propagation of updates until the next acquire operation. Scope Consistency (ScC) [9] proposes a memory consistency model (and associated protocol) that attempts to achieve the advantages of EC without having to explicitly bind data to synchronization objects. The ADSM protocol [11] implements a variation of EC that does not require explicit bindings either. Both the ScC and AEC protocols assume update-based coherence protocols, while ADSM only uses updates for single-writer data protected by locks.

SW-DSM protocols vary mainly in the way they manage the propagation of coherence information at the synchronization points; Munin [5], TreadMarks [2] and its Lazy Hybrid variation [6], and Midway [3] are important examples. AEC leads to much less communication than in Munin, since updates are only sent to the update set of the lock releaser, as opposed to all processors that shared the modified data. Like AEC, TreadMarks and Midway seek to avoid communication, but expose all the overhead of generating, fetching, and applying diffs to bring pages up-to-date. The Lazy Hybrid protocol avoids the overhead of fetching diffs by piggybacking them on a lock grant message when the last releaser of the lock has up-to-date data to provide and knows that the acquirer caches the data. AEC tackles the cost of diff handling more aggressively than these systems, using overlapped diffs and the LAP technique. In addition, AEC provides a simpler programming interface for EC than Midway.

The AEC protocol is based on a memory consistency model

216

equivalent to ScC. However, AEC differs from the ScC protocol in two important ways. AEC is a software-only algorithm, whereas the ScC protocol, as evaluated in [8], uses automatic update hardware (even though an all-software implementation of ScC is also possible). In addition, AEC tackles several overheads of traditional SW-DSMs by overlapping coherence and communication operations with useful work or other overheads. AEC [1] and ScC were developed simultaneously and independently.

AURC [8] and the protocol controller-based DSMs in [4] also seek to overlap communication and coherence overheads with useful computation. Both of these approaches also require a small amount of custom hardware.

The optimization of critical sections has also been the object of study in the context of cache-coherent multiprocessors. Trancoso and Torrellas [12] have studied the use of data prefetching and forwarding to reduce the number of cache misses occurring inside of critical sections. Forwarding in this context is used to send the data modified by a lock holder to the first processor waiting at the lock's queue; no data is sent out when there is no lock contention. Thus, their strategy has a similar effect to our LAP technique, but only when processors contend for lock access.

7 Conclusions

In this paper we proposed the AEC protocol, which relies heavily on the novel LAP technique and on overlapping diff generation and application overheads. Our analysis of the LAP technique showed that LAP is very successful at correctly predicting the next acquirer of a lock, which leads to a significant performance benefit to AEC. Hiding the generation of diffs behind synchronization overheads also improves performance significantly. However, most of the overhead of applying diffs is still exposed in AEC. A comparison against TreadMarks shows that AEC outperforms TreadMarks for 5 out of our 6 applications, mostly as a result of lower data access and synchronization overheads.

In summary, our main contributions have been the proposal and evaluation of AEC and LAP. AEC has been shown an efficient SW-DSM protocol. LAP is a general technique for predicting the lock acquisition order and can potentially be used for optimizing other update-based SW-DSMs.

Acknowledgements

The authors would like to thank Leonidas Kontothanassis and Raquel Pinto for their help with our simulation infrastructure. We would also like to thank Liviu Iftode, who helped us with applications. Luis Favre suggested the virtual queues technique, we thank him also. Finally, Raquel Pinto, Paula Maciel, and Luis Monnerat suggested modifications that helped improve the text.

References

[1] C. L. Amorim, C. B. Seidel, and R. Bianchini. The Affinity Entry Consistency Protocol. Tech. Report ES-388/96, COPPE Systems Engineering, Federal University of Rio de Janeiro, May 1996.

[2] C. Amza, A. Cox, S. Dwarkadas, H. Lu, R. Rajamony, W. Yu, and W. Zwaenepoel. TreadMarks: Shared Memory Computing on Networks of Workstations. *IEEE Computer*, 29(2), Feb 1996.

[3] B. N. Bershad, M. J. Zekauskas, and W. A. Sawdon. The Midway Distributed Shared Memory System. In *Proc. of the IEEE COMPCON'93 Conference*, Feb 1993.

[4] R. Bianchini, L. Kontothanassis, R. Pinto, M. De Maria, M. Abud, and C. L. Amorim. Hiding Communication Latency and Coherence Overhead in Software DSMs. In *Proc. of the 7th International Conference on Architectural Support for Programming Languages and Operating Systems*, Oct 1996.

[5] J. B. Carter, J. K. Bennett, and W. Zwaenepoel. Techniques for Reducing Consistency-Related Information in Distributed Shared Memory Systems. *ACM Transactions on Computer Systems*, 13(3), Aug 1995.

[6] S. Dwarkadas, P. Keleher, A. Cox, and W. Zwaenepoel. Evaluation of Release Consistent Software Distributed Shared Memory on Emerging Network Technology. In *Proc. of the 20th Annual International Symposium on Computer Architecture*, May 1993.

[7] K. Gharachorloo, D. Lenoski, J. Laudon, P. Gibbons, A. Gupta, and J. L. Hennessy. Memory Consistency and Event Ordering in Scalable Shared-Memory Multiprocessors. In *Proc. of the 17th International Symposium on Computer Architecture*, May 1990.

[8] L. Iftode, C. Dubnicki, E. W. Felten, and K. Li. Improving Release-Consistent Shared Virtual Memory Using Automatic Update. In *Proc. of the 2nd IEEE Symposium on High-Performance Computer Architecture*, Feb 1996.

[9] L. Iftode, J. P. Singh, and K. Li. Scope Consistency: A Bridge between Release Consistency and Entry Consistency. In *Proc. of the 8th Annual ACM Symposium on Parallel Algorithms and Architectures*, June 1996.

[10] P. Keleher, A. Cox, and W. Zwaenepoel. Lazy Release Consistency for Software Distributed Shared Memory. In *Proc. of the 19th International Symposium on Computer Architecture*, May 1992.

[11] L. R. Monnerat and R. Bianchini. ADSM: A Hybrid DSM Protocol that Efficiently Adapts to Sharing Patterns. Tech. Report ES-425/97, COPPE Systems Engineering, Federal University of Rio de Janeiro, March 1997.

[12] P. Trancoso and J. Torrellas. The Impact of Speeding up Critical Sections with Data Prefetching and Forwarding. In *Proc. of the 1996 International Conference on Parallel Processing*, Aug 1996.

[13] J. E. Veenstra and R. J. Fowler. MINT: A Front End for Efficient Simulation of Shared-Memory Multiprocessors. In *Proc. of the 2nd International Workshop on Modeling, Analysis and Simulation of Computer and Telecommunication Systems (MASCOTS '94)*, 1994.

[14] S. C. Woo, M. Ohara, E. Torrie, J. P. Singh, and A. Gupta. The SPLASH-2 Programs: Characterization and Methodological Considerations. In *Proc. of the 22nd Annual International Symposium on Computer Architecture*, May 1995.

Quantifying the Effects of Communication Optimizations[*]

Sung-Eun Choi   Lawrence Snyder

Department of Computer Science and Engineering
Box 352350
University of Washington
Seattle, WA 98195-2350

Abstract

Using a specially constructed machine independent communication optimizer that allows control over optimization selection, we quantify the performance benefit of three well known communication optimizations: redundant communication removal, communication combination, and communication pipelining. The numbers are shown relative to the base performance of benchmark programs using the standard communication optimization of message vectorization. *The effects on the number of calls to communication routines, both static and dynamic, are tabulated. We consider a variety of communication primitives including those found in Intel's NX library, PVM and the T3D's SHMEM library. The results show substantial improvement, with two combinations of optimizations being most effective.*

1 Introduction

In this paper, we quantify the effectiveness of three well-known communication optimizations: redundant communication removal, communication combination, and communication pipelining. In particular, each optimization is described in terms of how it improves performance. Though their descriptions are machine independent, the effectiveness of the optimizations can be influenced by machine specific characteristics. Consequently, we empirically evaluate these optimizations using three benchmark programs on two modern parallel machines, the Intel Paragon and the Cray T3D and two communication mechanisms, message passing and one-way communication (*i.e.*, T3D's SHMEM libraries). These benchmark programs are written in ZPL, a portable data parallel array language similar to the array subset of Fortran 90. We use an instrumented compiler where optimizations are performed in

a machine independent manner (ZPL source programs are compiled to SPMD ANSI C and linked with machine dependent libraries), allowing the same compiler output to be used for each set of experiments.

The paper is organized as follows. In Section 2, we review the goals of the three optimizations and comment on their effectiveness. In Section 3, we present an empirical evaluation of the optimizations. Finally, in Section 4, we give directions for future work and conclusions.

2 Review of Optimizations

Our language context eliminates the need for *message vectorization*, the most common communication optimization where in communication of individual array elements is hoisted outside of a loop nest and combined into a single communication of a slice of the array. Parallelizing compilers for scalar languages such as Fortran 77 must perform message vectorization since the unit of representation, and thus the unit of communication, is a single scalar value. Compilers for array languages can directly use arrays and array slices as the unit of representation [2], eliminating the need for message vectorization. Thus the baseline of comparison will be optimization using only message vectorization.

In our notation, we use i, j as subscripts to indicate whole array operations. For convenience, we will assume the compiler generates message passing code by emitting message sends and receives, though this is a simplification of what the ZPL compiler does [1]. For clarity of presentation, we omit the bounds information as well as the source and destination of the send and receive operations.

Figure 1(a) shows an example of naively generated communication. In the SPMD code shown here, for a given send/receive pair, a single processor is sending to processor p, while receiving from processor q where p and q are different processors, thus avoiding deadlock.

---

[*]This research was supported by ARPA Grant N00014-92-J-1824

(a)	(b)	(c)	(d)	(e)	(f)
$B_{i,j} \leftarrow f()$	$B_{i,j} \leftarrow f()$	$B_{i,j} \leftarrow f()$	$B_{i,j} \leftarrow f()$ **send** (B, E)	$C_{i,j} \leftarrow \ldots$	$C_{i,j} \leftarrow \ldots$
$\ldots$	$\ldots$	$\ldots$	$\ldots$	$\ldots$	$\ldots$
send (B) **receive** (B)	**send** (B) **receive** (B)	**send** (B, E) **receive** (B, E)	**receive** (B, E)	$B_{i,j} \leftarrow \ldots$	$B_{i,j} \leftarrow \ldots$ **send** (B, C)
$A_{i,j} \leftarrow B_{i,j+1}$	$A_{i,j} \leftarrow B_{i,j+1}$	$A_{i,j} \leftarrow B_{i,j+1}$	$A_{i,j} \leftarrow B_{i,j+1}$	$\ldots$	$D_{i,j} \leftarrow \ldots$ **send** (D)
$\ldots$	$\ldots$	$\ldots$	$\ldots$	$D_{i,j} \leftarrow \ldots$ **send** (B, C, D)	$\ldots$
send (B) **receive** (B)	$C_{i,j} \leftarrow B_{i,j+1}$	$C_{i,j} \leftarrow B_{i,j+1}$	$C_{i,j} \leftarrow B_{i,j+1}$	$\ldots$ **receive** (B, C, D)	**receive** (B, C)
$C_{i,j} \leftarrow B_{i,j+1}$	$\ldots$	$\ldots$	$\ldots$	$A_{i,j} \leftarrow B_{i,j+1}$	$A_{i,j} \leftarrow B_{i,j+1}$
$\ldots$	**send** (E) **receive** (E)			$\ldots$	$\ldots$
send (E) **receive** (E)	$D_{i,j} \leftarrow E_{i,j+1}$	$D_{i,j} \leftarrow E_{i,j+1}$	$D_{i,j} \leftarrow E_{i,j+1}$	$E_{i,j} \leftarrow C_{i,j+1}$	$E_{i,j} \leftarrow C_{i,j+1}$
$D_{i,j} \leftarrow E_{i,j+1}$				$\ldots$	$\ldots$ **receive** (D)
				$F_{i,j} \leftarrow D_{i,j+1}$	$F_{i,j} \leftarrow D_{i,j+1}$
(a) Naive insertion.	(b) Redundant communication removed.	(c) Combined communication.	(d) Pipelined communication.	(e) Maximized combining.	(f) Maintain latency hiding.

Figure 1: Example of communication optimizations: (a)-(d). Examples of combining communication: (e)-(f).

We now review the definition of the optimizations being considered and briefly describe the steps involved in their implementation.

Redundant communication removal. Communication is frequently not necessary because the non-local data has already been transmitted to the processor. Removing this redundant communication reduces the number of messages sent and the volume of data sent. In Figure 1(a), the second communication of B is redundant and can be removed as in Figure 1(b).

Communication combination. Several messages that are bound for the same processor may be *combined* into a single, larger message. Combining communication reduces the number but not the volume of data sent. For example, in Figure 1(c), the communication for B and E will have the same source and destination processors and can be combined.

Communication pipelining. Communication of messages may be *pipelined* such that the send is initiated earlier than the receive. This generally means that the receive is initiated immediately before the data is used while the send is initiated just after the last modification of the data. This optimization may hide the communication latency. Pipelining does not affect the number of messages sent or the volume of data sent (see Figure 1(d)).

Notice that the goals of combining and pipelining are sometimes at odds. Specifically, combining may reduce the "distance" between sends and receives, where distance is a measure of how much of the exposed communication latency can be hidden by computation. When combining communication, a compiler may choose to *maximize combining* or *maximize latency hiding potential* or even a hybrid solution based on machine and application characteristics. To maximize combining, messages are combined without regard for the distance

between the send and receive (see Figure 1(e)). To maximize latency hiding, only messages that are completely nested are combined (see Figure 1(f)).

3 Experimental Results

In this section, we present our methodology and the framework for evaluation. We then investigate the influence of machine characteristics. Finally, we empirically evaluate the optimizations for three benchmark programs.

3.1 Methodology and Framework

Experiments were run on two platforms: the Intel Paragon and the Cray T3D. On the Paragon, we use the native NX communication library routines. On the T3D we use a vendor optimized version of PVM and the native SHMEM library routines. The synthetic benchmark was run on two node dedicated partitions; all benchmark programs were run on 64 node dedicated partitions. Measured deviations were under 1% and therefore will not be reported. All timings were taken using each machine's native timer.

The benchmark programs are written in ZPL, a portable data parallel array language developed at the University of Washington. ZPL provides reductions, parallel prefix operators and other parallel operations, but for the purposes of this paper, we will concentrate on nearest-neighbor communication specified by the shift operator, @. The language's semantics guarantee static detection of communication and allow us to concentrate on optimizations.

In ZPL, arrays are first class citizens. Operations are performed on whole arrays and indexing is not allowed. The @ operator allows shifted accesses to arrays.

```
1 repeat
2     XX := X@east - X@west;
3     YX := Y@east - Y@west;
4     XY := X@south - X@north;
5     YY := Y@south - Y@north;

6     A := 0.250 * (XY * XY + YY * YY);
7     B := 0.250 * (XX * XX + YX * YX);
8     C := 0.125 * (XX * XY + YX * YY);

9     Rx := A*(X@east-2.0*X+X@west)
          + B*(X@south-2.0*X+X@north)
          - C*(X@se-X@ne-X@sw+X@nw);
10    Ry := A*(Y@east-2.0*Y+Y@west)
          + B*(Y@south-2.0*Y+Y@north)
          - C*(Y@se-Y@ne-Y@sw+Y@nw);
```

Figure 2: Code segment from Tomcatv SPEC benchmark written in ZPL.

@ is a binary operator with the following operands: an array (left operand) and a static offset vector (right operand). Figure 2 shows a code segment from the inner loop of the Tomcatv SPEC benchmark written in ZPL. At runtime, all arrays are trivially aligned (i.e., element (i, j) for all arrays resides on the same processor) and block distributed across a virtual processor mesh. Consequently, the use of an @ implies the need for nearest neighbor communication.

We now briefly explain the communication optimizations in the context of the ZPL compiler.

Redundant communication removal. Communication for @ expressions with the same array variable and same offset vector as a previous @ expression may be removed if the communication is redundant. In Tomcatv, the communication for X@east in line 9 is redundant because the non-local values have been cached earlier by the communication required for X@east in line 2.

Communication combination. Communication for @ expressions with the same offset vector but different array variable as a previous @ expression may be combined with that of the earlier expression if neither array variable is modified after the communication is completed and before the data is used. For example, the communication for Y@east in line 3 may be combined with that of X@east in line 2.

Communication pipelining. Communication may be pipelined within a basic block by pushing the send operation of a communication up as far as the most recent modification of the required array values or the top of the basic block, whichever occurs later. For example, the send operation for X@se in line 9 can be initiated at the top of the repeat loop.

Though the compiler considers all optimizations simultaneously, the optimizations can be turned on and off individually. To isolate the effects of combining communication, combining is *maximized* unless otherwise noted.

The ZPL compiler generates machine independent SPMD ANSI C code. The C code is compiled using the target machine's native C compiler and linked with the ZPL runtime libraries to produce an executable. More information on communication in ZPL can be found elsewhere [1, 3].

3.2 Influence of Machine Characteristics

Our first experiment is simply to determine the machine dependent characteristics that affect the optimizations on the Paragon and the T3D. We measure the software overhead, i.e., the *exposed* communication cost, for different communication primitives in our framework. On the Paragon, we use csend/crecv, basic message passing, isend/irecv, asynchronous message passing using the co-processor, and hsend/hrecv, message passing using callbacks. On the T3D, we use a vendor supplied version of PVM for basic message passing and SHMEM for asynchronous shared memory operations.

Figure 3 shows the observed software overhead of communication in our framework. The synthetic benchmark program sends a message from one node to another 10000 times. A busy loop is executed between any of the communication calls that require synchronization. The execution time of that loop is then subtracted from the total time.

The *knee* in the curves represents the message size for which combining messages begins to noticeably increase overhead. For both the Paragon and the T3D, the knee occurs at about 512 doubles (4K bytes). In other words, combining messages of 512 doubles or more degrades performance.

On the T3D, the SHMEM overhead is about 10% less than PVM. Though the difference is not as large as we hoped, it shows promise and we have already identified optimizations in our libraries that will improve these numbers. On the Paragon, we see that using the asynchronous primitives either does not reduce the exposed overhead, as in the case of isend/irecv, or increases it, as in case of hsend/hrecv. We also found that when we performed our full battery of tests using the benchmark suite on the Paragon, the asynchronous primitives saw little performance improvement or, in most cases, performance degradation. Consequently, we will not present the Paragon results of experiments to follow.

3.3 Whole Program Experiments

For our experiments, we chose three benchmark programs (see Figure 4). Each benchmark is substantial and requires a significant amount of communication.

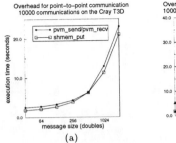

Figure 3: Exposed overhead of communication primitives on (a) the Cray T3D and (b) the Intel Paragon.

benchmark	description
TOMCATV	Thompson solver (SPECfp92)
SWM	Weather prediction (shallow water model)
SIMPLE	Hydrodynamics simulation (Livermore Labs)

Figure 4: Description of benchmark programs.

The plotted numbers are scaled to our baseline: naive communication generation with message vectorization.

Effectiveness of Eliminating Communication. Figure 5 shows the reduction in the number of communications (where a communication refers to a set of calls to perform a single data transfer) due to eliminating communications. The static counts are simply the number of communications in the text of the SPMD program. The dynamic counts are the actual number of communications performed during the execution of the program on a single processor.

The dynamic counts achieve nearly the same reduction as the static counts. Statically, the number of communications is between 55% and 20% that of the baseline; dynamically, between 70% and 33%. This implies that most of the communication occurs within the *main loop* of the program. Redundant communication removal accounts for the majority of the static improvement, while dynamically, communication combination accounts for more of the reduction. This suggests that a significant portion of the redundant communication occurs in *set up* code while the combined communication primarily occurs within the main loop of the program.

Performance of Benchmark Programs. In this section, we present the performance results of running each benchmark program on a 64 node partition of the Cray T3D. Figure 6 provides a key for the remaining graphs. For the first four, each experiment adds an optimization to the previous one (*e.g.*, "cc" is "rr" and combining). The "pl" experiments vary the communication mechanism (PVM *or* SHMEM) and the combin-

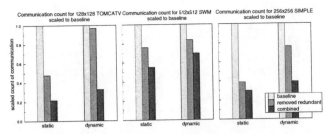

Figure 5: Reduction in the number communications due to redundant communication removal and communication combination.

experiment	description
baseline	message vectorization
rr	baseline with removing redundant
cc	rr with combining
pl	cc with pipelining
pl with shmem	pl using shmem_put, combining for maximum combining
pl with max latency	pl using shmem_put, combining for maximum latency hiding

Figure 6: Key for experiments performed.

ing heuristic (maximize combining *or* maximize latency hiding potential).

Performance using PVM. Figure 7(a) illustrates the reduction in execution times due to each optimization relative to the baseline. Execution times of fully optimized programs (pl) are as low as 72% of that of the baseline. Eliminating communication alone (cc), reduced running times to as low as 76% that of the baseline. In the case of TOMCATV, pipelining affects performance very little. Examination of the code reveals that a large amount of time is spent in two small loops that implement solvers. The opportunities for pipelining are limited by cross-loop dependences and the short code sequence itself. Compare this with the improvement for SIMPLE in which all communication occurs in the main body of the program. In general, each optimization impacts performance significantly.

Performance using SHMEM. Figure 7(b) illustrates the reduction in execution times of the fully optimized benchmark programs (relative to the baseline) using SHMEM's asynchronous shared memory primitives. The "pl with shmem" bar represents the performance of the same, fully optimized programs (pl) using shmem_put; for comparison, the "pl" bar is replicated from Figure 7(a). For SWM and SIMPLE, performance is noticeably improved. The running time of SIMPLE is reduced to almost 50% that of the baseline. TOMCATV experienced a degradation in performance. We have

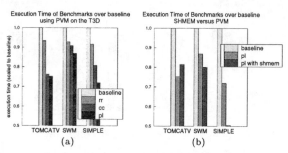

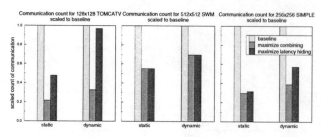

Figure 7: Performance of optimized benchmark programs (a) using PVM and (b) using SHMEM.

Figure 8: Reduction in the number communications due to different combining heuristics.

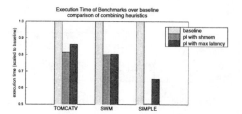

Figure 9: Comparison of combining heuristics.

identified this as a limitation of our implementation, as mentioned above. This is particularly detrimental when parts of the computation are inherently sequential, as in the TOMCATV solver. The PVM version is highly optimized and the penalties for sequential computation are less severe.

Comparing Combining Heuristics. In the previous section, we determined that the upper limit of message size for combining messages was 512 doubles. None of the above experiments combined messages as large as 512 doubles, so combining always improved performance. For those experiments, we use a heuristic that maximized combining. We now repeat the experiments for "pl with shmem" using the combining heuristic that maximizes latency hiding potential. Figure 8 shows the static and dynamic communication counts for the benchmarks when compiled using each of the combining heuristics. As expected, combining to maximize latency hiding potential does in some cases significantly increase the number of communications both statically and dynamically. For TOMCATV, the dynamic communication count is 97% that of the baseline, the same as for simply removing redundant communication (Figure 5). The only difference between the two versions is that the communication is pipelined. Figure 9 shows the scaled running times for this experiment. At runtime, the benchmark versions compiled for maximized combining always performed better than those compiled maximized latency hiding. Notice that the performance of TOMCATV when maximizing for latency hiding, effectively removing redundant communication and pipelining, is much better than that of simply removing redundant communication (Figure 7(a)), again showing that each optimization improves performance significantly.

4 Conclusions

We have quantified the effectiveness of three communication optimizations: redundant communication

removal, communication combination, and communication pipelining. We measured the exposed overheads of communication routines on the Intel Paragon and the Cray T3D and found that combining messages up to the size of 4K bytes does not affect the overhead significantly. More importantly, the asynchronous communication primitives provided by the NX library are extremely heavy-weight and showed no improvement over using the synchronous alternative. The T3D's SHMEM operations show promise for performance improvement over the message passing communication provided by PVM. The impact of each optimization is demonstrated using a suite of benchmark programs run on the T3D. We evaluated the effectiveness of each of the optimization and found that all three optimizations contribute significantly to decreasing running times versus the same benchmarks optimized using only message vectorization.

References

[1] Braford L. Chamberlain, Sung-Eun Choi, and Lawrence Snyder. IRONMAN: A machine independent parallel communication abstraction to replace message passing in compilers. Technical Report 97–04–04, University of Washington, 1997.

[2] Chamberlain *et al.* Factor-Join: A unique approach to compiling array languages for parallel machines. In *LCPC*, 1996.

[3] Sung-Eun Choi and Lawrence Snyder. Quantifying the effect of communication optimizations. Technical Report 97–04–05, University of Washington, 1997.

Reducing Overheads of Local Communications in Fine-grain Parallel Computation

Jin-Soo Kim   Soonhoi Ha   Chu Shik Jhon

Department of Computer Engineering
Seoul National University
Seoul 151-742, KOREA
{jinsoo, sha, csjhon}@comp.snu.ac.kr

Abstract

For fine-grain computation to be effective, the cost of communications between the large number of subtasks should be minimized. In this paper, we present an optimization technique which reduces overheads of communications between local subtasks by bypassing the network interface and transferring data directly from memory or registers to memory. On average, the optimization results in 35.6% improvement in total execution time on instruction-level simulations with six benchmark programs from 1 to 32 nodes.

1 Introduction

Fine-grain parallel computation has several advantages such as architecture independence, potential for exploiting parallelism, ease of use as a target for code generation, and capabilities of balancing loads and hiding communication latencies. An architecture that can exploit the fine-grain parallelism is a *multithreaded architecture*.

In parallel computation, communication latency between subtasks on different nodes is inevitable and keeping a certain number of subtasks in each node is necessary for multithreading to be useful. However, an operation that communication is expected at compile time may not generate any message at run time depending on the location of the target subtask. Those operations can not be determined statically because subtasks are created and destroyed dynamically and the number of subtasks itself is data-dependent. Moreover, the exact location of a subtask can not be predicted at compile time.

The proposed approach is to generate alternative codes at compile time that transfer data between local subtasks bypassing the network interface. Before generating a message, the program decides which code to execute according to the location of the destination. No message is generated in case of local communications and unnecessary context switching can be avoided.

2 A Model for Fine-grain Parallel Computation

In this paper, we are interested in a model of fine-grain multithreading, which can hide a long latency using a large number of threads. Also it is desirable for such model to be implementable using commodity microprocessors to exploit their high performance/price ratio. For these reasons, we have adopted the TAM (Threaded Abstract Machine) [1], a compiler-controlled multithreading model.

A TAM program consists of a collection of *code blocks*. Each code block represents a subtask, and typically specifies a function or a loop body. A code block is compiled into a set of *inlets* and *threads*. Inlets are short message handlers and threads are sequences of instructions that can not suspend. When a code block is invoked, a *frame* is allocated for storage of arguments, local variables, and a list of ready threads associated with the frame.

The TAM scheduling hierarchy consists of a two-level structure comprising a collection of frames, each containing one or more addresses of enabled threads in a region of the frame called the *remote continuation vector* (RCV). When a frame is activated, the list of ready threads in the RCV is copied into a special region called the *local continuation vector* (LCV). Threads are fetched and executed from the LCV until none remains, after which frame switching is performed. Any thread forked by other threads within the same frame is placed in the LCV rather than in the RCV. The set of threads executed in a single frame activation is called a *quantum*.

The TAM model enhances the parallelism of programs further by non-strict execution. Non-strict execution allows functions or arbitrary expressions to begin execution and possibly return results before all operands are computed. Non-strict execution also requires data structures able to be accessed while components are still being computed. In the TAM model, global data structures are based on I-structure [2] semantic, which provides synchronization on a per-element basis.

Several primitives are defined in the TAM model for

fine-grain multithreading. They are operations for message transfer (SEND, RECEIVE), frame management (FALLOC, FFREE), scheduling (SWAP, STOP), thread generation (FORK, SFORK, SWITCH, POST, SPOST), and I-structure management (IALLOC, IFREE, IFETCH, ISTORE). Those primitives, combined with ALU operations, form an intermediate language called TL0.

3 Reducing Overheads of Local Communications

We have identified three cases where communication is involved between subtasks; message sending, parallel function invocation, and I-structure accesses. Each case will be discussed in detail in the following subsections.

3.1 Message Sending

In our model of fine-grain computation, messages are primarily used to carry arguments and results between function activations. The TAM model uses a mechanism called *active messages* [3] for fine-grain communication. In active messages, each message contains at its head the address of a user-level handler which is executed on message arrival with the message body as the arguments. The role of the handler, or inlet, is to get the message out of the network and process the message by posting an appropriate thread.

For a message to be delivered, data should be copied from registers or frame slots to the network output buffer at the source node and from the network input buffer to frame slots at the destination node. Although the same mechanism can be used for local communications by providing a feedback path between the network input and output buffer, it is inefficient because the network interface becomes complex and unnecessary copying of data is performed.

To overcome these problems, we implement the LCV as a stack and extend it to be used for the linkage between sender and receiver in case of a local communication. For every inlet, we generate another version of codes, which extracts data from the LCV rather than from the network input buffer. We call this a *pseudo inlet*. Before sending a message, the program checks if the destination frame resides in the same node or not. If the communication is local, the program pushes arguments into the LCV with the address of the pseudo inlet. When the current thread reaches STOP, it fetches another enabled thread from the LCV, which is a pseudo inlet. The posted thread from the pseudo inlet is also put into the LCV. Therefore, the pseudo inlet and posted threads are executed within the context of the current frame without switching to the destination frame.

Frame accesses from threads or inlets are relative to the base address of the frame, or the frame pointer. In the original TAM model, all the threads in the LCV belong to the same frame. So the frame pointer is initialized only once when a frame switching occurs. On the other hand, the LCV in the proposed model holds the addresses of threads and pseudo inlets from different frames. Therefore, it is necessary to keep the frame pointer in the LCV and to initialize it whenever a thread is fetched from the LCV.

Table 1 shows an optimized implementation of SEND. **me** denotes my node number. **Node()** and **PseudoAddr()** are macros to find the node number for a given frame pointer, and an address of the pseudo inlet, respectively. At the beginning of a code block, there is a jump table that maps an inlet number to an actual address. Because a frame holds the base address of the corresponding code block, it is possible to find the address of an inlet or a pseudo inlet using a frame pointer and an inlet number.

Table 1. Optimized implementation of SEND

SEND $dest\_fp$, $dest\_inlet$, arg_0, ..., arg_n

if (**Node**($dest\_fp$) == **me**) {
    Push arg_0, ..., arg_n into the LCV;
    Push $dest\_fp$, **PseudoAddr**($dest\_fp$, $dest\_inlet$) into the LCV;
} else {
    Store $dest\_fp$, $dest\_inlet$, arg_0, ..., arg_n to the network output buffer;
    Send a message;
}

3.2 Parallel Function Invocation

TAM's function invocation consists of two phases. In the first phase, the caller sends a request for frame allocation using a FALLOC operation. The callee allocates a frame upon receiving the request, initializes the frame, and then returns the frame pointer back to the caller. In the second phase, if the caller receives the callee's frame pointer, it sends arguments to predefined inlets. Due to the non-strict execution, arguments are sent one by one as soon as its value is known to the caller.

Actually, FALLOC is handled by a run-time system (RTS). If a user issues a FALLOC, the RTS in the source node determines the node where the function is assigned, and then sends a request message to the RTS of the destination node on behalf of the user. In the destination node, the RTS allocates a frame and schedules inlet 0 with the caller's frame pointer, the return inlet number and the new frame pointer as the arguments. Inlet 0 initializes the frame and returns its frame pointer to the caller.

Normal messages are used to return the new frame pointer or to send arguments and results. Therefore, they can be avoided using the optimization described in section 3.1 if the callee is allocated to the same node as the caller. However, the request message sent by an RTS also should be avoided in case of a local invocation. This can be done by revising an RTS routine of FALLOC, as described in Table 2. If the callee is local, the RTS adjusts the LCV so that the pseudo inlet 0 of the new frame can be executed after the current thread. In Table 2, $fp denotes the register which holds the current frame pointer.

224

Table 2. Optimized implementation of FALLOC

FALLOC *code_block, return_inlet*
Determine *target_node*, where the code block is assigned.
if (*target_node* == **me**) {
Allocate a frame for *code_block*;
new_fp ← base address of the new frame;
Push \$fp, *return_inlet, new_fp* into the LCV;
Push *new_fp*, **PseudoAddr**(*new_fp*, 0) into the LCV;
} else
Send a request message to the RTS of *target_node*;

3.3 I-structure Accesses

I-structures are accessed by split-phase operations such as IALLOC, IFREE, IFETCH and ISTORE. IALLOC and IFREE allocate and deallocate I-structures and IFETCH reads an element by sending a message to the node containing the data which returns the value to an inlet. In particular, reads of empty elements are deferred until the corresponding write occurs. ISTORE writes a value to an element, resuming any deferred readers.

Table 3 shows an optimized implementation of IFETCH, which removes any local message if the element resides in the same node and if it has valid data. **Tag**() indicates whether the word contains data (FULL), or not (EMPTY), or it has any deferred readers (DEFERRED). Actual data can be accessed using the macro **Data**(). IALLOC, IFREE, and ISTORE also can be optimized similarly.

Table 3. Optimized implementation of IFETCH

IFETCH *return_inlet, heap_addr, element*
if (**Node**(*heap_addr*) == **me**)
switch (**Tag**(*heap_addr*[*element*])) {
case EMPTY:
case DEFERRED:
Insert <\$fp, *return_inlet*> to the deferred list;
break;
case FULL:
Push **Data**(*heap_addr*[*element*]) into the LCV;
Push \$fp, **PseudoAddr**(\$fp, *return_inlet*) into the LCV;
break;
}
else
Send a request message to the RTS of **Node**(*heap_addr*);

4 Experimental Evaluation

We have constructed an instruction-level simulator to evaluate the efficiency of the proposed optimization. The simulator was based on SPIM [4], an instruction-level simulator for MIPS instruction set, and was extended to parallel and multithreaded environments using a commercial event-driven simulator, SES/Workbench [5].

We have also implemented a translator which converts a TL0 program to MIPS assembly codes. The generated code consists of MIPS instruction set, assembly directives, and

Table 4. Benchmark programs

Benchmarks	Arguments	TL0 lines	Memory Sizes (KB)		
			ORG	OPT	% Increased
fib	20	361	1.88	2.55	35.6
qs	500	2773	16.65	21.84	31.2
mmt44	100.0	3964	25.93	34.20	31.9
dtw	100.0	3500	24.62	34.92	41.8
speech	10240 30	6766	45.98	60.83	32.3
paraffins	17	10324	66.90	88.11	31.7

several system calls. System calls are used to transfer control to the RTS for some multithreading primitives. Actually, the simulator handles these primitives as if there were an RTS on every node. The translator also performs register allocation, because TL0 language uses memory-to-memory ALU operations. For experiments, the translator generates two versions of codes for a given TL0 program; one without optimization (ORG), and the other with optimization (OPT).

The interconnection network is not simulated in detail. Instead, we assume that the network has a uniform communication latency of 100 instruction cycles. The local feedback of a message is also assumed to take 10 cycles.

Table 4 shows arguments and program sizes of six benchmark programs used in the experiment. These applications are originally written in Id, and compiled to TL0 programs by the TAM group[1].

We can observe that the code size increases by 34.1% on average when the optimization is performed. Additional pseudo inlets primarily contribute to the increase in the code size. Secondary factors include codes to check if the destination is local and codes to push arguments and the address of a pseudo inlet into the LCV in case of a local communication.

Figure 1 gives a relative speedup when the optimization is used. Optimized codes always result in shorter execution times in spite of added cost of checking the destination of messages for every SEND, and saving and restoring the frame pointer for all primitives that access the LCV. Most of the benchmarks except fib and paraffins follow the general trend that the relative speedup decreases as the number of nodes increases. This is because the number of allocated frames per each node decreases, reducing the possibility of local communications. On average, optimized codes run 1.55 times faster than unoptimized codes on a single node, where all communications are local. There is 35.6% improvement in total execution times when we average six benchmark programs from 1 to 32 nodes.

It can be easily found that the benefits of our optimization mainly come from eliminating local messages. Figure 2 shows the ratio of the total number of messages generated from optimized codes with respect to that of unoptimized codes. Note that no message is generated with a single node

---

[1]They are freely available by anonymous ftp at `ftp://ftp.cs.berkeley.edu/ucb/TAM/idtam-0.3.tar.Z`

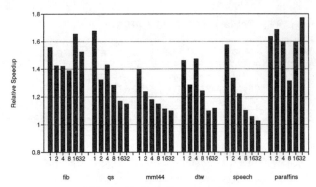

Figure 1. Relative speedup

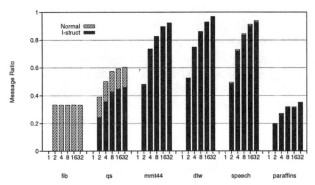

Figure 2. The reduction in total messages

are concentrated on a few nodes, most of IFETCH requests are remote. Issues of the optimal and balanced distribution of global data structures are beyond the scope of this paper and should be addressed as a separate research topic.

5 Concluding Remarks

In this paper, we have presented an optimization technique to reduce overheads of local communications in fine-grain parallel computation. Although the optimization increases the code size slightly, the code size hardly affects the total memory requirement because frames demand much more memory at run time.

The advantage of suggested optimization can be summarized as follows. First, the network interface can be simpler because local feedback path need not be provided. In addition, the number of total messages which should be handled by the network interface is significantly reduced. Second, the cost of a local communication can be reduced by avoiding unnecessary copying of data to and from the network buffers. Third, the scheduling cost can be reduced by executing pseudo inlets and locally posted threads within the context of the current frame.

From the experimental results, we have observed that it is important to distribute I-structures in a balanced way for better speedup. This problem can be alleviated by employing an I-structure cache [6]. Note that the suggested optimization can also be used with such I-structure caches by eliminating the need for sending a message if the designated I-structure element can be found on a local cache. We expect greater speedup by combining the proposed approach and I-structure caches.

using the optimized codes. The relatively low speedup of mmt44, dtw, and speech (see Figure 1), especially for the large number of nodes, is closely related to the low reduction in the number of messages.

We classify each message as *Normal* if it is generated by FALLOC or SEND, and as *I-struct* if it comes from I-structure operations. It is apparent from the figure that the number of I-structure messages is dominant. The reason that I-structure messages are not eliminated well in mmt44, dtw, and speech can be found from Table 5, which shows a dynamic statistics on I-structure operations.

Table 5. Statistics on I-structure operations

Benchmarks	IALLOC			IFETCH	ISTORE
	N	S	S/N	N	N
fib	0	0	-	0	0
qs	7885	15770	2.0	26540	14770
mmt44	10	30023	3002.3	507771	30023
dtw	14	40032	2859.4	2061000	40032
speech	157	45349	288.8	1565186	34909
paraffins	188272	615514	3.3	298632	608295

N denotes the total number of I-structure operations. S and S/N indicates the total size and the average size of I-structure elements requested by IALLOC, respectively. mmt44, dtw, and speech has a very large value of S/N, meaning that the large number of I-structure elements are allocated at once on a specific node. Because I-structures

References

[1] D. E. Culler, S. C. Goldstein, K. E. Schauser, and T. von Eicken, "TAM - A Compiler Controlled Threaded Abstract Machine," *J. of Parallel and Distributed Computing*, pp. 347–370, Jun. 1993.

[2] Arvind, R. S. Nikhil, and K. K. Pingali, "I-Structures: Data Structures for Parallel Computing," Tech. Rep. CSG Memo 269, MIT, Feb. 1987.

[3] T. von Eicken, D. Culler, S. Goldstein, and K. Schauser, "Active Messages: A Mechanism for Integrated Communication and Computation," in *Proc. 19th Int'l Symp. on Computer Architecture*, pp. 256–266, 1992.

[4] J. R. Larus, "SPIM S20: A MIPS R2000 Simulator," Tech. Rep. #966, University of Wisconsin-Madison, 1990.

[5] Scientific and Engineering Software Inc., *SES/Workbench 3.0 User's Manuals*. 1995.

[6] K. M. Kavi, A. R. Hurson, P. Patadia, E. Abraham, and P. Shanmugam, "Design of Cache Memories for Multi-Threaded Dataflow Architecture," in *Proc. 22th Int'l Symp. on Computer Architecture*, pp. 253–264, 1995.

Parallel Synchronization of Continuous Time Discrete Event Simulators*

Peter Frey, Harold W. Carter and *Philip A. Wilsey*
Dept. of ECECS, PO Box 210030, Cincinnati, OH 45221–0030

Abstract

Mixed-Mode simulation has been generating considerable interest in the simulation community and has continued to grow as an active research area. Traditional mixed-mode simulation involves the merging of digital and analog simulators in various ways. However, efficient methods for the synchronization between the two time domains remains elusive. This is due to the fact that the analog simulator uses dynamic time step control whereas the digital simulator uses the event driven paradigm. This paper proposes two new synchronization methods and presents their capabilities using a component-based continuous-time simulator integrated with an optimistic parallel discrete event simulator. The results of the performance evaluation leads us to believe that while both synchronization methods are functionally viable, one has superior performance.

1 Introduction

The need to join different simulation paradigms for mixed-mode simulation has resulted in a number of different time-synchronization approaches. The developments range from backplane approaches, which synchronize multiple separate simulators, to simple enhancements of specialized simulators. With the standardization of mixed-mode simulation languages, specialized tools capable of supporting all the different simulation paradigms, are being developed. These tools are able to exploit parallelism and make use of advanced synchronization protocols for performance enhancement.

The central design issue to be resolved first is, which of the two paradigms controls the other. This decision is of critical importance because the whole simulation will be controlled by this selection. However, the large variety of algorithms in a mixed-mode simulator, all with fundamentally different properties, increases the need for an in-depth study.

The remainder of this paper is organized as follows. Sections 2.1 and 2.2 describe the design decisions for each time domain. Section 2.3 summarizes the difficulties in the design of the mixed-mode simulator. Section 3 introduces two new synchronization protocols to coordinate the two simulation time domains. The paper concludes with an evaluation of performance of the two synchronization protocols.

2 Background

Before discussing the synchronization protocols, a review of the optimistic discrete event paradigm and the continuous-time simulation of algebraic differential equations, is presented.

2.1 Optimistic Parallel Discrete Event Simulation

A large variety of parallel discrete event simulation algorithms are available [3]. Parallel implementations are prefered because they reduce the huge computation time necessary to simulate today's large and complex systems. Also optimistic approaches are more promising because it

---

*This work was supported by the Defense Advanced Research Projects Agency under contracts J–FBI–93–116 and DABT63–96–C–0055.

can be shown that in the worst case a conservative method performs as poor as the sequential algorithms [14].

Optimistic discrete event simulation algorithms such as Time Warp [3, 4] employ asynchronous communication. These algorithms have no global clock and therefore the parallel processes are free to advance. This does not enforce an order on the event arrival times and therefore, a process may very well receive an event with a time stamp lower than it's local virtual time (LVT). If a parallel process receives an event with a time stamp lower than it's LVT, then a causality error is said to have occured. Optimistic approaches do not avoid causality errors, but instead detect them and invoke a recovery scheme (also known as rollback), to return the simulation to a state where causality is maintained. This allows the simulator to exploit parallelism in situations where causality errors that might occur do not [2].

The optimistic Time Warp simulator used in this study is the WARPED system [8] developed at the University of Cincinnati. The basic simulation object is called a physical process. One or more of these physical processes can be combined to form a logical process. Each logical process represents a heavy-weight process, that is run on one processor. Every physical process keeps a copy of the received events in the input queue and a copy of the out going events in the output queue. In addition, a copy of the simulation state associated with every local virtual time value is stored in the state queue. The periodically saved states in the state queue are used if the system has to rollback to a correct state. Events which result in a causality error are called straggler messages. Besides restoring the system state, the rollback has to undo the effects of all events with time stamps greater than that of the straggler. Thus a rollback of the input queue as well as the output queue needs to take place. The input queue just needs to be reset, whereas the output queue needs additional attention. Events which are no longer valid and were sent out, have to be "unsent". This is done by sending a negative event (anti-message) that annihilates the original positive message (causing the removal of the event from the receiver's input queue). If the receiving process has already processed the message, the incoming event is handled as a straggler which results in another rollback. Cascading rollbacks occur until all incorrectly generated messages are annihilated. Many different algorithms have been published to optimize these steps [11]. It can be shown that the recursive procedure terminates and that progress of the simulation [5] is guaranteed. Simulation progress results in the advancement of the global virtual time (GVT). GVT is the time stamp of the earliest unprocessed event message in the system. As GVT is a monotonically increasing quantity, a rollback to a time earlier than GVT is not possible. Calculation of GVT [5, 9] during simulation is necessary for simulation progress, as well as to handle irrevocable operations such as I/O, and garbage collection in the queues.

2.2 Continuous Simulation

Continuous simulation involves solving a set of differential equations describing a simulation model where the values are continuously changing. In circuit analysis, the most common form of continuous simulation is the transform analysis. Transform analysis calculates the circuit behavior depending on the input stimuli. This paper addresses the continuous transform analysis method only. Waveform relaxation methods [6], symbolic analysis & simulation [13] and behavioral simulation [1] are just a few of the many different algorithms with varying accuracy and performance.

Find the initial operating point (dc solution).
Choose a first time step (use the default).
   Discretize the derivatives (C's and L's) forming approximate models.
      Linearize the nonlinear elements forming approximate models.
         Form the linear equations associated with the
         approximate circuit.
         Solve the linear equations.
      Iterate until solution is found or reduce time step and try again.
   Check for accuracy.
If accurate, continue forward in time else reduce time step and try again.

Table 1. Standard Algorithm [7, Chapter 27]

Today's research in transform analysis is focussed towards performance enhancement without any accuracy loss. The development of parallel continuous simulators has been aided by the increased computation power of today's machines and the state-of-the-art developments in computer architectures. Due to the continuous simulator's high communication demands, shared memory implementations are generally preferred. This helps in the development of a generic interface between the continuous simulators and the surrounding environment. As soon as the model description is loaded, the continuous simulator now only needs the start and end time, to perform the computation.

Both the standard SPICE circuit simulator [10] and the object oriented implementation of the SPICE simulator developed at the University of Cincinnati, provide the same functionality for transfer analysis and maintain the interface discussed earlier. The only drawback is the limited set of differential equations supported by them. So the trade off is between performance and the range of differential equations. Differential equations are implemented as components in today's SPICE like simulators. This class of simulators is often referred to as the component-based simulators. Component-based solvers follow the standard method for solving circuit equations as shown in Table 1 [7, Chapter 27].

The standard method consists of multiple nested loops. The loop step size depends on the circuit description. Circuits with very small time constants (high slope) must be simulated with a small time step by the continuous simulator. In contrast, if the system exhibits a behavior that is relatively constant or changing slowly, a larger time step can be used. Circuits that exhibits phases of high and low activity, are known as stiff circuits. SPICE supports changing time steps to improve performance for stiff circuits. The performance improvement results from the fact that, the larger the time step chosen, the lesser the number of simulation time steps necessary. The optimal time step is the time step that satisfies all the tolerances. The time step modification is not done abruptly, instead it is increased slowly.

2.3 Mixed-Mode Simulation

This section deals with the design of a mixed-mode simulator that uses both the discrete and the continuous simulation paradigms. The task of simulation control is handled by the discrete event simulator as it usually handles less computationally intensive tasks than the continuous simulator. Two major problems arise when merging the two simulation paradigms.

- Continuous simulation processes can influence the next simulation cycle time. This implies that there is no lookahead, which results in poor performance of non-optimistic simulators. A lock step protocol for sequential and conservative simulators was developed by Tahawy *et al* [15]. Although optimistic simulators don't require lookahead, an in-depth study of the synchronization protocols is necessary.

- It is not possible to specify the exact stop time for the continuous simulator because the next event time is not known in optimistic simulations (*i.e.,* no lookahead). Short time intervals result in poor performance for the continuous simulator and large time intervals

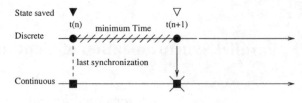

Continuous simulation with no event generation

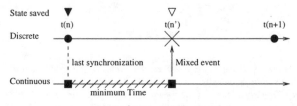

Continuous simulation with generation of an event

Figure 1. Minimum Time Step protocol

increase the risk of the continuous simulator receiving a causality error, resulting in a large penalty in terms of simulation time.

The synchronization protocols introduced in the following section avoid these issues while maintaining execution efficiency. This paper concentrates on the proposed protocols, and evaluates their efficiency and performance for some typical simulation models.

3 Synchronization Protocols

Three different synchronization protocols, between a continuous domain simulator and a parallel optimistic discrete event simulator, are dealt with in detail in this section. Named after their fundamental property of synchronization, the three synchronization protocols are (a) *Minimum Time Step* (MTS), (b) *N-event Synchronization* where N = 1 and (c) N = 2.

To aid the discussion of the protocols, a graphical representation similar to the one in [15] is used (see Figure 1). Modifications to the representation were necessary to represent the stored states of the continuous process in the optimistic discrete environment. Keep in mind that the picture represents one continuous process on top of an optimistic discrete event simulator. The discrete time line can be thought of as the discrete communication (input/output) of the process, with any other process in the system. On the continuous time line, the generation of intermediate values in the continuous simulator is marked as blocks on the time line and each of these blocks could potentially result in events.

3.1 Minimum Time Step protocol

This protocol prevents possible inconsistencies by restricting the execution time step of the continuous process. The value of the minimum time step is limited to the accuracy of the computer or is explicitly specified by the simulated processes. For example, in VHDL-AMS the smallest time unit is defined in the LRM, as one femtosecond.

Figure 1 illustrates the MTS protocol for a minimum time step where no event occurs in the continuous simulator during the interval, and the case where an event does occur.

In either case, the next possible event will be scheduled at time $t_n + minimum\ time\ step$. The continuous simulator will be automatically triggered by the next input event scheduled for this time. If the next input event is in the future, the continuous process will interrupt itself after the minimum time step has passed. In addition to a possible output event, it creates a dummy event and sends it to itself. Output events will only be

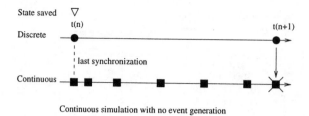

Continuous simulation with no event generation

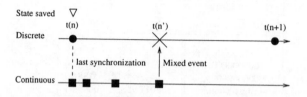

Continuous simulation with generation of an event

Figure 2. First Event Synchronization

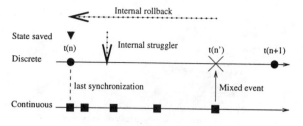

Internal straggler after or during simulation

Figure 3. First Event Synchronization error

created at the end of the interval so that the minimum time step assumption is not violated. A new synchronization point is created, whenever the minimum time step is passed. This happens regardless of an event in the future or the creation of the dummy event. The minimum time step ensures that no intermediate event occurs and therefore, all possible cases are covered. There is no need to consider events earlier than the last synchronization point. These will be handled automatically by the optimistic discrete event simulator (which is serving as global controller), which initiates a rollback to a synchronization point before the arrival time.

This protocol is suitable if the state, the execution speed and the communication overhead of the continuous simulator, can be kept small. An example would be a transfer function simulation available after symbolic analysis [13]. However, transfer functions cannot be used in all cases and are rather difficult to generate. Also if the transfer function has a lot of time dependent variables, the state can become large. To overcome these problems, and increase the accuracy, continuous simulators are commonly based on matrix solvers. These, however have large and frequently changing states and are computation extensive. To reduce computation time, variable step sizes are required which can not be supported in this protocol. This protocol is not considered in Section 4 because of this restriction.

3.2 First Event Synchronization protocol

In contrast to the MTS protocol, the N-event protocols do not restrict the execution of the event driven simulator. Consider the case where N = 1 (denoted as the First-Event Synchronization, FES). In this protocol, the continuous simulation engine is handled as a discrete event process. However, it has to handle some exceptions due to it's continuous nature.

Figure 2 gives a graphical representation of the FES protocol. The continuous process is activated by the first event (t_n). The last state stored contains the system state up to the event time (t_n). The continuous process tries to simulate to the time of the next scheduled event (t_{n+1}) of the process. If no event is generated, the continuous simulator calculates all intermediate values, stops computation at t_{n+1} and stores it's state. The state stored will be associated with the activation event (t_n) but it will contain the simulation state at time t_{n+1}. After the state is saved, a new synchronization point is reached. In case a threshold cross (event generation) occurs during computation of the continuous values, the FES protocol requires the storage of the state and an artificial event at time $t_{n'}$ to reach another synchronization point.

The protocol seems to be straight forward but multiple assumptions have to be satisfied to guarantee correct execution. The most obvious as-

sumption is that the protocol assumes the existence of the next event at time t_{n+1}. This can not be guaranteed. Therefore, if no further event is scheduled, a stop time has to be picked at random. This is not necessarily a problem, if we assume that the continuous process is the bottleneck of the simulated system and in general, the next event is available. A more serious problem arises from the use of the optimistic discrete event simulator. The optimistic protocol does not guarantee that all events arrive in order. As mentioned before, the optimistic simulation protocol takes care of events arriving before the current event (t_n). This, however is not enough in a mixed-mode simulation because the computation in the continuous domain has its own notion of time.

Figure 3 shows this case. Due to the event at time t_n, the continuous simulation is triggered to calculate the system behavior till $t_{n'}$ (the same error would occur if the continuous simulator did not cross the threshold). Now any event which arrives between the current event at t_n and the final time $t_{n'}$ (or t_{n+1}) would not result in a system rollback in the optimistic simulator, because the event would be in the future (*i.e.*, ahead of the local virtual time). On the other hand, the continuous time simulator has already advanced to the end time $t_{n'}$ (or t_{n+1}). This means that a rollback is necessary to restore correct initial conditions and to remove unwanted events. Therefore, by using FES the continuous process now has to recognize such internal stragglers and initiate a rollback by itself. This discussion shows that there is a relationship between the time interval given for simulation and the internal rollbacks. This makes the time step which is picked at random very crucial for performance considerations.

Another important fact of the FES protocol, is the necessity of an initial state. Because optimistic discrete-event simulators depend on saved states, a special first simulation cycle is required in the FES protocol. This simulation cycle does not advance time, but it is responsible for the creation of an initial state (synchronization point). Advancement of the simulation time will not guarantee the prevention of a rollback to an earlier state.

3.3 Second Event Synchronization protocol

The protocol with N = 2 (called Second Event Synchronization protocol (SES)) tries to overcome the necessity of picking at random, the next event arrival time. This is achieved by starting the continuous computation, with the second event marking the end of the simulation interval (*i.e.*, at time t_n). The general approach is shown in Figure 4.

The last executed event at time t_{n-1} marks the last synchronization point up to which the continuous process has simulated. The continuous process is reactivated by the event at time t_n and continues to simulate from t_{n-1} to t_n. If no threshold is crossed, the simulation reaches the time t_n and stops. A new synchronization point is automatically generated after the state is stored. In case an event is generated during this time interval, the continuous process has to be interrupted. An event at time $t_{n'}$ needs to be sent out and the state of the system has to be stored. Also the discrete event simulator has to be notified that the continuous process did not complete the calculations up to time t_n. A possible solution is to insert a dummy event at time $t_{n'}$ and make the system believe that the continuous

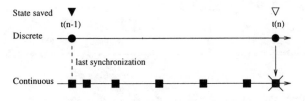

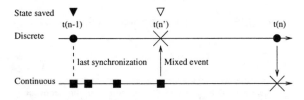

Continuous simulation without generation of an event

Continuous simulation with generation of an event

Figure 4. Second Event Synchronization

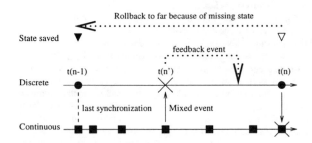

Figure 5. Second Event Synchronization error

Clock Generator on two processors		
	Timing values in seconds	
ext. Time Step	FES	SES
1000000 fs	286.12	278.55
100000000 fs	266.10	262.98
10000000000 fs	270.78	254.39
1000000000000 fs	255.83	237.53
max. (Infinity)	263.59	238.25
Two Clock Generators on two processors		
	Timing values in seconds	
ext. Time Step	FES	SES
10000000 fs	798.90	806.94
1000000000 fs	985.81	807.68
100000000000 fs	7215.03	5925.56
10000000000000 fs	4442.05	5188.90
max. (Infinity)	5017.95	6040.64

Table 3. Variation of maximum step sizes

4 Timing results

Because the examples were hand coded, only small models were used to evaluate the algorithms. The first circuit is a two-bit adder with an RLC circuit as delay line (Total number of processes = 11, number of continuous processes = 1, total simulation time = 40μs). The second is a clock generator consisting of a RC circuit connected to two not-gates [12, page 196] (5, 1, 13μs). To increase the system load, a third circuit, two clock generators in parallel, was used (8, 2, 40μs). All test circuits have two processes responsible for input and output. The set of circuits is considered to be large enough to see the effects mentioned above. This is especially true for the number of analog components inside the test circuit. The effect of increasing complexity in the analog part is easily achieved by restricting the analog computation time step.

Because the algorithms are designed for optimistic simulation, multiple parameters concerning the discrete event simulation environment have to be taken into account. The following parameters have to be considered to get a general performance overview of the synchronization algorithms.

- Number of processors: Even if the number of processes is relatively small, this parameter affects the behavior of the algorithms when the computational power is increased because of the cost of increased communication.

- Distribution of the processes: By keeping the number of processes constant, this parameter affects how much the synchronization protocol is dependent on the locality of the related processes.

The Table 2 displays the timings gathered with the different simulation protocols. All times represent the average of three different runs. The performance of the circuits were measured for three different initial configurations on two and three processors. There is only one initial configuration for the single processor case. The timing values are all taken on a four processor Sparc Center 1000 with 196 Mbyte of RAM.

The maximum time step, a continuous simulation process can advance without interruption, was set to 100ns, 1ns and 10ns for the RLC Adder, Clock Generator and the Two Clock Generator examples respectively. The maximum internal time step for the continuous calculation is 1/50 of the maximum time step values.

With the knowledge of the maximum internal time step, another set of measurements was taken. Table 3 shows the results of keeping the internal continuous time step constant (accuracy of the computation) and allowing the synchronization protocols, larger step sizes. To keep the number of measurements reasonable, the time step variation was only done on two of the above cases.

process was activated by it. This would also involve reactivating the event at time t_n. Changing the activation event as well as storing the state at $t_{n'}$ creates another synchronization point.

Because of the second event activation, there is no necessity of additional rollback detection. All rollbacks will be automatically detected by the optimistic simulator. But SES involves some additional processing overhead. As mentioned in the above paragraph, the state has to be saved if an event occurs during the continuous simulation. If not, the system can break as shown in Figure 5.

In this case, an event occurred at $t_{n'}$. However, no state was saved and the continuous simulator continued up to t_n. If the discrete event at time $t_{n'}$ is responsible for an event in the interval $[t_{n'}, t_n]$ to the continuous process, the system will lock up in an infinite loop. The initiated rollback will go back to the last saved state. This, however, removes both the event at time $t_{n'}$ and the feedback event, which initiated the rollback. The system will be in the same state as before (namely at time t_{n-1}) and the simulator will never be able to break this loop.

If the simulation interval increases, then there is a proportional increase in the probability of a rollback. Due to this phenomenon, the SES protocol has been implemented to support a maximum simulation interval. However, this value can be randomly set and is not as critical for performance as it was for the FES protocol. This is because there are no internal rollbacks and the nature of the simulation is more conservative than optimistic. But, it should be noted that the SES protocol becomes more complex as it supports this interval. Therefore, a special implementation of the SES protocol with no time step limit, was used for the measurements.

Num. of Proc.	Initial Config.	Timing values in seconds					
		RLC Adder		Clock Generator		Two Generators	
		FES	SES	FES	SES	FES	SES
1	1	193.76	157.62	302.83	308.22	1826.14	1773.85
2	1	177.09	170.76	277.26	285.43	1973.30	1728.37
	2	181.02	156.08	264.20	272.42	1256.25	930.92
	3	265.97	303.73	271.29	261.49	1158.35	863.38
3	1	312.62	213.81	271.85	263.00	883.59	784.49
	2	310.52	183.35	302.15	271.16	858.34	825.55
	3	329.91	167.01	326.17	283.80	1672.81	1575.86

Table 2. Performance values of the synchronization protocols

5 Performance Analysis

The performance values illustrated in Table 2, clearly favor the SES protocol in the case of a multiprocessor simulation. In all cases, the SES protocol out performs or equals the performance of the FES protocol. It can be clearly seen that the SES protocol is only marginally affected by the distribution of the connected processes. One of the reasons why SES proves to be more efficient over FES, could be due to the fact that a more conservative approach with the synchronization on the second event is performed. Unlike FES, where a lot of unnecessary computation is allowed, SES limits the number of such occurrences and thereby saves on wasted simulation time. This is a primary goal in parallel mixed-mode simulation.

The influence of the step size provides additional insight into the algorithms. The SES algorithm performs slightly better if the internal step size (accuracy) is fixed (independent from the external step size) and the algorithm is allowed to proceed in greater steps. However, as the second example shows, allowing synchronization time steps with a fixed internal step size, makes the synchronization protocol more vulnerable to the distribution of processes. In case of the FES protocol, too much unnecessary computation is permitted, whereas in the SES protocol, the event in the far future (high risk of rollback) is used as a trigger. Both these characteristics justify the poor performance in the last three measurements in Table 3, for the respective protocols.

6 Conclusion and Future Work

In this paper, a new protocol was introduced to synchronize an optimistic simulator with a continuous simulator. Two variations of the algorithm were implemented, and, with the help of empirical measurements, it was seen that one of the two variations performed better overall.

Experiences with the FES and the SES protocol show that both algorithms depend on the choice of an optimal step size. Further investigations are currently aimed at trying to establish an optimal step size. Efforts are also being taken to dynamically adjust the step size during simulation because a statically fixed value may not be suitable for different applications or different process distributions.

An informal description was given to justify the correctness of the algorithms. Part of the future work will be write a formal description of the algorithms and provide a formal proof of correctness. It will also be necessary to show the performance of the synchronization protocols together with other continuous solvers and more complex examples.

References

[1] B. A. A. Antao and A. J. Brodersen. Behavioral simulation for analog system design verification. *IEEE Transactions on VLSI Systems*, 3(3):417–429, Sep. 1995.

[2] O. Berry and D. Jefferson. Critical path analysis of distributed simulation. In *Distributed Simulation*, pages 57–60. Society for Computer Simulation, 1985.

[3] R. Fujimoto. Parallel discrete event simulation. *Communications of the ACM*, 33(10):30–53, Oct. 1990.

[4] D. Jefferson. Virtual time. *ACM Transactions on Programming Languages and Systems*, 7(3):405–425, July 1985.

[5] B. Kannikeswaran, R. Radhakrishnan, P. Frey, P. Alexander, and P. A. Wilsey. Formal specification and verification of the pGVT algorithm. In M.-C. Gaudel and J. Woodcock, editors, *FME '96: Industrial Benefit and Advances in Formal Methods*, volume 1051 of *Lecture Notes in Computer Science*, pages 405–424. Springer-Verlag, Mar. 1996.

[6] E. Lelarasmee, A. E. Ruehli, and A. L. Sangiovanni-Vincentelli. The waveform relaxation method for time-domain analysis of large scale integrated circuits. *IEEE Transactions on Computer-Aided Design of Integrated Circuits and Systems*, CAD-1(3):131–145, Jul. 1982.

[7] M. Lightner. *Computer Aided Circuit Simulation*. CRC Press, 1993.

[8] D. E. Martin, T. McBrayer, and P. A. Wilsey. WARPED: A time warp simulation kernel for analysis and application development, 1995. (available on the www at http://www.ece.uc.edu/ paw/warped/).

[9] F. Mattern. Efficient algorithms for distributed snapshots and global virtual time approximation. *Journal of Parallel and Distributed Computing*, 18(4):423–434, Aug. 1993.

[10] T. L. Quarles. *Analysis of Performance and Convergence Issues for Circuit Simulation*. PhD thesis, University of California, Berkeley, April 1989.

[11] R. Rajan and P. A. Wilsey. Dynamically switching between lazy and aggressive cancellation in a time warp parallel simulator. In *Proc. of the 28th Annual Simulation Symposium*, pages 22–30. IEEE Computer Society Press, Apr. 1995.

[12] R. Saleh, S.-J. Jou, and A. R. Newton. *Mixed-mode simulation and analog multilevel simulation*. Kluwer Academic Publishers, 1994.

[13] M. Sharif-Bakhtiar and M. A. Ahmad. Symbolic analysis of electronic circuits based on a tree enumeration technique. In *IEE Proceedings-G*, volume 140, pages 68–74, February 1993.

[14] L. P. Soulé and A. Gupta. An evaluation of the chandy-misra-bryant algorithm for digital logic simulation. *ACM Transactions on Modeling and Computer Simulation (TOMACS)*, 1(4):308–347, Oct. 1991.

[15] H. E. Tahawy, D. Rodriguez, S. Garcia-Sabiro, and J.-J. Mayol. VHD$_\varepsilon$LDO: A New Mixed Mode Simulation. *EURO DAC 1993*, 9/20–9/24 1993.

Session 4A

Data Distribution

Efficient Algorithms for Multi-dimensional Block-Cyclic Redistribution of Arrays [*]

Young Won Lim   Neungsoo Park   Viktor K. Prasanna

Department of EE-Systems, EEB200C
University of Southern California
Los Angeles, CA 90089-2562
http://ceng.usc.edu/~prasanna

Abstract

We present a uniform framework for a classical problem, redistribution of a multi-dimensional array. Using a generalized circulant matrix formalism, we derive efficient direct, indirect and hybrid contention-free communication schedules. Our indirect schedule reduces the number of communication steps significantly compared with the previous approaches. Our approach exploits the regularity of the block-cyclic redistribution to minimize the index computation overheads. For the case of 2-d redistribution, when the block size increases by factors of K_1 and K_2 along each dimension and the process topology remains fixed, our indirect schedule performs the redistribution in $O(\log(K_1 K_2))$ communication steps. For the case of fixed block size and the processor topology is transposed, our indirect schedule results in $O(\log(L/G))$ communication steps. Implementations of our algorithms on the IBM SP-2 show superior performance over previous approaches.

1 Introduction

Data distribution strongly influences the performance of an application on distributed memory parallel machines. In these machines, access to local data is much faster than access to remote data. These remote memory access overheads can be reduced by choosing data distributions that enhance data locality. The *block-cyclic distribution* matches the data access patterns of many High Performance Computing (HPC) applications. For example, the data distribution for radar and sonar signal processing [12, 10] can be viewed as a block-cyclic distribution. ScaLA-PACK, a mathematical software for dense linear algebra computations, also uses a block-cyclic distribution for good load balance and computation efficiency [6].

In many HPC applications, the data access patterns change during the computation. Hence, it is desirable to reorganize the data distribution at intermediate points of the computation to minimize the remote access overhead. This leads to scalable performance (for an example, see [13]).

Data distributions and redistribution can be specified at varying levels of detail in application programs. When parallelizing compilers are used, the programmer specifies data distributions using high level compiler directives. For example, parallel programs developed in HPF use the `ALIGN`, `DISTRIBUTE`, and `REDISTRIBUTE` directives [2]. If applications are developed using "explicit" parallel algorithms, then data distribution and data movement between the processors are managed by the programmer. Message passing calls (such as calls to MPI) are used to perform interprocessor communication. In either approach, efficient redistribution algorithms are needed. Otherwise, the overheads of redistribution would offset the performance benefits resulting from improved data locality.

The block-cyclic redistribution problem is a classical research problem and has been well studied [8, 7, 9, 4]. In the multi-dimensional block-cyclic redistribution, a process topology, *i.e.*, a Cartesian representation of process(or) assignment to each dimension, is specified. Thus, we have to consider changes in process topology as well as in block sizes. When the block sizes change, a multi-dimensional redistribution can be performed by repeatedly applying a *1-d* redistribution algorithm along each dimension of the array. However, this approach cannot be used when the process topology changes. This case includes corner turn (matrix transpose). Among others, the redistribution of 2-d arrays (matrices) attracts attention, since many scientific computations involve matrices. Some of the

---

[*]Work supported by DARPA under contract no. DABT63-95-C-0092.

Redistribution of n-d arrays		Direct Approach in [4]	Multi-phase Approach in [9]	Our Indirect Approach
Block sizes of each dimension are increased by a factor of K_i over $P_1 \times P_2 \times \cdots \times P_n$ process topology	For composite $K_i = \prod_{j=1}^{m_i} u_{i,j}$ $(i=1,2,\cdots,n)$	$\prod_{i=1}^{n} K_i$ $(i=1,2,\cdots,n)$	$\sum_{i=1}^{n}\sum_{j=1}^{m_i} u_{i,j}$	$\lceil \log(\prod_{i=1}^{n} K_i)\rceil$ $+\,n+1$
	For prime K_i $(i=1,2,\cdots,n)$		$\sum_{i=1}^{n} K_i$	
Processor topology is transposed $P_1 \times P_2 \to P_2 \times P_1$	$L=lcm(P_1,P_2)$ $G=gcd(P_1,P_2)$	L/G	—	$\lceil \log(L/G)\rceil + 1$

Table 1: Number of communication steps required in various approaches to perform n-d block-cyclic redistribution.

previous efforts for redistribution focus on reducing the index computation overhead, while others focus on reducing the actual communication cost of redistribution. Note that, without a proper communication schedule the redistribution overhead can be significant. Recently in [4], a communication schedule was proposed to avoid node contention. This can be classified as a direct schedule. In a direct schedule, array elements are sent directly to their destination. In [9], a multi-phase approach was proposed to reduce startup costs, using a tensor product formalism. Each phase corresponds to an intermediate block-cyclic redistribution. Within a phase, a direct schedule is used. All array elements are moved in each phase. The multiphase approach can offer superior performance when the block sizes increase by factors which are composite numbers. When the block sizes increase by prime numbers, it becomes a direct schedule. The matrix transpose problem has been studied in [5]. Both direct and indirect schedules have been proposed. However, their indirect schedule has excessive transmission costs compared with their direct schedule.

In this paper, we present a uniform framework for block-cyclic redistribution. The key idea of our approach lies in utilizing the notion of a generalized circulant matrix. Our approach fully exploits the regular characteristics of block-cyclic redistribution – the periodicities of the block assignment patterns and the underlying modulo systems arising from block-cyclic redistribution. This approach minimizes both the communication time and the index computation overhead. Efficient direct, indirect and hybrid schedules are derived from our uniform approach. The direct and indirect schedules belong to a class of hybrid schedules in our approach. Node contention is eliminated by reorganizing the communication events. Startup cost is reduced by reorganizing the communication pattern, *i.e.*, the array elements are sent to their destination through intermediate processors using an indirect schedule. The increase in the transmission costs

resulting from reorganizing the communication pattern is minimized, compared with those in [9, 1]. Our approach minimizes the redistribution overhead over a range of array size and the number of nodes by choosing an appropriate hybrid schedule.

Table 1 compares the performance of the proposed algorithms with the previous approaches. For example, consider 2-d redistribution where the block sizes of each dimension are increased by factors of K_1 and K_2 assuming $P_1 \times P_2$ process topology. Then, each processor sends its data to (as well as receives from) $\kappa = min(K_1 K_2, P_1 P_2)$ processors. Since $\kappa = P_1 P_2$ when $K_1 K_2 \geq P_1 P_2$, without loss of generality we only consider K_1 and K_2 such that $K_1 K_2 \leq P_1 P_2$. Then, our indirect schedule performs the redistribution in $O(\log(K_1 K_2))$[1] communication steps, while the direct schedule requires $K_1 K_2$ communication steps. Our experimental results show that reducing the number of communication steps significantly improves the redistribution time over a range of array size per processor. In the multi-phase approach [9], the communication steps can be reduced to $\sum_{j=1}^{m_1} u_{1,j} + \sum_{j=1}^{m_2} u_{2,j}$, only if K_1 and K_2 can be factored such that $K_1 = u_{1,1} \cdot u_{1,2} \cdots u_{1,m_1}$ and $K_2 = u_{2,1} \cdot u_{2,2} \cdots u_{2,m_2}$. If K_1 and K_2 are both prime numbers, then $K_1 + K_2$ steps are required. The approach in [8] performs the 2-d redistribution in two phases by performing two independent 1-d redistributions along each dimension. Thus, it requires $K_1 + K_2$ steps. Next, consider 2-d redistribution where the process topology $P_1 \times P_2$ is transposed. This redistribution is same as the matrix transpose problem. The direct schedule in [5] requires L/G steps, where $L = lcm(P_1, P_2)$ and $G = gcd(P_1, P_2)$. Our indirect schedule performs this redistribution in $O(\log(L/G))$ communication steps. Due to the lack of detailed information on how the approaches in [9, 8] are applied to this problem, we are unable to make detailed comparisons.

The rest of the paper is organized as follows.

---

[1]In this paper, log is $\log_2$.

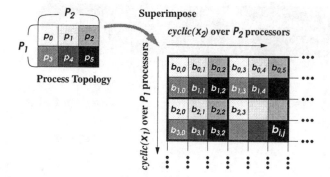

Figure 1: 2-d block-cyclic distribution.

In Section 2, we present the background for multi-dimensional block-cyclic redistribution. In Section 3, we present the key ideas of our algorithms. In Section 4, we report experimental results on IBM SP-2. Section 5 concludes the paper.

2 Background

For the sake of simplicity, we use the 2-d case to explain the multi-dimensional redistribution problems.

2.1 Definitions

A 2-d block-cyclic distribution is specified by four parameters: block size $x_1 \times x_2$ and process topology $P_1 \times P_2$. In the 2-d block-cyclic distribution, a given 2-d array of size $N_1 \times N_2$ is first partitioned into blocks of size $x_1 \times x_2$. Let $b_{i,j}$ denote the $(i,j)^{th}$ block, $0 \le i \le \frac{N_1}{x_1}$ and $0 \le j \le \frac{N_2}{x_2}$ [2]. These blocks are then distributed among $P = P_1 P_2$ processors in the following manner: The blocks are distributed as $cyclic(x_1)$ over P_1 processors along the first dimension. Similarly, the blocks are distributed as $cyclic(x_2)$ over P_2 processors along the second dimension. We can view the 2-d block-cyclic distribution as superimposing the process topology onto the 2-d array which is partitioned into blocks. (See Figure 1)

We denote the general 2-d redistribution problem as $\Re$: $D_i(x_1, x_2; P_1, P_2) \rightarrow D_f(y_1, y_2; Q_1, Q_2)$. $D_i(x_1, x_2; P_1, P_2)$ is the initial distribution where blocks of size $x_1 \times x_2$ are distributed as $cyclic(x_1)$ ($cyclic(x_2)$) over $P_1(P_2)$ processors along the first (second) dimension. In the final distribution $D_f(y_1, y_2; Q_1, Q_2)$, the blocks are similarly distributed. Usually, the process topology changes such that $P_1 P_2 = Q_1 Q_2$, since the array is redistributed among the same set of processors. However, this restriction is absent if, for example, task parallelism is used (see HPF-2), where array elements are redistributed between different sets of processors. In this paper, we

---

[2] For simplicity, we assume that x_1 and x_2 divide N_1 and N_2 respectively.

focus on the following cases that occur frequently:

1. n-d redistribution in which the block size changes by a factor along each dimension and the process topology remains fixed. This is denoted $\Re_B(K_1, K_2, \ldots, K_n; P_1, P_2, \ldots, P_n)$:
$$D_i(x_1, x_2, \ldots, x_n; P_1, P_2, \ldots, P_n)$$
$$\rightarrow D_f(K_1 x_1, K_2 x_2, \ldots, K_n x_n; P_1, P_2, \ldots, P_n).$$

2. 2-d redistribution in which the process topology is transposed and the block size of the corresponding dimension remains fixed. This is denoted $\Re_T(P_1, P_2)$:
$$D_i(x_1, x_2; P_1, P_2) \rightarrow D_f(x_2, x_1; P_2, P_1).$$

2.2 Cost of Redistribution

Redistribution incurs overheads in performing index computation and in interprocessor communication. An index computation overhead for each array element is incurred in calculating its destination processor and the location of the element within that processor. Each array element can be referenced by a global index and a local index. The global index is the index of an array element from the array point of view. From the global index, we can calculate the processor at which an array element is located as well as the local memory location in that processor, i.e., the local index. However, frequent computation of this information from the global index leads to significant index computation overhead. To reduce the index computation overhead, the regular structure of the block-cyclic array distribution must be utilized.

We have developed redistribution algorithms for block-cyclic redistribution based on a simple analytical model of distributed memory machines, the General purpose Distributed Memory (GDM) model [3, 12]. The model represents the communication time of a message passing operation using two parameters: the *startup time* τ_d and the *unit data transmission time* τ_d. The GDM model assumes that a processor can send at most one message and receive at most one message at a time. Messages originating from several source processors destined to the same processor, will compete with each other at the destination processor, i.e., node contention occurs. The impact of node contention as communication cost is more significant than link contention in current HPC machines. We avoid node contention by choosing the schedule in each communication step to be a permutation.

3 Key Ideas

In the redistribution of a 2-dimensional array, each block of the array moves from the one processor to another, i.e., the ownership is changed. The blocks of array in each processor's local memory are reorganized as well as the local memory location of each block is changed by redistribution. The reorganization pattern of a set of blocks repeats over all the blocks of a 2-dimensional array. Such a set of blocks is called a *superblock* [4]. Due to this periodic behavior, we only consider the first superblock in the following discussion. The first superblocks of the initial and final distributions are represented via a 2-dimensional table. In such a table, the actual local memory layout of the blocks can be depicted. By replacing the global block indices with the corresponding destination processor indices, we can represent all the required communication events using a table. The *destination processor table* (dpt) is defined as a table where the jth column contains all the destination processor indices of the blocks in processor p_j, ($0 \leq j < P$, where P denotes the total number of processors). Note that, if the redistribution parameters (the change in the block size along each dimension and the number of processors) and the global block index assignment order are given, then each block's location in the dpt can be determined. Redistribution can then be conceptually viewed as a table conversion process. As shown in the following, this provides a systematic way of computing the index sets and communication schedule. By allowing either column-wise or row-wise movement of blocks, the conversion process can be decomposed into column and row transformations. The column (row) transformations permute the entries in each column (row) of a table. While column transformation is a local operation in each processor's local memory, the row transformation incurs interprocessor communication. The key idea of our approach is to choose column transformations so that the resulting dpt is in the generalized circulant matrix form. Once the dpt is in generalized circulant matrix form, a class of efficient and contention free communication schedules can be derived. We first define a generalized circulant matrix.

Definition: An $m \times n$ matrix, $m \leq n$, is said to be a *circulant matrix* if row i = row 0 circularly right shifted i times, where $0 \leq i < m$.

Definition: Given an $\kappa \times P$ matrix, $\kappa \leq P$, suppose the matrix can be partitioned into blocks of size of $s \times t$, where $\kappa = m \cdot s$ and $P = n \cdot t$, for some $s, t > 0$ and $m \leq n$. Then, the matrix is said to be a *generalized circulant matrix* if, row block i = row block 0 circularly right shifted i times ($0 \leq i < m$) and each block is either a circulant matrix or is a generalized circulant matrix.

Our direct schedule performs the row transformations, by regarding the $(i, j)^{th}$ entry of dpt as the des-

tination processor of the ith communication event at processor p_j. Since every processor has a distinct destination processor in each communication event, node contention can be avoided. Our indirect schedule aligns diagonal entries vertically in logarithmic number of steps by cyclically shifting rows of dpt. Thus, the number of communication steps can be reduced. A hybrid schedule with degree of indirection d, performs the first d steps of the indirect schedule. Each of 2^d column entries that have the same destination are then transferred using a direct schedule. Theorem 1 shows the required number of communication steps of direct, indirect, and hybrid schedules. All communication steps are contention free, *i.e.*, communication pattern is a permutation. The proof of Theorem 1 is adapted from [11].

Theorem 1 *If the destination processor table of size $\kappa \times P$ is in generalized circulant matrix form and if every row is a permutation of $\{0, 1, \ldots, P-1\}$, the redistribution specified by the dpt can be performed in a contention free manner in (i) κ communication steps using a direct schedule, (ii) $\lceil \log \kappa \rceil + 2$ communication steps using an indirect schedule, and (iii) $d + \lceil \frac{\kappa}{2^d} \rceil$ communication steps using a hybrid schedule with d degree of indirection.*

Theorem 1 shows that the indirect schedule can perform a collective communication in $O(\log \kappa)$ communication steps, if the dpt of size $\kappa \times P$ can be transformed into a generalized circulant matrix form. Before discussing $\Re_B(K_1, K_2; P_1, P_2)$ and $\Re_T(P_1, P_2)$, let $G_1 = gcd(K_1, P_1)$, $G_2 = gcd(K_2, P_2)$, $K_1 = K_1' G_1$, $K_2 = K_2' G_2$, $G = gcd(P_1, P_2)$, $L = lcm(P_1, P_2)$, and $P = P_1 P_2$. The size of the dpt of $\Re_B(K_1, K_2; P_1, P_2)$ and $\Re_T(P_1, P_2)$ is $min(K_1 K_2, P) \times P$ and $P_1' P_2' \times P$ respectively. Theorem 2 shows that the initial dpt's of these cases can be transformed into the generalized circulant matrix form via operations within each column. Using Theorem 1, our algorithms perform $\Re_B(K_1, K_2; P_1, P_2)$ and $\Re_T(P_1, P_2)$ in $O(\log(K_1 K_2))$ and $O(\log(L/G))$ communication step, where $1 < K_1 K_2 < P$ and $1 < P_1' P_2' < P$. If $K_1 K_2 \geq P$ or $L/G = P$, then the dpt has size $P \times P$. In this case, our algorithms perform $\Re_B(K_1, K_2; P_1, P_2)$ and $\Re_T(P_1, P_2)$ in $O(\log P)$ steps.

Theorem 2 *The destination processor tables corresponding to $\Re_B(K_1, K_2; P_1, P_2)$ and $\Re_T(P_1, P_2)$, can be transformed into generalized circulant matrices by column transformations.*

Proof Sketch:
In the following, it is assumed that the blocks and the processors are numbered in row major order. The

ownership of the blocks in a superblock in the initial and final distributions are denoted by $\mathbf{S_b}$ and $\mathbf{R_b}$ respectively, *i.e.*, $\mathbf{S_b}(i,j)(\mathbf{R_b}(i,j))$ represents the processor which owns block $b_{i,j}$ before(after) the redistribution. A *run* in a table refers to a longest sequence of consecutive entries which are the same. A run can wrap-around in row major order. The length of a run is the number of entries in the run.

Case $\Re_B(K_1, K_2; P_1, P_2)$: Initially, $b_{i,j}$ belongs to processor $\mathbf{S_b}(i,j)$. After redistribution, it has to be moved to processor $\mathbf{R_b}(i,j)$. The initial *dpt* $\mathbf{P}$ is given by $\mathbf{P}(k, \mathbf{S_b}(i,j)) = \mathbf{R_b}(i,j)$ where $k = (i \text{ div } P_1)K_2 + (j \text{ div } P_2)$. Here, $x \text{ div } y$ denotes $\lfloor \frac{x}{y} \rfloor$, for integers x and $y > 0$. The size of the *dpt* is $K_1K_2 \times P$. In the following, the transformation of the initial *dpt* is described step by step. (See Example 1 below for an illustration.)

Step 1: Denote disjoint blocks of $\mathbf{P}$ of $K_2 \times P_2$ as a macroblock. $\mathbf{P}$ can be viewed as a table consisting of K_1P_1 macroblocks, where each consecutive K_1 macroblocks are the same in row major order. Thus, in $\mathbf{P}$, there are P_1 runs and each run consists of K_1 macroblocks. It can be shown that these K_1P_1 macroblocks can be reorganized into a generalized circulant matrix form.

Step 2: Consider the entries within a macroblock. Note that within each macroblock, there are exactly K_2P_2 distinct blocks. If we enumerate the K_2P_2 blocks in row major order, then there are P_2 runs of size K_2. The K_2P_2 blocks within a macroblock can be similarly reorganized into a generalized matrix form by column transformations.

Case $\Re_T(P_1, P_2)$: Assume without loss of generality $P_1 \leq P_2$. The $L \times P$ table $\mathbf{P}$ is obtained by $\mathbf{P}(k, \mathbf{S_b}(i,j)) = \mathbf{R_b}(i,j)$ and $k = (i \text{ div } P_1)P_2 + (j \text{ div } P_2)$.

Step 1: It is easy to verify that $\mathbf{P}$ contains $P_1'P_2'$ distinct rows and each distinct row repeats G times. By regarding these G rows as a single row, a compact *dpt* of size $P_1'P_2'(= L/G) \times P$ is obtained.

Step 2: Consider the following column transformation on the compact *dpt*. First, within each column, blocks are reorganized in the increasing order of the destination processor indices. This results in G^2 distinct columns. Each distinct column repeats $P_1'P_2'(= L/G)$ times. Then, the columns are reordered so that the compact *dpt* is partitioned into sets of columns, with each partition having a a distinct column. Each set has exactly L/G columns. Note that reordering the columns is not a row transformation.

Step 3: Consider L/G columns as a macroblock of size $L/G \times L/G$. The new *dpt* can be viewed as a ta-

0	0	0	0	1	1	0	0	0	0	1	1	0	0	0	0	1	1	6	6	6	6	7	7
1	1	2	2	2	2	1	1	2	2	2	2	1	1	2	2	2	2	7	7	8	8	8	8
3	3	3	3	4	4	3	3	3	3	4	4	3	3	3	3	4	4	9	9	9	9	10	10
4	4	5	5	5	5	4	4	5	5	5	5	4	4	5	5	5	5	10	10	11	11	11	11
6	6	6	6	7	7	6	6	6	6	7	7	12	12	12	12	13	13	12	12	12	12	13	13
7	7	8	8	8	8	7	7	8	8	8	8	13	13	14	14	14	14	13	13	14	14	14	14
9	9	9	9	10	10	9	9	9	9	10	10	15	15	15	15	16	16	15	15	15	15	16	16
10	10	11	11	11	11	10	10	11	11	11	11	16	16	17	17	17	17	16	16	17	17	17	17
12	12	12	12	13	13	18	18	18	18	19	19	18	18	18	18	19	19	18	18	18	18	19	19
13	13	14	14	14	14	19	19	20	20	20	20	19	19	20	20	20	20	19	19	20	20	20	20
15	15	15	15	16	16	21	21	21	21	22	22	21	21	21	21	22	22	21	21	21	21	22	22
16	16	17	17	17	17	22	22	23	23	23	23	22	22	23	23	23	23	22	22	23	23	23	23

(a) Initial Destination Processor Table $\mathbf{P}$

0	3	2	5	1	4	18	21	20	23	19	22	12	15	14	17	13	16	6	9	8	11	7	10
3	0	5	2	4	1	21	18	23	20	22	19	15	12	17	14	16	13	9	6	11	8	10	7
1	4	0	3	2	5	19	22	18	21	20	23	13	16	12	15	14	17	7	10	6	9	8	11
4	1	3	0	5	2	22	19	21	18	23	20	16	13	15	12	17	14	10	7	9	6	11	8
6	9	8	11	7	10	0	3	2	5	1	4	18	21	20	23	19	22	12	15	14	17	13	16
9	6	11	8	10	7	3	0	5	2	4	1	21	18	23	20	22	19	15	12	17	14	16	13
7	10	6	9	8	11	1	4	0	3	2	5	19	22	18	21	20	23	13	16	12	15	14	17
10	7	9	6	11	8	4	1	3	0	5	2	22	19	21	18	23	20	16	13	15	12	17	14
12	15	14	17	13	16	6	9	8	11	7	10	0	3	2	5	1	4	18	21	20	23	19	22
15	12	17	14	16	13	9	6	11	8	10	7	3	0	5	2	4	1	21	18	23	20	22	19
13	16	12	15	14	17	7	10	6	9	8	11	1	4	0	3	2	5	19	22	18	21	20	23
16	13	15	12	17	14	10	7	9	6	11	8	4	1	3	0	5	2	22	19	21	18	23	20

(b) Transformed Destination Processor Table $\mathbf{P_s}$

Figure 2: Transformations on *dpt* corresponding to $\Re_B(3, 4; 4, 6)$

ble consisting of G^2 macroblocks. Within each macroblock, all entries in a row are the same. Hence, each macroblock can be converted into a circulant matrix by diagonalizing each row.

The above is illustrated in Example 2 below. □

Example 1: $\Re_B(K_1, K_2; P_1, P_2)$

Consider the case when the block size is expanded by $K_1 \times K_2 = 3 \times 4$ while the process topology remains fixed as $P_1 \times P_2 = 4 \times 6$. Figure 2 (a) shows the initial *dpt*. Figure 2 (b) shows the column transformed *dpt* $\mathbf{P_s}$. Following *Step 1* in the proof, we consider $4 \times 6(= K_2 \times P_2)$ distinct blocks as a macroblock. There are $4(= P_1)$ runs in the *dpt* and each run has $3(= K_1)$ consecutive macroblocks as shown in Figure 2 (a). These K_1P_1 macroblocks are reorganized into a generalized circulant matrix form. There are K_1 identical macroblocks in a block diagonal. It takes $\lceil \log K_1 \rceil$ communication steps to align these diagonals into vertical lines.

In *Step 2*, within a macroblock there are P_2 runs of size K_2. P_2K_2 blocks in a macroblock is reorganized into a generalized circulant matrix form. Therefore, there are K_2' identical circulant matrices of size $G_2 \times G_2$ along these block diagonals. It takes $\lceil \log K_2' \rceil + \lceil \log G_2 \rceil$ steps to vertically align elements in each macroblock.

0	1	2	3	0	1	4	5	6	7	4	5	8	9	10	11	8	9	12	13	14	15	12	13
2	3	0	1	2	3	6	7	4	5	6	7	10	11	8	9	10	11	14	15	12	13	14	15
0	1	2	3	0	1	4	5	6	7	4	5	8	9	10	11	8	9	12	13	14	15	12	13
2	3	0	1	2	3	6	7	4	5	6	7	10	11	8	9	10	11	14	15	12	13	14	15
16	17	18	19	16	17	20	21	22	23	20	21	0	1	2	3	0	1	4	5	6	7	4	5
18	19	16	17	18	19	22	23	20	21	22	23	2	3	0	1	2	3	6	7	4	5	6	7
16	17	18	19	16	17	20	21	22	23	20	21	0	1	2	3	0	1	4	5	6	7	4	5
18	19	16	17	18	19	22	23	20	21	22	23	2	3	0	1	2	3	6	7	4	5	6	7
8	9	10	11	8	9	12	13	14	15	12	3	16	17	18	19	16	17	20	21	22	23	20	21
10	11	8	9	10	11	14	15	12	13	14	15	18	19	16	17	18	19	22	23	20	21	22	23
8	9	10	11	8	9	12	13	14	15	12	3	16	17	18	19	16	17	20	21	22	23	20	21
10	11	8	9	10	11	14	15	12	13	14	15	18	19	16	17	18	19	22	23	20	21	22	23

(a) Initial Destination Processor Table $\mathbf{P}$

0	0	0	0	0	0	1	1	1	1	1	1	4	4	4	4	4	4	5	5	5	5	5	5
2	2	2	2	2	2	3	3	3	3	3	3	6	6	6	6	6	6	7	7	7	7	7	7
8	8	8	8	8	8	9	9	9	9	9	9	12	12	12	12	12	12	13	13	13	13	13	13
10	10	10	10	10	10	11	11	11	11	11	11	14	14	14	14	14	14	15	15	15	15	15	15
16	16	16	16	16	16	17	17	17	17	17	17	20	20	20	20	20	20	21	21	21	21	21	21
18	18	18	18	18	18	19	19	19	19	19	19	22	22	22	22	22	22	23	23	23	23	23	23

(b) Compact form after reordering the columns

0	18	16	10	8	2	1	19	17	11	9	3	4	22	20	14	12	6	5	23	21	15	13	7
2	0	18	16	10	8	3	1	19	17	11	9	6	4	22	20	14	12	7	5	23	21	15	13
8	2	0	18	16	10	9	3	1	19	17	11	12	6	4	22	20	14	13	7	5	23	21	15
10	8	2	0	18	16	11	9	3	1	19	17	14	12	6	4	22	20	15	13	7	5	23	21
16	10	8	2	0	18	17	11	9	3	1	19	20	14	12	6	4	22	21	15	13	7	5	23
18	16	10	8	2	0	19	17	11	9	3	1	22	20	14	12	6	4	23	21	15	13	7	5

(c) Transformed Destination Processor Table $\mathbf{P_s}$

Figure 3: Transformations on *dpt* corresponding to $\Re_T(4,6)$.

Now, $\mathbf{P_s}$ is in the generalized circulant matrix form and each row is a permutation of the processor indices. Using Theorem 1, $\Re_B(K_1, K_2; P_1, P_2)$ can be performed in $K_1 K_2$ steps by a direct schedule and $\lceil \log K_1' \rceil + \lceil \log G_1 \rceil + \lceil \log K_2' \rceil + \lceil \log G_2 \rceil + 1 \leq \lceil \log(K_1 K_2) \rceil + 3$ by an indirect schedule.

Example 2: $\Re_T(P_1, P_2)$

In this example, the process topology $P_1 \times P_2 = 4 \times 6$ is transposed to 6×4. In Figure 3 (a), $\mathbf{P}$ contains $2 \cdot 3(= P_1' P_2')$ distinct rows and each distinct row repeats twice. In *Step 1*, a compact *dpt* is constructed from this initial *dpt*. In *Step 2*, the columns of this *dpt* are reordered. The compact form of *dpt* of size $12/2 \times 24(= L/G \times P)$ after reordering the columns is shown in Figure 3 (b). The *dpt* after column transformation in *Step 3* is shown in Figure 3 (c).

Corollary 1 $\Re_B(K_1, K_2; P_1, P_2)$ can be performed in a contention free manner in, (i) $K_1 K_2$ communication steps using a direct schedule, (ii) $\lceil \log K_1 K_2 \rceil + 3$ communication steps using an indirect schedule, and (iii) $d + \lceil \frac{K_1 K_2}{2^d} \rceil$ communication steps using a hybrid schedule with d degree of indirection.

Corollary 2 $\Re_T(P_1, P_2)$ can be performed in a con-

tention free manner in, (i) L/G communication steps using a direct schedule, (ii) $\lceil \log(L/G) \rceil + 1$ communication steps using an indirect schedule, and (iii) $d + \lceil \frac{L/G}{2^d} \rceil$ communication steps using a hybrid schedule with d degree of indirection.

To compute the index sets of 2-d redistribution, the index set computation approach for 1-d redistribution is applied to each dimension. In [11], we showed that the index sets can be computed in a distributed fashion at each node without interprocessor communication for the case of 1-d redistribution. The destination processor table (or processor send schedule table) and the corresponding send data schedule table for $cyclic(x)$ to $cyclic(Kx)$ redistribution on P processors are denoted as $\mathbf{P_s}^{(1)}[K, P]$ and $\mathbf{D_s}^{(1)}[K, P]$, in which the superscript is used to represent the number of dimensions. $\mathbf{P_s}^{(1)}[K, P](i, j)$ is the destination processor receiving data from processor j during communication step i and the corresponding $\mathbf{D_s}^{(1)}[K, P](i, j)$ is the local index of the data to be sent from processor j during communication step i (of the direct schedule). Theorem 3 shows how to compute the index sets for $\Re_B(K_1, K_2; P_1, P_2)$ of 2-d case. This is generalized to n-d case in Corollary 3. In the following, $x \bmod y$ is the remainder when x is divided by y, for integers x and y.

Theorem 3 *A destination processor table* $\mathbf{P_s}^{(2)}[K, P]$ *in generalized circulant matrix form and the corresponding send data schedule table* $\mathbf{D_s}^{(2)}[K, P]$ *for* $\Re_B(K_1, K_2; P_1, P_2)$ *can be constructed as follows:*

$$
\begin{aligned}
\mathbf{P_s}^{(2)}[K, P](i, j) &= \mathbf{P_s}^{(1)}[K_1, P_1](i_1, j_1) \cdot P_2 \\
&\quad + \mathbf{P_s}^{(1)}[K_2, P_2](i_2, j_2) \\
\mathbf{D_s}^{(2)}[K, P](i, j) &= \mathbf{D_s}^{(1)}[K_1, P_1](i_1, j_1) \cdot K_2 \\
&\quad + \mathbf{D_s}^{(1)}[K_2, P_2](i_2, j_2)
\end{aligned}
$$

where $0 \leq i < K$, $0 \leq j < P$, $i_1 = i \ div \ K_2$, $i_2 = i \bmod K_2$, $j_1 = j \ div \ P_2$, $j_2 = j \bmod P_2$, $P = P_1 \cdot P_2$, *and* $K = K_1 \cdot K_2$.

Proof Sketch:

The proof is based on the properties observed in the proof of Theorem 2 for the case of $\Re_B(K_1, K_2; P_1, P_2)$. In *Step 1* of the proof, a block of size $K_2 \times P_2$ is denoted as a macroblock. There are $K_1 \times P_1$ macroblocks. The reorganization operations on $K_1 \times P_1$ macroblocks can be looked upon as a 1-d $cyclic(x)$ to $cyclic(K_1 x)$ redistribution using P_1 processors. The corresponding 1-d processor send schedule table is $\mathbf{P_s}^{(1)}[K_1, P_1]$. As discussed in *Step 2*, there are $K_2 \times P_2$ blocks in

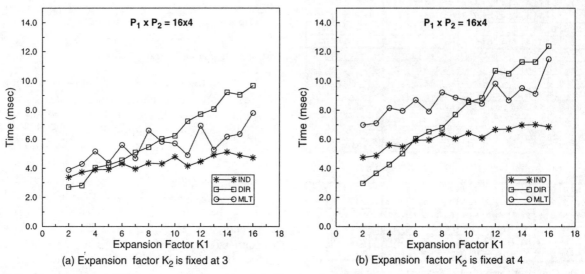

Figure 4: Comparison of direct, multi-phase, and indirect schedules for redistribution of 0.4 *Mbytes* array on a 64-node IBM SP-2.

a macroblock. The reorganization operation on the macroblock can be looked upon as a 1-*d cyclic(x)* to *cyclic*(K_2x) using P_2 processors. The corresponding 1-*d* processor send schedule table is $\mathbf{P_s}^{(1)}[K_2, P_2]$.

The processor index j is represented using P_2-radix system, *i.e.*, $j = P_2 j_1 + j_2$, where $0 \le j_1 < P_1$, and $0 \le j_2 < P_2$. The communication step i is represented using K_2-radix system, *i.e.*, $i = K_2 i_1 + i_2$, where $0 \le i_1 < K_1$, and $0 \le i_2 < K_2$.

We can compute the expressions for $\mathbf{P_s}^{(2)}[K, P](i, j)$ and $\mathbf{D_s}^{(2)}[K, P](i, j)$ by using the 1-*d* processor send schedule tables and the above representations. □

We can generalize the above index set computations to multi-dimensional redistribution:

Corollary 3 *A destination processor table* $\mathbf{P_s}^{(n)}[K, P]$ *in generalized circulant matrix form and the corresponding send data schedule table* $\mathbf{D_s}^{(n)}[K, P]$ *for* $\Re_B(K_1, K_2, \ldots, K_n; P_1, P_2, \ldots, P_n)$ *can be constructed as follows:*

$$\mathbf{P_s}^{(n)}[K, P](i, j) = \sum_{l=1}^{n} \mathbf{P_s}^{(1)}[K_l, P_l](i_l, j_l) \cdot \prod_{m=l+1}^{n+1} P_m$$

$$\mathbf{D_s}^{(n)}[K, P](i, j) = \sum_{l=1}^{n} \mathbf{D_s}^{(1)}[K_l, P](i_{l_l}, j_l) \cdot \prod_{m=l+1}^{n+1} K_m$$

where $P = \prod_{l=1}^{n} P_n$, $K = \prod_{l=1}^{n} K_l$, *and* $P_{n+1} = K_{n+1} = 1$.

The index of processor j, $0 \le j < P$, and communication step i, $0 \le i < K$, are decomposed along each

dimension. Therefore, indices for processor j are given by $j_n = j \bmod P_n$ and $j_l = j \operatorname{div} (\prod_{m=l+1}^{n} P_m)$, for $l = 1, 2, \ldots, n - 1$. Communication step i is decomposed into $i_n = i \bmod K_n$ and $i_l = i \operatorname{div} (\prod_{m=l+1}^{n} K_m)$, for $l = 1, 2, \ldots, n - 1$.

4   Experimental Results

This section shows preliminary timing results from the implementations of our 2-*d* redistribution algorithms. We are currently conducting experiments for $\Re_B(K_1, K_2; P_1, P_2)$ and $\Re_T(x_1, x_2; P_1, P_2)$. At the time of this writing, we have obtained experimental results for *cyclic*(x_1, x_2) to *cyclic*(K_1x_1, K_2x_2,) redistribution over $P(=P_1 \times P_2)$ processors. The algorithms were coded in C, and MPI function calls were used for interprocessor communication. We measured the turn around time for redistribution using `MPI_Wtime`.

While the multiphase algorithm improves on the direct algorithm for composite values of K_1 and K_2, it becomes the 2-phase approach when both K_1 and K_2 are prime numbers. Our indirect algorithm is uniformly applicable for both prime and composite K_1 and K_2. Apart from the fact that our algorithms use fewer communication steps, the amount of data moved in each step per processor is less than or equal to $\lfloor \frac{N}{2P} \rfloor$, where N is the total number of array elements and P is the total number of processors, *i.e.*, $N = N_1 \cdot N_2$ and $P = P_1 \cdot P_2$. In comparison, the multiphase approach moves the entire array in each phase and thus $\lceil \frac{N}{P} \rceil$ data is moved by each processor during each communication phase.

The experiments were performed using 64 processors on the IBM SP-2. The processor topology used in the present experiments was 16×4. The expansion factor K_2 was varied from 2 to 4 and K_1 was varied from 2 to 16. Figure 4 shows the redistribution times as K_1 is varied and K_2 is fixed at 3 and 4. The reported times include the time for index set computation, for buffer copy operations (*i.e.*, packing and unpacking) as well as for interprocessor communication. In Figure 4, our indirect algorithm outperforms the direct and multiphase algorithms as K_1 and K_2 increase. Due to limited space, we have not shown other experimental results. In general, we have observed that for other processor topologies, the indirect algorithm is superior to the direct and multiphase algorithms as the expansion factors increase.

5 Conclusion

In this paper, we have shown an efficient approach for the multi-dimensional block-cyclic redistribution problem. Our communication schedules are designed using the generalized circulant matrix formalism. The indirect schedule can be viewed as the process of aligning the diagonally located entries in a circulant matrix into a vertical line in logarithmic steps by cyclic shift operations. This concept is quite general so that it includes various forms of "combine-and-forward" techniques. The generalized circulant matrix formalism also provides a systematic way of computing index sets in each communication step. Many other data redistribution patterns arise in typical HPC applications. For example, in signal processing, it is required to redistribute data from a set of source processors to a different set of destination processors. This redistribution problem is different from those we have considered in this paper, where the data is reorganized among the same set of processors. However, our algorithms can be extended to perform this redistribution. We are developing efficient communication schedules for these patterns [14].

References

[1] J. Bruck, C.-H. Ho, S. Kipnis, and Weathersby. Efficient Algorithms for All-to-All Communications in Muti-Port Message-Passing Systems. In *6th Annual ACM Symp. on Para. Alg. and Arch.*, pages 298-309, July 1994.

[2] C. Koelbel, D. Loveman, R. Schreiber, G. Steele Jr., and M. Zosel. *The High Performance Fortran Handbook*. The MIT Press, 1994.

[3] C.-L. Wang, P.B. Bhat, and V.K. Prasanna. High-Performance Computing for Vision. *Proceedings of IEEE*, 84:931-946, 1996.

[4] D.W. Walker and S.W. Otto. Redistribution of Block-Cyclic Data Distributions using MPI. Technical Report ORNL/TM-12999, ORNL, June 1995.

[5] J. Choi, J. Dongarra, and D. Walker. Parallel Matrix Transpose Algorithms on Distributed Memory Concurrent Computers. Technical Report ORNL/TM-12309, ORNL, Oct 1993.

[6] J. Dongarra *et al.* ScaLAPACK: A Portable Linear Algebra Library of Distributed Memory Computers - Design Issues and Performance. Technical Report LAPACK Working Note 95, ORNL, 1995.

[7] S. Hiranandani, K. Kennedy, J. Mellor-Crummey, and A. Sethi. Compilation Techniques for Block-Cyclic Distributions. In *Proc. of Intl. Conf. on Supercomputing*, pages 392-403, July, 1994.

[8] R. Thakur, A. Choudhary, and G. Fox. Runtime Array Redistribution in HPF Programs. In *Proc. of Scalable High Performance Computing Conference*, pages 309-316, May 1994.

[9] S.D. Kaushik, C.-H. Huang, J. Ramanujam, and P. Sadayappan. Multiphase array redistribution: Modeling and Evaluation. Technical Report OSU-CISRC-9/94-TR52, September 1994.

[10] W. Liu, W. Kostis, and V.K. Prasanna. Communication Issues in Heterogeneous Embedded Systems. In *Proc. of Workshop on Para. and Dist. Real Time Sys.*, Apr, 1996.

[11] Y.W. Lim, P.B. Bhat, and V.K. Prasanna. Efficient Algorithms for Block-Cyclic Redistribution of Arrays. In *IEEE Symp. on Para. and Dist. Proc.*, Oct 1996.

[12] Y.W. Lim, P.B. Bhat, and V.K. Prasanna. Efficient Data Remapping Algorithms for Embedded Signal Processing Applications. In *10th Inter. Conf. High Perf. Comp.*, 1996.

[13] Y.W. Lim and V.K. Prasanna. Scalable Portable Implementations of Space-Time Adaptive Processing. In *10th Inter. Conf. High Perf. Comp.*, 1996.

[14] J. Suh and V.K. Prasanna. Portable Implementation of Real-Time Benchmarks on HPC. Submitted to *Supercomputing '97*.

Effects of Dynamic Task Distributions on the Performance of a Class of Irregular Computations*

Hemal V. Shah[†]and José A. B. Fortes

School of ECE, Purdue Univ., W. Lafayette, Indiana 47907. {hvs,fortes}@ecn.purdue.edu

Abstract

In this paper, a modified version of previously proposed quasi-barrier technique is developed. On distributed memory machines, relaxation with modified quasi-barriers can be used to perform basis computations that arise in symbolic polynomial manipulation. In this type of synchronous computation, the set of tasks is distributed across the processors. Each nonzero result of a task reduction dynamically generates a set of new tasks. The distribution of these newly generated tasks can have a significant impact on the overall execution time of the parallel computation. In this paper, four task distribution strategies, named modified block, modified sorted block, modified cyclic, and modified sorted cyclic are developed and their performances are comparatively evaluated. For the experiments performed on an 18-node IBM SP2, the modified cyclic distribution provides the best performance overall.

Keywords: *Task distribution, Distributed memory machines, Relaxation, Quasi-barrier, Symbolic polynomial manipulation*

1   Introduction

In symbolic polynomial manipulation, basis computations such as Gröbner basis computation [2] and ordered standard basis computation [4] are widely used in solving systems of polynomial equations, proving geometric theorems, checking the ideal membership of a polynomial, finding the Boardman symbol of a singularity, and many other applications. These basis computations are quite irregularly structured and their time and memory requirements can not be statically determined.

In sequential basis computations, a simplified set of polynomials (basis) is constructed from an initial set of polynomials by performing a sequence of task reductions. In each task reduction, a polynomial (representing the task) is rewritten with respect to the current basis. If the result of the task reduction is a nonzero polynomial, then the current basis and the set of tasks are updated. The selection of a task for reduction is heuristically guided. The computation terminates when there are no more tasks to be reduced.

In this paper, the previously proposed quasi-barrier technique [6] is modified to reduce unnecessary synchronizations and yet preserve the advantages of the quasi-barriers. On distributed memory machines, the relaxation approach [5] with modified quasi-barriers can be used to perform basis computations in a synchronous and decentralized fashion. In this parallel computation, the basis is replicated on each processor and kept consistent, while the set of tasks is distributed across the processors. The tasks are dynamically generated and distributed for each nonzero polynomial resulting from a task reduction. The execution time of the parallel computation is dependent upon the distribution of the tasks. In this paper, various strategies for distributing these tasks are developed. These strategies are modified versions of the block and cyclic distributions. The main contributions of this paper are 1) the modified quasi-barrier technique, 2) the study of the task distribution problem in parallel basis computations using relaxation with modified quasi-barriers including the development and performance evaluation of various dynamic task distribution strategies.

The organization of the rest of the paper is as follows. In Section 2, a class of basis computations that is considered here is discussed in brief. The relaxation approach and the quasi-barrier technique are discussed in Section 3. A modified quasi-barrier technique and a relaxation algorithm with modified quasi-barriers are developed in Section 3. In Section 4, four task distribution strategies are developed and discussed. Experimental results are provided in Section 5. Finally, in Section 6, conclusions are drawn.

2   A Class of Basis Computations

In this section, a class of basis computations that arise in symbolic polynomial manipulation is discussed. Sequentially, in this type of computation, a basis is computed from an initial set of polynomials by performing a sequence of task reductions. In each task reduction, a polynomial is reduced with respect to the current basis. The basis and the set of tasks is updated for each nonzero polynomial obtained from a task reduction. Gröbner basis computation [2] and ordered standard basis computation [4] are two examples of this type of computation.

The interesting properties of this type of basis computations are: 1) The computational and memory demands can not be determined statically. Furthermore, they depend on the order in which the tasks are reduced and the order in which the polynomials

---

* This research was supported in part by IBM SUR research grant, and NSF grants MIP-9500673 and CDA-9015696.

† Hemal V. Shah will be working for Intel corporation from June 1997.

are added to the basis. 2) The selection of a task is heuristically guided and there is a weak dependency of each task reduction on the results of the previously reduced tasks. 3) There are more than one execution path to obtain a basis from an initial set of polynomials. 4) Most of the execution time is spent in reductions and updates. 5) The ratio of the number of tasks that are reduced to zero to the number of tasks that are reduced to nonzero is $O(n)$ (where n is the number of polynomials in the computed basis). Even though application of task elimination criteria during updates can reduce this ratio, most of the tasks are still reduced to zero.

The time and memory demands imposed by these basis computations are often not efficiently met by the current sequential machines. In the next section, an abstract parallel algorithm to perform the basis computations on distributed memory machines is developed and the task distribution problem that is encountered in parallel basis computation is introduced.

3 Relaxation with Modified Quasi-barriers

The relaxation approach was developed in [5] to exploit coarse-grain parallelism in the basis computations. To achieve better computation to communication ratio, the working basis is replicated on each processor and the set of tasks is distributed across the processors. At every iteration, each processor reduces a local task if available, communicates the result of the task reduction and its status information, receives the results of the task reduction and status information from other processors, and updates the local set of tasks and basis. The computation terminates when each processor has no tasks left to be reduced. At every iteration, each processor does not start a new task execution until all tasks executed at that iteration are completely reduced. The idle time spent by each processor at every iteration can result in poor efficiency. This effect can be severe when during an iteration a few tasks take much longer time to complete than others. An algorithm-specific synchronization technique, named quasi-barrier technique, was developed in [6] to improve the load balance at each iteration. If NT_j $(1 \leq NT_j \leq$ number of processors $p)$ tasks are being reduced in parallel at j^{th} iteration, then instead of waiting for all NT_j tasks to complete, the results are communicated and the set of tasks and the basis are updated when q $(1 \leq q \leq NT_j)$ out of NT_j tasks are completely reduced. Quasi-barriers provide two advantages. First, they improve the load balance. Second, the early updates to the basis provided by them can speed up convergence to a solution. For more details on these techniques, the reader is referred to [5, 6].

When at a given iteration q tasks complete and polynomials representing these tasks are reduced to zero, no change in the state of the basis and the state of the local sets of tasks occurs. This results in an unnecessary quasi-barrier synchronization. In order to reduce unnecessary synchronizations, a modified quasi-barrier technique is developed next using the notion of

event: an *event* occurs when a processor starting with a nonempty local set of tasks generates a nonzero result or runs out of tasks. Let NT_j $(1 \leq NT_j \leq p)$ be the number of processors active after the jth synchronization. When q $(1 \leq q \leq NT_j)$ processors notify that each of them had an event occurrence, the processors synchronize for the $j + 1^{th}$ time. This is a modified quasi-barrier technique that preserves the advantages of the quasi-barrier and in addition reduces the number of unnecessary synchronizations.

Algorithm 1 : Parallel Relaxation Algorithm with Modified Quasi-barriers
Input: A set of polynomials $F = \{f_1, \cdots, f_m\}$.
Output: A set of polynomials (basis) $S = \{s_1, \cdots, s_n\}$.
parbegin
  Initialize T_k and S_k; $R_k \leftarrow \phi$
  while $(T_0 \neq \phi$ or $T_1 \neq \phi$ or $\cdots$ or $T_{p-1} \neq \phi$ or
           there is at least one processor with an
           incompletely reduced task) **do**
  Schedule tasks to be reduced in parallel
  Determine q for this iteration
  if $(T_k \neq \phi$ or t_k is not completely reduced) **then**
    if $(t_k$ is completely reduced)
      Select a new task t_k from T_k; $T_k \leftarrow T_k - \{t_k\}$
    end if
    while (q events have not occurred) **do**
      if $(t_k$ is not completely reduced) **then**
        $r_k \leftarrow Partially\_Reduce(r_k, t_k, S_k)$
      end if
      if $(t_k$ is completely reduced) **then**
        if $(r_k \neq 0$ or $T_k = \phi)$ **then**
          Notify processors of an event occurrence
          if $(r_k \neq 0)$ **then**
            Broadcast r_k to other processors
          end if
          Break the inner while loop
        else
          Select a new task t_k from T_k
          $T_k \leftarrow T_k - \{t_k\}$
        end if
      end if
    end while
  end if
  Gather results of the events occurred during this iteration and insert all nonzero results into R_k
  while $(R_k \neq \phi)$ **do**
    Select a polynomial r from R_k; $R_k \leftarrow R_k - \{r\}$
    if (r can not be reduced further) **then** $r^{'} \leftarrow r$
    else Reduce r further to $r^{'}$ **end if**
    if $(r^{'} \neq 0)$ **then** Update S_k, T_k **end if**
  end while
  Gather Status information of all processors
  end while
  $S \leftarrow Simplify(S_k)$
parend

Let S_k be the replicated basis on the kth processor and T_k be the local set of tasks of the kth processor. Let T be the global set of tasks that is distributed across the processors. Let there be p processors numbered from 0 to $p - 1$. Then, $S_0 = S_1 = \cdots = S_{p-1}$, $\bigcup_{k=0}^{p-1} T_k = T, T_i \bigcap T_j = \phi$ for $i \neq j, 0 \leq$

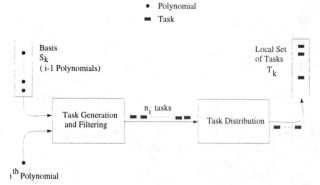

- • Polynomial
- ■ Task

Figure 1: Task generation and distribution for the ith added polynomial to the Basis

$i, j \leq p - 1$. A parallel algorithm based on relaxation with modified quasi-barriers is presented on the previous page (details of some of the operations are not provided here as they are beyond the scope of this paper).

In the relaxation algorithm with modified quasi-barriers, when the ith polynomial is added to the basis, it is used with the previous $i - 1$ polynomials (kept sorted in ascending order) to generate new tasks. These newly generated tasks are filtered by applying task elimination criteria. Thus, upon the addition of the ith polynomial to the basis, n_i new tasks are generated. These n_i tasks are then distributed across the processors and each processor adds the tasks distributed to it in its local set of tasks.

Figure 1 shows the kth processor's view of task generation and distribution. The task distribution can be performed in a decentralized fashion without any interprocessor communication due to consistent replicated basis on each processor. Furthermore, the local set of tasks of each processor and the basis are kept sorted throughout the computation. The distribution of these tasks can have significant impact on the execution time of the parallel computation as it determines the order in which the polynomials are added to the basis and the order in which the tasks are reduced. In the next section, different strategies for distributing the tasks are developed.

4 Task Distribution Strategies

In the previous section, the task distribution problem was introduced. The number of tasks should be evenly distributed across p processors. If n_i is an integer multiple of p, then each processor is assigned $\frac{n_i}{p}$ tasks when the ith polynomial is added to the basis. If $n_i = b \times p$, then there are $\frac{n_i!}{(b!)^p} = \frac{(b \times p)!}{(b!)^p}$ possibilities of distributing n_i tasks evenly across p processors. Table 1 provides some values of the number of possibilities for different b and p. Table 1 suggests that the number of possibilities grows faster than exponentially. For large b and large p, that number is approximately $O(p^{b \times p})$. It is practically impossible to explore all possible distributions. In this section, four different strategies that are intuitive and simple to implement are developed. Assume n_i tasks numbered from 0 to

	p=2	p=4	p=8	p=16
b=1	2	24	40320	20922789888000
b=2	6	2520	81729648000	≈ 4x10³⁰
b=3	20	369600	≈3.7x10¹⁷	≈4.4x10⁴⁸
b=4	70	63063000	≈2.4x10²⁴	≈1.05x10⁶⁷

Table 1: Value of Expression $\frac{(b \times p)!}{(b!)^p}$

$n_i - 1$. Let $n_i = b \times p + c$, where $0 \leq c \leq p - 1$.

Modified Block: In this strategy, when n_i tasks are generated upon the addition of ith polynomial to the basis, they are distributed in the following manner. Each of the first c processors is assigned $b + 1$ consecutive tasks and each of the remaining $p - c$ processors is assigned b consecutive tasks. For example, if $i = 15$, $n_i = 10$, $p = 4$, then processor 0 gets tasks numbered from 0 to 2, processor 1 gets tasks numbered from 3 to 5, processor 2 gets tasks numbered 6,7, and processor 3 gets tasks numbered 8,9.

Modified Sorted Block: Modified sorted block distribution is a variant of the modified block distribution. The newly generated n_i tasks are first sorted and then distributed in a block manner as described above. In Gröbner basis computation, the tasks are sorted in ascending order of the least common multiples of the leading power products of polynomials that construct the tasks. In ordered standard basis computation, the tasks are sorted in ascending order of the polynomials which represent the tasks.

Modified Cyclic[5, 6]: Let l be the number of the processor that was assigned the last task before the generation of the ith polynomial. Then, in modified cyclic strategy, the jth task ($0 \leq j \leq n_i - 1$) is assigned to the processor $(l + j + 1) \mod p$. If $i = 15$, $n_i = 10$, $p = 4$, $l = 1$, then processor 0 gets tasks numbered 2,6, processor 1 gets tasks numbered 3,7, processor 2 gets tasks numbered 0,4,8, and processor 3 gets tasks numbered 1,5,9.

Modified Sorted Cyclic: Modified sorted cyclic distribution is a variant of the modified cyclic distribution. The newly generated n_i tasks are first sorted in a similar order as described in modified sorted block distribution and then distributed in cyclic fashion as described for the modified cyclic distribution.

In the next section, the strategies introduced above are experimentally evaluated.

5 Experimental Results

In this section, some experimental results are provided. These experiments were performed on an 18-node IBM SP2 installed at PUCC (Purdue University Computing Center). The software used in these experiments is part of a prototype library developed by the authors for symbolic polynomial manipulation on distributed memory machines. The timings were averaged over 10 runs. The value of q in the relaxation algorithm with modified quasi-barriers was set to 1 in all experiments. Total degree reverse lexicographic ordering was used in computing Gröbner basis and total degree ordering as explained on pages 102-103 in [4] was used for ordered standard basis computation.

The speedup is defined here as the ratio of the time taken by the best known sequential algorithm to solve a problem to the time taken by the parallel algorithm

Example	Seq. Algo.	Relaxation Algorithm with Modified Quasi-barriers, Number of Processors $p = 4$			
		Modified Block	Modified Sorted Block	Modified Cyclic	Modified Sorted Cyclic
Gerdt	91	18.1	70.3	15.12	28.9
mat3-2-r	161.9	38.8	236.5	30.3	34.15
mat3-2-t	54.3	17.6	34.4	11.3	12.05
Schwarz7	18.6	9.78	8.5	4.42	5.02
Schwarz8	169.3	80.2	83.5	30.5	35.5
Valla	94.1	33.96	35.25	24.27	25.7

Example	Seq. Algo.	Relaxation Algorithm with Modified Quasi-barriers, Number of Processors $p = 8$			
		Modified Block	Modified Sorted Block	Modified Cyclic	Modified Sorted Cyclic
Gerdt	91	10.45	44.46	8.07	18.16
mat3-2-r	161.9	23.98	329.4	18.39	20.43
mat3-2-t	54.3	11.95	26.82	6.63	7.63
Schwarz7	18.6	6.64	5.33	2.45	3.07
Schwarz8	169.3	62.9	57.2	16.17	21.19
Valla	94.1	22.57	28.27	14.79	16.03

Table 2: Execution Times (in Seconds) Obtained for Gröbner Basis Computation of Some Examples

Example	Seq. Algo.	Relaxation Algorithm with Modified Quasi-barriers, Number of Processors $p = 4$			
		Modified Block	Modified Sorted Block	Modified Cyclic	Modified Sorted Cyclic
bjork60	502.98	151.9	210.7	204.6	141.9
ceva	700.22	251.9	291.5	215.9	217.6
maclane8	182.43	62.8	50.1	48.54	57.9
mod_bjork60_1	510.47	122.8	306.95	160.1	175.3
mod_bjork60_2	289.97	97.2	144.2	90.3	116.7
mod_pavelle7	852.03	244.6	257.4	229.8	220.2

Example	Seq. Algo.	Relaxation Algorithm with Modified Quasi-barriers, Number of Processors $p = 8$			
		Modified Block	Modified Sorted Block	Modified Cyclic	Modified Sorted Cyclic
bjork60	502.98	105.4	332	107.26	109.28
ceva	700.22	115.44	138.25	92.95	202.7
maclane8	182.43	22.35	45.48	27.27	27.26
mod_bjork60_1	510.47	83.22	211.48	52.21	59.07
mod_bjork60_2	289.97	66.7	76.79	54.85	73.02
mod_pavelle7	852.03	137.1	193.6	118.36	123.93

Table 3: Execution Times (in Seconds) Obtained for Ordered Standard Basis Computation of Some Examples

to solve the same problem on p processors. Several variants of Buchberger's algorithm for Gröbner basis computation exist in practice for efficiency reasons. It is hard to justify which variant is the best one because the computation is heuristically guided. One variant of Buchberger's algorithm, which keeps the set of tasks small by applying product and chain criteria when a new polynomial is added to the basis and set of tasks is updated, is considered here. This variant is implemented in GRÖBNER package [7] and has good performance in practice. In the sequential implementation of this variant, the basis and the set of tasks are kept sorted in ascending orders, the task whose least common multiple of the leading power products of polynomials is minimal is selected first for reduction, and the basis is inter-reduced in the end when no tasks are left for reduction.

In parallel basis computations, each processor keeps the basis and the local set of tasks sorted in ascending orders. From the local set of tasks, the task which is the most important (according to some heuristic) is selected first for reduction by each processor. Tables 2 and 3 show the execution times obtained on an 18-node IBM SP2 for Gröbner basis computation and ordered standard basis computation on 4 and 8

Example	Seq. Algo.	Relaxation Algorithm with Modified Quasi-barriers, Number of Processors $= p$							
		Modified Cyclic				Random			
		$p = 4$	$p = 8$	$p = 12$	$p = 16$	$p = 4$	$p = 8$	$p = 12$	$p = 16$
Gerdt	91	15.12	8.07	6.4	5.48	16.82	9.09	7.2	6.33
mat3-2-r	161.9	30.3	18.39	13.16	10.94	33.03	18.96	14.9	13.25
mat3-2-t	54.3	11.3	6.63	4.97	4.33	12.4	7.2	5.91	5.39
Schwarz7	18.6	4.42	2.45	2	1.66	5.4	2.85	2.28	2.06
Schwarz8	169.3	30.5	16.17	11.68	9.78	38.1	20.64	15.61	13.4
Valla	94.1	24.27	14.79	11.8	10.3	25.8	15.87	13.43	11.62

Table 4: Execution Times (in Seconds) Obtained for Gröbner Basis Computation of Some Examples

processors using the four distribution strategies developed in the previous section. Tables 2 and 3 suggest the following:

1. Out of four evaluated strategies presented in this paper, the modified sorted block distribution provides the worst performance overall. This is mainly due to the uneven distribution of tasks in terms of importance. In Gröbner basis computation, a particular task is more important than some other task if the least common multiple of the leading power products of the polynomials representing the task is less (with respect to the given ordering) than the least common multiple of the leading power products of the polynomials representing the other task. Similarly, in ordered standard basis computation a particular task is more important than some other task if the polynomial representing the task is less (with respect to the ordering used) than the polynomial representing the other task. Since the tasks are first sorted and then distributed in a block manner, important tasks tend to be distributed among a few processors. This can trigger an execution order where less important tasks are reduced early. This leads to poor performance. In fact, in some of the cases, the parallel execution times were more than the corresponding sequential execution times when modified sorted block distribution was used.

2. The variants of block distribution perform worse than the variants of the cyclic distribution in most cases. This can be mainly because blocking tends to distribute the important tasks unevenly across the processors.

3. Sorting the newly generated tasks before distributing them does not improve the performance in most cases. Only in a few cases, marginal improvement is achieved. Also, sorting introduces additional software overhead.

4. The modified cyclic distribution provides the best performance overall. The modified cyclic distribution introduces minimal overheads and tends to distribute the tasks evenly across the processors in terms of importance.

Table 4 provides a comparison of the modified cyclic distribution with a random distribution. In the random distribution considered here, a coordinator processor generates n_i random numbers and broadcasts them to other processors. If $r_i(j)$ is the jth ($0 \leq j \leq n_i - 1$) random number generated, then the jth task

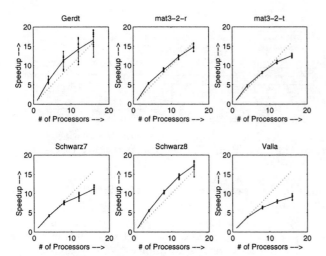

Figure 2: Speedups Achieved for Gröbner Basis Computation of Some Examples

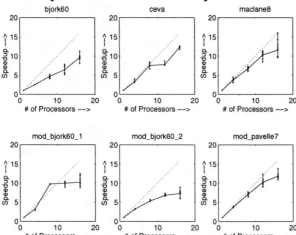

Figure 3: Speedups Achieved for Ordered Standard Basis Computation of Some Examples

is assigned to the $r_i(j)^{th}$ processor. From Table 4, it can be inferred that the modified cyclic distribution provides better performance than the random distribution. Though, the random distribution tends to distribute tasks evenly in terms of importance like the modified cyclic distribution, the software and communication overheads incurred in randomly distributing tasks are more than the same incurred in distributing tasks in the modified cyclic manner.

Figures 2 and 3 show the speedups achieved for Gröbner basis and ordered standard basis computations by the relaxation algorithm with modified quasi-barriers with modified cyclic distribution. The solid lines show the average speedups achieved over 10 runs. The dotted line in each plot represents the linear speedup curve. Each solid vertical line shows the range of speedups achieved over 10 sample runs for a fixed size of the set of processors. Each point on the vertical solid lines represents the speedup achieved for a particular run. The speedups are measured for $p = 4, 8, 12, 16$ number of processors. For Gröbner basis

computation, good speedups are achieved for *Gerdt*, *mat3-2-r*, *Schwarz8*, while reasonable speedups are achieved for *mat3-2-t*, *Schwarz7*, *Valla*. For ordered standard basis computation, reasonable speedups are achieved for all the examples considered here. The speedups achieved are fairly stable and increase with the number of processors. Since, the order in which the tasks are reduced and the order in which the polynomials are added to the basis in the parallel computation are different from those in the sequential computation, superlinear speedups are achieved in some cases. In those cases, the total work performed in finding a basis in the parallel computation is less than the total work performed to find a basis in the sequential computation.

6   Conclusion

A modified quasi-barrier technique was developed for a class of basis computations that arise in symbolic polynomial manipulation. The task distribution problem arising in performing these basis computations using the relaxation approach with modified quasi-barriers was considered. Four simple dynamic task distribution strategies were developed and their performances were comparatively evaluated. Out of four strategies, the modified cyclic distribution strategy performs the best overall. Due to large number of possibilities of distributing tasks, finding an optimal task distribution strategy in this type of computation still remains a challenging research issue. Nevertheless, the modified cyclic distribution strategy presented in this paper performs well in the practice.

Acknowledgments

The authors are thankful to research group at Research Institute for Symbolic Computation (RISC), Johannes Kepler University, Austria, for providing software packages *SACLIB* [3] and *GRÖBNER* [7] which were used in programming the parallel algorithm presented in this paper.

References

[1] B. Buchberger, "A Criterion for Detecting Unnecessary Reductions in the Construction of Gröbner-bases", *EUROSAM*, 1979, pp. 1–21.

[2] B. Buchberger, "Gröbner Bases: An Algorithmic Method in Polynomial Ideal Theory", *Recent Trends in Multidimensional Sys.*, 1985, pp. 184-232.

[3] B. Buchberger et.al., *SACLIB 1.1 User's Guide*, RISC-Linz Tech. Rep. No. 93-19, March 1993.

[4] R. G. Cowell, "Application of Ordered Standard Bases to Catastrophe Theory", *Journal of Symbolic Computation*, Vol. 13, 1992, pp. 101–115.

[5] H. V. Shah and J. A. B. Fortes, "Relaxation and Hybrid Approaches to Gröbner Basis Computation", *In Proc. of Int. Conf. on Parallel Processing*, Vol. III, August 1995, pp. 68-75.

[6] H. V. Shah and J. A. B. Fortes, "A Quasi-barrier Technique to Improve Performance of an Irregular Application", *Frontiers'96*, Oct. 1996, pp. 263–270.

[7] W. Windsteiger and B. Buchberger, *GRÖBNER: A Library for Computing Gröbner Bases Based on SACLIB*, RISC-Linz Tech. Rep. No. 93-72, 1993.

Session 4B

Memory Organizations

Hardware Versus Software Implementation of COMA

Adrian Moga, Alain Gefflaut*, and Michel Dubois

Department of Electrical Engineering - Systems
University of Southern California
Los Angeles, CA 90089-2562
(213)740-4475
{moga,dubois}@paris.usc.edu
http://www.usc.edu/dept/ceng/dubois/RPM.html

*Siemens AG
Public Communication Networks Group
München, Germany
Alain.Gefflaut@oenzl.siemens.de

Abstract

Traditionally, cache coherence in multiprocessors has been maintained in hardware. However, the cost-effectiveness of hardwired protocols is questionable. Virtual Shared Memory systems have highlighted the many advantages of software-implemented protocols, albeit at a performance price. The performance gap is narrowed by hybrid systems with the addition of hardware support for fine-grain sharing.

We have developed a software protocol for a COMA (Cache-Only Memory Architecture). We call the system SC-COMA for Software-Controlled COMA, to emphasize that the protocol engine is emulated by software executed on the main processor. Contrary to user-level protocols, the software handling coherence events in SC-COMA runs in sub-kernel mode, transparently providing the same services to applications as a hardware counterpart. The software emulation layer has been written and we compare SC-COMA to an idealized hardware COMA through detailed simulations.

Our results show that SC-COMA is competitive. On systems with 32 processors, it achieves a slowdown of 11-56% with respect to its hardware counterpart, across a range of applications and memory pressures. SC-COMA scales well, up to 32 nodes. A study on the impact of faster processors on SC-COMA's relative performance indicates a consistent improvement, but with a limitation due to the loosely-integrated design. We conclude that SC-COMA is a viable solution to easily transform networks of workstations into powerful multiprocessors.

1. Introduction

Several factors are motivating current research on Distributed Shared Memory (DSM) to investigate *hybrid* systems, which provide cache coherence with software-implemented protocols. In spite of achieving the best performance, hardware DSMs [16][3] are hard to build and costly, and lack flexibility. All these disadvantages are eliminated by software DSMs [17][7], at the cost of some performance degradation. Software-implemented protocols, however, can go to great lengths of complexity in order to improve protocol performance or hide remote access latency. The ever-increasing speed of processors drives the performance of software protocols even closer to hardware implementations [2]. To fight *false sharing* [6] effects, caused by the coarse, fixed-sized units of coherence (the pages), hybrid hardware/software systems rely on fine-grain access control. Apart from the performance aspects, hybrid systems are better suited for off-the-shelf components, which further improves their cost-effectiveness.

The contribution of this paper is to present the design of a hybrid COMA, where the protocol engine is emulated in software executed on the main processor, and to compare its performance to an idealized hardware implementation of the protocol. Our decision to explore a hybrid COMA solution is motivated, in part, by the intuition that a COMA maximizes node hit rates, reducing protocol overhead and protocol engine occupancy.

In the current version of our system, the targeted platform is a network of uniprocessor workstations. Hence, the protocol runs on the main processor, but the solution could easily be adapted if a dedicated processor is available. Fine-grain memory access checking support and the controller for a set-associative memory are incorporated in a single, relatively simple functional unit. This could be integrated in the memory controller or be plugged into the local bus, like in Typhoon-0 [21] or START-NG [5].

Our results show that a software-implemented protocol can perform very well, even when compared to an ideal hardware implementation. Addressing some concerns about performing protocol actions on the main processor [10][11], we show that efficient switching of the processor between application and protocol can be done without hardware support for fast context switching. We also show that the overhead of protocol actions does not disrupt application performance to a critical degree.

After describing the COMA and the coherence protocol in Section 2, we explain the issues involved in supporting a software protocol engine inside the main processor and we detail our solutions. The setup for comparing SC-COMA to an idealized hardware counterpart is presented in Section 4. Evaluation results follow in Section 5. The impact of processor speed is debated in Section 6. We end with a discussion of related work and our conclusions.

Funding for this work has been provided by the National Science Foundation under Grants MIP-9223812 and MIP-9633542.

248

2. Cache-Only Memory Architecture(COMA)

2.1. DSM hardware substrate

Figure 1 illustrates the composition of a generic DSM node. Processor P issues references, most of them satisfied by the internal and external caches. E-cache misses reach the Access Checking Device (ACD) for a possible completion of the access in the local memory. When memory contains a valid copy of the data, it sends it to the cache. Otherwise, the ACD signals a miss to the Protocol Engine (PE). The PE is responsible for completing the remote access by communicating with other nodes over the network. Request and reply packets, sent in accordance to a set of rules (the coherence protocol) and the information maintained in a distributed directory, are processed by the PEs to accomplish this task. When a reply packet contains data, the data can be transferred from the network interface (NI) buffers to the main memory or, in some cases, directly to the cache. Note that a COMA does not require the ability to transfer data between the E-cache and the NI.

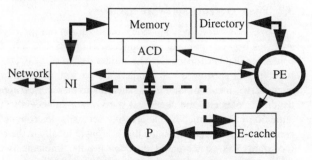

Figure 1. Hardware substrate for a DSM node

2.2. Memory organization in COMA

As shown in Figure 2, the portion of main memory hosting shared data in COMA is called the *attraction memory* (AM) and has a set-associative organization similar to a cache. A block of data in the AM is called a *line* and is identified by a tag stored in the Tag Table. Along with the tag in each table entry, several bits encode the state of the line, such as *Invalid, Shared, Exclusive*. The Tag Table is queried by the ACD on every AM access from the local processor and its information is used to signal a miss to the PE. It may also be queried by the PE during the processing of external requests or AM misses. The Tag Table is updated exclusively by the PE. Besides the AM, a private space, free of tags, hosts the stack and other non-shared data.

The COMA memory organization comes with a trade-off. On one hand, it provides support for automatic data replication and migration in memory, a great relief for programmers and operating systems. From a performance perspective, many cache capacity and conflict misses can be satisfied by the AM, thus improving the node hit ratio and average latency. On the other hand, it suffers from tag-checking overhead and the replacement problem. Searching the AM tags increases memory latency and delays the processing of misses. When replacing a line out of memory to make room for another, it is possible that no other copies of the replaced line exist in the system. Other nodes must be asked to accept this line in their memory. Replacements com-

plicate the coherence protocol and affect system performance. To allow data replication, the total allocated memory for the AMs should exceed application needs. The ratio between the total size of all shared data in the application and the size of all AMs is called *memory pressure*. Memory pressure has a direct effect on the rate of replacements.

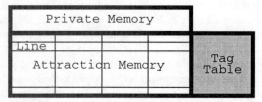

Figure 2. Memory organization in a COMA

2.3. Coherence protocol

The directory. We adopt the Flat COMA [13] organization, where a *home* node is statically associated with each page. The directory consists of the Owner and Copyset tables and is accessed only by the PE in the events of an AM miss or of an external request. The Owner Table at the home node for a line contains the pointer to the node currently owning the line. The size of a pointer is $\log N$ bits, N being the number of nodes. The Owner Table is indexed and dense. The owner node (not the home) for a line contains the presence bits in the Copyset Table, indicating the nodes with a copy of the line. While other presence representation methods are possible, we are assuming a full bitmap encoding. Thus, the size of a copyset is equal to the number of nodes and we need as many copysets as there are lines in the AM. The Copyset Table is indexed and sparse because not every line in a node is owned.

Protocol actions. We evaluate a write-invalidate protocol, very much like the one in DASH [16], with extensions for COMA and optimizations designed to improve performance when protocol actions are executed by the main processor. Currently, it implements a sequentially consistent memory access model with no prefetching; hence, no more than one request can be pending in each node at any time.

Each line in the AM can be in one of four stable states: *Exclusive, Master-Shared, Shared* and *Invalid*. The *Exclusive* (writable) and *Master-Shared* (read-only) states denote ownership of the line. The owner node must ensure that at least one copy of the line exists in the system. Thus, before replacing the line, it must *inject* it into another node. On a read miss, nodes acquire a line in state *Shared*.

After a miss in the AM, the PE sends a request to the line's home. If home is also the current owner, it replies to the request. If not, it forwards the request to the current owner, which will reply directly, bypassing the home. As opposed to DASH, the line owner (instead of home) maintains the current *copyset* (presence bits) for the line. Thus the owner can send invalidations without consulting the home node and the number of acknowledgments to be collected can be piggybacked on the reply, saving a message. Acknowledgments are sent directly to the originator of the request, which is idling anyway.

Keeping the copyset with the owner also allows us to implement *request buffering*. This technique is targeted at eliminating the retry (NACK) messages used by homes when the owner pointer is locked (usually, during transactions involving a change of ownership, such as write requests). Instead, the home always updates the Owner Table to point to the last writer and starts forwarding new requests to it. In case forwarded requests reach the new owner before the reply from the old owner, they are buffered. After receiving the reply, the new owner responds to buffered requests. When the PE is implemented in software, request buffering is inexpensive. This strategy reduces the number of messages exchanged by the nodes, as well as the number of interruptions on the main processor in the software implementation.

For replacements, the protocol picks a victim line in the set according to the priorities: (1) *Invalid*, (2) *Shared*, (3) *Exclusive/Master-Shared*. The replacement of a *Shared* line does not trigger a copyset update. *Exclusive/Master-Shared* lines are sent to their homes. If the home does not accept the injection, the request is forwarded from node to node until it finds a place. An injected line can only replace an *Invalid* or *Shared* line and does not generate other replacements in the visited nodes. During this injection, the owner pointer for the line at the home node is locked and requests for the line are NACKed. Pending replacements are the only situations where the protocol uses NACKs.

3. Software protocol implementation

We now describe the protocol engine implemented entirely in software executed on the main processor. Effectively, the processor is multiplexed between application and protocol modes. The protocol mode is a sub-kernel mode where the processor executes a thread with system-level privileges, having access rights to address ranges mapped to the directory, Tag Table, and the NI and ACD registers. The protocol threads run without interruptions and preserve atomicity with respect to remote references. In essence, the bare message-passing hardware and the coherence software handlers form a virtual machine having all the properties of a COMA (further extensions toward supporting virtual memory and I/O are required). With a careful design, this is accomplished with very low overhead.

3.1. Mechanisms

Referring back to Figure 1, the embedding of the PE into P requires several mechanisms at the processor interfaces with the ACD, NI, memory and cache in order to fully support the operations of the PE. The ACD access miss signal to the PE is implemented with a bus error transaction. This generates a synchronous data access exception trap, because we assume a processor with blocking loads and stores. (Store buffers and asynchronous data access traps could be accommodated by more complex fault handlers.) When the trap is shared by several events, such as MMU faults, status registers are queried to select the appropriate handler. The handler can retrieve information about the access, such as physical address and type, from the memory-mapped ACD registers. The processor trap is precise, so that the application can be safely restarted after the access fault.

When external requests and replies are received from the network, the NI signals the PE with asynchronous interrupts. Memory-mapped registers are used to communicate with the NI. DMA is available for data transfers between memory and the network, to off-load the processor and to bypass the caches.

The Tag Table and the directory are stored in main memory, for simplicity. Both of them reside in reserved areas. Because the ACD shares access to the Tag Table with the PE, the Tag Table cannot be cached. It could be cached, if the Tag Table can be accessed in write-through mode, but we do not assume this. However, the directory can be cached and it is cached.

Finally, when servicing external requests, the PE needs the ability to downgrade certain lines in the cache (we assume multiprocessor-ready caches), based on their physical address. Our assumption is that the processor and the cache controller support two special instructions: *Invalidate* and *Flush*. *Flush* is used to downgrade from *exclusive* to *shared*. Alternate Space Identifier (ASI) instructions in the SPARC architecture can be used to this purpose. Otherwise, the processor could program a bus device, namely the ACD, to issue the appropriate bus transactions.

3.2. The coherence software handlers

We now describe, in more detail, how the processor switches between protocol and application modes and how the coherence handlers operate. In the current design of SC-COMA, two types of coherence trap handlers are present, reflecting the client/server nature of the PE. A synchronous *memory exception* handler implements the client and starts when an access to the attraction memory misses. The missing access is not completed and will be re-executed after the line is brought locally in the correct state. The asynchronous *interrupt* handler implements the server and manipulates messages containing requests and replies issued by remote processors. At the time of an interruption, the processor can be either in application mode or in a memory exception and waiting for a reply.

The bulk of the trap handlers is written in C for ease of development. A prologue and an epilogue, in assembly language, are responsible to make the execution of the C routines transparent to the interrupted thread. When entering protocol mode, the prologue saves the current context entirely in processor registers (trap window locals) in most cases. This is made possible by SPARC's windowed registers and by forcing the compiled code for the C routines to avoid using global registers at no performance cost. The code for the prologue and the epilogue is highly optimized, adding an overhead of just 30 instructions to the C routines. Since this code is very likely to hit in the on-chip cache and data transfers are not involved, the transition to the C routines and back happens in about 30 cycles on average.

Memory exception handler. The memory exception handler is composed of three parts. First, the processor identifies the missing line, its current state in the memory, and the type of memory access (Read, Write, LoadStoreAtomic) by reading the ACD registers. Based on this information, the processor builds a request which is sent to the home node. If the AM has to make room for the requested line, a replacement is performed after sending the request. Thus, replacements are not on the critical path. Second, the processor enters a spinning loop waiting for a reply to its request. The third part of the memory exception handler starts as soon as the processor has received the reply to the request through an interruption (polling is another option). The processor can now restart its computation and re-execute the missing instruction. The different phases of a memory exception are depicted, in more detail, in Figure 3.

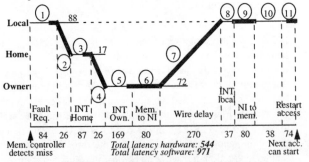

Figure 3. Anatomy of a remote miss

Thin lines are for software latencies and thick lines are for hardware latencies in 5ns cycles. After sending the request (1) the local processor idles. The request message traverses the network to the home node (2). Upon arrival, it interrupts the home, which performs a directory lookup (3). The request is forwarded to the owner and received (4). The owner node handles the request (5). After locating the line in its physical memory, invalidating/flushing it from the caches, the processor transfers the line to the network interface (6). The line crosses the network back to the local node (7). At reception, the local node is interrupted. The reply handler (8) precedes the transfer of the line from the NI to memory (9). After resuming the context of the waiting loop and exiting it (part of 10), the instruction is re-executed (11). The final events are checking for buffered requests, restoring the application context and returning from the fault handler; their penalty has been lumped into phase 10.

When a reply reaches a node, the pending memory access should be restarted and completed. However, between the time the interruption is completed and the time the instruction is restarted, another interruption for the same memory line could be raised and could remove the line from the memory; the restarting access then triggers a new memory exception. Two or more nodes competing for the same line could hence be tied in a live-lock situation where each node loses the line before the completion of its current memory access. The time window in which a memory line may be invalidated before the processor restarts accessing it is called the *window of vulnerability* [14]. To avoid livelocks and ensure forward progress, the window of vulnerability must be closed.

One approach [14] for closing the window of vulnerability, proposed for hardware coherence protocols consists of locking a cache line when it is loaded into the cache and deferring its invalidation until the processor effectively accesses it. When an interruption occurs and the line is locked, the request must be rejected so that the local processor can restart the access on the line before loosing it. Adapting such a solution to our implementation would require a new *locked* state for the lines of the AM as well as modifications of the ACD. To minimize hardware complexity, we have implemented a software solution in SC-COMA. The instruction generating the access fault is copied into the code of the memory exception handler in a dedicated slot and executed

with interruptions disabled after the reply is received. The instruction executes in exactly the same context as when the fault was generated, albeit in system mode and with a different program counter. After the epilogue, execution resumes with the following instruction. A distinct advantage of our software solution over associative locking is that it cannot create any deadlocks.

The interruption handler. Interruptions are triggered by the network interface when external messages (requests or replies) are received. When the message is a request, the handler simply treats the request and sends a reply message. If the message is a reply, the handler updates the line state and, if necessary, transfers the line into memory. Finally, the handler unlocks the waiting loop in the memory exception handler. No other interruption is allowed within an interruption handler.

4. Performance Evaluation Methodology

4.1. The two architectures

The ACD implements a 4-way set-associative AM with 128-byte lines. We have conducted extensive experiments to conclude that an associativity of four is necessary and sufficient for good performance [18]. The Tag Table is stored in DRAM, like all data. The tags and states for a set are packed in a single double word (8 bytes), which is fetched and checked in a full memory cycle, prior to the actual access. We do not assume memory interleaving or any fast page mode optimizations. Access checking to the code and private segments is disabled.

HW-COMA's PE is a hardware controller with zero occupancy. The PE has instantaneous access to the directory and the Tag Table. Hence, the latency of a remote access is due exclusively to data transfer delays and bus contention. SC-COMA's PE is implemented in software. The duration of the PE operations is variable. The directory is stored in main memory and is cacheable. Accesses to the Tag Table are uncached. When handlers search for a line in the AM, the ACD provides assistance, so that the cost is slightly more than an uncached read. Although we still simulate arbitration for the local bus, there is no longer contention with external requests.

The simulated architectures consist of 32 nodes, each with a 200 MHz SPARC processor. The 16KB first-level cache (FLC) is direct-mapped and write-through. The second-level cache (SLC) is four-way set-associative. The SLC size is scaled down to reflect the small data set size of the benchmarks. 64KB is enough for the primary working set WS1 of the benchmarks [28], while at the same time yielding a reasonable ratio of memory versus cache sizes. (The shared memory size per processor in these runs varies between 100KB and 4MB). The SLC connects to the memory by a 128-bits local bus running at 100 MHz. The memory has a 16-byte wide interface and an access time of 28 cycles (140 ns). The critical word of the line is fetched first. Read latencies are given in Table 1. The network interface is controlled through a set of memory-mapped registers. A line is transferred between network buffers and main memory in 80 cycles, assuming DMA assistance. The simulated network is an 8-bit wide crossbar clocked at 100 MHz. The transfer of a request (8 bytes) takes 16 cycles and the transfer of a message containing a line (128 bytes) takes 272 cycles. Ten cycles are added for processing at the reception.

Read Requests	Latency (pclocks)
Hit in FLC	0
Hit in SLC	6
Hit in local memory	46
Hit in attraction memory	46+28=74
Uncacheable access	40

Table 1: Read latencies

4.2. The simulator

We have developed a flexible simulation environment for hybrid and hardware DSM architectures. Common modules include a processor simulator, MMU, two levels of caches, physical memory, a FIFO message-passing substrate, and a custom event scheduler implementing the multiprocessor features. System-specific modules interface the cache to main memory. The code implementing the coherence protocol can be linked either with the application or with the simulator by simply modifying some macros. The former case corresponds to hybrid DSMs. In the latter case, we simulate an ideal hardware implementation where protocol handlers take zero time to execute. The processor simulator is a SPARC interpreter. With every invocation, the simulated processor advances exactly by one instruction, as we do not simulate the details of the instruction pipeline. Load and store instructions are both blocking.

4.3. The benchmarks

The SPLASH-2 benchmarks are compiled for SPARC V7 using gcc-2.7.2 -O2, and linked with the system libraries of Solaris 2.5. Support for efficient synchronization is included in the form of queue-based locks and hardware barriers. The simulator detects special load-store atomic (LDSTUB) instructions used in synchronization routines and suspends/resumes execution for processors, as appropriate. The trap table and software handlers are linked together with the application to create an executable used for simulation of both the hybrid architecture and its hardware counterpart. The characteristics of the benchmarks are given in Table 2.

Benchmark	Parameters	Shared memory
Barnes	16K particles	3.96 MB
FFT	64K points	3.54 MB
LU	512 x 512	2.16 MB
Ocean	258 x 258	15.52 MB
Radix	1M integers	9.87 MB
Raytrace	car	34.87 MB

Table 2: Characteristics of the benchmarks

The data placement strategy is round-robin with a 4KB page as the allocation unit. We point out that other placements, optimized for locality, lead to slightly better performance for all benchmarks. However, it is an advantage of COMA that uninformed placement strategies perform almost as well as optimized strategies. When comparing the performance of SC-COMA to an ideal hardware implementation, a less efficient placement is less favorable to SC-COMA, as the number of interrupts, hence the software overhead, increases due to request forwardings.

5. Simulation Results

5.1. Miss Latencies

To understand where time is spent during a miss in SC-COMA, we have run a set of micro-benchmarks, each targeting a particular situation such as a read miss or a write miss with zero, one or two invalidations. For each of these cases, we measure the time spent in the different software handlers and in the network. In Figure 4, each stacked bar gives the time breakdown in cycles for the activities of a request. All handler times include the time to save and restore the context of the processor. The memory exception handler time also includes the time to re-execute the faulted instruction. For write misses with invalidations, the invalidation acknowledgment handler time is the average sum of all the times spent in processing acknowledgments. The bar on the right of each stacked bar gives the latency experienced by the requester. They are shorter than the sums of the times for all activities because some activities overlap.

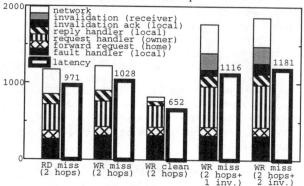

Figure 4. Breakdown of latencies for simple requests (micro-benchmarks)

The most important component of the latency is the remote read or write interruption handler at the owner. The owner must identify the location of the line, using hardware assistance, and reply to the request. On average, this takes 280 cycles when no line is sent back and 330 cycles when the reply contains a line. For write requests, the first invalidation sent by the owner increases the handler time by 246 cycles (on a 32-node configuration); each additional invalidation adds 22 cycles.

On a node with a Shared copy of a line, the invalidation interruption time is 218 cycles (we only show the time for one invalidation interruption, since all the invalidations handlers are executed in parallel.) A big part of this latency is hidden, however, since the invalidation acknowledgment message is sent before searching for the line and invalidating it. Receiving an invalidation acknowledgment at the local node consumes 65 cycles, except for the last one (76 cycles).

By looking at the latency times experienced by the local node (right bars for write miss cases), we see that the global cost per invalidation is 65-88 cycles. Since the number of simultaneous copies of a line is usually low in typical programs we do not think that dispatching invalidations and collecting invalidation acknowledgments in hardware, as advocated for software-extended protocols [4], would yield a large performance improvement, except for benchmarks with wide sharing.

5.2. Execution Times

In this section we present the overall performance of SC-COMA by comparing it to an ideal hardware implementation, called HW-COMA. HW-COMA uses exactly the same coherence protocol as SC-COMA, but incurs no penalty for the (software) execution of coherence actions, as if they were performed by an extremely fast hardware controller. HW-COMA's controller is arbitrated between the local cache and the network interface and is occupied by a request for a duration of time involving mostly data transfers between memory and the network interface or the cache.

Figure 5 shows execution times on SC-COMA normalized with respect to HW-COMA, for three memory pressure points: 25%, 50% and 75%. The execution times are broken down into several components. The *busy* time corresponds to the effective instruction processing time of the processor. The processor is stalled during *synchronization* events and whenever it misses in the FLC. When the access hits in the SLC or local memory, the delay is counted as *local* stall. In SC-COMA, this corresponds to accesses performed without software intervention. Attraction memory misses contribute to the *remote* stall. An additional component of the execution time in SC-COMA is due to the processing of external requests which *interrupt* the application thread. This category excludes the overhead of requests occurring while the processor spins at a synchronization point or while a remote access is pending. SC-COMA's slowdown ranges from 11-37% at low memory pressure to 21-56% at high pressure. In spite of almost identical cache and memory hit ratios for the two architectures, the local stall is higher in HW-COMA. This is explained by the increased delay in processing cache misses, when HW-COMA's controller is busy with external requests. By contrast, SC-COMA's cache controller has exclusive access to the bus and the memory.

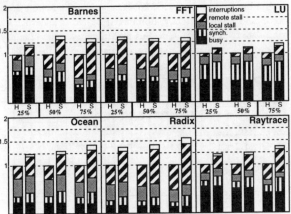

Figure 5. Execution times. SC-COMA time is normalized with respect to HW-COMA at the same memory pressure.

The amount of remote stall in SC-COMA, as compared to

HW-COMA, roughly scales up by the ratio of the remote read/write miss latencies, shown in Figure 3. The reason is that the node miss ratio remains practically constant in the two architectures and, except for LU, there is no significant component of upgrade (ownership) misses. Compared to read misses, the overheads of SC-COMA for upgrade misses are relatively bigger, hence LU shows a higher scale-up factor for the remote latency. Other factors of fluctuation from this approximate ratio are the amount of request forwarding and contention for certain nodes, which increases queuing delays. The number of forwarded requests should decrease with better placement strategies, leading to a reduction of the average latency which is more significant in SC-COMA. The likelihood of contention goes up with the memory pressure, as processors become interrupted more frequently. This explains why the ratio between the amounts of remote stalls increases slightly with the memory pressure.

The activity of the coherence handlers affects the synchronization stall indirectly. The increased synchronization penalty in the context of software-implemented protocols has been attributed by Grahn and Stenström [8] to node activity imbalances due to uneven distributions of coherence requests. This is more serious at high memory pressure, when the protocol overhead is more pronounced.

Finally, SC-COMA has a component of overhead due to interrupts disturbing the application. Overall, this is quite small, indicating that a potential communication coprocessor would be underutilized. As memory pressure increases and replacements become more frequent, this component becomes more significant, but never critical. An interesting effect in some applications is the occurrence of external requests when the processor is stalled anyway, either in synchronization or because of a pending miss. LU, with a high synchronization penalty, is able to overlap the processing of some external requests with barrier synchronization. On the other hand, FFT, Radix and Ocean exhibit clustered misses during data exchange phases, when processors are cross-servicing misses, and some of the overhead due to interrupts is again absorbed in the remote stall.

5.3. Speedups

In Figure 6 we present speedups for up to 32 processors. The algorithmic speedup is derived for a perfect memory system (no stalls). To gain insight into the behavior of the COMAs, we show the speedup at three different memory pressures. The total amount of memory in the system is kept constant and is divided equally among the processors. In all configurations, processors have a 64KB cache. The tag-checking overhead in shared memory accesses is removed for simulations of the uniprocessor case. This explains why the slope of the speedup is smaller than one right from the start (i.e. for just a few processors), especially in applications with high cache miss ratios: Radix, Ocean, and FFT.

The main observation is that, while SC-COMA does show some slowdown, it does not introduce any bottlenecks accentuating the speedup saturation. The communication-to-computation characteristic of an application dictates when saturation occurs. The higher remote latency in SC-COMA makes it's speedup diverge from HW-COMA's, but the speedup still remains almost linear when memory pressure is low. Radix is the only application with a traffic so large to show rapid saturation for both COMAs. At higher memory pressures, the replacements and the capacity traffic start to pick up, deteriorating the speedups. Capacity traffic increases mostly in Barnes and Raytrace. In Raytrace, where data is mostly-read, the rate of replacements is small and the combined effect on the speedup is lesser.

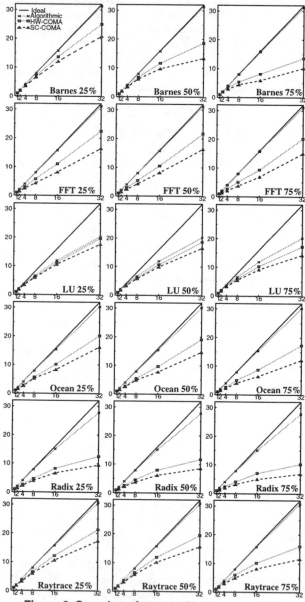

Figure 6. Speedups for up to 32 processors (three memory pressure points)

5.4. Effects of processor speed

It is expected that, with increasing processor speeds, the overhead of coherence-related software and the contribution of software-implemented actions to the remote latency should be relatively diminished, if the memory and network speeds are kept constant. In order to quantify this intuition, we have performed simulations for SC-COMA and HW-COMA using varying pro-

cessor clock frequencies, from 100MHz to 1GHz. These simulations are performed at 75% memory pressure, where the software overhead is higher, due to more frequent replacements, and the impact of faster processors is more significant. Our indicator is SC-COMA's slowdown, the ratio of execution times t_{ex}^{SC}/t_{ex}^{HW}.

Indeed, as shown in Figure 7, there is an obvious trend for a relative improvement of SC-COMA as the processor is clocked faster. However, the slowdown never approaches one. This is because of the overly optimistic timings of HW-COMA, which is assumed to have instantaneous access to all the resources, whereas SC-COMA must perform costly uncached accesses to program the NI and update the Tag Table. The absolute penalty of uncached accesses is constant, regardless of processor speed.

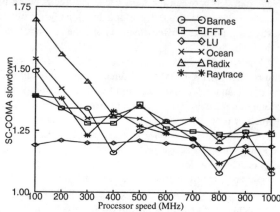

Figure 7. SC-COMA's slowdown for different processor speeds (75% pressure)

Barnes	FFT	LU	Ocean	Radix	Raytrace
1.08	1.24	1.19	1.25	1.31	1.10

Table 3: Asymptotic slowdown for SC-COMA

Table 3 lists the estimated value (at 1GHz) where SC-COMA's slowdown is converging. Because of the saturation, this is approximately the ratio of the *average* remote latencies for SC-COMA, when the overhead of executing software handlers is negligible, and for HW-COMA. Read and write remote accesses have very similar latency, dominated by the delays of transferring data over the network, bus and memory, hence the asymptotic slowdown can be roughly approximated by the ratio of the remote read/write latencies.

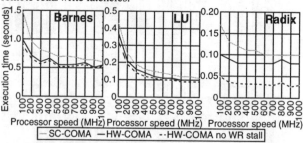

Figure 8. Execution times for SC-COMA and HW-COMA with varying processor speeds

To better understand the prospects of SC-COMA in the future world of fast processors, we plot in Figure 8 the absolute

254

execution times for some benchmarks using processors clocked up to 1GHz. The results for the other three benchmarks are similar to Barnes and LU. The curves for LU show that a 275 MHz SC-COMA performs like a 200 MHz HW-COMA. The same is true for a 450 MHz SC-COMA and a 300 MHz HW-COMA. In essence, this indicates that SC-COMA could be a very viable solution for the present and near-future. The release of a hardware COMA using 300 MHz processors could take as long as the development of a next-generation, 450 MHz processor, which can be used immediately by a software COMA, at virtually no costs.

The current version of SC-COMA runs on a sequentially consistent hardware. Thus, the store buffers are disabled. In Figure 8, a third curve is plotted for a HW-COMA where all write stalls have been eliminated. At 200 MHz, SC-COMA shows a slowdown between 1.36 for LU and 3.25 for Radix, as compared to this HW-COMA with ideal release consistency. However, the software protocol in SC-COMA could be upgraded as well to run on a release consistent substrate. This would involve the software ability to recover pending stores from the buffer (address and data), after they are faulted, and to complete them, using untranslated stores.

Obviously, future processors will incorporate features to fight the memory wall [23], such as bigger on-chip caches, simultaneous multithreading, out-of-order execution. At the same time, limited improvements in memory speed are also expected. Therefore, our results plotted for processor speeds higher than 500 MHz are highly speculative.

6. Related Work

Research on the hardware implementations of COMA begun with the DDM [9], which used hierarchical directories. As demonstrated by the KSR-1 [3], hierarchical directories increase the latency of remote accesses. This would become even worse with software-implemented directory management. The Flat COMA, COMA-F [13], was proposed to eliminated hierarchical directories. We do not know of any working prototype of a Flat COMA. The Illinois Aggressive COMA (I-ACOMA) [27] group is currently building one. A variation of the COMA, using a page grain in the allocation policy, is the Simple COMA [22]. S3.mp [19] has provided a testbed for its implementation.

A variety of DSM systems have used the main processor for protocol processing. Alewife [4] was first to experiment with software extensions to a NUMA protocol implemented mostly in hardware. The software protocol actions were written in C and executed on the main processor, equipped with support for fast context switching.

On the heels of the Alewife study, Grahn and Stenström evaluated various implementations of a NUMA protocol with software-only management of the directory on a NCC-NUMA substrate [8]. A custom node controller provides support for remote put/get operations and implements a good part of the protocol actions. Other protocol actions are running on the main processor. The necessity to handle requests while an access is pending requires the provision of high-availability interrupts.

Blizzard-E [25], a cross between VSM and hybrid systems, uses the virtual memory system to trap shared writes and the error-correcting codes (ECC) to implement a memory line valid bit and support fine grain sharing for read-only pages. Protocol actions run at user level, taking advantage of CM5's user-level NI. The overhead of kernel traps was reduced by careful recoding. Faulted accesses are re-executed after the trap handler terminates. There is no detail on how forward progress is guaranteed.

All VSM systems implement the coherence protocol in software running at user-level on the main processor, albeit using coarse-grain sharing. More recently, user-level software-only systems with support for fine-grain sharing have been proposed by Blizzard-S [25] and Shasta [24]. They do, however, incur a penalty for performing access checking in software for every potential access to shared memory. This category of DSM has COMA-like features, by accumulating the working set in the local memory. However, the replacement algorithm must dispense of a whole page, which could be too large a grain in some cases, and adds the overhead of page faults.

Typhoon [20] is one of the first proposals for hybrid DSMs with high levels of integration. Its network device contains a processor dedicated to user-level protocol handling. Coherence events, snooped from the bus or signaled by the network interface, invoke user-level procedures. Bus addresses must be passed through a reverse TLB which adds to the complexity. The memory organization is inspired from Simple COMA.

The Stanford FLASH [16] is the most aggressive proposal for a DSM with software-implemented coherence. A custom node controller, the MAGIC chip, contains the processor running the coherence protocol. Currently, like SC-COMA, FLASH does not allow user-level handlers and runs protocol handlers at system-level. Although a COMA protocol is planned for evaluation, the only reports [10] available are for a NUMA protocol with a directory structure using dynamic pointer allocation.

Typhoon-0 [21], START-NG [5] run the protocol on one of the processors in a standard SMP cluster. Fine-grain sharing is supported by the addition of a custom access checking device on the local bus. Both run user-level protocols. While Typhoon-0 uses a Simple COMA memory organization, START-NG manages a level-3 cache in software, requiring intervention on all level-2 cache misses.

7. Conclusions

We have presented a COMA architecture with the coherence protocol executed in software on the main processor. The hardware substrate is very close to a generic network of workstations. We rely on a custom hardware device, acting at the local bus level of every node, to organize and control a fine-grained attraction memory using standard DRAMs. Misses in the attraction memory are faulted on the bus and trigger protocol actions on the main processor. Packets received from the network are flagged with asynchronous interrupts and are handled similarly. The protocol handlers run in kernel mode and are lightweight. These handlers can be integrated into a standard OS kernel with minor modifications. SC-COMA's approach and several optimizations allow it to achieve a software overhead of just 430 cycles for a three-hop remote read.

The protocol engine occupancy, relative to measurements in FLASH [10], is reduced by several effects. The number of accesses hitting in the local memory is maximized by the COMA organization and such accesses bypass the protocol engine, generating zero occupancy, unlike in FLASH. When the main processor is blocked in a remote access or even for synchronization, servicing external requests also produces zero occupancy.

The performance of SC-COMA compares favorably with an idealized hardware-implemented COMA. Execution times on 32 nodes for six benchmarks indicate a slowdown of 11-37% at 25% memory pressure and 21-56% at 75% memory pressure. SC-COMA scales well up to 32 processors. Our investigation on the effects of faster processors, relative to memory and network speeds, revealed that SC-COMA's slowdown is reduced as the overall contribution of the software overhead to the remote latency shrinks. However, the slowdown cannot pass below a certain threshold due to SC-COMA's loose integration of the protocol engine with the network interface and the Access Checking Device. The results we have presented are encouraging given the simplicity of the current protocol. We can expect improvements from further optimizations and extensions, such as ownership hints [1], application-specific protocols, and adaptive sequential prefetching.

8. References

[1] M. Björklund, F. Dahlgren, P. Stenström. Using Hints to Reduce the Read Miss Penalty for Flat COMA Protocols. *Proc of the 28th Hawaii International Conference on System Sciences*, pp. 242-251, 1995.

[2] W.J. Bolosky. Software Coherence in Multiprocessor Memory Systems. PhD. Thesis. University of Rochester, 1993.

[3] H. Burkhardt III et al. Overview of the KSR-1 Computer System. Technical Report KSR-TR-9202001, Kendall Square Research, Feb. 1992.

[4] D. Chaiken, A. Agarwal. Software Extended Coherent Shared Memory: Performance and Cost. *Proc. of the 21st Int. Symposium on Computer Architecture*, pp. 314-324, May 1994.

[5] Derek Chiou et al. StarT-NG: Delivering Seamless Parallel Computing. *Euro-Par'95*, Aug. 1995.

[6] M. Dubois, J. Skeppstedt, P. Stenström. Essential Misses and Data Traffic in Coherence Protocols. *Journal of Parallel and Distributed Computing*, Vol. 29, No. 2, pp. 108-125, Sep. 1995.

[7] S. Dwarkadas, P. Keheler, A.L. Cox, W. Zwaenepoel. Evaluation of Release Consistent Software Distributed Shared Memory on Emerging Network Technology. *Proc. of the 20th Annual Int. Symp. on Computer Architecture*, pp. 144-155, 1993.

[8] H. Grahn, P. Stenström. Efficient Strategies for Software-Only Directory Protocols in Shared-Memory Multiprocessors. *Proc. of the 22nd Annual International Symposium on Computer Architecture*. Santa Margherita, Italy, Jun. 1995.

[9] E. Hagersten, A. Landin, S. Haridi. DDM-A Cache-Only Memory Architecture. *IEEE Computer*, Vol. 25, No. 9, pp. 44-54, Sep. 1992.

[10] M. Heinrich et al. The Performance Impact of Flexibility in the Stanford FLASH Multiprocessor. *Proc. of the Sixth Int. Conf. on Arch. Support for Programming Languages and Operating Systems*, pp 274-285, 1994.

[11] C. Holt, M. Heinrich, J.P. Singh, E. Rothberg, J.Hennessy. The Effects of Latency, Occupancy, and Bandwidth in Distributed Shared Memory Multiprocessors. Technical Report CSL-TR-95-660, Computer Systems Laboratory, Stanford University, Jan. 1995.

[12] M. Horowitz, M. Martonosi, T.C. Mowry, M.D. Smith. Informing Memory Operations: Providing Memory Performance Feedback in Modern Processors. *Proceedings of the 23rd Annual Symposium on Computer Architecture*, pages 260-270, 1996.

[13] T. Joe. COMA-F: a Non-Hierarchical Cache Only Memory Architecture. PhD. Thesis, Stanford University, Mar. 1995.

[14] J. Kubiatowicz, D. Chaiken, A. Agarwal. Closing the Window of Vulnerability in Multiphase Memory Transactions. *Proc. of the 5th International Conference on Architectural Support for Programming Languages and Operating Systems.* ACM Sigplan Notices, Volume 27, Number 9, Sep. 1992.

[15] J. Kuskin et al. The Stanford FLASH Multiprocessor. *Proc. of the 21st Annual International Symposium on Computer Architecture.* Apr. 1994.

[16] D.E. Lenoski et al. The Directory-Based Cache Coherence Protocol for the DASH Multiprocessor. *Proc. of the 17th Annual Int. Symp. on Computer Architecture*, pp 148-159, 1990

[17] K. Li. IVY: A Shared Virtual Memory System for Parallel Computing. *Proc. of the Int. Parallel Processing Conference* pp. 94-101, 1988.

[18] A. Moga, A. Gefflaut, M. Dubois. Hardware versus Software Implementation of COMA. Technical Report CENG 97-03. University of Southern California. Jan. 1997.

[19] A. Nowatzyk et al. The S3.mp Scalable Shared Memory Multiprocessor. *Proc. of the Int. Parallel Processing Conference*, pp. I-1-I-10, 1995.

[20] S.K. Reinhardt, J.R. Larus, D.A. Wood. Tempest and Typhoon: User-level Shared Memory. *Proc. of the 21st Annual International Symposium on Computer Architecture*, pages 325-337, Apr. 1994.

[21] S.K. Reinhardt, R.W. Pfile, D.A. Wood. Decoupled Hardware Support for Distributed Shared Memory. *Proc. of the 23rd International Symposium on Computer Architecture*, May 1996.

[22] A. Saulsbury, T. Wilkinson, J. Carter and A. Landin. An Argument for Simple COMA. *Proc. of the 1st Symposium on High-Performance Computer Architecture*, pages 276-285, Raleigh, Jan. 1995.

[23] A. Saulsbury, F. Pong, A. Nowatzyk. Missing the Memory Wall: The Case for Processor/Memory Integration. *Proc. of the 23rd Annual Int. Symp. on Computer Architecture*, 1996.

[24] D.J. Scales, K. Gharachorloo, C.A. Thekkath. Shasta: A Low Overhead, Software-Only Approach for Supporting Fine-Grain Shared Memory. *Proceedings of the 3rd International Symposium on High-Performance Computer Architecture*, 1997.

[25] I. Schoinas, B. Falsafi, A.R. Lebeck, S.K. Reinhardt, J.R. Larus and D.A. Wood. Fine-grain Access Control for Distributed Shared Memory. *Proc. of the 6th International Conference on Architectural Support for Programming Languages and Operating Systems.* Oct. 1994.

[26] P. Stenström, T. Joe, A. Gupta. Comparative Performance Evaluation of Cache-Coherent NUMA and COMA architectures. *Proc. of the 19th Annual Symposium on Computer Architecture*, pages 80-91, May 1992.

[27] J. Torrellas, D. Padua. The Illinois Aggressive COMA Multiprocessor Project (I-ACOMA). *6th Symposium on the Frontiers of Massively Parallel Computing*, Oct. 1996.

[28] S. Woo et al. The SPLASH-2 Programs: Characterization and Methodological Considerations. *Proc. of the 23rd Int. Symp. on Computer Architecture*, pp. 24-36, 1995.

Performance and Configuration of Hierarchical Ring Networks for Multiprocessors

V. Carl Hamacher*
Department of Electrical and
Computer Engineering
Queen's University
Kingston, Ontario, Canada K7L 3N6

Hong Jiang[†]
Department of Computer Science
and Engineering
University of Nebraska-Lincoln
Lincoln, Nebraska 68588-0115

Abstract

Analytical queueing network models for expected message delay in 2-level and 3-level hierarchical-ring interconnection networks (INs) are developed. Such networks have recently been used in commercial and research prototype multiprocessors. A major class of traffic carried by these INs consists of cache line transfers, and associated coherency control messages, between processor caches and remote memory modules in shared-memory multiprocessors. Memory modules are assumed to be evenly distributed over the processor nodes. Such traffic consists of short, fixed-length messages. They can be conveniently transported using the slotted ring transmission technique, which is studied here. The message delay results derived from the models are shown to be quite accurate when checked against a simulation study. The comparisons to simulations include heavy traffic situations where queueing delays in ring crossover switches are significant for ring utilization levels of 80 to 90%. As well as facilitating analysis, the analytical models can be used to determine optimal sizes for the rings at different levels in the hierarchy under specified traffic distributions in a system with a given total number of processor nodes. Optimality is in terms of minimizing average message delay. A specific example of such a design exercise is provided for the uniform traffic case.

1 Introduction

A main hardware component in a multiprocessor system is the interconnection network (IN) that connects together processors and remote memory modules. One such IN structure, hierarchical slotted rings, is an interesting base on which to build large scale shared-memory multiprocessors. They have received a great deal of attention recently, both in academia [12, 17, 14, 5, 7, 10, 6] and in industry [16, 3, 4]. The salient features of this class of INs are: (1) the physical locality of hierarchical rings blends naturally with that of computational locality of shared-memory multiprocessing [12, 7], (2) the hierarchical ring structure

provides natural and efficient broadcasting and multicasting capabilities that are crucial for process coordination and cache coherence protocols [5], and (3) hierarchical rings have an inherent and unique capability of "diluting" the impact of hot-spot traffic [17, 7]. Nevertheless, a more popular choice for INs seems to be meshes. This, as noted in [12], may stem from the fact that mesh-connected systems are relatively easy to build using off-the-shelf routers and processors and have good scalability characteristics. While meshes have superior scaling characteristics relative to hierarchical rings, both of the only two comparative studies of hierarchical rings and meshes in the literature, one based on an approximate modeling [6] and the other based on detailed execution-driven simulations [12], concluded that hierarchical rings outperform meshes under some practical workloads. More specifically, [12] found that hierarchical rings perform significantly better than meshes for system sizes up to 121 processors if the workload exhibits moderate to high memory access locality. Even if there is no memory locality, [12] observed that hierarchical ring systems perform better than meshes for systems with large cache lines either if the system is small, or if the global ring has double the normal bandwidth.

Exact analytical modeling of hierarchical slotted-ring networks is intractable because of the phenomenon of "clustering" of occupied slots in the ring as observed in [11, 1]. As a result, analytical studies of such networks have been based on approximation techniques [11, 1, 17]. With the exception of [17], which analyzed 2-level structures, hierarchical ring structures have not been studied analytically so far despite the existence of many analytical studies in the literature on single-level rings [11, 1]. Paper [17] evaluated the performance of two-level ring structures under cache-coherent traffic in the form of hot-spot patterns. It considered the source removal transmission protocol. Two other recent performance studies on hierarchical ring networks were based entirely on simulations [7, 12].

In this paper, we use approximate analytical techniques to model the message delay performance of 2-level and 3-level hierarchical ring networks that operate under a destination removal protocol, as opposed to source removal. The former is more efficient in terms of network channel utilization and has been em-

---
*Supported by an NSERC (Canada) Research G rant

[†]Supported in part by a Nebraska Research Initiative (NRI) Research Grant

ployed in recent research prototypes [15, 14]. We consider both uniform and localized traffic patterns that are typical of shared-memory multiprocessing applications. A main objective of the paper is to gain important insights based on the performance measures obtained analytically, into the optimal design of hierarchical ring systems. That is, for a given total node size and traffic environment, how should one determine the size of rings on different levels to minimize the expected message delay?

The paper is organized as follows. Section 2 presents a description of the hierarchical interconnection network model, including enough structural and operational detail for performance evaluation purposes. Section 3 presents message delay models using queueing models to capture the effect of contention. The analytical models developed are validated through extensive simulations and accuracy of the analytical models is assessed in Section 4. Section 5 addresses the issue of optimal configuration using the analytical models developed in Section 3. Finally, some concluding remarks and prospects for future work are made in Section 6.

2 Hierarchical Ring Networks

The hierarchical slotted-ring IN studied here consists of unidirectional rings, as employed in [3, 4]. Processor node clusters are only connected to local rings, as shown in Figure 1. Each segment, called a station, connects one cluster into the ring. The station switch, S, removes an incoming ring message into its cluster interface if it is the destination, or sends the message on around the ring otherwise. This message-handling protocol is the same as that used in destination-remove, slotted, Local Area Networks (LANs) [11]. A switch introduces a pending transmit message from its cluster interface into the downstream station as soon as it observes its own ring input side to be empty. Ring traffic is thus never blocked. In the context of memory read/write messages in shared-memory multiprocessors, operations can be described briefly as follows. At the destination station, the message has priority on the cluster bus. If the target memory module is free to handle the request, it starts the operation (a read or a write), and immediately sends a positive acknowledgment message back to the source station, where the acknowledgment is removed by the source station switch. A negative acknowledgement is returned if the target memory module is busy, and the read/write request message will need to be tried again later by the source. If the destination memory module is free, a write operation requires a request and acknowledgement message. A read operation requires three messages: one to send the read request, an acknowledgement, and a later one from the destination station to return the requested data. These details are not actually needed for the network performance modeling done later, but they explain the use of the destination-remove protocol in the shared-memory application. Efficiency is enhanced if acknowledgements immediately use the slot vacated by the request. This operational possibility is modeled in the analytic and simulation study reported here.

The bit width of the local ring is assumed to be enough to carry full information for a memory word write message or a two-word reply message to a read request. This wide-slot format is used in both [3] and [4].

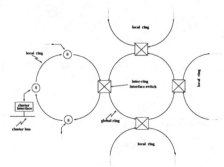

Figure 1: A 2-Level Hierarchically Structured Multiprocessor

A local ring can be expanded to any desired number of segments because each station is a regenerative repeater in the electrical sense. However, from a performance standpoint, message transfer delay will increase linearly, degrading performance. To alleviate the performance problem, a higher level ring can be added in the form of a global segmented ring that is used to interconnect local rings, as shown in Figure 1. It operates much like a local ring, with its source and destination stations being local ring interfaces instead of cluster interfaces. This structure can be extended to even higher levels. Message blocking can occur at the crossover switch between two rings. For example, in a 2-level system, if a message from a local ring needs to move up to the global ring at the same time that a continuing message on the global ring arrives at the crossover switch, there is contention for the downstream link on the global ring, and only one message can proceed. The other message must be temporarily buffered in the crossover switch to insure that messages are never lost in the network. Details will be given in Section 3.2.

3 Contention (Queueing) Model for Message Delay

In [6, 10] we developed message delay and throughput performance measures for hierarchical rings in the light traffic (no contention) situation. While contention-free models are easy to develop and useful for rough network comparison purposes, any detailed evaluation of a network must consider contentions that occur. Further, only contention models can identify potential system performance bottlenecks. In this section, analytical models will be developed to capture the effect of contention under the full range of the applied loads.

3.1 Message Destination Distribution

Applications that run on shared-memory multiprocessors will have different patterns of message destination locality as the processor clusters (containing one or more processors) make memory read/write requests to remote memory modules. These patterns may range from situations where a cluster references mainly only a small number of other cluster memories (high locality) to situations where references are are uniformly distributed over all other clusters (low/no locality). In the first case, clusters that reference each other often should be located on the same local ring. Conversely, if such situations dominate, the size of the local ring in a hierarchical ring network can be chosen to best match the size of the typical locality sets. If applications tend to have uniform destination distributions, then for a fixed total number of clusters, the various ring sizes can be chosen to minimize average message delay. An example of this network design optimization is given in Section 5.

In the models to be developed, the following parameters reflect message destination locality. In H2 (2-level systems), P is the probability that a message is destined for a cluster on the same local ring, with $1 - P$ being the probability that it will need to move over the global ring to a different local ring. In H3 (3-level systems), P_L is the probability of a "same local ring" destination. P_M is the probability that the message is destined for another local ring attached to the same intermediate ring; while $P_G = 1 - (P_L + P_M)$ is the probability that the message must move all the way up through the global ring, eventually moving down through the hierarchy to a local ring on a different intermediate ring.

3.2 Queues in the Network

FIFO queues are associated with each local ring station interface and inter-ring interface, as shown in Figure 2 and Figure 3, respectively. At a station interface, shown in Figure 2, the message packet at the head of the queue waits until an empty slot passes by, or a full slot destined to the local station arrives and the packet is removed from the slot by the station, at which time the head packet is transmitted onto the slot. Thus, a slot is deemed *empty* if it (1) contains no valid packet, or (2) contains a packet destined to the local station and will be removed by it. The transmitted packet will then travel to its destination station unblocked if the destination is on the local ring, or to the inter-ring interface otherwise. At the inter-ring interface, shown in Figure 3, the packet joins the FIFO queue for the higher level ring. Once at the head of the queue, the packet follows similar steps as in the case of a local station interface; that is, the packet rides on the first empty slot to join the FIFO queue at another inter-ring interface connecting down to the destination ring, or up to a higher-level ring, depending on the destination. Ultimately, the packet is removed from the ring by the destination station. Thus, the message delay, d (see Figure 2), of a packet is the sum of (1) *queueing delays* at all FIFO queues on its entire path from source station to destination station, (2) *slot access time* at all interfaces on its path, that is, the time between when the packet reaches the head of a FIFO queue and when it gets an empty slot, (3) *slot traverse time*, the total time the packet spends moving through ring segment slots on its entire path, and (4) a final time step into the destination station bus buffer.

Part (3) of the message delay is uniquely determined by the source and destination addresses and the net-

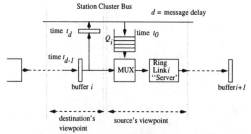

Figure 2: Structure of Local Station Interface

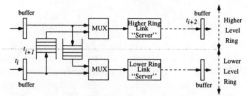

Figure 3: Structure of Inter-Ring Interface

work configuration, independent of traffic density and contention. Clearly parts (1) and (2) of the message delay capture the effect of contention, and hence are traffic density dependent. Unfortunately, it is extremely difficult to model the contention exactly, due to the dependence among *full slots*. This dependence, also known as "clustering of full slots", has been observed in [11, 1, 17], where, as traffic intensifies, full slots tend to cluster together to form "trains" of slots, as opposed to full slots being uniformly distributed on the rings. This dependence makes an exact analysis intractable [9]. A second factor that complicates the exact analysis is the issue of finite buffers. To make the analysis tractable and simple, we circumvent the problems by making two main simplifying assumptions. First, we assume that the event of a slot being full is independent of that of other slots. Second, we assume the FIFO buffers at all interfaces are infinite in size. Fortunately, these assumptions have been shown to be not problematic as shown in [11, 1, 17] and by our own simulation validation studies.

With the above assumptions, we model the contention in parts (1) and (2) of message delay using the M/G/1 queueing center model, similar to the approach in [1] and [17] where source-remove one-level and two-level rings, respectively, are analyzed. The key in this method lies in finding the expected service time of the M/G/1 service center which models a particular interface FIFO queue. This expected service time is effectively the expected time that a packet at the head of the queue waits before it gets an empty slot. In what follows we first define the necessary parameters and list assumptions for the analysis and then give a detailed description of the analytical model.

It should also be noted that, from the modeling viewpoint, there is also a buffer, called a *ring link buffer*, associated with each ring link in the system, as shown in Figures 2 and 3 in narrow bars. It only needs to have capacity of 1 because:

i) arrivals occur only at discrete time points, and

the associated ring link "server" has a constant service time of 1 discrete time step; and

ii) this ring link buffer has priority over station FIFO queues and inter-ring crossover queues in competing for access to the ring link "server". This priority policy is consistent with the implementations of the NUMAchine [14, 12] and KSR [4].

We will not need a specific notation to identify these buffers because their total occupancies can be derived from ring utilization, which can be calculated directly from input message traffic and message travel patterns. This will become clear later.

3.3 Definitions and Assumptions

Time is discretized into clock ticks, where one tick is the time needed for a packet to move between adjacent slot segments in any ring. The models to be developed are based on the following system parameters:

1. λ: identical traffic arrival rate at each local station, i.e., number of independent message packets per clock tick arriving at a local ring station FIFO queue.
2. message destination locality in H2 is determined by probability P as defined in Section 3.1.
3. message destination locality in H3 is determined by probabilities P_L and P_M as defined in Section 3.1.
4. N: total number of local stations in the network.
5. L: number of stations on a local ring.
6. M: number of local rings on an intermediate ring in the case of 3-level ring network.
7. G: number of lower-level rings connected to the global ring. Note that $G = \frac{N}{L}$ in 2-level ring networks and $G = \frac{N}{LM}$ in 3-level ring networks.

Furthermore, we make the following assumptions:

1. The traffic arrival rate at each station and inter-ring interface FIFO follows a Poisson process.
2. One message packet can be completely carried by one slot.
3. A packet is removed from the network by the destination immediately after it reaches the destination station cluster bus buffer (see Figure 2).

3.4 General Model

The basic idea of this analysis is to solve the M/G/1 queueing model for all FIFO queues (local stations and inter-ring interfaces), which will give rise to expected queue lengths at all FIFO queues. We also need ring utilizations. Using Little's result [13], these results can then be used to derive expected message delays as follows.

Let Q_i, $1 \le i \le N$, denote the queue length of local station $S(i)$, and let $Q_{L-G(i)}$ and $Q_{G-L(i)}$ denote, respectively, the local-ring to global-ring FIFO queue length and the global-ring to local-ring FIFO queue length of the inter-ring interface i, $1 \le i \le \frac{N}{L}$ for the 2-level ring. Similarly, for the 3-level ring,

let $Q_{M-L(i)}$, $Q_{L-M(i)}$, $Q_{G-M(j)}$, and $Q_{M-G(j)}$ denote, respectively, the middle-ring to local-ring, local-ring to middle-ring, global-ring to middle-ring, and middle-ring to global-ring FIFO queue lengths. Here, $1 \le i \le \frac{N}{L}$ and $1 \le j \le \frac{N}{LM}$. Further, let U_L, U_M, and U_G represent the ring utilizations at local, intermediate, and global rings, respectively. In steady state, Little's result applies and the expected message delays for H2 and H3, T_{H2} and T_{H3}, are:

$$
\begin{aligned}
T_{H2} &= \frac{\text{Average Number of Packets in System}}{\text{System Throughput}} = \frac{\overline{n}}{\overline{X}} \\
&= \frac{\sum_{i=1}^{N} \overline{Q}_i + \sum_{i=1}^{\frac{N}{L}} (\overline{Q}_{G-L(i)} + \overline{Q}_{L-G(i)})}{N\lambda} \\
&\quad + \frac{(N + \frac{N}{L})U_L + \frac{N}{L}U_G}{N\lambda}
\end{aligned}
\tag{1}
$$

$$
\begin{aligned}
T_{H3} &= \frac{\text{Average Number of Packets in System}}{\text{System Throughput}} = \frac{\overline{n}}{\overline{X}} \\
&= [\sum_{i=1}^{N} \overline{Q}_i + \sum_{i=1}^{\frac{N}{L}} (\overline{Q}_{M-L(i)} + \overline{Q}_{L-M(i)}) \\
&\quad + \sum_{i=1}^{\frac{N}{LM}} (\overline{Q}_{M-G(i)} + \overline{Q}_{G-M(i)}) + (N + \frac{N}{L})U_L \\
&\quad + (\frac{N}{L} + \frac{N}{LM})U_M + \frac{N}{LM}U_G] \times \frac{1}{N\lambda}
\end{aligned}
\tag{2}
$$

In each equation, $\overline{Y}$ denotes the expected value of the variable Y, the numerator represents the total population (number of packets) in the network, including all FIFO queues and those in the rings. The latter quantity, packets in all rings, is derived from the ring utilizations. The denominator represents the system throughput. An implicit assumption here is that the system is non-saturated and in steady state, making the system throughput equal to the total packet arrival rate.

3.5 Ring Utilizations

In H2 and H3, all local rings have $L + 1$ links, with the extra link being needed to incorporate the inter-ring interface to the intermediate level ring. All global rings have G links; while in H3, intermediate rings have $M + 1$ links, with the extra link incorporating the interface to the global ring.

Because of the destination-remove protocol, it is easy to see that, on average, a message traverses half of the links on any ring it moves over to reach its destination. This assumes that destinations are uniformly distributed inside the local, intermediate, and global sets of messages.

H2: Assuming symmetry over all stations, there are two types of utilizations: U_L for all local rings, and U_G for the global ring.

U_L: To derive U_L, consider a period of T time steps. During this time, there are two sources of traffic onto each local ring: one from local stations Q_i and the other from the global ring through Q_{G-L}. Traffic from

Q_i can be further divided into two parts, namely, those packets staying in the same local ring with probability P, and those going up to the global ring with probability $1 - P$. They all use $(L+1)/2$ links on average. Thus traffic from Q_i uses $L\lambda T(L+1)/2$ links over time T.

The total traffic from global ring Q_{G-L} can be calculated as:

$$\lambda_{G-L} = \sum_{1}^{G-1} \frac{L\lambda(1-P)}{(G-1)} = L\lambda(1-P),$$

because $1/(G-1)$ of the global packets from each of the $G-1$ other local rings will be destined for any local ring. Of this traffic, each message uses $(L+1)/2$ links on average. Total number of links used by this traffic over T is $L\lambda(1-P)T(L+1)/2$. Since there are $(L+1)T$ links available over T, we have

$$U_L = \frac{L\lambda}{2} + \frac{L\lambda(1-P)}{2} = \frac{L\lambda(2-P)}{2} \quad (3)$$

U_G: Each global message uses $G/2$ links on average, and there are GT links available over T. There are a total of $N\lambda(1-P)T$ messages over T, thus

$$U_G = N\lambda(1-P)T\frac{G}{2} \times \frac{1}{GT} = \frac{N\lambda(1-P)}{2} \quad (4)$$

Also note that

$$\lambda_{L-G} = \lambda_{G-L} = L\lambda(1-P) \quad (5)$$

H3: As in H2, consider a period of time T. We define the following locality terms:

"Local": all source traffic staying on the local ring with probability P_L;

"Middle": all source traffic going L → M → L with probability P_M; and

"Global": all source traffic going L → M → G → M → L with probability $1 - P_L - P_M$.

U_L: Over T time steps, there are two sources of traffic going onto each local ring: Q_i and Q_{M-L}. All messages from Q_i, whether L, L → M → L, or L → M → G → M → L bound, use $(L+1)/2$ links on average. Thus traffic from Q_i uses a total of $L\lambda T(L+1)/2$ links over T.

Messages coming down from Q_{M-L} can be divided into two groups:

i) L → M → L messages from other local rings attached to the same intermediate ring. There are $M-1$ such local rings; and each of them sends $1/(M-1)$ of their L → M → L traffic to any particular local ring; and each such message uses $(L+1)/2$ links. Hence, over T the number of links used by these messages are:

$$A1 = \sum^{M-1} L\lambda P_M \frac{(L+1)}{2(M-1)}T = L\lambda P_M T\frac{(L+1)}{2}$$

ii) L → M → G → M → L messages from all $(N/L)-1$ other local rings; and, arguing as in i), over T the number of links used by these messages are:

$$B1 = \sum^{N/L-1} L\lambda(1-P_M-P_L)\frac{(L+1)}{2(N/L-1)}T$$

$$= L\lambda(1-P_M-P_L)T\frac{(L+1)}{2}$$

But there are $(L+1)T$ links available over T. Therefore, combining link usage from Q_i traffic with $A1$ and $B1$, we have

$$U_L = L\lambda T\frac{L+1}{2} + \frac{A1+B1}{(L+1)T} = \frac{L\lambda(2-P_L)}{2} \quad (6)$$

Note that

$$\lambda_{Q_{M-L}} = \lambda_{Q_{L-M}} = L\lambda(1-P_L) \quad (7)$$

U_M: There are two sources of traffic going onto each intermediate ring: (1) Up from all M local rings attached to it, through each Q_{L-M}, and (2) Down from the global ring, through Q_{G-M}. Since both L → M → L and L → M → G → M → L traffic classes use $(M+1)/2$ links, the number of links used by the first traffic source (1) over T is:

$$A2 = LM\lambda[P_M + (1-P_M-P_L)]T\frac{(M+1)}{2}$$

$$= LM\lambda(1-P_L)T\frac{(M+1)}{2}$$

The second traffic source is the L → M → G → M → L traffic from other intermediate rings; there are $G-1$ of them, and each one sends $1/(G-1)$ of its global traffic to each other intermediate ring. Each such message uses $(M-1)/2$ links. Hence, over T the number of links used by the second traffic source (2) is:

$$B2 = \sum^{G-1} LM\lambda(1-P_M-P_L)\frac{(M+1)}{2}\frac{1}{(G-1)}T$$

$$= LM\lambda T(1-P_M-P_L)\frac{(M+1)}{2}$$

But there are $(M+1)T$ links available over T. Therefore, combining $A2$ and $B2$ we have:

$$U_M = \frac{A2+B2}{(M+1)T} = \frac{LM\lambda}{2}(2-2P_L-P_M) \quad (8)$$

Also note that

$$\lambda_{Q_{L-M}} = \lambda_{Q_{M-L}} = L\lambda(1-P_L) \quad \text{and} \quad (9)$$

$$\lambda_{Q_{G-M}} = \lambda_{Q_{M-G}} = LM\lambda(1-P_M-P_L) \quad (10)$$

U_G: Over T there are $N\lambda(1-P_M-P_L)T$ L → M → G → M → L messages, each of which uses $G/2$ links; but GT links are available, thus

$$U_G = \frac{N\lambda(1-P_L-P_M)}{2} \quad (11)$$

3.6 Derivation of Average Queue Lengths

Now, we need average queue lengths, $\overline{Q}$, everywhere, for both H2 and H3 systems.

H2:

$\overline{Q}_i$: Waiting (queueing) time at a local station, before getting into the ring link "server" (see Figure 2) will be zero if the upstream link buffer is empty at the time the packet arrives at the head of the line (HOL) position. Service in the first link traversed is counted in the U_L part of the $\overline{n}$ expression in 1, because technically, as soon as the HOL entry starts to get service in the first link, it can be considered that it has been dropped into the empty upstream link buffer.

If p is the probability that a slot is full AND continuing past the current point, then waiting time for the HOL message is:

$$s \triangleq \sum_{j=1}^{\infty} p^j(1-p)j = \frac{p}{1-p}$$

Now, applying Little's Law we get $\overline{Q}_i = W\lambda$, where W is the average waiting time in queue. When a new message arrives, it must wait s time units for each item ahead of it, and then wait s more units. Because of the memoryless property of the stochastic process, we have $W = s + s\overline{Q}_i$. Therefore

$$\overline{Q}_i = (s + s\overline{Q}_i)\lambda$$

$$\overline{Q}_i = \frac{s\lambda}{1 - s\lambda}, \text{ for } s = \frac{p}{1-p} \quad (12)$$

Now, $p = U_L \frac{L-(1+P)}{L}$, where P is locality. This expression for p takes into account the fact that a released slot at either a local station or a inter-ring switch is allowed to be used immediately. Substituting this expression of p into 12, we have

$$\overline{Q}_i = \frac{U_L(L-1-P)\lambda}{L - U_L(L-1-P)(1+\lambda)} \quad (13)$$

$\overline{Q}_{L-G(i)}$: Similar to local station queue Q_i, the average queue length of the inter-ring switch is:

$$\overline{Q}_{L-G(i)} = \frac{s_x \lambda_{L-G}}{1 - s_x \lambda_{L-G}} \quad (14)$$

Where $s_x = 1 + \frac{p}{1-p} = \frac{1}{1-p}$. This modification to s is needed for the following reason. One extra unit must be added to the waiting time of every message crossing between rings to denote the step into $Q_{L-G(i)}$ from the adjacent ring link buffer (because it is not accounted for in either U_L or U_G).

Similar to the Q_i discussion, $p = U_G \frac{N/L-2}{N/L}$ and substituting in 14, we have

$$\overline{Q}_{L-G(i)} = \frac{N\lambda_{L-G}}{N(1 - \lambda_{L-G}) - U_G(N - 2L)} \quad (15)$$

$\overline{Q}_{G-L(i)}$: We have $p = PL\lambda/2$ because the only traffic continuing on the local ring through the interface switch is local traffic, leading to

$$\overline{Q}_{G-L(i)} = \frac{2\lambda_{G-L}}{2 - PL\lambda - 2\lambda_{G-L}} \quad (16)$$

H3: Message destination localities are given in terms of the probabilities P_L, P_M, and P_G, where $P_G = 1 - P_L - P_M$. In terms of these probabilities, and using reasoning similar to that used for H2 systems, the resulting average queue lengths in H3 systems are:

$$\overline{Q}_i = \frac{U_L(L-1-P_L)\lambda}{L - U_L(L-1-P_L)(1+\lambda)} \quad (17)$$

$$\overline{Q}_{L-M(i)} = \frac{\lambda_{Q_{L-M}}}{1 - U_M \frac{M-1-\frac{P_M}{P_M+P_G}}{M} - \lambda_{Q_{L-M}}} \quad (18)$$

$$\overline{Q}_{M-L(i)} = \frac{2\lambda_{Q_{M-L}}}{2 - P_L L\lambda - 2\lambda_{Q_{M-L}}} \quad (19)$$

$$\overline{Q}_{M-G(i)} = \frac{\lambda_{Q_{M-G}}}{1 - U_G(G-2)/G - \lambda_{Q_{M-G}}} \quad (20)$$

$$\overline{Q}_{G-M(i)} = \frac{\lambda_{Q_{G-M}}}{1 - LM\lambda P_M/2 - \lambda_{Q_{G-M}}} \quad (21)$$

3.7 Expected Message Delay

The expressions for ring utilizations and average queue lengths, developed in Sections 3.5 and 3.6, can now be used in the general model, described in Section 3.4, to derive expressions for the expected message delay in both the 2-level and 3-level ring structures.

Substituting from expressions 3 and 4 for U_L and U_G, from expressions 13, 15, and 16 for average queue lengths, and from the expression 5 for message rates λ_{G-L} and λ_{L-G}, into expression 1 for expected message delay T_{H2}, and performing a number of algebraic rearrangements and simplifications of terms, leads to:

$$T_{H2} = T_1 + PT_2 + (1-P)(T_3 + T_4 + T_5) + 1 \quad (22)$$

where $T_1 = \frac{X}{1 - X(1+\lambda)}$, for $X = (\lambda/2)(2-P)(L-1-P)$, $T_2 = \frac{L+1}{2}$, $T_3 = \frac{1}{1-N\lambda(1-P)/2}$, $T_4 = \frac{1}{1-L\lambda(2-P)/2}$, and $T_5 = (L+1) + \frac{G}{2}$.

In this form, T_1 represents average waiting time in the local (source) station interface queue, Q_i; T_2 represents average path length for a local message; T_3 represents average waiting time in $Q_{L-G(i)}$ for a remote message moving up from a (source) local ring to the global ring; T_4 represents average waiting time in $Q_{G-L(i)}$ for a remote message moving down from the global ring to a (destination) local ring; and T_5 represents average path length for a remote message. The final "1" term in the T_{H2} expression 22 represents the time step needed to move a message from the ring buffer at the destination station into the station interface, as indicated in Figure 2. (This term was not accounted for in the earlier expression 1 for T_{H2}.)

A similar sequence of substitutions (using expressions 6, 8, and 11 for ring utilizations, expressions 17, 18, 19, 20, and 21 for average queue lengths, and expressions 7, 9, and 10 for message rates at crossovers) and algebraic rearrangements and simplifications can be used to derive the following expression for expected message delay in 3-level ring structures. The final result is:

$$T_{H3} = T_6 + P_L T_7 + P_M(T_8 + T_9 + T_{10}) + P_G(T_8 + T_9 + T_{11} + T_{12} + T_{13}) + 1 \quad (23)$$

where $T_6 = \frac{Y}{1-Y(1+\lambda)}$, for $Y = \frac{\lambda}{2}(2 - P_L)(L - 1 - P_L)$, $T_7 = \frac{L+1}{2}$,

$$T_8 = \frac{1}{1 - [\frac{L\lambda}{2}(2P_G + P_M)(M - 1 - \frac{P_M}{P_M+P_G}) + L\lambda(P_M + P_G)]},$$

$T_9 = \frac{1}{1-L\lambda(2-P_L)/2}$, $T_{10} = (L + 1) + \frac{M+1}{2}$, $T_{11} = \frac{1}{1-N\lambda P_G/2}$, $T_{12} = \frac{1}{1-LM\lambda(2P_G+P_M)/2}$, and $T_{13} = (L + 1) + (M + 1) + G/2$.

As with the T_{H2} expression 22, each of the terms in 23 for T_{H3} has an interpretation that is directly related to the network. Briefly, T_6 represents local station queueing delay; T_7, T_{10}, and T_{13} represent path lengths for local, intermediate, and global messages, respectively; T_8 and T_9 represent the up-queue and down-queue delays in switches between local ring and intermediate rings; and T_{11} and T_{12} represent up and down queueing delays between intermediate rings and the global ring.

4 Validation of the Analytical Models via Simulations

In this section we validate our analytical model through extensive simulations. In the simulation study, reported in [8], an event-driven simulator was used to study 2-level and 3-level hierarchical ring systems. All the simulation results presented here have very small 95% confidence intervals and so these intervals are not shown.

In Figure 4, results for an H2 system are plotted to show expected packet delay as a function of λ and locality. Since the global ring saturates faster than any other ring in the system, we also included its utilization. We were not able to compare the case of $P = 0.2$ and $\lambda > 0.004$ because the system entered saturation soon after that point. Nevertheless, it is clear from the figure that our model is very accurate with the exception of two points where errors of 7% and 14% occur at global utilizations of 80% and 90%, respectively. This discrepancy can be explained as a result of our model's inability to capture the "train effects" (see Section 3.2) at the near-saturated global ring conditions.

Figure 5 shows a comparison between our model and the simulations for an H3 system. Consistent with the case of H2, our model agrees very well with the simulation. In fact, the agreement in this case is better

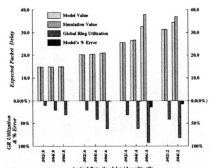

Figure 4: Comparison between the Model and Simulation for an H2 system where $N = 512$ and $L = 16$; that is, 32 local rings with 16 stations each.

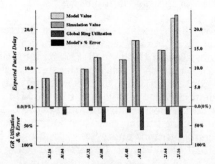

Figure 5: Comparison between the Model and Simulation for an H3 system where $N = 504$, $L = 7$, $M = 6$, $G = 12$ and $\lambda = 0.005$.

than H2. The improved accuracy may be viewed as a result of the "diluting" effect of the 3-level rings that alleviates the "train effects", thus making our model more accurate.

Our final comparison between model and simulation is shown in Figure 6, again revealing very good agreement except at high global ring utilization levels.

The more important point brought out by Figure 6, however, relates to the relationship between average message delay performance and network configuration at different traffic levels. Consider the following. Assume a distribution of message packet destinations that is characterized by the application, not related to network configuration. For example, in the uniform distribution, all processor nodes are equally likely as destination of a message packet. This presents the most demanding case for any multiprocessor network. There is no locality that can be exploited.

Figure 6 shows such a case. N is close to 400 for all three configurations. As the configurations (L, M, G) vary, P_L, P_M, and P_G, must also vary to properly reflect a uniform message destination distribution.

The figure reveals that for light traffic ($\lambda = 0.001$), the $(L, M, G) = (6, 6, 11)$ configuration provides a lower average message delay than the $(10, 10, 4)$ configuration; while for heavy traffic ($\lambda = 0.005$, and global ring utilizations upwards of 75%), the opposite is true. In general, we have shown earlier [6] that the configuration leading to the lowest maximum distance be-

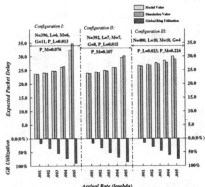

Figure 6: Comparison between the Model and Simulation for three H3 configurations, with a uniform distribution of message destinations.

tween any pair of nodes (the minimum diameter network) has L, M, and G sizes in proportions $1:1:2$. This is consistent with the $(6,6,11)$ configuration having the lowest average delay in the light traffic (and thus low contention) case. Correspondingly, in [12] an independent detailed simulation study of H3 systems showed that the best configurations for the heavy uniform traffic case (under their method for developing feasible configurations under heavy traffic) all had relatively small global rings. In particular, they derived $(L,M,G) = (6,3,3)$ for a particular $N = 54$ network, and $(12,3,3)$ for an $N = 108$ network. This tendency is qualitatively similar to our result that $(10,10,4)$ is better than $(6,6,11)$ for the heavy traffic case.

We will expand on this use of the model in configuration design in the next section.

5 Optimal Configurations

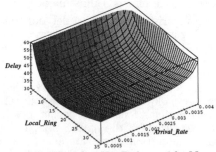

Figure 7: 3-D Plot for H2 Delay with $N = 500$ and Uniform Message Destination Distributions

One very important issue in the design of hierarchical-ring systems is that of configuration. Our analytical model can predict expected packet delay accurately. It can now be used to answer the logical question: What is the best configuration for the hierarchical-ring network to minimize the average delay, given a particular application-based traffic pattern and system size? A quick answer to this question can be very helpful in enabling the system architect/designer to make sensible design decisions. The answer to the question may be found by deriving optimal values for L in H2, and L and M in H3, that minimize T_{H2} and T_{H3}, respectively.

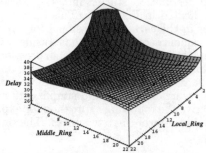

Figure 8: 3-D Plot for H3 Delay with $N = 500$, $\lambda = 0.002$ and Uniform Message Destination Distributions

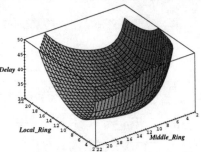

Figure 9: 3-D Plot for H3 Delay with $N = 500$, $\lambda = 0.004$ and Uniform Message Destination Distributions

The expressions for T_{H2} and T_{H3} are closed form functions of N, L, M, and traffic, which is uniquely defined by values of λ and locality (P, P_L, and P_M). Therefore, if one has some knowledge of the density (λ) and pattern (locality) of the traffic which the future system will likely be subject to, then for a given system size (N) it is possible to find values of L (for H2) and L and M (for H3) that minimize T_{H2} and T_{H3}, respectively, for given values of λ and application-based traffic locality. In this section, we show how expressions 22 and 23 can be used to find optimal values of L and M. All 3-D plots in this section were generated using the Maple-V software [2]. The design optimization question, as we have posed it, only makes sense if we are able to show how the physical network locality parameters P_L, P_M, and P_G ($= 1 - P_L - P_M$), are functionally related to N, L, M, and $G = N/LM$, for a given application-based locality specification. As an example, we will deal with the uniform message destination case here. This is simply the case in which all other $N - 1$ nodes are equally likely as message destinations from any particular source node. This traffic distribution is reflected in the following functional relationships: In H2, $P = (L-1)/(N-1)$; and in H3, $P_L = (L-1)/(N-1)$, $P_M = (M-1)L/(N-1)$, and $P_G = 1 - P_L - P_M = (G-1)LM/(N-1)$. These substitutions are made in T_{H2} and T_{H3} before plotting the Maple-V surfaces.

Figure 7 shows a 3-D plot of T_{H2} as a function of L and λ while the traffic pattern is uniform and $N = 500$. In this figure, traffic density λ ranges from 0.0005, representing light traffic, to 0.004, representing the heavier traffic. As can be seen in the figure, there is an optimum of L for each λ value. For light traffic, L

is optimal near 16, shifting to larger values as λ increases.

In Figures 8 and 9 we plot T_{H3} as a function of L and M for $\lambda = 0.002$ and $\lambda = 0.004$, respectively, while keeping the traffic pattern uniform and $N = 500$. As expected, for each λ value there is a pair of optimal L and M values. In fact, for $\lambda = 0.002$ the optimal values for L and M are 6 and 7, respectively; whereas for $\lambda = 0.004$ values of 9 and 10 for L and M, respectively, minimize T_{H3}.

6 Concluding Remarks

Network configuration, that is, appropriate choices for the size of local, intermediate, and global rings, can be quickly and easily estimated by using the queueing models developed here, without resorting to time-consuming simulations, assuming that minimizing average message delay is the important criterion. We gave an example of such a design study in the previous section. As we noted, network optimization is only meaningful relative to a specified traffic intensity and message destination distribution that is determined by the application. In Section 5 we used a uniform distribution, which is easy to incorporate into the model. For more general application-based distributions, such as those described in [7], we have shown in [8] how to incorporate them into a simple model that is, however, only valid for very light traffic (no significant contention at crossover switches). We are currently incorporating the general distribution specifications into the queueing models, enabling wider use of the models in design evaluations.

References

[1] L. N. Bhuyan, D. Ghosal, and Q. Yang. Approximate analysis of single and multiple ring networks. *IEEE Transactions on Computers*, C-38(7):1022–1040, July 1989.

[2] B.W. Char, K.O. Geddes, G.H. Gonnet, B.L. Leong, M.B. Monagan, and S.M. Watt. *Maple V Language Reference Manual*. Spring-Verlag and Waterloo Maple Publishing, 1991.

[3] D. R. Cheriton, H. A. Goosen, and P. D. Boyle. Paradigm: A highly scalable shared- memory multicomputer architecture. *Computer*, 24(2):33–46, February 1991.

[4] T. H. Dunigan. Multi-ring performance of the kendall square multiprocessor. *Oak Ridge National Laboratory Report TM-12331*, October 1994.

[5] K. Farkas, Z. Vranesic, and M. Stumm. Scalable cache consistency for hierarchically structured multiprocessors. *The Journal of Supercomputing*, 8:345–369, June 1995.

[6] V. C. Hamacher and H. Jiang. Comparison of mesh and hierarchical networks for multiprocessors. *Proceedings of 1994 International Conference on Parallel Processing*, I:67–71, August 1994.

[7] M. Holliday and M. Stumm. Performance evaluation of hierarchical ring-based shared memory multiprocessors. *IEEE Transactions on Computers*, C-43(1):52–67, January 1994.

[8] H. Jiang, C. Lam, and V.C. Hamacher. On some architectural issues of optical hierarchical ring networks for shared-memory multiprocessors. *Proceedings of The Second International Conference on Massively Parallel Processing Using Optical Interconnections (MPPOI)*, pages 345–353, October 23-24 1995.

[9] P. J. B. King and I. Mitrani. Modeling a slotted ring local area network. *IEEE Transactions on Computers*, C-36(5):554–561, May 1987.

[10] C. Lam, H. Jiang, and V. C. Hamacher. Design and analysis of hierarchical ring networks for multiprocessors. *Proceedings of 1995 International Conference on Parallel Processing*, I:46–50, August 14-19 1995.

[11] W. M. Loucks, V. C. Hamacher, B. R. Preiss, and L. Wong. Short-packet transfer performance on local area ring networks. *IEEE Transactions on Computers*, C-34(11):1006–1014, November 1985.

[12] G. Ravindran and M. Stumm. A performance comparison of hierarchical ring- and mesh-connected multiprocessor networks. *Proceedings of 1997 International Symposium on High Performance Computer Architecture*, pages 58–69, February 1997.

[13] T.D. Todd and A.M. Bignell. Performance modeling of the SIGnet MAN backbone. *Proc. IEEE INFOCOM'90*, 1:192–199, June 1990.

[14] Z. Vranesic, S. Brown, and M. Stumm. The NUMAchine Multiprocessor. *Technical Report, Department of Electrical and Computer Engineering, University of Toronto*, June 1995.

[15] Z. G. Vranesic, M. Stumm, D. M. Lewis, and R. White. Hector: A hierarchically structured shared-memory multiprocessor. *IEEE Computer*, 24(1):72–79, January 1991.

[16] A. W. Wilson. Hierarchical cache/bus architecture for shared memory multiprocessors. In *Proceedings of the 14th Annual International Symposium on Computer Architecture*, page 1987, 1987.

[17] X. Zhang and Y. Yan. Comparative modeling and evaluation of CC-NUMA and COMA on hierarchical ring architectures. *IEEE Transactions on Parallel and Distributed Systems*, 6:1316–1331, December 1995.

An Effective Memory–Processor Integrated Architecture for Computer Vision

Youngsik Kim, Tack–Don Han, Shin–Dug Kim, and Sung–Bong Yang
Dept. of Computer Science, Yonsei University,
Seoul, 120-749, Korea.
{yskim,hantack,sdkim,yang}@kurene.yonsei.ac.kr

Abstract

In this paper an effective memory–processor integrated architecture, called memory_based processor array (MPA), for computer vision is proposed. The MPA can be easily attached into any host system via memory interface. In order to measure the impact of the memory interface structure an analytical model is derived. The performance improvement on the proposed model for the memory interface architecture of the MPA system can be 6% ∼ 40% for vision tasks consisting of sequential and data parallel tasks. The asymptotic time complexities of the mapping algorithms are evaluated to verify the cost–effectiveness and the efficiency of the MPA system.

1 Introduction

Because the current memory technology can support the gigabit DRAMs, a single memory chip would cover the memory volume needed for the computer systems in the future. A number of studies for the memory–logic integration have utilized both high internal memory bandwidth and the available chip density [1, 2, 3, 4, 5, 6]

In this paper an effective memory–processor integrated architecture, called memory_based processor array (MPA), for computer vision is proposed. It is an effective SIMD array which is based on the memory–processor integration structure. Thus, it can be easily attached into any host system from a personal computer to a multiprocessor. It can be considered as a portion of the single linear address space given for the host system. The MPA approach is to design a hybrid system that can be performed selectively for different levels of processing steps in vision tasks cost–effectively.

Especially, a couple of machine architectures for both the low level vision tasks and the intermediate to high level vision tasks are chosen as the MPA and the host system, respectively. These are integrated into a single machine tightly coupled via a single system bus. The low level and data parallel processing steps are executed by the MPA and the intermediate to high level processing steps with complex or sequential processing can be executed by the host system selectively. Furthermore any interaction by the program and the shared data between the host system and the MPA can be resolved by means of simple memory reads and

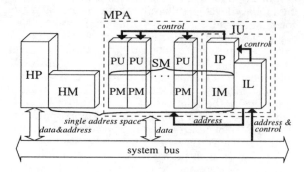

Figure 1: The MPA system architecture.

writes. In this paper, parallel algorithms for thresholding by the best threshold (TBT) mapped onto the MPA are presented and the asymptotic time complexities of the algorithms are estimated with the big–oh notation. Also, the MPA system shows a significant performance improvement, illustrated with the proposed analytical model for the impact of the memory interface structure.

2 The MPA System

In this section, the MPA system architecture is described. An effective interfacing mechanism with any host system is specified as the basic building block of a complete system construction.

2.1 The Structure and Configuration

In the memory–processor integrated array approach, a complete MPA system structure consists of a host processor (HP), the HP memory module (HM), a system bus, and an MPA as shown in Figure 1. The MPA can be configured as the two different operational modes, i.e., simply as the memory and as the SIMD array.

In the MPA, a set of m PMs forms a pool of two-dimensional memory cells as shown in Figure 2. When the MPA system is used simply as for memory, the top and local decoders in Figure 2 can be operated as the conventional memory decoder and the HP can access every memory cell by the conventional memory row and column addresses. Each PU is constructed as an ALU including an adder and a shifter, a set of registers, and two bidirectional links to its immediate left and right neighboring PUs.

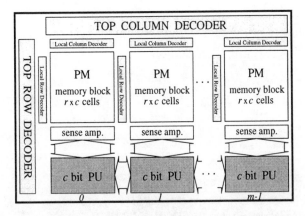

Figure 2: A memory_based processor array chip.

For algorithm mapping examples, the following variables are defined to explain the configuration of the complete MPA system.

- $N \times N$: the number of the pixels with G gray level intensities in the input image array $I[0..N-1, 0..N-1]$. Notice that $I[0,0]$ is in the topmost left corner of the image array.

- m : the number of PMs and the number of PUs for an MPA chip.

- P : the number of PUs for the MPA system. P is a power of two. The single– or multi–chip MPA system can perform any processing given to a single image and each PU can perform any operation assigned to an image pixel column. If $(m < N)$, the MPA system can be constructed by using the $\lceil \frac{N}{m} \rceil$ MPA chips. Therefore, $P = m\lceil \frac{N}{m} \rceil$ and $N \le P \le N^2$.

- $r \times c$: the number of memory cells for each PM, where r and c are defined as the numbers of memory cell rows and columns, respectively. Thus an MPA chip should have the entire $m \cdot r \cdot c$ memory cells and the number of memory cell columns for a PM should be formed as the width of a data path for a PU.

2.2 A Model for the Memory Interface

In the conventional SIMD systems or in the complete MPA system, any specific application program can be divided into a set of data parallel code blocks ($\mathcal{A}$) to be executed by the SIMD system or the MPA system and a set of non–data parallel code blocks ($\mathcal{B}$) such as sequential code or medium to coarse grain parallel code blocks to be executed by the host system.

In order to evaluate the performance of the SIMD system more precisely, a performance model must consider not only the computation and communication time τ^S on the SIMD array system, but also the execution time τ^H by the host system, and the time τ^T to send or receive the program and the shared data between the host system and the SIMD machine. Therefore, the overall time τ required to execute any application program by the complete SIMD system can be defined as

$$\tau = \tau^H + \tau^S + \tau^T. \tag{1}$$

A model describing the impact of the memory interface can be derived from the operational model for the MPA system. Thus, the following variables are defined to develop this analytical model.

Definitions

The code and data blocks need to be defined to represent the size of code and the amount of data. Conceptually, the size in time corresponds to the amount of the time to execute any code block, divided by the execution time of a unit instruction.

- $|\mathcal{A}'|$: the number of bytes in data parallel code blocks of high level instruction words.

- $|\mathcal{A}|$ and $|\mathcal{B}|$: the number of machine instructions required to execute the data parallel code blocks and the non–data parallel code blocks, respectively.

- $|\mathcal{A}^{\mathcal{D}}|$ and $|\mathcal{B}^{\mathcal{D}}|$: the number of bytes in the data needed in the $\mathcal{A}$ code blocks and the $\mathcal{B}$ code blocks, respectively.

- $|\mathcal{A}^{\mathcal{D}} \cap \mathcal{B}^{\mathcal{D}}|$: the number of bytes in the shared data between $\mathcal{A}^{\mathcal{D}}$ and $\mathcal{B}^{\mathcal{D}}$.

A set of system parameters is defined as follows.

- T_{ex}^S : the time that a PU for both the conventional SIMD array and the MPA executes a basic operation. It is assumed that the PU executes complex operations such as multiplication and division in multiples of T_{ex}^S, i.e., $8T_{ex}^S$ and $16T_{ex}^S$, respectively.

- T_{ex}^H: the time that the HP executes a basic arithmetic or logic operation. The time for the complex operation is assumed to be a multiple of T_{ex}^H. In this research, it is also assumed that the floating point unit (FPU) in the HP executes the 32–bit floating point number addition, multiplication, and division in $3T_{ex}^H$, $4T_{ex}^H$, and $16T_{ex}^H$, respectively, by the pipelining and radix–4 SRT divider.

- T_{tr}: the time to send or receive a unit of data (one byte) between the host system and the SIMD system only for the conventional SIMD systems.

Each of T_{ex}^S for each PU, T_{ex}^H for the HP, T_{tr} cannot exceed $O(1)$. However, in order to evaluate the analytical model the ratio of T_{ex}^H to T_{ex}^S and the ratio of T_{tr} to T_{ex}^S are defined as r_1 and r_2, respectively.

To show how effective the interaction mechanism between the HP and the MPA is, two timing parameters, the T_{ex}^S and T_{ex}^H of the MPA system are assumed to be equal to those of the conventional SIMD system, respectively. Parallel execution time τ^{C-SIMD} by the conventional SIMD systems for any pair of code blocks, i.e., $\mathcal{A}$ and $\mathcal{B}$ can be obtained as

$$\tau^{C-SIMD} = \overbrace{|\mathcal{B}|T_{ex}^H}^{\tau^H} + \overbrace{|\mathcal{A}|T_{ex}^S}^{\tau^S} + \overbrace{\left(|\mathcal{A}'| + |\mathcal{A}^{\mathcal{D}} \cap \mathcal{B}^{\mathcal{D}}|\right)T_{tr}}^{\tau^T}, \tag{2}$$

where $|\mathcal{A}^{\mathcal{D}} \cap \mathcal{B}^{\mathcal{D}}|$ is a portion of $\mathcal{A}^{\mathcal{D}}$ for the host system and a portion of $\mathcal{B}^{\mathcal{D}}$ for the SIMD array. Parallel execution time τ^{MPA} by the MPA system for any pair of $\mathcal{A}$ and $\mathcal{B}$ can be represented as

$$\tau^{MPA} = \overbrace{|\mathcal{B}|T_{ex}^H}^{\tau^H} + \overbrace{|\mathcal{A}|T_{ex}^S}^{\tau^S}. \qquad (3)$$

By the impact of the memory interface, the performance improvement (PI) of the MPA system comparing with the conventional SIMD systems can be specified as

$$
\begin{aligned}
PI &= \frac{\tau^{C-SIMD} - \tau^{MPA}}{\tau^{C-SIMD}} \times 100 \\
&= \frac{\left(|\mathcal{A}'| + |\mathcal{A}^{\mathcal{D}} \cap \mathcal{B}^{\mathcal{D}}|\right) T_{tr}}{|\mathcal{B}|T_{ex}^H + |\mathcal{A}|T_{ex}^S + \left(|\mathcal{A}'| + |\mathcal{A}^{\mathcal{D}} \cap \mathcal{B}^{\mathcal{D}}|\right) T_{tr}} \times 100 \\
&= \frac{\left(|\mathcal{A}'| + |\mathcal{A}^{\mathcal{D}} \cap \mathcal{B}^{\mathcal{D}}|\right) r_2}{|\mathcal{B}|r_1 + |\mathcal{A}| + \left(|\mathcal{A}'| + |\mathcal{A}^{\mathcal{D}} \cap \mathcal{B}^{\mathcal{D}}|\right) r_2} \times 100. \qquad (4)
\end{aligned}
$$

The performance improvement on the impact of the memory interface is exemplified by considering a mixed set of vision tasks consisting of parallel and sequential tasks in Section 3.2 later.

3 Low Level Computer Vision Tasks

To clarify the impact of the memory interface structure, a detailed discussion of a vision task, called *thresholding by the best threshold* (TBT) [7], is presented.

Some of the assumptions made for the applications are first described. Each PU can process $N \times 1$ partitioned subimage. In the striped partitioning, the image pixels are divided into groups of complete columns, each MPA chip module is assigned for one such group, and each PU is assigned for the pixels of a column.

TBT considered in this paper is composed of a couple of parallel tasks and a sequential task. The parallel tasks are histogramming and thresholding required to be executed by the MPA and the sequential task is to find the best threshold required to be executed by the HP. Algorithm 2 of Figure 3 to execute TBT on the MPA system calls sequentially three procedures, *Histogramming-MPA*, *Finding-Best-Threshold-HP*, and *Thresholding-MPA*.

Histogramming, which is not a window processing, is a time consuming task. The procedure, *Histogramming-MPA*, represented in data parallel codes is shown in lines 4~16. *Histogramming-MPA* is based on the algorithm presented in [9]. Specifically, the number $\tau_{MPA}^{histogram}$ of computation steps to execute histogramming by the MPA system with P PUs, $P = N$, is obtained as

$$
\begin{aligned}
&\tau_{MPA}^{histogram} \\
&= N \left\{ \overbrace{T_{ex}^S}^{memory} + \overbrace{16T_{ex}^S}^{divide} + N \left(\overbrace{T_{ex}^S}^{compare} + \overbrace{T_{ex}^S}^{add} + \overbrace{T_{ex}^S}^{comm.} \right) \right\} \\
&= O(N^2). \qquad (5)
\end{aligned}
$$

The procedure *Finding-Best-Threshold-HP* is a sequential order of calculations followed by the computation of the best threshold (BT) executed by the HP

Algorithm 2. Thresholding by the Best Threshold
Input: Image Pixels $I[0..N-1, 0..N-1]$.
Output: Image Pixels $O[0..N-1, 0..N-1]$.

```
1    Histogramming-MPA (I);
2    Finding-Best-Threshold-HP (R);
3    Thresholding-MPA (I, BT);

4    procedure Histogramming-MPA
     Input: Image Pixels I[0..N-1, 0..N-1].
     Output: Histogram Probabilities R[1..G].
5    for all 0 ≤ c ≤ P - 1 do
6    parbegin
7      for r = 0 to N - 1 do
8        • PU[c] reads I[r, c];
9        for i = 0 to N - 1 do
10         if c = I[r, c - i] then PU[c] computes R[c] + +;
11         • PU[c] shifts right I[r, c - i] to PU[c + 1];
12       endfor {line 9 for }
13     endfor {line 7 for }
14     • PU[c] computes R[c] = R[c]/N²;
15   parend {line 6 parbegin}
16   endprocedure {Histogramming-MPA}

17   procedure Finding-Best-Threshold-HP
     Input: Histogram Probabilities R[1..G].
     Output: Best Threshold BT.
18   • Calculate the total mean μ = Σ(i=1 to G) R[i]/G.
19   • Initial condition: when BT = t = 0,
       q₁[0] = 0, q₂[0] = 1, μ₁[0] = 0, μ₂[0] = μ, and σ²_B[0] = 0.
20   for t = 1 to G do
21     • q₁[t] is obtained by q₁[t] = q₁[t - 1] + R[t].
22     • μ₁[t] is obtained by μ₁[t] = (q₁[t - 1]μ₁[t - 1] + tR[t])/q₁[t].
23     • μ₂[t] is obtained by μ₂[t] = (μ - q₁[t]μ₁[t])/(1 - q₁[t]).
24     • σ²_B[t] is obtained.
25     • Find the best threshold, BT, maximizing σ²_B[t].
         if σ²_B[t] > σ²_B[BT] then BT = t;
26   endfor {line 20 for}
27   endprocedure {Finding-Best-Threshold-HP}

28   procedure Thresholding-MPA
     Input: Image Pixels I[0..N-1, 0..N-1], Best Threshold BT.
     Output: Image Pixels O[0..N-1, 0..N-1].
29   for r = 0 to N - 1 do
30     for all 0 ≤ c ≤ P - 1 do
31     parbegin
32       • PU[c] reads I[r, c];
33       if Threshold ≤ I[r, c] then O[r, c] = 0
34       else O[r, c] = 1;
35     parend {line 31 parbegin}
36   endfor {line 29 for}
37   endprocedure {Thresholding-MPA}
```

Figure 3: An algorithm for TBT implemented on the MPA system.

as in lines 17~27 of Figure 3. Finding the BT in this procedure is based on Otsu's algorithm [8]. Let $R[1], ..., R[G]$ represent the histogram probabilities of the observed gray values $1, ..., G$, respectively. Here, the BT is the threshold which is chosen in such a way that the weighted sum of the group variances should be minimized.

Therefore, the number τ_{HP}^{FBT} of computation steps in finding the BT on the HP is obtained as

$$
\begin{aligned}
\tau_{HP}^{FBT} &= \overbrace{(7G-1)3T_{ex}^H}^{FP\_add} + \overbrace{(6G)4T_{ex}^H}^{FP\_multiply} + \overbrace{(2G+1)16T_{ex}^H}^{FP\_divide} \\
&\quad + \overbrace{7T_{ex}^H}^{assign} + \overbrace{GT_{ex}^H}^{compare} = O(G). \qquad (6)
\end{aligned}
$$

To perform the thresholding for the MPA system, a parallel algorithm in a pseudo code is shown in lines 28~37. Therefore, the number $\tau_{MPA}^{threshold}$ of computa-

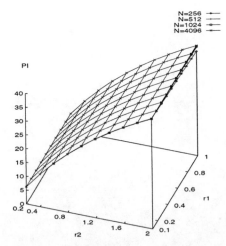

Figure 4: The performance improvement as r_1, r_2, and N vary.

tion steps to execute thresholding on the MPA system with P PUs, $P = N$, is obtained as

$$\tau_{MPA}^{threshold} = N \left(\overbrace{T_{ex}^S}^{memory} + \overbrace{T_{ex}^S}^{compare} + \overbrace{T_{ex}^S}^{assign} \right) = O(N). \quad (7)$$

The MPA system could gain the performance improvement from the effect of the memory interface structure over the conventional back–end interfacing system for SIMD system configuration. The original image data (N^2) and the histogram data ($G\lceil \frac{\log_2 N^2}{8} \rceil = O(G \log_2 N)$) are shared between the HP and the SIMD system. Thus the ratio of the shared data to all the data is about 50 % for any N from 256 to 4096, since the ratio is $\frac{|\mathcal{A}^{\mathcal{D}} \cap \mathcal{B}^{\mathcal{D}}|}{|\mathcal{A}^{\mathcal{D}}| + |\mathcal{B}^{\mathcal{D}}|}$ which can be reduced to $\frac{N^2 + G\lceil \frac{\log_2 N^2}{8} \rceil}{2N^2 + G\lceil \frac{\log_2 N^2}{8} \rceil}$. In the conventional SIMD systems environment, the SIMD array needs the additional time to fetch the original image data from the host system. Also, the host system needs the additional $G\lceil \frac{\log_2 N^2}{8} \rceil$ data transfer time before executing of the procedure *Finding-Best-Threshold-HP*. However, the HP of the MPA system needs not transfer the shared data to the local memory because MPA system can be operated as a passive memory structure.

The execution times, τ^{C-SIMD} and τ^{MPA}, of TBT in Algorithm 2 by the conventional SIMD system and the MPA system can be calculated as following components.

$$\tau^H = \tau_{HP}^{FBT}, \quad (8)$$

$$\tau^A = \tau_{MPA}^{histogram} + \tau_{MPA}^{threshold}, \quad (9)$$

and $$\tau^T = \left(|\mathcal{A}'| + N^2 + G\lceil \frac{\log_2 N^2}{8} \rceil \right) T_{tr}. (10)$$

Since $|\mathcal{A}'|$ is very small, it can be ignored in the calculation. Thus, the performance improvement from

the memory interface structure for Algorithm 2 can be expressed using equations (8), (9), and (10) as

$$PI = \frac{\tau^{C-SIMD} - \tau^{MPA}}{\tau^{C-SIMD}} \times 100 = \frac{\tau^T}{\tau^H + \tau^S + \tau^T} \times 100$$

$$= \frac{\left(N^2 + G\lceil \frac{\log_2 N^2}{8} \rceil \right) r_2 \times 100}{N(3N + 20) + (78G + 20)r_1 + \left(N^2 + G\lceil \frac{\log_2 N^2}{8} \rceil \right) r_2}. (11)$$

Figure 4 shows that PI rises drastically as r_2 increases from 0.2 to 2.0 and PI rises very slowly as r_1 decreases from 1.0 to 0.1 while N increases from 256 to 4096. Thus for a given problem PI is dominated by r_2 which can emphasize the additional transfer time of the shared data only for the conventional SIMD system. The performance improvement according to the memory interface architecture of the MPA system can be 6% $\sim$ 40% while N varies from 256 to 4096. Thus, the MPA system can achieve a performance gain from the memory interface structure in performing a conventional program composed of a mixed set of code blocks.

4 Conclusions

The MPA system is to design a hybrid parallel system that can perform selectively for different types of parallelism in computer vision tasks. The MPA system is constructed by integrating two different types of parallel architectures tightly into a single machine. Operational interaction between these two systems can be performed via the conventional subroutine calling mechanism to execute data parallel code on the MPA. This research is to design an underlying base architecture that can be executed for a broad range of vision tasks from the low level to the high level processing. The MPA has been shown to provide significant performance improvement and cost effectiveness for parallel applications having a mixed set of tasks.

References

[1] D. Patterson, et. al, "Intelligent RAM(IRAM): Chips that remember and compute," *ISSCC97*.

[2] K. Murakami, et. al, "Parallel processing RAM chip with 256Mb DRAM and quad processors," *ISSCC97*.

[3] T. Shimizu, et. al, "A multimedia 32b RISC microprocessor with 16Mb DRAM," *ISSCC96*, pp. 216 $\sim$ 217.

[4] D. Elliott, M. Snelgrove, and M Stumm, "Computational RAM: a memory-SIMD hybrid and its application to DSP," *IEEE 1992 Custom Integrated Circuit Conference*, pp. 30.6.1 $\sim$ 30.6.4, 1992.

[5] P.M. Kogge "Execube – a new architecture for scalable MPPs," *1994 ICPP*, pp. I.77 $\sim$ I.84.

[6] M. Gokhale, B. Holmes, and K. Iobst, "Processing in memory: the terasys massively parallel PIM array," *IEEE Computer*, Vol. 28, No. 4, pp. 23 $\sim$ 31, Apr. 1995.

[7] R.M. Haralick and L.G. Shapiro, *Computer and robot vision*, Addison–Wesley Publishing Company, 1992.

[8] N. Otsu, "A threshold selection method from gray–level histograms," *IEEE Trans. on Systems, Man, and Cybernetics*, Vol. SMC-9, pp.62 $\sim$ 66, 1979.

[9] T.Kushner, A.Y. Wu, and A. Rosenfeld, "Image processing on MPP," *Pattern Recognition*, Vol. 15, pp. 121 $\sim$ 130, 1982.

Session 4C

Load Balancing and Scheduling

Load Balancing and Work Load Minimization of Overlapping Parallel Tasks

Venkatram Krishnaswamy
Intel Corp.
JFT-103
2111 NE 25th Ave
Hillsboro,
OR 97225
vkrishna@ichips.intel.com

Gagan Hasteer
Coord. Science Lab.,
University of Illinois
Urbana-Champaign,
1308 W Main St.,
Urbana IL 61801
hasteer@crhc.uiuc.edu

Prithviraj Banerjee
ECE Department,
Northwestern University,
4386 Tech. Institute,
2145 Sheridan Rd,
Evanston IL 60208
banerjee@ece.nwu.edu

May 26, 1997

Abstract

In this paper, we propose a unique problem in the assignment of overlapping tasks to processors on a parallel machine, with the twin objectives of minimizing workloads while maintaining good load balance. This problem arises in some applications in VLSI CAD, e.g. parallel compiled VHDL simulation. We assume that the parallel application can be decomposed into a set of tasks, each in turn comprising a finite number of subtasks. Overlapped computations arise as a result of replication of subtasks across tasks in order to reduce the amount of communication performed in fine grained parallel applications. The uniqueness of the problem stems from the fact that overlapping computation on tasks assigned to the same processor is only performed once. Theoretical results on NP-hardness and bounds on the utilization of overlap are provided. A heuristic solution is also proposed. An important application area in VLSI-CAD, parallel compiled event driven VHDL simulation is introduced. Results of the application of our heuristics to this problem are reported on a SUN Sparcserver 1000 multiprocessor.

1 Introduction

This paper deals with load balancing and workload minimization of a class of parallel problems which are decomposed into tasks having some overlapping computations. Each task comprises several subtasks. Overlapping computations arise when the same subtasks are assigned to different tasks. Typically, there are more tasks than processors. The uniqueness of our problem is due to the fact that overlapped computations between tasks assigned to the same processor are only performed once. Hence the total amount of computation performed is less than or equal to the sum of the workloads of the individual tasks. The equality only occurs in the worst case when there is no overlap between any of the tasks assigned to any processor.

This class of problems arises in extremely fine grained parallel applications for example, in parallel compiled VHDL simulation. The fine granularity of these applications makes the overhead of communication prohibitively expensive. We assume that the parallel applications can be decomposed into a set of tasks. Rather than communicate values across tasks all the time, it is more profitable to compute some of these values locally. Thus, some of the computation is replicated across tasks. While this method provides speedups, the scalability is limited by the amount of overlapped computation performed.

Our assumption is that overlapped computation on tasks assigned to the same processor can be collapsed. This implies that overlapped computation across tasks assigned to the same processor needs to be performed only once. Hence, by assigning tasks to processors in an intelligent manner, it is possible to reduce the amount of overlapped computation performed. However, at the same time, it is important to ensure that load is balanced across processors, in order to maximize their utilization.

In this paper, we formulate this problem, and prove its NP-hardness. In addition lower and upper bounds on the amount of overlapped computation which can be exploited are shown. We then describe a heuristic which we have im-

This research was supported in part by the Semiconductor Research Corporation under contract SRC 95-DP-109 and the Advanced Research Projects Agency under contract DAA-H04-94-G-0273 administered by the Army Research Office. Venkatram Krishnaswamy was at the University of Illinois at Urbana-Champaign when this research was conducted.

272

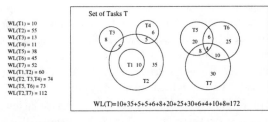

WL(T1) = 10
WL(T2) = 55
WL(T3) = 13
WL(T4) = 11
WL(T5) = 38
WL(T6) = 45
WL(T7) = 52
WL(T1,T2) = 60
WL(T2, T3,T4) = 74
WL(T5, T6) = 73
WL(T2,T7) = 112

Set of Tasks T

$WL(T)=10+35+5+5+6+8+20+25+30+6+4+10+8=172$

Partition 1	Partition 2	Overlap Utilized	System Workload	Unutilized Overlap
T1 T4 T7	T2 T3 T5 T6	5+6+4=15	MAX(73,136)=136	73+136-172=37
T1 T2 T3 T4	T5 T6 T7	10+5+5+6+4+10+8=48	MAX(69,103)=103	69+103-172=0
T1 T2 T4 T5	T3 T6 T7	10+5+10=25	MAX(99,96)=99	99+96-172=23

Figure 1: An instance of WMOT on 2 processors.

plemented and compare its performance with the bounds.

We have encountered an instance of this class of problems in parallel compiled event driven VHDL simulation [1]. The extremely fine granularity of VHDL simulations leads us to partition simulations using the fanin cone strategy [2, 3]. This strategy causes replicated computations across partitions. This problem is an ideal application for the methods described in this paper. We report results in terms of improvements to simulation runtimes brought about by the assignment techniques reported here.

The remainder of this paper is organized as follows. Section 2 contains the problem formulation, and a proof of its NP-hardness. Upper and lower bounds are calculated in Section 4. Our heuristic algorithm is described in Section 5. We introduce our application domain briefly in Section 6. Results and presented and discussed in Section 7. Related work is discussed in Section 8. We conclude in Section 9.

2 Problem Formulation

In this section, we formulate the workload minimization problem for a set of overlapping tasks(WMOT) and prove that it is NP-hard. The problem of assigning cones to processors such that overlap is maximized while load balance is maintained is an instance of WMOT.

Consider a system of K processors computing a set of overlapping tasks in parallel. The *system workload* is defined as the largest amount of computation (workload) assigned to any processor in the system. *Total workload* is defined as the sum of the workloads on each processor. In order to achieve load balance, we endeavor to assign roughly the same workloads to each processor in the system. Note that this is done on the basis of a static estimation of the dynamic load. We do not deal with dynamic load balancing.

Figure 1 illustrates an instance of WMOT with number of processors $K = 2$. It shows a set T of 7 over-

lapping tasks in the form of a Venn diagram. Each number represents the amount of computation to be performed for that region or simply the workload of that region. The workload of a task is the sum of the numbers in the region representing it e.g. the workload of T_2 is the sum of its overlaps with other tasks and its exclusive workload. $WL(T_2) = 35 + 5 + 5 + 10 = 55$. Workloads of all tasks are defined similarly. The workload of a region is defined as the workload of the union of the tasks in that region. Thus if a single processor was to compute all the tasks its workload would be $WL(T) = WL(\bigcup_i T_i) = 172$. If K processors perform the computation for these tasks in parallel, then $\frac{WL(T)}{K}$ would be the work performed by each processor in the ideal case. In order to achieve this, it is necessary to communicate results for the overlapping regions across processors. Since we restrict our attention to fine grained parallel applications, communications overheads become very significant. It is preferable to compute values locally on processors by replicating subtasks across them, rather than incur the overhead of frequent communication. This approach leads to speedups, although the scalability is limited by the amount of replication. Thus the WMOT problem involves partitioning the tasks among processors to minimize the system workload by utilizing the overlaps between tasks to reduce the total workload. Figure 1 shows three possible partitions of tasks between two processors. The second partition utilizes the task overlaps completely and results in minimum total workload which is equal to the workload of $T(69+103=172)$. However, the system workload is not optimal because of the skew in the loads on individual processors. System workload=$MAX(69, 103) = 103$. The third case shows that a better load balance can be achieved by sacrificing some overlap between tasks. This leads to some redundant computation (23 units) compared to the uniprocessor run but reduces the system workload from 103 to 99.

The WMOT problem is related to the traditional scheduling problem of tasks with interprocessor communication onto a number of processors. In that problem, the cost of interprocessor communication between tasks becomes zero when two tasks get mapped to the same processor. Our problem is implicitly modeling either the task redundancies or interprocessor communication. The only thing we do not model is the task precedences. We assume that all tasks are independent.

As shown in Figure 1 exploiting overlapping computation between different tasks does not translate to better load balance. WMOT may be viewed as a two dimensional optimization problem where the goal is to minimize the system workload and maximize task overlap utilization.

In case of a conflict, the former takes precedence. The WMOT problem is formally defined as follows.

Given a finite set T of overlapping tasks, a workload $w(T_i) \in Z^+$ for each $T_i \subset T$, and number of processors K ($w(T_i)$ represents the sum of workloads of the set of subtasks $t \in T_i$). Partition T into disjoint sets $T_1, T_2, ..., T_K$ such that the resulting workload of the system is minimized. We prove that WMOT is NP-hard by a straightforward reduction from the Bin Packing (BP) problem which is known to be NP-complete.

BP is formally defined as follows. *Given a finite set U of items, a size $s(u) \in Z^+$ for each $u \in U$, and a positive integer K. Is there a partition of U into disjoint sets $U_1, U_2, ..., U_K$ such that the sum of the sizes of the items in each U_i is minimized?*

Theorem 1: *Bin Packing Problem is NP-Complete* [4].

Theorem 2: *Workload Minimization of Overlapping Tasks is NP-hard.* [5]

3 Bounds on the System Workload

A good system workload can be achieved by exploiting overlap between tasks efficiently. The complexity of workload minimization with maximum overlap utilization warrants fixing one of the two variables and analyzing the effect of the other.

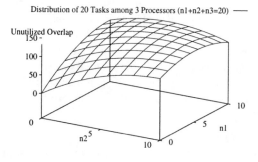

Figure 2: Unutilized Overlap for 20 tasks on 3 Processors

In the following analysis we derive upper and lower bounds on the amount of overlap that can be realized for a given set of tasks T on K processors by using a counting argument. The upper and lower bounds on the overlap translate directly into lower and upper bounds for the total workload of the system respectively. In deriving the bounds we consider pairwise overlaps only and ignore

overlaps of 3 or more tasks. Due to combinatorial explosion, the calculation of the bounds becomes intractable and of not much practical use. However, the analysis can easily be extended to overlaps of 3 or more tasks.

Since $WL(T)$ is the trivial lower bound on the total workload, a perfectly load balanced system would have a system workload $\geq \frac{WL(T)}{K}$. Thus $\frac{WL(T)}{K}$ is a trivial lower bound for system workload. This bound assumes that all the overlaps are utilized completely and that there is no redundant computation. Thus we assume that the tasks will be partitioned over the K processors such that each processor does at least $\frac{WL(T)}{K}$ work. We have computed tighter bounds on overlap utilization, and system workloads [5], a summary of which is shown in Table 1.

4 Heuristic Solution to WMOT Problem

In this section, we present a heuristic solution to the WMOT problem. We compare the solutions it generates to an iterative naive round robin algorithm. Each iteration of the loop simply assigns the next task to a new processor. Thus, each processor gets the same roughly the same number of tasks. Neither the computational weight of a task nor the computation shared with other tasks is taken into account in this routine.

Our heuristic for solving WMOT, HMOT appears in Figure 3. The analysis presented in the previous section for computation of bounds only considers pairwise overlaps between tasks. In contrast, the heuristic presented here considers all interactions between tasks. The algorithm proceeds in two phases; the first is a seeding phase, where tasks are chosen from which to grow partitions. In the second phase, the partitions are grown from the seeds.

The initial phase is a seeding phase. In this, K seeds are identified from the set of tasks, with the intention of growing partitions from them, where K is the number of processors. In order to maximize the gain from utilizing overlapping computations, the seeds are chosen such that they have minimum overlap.

Each task is represented by a data structure, whose components include an array containing pairwise overlaps with other tasks. The sum of these array elements is computed for each task. This sum is a measure of the overlaps of the task with all other tasks in the system. The task with least element sum is chosen as the seed for the first partition. We have now to come up with $K - 1$ other seeds such that they have least common computation with one another. This is accomplished in lines 1 through 15 of Figure 3. Another array of integers, *seedArray*, comprising

Table 1: Summary of Bounds on Workloads (System and Total), and Overlap Utilized

Quantity	Upper Bound	Lower Bound
Total Workload (trivial)	$\Sigma WL(T_i)$	$\Sigma WL(T)$
Total Workload (tight)	$\Sigma WL(T_i) - \Sigma_{i=1}^{\frac{N(N-K)}{2K}} w(e_i)$	$\Sigma WL(T) + \Sigma_{i=1}^{i=q} w_i$
System Workload (trivial)	$\frac{\Sigma WL(T_i)}{K}$	$\frac{WL(T)}{K}$
System Workload (tight)	$\Sigma WL(T_i) - \frac{(K-1)*WL(T)}{K}$	$\Sigma_{i=1}^{i=m} w_i$
Overlap Utilized	$\Sigma WL(T_i) - \Sigma WL(T) - \Sigma_{i=1}^{i=q} w_i$	$\Sigma_{i=1}^{\frac{N(N-K)}{2K}} w(e_i)$

```
HMOT()
 1   seedArray = minConeArray;
 2   proc[0].add(curMinCone);
 3   seedArray[curMinCone] = ∞;
 4   for i in 1 to numProcessors
 5   do
 6      newCone = findMin(seedArray);
 7      Sum(seedArray, i);
 8      proc[i].add(newCone);
 9      seedArray[newCone] = ∞;
10
11   //seeding over, now initialize to grow partitions
12   for i in 0 to numProcessors
13   do
14      for k in 0 to numProcessors
15      do
16         sumArray[k][proc[i].task[0]] = -∞;
17
18   //initialization over, grow partitions
19   while unassigned tasks remain
20      do
21         for i in 0 to numProcessors
22         do
23            if unassigned tasks remain
24            then
25               if procs[i].Weight - minProcWeight <= 0
26               then
27                  newCone = findMax(sumArray[i]);
28                  Sum(sumArray[i], i);
29                  for k in 0 to numProcessors
30                  do
31                     sumArray[k][newCone] = -∞;
32
33                  procs[i].add(newCone);
34                  procs[i].Weight = exclusiveWeight(i);
35
```

Figure 3: Heuristic Minimization of Overlapping Tasks (HMOT).

as many elements as tasks, is used to hold a running metric of overlapping computation. The running metric is updated by the routine Sum.

Sum accepts an array and an integer as inputs. The integer input is used to index into an array of processor descriptors. All entries other than those set to ∞ or $-\infty$ are initialized to 0. This excludes tasks which have already been assigned. Then, for every subtask in the system, we check whether there is some common computation with every task already assigned to the current processor. If N_0 through N_k tasks have been assigned to the current processor, then the overlap value being computed for task N_{k+1} is the weight of $(\bigcup_{i=0}^{k} N_i) \cap N_{k+1}$. This takes into account all overlap interactions between all tasks in the system, in contrast to the pairwise interactions used to simplify the analysis of bounds in the previous section.

The functions $findMin$ and $findMax$ on lines 6 and 25 respectively of Figure 3 simply return the index of the minimum and maximum value in the array passed as a parameter. This allows HMOT to determine the next task to be assigned to the current processor. The $exclusiveWeight$ function on line 30 returns the weight of a partition P computed as $|\bigcup N_i|$ where N_i are tasks allocated to P.

The partition growth phase of HMOT (lines 17 through 32) iterates until all tasks have been assigned. The algorithm iterates over the processors, and decides whether to add a task based on whether the weight of the current processor is less than the minimum processor weight seen on the current iterations (the maintenance of the value $minProcWeight$ is not shown for brevity). This allows maintenance of load balance. When a processor decides to add a task, it finds the unassigned task with maximum common computation, as determined by the $findMax$ function, and adds it to its pool of tasks.

5   Problem Domain

In this section we will describe a real application from the domain of VLSI CAD that can be modeled as the WMOT problem. The design of complex digital systems begins with conceptualization using behavioral or RTL (Register Transfer Level) descriptions in a Hardware Description Language (HDL) such as Verilog or VHDL. Therefore simulation of these descriptions becomes a bottleneck in the design cycle, which requires alleviation. Parallelization is an appropriate method of doing this, since modern design styles incorporate use of superpipelining and multiple functional units. Hence, it is reasonable to expect that several modules in the design will be concurrently active, and this concurrency may be exploited to speedup simulation. In addition, use of memory scalable parallel algorithms enables simulation of descriptions which may be too large to execute on uniprocessor machines.

Our early work in parallel simulation for VHDL [6] showed us that there was room for improvement in both sequential algorithms for simulation, as well as in parallel algorithms. Therefore, we chose to implement an efficient sequential algorithm based on that of French *et al.* [7]. The advantage of this compiled event driven simulation algorithm over traditional event driven simulation is that the complexity of event scheduling is moved from runtime into compile time. This opens up possibilities for aggressive compiler optimizations to improve the quality of the simulation code. Our experience with parallelization of VHDL simulation has been that the fine computational granularity poses unique problems. In the worst case, a piece of RTL code representing an AND gate may have to communicate after 3 machine instructions. Hence, asynchronous parallel simulation algorithms such as Time Warp [8] are not well suited to this application. Since the synchronization costs are high, the computational granularity must be large in order for parallelization to pay off.

We have investigated static parallelization techniques with respect to compiled event driven simulation in [1]. The first of these techniques relied on static list scheduling of a conservative estimation of the path taken by the simulation, as estimated at compile time. This estimation is abstracted as a directed graph which is then scheduled using a list scheduling [9] algorithm onto the desired number of processors. Even though we generated code targetted towards symmetric shared memory multiprocessors (SMPs), it turned out that the granularity of computation between synchronizations was too fine for profitable exploitation of parallelism. We therefore used a partitioning technique based on fanin cones [2, 3] which traded off performing redundant communication on processors against frequent communication. This technique provides good speedups. However the scalability of simulations is bounded by the amount of redundant computation performed.

5.1 Parallelization of Compiled Event Driven Simulation

In this section we describe parallel compiled event driven VHDL simulation using partitioning based on a fanin cone algorithm [2, 3]. We extract a flattened execution graph from the circuit description. The vertices comprising the execution graph are execution blocks representing non-preemptably executing sections of the source VHDL. Edges between execution blocks represent precedence constraints. Fanin cones are grown from output nodes in the execution graph, and from the inputs of latches. This is an efficient, linear algorithm (since it follows depth first search order) which places each primary output in a separate partition. It then traces recursively backwards through the input arcs to the primary inputs, or the outputs of latches, placing nodes in the partition as it does so. Back edges are not followed to avoid getting stuck in cycles.

Execution blocks may appear on multiple cones, representing overlapping computation. The fanin cones are assigned to processors using an assignment strategy (either the round robin algorithm or HMOT). Static simulation is performed on the cones assigned to each processor, and code is generated for each partition. Static simulation yields a static approximation of the path followed by the simulation at runtime. Runtime event driven behavior is provided by predicating the execution of EB's on boolean triggers. The code is multithreaded, and threads synchronize at clock boundaries.

Clearly, nodes may be resident on multiple partitions, resulting in redundant work being performed across cones (partitions). This redundancy is the overhead of parallelization. In the simplest case, where the algorithm backtraces from the primary outputs all the way to the primary inputs, the redundancy is high. However, there is no need for communication between cones. Methods for reducing the amount of redundancy at the cost of increasing communication are being investigated.

Initially we generated a class for each cone, with its own copies of variables and signals. Cones were then assigned to threads which are executed in parallel. Since there is no communication between cones, we can serially execute cones on a thread. However, as shown in Figure 4 there are two levels of redundancy; there is redundancy between cones assigned to different processors, about which nothing can be done, and there is redundancy across all cones assigned to the same processor. In order to take care of the second level of redundancy, i.e. that between all cones assigned to the same processors, we modified the code generator, so that a single class is generated for each thread. The code generator is intelligent enough to check for re-

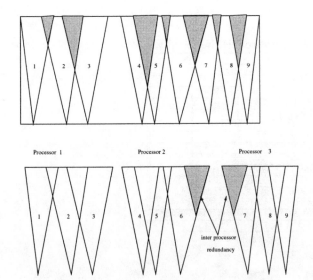

Figure 4: In this graph, there are 9 outputs, and therefore 9 cones. The hatched areas in the figure above denote redundant components across overlapping cones. The figure below shows the assignment of these cones to 3 processors. As shown, intra processor redundancy is removed and we have only to live with inter processor redundancies.

dundancies within a thread, and the code it produces for a give thread is irredundant. As can be seen, the assignment of cones to processor is an instance of the WMOT problem, wherein each cone is a task. The redundancy across cones is the overlapping computation across tasks. Redundant computation across tasks assigned to the same processor is collapsed, as is true of the definition of WMOT.

After invoking HMOT, we perform a constant number of iterations of random pairwise exchanges of cones across processors. A greedy acceptance policy is used, with improvement in system workload being the cost function.

6 Results

In this section, we show experimental results for parallelization of compiled event driven simulations, including partitioning and assignment statistics.

In evaluating the parallel compiled event driven simulation, we have tried to use a spectrum of benchmarks with different circuit characteristics, and different levels of modeling abstraction. The bulk of the circuits come from the ISCAS suite of sequential and combinational benchmarks [10, 11]. In addition, we have used a 32 bit transceiver, XCVR from the RASSP suite of VHDL models [12], an implementation of the DLX processor [13] from the University of Stuttgart [14], and a pipelined mul-

tiplier developed inhouse. The sequential sizes are computed as the number of lines of C++ for each execution block in the execution graph of the circuit.

We present the results obtained by our heuristic assignment routine, HMOT, and the improvements brought about by iteratively accepting pairwise. As mentioned in Section 7, we use a greedy acceptance criterion. Any move which brings about an improvement in system workload is accepted, while all others are rejected. This has the danger of entering local minima. Table 2 shows the results obtained by HMOT for our benchmark circuits in terms of overlap utilized. The columns labeled NA are results obtained by the naive assignment strategy, while those labeled HA are those achieved by HMOT. Notice that sometimes less overlap is utilized than HMOT than the Naive Algorithm. This is because HMOT is biased in favor of load balance. However the system workloads using HMOT are always superior to the Naive Algorithm as shown in Table 3, contains statistics obtained by 1000 iterations of exchanges after performing HMOT. As before, NA stands for Naive Assignment, HA for HMOT Assignment, and II for Iterative Improvement, which is performed after HMOT. The speedups which can be achieved in the ideal case are $\frac{SWL(1)}{SWL(8)}$.

Table 4 shows runtimes in seconds for ISCAS benchmarks running on a SparcServer 1000 using POSIX pthreads. The columns are labeled NA for Naive Assignment, HA for HMOT Assignment, II for Iterative Improvement, and CS for clock suppressed synchronization after II. In the last scheme, barrier synchronizations are only performed on active phases of the clock instead of on every event on the clock signal. This optimization requires that the designer specify clock related information. This optimization is therefore only applicable to synchronous circuits. The speedups of combinational benchmarks are clearly dominated by the size of the dominant cones. XCVR scales well since it is partitioned into evenly sized cones. The sequential circuits show better scaling characteristics than the combinational circuits, but owing to barrier synchronizations, the load balance is a limiting factor. Larger circuits show speedups of 3 to 4 on 8 processors when completely optimized, which agree with the ratios of uniprocessor load to system workloads on 8 processors. This shows that we are achieving the maximum possible speedup, given the partition and assignment. The pipelined multiplier is seen to benefit from the HMOT seeding policy which results in different pipeline stages being assignmed to different processors. In this way it is possible to extract the entire parallelism exposed to the simulator by pipelined design styles. DLX is disappointingly restricted by the size of its largest cone.

Table 2: Overlap Utilization Statistics from HMOT.

circuit	1 Proc	2 Procs		4 Procs		8 Procs	
	NA/HA	NA	HA	NA	HA	NA	HA
c432	3633	2810	2821	1260	1260	0	0
c499	21436	20536	20536	18736	18736	15648	15648
c1908	7938	7395	7395	6351	6355	4404	4290
c2670	19789	16961	17194	15474	15201	13033	12996
c5315	109945	102912	103221	91061	92314	77975	83540
s1423	32738	31520	31573	29185	29441	25787	25743
s1488	3718	3313	3383	2763	2858	1895	1995
s5378	61519	56676	58174	49240	53665	40272	45902
s4863	99207	90259	98962	76558	88181	58175	71028
s13207	91672	86615	86873	83540	82280	78311	77380
s15850	217664	209674	210936	197090	201208	174390	179802
XCVR	4729	4402	4418	4260	4260	3976	3976
dlx	109686	107224	107552	103657	104514	98093	98825
pmult	6085	5531	5917	5355	5724	5003	5179

Table 3: System Workload Statistics.

circuit	1 Proc	2 Proc			4 Proc			8 Proc		
		NA	HA	II	NA	HA	II	NA	HA	II
c499	1220	1060	1060	1060	980	980	980	876	876	876
c1908	2276	1595	1423	1412	1157	979	968	933	925	901
c5315	10851	9448	8789	7836	8087	7197	6581	7658	6636	4577
s1423	3734	2579	2457	2393	1920	1774	1668	1583	1379	1331
s1488	3495	2058	1916	1916	1292	1138	1107	834	730	676
s5378	13216	9196	8281	7905	6973	5282	5023	5033	3803	3584
s4863	12431	10672	6344	6313	9594	6828	5481	8838	6816	4676
s13207	20524	14214	12662	12662	10806	7502	7502	9273	6445	6390
s15850	25246	17450	15995	15967	12178	10432	10428	9222	7895	7890
dlx	2837	2688	2500	2500	2560	2022	2022	2357	2022	2022
pmult	741	650	456	405	405	278	254	229	211	207

Table 4: Runtimes in seconds of 4-valued simulations on SparcServer1000E using pthreads

ckt	1 proc	2 proc				4 proc				8 proc			
		NA	HA	II	CS	NA	HA	II	CS	NA	HA	II	CS
c432	249.5	197.3	193.8	193.8	na	217.6	227.4	227.4	na	236.4	236.4	236.4	na
c499	266.1	226.3	225.8	226.0	na	255.8	239.2	237.9	na	244.8	257.3	243.6	na
c1908	61.6	44.4	40.9	38.6	na	34.7	32.3	28.6	na	34.2	28.2	31.9	na
c5315	100.2	80.4	83.7	77.2	na	68.8	87.9	70.5	na	79.7	70.2	65.6	na
XCVR	52.2	48.3	47.4	27.6	na	25.7	25.5	25.5	na	16.7	16.7	16.8	na
s1423	518.8	345.6	326.8	344.8	335.4	251.2	237.6	232.0	231.7	252.8	29.5	248.3	190.1
s1488	125.2	79.6	72.1	76.0	69.1	57.6	56.7	52.2	45.4	61.2	61.6	60.9	58.3
s5376	638.3	397.5	413.7	420.7	411.8	356.3	273.7	272.4	262.6	341.8	285.3	272.6	258.2
s4863	2851.3	2467.4	1662.3	1680.9	1669.1	1049.0	1731.1	1471.2	1412.9	1142.8	926.7	785.7	716.9
s13207	756.4	634.6	623.7	623.4	616.6	552.5	441.9	441.9	420.5	560.6	422.3	416.2	405.1
s15850	3986.8	3254.4	3179.1	3170.6	3028.2	2556.2	2055.6	2053.8	1974.4	1986.0	1462.7	1440.9	1370.5
dlx	266.3	287.5	237.2	237.2	230.4	212.7	180.1	180.1	164.2	216.0	188.3	188.3	170.4
pmult	1858.14	1444.7	1284.3	1212.62	1160.4	936.7	867.3	820.4	792.6	953.7	837.6	834.1	614.4

7 Related Work

Our sequential simulation algorithm is based on the work of French *et al* [7]. While there is a large body of work in the parallel simulation of VHDL, much of it is concerned with asynchrounous parallel discrete event simulation algorithms. Some of this work includes that of Wilsey *et al* [15] in Time Warp simulation of VHDL. Hartrum *et al* [16] have reported a VHDL simulator based on a conservative synchronization algorithm.

8 Conclusions

In this paper, we have proposed the problem of Workload Minimization of Overlapping tasks to achieve load balance. In addition to proving its NP-Hardness, we have provided upper and lower bounds on the amounts of overlap which may be utilized. We have proposed a heuristic algorithm for solving the problem. An application of this problem has been shown in parallel compiled event driven simulation of VHDL models. This is an important task in Computer Aided Design for digital systems, which benefits greatly from the use of parallel processing. The efficiency of our heuristic in improving the scalability of this application has been demonstrated. From the viewpoint of design styles, it is evident that pipelined designs are particularly suited for parallel simulation using our partitioning and assignment strategies. Intuitively, the reason for this is that pipelined designs comprise combinational subcircuits separated from one another by means of registers. These independent subcircuits have no overlap and are therefore assigned to different processors by the seeding phase of HMOT. Thus the parallelism exposed by pipelining designs is fully exploited.

References

[1] V. Krishnaswamy and P. Banerjee, "Parallel compiled event driven simulation," tech. rep., University of Illinois, 1996. under preparation.

[2] E. Smith, B. Underwood, and M. Mercer, "An analysis of several approaches to circuit partitioning for parallel logic simulation," in *Proc. of Int'l Conf. on Computer Design*, pp. 664–667, IEEE, 1987.

[3] R. Mueller-Thuns, D. Saab, R. Damiano, and J. Abraham, "VLSI Logic and Fault Simulation on General Purpose Parallel Computers," *IEEE Transactions on CAD of Integrated Circuits and Systems*, vol. 12, pp. 446 – 460, March 1993.

[4] M. R. Garey and D. S. Johnson, *Computers and Intractability*. W.H. Freeman and Company, 1979.

[5] V. Krishnaswamy, *Parallel Algorithms for VHDL Simulation*. PhD thesis, University of Illinois at Urbana-Champaign, 1997.

[6] V. Krishnaswamy and P. Banerjee, "Actor Based Parallel VHDL Simulation Using Time Warp," in *Proceedings of the 10th Workshop on Parallel and Distributed Simulation*, May 1996.

[7] R. French, M. Lam, J. Levitt, and K. Olukotun, "A General Method for Compiling Event Driven Simulations," in *Proceedings of 1995 Design Automation Conference*, pp. 151 – 156, 1995.

[8] D. Jefferson, "Virtual Time," *ACM Transactions on Programming Languages and Systems*, vol. 7, no. 3, pp. 404–425, 1985.

[9] T. C. Hu, "Parallel Sequencing and Assembly Line Problems," *Operations Research*, no. 9, pp. 841 – 848, 1961.

[10] F. Brglez and H. Fujiwara, "A Neutral Netlist of 10 Combinational Benchmark Circuits and a Target Translator in Fortran," *IEEE Intl. Symp. on Circuits and Systems*, vol. 3, June 1985.

[11] F. Brglez, D. Bryan, and K. Kozminski, "Combinational Profiles of Sequential Benchmark Circuits," *IEEE Intl. Symp. on Circuits and Systems*, pp. 1929–1934, May 1989.

[12] RASSP, "RASSP VHDL models." http://rassp.scra.org/information/public-vhdl/models/models.html.

[13] J. Henessey and D. Patterson, *Computer Architecture : A Quantitative Approach*. Morgan Kaufmann, 2 ed., 1995.

[14] M. Gumm, M. Buehler, and U. Baitinger, "VHDL and Synthesis Based Design of a 32-bit RISC processor in a Four Months Course," in *Proceedings of the European Workshop on Microelectronics Education*, (Grenoble, France), Feb 1996.

[15] T. J. McBrayer and P. A. Wilsey, "Process Combination to Increase Event Granularity in Parallel Logic Simulation," in *Proceedings of Int. Parallel Processing Symposium*, April 1995.

[16] K. L. Kapp, T. C. Hartrum, and T. S. Wailes, "An Improved Cost Function for Static Partitioning of Parallel Circuit Simulations Using a Conservative Synchronization Protocol," in *Proc. of 9th Workshop on Parallel and Distributed Simulation*, pp. 78 – 85, June 1995.

Good Processor Management = Fast Allocation + Efficient Scheduling[*]

Byung S. Yoo and Chita R. Das
Department of Computer Science and Engineering
The Pennsylvania State University
University Park, PA 16802
E-mail: {yoo | das} @cse.psu.edu

Abstract

Fast and efficient processor allocation and job scheduling algorithms are essential components of a multi-user multicomputer operating system. In this paper, we propose two novel processor management schemes which meet such demands for mesh-connected multicomputers. A stack-based allocation algorithm that can locate a free submesh for a job very quickly using simple coordinate calculation and spatial subtraction is proposed. Simulation results show that the stack-based allocation algorithm outperforms all the existing allocation policies in terms of allocation overhead while delivering competitive performance. Another technique, called group scheduling, schedules jobs in such a way that the jobs belonging to the same group do not block each other. The groups are scheduled in an FCFS order to prevent starvation. This simple but efficient scheduling policy reduces the response time significantly by minimizing the queueing delay for the jobs in the same group. These two schemes, when used together, can provide faster service to users with very little overhead.

Index Terms - Group scheduling policy, mesh-connected multicomputers, operating systems, processor management, stack-based allocation algorithm

1 Introduction

An important attribute of a multicomputer OS is that it should support a multi-user environment via efficient management of system resources. The underlying allocation and scheduling algorithms of the OS provide this functionality. While both these schemes complement each other in providing better system performance, most of the research has centered around job allocation because of its nontrivial nature. The non-triviality implies that it is extremely difficult to develop an allocation scheme that can provide maximum achievable performance without incurring too much overhead. Thus, the allocation algorithms proposed for large multicomputers exhibit various tradeoffs between performance and complexity.

The main focus of this paper is on developing a fast contiguous processor allocation algorithm for low-dimensional mesh architectures. Prior research indicates that better submesh recognition ability of an allocation algorithm provides only incremental performance gain at the cost of high run-time overhead [1, 4, 11]. It is therefore important to develop a faster allocation algorithm than to improve the recognition ability of the algorithm. Further performance improvement can be achieved by using a scheduling scheme other than the usual FCFS method.

An allocation algorithm can use either the bitmap or list representation approach to maintain node availability information. In the bitmap approach, each node is represented by a bit and hence the search space is a function of the number of nodes in the system. With the list representation, the available or allocated nodes are maintained as a list of free or busy submeshes. The search space is hence limited to the length of the list. It turns out that list-based algorithms are better candidates than bitmap-based algorithms for optimizing the speed. In this paper we present such an algorithm for mesh-connected multicomputers. The proposed algorithm is faster than any of the existing submesh allocation schemes and can provide competitive performance.

The algorithm maintains a list of the allocated submeshes, called busy list. Using the busy list, requested submesh size, and the architectural limitations, the algorithm quickly determines all the nodes that cannot be assigned to the request. Then, these nodes are spatially subtracted from the entire mesh system to find a free submesh for the job. The algorithm uses a stack (hence called *stack-based allocation algorithm*) to speed up this search process. In addition, we propose a simple scheduling algorithm as an alternative to FCFS scheduling. We call it *group scheduling* in this paper as the incoming jobs are grouped based on a predetermined group size. Jobs in the same group do not block each other as in FCFS scheduling. The groups are scheduled in an FCFS order to avoid starvation.

In-depth performance analysis of the two proposed

---

[*]This research was supported in part by the National Science Foundation under Grant No. MIP-9406984.

techniques are conducted via simulation. Two schemes, the first fit (FF) algorithm [13] that has been referred in most prior studies and the more recent quick allocation (QA) algorithm [12] that has been shown to be the fastest allocation algorithm, are used for comparison in our study. It is shown that the stack-based allocation method outperforms all the existing allocation policies in terms of allocation overhead while providing comparable performance. Moreover, the allocation overhead of the prior allocation policies can be significantly reduced if they are implemented using the proposed stack approach. The group scheduling strategy reduces the response time considerably compared to the FCFS scheduling. We also studied the impact of the group size on job response time. It is shown that both the proposed schemes together can provide better performance over a wide range of workloads.

The rest of the paper is organized as follows. Section 2 presents the pertinent preliminaries, and the proposed schemes are described in Section 3. In Section 4, performance results are reported followed by the concluding remarks in Section 5.

2 Preliminaries

2.1 Nomenclature

A two-dimensional mesh, denoted as $M(w, h)$, consists of $w \times h$ nodes (or processors) arranged in a $w \times h$ two-dimensional grid. The node in column i and row j is identified by its address $<i, j>$. Each node is connected to its four neighbors, $<i \pm 1, j>$ and $<i, j \pm 1>$, for $0 \le i < w$ and $0 \le j < h$, through direct communication links.

Definition 1 A (two-dimensional) *submesh* $S(a, b)$ in the mesh $M(w, h)$ is a subgrid $M(a, b)$ such that $1 \le a \le w$ and $1 \le b \le h$. A submesh S is identified by its *base* and *end* and is denoted by $S[base, end]$. The base and end refer to the processors at the lower-left and upper-right corners of S, respectively. A submesh is *busy* when all of its nodes are allocated to a job. Similarly, a submesh is *free* when all of its nodes are available. The *busy list* refers to a set of all the busy submeshes in the system.

Definition 2 The *coverage* of a busy (allocated) submesh β with respect to a job J, denoted as $\xi_{\beta, J}$, is a set of processors such that the use of any node in $\xi_{\beta, J}$ as the base of a free submesh for the allocation of the job will make the job to be overlapped with β. The *coverage set* with respect to J, denoted as C_J, is a set of the coverages of all the busy submeshes.

Definition 3 The *reject area* with respect to a job J, R_J, is a set of processors such that the use of any node in R_J as the base of a free submesh for the allocation of the job will make the job to cross the boundary of the mesh.

Definition 4 The *base set* with respect to a job J, B_J, is a set of processors that can be used as the bases of free sub-

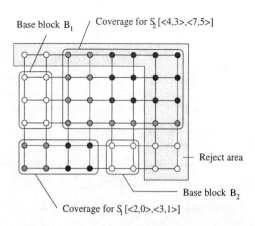

Figure 1: Base blocks, coverage set, and reject area in an $M(8, 6)$ with respect to a $J(3, 2)$.

meshes to accommodate the job J. A base set consists of disjoint *base blocks*, each of which is a submesh containing eligible bases for J.

The coverages of two allocated submeshes, the reject area, and two base blocks with respect to a $J(3, 2)^1$ are shown in Fig. 1. The busy nodes are represented by dark circles and the (free) nodes that belong to the coverages are depicted as shaded circles. The reject area is represented by a shaded region. The node addresses are not shown in the figure for clarity. Here, the coverages of busy submeshes, $S_1[<2, 0>, <3, 1>]$ and $S_2[<4, 3>, <7, 5>]$, are $\xi_{S_1, J}[<0, 0>, <3, 1>]$ and $\xi_{S_2, J}[<2, 2>, <7, 5>]$, respectively. The base set, B_J, consists of two base blocks, $B_1[<0, 2>, <1, 4>]$ and $B_2[<4, 0>, <5, 1>]$. Any node in the base blocks can serve as the base of a free submesh to accommodate J.

The reject area and the coverage set can be determined quite easily through a simple address calculation. The reject area of a mesh $M(w, h)$ with respect to $J(a, b)$ consists of processors with address $< i, j >$ such that $w - a + 1 \le i < w$ or $h - b + 1 \le j < h$. We refer to the processor $<w - a + 1, h - b + 1>$ as the *sink* of the reject area. A coverage set with respect to the job J is constructed by dilating each busy (allocated) submesh. Given a busy submesh $\beta[<x_b, y_b>, <x_e, y_e>]$, its coverage with respect to a $J(a, b)$ is $\xi_{\beta, J}[<x_c, y_c>, <x_e, y_e>]$, where $x_c = \max(0, x_b - a + 1)$ and $y_c = \max(0, y_b - b + 1)$.

It is important to note that, given a job J for allocation, the union of C_J and R_J represents a set of processors each of which cannot serve as the base of a free submesh to accommodate J. This implies that the base set for J, B_J, is simply $B_J = U - R_J - C_J$, where U represents the set of all the processors in the system. Once R_J and C_J are constructed for a job J, then the submesh allocation is reduced

---

[1]A job requesting an $a \times b$ submesh is denoted by $J(a, b)$ in this paper.

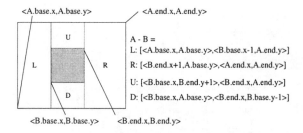

$A - B =$
L: [<A.base.x,A.base.y>,<B.base.x-1,A.end.y>]
R: [<B.end.x+1,A.base.y>,<A.end.x,A.end.y>]
U: [<B.base.x,B.end.y+1>,<B.end.x,A.end.y>]
D: [<B.base.x,A.base.y>,<B.end.x,B.base.y-1>]

Figure 2: Spatial subtraction between two submeshes.

to the problem of finding the base set B_J and selecting a node in B_J as the base of a free submesh for J.

2.2 Related Work

Two (submesh) allocation algorithms of interest, *first fit* (FF) [13] and *quick allocation* (QA) [12], are briefly discussed in this subsection. We have selected these policies for comparison because they represent simple, fast, and efficient bitmap-based (first fit) and list-based (quick allocation) algorithms. Other existing allocation algorithms are not described here due to space limitation. These algorithms are described in detail in [2, 3, 5, 6, 7, 8].

First Fit (FF) The first fit strategy [13] can be used for meshes of arbitrary sizes and incurs no internal fragmentation. It maintains a *busy array* representing the allocation status of the mesh. With respect to a job to be allocated, the busy array is searched to construct a *coverage array*, which represents a coverage set. The first available node (not belonging to the coverage array) is selected as the base of a free submesh. The FF scheme is simple and efficient and can provide relatively good performance. However, it is not a recognition-complete algorithm since it considers only a fixed orientation of a submesh request. Another drawback of the algorithm is its excessive run-time overhead due to the manipulation of the bitmap arrays. This high run-time overhead renders the algorithm (and any bitmap-based algorithms) unattractive, especially when the mesh system is large or a fast submesh allocation is required.

Quick Allocation (QA) This recently proposed allocation scheme aims at providing complete submesh recognition ability with minimal run-time overhead [12]. The basic idea of the QA scheme is very similar to that of the FF strategy. In an effort to reduce search overhead, the QA scheme identifies a set of adjacent processors, called *covered segment*, for each row. Each covered segment indicates if the corresponding row has a potential base of a free submesh (and its position as well). With the covered segment, it is not necessary to check the state of each node in the mesh. Furthermore, the column wise scan employed by many bitmap-based algorithms can also be avoided. It has been shown that the QA algorithm is the fastest and

the most efficient of all the allocation policies reported in the literature [12]. However, the construction of the covered segments requires a sorting operation whose cost is relatively expensive (but not as expensive as bitmap operations). In addition, the allocation overhead of the QA scheme linearly increases as number of rows in the mesh increases. The reader should refer to [12] for the detailed discussion of the QA algorithm.

3 Proposed Processor Management Schemes

3.1 Processor Allocation

The basic idea of our approach is to find a base set for allocation of a job. To speed up this allocation process, the search space should be minimized and any unnecessary search should be avoided in an attempt to find such a base set. The proposed allocation scheme quickly finds the base set through simple address calculation and spatial subtraction. First, we determine a reject area (R_J) and coverage set (C_J) with respect to a job J to be allocated using the busy list, job size, and the system size. Then we spatially subtract R_J and C_J from a set of candidate base blocks to find a base set B_J. The list of candidate (base) blocks is referred to as *candidate list* in this paper. If the candidate list is empty after all the subtractions are completed, then the allocation fails. Otherwise, the candidate list obtained represents the base set for J. A node in one of the base blocks is selected as the base for J. Each block in the candidate list is represented by its base and end addresses.

The proposed allocation scheme first determines $U - R_J$ and inserts the set difference into the candidate list as an initial candidate base block. Given an R_J with a sink $<x_s, y_s>$, the initial candidate block is a submesh $I_f[<0,0>, <x_s - 1, y_s - 1>]$. The coverages in C_J are then spatially subtracted from the initial candidate block. After subtracting a coverage from a candidate block, a new candidate blocks are generated. Then the candidate list is updated by replacing the old candidate block with these newly created candidate blocks. After a coverage is subtracted from all the candidate blocks, the next coverage is subtracted from the updated candidate list. This continues until the coverages in C_J are depleted.

A spatial subtraction operation between two submeshes is illustrated in Fig. 2. The shaded and white rectangles in the figure represent a subtrahend and a minuend submeshes, respectively. Here, the subtrahend chips off the minuend block into smaller disjoint blocks. These smaller blocks with their base and end addresses are shown in Fig. 2. Depending on the configuration of the two submeshes, there may be less than four blocks generated by a spatial subtraction.

As explained earlier, the newly created candidate blocks after a spatial subtraction replace the old candidate block in the candidate list. When more than one candidate blocks

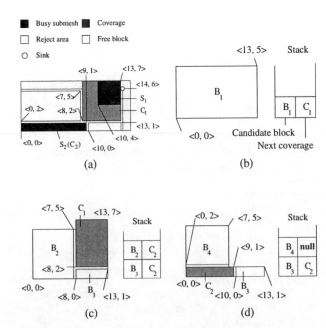

(a)

(b)

(c)

(d)

Figure 3: Allocation of a 3×3 job in $M(16,8)$.

are generated after a subtraction, the length of the candidate list increases and so does the search space. However, to allocate a job we need to find only one base block, which is disjoint with all the coverages. Through the clever implementation of this idea, we can further improve the speed of the already fast algorithm.

The key idea is to implement the candidate list as a stack. A candidate block on top of the stack is always checked to see if it intersects with the next coverage in the coverage set. When a new set of candidate base blocks is generated due to a spatial subtraction, these new candidate blocks are pushed onto the stack replacing the top element. Associated with each candidate base block is a pointer to the next coverage that the candidate block must be checked against. When a new candidate block is created, the next coverage which the new candidate block will be checked against is determined, and they are pushed onto the stack together. The coverages are selected in an arbitrary order. When a candidate block with a null pointer appears on top of the stack, the desired base block is obtained. The node at the lower-left corner of the base block is returned as the base of a free submesh. If no such candidate block is found (that is, when the stack becomes empty), then the allocation fails.

The allocation of $J(3,3)$ using this stack-based algorithm is illustrated in Fig. 3, where an $S_1(4,4)$ and an $S_2(10,2)$ (depicted as dark rectangles) are allocated in an $M(16,8)$. The nodes and links are not shown in the figure for clarity. The coverages of these two busy submeshes are represented as shaded rectangles. First, the reject area R_J with sink $< 14, 6 >$ is determined. Using the sink,

then, an initial candidate block $B_1[< 0, 0 >, < 13, 5 >]$ is pushed onto the stack with C_1 as the next coverage to be checked against as shown in Fig. 3.b. Here, B_1 represents $U - R_J$. Since B_1 and C_1 intersect with each other, a spatial subtraction is carried out and two new candidate blocks, $B_2[<0, 0>, <7, 5>]$ and $B_3[<8, 0>, <13, 1>]$ with the next coverage C_2 are pushed onto the stack as shown in Fig. 3.c. B_2 intersects with C_2, and hence a new candidate block $B_4[<0, 2>, <7, 5>]$ is created after spatially subtracting C_2 from B_2. This is shown in Fig. 3.d. Because there are no more coverages to be checked, a null pointer is pushed with B_4, implying that B_4 is the first base block obtained. Any node in B_4 can be used as a base for J. The lower-left corner of B_4, $<0, 2>$, is returned as the base of a free submesh to accommodate J.

The algorithm also consider all possible orientations of a submesh request to provide complete submesh recognition ability. Detailed steps of the stack-based allocation algorithm are described below.

Stack-based Allocation Algorithm: Stack(J)
Notations:
1. $C_J[i]$ denotes the ith coverage in a coverage set C_J.
2. $f_{coverage}$ denotes the current coverage that a candidate block f needs to be checked against.
3. $stacktop$ represents the candidate base block on top of the stack.
4. $next(k)$ returns $k + 1$ if $C_J[k + 1]$ exists. Otherwise, it returns **null**.

Allocation:
1. Construct the coverage set C_J with respect to J.
2. Determine the initial candidate block and push it with the next coverage onto the stack.
3. While the stack is not empty do
   If $stacktop_{coverage}$ is **null**, then return the base of $stacktop$. Otherwise, $k \leftarrow stacktop_{coverage}$.
   If $stacktop$ intersects with $C_J[k]$ then
      Pop up $stacktop$ from the stack.
      Create new candidate blocks and for each new candidate block f do
         $f_{coverage} \leftarrow next(k)$.
         Push f into the stack.
   Else $stacktop_{coverage} \leftarrow next(stacktop_{coverage})$.
4. If all the orientations of J are considered, then return **fail**. Otherwise, rotate the orientation of J and go to step 1.

Deallocation:
1. Remove the released submesh from the busy list.

The most expensive operation in above algorithm is step 3, in which all of the candidate blocks in the stack must be checked against all the coverages in the worst case. Since there is one coverage for each busy submesh, the number of coverages to be checked is the same as the number of the busy submeshes. Therefore, assuming that the stack length is a constant, the overall time complexity of above algorithm is $O(B)$, where B is the length of the busy list.

The time complexity and other performance characteristics of the proposed algorithm and other existing schemes are compared in [10].

It is interesting to note that the stack-based allocation scheme is versatile in the sense that it can emulate other existing allocation schemes. By manipulating the order in which candidate blocks are pushed into the stack and by using a fixed location in a selected base block as a base, some of the prior algorithms can be emulated with significantly reduced search time. For example, the FF strategy [13] (QA strategy [12]) can be emulated by ordering the candidate blocks in such a way that a block with a base $<x_1, y_1>$ precedes a block with a base $<x_2, y_2>$ when $x_1 < x_2$ or $x_1 = x_2$ and $y_1 > y_2$ ($y_1 < y_2$ or $y_1 = y_2$ and $x_1 < x_2$) and by returning the upper-left (lower-left) corner of the selected base block as a base.

3.2 Job Scheduling

In this subsection, a simple, efficient and starvation-free scheduling policy called *group scheduling* is described. Many previous processor management schemes schedule jobs using the FCFS policy. The major drawback of the FCFS policy is its 'blocking' property. That is, a job that is not allocatable blocks other jobs, which may be serviceable. This unnecessarily increases the queueing delay of the blocked jobs resulting in high response time. The proposed scheduling policy resolves this limitation of FCFS scheduling. The idea is to eliminate such blocking property among a limited number of jobs. The policy collects a number of incoming jobs into a group and schedules the groups in an FCFS order. The number of jobs in a group is referred to as group size and is denoted by Δ. The jobs in a group are considered for allocation in a smallest job first (SJF) order. The size of a job is defined as the number of processors the job requests. The jobs in the same group are maintained in an increasing order of job sizes using a balanced tree data structure. It is important to note that in a submesh allocation failure to allocate a job does not necessarily imply that any job of bigger size cannot be allocated. Due to aspect ratio, for instance, a 2×5 job can be allocated while a 8×1 job may be rejected. Each job in a group has equal priority. That is, a job does not block other jobs in the same group in any circumstances, implying that a failure to allocate a job does not force other jobs in the same group to wait. With the SJF-order allocation and equal priority scheduling, the proposed scheduling scheme increases the parallelism and reduces the average waiting delay for the jobs in the same group.

In the group scheduling policy, an incoming job joins the last group in the system queue. If such a group does not exist or the size of the last group reaches Δ, a new group is created in the queue and the job joins the new group. Since groups are scheduled in an FCFS order, jobs in the head (first) group block incoming jobs as well as the jobs in the

system queue. When a job departs releasing an assigned submesh, the jobs in the head group are considered for allocation (in an SJF order). After all the jobs in the head group are allocated, the group is removed from the queue and the jobs in the next group are considered for allocation. Because a job in the group has higher priority than the jobs in the following groups, no jobs suffer from starvation. The group scheduling scheme can be used with any submesh allocation algorithm. What follows is the detailed description of the group scheduling policy.

Group Scheduling

Notations:
  1. J denotes an incoming job.
  2. $Group_{head}$ denotes the group at the head of system queue. Similarly, $Group_{tail}$ denotes the group at the end of the queue.
  3. insert(J) inserts job J into $Group_{tail}$. When $Group_{tail}$ does not exist or its size has reached Δ, a new group G' is created and J joins G'. G' becomes a new $Groupd_{tail}$.
  4. delete() removes the $Group_{head}$ from the system queue.
  5. allocated(G) returns the number of allocated jobs in group G.

Job Arrival:
  1. insert(J).
  2. If $Group_{head} = Group_{tail}$ and J is allocatable then Allocate J.
     If allocated(G_{head}) = Δ, then delete().

Job Departure:
  1. Allocate the jobs in $Group_{head}$ in an SJF order.
  2. If allocated($Group_{head}$) = Δ then
     delete().
     Go to step 1.

The scheduling algorithm presented above is very simple. The most time-consuming operation is the processor allocation. Since Δ is a constant, the overall time complexity of of the scheduling algorithm is the same as that of the allocation algorithm used.

4 Performance Study

4.1 System Model and Workload Characterization

We have conducted a simulation study to evaluate the performance of the proposed allocation and scheduling schemes. The model simulated is a 32×32 two-dimensional mesh. The workload is characterized by the distribution of job interarrival time, the distribution of job service time, and the distribution of job size. The job interarrival time is assumed to follow an exponential distribution with a mean $\frac{1}{\lambda}$. The job service time (or demand) follows a bimodal hyperexponential distribution, which is considered as the most probable distribution for the processor service time [9], with a mean $\frac{1}{\mu}$. The service demand of a job is computed based on the system load (ρ). The

284

system load is defined as $\rho = \frac{\lambda}{\mu}$, where μ is the mean job service rate and λ is the mean job arrival rate. The mean job service rate is calculated for a given system load and a mean job arrival rate ($\mu = \frac{\lambda}{\rho}$).

Each side of a submesh request is calculated following a uniform, normal, or bimodal uniform distribution. In a bimodal uniform distribution, each side of a submesh request is uniformly selected from an interval $[1, m]$ with a probability φ and selected from an interval $[m+1, l]$ with a probability $(1-\varphi)$ for some integer m ($1 \leq m < l$), where l represents the length of the corresponding side of mesh system.

Three performance parameters are measured in this study: allocation overhead, mean job response time, and processor utilization. The first parameter is an indication of of the speed of the algorithm while the other two parameters are the indicators of actual performance. Allocation overhead is defined as the average run time that the algorithm takes per each allocation. We measure the actual execution time of a simulation run, in which 50000 jobs are allocated using an underlying allocation algorithm and FCFS scheduling. We then divide the measured execution time by the total number of allocation trials to obtain the allocation overhead. Overhead due to simple FCFS scheduling is minimal and hence negligible. For obtaining steady state performance parameters, each run of the simulation continues until 2000 jobs complete execution. Using the independent replication, all the experiments are conducted until 90% confidence level of the results is within 10% of the mean.

4.2 Simulation Results

The performance of the proposed stack-based allocation algorithm is analyzed in Fig. 4 through Fig. 7. The FCFS scheduling policy is used in this study. First, we demonstrate the versatility and the usefulness of the proposed allocation algorithm by comparing the allocation overhead of the bit-map based first fit (BFF) [13] scheme to that of the emulated first fit (EFF). The EFF scheme is simply the BFF policy emulated by our stack-based allocation scheme using the method explained in Section 3.1. Obviously, both algorithms have the same response time behavior. The allocation overhead of both strategies are plotted in Fig. 4 with respect to system load. Job sizes follow a uniform and a bimodal uniform distributions in Fig. 4.a and Fig. 4.b, respectively. As shown in the figure, the allocation overhead of the EFF scheme is negligible compared to the BFF policy. This implies that the same BFF scheme that has been compared and contrasted against many policies can run more efficiently using our stack-based implementation. Such a significant speedup can be attributed to the fact that the proposed stack-based scheme reduces the search space significantly through the use of spatial subtraction. We believe that our allocation scheme can emulate other bitmap-

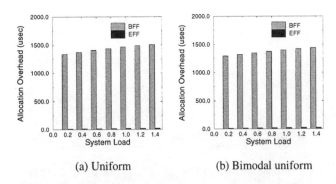

(a) Uniform   (b) Bimodal uniform

Figure 4: Allocation overhead of BFF and EFF algorithms ((b) $\varphi = 0.5$ and $m = 10$).

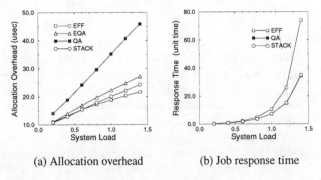

(a) Allocation overhead   (b) Job response time

Figure 5: Performance evaluation of four allocation schemes for a uniform job size distribution.

based allocation schemes with very little allocation overhead.

Since it is evident that the allocation overhead of the bitmap-based FF scheme is considerably higher than its stack-based counterpart, we will not evaluate the performance of the BFF scheme any more in this simulation study. In what follows, the performance of the QA allocation scheme is compared with that of the stack-based allocation algorithm (STACK). Other allocation schemes are not considered in this paper simply because the QA scheme is the fastest of all the allocation algorithms reported in the literature [12]. The QA algorithm is emulated by the stack-based algorithm (hence called emulated quick allocation (EQA) scheme) and its performance is compared to show that the proposed allocation scheme can emulate the QA scheme with far less overhead. The performance of the EFF scheme is also compared to that of the QA algorithm. The only difference between the STACK and its variants (EQA and EFF) is that the variant algorithms need the stack to be arranged in a certain order.

In Fig. 5 and Fig. 6, the performance of the stack-based algorithms, STACK, EQA, and EFF, is compared with that of the QA [12] scheme, when the job size follows a uniform and a bimodal uniform distribution, respectively. The

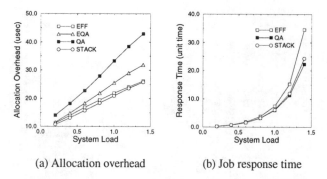

(a) Allocation overhead   (b) Job response time

Figure 6: Performance evaluation of four allocation schemes for a bimodal uniform job size distribution ($\varphi = 0.5$ and $m = 10$).

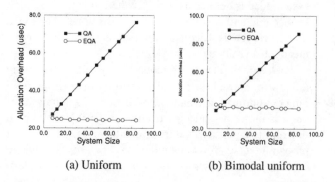

(a) Uniform   (b) Bimodal uniform

Figure 7: Effect of system size on the performance of QA and EQA scheme ((b) $\varphi = 0.5$ and $m = 10$).

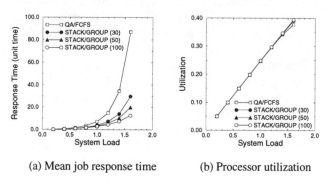

(a) Mean job response time   (b) Processor utilization

Figure 8: Performance evaluation of the Group and the FCFS scheduling policies for uniform job size distribution.

allocation overhead and mean job response time of four policies are plotted with respect to system load. The response time curve of the EQA scheme is identical to that of the QA scheme and hence not shown in the figure. The reader should note that the proposed STACK algorithm reduces the allocation overhead considerably (and hence provides much faster service) compared to the QA algorithm, while providing comparable performance. The allocation overhead reduces by as high as 47% using the STACK algorithm as indicated by Fig. 5.a and Fig. 6.a when the load is high.

The EFF and the EQA schemes also incur much less allocation overhead than the QA policy. The allocation overhead can be reduced by more than 50% (EFF) and 40% (EQA) compared to the QA scheme. Such significant reduction in allocation overhead achieved by the STACK algorithm and its two variants is due to the fact that, unlike the QA scheme, these stack-based algorithms do not need to sort any submeshes. The EFF scheme shows the worst performance, because the EFF scheme considers only a fixed orientation of submesh requests. The effect of the fixed-orientation method on the performance is shown in in Fig. 5.b and Fig. 6.b. Similar performance trend is observed when the job size follows a normal distribution with various means. The results are not shown here due to space limitation.

The effect of system size on the speed of the QA and the EQA schemes is evaluated in Fig. 7. The job size follows a uniform and a bimodal uniform distribution. Square meshes are considered in this experiment for simplicity of plotting graphs. As Fig. 7 indicates, the overhead of the QA algorithm linearly increases as the system size increases, while that of the EQA scheme remains constant. This is because the QA scheme has to find a covered segment for each row, whereas the system size does not affect the speed of the EQA scheme. This implies that the stack-based allocation algorithm (EQA) is highly attractive espe-

cially for large meshes.

The performance of the group scheduling policy is compared to that of FCFS scheduling in Fig. 8 and Fig. 9. The job size follows a uniform and a bimodal uniform distribution in Fig. 8 and Fig. 9, respectively. The QA scheme is used with the FCFS scheduling policy, whereas the STACK algorithm is used with the group scheduling. For group scheduling, three different group sizes (30, 50, and 100) are considered. As the graphs indicate, the group scheduling scheme shows far better response time behavior than the FCFS scheduling policy with even a small group size. With this policy, the response time improves by more than 80% compared to FCFS scheduling under moderate to heavy load. The fact that the group scheduling even with a small group size (30) can achieve significant improvement in response time over FCFS scheduling reveals the negative effect of the blocking property of the FCFS policy. The proposed scheduling policy eliminates any waiting time (or queueing delay) due to the blocking for the jobs in the same group. Since the queueing delay due to blocking is far greater than the actual execution time in most cases (especially when the system load is high), the elimination of such unnecessary queueing delay even for a small number of jobs improves the overall job response time consid-

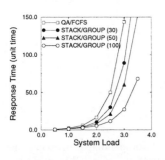 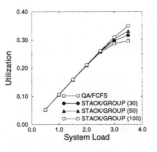

(a) Mean job response time   (b) Processor utilization

Figure 9: Performance evaluation of the Group and the FCFS scheduling policies for bimodal uniform job size distribution ($\varphi = 0.5$ and $m = 10$).

erably. The improvement in processor utilization due to group scheduling is not as significant as the improvement in response time. This is because the groups are scheduled using the FCFS scheduling policy and hence a job may block other serviceable jobs in following groups. Due to this blocking between groups, the overall completion time does not improve much and neither does the processor utilization. The effect of group size on the response time has also been analyzed. However, in the interest of brevity, these results are not presented here. Interested readers may refer to [10].

5 Conclusions

It has been observed that the performance gain obtained by improving the efficiency of an underlying allocation algorithm, at the expense of high run-time overhead, is insignificant and that job scheduling plays an equally important role in improving the system performance. In an effort to resolve such limitations, we propose two novel processor management techniques for two-dimensional mesh-connected multicomputers in this paper.

First, an allocation algorithm that uses a stack (hence called the stack-based allocation algorithm) is proposed for fast and efficient processor allocation. The algorithm can find a free submesh very quickly by the use of simple coordinate calculation and spatial subtraction. Simulation results reveal that the stack-based allocation algorithm is faster than any other existing allocation schemes and can still deliver comparable performance.

Next, a simple but efficient scheduling policy, called group scheduling, is proposed. This policy schedules groups of jobs in an FCFS order in such a way that the jobs in the same group do not block each other. The simulation results indicate that, even with a small group size, the group scheduling strategy reduces response time considerably compared to the conventional FCFS scheduling policy. The stack-based allocation and group scheduling,

when used together, can provide faster service to users with very little overhead.

Acknowledgment

The authors would like to thank S. Yoo for providing source code for his approach [12].

References

[1] D. Babbar and P. Krueger, "A Performance Comparison of Processor Allocation and Job Scheduling Algorithms for Mesh-Connected Multiprocessors," *Proc. 6th IEEE Symp. on Parallel and Distributed Processing*, pp. 46-53, Oct. 1994.

[2] P. J. Chuang and N. F. Tzeng, "An Efficient Submesh Allocation Strategy for Mesh Computer Systems," *Proc. Int'l Conf. on Distributed Computing Systems*, pp. 256-263, May 1991.

[3] J. Ding and L. N. Bhuyan, "An Adaptive Submesh Allocation Strategy for Two-Dimensional Mesh Connected Systems," *Proc. Int'l Conf. on Parallel Processing*, Vol. II, pp. 193-200, Aug. 1993.

[4] P. Krueger, T. H. Lai and V. A. Radiya, "Job Scheduling Is More Important than Processor Allocation for Hypercube Computers," *IEEE Trans. on Parallel and Distributed Systems*, Vol. 5, pp. 488-497, May 1994.

[5] K. Li and K. H. Cheng, "A Two Dimensional Buddy System for Dynamic Resource Allocation in A Partitionable Mesh Connected System," *Proc. ACM Computer Science Conf.*, pp. 22-28, Feb. 1990.

[6] T. Liu, W. Huang, F. Lombardi and L. N. Bhuyan, "A Submesh Allocation Scheme for Mesh-Connected Multiprocessor Systems," *Proc. Int'l Conf. on Parallel Processing*, Vol. II, pp. 159-163, Aug. 1995.

[7] W. Liu, V. Lo and B. Nitzberg, "Non-contiguous Processor Allocation Algorithms for Distributed Memory Multicomputers," *Proc. Supercomputing '94*, pp. 227-236, 1994.

[8] D. Das Sharma and D. K. Pradhan, "A Fast and Efficient Strategy for Submesh Allocation in Mesh-Connected Parallel Computers," *Proc. 5th IEEE Symp. on Parallel and Distributed Processing*, pp. 682-689, Dec. 1993.

[9] K. S. Trivedi, *Probability and Statistics with Reliability, Queuing, and Computer Science Applications*, Prentice-Hall Inc., 1982.

[10] B. S. Yoo and C. R. Das, "A Fast and Efficient Processor Management Scheme for Mesh-Connected Multicomputer Systems," Technical Report, CSE-97-002, Dept. of Computer Science and Engineering, The Pennsylvania State University, May 1997.

[11] B. S. Yoo, C. R. Das and C. Yu, "Processor Management Techniques for Mesh-Connected Multiprocessors," *Proc. Int'l Conf. on Parallel Processing*, Vol. II, pp. 105-112, Aug. 1995.

[12] S. M. Yoo and H. Y. Youn, "An Efficient Task Allocation Scheme for Two-Dimensional Mesh-Connected Systems," *Proc. Int'l. Conf. on Distributed Computing Systems*, pp. 501-508, May 1995.

[13] Y. Zhu, "Efficient Processor Allocation Strategies for Mesh-Connected Parallel Computers," *Journal of Parallel and Distributed Computing*, Vol. 16, pp. 328-337, Dec. 1992.

Automatic Parallelization and Scheduling of Programs on Multiprocessors using CASCH

Ishfaq Ahmad[1], Yu-Kwong Kwok[1], Min-You Wu[2] and Wei Shu[2]

[1]Department of Computer Science, The Hong Kong University of Science and Technology, Hong Kong
[2]Department of Computer Science, State University of New York at Buffalo, New York
Email: {iahmad, csricky}@cs.ust.hk, {wu, shu}@cs.buffalo.edu

Abstract[†]

The lack of a versatile software tool for parallel program development has been one of the major obstacles for exploiting the potential of high-performance architectures. In this paper, we describe an experimental software tool called CASCH (Computer Aided SCHeduling) for parallelizing and scheduling applications to parallel processors. CASCH transforms a sequential program to a parallel program with automatic scheduling, mapping, communication, and synchronization. The major strength of CASCH is its extensive library of scheduling and mapping algorithms representing a broad range of state-of-the-art work reported in the recent literature. These algorithms are applied for allocating a parallelized program to the processors, and thus the algorithms can be interactively analyzed, tested and compared using real data on a common platform with various performance objectives. CASCH is useful for both novice and expert programmers of parallel machines, and can serve as a teaching and learning aid for understanding scheduling and mapping algorithms.

1 Introduction

Parallel machines provide tremendous potential for high performance but their programming can be a tedious task. The software development process for parallel processing includes designing a parallel algorithm, partitioning the data and control, communication, synchronization, scheduling, mapping, and identifying and interpreting various performance measures. While an efficient implementation of some of these tasks can only be done manually, a number of tedious chores, such as scheduling, mapping, and communication can be automated.

Several research efforts have demonstrated the usefulness of program development tools for parallel processing. Essentially, these tools can be classified into two types. The first type of tools are mostly commercial tools which provide software development and debugging environments [5], [6], [10]. Some of these tools also provide performance tuning and other program development facilities [3], [11], [19]. A major drawback of some of these tools is that they are essentially simulation environments. While they can help in understanding the operation and behavior of scheduling and mapping algorithms, they are inadequate for practical purposes. The second type of tools performs some program transformation through program restructuring [7], [9], [13], [17], [22], [23], [24]. However, these tools are usually not well integrated with sophisticated scheduling algorithms.

In this paper, we describe a software tool called CASCH (Computer Aided SCHeduling) for parallel processing on distributed-memory multiprocessors. CASCH can be considered to be a super set of tools such as PAWS [19], Hypertool [23], PYRROS [24], and Parallax [17], since it includes the major functionalities of these tools at a more advanced and comprehensive level and also offers additional useful features. CASCH is aimed to be a complete parallel programming environment including parallelization, partitioning, scheduling, mapping, communication, synchronization, code generation, and performance evaluation. Parallelization is performed by a compiler that automatically converts sequential applications into parallel codes. The parallel code is optimized through proper scheduling and mapping, and is executed on a target machine. CASCH provides an extensive library of state-of-the-art scheduling algorithms from the recent literature. The library of scheduling algorithms is organized into different categories which are suitable for different architectural environments.

The scheduling and mapping algorithms are used for scheduling the task graph generated from the user program. The weights on the nodes and edges of the task graph are computed using a database that contains the timing of various computation, communication, and I/O operations for different machines. These timings are obtained through benchmarking. An attractive feature of CASCH is its easy-to-use GUI for analyzing various scheduling and mapping algorithms using task graphs generated randomly, interactively, or directly from real programs. The best schedule generated by an algorithm can be used by the code generator for generating a parallel program for a particular machine—the same process can be repeated for another machine.

The rest of this paper is organized as follows. Section 2 gives an overview of CASCH and describes it major functionalities. Section 3 includes the results of the experiments conducted on the Intel Paragon using CASCH. The last section includes a discussion of the future work and some concluding remarks.

2 Overview of CASCH

The overall organization of CASCH is shown in Figure 1. The main components of CASCH includes:
- A compiler which includes a lexer and a parser;
- A DAG (directed acyclic graph) generator;
- A weight estimator;
- A scheduling/mapping tool;
- A communication inserter;
- An interactive display unit;
- A code generator;
- A performance evaluation module.

These components are described below.

User Programs: Using the CASCH tool, the user first writes a sequential program from which a DAG is generated.

---

†. This research was partly supported by a grant from the Hong Kong Research Grants Council under contract number HKUST 734/96E and HKUST RI 93/94.EG06.

To facilitate the automation of program development, we use a programming style in which a program is composed of a set of procedures called from the main program. A procedure is an indivisible unit of computation to be scheduled on one processor. The grain sizes of procedures are determined by the programmer, and can be modified with CASCH.

The control dependencies can be ignored, so that a procedure call can be executed whenever all input data of the procedure are available. Data dependencies are defined by the single assignment of parameters in procedure calls. Communications are invoked only at the beginning and the end of procedures. In other words, a procedure receives messages before it begins execution, and it sends messages after it has finished the computation.

Lexer and Parser: The lexer and parser analyze the data dependencies and user defined partitions. For a static program, the number of procedures are known before program execution. Such a program can be executed sequentially or in parallel. It is system independent since communication primitives are not specified in the program. Data dependencies among the procedural parameters define a macro dataflow graph.

Weight Estimator: The weights on the nodes and edges of the DAG are inserted with the help of an estimator that provides timings of various instructions as well as the cost of communication on a given machine. The estimator uses actual timings of various computation, communication, and I/O operations on various machines. These timings are obtained through benchmarking using an approach similar to [19]. Communication estimation, which is obtained experimentally, is based on the cost for each communication primitive, such as *send*, *receive*, and *broadcast*.

DAG Generation: A macro dataflow graph, which is generated directly from the main program, is a directed graph with a start and an end point. Each node corresponds to a procedure, and the node weight is represented by the procedure execution time. Each edge corresponds to a message transferred from one procedure to another procedure, and the weight of the edge is equal to the transmission time of the message. When two nodes are scheduled to a single processor, the weight of the edge connecting them becomes zero. The execution time of a node is obtained by using the estimator. The transmission time of a message is estimated by using the message start-up time, message length, and communication channel bandwidth.

Scheduling/Mapping Tool: A common approach to distributing workload to processors is to partition a problem into P tasks and perform a one-to-one mapping between the tasks and the processors. Partitioning can be done with the "block", "cyclic", or "block-cyclic" pattern [10]. Such partitioning schemes are suitable for problems with regular structures. Simple scheduling heuristics such as the "owner compute" rule work for certain problems but could fail for many others, especially for irregular problems, as it is difficult to balance load and minimize dependencies simultaneously. The way to solve irregular problems is to partition the problem into many tasks which are scheduled for a balanced load and minimized communication. In CASCH, a DAG generated based on this partitioning is scheduled using a scheduling algorithm. However, one scheduling algorithm may not be suitable for a certain problem on a given architecture.

CASCH includes various algorithms (see Figure 1) which are suitable to various environments. Currently, CASCH includes three classes of algorithms [2]: the *UNC (unbounded number of clusters)*, the *BNP (bounded number of processors)*, and the *APN (arbitrary processor network)* scheduling algorithms. The UNC scheduling algorithms, which are mostly based on clustering techniques, are designed for scheduling with unlimited number of processors. The BNP scheduling algorithms, which are based on the *list*

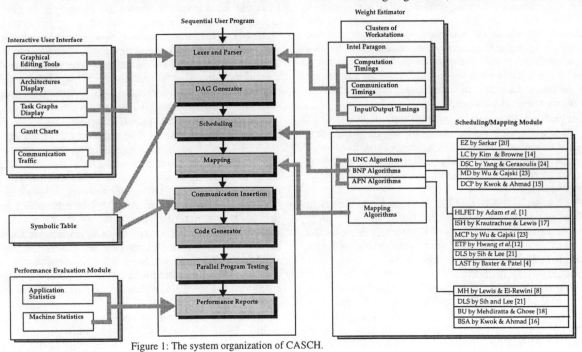

Figure 1: The system organization of CASCH.

scheduling technique [1], are suitable for scheduling when only a limited number of processors are available. The APN scheduling algorithms, which take into consideration link contention and the topology of target processor network, are useful for scheduling a distributed system.

Communication Insertion and Code Generation: Synchronization among the tasks running on multiple processors is carried out by communication primitives. The basic communication primitives for exchanging messages between processors are *send* and *receive*. They must be used properly to ensure a correct sequence of computation. These primitives are inserted automatically, reducing a programmer's burden and eliminating insertion errors. The procedure for inserting communication primitive is as follows. After scheduling and mapping, each node in a macro dataflow graph is allocated to a processor. If an edge leaves from a node to another node which belongs to a different processor, the *send* primitive is inserted after the node. Similarly, if an edge comes from another node in a different processor, the *receive* primitive is inserted before the node. However, if a message has already been sent to a particular processor, the same message does not need to be sent to the same processor again. If a message is to be sent to many processors, *broadcasting* or *multicasting* can be applied instead of separate message. After the communication primitives are properly inserted, parallel code is generated by including appropriate library procedures from a standard package such as the NX of the Intel Paragon.

3 Performance Results

CASCH runs on a SUN workstation that is linked through a network to an Intel Paragon. We have parallelized several applications on CASCH by using the scheduling algorithms described above (see Figure 1). In this paper we discuss the performance of two applications: Gaussian elimination and Laplace equation solver. The objective of including these results is to demonstrate the viability and usefulness of CASCH as well as to make a comparison among various scheduling algorithms. For reference, we have also included the results obtained with manually generated code. A manual code is generated by first partitioning the data among processors in a fashion that reduces the dependencies among these partitions. Based on this partitioning, an SPMD-based code is generated for each processors.

The performance measures include the program execution time (the maximum finish time out of all processors) measured on the Intel Paragon, the number of processors used by the schedule (and hence by the application program) generated by the scheduling algorithm, and the running time of the scheduling algorithm.

The first set of results (see Figure 2) are for the Gaussian elimination application with four different sizes of input matrix dimensions: 4, 8, 16, and 32. Figure 2(a) shows the execution times for various data sizes using different algorithms. We observe that the execution times vary considerably with different algorithms. Among the UNC algorithm, the DCP algorithm yields the best performance due to its superior scheduling method. Among the BNP algorithms, MCP and DLS are in general better, primarily because of their better task priority assignment methods. Among the APN algorithms, BSA and MH perform better,

Algorithm	Matrix Dimension			
	4	8	16	32
Manual	0.14	0.42	2.42	4.52
DCP	0.10	0.11	0.28	1.21
DSC	0.11	0.14	N.A.	N.A.
EZ	0.12	0.15	0.32	1.38
LC	0.10	0.13	0.32	1.42
MD	0.11	0.13	0.30	1.29
ETF	0.11	0.13	0.31	1.34
HLFET	0.11	0.14	0.35	2.47
ISH	0.11	0.14	0.34	1.29
LAST	0.12	0.16	0.33	1.50
MCP	0.11	0.16	0.30	1.28
DLS	0.11	0.14	0.29	1.30
BSA	0.11	0.13	0.32	1.42
BU	0.11	0.34	0.35	1.52
DLS	0.11	0.23	0.34	1.39
MH	0.12	0.26	0.33	1.28

(a) Execution Times (sec.) on the Paragon.

Algorithm	Matrix Dimension			
	4	8	16	32
Manual	4	8	16	32
DCP	3	7	10	22
DSC	5	22	95	128
EZ	1	2	15	33
LC	8	16	32	64
MD	2	3	4	7
ETF	3	7	16	32
HLFET	3	7	16	32
ISH	2	9	21	56
LAST	1	5	13	29
MCP	3	7	16	32
DLS	3	7	16	32
BSA	3	6	12	32
BU	8	20	38	48
DLS	3	7	12	16
MH	1	2	6	17

(b) Number of processors used.

Algorithm	Matrix Dimension (No. of Tasks)			
	4 (20)	8 (54)	16 (170)	32 (594)
DCP	6.22	6.48	13.29	281.54
DSC	0.04	0.05	0.09	0.23
EZ	6.19	6.50	14.81	330.15
LC	0.05	0.06	0.08	0.27
MD	6.21	6.84	38.91	2671.4
ETF	0.05	0.07	0.21	2.26
HLFET	0.06	0.07	0.15	0.69
ISH	0.05	0.07	0.08	0.32
LAST	0.05	0.08	0.24	2.23
MCP	0.05	0.07	0.09	0.40
DLS	0.04	0.08	0.28	2.84
BSA	0.74	1.96	13.57	224.05
BU	0.36	0.37	0.43	0.97
DLS	1.74	15.33	301.66	7459.3
MH	0.75	1.38	10.14	364.75

(c) Scheduling times (sec.) on a SPARC Station 2.

Figure 2: Execution times, number of processors used and scheduling times for the Gaussian elimination application.

due to their proper allocations of tasks and messages. All algorithms perform better than manually generated code: Compared to the manual scheduling, the level of performance improvement is up to 400%. The number of processors used by these algorithms is shown in Figure 2(b). The BU algorithm has a tendency of using a large number of processors. The times taken by various scheduling algorithms for generating the schedules for the Gaussian elimination example are included in Figure 2(c). We notice that these scheduling times vary drastically. The MD and DLS algorithms take considerably longer time to generate solutions while DSC and MCP are much faster.

Our second application is a Gauss-Seidel based algorithm to solve Laplace equations. The 4 matrix sizes used are 4, 8, 16, and 32. The application execution times using various algorithms and data size are shown in Figure 3(a). Again, using the best algorithms, such as DCP, more than 400% improvement over manually generated code is obtained. The UNC algorithms in general yield better schedules (mainly because they tend to use large numbers of processors). The numbers of processors used by these algorithms are shown in Figure 3(b). Again, the number of processors used by the DSC algorithm is quite large as compared to the other algorithms. The running times of the scheduling algorithms are shown in Figure 3(c) which are consistent with our earlier observations.

A number of conclusions can be made from the above results. First, in general UNC algorithms generate shorter schedules but uses more processors than BNP and APN

	Matrix Dimension						Matrix Dimension			
Algorithm	4	8	16	32		Algorithm	4	8	16	32
Manual	0.72	2.89	24.12	72.32		Manual	2	4	8	16
DCP	0.72	1.06	6.08	16.02		DCP	1	4	4	8
DSC	0.72	1.34	6.30	16.42		DSC	1	7	4	14
EZ	0.72	1.44	6.95	18.28		EZ	1	8	2	39
LC	0.54	1.25	6.95	18.81		LC	2	4	4	8
MD	0.72	1.25	6.52	17.08		MD	1	4	3	6
ETF	0.72	1.25	6.73	17.75		ETF	1	4	4	6
HLFET	0.72	1.34	7.60	32.71		HLFET	1	4	4	7
ISH	0.72	1.34	7.39	17.08		ISH	1	5	4	14
LAST	0.72	1.54	7.17	19.87		LAST	1	3	2	5
MCP	0.72	1.54	6.52	16.95		MCP	1	4	4	7
DLS	0.72	1.34	6.30	17.22		DLS	1	4	4	6
BSA	0.72	1.25	6.95	18.81		BSA	1	5	4	7
BU	0.59	3.26	7.60	20.13		BU	2	5	5	5
DLS	0.72	1.92	8.69	23.25		DLS	1	1	1	1
MH	0.72	1.92	8.69	23.25		MH	1	1	1	1

(a) Execution Times (sec.) on the Paragon. (b) Number of processors used.

	Matrix Dimension (No. of Tasks)			
Algorithm	4 (18)	8 (66)	16 (258)	32 (1026)
DCP	8.58	7.03	9.60	44.95
DSC	0.07	0.04	0.10	0.29
EZ	8.63	7.15	9.71	35.00
LC	0.06	0.07	0.09	0.16
MD	8.58	7.65	10.01	111.99
ETF	0.05	0.07	0.10	0.30
HLFET	0.08	0.09	0.11	0.29
ISH	0.04	0.08	0.09	0.35
LAST	0.08	0.10	0.15	0.82
MCP	0.03	0.04	0.10	0.19
DLS	0.05	0.07	0.10	0.36
BSA	1.07	2.81	4.92	27.99
BU	0.47	0.37	0.50	0.73
DLS	1.66	7.81	10.86	75.90
MH	1.00	2.41	3.25	16.29

(c) Scheduling times (sec.) on a SPARC Station 2.

Figure 3: Execution times, number of processors used and scheduling times for the Laplace equation solver application.

algorithms. Thus, UNC algorithms are more suitable for MPPs. Second, BNP algorithms require less time for scheduling than UNC and APN algorithms and therefore are more suitable for scheduling under time constraint. Finally, APN algorithms tend to use less processors, due to its consideration of link contention, but generate slightly longer schedules for the Intel Paragon which has a fast network. Thus, APN algorithms are more suitable for distributed systems such as a network of workstations (NOW).

4 Conclusions and Future Work

The main objectives of CASCH are automatic parallelization and scheduling of applications to parallel processors. CASCH achieves these objectives by providing a unified environment for various existing and conceptual machines. Users can optimize their code by choosing the best algorithm. We are currently working on extending the capabilities of CASCH by including the following:

- including support for distributed computing systems such as a collection of diverse machines working as a distributed heterogeneous supercomputer system;
- extending the current database of benchmark timings by including more detailed and lower level timings of various computation, communication and I/O operations of various existing machines;
- including debugging facilities for error detection and global variable checking, etc.;
- expressing various kinds of parallelism, use a functional or logic programming language or object oriented language such as C++;

- designing a partitioning module for automatic or interactive partitioning of programs.

References

[1] T.L. Adam, K.M. Chandy, and J. Dickson, "A Comparison of List Scheduling for Parallel Processing Systems," *Comm. of the ACM*, vol. 17, pp. 685-690, Dec. 1974.

[2] I. Ahmad, Y.-K. Kwok, and M.-Y. Wu, "Analysis, Evaluation and Comparison of Algorithms for Scheduling Task Graphs to Parallel Processors," Proc. of *the 1996 Int'l Symposium on Parallel Architecture, Algorithms and Networks*, Beijing, China, Jun. 1996, pp. 207-213.

[3] B. Appelbe and K. Smith, "A Parallel-Programming Toolkit," *IEEE Software*, pp. 29-38, Jul. 1989.

[4] J. Baxter and J.H. Patel, "The LAST Algorithm: A Heuristic-Based Static Task Allocation Algorithm," Proc. *ICPP*, vol. II, pp. 217-222, Aug. 1989.

[5] Cray Research Inc., *UNICOS Performance Utilities Reference Manual*, sr2040 6.0 edition, 1991.

[6] Digital Equipment Corp., *PARASPHERE User Guide*.

[7] J.J. Dongarra and D.C. Sorensen, *Schedule Users Guide*, Tech. Rep. Version 1.1, Argonne National Lab., Jun. 1987.

[8] H. El-Rewini and T.G. Lewis, "Scheduling Parallel Programs onto Arbitrary Target Machines," *J. of Parallel and Dist. Computing*, vol. 9, no. 2, pp. 138-153, Jun. 1990.

[9] B.C. Gorda and E.D. Brooks III., "Gang Scheduling a Parallel machine," Technical Report UCRL--JC--107020, Lawrence Livermore National Laboratory.

[10] High Performance Fortran Forum, *High performance fortran language specification*, Technical Report Version 1.0, Rice University, May 1993.

[11] M.T. Heath and J.A. Etheridge, "Visualizing the Performance of Parallel Programs," *IEEE Software*, 8(5):29-39, 1991.

[12] J.J.Hwang, Y.C. Chow, F.D. Anger and C.Y. Lee, "Scheduling Precedence Graphs in Systems with Interprocessor Communication Times," *SIAM Journal of Computing*, vol. 18, no. 2, pp. 244-257, Apr. 1989.

[13] K. Kennedy, K.S. McKinley, and C. Tseng, "Interactive Parallel Programming Using the Parascope Editor," *IEEE Trans. Parallel and Dist. Systems*, 2(3):329--341, 1991.

[14] S.J. Kim and J.C. Browne, "A General Approach to Mapping of Parallel Computation upon Multiprocessor Architectures," Proc. *ICPP*, vol. II, pp. 1-8, Aug. 1988.

[15] Y.-K. Kwok and I. Ahmad, "Dynamic Critical-Path Scheduling: An Effective Technique for Allocating Task Graphs to Multiprocessors," *IEEE Trans. on Parallel and Distributed Systems*, vol. 7, no. 5, May 1996, pp. 506-521.

[16] —, "Bubble Scheduling: A Quasi Dynamic Algorithm for Static Allocation of Tasks to Parallel Architectures," Proceedings of the *7th IEEE Symposium on Parallel and Distributed Processing*, Oct. 1995, pp. 36-43.

[17] T.G. Lewis and H. El-Rewini, "Parallax: A Tool for Parallel Program Scheduling," *IEEE Parallel & Distributed Technology*, vol.1, no. 3, pp. 62-72, May 1993.

[18] N. Mehdiratta and K. Ghose, "A Bottom-Up Approach to Task Scheduling on Distributed Memory Multiprocessor," Proc. *ICPP*, vol. II, pp. 151-154, Aug. 1994.

[19] D. Pease, A. Ghafoor, I. Ahmad, K. Foudil-Bey, D. Andrews, T. Karpinski, M. Mikki and M. Zerrouki, "PAWS: A performance Assessment Tool for Parallel Computing Systems," *IEEE Computer*, vol. 24, no. 1, pp. 18-29, Jan. 1991.

[20] V. Sarkar, *Partitioning and Scheduling Parallel Programs for Multiprocessors*, MIT Press, Cambridge, MA, 1989.

[21] G.C. Sih and E.A. Lee, "A Compile-Time Scheduling Heuristic for Interconnection-Constrained Heterogeneous Processor Architectures," *IEEE Trans. on Parallel and Distributed Systems*, vol. 4, no. 2, pp. 75-87, Feb. 1993.

[22] M. Wolfe, "The Tiny Loop Restructuring Research Tool," Proc. *ICPP*, vol. II, pp. 46-53, Aug. 1991.

[23] M.-Y. Wu and D.D. Gajski, "Hypertool: A Programming Aid for Message-Passing Systems," *IEEE Trans. Parallel and Distributed Systems*, 1(3):330-343, Jul. 1990.

[24] T. Yang and A. Gerasoulis, "PYRROS: Static Task Scheduling and Code Generation for Message-Passing Multiprocessors," *The 6th ACM Int'l Conf. on Supercomputing*, Jul. 1992.

Probabilistic Rotation: Scheduling Graphs with Uncertain Execution Time[†]

Sissades Tongsima[‡]   Chantana Chantrapornchai[‡]   Edwin H.-M. Sha[‡]   Nelson Passos[§]

Abstract

This paper proposes an algorithm called probabilistic rotation scheduling which takes advantage of loop pipelining to schedule tasks with uncertain times to a parallel processing system. These tasks normally occur when conditional instructions are employed and/or inputs of the tasks influence the computation time. We show that based on our loop scheduling algorithm the length of the resulting schedule can be guaranteed to be satisfied for a given probability. The experiments show that the resulting schedule length for a given probability of confidence can be significantly better than the schedules obtained by worst-case or average-case scenario.

1 Introduction

In many practical applications such as interface systems, fuzzy systems, and artificial intelligence systems, etc., many tasks from these applications normally have uncertain computation time. Such tasks normally contain conditional instructions and/or operations that may take different computation time when calculating different inputs. A dynamic scheduling scheme may be considered to address the problem; however, the decision of the run-time scheduler which depends on the local on-line knowledge may not give a good overall schedule. Although many static scheduling techniques can thoroughly check for the best assignment for dependent tasks, the existing methods are not able to deal with such an uncertainty. Therefore, either worst-case or average-case computation for the task (may not reflect the real operating situation) is usually assumed.

For iterative applications, the statistics of a computation time of those uncertain tasks are not difficult to be collected. In order to take advantage of these statistical data and loop pipelining, a novel loop scheduling algorithm, called *probabilistic rotation scheduling* (PRS), is introduced in this paper. This algorithm attempts to expose the parallelism of those certain and uncertain tasks (collectively called *probabilistic tasks*) within each iteration. The synchronization is then applied at the end of each iteration. Such a parallel computing style is also known as *synchronous parallelism* [2, 11]. The proposed algorithm takes an input application which is modeled as a hierarchical data-flow graph (DFG) where a node corresponds to a task, e.g., a collection of statements, and a set of edges represents dependencies

between these tasks. The dependency distances, also called *delays*, between tasks in different iterations is represented by short bar lines on those edges. The computation time of these nodes can be either fixed or varied. A probability model is employed to represent the timing of the probabilistic tasks.

Considerable research has been conducted in the area of scheduling directed-acyclic graphs (DAGs) to the multiple processing system. Such graphs are obtained by ignoring edges containing one or more delays. Many heuristics have been proposed, e.g., list scheduling, and graph decomposition [5, 6], to schedule the DAG. These methods consider neither exploring the parallelism across iterations nor addressing the problem with the probabilistic tasks. In [7, 8], Ku and De Micheli proposed the relative scheduling method which handles tasks with unbounded nodes. Their approach, however, considers DAG as an input graph and does not explore the parallelism across iterations. Furthermore, if the statistics of the computation time of uncertain nodes can be collected, their method will not use these statistical information. For the class of global scheduling, software pipelining [9] is used to overlap instructions, i.e., exposing the parallelism across iterations. This technique, however, expands the graph by unfolding it. Furthermore, such an approach is limited to solving the problem without considering the uncertainty of the computation time [3, 9].

A rotation scheduling technique was developed by Chao, La-Paugh and Sha [1] This technique assigns nodes from a DFG to the system with limited number of functional units. It implicitly explores traditional retiming [10] in order to reduce the total computation time of the nodes along the longest paths, (also called the critical paths) in the DFG. In this paper, the rotation scheduling technique is extended so that it can deal with those uncertain tasks. An application with probabilistic execution time is transformed to a graph model, called the *probabilistic data-flow graph* (PG), which is a generalization of the DFG model. After the initial execution order and functional unit assignment are given. The probabilistic rotation scheduling is applied so that the total computation time of the final schedule above a given probability can be reduced by exploring parallelism across iterations. As an example, Figures 1(a) and 1(b) show a PG and its corresponding computation times distribution for each node.

Since the computation times in PG are random variables, the total computation time of the graph is also a random variable. The concept of a *control step*, i.e., the synchronization time of the tasks within each iteration, is no longer applicable. A schedule conveys only the *execution order*, of the tasks being executed in a functional unit and/or between different units. Our technique

[†] This work was supported in part by the NFS grant MIP 95-01006.

[‡] Dept. of Computer Sci. and Engr., Notre Dame, IN 46556.

[§] Midwestern State University, Wichita Falls, TX 76308.

Time	Nodes			
	A	B	C	D
1	0	0	0	0
2	1	0.80	1	0.75
3	0	0	0	0
4	0	0.20	0	0.25

(a) PG   (b) Its computation time

Fig. 1: PG and its computation time

will give a good initial schedule whose length is guaranteed for a given probability. Therefore, the resulting schedule is most likely satisfied the system constraints and the number of redesign cycles can be reduced. In order to compute the total computation time of this order, a *probabilistic task-assignment graph* (PTG) is constructed. Such a graph is obtained from the original PG in which non-zero delay edges are ignored and each node is assigned to a specific functional unit in the system. The PTG also contains some extra edges, called *flow-control* edges, and each of which is established between two independent tasks u and v where u is executed right before v within the same functional unit.

2 Background

A probabilistic data flow graph (PG) is a vertex-weighted, edge-weighted, directed graph $G = \langle V, E, d, T \rangle$, where V is the set of vertices representing tasks, E is the set of edges representing the data dependencies between vertices, d is a function from E to $\mathbb{Z}^+$, the set of positive integers, representing the number of delays on an edge, and T_v is a random variable representing the computation time of a node $v \in V$. Note that an ordinary DFG is a special case of the PG. A *probability distribution* of T is assumed to be discrete in this paper. The granularity of the resulting probability distribution, if necessary, depends on the need of accuracy. The notation $\mathcal{P}(T = x)$ is read "the probability that the random variable T assumes the value x". The *probability function* is a function that maps the possible value x to its probability, i.e., $p(x) = \mathcal{P}(T = x)$. Each vertex $v \in V$ from the PG is weighted with the probability distribution of the computation time, T_v, where T_v is a discrete random variable associated with the set of possible computation time of the vertex v such that $\sum_{\forall x} \mathcal{P}(T_v = x) = 1$. For those nodes with only one computation time t in the PG, $\mathcal{P}(T = t) = 1$. An edge $e \in E$ from nodes u to v, is denoted by $u \xrightarrow{e} v$ and a path p starting from node u and ending at node v is indicated by the notation $u \xrightarrow{p} v$.

An *iteration* is the execution pattern of each node in V exactly once. Iterations are identified by an index i starting from 0. Inter-iteration dependencies are represented by weighted edges. An iteration is associated with a static schedule. A static schedule must obey the precedence relations defined by the data flow graph. For any iteration j, an edge e from u to v with delay $d(e)$ conveys that the computation of node v at iteration j depends on the execution of node u at iteration $j - d(e)$. An edge with no delays represents a data dependency within the same iteration. A legal data flow graph must have a strictly positive delay cycles,

i.e., the summation of the delay functions along any cycle cannot be less than or equal to zero.

The execution order of the PG can be defined as: A probabilistic task-assignment graph (PTG) $G = \langle V, E, w, T, b \rangle$, is a vertex-weighted, edge-weighted, directed acyclic graph, where V is the set of vertices representing tasks, E is the set of edges representing the data dependencies between vertices, w is a edge-type function from $e \in E$ to $\{0, 1\}$, where 0 represents the type of dependency edge and 1 represents the type of flow-control edge, T_v is a random variable representing the computation time of a node $v \in V$, and b is a processor binding function from $v \in V$ to $\{PE_i, 1 \leq i \leq n\}$, where PE_i is processing element i and n is the total number of processing elements. For example, Figure 2 shows a PTG and its corresponding execution order while two processing elements are available. Nodes B and D are assigned to PE_0. That is $b(B) = b(D) = PE_0$. Meanwhile $b(C) = b(A) = PE_1$. Edges consists of $C \xrightarrow{e_1} A$, $C \xrightarrow{e_2} D$, $B \xrightarrow{e_3} D$ where $w(e_1) = 1$ and $w(e_2) = w(e_3) = 0$.

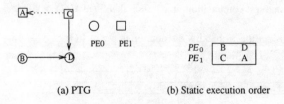

(a) PTG   (b) Static execution order

Fig. 2: A PTG and its execution order

3 Probabilistic Rotation Scheduling (PRS)

Recall the definition of a probabilistic data flow graph (PG) found in Section 2. Since the computation time of each vertex of a PG is a random variable, the traditional notion of a fixed global cycle period, $\Phi(G)$, for PG G is no longer valid. Therefore, the random variable called the maximum reaching time (mrt) is introduced. The notation $\mathrm{mrt}(u, v)$ represents the probabilistic critical path length for the portion of the graph between nodes u and v. Likewise, $\mathrm{mrt}(G)$ is the maximum reaching time of graph G, which represents the probabilistic cycle period for graph G, i.e., the probabilistic schedule length of G.

Note that the mrt of PTG represents the probabilistic cycle period, i.e., the probabilistic schedule length of the PTG. Algorithm 3.1 calculates the mrt for a PTG. In order to simplify the calculation, two dummy vertices with zero computation time, v_s and v_d, are added to the graph. A set of zero delay edges is used to connect vertex v_s to all root-nodes, and to connect all leaf-nodes to vertex v_d. Therefore, the $\mathrm{mrt}(v_s, v_d)$ gives the overall maximum reaching time of the graph and will be used to compute the schedule length of the given PTG. This schedule length implies possible computation time of the graph.

Algorithm 3.1 (Maximum reaching time)
Input : PTG $G = \langle V, E, w, T, b \rangle$
Output: $\mathrm{mrt}(G) = \mathrm{mrt}'(v_s, v_d)$

1   $G_0 = \langle V_0, E_0, d, T \rangle$ such that $V_0 = V + \{v_s, v_d\}$,

2   $E_0 = E + \{v_s \xrightarrow{e} v \in V_r, u \in V_l \xrightarrow{e} v_d\}$

3   $\forall u \in V_0, \mathsf{mrt}'(v_s, u) = 0, T_{v_s} = T_{v_d} = 0, Queue = v_s$

4   **while** $Queue \neq \emptyset$ **do**

5      $get(u, Queue)$

6      $\mathsf{mrt}'(v_s, u) = \mathsf{mrt}'(v_s, u) + T_u$

7   **foreach** $u \xrightarrow{e} v$ **do**

8        $indegree(v) = indegree(v) - 1$

9        $\mathsf{mrt}'(v_s, v) = \max(\mathsf{mrt}'(v_s, u), \mathsf{mrt}'(v_s, v))$

10   **if** $indegree(v) = 0$ **then** $put(v, Queue)$ **fi**

11   **od**

12   **od**

In this algorithm, the graph is traversed in topological order and the mrt of each node v is computed with respect to v_s. The mrt' for node v, originally set to zero, is updated as the parent of v is dequeued. Note that operations "+" and max in Line 6 and 9 operate between two random variables. Finally, when v_d is extracted from the queue, the $\mathsf{mrt}(G)$ is computed.

Using the mrt, the concept of a *probabilistic schedule length* ($\mathsf{psl}(G, \theta)$) can be defined with respect to a confidence level θ, as the smallest computation time c such that $\mathcal{P}(\mathsf{mrt}(G) > c) < 1 - \theta$.

Consider the probability distribution of the $\mathsf{mrt}(G)$:

	Possible computation time			
	...	13	14	15	16
Prob.	...	0.18194	0.04365	0.02293	0.00875

With $\theta = 0.8$, $\mathsf{psl}(G, 0.8)$ is 14 because the smallest possible computation time is 14 where $\mathcal{P}(\mathsf{mrt}(G) > 14) < 0.2$ ($0.04365 + 0.02293 + 0.00875 = 0.07818 < 0.2$). Note that c could be 15 and 16 but 14 is the smallest one. Therefore with above 80% confidence, the computation time of G is less than 14.

In traditional rotation scheduling, a re-mapping heuristic (or re-scheduling phase) plays an important role in reducing the schedule length. For probabilistic rotation scheduling, *Template scheduling*(TS) heuristic is applied to find a place to re-schedule a task. In such an approach, a weight, called *degree of flexibility*, is assigned to each node in the PTG. In order to compute such a weight, the expected computation time of each node is computed to build up a template. This template implies not only the execution order but also the control step assignment for each task. By observing this template, one can expect how long (number of control steps) each processing element would be idle. Therefore, the template scheduling scheme should be able to decide where to re-scheduled a node.

In order to determine an *degree of flexibility* ($\mathsf{dflex}(u, i)$) we first compute an expected control step of each node ($\mathsf{Ecs}(v)$). By traversing the PTG in the topological order, we compute ($\mathsf{Ecs}(v)$) as $\mathsf{Ecs}(v) = \max_i(\mathsf{Ecs}(u_i) + ET_{u_i})$, where $u_i \xrightarrow{e} v \in E$, ET_u represents the expected computation time of node u and $\mathsf{Ecs}(v_i) = 0$ for all root nodes $v_i \in V$. We assume here that node v can start execution right after all of their parents finish their executions. Then, $\mathsf{dflex}(u, i)$, is computed by: $\mathsf{dflex}(u, i) = \mathsf{Ecs}(v) - \mathsf{Ecs}(u) - ET_u$ where $u \xrightarrow{e} v \in E$ and u and v are assigned to PE_i.

Note that the degree of flexibility of a node, which is executed at last in any PE, is undefined. The template scheduling, de-scribed in Algorithm 3.2, seeks the best processing element that results in the shortest possible psl to re-schedule a node.

Algorithm 3.2 (Template scheduling)

Input : PTG $G = \langle V, E, w, T, b \rangle$ with pre-computed $ET_u, \forall u \in V$, re-mapped node v, and θ

Output: New G with the assignment of v

1   compute $\mathsf{Ecs}(u), \forall u \in V$

2   compute $\mathsf{dflex}(u), \forall u \in V$

3   $G_{\text{temp}} = G$; $G_{\text{best}} = $ **NULL**

4   **for** $PE_i := PE_0$ **to** PE_n **do**

5      $x = $ node v with $\max_{PE(v)=i} \mathsf{dflex}(v, i)$

6      $G_{\text{temp}} = $ temporarily assign v after x

7   **if** $\mathsf{psl}(G_{\text{temp}}, \theta) < \mathsf{psl}(G_{\text{best}}, \theta)$

8   **then** $G_{\text{best}} = G_{\text{temp}}$ **fi**

9   remove the assignment and retry on the next PE **od**

10   **return**(G_{best})

Algorithm 3.3 presents the probabilistic rotation scheduling (PRS).

Algorithm 3.3 (Probabilistic Rotation Scheduling)

Input : PG $G = \langle V, E, d, T \rangle$, and θ

Output: a shortest possible PTG $G_s = \langle V, E, w, T, b \rangle$

1   compute $ET_u, \forall u \in V$

2   $G_s = Init\_Schedule(G)$ // construct the initial schedule (DAG)

3   $G_{\text{best}} = G_s$

4   **for** $i = 1$ **to** $2|V|$ **do**

5      $R = Extract\_Roots(G_s)$

6      $(G_s, G, u) = Select\_Rotate(R, G_s)$// select a node and retime it

7      $G_s = Re\text{-}map(G_s, u, \theta)$ // template scheduling

8   **if** $\mathsf{psl}(G_s, \theta) < \mathsf{psl}(G_{\text{best}})$

9   **then** $G_{\text{best}} = G_s$ **fi od**

10   **return**(G_{best})

Line 2 constructs an initial schedule using any DAG scheduling, e.g., list scheduling which needs to be modified in order to return a PTG. The rotation phase begins in Lines 4–9. This phase loops $2|V|$ times with hope that all nodes in the graph will have a chance to be rescheduled at least once. *Extract_Roots* returns a set of roots which can be legally retimed. Then *Select_Rotate* selects node u to be rotated using any priority function. In this routine, one delay is drawn from all incoming edges of node u and pushed to all outgoing edges of node u. Meanwhile, the PTG G_s is also updated, i.e., the flow-control and dependency edges are modified. Then a node is re-mapped using the TS heuristic proposed in the previous subsection. If the obtained probabilistic schedule is better than the current one, it saves the better PTG and the rotation iteration continues.

4 Experiments

In order to be more realistic and easy to compare with traditional rotation scheduling, we tested the PRS algorithm on some well-known benchmarks: (1) differential equation, (2) 3 stage-IIR filter, (3) lattice filter, (4) Volterra filter, and (5) the 5th elliptic filter. The computation time of each node from those benchmark graphs is obtained from [4].

Table 1 demonstrates the effectiveness of our approach on both 2-adder, 1-multiplier and 2-adder, 2-multiplier systems. The

Spec.	Ben.	$\theta = 0.9$				$\theta = 0.8$			
		PL	PRS			PL	PRS		
			AS	ET	TS		AS	ET	TS
2 Adds. 1 Mul.	(1)	169	152	133	**133**	165	147	131	**131**
	(2)	188	184	151	**151**	184	179	147	**147**
	(3)	229	225	142	**141**	225	220	138	**138**
	(4)	526	468	361	**361**	519	461	354	**354**
	(5)	318	298	293	**293**	314	294	289	**289**
2 Adds. 2 Muls.	(1)	120	103	**83**	90	117	100	**83**	91
	(2)	124	120	87	**87**	120	110	83	**82**
	(3)	229	225	140	**139**	225	220	136	**136**
	(4)	359	270	**237**	259	353	265	**221**	256
	(5)	288	288	274	**271**	284	274	270	**267**

Table 1: List scheduling vs. PRS

Ben.	worst case		$\theta = 0.9$			$\theta = 0.8$		
	L	R	PL	PRS		PL	PRS	
				TS	Exp		TS	Exp
(1)	228	180	169	**133**	136	165	**131**	131
(2)	252	204	188	**151**	163	184	**147**	179
(3)	312	204	229	**141**	153	225	**138**	149
(4)	750	510	526	**361**	526	519	**354**	519
(5)	438	396	318	**293**	299	314	**289**	294

Table 2: Worst case, average case, vs. probabilistic case

performance of PRS is evaluated when the algorithm applies three different re-mapping heuristics: template scheduling (TS), exhaustive trial (ET) and as-late-as-possible scheduling (AS). The ET approach strives to re-map a node to all possible legal location and returns the assignment which yields the minimum $psl(G, \theta)$. The AS method attempts to schedule a task once at the legal farthest position in each functional unit (adder or multiplier) while the TS heuristic legally places a task after the node with the highest degree of flexibility in each functional unit.

Columns $\theta = 0.8$ and $\theta = 0.9$ show the result when considering probabilistic situation with the confidence probability 0.8 and 0.9. Column "PL" presents the psl after list scheduling is applied to the benchmarks. After running PRS using the re-mapping heuristics ET, AS and TS, Columns *ET*, *AS* and *TS* show the resulting psl. Among these three heuristics, the TS scheme produces better results than AS which uses the simplest criteria. Further, it yields as good as or sometimes even better results than what gives by the ET approach, while TS takes less time to select a re-scheduled position for a node. This is because in each iteration the ET method finds the local optimal place; however, scheduling nodes to these positions does not always result in the global optimal schedule length.

In Table 2, based on the system that has 2 adders and 1 multiplier, we present the comparison results obtained from applying list scheduling, traditional rotation scheduling, probabilistic rotation scheduling using TS, and traditional rotation scheduling considering expected computation times, to the benchmarks. Columns "L" and "R" show the schedule length obtained from applying list scheduling and traditional rotation scheduling using TS when considering the worst case scenario. Obviously, considering the probabilistic case gives the significant improvement of the schedule length over the worst case scenario.

Also, column "PL" presents the initial schedule lengths obtained from using the list scheduling approach when considering the underlying probabilistic computation time. The results in column *TS* are obtained from Table 1. In column "Exp", the psl is computed by using the PG configuration retrieved from running traditional rotation to the benchmarks where the expected computation time is used for a node rather than its probability distribution. These results demonstrate that considering the probabilistic situation while performing rotation scheduling can consistently give better schedules than considering only worst-case or average-case scenario.

5 Conclusion

We have presented the probabilistic rotation scheduling algorithm which the probabilistic concept and loop pipelining are integrated so as to optimize a task schedule. A probabilistic data flow graph is used to model an application, which allows the probabilistic computation time. The concept of probabilistic schedule length is presented to measure the total computation time of these tasks being scheduled in one iteration. Probabilistic rotation scheduling is applied to the initial schedule in order to optimize the schedule. It produces the best optimized schedule with respect to the confidence probability. The re-mapping heuristic, template scheduling, is incorporated in the algorithm in order to find the scheduling position for a node.

REFERENCES

[1] L. Chao, A. LaPaugh, and E. Sha. Rotation scheduling: A loop pipelining algorithm. In *30th DAC*, pp. 566–572, June 1993.

[2] I. Foster. *Designing and building parallel program: concepts and tools for parallel software engineering*. Addison-Wesley Publishing Co., 1994.

[3] E. M. Girczyc. Loop winding—a data flow approach to functional pipeline. In *ISCAS*, pp. 382–385, May 1987.

[4] Texas Instruments. *The TTL data book*, volume 2. Texas Instruments Incorporation, 1985.

[5] R. A. Kamin, G. B. Adams, and P. K. Dubey. Dynamic list-scheduling with finite resources. In *ICCD*, pp. 140–144, Oct. 1994.

[6] A. A. Khan, C. L. McCreary, and M. S. Jones. A comparison of multiprocessor scheduling heuristics. In *ICPP* , pp. 243–250, 1994.

[7] D. Ku and G. De Micheli. *High-Level synthesis of ASICS under Timing and Synchronization constraints*. Kluwer Academic, 1992.

[8] D. Ku and G. De Micheli. Relative scheduling under timing constraints: Algorithm for high-level synthesis. *IEEE trans. CAD/ICAS*, pp. 697–718, June 1992.

[9] M. Lam. Software pipelining. In *ACM SIGPLAN'88*, pp. 318–328, June 1988.

[10] C. E. Leiserson and J. B. Saxe. Retiming synchronous circuitry. *Algorithmica*, 6:5–35, 1991.

[11] B. P. Lester. *The art of parallel programming*. Prentice-Hall, Inc., Englewood Cliffs, New Jersey 07632, 1993.

Session 5A

Profetching in Multiprocessors

Hybrid Compiler/Hardware Prefetching for Multiprocessors Using Low-Overhead Cache Miss Traps

Jonas Skeppstedt

Dept. of Computer Engineering
Chalmers University of Technology
SE-412 96 Gothenburg, SWEDEN
jonas@acm.org

Michel Dubois

Dept. of Electrical Engineering-Systems
University of Southern California
Los Angeles, CA 90089-2562, USA
dubois@paris.usc.edu

Abstract

We propose and evaluate a new data prefetching technique for cache coherent multiprocessors. Prefetches are issued by a prefetch engine which is controlled by the compiler. Second-level cache misses generate cache miss traps, and start the prefetch engine in a trap handler generated by the compiler. The only instruction overhead in our approach is when a trap handler terminates after data arrives. We present the functionality of the prefetch engine and a compiler algorithm to control it. We also study emulation of the prefetch engine in software. Our techniques are evaluated on six parallel applications using a compiler which incorporates our algorithm and a simulated multiprocessor. The prefetch engines remove up to 67% of the memory access stall time at an instruction overhead less than 0.42%. The emulated prefetch engines remove in general less stall time at a higher instruction overhead.

1 Introduction

Data prefetching is a promising approach to hide memory access latencies in cache coherent multiprocessors. Both compiler-based and hardware-based prefetch techniques have been studied which are effective for regular array accesses [5, 7, 8, 13, 14, 15]. In traditional compiler-based prefetching, the compiler tries to predict which memory accesses will suffer cache misses and it then inserts prefetch instructions for that data. Instruction overhead is a fundamental limitation of traditional compiler-based prefetching, and in [15] the importance of limiting the prefetching to accesses which are likely to experience cache misses was shown. Unfortunately, both the cache size and the input data set size (or loop iteration count) must be known at compile-time to predict cache misses accurately. In contrast, hardware-based prefetch techniques execute in parallel and do not cause any instruction overhead. Stride prefetching in hardware identifies the stride by comparing the sequence of addresses generated by each memory access instruction. However, the stride-detection phase requires quite complex hardware.

The problems with the previous techniques have motivated us to consider a hybrid prefetching technique which can take advantage of static compiler analysis to determine what to prefetch while still being able to issue prefetches with very little instruction overhead, and in particular, *no*

instruction overhead cost at all when memory accesses hit in the cache.

In this paper we propose and evaluate a new prefetching technique, which is based on static compiler analysis, memory access traps, and a prefetch engine which issues prefetch requests. Our approach uses low-overhead cache miss traps as proposed in [10]. For certain memory access instructions, we let a miss in the second-level cache generate a *cache miss trap*. Each such memory access instruction has a corresponding trap handler which is generated by the compiler. The prefetch engine is started by trap handlers.

We also study whether one could emulate the prefetch engine in software by a loop in the trap handler which issues prefetches using ordinary prefetch instructions.

To evaluate our techniques we have implemented the prefetch engine in a detailed architectural simulator of a sequentially consistent cache-coherent multiprocessor and compiled six parallel scientific and engineering applications using an optimising compiler which incorporates our algorithm to generate cache miss trap handlers. We find that the prefetch engine removed up to 67% of the memory access stall time at an instruction overhead less than 0.42%. The emulated prefetch engine removes in general less stall time at a higher instruction overhead.

The rest of the paper is organised as follows. In Section 2 we give an overview of our prefetching technique. In Section 3 we present the functionality of the prefetch engine and in Section 4 we describe a compiler algorithm that generates the cache miss trap handlers to control prefetching. In Section 5 we present the experimental methodology, and we show the simulation results in Section 6. We discuss our results and relate them to work by others in Section 7. Finally, we conclude the paper in Section 8.

2 Prefetching Approach

The purpose of this section is to give the reader an idea of the types of memory access patterns which are handled by our prefetching approach.

The compiler marks certain memory instructions in a program to generate a low-overhead trap on a second-level cache miss. Such a memory access instruction is called a *faulting* memory access instruction, and for each faulting memory access instruction, there is a corresponding cache miss trap handler. Upon a cache miss trap, a prologue code sequence saves a small number of the general purpose registers, locates the faulting instruction's trap handler using the saved program counter in a hash table, and jumps to the trap handler. After the trap handler has completed, an epilogue restores the saved registers and re-executes the faulted instruction. If the faulted instruction gets a second cache miss when it is re-executed, it does not generate a new trap.

The compiler controls a prefetch engine by specifiying the following prefetch parameters: *Count* is the number of prefetches to issue using direct addressing, *Stride* is the distance in bytes between blocks that are prefetched, *Indirect* is the number of prefetches to issue using indirect addressing, *Cache state* specifies whether a block is expected to be read only or also modified, and finally, *Address* is the byte address of the first prefetch. So, the task of the compiler is to extract these parameters for each stride access in a loop.

To illustrate the operation of a prefetch engine, we will use C code fragments and show how the engine should be controlled. In the examples below we assume that the cache block size is B bytes.

```
for (i = 0; i < n; i = i + D)
    x = x + a[K*i];
```

Figure 1: Example code which reads an array.

In the code in Figure 1, a number of elements of an array a are read. A trap handler is associated with the instruction that loads a[K*i], and will be invoked when the load instruction generates a cache miss trap. The information that the compiler extracts from the code in Figure 1 is the stride of a[K*i], the number of blocks to prefetch, and the starting address. While the stride is constant and is required to be known at compile-time, the number of prefetches to issue is computed in the trap handler. The number of prefetches depends on the value of the loop index i when a miss occurs. The task for the compiler is to generate code for the trap handler that computes this by comparing i and n. The index i is incremented by D in each loop iteration, and the number of iterations remaining in the loop is $(n - i)/D$. An address-expression with a stride must contain a variable that is incremented by a constant in each loop iteration. In Figure 1, this variable is i. Assuming that the size of an array-element is E, the stride S of the instruction loading a[K*i] then becomes $K \times D \times E$. If the stride S is equal to or greater than the cache block size B, then $N = (n - i)/D$ blocks will be accessed. On the other hand, if S is less than B, the number of cache blocks that will be accessed becomes $N = \lceil (n - i) \times S/(D \times B) \rceil$ (assuming i refers to the beginning of a cache block). We should prefetch one block less than N since the missing load instruction requests the first block itself.

In Figure 2 we give an example of indirect prefetching. a is an array of pointers to integers and each loop iteration dereferences one pointer. In this case the prefetch engine is set up to do indirect prefetching. When the engine has prefetched one cache block of the array a using direct addressing, it will prefetch the pointed-to blocks as well. While we not describe the details, indirect addressing can also be used to prefetch blocks pointed-to by record fields.

```
int     *a[];

for (i = 0; i < n; i++)
    x = x + *a[i];
```

Figure 2: Here indirect addressing is used.

To emulate prefetch engines in trap handlers, a trap handler issues prefetches using ordinary prefetch instructions in a loop. In order to reduce the risk of hot-spots in the memory system, the number of prefetches is limited to four. Indirect addressing prefetch is not emulated by trap handlers. Apart from this, the compiler analysis to generate trap handlers is identical regardless of whether the trap handler will start a prefetch engine or it will emulate a prefetch engine.

3 Prefetch Engine Functionality

This section describes the state variables and the operation of the prefetch engine that we have evaluated. A processor has multiple prefetch engines, and the exact number is implementation-defined. Before the compiler can specify prefetch parameters, one prefetch engine must first be chosen. This is done with a *reset* command which selects one prefetch engine. Subsequent parameters up to and including the start address will implicitly refer to the most recently selected engine.

3.1 Prefetch buffer

The purpose of the prefetch buffer is to control the prefetch issue pace. Each prefetch engine has a prefetch buffer with four entries and a prefetch cannot be issued unless there is a free entry. The motivation for using four entries is that, according to Mowry's measurements [13], it does not pay to allow for more than four outstanding prefetches. The state for each entry is shown in Table 1. A prefetch request allocates an entry and records the block address. An entry is deallocated when two conditions are satisfied: data has arrived and it has been requested by the processor. A replacement or an invalidation also deallocates an entry. A reset command deallocates entries whose data has arrived but that has not yet been accessed (otherwise, a useless prefetch would occupy an entry until the entry is deallocated by a replacement or an invalidation). The *Accessed*-flag is set when an access refers to a block with a pending prefetch, and is reset when an entry is allocated.

Name	Description
Free	True if entry is not in use
Accessed	True if block has been accessed
Block	Prefetched block number

Table 1: Prefetch buffer entry.

3.2 Prefetch engine state

In Table 2 we show which state variables a prefetch engine uses. There are three groups of state variables. The first group, *Operating* and *Stride*, is used both for direct and indirect address prefetching. The next group, *Address*, *Count*, and *DState*, is used only for direct addressing, and the last group *Pointer*, *Indirect*, and *IState*, is used only for indirect addressing. We will now describe the purpose of each variable.

To start with the first group, *Operating* is true when the engine has valid prefetch parameters. *Stride* is the amount that both *Address* and *Pointer* will be incremented for the next prefetch using direct addressing. In the next group, *Address* is the byte address of the next block to prefetch using direct addressing, and *Count* is the number of remaining prefetches to issue. *DState* controls whether shared or exclusive mode prefetches should be issued for direct addressing. In the last group, *Pointer* is the byte address of a pointer in the program. To issue a request using indirect addressing, the data that contains the address must (of course) be present in the cache first. *Indirect* is the number of blocks to prefetch starting at the memory (cache) contents at *Pointer*, and *IState* specifies whether shared or exclusive mode prefetches should be used. *Indirect* specifies the number of sequential blocks to prefetch using indirect addressing. We will now describe how direct and indirect prefetching is carried out.

Name	Description
Operating	True if parameters are valid
Stride	Byte stride
Address	Next address to prefetch
Count	Remaining prefetches to issue
DState	Direct addressing cache state
Pointer	Next address to prefetch indirectly
Indirect	Number of indirect prefetches
IState	Indirect addressing cache state

Table 2: State variables in each prefetch engine.

3.3 Prefetch engine operation

A reset selects an engine, deallocates the engine's prefetch buffer entries as discussed in Section 3.2, clears all state variables of that engine, and initialises the following default values: *Stride* is set to the cache block size, the addressing mode is set to direct addressing by setting *Indirect* to zero, *Count* is set to a maximum value (we use the number of cache blocks in a page), and both direct and indirect addressing prefetch are set to use shared state. After a reset, the default values may be overridden by giving new values. Finally, when the *Address* parameter is specified, the *Address* and *Pointer* state variables are set to this address and *Operating* is set to true. An operating prefetch engine issues prefetches using direct addressing until its *Count* becomes zero or it is selected by another reset command. We will first describe the operation of direct addressing prefetch and then indirect addressing prefetch. A new prefetch request can be issued by an engine when a free entry in the prefetch buffer is available.

The *Address* state variable contains the byte address of the next block to prefetch. This block is looked-up in the second-level cache and if it is not present, the block is requested and a prefetch buffer entry is allocated. If the block was prefetched or present, the *Address* variable is incremented by *Stride* and *Count* is decremented by one.

Address and *Count* do not change if the block was absent but there was no available buffer entry. If *Address* crosses a physical page, *Count* is set to zero. This will generate a new trap at a cache miss in the new page and prefetching will start again.

The state variable *Pointer* contains the byte address of a pointer in the program, and is initialised to the same value as *Address*. If the block of the pointer is not present in the cache, indirect addressing prefetching is paused until that block arrives, eg as a result of direct addressing prefetch. When the block is present, the cache content at the memory address *Pointer* is read and is treated as a virtual address *VA*. *VA* is translated to a physical address and then a prefetch is issued when a free entry becomes available. Note that indirect prefetch requires interaction with the virtual memory system.

To limit the prefetching activity, an engine has only four prefetch buffer entries. Both direct and indirect addressing compete for these four entries and we give indirect addressing higher priority to be granted an entry.

4   Compiler Algorithm

This section gives an overview of a compiler algorithm for automatically generating cache miss trap handlers for prefetching. The analysis performed by the compiler is based on natural loop analysis, induction-variable analysis, and a dataflow analysis similar to live-variables analysis [1]. In general, our algorithm can detect stride accesses in loops if an induction-variable is part of an access's address-expression.

Direct addressing engine prefetch

Assume a memory access A belongs to a natural loop L. If A will generate addresses that differ by a constant S (known at compile-time) in subsequent iterations of L, then A is a *stride access*. The constant S denotes the *stride*. A trap handler is generated for every stride access. If L has a loop-termination condition of the form $i < n$, the remaining number of loop iterations can be computed and from that the number of prefetches to issue. Assume i is incremented by D in each iteration. As we discussed in Section 2, if the stride S is equal to or greater than the cache block size B, the number of direct addressing prefetches, N, is set to $(n - i)/D - 1$. Otherwise, if S is less than B, N is set to $(n - i) \times S/(B \times D) - 1$. Here i and possibly n are variables, and D, B, and S are compile-time constants. The number of prefetches is not computed using multiply and divide instructions, which can be too time-consuming, instead we approximate the number using shifts.

If the number of prefetches to issue cannot be computed at runtime, a default number is used instead.

Indirect addressing engine prefetch

For indirect addressing prefetch, the compiler must analyse the use of data read by a load instruction. If the data read by one load instruction A_1 is used as a base address by another memory access instruction A_2, then A_1 is said to be a *parent* of A_2, which is said to be a *child*. When the parent is a stride access, then indirect engine prefetching is started in the trap handler of the parent. The engine parameter *Indirect* is determined by considering which blocks are accessed using the base pointer loaded by the parent instruction.

5 Experimental Methodology

To evaluate our prefetch technique, we have incorporated the prefetch algorithm in a compiler. We have then compiled and run six parallel applications on a simulated cache-coherent NUMA multiprocessor. First we present the compiler and the benchmarks we have used. Then we present the multiprocessor architectures we have simulated to evaluate effects on execution time and traffic.

5.1 Compiler and benchmark programs

We have incorporated the compiler algorithms in an optimising C compiler [17] which compiles parallel applications using the ANL macros [2] and generates code for shared-memory multiprocessors based on SPARC processors. We have used a set of six applications developed at Stanford University (Water, Cholesky, LU, MP3D, Barnes-Hut, and PTHOR), of which all but LU are part of the SPLASH-1 suite [16]. We used the data set sizes that are shown in Table 3.

Table 3: Benchmark Programs, Data Set Sizes used.

Benchmark	Data Sets
Water	244 molecules, 3 time steps
Cholesky	matrix bcsstk14
MP3D	50,000 particles, 5 time steps
LU	200 x 200 matrix
Barnes-Hut	128 bodies
PTHOR	RISC circuit

5.2 Metrics of Detection Efficiency

To understand how close to the optimum the prefetch efficiency of the compiler algorithm is, we have measured the number of second-level cache misses in an execution that were removed because the data was prefetched. Unless the processor was stalled waiting for a prefetched block B, when B is loaded into the second-level cache (SLC), a PF-flag is set in the simulator's cache block. When the block is accessed, invalidated, or replaced, the flag is reset. Let M be the number of SLC misses which request data from memory (this excludes misses to blocks that have a pending prefetch and also re-executed faulted instructions). Let H be the number of SLC accesses where the PF-flag is true and P be the number of SLC accesses to blocks which have a pending prefetch. Consequently, H is the number of memory accesses whose latency was hidden, and P is the number of memory access whose latency was partly hidden, and they count the number of misses which are covered by prefetches. We define the *coverage* to be $C = (H + P)/(H + P + M)$.

A prefetch request sent to memory which does not cover a cache miss is useless. We define the *degree of bad prefetches* to be the number of useless prefetch requests divided by the number of prefetch requests sent to memory.

The measurements coverage, useless, execution-time, and traffic have all been carried out by executing the compiled applications on a detailed architectural simulator which we will describe next.

5.3 Simulated architectures

We have developed two detailed architectural simulation models: first a basic write-invalidate protocol which constitutes the baseline architecture and second the baseline extended with load and store instructions that can generate a cache-miss trap and with prefetch engines. These models are described in detail below. The simulation platform consists of a functional simulator of SPARC processors which generate memory references to an attached memory system architectural simulator with a detailed timing model [3]. Since the executing processors are delayed according to the latencies encountered by each memory reference, the same interleaving of memory references will be encountered as in the target architecture.

Baseline architecture

The overall organisation of the baseline architecture is shown in Figure 3. It consists of 16 processing nodes. Apart from the local portion of the shared memory, each processing node also contains a two-level cache hierarchy whose organisation is shown in Figure 4. It consists of a write-through, direct-mapped first-level cache (denoted FLC) with an associated first-level write buffer denoted $FLWB$. In the baseline, the $FLWB$ buffers requests to a copy-back, second-level cache (SLC). Since the processor is stalled on loads that miss in the FLC and on stores, the $FLWB$ is not needed in the baseline architecture. As we will see below, it is used to buffer requests that do not need to stall the processor, namely, requests related to prefetching.

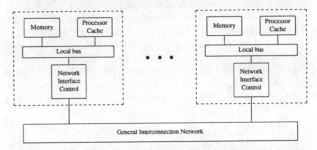

Figure 3: Organisation of a cache coherent multiprocessor.

System-level cache coherence between the second-level caches is maintained by a Censier and Feautrier write-invalidate protocol which associates a bit vector with each memory block [4]. Virtual pages are 4KB and are mapped to physical memory modules using a round-robin policy that interprets the four least significant bits of the virtual page number as the node identity. The node in which a certain page is mapped is called the *home* of all blocks in that page.

Loads that miss in the FLC and the SLC cause a miss request to be sent to home. If the copy is present at home, and if home is the local node, the miss is serviced locally. Otherwise, two or four node-to-node traversals are required to fill the cache.

Stores are written through the FLC. If the SLC copy is exclusive, the store can be carried out locally. Otherwise, ownership has to be acquired. The coherence protocol in both the baseline and the extended architecture we evaluate, implements *sequential consistency* by stalling the processor

301

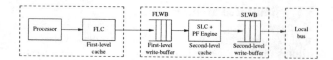

Figure 4: The two-level cache hierarchy in each processing node. The prefetch engine is part of the SLC.

until ownership is granted. Depending on the location of home and whether another node has an exclusive copy, ownership acquisition may encounter zero, two, or four node-to-node traversals.

In Figure 4, a write buffer is also associated with the *SLC*, denoted *SLWB*. Since the processor is stalled on every global store, this buffer is not needed in the baseline architecture.

Faulting memory access instructions

We evaluate the effectiveness of our compiler algorithms by replacing marked memory accesses by special instructions denoted *faulting memory access instructions*. Unlike ordinary memory access instructions, they generate a hardware cache miss trap on a second-level cache miss.

The actions taken by the cache hierarchy when an ordinary load or store instruction executes are identical to those of the baseline. The actions taken by the cache hierarchy when a faulting memory access instruction executes are as follows. If the block is present in the *FLC*, the behaviour is identical with that of the baseline. If the block is not present in the *FLC*, however, the processor has to stall, and the memory request is buffered in the *FLWB*. If the *SLC* has a copy, the behaviour again is identical with that of the baseline. Conversely, if the block is not present in the *SLC* and there is no pending request in the *SLWB* (or in a prefetch buffer), a *cache miss trap* is generated.

The request of the cache miss which generated the trap is recorded in the *SLWB*, the request is sent to home, and the processor continues execution in a trap handler prologue. To support faulting memory access instructions, the *SLWB* should have at least two entries; one entry for the faulted access and one entry if an access in the trap handler would experience another second-level cache miss. A cache miss trap is a low-overhead trap [9], and a trap does not need service from the operating system. During execution of a trap handler, new memory access traps are disabled, and when an instruction is re-executed, it behaves exactly as in the baseline architecture.

Support for prefetch engines

An *SLC* is extended with four prefetch engines where each engine has a prefetch buffer with four entries. To issue a prefetch by an engine, the request must first be allocated a prefetch buffer entry. An engine request cannot allocate an entry whose block has not been accessed; the purpose of this is to control the prefetch issue pace. Indirect prefetch requires a TLB access. In this study, we do not model any cost for doing this translation. Instructions to control the

prefetch engine and ordinary prefetch instructions do not stall the processor; rather, they are buffered in the *FLWB*.

Support for emulated prefetch engines

The hardware support required to emulate prefetch engines in trap handlers is as follows: faulting memory access instructions, a lockup-free *SLC*, and ordinary prefetch instructions included in modern instruction set architectures. To make the *SLC* lockup-free, pending prefetch requests are buffered in the *SLWB*. A prefetch request, either from a prefetch engine or an ordinary prefetch instruction, first checks that a block is not in the *SLC* already or has a pending request.

Architectural parameters

In our simulations we assume that the *FLWB* and the *SLWB* contain 8 and 16 entries, respectively. The architectural parameters we assume for all three architecture variations are as follows. Each node contains a SPARC processor clocked at 200MHz (1 pclock = 5ns). We model a 4KB *FLC* and a 64KB *SLC*, both direct mapped and with a block size of 16 bytes. *FLC*, *SLC*, and local memory access times are 1, 6, and 30 pclocks, respectively. The nodes are interconnected with a network with a fixed node-to-node latency of 54 pclocks. Each control message is 5 bytes, and each data message is 21 bytes. Only shared references in the applications' parallel section are modelled with these parameters. Other memory accesses are assumed to hit in the *FLC*.

6 Simulation Results

In this section we first show the detection efficiences and then as a case study show the effects on the execution-times.

6.1 Detection Efficiency

The diagrams of Figure 5 show the coverages (top) and degrees of bad prefetches (bottom) for the applications we have studied. For each application we show five bars that from left to right correspond to the following prefetch techniques: prefetch engine using direct addressing only is *DH*, *DH* extended with indirect addressing prefetch is *IH*, *IH* extended with exclusive mode prefetching is *EH*, emulated prefetch engine using direct addressing is *DS*, and finally *DS* extended with exclusive mode prefetching is *ES*. We will also collectively refer to *DH*, *IH*, and *EH* as *HW*, and *DS* and *ES* as *SW*.

For three of the applications (Water, Cholesky, and LU), most cache misses are to arrays accessed with direct addressing. MP3D is an application with both regular array accesses and indirect accesses. Finally, the last two applications (Barnes-Hut and PTHOR) have many pointer dereferences. The compiler used indirect addressing prefetch only for three of the applications, namely, MP3D, Barnes-Hut, and PTHOR. So, for Water, Cholesky, and LU, the simulation results for *DH* and *IH* are identical.

We expect that the detection efficiency for *HW* should be somewhat better than for *SW* since *SW* is limited to prefetch at most four cache blocks per cache miss. An upper bound of the coverage for *SW* is therefore 80%, which is achieved when one miss causes four useful prefetches.

302

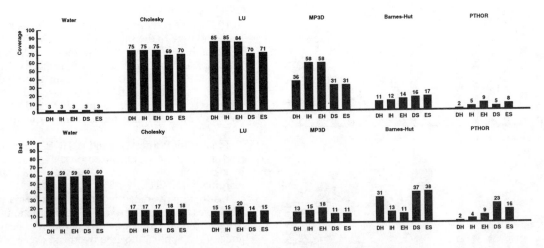

Figure 5: Coverage and degree of bad prefetches in percent.

To start with Water, the number of prefetches issued is low for each technique[1]. Of the few issued prefetches less than half were useful: each technique covered only 3% of the misses. We found two situations that limited the coverage. The first is in the procedure INTERF where one variable comp is used to index array elements in a loop. Although the value of comp normally is incremented by one for each iteration, in some cases its value is set modulo another variable, which prevents our compiler from using a prefetch engine for these accesses. The second situation which our compiler currently cannot handle is when the surrounding loop is in one source file and the array accesses are in another. With interprocedural analysis at the file level this situation could be handled. A significant fraction of the prefetched data was invalidated resulting in high degrees of bad of 59% for HW, and 60% for SW.

Continuing with Cholesky, all techniques use prefetching extensively and are quite successful. HW covers 75%, DS covers 69%, and ES covers 70% of the misses. The degrees of bad are 17% for HW and 18% for SW. These useless prefetches were due to prefetched data that was either replaced or invalidated.

For LU, prefetching is also used extensively. HW has a coverage which exceeds the upper bound that SW can reach. DH covers 85% and EH covers 84%. We analysed the reason why HW did not reach an even higher coverage and found it is mainly due to a limitation in our coherence protocol. When one processor has produced a column, then all processors waiting for this column will prefetch the cache blocks of that column. However, our coherence protocol permits only one prefetch request to wait for home to become clean. The other nodes receive a negative acknowledgement (nack) of their prefetch request. This limitation can be removed by a more sophisticated coherence protocol. These nacks constitute the majority of the useless prefetch requests both for HW and for SW. The remaining misses in LU were mostly to the synchronisation structure Global->done.

There are two data structures in MP3D, one array of particle records and one array of cell records. Each particle has a pointer to a cell. The cells are migratory objects and most misses are to the cells. With DH and SW, only the particles are prefetched, and therefore their coverages become only 36% and 31%, respectively. With IH, an engine prefetches the pointed-to cells as well, and a coverage of 58% is reached. The misses that remain are mostly due to prefetched cells that were invalidated before they were accessed, and to cells when a particle moves from one cell into another. As expected, SW has a lower degree of bad prefetches than HW since SW only prefetches particles (which are seldom invalidated).

Barnes-Hut is an application whose main data structure is recursive and is operated on by recursive procedure calls, which limit the prefetching. For DH and SW, typically only the array of subnode pointers are prefetched — but not the subnodes themselves. IH does prefetch subnodes using indirect addressing in the recursive procedure walksub() and reaches a marginally higher coverage of 12%. However, many misses remain that could not be handled by our algorithm.

PTHOR is also an application whose main data structure is recursive and is a graph of circuit elements. There are more prefetches issued for exclusive mode prefetching, which indicates that EH and ES create new misses. For this application DH and IH only cover 5% of the misses. The degree of bad prefetches for ES is 16%.

In summary, we find that the prefetch engine reaches high coverages for codes with regular array accesses, namely LU and Cholesky, and that the emulated engines reach coverages which are quite close to their upper bounds of 80%. The degrees of bad are around 20%. We also see that indirect engine prefetch could contribute significantly to the coverage for one application with pointer dereferences (MP3D), but many misses due to pointer dereferences that could not be handled by our algorithm remain. One other reason for not having an even higher coverage was a limitation in the coherence protocol we used, namely, that multiple prefetch requests for a block were allowed while home was waiting for becoming clean. Another limitation was related to the scheduling of prefetches. Some blocks were invalidated before they were used. We will next consider the effects on the execution time and traffic of our prefetch technique.

---

[1]The total number of prefetches cannot be derived from coverage and degree of bad but we measured that separately.

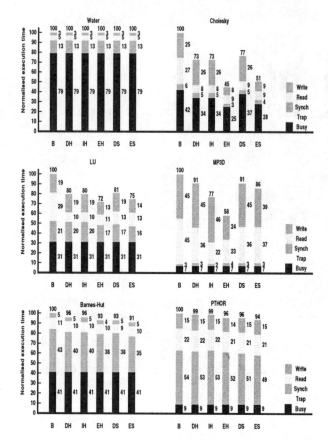

Figure 6: Normalised execution times.

6.2 Effects on Execution Time

In this section we present the execution times for the applications in Figure 6. For each application we show six bars where *B* is the baseline in addition to *DH*, *IH*, *EH*, *DS*, and *ES*, which are the same as in Section 6.1. We will again collectively refer to *DH*, *IH*, and *EH* as *HW*, and *DS* and *ES* as *SW*. The normalised execution times for each application is broken down into the following components from bottom to top: the busy time, the trap handler time, synchronisation and buffer stall, the read stall, and the write stall. We define the trap handler time as the execution time a processor is executing in a trap handler *after* that the data has arrived.

To start with Water, no prefetch technique has any effect on the the execution-time. This was due to the compiler could detect very few stride accesses, as discussed in Section 6.1.

Continuing with Cholesky, we see that the memory access stall accounts for more than half of the execution time in *B*. *DH* reduces the read stall time from 27% down to 8%. The synchronisation stall time is also reduced from 6% to 5%. *EH* reduces the write stall time from 25% to 8%. However, *E* has a somewhat longer read stall time than *DH*, 9% versus 8%. Although the execution time has dropped to 45% for *EH*, part of this is due to the application's scheduling which in this case reduces the busy time significantly.

For LU, *DH* and *DI* reduce the read stall time from 29%

to 10%, and *EH* reduces it to 11%. *SW* does not reduce the read stall time to the same extent as *HW*, but still cuts it to less than half. *EH* and *ES* also reduce the write stall time from 19% down to 13% and 14%, respectively.

For MP3D, *DH* and *SW* are not expected to reduce the read stall time significantly because indirect addressing prefetch is required. *IH* on the other hand reduces it from 45% to 22%. *EH* also reduces the write stall time from 45% to 24%.

Finally, for Barnes-Hut and PTHOR, we see that both the read stall and the synchronisation stall are reduced slightly by each technique, and the write stall time is also reduced marginally for *EH*.

Instruction overhead is introduced when a trap handler completes after data arrives. The instruction overhead is defined to be the trap time divided by the busy time. For none of the applications the overhead exceeds 0.42%, and this is why the trap times don't appear in the diagrams. We also measured the amount of generated traffic and found that it is not affected much by our prefetch techinques. By removing separate ownership requests, for Cholesky, LU, MP3D, and Barnes-Hut, *EH* could reduce the traffic between 1% and 4%, while the worst increase for any technique and application was an increase by 10% for *ES* for Barnes-Hut. In summary, we see that data prefetching using prefetch engines —either implemented in hardware or emulated in software— are successful at reducing both the read and write stall time at very little instruction overhead and increased traffic.

7 Related Work

Compiler-based data prefetching has been studied extensively by Mowry in [13]. As mentioned in Section 1, one goal of this paper is to overcome the problem of instruction overhead present in his approach. The instruction overhead limits his approach to source codes where the compiler can predict that misses will occur. In our approach on the other hand, there is instruction overhead only in the trap handlers, but as we saw in Section 6, this overhead is very small, and more importantly is only present when misses occur. In our approach, there is no need to restrict the compiler's use of data prefetching.

In recent work, Luk and Mowry [12] have evaluated a compiler algorithm to prefetch recursive data structures. We expect that the prefetch engine approach presented in this paper will not be useful at prefetching recursive data structures, because of the difficulty at generating addresses to prefetch without actually traversing a recursive data structure, which our prefetch engines are not intended to do.

To reduce the complexity of pure hardware-based stride prefetchers is another motivation of this work. The stride-prefetcher proposed by Chen and Baer [5] includes complex hardware to analyse the string of accesses to detect strides, and the hardware includes a reference prediction table [5]. Our simulations indicate that this complexity is not necessary. Chen [6] has proposed an on-chip prefetch engine which works with the first-level cache and is programmed by a compiler before a loop is entered (although the compiler's task was done by hand in [6]). A difference between that work and ours is that our technique suffers no instruction overhead when there are no misses. However, Chen's prefetch engines can, of course, also exploit low-overhead cache miss traps proposed in [10] and the compiler-generated trap-handlers proposed in this paper.

8 Conclusion

The contributions of this paper are the design and evaluation of a new approach to do data prefetching in multiprocessors. The components of our approach are a prefetch engine that issues prefetch requests, memory access instructions that trap on a second-level cache miss, and a compiler algorithm that automatically generates trap handlers. The prefetch engine is initialised by trap handlers with the number of blocks to prefetch, the access stride, and an address to start prefetching. Once started, the prefetch engine executes autonomously and creates no instruction overhead. We also evaluated the possibility of emulating the prefetch engine in a software loop in the trap handler. To evaluate our designs, we have implemented the prefetch engine in a detailed multiprocessor simulator, incorporated the compiler algorithm in an optimising compiler, and compiled and run six parallel applications. We find that the memory access stall time could be reduced by up to 67%, at an instruction overhead of less than 0.42% and very little additional memory traffic.

Although we have evaluated the prefetch engine in the context of a cache coherent NUMA, we expect that the prefetch engine can have a potential to reduce memory access latencies also in uniprocessors. We also expect that distributed virtual shared memory systems [11] could take advantage of our stride prefetching because each miss takes a large number of cycles. In this case, it might be good to "batch" the prefetches, so that they cause one single interruption on their way back.

To conclude, we have shown that with proper hardware support, it is possible to exploit an optimising compiler's static analysis in order to do accurate data prefetching at very little instruction overhead. In addition, we find that the emulated prefetch engine is competitive with prefetch engines while not requiring any hardware support beyond cache miss traps and prefetch instructions.

Acknowledgements

This research has been supported by a grant from the Swedish Research Council on Engineering Science (TFR) under the contract number 94-315.

References

[1] Alfred Aho, Ravi Sethi, and Jeffrey Ullman. *Compilers: Principles, Techniques, and Tools*. Addison-Wesley, Reading, Mass., 1986.

[2] J. Boyle, R. Butler, T. Diaz, B. Glickfield, E. Lusk, R. Overbeek, J. Patterson, and R. Stevens. *Portable Programs for Parallel Processors*. Holt, Rinehart, and Winston, New York, 1987.

[3] Mats Brorsson, Fredrik Dahlgren, Håkan Nilsson, and Per Stenström. The CacheMire Test Bench - A flexible and effective approach for simulation of multiprocessors. In *Proceedings of the 26th IEEE Annual Simulation Symposium*, pages 41–49. IEEE, New York, March 1993.

[4] Lucien Censier and Paul Feautrier. A new solution to coherence problems in multicache systems. *IEEE Trans. Comput.*, 27(12):1112–1118, 1978.

[5] T.-F. Chen and J.-L. Baer. A Performance Study of Software and Hardware Data Prefetching Schemes. In *Proceedings of 21st Annual International Symposium on Computer Architecture*, pages 223–232, 1994.

[6] Tien-Fu Chen. An effective programmable prefetch engine for on-chip caches. In *Proceedings of the 28th Annual International Symposium on Microarchitecture*, pages 237–242, 1995.

[7] Fredrik Dahlgren, Michel Dubois, and Per Stenström. Sequential Hardware Prefetching in Shared-Memory Multiprocessors. *IEEE Transactions on Parallel and Distributed Systems*, 6(7):733–746, 1995.

[8] Eric Hagersten. *Toward Scalable Cache Only Memory Architectures*. PhD thesis, Royal Institute of Technology, Stockholm, Sweden., October 1992.

[9] Mark Horowitz, Margaret Martonosi, Todd Mowry, and Mike Smith. Informing Loads: Enabling Software to Observe and React to Memory Behavior. CSL-TR-95-673, Computer Systems Laboratory, Stanford Univ., July 1995.

[10] Mark Horowitz, Margaret Martonosi, Todd Mowry, and Mike Smith. Informing Memory Operations: Providing Memory Performance Feedback in Modern Processors. In *Proceedings of the 23rd International Symposium on Computer Architecture*, pages 260–270. ACM, New York, 1996.

[11] K. Li and P. Hudak. Memory coherence in shared virtual memory systems. *ACM Trans. Comput. Syst.*, 7(4):321-359, November 1989.

[12] Chi-Keung Luk and Todd C. Mowry. Compiler-based prefetching for recursive data structures. In *Proceedings of the Seventh International Conference on Architectural Support for Programming Languages and Operating Systems*, pages 222–233. ACM, New York, 1996.

[13] Todd Mowry. *Tolerating Latency Through Software-Controlled Data Prefetching*. PhD thesis, Stanford Univ., Computer Systems Laboratory, Stanford, Calif., March 1994.

[14] Todd Mowry and Anoop Gupta. Tolerating latency through software-controlled prefetching in scalable shared-memory multiprocessors. *J. Parallel Distrib. Comput.*, 2(4):87–106, 1991.

[15] Todd Mowry, Monica Lam, and Anoop Gupta. Design and evaluation of a compiler algorithm for prefetching. In *Proceedings of the Fifth International Conference on Architectural Support for Programming Languages and Operating Systems*, pages 62–73. ACM, New York, 1992.

[16] Jaswinder Pal Singh, Wolf-Dietrich Weber, and Anoop Gupta. SPLASH: Stanford Parallel Applications for Shared-Memory. *Comput. Arch. News*, 20(1):5–44, 1992.

[17] Jonas Skeppstedt. The design and implementation of an optimizing ANSI C compiler for SPARC. Technical report, Dep. of Computer Science, Lund Univ., Lund, Sweden, April 1990.

An Adaptive Sequential Prefetching Scheme in Shared-Memory Multiprocessors

Myoung Kwon Tcheun, Hyunsoo Yoon, Seung Ryoul Maeng
Department of Computer Science, CAIR
Korea Advanced Institute of Science and Technology (KAIST)
373-1 Kusong-Dong Yusung-Gu, Taejon 305-701, Korea
E-mail: {tcheun,hyoon,maeng}@camars.kaist.ac.kr

Abstract

The sequential prefetching scheme is a simple hardware-controlled scheme, which exploits the sequentiality of memory accesses to predict which blocks will be read in the near future. We analyze the relationship between the sequentiality of application programs and the effectiveness of sequential prefetching on shared-memory multiprocessors. Also, we propose a simple hardware scheme which selects the prefetching degree on each miss by adding a small table(PDS: Prefetching Degree Selector) to the sequential prefetching scheme. This scheme could prefetch consecutive blocks aggressively for applications with high sequentiality and conservatively for applications with low sequentiality.

1 Introduction

In large-scale multiprocessors with a general interconnection network, the program execution time significantly depends on the shared-memory access latency. The latency consists of the memory latency and the network latency. Caches are quite effective to reduce and hide the shared-memory access latency by reducing the number of shared-memory accesses. However, the remained shared-memory accesses are still serious bottleneck to achieve high performance computing because the cache miss penalty reaches to tens to hundreds of processor cycles with the advent of very fast uniprocessors and massively parallel systems [1, 2].

Prefetching is an attractive scheme to reduce the cache miss penalty by exploiting the overlap of processor computations with data accesses. Especially for multiprocessors, cache miss penalty can be decreased significantly by overlapping the network latency of fetched block with those of prefetched blocks. Many prefetching schemes based on software or hardware have been proposed. Software prefetching schemes [3, 4, 5, 6] perform static program analysis and insert explicitly prefetch instructions into the program code, which increases the program size. In contrast, hardware prefetching schemes control the prefetch activities according to the program execution by only hardware. Several hardware prefetching schemes [7, 8, 9] prefetch blocks if a regular access pattern is detected. These schemes require complex hardware to detect a regular access pattern. One block lookahead schemes (OBL)[10] are simple hardware prefetching schemes, where the next one block is only concerned upon referencing a block. There are three types of OBL schemes: *Always prefetch* prefetches the next block on each reference, so it makes excessive cache lookups. *Tagged*

prefetch prefetches the next block if referenced block is accessed for the first time. This scheme requires an extra bit per cache block. *Prefetch on misses* prefetches the next block only on the miss. Since this scheme requires no extra bit per cache block and no prefetch activities on cache hits, it is simple to implement. However, this scheme is too conservative to need a cache miss to prefetch one block.

The *sequential prefetching schemes* [10, 11, 12, 13] are an extension of *prefetch on misses*. They prefetch several consecutive blocks following the missed block in the caches on each miss. Fu and Patel [11] show that the performance of sequential prefetching is enhanced with increasing the number of blocks to prefetch. Their scheme prefetches several blocks on misses which access a scalar or a short stride vector, while it does not prefetch on misses which access a long stride vector. This scheme uses the stride information carried by vector instructions. For scalar processor, it requires complex hardware to get the stride information. Dahlgren, Dubois, and Stenstrom [12] mention that sequential prefetching, which prefetches more than one block on each miss, could be useful if the system use the high bandwidth network. They propose an adaptive sequential prefetching scheme, where the prefetching degree, i.e., the number of blocks to prefetch on each miss, is controlled by the prefetch efficiency. The prefetch efficiency is measured by counting the prefetched blocks that are useful. To count the useful prefetches, this scheme uses two extra bits for each cache block and needs some activities on cache hits. Bianchini and LeBlanc [13] simulate the performance of sequential prefetching scheme with various prefetching degrees on various memory and network latency and analyze the effect of fine-grain sharing and write operations. While aggressive sequential prefetches many blocks on each miss and improves the miss rates of application programs, it may not result in reduction of the stall time. In some cases, prefetching only one block increases the execution time for application programs with fine-grain sharing and lots of write operations. They propose Hybrid prefetching scheme combining hardware and software supports for stride-directed prefetching. The compiler assigns the number of blocks to prefetch for each instructions according to the data type. One block is assigned for instructions which access fine-grain sharing data and several blocks are assigned for the other instructions.

Each of these studies concludes that the performance of sequential prefetching depends on several factors, such as the characteristics of application programs, the prefetching degree, and the memory and network latency.

In this paper, we analyze the relationship between the sequentiality of application programs and the effectiveness of sequential prefetching on various memory and network latency, and we propose a new simple adaptive sequential prefetching scheme which does not need compiler assistance and extra activity on cache hits. This scheme prefetches many blocks on cache misses in long sequential streams and a few blocks on misses in short sequential streams by adjusting the prefetching degree according to the length of sequential streams. Therefore, for application programs with high sequentiality, the proposed scheme can prefetch blocks aggressively and shows better execution time than the sequential prefetching scheme with the prefetching degree of one. Also, the proposed scheme shows better execution time in low bandwidth than the adaptive sequential prefetching scheme proposed by Dahlgren et al. For application programs with low sequentiality, this scheme prefetches blocks conservatively and can avoid prefetching of useless blocks. The proposed scheme shows similar execution time to the sequential prefetching scheme with the prefetching degree of one and shows better execution time in high bandwidth than the adaptive sequential prefetching scheme proposed by Dahlgren et al.

The remainder of this paper will be organized as follows. Section 2 describes the overview and implementation of the new adaptive sequential prefetching scheme. In Section 3, we present the simulation methodology and workloads used in this study. We analyze the relationship between the sequentiality of application programs and the effectiveness of sequential prefetching in Section 4. In Section 5, the proposed scheme is compared with the other simple hardware sequential prefetching schemes. Finally, conclusions are presented in Section 6.

2 An Adaptive Sequential Prefetching Scheme

2.1 Overview

When a cache miss occurs, the processor accesses the memory. If the cache misses are occurred on to the consecutive blocks, the processor accesses the blocks in the memory sequentially. We define the sequence of these memory accesses as *a sequential stream*, and the number of consecutive blocks as *the length of sequential stream*. The effectiveness of sequential prefetching depends on the length of sequential streams and the prefetching degree. In a long sequential stream, aggressive prefetching reduces the miss rate efficiently. The miss penalty can be also decreased significantly by overlapping the network latency of fetched block with those of prefetched blocks. However, aggressive prefetching in a short sequential stream increases the traffic for useless blocks and may increase the network latency.

The proposed scheme increases the prefetching degree according to the length of sequential stream. Since the length of the sequential stream is not known, the prefetching degree is increased one by one on each miss in a sequential stream as shown in Figure 1. After K misses have been occurred in a sequential stream, $K + 1$ blocks are prefetched on the next miss in the sequential stream. Thus, many blocks can be prefetched on a miss in a long sequential stream.

Since the sequential streams can be interleaved, this scheme detects misses in the same sequential stream by using a small table containing addresses on which the next

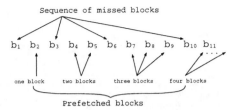

$b_{i+1} = b_i + 1$: the sequence of b_i is sequential
b_i : the ith block address of a sequential stream

Figure 1: Missed block sequence

miss will be occurred. When there is a miss on the first block in a sequential stream, this scheme stores the third block address with the prefetching degree of 2 in the table. The prefetching degree is stored in the table to keep the increased prefetching degree for each stream. A block is considered to be the first in a sequential stream if there is no previous miss in the same sequential stream. In implementation, the first miss is detected by checking the existance of the missed block address in the table. If a miss really belongs to a sequential stream, there will be references to the second block, the third block, and so on. A reference to the second block becomes a cache hit because the second block is already prefetched. When a miss on the third block occurs, this scheme compares the miss address with the stored addresses in the table. Since there exists third block address with the prefetching degree of 2, this scheme prefetches two consecutive blocks, the fourth and fifth blocks, following the third block. The third block address is replaced with the sixth block address, and the prefetching degree is increased to 3. The misses will occur on the 1st, the 3rd, the 6th, and the 10th blocks of a sequential stream in the proposed scheme because the prefetching degree is increased one by one as shown in Figure 1. When the reference reaches to the end of the sequential stream, the processor would not access the saved address in the near future. Since the table size is finite, the saved address and the increased prefetching degree would be replaced by the first address of the other sequential stream. Each entry in the table keeps different prefetching degree for the recent sequential streams. The proposed scheme prefetches one block on first misses in sequential stream which may access a long stride vector or fine-grain sharing data, and several blocks on the other misses in sequential stream which access scalar variables or a short stride vector. Thus, there is no need to decrease the prefetching degree.

2.2 Processing Node Architecture

The processing node shown in Figure 2.a consists of a processor, a cache, a prefetching unit, a prefetching degree selector (PDS), and a network interface. Figure 2.a except for PDS shows the mechanism of a sequential prefetching scheme. The processor is blocked only during the time when it takes to handle the read miss. A cache read miss for the block address A issues a fetch request to the network interface and activates the prefetching unit. The prefetching unit increases the block address A to $A + 1$ and lookups the cache for the block address $A + 1$. If the block is not present in the cache, the prefetching unit issues a prefetch request to the network interface. During this time, the block address $A + 1$ is increased to $A + 2$. In the next cache

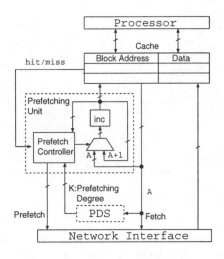

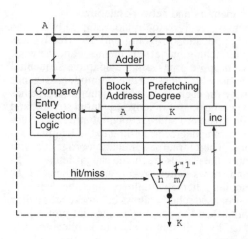

a. Processing node architecture	b. Prefetching Degree Selector (PDS)

Figure 2: Prefetching mechanism

cycle, a cache lookup is made for block address $A + 2$. If the block is not present in the cache, a prefetch request is issued to the network interface. K cache lookups are made for K consecutive blocks, and prefetch requests are issued for the blocks which are not present in the cache. K is the prefetching degree. The Prefetch Controller controlls the number of cache lookups and issues prefetch requests depending on the result of each cache lookup.

Since the prefetch requests are issued one at a time and are pipelined in the network and memory system, they can be overlapped with the fetch request. The Prefetching Degree Selector (PDS) selects a prefetching degree for a cache miss and sends the selected prefetching degree to the prefetching unit.

2.3 Prefetching Degree Selector

PDS uses a table to increase the prefetching degree one by one on each miss in a sequential stream. Each entry of the table contains a block address to detect the next miss in the same sequential stream and a prefetching degree to increase the prefetching degree for the next miss. Figure 2.b shows the block diagram of PDS. The compare logic compares the miss address A with the addresses stored in the table. If there is a hit, the associated prefetching degree K is selected, and the entry (A, K) is replaced with $(A + K + 1, K + 1)$. The prefetching degree K is increased to $K + 1$, and the address is added to the increased prefetching degree. If the address $(A + K + 1)$ also exists in the table, PDS invalidates the entry. However, if the miss address does not exist in the table, an entry $(A + 2, 2)$ is inserted into the table. If the address $(A + 2)$ exists in the table, the entry is replaced by the entry $(A + 2, 2)$. Since the table is finite, the new entry might cause the least recently used (LRU) entry to be replaced by an entry selection logic. The number of entries affects the performance of the proposed scheme. Our experimental results suggest that a table of four entries is appropriate.

Consider an arbitrary sequence.

$$a_1, a_2, b_1, b_2, c_1, c_2, d_1, d_2, b_3, b_4, b_5, b_6, e_1, e_2, e_3$$

Each sequence of x_i is sequential, i.e., $x_{i+1} = x_i + 1$. x_i is an address of ith block of each sequential sequence of x_i.

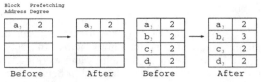

a. On the miss of block a_1	b. On the miss of block b_3

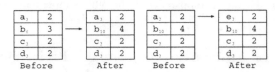

c. On the miss of block b_6	d. On the miss of block e_1

Figure 3: Update entries in the table

For example, a_1 is the first block address of sequential stream a_1, a_2, and b_3 is the third block address of sequential stream $b_1, b_2, b_3, b_4, b_5, b_6$. Five sequential streams, sequences of a_i, b_i, c_i, d_i, and e_i, are interleaved. The read miss on a_1 will prefetch a_2 and will insert address a_3 and the prefetching degree of 2 into the table (Figure 3.a). A reference to a_2 is a hit, because a_2 is already prefetched. Read misses b_1, c_1, d_1 will also prefetch b_2, c_2, d_2 and will insert addresses b_3, c_3, d_3 and prefetching degrees of 2. A read miss on b_3 will prefetch b_4, b_5 because the prefetching degree in the table is 2. The address b_3 is replaced with b_6 and the prefetching degree increases to 3 from 2 (Figure 3.b). After references to b_4 and b_5, a miss to block b_6 will be occurred. This miss replaces b_6 and 3 with b_{10} and 4 (Figure 3.c). A miss to block e_1, which is the first block of e_1, e_2, e_3 stream, replaces the entry a_3 and 2 with e_3 and 2 (Figure 3.d).

3 Simulation Environment

We make the architectural simulation model using MINT [14]. The architecture is a scalable direct-connected multiprocessor with 16 nodes. Cache coherence is maintained by the full directory protocol [15] distributed among the mem-

308

Table 1: Benchmark Programs

Program	Description	Data Sets
LU	decompose a dense matrix	200×200 matrix
FFT	FFT algorithm	32 K complex data points
Radix	Integer radix sort algorithm	1024 radix, 262144 keys
MP3D	simulate rarefied hypersonic flow	10 K parts, 10 time steps
Ocean	simulate eddy currents in an ocean basin	128×128
PTHOR	simulate a digital circuit at the logic level	iRISC circuit, 1000 time steps

Table 2: The Characteristics of Application Programs

a. The Distribution of Sequential Stream Lengths (Unit %)

Program	The length of sequential streams						
	1-5	6-10	11-15	16-20	21-25	26-30	>31
FFT	58.6	36.2	0.2	0.1	0.1	0.2	4.4
LU	89.8	3.0	1.3	2.6	0.0	1.6	2.6
Radix	94.9	0.6	0.2	0.2	0.2	1.5	2.1
MP3D	95.0	4.5	0.1	0.2	0.0	0.0	0.0
Ocean	98.3	1.6	0.0	0.0	0.0	0.0	0.0
PTHOR	99.9	0.0	0.0	0.0	0.0	0.0	0.0

b. The Fraction of Misses in Sequential Streams

	Read misses belonging to sequential streams of length one	Read misses belonging to sequential streams of length greater than 30	Average length of sequential streams
FFT	7%	52%	7.85
LU	13%	42%	4.25
Radix	26%	41%	2.98
MP3D	44%	1%	1.64
Ocean	59%	0%	1.39
PTHOR	88%	0%	1.06

ory modules. Prefetched data are loaded into the caches so that the data can be invalidated by the cache coherence protocol. The page size is 4 Kbytes, and the pages are allocated in a round-robin fashion. The interconnection network is a bi-directional wormhole-routed mesh with dimension-ordered routing. We simulate in different memory and network bandwidths to explore the effect of the bandwidth. We use memory and network bandwidths used in [13]. The latency of a memory module is 24 processor cycles. The memory transfer rates are 0.5 cycles, 2 cycles, and 4 cycles per word for high, medium, and low bandwidths, respectively. Network latency per link and latency per switch are 1 cycles and 5 cycles. Path widths are 128 bits, 32 bits, and 16 bits for high, medium, and low bandwidths, respectively. In simulation, high handwidth means high transfer rate and high path width. Also, medium and low bandwidth mean each memory transfer rate and path width.

Six benchmark programs are considered for the simulation. Four of them (LU, FFT, Radix and Ocean) are taken from the SPLASH-2 suite [16], and the other two programs(MP3D and PTHOR) from SPLASH suite [17]. We summarize them in Table 1.

Simulations are carried out with caches of 16 Kbytes and a block size of 32 bytes. We will focus on four different metrics: the read miss rate, the prefetch efficiency, the number of transferred blocks, and the execution time. The read miss rate is computed solely with respect to shared references. The purpose of prefetching is to reduce the cache misses. So the read miss rate is a proper metric. Cache pollution is one of the cost of prefetching. We use the prefetch efficiency to measure how many prefetched blocks are useful. The prefetch efficiency is defined as the number of prefetched and useful blocks divided by the total number of prefetched blocks. The prefetched and useful blocks are prefetched blocks that are accessed later. The traffic for prefetched blocks is the other cost of prefetching. The high traffic may increase the memory access latency. We use the number of transferred blocks to measure the traffic for read cache misses and prefetches.

4 The Impact of Sequentiality to Sequential Prefetching

The performance of the sequential prefetching schemes depends on the distribution of sequential stream lengths of application programs because the effectiveness of sequential prefetching depends on the length of sequential streams. Table 2.a shows the distribution of sequential stream lengths, and Table 2.b shows the fraction of misses belonging to sequential streams of length one, the fraction of misses belonging to sequential streams of length greater than 30, and the average length of sequential streams. If the length of sequential stream is one, most of prefetched blocks will be useless, while for a long sequential stream, many useful blocks can be prefetched on each miss. We define *the sequentiality of application program* as the average length of sequential streams of application program.

FFT, LU, and Radix show high sequentiality because large fraction of all misses belong to the sequential streams of length greater than 30, while MP3D, Ocean, and PTHOR show low sequentiality because large fraction of all misses belong to the sequential streams of length one.

Benchmark programs are simulated with the prefetching degree of 1, 2, 4, 8, 16, and no prefetching to examine the impact of sequentiality to sequential prefetching with various prefetching degrees. Figure 4.a shows the reduction of misses. The number of misses is normalized to no prefetching. The reduction of misses is larger for application programs with higher sequentiality for most of the prefetching degrees.

Figure 4.b shows that the prefetch efficiency is higher for application programs with higher sequentiality. Figure 4.c shows the number of transferred blocks which is normalized to no prefetching. As can be seen, the increase of transferred blocks is larger for application programs with lower sequentiality.

Figure 5 shows the execution times which are normalized to no prefetching. The execution times as a function of the prefetching degree follow U-shaped curves. The execution time depends on various factors, i.e., cache size and cache block size, the memory access latency, the memory and network bandwidth, the sequentiality of application programs,

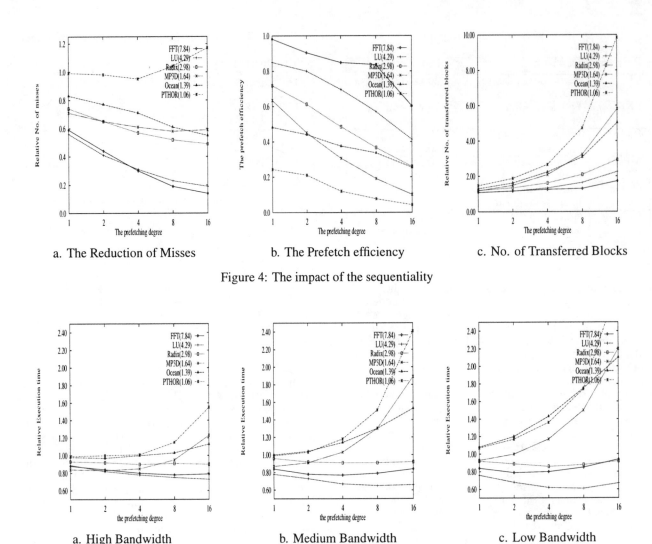

a. The Reduction of Misses   b. The Prefetch efficiency   c. No. of Transferred Blocks

Figure 4: The impact of the sequentiality

a. High Bandwidth   b. Medium Bandwidth   c. Low Bandwidth

Figure 5: The execution time

and the number of write operations. In this paper, we concentrate on the sequentiality of application programs and the memory and network bandwidth. Figure 5.b and Figure 5.c clearly show the distinction between application programs with high sequentiality and application programs with low sequentiality. For application programs with high sequentiality, the reductions of execution time are high. This is expected because the reduction of misses is high and the traffic is slightly increased. The reduction of execution time of FFT is smaller than that of LU in spite of higher reduction of read misses and higher prefetch efficiency. The reason for this is that the stall time for FFT increases more than that for LU because the write traffic for FFT is much higher than that for LU.

In general, application programs with high sequentiality show high reduction of misses, high prefetch efficiency, and small increase of transferred blocks. Therefore, aggressive sequential prefetching works well for application programs with high sequentiality. On the other hand, for application programs with low sequentiality, sequential prefetching de-

grades the execution time in some cases.

5 Comparison with Other Sequential Prefetching Schemes

In this section, we compare the proposed scheme with the other simple hardware sequential prefetching schemes, i.e., the sequential prefetching scheme with the prefetching degree of one and the adaptive sequential prefetching scheme proposed by Dahlgren et al. We refer to these two sequential prefetching schemes as SP1 and ASP1. We also refer to the adaptive sequential prefetching scheme proposed by ours as ASP2.

SP1 is the most simplest hardware sequential prefetching scheme. The sequential prefetching scheme with the prefetching degree greater than one needs hardware to count the number of prefetch requests on each miss. In the previous section, higher prefetching degree shows better execution time for application programs with high sequentiality, but SP1 shows the best execution time for application pro-

310

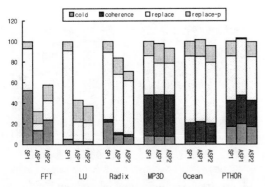

Figure 6: The miss rates

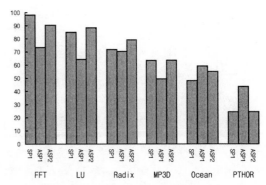

Figure 7: The prefetch efficiency

Table 3: Characteristics of sequential prefetching schemes

	SP1	ASP1	ASP2
Needs Extra Hardware	No	Yes • Two bits per cache line (1Kbits for 16 Kbytes cache)	Yes • A small table (4 X 32bits for 4 entry table)
The activities on cache hit	No activity	Activities • set the bits in the cache and count useful blocks	No Activity

Differentiate the misses	No	No	Yes
			• sequential
			  - scalar variables
			  - short stride vector
			• non-sequential
			  - long stride vector
			  - fine-grain sharing data

grams with low sequentility.

ASP1 controls the prefetching degree to make the prefetch efficiency lie between two predefined values. We use 75% and 50% for these two values in simulations. Those are the same values used in [12]. As shown in the previous section, the prefetch efficiency is decreased with increasing the prefetching degree. When the prefetch efficiency is high, ASP1 increases the prefetching degree and when the prefetch efficiency is low, ASP1 decreases the prefetching degree. In some case, prefetching can be stopped. This scheme needs two extra bits for each cache block and some activities on cache hits to count the useful prefetches. 1 Kbits are needed for 16 Kbytes cache with 32 byte block size.

ASP2 increases the prefetching degree to prefetch many blocks on misses in long sequential streams. A small table is required to increase the prefetching degree. Each entry in the table consists a block address and a prefetching degree. A block address needs 27 bits for the block of 32 bytes and the prefetching degree needs 5 bits to increase from 1 to 32. 5 bits are sufficient to cover the longest sequential stream of six application programs. Since 32 bits are used for one entry, 4 × 32 bits are required for a table with four entries. This scheme differentiates the misses according to the sequentiality. The characteristics of the above three prefetching schemes are summarized in Table 3.

Figures 6-11 show the simulation results. Figure 6, Figure 7, and Figure 8 show the miss rates, the prefetch ef-

ficiencies, and the numbers of transferred blocks in high bandwidth. These results are similar with the results in medium and low bandwidth.

Figure 6 shows the relative numbers of misses which are normalized to SP1. Each bar consists of four sections that, from the bottom to the top, correspond to cold misses, coherence misses, replace misses, and replace_p misses. A miss is classified as a cold miss if it has never been fetched into the cache, coherence miss if it was invalidated by cache coherence protocol, and a replace miss if it was replaced out from the cache. A read miss to a block that was replaced out from the cache by prefetched block is classified as a replace_p miss.

As expected, the reduction of miss rates of ASP2 for FFT, LU, and Radix is high, because the sequentiality is high. On the other hand, for application programs like MP3D, Ocean, and PTHOR, the miss rates are slightly lower than those of SP1, because these application programs have low sequentialities. Also, the reduction of miss rates of ASP1 for FFT, LU, and Radix is high, because the prefetch efficiency is high. Since the prefetch efficiencies of FFT is very high as shown in Figure 4.b, the miss rate of ASP2 is higher than that of ASP1 for FFT.

Figure 7 shows the prefetch efficiency. The prefetch efficiency of ASP2 is better than that of SP1 for all programs except FFT, because ASP2 prefetches many blocks on misses in long sequential streams. For FFT, although the prefetch efficiency of ASP2 is worse than that of SP1, it is still high as 90.4%. The prefetch efficiency of ASP1 is worse than that of SP1 for four of six application programs because ASP1 makes the prefetch efficiencies of those application programs lie between 75% and 50%. For Ocean and PTHOR, the prefetch efficiency of ASP1 is better than that of SP1, because the prefetch efficiencies are lower than 50% for most of the prefetching degrees.

Figure 8 shows the number of transferred blocks. We have broken down the transferred blocks into three components that, from bottom to the top, correspond to the prefetched and useful blocks, the prefetched but useless blocks, and the fetched blocks. A prefetched but useless block means a block which is replaced or invalidated before accessed.

The number of transferred blocks of ASP2 is slightly higher than that of SP1. For FFT, LU, and Radix, the por-

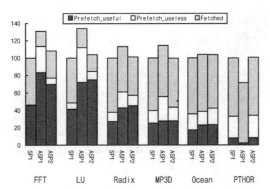

Figure 8: The number of transferred blocks

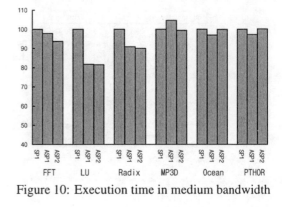

Figure 10: Execution time in medium bandwidth

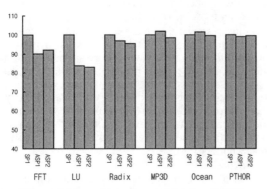

Figure 9: Execution time in high bandwidth

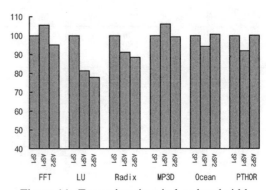

Figure 11: Execution time in low bandwidth

tion of fetched blocks of ASP2 is smaller than that of SP1 since the miss rates are reduced significantly. The portion of useful prefetched blocks is larger than that of SP1 because the sequentiality is high. For MP3D, Ocean, and PTHOR, each portion is similar with that of SP1. The number of transferred blocks of ASP1 is larger than that of ASP2 for all application programs except PTHOR. PTHOR shows extremely small portion of prefetched blocks because the prefetch efficiency is extremely low. For FFT, LU, Radix, and MP3D, the portion of useless blocks under ASP1 is much larger than that under ASP2 because the prefetch efficiencies are high. For PTHOR, the portion of useless blocks under ASP1 is smaller than that under ASP2, because the prefetch efficiency is extremely low. These results are similar with the results in medium and low bandwidth except Ocean. For Ocean, ASP2 transfers more blocks than ASP1 in in medium and low bandwidth.

Figures 9-11 show the relative execution times which are normalized to SP1, respectively according to the bandwidth. The execution time depends on the miss rate, the number of transferred blocks. The blocked time is in propotion to the miss rate, while the memory access latency is affected by the number of transferred blocks.

For application programs with high sequentiality, ASP2 shows much lower miss rate than SP1 and transfers sim-

ilar number of blocks to SP1. Thus, ASP2 shows better execution time than SP1. For LU, the execution time of ASP2 is reduced to 77% of SP1. For application programs with low sequentiality, ASP2 shows similar execution time to SP1. For MP3D, ASP2 shows slightly better execution time because ASP2 shows slightly lower miss rate than SP1 and transfers similar number of blocks to SP1. For Ocean, ASP2 shows similar execution time to SP1 because ASP2 shows slightly lower miss rate but slightly higher number of transferred blocks than SP1. For PTHOR, ASP2 shows similar execution time to SP1 because ASP2 and SP1 shows similar miss rate and similar number of transferred blocks.

ASP2 shows better execution time than ASP1 in some cases while ASP1 shows better execution time than ASP2 in other cases. For FFT, ASP2 shows better performance than ASP1 in low bandwidth while ASP1 shows better execution time than ASP2 in high bandwidth. The reason is that ASP1 shows much lower miss rate than ASP2 but transfers much more blocks than ASP2, and the execution time is more sensitve to the miss rate than the number of transferred blocks in high bandwidth, but more sensitive to the number of transferred blocks in low bandwidth. LU, Radix, and MP3D show better execution times under ASP2 in all bandwidth because ASP2 shows similar miss rate with small number of transferred blocks. Ocean shows better execution times under ASP2 in high bandwidth because ASP2 shows lower miss rate with small number of transferred blocks. But, in medium and low bandwidth, ASP2 shows slightly worse execution time than ASP1 because ASP2 shows lower miss rate but transfers much more blocks than ASP1. PTHOR prefetches very small number of blocks because this program shows extremely low sequentiality. ASP2 shows slightly lower miss rate, but prefetches more blocks than ASP1. Thus, ASP1 shows better execution time in all bandwidth.

As expected, ASP2 shows better execution time than SP1 for application programs with high sequentiality and similar execution time to SP1 for application programs with low sequentiality. For four out of six application programs, ASP2 shows higher prefetch efficiency and better execution time than ASP1 because ASP2 prefetches useless blocks less than ASP1.

6 Conclusion

In this paper, we have analyzed the impact of sequentiality on the sequential prefetching scheme. For application programs with high sequentiality, it is shown that aggressive sequential prefetching can reduce miss rate significantly and keep prefetch efficiency high with small increase of transferred blocks. Therefore, we can conclude that aggressive sequential prefetching works well for application programs with high sequentiality. On the other hand, for application programs with low sequentiality, it is shown that aggressive sequential prefetching degrades prefetch efficiency with high increase of transferred blocks and results in a small reduction of miss rate.

We have also proposed a simple hardware sequential prefetching scheme which can increase the prefetching degree according to the length of sequential streams. Simply adding a small table to the sequential prefetching scheme, it is shown that the proposed scheme can reduce the execution time upto 77% of the sequential prefetching scheme with the prefetching degree of one. For four out of six application programs, the proposed scheme shows better execution time than the scheme proposed by Dahlgren et al.

References

[1] A. Gupta, J. Hennessy, K. Gharachorloo, T. Mowry, and W.-D. Weber, "Comparative Evaluation of Latency Reducing and Tolerating Techniques," in *Proc. of the 18th Annual International Symposium on Computer Architecture*, pp. 254–263, 1991.

[2] D.Lenoski, J.Lauden, K.Gharachorloo, A.Gupta, and J.Hennessy, "The directory-based cache coherence protocol for the dash multiprocessor," in *Proc. of the 17th Annual International Symposium on Computer Architecture*, pp. 148–159, 1990.

[3] E. Gornish, E. Granston, and A. Veidenbaum, "Compiler-directed data prefetching in multiprocessors with memory hierarchies," in *Proc. 1990 International Conference on Supercomputing*, pp. 354–368, 1990.

[4] D. Callahan, K. Kennedy, and A. Porterfield, "Software prefetching," in *Proc. of the 4th Intl. Conf. on Architectural Support for Programming Languages and Operating Systems*, pp. 40–52, 1991.

[5] T. Mowry and A. Gupta, "Tolerating latency through software-controlled prefetching in shared-memory multiprocessors," *Journal of Parallel and Distributed Computing*, vol. 12, no. 2, pp. 87–106, 1991.

[6] T. Mowry, M. Lam, and A. Gupta, "Design and evaluation of a compiler algorithm for prefetching," in *Proc. of the 5th Intl. Conf. on Architectural Support for Programming Languages and Operating Systems*, pp. 62–73, 1992.

[7] J. Baer and T. Chen, "An effective on-chip preloading scheme to reduce data access penalty," in *Proc. of Supercomputing '91*, pp. 176–186, 1991.

[8] J. Baer and T. Chen, "Reducing memory latency via non-blocking and prefetching caches," in *Architectural Support for Programming Languages and Operating Systems*, pp. 51–61, 1992.

[9] J. Fu, J. Patel, and B. Janssens, "Stride directed prefetching in scalar processors," in *Proc. of the 25th International Symposium on Microarchitectute*, pp. 102–110, 1992.

[10] A. Smith, "Cache memories," *ACM Computing Surveys*, vol. 14, pp. 473–530, Sep. 1982.

[11] J. Fu and J. Patel, "Data prefetching in multiprocessor vector cache memories," in *Proc. of the 18th Annual International Symposium on Computer Architecture*, pp. 54–63, 1991.

[12] F. Dahlgren, M. Dubois, and P. Stenstrom, "Fixed and Adaptive sequential prefetching in shared memory multiprocessors," in *Proc. of the International Conference on Parallel Processing*, pp. 56–63, 1993.

[13] R. Bianchini and T. LeBlanc, "A preliminary evaluation of cache-miss-initiated prefetching techniques in scalable multiprocessors," in *tech. rep. 515, University of Rochester*, 1994.

[14] J. Veenstra, "Mint Tutorial and User Manual," in *tech. rep. 452, Department of Computer Science, University of Rochester*, July 1993.

[15] L.Censier and P.Feautrier, "A new solution to coherence problems in multicache systems," *IEEE Transactions on Computers*, vol. C-27, no. 12, pp. 1112–1118, 1978.

[16] S. C. Woo, M. Ohara, E. Torrie, J. P. Singh, and A. Gupta, "The SPLASH-2 Programs: Characterization and Methodological Considerations," in *International Symposium on Computer Architecture*, 1995.

[17] J.P.Singh, W.D.Weber, and A.Gupta, "SPLASH: Stanford Parallel Applications for Shared-Memory," *Computer Architecture News*, vol. 20, pp. 5–44, Mar. 1992.

Stride-directed Prefetching for Secondary Caches *

Sunil Kim
IBM (MS 4305)
11400 Burnet Road
Austin, TX 78758
skim@austin.ibm.com

Alexander V. Veidenbaum
Department of EECS
University of Illinois at Chicago
Chicago, IL 60607-7053
alexv@eecs.uic.edu

Abstract

This paper studies hardware prefetching for second-level (L2) caches. Previous work on prefetching has been extensive but largely directed at primary caches. In some cases only L2 prefetching is possible or is more appropriate. By studying L2 prefetching characteristics we show that existing stride-directed methods [1, 8] for L1 caches do not work as well in L2 caches. We propose a new stride-detection mechanism for L2 prefetching and combine it with stream buffers used in [16]. Our evaluation shows that this new prefetching scheme is more effective than stream buffer prefetching particularly for applications with long-stride accesses. Finally, we evaluate an L2 cache prefetching organization which combines a small L2 cache with our stride-directed prefetching scheme. Our results show that this system performs significantly better than stream buffer prefetching or a larger non-prefetching L2 cache without suffering from a significant increase in the memory traffic.

1 Introduction

Advances in processor architecture and its implementation technology make memory latency an ever increasing problem for high-performance systems. A two-level cache hierarchy is typically used to deal with the problem and the approach is quite successful for many types of applications. However, programs with large data sets or low data reuse, such as scientific applications, often have high miss rates. Combined with longer access times for the secondary caches and main memory this results in poor cache performance.

Several solutions have been advanced as a way to tolerate these long latencies. A solution we will concentrate on in this paper is data prefetching. Prefetching attempts to predict future data accesses and move the data to the upper levels of the memory hierarchy before it is referenced. This either eliminates or reduces the memory latency.

Both hardware and software prefetching approaches have been studied extensively. Software prefetching, which has been investigated in [3, 9, 13, 15], uses a compiler to analyze memory references and insert prefetch instructions accordingly. The prefetch instructions fetch data into caches or prefetch buffers for future memory accesses.

In hardware prefetching, special-purpose hardware monitors data access patterns and prefetches data according to the observed memory access patterns. The simplest hardware prefetching schemes are the *one block lookahead* (OBL)

schemes [18], where only cache line $l + 1$ is considered for prefetching when line l is accessed. These schemes differ in ways a prefetch of a line is triggered, namely *always prefetching, prefetching on misses*, and *tagged prefetching*. Another prefetching method is stream buffers, proposed in [12]. In this method a stream buffer is assigned on a cache miss and the stream buffer prefetches successive cache lines starting at the miss address. Both of these methods cannot handle strides longer than a cache line.

More sophisticated hardware prefetching schemes use *stride-directed* prefetching and are described in [1, 8, 11, 16]. These can handle arbitrary constant strides and are discussed in more detail later.

Finally, it is possible to attack the problem through a combination of hardware and software. A general prefetch engine using software instructions to supply the stride and start prefetching for a stream is proposed in [4]. A different integrated hardware/software prefetching approach is proposed in [10].

We will focus on hardware-based prefetching in this paper. We further limit our study to secondary cache prefetching only while assuming no prefetching in the primary cache. There are several reasons for performing prefetching only at second-level caches (L2 prefetching). First, system designers have an opportunity to add prefetching hardware to an off-chip secondary cache which may not be possible in an on-chip primary cache. Prefetching logic added to primary cache increases complexity and may increase processor cycle time. Finally, a larger L2 cache can tolerate more cache pollution caused by prefetching than a small primary cache can.

Simple hardware prefetching such as tagged prefetching and stream buffers can be used for L2 prefetching. These methods are attractive for L2 prefetching because of their simplicity and/or when only L1 cache miss addresses are available. However, these methods are not effective for memory accesses with strides longer than a cache line which occur in most scientific applications. Stride-directed prefetching is much more appropriate in such programs.

In stride-directed prefetching, a *memory reference stream*, i.e. a sequence of data addresses generated by a given memory access instruction, is detected by hardware and its stride calculated. The calculated stride is used to predict and prefetch future memory accesses.

In most previous studies [1, 8, 11], a memory reference stream is detected by using instruction addresses. This approach, denoted an *instruction-address-based* prefetching, is quite successful in L1 prefetching. However, it has not been shown whether instruction-address-based or stride-directed prefetching is effective at L2 cache level. There

*This work was supported in part by the National Science Foundation under Grant No. NSF 89-20891.

are several possible reasons why they may not be. First, the stride detector at L2 does not see all data addresses, just L1 cache misses. This makes it difficult to detect a constant stride due to locality or due to cache conflicts in L1 cache. The former makes a hit address invisible to the stride detector, the latter causes *extra* misses to be seen by the stride detector. We refer to this as an L1 cache *screening* effect. Second, instruction addresses may be difficult or costly to obtain outside of a processor chip for system-level L2 cache implementation. Thus it is desirable to have an L2 prefetching method capable of detecting memory reference streams without instruction addresses.

L2 prefetching proposed in [16] combines stream buffers with non-unit stride detection. This is the only method specifically aimed at L2 prefetching and it does not use instruction addresses. Two heuristic approaches to non-unit stride detection are proposed. In one a program address space is partitioned into separate *concentration zones*. References falling into the same zone are considered to be in the same stream and are used to calculate the stride. Prefetching performance is shown sensitive to the zone size. The choice of the right zone size is delegated to either a compiler or a programmer. A second heuristic is a *minimal delta* scheme which detects a stream by finding two memory references with the smallest address distance among last few memory references. It was found to work as well in [7] but needed more complex hardware. However, these methods are not as accurate as L1 instruction-address-based method in detecting memory reference streams and can stand improvement.

In this paper, we propose a new stride detection method for L2 caches, called *loop-based prefetching*. This scheme does not need instruction addresses to identify a memory reference stream and requires only modest hardware. We compare loop-based prefetching with stream buffers and instruction-address-based prefetching. We also analyze L2 prefetching characteristics which profoundly affect the relative performance of different prefetching methods.

L2 prefetching has been proposed with and without caches. Only stream buffers and other prefetching hardware are used in [16], whereas a small L2 cache is added to prefetching hardware in [14]. However these two different architectures have not been directly compared. In this study we add a small cache to prefetching hardware and compare it with a traditional cache (cache-only), stream buffer prefetching without a cache (prefetching-only), and prefetching with a small cache.

The rest of this paper is organized as follows. The next section describes loop-based prefetching. Section 3 presents our evaluation methodology and prefetching architectures. Section 4 discusses our results. Section 5 concludes this paper.

2 Loop-Based Prefetching and Its Implementation

Our goal is an L2 prefetching which can detect memory references streams without using instruction addresses. We will use it in conjunction with stride calculation units to perform stride detection and prediction. We call our proposed scheme *loop-based prefetching*. The method incurs only a modest hardware increase compared to other proposed methods.

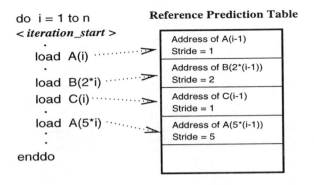

Figure 1: Memory reference stream detection in Loop-Based Prefetching

2.1 The approach

Memory references with a constant stride are usually generated by load/store instructions which are repeatedly executed in a loop. During the execution of a loop body, the execution order of load/store instructions inside the loop body remains constant from one iteration to the next (assuming in-order execution with respect to other loads/stores and absence of branches). If a start of an iteration can be detected, it is possible to identify a memory reference stream by its appearance relative to the start of an iteration as shown in Figure 1.

An iteration of a loop provides the prefetching unit with an *iteration start* signal. Subsequent loads are identified by their relative position with respect to the iteration start signal. The relative position of a load within an iteration is used by the prefetching unit as an index into the *Reference Prediction Table(RPT)*. An entry at the indexed position contains a stride and prefetch address for the load instruction. The prefetching unit resets the index to zero on each iteration start signal. Thus a simple counter is sufficient to identify a stream and access an RPT entry. The stride is used to prefetch ahead of the L1 requests once it is computed.

An overflow occurs if there are more loads than the total number of entries in the RPT. Such a case is easily detected as the counter overflows, and subsequent loads until the next iteration start signal are ignored and are not prefetched. Other RPT operations, such as updating memory access history and computing strides, can be implemented in ways similar to previous proposals [1, 8, 11]. The iteration start signal can be generated by a memory-mapped instruction accessing a particular memory address, a new instruction, or by an instruction unit detecting a backward branch. In either case, only one such instruction is needed per iteration in contrast to some schemes requiring an instruction per memory reference.

In L2 loop-based prefetching load accesses that hit in the L1 cache are not seen by prefetching hardware. Therefore, the L2 prefetching unit uses only L1 misses to increment the index to RPT and keeps trying to acquire a constant stride from L1 misses mapped to the same RPT entry. Thus loop-based prefetching may suffer from the L1 screening effect just as other stride-directed prefetching methods do. But as we will show, this simple approach is quite effective for stride detection.

The method can be extended to handle multiply-nested

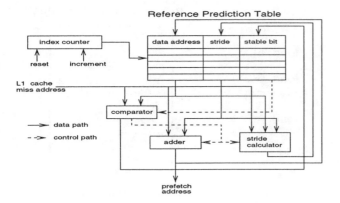

Reference Prediction Table

index counter

reset   increment

data address | stride | stable bit

L1 cache
miss address

comparator

adder

stride
calculator

→ data path
- -▹ control path

prefetch
address

Figure 2: Loop-Based Stride Detection Unit

loops and branches inside loops. By providing additional loop execution information, such as *loop start*, *loop exit*, and *branch taken* it is possible to accurately identify any memory reference stream generated in a loop. However, the prefetching unit becomes more complex. In this study we use a simple RPT hardware mechanism ignoring branches and concentrating on *innermost* loops only because they account for most of the memory accesses in a program (see statistics in Table 1).

2.2 Implementation

The organization of a stride detection unit for loop-based prefetching is shown in Figure 2. We refer to it as *loop-based stride detection unit*. It consists of a Reference Prediction Table (RPT), an RPT index counter, a comparator, an address adder, and a stride calculator. Each RPT entry contains a data address (DA_l) and a stride (St_l) for a reference stream.

An RPT entry pointed by the RPT index counter is accessed with an L1 miss address (M_a), and the stride is computed. As soon as a *constant stride* is detected, that is, a newly calculated stride is equal to the old stride, the information (data address and stride) is sent to a prefetching engine such as stream buffers. The stream buffer will generate a prefetching request for the stream. The following algorithm describes the operation of the prefetching unit.

> if $M_a == DA_l$ and Stable then
>   /* constant stride detected */
>   allocate a stream buffer with
> $DA \leftarrow DA_l + St_l$; $St \leftarrow St_l$.
>   issue a prefetch for DA.
> else
>   /* set stable bit and calculate a new stride */
> $Stable \leftarrow St_l == M_a - (DA_l - St_l)$.
> $St_l \leftarrow M_a - (DA_l - St_l)$.
> endif
> $DA_l \leftarrow M_a + St_l$.   /* update data address */

3 Performance Evaluation Methodology

3.1 Simulation

We used trace-driven simulation for performance evaluation. Benchmark programs were executed and memory ad-

dresses referenced by loads were obtained via program instrumentation. Programs were instrumented by a tracing tool [5] we developed for MIPS R3000 processors, compiled with a MIPS optimizing Fortran compiler, and executed on a MIPS M120 system with a R3000/3010 processor. The address traces drive prefetching architecture simulators developed for this study.

Instructions fetches are ignored by assuming an instruction cache with a perfect hit rate. The first and second-level data caches are direct-mapped, write-through, and no-write-allocate. A cache line size is 4 words, and a word is 8 bytes in each case (32-byte line). We use an 8 Kbyte L1 data cache throughout our experiments while L2 cache size and organization vary.

Only loads are prefetched. An L2 cache, if present, is searched before a prefetching unit issues a prefetch request to memory. The prefetch request is discarded on hit. We do not employ timing simulation and therefore assume that prefetched data is available to subsequent memory references without any delay.

The *iteration start* signal for a loop is obtained by inserting a special command inside the loop. From this command the MIPS tracing tool generates a special instruction that is recognized as an iteration start by the simulator.

3.2 Benchmarks

Table 1 shows the characteristics of the benchmarks used. All are computationally intensive numerical applications. These applications usually exhibit large data set sizes. Except for ARC3D, they are selected from among the PERFECT [6] and NAS benchmarks [2]: DYFESM, FLO52, MDG, OCEAN and TRFD are PERFECT benchmarks, and APPBT, APPSP, CG, and MGRID are NAS benchmarks.

Benchmark statistics were collected dynamically during program execution. They include percentage of innermost loads, e.g. loads generated inside innermost loops, and of loads with constant stride. Percentage of constant *long* stride loads, e.g. strides longer than a cache line size (positive or negative), in the total number of constant stride loads is also shown. Notice a large number of long stride accesses for some benchmarks.

For programs other than MDG, the innermost loads account for most of the load accesses in a program. MDG shows a noticeably lower innermost load percentage, 65.4 %, as compared to the other benchmarks. Note that CG and DYFESM have relatively low constant stride load access ratios, and APPBT, APPSP, ARC3D, OCEAN and TRFD have higher long stride ratios. CG and DYFESM showed such low constant stride ratios because they have a large number of array indirections.

3.3 Performance Metrics

A cache miss (hit) rate is our main performance metric. In addition, prefetch prediction miss rate (PPMR) is used to evaluate how well future data accesses are predicted by prefetching units. This metric is defined as

$$PPMR = (1 - \frac{\text{The number of memory accesses that hit in a prefetching unit}}{\text{The number of prefetch requests generated}}) \times 100$$

316

Benchmark	Description	Load Access (M)	Load Hit Rate (L1) (%)	Innermost Load (%)	Const. Stride Load (%)	Const. Long Stride Load (%)
APPBT	BT simulated CFD	17.47	93.2	86.6	80.51	57.88
APPSP	SP simulated CFD	16.49	86.1	95.7	86.41	44.6
ARC3D	3-D CFD	20.33	86.8	86.1	83.37	31.87
CG	Conjugate gradient	14.4	67.5	95.5	61.55	0.05
DYFESM	Structural dynamics	18.08	87.0	89.3	71.92	5.97
FLO52	2-D fluid dynamics	15.03	82.5	99.5	92.64	5.75
MDG	Molecular dynamics	20.70	96.9	65.4	82.47	2.64
MGRID	Multigrid kernel	14.53	94.8	99.9	92.49	0.40
OCEAN	2-D fluid dynamics	13.21	76.3	99.3	96.93	31.9
TRFD	Molecular dynamics	15.39	92.0	97.6	87.16	49.49

Table 1: Benchmark Characteristics

Finally, we measure memory traffic, that is, the total number of memory requests generated by cache misses and prefetch requests. Prefetching may increase the memory traffic and lead to a higher overall memory latency.

We do not measure execution time because it requires detailed timing information about the memory subsystem and the processor. The above metrics, on the other hand, are timing independent. The absence of timing evaluation may produce optimistic results for prefetching when compared with caches. It demonstrates the upper bound of performance improvement with prefetching. However, PPMR and total memory traffic are sufficient performance metrics for uniform comparison of prefetching architectures.

3.4 Prefetching Architecture

A general system organization for L2 prefetching used in this study includes a CPU, an L1 and an (optional) L2 caches, and an L2 prefetching unit. An L2 cache and/or an L2 prefetching unit are directly connected to an L1 cache. We investigate three prefetching unit architectures:

1. *Stream buffers* and a *miss table unit* (similar to the unit-stride filter [16]) is our baseline prefetching architecture called *miss table prefetching (MTP)* architecture.

2. *Loop-based prefetching architecture (LBP)* uses our new stride detection unit to detect memory reference streams and compute their strides based on the knowledge of program loop iterations. The unit is added to the baseline architecture.

3. *Instruction-address-based architecture (IAP)* uses an instruction address (PC) to identify memory access streams and compute their strides for prefetching.

The baseline architecture is chosen because it is simple, does not use memory reference stream and stride detection, and has been shown effective in L2 prefetching [16]. The loop-based stride detection unit replaces the heuristic non-unit stride filter used in [16] and is mainly used for long stride detection. Note that we do not use the loop-based stride detection unit alone, which will be explained later. Figure 3 shows the baseline prefetching architecture

(inner dotted box) and the loop-based prefetching architecture(outer dotted box).

The stream buffers are based on the model used in [16]. The stream buffers are fully-associative, and LRU allocation is used. A stream buffer is allocated with *data address* and *stride* supplied by the miss table unit or the loop-based stride detection unit, and a line containing the data address is fetched into the stream buffer. When an L1 miss hits on a stream buffer, the stream buffer fetches the next line that contains a word at the data address plus stride and increases its data address by the stride.

When no stream buffers are found to contain the L1 miss address, the L1 miss address is sent to the miss table unit. The miss table is fully-associative and contains a *next line* address for each previously seen L1 miss. The miss table sees only L1 misses that miss the stream buffers. If the L1 miss address hits in the miss table, a stream buffer is allocated with a data address and a stride equal to the line size. The data address is the starting address of the next line to the L1 miss. If the L1 miss address misses in the table, an entry is allocated for the miss in FIFO order. The miss table detects short stride memory accesses.

The loop-based stride detection unit is added to MTP to detect long stride memory accesses. The operation of the detection unit is described in Section 2.2. Note that the detection unit only sees L1 misses that miss in both stream buffers and miss table unit. Stream buffer and miss table hits filter out unit-stride references which otherwise may *confuse* the stride detector.

The instruction-address-based architecture is based on the model proposed by Baer and Chen [1]. L1 misses are directly sent to the reference prediction table (RPT) with their instruction address. The RPT is fully-associative and indexed by the instruction address. If the instruction address misses in the RPT, an LRU entry is allocated with the L1 miss address and the instruction address. If it is a hit, the RPT stores the miss address and compares it with a previously stored miss address to compute the stride. If a *constant* stride is obtained, the unit will prefetch the line containing the miss address increased by the stride.

We use two different L2 memory organizations: one with an L2 cache and one without an L2 cache. In the latter case only stream buffer storage is used for data. In the former case data is stored in the L2 caches itself, and the

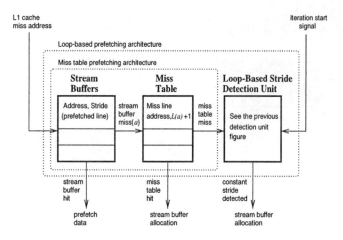

Figure 3: L2 Prefetching Architectures

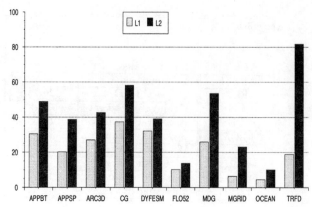

Figure 4: IAP L1 and L2 Prefetching Prediction Miss Rate (PPMR), RPT size = 256

stream buffers only generate and test address information for prefetching. For instruction-address-based prefetching architecture data is stored in separate additional storage associated with each Reference Prediction Table (RPT) entry. RPT is thus similar to stream buffers in this sense. The difference is that data is accessed with instruction addresses in RPT.

4 Experimental Results and Analysis

Let us start by examining the effectiveness of L2 stride-directed prefetching. First, we compare the IAP prediction miss rates for L1 and L2 caches. Figure 4 shows the prefetch prediction miss rate (PPMR) for the two cases using a large RPT (256 entries). Although we use the same prefetching method by supplying instruction addresses to the L2 IAP unit, for most benchmarks the prefetch prediction miss rate of the L2 IAP is much higher than that of the L1 IAP method. This high PPMR is caused by the difficulty in detecting a constant stride at L2 cache. The screening effect of L1 caches and conflict misses perturb miss address streams which otherwise would be consistently visible to L2 prefetching units. The results indicate that stride-directed prefetching may not be as effective at L2 as at L1, even if memory reference streams are accurately detected.

4.1 Stream Buffer Prefetching

The effect of the number of stream buffers on performance for all three prefetching methods (IAP, LBP, and MTP) is evaluated next. Data is stored in stream buffers for the MTP and LBP and in the RPT data space in each table entry for the IAP. Thus the RPT and stream buffers are similar in their overall function and organization and we use the term *stream buffer* for both, unless stated otherwise. There is no conventional L2 cache in this case.

The results for 16, 64, and 256 stream buffers (RPT size) are presented. Even the smallest size used here is larger than what has been previously studied since we believe that extra locality can be exploited with more buffers. The miss table size was determined in other experiments and set to 32 entries. Increasing the size beyond 32 did not improve the prediction miss rate significantly but hurt the

performance in some cases. Stream buffers and miss tables need to be fully associative and it may not be practical to increase their size beyond 64. The larger size is used to confirm our locality conjecture.

In addition to the stream buffers and the miss table, the LBP method needs an RPT for loop-based stream detection. In the experiments, the size of this additional RPT is fixed at 64 entries. We observed that no more than 33 entries were used in any of our benchmarks. Note that the RPT for loop-based prefetching is used only for stream detection and does not issue prefetch requests as done by the stream buffers or the RPT in the IAP method.

Figures 5 shows stream buffer miss rates for each benchmark. The stream buffer miss rate is the number of stream buffer misses over the total number of stream buffer accesses. The latter is the same as L1 cache misses. The stream buffer miss rate steadily decreases, in most cases, as the number of stream buffers is increased. Increasing the number of stream buffers is beneficial because it provides more storage for prefetched data and thus the opportunity for reuse. In addition, it allows more opportunities to initiate prefetches.

LBP shows equal or lower stream buffer miss rates than MTP for all benchmarks and parameters. LBP improves noticeably over MTP by detecting long stride accesses for APPSP, ARC3D, and OCEAN and by detecting streams more accurately for MDG. These benchmarks except for MDG have a relatively large portion of long stride accesses as shown in Table 1. This result shows that the loop-based stride detection unit is effective at L2 prefetching for long stride accesses and in some cases for short stride accesses.

Two other benchmarks, APPBT and TRFD, with many long stride accesses do not have much improvement with LBP. More than 60 % of long-stride misses in APPBT have strides less than 2 cache line sizes. The miss table can also successfully capture such accesses and allocate stream buffers not leaving much room for improvement from LBP. TRFD has a large percentage of true long stride accesses, but shows only small improvements with LBP or IAP because they fail to detect a constant stride. This is due, in part, to conflict misses in L1. We confirmed in additional experiments that TRFD performance improves noticeably with a 4KB, 2-way set-associative L1 cache.

Previous results showed that stride-direct prefetching

318

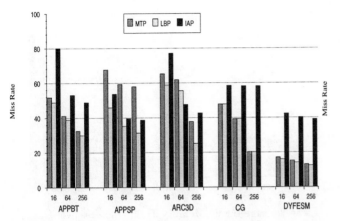
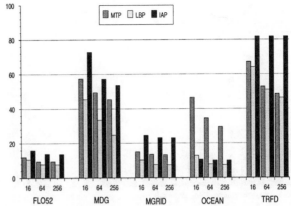

Figure 5: Stream Buffers Miss Rates. The X-axis numbers represent the number of stream buffers.

can be effective at L2. However, IAP while theoretically capable of detecting memory streams more accurately than the loop-based stride detection unit performs worse than MTP and LBP in most cases. One of the reasons for loss of performance in IAP is that data in the stream buffers is looked up by a data address in MTP and LBP, whereas it is looked up by an instruction address in IAP. A more important reason is a different approach to prefetching. IAP is based on memory access patterns of each memory reference stream, whereas MTP and LBP can exploit memory access patterns with good spatial locality across several memory reference streams. We quantify this more precisely in the next section.

4.2 Cross-stream locality

A stream buffer allocation by a miss table or a loop-based stream detection unit is caused by a series of L1 cache misses. The misses causing the allocation may actually belong to the same or a different memory reference stream. If they do belong to the same memory reference stream we say that a stream buffer is *exactly allocated* for the memory reference stream and *belongs to* the memory reference stream. When a miss address hits on a stream buffer, the miss address and stream buffers may belong to the same or a different memory reference stream, or the stream buffer is not even exactly allocated. Based on these observations we classify stream buffer hits as follows:

- Type 1 hit: the stream buffer is *not* exactly allocated.

- Type 2 hit: the stream buffer is exactly allocated, but the L1 cache miss and the stream buffer belong to different memory reference streams.

- Type 3 hit: the stream buffer is exactly allocated, and the L1 cache miss and the stream buffer belong to the same memory reference stream.

The type 1 and type 2 hits indicate a *cross-stream* locality, the locality among different memory reference streams. The type 3 hit implies successful prefetching based entirely on memory access patterns of a *single* memory reference stream.

The type distribution of stream buffer hits for MTP and LBP is shown in Figure 6. It shows that a large portion of

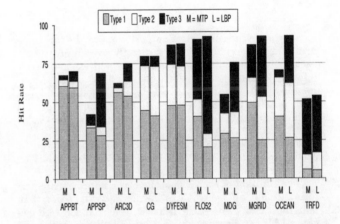

Figure 6: Distribution of Stream Buffer Hits for MTP and LBP with 256 Stream Buffers

stream buffer hits is contributed by type 1 and type 2 hits. A similar behavior is observed for MTP except that type 3 hit contribution is not as large as for LBP. Under IAP only type 3 hits are possible since the RPT is indexed by an instruction address both when memory access patterns are detected and data is accessed. Since IAP can have only type 3 hits, IAP showed worse performance than MTP and LBP. Furthermore, the results in the next section show (see Figure 7) that when IAP is used to prefetch into an L2 cache and type 2 hits are exploited the performance for most benchmarks is still worse than that of MTP and LBP. This implies that an ability to exploit type 1 hits is very important to the success of L2 prefetching.

Stride detection is more difficult at L2 and not as effective as at L1 because L1 misses which arrive at L2 may not have a constant stride. Therefore, prefetching methods which can take advantage of good cross-stream spatial locality should be used for L2 prefetching.

4.3 Prefetching with Caches

Previous experiments showed that a large number of stream buffers improved the performance by exploiting memory reference locality. In this section, we add a small L2 cache to the prefetching architectures to take advantage of the

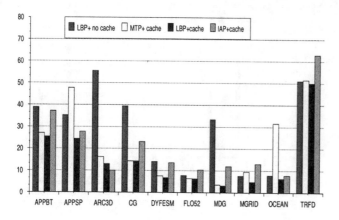

Figure 7: Miss rates for Prefetching with and without 32KB L2 caches: 64 Stream Buffers for LBP, MTP and IAP

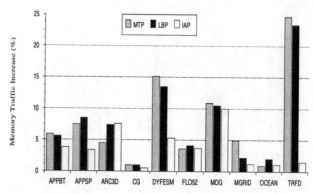

Figure 9: Prefetching Memory Traffic Increase over Cache-only System: MTP, LBP, and IAP use a 32KB L2 Cache and 64 Stream Buffers. The Cache-only System uses a 32KB L2 cache.

locality and study the effect on performance. In this organization, the prefetched data is directly stored into the L2 cache. Stream buffers only store data address and stride information and issue prefetch requests. A 32KB, direct-mapped, write-through L2 cache is used in this study. A line contains four 8Byte words. The number of stream buffers and the RPT size of IAP is 64, and the miss table size is 32.

The L2 miss rates of LBP without a cache and the L2 cache miss rate of MTP, LBP, and IAP with a 32KB L2 cache are shown in Figure 7.

The addition of even a small L2 cache improves the performance for all benchmarks, significantly in more than half the cases. The cache is most beneficial for IAP because IAP can now have type 2 hits. However, MTP and LBP with a cache still show better performance than IAP with a cache for most benchmarks due to their ability to utilize type 1 hits. Although not shown here, the number of stream buffers is not as important in this case, even a smaller number is very effective with a small L2. Also not shown is the fact that the small L2 cache suffers from conflict misses in some benchmarks. Once the set-associativity of the small L2 cache is increased, the cache miss rate is dramatically reduced.

Next, the hit rates of non-prefetching L2 caches and prefetching with a small cache are compared while varying the non-prefetching cache size. Figure 8 shows that the cache hit rate difference between LBP with a 32KB L2 cache and conventional L2 caches of size 32K, 128K, 256K, 512K, 1M, and 2M Bytes. A negative value in the figure means the LBP system has a higher hit rate than the non-prefetching L2 cache by the amount shown. In general, as the L2 cache size increases, the hit rate of a non-prefetching L2 cache becomes higher than that of the LBP system with a small cache. For all benchmarks except TRFD, L2 caches need to be two to four times larger (64 to 128K) than the cache used with LBP to match the hit rate. The LBP system can attain up to 40 % higher hit rates in half of the benchmarks than a 16-times larger non-prefetching L2 cache (512K).

TRFD has the worst LBP performance because LBP suffers from L2 cache conflict misses. We have verified that performance of LBP improves significantly when the

associativity of the L2 cache is increased.

These results are consistent with [16] which has shown that stream buffers alone can perform better than an L2 cache for some scientific codes with large data sets. Our results show that adding a small L2 cache to LBP can significantly boost the performance. It also requires a smaller number of stream buffers for most benchmarks. This combined organization is a better choice than stream buffers alone and, in many cases, non-prefetching L2 cache alone.

4.4 Traffic increase under prefetching

One problem associated with prefetching is a memory traffic increase. We compare memory traffic increase of MTP, LBP, and IAP with respect to the memory traffic generated with a 32 Kbyte L2 cache. Figure 9 shows the memory traffic increase for each prefetching method and benchmark. In most cases the increase is less than 10%. Only DYFESM, MDG and TRFD show a 15 %, 11 %, and 24 % increase, respectively. The low increase is due to the fact that prefetches are not started until a stable stride is detected and only one cache line is prefetched each time. For most benchmarks, IAP shows the smallest increase because it does not prefetch much data due to low stream buffer hit rates. LBP has a lower memory traffic increase than MTP for APPBT, DYFESM, MGRID and TRFD. Lower miss rates and a relatively small memory traffic increase makes LBP with a small cache the most efficient architecture among the various L2 memory organizations we studied.

5 Conclusions

We have shown that second-level (L2) prefetching has different characteristics compared to first-level (L1) prefetching. In particular, prefetching that relies solely on constant stride detection of a memory reference stream was shown to be less effective. An L2 prefetching architecture should take advantage of cross-stream locality to be effective. Stream buffers and the miss table prefetching (MTP) are one of such L2 prefetching methods. However, these methods still leave room for improvement for long stride accesses.

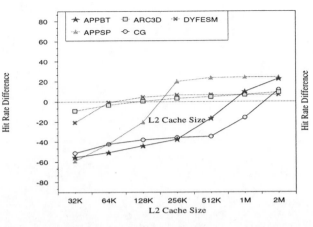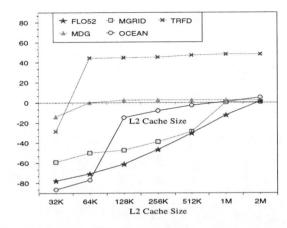

Figure 8: Hit Rate Difference Between Loop-Based Prefetching versus Secondary Caches: LBP uses 64 Stream Buffers, a 32-entry Miss Table, a Loop-Based Stream Detection Unit and a 32K L2 Cache. L2 Cache-only uses 32K, 64K, 128K, 256K, 512K, 1M, and 2M Caches.

We proposed loop-based prefetching (LBP) to perform prefetching for long stride accesses at L2 as a way to improve on existing heuristics. Loop-based prefetching relies on loop execution information and does not need instruction addresses to identify memory reference streams. When we combined loop-based stride detection with MTP prefetching, it significantly improved performance particularly for applications with long stride accesses. This combined architecture (LBP architecture) was the best method improving over both MTP and IAP architectures.

We have also shown that additional locality can be exploited by increasing the number of stream buffers when prefetched data is store in the buffers only. Finally, by using a small L2 cache for prefetched data storage we were able to improve the performance of LBP architecture even further. This organization was competitive with much larger non-prefetching caches in many benchmarks. The combined LBP architecture exhibited only a small increase in memory traffic due to prefetching compared to other prefetching architectures we investigated.

References

[1] Jean-Loup Baer and Tien-Fu Chen. An effective on-chip preloading scheme to reduce data access penalty. In *Supercomputing*, pages 176–186. IEEE, November 1991.

[2] D. Bailey, H. Simon, J. Barton, and T.Lasinski. The NAS parallel benchmarks. Technical Report RNR-91-02, NASA Ames Research Center, 1991.

[3] David Callahan, Ken Kennedy, and Allan Porterfield. Software prefetching. In *Architectural Support for Programming Languages and Operating Systems*, pages 40–52, April 1991.

[4] Tien-Fu Chen. *An Effective Programmable Prefetch Engine for On-Chip Caches*. In *International Symposium on Microarchitecture (Micro-28)*, pages 237–242, November 1995.

[5] Yung-Chin Chen. *Cache Design and Performance in a Large-Scale Shared-Memory Multiprocessor System*. PhD thesis, University of Illinois at Urbana-Champaign, 1993.

[6] G. Cybenko, L. Kipp, L. Pointer, and D. Kuck. Supercomputer performance evaluation and the perfect benchmarks. In *International Conference on Supercomputing*, 1990.

[7] Keith Farkas and Norman Jouppi. How Useful Are Non-Blocking Loads, Stream Buffers and Speculative Execution in Multiple Issue Processors? In *High-Performance Computer Architecture*, pages 78–89, January 1995.

[8] John W.C. Fu, Janak H. Patel, and Bob L. Janssens. Stride directed prefetching in scalar processors. In *International Symposium on Microarchitecture*, pages 102–110, December 1992.

[9] Edward H. Gornish, Elana D. Granston, and Alexander V. Veidenbaum. Compiler-directed data prefetching in multiprocessors with memory hierarchies. In *International Conference on Supercomputing*, pages 354–368, June 1990.

[10] Edward H. Gornish and Alexander V. Veidenbaum. An Integrated Hardware/Software Data Prefetching Scheme for Shared-Memory Multiprocessors In *International Conference on Parallel Processing*, Aug. 1994.

[11] Y. Jegou and O. Temam. Speculative prefetching. In *Supercomputing*, 1993.

[12] Norman P. Jouppi. Improving direct-mapped cache performance by the addition of a small fully-associative cache and prefetch buffers. In *International Symposium on Computer Architecture*, pages 364–373, May 1990.

[13] Alexander C. Klaiber and Henry M. Levy. An architecture for software-controlled data prefetching. In *International Symposium on Computer Architecture*, pages 43–53, May 1991.

[14] K. Krishnamohan. Applying rambus technology to desktop computer main memory subsystems, March 1992.

[15] Todd C. Mowry, Monica S. Lam, and Anoop Gupta. Design and evaluation of a compiler algorithm for prefetching. In *Architectural Support for Programming Languages and Operating Systems*, pages 62–73, 1992.

[16] Subbarao Palacharla and R. E. Kessler. Evaluating stream buffers as a secondary cache replacement. In *International Symposium on Computer Architecture*, pages 24–33, May 1994.

[17] Steven A. Przybylski. *Cache and Memory Hierarchy Design*. Morgan Kaufmann Publishers, Inc., 1990.

[18] Alan Jay Smith. Cache memories. *Computing Surveys*, 14(3):473–530, September 1982.

Session 5B

Local Area and Wireless Networks

Design of Scalable and Multicast Capable Cut-Through Switches for High-Speed LANs *

Mingyao Yang and *Lionel M. Ni*

Department of Computer Science
Michigan State University
East Lansing, MI 48824-1226
{yangming,ni}@cps.msu.edu

Abstract

High-speed switches play an important role in building switched LANs. Among different techniques used in switch design, cut-through switching promises short latency delivery and thus is well suited to distributed/parallel applications. The back pressure flow control of cut-through switching also prevents packet loss due to buffer overflow. This paper presents an incremental switch design based on modular building blocks using cut-through switching technique. The switch can be either nonblocking with full configuration and deterministic routing, or blocking but having more flexibility in configuration and fault tolerance. A kind of switch configuration that fits the client/server computing paradigm is presented. Simulation results are given for various switch configurations and traffic loads. The switch also has built-in hardware multicast capability. Issues of physical layout and integration into practical LANs are also discussed.

1 Introduction

Switch-based networks are becoming popular to meet the increasing demand for higher network performance. Traditional shared-medium Local Area Networks (LANs) do not provide satisfactory throughput and latency for some communication intensive applications, especially those emerging multimedia applications. Switch-based networks make such applications possible by providing virtual point-to-point communication. Therefore, higher bandwidth and lower latency can be achieved. Security is improved than that of share-medium networks because data on the physical link is no longer always available to every host on the subnet. Switched LAN is also an incremental approach to

---
* This work was supported in part by NSF grants MIP-9204066 and MIP-9528903, DOE grant DE-FG02-93ER25167 and a grant from Hewlett-Packard Co..

upgrade LAN performance since the investment in existing adapters, cables, and drivers are preserved and switched LANs still conform to widely accepted network standards. Many problems existing in shared-medium networks also occur in the switches. Therefore, good switch design plays a significant role in improving LAN performance to better support distributed multimedia applications or high performance computing based on networks of workstations.

Various switching hubs are getting applied in switched LANs. Commercial products have been developed for Ethernet, Fast Ethernet, FDDI, FCS (Fiber Channel Standard), Myrinet, and ATM. The data unit to be switched in ATM networks is a fixed-size cell of 53 bytes. The data unit to be switched in traditional networks is usually a frame, which tends to be much larger than a cell. For example, the MTU (maximum transmission unit) for Ethernet and FDDI is 1500 bytes and 4352 bytes, respectively, not including the link layer header and trailer. A Myrinet [1] data packet can be an arbitrary-length byte stream constrained by the memory capacity on the host interface card.

There are two common switching techniques used in building LAN switches: store-and-forward and cut-through. Store-and-forward must keep a whole frame of data buffered before forwarding the data. The disadvantages of this approach include increased latency and buffer space, especially for frame-switching networks. Cut-through switching can forward partially received data as long as the packet header is received and decoded, thus promises low-latency delivery and relieves the burden on buffer space. Packets are sent in a pipeline fashion with cut-through switching. Furthermore, cut-through switching can provide primitive link-to-link flow control capability due to the back pressure mechanism in each link. Store-and-forward can make better decisions for corrupted or truncated frames by receiving a whole packet. Cut-through switching just propagates a frame all the way to its destination. If a frame is corrupted or truncated, it may not be able to be fully removed from the network until it reaches the destination, thus wasting network bandwidth. However, in a local network environment the error rate for a data frame is generally very low. Therefore, latency-sensitive applications such as high performance computing will greatly benefit from cut-through switching because of its shorter latency. Cell-switching networks such as ATM also pipeline data due to small fixed cell size. However, there is more overhead involved in transmitting a packet since each cell carries a fixed-size header besides payload data. In contrast, frame-switching networks allow variable packet size and have relatively less overhead incurred by headers if the frame size is large. Many new generation switches support cut-through switching, such as the DEC GIGAswitch [2] for FDDI networks, and the Myricom Myrinet [1]. Note that cut-through switching is different from virtual cut-through switching, where a large buffer will hold the entire packet when the outgoing channel is in use.

The objective of this paper is to identify those issues in the design of a cut-through switch, which will be discussed in Section 2, and to propose a scalable and multicast capable switch design, which will be covered in Section 3 and Section 4. Section 5 shows the simulation results for performance evaluation. Issues of physical layout and LAN integration are discussed in Section 6. Section 7 concludes the paper.

2 Design considerations

A high-level view of a cut-through switch architecture is shown in Figure 1. Its function is to switch packets from input ports to output ports. The switch fabric is based on many small switching elements. Switch modules are built from switching elements, where a switch module is usually a physical chip. A switch board is built from a number of interconnected switch modules. A switch consists of many stacked switch boards, where the number of switch boards is determined by the switch capacity, i.e., the number of ports. A practical engineering issue of packaging deserves consideration.

Packets which cannot be delivered immediately due to channel contention inside the switch can be buffered at the input FIFO buffers. Some output FIFO buffers are available to accommodate network links of different speed. Each switching element also has a number of small buffers, thus with cut-through switching a packet is pipelined through a number of switching elements in one or more switches.

2.1 Link-level back pressure flow control

When the input buffers or the buffers within switching elements are nearly full, back pressure can be generated. The sending source is throttled when back pressure is propagated to it. If this mechanism is utilized, there will be less packet loss caused by buffer overflow which is the major reason for losing packets in a local network environment. Myrinet [1] is an example which uses cut-through switching with flow control on every communication channel.

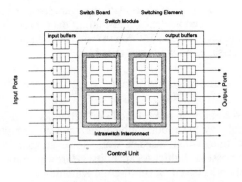

Figure 1. A high-level view of a cut-through switch.

2.2 Scalability and incremental expandability

A scalable switch means that the same switch architecture can be applied when higher performance is demanded from the switch. To achieve good expandability in switches, modular design is usually followed. A switch is constructed from switch boards which are also built from some building modules. Ideally the minimum requirement to expand a switch to the next allowed configuration is a single switch board.

2.3 Deadlock-free routing

Deadlock is a well known issue in cut-through switching with back pressure flow control. Because a message can hold some channels and wait for another channel, deadlock may occur if there is a cycle in the channel dependency graph [3, 4].

There are two levels of deadlock freedom in a switch-based network. One guarantees that within a switch the routing is deadlock free, i.e., if the whole network is connected to a single switch, deadlock never happens. This may be referred to as *intra-switch deadlock freedom*. The other guarantees that the switching in a network which is interconnected by more than one switch is deadlock free. This may also be referred to as *inter-switch deadlock freedom*. In order to achieve inter-switch deadlock freedom, network topology and global routing algorithm need to be carefully designed.

This paper will focus on intra-switch deadlock freedom (including multicast deadlock freedom). Interested readers may refer to [5, 6, 7] for inter-switch deadlock-free routing. All deadlock freedom mentioned later in the paper refers to intra-switch deadlock freedom unless otherwise specified.

2.4 Nonblocking vs. blocking

Nonblocking switch guarantees that any routing request to any free output port can be supported without interference with other packets being routed. Nonblocking switches have dedicated bandwidth for each port and is helpful to guarantee the quality of service for some applications.

Nonblocking switch is also important to inter-switch deadlock freedom when transmitting data through several interconnected cut-through switches without buffering messages between switches [8].

2.5 Hardware multicast

Conventional shared-medium networks have very natural way to support multicast/broadcast communications. In a switch-based network, however, each switch must possess multicast capability. Hardware multicast in networks based on cut-through switching is not a trivial task because it is very difficult to prevent deadlock.

2.6 Packaging and layout issues

For ease of maintenance and expandability, the switch design must follow a modular approach. There may be many hierarchies of modules, from chips to switch boards. How to efficiently design 2D layout on a board and stack switch boards in 3D is a critical engineering issue. When a switch is expanded or reconfigured due to fault, it is desirable that minimum number of rewiring is required. Packaging of a switch decides the physical space consumed, wiring complexity, wire length, whether a switch is stackable, easy to configure and maintain, and ready for expansion.

2.7 Fault tolerance

It is likely that one or more of the building modules of a switch are faulty sometime. A fault tolerant switch either can continue to function well regardless of the faulty module(s), or is able to function well by making minimal reconfiguration to the existing boards, without adding new good boards. We call the former *on-line fault tolerance* and the latter *board-level fault tolerance*. On-line fault tolerance can afford faulty boards without loss of service. Board-level fault tolerance may lose some service upon failure but allows quick and easy recovery.

3 Proposed switch architecture

Cut-through switching has been the major switching technique used in multicomputer systems [3, 4]. Crosspoint switching matrix has simple routing function and possesses good modularity. Therefore, we choose to use 2D matrix with built-in cut-through switching function as building modules for our switch design.

One such building module is shown in Figure 2(a). It can be treated as a switch with eight input ports, namely $i_0, i_1, \ldots, i_7$ and eight output ports, namely $o_0, o_1, \ldots, o_7$. The unused channels can be used to expand the switch. Figure 2(b) shows a 16×16 switch built from 8×8 modules. In order to guarantee deadlock freedom, XY routing is generally used [3, 4]. In XY routing, a special case of dimension order routing, a

message first goes in X direction then turns into Y direction. ATOMIC project [9] basically used the above approach. However, this kind of design suffers from deadlocks if it wants to support multicast. Figure 3 shows an example. Suppose a multicast from i_0 to o_5 and o_6 and another multicast from i_4 to o_5 and o_6 starts simultaneously, and there is no other traffic in the switch, mutual blocking situation may occur. Deadlock can also occur if fully adaptive routing is used in the switch. Figure 4 illustrates a potential circle of channel dependency.

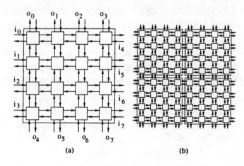

Figure 2. Traditional 2D meshes as building modules.

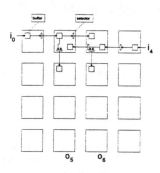

Figure 3. An example of deadlock situation with two multicast in a 2D mesh.

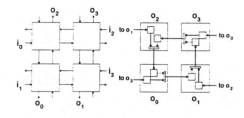

Figure 4. An example of deadlock situation resulted from fully adaptive routing.

To support multicast capability and be able to use fully adaptive routing, we choose to use the building module shown in Figure 5. The building module shown has two input ports and two output ports with four additional channels to interconnect with other building modules. It looks like a crossbar. The main difference between it and a crossbar is its use of cut-through switching in each crosspoint switching element instead of establishing a connection between an input and an output. So there is no need to maintain connection information between inputs and outputs since all channels are allocated on the fly. Figure 6 shows a way of using 2×2 modules with additional channels for expansion to build a 4×4 switch.

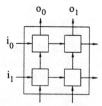

Figure 5. The building module used in our design.

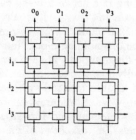

Figure 6. Use building modules to build a larger switch.

The new crossbar-like switch also simplifies switching logic. Each switching element has two inputs and two outputs instead of four inputs and four outputs. Figure 7 shows a switching element. It has two small buffers. Back pressure is generated if the buffers are full. Two channel selectors decide which outgoing channel is granted for the data in a buffer. For simplicity, the control circuit for internal routing control and the external wires for handshaking between adjacent switching elements are not shown.

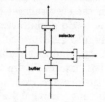

Figure 7. A switching element.

Cut-through routing switches a message along a network by dividing the message into small units. Each unit is no bigger than the small buffer in each switching element. The header unit (routing tag) of a packet governs the route and reserves channels. As the header unit advances along the specified route, the remaining units follow in a pipeline fashion. A trailer signal or special character releases the reserved channels [3, 4].

Routing in the proposed switch can be XY routing to guarantee deadlock freedom. XY routing also guarantees switches to be nonblocking and has low hardware complexity for routing decisions.

However, the restriction on routing in the proposed switch can be much looser. The theorem below shows that fully adaptive routing in the switch is also deadlock free. Fully adaptive routing allows a message to take any possible path from an input to an output. In our switch, all possible paths under fully adaptive routing are minimal.

Theorem 1 *Fully adaptive routing in the proposed cut-through switch is deadlock free.*

Fully adaptive routing has some advantages over XY routing. Figure 8 shows an example that message M3 can be delivered to its destination without waiting for message M2 which is blocked by message M1 if message M2 is short enough to be absorbed in the switch totally. This case is possible if the message is short and the switch is large.

Fully adaptive routing allows some degree of fault tolerance if some links or switching elements are faulty. In Figure 8, if link c is down, message M3 can still be routed to the destination port. Fully adaptive routing also allows the topology of the switch to be an incomplete mesh [10], as shown in Figure 9. So when the switch is short of boards, e.g., when some boards are faulty, it is still possible to reconfigure the system to make it work. Therefore, fully adaptive routing allows both on-line fault tolerance and board-level fault tolerance.

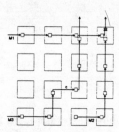

Figure 8. Example of adaptive routing in the switch.

A switch of incomplete mesh topology still has the property of low latency in cut-through switching. When the load of the switch goes high, the bandwidth may be a problem because the reduced number of channels produce bottlenecks. If each switch board is $m \times m$, an $n \times n$ switch needs $(2 \times \lceil \frac{n}{m} \rceil - 1)$ number of boards to begin functioning if fully adaptive routing is used, compared to $\lceil \frac{n}{m} \rceil^2$ number of boards using XY routing.

Fully adaptive routing does not guarantee a switch to be nonblocking. Figure 10 shows an example. Four messages go from i_0 to o_2, from i_1 to o_3, from i_2 to o_1, and from i_3 to o_0, respectively. When fully adaptive routing is used, messages may be blocked as shown in the figure. Therefore, fully adaptive routing may produce unnecessary blocking if a message is allowed to

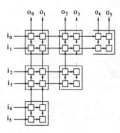

Figure 9. A switch of incomplete mesh topology.

turn randomly when it can go in either X or Y dimension. The switching elements in the southeast part of the switch are also less likely to be utilized. Some mechanism is necessary to decide which route is favored under adaptive routing. A simple mechanism is used below. A packet tries to follow XY routing unless it is forced to use Y channels because X channels are not physically existing. Therefore, X channels are favored over Y channels even if X channels are occupied by other packets. A packet uses Y channels only when X dimension routing is finished or its favored X channel is an open link. It is possible for hardware to detect an open link, which is done in Myrinet [11]. Figure 11 illustrates the route under this routing algorithm for the switch configuration shown. We call the routing algorithm *relaxed XY routing*. A message only turns when absolutely necessary under this routing algorithm. Relaxed XY routing for incomplete switch configurations is not guaranteed to be nonblocking.

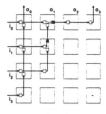

Figure 10. A blocking example for fully adaptive routing.

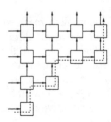

Figure 11. Relaxed XY routing.

Fully adaptive routing and XY routing can be combined into one switch. One way of doing it is by allowing two routing modes within the switch. Choosing XY routing or fully adaptive routing is achievable by switching the routing mode. Another way of integrating

XY routing and fully adaptive routing is by using virtual channels. In such a switch, there are two planes of switching elements, corresponding to two sets of virtual channels. One plane uses XY routing and the other uses fully adaptive routing. Messages are first routed in XY routing plane. It enters fully adaptive routing plane upon being blocked and continues its routing within the new plane. A message will not return to XY routing plane if it has entered fully adaptive routing plane. It can be easily seen that such routing scheme is deadlock free. The above two approaches combines the advantages of both XY routing and fully adaptive routing such as nonblocking, fault tolerance, flexibility in configuration. However the switch becomes more complicated and costly.

4 Multicast support

Multicasting in a network using cut-through switching technique is not trivial. It is very difficult to guarantee deadlock freedom. We will present a switch design based on the building blocks introduced in Section 3 and prove that multicast in such switches is deadlock free under fully adaptive routing.

Multicast in our proposed switches is performed in the following way. A frame of data can be duplicated in a switching element and forwarded along two outgoing channels, i.e., one head of the message can fork into two heads for two outgoing channels as shown in Figure 7. No head of the message will proceed unless it is pushed by the source of the message. However, the source will not push the message unless every head is able to proceed, which means the channel that the head is going to use is free. Note that a head can reserve a free channel and feedback the information to the source but no data will be put on the channel until the source pushes the message. This signaling scheme was used in the nCUBE-2 to support hardware broadcast. Therefore, different branches of a message move forward synchronously. A head is allowed to go adaptively to northeast in our proposed switch.

Allowing a message head to fork freely can lead to deadlock and inefficient usage of channels. Figure 12 shows three way to do a multicast. The cases in Figure 12(b) and Figure 12(c) are allowed. Figure 12(c) also has the minimum number of channels required to do the multicast. The case in Figure 12(a) is not allowed, where a multicast message from i_3 destined to o_2 and o_3 forks at switching element S and the forked heads converge at switching element I. Only one head is able to proceed if there is no virtual channel. But the source will not push the message forward unless both heads can proceed, thus deadlock occurs. We need to introduce the restriction that a message head can only fork when one of its destinations is exactly to the north of the head and the branch forked to the north cannot fork further. Under this restriction, only heads from different messages can compete for one channel, namely a message will never be blocked by itself.

Another issue needs to be solved is if there are two

328

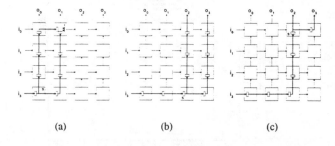

(a)   (b)   (c)

Figure 12. Different message forking patterns.

heads competing for one free outgoing channel, which head will occupy the channel. There should be some tie-breaking mechanism. A good tie-breaking mechanism is critical to multicast since deadlock can result from some tie-breaking mechanisms. For instance, randomly granting access to one of the two messages competing for one free channel may cause deadlock in multicast communication. Figure 13 shows a case. Messages M1 and M2 are both competing for channels c_1 and c_2. If by random selection, M1 reserves c_1 and M2 reserves c_2, deadlock occurs. We will use a simple mechanism to break ties by comparing the priority of each message, if there is a unique level of priority assigned to each message. One scheme is to assign priority to be the input port number of the message plus a timestamp. The message that has higher priority will grab the channel.

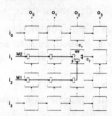

Figure 13. Deadlock resulted from random tie-breaking.

In short, each switching element can duplicate a message from one input to both outputs. A message head can fork into two heads when one of its destination is to its north and all heads of a message proceed synchronously. There is a unique priority associated with each message and when two messages compete for a channel, the message with higher priority grabs the channel.

Theorem 2 *The above multicast scheme is deadlock free under fully adaptive routing.*

The proof of the above theorem can be found in [8]. The approach guarantees intra-switch deadlock freedom for cut-through switches. Interested readers may refer to [12] for some work on inter-switch multicast.

5 Performance evaluation

A simulator has been developed to study the performance of unicast traffic in the proposed switch architecture. The following factors were considered in the performance evaluation: switch configurations, traffic patterns, workloads, packet sizes, routing algorithms and output arbitration schemes of each switching element.

The size of each small buffer in a switching element (Figure 7) is two bytes. All the data were collected after a warm-up period of at least 1,000,000 cycles and until steady state was reached. The latency is counted as the lapse of time between the first byte of a message arriving at the switch and the last byte of the message leaving the switch. The packet interarrival time for each port is exponentially distributed. Figure 14 illustrates the three switch configurations used in the simulation, which cover the maximum and the minimum switch configurations and an intermediate switch configuration.

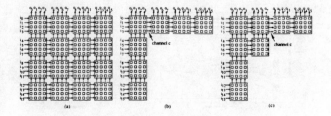

Figure 14. Three switch configurations used in the simulation.

One important factor that can greatly affect the performance was found to be the output arbitration scheme of each switching element. When the headers of two messages compete for one output channel in a switching element, an arbitration scheme is used to decide which message is granted the output channel. Some commonly found arbitration schemes include random or round-robin selection. However, it was found that such schemes produce unfair performance for different switch ports. Figure 15(a) show the average latencies of messages sent from each port for the switch configuration shown in Figure 14(a). Assume each input port is 50% loaded, XY routing is used and message size is 128 bytes. Figure 15(b) shows the average latency of messages sent from each port for the switch configuration shown in Figure 14(b). Assume each port is 5% loaded, relaxed XY routing is used and message size is 128 bytes. The destination port of a message is uniformly distributed across all output ports. It can be seen that random or round-robin arbitration schemes result in unfair results for different ports and higher variances of latencies. The reason for that is that the proposed switch architecture is not symmetric. Messages sent from different ports will traverse different number of channels on the average and thus will have different chances of being blocked, which cause unfair results.

To solve the problem, an arbitration scheme based on

329

timestamps of messages is used. Each message is assumed to carry a timestamp with it and an older message has higher priority to be selected for an output channel when competing with a younger message. Figures 15(a) and (b) also show the performance of this scheme. The results are fair for different ports and the latency of a message is more predictable regardless of the port from which the message is sent. Figures 15 (b) also shows under the same traffic load on all ports of the switch shown in Figure 14 (b), the switch ports fall into two groups. Ports 0-2 have superior averages latencies to those of ports 4-15. Port 3 falls between the two groups but is more similar to ports 3-15. Timestamp-based arbitration scheme does not involve much hardware complexity since a message only needs to carry the clock information local to each switch and no global clock is required. Carrying timestamps is also transparent to hosts, thus no constraint is put on packet format seen by hosts. Our later performance study will be based on this timestamp-based arbitration scheme.

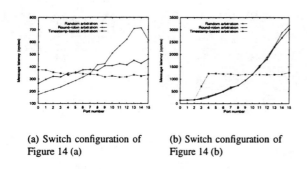

(a) Switch configuration of Figure 14 (a)

(b) Switch configuration of Figure 14 (b)

Figure 15. Average message latency of each switch input port under different arbitration schemes.

For the full switch configuration shown in Figure 14(a), the throughput can reach 62% under XY routing for message size of 128 bytes, which is close to the theoretical upper bound $(1 - e^{-1} = 0.632)$ for a nonblocking switch with HOL (Head of Line) blocking [13]. If the message size is very small, the throughput can be higher due to the ease of HOL blocking since a message can be fully absorbed within the switch. For example, if the message size is 8 bytes, the throughput can reach 79%. The throughput-latency relations are shown in Figure 16 for message sizes of 8, 128, 1024 bytes respectively. Here the latencies are calculated with all ports included since the average latencies for different input ports are similar to each other. A breakdown of latencies for different input ports was shown previously in Figure 15(a) for 128-byte messages and 50% input port load. The performance of fully adaptive routing is worse than XY routing since a message can make unnecessary turns and block other messages unnecessarily. The simulator shows that the throughput can only reach 24% under fully adaptive routing with random turns for message size of 128 bytes.

For incomplete switch configurations, relaxed XY

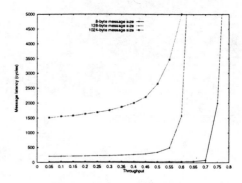

Figure 16. Throughput-latency relations for various message sizes.

routing can be used. One configurations is given in Figure 14(b). This kind of configuration is well suited to client/server computing. Ports 0-2 serve servers and ports 3-15 serve clients. Ports 0-2 are nonblocking ports since messages sent from ports 0-2 can only be blocked due to output port contention. Ports 3-15 are blocking ports since channel c is shared for messages sent from input ports 3-15 to output ports 3-15. Suppose three servers are connected to ports 0-2 and 13 clients are connected to ports 3-15. Assume the destination port of a packet sent from a server is uniformly distributed across ports 0-15, and the destination of a packet sent from a client has 50% probability of going to one of the three servers and 50% probability of going to one of the thirteen clients. Under this traffic pattern, each input port of 3-15 cannot be loaded more than $\frac{1}{13 \times 0.5 \times \frac{12}{13}}$, or 16.7%, because channel c is a bottleneck. Each input port of 0-2 can be heavily loaded. Figure 17(a) shows the average latency of packets sent from each port, where ports 0-2 are each 80% loaded and ports 3-15 are each 12% loaded. Message size is 128 bytes.

For the switch configuration shown in Figure 14(c), ports 0-2 are nonblocking ports. Ports 3-6 are blocking but can offer higher bandwidth than ports 7-15. If the previous traffic loads are unchanged for input ports 0-2, which is each 80% loaded and input ports 7-15, which is each 12% loaded, each load of input ports 3-6 cannot exceed 54% (which can be calculated from the bottleneck produced by channel c). Figure 17(b) shows the simulation results corresponding to this configuration, where ports 0-2 are each 80% loaded, ports 3-6 are each 35% loaded and ports 7-15 are each 12% loaded.

Therefore, an incomplete switch configuration may well satisfy the requirement in a client/server computing environment. A full switch configuration for maximum network performance is easily achievable by adding more switch boards.

6 Physical layout and LAN integration

Physical layout of switch boards in building large-scale switches is a practical engineering issue. A good layout makes a switch stackable. It also decides whether

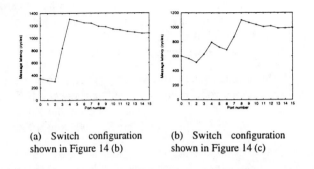

(a) Switch configuration shown in Figure 14 (b)

(b) Switch configuration shown in Figure 14 (c)

Figure 17. Message latency of each input port.

a switch is easy to install and maintain. This section discusses issues in mapping logical 2D switch boards into 3D space.

Figure 18 shows the general physical outlook of a switch board and the corresponding logical switch board. It has groups of input pins (group I), Output pins (group O) and others for interconnections between boards (groups A and B). On the boards there is a mesh of switch modules (chips), which are arrays of 2-by-2 switching elements. Basic building blocks are arranged on a board to build a switch. Furthermore, switch boards are inserted into some interconnected slots to build an even larger switch. To save space, switch boards can be laid in parallel with the interconnection board but with different heights to allow one switch board on top of the other.

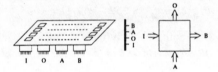

Figure 18. A switch board.

Figure 19 is an example of a large-scale switch built from 16 switch boards shown in Figure 18. The interconnection between boards is simple and regular. Those links between slots can be either hardwired or be ribbon cables which prove to be reliable enough [14]. The inputs and outputs of the whole switch are labeled with I and O, respectively.

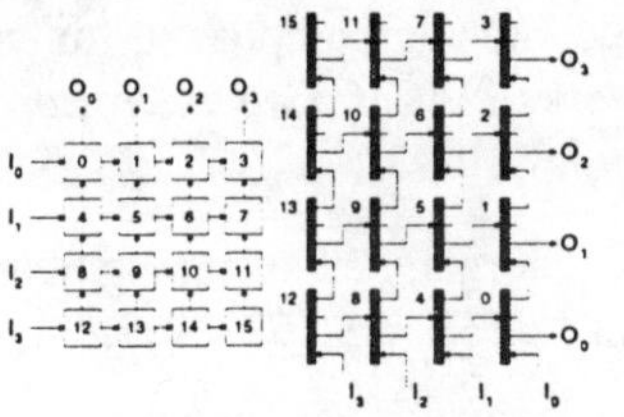

Figure 19. A large switch built from switch boards plugged into one interconnection board.

A switch has the same number of input ports and output ports since an input port and an output port form one full duplex connection for a host. Usually a simple switch can be constructed from a single board which has the same number of input ports and output ports. However, for a switch built from more than one switch board, each switch board does not need to be a square mesh. One 32-port switch can be built from eight 8-by-16 switch boards. This kind of switch boards may be more appropriate in realistic situations depending on the distance between neighboring slots and the width of a slot. Multi-layer layout can be configured when the scale of a switch is large. An example is shown in [8].

If adaptive routing (or relaxed XY routing) is used, it is not necessary for the switch to be a complete mesh. Figure 20 shows such an example with its physical layout. Adaptive routing allows very flexible switch configuration. If one board is faulty, either without reconfiguration or just by rearranging some boards, the switch can still function. Adaptive routing offers both on-line fault tolerance and board-level fault tolerance. Incomplete switch architecture is also suited to non-uniform communication pattern in client/server computing.

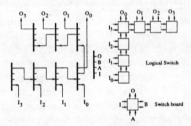

Figure 20. Layout of a switch which uses adaptive routing.

Currently there are a lot of LANs using unshielded twisted pairs to connect hosts with switches. If the interboard links are parallel lines, a serial to parallel conversion is done before data are switched. Also logical inputs and outputs are combined into individual physical ports. However, it is also possible to allow fully-duplex transmission with separately inputs and outputs if hosts accept fully-duplex traffic.

The switch presented can be easily integrated into practical products. A data frame is injected into the network by a host. When the frame enters a switch, the destination MAC address is first captured. Then that MAC address is used to lookup CAM (content addressable memory) for the internal routing tag. The routing tag can be one $(\Delta x, \Delta y)$ pair for a unicast address and more than one for a multicast address. $(\Delta x, \Delta y)$ is the offsets between input port and output port in X dimension and Y dimensions. The routing tag can also include other information such as an internal timestamp. After attaching the routing tag as the message header, the message is routed through the switch to an output port. At the output port, the internal routing tag is stripped and the frame is delivered to the destination host or another switch.

If the buffer of an input port is nearly full, usually because a message is blocked during cut-through switching and more data is coming, back pressure flow control propagates back pressure to the sending source and hints it not to inject more frames of data into the network, e.g., by faking CSMA/CD MAC-layer collision-detection signals to let the sending host back off the attempt to send another packet [15].

7 Conclusions

We have proposed a design of cut-through switches for an intra-switch LAN environment where a single switch serves all the network communications of a LAN. The modular construction endows switches with scalability and extendibility. The building module is chosen to facilitate deadlock free routing and multicast. Two routing schemes are discussed: XY routing which guarantees switches to be nonblocking and adaptive routing which gives the switch more flexibility and fault tolerance. One can even build a switch with two routing modes and choose the appropriate routing accordingly or using two sets of virtual channels for two different routing respectively. Under relaxed XY routing, the switch can be configured for distributed systems of clients and servers with dedicated bandwidth for servers. Simulation results have shown that local timestamp-based arbitration scheme in the output selectors of each switching element provides good fairness for different ports of the switch, and incomplete switch configurations may be adequate to meet the requirement for network performance in client/server computing. Hardware multicast is also possible in the designed switches without causing deadlock. Packaging issue of physically stacking switch boards in 3D space is discussed. The switch is easy to be integrated into a practical LAN based on existing equipments. Performance of multicast communications in the switch will be studied in the future for pure multicast traffic or mixed unicast and multicast traffic under various workloads.

References

[1] N. J. Boden and et al., "Myrinet – a Gigabit-per-second local area network," *IEEE Micro*, vol. 15, pp. 29 – 36, Feb. 1995.

[2] R. J. Souza and et al., "The GIGAswitch system: A high-performance packet switching platform," *Digital Technical Journal*, vol. 6, Jan. 1994.

[3] W. Dally and C. Seitz, "Deadlock-free message routing in multiprocessor interconnection networks," *IEEE Transactions on Computers*, vol. C-36, pp. 547 – 553, May 1987.

[4] L. M. Ni and P. K. McKinley, "A survey of wormhole routing techniques in direct networks," *IEEE Computer*, vol. 26, pp. 62 – 76, Feb. 1993.

[5] M. Schroeder and et al., "Autonet: a high-speed, self-configuring, local area network using point-to-point links," *IEEE Journal on Selected Areas in Communications*, vol. 9, Oct. 1991.

[6] W. Qiao and L. M. Ni, "Adaptive routing in irregular networks using cut-throughput switches," *IEEE Proc. of the 1996 International Conference on Parallel Processing*, vol. I, pp. 52 – 60, Aug. 1996.

[7] F. Silla and et al., "Efficient adaptive routing in networks of workstations with irregular topology," *First Internationsl Workshop on Communication and Architetural Support for Network-Based Parallel Computing*, pp. 46 – 60, Feb. 1997.

[8] M. Yang and L. M. Ni, "Design of scalable and multicast capable cut-through switches for high-speed lans," Tech. Rep. MSU-CPS-ACS-97-01, Michigan State Univ., Dept. of Computer Science, E. Lansing, MI, Jan. 1997.

[9] D. Cohen and G. Finn, "ATOMIC: A low-cost, very-high-speed, local communication architecture," in *Proceedings of the 1993 International Conference on Parallel Processing*, vol. I, pp. 39 – 46, Aug. 1993.

[10] M. Yang and L. M. Ni, "Incremental design of scalable interconnection networks using basic building blocks," *Symposium of Parallel and Distributed Processing*, pp. 252 – 259, Oct. 1995.

[11] Myricom, "Myrinet link specification," *http://www.myri.com/products/documentation/link/*.

[12] R. Sivaram, D. K. Panda, and C. B. Stunkel, "Multicasting in irregular networks with cut-through switches using tree-based multidestination worms," *Parallel Computing, Routing, and Communication Workshop*, 1997.

[13] J. Y. Hui, *Switching and Traffic Theory for Integrated Broadband Networks*. Kluwer Academic Publishers, 1990.

[14] D. Cohen and et al., "The use of message-based multicomputer components to construct gigabit networks," *ACM Computer Communication Review*, July 1993.

[15] T. W. Giorgis, "29 switching hubs save the bandwidth," *BYTE*, pp. 162 – 169, July 1995.

Session 5C

Fault-Tolerant Networks

Performance Evaluation of Fault Tolerance
for Parallel Applications in Networked Environments

Pierre SENS* and Bertil FOLLIOT**

LIP6 Laboratory , University Paris VI*, University Paris VII**

email: {sens,folliot}@masi.ibp.fr

Abstract

This paper presents the performance evaluation of a software fault manager for distributed applications. Dubbed STAR, it uses the natural redundancy existing in networks of workstations to offer a high level of fault tolerance. Fault management is transparent to the supported parallel applications. STAR is application independent, highly configurable and easily portable to UNIX-like operating systems. The current implementation is based on independent checkpointing and message logging. Measurements show the efficiency and the limits of this implementation. The challenge is to show that a software approach to fault tolerance can efficiently be implemented in a standard networked environment.

1. Introduction

Few distributed computing environments offer fault management using the natural redundancy of the distributed system and requiring no specific hardware support [1, 14, 17]. STAR was developed to add to the filling of this gap and is built totally outside the operating system. It also answers to the challenge to show that software fault tolerance can be efficiently implemented in a standardized environment.

Checkpointing and rollback recovery are well-known techniques to provide fault tolerance in distributed systems [11, 12, 13]. With *coordinated checkpointing*, processes coordinate their checkpointing actions such that the collection of checkpoints represents a consistent state of the whole system [5]. When a failure occurs, the system restarts from these checkpoints. Looking at the results of [2], [7], and [13], the main drawback of this approach is that the messages used for synchronizing a checkpoint are an important source of overhead. In *independent checkpointing*, each process independently saves its state. Because processes do not synchronize themselves for checkpointing, this method generally provides low run-time overhead. However, since the set of checkpoints may not define a consistent global state, the failure of one process may lead to the rollback of other processes (well-known as the domino effect [5]).

In the STAR implementation, an independent checkpointing mechanism is used to recover processes [4, 16, 21]. Our recovery protocols are based on *message logging* [4, 8, 10, 19] to avoid the domino effect. In the general approach, processes log their received messages. A process may recover by restarting from its last checkpoint and then replaying from the log the sequence of messages it originally received. We also present an evaluation of *optimistic message logging* [1, 18, 20] where received messages are buffered in volatile storage and logged to stable storage asynchronously. Unlike pessimistic message logging, this approach allows a process to continue execution before the message is logged.

To improve the response time of fault-tolerant applications, STAR includes several optimizations. First, it implements non-blocking and incremental checkpointing to perform an efficient backup of process state. Secondly, we developed an optimized stable storage based on replicated file system. It appears from other works and our experience, that these optimization methods are very important [7]. These techniques lead to a drastic reduction of the overhead for classical parallel applications.

STAR was implemented on a set of Sparc stations connected by Ethernet. The results demonstrate that independent checkpointing is an efficient approach for providing fault tolerance for the chosen applications, namely long-running ones with small message exchanges. We show that a software based fault tolerant management is an interesting alternative to specialized hardware or kernel-integrated fault tolerance. Results from [13,14] as well as our own instrumentation of several parallel applications corroborate this claim.

The remainder of this paper is organized as follows. Section 2 presents the application, environment and failure models. Sections 3 and 4 describe the mechanism of failure detection and the process recovery strategy. Our implementation of the stable storage is presented in section 5. Then, Section 6 gives the performance of STAR in a real academic environment. We conclude in Section 7.

2.   Environment

STAR manages fault of processes already allocated by an allocation manager. To provide a complete management of parallel applications STAR was integrated in the Gatos process allocation manager [9]. An application is a dynamic set of communicating processes which may use any resource of the network (mostly CPU and files). The only way to exchange information between processes is through message passing. A further assumption is made that processes involved in the parallel computation are *deterministic*. The state of a process is determined by its starting state and by the sequence of messages it has received [5]. This assumption is met by many applications, but excludes for example all programs relying on the values of the local time. To handle some nondeterminism, we can extend the message logging scheme by treating each nondetermisnistic function as a message, logging it and replaying it during recovery [8].

User applications rely on a *fault-tolerant software layer* providing a reliable access to all external components (processes and files). This layer allows the recovery of processes affected by a host failure in a transparent way on any remaining valid and compatible host. It provides a *global naming space* for processes and files independent of the location. The STAR communication protocol relies on this global naming space to find the location of the target process. This knowledge is updated after each process recovery.

STAR lies on top of a Unix operating system including network facilities (SunOS). It works on a set of workstations (hosts) connected by a local area network (Ethernet). We assume that the underlying transport layer provides reliable, sequenced point-to-point communication. The system is composed of fail-silent processors where a failed node simply stops and all the processes on the node die.

STAR consists of a set of servers and a client library. There are three main servers: the *recovery server* in charge of failure management, the *file server* implementing the stable storage by means of replicated files, and the *communication server* managing interactions between application processes.

Each application program must be linked to the STAR library which contains the following functions

- Checkpoint and restoration: the **checkpoint** function is either periodically called or explicitly indicated in the source code. When a process is restarted the **restore** function is automatically called.
- File access functions: these functions provide a Unix-like interface to the STAR file manager.
- Communication functions: these functions allow reliable message exchanges implementing message logging strategies.

3.   Failure Detection

The software approach to detect a host crash is often realized by using the normal communication traffic. This method has no overhead, in terms of number of messages, but the failure processing can only occur when one needs to use the faulty host. Thus, the recovery time in case of failure can be very high. Such a method only based on normal communication traffic is not appropriate for a fault manager.

Another solution consists in periodically checking the hosts states [4]. The recovery is invoked as soon as a host does not respond to the checker. This technique allows a fast recovery, but introduces an overhead in the network traffic. This overhead is proportional to the checking rate.

STAR uses a combination of the two methods. The normal traffic is used as in the first method, but in addition, when there is no traffic during a given time slice, a specific detection message is generated. A naive implementation of this detection would be for each host to check all other active ones. This solution is not suitable for complex systems with many hosts, since the network would become rapidly overcrowded by detection messages. In order to get an efficient detection message traffic, we organize all the hosts in a *logical ring*. Periodically, each host *only* checks its immediate successor on the ring. The checking process is straightforward and the cost in messages is very low. However, to insure the coherence of the ring, a two-phase reconfiguration protocol is executed when adding or removing a host. The cost of the reconfiguration protocol is not significant since host crashes are uncommon events.

On each host, the recovery server maintains a global view of the ring. In case of failure, the predecessor of the faulty host can locally determine its new successor. Host insertion in the ring is done in three steps: broadcast of an insertion message, update of the global knowledge, and transmission of the knowledge to the new host. The new host takes place in the ring according to its own host identification. This method supports an arbitrary number of simultaneous failures

The implementation of the logical ring is as follows. Each recovery server is linked to its predecessor and successor using the TCP communication protocol. Periodically, the server checks if a normal message has been received from its successor. If no message has been received, it sends a detection message to its successor. If this sending fails, the successor is considered faulty and the server initiates the recovery step. At present, we make no attempt to detect individual process failures on a node. Future versions of the STAR software will handle also finer-grained failures.

4. Process Recovery

The recovery step is invoked as soon as a failure is detected. Processes affected by the failure are immediately restarted on a valid host unlike some other fault managers where processes can only be restarted after the faulty host is rebooted (as in DAWGS [6] or Arjuna [17]). The process recovery in STAR is done by (1) checkpointing process on a stable storage, (2) restarting the process on a hardware compatible valid host, and (3) redirecting communications to the new process location.

4.1. Checkpointing a single process

The checkpoint of a single process is a snapshot of the process address space at a given time. Each checkpoint is saved on a stable storage capable of surviving to a given number of host failures. To reduce the cost of checkpointing, STAR's checkpoint mechanism uses both incremental and non-blocking checkpointing.

The Unix fork() primitive provides exactly the mechanism needed to implement non-blocking checkpointing. When checkpointing, the STAR library forks a child process which performs its context backup

while the parent process returns to executing the application. The fork system call creates a new process with the same address space as the caller. Many implementations of fork use a copy-on-write mechanism to optimize the copying of the parent's address space.

To perform incremental checkpointing, the new child process compares through a pipe its address space with the space of the child process created at the previous checkpoint then it saves only data that have been modified. We show in Section 5 that these two techniques considerably reduce the cost of checkpointing. However, they require a larger amount of memory and result in increased multiprogramming.

4.2. Recovery schemes for communicating processes

When processes exchange messages, the simple approach to recovery for independent processes is no longer adequate. In particular, attempts by individual cooperating processes to achieve backward error recovery can result in the well-known domino effect [15].

The current implementation of STAR is based on independent checkpointing with message logging. This technique is tailored to applications consisting of processes exchanging small streams of data. This method totally suppresses the domino-effect and consequently only one checkpoint is needed for each process. We have implemented pessimistic and optimistic message logging to allow application designers to choose the logging algorithm according to their application requirements.

These benefits are obtained at the expense of the space and time required for logging messages. The space overhead is reasonable given the current large disk capacities. Furthermore, at each new checkpoint all messages are deleted from the associated backup (a log is completely deleted after each checkpoint). The main drawback is the Input/Output overhead (i.e., the latency accessing the stable storage, see Section 6).

4.3 Communication management

The STAR communication protocol relies on the confining principle: *"a recovered process has no interaction with the others until it reaches the last state before the failure"* and consequently avoids the domino effect. All communications done between the checkpoint and the fault point are locally simulated. Thus, any process may be independently rolled back. To comply with this principle, we use the following techniques:

- Each process *saves all input messages* (message logging, see Section 4.3). A recovered process refers to this backup to access old messages. Thus, old valid senders are not concerned by the recovery of a process. All requests to receive messages are transparently transmitted to the local fault-tolerance layer. This layer directly accesses the backup or waits for messages according to the process state (recovered or not). At the process level there is no difference between receiving a message from the network or from the backup.

- Because processes are deterministic, a recovered process sends again all messages since its last checkpoint. A timestamp on each message allows to detect these retransmissions. Each message has a unique timestamp and is retransmitted with the same timestamp in case of failure. The fault-tolerant layer detects the retransmission by comparing the timestamp of a message with the stamp of the last transmitted message to discard already received messages.

In the optimistic scheme, messages are not directly saved on the stable storage but are kept on the main memory of the sending host. Periodically (when `MaxTransit` messages have been sent), the sending host asynchronously saves all messages on the stable storage. In case of failure, messages addressed to faulty processes are found either on the stable storage or on the main memory of the sending hosts. STAR also provides a sender-based algorithm where all messages are kept in the sending queue and are never saved on stable storage.

5. Stable Storage

Stable storage is a key feature in a fault manager. In STAR, a reliable file manager implements stable storage. It is used for file accesses, message backups and checkpoint storage.

In STAR, each file is replicated on separate disks on different hosts. The number of replicated copies is maintained in case of failure (obviously, only if the number of remaining disks is sufficient). Because failures are uncommon events, only a small number of copies is usually necessary (usually 2 for a network of 20 involved workstations). This number is set by the network administrator or by the application designer according to the fault tolerance and performance requirements. To ensure consistency of all copies, the file manager performs a reliable broadcast protocol [3]. A file update is reliably broadcast to all managers having a copy. A read operation is locally done whenever possible.

A reliable file is composed of a set of standard UNIX files replicated on a set of disks. On each host where copies are present, a file server manages accesses to copies. When a file server host fails, the files are copied from a valid host to a new file server thus maintaining the initial replication degree.

Performance of STAR directly depends on the stable storage management. To provide an efficient replicated file access, we take advantage of the pseudo-parallelism offered by the underlying system. Any access to a remote file server is achieved by a specific process located in the client host: the file server proxy. One proxy is associated with each remote server. Local clients and proxies exchange information through a local shared segment of memory. When a client wants to send a request to N servers, it puts the request arguments in the local memory and wakes up the proxies corresponding to the remote servers. Then, proxies read and transmit the request in a pseudo-parallel way.

6. Performance Evaluation of STAR

Fig. 1 shows the performance of the STAR file system (SFS) according to different replication degrees for writing and reading a file of 1 Megabyte. These measures were done on a set of Sun 5 and 10 workstations with 32 Mb of memory. A replication degree of 4 means that the file is saved on 4 disks on 4 hosts. We also illustrate the performance of NFS when data are in cache or not. Naturally, NFS measurements do not depend of the replication degree. SFS read has not been optimized since it is only used when recovering. On the other hand, SFS write is especially stressed since it is used during normal running for checkpointing and message logging. We see that in every case SFS writing is very efficient compared to NFS. These good performances are essentially due to the parallelization of servers accesses.

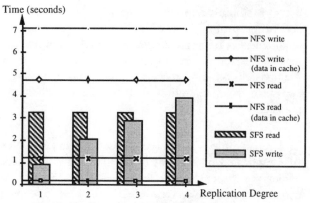

Fig. 1: Performance of the Star File System

Fig. 2 illustrates the cost of the optimistic message logging according to the size of the queue on the sending host. 0 means that messages are directly saved on stable storage before delivery. 500 means that messages are queued at the sending host and are asynchronously saved when the queue contains 500 messages. 0 queue size is equivalent to the pessimistic strategy. We also indicate the time to send messages with the sender-based algorithm where all messages are kept in the queue and are never saved on stable storage. These measures were done for 1024 messages of one kilobyte transmitted between two users processes. Messages are saved on two different hosts. The sender-based protocol seems more efficient but in fact it uses too much memory to be applicable in real applications.

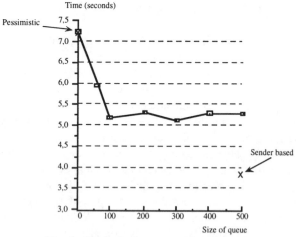

Fig. 2: Optimistic message logging cost

Additional experiments were run with STAR ported to a Sun IPC network with an approximate computing power of 12 VAX MIPS and 24 Mb of memory. Figures 3 and 4 present the running times for two independent

checkpointing implementations: full checkpointing where all data are written in stable storage and the process is blocked until the checkpoint is over and incremental non-blocking checkpointing where application continues while the checkpoint is written on stable storage and the amount of data to be written is reduced. The cost of checkpointing was measured with different replication degrees (from 1 to 4) and with different process sizes (from 100 to 1150 kilo-bytes). Programs run with a 20 seconds checkpointing interval, a rather short interval. In practice, longer intervals should be used. In that sense, we overestimate the cost of checkpointing and we stress the checkpoint mechanism.

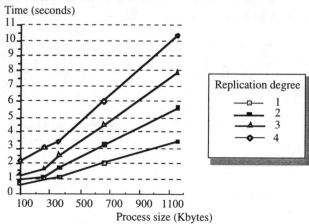

Fig. 3: Full checkpoint cost

Fig. 3 shows the cost of full checkpointing, where data and stack segments are entirely copied on stable storage. The process memory usage (i.e., process locality) is not taken into account. The cost linearly depends on the process context size. The time to save 1150 kilo-bytes on four replicated files takes 10.3 seconds. This is about three times slower than to write the same amount of data on a single file (3.4 seconds). The measured time can appear high compared to the performance of the STAR file server presented above. This is mainly due to the difference of machines in term of processing power. Moreover, the short checkpoint period overloads the file servers.

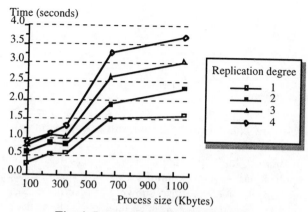

Fig. 4: Incremental checkpoint cost

the ring, create a new process, restore its context and finally update the global knowledge.

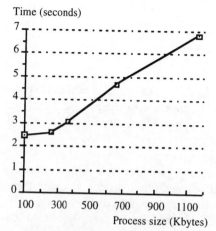

Fig. 5 : Restore context cost

Fig. 4 presents the cost obtained with non-blocking and incremental checkpointing. In the previous checkpointing methods, the amount of data written on stable storage was important whereas a small part of the data changes between two checkpoints. We observe a sizeable reduction of the checkpoint overhead. An incremental checkpoint is about three times faster than a full one. For the smallest program the checkpoint cost is below 1 second for all the replication degrees. Note that the curves are not linear because the time to take a checkpoint depends on the process memory usage.

The performance figures shown above are quiet good compared to that of other software fault managers. For a 2.6 megabytes program (a matrix multiplication) the mean time to perform a checkpoint is in STAR 4 times faster than libckpt [14]. This difference is mainly due to the use of the inefficient mprotect system call to implement incremental checkpointing. The system DAWGS [6] does checkpointing with only replication of degree one. In a network of 10 workstations with an approximate computing power of 3 VAX MIPS, the checkpoint time is about 1.84 seconds for 25 Kbytes.

Fig. 5 presents the recovery time of a process after a failure. This time includes the time to relaunch a process and to recover its state from its last checkpoint. This time is close to linear with the process size. For a 100 Kbytes process, it is 2.5 seconds, and for a 1150 Kbytes process, it is 6.8 seconds.

The restoration time can appear important compared to the checkpoint cost. In fact, the restoration step is much more complex. It must identify the process, reconfigurate

To tally the performance of STAR under a working load we chose three long-running, compute-intensive applications representing different memory usage and communications patterns:

- The gauss application performs gaussian elimination with partial pivoting on a 1024 x 1024 matrix. The matrix is distributed among several processes. At each iteration of the reduction, the process which holds the pivot sends the pivot column to all other processes.
- The multiplication application, called matmul, multiplies two square matrixes of size 1024 x 1024. The computation is distributed among several processes. No communication is required other than reporting the final solution.
- The fft application computes the Fast Fourier Transform of 32768 data points. The problem is distributed by assigning each process an equal range of data points. Like the previous application, no communication is required other than reporting the final solution.

Table 1 presents running time, communication, and memory requirements for the three applications when run without fault-tolerant management (without checkpointing and message logging). Gauss and matmul require a sizeable amount of data stressing the checkpoint mechanism. Moreover, the gauss application exhibits a large amount of communications especially stressing the message logging. The fft application is long-running and requires a medium amount of data.

Application	Running Time (seconds)	Per Process Memory (Kbytes)	Per Process communication (Kbytes)
gauss	344	1704	2700
matmul	723	2688	0.06
fft	1177	1200	0.06

Table 1: Application requirements

Table 2 presents the running times of the applications programs when run with independent checkpointing and message logging. Applications run with a 2-minutes checkpointing interval. Checkpoints and logs are duplicated. For the three applications, incremental checkpointing provides a sizeable reduction of the overhead. Comparing to the non-blocking checkpointing, we obtain a reduction of the overhead from 42% to 190%. Applications can be divided into two categories: applications with an address space that is modified with high locality (matrix multiplication and fft applications) and applications with an address space that is modified almost entirely between any two checkpoints (gauss application). For the applications in the first category, incremental checkpointing is very successful (more than 77 % of reduction for matrix multiplication and 190 % of reduction for fft). For the applications in the last category, incremental checkpointing is less effective (about 42 % of reduction for the gauss application). Furthermore, the cost of message logging for the gauss application represents a half of the global overhead.

7. Conclusions

This paper has presented an evaluation of the STAR fault manager for distributed applications in a standard workstation environment. The current implementation is based on independent checkpointing, and avoids the domino effect by using message logging. From the basic components, other fault-tolerant techniques can be implemented according to the needs of the supported parallel applications.

We reported performance measurements of the basic software components. The results demonstrate that independent checkpointing is an efficient approach for providing fault tolerance for the specific studied applications, i.e., long-running ones with small message exchanges. We have also shown that a software based fault tolerant management is an interesting alternative to specialized hardware or kernel-integrated fault tolerance. Results from [13] as well as own instrumentation of distributed applications corroborate this claim.

References

[1] L. Alvisi, K. Marzullo. Message Logging: Pessimistic, optimistic, and Causal. In *Proc. of the 15th International Conference on Distributed Computing System, June 1995*.

[2] B. Bhargava, S-R. Lian, and P-J. Leu. Experimental Evaluation of Concurrent Checkpointing and Rollback-recovery Algorithms. In *Proc. of the International Conference on Data Engineering*, pp. 182-189, March 1990.

[3] K.P. Birman and T. Joseph. Reliable Communication in the Presence of Failures. *ACM Transactions on Computer Systems*, 5:47-76, February 1987.

[4] A. Borg, W. Blau, W. Craetsch, F. Herrmann, and W. Oberle. Fault Tolerance under UNIX. *ACM Transactions on Computer Systems*, 7(1):1-24, February 1989.

[5] K.M. Chandy and L. Lamport. Distributed Snapshots: Determining Global States of Distributed Systems. *ACM Transactions on Computer Systems*, 3(1):63-75, 1985.

	Full checkpoint		Non-blocking checkpoint		Incremental checkpoint	
	Running Time (sec.)	Percentage of overhead	Running Time (sec.)	Percentage of overhead	Running Time (sec.)	Percentage of overhead
gauss	567	64.92	505	46.80	457	32.85
matmul	844	16.79	768	6.34	748	3.57
fft	1244	5.75	1228	4.36	1194	1.50

Table 2: Parallel Applications Evaluation

[6] H. Clark and B. McMillin. DAWGS - a Distributed Compute Server Utilizing Idle Workstations. *Journal of Parallel and Distributed Computing*, 14:175-186, February 1992.

[7] E.N. ELnozahy, D.B. Johnson, and W. Zwaenepoel. The Performance of Consistent Checkpointing. In *Proc. of the 11th Symposium on Reliable Distributed Systems*, October 1992.

[8] E.N. Elnozahy, W. Zwaenepoel. On the Use and Implementation of Message Logging. In *Proc. of the 24th International Symposium on Fault-Tolerant Computing Systems*, pp. 298-307, Austin, Texas (USA), June 1994.

[9] B. Folliot and P. Sens. GATOSTAR: A Fault-tolerant Load Sharing Facility for Parallel Applications. In *Proc. of the First European Dependable Computing Conference*, Berlin, Germany, October 1994, K. Echtle, D. Hammer, D. Powell (Ed), Lecture Notes in Computer Science 852, pp. 581-598, 1994.

[10] D. B. Johnson and W. Zwaenepoel. Sender-Based Message Logging. In *Proc. of the 7th Symposium on Fault Tolerant Computing Systems*, pp. 97-104, June 1990.

[11] D.B. Johnson and W. Zwaenepoel. Recovery in Distributed Systems using Optimistic Message Logging and Checkpointing. *Journal of Algorithms*, 11(3):462-491, September 1990.

[12] R. Koo and S. Toueg. Checkpointing and Rollback-Recovery for Distributed Systems. *IEEE Transactions on Software Engineering*, SE-13(1):23-21, January 1987.

[13] G. Muller, M. Hue, N. Peyrouze. Performance of Consistent Checkpointing in a modular Operating System: results of the FTM Experiment. In *Proc. of the First European Dependable Computing Conference*, Berlin, Germany, October 1994, K. Echtle, D. Hammer, D. Powell (Ed), Lecture Notes in Computer Science 852, pp. 491-508, 1994.

[14] J.S. Plank, M. Beck, G. Kingsley, K. Li. Libckpt: Transparent Checkpointing under Unix. In *Proc. of USENIX Winter 1995 Technical Conference* , New Orleans, Louisiana(USA), January 1995.

[15] B. Randell. Design Fault Tolerance. *The Evolution of Fault-Tolerant Computing Vol. 1*, A. Avizienis, H. Kopetz, J-C. Laprie (Ed), Springer-Verlag, pp. 251-270, 1987

[16] P. Sens. The Performance of Independent Checkpointing in Distributed Systems. In *Proc. of the 28th Hawaii International Conference on System Science*, pp. 525-533, Maui, Hawaii, January 1995.

[17] S.K. Shrivastava, D.L. McCue. Structuring Fault-Tolerant Object Systems for Modularity in a Distributed Environment. *IEEE Transactions on Parallel and Distributed Systems*, pp. 421-432, April 1994.

[18] S.W. Smith, D.B. Johnson, J.D. Tygar. Completely Asynchronous Optimistic Recovery with Minimal Rollbacks. In *Proc. of the 25th Annual International Symposium on Fault-Tolerant Computing*, Pasadena, CA (USA), June 1995

[19] R.E. Strom and S.A. Yemini. Optimistic Recovery in Distributed Systems. *ACM Transactions on Computer Systems*, 3(3):204-226, August 1985.

[20] Y.M. Wang, W.F. Fuchs. Optimistic Message Logging for Independent Checkpointing in Message-Passing Systems. In *Proc. of the IEEE 11th Symposium on Reliable Distributed Systems*, pp. 147-154, October 1992.

[21] J. Xu, R.H.B Netzer. Adaptive Independent Checkpointing for Reducing Rollback Propagation. In *Proc. of the 5th IEEE Symposium on Parallel and Distributed Processing*, pp. 754-761, December 1993.

Design of a Circuit-Switched Highly Fault-Tolerant k-ary n-cube

Baback A. Izadi
Elect. Eng. Tech. Dept.
DeVry Institute of Technology
Columbus, Ohio 43209   U.S.A.
bai@devrycols.edu

Füsun Özgüner
Dept. of Elect. Eng.
The Ohio State University
Columbus, Ohio 43210   U.S.A.
ozguner@ee.eng.ohio-state.edu

Abstract

In this paper, we present a strongly fault-tolerant design for the k-ary n-cube multiprocessor and examine its reconfigurability. Our design augments the k-ary n-cube with $\left(\frac{k}{j}\right)^n$ spare nodes; each set of j^n regular nodes is connected to a spare node and the spare nodes are interconnected as a $\left(\frac{k}{j}\right)$-ary n-cube. Our approach utilizes the circuit-switched capabilities of the communication modules of the spare nodes to tolerate a large number of faulty nodes and faulty links without any performance degradation. Both theoretical and simulation results are presented.

1 Introduction

As the size of the k-ary n-cube multicomputer grows, due to its complexity, the probability of node and/or link failures become high. Therefore, it is crucial that such systems be able to withstand a large number of faults. To sustain the same level of performance, some researchers have investigated hardware schemes for the k-ary n-cube where spare nodes and/or spare links are used to replace the faulty ones. In the literature, a hardware scheme that retains the same service level, as well as keeping the same system topology after the occurrence of faults, is referred to as a *strongly fault-tolerant* system. Two classes of hardware schemes have been proposed in the literature. Some researchers have examined local reconfiguration techniques where a spare node can only replace a faulty node within a given subset [7, 1]. A common drawback of these approaches is low utilization of spare nodes. Moreover, the schemes do not tolerate any faulty link and generally are not strongly fault tolerant. The second class of approaches uses a global reconfiguration scheme and is based on creating a supergraph of the target topology [2, 4, 3]. The schemes are strongly fault tolerant. However, they are mostly node-minimal and suffer from large node degrees.

In this paper, we propose a global reconfiguration scheme that utilizes circuit-switched communication to make the k-ary n-cube strongly fault tolerant. Both theoretical and simulation results are presented. Our theoretical result indicates that the enhanced cluster k-ary n-cube tolerates $2n + 1$ faulty nodes regardless of the fault distribution; proofs of our theorems are omitted due to space limitation [5]. Our simulation results, based on random distribution of up to $\left(\frac{k}{j}\right)^n$ faulty nodes, have yielded 100% fault coverage.

The following notations are used throughout the paper. Each node of a k-ary n-cube is identified by n-tuple $(a_{n-1} \cdots a_i \cdots a_0)$, where a_i is a radix k digit and represents the node's position in the i-th dimension. Each node is connected along the dimension i to the neighboring nodes $(a_{n-1} \cdots a_{(i \pm 1 \bmod k)} \cdots a_0)$. Each spare node, in addition to n digits, is labeled with a prefix S, *i.e.* $Sa_{n-1} \cdots a_i \cdots a_0$. The link connecting any two nodes P and Q is represented by $P \rightarrow Q$. A cluster whose local spare is labeled $Sa_{n-1} \cdots a_i \cdots a_0$ is called *cluster* $a_{n-1} \cdots a_i \cdots a_0$.

2 Overview of the Approach

An enhanced cluster k-ary n-cube (ECKN) is constructed by assigning one spare node to each group of j^n regular nodes, called a cluster; each spare node is connected to every regular node of its cluster via an intra-cluster spare link. Hence, there exist $\frac{k^n}{j^n}$ spare nodes. Furthermore, the spare nodes of neighboring clusters are interconnected using inter-cluster spare links; two clusters are declared neighbors if there exists at least one regular node in each with a direct link between them. Therefore, the topology that interconnects the spare nodes (spare network) is the $\frac{k}{j}$-ary n-cube ($j \neq \frac{k}{2}$; see [5] for $j = \frac{k}{2}$). Figure 1 depicts an enhanced cluster 6-ary 2-cube where $j = 2$. Note that the spare network is a 3-ary 2-cube. The resultant structure consists of k^n regular nodes and $\left(\frac{k}{j}\right)^n$ spare nodes. The degree of each regular node and spare node is $2n + 1$ and $2n + j^n$ respectively.

We assume that faulty nodes retain their ability to communicate. This assumption may be avoided by duplicating the communication module in each node. In the k-ary n-cube with circuit-switched communication modules, the cost of communication is nearly constant between any two

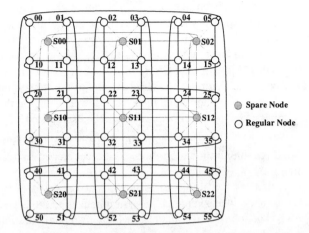

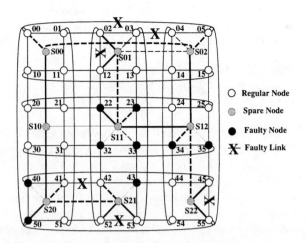

Figure 1: An enhanced cluster 6-ary 2-cube with $j = 2$

Figure 2: Reconfiguration of an ECKN.

given nodes. The regular node router consists of $2n + 1$ routing channels, connecting it to its $2n$ neighboring regular nodes as well as its local spare node. The spare node router is made of $2^n + j^n$ routing channels, connecting it to its 2^n local regular nodes and its j^n neighboring spare nodes. Each routing channel consists of one channel in and one channel out.

We next describe how the ECKN tolerates faulty nodes and faulty links. Connecting a spare node to a regular node is done to tolerate a node failure. If the spare node resides in the cluster of the faulty node, the appropriate communication channel of the spare node is merged with the communication module of the faulty node. If the assigned spare node and the faulty node belong to different clusters, a dedicated path to connect them needs to be established. Once such a path is established, due to the capabilities of the circuit-switched routing modules, the physical location of the faulty node and its assigned spare node is irrelevant. Moreover, no modification of the available computation or communication algorithm is necessary. Faulty links are bypassed by establishing parallel paths using spare links. Figure 2 illustrates reconfiguration of an ECKN with $k = 6$ and $n = j = 2$ in the presence of indicated faulty nodes and faulty links. For the sake of clarity, only active spare links are shown in the figure. Note that by utilizing the intermediate spare nodes, in effect 4 logical spare nodes are present in cluster 11. Figure 3 shows how appropriate communication channels of various spare nodes are merged with the communication module of node 22 so that the spare node $S02$ could replace the faulty node 22.

3 Reconfiguration of the ECKN

Let's define a cluster with one or more faulty nodes as a faulty cluster. Since within a cluster, the local spare node is directly connected to every regular node, the number of edge-disjoint paths between the faulty nodes of a cluster

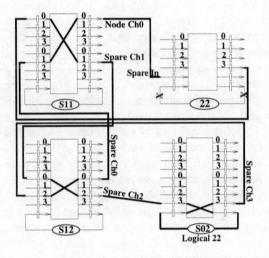

Figure 3: Tolerating faulty node 22 with spare node S02

and unassigned spare nodes in other clusters is the same as the number of edge-disjoint paths between the local spare node of the faulty cluster and unassigned spare nodes. The reconfigurability of the ECKN is then a function of the number of dedicated and edge-disjoint paths, within the spare network, that can be established between the local spare node of a cluster with multiple faulty nodes and the available spare nodes in the fault-free clusters. We define the number of such edge-disjoint paths that must be constructed from a spare node as the *connection requirement* (C_R) of that spare node. For example, in Figure 2, since 3 out of 4 logical spare nodes of cluster 11 physically belong to other clusters, the C_R of the spare node $S11$ is 3. Note that the C_R of a spare node is equal to the number of faulty nodes in its cluster minus one. The following theorems establish the number of faulty nodes that can be tolerated by the ECKN.

343

Theorem 1 *The upper bound on the number of faulty nodes that an enhanced cluster k-ary n-cube ($k \neq 2$) can tolerate in a cluster is $2n + 1$.* ∎

Theorem 2 *In an enhanced cluster k-ary n-cube ($k \neq 2$), a total of $2n + 1$ faulty nodes can be tolerated regardless of fault distribution.* ∎

Let's group the spare nodes into three sets: S_S (set of source nodes), S_U (set of used nodes), and S_T (set of target nodes). A source node is a spare node in a cluster with multiple faulty nodes. The set S_S then represents the spare nodes with a C_R greater than 0. S_T is the set of unassigned spare nodes, and S_U consists of spare nodes that have been assigned to faulty nodes and have a C_R of 0. For example, considering only the faulty nodes in Figure 2, after assigning the local spare node to a local faulty node in each faulty cluster, $S_S = \{S11, S12, S20\}$, $S_U = \{S21\}$, and $S_T = \{S00, S01, S02, S10, S22\}$. During our reconfiguration algorithm, which is discussed later in this section, the spare nodes are dynamically assigned to the various sets. To illustrate this, suppose the C_R of a spare node $\alpha \in S_S$ is greater than 0 and there exists a dedicated path from α to $\beta \in S_T$. Consequently, β replaces a faulty node in the cluster of α. β is then called used and is assigned to S_U. Also, the C_R of α is reduced by one. If the C_R of α becomes zero, it is also marked as used and is assigned to S_U. The ECKN is reconfigured when S_S becomes an empty set.

As mentioned before, the reconfigurability of the ECKN is a function of the number of edge-disjoint paths, within the spare network, that can be established between the local spare nodes (nodes in S_S) of the clusters with multiple faulty nodes and the available spare nodes (nodes in S_T) of the fault-free clusters. However, spare nodes do not have to be interconnected as a $\frac{k}{j}$-ary n-cube. Obviously, if the spare network is a complete graph, the ECKN can tolerate $\left(\frac{k}{j}\right)^n$ faulty nodes regardless of the fault distribution. Hence, the reconfigurability of the ECKN is a direct consequence of the connectivity of the topology of the spare network. Let's denote the topology of the graph connecting the spare nodes by $G = (V, E)$, where $V = S_S \bigcup S_U \bigcup S_T$ and E represents the appropriate spare links. Let the C_R of a node $n \in S_S$ be represented by $C_R(n)$ and denote the sum of the C_R's of all nodes in a set P as $\sum_{n \in P} C_R(n)$. The next theorem examines the connectivity of G as it pertains to the reconfigurability of the ECKN.

Theorem 3 *Consider a graph $G(V,E)$, where $V = S_S \bigcup S_U \bigcup S_T$. The necessary and sufficient condition for every node $n \in S_S$ to have $C_R(n)$ edge-disjoint paths to $C_R(n)$ nodes in S_T is that the minimum number of edges leaving any subset of nodes $P \subseteq V$ be greater than or equal to $\sum_{n \in (P \bigcap S_S)} C_R(n) - |P \bigcap S_T|$.* ∎

Based on Theorem 3, the ECKN can tolerate a given distribution of faulty nodes provided the sum of the C_R's of any set of spare nodes (with non-zero C_R) is smaller than the number of edges leaving the set. However, for a given dimension of the ECKN, one can always find a radix that violates Theorem 3. Therefore, under the maximum number of faulty nodes, no theoretical lower bound on the number of faulty nodes per cluster can be established.

We next present our reconfiguration algorithm. An optimal reconfiguration algorithm can be developed by utilizing the maxflow/mincut algorithm. Here, optimality is measured as the ability to assign a spare node to every faulty node whenever such an assignment is feasible vis-a-vis Theorem 3. The main drawback to reconfiguration using the above algorithm is that a digraph representation of the spare network has to be constructed [5] and the spare node assignment has to be done by the host processor. To overcome these deficiencies, we next present a near optimal reconfiguration algorithm, which is called *Alloc-Spare*. The algorithm consists of three parts as specified below:

1. Early Abort: The following solvability checks are performed to determine whether the reconfiguration is feasible. If the total number of faulty nodes is greater than the number of spare nodes ($(\frac{k}{j})^n$), the reconfiguration fails. If the C_R of a spare node is greater than $2n$, the reconfiguration fails due to Theorem 1. The reconfiguration also fails if the sum of the C_R of any two neighboring spare nodes in the spare network is greater than $4n - 2$ (Theorem 3).

2. Local Assignment: The local spare node of every faulty cluster is assigned to a faulty node within the cluster. If all faulty nodes are covered, the ECKN is reconfigured.

3. Non-Local Assignment: To find a set of candidate spare nodes that can be assigned to a faulty node, we utilize Lee's path-finding algorithm [6]. The algorithm begins by constructing a breadth-first search of the minimum depth d ($1 \leq d \leq (\frac{k}{j})^n - 1$) in the spare network from the local spare node of a faulty cluster with a non-zero C_R. If a free spare node is found, a path to the source node is formed. The algorithm guarantees that a path to a spare node will be found if one exists and the path will be the shortest possible [6]. Once a path is formed, the links associated with that path are deleted from the spare network, resulting in a new structure. If there still remain some uncovered faulty nodes, a solvability test to check the C_R of neighboring spare nodes, similar to Early Abort, is performed on the new structure and Step 3 is repeated for a higher depth d. Reconfiguration fails if $d > (\frac{k}{j})^n - 1$, which is the longest acyclic path in the spare network. ∎

We implemented the algorithm Alloc-Spare for an ECKN with $k = 24$, $n = 4$, and $j = 6$ (256 spare nodes). The simulation result for up to 256 randomly placed faulty

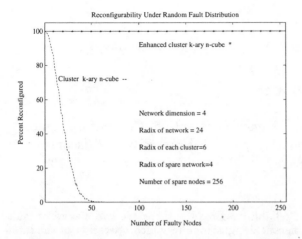

Figure 4: The ECKN under random faulty nodes

nodes is shown in Figure 4. The other plot in the figure pertains to the result of our local reconfiguration scheme, called the cluster scheme [5], whose performance is similar to the scheme proposed in [7]. The result indicates 100% reconfigurability for the ECKN under up to 256 randomly placed faulty nodes. Our simulation result further reveals that on the average about one spare link per spare node is used to reconfigure the ECKN. Hence, the spare network of the ECKN is a well connected graph even after the reconfiguration. To examine the limitation of the ECKN under random fault distribution, we next assumed that the number of faulty nodes in the ECKN is the maximum $((\frac{k}{j})^n)$. Furthermore, we assumed that each faulty cluster contains a fixed number of faulty nodes. Since by Theorem 1, a faulty cluster may have up to $2n + 1$ faulty nodes, simulation runs for 1 to $2n + 1$ faulty nodes per cluster were carried out. The faulty clusters were then randomly allocated in an ECKN with $k = 66$, $j = 11$, and $n = 3$ (216 spare nodes). Our simulation result indicates that nearly 100% reconfiguration is achieved (all 216 faulty nodes are tolerated) for up to 4 faulty nodes per cluster. Moreover, on the average less than half of the 6 spare links per spare node were needed to make the reconfiguration feasible. Additional simulations were carried out to measure the effect of the radix size and the dimension of the ECKN on its fault tolerance. The results suggest that for a given dimension, the radix of the spare network is inversely proportional to its reconfigurability. Furthermore, a lower dimensional spare network uses a higher percent of its spare links to reconfigure and therefore is less fault tolerant.

We implemented two algorithms to tolerate faulty links. In the first one (MPP), if any one of the spare links of a parallel path to any faulty link is unavailable, the reconfiguration fails. The second algorithm (dilation 2) considers more than one parallel path to an inter-cluster faulty link. For example, in Figure 1, if the spare link $S01 \rightarrow S02$ is not available, the faulty link $03 \rightarrow 04$ can still be replaced by the parallel path $03 \rightarrow S01 \rightarrow S11 \rightarrow S12 \rightarrow S02 \rightarrow 04$. The simulation results for an ECKN with $n = j = 4$ and $k = 24$ is shown in Figure 5. The results indicate that 90% of the time, the given ECKN can tolerate nearly 40 faulty links under MPP algorithm and nearly 50 faulty links under dilation 2 algorithm.

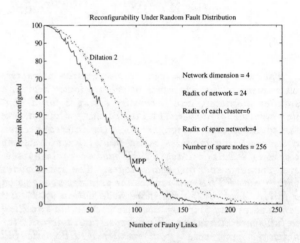

Figure 5: Tolerating link failures only

By combining the reconfiguration algorithms which tolerate node failures and link failures, a combination of faulty links and faulty nodes is tolerated [5].

References

[1] M. Alam and R. Melhem. Routing in modular fault-tolerant multiprocessor systems. In *IEEE Transactions on Parallel and Distributed Systems*, volume 6, pp. 1206–1220, November 1995.

[2] J. Bruck, R. Cypher, and C. T. Ho. Efficient fault-tolerant mesh and hypercube architectures. *Proceedings of the 22nd Annual International Symposium on Fault Tolerant Computing*, pp. 162–169, July 1992.

[3] J. Bruck, R. Cypher, and C. T. Ho. Fault-tolerant meshes with small degree. *Proceeding of 5th ACM Symposium on Parallel Algorithm and Architectures*, pp. 1–10, June 1993.

[4] S. Dutt. Fast polylog-time reconfiguration of structurally fault-tolerant multiprocessors. *IEEE Symposium on Parallel and Distributed Processing*, pp. 161–169, 1993.

[5] B. Izadi. Design of fault-tolerant distributed memory multiprocessors. *Ph.D. thesis, the Ohio State University*, 1995.

[6] C. Y. Lee. An algorithm for path connection and its applications. *IRE Transactions on Electronic Computers*, ec-10:346–365, 1961.

[7] A. D. Singh. Interstitial redundancy: An area efficient fault tolerance scheme for large area VLSI processor arrays. *IEEE Transactions on Computers*, 37(11):1398–1410, November 1988.

Design and Analysis of Fault-Tolerant Star Networks

Chungti A. Liang

Mail Station P324
IBM Corporation
Poughkeepsie, NY 12601

Sourav Bhattacharya

Dept. of Computer Science
Arizona State University
Tempe, AZ 85287

Jack Tan

Dept. of Computer Science
University of Wisconsin
Eau Claire, WI 54702

Abstract

The star graph has been proposed as an attractive alternative to the hypercube offering a lower degree, a smaller diameter, and a smaller distance for a similar number of nodes. In this paper, we investigate the fault-tolerant design for the Star interconnection networks using modules called fault tolerant building blocks (FTBBs). Each FTBB module contains several primary and few spare nodes. The spare nodes within each FTBB can replace the primary nodes when a failure occurs. If each spare node within an FTBB can replace any primary node we ascribe the situation to full spare utilization. We propose fault tolerant Star networks constructed from smaller FTBBs with full spare utilization and a fault-tolerant routing scheme to reconfigure the system when a failure occurs.

1 Introduction

The star graph has been proposed as an attractive and viable alternative to the hypercube topology for the design and development of distributed memory architectures [1, 4]. The star graph has a hierarchical structure, is vertex and edge symmetric, has a lower degree, a smaller diameter, and a smaller distance for a similar number of nodes.

An $n-$star graph [1], denoted as S_n, is an undirected graph consisting of $n!$ vertices labelled with $n!$ permutation of the n symbols. Let the n symbols be $1, 2, \cdots, n$. Two vertices are connected by an edge *iff* the label of one of the nodes can be obtained from the label of the other node by exchanging the first(leftmost) symbol with any one of the other $n - 1$ symbols. For example, in S_4 the node 1234 is adjacent to node 2134, 3214 and 4231 by exchanging the first symbol '1' with the 2nd, 3rd and 4th symbols respectively. Every node of S_n has $n - 1$ edges incident to it, corresponding to the $n - 1$ symbols with which the first symbol can exchange. Thus, S_n is regular graph of degree $n-1$; and is both vertex and edge symmetric.

Formally, for each node $p = p_1 p_2 \cdots p_n$ and for each i, $2 \le i \le n$, we denote by $ADJ_i(p)$ for the adjacent node to p by exchanging p_1 with p_i in p. The edge $(p, ADJ_i(p))$ is called an $i - edge$. Each node p has $n - 1$ ports numbered $2, 3, \cdots, n$ corresponding to its $n - 1$ edges.

Fault-tolerant design of interconnection networks is an important problem, since the fault-tolerance of a network topology provides a higher (or desired) degree of reliability. Broadly, there are two classes of fault-tolerant designs: one in which operation of the interconnection network is adapted to bypass the faulty units using fault-tolerant routing [5, 6]. and the other in which redundant hardware modules are incorporated into the topology, where such redundant units substitute primary modules in the event of a failure.

The later approach, namely the redundant modular design and failure-replacement technique, has several advantages such as: 1) local and fast fault detection and reconfiguration, 2) ease of construction and fault replacement, 3) scalability of the design, and 4) simple fault-tolerant routing algorithms. Such modular reconfiguration techniques have been previously proposed for binary trees [7] and hypercubes [2].

We propose a fault-tolerant building block (FTBB) design for the Star interconnection network. Modular reconfiguration techniques, that efficiently utilize the spare nodes (to achieve fault tolerance), are investigated. We propose a method to preserve the physical adjacency between the active nodes, once the reconfiguration takes place. Finally, we present analytical estimates of the degree of fault-tolerance (i.e., reliability) achieved using the proposed design.

2 Fault-Tolerant Building Block

A fault-tolerant building block (FTBB), originally proposed by [2] is a module consisting of some primary and spare nodes. For a spare node S, the primary set $PS(S)$ is the set of primary nodes that S can replace, when a failure occurs. The flexibility, flex(S), is the number of primary nodes S can replace, i.e., the cardinality of $PS(S)$. For a primary node P, the spare set $SS(P)$ is the set of spare nodes that can replace P. The degree of coverage deg(P) is the number of spare nodes that can replace P, i.e., the cardinality of $SS(P)$. For a system, if flex(S) is constant for each spare node S, and deg(P) is constant for each primary node P; then we refer to these constants by 'flex' and 'deg' respectively.

If each spare node in an FTBB can replace any primary node from that FTBB, then we refer to it as a *full spare utilization*. An FTBB is designed such that the set of nodes F in the FTBB is the minimal set of nodes satisfying the following property:

Definition 1 *For any primary node P the nodes $SS(P)$ are in F and for any spare node S the nodes*

PS(S) are in *F*.

The size of an FTBB is denoted by a tuple (M, K) where M and K $(F = M + K)$ are the number of primary nodes and spare nodes within this FTBB respectively. In an FTBB of size (M, K), *full spare utilization* is achieved if flex $= M$ and deg $= K$, i.e., every spare node S can replace all($=M$) primary nodes and every primary node P can be replaced by all($=K$) spare nodes. In this case, the FTBB with size (M, K) is K-fault tolerant, since it can tolerate any combination of up to K faults. Figure 1a and 1b show FTBBs with size (6,1) and (6,2) respectively.

3 Fault Tolerant Star Networks

We propose fault tolerant Star networks constructed from smaller size FTBBs with *full spare utilization*. We prove that the fault-tolerant n-star networks constructed using FTBB of size $(k!, 1)$ where $3 \leq k \leq n$ can tolerate upto $\frac{n!}{k!}$ node failures after reconfiguration. We measure the link and node overhead as well the system reliability of the fault tolerant star networks constructed from different sizes of FTBBs.

3.1 Construction Rules

Fault-tolerant links are categorized into intra-FTBB and inter-FTBB links. Intra-FTBB links are used to construct each FTBB$(k!, 1)$, which has $k!$ primary nodes and 1 spare node. From the *full spare utilization* and modularity properties, we know that the spare node must connect to each primary node and none of the primary nodes must connect to any *other* spare node beyond that of the host FTBB.

Inter-FTBB links are used to link the individual FTBB$(k!, 1)$ units. For an n-star, there will be $\frac{n!}{k!}$ such FTBB units. The primary nodes of the n-star will interconnect following the star connectivity property.

An inter-FTBB link will only be between the spare nodes of two FTBB units. This is because, a primary node, will only connect to the spare node of its own FTBB; and hence a primary node cannot participate in the connectivity of an inter-FTBB link. Two spare nodes (S_1 and S_2) from two different FTBBs will require to be connected, if *any* primary node of S_1 is Star-interconnected[1] to *any* primary node of S_2 and vice versa. This is because, if the respective primary nodes for S_1 and S_2 fail, then S_1 and S_2 must take over and replace their connectivity. These lead to the following construction rules.

1. For an n-star, we decompose the n-star into $\frac{n!}{k!}$ k-stars.

2. To construct an FTBB of size $(M, 1)$, add one spare node S to a k-star, where $M = k!$ and connect S to each of the M nodes in a k-star.

3. For spare nodes S_i and S_j in two different FTBBs, namely $FTBB_i$ and $FTBB_j$, we connect S_i and S_j *iff* there exists at least one primary node P_i in

---

[1]By the term "Star-interconnected" we imply a connectivity between the two nodes following the Star graph connectivity pattern, refer Section ??.

$FTBB_i$ that is connected to at least one primary node P_j in $FTBB_j$.

Figure 2 shows a fault-tolerant 4-star with FTBBs of size (6,1). By Rule 1, the 4-star is decomposed into four 3-stars. By Rule 2, one spare node is added to each 3-star and 6(=3!) links connect the spare node to each of the primary nodes. By Rule 3, the spare nodes are fully connected since there are links between the primary nodes of any pair of the four 3-stars.

3.2 Redundant Links and Nodes

- **Redundant nodes:**

  – Number of redundant nodes at each FTBB$(k!, 1) = 1$

  – Total number of redundant nodes $= \frac{n!}{k!}$.

- **Redundant links:**

  – Number of redundant intra-links at each FTBB$(k!, 1) = k!$

  – Number of redundant inter-links out of each FTBB$(k!, 1) = (n - k)k$.

  – Total number of redundant links for the n-star $= \frac{n!}{k!} \times k! + \frac{n!}{k!} \times \frac{(n-k)k}{2} = n! + \frac{n!}{k!} \times \frac{(n-k)k}{2}$.

3.3 Fault Tolerant Reconfiguration and Routing

We propose a reconfiguration scheme such that when a primary node P in an FTBB fails, it is replaced by a spare node S within that FTBB and its address is inherited by S. Instead of changing the physical connections to preserve physical adjacency, a fault-tolerant routing algorithm, *Algorithm I*, is proposed for the n-star network built from FTBB$(k!, 1)$ modules such that any message destined to P is routed to S. Let us consider a message in the n-star from source node $p = p_1 p_2 \cdots p_n$ to destination node $d = d_1 d_2 \cdots d_n$. Suppose, in the absence of any fault the message requires to traverse the following sequence of dimensions: $e_1, e_2, e_3 \cdots e_{X-1}, e_X$; where $1 \leq X \leq \lfloor \frac{3}{2}(n-1) \rfloor$ and $2 \leq e_i \leq n$. The sequence of dimensions can be partitioned into G groups such that:

- The dimensions in each of the first $G - 1$ groups, namely $e_{t+1}, e_{t+2}, \cdots e_{t+\Delta-1}, e_{t+\Delta}$ where $\Delta \geq 1$ and $0 \leq t \leq X - \Delta$. The e_is have the following characteristics:

- $e_i \in \{2, 3, \cdots, k-1, k\}$ for $t + 1 \leq i \leq t + \Delta - 1$ and $\Delta > 1$, and

- $e_{t+\Delta} \in \{k+1, k+2, \cdots, n-1, n\}$.

In other words, the sequence of dimensions in each of the first $(G - 1)$ groups is either the *intra*-FTBB dimensions (if any) within a specific FTBB followed by an *inter*-FTBB dimension $e_{t+\Delta}$ when $\Delta > 1$, or just an *inter*-FTBB dimension e_{t+1} when $\Delta = 1$. Note that when $\Delta = 1$, it means there is no *intra*-FTBB dimensions needed in a specific FTBB.

The sequence of dimensions in the G-th group is the *intra*-FTBB dimensions needed to reach the destination d. Let the FTBB which contains the destination node be termed as $FTBB_d$. However, the number of dimensions in the $G - th$ group may be zero, i.e. no *intra* $- FTBB$ dimensions are needed in the destination's $FTBB$.

Specifically, *Algorithm I*, has three phases as formalized next.

- Phase 1: If the message is currently at some node x in FTBB F_x, where $F_x \neq F_d$, then send the message to the node x_1 via *intra*-FTBB dimensions $e_{t+1}, e_{t+2}, \cdots e_{t+\Delta-1}$ such that node x_1 is adjacent to node y in another FTBB across dimension $e_{t+\Delta}$.

- Phase 2: Send the message from node x_1 to node y via the *inter*-FTBB dimension j where $j = e_t + \delta$. If node y is a spare node without the inheritance of the address of node $ADJ_j(x_1)$, i.e., $y \neq ADJ_j(x_1)$, then send the message from node y to node $ADJ_j(x_1)$ via the redundant link between them.

  If FTBB of the node $y \neq$ FTBB of the node d, then goto Phase 1.

- Phase 3: Route the message to node d within FTBB of F_d by the sequence of the *intra* $- FTBB$ dimensions in the $G - th$ group.

Theorem 1 *Algorithm I can always route messages from any source to any destination in a functional fault-tolerant n-star networks built from $FTBB(k!, 1)$.*

Theorem 2 *The fault tolerant star networks constructed from FTBBs of size $(k!, 1)$ can tolerate x node failures, where $1 \leq x \leq \frac{n!}{k!}$, as long as each FTBB contains no more than one fault.*

4   Fault Tolerance Analysis

In this section, we measure the overhead of spare nodes/links, and system reliability of different sizes of fault tolerant star networks constructed from different sizes of fault tolerant building blocks. We use the probability of continuous operation, namely *survival rate* as the measurement for system reliability.

1. Overhead ratio of redundant nodes = $\frac{n!/k!}{n!} = \frac{1}{k!}$

2. Overhead ratio of redundant links = $\frac{\frac{(n!/k!)*(n-k)k}{2}+n!}{n!*(n-1)/2} = \frac{n-k}{(n-1)(k-1)!} + \frac{2}{n-1}$

3. Survival rate = $\prod_{i=1}^{x} \frac{N-(i-1)(k!+1)}{N-(i-1)}$, where $N = n! + n!/k!$ and $1 \leq x \leq n!/k!$.

Figure 3 shows the relative overheads in the number of nodes and number of links in the n-star when using FTBB$(k!, 1)$ modules. Figure 4 shows the survival probabilities for different (n, k) value pairs. We make the following observations from these plots.

- The overhead ratio for redundant nodes is independent of n, The overhead ratio decreases rapidly with increasing k, and is negligible beyond $k = 4$ or so.

- The overhead ratio for redundant links is independent of n and it decreases with increasing k. The decline is sharper when k is small, and the link-overhead eventually approaches a constant.

- For a larger n, the link-overhead is smaller for a given k. This implies that for a fixed size of FTBB, the link-overhead ratio is lower if the star size is larger.

- The survival probability increases with decreasing k. This is expected since the lower the k is, the higher the fault coverage the design would be. Likewise, with increasing number of failures the survival probability decreases.

References

[1] S.B. Akers, D. Harel, and B. Krishnamurthy, "The Star Graph: An Attractive Alternative to the n-cube" *Proc. International Conference on Parallel Processing*, 1987, pp. 393-400.

[2] M. Sultan Alam and Rami G. Melhem, "An Efecient Modular Spare Allocation Scheme and Its Application to Fault Tolerant Binary Hypercubes" *IEEE Trans. on Computers*, Vol. 2, No. 1, January 1991, pp117-126.

[3] K. Day and A. Tripathi, "A Comparative study of topological properties of hypercubes and star graphs" *IEEE Trans. Parallel and Distributed Systems*", to appear.

[4] C. Liang, S. Bhattacharya and J. Tan, "Performance Evaluation of Fault-Tolerant Routing on Star Networks" *Proc. of Scalable High-Performance Computing Conference*", pp. 650-657, May 23-25, 1994.

[5] C. Liang, S. Bhattacharya and W. T. Tsai, "Distributed Fault-Tolerance Routing on Hypercubes: Algorithms and Performance Study" *Proc. of 3rd IEEE Symposium on Parallel and Distributed Processing*", pp. 474-481, Dec 1991.

[6] A. S. M. Hassan and V. K. Agrawal, "A fault-tolerant modular architecture for binary trees" *IEEE Trans. on Computers*, Vol. C-35, No. 4, April 1986, pp. 356-361.

[7] C. Liang, S. Bhattacharya, J. Tan, "Design and Analysis of A Fault-Tolerant Modular Architecture for Star Networks", IBM Technical Report, TR 00.3761, 1995.

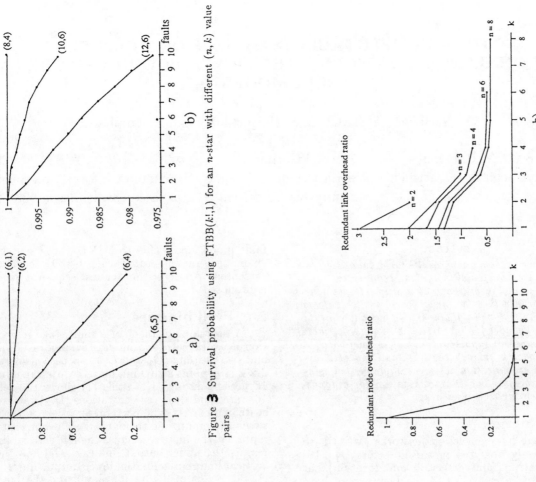

Figure **3** Survival probability using FTBB($k!,1$) for an n-star with different (n,k) value pairs.

Figure **4** Overhead using FTBB($k!,1$) in an n-star: a) node overhead ratio, b) link overhead ratio.

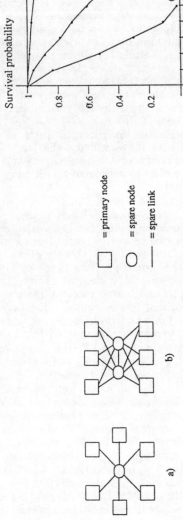

= primary node
= spare node
= spare link

Figure 1: Fault-tolerant Building Block (FTBB) Illustrations: a) FTBB(6,1), b) FTBB(6,2).

Figure 2: Fault-tolerant Star network illustrations, with $n = 4$ and FTBB($3!, 1$).

ON THE MULTIPLE FAULT DIAGNOSIS OF MULTISTAGE INTERCONNECTION NETWORKS: THE LOWER BOUND AND THE CMOS FAULT MODEL *

Y.-N. Shen[+], X.-T. Chen, S. Horiguchi[++] and F. Lombardi

Texas A&M University	[+] Actel Corporation	[++] JAIST
Computer Science Department	955 East Arques Avenue	School of Information Science
College Station, TX 77843	Sunnyvale CA 94086	Tasunokuchi, Ishikawa 923-12, JP

Abstract

This paper presents new results for diagnosing (detection and location) multistage interconnection networks (MINs) in the presence of multiple faults. Initially, it is proved that the lower bound in the number of tests for multiple fault diagnosis (independent of the assumed fault model for the MIN) is $2 \times \log_2 N$, where N is the number of inputs/outputs of the network. A new fault model is introduced; this fault model is applicable to interconnection networks implemented using CMOS technology. The characterization for diagnosing stuck-open faults is presented.

1 Introduction.

Multistage interconnection networks (MIN) have been extensively analyzed in the literature [1]. Diagnosis of MINs (fault detection and location) has been analyzed extensively [1,4,7]. Few papers have addressed fault diagnosis of multistage interconnection networks under multiple faults [1,4,7,8]. In [1], it has been proved that $2(1+\log_2 N)$ tests (Figure (1) shows a MIN for $N=16$) may detect in most cases multiple faults under an unrestricted combinatorial fault model for the switching elements and a stuck-at model for the links. [7] has presented an algorithm for multiple fault diagnosis in interconnection networks made of baseline switching elements. This approach requires the execution of two phases, each made of $1+\log_2 N$ tests. However, previous approaches are based on a fully combinatorial functional fault model in which each faulty switching elements is analyzed based on the responses at its outputs (and hence, by applying the stuck-at fault model) and its switching modes [1,4,7]. These approaches are independent of the technology used in manufacturing the switching element and the MIN. However, current technology (such as CMOS) shows faulty modes and behavior (such as stuck-open faults) which have not been analyzed in previous papers [1,7].

The objective of this paper is to present novel results for diagnosis in the presence of multiple faults. Initially, the lower bound on the number of tests for multiple fault diagnosis is proved. Then, a new

---

*This research is supported in part by TARP and the Japan Ministry of Culture and Educ.. Contact: tel (409) 845-5464; Email lombardi@cs.tamu.edu.

fault model applicable to MINs, whose switching elements are manufactured using CMOS technology, is presented. An algorithm for test sequence generation is proposed.

2 Preliminaries.

A switching element of a multistage interconnection network with two inputs (denoted as I_1 and I_2) and two outputs (O_1 and O_2) can be considered as a 2×2 crosspoint switching matrix with a maximum of 16 possible states [1]. Table (1) shows the set of all 16 states and their representations [1]. The crosspoint switching matrix symbols represent the connection between the inputs and the outputs. The horizontal lines represent the inputs, whereas the left vertical line represents the upper output link (i.e. O_1) and the right vertical line represents the lower output link (i.e. O_2) [1]. It is assumed that for simplicity, the fanin (the number of input links of a switching element) and the fanout (the number of output links of a switching element) are both equal to 2.

The valid states of a baseline switching element in a MINs are S_5 and S_{10}, i.e. $SW=S_5$ or S_{10}. The fault model of [1] assumes that a faulty switching element can be in any one of the 16 states from a given valid state. In the fault model of [1], only permanent faults are considered; there are two types of faults: link-stuck fault and switching element fault. There are four cases for the switching element fault: one-response fault, separated two response fault, nonseparated two response fault and multiple response fault. Two types of test vectors are permitted [1]. These are denoted as t (of value 01) and t' (the complement value of t). The logically erroneous output and the logically unidentified output are denoted as "#" and "-" respectively. In each faulty switching element, an input (or output) line must be connected to at least one output (or input) line. Else, *separation* is said to occur. Hence, the incorrect states of faulty switching elements are given by S_7, S_{11}, S_{13}, S_{14} and S_{15}.

The following assumptions are applicable in the analysis presented in the next sections. 1. It is assumed that link failures can be collapsed to the switching elements directly connected to it. 2. Valid faulty (permanent) values appear at the outputs of the faulty switching elements (as permitted in the assumed fault

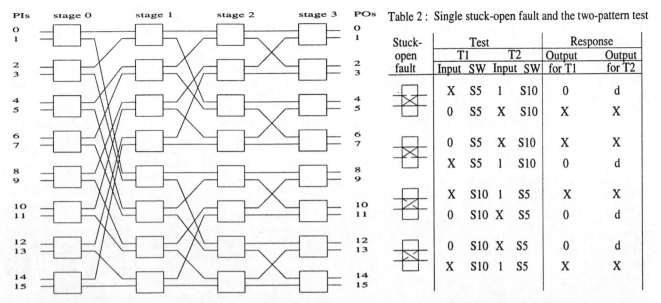

Figure 1: Multistage Interconnection Network (for N=16)

Table 2 : Single stuck-open fault and the two-pattern test

Stuck-open fault	Test				Response	
	T1		T2		Output for T1	Output for T2
	Input	SW	Input	SW		
	X	S5	1	S10	0	d
	0	S5	X	S10	X	X
	0	S5	X	S10	X	X
	X	S5	1	S10	0	d
	X	S10	1	S5	X	X
	0	S10	X	S5	0	d
	0	S10	X	S5	0	d
	X	S10	1	S5	X	X

Table 1 : Modes of a Switching Element

State Name	S0	S1	S2	S3
Switch elem. symb.				
State Name	S4	S5	S6	S7
Switch elem. symb.				
State Name	S8	S9	S10	S11
Switch elem. symb.				
State Name	S12	S13	S14	S15
Switch elem. symb.				

Table 3 : Responses for the Tests

SW S5S10S5 Set	IN	reponse for fault-free switch	response for stuck-at fault			
Tb0	000	000	000	000	000	000
	000	000	000	000	000	000
Tb1	000	101	1u1	101	101	10d
	111	010	010	0d0	01u	010
Tb2	111	101	1d0	010	010	01u
	000	101	101	1u1	10d	101
Tb3	111	111	111	111	111	111
	111	111	111	111	111	111
Tb4	010	010	0d0	010	010	01u
	010	010	010	0d0	01u	010
Tb5	101	101	1u1	101	101	10d
	101	101	101	1u1	10d	101

model) for faults to be diagnosed. 3. Multiple faults can be present in a switching element as well as in the MIN.

3 The Lower Bound For Multiple Fault Diagnosis.

Prior to presenting the proposed approach to determine the lower bound on the number of tests for multiple fault diagnosis, some definitions must be introduced. The *string* of an input (output) line is defined as the series of the 0 or 1 states which appear at that line for a given test sequence. For example, if the states of the third primary output line of a MIN are 010 under a given test sequence, then 010 is referred to as a string. The sets of strings for all inputs (or

outputs) of the MIN is referred to as the *pattern* of inputs (or outputs).

The following Theorem establishes the lower bound for fault diagnosis (detection and location) of a MIN under multiple faults.

Theorem 1. The lower bound for the length of the test sequence for multiple fault diagnosis of a MIN with N inputs, is $2 \times k$ where $k = \log_2 N$.

Proof: The proposed approach consists of proving the existence of at least two different faulty machines (corresponding to the MINs), such that they have the same outputs for any test sequence of length k-1. This is equivalent to the following statement: given an arbitrary test sequence of length k-1 and a faulty machine, it is always possible to design another machine such that it produces the same pattern as the original faulty machine. For sake of simplicity, let the faulty model be limited to multiple stuck-at-S_5 faults. Then, if it

351

is possible to prove that a test sequence of length k-1 is not sufficient to diagnosis this machine, then this sequence is also not sufficient in the general case. Assume that there is a test sequence of length k-1, then the number of strings for each primary input and output of the MIN under any possible test sequence is at most $2^{\log_2 N-1}=\frac{N}{2}$. Given a faulty machine, then there exist at least two outputs for any test sequence such that these outputs have the same output string (because the number of outputs is N). The primary outputs with this property can be then selected; let these outputs be O_i and O_j and their string be C. Attach (or concatenate) a $0(1)$ to O_i (O_j), i.e. the strings of O_i and O_j are 0 & C and 1 & C, respectively (where & indicates concatenation and C is the original string). Also, attach all 0's (or 1's) to all other outputs. After this process is completed, the number of strings is no more than $2^{k+1}+1<N$. As two primary inputs I_{i1} and I_{i2} can be connected to two primary outputs O_i and O_j in the faulty machine, then add one bit to the original test sequence to make the output pattern the same as the previous case (this output pattern is just a permutation of the input pattern and the number of strings is less than N). Then, swap the attached bits to O_i and O_j, i.e. the strings of O_i and O_j are 1 & C and 0 & C' respectively, while not changing the strings of the other outputs (the output pattern is just another permutation of the input pattern). By [1,7], it is possible to find another arrangement of switching modes for the switching elements of the MIN (i.e. another machine) which can implement this permutation. However, if only the last k-1 bits of the output pattern are considered, then the two faulty machines are indistinguishable. The two faults cannot be distinguished by a test sequence of length k-1, i.e. no fault diagnosis is possible. This implies that k is the lower bound for stuck-at-S_5. This process is also applicable to stuck-at-S_{10} (by symmetry of the MIN). Therefore, the length of the test sequence which corresponds to the lower bound, is $2\times k$.

4   The CMOS Fault Model.

CMOS has unique properties which distinguish this technology from others. It has been proved that the traditional stuck-at fault model is inadequate for CMOS circuits [2]. For CMOS technology, two new types of fault are possible [2,3]: 1. Stuck-open. 2. Stuck-on. The combinatorial switching fault model (consisting of 16 different modes) can be thought as equivalent to a stuck-at-0(1) fault on the control lines of the switching element. This model is therefore not applicable to CMOS and a new diagnosis approach must be formulated.

Consider initially the stuck-on fault. It is easy to prove that a stuck-on fault is equivalent to a stuck-at-S_i (i=5 or 10 for a baseline switching element) and can be diagnosed using previous approaches [1,7]. Table (2) shows the faulty behavior due to a single stuck-open fault in a switching element. The faulty behavior of this element can be analyzed as follows: let the switching mode be given by S_5 and the input signal (referred to as state) at its input line I_2 be 0. The stuck-open fault affects the switching element only

when it is in S_{10}; hence, no faulty output appears at the output O_1 for an input of 0. If the switching mode is changed to S_{10} and a 1 is applied to I_1, then O_1 is 1 (as in the fault free case). In this case, the stuck-open fault isolates the connection between I_1 and O_1 in the switching element and the charge in the capacitor of the output line remains as in the previous state [3,5]. As for CMOS circuits [5,6], a stuck-open fault is detected by a two-pattern test $<T_1,T_2>$ where T_1 is referred to as the initializing input and T_2 is referred to as the test input. All single stuck-open faults in a switching element of a MIN and the two-pattern tests for detecting them are shown also in Table (2). The entries of this table are defined as follows: 1. d represents the condition (10), i.e. the output is 1 under fault free conditions and 0 in the faulty case. 2. u represents the condition (01), i.e. the output is 0 under fault free conditions and 1 in the faulty case. 3. A "1" or a "0" in this table represent the (11) or (00) condition, respectively, i.e. the output is 1 (or 0) in both the fault free and faulty cases. 4. x (corresponding to an undetermined value) represents the condition (xx), i.e. the output is x in both the fault free and faulty cases. Among these five states (d, u, 1, 0 and x) for each input/output line, a fault is detected if either u or d appears at the output of a switching element and it can be propagated and observed at the primary outputs of the MIN.

A new test set referred to as the *basic input set*, is proposed for diagnosing stuck-open faults. The basic input set can be defined as $T=\{T_{b0},\,T_{b1},\,T_{b2},\,T_{b3}\}$; each T_{bi} is a two-pattern test $T_{bi}=(T_1,\,T_2)$ where every T_j is applied to the I_j of a switching element and consists of three consecutive vectors, i.e. $T_j=t_{j1}t_{j2}t_{j3}$ for j=1,2. T is therefore given by $T_{b0} = (000, 000)$, $T_{b1} = (000, 111)$, $T_{b2} = (111, 000)$, $T_{b3} = (111, 111)$. T can be used to detect the four different single stuck-open faults, as shown in Table (2). The responses for the basic test set are shown in Table (3); from Table (2), T_{b1} and T_{b2} detect the four single stuck-open faults, while T_{b0} and T_{b3} hide all four single stuck-open faults.

5   Multiple Fault Diagnosis under the CMOS Fault Model.

The algorithm for test sequence generation is as follows (MOD(x) stands for the modulus operation over x).

Algorithm 1: Test Sequence Generation.
```
BEGIN
FOR i= 1 TO k-1 DO /* k=log₂N */
BEGIN
/* TSᵢ₋₁ */
put the elements in switching mode S₅
FOR j=1 TO N DO
input[j,3×i-3]=jMOD(2^(k-i));
put the elements in switching mode S₁₀
FOR j=1 to N DO
input[j,3×-2]=1-(jMOD(2^(k-i)));
put the elements in switching mode S₅
FOR j=1 TO N DO
input[j,3×i-1]=iMOD(2^(k-i));
END
```

END

As an example, consider a MIN with $N=16$; in this case, Table (4) shows the test sequence generated using Algorithm (1). Four test sets (denoted to as TS_i for $i=0,1,2,3$) are generated. Note that all test vectors in each TS_i are the same and the first and third (second) test vectors have S_5 (S_{10}) as switching mode.

Table 4:

Test Set	Switching Mode	Test Vector
TS_0	S_5	0000000011111111
TS_0	S_{10}	0000000011111111
TS_0	S_5	0000000011111111
TS_1	S_5	0000111100001111
TS_1	S_{10}	0000111100001111
TS_1	S_5	0000111100001111
TS_2	S_5	0011001100110011
TS_2	S_{10}	0011001100110011
TS_2	S_5	0011001100110011
TS_3	S_5	0101010101010101
TS_3	S_{10}	0101010101010101
TS_3	S_5	0101010101010101

Multiple fault diagnosis under the CMOS fault model presented in the previous section, follows the same process as in [7]. The process of fault location in particular, is similar to [7] because it exploits the property of the basic input set by testing one stage at a time. As an example consider a generalized cube MIN with $N=16$ and the test sets of Table (4). Stuck-open faults in stages 0, 1 and 2 are hidden and only the faults in stage 3 are directly observable through the primary outputs of the MIN. Therefore, the faults in the switching elements of stage 3 can be detected by applying ST_0. If faults are detected (at least a d or u appears at the primary outputs), the faults can be promptly located in at least one switching element in stage 3. Similarly ST_1, ST_2 and ST_3 can locate faults in the switching elements at stages 2, 1, 0 respectively.

The following definitions can be introduced. The *control path* is defined as the path along which a signal (in this case a test) can propagate from a primary input of the MIN to the designated input of the switching element in the stage under test. The *observation path* is defined as the path along which the response of each of the outputs of a switching element in the stage under test can be propagated to a primary output.

As proved in [7], there is no problem in locating a single stuck-open fault. For multiple faults, the so-called *fault masking problem* may arise. This occurs when the fault is located either directly before the switching element under test (thus blocking the control path), or just after the switching element under test to block the observation path. Note that usually fault masking depends on the choice of tests.

Consider the case of multiple stuck-open faults within a switching element. Two cases are possible in a switching element: 1. There is no path which connects an output to an input. 2. The output has still at least one path which is connected to an input

for either S_5 or S_{10}. The following Lemma gives the conditions for fault masking for stuck-open faults.

Lemma 1. If the inputs of a switching element in a (generalized cube) MIN are given by T_{b0} (T_{b3}) then the outputs of this element are always given by T_{b0} (T_{b3}) regardless of the number of stuck-open faults, i.e. unaltered propagation of T_{b0} (T_{b3}) is always possible, independently of the status of the switching element.

A further test set can be defined. This test set consists of two elements for accomplishing multiple fault location in a MIN. This set denoted as T', consists of $T_{b4}=(010,010)$ and $T_{b5}=(101,101)$, where T_{b4} and T_{b5} are defined in a similar manner as the elements of T.

Lemma 2. Let the inputs of a switching element be given by T_{b4} (T_{b5}). If d or u appears at one of the inputs, then d or u will appear in at least one of the outputs, regardless of any stuck-open faults in the element.

The following Theorems establish the conditions for multiple fault diagnosis in a generalized cube MIN.

Theorem 2. The test sequence generated by Algorithm (1) diagnose all multiple stuck-open in faulty switching elements of a generalized cube MIN, i.e. no masking occurs.

Theorem 3. Multiple fault diagnosis of a MIN with baseline switching elements arranged in $\log_2 N$ stages, can be accomplished under the CMOS model using $6 \times \log_2 N$ tests.

6. References.

[1] Wu, C. and T. Feng, "Fault Diagnosis for a Class of Multistage Interconnection Networks," *IEEE Trans. on Comput.*, Vol. C30, No. 10, pp. 743-758, 1981.

[2] Wadsack, R.L., "Fault Modeling and Logic Simulation of CMOS and MOS Integrated Circuits," *Bell Syst. Tech.J.*, Vol. 57, No. 2, pp 1449-1474, 1978.

[3] Mc Cluskey, E.J., "Logic Design Principles: With Emphasis on Testable Semicustoms Circuits," Prentice-Hall, Englewood Cliffs, N.J., 1986.

[4] Lombardi, F. and W-K. Huang, "On The Constant Diagnosability of Baseline Interconnection Networks," *IEEE Trans. on Comput.* Vol. C39, No. 12, pp. 1485-1488, 1990.

[5] Reddy, S.M. and M.K. Reddy, "Testable Realization for FET Stuck-Open Faults in CMOS Combinational Logic Circuits," *IEEE Trans. on Comp.*, Vol. C35, No. 8, pp. 742-754, 1986.

[6] Chandramouli, R., "On Testing Stuck-Open Faults," *Proc. IEEE FTCS*, pp. 258-265, 1983.

[7] Feng, C., F. Lombardi and W.-K. Huang, "Detection and Location of Multiple Faults in Baseline Interconnection Networks," *IEEE Transactions on Computers*, Vol. C41, No. 10, pp. 1340-1344, 1992.

[8] Park, N., F. Lombardi and S. Horiguchi, "On the Multiple Bridge Fault Diagnosis of Baseline MINs," *Trans. on Inf. and Syst. of the Inst. of Elect and Comp. Eng. of Japan*, Vol. E79D, No. 8, pp. 1151-1162, 1996.

Panel 2

In Search of the "Killer Application"

Moderator and Organizer

M.T. O'Keefe
University of Minnesota

Panel 3

Of Languages and Libraries

Moderator and Organizer

David Padua
University of Illinois

Session 6A

Load Balancing

Adaptive Load-Balancing Algorithms using Symmetric Broadcast Networks: Performance Study on an IBM SP2

Sajal K. Das and Daniel J. Harvey

Department of Computer Sciences
University of North Texas
P.O. Box 13886
Denton, TX 76203-6886
E-mail:{das,harvey}@cs.unt.edu

Rupak Biswas

MRJ Technology Solutions
NASA Ames Research Center
Mail Stop T27A-1
Moffett Field, CA 94035-1000
E-mail: rbiswas@nas.nasa.gov

Abstract

In a distributed-computing environment, it is important to ensure that the processor workloads are adequately balanced. Among numerous load-balancing algorithms, a unique approach due to Das and Prasad defines a symmetric broadcast network (SBN) that provides a robust communication pattern among the processors in a topology-independent manner. In this paper, we propose and analyze three SBN-based load-balancing algorithms, and implement them on an SP2. A thorough experimental study with Poisson-distributed synthetic loads demonstrates that these algorithms are very effective in balancing system load while minimizing processor idle time. They also compare favorably with several existing techniques.

1 Introduction

To maximize the performance of a multicomputer system, it is essential to evenly distribute the load among the processors. In other words, it is desirable to prevent, if possible, the condition where one node is overloaded with a backlog of jobs while another processor is lightly loaded or idle. The load-balancing problem is closely related to scheduling and resource allocation, and can be static or dynamic. A *static* allocation [12] relates to decisions made at compile time, and compile-time programming tools are necessary to adequately estimate the required resources. On the other hand, *dynamic* algorithms [1, 5] allocate/reallocate resources at run time based on a set of system parameters that are maintained. Determining these parameters and how to broadcast them are important considerations.

In this paper, we consider general-purpose distributed memory parallel computers where processors (or nodes) are connected by a point-to-point network topology and the nodes communicate with one another using message passing. Responsibility for load balancing is decentralized, and processor workload is determined by the length of the local job queue of a node. The network is assumed to be homogeneous and any job can be processed by any node. However, jobs cannot be rerouted once execution begins.

Das et al. [3, 4] have suggested a different approach to load balancing, by introducing a logical topology-independent communication pattern called a *symmetric broadcast network* (SBN). We refine this approach and propose three novel and efficient load-balancing algorithms, one of which is adapted for use on a hypercube architecture. Based on [13], our SBN-based algorithms can be classified as:

Adaptive: performance adapts to the system load;
Symmetric: senders and receivers initiate balancing;
Stable: excessive balancing traffic is avoided;
Effective: balancing does not degrade performance.

The three algorithms proposed in this paper have been implemented on an IBM SP2 using the Message-Passing Interface (MPI). Performance of the SBN algorithms are analyzed by an extensive set of experiments with Poisson-distributed synthetic loads. The results are compared with other existing techniques such as Random [5], Gradient [9], Sender Initiated [6], Receiver Initiated [6], and Adaptive Contracting [6]. Our experiments demonstrate that a superior quality of load balancing is achieved by the SBN approach with respect to such metrics as the total jobs transferred, total completion time, message traffic per node, and maximum variance in node idle time. Additional experiments where the SBN-based load balancing is applied to dynamic mesh adaptation problems using actual load data further confirm these conclusions [2].

This paper is organized as follows. Section 2 reviews a few existing approaches for load balancing that will be used for comparison purposes. Section 3 defines symmetric broadcast networks. Section 4 discusses general characteristics common to all of the proposed algorithms. Section 5 presents three SBN-based load-balancing schemes while Section 6 summarizes the experimental results, comparing SBN algorithms to other load-balancing techniques. The final section concludes the paper.

2 Previous Work

Among various approaches for comparing load-balancing algorithms, three categories of analysis predominate: (a) mathematical modeling, (b) solving well-known problems in a multiprocessor environment, and (c) simulation. For example, in [11], the probability of load-balancing success is computed analytically. In [7], several load-balancing methods are compared by implementing Fibonacci number generation, the N-Queens problem, and the 15-puzzle on a network; whereas the simulation approach has been employed in [8].

In this paper we perform experiments on an IBM SP2 multiprocessor, using the simulation approach with synthetically-generated random loads according to Poisson distributions. A mathematical analysis of the alorithms and results of additional experiments that utilize actual load data from a dynamic mesh application are reported in [2].

In general, load-balancing algorithms are very susceptible to the choice of system thresholds [10]. We have also noticed that proper selection of threshold values optimizes the proposed SBN-based algorithms. The following load-balancing algorithms will be compared with ours.

Random [5]: Jobs are randomly distributed among processors (or nodes) as they are generated. Once a job originating at a node is received by another node, it is processed.

Gradient [9]: Jobs migrate from overloaded to lightly-loaded nodes. This is accomplished by a maintaining a gradient at all nodes of the network. The gradient specifies the distance of the nearest lightly-loaded node through each neighbor. This requires frequent broadcasts between neighboring nodes.

Receiver initiated [6]: Load balancing is triggered by a lightly-loaded node. If the load value of a node falls below the system threshold, it broadcasts a job request message to its neighbors. The node's job queue length is "piggy backed" to the request message. To prevent instability in light system load conditions, a node waits one second before initiating additional requests.

Sender initiated [6]: Messages are directed to lightly-loaded neighbors from overloaded nodes. To prevent instability under heavy system loads, nodes exchange load information with their neighbors when local job queue sizes are halved or doubled.

Adaptive contracting [6]: When jobs are generated, the originating node distributes bids to its neighbor nodes in parallel. The neighbors in turn respond with a message containing the number of jobs in their respective local queues. The originating node then appropriately distributes jobs to its neighbors.

3 Preliminaries on SBN

A *symmetric broadcast network* (SBN) defines a communication pattern (logical or physical) among the P processors in a multicomputer system [3, 4]. An SBN of dimension $d \geq 0$, denoted as SBN(d), is a $d + 1$-stage interconnection network with $P = 2^d$ processors in each stage. It is constructed recursively as follows:

- A single node forms the basis network SBN(0).
- For $d > 0$, an SBN(d) is obtained from a pair of SBN($d - 1$)s by adding a communication stage in the front and additional interprocessor connections as follows:

  (a) Node i in stage 0 is connected to node $j = (i + P/2) \bmod P$ in stage 1; and

  (b) Node j in stage 1 is connected to the node in stage 2, that was the stage 0 successor of node i in SBN($d - 1$).

An example of how an SBN(2) is formed from two SBN(1)s is shown in Fig. 1. The SBN approach defines unique communication patterns among the nodes in the network. For any source node at stage 0, there are $\log P$ stages of communication with each node appearing exactly once. The successors and predecessors of a node are uniquely defined by the message originating node and the communication stage.

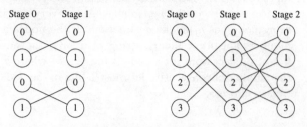

Figure 1: Construction of SBN(2) from two SBN(1)s

As an example, consider the two communication patterns for SBN(3) shown in Fig. 2. The paths in Fig. 2(a) are used to route messages originating from node 0, while those in Fig. 2(b) are for messages originating from node 5. Now if n_5^s denotes a node at

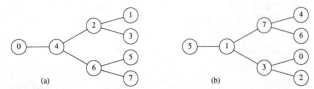

Figure 2: SBN communication patterns in SBN(3)

stage s in Fig. 2(b) and n_0^s is the corresponding node in Fig. 2(a), then $n_5^s = n_0^s \oplus 5$, where $\oplus$ is the exclusive-OR operator. In general, if n_x^s is the corresponding node in the communication pattern for messages originating from source node x, then $n_x^s = n_0^s \oplus x$. Thus, all SBN communication patterns can be derived from the template with node 0 as the root. The predecessor and two successors to n_0^s can be computed as follows:

Predecessor $= (n_0^s - 2^{d-s}) \vee 2^{d-s+1}$,

where $\vee$ is the inclusive-OR operator.

Successor_1 $= n_0^s + 2^{d-s-1}$ for $0 \leq s < d$,

Successor_2 $= n_0^s - 2^{d-s-1}$ for $1 \leq s < d$.

Figure 2 illustrates two possible SBN communication patterns, but many others can easily be derived based on network topology and application requirements.

For example, a *modified binomial spanning tree*, which is two binomial trees connected back to back, can be obtained. Figure 3 shows such a communication pattern for a 16-node SBN network which routes messages from node 0. The solid lines represent the actual SBN pattern, whereas the dashed lines are used to gather load-balancing messages at the destination node 15.

The modified binomial spanning tree is particularly suitable for adapting an SBN-based algorithm to the hypercube architecture. It ensures that all successor and predecessor nodes at any communication stage are adjacent nodes in the hypercube. Also, every originating node has a unique destination. If the nodes are numbered using a binary string of d bits, the number of predecessors for a node is max $\{1, b\}$ where b is the number of consecutive leftmost 1-bits in the node's binary address.

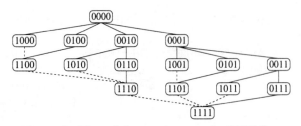

Figure 3: Binomial spanning tree in SBN(4)

4 Load Balancing Characteristics
4.1 System Thresholds

All SBN-based load-balancing algorithms adapt their behavior to the system load. Under heavy (light) loads, the balancing activity is primarily initiated by processors that are lightly (heavily) loaded. This activity is controlled by two system thresholds, MinTh and MaxTh, which are respectively the minimum and maximum system load levels. The system load level, SysLL, is the average number of jobs queued per processor. If a processor has a queue length, QLen, below MinTh, a message is initiated to balance load. If QLen > MaxTh, extra jobs are distributed through the network. If this distribution overloads other processors, load balancing is triggered.

Algorithm behavior is affected by the values chosen for MinTh and MaxTh. For instance, MinTh must be large enough to receive sufficient jobs can be received before a lightly-loaded processor becomes idle. However, the value should not be so large as to initiate unnecessary load balancing. If MaxTh is too small, it will cause an excessive number of job distributions. If it is too large, jobs will not be adequately distributed under light system loads. Moreover, once there is sufficient load on the network, very little load-balancing activity should be required.

4.2 Message Communication

Two types of messages are processed by the SBN approach. The first type is the balancing message which is sent through the network to indicate unbalanced system load. These messages are originated from an unbalanced node and then routed through the SBN. As these balancing messages pass through the network, the cumulative total of queued jobs is computed to obtain SysLL. The second message type for job distribution is used for three purposes. First, they are used to route the SysLL through the network. Each node, upon receipt of such a message, updates its local values for MinTh, MaxTh, and SysLL. Second, job distribution messages are used to pass excess jobs from one node to another. This action can occur whenever a node has more jobs than its MaxTh. Third, jobs can be distributed when a node responds to another node's need for jobs. This need is embedded in both load-balance messages and distribution messages. To reduce message traffic, a node does not initiate additional load-balancing activity until all previous balancing-related messages that have passed through the node have been completely processed.

4.3 Common Procedures

All of our SBN-based load-balancing algorithms consist of four key procedures. The first two, *Get-*

Distribute and *GetBalance*, are used to respectively process distribution and balance messages that are received. Similarly, the procedures, *Distribute* and *Balance*, respectively route distribution and balance messages to the SBN successor nodes. Details of these procedures depend on the particular load-balancing algorithm used. Figure 4 presents the pseudo code that is common to all of the SBN based load-balancing algorithms.

Procedure *Main Line Processing*
Repeat forever
  Call *GetBalance* to receive load-balance messages
  Call *GetDistribute* to receive distribution messages
  If (QLen > MaxTh)
    Call *Distribute* to send excess jobs through SBN
  If (QLen < MinTh)
    Call *Balance* to initiate load-balancing operation
    Call *UpdateLoad*(TotalJobsQueued) to set SysLL
  Normal Processing
End Repeat

Procedure *UpdateLoad*(LoadLevelEstimate)
  SysLL = $\lceil$LoadLevelEstimate$/P\rceil$
  MaxTh = SysLL + $2^{\lfloor \text{SysLL}/\text{ConstantValue} \rfloor}$
  If (SysLL $\geq$ ConstantValue)
    MinTh = ConstantValue
  else
    MinTh = SysLL -1
Return

Figure 4: Pseudo code for all SBN algorithms

5 Proposed algorithms
5.1 Standard SBN Algorithm

In the standard SBN algorithm, load-balancing messages are routed through the SBN from the source to the processors at the last stage. Load-balance messages are then routed back towards the original source so the total number of jobs in the system can be computed. The originating node thus has an accurate value of SysLL. Distribution messages are then sent to all nodes along with SysLL. All nodes update their local SysLL, MinTh, and MaxTh. Excess jobs are routed as part of this distribution to balance the system load. In addition, if a processor has QLen < SysLL, the need for jobs is indicated during the distribution process. Successor nodes respond by routing back an appropriate number of excess jobs. Figure 5 provides pseudo code of the standard SBN algorithm.

For illustration, consider SBN(3) in Fig. 6(a) which depicts the id and QLen for each node. For example, node 6 has three jobs queued for processing, indicated as $Q3$. The initial values of the SysLL, MinTh,

Procedure *GetBalance*
While there are balance messages to receive
  Route needed jobs to predecessor node if possible
  If balancing messages are to be gathered, **Break**
  If this is the final SBN stage
    Route distribution and SysLL to originator node
  If this is the originator of the load balancing
    Decrement number of active balance operations
    Call *UpdateLoad*(TotalJobsQueued)
    Distribute excess jobs and SysLL through SBN
  else
    Increment load-balancing operations in process
    Route the balance message to the next SBN stage
End While
Return

Procedure *GetDistribute*
While there are distribution messages to receive
  Enqueue any jobs received
  If predecessor node needs jobs, route excess jobs
  If load balancing is complete
    Decrement number of active balancing operations
    Call *UpdateLoad*(TotalJobsQueued)
  If this message completes a distribution
    If (QLen > MaxTh)
      Trigger load balancing
  else
    Call *Distribute* to route excess jobs through SBN
end While
Return

Procedure *Balance*
If this is the final stage, **Return**
If this is a new balance operation
  If load balancing is in process, **Return**
  Increment number of active balance operations
  Compute number of distribution messages expected
Compute number of jobs needed
Route the balance message to the next SBN stage
Return

Procedure *Distribute*
If this is the final SBN stage, **Return**
If a normal distribution and load balancing is active
  Inhibit the distribution and **Return**
Compute number of excess jobs and jobs needed
Dequeue the jobs to be distributed
Distribute jobs and forward SysLL data to successors
Return

Figure 5: Standard SBN algorithm pseudo code

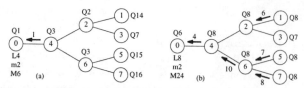

Figure 6: Standard SBN algorithm load-balancing

and `MaxTh` at node 0 are 4, 2, and 6, respectively (indicated as $L4$, $m2$, and $M6$). After a load-balancing request is sent through the SBN and then routed back to node 0, these values are updated as 8, 2, and 24, respectively, using:

$$\texttt{SysLL} = \lceil \texttt{TotalJobsQueued} / P \rceil$$
$$\texttt{MinTh} = \min\{\texttt{ConstantParameter}, \texttt{SysLL} - 1\}$$
$$\texttt{MaxTh} = \texttt{SysLL} + 2^{\lfloor \texttt{SysLL/ConstantParameter} \rfloor}$$

Note that when the balancing is initiated, node 4 distributes half of its `QLen` jobs, i.e. $\lfloor 3/2 \rfloor$, back to node 0 which had a need for jobs. This distribution is shown by a label on the arrow in Fig. 6(a).

Distribution messages are then used to route excess jobs to the successor nodes or to indicate a need for jobs if the local `QLen` is less than `SysLL`. Jobs are routed back to the predecessors when appropriate. Figure 6(b) shows the result of this distribution. The arrows indicate the number of jobs routed between nodes.

To balance loads of P processors, $P-1$ balance messages are sent through the SBN. Then $P-1$ distribution messages are routed back to the originating node with the `SysLL` value. Finally, another $P-1$ distribution messages are sent to complete the operation. Thus, a total of $3P-3$ messages have to be processed, requiring a total time of $O(\log P)$ for this operation.

5.2 Hypercube Variant

The SBN approach can be adapted for implementation on a hypercube topology, using the modified binomial spanning tree sketched in Fig. 3. It operates in a manner similar to the standard SBN algorithm with the following differences:

- The value of `SysLL` is computed when all balance messages arrive at the destination. This is possible because there is a unique destination node for every originating node. Distribution messages are then routed back to complete the load balancing. Since there are $P-1+\frac{P}{2}-1$ interconnections in the modified binomial spanning tree, a load-balancing operation requires $3P-4$ messages to be processed in $O(\log P)$ time.

- Nodes in the SBN need to gather all balancing messages from their predecessors before routing the updated `SysLL` to the successors.

- The network topology is such that the number of predecessor and successor nodes vary at the different stages of communication.

5.3 Heuristic SBN Algorithm

Both of the previous algorithms are expensive since a large number of messages has to be processed to accurately maintain the `SysLL`. The heuristic version attempts to reduce the amount of processing by terminating load-balancing operations as soon as enough jobs are found that can be distributed. In general, this strategy reduces the number of messages although $O(P)$ messages are needed in the worst case.

In the heuristic algorithm, a processor estimates `SysLL` by averaging `QLen` for the processors through which the balance message has passed. An appropriate number of jobs is then returned to the predecessor nodes as follows:

$$\texttt{ExJobs} = \begin{cases} 0 & \text{if} \quad \texttt{QLen} < 3 \\ \lfloor \texttt{QLen}/2 \rfloor & \text{otherwise.} \end{cases}$$

If `ExJobs` $= 0$ or if `SysLL` > 2 when `ExJobs` $= 1$, the balance message is forwarded to the next stage. Otherwise, the load balancing is terminated. The justification for this strategy is discussed in [2].

Job distribution is also processed differently in the heuristic SBN algorithm. For example, consider the network SBN(3) that has a processor with `MaxTh` $= 15$ and `QLen` $= 24$. The number of jobs to be distributed is computed by dividing `QLen` by the total number of stages. Thus, six jobs are distributed in this case. `SysLL` is then set to $24 - 6 = 18$. The processor that receives these jobs divides the number of jobs received by the remaining number of stages and adds the result to the `SysLL` stored at that node. The pseudo code in Fig. 7 gives the operational details of the heuristic SBN algorithm.

5.4 Remarks

A significant advantage of the heuristic variant is that the load-balancing messages do not have to be gathered until `SysLL` can be estimated. This reduces the interdependencies associated with the communication. If a processor fails, load balancing can still be accomplished utilizing the remaining processors.

An additional improvement has been obtained for all three load-balancing algorithms by using multiple SBN communication patterns. Each time a message is initiated, one of the SBN patterns is randomly chosen. Each message includes the source node, the pattern used, and the stage to which the message is being routed. Since all nodes have the SBN template associated with messages originating from node 0, the required SBN communication pattern can be determined. Multiple randomly-selected SBN patterns distribute messages more evenly, enhance network reliability, and allow various applications to be written using different communication patterns.

Procedure *GetBalance*
While there are balance messages to be processed
    Calculate the estimated `TotalJobsQueued`
    Call *UpdateLoad*(`TotalJobsQueued`)
    Distribute excess jobs to predecessor node
    If jobs distributed $= 0$ (or one job when `SysLL` > 2)
        Route the balance message to the next SBN stage
End While
Return

Procedure *GetDistribute*
While there are distribution messages to be processed
    If this distribution is in response to load balancing
        `NewLL` $=$ `SysLL` $+\lceil$ `JobsReceived`$/($`Stage` $+1)\rceil$
    else
        `NewLL` = `QLen` + $\lceil$`JobsReceived`$/(2^{d-\text{Stage}} - 1)\rceil$
    Call *UpdateLoad*($P\times$ `NewLL`)
    Enqueue received messages
    Continue the distribution to the next SBN stage
End While
Return

Procedure *Balance*
If this is the final stage, **return**
Route the Balance message to the next SBN stage
Return

Procedure *Distribute*
If this is the final SBN stage, **return**
If this is a response to a load-balancing operation
    If (`QLen` < 3)
        `ExJobs` $= 0$
    else `ExJobs` $= \lfloor$`Qlen`$/2\rfloor$
else `ExJobs` $=$ `QLen` $-$ `MaxTh`
If the last job is to be distributed, `ExJobs` $= 0$
Dequeue the jobs to be distributed
Distribute the `ExJobs` among adjacent SBN nodes
Return(`NumberOfJobsDistributed`)

Figure 7: Heuristic SBN algorithm pseudo code

6 Experimental Results

The three SBN-based load-balancing algorithms have been implemented using MPI and tested with synthetically-generated workloads on the SP2 located at NASA Ames Research Center. The simulation program spawns the appropriate number of child processes and creates the desired network. The list of all process ids and an initial distribution of jobs is routed through the network.

In addition to the initial load, each node dynamically generates additional job loads to be processed. Namely, 10 job creation cycles are processed. The number of jobs generated at each node during each cycle follows a Poisson distribution. By randomly picking different values of λ, varying numbers of jobs are created. Therefore, both heavy and light system load conditions are dynamically simulated. Jobs are processed by "spinning" for the designated time period. The simulation terminates when all jobs have been processed. Two test runs are reported here.

Heavy system load (cf. Fig. 8): Initially, 10 jobs per node are randomly distributed throughout the network. The jobs generated during execution are more than the network can process. Job duration averages one second.

Light system load (cf. Fig. 9): A small number of jobs are initially distributed to a small subset of nodes. A light load of jobs are created as the algorithms execute.

An additional experiment in which the system load transitions from heavy to light is reported in [2].

The performance of the SBN-based algorithms are compared with several popular algorithms (e.g. Random, Gradient, Sender Initiated, Receiver Initiated, Adaptive Contracting). The same simulation tests are also run without load balancing.

The line charts included in Figs. 8-9 measure the comparative performance of the various load-balancing algorithms on an SP2. The X-axis of the line charts show the number of processors used. The Y-axis tracks the following variables:

(a) **Message Traffic Comparison by Node**:
Measures the maximum total number of load-balancing messages sent by a node.

(b) **Total Jobs Transferred**:
Measures the total number of job transfers that occurred from one node to another.

(c) **Maximum Variance by Node in Idle Time**:
Measures processing difference between the most busy node and the least busy node.

(d) **Total Time to Complete**:
Measures the total amount of elapsed time in seconds before all jobs are fully processed.

As expected, the program with no load balancing (*nobal*) performs by far the worst. The *random* algorithm, although providing significant improvement in minimizing idle time, nevertheless is less effective than the remaining algorithms.

The Sender Initiated (*send*) algorithm more evenly balances the load than *random*; however, the Receiver

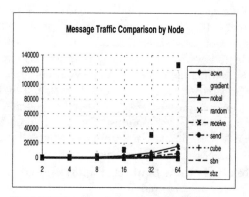

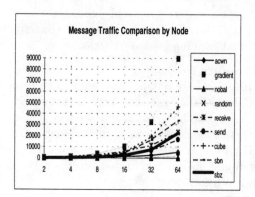

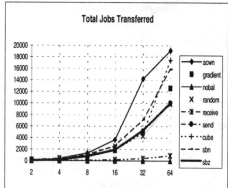

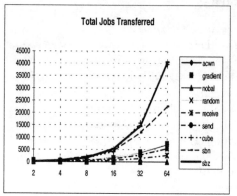

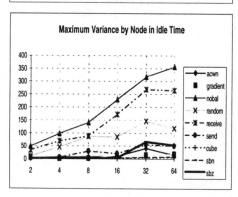

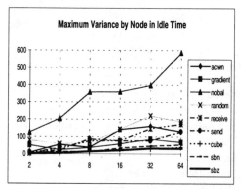

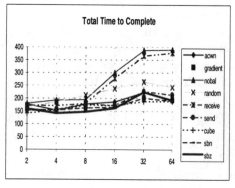

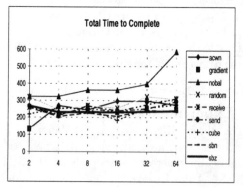

Figure 8: Heavy system load

Figure 9: Light system load

Initiated (*receive*) algorithm does better only when the system load is light. For light to moderate loads, *receive* generates more network traffic because all nodes poll neighbors to find jobs they can process. To overcome this deficiency, a time delay of one second has been introduced after a polling operation at the cost of increasing the idle time. At heavy system loads, *send* can cause job thrashing. This has been overcome by reducing the number of job transfers that are done at high load levels. However, it can cause one or more nodes to remain lightly loaded.

The Gradient (*gradient*) algorithm balances the load quite well without any of the above deficiencies. Unfortunately, lightly-loaded nodes can sometimes receive too many messages from the overloaded nodes. Also, message communication required to update neighbor node information is significant and often results in excessive network traffic. The Adaptive Contracting (*acwn*) algorithm performs the best in periods of heavy system loads. However, as for the *gradient* algorithm, an increased system traffic and the number of jobs migrated is observed.

Both the standard SBN (*sbn*) algorithm and its hypercube variant (*cube*) were able to balance the system load more evenly than other algorithms. Their performance characteristics are very similar. They require less message traffic than the *gradient* algorithm but cause a higher number of job migrations, especially in periods of light system loads.

The heuristic SBN algorithm (*sbz*) performs well in minimizing idle time in light system loads. Although its performance during periods of heavy loads is relatively good, it does not balance the generated system load as well as the *cube* or *sbn*. This is because its estimate of SysLL is not necessarily accurate. Note that for light loads, *sbz* requires many more job transfers than the other algorithms. However, it consistently requires fewer messages than *gradient*, *sbn*, or *cube*.

7 Conclusions

Empirical results have shown that our approach to load balancing using the concept of a symmetric broadcast network (SBN) is effective and superior to several other schemes. All three proposed algorithms that we propose successfully balance the system load and minimize processor idle time. In addition, the heuristic variant reduces the overhead associated with balancing message traffic.

The research presented in this paper could be extended in different directions. Further adaptations of our SBN-based load balancing approach to a wide variety of topological interconnections (and hence multicomputer configurations) would make our scheme even more versatile and architecture-independent. This simply means how effectively SBNs can be mapped onto existing topologies like meshes, fat trees, etc. Another important topic is to analyze the effect of altering the definition of "system load". In the standard SBN algorithm, we have assumed that the local queue size determines system load. In the dynamic mesh adaptation reported in [2], a weighted queue length was used. However, other parameters such as processor resource allocation and execution dependencies could greatly alter how load balancing should be accomplished.

References

[1] G. Cybenko, "Dynamic Load Balancing for Distributed Memory Multiprocessors," *Journal of Parallel and Distributed Computing*, Vol. 7, No. 2, pp. 279–301, Oct. 1989.

[2] S.K. Das, D.J. Harvey, and R. Biswas, "Adaptive Load-Balancing Algorithms Using Symmetric Broadcast Networks," *NASA Ames Research Center Technical Report*, NAS-97-014, May 1997.

[3] S.K. Das and S.K. Prasad, "Implementing Task Ready Queues in a Multiprocessing Environment," *Proc. of the International Conference on Parallel Computing*, Pune, India, pp. 132–140, Dec. 1990.

[4] S.K. Das, S.K. Prasad, C-Q. Yang, N.M.Leung, "Symmetric Broadcast Networks for Implementing Global Task Queues and Load Balancing in a Multiprocessor Environment," *UNT Technical Report*, CRPDC-92-1, 1992.

[5] D.L. Eager, E.D. Lazowska, and J. Zahorjan, "Adaptive Load Sharing in Homogeneous Distributed Systems," *IEEE Transactions on Software Engineering*, Vol. SE-12, No. 5, pp. 662–675, May 1986.

[6] D.L. Eager, E.D. Lazowska, and J. Zahorjan, "A Comparison of Receiver-Initiated and Sender-Initiated Adaptive Load Sharing," *Performance Evaluation*, Vol. 6, No. 1, pp. 53–68, Mar. 1986.

[7] M.D. Feng and C.K. Yuen, "Dynamic Load Balancing on a Distributed System," *Proc. of the Symposium on Parallel and Distributed Processing*, Dallas, TX, pp. 318–325, Oct. 1994.

[8] L.V. Kale, "Comparing the Performance of Two Dynamic Load Distribution Methods," *Proc. of the International Conference on Parallel Processing*, Vol I, pp. 8–12, 1988.

[9] F.C.H. Lin and R.M. Keller, "The Gradient Model Load Balancing Method," *IEEE Trans. on Software Engineering*, SE-13, pp. 32–38, 1987.

[10] S. Pulidas, D. Towsley, and J. A. Stankovic, "Embedding Gradient Estimators in Load Balancing Algorithms," *Proc. of the International Conference on Distributed Computing Systems*, pp. 482–490, 1988.

[11] C.G. Rommel, "The Probability of Load Balancing Success in a Homogeneous Network," *IEEE Transactions on Software Engineering*, pp. 922–923, Sept. 1992.

[12] V. Sarkar and J. Hennessy, "Compile-time Partitioning and Scheduling of Parallel Programs," *Scheduling and Load Balancing in Parallel and Distributed Systems*, IEEE Computer Society Press, Los Alamitos, CA, pp. 61–70, 1995.

[13] N.G. Shivaratri, P. Krueger, and M. Singhal, "Load Distributing for Locally Distributed Systems," *Computer*, pp. 33–44, December 1992.

Session 6B

Multicast Communication

Optimal Multicast with Packetization and Network Interface Support *

Ram Kesavan and Dhabaleswar K. Panda
Department of Computer and Information Science
The Ohio State University, Columbus, OH 43210-1277
Email: {kesavan,panda}@cis.ohio-state.edu

Abstract: *Modern networks typically limit the size of the largest packet for efficient communication. Thus, long messages are packetized and transmitted. Such networks also provide network interface support for nodes, which typically includes a coprocessor and memory, to implement the lower layers of the communication protocol. This paper presents a concept of smart network interface support for packetization and an optimal multicast algorithm for systems with such support. Two implementations of smart network interface, First-Child-First-Served (FCFS) and First-Packet-First-Served (FPFS), are studied and compared. It is shown that the FPFS network interface support is more practical and efficient. Next, the components of multicast latency under FPFS implementation are analyzed by using a pipelined model. A concept of k-binomial tree is introduced, and proved to be optimal for multicasting under the FPFS scheme. A method to construct contention-free k-binomial trees on contention-free orderings of the nodes is presented. For a 64-node system with irregular network, simulation results indicate that the optimal k-binomial tree is upto 2 times better than the conventional binomial tree for a range of multicast set sizes and message lengths. Thus, these results demonstrate significant potential to be applied to current and future generation high performance systems including MPPs and NOWs, where network interface support for multicast is provided.*

1 Introduction

Multicast/broadcast is a common collective communication operation as defined by the MPI standard. Parallel systems supporting distributed memory or distributed-shared memory programming paradigms require fast implementation of multicast and broadcast operations in order to support various application and system level data distribution functions. There have been many multicast/broadcast algorithms proposed in the literature in recent years [5, 6, 9, 11]. All these algorithms are designed assuming arbitrarily long single-packet messages. Typically, modern networks limit the size of the largest packet to minimize network contention and support efficient buffer utilization in the network and the network interfaces. Therefore, large messages are broken up and transmitted as multiple packets. Modern networks also provide network interface support associated with each node. Such support, which includes a coprocessor and a small amount of memory, implements the lower layers of

the communication protocol. This is true of nodes on a NOW, as well as on systems like the IBM SP2.

Recently, a solution for implementing multicast under packetization has been proposed in [2]. However, this work assumes host processor handling of packetization and user/system control of determining optimal packet size for a given multicast set and message length. Thus, this result is not practical for modern systems with fixed packet lengths and network interface support for packetization. This leads to the challenge of designing optimal multicast algorithms under packetization using network interface support.

In this paper we take on this challenge. First, the features of conventional and smart network interfaces are analyzed. Next, two implementations of smart network interface, First-Child-First-Served (FCFS) and First-Packet-First-Served (FPFS), are investigated for packetized multicast. It is shown that the FPFS network interface support is more practical and efficient in terms of buffer requirement. It is also shown that the binomial tree is not optimal for an arbitrary multicast set size and an arbitrary number of packets using the FPFS implementation. In order to calculate multicast latency a pipelined model of multi-packet multicast is built for the FPFS implementation. Then, a new concept of k-binomial tree is defined and shown to be optimal for multi-packet multicast. A method to construct contention-free k-binomial trees is developed using the concept of contention-free ordering of nodes [9]. The k-binomial tree is evaluated and compared to the conventional binomial tree on a 64-node irregular switch-based network using simulation experiments. Results show an improvement by a factor of 2 when using the k-binomial tree. Also, the benefit of using the k-binomial tree is shown to increase with increase in number of packets of a multicast. These results are quite general and can be used in any kind of network (regular or irregular) which provides network interface support for multicast packetization.

The rest of the paper is organized as follows. Section 2 reviews packetization and network interface. Section 3 discusses FCFS and FPFS implementations of smart network interface support, and compares them. Section 4 presents the optimal multicast algorithm. Performance analysis results are presented in Section 5.Related work is described

*This research is supported in part by NSF Grant MIP-9309627 and NSF Career Award MIP-9502294.

in Section 6, and concluding remarks are made in Section 7.

2 Packetization and Network Interface Support

In this section, we discuss multicast of packetized messages over conventional and smart network interfaces, and show that existing multicast algorithms are not optimal on systems with smart network interface support.

2.1 Packetization

Modern day networks typically limit the size of the largest packet. This is done to minimize network contention and support efficient buffer utilization in the network and the network interfaces. If a node needs to send a large message to another node, the message is broken up into packets of fixed size. Typically, the maximum packet size is dictated by the design of the network and the associated communication protocol. The sender fragments the message and sends out the individual packets into the network. The packets are routed as individual messages to the destination depending on the routing information contained in the headers. The destination collects the packets and assembles them into the complete message.

Communication support can be provided at one of two levels in a typical high performance node: system level or network interface level. System level support involves host processors at the sender and receiver sides executing some software to accomplish the above tasks. Such support is inefficient due to the large overheads of software execution, buffer copying, and loss of computing time at the host processor. To improve performance, modern network systems provide a network interface associated with each node. The network interface, which includes a co-processor and a small amount of memory, implements the lower layers of the communication protocol.

2.2 Conventional Network Interface Support

Let us consider the conventional network interface support for message transfer in a typical high performance system. Figure 1 shows a generic network interface at a host node. The interface contains a coprocessor, send/receive queues to store packets that are being sent to or received from the network, DMA engines to transfer the packets between the host memory and the send/receive queues, and other hardware to interface with the network.

An application is typically linked to a communication library in the host, and a portion of the host memory is allocated for DMA to and from the network interface. Recent implementations of high performance messaging systems show a trend of circumventing the operating system and providing applications direct access to the network device [3, 8, 10]. This reduces the send and receive overheads for messaging, so that the low latency and high bandwidth

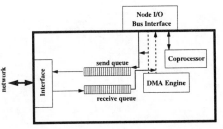

Figure 1: Generic diagram of a typical network interface at a host node.

requirements of cluster computing can be achieved. The programmable coprocessor at the network interface controls the actual sending and receiving of the messages.

A typical message transfer in these systems is done in the following way. At the sender side, one of two schemes is used. The host processor at the sender fragments the message into fixed size packets and transfers them to the send queue of the network interface [10]. Alternatively, the host processor copies data into the host DMA memory, writes the message pointers to the network interface, and the coprocessor uses DMA to copy the packets to the send queue [3]. Subsequently, the software executing at the co-processor detects entries in the send queue, and sends the packets out to the network channel. At the receiver side, the incoming packets join the receive queue at the network interface. The coprocessor detects the received packets and uses DMA to copy them to the host memory. The discussions in this paper are applicable with either scheme at the sender side.

2.3 Multicasting over Conventional Network Interface

When a multicast tree is implemented on a high performance system, some destinations serve as intermediate sources. This means that when they receive a message, they forward copies of it to other destinations. Let us consider the multicast of a large message spanning multiple packets. Figure 2 shows the forwarding of a 2-packet multicast message at an intermediate node of a multicast tree. All the packets of the message are received at the network interface and copied to host memory using DMA. The host processor at the intermediate node receives the complete message and then initiates send operations to each of its children in the multicast tree. For each of the send operations, a copy of the message is sent to the network interface, from where it is sent into the network. Therefore, an intermediate node undergoes the message send overhead for every copy of the message that it forwards to other destinations. This overhead includes the software start-up overhead and the overhead at the network interface for each packet transmission. Smart network interface support can reduce this overhead for multicast of large messages.

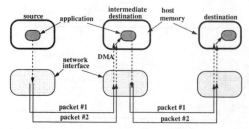

Figure 2: Forwarding of a 2-packet long multicast message by intermediate node using conventional network interface support.

2.4 Smart Network Interface Support

Here, the forwarding process at the source and intermediate nodes is completely handled by the software running at the network interface coprocessor. This software is given the capability to identify a multicast packet. If the next outgoing packet in the send queue of the source node is a multicast packet, the network interface coprocessor forwards replicas of the packet to the nodes adjacent to the root of the multicast tree. When a multicast packet is received at the network interface of an intermediate node, the network interface coprocessor, after it starts copying (using DMA) of the packet to host memory, forwards replicas of the packet to its children in the multicast tree. Figure 3 shows such forwarding.

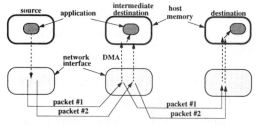

Figure 3: Forwarding of a 2-packet long multicast message by intermediate node using smart network interface support.

2.5 Multicasting over Smart Network Interface

Let us estimate the latency of a multicast operation using smart network interface support. The software start-up overhead, t_s, is incurred once at the host processor of source of the multicast to transfer the data to the network interface memory. Consequently, the multicast tree is implemented at the network interfaces of the participating processors. The host processor at each destination undergoes the software overhead, t_r, for receiving the message. Although, these software overheads are large, they are independent of the choice of the multicast tree. However, the overhead incurred at the network interfaces of the participating nodes depends on the choice of the multicast tree. Therefore, the latency of a multicast tree is determined by the time required for the actual transmission of all the packets of the multicast message to the network interfaces of the destinations. Hereafter, we refer to the transmission of

a packet from the network interface of one processor to another as a *step*. This time, denoted t_{step}, includes the overhead at the sender network interface for sending a packet, propagation overhead, and the overhead at the receiver network interface for receiving the packet.

Let us take a simple example of a single-packet multicast using a binomial tree over three destinations to illustrate the advantage of using smart network interface support. Figures 4(a) and 4(b) show the multicast over conventional and smart network interface, respectively. It can be easily observed that the multicast latencies using conventional and smart network interfaces are $2(t_s + t_{step} + t_r)$ and $(t_s + 2t_{step} + t_r)$, respectively. For an arbitrary multicast set size of n nodes, these values will be $\lceil log_2 n \rceil (t_s + t_{step} + t_r)$ and $(t_s + \lceil log_2 n \rceil t_{step} + t_r)$, respectively. Therefore, multicast latency can be lowered by using smart network interface support.

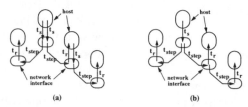

Figure 4: Performance benefits of the smart network interface: (a) binomial single-packet multicast tree over the conventional network interface and (b) binomial single-packet multicast tree over the smart network interface.

This improvement in performance is due to two main reasons. First, the host processor at the intermediate node is not involved in the forwarding of multicast packets, thereby reducing the forwarding overhead. Second, an intermediate node can forward a packet of the message as soon as it arrives, independent of the arrival of the remaining packets. As it can be observed, such network interface support requires buffering of multicast packets at the network interface. This is because each packet is forwarded to multiple destinations, and the packet data requires buffering at the network interface until the network interface coprocessor has injected all required copies of it into the network. An example of the use of such smart network interface has been described in [12].

2.6 Optimal Multicast Trees over Smart Network Interface

Prior work in the literature has shown the binomial tree to be optimal (in terms of number of start-ups) for multicast on systems with conventional network interface support [9]. However, it is not clear whether this is true for systems with smart network interface. Let us consider an example multicast of a 3-packet long message to three destinations on a system with smart network interface support. Figures 5(a) and 5(b) show the number of steps taken to complete such a multicast using a binomial and a linear tree, respectively. In the figures, the numbers in brackets indicate the step numbers and the subscripts indicate the packet numbers. For example $[4]_2$ indicates the second packet being transmitted in the fourth time step. It can be easily observed that the binomial tree takes 6 steps and the linear tree takes 5 steps. The multicast latency for the binomial tree is $(t_s + 6 * t_{step} + t_r)$, and the multicast latency for the linear tree is $(t_s + 5 * t_{step} + t_r)$. This simple example shows that the binomial tree is not the optimal tree for multicast of packetized messages with smart network interface support.

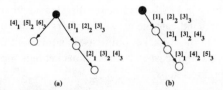

Figure 5: The number of steps to complete multicast of a 3-packet long message to 3 destinations using: (a) a binomial tree and (b) a linear tree.

3 Implementations of Smart Network Interface Support

In this section, we describe two implementations of smart network interface support for multicast: First-Child-First-Served (FCFS) and First-Packet-First-Served (FPFS). We compare both implementations, and show why the FPFS implementation is more efficient and practical.

3.1 First-Child-First-Served (FCFS) Implementation

In this implementation, the network interface at the source node sends all packets of the multicast message to its first child in the multicast tree, then to its second child, and so on. When the network interface of an intermediate node receives the first packet of a multicast message, it forwards the packet to its first child. When the second packet of the multicast message arrives at the network interface, it also forwards this packet to the first child. Similarly, the complete multicast message is forwarded, one packet at a time, to the first child. Subsequently, the network interface forwards the message to the second child, followed by the third child, and so on. Figure 6 formally expresses this implementation in a pseudo-code format.

3.2 First-Packet-First-Served (FPFS) Implementation

In this implementation, the network interface forwards the message on a per-packet basis. The network interface at the source node sends the first packet to all the children of the source, then sends the second packet to all the children of the source, and so on. When the first packet of the multicast message arrives at the network interface of

Sender	Receiver with Forwarding (Intermediate Node)

for i = 1 to num_children {
  for j = 1 to num_packets {
    send(child_i, packet_j);
  }
}
 	
Receiver
for j = 1 to num_packets {
  receive(packet_j);
}
	for i = 1 to num_children {
	  for j = 1 to num_packets {
	    if (i == 1)
	      receive(packet_j);
	    send(child_i, packet_j);
	  }
	}

Figure 6: Pseudo-code description of the FCFS implementation of the smart network interface for multicast.

an intermediate node, it forwards the packet to each of the children of the intermediate node. Subsequently, when the second packet of the multicast message arrives at the network interface, it forwards the packet to each of the children, and so on till the last packet is forwarded. Figure 7 formally expresses this implementation in a pseudo-code format.

Sender	Receiver with Forwarding (Intermediate Node)

for j = 1 to num_packets {
  for i = 1 to num_children {
    send(child_i, packet_j);
  }
}
 	
Receiver
for j = 1 to num_packets {
  receive(packet_j);
}
	for j = 1 to num_packets {
	  receive(packet_j);
	  for i = 1 to num_children {
	    send(child_i, packet_j);
	  }
	}

Figure 7: Pseudo-code description of the FPFS implementation of the smart network interface for multicast.

3.3 Comparison of FCFS and FPFS Implementations

Let us evaluate and compare these two implementations of smart network interface support with respect to ease of implementation and buffer requirement.

3.3.1 Ease of Implementation

The FPFS is an easier implementation than the FCFS. Let us consider packets of multiple messages coming into the receive queue of the network interface at an intermediate node. To implement FCFS, the network interface processor has to maintain a counter for each incoming message. Each arriving packet increments the counter corresponding to its message. When the counter value becomes equal to the message length, all the packets are sent to the remaining children. To implement FPFS, the network interface processor handles the forwarding of the multicast message on a per-packet basis. When the network interface processor reads the header of a multicast packet from the receive queue, it forwards the packet to all the children in the multicast tree. The processor does not have to maintain a counter for each incoming multicast message. Therefore, the FPFS is an easier implementation than the FCFS.

3.3.2 Buffer Requirement at the Network Interface

It can be quantatively shown that the FPFS implementation is more efficient than the FCFS implementation in terms of buffer requirement. Let us take an example of an intermediate node with k children in the multicast tree of a p-packet multicast. Let t_{ns} be the time for a copy of a packet to be sent out from the queue to the network adaptor. Let us consider the time interval starting from when the network interface coprocessor reading an incoming packet until all copies of this packet have been sent to its children. Let T_c and T_p denote this time interval for FCFS and FPFS implementations, respectively.

Let us assume the best case of zero time delay between incoming packets. In the FCFS implementation a packet needs to be buffered at the network interface of an intermediate node until all packets of the corresponding message have been forwarded to all the children of the node. Thus, the ith packet needs to be buffered till the ith packet and the remaining $(p - i)$ packets are forwarded to the first child of the intermediate node, all p packets are forwarded to the next $(k - 2)$ children, and the first i packets are forwarded to the kth child. This leads to $T_c = (p - i + 1)t_{ns} + (k - 2)pt_{ns} + it_{ns}$.

In the FPFS implementation, a packet only needs to be buffered at the network interface of an intermediate node until it has been forwarded to all the children of the node. Thus, the ith packet needs to be buffered only until it is forwarded to the k children of the intermediate node. This leads to $T_p = kt_{ns}$.

Here we have assumed the best case conditions of zero delay between incoming packets for both implementations. If there is delay between incoming packets, each packet requires longer buffering in the FCFS implementation. It can be easily observed that even with the best case assumptions, $T_p < T_c$. This translates to larger buffer requirement for the FCFS implementation as compared to the FPFS implementation.

The above discussion shows that the FPFS implementation is a more practical and efficient approach. In the next section, we take on the challenge of developing optimal multicast trees for systems with such FPFS network interface support.

4 Optimal Multicast with FPFS

In this section, we propose an optimal multicast tree on a system with FPFS network interface support and discuss the related implementation issues.

4.1 A Pipelined Model for Estimating Multicast Latency

The discussion in Section 2.5 clearly shows that multicast latency for a single packet on a system with smart network interface support can be written as $(t_s + num\_steps *$

$t_{step} + t_r)$. The same formula can be extended to multi-packet multicast latency where t_s (t_r) can denote the send (receive) overhead at the host processor to transfer all packets of the message to (from) the network interface. In this section, we analyze multicast latency in terms of *steps* occuring at the network interface layer, as discussed in Section 2.5.

Let us model the multicast latency at the network interface layer assuming the FPFS implementation. The multicast of the complete message can be treated as a sequence of single-packet multicasts following one another. Figure 8 shows the break up of the multicast of a 3-packet message to 7 destinations over an example binomial multicast tree. The numbers in brackets indicate the step numbers, and the subscripts indicate the packet numbers. It can be easily observed that the 3-packet multicast is equivalent to three single-packet multicasts where each packet lags the previous one by three steps.

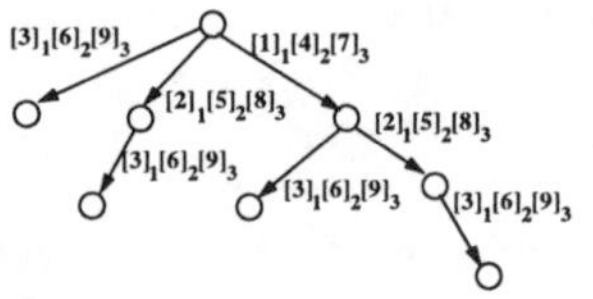

Figure 8: The break up of a 3-packet multicast over 7 destinations using a binomial multicast tree.

Let T be a multicast tree, and let δ_r be the number of children of the root of T. Let the multicast begin at time zero. Let L_i denote the time at which the multicast of the ith packet is completed, i.e. the time at which the ith packet has been received by the network interface of each destination. Then, the following theorem can be derived.

Theorem 1 *The time interval $(L_{i+1} - L_i)$, i.e. the time between the completions of multicast of any two successive packets, for a multicast tree is given by δ_r.*

Proof: Due to lack of space, we are not able to present this proof here. Interested readers are requested to read [7] for the detailed proof. ∎

From Theorem 1 it can be observed that the time interval $(L_{i+1} - L_i)$ is independent of i. Also, each successive packet completes its multicast δ_r steps after the completion of the previous one. Therefore, an m-packet multicast can be modeled as m single-packet pipelined multicasts. This leads to the following theorem.

Theorem 2 *The time for completion of these m pipelined single-packet multicasts is $L_1 + (m - 1)\delta_r$ steps.*

It can also be observed from Fig. 8 that the multicast of each packet lags the previous one by exactly 3 steps, which is equal to the number of children of the root. Also, the complete multicast takes 9 steps, which is $3 + (3 - 1) * 3$.

4.2 Deriving Optimal Multicast Tree

The optimal multicast tree is one that produces the minimum value for the expression $L_1 + (m-1)\delta_r$. Let us consider a multicast set of size n nodes. The value of δ_r in a multicast tree determines the value of L_1. In the case of a linear tree (Fig 5(b) for example), $\delta_r = 1$ which leads to $L_1 = (n-1)$. If δ_r of a tree is increased, the value of L_1 decreases. In the case of the binomial tree [9] where $\delta_r = \lceil log_2 n \rceil$, L_1 reaches a minimum of $\lceil log_2 n \rceil$ since this tree recursively doubles the number of destinations covered in each step. However, on further increase of δ_r of a multicast tree beyond $\lceil log_2 n \rceil$, the value of L_1 increases. Therefore, for getting the minimum value for $L_1 + (m-1)\delta_r$, we need to only consider the interval $[1, \lceil log_2 n \rceil]$ to compute the optimal value of δ_r. If δ_r of a tree is less than $\lceil log_2 n \rceil$, we get the special case of a restricted binomial tree. Let us call this tree a k-binomial tree.

Definition 1 *A k-binomial tree is defined as a recursively doubling tree where each vertex has atmost k children, i.e. $\delta_r \leq k$.*

Figures 9(a) and 9(b) show examples of 3-binomial and 4-binomial trees with multicast set size of 16. To calculate the optimal value of δ_r which produces the minimum value for $L_1 + (m-1)\delta_r$, let us derive a relationship between L_1 and δ_r using the k-binomial tree.

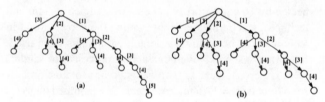

Figure 9: Examples of k-binomial trees on a multicast set size of 16: (a) the 3-binomial tree, and (b) the 4-binomial tree.

Lemma 1 *Let $N(s,k)$ denote the number of nodes covered in s steps by a k-binomial multicast tree. The value of $N(s,k)$ is given by*

$$N(s,k) = \begin{cases} 2^s & \text{if } s \leq k \\ 1 + N(s-1,k) + N(s-2,k) + \\ \quad \ldots + N(s-k,k) & \text{if } s > k \end{cases}$$

Proof: If $s \leq k$, the k-binomial tree is like a binomial tree, so $N(s,k) = 2^s$. For the case of $s > k$, Fig. 10 illustrates the structure of a k-binomial tree after s steps. The root has k subtrees, and each of the subtrees is recursively a k-binomial tree. It can be seen that after s steps the number of nodes in the first subtree is given by $N(s-1,k)$ since the depth of this subtree is $(s-1)$. Similarly, the number of nodes in the second subtree is given by $N(s-2,k)$, and so on. Therefore, $N(s,k)$ is equal to the summation of the nodes in each of the subtrees, and one (the source). ∎

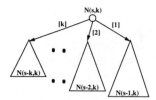

Figure 10: The number of nodes covered by a k-binomial tree in s steps when $s > k$. The number of nodes in the ith subtree from right is given by $N(s-i,k)$.

Thus, for a given δ_r and n, the value of L_1 is the minimum value of s such that $N(s, \delta_r) \geq n$. Using this relation, the optimal multicast tree for a given n and m can be calculated as follows.

Theorem 3 *Given n and m, the k-binomial tree which produces the minimum value of $L_1 + (m-1)k$ is the optimal multicast tree, where $1 \leq k \leq \lceil log_2 n \rceil$, and L_1 is equal to the minimum value of s for which $N(s,k) \geq n$.*

4.3 Implementation Issues

There are two major issues for implementing k-binomial trees for packetized multicast in a given system. These issues are: a) computing the optimal value of k for given n and m, and b) constructing contention-free k-binomial multicast trees on the interconnection network of the system.

4.3.1 Computing Optimal k

For given n and m, it can be shown using Theorem 3 and Lemma 1 that there is no closed form solution for the optimal value of k which produces the minimum value for $L + (m-1)k$. However, this value can be easily computed by checking all possible values of k in the interval $[1, \lceil log_2 n \rceil]$ Thus, the optimal value of k can be precomputed and stored in a table for all possible values of n and m. As we will see in Section 5.1, the optimal value of k is identical for a range of m values and the optimal value of k converges to 1 with increase in m. Thus, this table requires less than $O(mn)$ memory. Therefore the precomputation of the optimal value of k for n and m is a feasible implementation.

4.3.2 Constructing Contention-free k-binomial Trees

For optimal multi-packet multicast performance, the multicast tree should be *depth contention-free* [9]. This means that the paths that the tree edges get mapped to in the network should be edge-disjoint with respect to each other. The concept of contention-free ordering of nodes in a system has been used to construct contention-free binomial trees [9]. A similar approach can be used to construct contention-free k-binomial trees.

Let the n participating nodes of a multicast be ordered, and let the symbol $<_d$ denote the ordering. An ordering is said to be contention-free if $\forall w, x, y, z$ in the ordered chain such that $w <_d x <_d y <_d z$, messages between processors w and x do not contend for any links with messages between processors y and z. Without loss of generality, let us assume that the source of the multicast is the first node in the ordering. Figure 11 gives a pictorial representation of the construction of a contention-free, k-binomial tree on this ordering in a recursive manner. In the first step, the source sends the message to the node, a, which is $N(s-1, k)$ places from the right end of the chain, where s is computed from Theorem 3. In the second step, the source sends the message to the node, b, which is $N(s-2, k)$ places away from the previous recipient. Similarly, the source sends messages to $k-2$ other nodes. The intermediate nodes, like a and b cover the destinations to their right by building k-binomial trees in a recursive fashion.

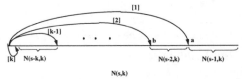

Figure 11: The construction of contention-free k-binomial tree from a given contention-free ordering of participating nodes.

This construction can be applied to different types of systems. For k-ary n-cubes, the dimension-ordered chain [9] can be used to construct contention-free k-binomial trees. For irregular networks, we have recently shown that no contention-free ordering exists for *up*/down** routing[5]. A concept of Partial Ordered Chain (POC) has been proposed to create an ordering with minimal contention on these networks. Such ordering can be used to construct k-binomial trees with minimal contention on irregular switch-based networks.

5 Performance Analysis

In this section, we present the results which show the behavior of the optimal value of k with varying n (multicast set size) and m (number of packets in the multicast message). We also present simulation results comparing the performance of the k-binomial tree with the binomial tree for multicast.

5.1 Optimal k

We analytically studied the variation of the optimal value of k with change in multicast set size, n, and number of packets, m. We conducted two experiments. The value of m was first fixed, and the multicast set size was varied. Then, the value of n was fixed, and the number of packets in the multicast message was varied. Figures 12(a) and 12(b) show the results of these experiments, respectively. It can be observed from Fig. 12(a) that for $m = 1$, the optimal value of $k = \lceil log_2 n \rceil$. As the value of m is increased, the value of k comes down. After a certain point, $k = 1$ (i.e., the linear tree) becomes optimal. For $k = 1$,

the multicast latency $ML_1 = (n - 1) + (m - 1)$ and for $k = 2$, the multicast latency $ML_2 = O(logn) + 2(m - 1)$. A crossover occurs at the minimum value of m for which $ML_2 > ML_1$. It can be easily seen that smaller the value of n, the smaller the value of m at which $ML_2 > ML_1$. This can be seen in Fig. 12(a) where the optimal k for multicast set size 16 (number of destinations = 15) becomes 1 before multicast set size 32. It can also be observed in Fig. 12(b) that for multicast messages of length of 4 or 8 packets, the optimal value of k is 2 as the multicast set size is increased. Even for messages with 4 or 8 packets, it can be analytically determined the optimal value of k increases with increase in n beyond 64.

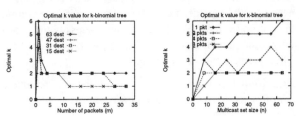

Figure 12: Variation of the optimal value of k: (a) with fixed n and changing m, and (b) fixed m and changing n.

5.2 Multicast Latency

For comparing multicast latency of k-binomial trees with binomial trees, we simulated these algorithms an irregular switch-based network with 64 processors connected by 16 eight-port switches. We assumed system and technological parameters representing the current trend in technology. The following default parameters were used: t_s (software start-up overhead at host processor of sender) = 12.5 microseconds, t_r (software overhead at host processor of receiver) = 12.5 microseconds. We assumed 64 bytes packet size, t_{ns} (overhead at network interface for sending a packet) = 3.0 microseconds, and t_{nr} (overhead at network interface for receiving a packet) = 2.0 microseconds. For each data point, the multicast latency was averaged over 30 different random sets of destinations for each of 10 different random network switch interconnection topologies. We used the Chain Concatenated Ordering (CCO), described in [5], as the base ordering for irregular switch-based networks.

First, we studied the multicast latency for the k-binomial tree (using the optimal values of k from the previous study) for varying m and n. Figures 13(a) and 13(b) show the results of these experiments, respectively. It can be observed that increase in multicast latency is less when the corresponding optimal value of k reduces. In Fig. 13(a), the slope for the graph for 15 destinations reduces when $k = 1$. Similarily, the slopes of the graphs in Fig. 13(b) reduce when k converges to 2.

Next, we compared the performance of the k-binomial trees with the standard binomial trees. Figures 14(a) and

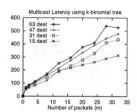
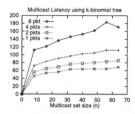

Figure 13: Multicast latency (in microseconds) using the optimal k-binomial tree: (a) with fixed n and changing m, and (b) fixed m and changing n.

14(b) show the results of the comparison. It can be clearly observed in Fig. 14(a) that the performance of the k-binomial tree is better by a factor of up to 2 when compared to the binomial tree. From Fig. 14(b), it can also be observed that with increase in number of packets in the message, the performance improvement of k-binomial tree over the binomial tree increases.

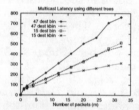
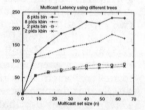

Figure 14: Comparison of multicast latencies (in microseconds) using k-binomial and binomial trees: (a) with fixed n and changing m, and (b) fixed m and changing n.

6 Related Work

A recent work [4] studies the efficient implementation of collective communication operations on a NOW over ATM using the network interface support. Since ATM switches provide hardware multicast capability, the network interface support in this work is primarily geared towards achieving reliable multicast over the unreliable ATM layer. Another recent work [12] describes an implementation of packetized multicast over the Myrinet network interface [1]. This work is also geared towards development of a reliable multicast communication layer and does not provide any formal multicast algorithms.

7 Conclusions

In this paper we have analyzed the features of network interface to support packetized multicast. Two implementations, FCFS and FPFS, using smart network interface support have been presented. The FPFS scheme has been shown to be more practical and efficient than the FCFS. Next, we have shown that the binomial tree is not optimal for an arbitrary multicast set size and an arbitrary number of packets using the FPFS implementation. Components of multicast latency using FPFS implementation have been analyzed. A new concept of k-binomial tree has been introduced and it has been proved that the k-binomial tree is

optimal for multi-packet multicast. A method to construct contention-free k-binomial tree has been proposed. The k-binomial algorithm has been evaluated through simulation and its performance has been shown to be better than that of the conventional binomial tree. These results demonstrate significant potential to be applied to current and future generation of high performance systems with network interface support.

In this paper we have proposed an optimal algorithm for multicast on networks with network interface and packetization. It will interesting to see how this framework can be mapped to different network topologies and routing schemes in a contention-free manner. It will also be challenging to design optimal algorithms for other collective communication operations with such packetization and network interface support.

Additional Information: A number of related papers and technical reports can be obtained from the home page of *Parallel Architecture and Communication* (PAC) research group. The URL is *http://www.cis.ohio-state.edu/~panda/pac.html*.

References

[1] N. J. Boden, D. Cohen, and et al. Myrinet: A Gigabit-per-Second Local Area Network. *IEEE Micro*, pages 29–35, Feb 1995.

[2] L. De Coster, N. Dewulf, and C.-T. Ho. Efficient Multipacket Multicast Algorithms on Meshes with Wormhole and Dimension-Ordered Routing. In *ICPP*, pp III:137–141, Aug 1995.

[3] T. V. Eicken, A. Basu, V. Buch, and W. Vogels. U-Net: A User-level Network Interface for Parallel and Distributed Computing. In *ACM SOSP*, 1995.

[4] Y. Huang and P. K. McKinley. Efficient Collective Operations with ATM Network Interface Support. In *ICPP*, pp I:34–43, Aug 1996.

[5] R. Kesavan, K. Bondalapati, and D. K. Panda. Multicast on Irregular Switch-based Networks with Wormhole Routing. In *HPCA-3*, pp 48–57, Feb 1997.

[6] R. Kesavan and D. K. Panda. Minimizing Node Contention in Multiple Multicast on Wormhole k-ary n-cube Networks. In *ICPP*, pp I:188–195, Aug 1996.

[7] R. Kesavan and D. K. Panda. Optimal Multicast with Packetization and Network Interface Support. Technical Report OSU-CISRC-2/97-TR10, Jan 1997.

[8] R. P. Martin. HPAM: An Active Message Layer for a Network of HP Workstations. In *Proceedings of the Hot Interconnectes Symposium*, 1994.

[9] P. K. McKinley, H. Xu, A.-H. Esfahanian, and L. M. Ni. Unicast-based Multicast Communication in Wormhole-routed Networks. *IEEE TPDS*, 5(12):1252–1265, Dec 1994.

[10] S. Pakin, M. Lauria, and A. Chien. High Performance Messaging on Workstations: Illinois Fast Messages (FM). In *Proceedings of the Supercomputing*, 1995.

[11] J. Y. L. Park, H. A. Choi, N. Nupairoj, and L. M. Ni. Construction of Optimal Multicast Trees Based on the Parameterized Communication Model. In *ICPP*, Aug 1996.

[12] K. Verstoep, K. Langendoen, and H. Bal. Efficient Reliable Multicast on Myrinet. In *ICPP*, pp III:156–165, Aug 1996.

An Euler Path Based Technique for Deadlock-free Multicasting

Nidhi Agrawal and C.P.Ravikumar
Department of Electrical Engineering
Indian Institute of Technology
New Delhi - 110016
{nidhi,rkumar}@ee.iitd.ernet.in

Abstract

The existing algorithms for deadlock-free multicasting in interconnection networks assume the Hamiltonian property in the networks topology. However, these networks fail to be Hamiltonian in the presence of faults. This paper investigates the use of Euler circuits in deadlock-free multicasting. Not only are Euler circuits known to exist in all connected networks, a fast polynomial-time algorithm exists to find an Euler circuit in a network. We present a multicasting algorithm which works for both regular and irregular topologies. Our algorithm is applicable to store-and-forward as well as wormhole-routed networks. We show that at most two virtual channels are required per physical channel for any connected network. We also prove that no virtual channels are required to achieve deadlock-free multicasting on a large class of networks. Unlike other existing algorithms for deadlock-free multicasting in faulty networks, our algorithm requires a small amount of information to be stored at each node. The potential of our technique is further illustrated with the help of various examples. A performance analysis on wormhole-routed networks shows that our routing algorithm outperforms existing multicasting procedures.

1 Introduction

Multicasting is an important communication pattern where message originating at a source node Src must be delivered to a set of destination nodes $Dest$. Various parallel applications like parallel search and barrier synchronization demand multicast communication. While it is straightforward to implement a k-way multicast as a set of k unicasts, such an approach is wasteful of network resources and creates too much additional traffic. This disadvantage of unicast-based multicasting is overcome in tree-based multicasting; which is based on finding a spanning tree with source node as the root. The copies of the message are routed along the spanning tree; at any intermediate node copies of the message are made and delivered to each child. Many tree-based multicast routing algorithms exist in the literature[7, 8, 9, 12]. Such techniques are best suited for packet switched networks, but are inefficient for multicomputers based on wormhole routing[2,10]. Lin et.al.[10] have shown that path based multicasting is suitable for wormhole

routed networks. In path-based multicasting a path is found which originates at the source node Src and includes all the destination nodes in $Dest$. Several algorithms have been proposed in the literature for path based deadlock-free multicasting[4,10,11,14]. The algorithm in[10] numbers the nodes in the network using a Hamiltonian path, and decomposes the network into two directed acyclic subnetworks. The *lower* network includes all edges of the form (i, j) where $H(i) > H(j)$, $H(i)$ being the Hamiltonian number of node i. Similarly, the *higher* network consists of all edges of the form (i, j) such that $H(i) < H(j)$. The destination set $Dest$ is decomposed into $Dest_L$ and $Dest_H$, where $Dest_L$ includes destination nodes whose Hamiltonian number is smaller than $H(Src)$. $Dest_H$ is similarly defined. A path can be found from Src in the *lower* network to span all the nodes in $Dest_L$; similarly, a path can be found from Src in the *higher* network to span all nodes in $Dest_H$. Since *higher* and *lower* networks are acyclic, routing in either of these subnetworks is deadlock-free.

The limitation of dual path multicasting described above is that it finds no immediate extension in a faulty network. Duato[4] extended the dual-path algorithm to achieve adaptivity in a 2-D mesh by adding virtual channels[3]. It is well known that testing for Hamiltonian property in a network is NP-complete[6]. Even when a network is known to be Hamiltonian, embedding a Hamiltonian path in the network is a difficult problem. To deal with multicasting in non-Hamiltonian networks, Tseng et.al.[14] proposed a *trip* based algorithm. A trip is a path in the network which spans all the nodes in the network at least once, but may visit some nodes more than once. Through the use of a special class of trips, called *skirt based trips*, it is possible to achieve deadlock-free multicasting using two virtual channels. The construction of a trip is by itself complex. Trip-based multicasting assumes a lot of information to be stored at each node in the form of a table which is significantly large for massively parallel multicomputers. Specifically, there is a need to store a table with $n^2 + 2n + 4d$ entries, where n is the number of nodes and d is the maximum degree.

In this paper, we present a simple, adaptive and deadlock free multicasting algorithm which works for all classes of networks. Our algorithm eliminates the limitations of earlier schemes[4,10,11,14]. The routing is deadlock-free without using any virtual channels for a large class of networks, and gives better performance in comparison to other existing schemes for irregular networks. Our algorithm is based on finding an Euler circuit in the network. Euler circuits are known to exist in any graph where all nodes have even degree. Since bidirectional physical channels can be viewed as two unidirectional channels connected back to back, each node in this directed graph has equal in-degree and out-degree. Such networks are known to have Euler circuits. A simple $(O|E|)$ algorithm exists to find an Euler circuit in these networks[6]. Our multicasting algorithm is based on numbering the channels according to the Euler number and restricting the routing in the increasing order of channel numbers to achieve deadlock freedom. The details of virtual channels and wormhole routing can be found in [2,3]. Survey of adaptive, deadlock-free wormhole routing can be found in [1,5,13].

The rest of this paper is organized as follows. Section 2 gives the concepts of Euler circuits and channel numbering. Section 3 describes the header preparation procedure and routing algorithm. In Section 4, we give a deadlock-free routing algorithm which does not require virtual channels. Section 5 describes the dynamic performance of our algorithm on both faulty and non-faulty meshes. Conclusions are discussed in Section 6.

2 Euler circuits and channel numbering

Let a network be denoted by an undirected graph $G = (V, E)$, where V is the set of nodes and E is the set of edges. Let $G' = (V, E')$ be the digraph obtained by replacing each edge in E by a pair of directed edges in the opposite directions. G' is guaranteed to contain an Euler circuit. Let $NS = \{n_1, n_2, ...n_m, n_1\}$ be the sequence of nodes traversed by an Euler circuit, where m is the size of the Euler circuit. A reverse node sequence $\overline{NS}$ is obtained by traversing the nodes in the reverse order. Thus $\overline{NS} = \{n_1, n_m, ..., n_2, n_1\}$. We divide G' into two virtual networks, a Forward Virtual Network (FVN) and a Backward Virtual Network(BVN). The channels of FVN are numbered according to the node sequence NS. The channels of BVN are marked according to the node sequence $\overline{NS}$.

Definition 1 *A mapping function* $LOW_{NS} : V \rightarrow \{1, 2, ..., m\}$, $LOW_{NS}(i) = min(j : NS[j] = i)$.

Definition 2 *A mapping function* $HIGH_{NS} : V \rightarrow \{1, 2, ..., (m+1)\}$, $HIGH_{NS}(i) = max(j : NS[j] = i)$.

Definition 3 *The mapping function Euler is defined as* $Euler_{NS} : E' \rightarrow \{1, 2, ..., m\}$, $Euler_{NS}(i, j) = k$ *if* $NS[k] = i$ *and* $NS[k + 1] = j$.

Figure 1(a) shows a graph corresponding to a 2×3 faulty mesh. In the corresponding network of figure 1(b), $NS = \{3, 4, 5, 6, 3, 6, 5, 4, 3, 2, 1, 2, 3\}$. Then $\overline{NS} = \{3, 2, 1, 2, 3, 4, 5, 6, 3, 6, 5, 4, 3\}$ is another euler circuit as seen in Figure 1(c). The edges of FVN

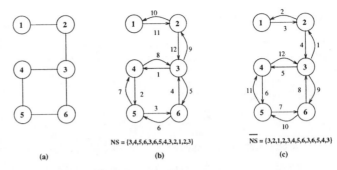

Figure 1: (a)A faulty mesh (b)Forward Virtual Network (c)Backward Virtual Network

are marked according to the node sequence NS as shown in Figure 1(b) and the edges of BVN are marked according to the node sequence $\overline{NS}$ as shown in Figure 1(c). In this example $LOW_{NS}(2) = 10$, $LOW_{\overline{NS}}(2) = 2$, $HIGH_{NS}(4) = 8$, $HIGH_{\overline{NS}}(4) = 12$ and $Euler_{NS}(6, 5) = 6$.

2.1 Reachability Conditions

Lemma 1 *For two distinct nodes* i *and* j, *if* $LOW_{NS}(i) > HIGH_{NS}(j)$ *then* $LOW_{\overline{NS}}(i) < HIGH_{\overline{NS}}(j)$.

Proof: By the definition of LOW_{NS}, $LOW_{NS}(i) = (m + 1) - HIGH_{\overline{NS}}(i) + 1$. Similarly $HIGH_{NS}(j) = (m + 1) - LOW_{\overline{NS}}(j) + 1$. Given that $LOW_{NS}(i) > HIGH_{NS}(j)$, we see $(m + 2) - HIGH_{\overline{NS}}(i) > (m + 2) - LOW_{\overline{NS}}(j)$. Hence the lemma. ♣

Lemma 2 *Let* NS *be a node sequence as defined above. Given two node* i *and* j, *there exists a path from* i *to* j *strictly in the increasing order of Euler numbers if and only if* $LOW_{NS}(i) < HIGH_{NS}(j)$.

Proof :
"If" : (By Contradiction). Let there be no path from i to j in the increasing order of channel numbers. If we start traversing from $LOW_{NS}(i)$, to the right on NS, the path traversed follows the channels in increasing order of channel numbers with an increment of 1 each time. Since there is no path to j in the increasing order, j must not be encountered while traversing to the right. Thus the node j is to the left of i on the node sequence NS. This leads to the conclusion $HIGH_{NS}(j) < LOW_{NS}(i)$, a contradiction.
"Only if": (By Contradiction).
Assume $LOW_{NS}(i) > HIGH_{NS}(j)$. If we start traversing from $LOW_{NS}(i)$, to the right on NS, then node j must not be encountered. Thus there must not be any path from i to j in the increasing order of Euler numbers, a contradiction.♣

Lemma 3 *Let* $\overline{NS}$ *be a node sequence as defined above. Given two nodes* i *and* j, *there exists a path from* i *to* j *strictly in the increasing order of channel numbers marked according to* $\overline{NS}$, *if and only if* $LOW_{\overline{NS}}(i) < HIGH_{\overline{NS}}(j)$.

Theorem 1 *There always exists a path from any node i to any other node j, strictly in the increasing order of the forward virtual channel numbers or in the increasing order of the backward virtual channel numbers.*

Proof: Given two distinct nodes i and j, at least one of the following is true (see Lemma 1)

1. $LOW_{NS}(i) < HIGH_{NS}(j)$: In this case j is reachable from node i in strictly increasing order of the virtual channel numbers on FVN.

2. $LOW_{\overline{NS}}(i) < HIGH_{\overline{NS}}(j)$: In this case j is reachable from i in strictly increasing order of the virtual channel numbers on BVN. ♣

Our multicast routing algorithm is based on Theorem 1. Two virtual channels (one for FVN and another for BVN) are sufficient to achieve deadlock-free multicasting.

3 Routing Algorithm
3.1 Header Preparation

The destination set $Dest = \{d_1, d_2, ..., d_N\}$ is divided into three subsets D_F, D_B and D_C based on the reachability conditions of Lemma 2 and 3. D_F is the set of destination nodes which can be routed to only on FVN and D_B is the set of destination nodes which can be routed only on BVN. D_C is the set of destination nodes which can be routed on both FVN and BVN.

1. $D_F = \{i \in Dest : HIGH_{\overline{NS}}(i) < LOW_{\overline{NS}}(Src)\}$

2. $D_B = \{i \in Dest : HIGH_{NS}(i) < LOW_{NS}(Src)\}$

3. $D_C = Dest - \{D_B \cup D_F\}$

Let d be the degree of the source node. To send message to the destination set $D_F(D_B)$ on FVN(BVN), at most d worms can be started, one through each of the neighboring nodes. D_F is further divided into subsets $D_F[1], D_F[2], ..., D_F[d]$, as follows.

```
for each x ∈ D_F
{
    S_x = {}
    ∀i, 1 ≤ i ≤ d
    {
    if(Euler_NS(Src, Neighbor[i]) ≤ HIGH_NS(x))
    S_x = S_x ∪ {i}
    }
    Select  some j ∈ S_x /* Adaptively permissible */
    D_F[j] → D_F[j] ∪ {x};
}
```

The above procedure partitions D_F into d subsets; a similar procedure is used to partition D_B. The procedure to partition D_C is similar, except that S_x consists of all possible neighboring nodes on FVN as well as on BVN. One of the neighboring node on FVN or BVN can be chosen adaptively, if k^{th} neighbor on FVN

is selected then $x \in D_C$ is included in the destination set $D_F[k]$. The procedure *Select* chooses one of the neighbors from S_x depending upon the distance (and/or congestion). Alternate heuristics may be used that balance the load on both the virtual networks. Consider a multicasting example on the network of Figure 1, where $Src = 2$ and $Dest = \{1, 3, 5, 6\}$. $Dest$ is divided to give $D_F = \{\}, D_B = \{5, 6\}$ and $D_C = \{1, 3\}$. Using the distance based heuristic D_C is further divided. The destination node 1 has equal distance from both forward network neighbor and backward network neighbor. Randomly we select the forward network neighbor and 1 is included in $D_F[1]$. The load balancing heuristic also includes the destination node 1 to $D_F[1]$. The resulting sets are $D_F[1] = \{1\}, D_F[2] = \{\}, D_B[1] = \{\}$ and $D_B[2] = \{6, 5, 3\}$. The subsets $D_F[1], D_F[2], ..., D_F[d]$ are sorted in the ascending order of $HIGH_{NS}$. $D_B[1], D_B[2], ..., D_B[d]$ are sorted in the ascending order of $HIGH_{\overline{NS}}$ to ensure the reachability. For our example $D_B[2]$ is sorted and the resulting set is $\{6, 5, 3\}$. Two worms are started one along FVN and other along BVN.

Theorem 2 *The time complexity of header preparation is $O(MAX(Nd, N \log N))$, where N is the size of the destination set Dest and d is the degree of the source node Src.*

Proof:

1. Division of $Dest$ into D_F, D_B and D_C takes $O(N)$ time.

2. Division of D_F takes $|D_F| \times d$ time units. Similarly, to divide $|D_B|$ and $|D_C|$ takes $|D_B| \times d$ and $|D_C| \times 2d$ time units respectively; thereby accounting for total $O(Nd)$ time complexity in the worst case.

3. Sorting of all the $2d$ destination sets $D_F[1], D_F[2], ..., D_F[d]$ and $D_B[1], D_B[2], ..., D_B[d]$ takes $O(N \log N)$ time in the worst case.

Thus the time complexity of header preparation is $O(MAX(Nd, N \log N))$ in the worst case. ♣

3.2 Routing function

The heuristic of the previous section divides the destination set into at most $2d$ subsets. To send a message M to $D_F[i]$(or $D_B[i]$), a worm is initiated along the ith neighboring node of Src on FVN(or BVN). We define the routing rules $\Re_f$ and $\Re_b$ to route on FVN and BVN respectively.

$\Re_f$: *When a message destined for a node x reaches a node j along the forward virtual channel $< i, j >$, the message can be routed to a neighbor k, along the forward virtual channel $< j, k >$, provided $Euler_{NS}(i, j) < Euler_{NS}(j, k)$ and $Euler_{NS}(j, k) \leq HIGH_{NS}(x)$.*

$\Re_b$: *When a message destined for a node x reaches a node j along the backward virtual channel $< i, j >$, the message can be routed to a neighbor k, along the backward virtual channel $< j, k >$, provided*

$Euler_{\overline{NS}}(i,j) < Euler_{\overline{NS}}(j,k)$ and $Euler_{\overline{NS}}(j,k) \leq HIGH_{\overline{NS}}(x)$.

When there is a choice in the selection of the next channel $<j,k>$, the router at node j selects a channel based on the distance heuristic and/or congestion on $<j,k>$. In our example, on the network of Figure 1, to route on BVN from node 3 to destination node 5, alternate paths available are $3 \to 4 \to 5$ and $3 \to 6 \to 5$.

Theorem 3 *A routing algorithm which applies the routing function $\Re_f$ ($\Re_b$) in the forward virtual network (backward virtual network) is deadlock free and livelock free.*

4 Multicasting without virtual channels

4.1 Necessary and sufficient condition

If, for any node sequence NS, the condition $\forall i, j \in V$, $LOW_{NS}(i) < HIGH_{NS}(j)$ is satisfied, then deadlock-free routing is assured without virtual channels. For example in figure 1, consider the Euler circuit defined by the node sequence $NS = \{1,2,3,4,5,6,3,6,5,4,3,2,1\}$. For all the nodes, the LOW value of each node on NS is less than the $HIGH$ value of all other nodes. For example $LOW_{NS}(5) < HIGH(j), \forall j \in \{1,2,3,4,5,6\}$. Thus deadlock-free routing is possible.

Lemma 4 *For a node sequence $NS = \{n_1, n_2, .., n_m, n_1\}$ corresponding to an Euler circuit, if there exists a position p such that $\forall i \in V$, $i \in \{n_1, n_2, ..., n_p\}$ and $i \in \{n_p, n_{p+1}, .., n_m, n_1\}$, then deadlock free routing can be implemented without using virtual channels.*

Proof :

- $i \neq n_p$: From the definition of LOW we have $LOW_{NS}(i) < p$. Since $i \in \{n_p, n_{p+1}, ...n_m, n_1\}$, it follows from the definition of $HIGH$ that $HIGH_{NS}(i) \geq p$. Thus for any $i \neq j$, we have $LOW_{NS}(i) < HIGH_{NS}(j)$.

- $i = n_p$: If $LOW_{NS}(i) = p$, then either $HIGH_{NS}(i) = p$ or $HIGH_{NS}(i) > p$. When $LOW_{NS}(i) = HIGH_{NS}(i) = p$, $\forall j \neq i$, we have $HIGH_{NS}(j) > p$. Thus $\forall i, j$, $HIGH_{NS}(j) > LOW_{NS}(i)$. Consider the case when $HIGH_{NS}(i) > p$ and $\forall i \in V$, $LOW_{NS}(i) \leq p$. In this case also, $LOW_{NS}(i) < HIGH_{NS}(j)$. ♣

4.2 Multicasting on Hamiltonian Graphs

Claim 1 : *If the undirected graph $G = (V,E)$ corresponding to a given network is Hamiltonian, deadlock free routing is possible without using virtual channels.* Let $HP = \{n_1, n_2, ...n_{|V|}\}$ be a Hamiltonian path in G and G' be the diected graph corresponding to the network. HP will also be a Hamiltonian path for the

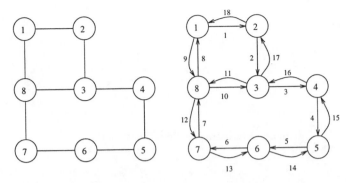

Figure 2: Deadlock free Node Sequence in a Hamiltonian graph

digraph G'. Using the procedure given below, an Euler circuit C can be found in the network G' (with bidirectional links) such that the condition of Lemma 4 is satisfied.

$FindEuler_H(G')$ {

1. Traverse from n_1 to $n_{|V|}$ along HP in G', and include the edges $<n_1, n_2>$, $<n_2, n_3>$, $...$, $<n_{|V|-1}, n_{|V|}>$ in C.

2. Starting from $n_{|V|}$, traverse back along the sequence $n_{|V|}$, $n_{|V|-1}$, $...,n_2$ in G'. During this traversal at any node i, if we encounter a pair of edges $<n_i, n_j><n_j, n_i>$ connected back to back which are not included in C then include $<n_i, n_j>$ and $<n_j, n_i>$. Include $<n_i, n_{i-1}>$.

}

Theorem 4 *The procedure $FindEuler_H()$ generates an Euler circuit C in a network corresponding to the Hamiltonian graph $G = (V, E)$, such that C satisfies the condition of Lemma 4.*

In the graph of Figure 2(a), the path $1 \to 2 \to 3 \to 4 \to 5 \to 6 \to 7 \to 8$, is Hamiltonian. An Euler circuit is found based on the procedure $FindEuler_H()$; the corresponding node sequence is $NS = \{1,2,3,4, 5,6,7,8,1,8,3,8,7,6,5,4,3,2,1\}$. Figure 2(b), shows the Euler circuit based on the Hamiltonian path. Since all the nodes are visited once before traversing back, there exists a position p such that all the nodes appear both on the right as well as left of p. In this example $p = 9$. Consider an example of multicasting from 2 to the destination set $Dest = \{4,6,8\}$. The header preparation procedure divides the destination $Dest$ into $D_1 = \{\}$ and $D_3 = \{4,6,8\}$. After sorting D_1 and D_3 in the ascending order of $HIGH_{NS}$, we get $D_1 = \{\}$ and $D_3 = \{8,6,4\}$. The path followed is $2 \xrightarrow{2} 3 \xrightarrow{11} 8 \xrightarrow{12} 7 \xrightarrow{13} 6 \xrightarrow{14} 5 \xrightarrow{15} 4$. The channel numbers, as marked on the top of the arrows are strictly in the increasing order; thus the routing is deadlockfree.

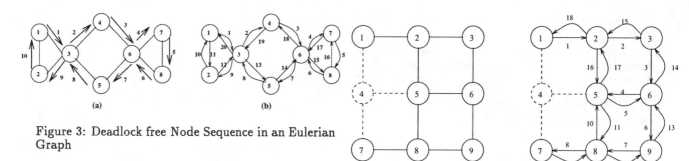

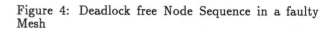

Figure 3: Deadlock free Node Sequence in an Eulerian Graph

4.3 Multicasting on Eulerian Graphs

Claim 2 : *If the undirected graph $G = (V, E)$ corresponding to a given network is Eulerian, then deadlock-free routing is possible without using virtual channels.*

Let G' be the directed graph corresponding to the network and EP be an Euler path in the undirected graph G. The following procedure $FindEuler_E()$ finds an Euler circuit C in G' such that C satisfies the condition of Lemma 4.

$FindEuler_E(G') : \{$

1. Traverse along EP in G' and include all edges encountered in C.

2. Traverse back on EP and include all edges encountered in C.

$\}$

Theorem 5 *The procedure $FindEuler_E()$ described above generates an Euler circuit C in a network corresponding to the undirected Eulerian graph $G = (V, E)$, such that C satisfies the condition of Lemma 4.*

The graph in Figure 3(a) is Eulerian (but not Hamiltonian). An Euler path in the graph is $1 \to 3 \to 4 \to 6 \to 7 \to 8 \to 6 \to 5 \to 3 \to 2 \to 1$. Applying the above procedure, we find that $NS = \{1, 3, 4, 6, 7, 8, 6, 5, 3, 2, 1, 2, 3, 5, 6, 8, 7, 6, 4, 3, 1\}$, is an Euler circuit in the network of Figure 3(b). Consider routing from 7 to 2 on the network of Figure 3. The deadlock free path is $7 \xrightarrow{5} 8 \xrightarrow{6} 6 \xrightarrow{7} 5 \xrightarrow{8} 3 \xrightarrow{9} 2$. The channel numbers are marked on the top of the arrows which represent channels. Note that these numbers are strictly in the increasing order.

4.4 Multicasting on other Graphs

Even for many graphs which are neither Eulerian nor Hamiltonian, an Euler circuit may be found in the network to satisfy the condition of Lemma 4. Consider the graph and the network for a faulty mesh shown in Figure 4. Neither a Hamiltonian nor an Eulerian path exists in the network. If the nodes are traversed in the sequence shown in Figure 4(b), we get the Euler circuit $\{1, 2, 3, 6, 5, 6, 9, 8, 7, \mathbf{8}, 5, 8, 9, 6, 3, 2, 5, 2, 1\}$. In this Euler node sequence, all the nodes appear at least once on the right as well as left of $n_{10} = 8$.

(a)　　　　　　　　　　(b)

Figure 4: Deadlock free Node Sequence in a faulty Mesh

Conjecture : *In an undirected graph G corresponding to any network, if the edge connectivity of G is greater than or equal to 2, an Euler circuit can be found to satisfy the condition of Lemma 4.*

5 Simulation Experiments and Results

We evaluated the performance of the proposed algorithm on an 8×8 mesh. Each physical channel is assumed to be divided into two virtual channels. The header is assumed to be 1 flit long. It takes one unit of time each to transmit a flit across a physical channel and to make a routing decision. Each experiment was conducted 100 times by varying the seed value for the random number generator.

5.1 Synchronous Model

In this model, all the multicast patterns are started synchronously. The number of sources is kept constant and the size of the destination set is varied in one set of experiments. We repeat the experiment, keeping the number of destinations fixed and varying the number of sources. Sources and destinations are generated randomly. The performance metric is the *mean delay*. Delay for any multicast set is measured as the difference in time taken by the message to reach the last destination node from the time at which it originated at the source node. Average of all the delays over all the multicast patterns is the *mean delay*. The messages were generated with lengths varying uniformly between 1 and 40 flits. As can be seen from Figure 5 the mean delay increases with the size of the destination set. It may be observed that there is only marginal increase in mean delay for faulty meshes. It can be noted from Figure 6 that for non-faulty meshes mean delay due for Euler based routing is significantly less than that due to Trip based.

In our second experiment, the number of destination nodes is kept fixed and the number of sources is varied from 5 to 40. It is observed that when the number of sources is larger there is a sharp increase in mean delay. Typically, for a non-faulty 8×8 mesh, the value of the mean delay with 8 sources and 25 destinations is in the range of 150 time units while for 25 sources and 8 destinations the value is approximately

230. The mean delay is more sensitive to the number of sources than the number of destinations. Figure 7 shows the variation of mean delay for faulty and non-faulty meshes with the number of sources, keeping the number of destinations fixed at 8. It may be observed that there is a marginal increase in mean delay for faulty meshes, when the number of sources is in the range of 5 to 25. We also compared the values of mean delay for the Euler and Trip based algorithms, when the number of destinations is fixed and the number of sources is increased. Figure 8 shows the comparison for an 8×8 mesh. The number of sources are fixed at 8. Our algorithm performs better than the trip based algorithm of[14].

5.2 Poisson Model

Here, we consider a more realistic model for multicasting. We assume that each node generates messages with Poisson distribution. The values of the mean arrival rate (Lambda) are assumed to vary between 0.05 and 0.80. Each node generates 90% of the time unicast messages and 10% of the time multicast messages. The size of the multicast destination sets is assumed to vary uniformly between 2 and 63. The messages are assumed to be of the length 16 flits. The performance metric considered here is *throughput*. *Throughput* is the mean number of messages going out of the network per node per time unit. For multicasting, when the message is passed on to all the destinations within the multicast set, the message is considered as completely consumed. The results are taken for 1000 messages and the initial 500 messages are discarded (warm up period).

Figure 9 shows the throughput due to the two multicasting algorithms. It is interesting to note that our Euler based multicasting gives much better throughput. While the throughput for Euler based routing saturates at 13%, throughput saturates at 5% for the trip based routing. Furthermore, it is clear from Figure 10 that for faulty meshes, the throughput does not reduce.

6 Conclusions

we have presented a multicasting algorithm which assures deadlock-free routing without the use of virtual channels in the following classes of network topologies; (a) Hamiltonian graphs, and (b) Eulerian graphs. There also exist graphs which are neither Hamiltonian or Eulerian and still permit deadlock-free multicasting without virtual channels using our algorithm. Our multicasting algorithm can be used on all connected topologies with bidirectional links using at most two virtual channels. Our algorithm is inherently adaptive and performs better than some of the existing algorithms for multicasting in faulty networks.

References

[1] R.V.Bopanna and S.Chalasani, "A comparison of Adaptive wormhole routing algorithms", *International Symposium on Computer Architecture*, 1993, pages $351 - 360$.

[2] W.J. Dally and C.L.Seitz, "Deadlock-free Message routing in multicomputers", *IEEE transactions on computer*, Vol.C-36, 1987, pages $547 - 553$.

[3] W.J.Dally, "Virtual channel flow control", *IEEE transactions on Parallel and Distributed Systems*, Vol.3, 1992, pages $194 - 205$.

[4] J.Duato, "A new theory of deadlock-free adaptive multicast routing in wormhole networks", *Symp. on Parallel and Distributed Processing*, 1993, pages $64 - 71$.

[5] P.T.Gaughan and S.Yalamanchili, "Adaptive Routing Protocol for Hypercube Interconnection Networks", *IEEE Computer*, May 1993, pages $12 - 22$.

[6] A.F.Harary, "Graph Theory" Addison Wesley, 1969.

[7] Y.Lan, "Multicast in faulty hypercubes", *International Conference on Parallel Processing*, 1992, pages $I - 58 - 61$.

[8] Y.Lan, "Adaptive Fault-tolerant Multicast in Hypercube Multicomputers", *Journal of Parallel and Distributed Computing*, Vol.23, 1994, pages $80 - 93$.

[9] Y.Lan, A.H.Esfahanian, and L.M.Ni, "Multicast in hypercube multiprocessors", *Journal of Parallel and Distributed Computing*, Vol.23, 1990, pages $30 - 41$.

[10] X.Lin, P.K.McKinley and L.M.Ni, "Deadlock-free multicast wormhole routing in 2D mesh multicomputers", *IEEE Trans. on Parallel and Distributed Systems*, Vol.5, no.8, 1994, pages $793 - 804$.

[11] X.Lin, P.K.McKinley and A.H.Esfahanian, "Adaptive Multicast Wormhole routing in 2D mesh multicomputers", *Journal of parallel and Distributed Computing*, Vol.28, 1995, pages $19 - 31$.

[12] J. Misic, "Multiast Communication algorithm on a Wormhole-Routed Star Graph Interconnection Network", *Proceedings of IEEE international conference on high performance computing*, 1996, pages $322 - 329$.

[13] L.M.Ni and P.K.McKinley, "A survey of wormhole routing techniques in Direct Networks", *IEEE Computer*, Feb.1993, pages $62 - 76$.

[14] Y.C Tseng, D.K. Panda and T.H.Lai, "A Trip-based Multicasting Model in Wormhole-routed Networks with Virtual Channels", *IEEE Trans. on Par. and Dist. Sys.*,1996 ,Vol.7,No.2,pages $138 - 150$.

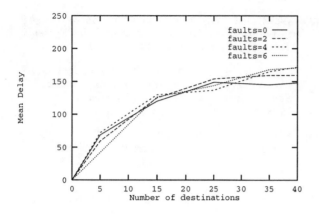

Figure 5: Mean delay of multicasting when number of sources=8

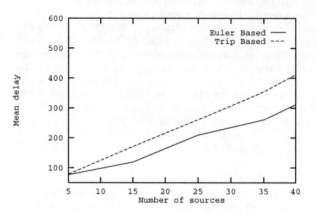

Figure 8: Comparison of mean delay with 8 destinations for non-faulty 8 × 8 mesh

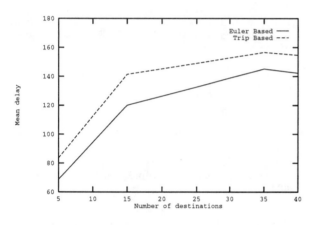

Figure 6: Comparison of mean delay due to the two algorithms with sources=8

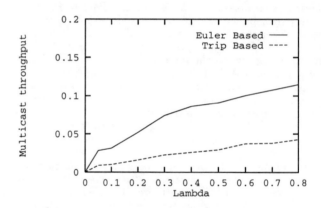

Figure 9: Comparison of throughput on 8 × 8 mesh

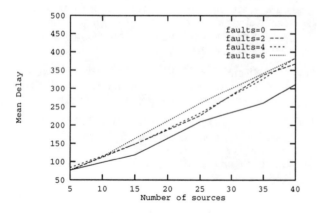

Figure 7: Mean delay for number of destinations=8

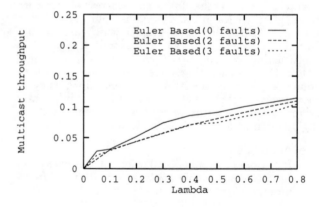

Figure 10: Throughput for faulty and non-faulty 8 × 8 mesh

Performance Analysis and Simulation of Multicast Networks

Yuanyuan Yang*
Department of Computer Science
University of Vermont
Burlington, VT 05405
yang@cs.uvm.edu

Jianchao Wang
GTE Laboratories
40 Sylvan Road
Waltham, MA 02254
jwang@gte.com

Abstract

In this paper, we look into the issue of supporting multicast in the well-known three-stage Clos network or $v(m, n, r)$ network. We first develop an analytical model for the blocking probability of the $v(m, n, r)$ multicast network, and then study the blocking behavior of the network under various routing control strategies through simulations. Our analytical and simulation results show that a $v(m, n, r)$ network with a small number of middle switches m, such as $m = n + c$ or dn, where c and d are small constants, is almost nonblocking for multicast connections, although theoretically it requires $m \geq \Theta\left(n \frac{\log r}{\log \log r}\right)$ to achieve nonblocking for multicast connections. We also demonstrate that routing control strategies are effective for reducing the blocking probability of the multicast network. The best routing control strategy can provide a factor of 2 to 3 performance improvement over random routing. The results indicate that a $v(m, n, r)$ network with a comparable cost to a permutation network can provide cost-effective support for multicast communication.

1 Introduction

Multicast communication is one of the most important collective communication operations[1] and is highly demanded in parallel applications as well as in other communication environments. Some examples of such applications are barrier synchronization and write update/invalidate in directory-based cache coherence protocols. It has become increasingly important to support multicast communication in scalable parallel computers. In general, providing multicast support at hardware/interconnection network level is the most efficient way supporting such communication operations[2]. In this paper, we look into the issue of supporting multicast in the well-known three-stage Clos network[3]. Clos-type networks have been widely used in various interconnection problems. Some recent applications include the NEC ATOM switch designed for BISDN, the IBM GF11 multiprocessor, and ANSI Fibre Channel Standard for interconnection of processors to the I/O system. More recently, it was shown[4] that the network in the IBM SP2 is functionally equivalent to the Clos network.

A three-stage Clos network or a $v(m, n, r)$ network[3] has r ($n \times m$) switches in the first stage (or input stage), m ($r \times r$) switches in the middle stage, and r ($m \times n$) switches in the third

*Supported by the U.S. National Science Foundation under Grant No. OSR-9350540 and MIP-9522532, and by the U.S. Army Research Office under Grant No. DAAH04-96-1-0234.

stage (or output stage). Figure 1 illustrates a general schematic of a $v(m, n, r)$ network. The main focus of the study for this type of network is to determine the minimum value of the network parameter m for a certain type of connecting capability to achieve the minimum network cost.

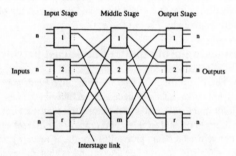

Figure 1: An $N \times N$ $v(m, n, r)$ network with $N = nr$.

When the $v(m, n, r)$ network is considered for supporting multicast, it is reasonable to assume that every switch in the network has multicast capability. Then a *multicast connection* from an input port can be simply expressed in terms of output switches it connects to. The number of output switches in a multicast connection is referred to as the *fanout* of the multicast connection.

Several designs have been proposed for this type of multicast network[5, 6, 7]. The most recent design[7] showed that a $v(m, n, r)$ network is *nonblocking* for arbitrary multicast connections if the number of middle switches $m \geq 3(n - 1)\frac{\log r}{\log \log r}$. Although the new condition significantly improved the previous sufficient condition[5, 6], it is still much larger than that for a nonblocking permutation network which requires only $m \geq 2n - 1$[3]. On the other hand, a necessary condition, $m = \Theta\left(n \frac{\log r}{\log \log r}\right)$, was obtained[8] for this type of multicast network to be nonblocking under three typical routing control strategies, which matches the sufficient condition in [7]. This suggests that there is little room for further improvement on the nonblocking condition for multicast connections. However, note that the previous work has primarily focused on the analysis of nonblocking conditions. Little has been done on the behavior of the $v(m, n, r)$ multicast network with only a comparable network cost to a permutation network. In this paper, we study this issue along two parallel lines: (1) develop an analytical model for the blocking probability of the $v(m, n, r)$ multicast networks; (2) look into the blocking behavior of the networks under various routing control strategies through simulations.

0190-3918/97 $10.00 © 1997 IEEE

2 Analysis of Multicast Blocking Probability

In general, determination of blocking probability in a multistage network (even for permutation networks) is inherently complex and difficult. This is due to the fact that there are many possible paths to consider in a typical large network, and the dependencies among links in the network lead to combinatorial explosion problems. To the best of our knowledge, previous work on blocking probability of $v(m, n, r)$ networks was done only for permutation networks. Several analytical models have been proposed in the literature, for example, [9, 10, 11]. C.Y. Lee[9, 10] gave the simplest method for analyzing the blocking probability for the $v(m, n, r)$ permutation network, in which the events that individual links are busy are assumed to be independent. Let the probability that a typical input port or output port is busy be a, and assume that the incoming traffic is uniformly distributed over the m interstage links. Then the probability that an interstage link is busy is given by $p = \frac{an}{m}$, and is idle is given by $q = 1 - p$. With the link independence assumption, the probability that no idle path is available for making the connection between a given input and output, or the blocking probability, is given by $P_B = (1 - q^2)^m$.

2.1 Blocking probability of multicast networks

However, it is difficult to directly generalize Lee's approach to multicast networks. This is because that multicast trees are not link disjoint and the dependencies among the multicast trees make the problem almost intractable. We employ a different approach here to derive the blocking probability for the $v(m, n, r)$ multicast networks. We still follow Lee's assumption that the events that individual links are busy are independent.

Consider the subnetwork in Figure 2. Let ε be the event that a connection request with fanout f cannot be realized in the subnetwork. Denote the event that link a_i is busy as $\mathbf{a}_i$ and the event that link a_i is idle as $\bar{\mathbf{a}}_i$ for $1 \leq i \leq m$. Let σ represent the state of the input-middle interstage links $a_1, a_2, \ldots, a_m$, $P(\varepsilon|\sigma)$ be the conditional blocking probability in this state, and $P(\sigma)$ be the probability of being in state σ. If in state σ, k a_i's are idle and the rest of a_i's are busy, by the link independence assumption we have $P(\sigma) = q^k p^{m-k}$. Considering all states of input-middle interstage links $a_1, a_2, \ldots, a_m$, and using symmetry of the states, it is apparent that the *blocking probability for a multicast connection with fanout* f is given by

$$P_B(f) = P(\varepsilon) = \sum_{\sigma} P(\sigma)P(\varepsilon|\sigma)$$

$$= \sum_{k=0}^{m} \binom{m}{k} q^k p^{m-k} P(\varepsilon|\bar{\mathbf{a}}_1, \ldots, \bar{\mathbf{a}}_k, \mathbf{a}_{k+1}, \ldots, \mathbf{a}_m) \ (1)$$

Under the condition that $a_{k+1}, \ldots, a_m$ are busy and rest of a_i's are idle, finding the blocking probability of the network is equivalent to finding the blocking probability of a smaller subnetwork shown in Figure 2 by dashed lines. We have the following lemma concerning the blocking property of this subnetwork.

Lemma 1 *Assume that the interstage links $a_1, a_2, \ldots, a_k$ in the subnetwork in Figure 2 are idle. A multicast connection from an input of the input switch to f distinct output switches cannot be realized iff there exists an output switch whose all k inputs are busy.*

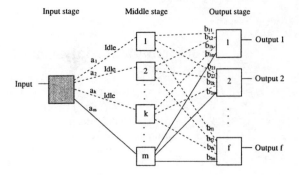

Figure 2: The subnetwork associated with a multicast connection with fanout f. Dashed lines indicate the idle link subnetwork.

Proof. If there exists an output switch whose all k inputs are busy, then there is not any idle path to connect the input switch to this output switch. On the other hand, if there exists at least one idle input on each of the f output switches, noticing that all input-middle interstage links $a_1, a_2, \ldots, a_k$ are idle, then there exist idle paths from the input switch to all the f output switches and these paths form a multicast tree which can be used to realize the connection□

Let ε' be the event that the connection request with fanout f cannot be realized in the subnetwork in Figure 2. We have

$$P(\varepsilon') = P(\varepsilon|\bar{\mathbf{a}}_1, \ldots, \bar{\mathbf{a}}_k, \mathbf{a}_{k+1}, \ldots, \mathbf{a}_m) \quad (2)$$

On the other hand, for a middle-output interstage link b_{ij} which is an input to the ith output switch in Figure 2, let $\mathbf{b}_{ij}$ be the event that b_{ij} is busy, where $1 \leq i \leq f$ and $1 \leq j \leq k$. From Lemma 1, event ε' can be expressed in terms of events $\mathbf{b}_{ij}$'s as follows.

$$\varepsilon' = (\mathbf{b}_{11} \cap \mathbf{b}_{12} \cap \cdots \cap \mathbf{b}_{1k}) \cup (\mathbf{b}_{21} \cap \mathbf{b}_{22} \cap \cdots \cap \mathbf{b}_{2k}) \cup \cdots$$
$$\cup (\mathbf{b}_{f1} \cap \mathbf{b}_{f2} \cap \cdots \cap \mathbf{b}_{fk}) \quad (3)$$

By the link independence assumption, for any $i \neq i'$ or $j \neq j'$, events $\mathbf{b}_{ij}$ and $\mathbf{b}_{i'j'}$ are independent, and for any $i \neq i'$, events $(\mathbf{b}_{i1} \cap \mathbf{b}_{i2} \cap \cdots \cap \mathbf{b}_{ik})$ and $(\mathbf{b}_{i'1} \cap \mathbf{b}_{i'2} \cap \cdots \cap \mathbf{b}_{i'k})$ are independent since there are not any shared links. Therefore, from (3) and by De Morgan's laws, the probability of event ε' is given by

$$P(\varepsilon') = 1 - \prod_{i=1}^{f} P(\overline{\mathbf{b}_{i1} \cap \mathbf{b}_{i2} \cap \cdots \cap \mathbf{b}_{ik}})$$

$$= 1 - \prod_{i=1}^{f} [1 - P(\mathbf{b}_{i1} \cap \mathbf{b}_{i2} \cap \cdots \cap \mathbf{b}_{ik})]$$

$$= 1 - \prod_{i=1}^{f} (1 - p^k) = 1 - (1 - p^k)^f \quad (4)$$

Combing (1), (2) and (4), we obtain the blocking probability for a multicast connection with fanout f

$$P_B(f) = \sum_{k=0}^{m} \binom{m}{k} q^k p^{m-k} [1 - (1 - p^k)^f] \quad (5)$$

In particular, letting $f = 1$, we have

$$P_B(1) = \sum_{k=0}^{m} \binom{m}{k} q^k p^{m-k} [1 - (1 - p^k)] = p^m \sum_{k=0}^{m} \binom{m}{k} q^k$$

$$= p^m (1 + q)^m = (1 - q)^m (1 + q)^m = (1 - q^2)^m.$$

This is exactly Lee's blocking probability for the $v(m, n, r)$ permutation network[9, 10]. Figure 3 gives some numerical examples of $P_B(f)$ in (5). From Figure 3 we can see that, for a fixed m the blocking probability increases as the fanout gets larger, and for a fixed fanout, the blocking probability decreases sharply as m gets larger.

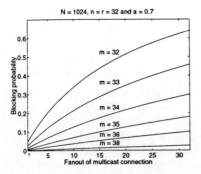

Figure 3: Blocking probabilities for $v(m, 32, 32)$ network with fanouts between 1 and 32.

In general, we may be more interested in the typical behavior of the blocking probability and ask about its "average" value over all fanouts. Suppose the probability distribution for different fanouts in a multicast connection is

$$\{w_f | 0 \leq w_f \leq 1, 1 \leq f \leq r, \sum_{i=1}^{r} w_i = 1\}.$$

The "average" value of the blocking probability can be written as

$$P_B = \sum_{f=1}^{r} P_B(f) \cdot w_f \quad (6)$$

Suppose the fanout is uniformly distributed over 1 to r. (6) becomes

$$P_B = \frac{1}{r} \sum_{f=1}^{r} P_B(f) = \frac{1}{r} \sum_{f=1}^{r} \sum_{k=0}^{m} \binom{m}{k} q^k p^{m-k} [1 - (1 - p^k)^f] \quad (7)$$

In the rest of the paper, we simply refer to P_B as the *blocking probability of the $v(m, n, r)$ multicast network*.

2.2 Asymptotic bound on the blocking probability

Since there is (apparently) no closed form for the blocking probability P_B in (7), it is appropriate that we derive a closed form for the asymptotic bound on it.

We are interested in the networks with small m values and consider the following two cases:
Case 1: $m = n + c$, for some constant integer $c > 1$.
Case 2: $m = dn$, for some constant $d > 1$.

In our analysis, we need the following inequality

$$1 - (1 - x)^l < lx, \quad (8)$$

where $0 < x < 1$, and l is an integer ≥ 1.

By applying (8) to (7), we can obtain an upper bound on P_B:

$$P_B < \frac{1}{r} \sum_{f=1}^{r} \sum_{k=0}^{m} \binom{m}{k} q^k p^{m-k} \cdot f \cdot p^k$$

$$= \frac{1}{r} (1 - q^2)^m \sum_{f=1}^{r} f = \frac{r+1}{2} [1 - (1-p)^2]^m \quad (9)$$

Consider Case 1 first. Suppose $m = n + c$ for some constant integer $c > 1$. As discussed in Section 2, we have $p = \frac{an}{m}$, where a is a constant and $0 \leq a < 1$. Then

$$[1 - (1-p)^2]^m = \left[1 - \left(1 - \frac{an}{m}\right)^2\right]^m < [1 - (1-a)^2]^m$$

which implies $P_B = O(r \cdot \delta^m)$, where $\delta = 1 - (1-a)^2$. Clearly, δ is a constant such that $0 < \delta < 1$.

Now consider Case 2. Suppose $m = dn$ for some constant $d > 1$. Since $p < \frac{n}{m} = \frac{1}{d}$, (9) becomes

$$P_B < \frac{r+1}{2} \left[1 - \left(1 - \frac{1}{d}\right)^2\right]^m = O(r \cdot \delta'^m),$$

where $\delta' = 1 - (1 - \frac{1}{d})^2$. Similarly, δ' is a constant such that $0 < \delta' < 1$.

Notice that, in both cases, if $r = O(n)$ we obtain $P_B = O(e^{-\epsilon n})$, where ϵ is a constant > 0. We can see that the blocking probability tends to zero very quickly as n increases. In other words, for a sufficiently large n, the network is almost nonblocking for multicast connections. This suggests that, in practice, even when the network parameter m is as small as dn or $n + c$, the network performance is still fairly good. Such m values are much smaller than the theoretical bound $\Theta(n \frac{\log r}{\log \log r})$ given in [7, 8].

3 Experimental Study of the Blocking Behavior of Multicast Networks

Our model in previous section indicates that the blocking probability is very low even for small m. In this section, we look into this issue through the simulation of real networks. As discussed in [7], a routing control strategy plays an important role in reducing the non-uniformity of multicast connections, and in turn reducing the blocking probability of the $v(m, n, r)$ multicast network. Therefore, it is more appropriate to study the blocking behavior of the network under a good routing control strategy. In our simulation, we employ seven different routing control strategies and compare the blocking probabilities under all these control strategies.

3.1 A generic routing algorithm

We start from describing a generic routing algorithm in which different routing control strategies can be embedded. In a $v(m, n, r)$ network, for any input port, we refer to the set of middle switches with currently unused links to the input switch associated with the input port *available middle switches*. For any middle switch, we refer to the subset of output switches to which the middle switch is currently providing connection paths from the input ports *destination set* of the middle switch. Given a $v(m, n, r)$ multicast network with destination sets and a new connection request, the main function of a routing algorithm is to choose a set of middle switches which can satisfy the connection request. The routing algorithm can be described as follows.

Algorithm:

Step 1: If no available middle switches for the current connection request, then exit without making the connection (blocking), otherwise go to Step 2.

Step 2: Choose a non-full middle switch (i.e. a middle switch with at least one idle output link) among the available middle switches for the connection request according to some control strategy. If no such middle switch exits, then exit without making the connection (blocking).

Step 3: Realize as large as possible portion of the connection request in the middle switch chosen in Step 2.

Step 4: Update the connection request by discarding the portion that is satisfied by the middle switch chosen in Step 2.

Step 5: If the connection request is non-empty, go to Step 1.

3.2 Routing control strategies

In Step 2 of the above generic routing algorithm, there are many ways to choose middle switches among available middle switches. Due to the non-uniform nature of multicast connections, if no control strategy is employed, we can expect that the number of middle switches required for nonblocking becomes large. Hence, we must employ some kind of "intelligent" control strategy to reduce such non-uniformity of multicast connections. In the following, we describe seven control strategies for choosing middle switches from the available middle switches in a $v(m, n, r)$ multicast network.

- *Smallest Absolute Cardinality Strategy:* Choose a middle switch whose destination set has the smallest cardinality.

- *Largest Absolute Cardinality Strategy:* Choose a middle switch whose destination set has the largest cardinality.

- *Average Absolute Cardinality Strategy:* Choose a middle switch such that the cardinality of its destination set is equal to the average cardinality of all available middle switches.

- *Smallest Relative Cardinality Strategy:* Choose a middle switch whose destination set has the smallest cardinality with respect to the connection request.

- *Largest Relative Cardinality Strategy:* Choose a middle switch whose destination set has the largest cardinality with respect to the connection request.

- *Average Relative Cardinality Strategy:* Choose a middle switch such that the cardinality of its destination set with respect to the connection request is equal to the average cardinality of all available middle switches with respect to the connection request.

- *Random Strategy:* Choose a middle switch at random.

3.3 The network simulator

We have developed a discrete event simulator which simulates the $v(m, n, r)$ multicast network to study the blocking behavior of the network under these routing control strategies.

The discrete event simulator used to evaluate the performance of $v(m, n, r)$ multicast network is based on the following assumptions.

- Uniform traffic and Poisson traffic are considered.

- The network is considered as a multiple-server queueing system with the number of servers varies from n to N depending on the network state.

- In the steady state, the arrival rate of the connection requests is equal to the departure rate (service rate) of the connections.

- A new multicast connection request is randomly generated among all idle network input ports and output ports.

- During the network operation, a certain workload is maintained. The workload is measured by the network utilization (the ratio of the total number of busy output ports to N).

The simulator has three main components: *network initializer, connection/disconnection handler,* and *data collector. Network initializer* module initializes the network to a prespecified utilization ratio. *Connection/disconnection handler* module performs basic network operations, such as generating connection requests, realizing and releasing connections. The *data collector* module records all information regarding the network blocking behavior. For each network size, control strategy and traffic model, the network is simulated for five runs with different initial network states, and the final results are average over these five runs. In each run, 5000 connection requests are handled and 95% confidence interval is achieved.

3.4 The simulation results

Extensive simulations were carried out on the $v(m, n, r)$ multicast networks for different m values under seven routing control strategies. We present and discuss the simulation results for the following two network configurations.

Configuration 1: $N = 1024, n = r = 32$, and $32 \leq m \leq 42$.

Configuration 2: $N = 4096, n = r = 64$, and $64 \leq m \leq 76$.

In Figure 4, we plotted the blocking probability for configurations 1 and 2 under seven routing control strategies. The results were obtained for both uniform traffic and Poisson traffic with initial utilization = 90%. From Figure 4, we observe that, in configuration 1, when $m = 32 = n$ the blocking probability is relatively high under all seven control strategies, and as the number of middle switches increases the blocking probability tends to zero quickly. Specially, when $m \geq 42 = n + 10 \approx 1.31n$, no blocking cases were found among 25,000 connection requests for each strategy. We also see that, under uniform traffic, *smallest relative, average relative,* and *largest absolute* strategies lead to a lower blocking probability, and the rest of strategies have a higher blocking probability. Under Poisson traffic, *smallest relative* strategy has the lowest blocking probability and *random* strategy has the highest blocking probability in most cases. Moreover, under Poisson traffic, the blocking probability is sightly lower than that under uniform traffic for the same strategy. In configuration 2, it shows a similar general trend. In this case, when $m \geq 76 = n + 12 \approx 1.19n$, no blocking cases were found among 25,000 connection requests for each strategy. Under uniform traffic, the *largest relative* strategy joins the lower blocking probability strategy group, and under Poisson traffic, *smallest relative, largest absolute, average relative* and *largest relative* have a lower blocking probability. Finally, we observe that, in both configurations and under two types of traffic distributions, a "better" strategy, such as *smallest relative* strategy, can approximately provide a factor of 2 to 3 performance improvement over other "poorer" strategies, such as *random* strategy.

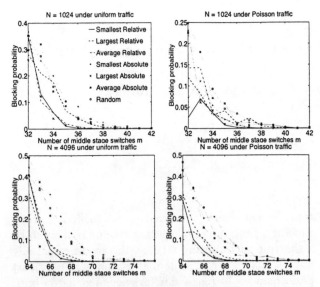

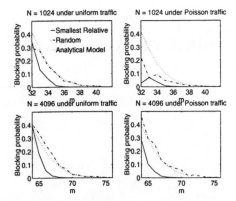

Figure 4: The blocking probability of the $v(m, n, r)$ multicast network under seven routing control strategies.

Figure 5: The comparison between the analytical model and the simulation results.

4 Comparison between Analytical Model and Simulation Results

In this section, we compare the analytical model with the simulation results. For simulation results, it is reasonable that we choose two typical routing control strategies: *smallest relative* and *random*.

Figure 5 depicts the comparisons between the analytical blocking probability P_B in (7) and the simulation results under *smallest relative* and *random* control strategies for configuration 1 and configuration 2. From Figure 5, we observe that, in configuration 1 the analytical blocking probability approaches zero when $m \geq 42 \approx 1.31n$, and in configuration 2 it approaches zero when $m \geq 76 \approx 1.19n$. We can see that the analytical model matches well with the simulation result under *random* strategy. As discussed in the previous section, *random* strategy has higher blocking probability in most cases than other strategies. Thus, the analytical model can be approximately used as an upper bound on the real blocking probability. Finally, we can see that, although the analytical model and the simulation results were obtained under different assumptions, they reveal the same trend in the blocking behavior of the $v(m, n, r)$ multicast network: when m gets slightly larger than n, the network becomes almost nonblocking.

5 Conclusions

We have studied the blocking behavior of the $v(m, n, r)$ multicast networks along two parallel lines: (1) developed an analytical model for the blocking probability of the $v(m, n, r)$ multicast network; (2) studied the blocking behavior of the network under various routing control strategies through simulations. Our observations can be summarized as follows. A network with a small m, such as $m = n + c$ or dn, where c and d are small constants, is almost nonblocking for multicast connections, although theoretically it requires $m \geq \Theta \left(n \frac{\log r}{\log \log r} \right)$ to achieve nonblocking for multicast connections. Routing control strategies are effective for reducing

the blocking probability of the multicast network. The best routing control strategy can provide a factor of 2 to 3 performance improvement over random routing. The results indicate that a $v(m, n, r)$ network with a comparable cost to a permutation network can provide cost-effective support for multicast communication.

References

[1] D.K. Panda, "Issues in designing efficient and practical algorithms for collective communication on wormhole-routed systems," *ICPP'95 Workshop on Challenges for Parallel Processing*, pp. 8-15, 1995.

[2] L.M. Ni, "Should scalable parallel computers support efficient hardware multicast?" *ICPP'95 Workshop on Challenges for Parallel Processing*, pp. 2-7, 1995.

[3] C. Clos, "A study of non-blocking switching networks," *BSTJ*, vol. 32, pp. 406-424, 1953.

[4] M.T. Bruggencate and S. Chalasani, "Equivalence between SP2 high-performance switches and three-stage Clos networks," *ICPP'96*, pp. I-1–I-8, 1996.

[5] G.M. Masson and B.W. Jordan, "Generalized multi-stage connection networks," *Networks*, vol. 2, pp. 191-209, 1972.

[6] F.K. Hwang and A. Jajszczyk, "On nonblocking multiconnection networks," *IEEE Trans. Comm.*, vol. COM-34, pp. 1038-1041, 1986.

[7] Y. Yang and G.M. Masson, "Nonblocking broadcast switching networks," *IEEE Trans. Comp.*, vol. C-40, pp. 1005-1015, 1991.

[8] Y. Yang and G.M. Masson, "The necessary conditions for Clos-type nonblocking multicast networks," *IPPS'96*, pp. 789-795, 1996.

[9] C.Y. Lee, "Analysis of switching networks," *BSTJ*, vol. 34, no. 6, Nov. 1955, pp. 1287-1315.

[10] Mischa Schwartz, *Telecommunication Networks: Protocols, Modeling and Analysis*, Addison-Wesley Publishing, 1987.

[11] Y. Mun, Y. Tang and V. Devarajan, "Analysis of call packing and rearrangement in a multi stage switch," *IEEE Trans. Comm.*, vol. 42, No. 2/3/4, pp. 252-254, 1994.

Sufficient Conditions for Optimal Multicast Communication

Barbara D. Birchler, Abdol-Hossein Esfahanian, and Eric Torng
Department of Computer Science
Michigan State University
East Lansing, MI 48824-1266
{birchler,esfahani,torng}@cps.msu.edu

Abstract

*In this paper, we give a general technique for computing **optimal** multicast calling schedules in **any** multiprocessor system that utilizes a direct network interconnection structure as long as a few simple conditions are satisfied. Since almost any real system will satisfy these conditions, this result essentially means that multicast can **always** be performed in $\lceil \log(d+1) \rceil$ phases where d is the number of multicast destinations. In particular, previous results on optimal multicast algorithms in specific direct network topologies [1, 2, 3] are simply corollaries of our result.*

1 Introduction

Multicast communication has been studied under a wide variety of models for parallel and distributed computing [1, 2, 3, 4, 5, 6, 7, 8]. In this paper, we present sufficient conditions that allow optimal time unicast-based multicast in direct network systems that employ a cut-through routing technique such as wormhole routing. This result provides a *general* technique for constructing optimal time multicast algorithms for *arbitrary* topologies. It also explains the theoretical basis that enabled previous optimal multicast algorithms to be developed for specific routing strategies in specific topologies [1, 2, 3].

We assume that the direct network can be modeled as a graph $G(V, E)$, where $V(G)$ represents the nodes of the network, and $v_i v_j \in E(G)$ if nodes v_i and v_j have a direct communication link between them. In particular, if $e = v_i v_j$, we assume that both v_i and v_j can send messages along edge e, but not at the same time. The undirected graph model G is equivalent to a symmetric digraph D in which each edge $v_i v_j$ in G is replaced by two arcs $a_1 = v_i v_j$ and $a_2 = v_j v_i$ in D. In the digraph model, the two arcs a_1 and a_2 can not be used simultaneously.

Within this context, we show that *any* routing scheme that uses *shortest paths* to deliver messages between all pairs of nodes in the network allows op-timal unicast-based multicast in any arbitrary graph topology. Since any real routing scheme is likely to be a shortest path routing scheme, this result essentially implies that *any* real system allows optimal multicast performance. In particular, previous results on optimal multicast algorithms for specific routing strategies in specific topologies [1, 2, 3] are corollaries of our result.

The remainder of the paper is organized as follows. Section 2 explains the background and the framework in which multicast is done. Section 3 contains the proofs of our results. Due to lack of space, we provide only proof sketches in many cases. Section 4 discusses the implications of our result.

2 Background

A *multicast* request, denoted by $M = (s, D)$, signifies that a single message must be sent from a *source* node s in a communication network to some subset D of *destination* nodes in the network. Two special cases of multicast are *unicast* (one-to-one communication) and *broadcast* (one-to-all communication). Because multicast communication is a fundamental component of many parallel and distributed computing applications, efficient multicast implementation is an important issue in the high performance computing arena.

2.1 UBM Implementation

Due to the complexity of hardware implementations of one-to-many communication, most existing direct network systems only support unicast communication in hardware. Thus, multicast must be provided in software. Several authors have addressed a software technique called Unicast-Based Multicast (UBM) [1, 2, 3, 6]. A UBM *schedule* for implementing $M = (s, D)$ consists of several time steps in which one or more informed nodes send the message to uninformed nodes in D. Cut-through switching allows us to assume that each step of the UBM schedule requires unit time regardless of the number of calls that are made during that step [9].

There are three conditions that a UBM schedule must satisfy in order to be a *legal* implementation for M. First, only nodes in D can receive the message. Second, all nodes in D must eventually receive the message. Third, the hardware must allow simultaneous use of all the paths that are used to send messages in a single time step. In the direct network system that we consider, a node can switch multiple incoming messages as long as the output ports needed are not the same; this is equivalent to requiring that all paths used in a single time step are edge disjoint. This is referred to as the *line-switching* model of communication [1, 6].

The *length* of a UBM schedule is the number of time steps in which calls are made. Because the number of informed nodes can at most double in each step, the minimum length of a UBM schedule is $\lceil \log(|D|+1) \rceil$.

2.2 Routing Schemes

A routing scheme R of a direct network is a collection of all permissible paths along which a message can be delivered for each pair of nodes in the network. If a routing scheme R includes *every* (u,v)-path for each u and v, the system is said to use *free* routing [2]. If, on the other hand, R includes *exactly one* path for every pair of nodes, the system is said to use *oblivious* routing or *restricted* routing [2].

In practice, parallel systems use oblivious routing rather than free routing. For example, current systems based on mesh and hypercube topologies use an oblivious routing scheme called dimension-ordered routing.

3 Shortest Path Routing Schemes

The lower bound on the number of steps required to complete a multicast request is $\lceil \log(|D|+1) \rceil$. Thus, a multicast schedule with length $\lceil \log(|D|+1) \rceil$ is optimal. Ideally, we want to find an optimal multicast schedule for any multicast request in any direct network topology. Optimal UBM algorithms have been designed for arbitrary network topologies that employ free routing, for mesh topologies that use xy-routing, for hypercube topologies that use e-cube routing, and for torus topologies that use dimension ordered routing [2, 3]. Unfortunately, multicast cannot always be performed in $\lceil \log(|D|+1) \rceil$ steps. A natural question to ask is, "Under what conditions can UBM be done in $\lceil \log(|D|+1) \rceil$ time steps?" In this section, we show that any routing scheme that includes a shortest path for all pairs of nodes allows optimal line-switching UBM in any symmetric digraph. First, some definitions are needed to prove the result.

Definition 3.1 *Let $dis_G(u,v)$ be the length of a shortest uv-path in G.*

Definition 3.2 *A routing scheme R is called a shortest path routing scheme if for every pair of nodes u and v, R contains a routing path of length $dis_G(u,v)$.*

Definition 3.3 *Let $|p(u,v)|$ denote the length of path $p(u,v)$.*

The following Lemma is the key for finding edge disjoint routing paths needed to create a legal line-switching multicast schedule.

Lemma 3.1 *Let R be a shortest path routing scheme for a direct network system represented by a symmetric digraph $D(V,A)$. Further, let $p_R(s,d)$ be the path used by R to send a message from node s to node d. If there are two routing paths $p_R(s_1,d_1)$ and $p_R(s_2,d_2)$ that contain a common underlying edge, then either $|p_R(s_1,s_2)| + |p_R(d_1,d_2)| < |p_R(s_1,d_1)| + |p_R(s_2,d_2)|$, or $|p_R(s_1,d_2)| + |p_R(s_2,d_1)| < |p_R(s_1,d_1)| + |p_R(s_2,d_2)|$.*

Proof: Suppose that both $p_R(s_1,d_1)$ and $p_R(s_2,d_2)$ contain an underlying edge xy. WLOG, assume that $p_R(s_1,s_2)$ contains arc xy. Then there are two cases to consider,

1. $p_R(s_2,d_2)$ contains arc xy (see Figure 1(a)).

2. $p_R(s_2,d_2)$ contains arc yx (see Figure 1(b)).

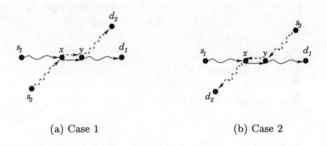

(a) Case 1   (b) Case 2

Figure 1: Two conflicting paths.

It is easy to see that in the first case, $|p_R(s_1,d_1)| + |p_R(s_2,d_2)| > |p_R(s_1,s_2)| + |p_R(d_1,d_2)|$, and in the second case, $|p_R(s_1,d_1)| + |p_R(s_2,d_2)| > |p_R(s_1,d_2)| + |p_R(s_2,d_1)|$. $\square$

We will illustrate the use of Lemma 3.1 to find pairwise edge disjoint shortest paths between pairs of vertices. Suppose that a 2D-mesh uses xy-routing. Consider the following set of vertices: $s_1 = (4,2)$, $s_2 = (4,1)$, $s_3 = (2,4)$, $d_1 = (2,3)$, $d_2 = (1,4)$, and $d_3 = (1,2)$. Figure 2(a) shows the xy-routing paths used for each (s_i, d_i) pair. Because both $p(s_1,d_1)$ and $p(s_2,d_2)$ contain the edge from $(4,2)$ to $(4,3)$, these

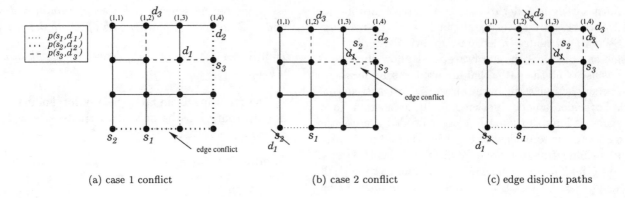

(a) case 1 conflict   (b) case 2 conflict   (c) edge disjoint paths

Figure 2: Using Lemma 3.1.

paths cannot be used during the same step of a legal line-switching schedule. Since the conflict between $p(s_1, d_1)$ and $p(s_2, d_2)$ is as described by case 1 of the proof of Lemma 3.1, swapping d_1 and s_2 will result in paths whose sum is less than 9 (the original sum of the path lengths). Figure 2(b) shows that the sum of the new paths is 3.

Now, in Figure 2(b) $p(s_2, d_2)$ and $p(s_3, d_3)$ have an edge conflict as described by case 2 of the proof of Lemma 3.1. Again, the line-switching model does not allow these paths to be used to deliver messages during the same step. By Lemma 3.1, swapping d_2 and d_3 will result in paths whose sum is less than 5. Figure 2(c) shows that the sum of the lengths of the new paths is 3. Notice that all the paths in Figure 2(c) are edge disjoint. Lemma 3.1 leads naturally to a method for resolving all edge conflicts in a shortest path routing scheme.

Lemma 3.2 *Let R be a shortest path routing scheme, X be a set of nodes, and $k = \lfloor \frac{|X|}{2} \rfloor$. Then there exists a set P of k pairwise edge disjoint paths from R such that all the $2k$ endpoints of the paths in P are distinct nodes in X.*

Proof: Let $X = \{x_1, \ldots, x_n\}$, and let $p_R(x_i, x_j)$ be a shortest routing path from R. We initialize $M(0)$ to be a set of paths between k arbitrary pairs of vertices in X. WLOG, let $M(0) = \cup_{i=1}^{k} p_i$, where $p_i = p_R(x_i, x_{k+i})$.

Initially, $M(0)$ may not contain pairwise edge-disjoint paths. We describe a procedure that transforms $M(0)$ into a set of pairwise edge-disjoint paths. Let $M(i)$ be the set of paths associated with iteration i in the procedure, and assume the path p_j has source s_j and destination d_j. We transform $M(0)$ into a pairwise edge-disjoint set of paths as follows:

1. Let $iteration = 0$
2. If $p_i = p_R(s_i, d_i)$ and $p_j = p_R(s_j, d_j)$ from $M(iteration)$ contain underlying edge xy, then increment $iteration$ and use Lemma 3.1 to modify $M(iteration)$ as follows:
   If arc $xy \in p_i$ and arc $xy \in p_j$, then
   $$M(iteration) = M(iteration - 1) - p_i - p_j$$
   $$+ p(s_i, s_j) + p(d_i, d_j)$$
   Else if arc $xy \in p_i$ and arc $yx \in p_j$, then
   $$M(iteration) = M(iteration - 1) - p_i - p_j$$
   $$+ p(s_i, d_j) + p(s_j, d_i)$$
   Else there is no edge contention. STOP.
3. Repeat step 2.

If the procedure terminates with $iteration = i$, all k paths in $M(i)$ are pairwise edge disjoint. Thus, we only need to show that the procedure terminates.

Define $size[M(i)] = \sum_{p \in M(i)} |p|$. Because each path p in $M(i)$ must contain at least one edge,

$$\forall i \quad size[M(i)] \geq k. \qquad (1)$$

By Lemma 3.1,

$$\forall i \quad size[M(i+1)] < size[M(i)]. \qquad (2)$$

Combining the facts in Equations 1 and 2 guarantees that the procedure must terminate. □

Theorem 3.1 *There is an optimal line-switching UBM implementation for any shortest path routing scheme in any arbitrary direct network topology that can be represented as a symmetric digraph $D(V, A)$.*

Proof: We describe a method to create a UBM schedule of length $\lceil \log(|D| + 1) \rceil$ for any multicast request $M = (s, D)$ in any symmetric digraph that employs a shortest path routing scheme R. Let $p_R(s, d)$

be the routing path used by R to send a message from node s to node d.

In order to achieve multicast in $\lceil \log(d + 1) \rceil$ time steps, the number of informed nodes must double in each time step. Thus, in the last step, half of the destination nodes are already informed and must make calls to the other half of the destinations. This is the underlying principle of the technique that we describe.

A UBM schedule is built from the bottom up. That is, the calls in time step $\lceil \log(|D| + 1) \rceil$ are scheduled first, then the calls in step $\lceil \log(|D| + 1) \rceil - 1$, and so on. Because R is a shortest path routing scheme, we can use Lemma 3.2 to find a set P_1 of $k = \lfloor \frac{|s \cup D|}{2} \rfloor$ pairwise edge disjoint routing paths between pairs of nodes in $X = s \cup D$. Let $P_1 = \{p_R(s_t, d_t) | 1 \le t \le k\}$. The paths in P_1 represent the calls that will be made in step $\lceil \log(|D| + 1) \rceil$ of the UBM schedule. Let $S = \cup_{i=1}^{k} s_i$. Since the nodes in S are sources of unicast calls in step $\lceil \log(|D| + 1) \rceil$, these nodes must be informed in $\lceil \log(|D| + 1) \rceil - 1$ steps. Essentially, we have a new multicast request $M' = (s, D')$, where $D' = S - \{s\}$. Again, we use Lemma 3.2 to find a set P_2 of pairwise edge-disjoint paths for $s \cup D'$, and we use the paths in P_2 to make unicast calls during step $\lceil \log(|D| + 1) \rceil - 1$.

In general, for $\lceil \log(|D| + 1) \rceil$ steps, we recursively repeat the process of finding a set P_i of pairwise edge disjoint paths between pairs of vertices in $X = \cup_{i=1}^{k} s_i$. At each step i, the paths in P_i represent the unicast calls made in step $\lceil \log(|D| + 1) \rceil - (i - 1)$ of the UBM schedule. $\square$

4 Implications of Our Result

Theorem 3.1 tells system designers that as long as they utilize a shortest path routing scheme, their systems will allow optimal multicast performance. Fortunately, most system designers use shortest path routing schemes anyways because shortest paths can reduce overall message transmission latency and network traffic. In addition, shortest paths require the least amount of space to encode in routing tables.

In essence, Theorem 3.1 implies that *any* real system will allow optimal multicast performance. In particular, the following results presented in [1, 2, 3] are simply corollaries to Theorem 3.1.

Corollary 4.1 *There is an optimal line-switching UBM implementation for all $M = (s, D)$ in an arbitrary topology that employs free routing.*

Corollary 4.2 *There is an optimal line-switching UBM implementation for all $M = (s, D)$ in any mesh topology that employs xy-routing.*

Corollary 4.3 *There is an optimal line-switching UBM implementation for all $M = (s, D)$ in any hypercube topology that employs e-cube routing.*

Corollary 4.4 *There is an optimal line-switching UBM implementation for all $M = (s, D)$ in any torus topology that employs dimension-ordered routing.*

References

[1] A. M. Farley, "Minimum-time line broadcast networks," *Networks*, vol. 10, pp. 59–70, 1980.

[2] P. K. McKinley, H. Xu, A-H. Esfahanian, and L. M. Ni, "Unicast-based multicast communication in wormhole-routed networks," *IEEE Transactions on Parallel and Distributed Systems*, vol. 5, pp. 1252–1265, December 1994.

[3] D. F. Robinson, P. K. McKinley, and B. H. Cheng, "Optimal multicast communication in wormhole-routed torus networks," in *1994 International Conference on Parallel Processing*, pp. I–134–I–141, 1994.

[4] G. T. Byrd, N. P. Saraiya, and B. A. Delagi, "Multicast communication in multiprocessor systems," in *1989 International Conference on Parallel Processing*, pp. I–196–I–200, 1989.

[5] H. Xu, Y.-D. Gui, and L. M. Ni, "Optimal software multicast in wormhole-routed multistage networks," in *Proceedings of the 1994 Supercomputing Conference*, pp. 703–712, November 1994.

[6] B. D. Birchler, A-H. Esfahanian, and E. Torng, "Information dissemination in restricted routing networks," in *The International Symposium on Combinatorics and Applications*, (Tianjin, China), pp. 33–43, June 1996.

[7] Y.-C. Tseng, D. K. Panda, and T.-H. Lai, "A trip-based multicasting model in wormhole-routed networks with virtual channels," *IEEE Transactions on Parallel and Distributed Systems*, vol. 7, pp. 138–150, February 1996.

[8] J.-Y. L. Park, H.-A. Choi, N. Nupairoj, and L. M. Ni, "Construction of optimal multicast trees based on the parameterized communication model," in *1996 International Conference on Parallel Processing*, 1996.

[9] L. M. Ni and P. K. McKinley, "A survey of wormhole routing techniques in direct networks," *IEEE Computer*, vol. 26, pp. 62–76, February 1993.

Session 6C

Compilers II
Analysis, Allocation, and Mapping

False Sharing Elimination by Selection of Runtime Scheduling Parameters

Jyh-Herng Chow
IBM Santa Teresa Laboratory
555 Bailey Avenue
San Jose, California 95141
Phone: 408-927-1751
Email: chowjh@vnet.ibm.com

Vivek Sarkar
MIT Laboratory for Computer Science
545 Technology Square, NE43-206
Cambridge, Massachusetts 02139
Phone: 617-253-6035
Email: vivek@lcs.mit.edu

Abstract

False sharing can be a source of significant overhead on shared-memory multiprocessors. Several program restructuring techniques to reduce false sharing have been proposed in past work. In this paper, we propose an approach for elimination of false sharing based solely on selection of runtime schedule parameters for parallel loops. This approach leads to more portable code since only the schedule parameters need to be changed to target different multiprocessors. Also, the guarantee of elimination (rather than reduction) of false sharing in a parallel loop can significantly reduce the bookkeeping overhead in some memory consistency mechanisms. We present some preliminary experimental results for this approach.

1 Introduction

False sharing occurs when two processors attempt to concurrently write to distinct memory locations in the same cache line. The false sharing is *self-variable* if the two memory locations belong to the same (array or structure) variable; otherwise, it is *cross-variable*. Consider a self-scheduled [16] execution of the following parallel (DOALL) loop:

```
REAL*4 A(N)
DOALL I=1,N
    A(I)=I
ENDDO
```

Because a cache line can contain more than one element, self-variable false sharing can occur in the above loop even though different processors update different array elements.

For the following loop, cross-variable false sharing can occur in addition to self-variable false sharing if the last element of A and the first element of B are mapped to the same cache line:

```
REAL*4 A(N),B(N)
DOALL I=1,N
    A(I)=I
    B(I)=I
ENDDO
```

Consider a machine with hardware supported cache coherence (e.g., a snooping bus or a directory-based memory consistency mechanism [15]). When a processor writes to a location, a write-invalidate protocol will invalidate all cache line copies on other processors that contain the same location. Thus, other processors will incur a cache miss when they attempt to write to a different location that is mapped to the invalidated cache line.

False sharing has two debilitating effects on performance. First, performance is degraded due to an increase in the number of cache misses. Second, performance can be degraded due to cache line ownership becoming a serial bottleneck thus increasing the miss penalty by the waiting time for ownership. The increase in memory traffic caused by "ping-ponging" of cache lines due to false sharing has been studied by several researchers, e.g., [18, 8, 5]. False sharing can also lead to an anomaly in which increasing the cache line size leads to an increase in the number of cache misses observed in parallel programs, even though the programs may have good spatial locality [6].

In most currently implemented memory consistency mechanisms, the false sharing phenomenon also occurs between a read access and a write access to distinct memory locations in the same cache line. However, this form of read-write false sharing can be avoided. Newer memory consistency mechanisms (for weaker memory consistency models [4]) recognize that, in the absence of synchronization, a write in a cache line on one processor need not interfere with a read from the same cache line on another processor. So, we use the term "false sharing" to only refer to write-write interference. If needed, the techniques described in this paper can be extended to address read-write false sharing by considering read references in conjunction with write references, though doing so may decrease the set of loops for which false sharing elimination is guaranteed.

The techniques that have been proposed in the past for reducing false sharing fall into one of the following approaches [18, 8, 5]:

Changing loop structures : Transform program loops, e.g., by blocking, alignment, or peeling, so that iterations in a parallel loop access disjoint cache lines [19, 8, 7].

Changing data structures : Change the layout of data structures, e.g., by array alignment and padding [18, 1]. Array alignment is the insertion of dummy space so as to change the starting address of an array variable. Array padding is an increase in the allocated dimension size of an array variable.

Copying data : Copy the data to be updated by the loop into a temporary data structure that does not exhibit false sharing and is well suited to the data access patterns in the loop [5, 11, 17]. After the parallel loop completes execution, the temporary data structure is copied back to the original structure. The copy back may exhibit false sharing, however.

Changing schedule parameters : Schedule the loop iterations so that concurrently executed iterations access disjoint cache lines, e.g., [14].

The first three approaches rely on extensive program restructuring. The fourth approach is less intrusive – it only involves selecting specific runtime schedule parameters or a specific runtime scheduling algorithm for a given parallel loop and target multiprocessor.

In this paper, we pursue the fourth approach and address the problem of *eliminating false sharing by the selection of runtime schedule parameters*. Our solution is complementary to the other three approaches. If any program restructuring is performed to reduce false sharing, it should be performed prior to our selection of runtime schedule parameters. For example, cross-variable false sharing can be eliminated by aligning the first word of each array variable with a cache line boundary, and is therefore a useful pre-pass to our approach. We are interested in the approach of selecting runtime schedule parameters so as to make the code portable. Rather than restructure, and hence specialize, the program for a specific machine architecture, we use a common code representation (a parallel loop) for different architectures and instead set runtime schedule parameters to

control optimization of false sharing for the architecture that the parallel program is executing on. In addition to portability, this approach has the advantage of reducing compile-time by avoiding program restructuring.

The focus of this paper is on solutions that can guarantee an elimination (rather than a reduction) of false sharing for a parallel loop because we believe that memory consistency schemes in future distributed-shared-memory multiprocessors will work more efficiently in program regions for which the consistency mechanism is informed that no false sharing is possible. This is certainly true for software-based distributed shared memory schemes [10, 9]; if the consistency mechanism knows that false sharing is guaranteed to not occur for a specified cache line (i.e., that the cache line will have a single writer between synchronization points), then the fixed overheads of making a clone/twin copy of the cache line can be avoided. In addition, solutions for eliminating false sharing are necessary to guarantee correct execution on shared-memory multiprocessors that have no automatic (hardware or software) support for cache consistency (e.g., as in [13]).

The rest of the paper is organized as follows. Section 2 defines our machine and program model. Section 3 describes how to eliminate false sharing by selecting values for the CHUNKSIZE and CHUNKSTRIDE loop scheduling parameters. Section 4 shows how false sharing can also be eliminated by setting the PEEL parameter. Section 5 contains some preliminary experimental results showing the CHUNKSTRIDE values needed to eliminate false sharing in the SPECfp92 and the Perfect Club benchmarks. This section also uses a simple test program to illustrate the run-time improvement that can be obtained by elimination of false sharing. Section 6 summarizes related work, and section 7 contains our conclusions.

2 Machine and Program Model

The machine architecture is assumed to be a shared-memory multiprocessor with private L1 and L2 caches and an automatic memory consistency mechanism. We assume that all memory data accesses go through cache i.e., there is no provision for eliminating false sharing by making data non-cachable. For convenience, we assume in this paper that all array variables have an element size of one word; the extension to variable element sizes is straightforward. Let w be the number of words (array elements) that can fit in a cache line for the target architecture. We will refer to individual words in a cache line by their offsets, which are numbered $0, 1, 2, \ldots, w - 1$.

The program model is as follows. We address the problem of false sharing elimination for a single DOALL

```
DOALL I₀ = L₀, U₀
    ⋮
    DO I₁ = L₁, U₁
        ⋮
        DO I_d = L_d, U_d
            A₁(f̄₁(I₀,I₁,...,I_d)) = ...
                ⋮
            A_r(f̄_r(I₀,I₁,...,I_d)) = ...
        ENDDO
    ENDDO
ENDDO
```

Figure 1: **Program model**

construct (loop I_0) as shown in Figure 1. Iterations of the DOALL are independent and can be executed in any order. A barrier synchronization is assumed at the end of a DOALL execution. A single iteration of the DOALL contains $d \geq 0$ sequential DO loops $(I_1, \ldots, I_d)$ that need not be perfectly nested. We allow conditionals to be present in the loop body of the DOALL even though they are not explicitly shown in Figure 1. Our analysis for false sharing elimination conservatively assumes that an array reference guarded by a conditional may execute in every iteration of its surrounding loops.

Since we only need to consider write-write interference in false sharing, we restrict our false sharing analysis to writes of array variables, (say) $A_1, \cdots, A_r$, as shown in Figure 1. Scalar variables that are updated either prevent the loop from being parallelized or are recognized and allocated as private variables; they do not contribute to false sharing in either case. Our analysis is restricted to the (common) case in which all writes to an array variable in a parallel loop have the same index expression. In Figure 1, the index expression of array variable A_k is denoted by a vector of subscript expressions, $\overline{f}_k$, where $|\overline{f}_k|$ equals the number of dimensions of A_k and each element of the vector contains the subscript expression for the corresponding dimension of A_k. As in [17], we restrict the individual subscript expression for each dimension to either be of the form $c_1 I_1 + c_2 I_2 + \cdots + c_d I_d + \lambda$ or the form $c_0 I_0 + \lambda$ i.e., we do not allow the index variable of the DOALL loop, I_0, to appear in the same dimension subscript expression as an index variable on an inner sequential DO loop. This restriction is not severe in practice. Recall that the restriction only applies to array writes, e.g., an array reference on the left-hand-side of an assignment statement. It is highly unlikely for the I_0 loop to be parallelizable if it violates this restriction.

For simplicity, we assume that the coefficients of the parallel loop index appearing in array subscripts are positive ($c_0 \geq 0$), arrays are stored in column major format, and all array dimensions have lower bound = 1.

It is straightforward to extend our approach to remove these restrictions. The cache line offset for a data element e is denoted by $o(e)$, and the offset of the starting address of an array A is denoted by A^*, so we can write $A^* = o(A[1, 1])$.

For the execution of parallel loops, we assume that the runtime system supports the following three parameters:

- CHUNKSIZE: the chunk size specifies the number of contiguous iterations a participating processor picks up at a time when executing the DOALL loop.

- CHUNKSTRIDE: the chunk stride specifies the degree of interleaving for mapping chunks to processors. The default is CHUNKSTRIDE = 1 in which processors pick up chunks of iterations in a self-scheduled fashion. For CHUNKSTRIDE = 2, the execution of chunks is partitioned into a sequence of two phases. In the first phase, processors only execute even-numbered chunks (assuming that chunk numbering starts at 0). In the second phase, processors only execute odd-numbered chunks. Scheduling with CHUNKSTRIDE = 2 has also been referred to as "red-black scheduling" in the literature.

  In general, for CHUNKSTRIDE = m, execution is partitioned into a sequence of m phases such that chunks that are congruent (mod m) to i are executed in phase i, for $0 \leq i < m$. The sequencing of phases can be enforced by inserting barrier synchronizations between consecutive phases. As we will see later, a CHUNKSTRIDE > 1 value can be used to ensure that two chunks that might have falsely shared a cache line in the original DOALL construct now execute in different phases. Since the phases are executed in sequence, the writes will not occur concurrently thus eliminating the false sharing. In general, a smaller CHUNKSTRIDE value is more desirable so as to avoid the increase in overhead and decrease in parallelism that results from the extra sequencing, and a possible adverse impact on data locality.

- PEEL: the number of initial iterations of the DOALL loop to be "peeled" by the runtime system i.e., to be executed as a special first chunk with PEEL iterations. The remaining chunks (except possibly the last chunk) have CHUNKSIZE iterations each. The PEEL parameter has the same effect as the alignment factor in generalized loop blocking [7]. The default value is PEEL = 0.

We assume that the compiler translates a DOALL construct by generating appropriate calls to the runtime library. The three parameters listed above (CHUNKSIZE, CHUNKSTRIDE, PEEL) can be computed at compile-time or at runtime and are then passed on to the runtime library. Note that the structure of the code remains unchanged for different parameter values, hence satisfying our goal of portability.

3 False Sharing Elimination using CHUNKSIZE and CHUNKSTRIDE Parameters

Recall that our goal is to eliminate false sharing by choosing appropriate scheduling parameters, without changing the program structure. In this section, we describe how false sharing can be eliminated by selecting CHUNKSIZE and CHUNKSTRIDE parameters.

```
(a)   ! CHUNKSIZE=16, CHUNKSTRIDE=1
      DOALL I=1,100
         A(I) = ...
      ENDDO
(b)   ! CHUNKSIZE=8, CHUNKSTRIDE=1
      DOALL I=1,100
         A(2*I-1) = ...
      ENDDO
(c)   ! CHUNKSIZE=16, CHUNKSTRIDE=2
      DOALL I=2,100
         A(I) = ...
      ENDDO
(d)   ! CHUNKSIZE=8, CHUNKSTRIDE=2
      DOALL I=1,100
         A(2*I+1) = ...
      ENDDO
```

Figure 2: **Examples of preventing false sharing**

As an example, consider the case when there is only one array reference in the loop (to array variable A, say) that is being written, as in loops (a), (b), (c), (d) in Figure 2. We will show how the CHUNKSIZE and CHUNKSTRIDE values can be set to avoid false sharing in these four different loops (the CHUNKSIZE and CHUNKSTRIDE values in Figure 2 assume that the cache line size is $w = 16$). Assume $A^* = 0$, i.e., array A is aligned with a cache line boundary. If we choose a chunk size so that each chunk works on disjoint cache lines, then false sharing cannot occur. Specifically, a chunk size of multiple cache lines for loop (a), i.e., CHUNKSIZE $= k \times w$ for some integer $k \geq 1$, will prevent false sharing since $A^* = 0$.

Loop (b) is similar to loop (a) in that the element written by the first iteration is still A(1) and hence aligned with a cache line boundary. However, a value of CHUNKSIZE $= k \times w/2$ is sufficient to prevent false sharing in loop (b) because the array reference has stride $= 2$.

Note that selecting CHUNKSIZE $= k \times w$ will not prevent false sharing in loop (c) or loop (d) in Figure 2,

because in both cases the word written by the first iteration is not aligned with a cache line boundary. In this section, we show how setting the CHUNKSTRIDE parameter can prevent false sharing for these two cases, and in the next section we show how the PEEL parameter can also be used to prevent false sharing.

If CHUNKSIZE is selected so that the size of the array section written by every chunk (except possibly the last one) is $\geq w$, then we can set CHUNKSTRIDE $= 2$ to avoid false sharing in loop (c) and loop (d). We use CHUNKSTRIDE $= 2$ because the same cache line can only be written by consecutive chunks in this case, and CHUNKSTRIDE $= 2$ ensures that any two consecutive chunks are not executed concurrently. For an array subscript $cI + \lambda$, the CHUNKSIZE constraint can be enforced by setting CHUNKSIZE $\geq \lceil \frac{w}{c} \rceil$.

The above observations for loops (c) and (d) lead us to the following theorem.

Theorem 1 *False sharing can be eliminated for the following kind of* DOALL *loop containing writes to r distinct array variables, $A_1 \ldots, A_r$, by setting* CHUNKSIZE$\geq \lceil \frac{w}{min(c_1, \cdots, c_r)} \rceil$ *and* CHUNKSTRIDE$=2$. *Further, if* $\lceil \frac{w}{min(c_1, \cdots, c_r)} \rceil = 1$, *false sharing can be eliminated by just setting* CHUNKSIZE ≥ 1 *and* CHUNKSTRIDE $= 1$.

```
DOALL I = L, U
   A₁ (c₁ I+λ₁) = ...
      ⋮
   Aᵣ (cᵣ I+λᵣ) = ...
ENDDO
```

In the case when $\lceil \frac{w}{min(c_1, \cdots, c_r)} \rceil = 1$, we know that each array reference has a memory stride in contiguous iterations that is $\geq w$ words. Therefore, there is no false sharing in this case and we can use CHUNKSTRIDE$=1$ with any CHUNKSIZE.

The solution in Theorem 1 correctly prevents false sharing by using CHUNKSTRIDE$=2$. Since CHUNKSTRIDE$=2$ requires a sequencing between its two phases, we prefer to use CHUNKSTRIDE$=1$ whenever possible. We say a loop satisfies the C.L.B. (Cache Line Boundary) condition if for every array variable written in the loop, the element written in the first iteration is aligned with a cache line boundary. For example, the following loop

```
DOALL I=L, U
   A(c*I+λ) = ...
ENDDO
```

satisfies the C.L.B. condition if $(A^* + cL + \lambda - 1) \bmod w = 0$.

Theorem 2 *If the* DOALL *loop in Theorem 1 satisfies the C.L.B. condition, then false sharing can be prevented by setting* CHUNKSIZE $= k \times \frac{w}{gcd(w, c_1, \cdots, c_r)}$ *and* CHUNKSTRIDE$=1$.

We now turn our attention to multi-dimensional array variables and nested loops. Consider the following two cases, which we call R1-type and R2-type references:

```
      REAL*4 A(N1,N2)
      DOALL I=L₁,U₁
        DO J=L₂,U₂
R1:       A(c₁J+λ₁,c₂I+λ₂) =
        ENDDO
      ENDDO
      DOALL I=L₁,U₁
        DO J=L₂,U₂
R2:       A(c₁I+λ₁,c₂J+λ₂) =
        ENDDO
      ENDDO
```

For reference R1, the linearized subscript is $(c_2 N_1 I + c_1 J + \lambda')$, for some λ'. We can compute the difference between the address of the last element accessed in ith iteration and that of the first element accessed in $(i+1)$th iteration. If it is greater than or equal to w, then no false sharing can occur. This leads to the following test for false sharing due to an R1-type reference:

$$c_2 N_1 - c_1(U_2 - L_2) \geq w.$$

If the test fails, there may be false sharing. Analogous to Theorem 1, false sharing can be prevented in this case by setting CHUNKSIZE$\geq \lceil \frac{w}{c_2 N_1} \rceil$ and CHUNKSTRIDE$=2$. Furthermore, if the loop satisfies the C.L.B. condition and the array column size is a multiple of w, then false sharing can be prevented by setting CHUNKSTRIDE$=1$ with CHUNKSIZE$=k \times \frac{w}{gcd(w,c_2 N_1)}$ (analogous to Theorem 2).

For reference R2, the linearized subscript is $(c_1 I + c_2 N_1 J + \lambda'')$. If the array column size is a multiple of w, then false sharing can be prevented by setting CHUNKSIZE$\geq \lceil \frac{w}{c_1} \rceil$ and CHUNKSTRIDE$=2$.

The above solutions can be extended to higher-dimensional arrays by assuming that the first dimension size is a multiple of w as in the two-dimensional case.

4 Selection of PEEL parameter

In this section, we describe how the PEEL parameter can be used to eliminate false sharing. Recall that the PEEL parameter specifies the number of initial iterations of the DOALL loop to be "peeled" by the runtime system i.e., to be executed as a special first chunk with PEEL iterations. Our goal is to set the PEEL parameter to the smallest value that enables the $(\text{PEEL}+1)^{th}$ iteration to satisfy the C.L.B. condition, thus allowing us to then set CHUNKSTRIDE $= 1$, and CHUNKSIZE as specified in Theorem 2.

Consider the following DOALL loop:

```
      DOALL I=L,U
        A(cI+λ)=
      ENDDO
```

```
 0  1  2  3  4  5  6  7  8  9 10 11 12 13 14 15
+---------------------------------------------------+
|  .  .  .  .  .  .  .  .  .  .  .  .  .  3  .  . |
|  .  4  .  .  5  .  .  6  .  .  7  .  .  8  .  . |
|  9  .  . 10  .  . 11  .  . 12  .  . 13  .  . 14 |
|  . 15  .  . 16  .  . 17  .  . 18  .  . 19  .  . |
|  . 20  .  . 21  .  . 22  .  . 23  .  . 24  .  . |
| 25  .  . 26  .  . 27  .  . 28  .  . 29  .  . 30 |
|  . 31  .  . 32  .  .  .  .  .  .  .  .  .  .  . |
+---------------------------------------------------+
```

Figure 3: **Footprint for Example 1**

Let $I=x$ be an iteration that satisfies the C.L.B. condition, $(A^* + cx + \lambda - 1) \mod w = 0$. We can then set PEEL $= x-L+1$ to ensure that normal chunking begins at iteration $I=x$. The set of possible values for x are the integer solutions of x in the following equation:

$$wy - cx = A^* + \lambda - 1, \qquad L \leq x \leq U \text{ and } y \geq 0.$$

We want to find the smallest solution for x in the above equation. Note that a solution exists only when $gcd(w,c)|(A^* + \lambda - 1)$.

Example 1 Consider the following loop:
```
      REAL*4 A(N)
      DOALL I=3,32
        A(3*I+1)=
      ENDDO
```
Assume $A^* = 5$ and $w = 16$. The footprint of the accesses on the cache for Example 1 is shown in Figure 3. The line on teh top identifies cache line offsets $(0, \ldots, 15)$, and the numbers inside the box denote loop iterations; for example, iteration 6 accesses an element that resides in cache line offset 7. Since $gcd(16,3) = 1$, there are integer solutions in $16y - 3x = 5$, and $\langle y, x \rangle = \langle 2, 9 \rangle$ is one solution. As shown in the footprint, iteration 9 indeed satisfies the C.L.B. condition which suggests setting PEEL $= 9 - 3 + 1 = 6$. ∎

The next theorem gives a more general condition for setting the PEEL parameter so as to prevent false sharing; it works even when the above equation has no solution.

Theorem 3 *To use* CHUNKSTRIDE$=1$ *for the program*
```
      DOALL I=L,U
        A(cI+λ)=
      ENDDO
```
Let $d = gcd(w,c)$, *and* $e = (A^* + cL + \lambda - 1) \mod w$. *If* $e < c$, *then false sharing is prevented by just setting* CHUNKSIZE$=k \times \frac{w}{d}$ *(*PEEL *can remain $= 0$). Otherwise, false sharing can be prevented by setting* PEEL $= \lceil \frac{w-e}{c} \rceil$ *with* CHUNKSIZE$=k \times \frac{w}{d}$.

Example 2 Consider the following loop:

```
   0  1  2  3  4  5  6  7  8  9 10 11 12 13 14 15
+-------------------------------------------------+
|  .  .  .  .  .  .  .  .  .  4  .  .  .  .  .  5  |
|  .  .  .  .  .  6  .  .  .  .  .  7  .  .  .  .  |
|  .  8  .  .  .  .  .  9  .  .  .  .  . 10  .  .  |
|  .  .  . 11  .  .  .  .  . 12  .  .  .  .  . 13  |
|  .  .  .  .  . 14  .  .  .  .  . 15  .  .  .  .  |
|  . 16  .  .  .  .  . 17  .  .  .  .  . 18  .  .  |
|  .  .  . 19  .  .  .  .  . 20  .  .  .  .  .  .  |
+-------------------------------------------------+
```

Figure 4: Footprint for Example 2

```
REAL*4 A(N)
DOALL I=4,20
   A(6*I+1)=
ENDDO
```

Assume $A^* = 1$ and $w = 16$. The footprint of the accesses on the cache for Example 2 is shown in Figure 4. Note that no value of PEEL can make the loop satisfy the C.L.B. condition. However, since $e = (1 + 6 \times 4 + 1 - 1) \bmod 16 = 9$, we can still set PEEL $= \lceil \frac{16-9}{6} \rceil = 2$ and CHUNKSIZE$=\frac{16}{gcd(16,6)} = 8$ to prevent false sharing. ∎

The PEEL parameter can also be used to prevent cross-variable false sharing. Consider the following loop:

```
COMMON // A(N),B(N)
DOALL I=1,N
   A(I)=I
   B(I)=I
ENDDO
```

Suppose array variable B cannot be aligned with a cache line boundary. Cross-variable false sharing occurs if the last k elements of A and the first h elements of B fall in the same cache line. We can then prevent cross-variable false sharing by setting PEEL $= h$. If the runtime library also supports a LASTPEEL parameter that specifies the number of final iterations of the DOALL loop to be "peeled" by the runtime system, then we can alternatively prevent false sharing by setting LASTPEEL $= k$.

Now consider a 2D loop with a 2D array, with a R1-type reference and an R2-type reference as outlined in the previous section. Consider the R1-type reference first. Let $x = w - N_1 \bmod w$. If $ix + A^* = wj$ has an integer solution for $L_1 \leq i \leq U_1$, and $j \geq 0$, then we can adjust the loop to prevent false sharing, with block size $k \times \frac{w}{gcd(x,w)}$. False sharing can be prevented by setting PEEL $= i - L_1 + 1$, where i is a positive integer solution to the equation (it would be desirable to select the smallest such solution). If the first dimension size of A is a multiple of w, then this is the same case as that in Section 3 and we can leave PEEL=0.

For the R2-type reference, if the first dimension size of A is a multiple of w, the J loop can be ignored with the same reasoning as in Section 3. Thus the solution for a single loop can be applied.

5 Preliminary Experimental Results

5.1 Analysis of CHUNKSTRIDE parameters

We statically analyzed the SPECfp92 and Perfect Club benchmarks to count the number of parallel loops in which false sharing can be eliminated for CHUNKSTRIDE $= 1$ or CHUNKSTRIDE $= 2$, assuming PEEL=0. The results are shown in Figure 5. This analysis assumed that each array variable is aligned to start at a cache line boundary, except for cases in which the Fortran 77 storage association semantics would prevent realignment. The results show that there is no false sharing for a significant number of DOALL loops when CHUNKSTRIDE $= 1$. However, a larger number of loops require CHUNKSTRIDE $= 2$ for false sharing elimination[1].

A common case that requires CHUNKSTRIDE $= 2$ for false sharing elimination is when the first iteration of the parallel loop does not access the first element in the array e.g., when the lower bound of the parallel loop is 2 instead of 1. As discussed in section 4, false sharing can be eliminated in this case with the more efficient CHUNKSTRIDE $= 1$ by setting the PEEL parameter appropriately.

5.2 Runtime measurements for a simple example

In this section, we present runtime measurements for a simple parallel loop executed with different schedule parameters. The performance measurements were made using the beta version of the IBM XL Fortran SMP compiler on an IBM RS/6000 model J30 SMP workstation containing four 133MHz PowerPC 604 processors. A description of an early version of the beta compiler can be found in [3].

The example program is shown in figure 6, along with runtime measurements obtained by scheduling the DOALL loop with different schedule parameters. The timings in figure 6 are for a single call to subroutine TEST with $N1 = N2 = 8$. We intentionally chose a small array size so that this example would have only compulsory cache misses and false sharing cache misses (i.e., no capacity misses or collision misses). The execution times reported are the smallest times measured

---

[1] The results for the spice2g6 benchmark in SPECfp92 and the SPICE benchmark in Perfect are different because some short subroutines, e.g., ZERO8, are written in C in spice2g6 and in Fortran in SPICE.

SPECfp92	stride=1	stride=2	total
spice2g6	9	7	16
doduc	157	29	186
mdljdp2	8	0	8
wave5	27	127	154
tomcatv	4	5	9
ora	1	2	3
mdljsp2	8	0	8
swm256	12	3	15
su2cor	25	18	43
hydro2d	7	56	63
nasa7	2	34	36
fpppp	6	2	8
TOTAL	266	283	576

PERFECT	stride=1	stride=2	total
ADM	13	71	84
ARC2D	3	92	95
BDNA	21	9	30
DYFESM	30	26	56
FLO52	33	31	64
MDG	6	3	9
MG3D	15	21	36
OCEAN	11	47	58
QCD	16	56	72
SPEC77	74	76	150
SPICE	13	7	20
TRACK	17	1	18
TRFD	3	9	12
TOTAL	255	449	704

Figure 5: **Number of DOALL loops for which false sharing can be eliminated for CHUNKSTRIDE=1 and CHUNKSTRIDE=2 assuming PEEL=0.**

over twenty runs for each case, and the total CPU time includes the user and system times reported by the time command. Both the CHUNKSTRIDE = 1 and CHUNKSTRIDE = 2 cases were measured for PEEL = 0.

For this example, we see that elimination of false sharing by setting CHUNKSTRIDE = 2 resulted in a wallclock execution time that is 15% better than the CHUNKSTRIDE = 1 case. Since this SMP is a small-scale tightly-coupled multiprocessor, we would expect to see larger overheads due to false sharing on loosely-coupled multiprocessors such as clusters of workstations.

6 Related Work

Due to space limitations, we only provide a brief summary of past work that is most relevant to our paper.

Generalized loop blocking [7] is a technique that prevents false sharing by blocking the DOALL loop with a non-integer block size such that each iteration in the blocked loop will cover disjoint cache lines. The parallel loop is blocked with a blocking factor $b = k \times \frac{w}{c}$ and

```
SUBROUTINE TEST(A, N1, N2)
PARAMETER(M=100,N=100000)
REAL*4 A(N1,N2)
DO K = 1, M
    DOALL I = 1, N2
        DO J = 1, N
            DO L = 1, N1
                A(L,I) = A(L,I) + 1
            END DO
        END DO
    END DO
END DO
```

Schedule parameters	Number of processors	Wallclock time	Total CPU time
Sequential	1	31.2s	31.0s
CHUNKSTRIDE = 1 (CHUNKSIZE = 2)	4	10.7s	35.5s
CHUNKSTRIDE = 2 (CHUNKSIZE = 1)	4	9.3s	27.2s

Figure 6: **Example program and runtime measurements for different schedule parameters.**

aligned with an alignment factor $\phi = \frac{(A^* + \lambda) \bmod (kw)}{c}$, where k is an adjustable parameter. The effect of generalized loop blocking is that each iteration (except possibly the first and the last iteration) of the blocking (outer) loop will cover disjoint k cache lines; thus, no false sharing is possible. Note that if c does not divide w, the blocking factor b may not be an integer and the number of iterations executed in the inner loop is not constant.

Another scheduling algorithm for preventing false sharing (different from the CHUNKSTRIDE = 2 approach) can be found in [14]. Given a single parallel loop L, iteration interference distance d, and the number of processors p, the algorithm determines a schedule S which orders the iterations such that any two concurrent iterations in S will have pairwise separation of at least d. The interference distance d is selected to ensure elimination of false sharing. The schedule constructed by this algorithm is similar to a schedule with CHUNKSTRIDE=d and CHUNKSIZE=1. An important difference is that the schedule from [14] requires at most two synchronizations per iteration, while a CHUNKSTRIDE=d schedule requires d barrier synchronizations. Additionally, if p is unknown at compile-time, the schedule from [14] will have to be constructed at runtime, with proper synchronizations inserted for each iteration.

The false sharing problem also occurs in distributed shared memory machines [12] where a shared memory abstraction is implemented above physically distributed memories. On these machines, multiple copies of the same memory page can co-exist to facilitate local accesses. Memory consistency is maintained at the page level. Since the unit of "caching" is a page, false sharing can pose an even bigger problem for these machines.

7 Conclusion and Future Work

In this paper, we have presented an approach for elimination of false sharing solely by the selection of runtime schedule parameters. The techniques presented can be useful for machines with hardware supported cache coherence, because cache misses and memory traffic caused by false sharing can be reduced. These techniques can also be used in a distributed shared memory environment to reduce the overhead of maintaining memory coherence.

Some of our methods require knowledge of the cache line alignment of an array variable. This information is hard to obtain at compile-time. However, as we have shown, it is possible to generate code that sets the schedule parameters at runtime based on the offset of the starting address of array variables.

Further studies are necessary to understand the interaction between blocking for cache locality and chunking for false sharing elimination, as well as the interaction between array dimension padding for reducing cache set conflicts suggested in [2] and the array dimension padding (to a multiple of w, which is a power of two) discussed in this paper.

Acknowledgments

The authors would like to thank Barbara Simons for her feedback on an earlier version of this paper, and the members of the Parallel Development group in IBM Toronto for their ongoing work on the IBM XL Fortran SMP compiler used to obtain our experimental results.

References

[1] David F. Bacon, Jyh-Herng Chow, Dz ching R. Ju, K. Muthukumar, and Vivek Sarkar. A Compiler Framework for Restructuring Data Declarations to Enhance Cache and TLB Effectiveness. *CASCON '94 conference*, November 1994.

[2] David H. Bailey. Unfavorable Strides in Cache Memory Systems. *Scientific Programming*, 4:53–58, 1995. RNR Technical Report RNR-92-015, NASA Ames Research Center.

[3] Jyh-Herng Chow, Leonard E. Lyon, and Vivek Sarkar. Automatic Parallelization for Symmetric Shared-Memory Multiprocessors. *CASCON '96 conference*, November 1996.

[4] Michel Dubois, Christoph Scheurich, and Faye A. Briggs. Synchronization, Coherence, and Event Ordering in Multiprocessors. *IEEE Computer*, 21(2), February 1988. Survey and Tutorial Series.

[5] Susan J. Eggers and Tor E. Jeremiassen. Eliminating False Sharing. In *International Conference on Parallel Processing*, 1991.

[6] Susan J. Eggers and Randy H. Katz. The Effect of Sharing on the Cache and Bus Performance of Parallel Programs. In *ACM International Conference on Architectural Support for Programming Languages and Operating Systems*, pages 257–270, 1989.

[7] Elana D. Granston. Toward a Compile-Time Methodology for Reducing False Sharing and Communication Traffic in Shared Virtual Memory Systems. In *Proc. of Sixth Workshop on Language and Compilers for Parallel Computing*, 1993.

[8] Manish Gupta and David A. Padua. Effects of Program Parallelization and Stripmining Transformation on Cache Performance in a Multiprocessor. In *International Conference on Parallel Processing*, pages I.301–I.304, 1991.

[9] Alan H. Karp and Vivek Sarkar. Data Merging for Shared-Memory Multiprocessors. *Proceedings of the 26th Hawaii International Conference on System Sciences, Wailea, Hawaii, Volume I (Architecture)*, pages 244–256, January 1993.

[10] Pete Keleher, Alan L. Cox, and Willy Zwaenepoel. Lazy Release Consistency for Software Distributed Shared Memory. In *Proc. of the 19th Annual International Symposium on Computer Architecture*, pages 13–21, May 1992.

[11] Monica S. Lam, Edward E. Rothberg, and Michael E. Wolf. The Cache Performance and Optimizations of Blocked Algorithms. In *ACM International Conference on Architectural Support for Programming Languages and Operating Systems*, pages 63–74, 1991.

[12] Bill Nitzberg and Virginia Lo. Distributed Shared Memory: A Survey of Issues and Algorithms. *IEEE Computer*, 24(8):52–60, 1991.

[13] *IBM Shared Memory System POWER/4 User's Guide and Technical Reference*, 1993.

[14] Barbara Simons, Vivek Sarkar, Jr. Mauricio Breternitz, and Michael Lai. An Optimal Asynchronous Scheduling Algorithm for Software Cache Consistency. *Proc. Hawaii International Conference on System Sciences*, January 1994.

[15] Per Stenström. A Survey of Cache Coherence Schemes for Multiprocessors. *IEEE Computer*, 23(6):12–24, 1990.

[16] Peiyi Tang and Pen-Chung Yew. Processor Self-Scheduling for Multiple-Nested Parallel Loops. *Proc. of the 1986 Int'l Conf. on Parallel Processing*, February 1986.

[17] Olivier Temam, Elana Granston, and William Jalby. To Copy or Not to Copy: A Compile-Time Technique for Assessing When Data Copying Should be Used to Eliminate Cache Conflicts. In *Proc. Supercomputing '93*, pages 410–419, 1993.

[18] Josep Torrellas, Monica S. Lam, and John L. Hennessy. Shared Data Placement Optimizations to Reduce Multiprocessor Cache Miss Rates. In *International Conference on Parallel Processing*, pages II.266–II.270, 1990.

[19] Michael E. Wolf and Monica S. Lam. A Data Locality Optimization Algorithm. *Proceedings of the ACM SIGPLAN Symposium on Programming Language Design and Implementation*, pages 30–44, June 1991.

A Register Allocation Technique Using Register Existence Graph

A. Koseki

School of Science & Engineering
Waseda University
3-4-1 Okubo, Shinjuku-ku
Tokyo 169, Japan
koseki@fuka.info.waseda.ac.jp

H. Komastu

Tokyo Research Laboratory
IBM Japan, Ltd.
1623-14 Shimotsuruma, Yamato-shi
Kanagawa 242, Japan
komatsu@trl.ibm.co.jp

Y. Fukazawa

School of Science & Engineering
Waseda University
3-4-1 Okubo, Shinjuku-ku
Tokyo 169, Japan
fukazawa@fuka.info.waseda.ac.jp

Abstract

Optimizing compilation is very important for generating code sequences in order to utilize the characteristics of processor architectures. One of the most essential optimization techniques is register allocation. In register allocation that takes account of instruction-level parallelism, anti-dependences generated when the same register is allocated to different variables, and spill code generated when the number of registers is insufficient should be handled in such a way that the parallelism in a program is not lost. In our method, we realized register allocation using a new data structure called the register existence graph, in which the parallelism in a program is well expressed.

1 Introduction

The number of registers in a processor is limited; therefore, variables and pseudo-registers in the intermediate code used by a compiler (symbolic registers) should be mapped to a restricted number of registers. This mapping is called register allocation [1, 2, 3, 4, 5]. In a register allocator, the most important consideration is how symbolic registers are used and how many of them are live at the same time. Symbolic registers live at the same time cannot be mapped to the same registers; therefore, if the number of such symbolic registers exceeds the number of registers, some code changes are needed to decrease their number.

The mapping process has hitherto been performed by algorithms using a register interference graph [1, 2] that expresses the overlap of the lifespans of symbolic registers. It can map symbolic registers and decrease their number by spilling them out and in. In this process, anti-dependence, which arises when symbolic registers are mapped, and spill code are generated.

Register allocation using a register interference graph gives better code for scalar processors. However, register interference graphs cannot express parallelism among instructions [6]; therefore, it is difficult to handle the generation of spill code and anti-dependence without losing the parallelism.

This paper describes a new register allocation technique using a register existence graph that can express the interference among symbolic registers and the par-

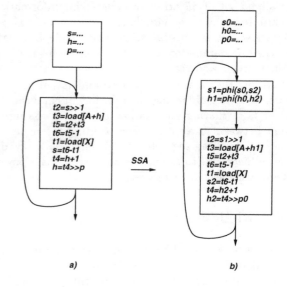

Figure 1: Source Program and SSA Transformation

allelism among instructions in a program simultaneously.

2 Background

Generally, registers are allocated by coloring a register interference graph with the number of the registers. Register interference graphs are produced by scanning instructions in a program and by adding edges between nodes that indicate symbolic registers live at the same time.

Fig. 1 shows an example of the construction of a register interference graph.

Fig. 1a) shows the source program, and Fig. 1b) shows the target program after applying SSA (Static Single Assignment) transformation [7]. We assume the use of the hierarchical register allocation proposed by Callahan and Koblenz [3], so the target code should comprise the instructions in the innermost loop.

Then, we obtain a register interference graph by

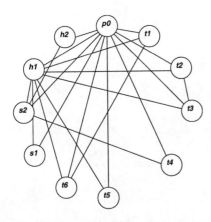

Figure 2: Register Interference Graph

```
h1:r1 p1:r2 s1:r3

r3=r3>>1
r4=load[A+r1]
r3=r3+r4
r4=r3-1
r3=load[X]
r3=r4-r3
r4=r1+1
r1=r4>>r2
```

Figure 3: Possible Register Allocation

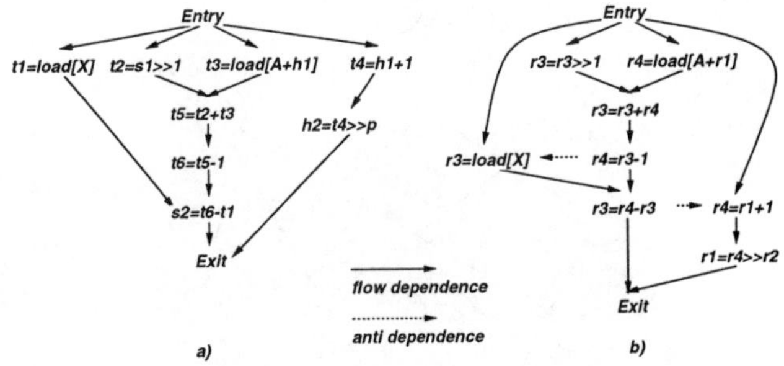

Figure 4: Loss of Parallelism

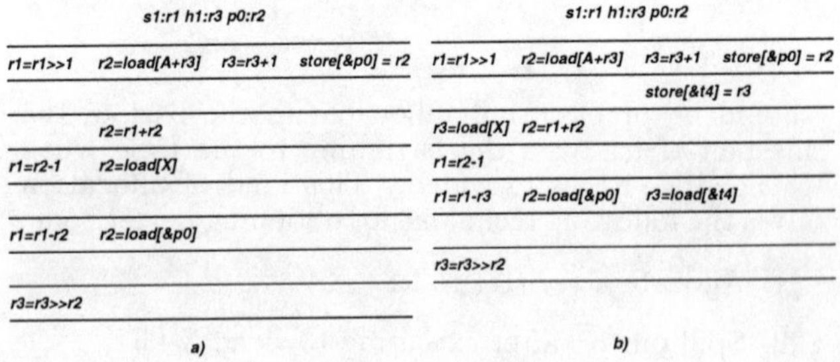

Figure 5: Utilizing Spill Code

scanning the code. Fig. 2 shows the register interference graph.

Fig. 3 shows the result of a possible register allocation, assuming that four registers are available.

Coloring a register interference graph produces a maapping of physical registers to symbolic registers. It works in order to obtain the lowest number of symbolic registers that should be spilled. On scalar processors, decreasing the ammount of spill code improves the performance of computing. Therefore, register allocation by coloring is very effective for producing better code for scalar processors, and has contributed to speedups of the execution of programs. However, taking account of instruction-level parallel processors, it cannot fully utilize the parallelism in a processor. We can demonstrate these three problems in conventional register allocators using a register interference graph.

1. Loss of Parallelism Due to Generation of Anti-dependence

Fig. 4a) shows a data dependence DAG of the target code in Fig 1b). Fig. 4b) shows a DAG after the allocation of registers as shown in Fig. 3 and the addition of edges expressing anti-dependence. Assuming the delay of load instructions to be 2 cycles and the delay of the others to be 1 cycle, the code shown in Fig. 4a) can be executed in 5 cycles on an instruction-level parallel processor that has sufficient ALUs. However, the code after register allocation in Fig. 4b) needs 2 more cycles, because of the generation of anti-dependence. The generation of anti-dependence is in-

evitable, but it is important to consider ways of generating anti-dependence without losing the parallelism in a program.

2. No Consideration of Spill Code That Gives Higher Parallelism

Fig. 5 shows the result of allocating 3 registers and scheduling instructions to obtain the minimum execution time. Fig. 5a) shows that 8 cycles are needed and that 1 symbolic register is spilled out. However, the code shown in Fig. 5b) has 2 symbolic registers that are spilled and the necessary execution time is 7 cycles. This is because spill code can be simultaneously executed with other instructions. This example indicates that there are some cases in which optimizations that take account of parallel execution of spill code and other instructions are needed when a program is executed on an instruction-level parallel processor.

3. No Consideration of Reference Differences of Symbolic Registers in Different Contexts

If the same symbolic register is referred to in several different places, these references have different importance. For example, "h1" in Fig. 4 is referred to by t3=load[X+h1] and t4=h1+1. Conventional register allocators do not take account of the difference between the reference to h1 in t3=load[X+h1] and the reference in t4=h1+1. However, Fig. 4 obviously shows that the reference to h1 in t3=load[X+h1] is more important than that in t4=h1+1, because the execution of t3=load[X+h1] is more critical to the total execution time of the program. Therefore, a register

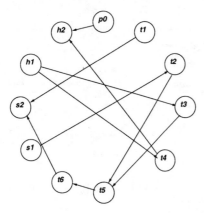

Figure 6: DAG

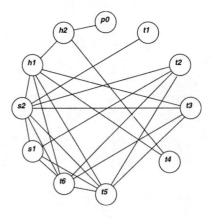

Figure 7: Transitive Closure

should be preferentially allocated to the part of the lifespan of h1 from the beginning to the time when t3=load[X+h1] is executed. This kind of allocation gives the following technique for obtaining better code:

1. Allocate a register to h1.

2. Spill out h1 after executing t3=load[X+h1].

3. Spill in h1 before executing t4=h1+1.

3   Recent Approaches

To solve the problem of generating anti-dependence, several approaches have been suggested.

The methods of Pinter [8] and Norris and Pollock [9] consider the parallelism in a program in such a way that not only the interferences between symbolic registers obtained by scanning code lexically but also possible interferences that may appear when instructions are reordered by the code scheduler are used.

This is performed as follows. First, make a DAG from a source code (Fig. 6).

Next, make the transitive closure of the graph, and eliminate the edge directions (Fig. 7).

In this graph, there is no flow-dependence between nodes not connected by edges. Therefore, allocating the same register to symbolic registers represented by these nodes may cause the generation of anti-dependence that results in the loss of parallelism in a program.

Finally, add edges between the nodes in a register interference graph that are not connected by edges in the non-directed transitive closure of a DAG (Fig. 8). Pinter called this graph a parallelized register interference graph [8]. A similar graph is obtained by the method of Norris and Pollock. Register allocation based on this kind of graph allows code schedulers to extract the parallelism in a program despite the generation of anti-dependence.

Theoretically, register allocators that use parallelized register interference graph coloring give a better code if a very large number of registers are available. However, a parallelized register interference

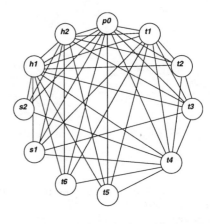

Figure 8: Interference Graph Considering Parallelism

graph contains too many edges, and therefore produces unnecessary spill code and impairs the code if the number of registers is not very large.

Pinter, and also Norris and Pollock, attempted to avoid this problem by removing edges from a parallelized register interference graph. However, removing edges after adding them makes allocation more complicated and results in futile processes. Moreover, removing processes does not ensure the retention of parallelism in the graph. The method of Norris and Pollock can possibly maintain the parallelism, but how it does so was not mentioned.

4   Our Approach

This section describes a new approach to register allocation that is very different from existing approaches based on register interference graph coloring. We introduce a data structure for register allocation in which the parallelism in a program and data flows over symbolic registers can be well described. The data structure is called a **Register Existence Graph**.

Section 4.1 describes the method of constructing a

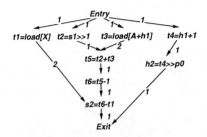

Figure 9: Weighed Data Dependence DAG

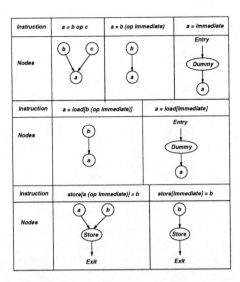

Figure 10: Making Nodes in a Register Existence Graph

register existence graph. Section 4.2 explains how the interference among symbolic registers is expressed in a register existence graph. Then, section 4.3 presents a register allocation model using a register existence graph. After a description of the method of handling spill code in section 4.4, the specifications of the register allocation algorithm are given in section 4.5.

4.1 Making a Register Existence Graph

This section describes the construction of a register existence graph. First, a data dependence DAG is made from source code in which nodes express instructions and edges express data dependence. Then, each edge is weighted according to the delay needed to execute the instructions that the nodes connected by the edge represent. Fig. 9 shows a DAG of Fig. 1b). For example, there is a delay of 2 cycles between instruction t3=load[A+h1] and instruction t5=t2+t3, so the weight of the edge is 2.

In this DAG, the distance between nodes is defined as the largest total weight of nodes in the path. The path that has the largest distance is called the critical path. When the code expressed by a DAG is executed on processors that have a sufficient number of ALUs, it needs at least as many cycles as the critical path, so the execution time of a program should be determined by the length of the critical path [10]. Using this length as an index for optimizing elements such as register allocator and code scheduler is obviously effective.

Next, make a register existence graph from the obtained DAG. Except in some cases, in register existence graphs, nodes represent symbolic registers and edges represent the use of data in symbolic registers. For example, if data in a symbolic register b are defined by data in a symbolic register a, add an edge from a to b. Each node in a register existence graph is weighted by the delay needed to generate data in the symbolic register that the node represents.

The method for obtaining a register existence graph from a DAG is as follows:

- Put Entry and Exit as the source and the sink of the register existence graph, respectively.

- Analyze symbolic registers that are live in the entrance of the code, put nodes that represent the

symbolic registers, and then put edges from Entry to the nodes.

- Analyze symbolic registers that are live in the exit of the code, put nodes that represent the symbolic registers, and then put edges from the nodes to Exit.

- For each instruction in the DAG, apply the transformation shown in Fig. 10.

Fig. 11 shows a register existence graph made by these processes.

4.2 How a Register Existence Graph Expresses Interference among Symbolic Registers

Consider the register existence graph in Fig. 12, in which two thick lines are drawn.

These lines divide the graph into two planes: one includes Entry and the other includes Exit. A line of this kind indicates the following:

- A result of code scheduling exists in which the symbolic registers represented by nodes crossed by the line are live at the same time.

Fig. 12b) shows the result of code scheduling. Symbolic registers t2, h1 and p0 are crossed by line1 and are simultaneously live between cycles n and n+1. In addition, symbolic registers t1, t5, t4 and p0 are crossed by line2 and are simultaneously live between cycles n+3 and n+4.

We call these lines **con-time lines** in the sense that the line indicates the time at which the symbolic registers in the nodes that the line crosses are live simultaneously. The existence of the possibility of drawing

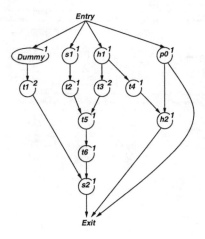

Figure 11: Register Existence Graph

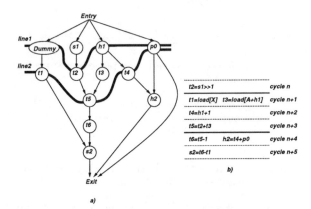

t2=s1>>1	cycle n
t1=load[X] t3=load[A+h1]	cycle n+1
t4=h1+1	cycle n+2
t5=t2+t3	cycle n+3
t6=t5-1 h2=t4+p0	cycle n+4
s2=t6-t1	cycle n+5

b)

a)

Figure 12: Cutting a Register Existence Graph

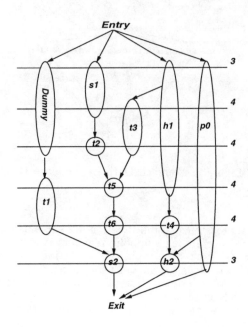

Figure 13: Leveling a Register Existence Graph

such a line means that there exists a possible interference among the symbolic registers in the nodes that the line crosses, so does a result of code scheduling that produces such interference.

4.3 Register Allocation and Code Scheduling in a Register Existence Graph

As mentioned in the previous section, the drawing of a con-time line is related to the interference among symbolic registers and the results of code scheduling. Therefore, drawing con-time lines as follows on a register existence graph somewhat restricts the allocation of registers and scheduling of instructions.

- Con-time lines never cross each other.

- For each node, one or more con-time lines representing weights equivalent to or greater than that of the node are drawn horizontally.

We call this process **leveling**. Leveling fixes the overlaps of the lifespans of symbolic registers for the entire code, in other words, it determines which symbolic registers interfere with each other at the same time. Thus, leveling means performing a part of the register allocation and a part of the code scheduling.

Fig. 13 shows an example of leveling.

Here, the number put on each line indicates the number of symbolic registers the line crosses. This indicates the number of symbolic registers that are live simultaneously. Therefore, we call the number "the degree of interference of symbolic registers." Leveling determines the degrees of interference of symbolic registers for each con-time line. The maximum degree means the smallest number of physical registers the code needs after leveling without spilling. In this example, 4 registers can be mapped to the symbolic registers without spilling.

4.4 Handling Spill Code in a Register Existence Graph

This section describes the method of spilling out and in symbolic registers on a register existence graph. The symbolic registers are spilled out and in by inserting nodes that express spilled symbolic registers into the register existence graph. These nodes are called spill nodes, and do not produce an increase in the degree of interference among symbolic registers, even if a con-time line goes through the nodes.

Spill nodes are inserted as shown in Fig. 14.

Fig. 14 a) shows an example in which a temporal register used in an intermediate code is spilled out and in. The lifespan of the temporal register is within the code expressed by the register existence graph, so the register is not live at either the top or the bottom of

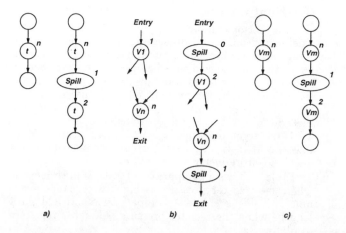

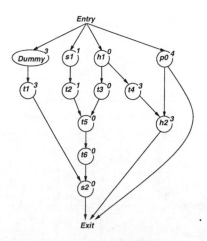

Figure 14: Inserting Spill Nodes

Figure 15: Slackness of Nodes

the code. In this case, after duplication of the node that expresses the symbolic register being spilled, a spill node is inserted between the duplicated nodes. Thus, the degree of interference is decreased by making the con-time lines that used to go through the temporal register go through the spill node.

Figs. 14 b) and c) are examples in which a variable (transformed into SSA form) is spilled out and in. Its lifespan is not within the code expressed by a register existence graph, so it is live at both the top and bottom of the code. Here, we have two cases of inserting a spill node. One is a case in which data in the variable that are live over the iteration, i.e., live at both the top and bottom of the code, are spilled. The other is a case in which other data in the variable are spilled. For a variable "V" transformed as V1, V2 ..., Vn, the datum defined first is V1 and that defined last is Vn, and edges are put from Entry to V1, and from Vn to Exit. In this case, V1 and Vn are live over the iteration. V1 and Vn are spilled out and in as shown in Fig. 14 b). Others are spilled out and in as shown in Fig. 14 c).

All nodes inserted are weighted as in Fig. 14.

4.5 Required Specifications of the Register Allocation Algorithm

The specification of register allocation with leveling a register existence graph is as follows:

- Leveling and the insertion of spill nodes are performed to ensure that every node is crossed by as many or more lines than its weighted value, and to ensure that the degree of interference on every con-time line does not exceed the number of available registers.

An algorithm that satisfies this specification will be described in Section 5.

4.6 Information for Leveling Derived from a Register Existence Graph
Number of con-time lines

We have shown that the distance of the critical path of a DAG can be considered as the execution time of a program, and its utilization as an index of optimization techniques using DAG is effective.

Since a register existence graph is a type of transformation of a DAG, it includes some information that corresponds to the distance of the critical path of a DAG. In a register existence graph, this information is the number of con-time lines that satisfy the restriction mentioned in Section 4.3. Therefore, since this number can be considerd as the execution time of a program, an algorithm using a register existence graph should work in such a way that it does not increase this number.

Slackness of a node

The slackness of a node is defined as the maximum weight that can be added to the node without an increase in the number of con-time lines. Taking Fig. 15 as an example, the addition of one weight to node s1, whose weight is 1, does not increase the number of con-time lines. Therefore, the slackness of the node is 1. Fig. 15 shows the slackness of each node in Fig. 11. This information is useful for minimizing the increase in the number of con-time lines, which is achieved by allocating hardware resources preferentially to less slack nodes and spilling symbolic registers expressed by slacker nodes.

5 An Example of an Algorithm

This section presents an algorithm for leveling a register existence graph. The algorithm works at the order of n^2, where n is the number of nodes.

```
Nodes = choose-successors(Entry);
Level = 1;

while(Nodes != {Exit}){
  if(the degree of interference exceeds
     the number of registers){
```

409

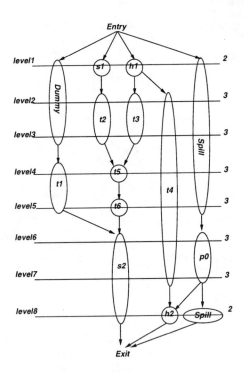

Figure 16: Result of Leveling

```
Nodes = sort-nodes-by-slackness(Nodes);
ChosenNodes = choose-as-many-nodes-as-
              the-number-of-registers-
              from-the-top(Nodes);
finished[Level++] = ChosenNodes;
spill nodes except ChosenNodes
}else{
  ChosenNodes = Nodes;
}
Remains = Null;
foreach(Node in ChosenNodes){
  Node.weight--;
  if(Node.weight > 0)
    Remains = Remains + Node;
}
Nodes = Null;
foreach(Node in ChosenNodes){
  Nodes = choose-successors(Node)
  if (exists Successor1 and Successor2
      in Nodes such that
      Successor1 is the successor
      of Successor2)){
    Nodes = Nodes + Node;
    Nodes = Nodes - Successor1;
  }
}
Nodes = Nodes + Remains;
}
```

The result of leveling the code is shown in Fig. 16.

6 Evaluation

This section compares our approach using a register existence graph, an ordinary register allocation using a register interference graph, and a register allocation using the parallelized interference graph described in section 3. We selected some programs from the Stanford Benchmark for evaluation, and the lengths of their critical paths after register allocation using each method and code scheduling are listed in Tables 1 and 2. Our target machine is a VLIW that can execute fixed-point instructions in 1 cycle, and floating-point and load/store instructions in 2 cycles.

Table 1 shows a comparison of critical path lengths when the register pressure is high (8 registers available). Table 2 shows a comparison of critical path lengths when the register pressure is low (32 registers available).

If the register pressure is high, our method gives better results than the other two methods. Consequently, it performs 2.01 times better on average than the method using a parallelized interference graph, and 2.17 times better on average than the method using an interference graph. Table 1 shows that the ratio of performance improvement with the method using a parallelized interference graph is higher when the number of available ALUs is larger. This is because that method increases the edges of the interference among symbolic registers so much that it is difficult to determine which edges should be deleted. Table 1 also shows that the ratio of performance improvement with the method using an interference graph is higher when the number of available ALUs is smaller. This is because that method increases the number of instructions by inserting spill code to decrease the interference among symbolic registers.

If the register pressure is low, our method gives almost the same result as that using an interference graph because, spill code is rarely generated. As a result, it performs 1.28 times better on average than the method using a parallelized interference graph, and 1.02 times better on average than the method using an interference graph. The method using a parallelized interference graph gives the worst results, because of an increase in the number of edges of the interference. In the method using a parallelized interference graph, it is imporntant to improve the method of deleting the added edges if the register pressure is not very high.

In our method, the interference among symbolic registers changes during leveling. This method of handling the interference, using a register existence graph, allows us to consider the parallelism among instructions and to handle the interference according to the number of registers available.

7 Conclusions

We have introduced a register existence graph that can express the interference among symbolic registers and the parallelism among instructions in a program. We have also shown that leveling a register existence graph realizes the generation of anti-dependence and spill code taking account of the parallelism in a program, which existing methods rarely do. We are now

410

Table 1: Comparison When Register Pressure Is High (8 Registers Available)

Number of ALUs	Our method					Method using a parallelized interference graph					Method using an interference graph				
	1	2	4	8	∞	1	2	4	8	∞	1	2	4	8	∞
Bubble	39	22	14	11	11	53	37	37	37	37	59	32	19	18	18
Exptab	67	37	22	18	18	105	91	91	91	91	162	49	43	24	24
Fit	86	63	62	62	62	88	73	70	70	70	249	150	148	148	148
Initarr	79	41	32	32	32	106	96	96	96	96	164	84	56	56	56
Initmat	89	51	29	28	28	150	110	110	110	110	310	77	74	74	74
Permute	33	19	15	15	15	33	25	24	24	24	74	40	29	29	29
Qsort	40	26	19	18	18	46	34	34	34	34	77	45	31	28	28
Remove	81	46	44	44	44	99	83	83	83	83	243	106	104	104	104
Try	109	62	44	42	41	163	137	137	137	137	290	86	85	79	79

Table 2: Comparison When Register Pressure Is Low (32 Registers Available)

Number of ALUs	Our method					Method using a parallelized interference graph					Method using an interference graph				
	1	2	4	8	∞	1	2	4	8	∞	1	2	4	8	∞
Bubble	39	22	14	11	11	39	26	24	23	23	39	22	14	11	11
Exptab	62	35	18	11	10	62	38	33	33	33	62	35	18	11	11
Fit	86	63	62	62	62	86	71	69	69	69	86	63	62	62	62
Initarr	75	39	32	32	32	75	51	49	49	49	75	39	32	32	32
Initmat	89	51	29	28	28	96	62	58	58	58	96	51	29	28	28
Permute	33	19	15	15	15	33	25	24	24	24	33	19	15	15	15
Qsort	38	25	19	17	17	38	25	23	23	23	38	24	19	17	17
Remove	81	46	44	44	44	81	59	57	57	57	81	46	44	44	44
Try	76	61	44	39	39	105	69	66	66	66	105	61	44	39	39

considering the ways of improving the leveling algorithm and allowing cooperation between a spill code generator and a code scheduler.

References

[1] G.J.Chaitin, M.A.Auslander, A.K.Chandra, J.Cocke, M.E.Hopplins and P.W.Markstein, "Register Allocation via Coloring," Computer Languages 6 (1981), pp.47-57.

[2] G.J.Chaitin, "Register Allocation & Spilling via Graph Coloring," Proceedings of the ACM SIGPLAN '82 Symposium on Compiler Construction (Jun. 1982), pp.98-105.

[3] D.Callahan and B.Koblenz, "Register Allocation via Hierarchical Graph Coloring," Proceedings of the ACM SIGPLAN '91 Conference on Programming Language Design and Implementation (Jun. 1991), pp.192-203.

[4] A.Koseki, H.Komatsu and Y.Fukazawa "A Register Allocation Technique Using Guarded PDG," Proceedings of the International Conference on Supercomputing (May 1996), pp.270-277.

[5] J.R.Goodman and W.C.Hsu, "Code Scheduling and Register Allocation in Large Basic Blocks," International Conference on Supercomputing (Jul. 1988), pp.442-452.

[6] J.R.Ellis, "Bulldog: A Compiler for VLIW Architectures," The MIT Press (1985).

[7] R.Cytron, J.Ferrante, B.K.Rosen, M.N.Wegman and F.K.Zadeck, "An Efficient Method of Computing Static Single Assignment Form," Conference Record of the Sixteenth ACM Symposium on the Principles of Programming Languages (Jan. 1989), pp.25-35.

[8] S.S.Pinter, "Register Allocation with Instruction Scheduling: A New Approach," Proceedings of the ACM SIGPLAN '93 Conference on Programming Languages Design and Implementation (1993), pp.248-257.

[9] C.Norris and L.L.Pollock, "A Scheduler-Sensitive Global Register Allocation," Proceedings of the ACM SIGPLAN '93 Conference on Supercomputing (1993), pp.804-813.

[10] E.B. Fernandez and B. Bussel, "Bounds on the Number of Processors and Time for Multiprocessor Optimal Schedules," IEEE Trans. Computers, Vol.C22, No.8, pp.745-751 (1973).

Precise Call Graph Construction for OO Programs in the Presence of Virtual Functions*

Deepankar Bairagi, Sandeep Kumar[†]and Dharma P. Agrawal
Department of Electrical and Computer Engineering
North Carolina State University
Raleigh, NC-27695.
{dbairag,skumar,dpa}@eos.ncsu.edu

Abstract

Several intra- and inter-procedural program analysis techniques form the backbone of an optimizing and parallelizing compiler. The efficacy of these analyses depends upon how precise the call graph is. However, due to lack of exact type information for objects in an object-oriented (OO) program, the existing call graph construction algorithms are rendered imprecise. In this paper, we present an algorithm for constructing a more precise call graph by exploiting the static class hierarchy of an OO program. The information collected during the class hierarchy analysis helps in avoiding unnecessary addition of many spurious call graph edges for virtual-function calls. We have implemented our algorithm for handling C++ programs within a restructuring tool, Sage++. With our precise algorithm for call graph construction, the percentage reduction in the number of nodes and edges in the call graphs for the benchmark programs we had selected, ranged between 4% to 56% and between 22% to 58%, respectively.

1 Introduction

Detection of parallelism from a program written in any language typically requires precise control and data dependence analyses. While established dependence analysis techniques for conventional languages still form the basis for parallelizing OO programs, certain OO language features make these analyses imprecise, or practically useless. The OO language features which ease the programming effort namely, inheritance, virtual functions, pointers and dynamic binding, severely hinder opportunities for program optimization and parallelization.

Interprocedural analysis is extremely critical in exposing parallelism beyond procedural boundaries. The purpose of interprocedural analysis is to increase the precision of flow and data dependence analyses by summarizing the side-effects of procedure calls. Interprocedural analysis begins with the construction of a call

graph. A call graph is a directed graph representing the calling relationships between the procedures of a program [12]. The nodes of a call graph represent the procedures in a program and the directed edges represent the caller-callee relationship.

In OO languages such as C++, construction of a precise call graph is limited by the presence of virtual functions. Virtual function is a construct which allows the programmer to declare functions in a base class that are possibly redefined (or specialized) in its derived classes. Recent studies [1] have shown that the function calls in C++ programs tend to have very small number of instructions (about 80 per function call and 5-8 instructions per basic block). 63% of the called functions are attributed to calls to methods and 23% are attributed to indirect function calls. The observations of this study [1] indicate that OO programming style encourages the use of virtual functions. These observations stress the need for precise interprocedural analysis and proper handling of virtual function calls in OO programs. It is important to note that in C programs, basic blocks contain a degree of parallelism no more than 3 or 4 [11]. Moreover, inclusion of large class libraries results in very large OO programs, of which, a lot of code is never reached at run-time. A precise call graph can help eliminate a lot of unreachable procedures from OO programs [9].

Techniques for construction of call graphs have been explored in detail for languages like Fortran and C [2, 7, 4]. A pioneering approach to precise call graph construction is described in the work by Ryder [7]. A more precise and efficient algorithm is presented by Hall and Kennedy [4]. However, these call graph construction techniques for procedural languages are unable to build a precise call graph for OO programs in the presence of virtual functions. The following example shows how the presence of virtual functions can result in an incorrect or an imprecise call graph using the traditional techniques.

```
class A{                class B : public A{
  virtual foo();          foo();
  virtual bar();        }
}
class C : public B{     class D{
  bar();                  virtual foo();
}                         virtual bar();
```

---

*This work has been supported in part by the Army Research Office under contract DAAH04-94-G-0306.

[†]Currently this author is with Hewlett-Packard Laboratories, 1 Main Street, 10th Floor, Cambridge, MA 02142

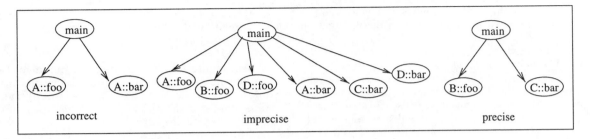

Figure 1: Call graph in the presence of virtual functions

```
                                    }

main(){
    A *objA;
    B *objB;
    C *objC;
    D *objD;
    objA = objB;
    objA->foo();   // call 1
    objB = objC;
    objB->bar();   // call 2
}
```

The declared types of objA and objB are A and B respectively. Therefore, a traditional call graph construction technique would bind call 1 to A::foo and call 2 to A::bar (B inherits bar from A). This would result in an incorrect call graph as shown in the figure. But if we look at the preceding assignments, call 1 actually invokes B::foo and call 2 invokes C::bar. This is due to lack of program-point-specific type information [5]. We cannot always statically determine the types assumed by objects at various program points. It has been proven that precise program-point type determination for a language like C++ is NP-hard [6]. An approach which ensures correctness would be to add an edge to all the virtual functions with the same name. The resulting imprecise call graph with a lot of redundant edges is shown in Figure 1.

In this paper, we present an algorithm which circumvents the problem posed by virtual functions by incorporating Class Hierarchy Analysis (CHA) during call graph construction. We identify a minimal set of classes that an object could belong to by analyzing the class hierarchy graph (CHG), and consequently, identify only the relevant subset of candidates for a virtual function. We have implemented our algorithm for C++ programs and obtained precise call graphs for several benchmark programs. We compare our call graph with the call graph as would be obtained by a naive approach, i.e., when the target of a virtual function call could be any virtual function with the same name, and we have obtained considerable improvement in the precise construction of the call graphs.

The rest of the paper is organized as follows. In the next section, we discuss class hierarchy analysis and present our algorithm in detail. In Section 3 we discuss some of the implementation issues and present our results. Finally in Section 4 we derive conclusions from this work.

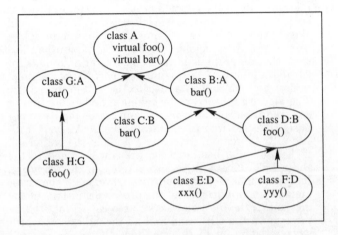

Figure 2: A Class Hierarchy Graph

2 Our approach

A CHG represents the inheritance relationship between classes defined in a program. Precise information gathered after class analysis not only exposes hidden parallelism, which is our final goal, but also creates opportunities for other compiler optimizations, such as inlining of messages, minimizing the number of dispatches, procedure cloning, code motion, etc.. The compiler can assimilate valuable static information about the possible classes of objects of each method being compiled by exploiting the information about the structure of the CHG, including where methods are defined[10]. The CHA done by Dean et. al. [3] as implemented for Cecil programs in the Vortex compiler has motivated us to some extent to employ CHA to construct more precise call graphs for C++ programs.

The following example shows how a virtual function can be accurately predicted using CHA [3]. Consider a situation, as shown in Figure 2, where the definition of a method foo() in class D contains a call to a method bar(). Assume that the method bar() has been declared as a virtual function, and multiple definitions of bar() exist in the subclasses of A. However, only one such method definition of bar() would be invoked at the run-time. Static interprocedural analysis without class hierarchy information is unable to bind this call to one single definition of bar (or to a subset of many defintions of bar()). However, by simply examining the CHG, it is obvious that as there are no overriding definitions of bar() in any of the subclasses of D, the call to bar() in D::foo() can be replaced by a direct function call to B::bar(). In turn such an observation also indicates that only one edge should be added to the call graph. The above example shows that in order to obtain precise interprocedural summary information, the CHA complements the determination of types.

Our three-step approach to precise construction of call-graphs in the presence of virtual functions is outlined below. In the first step, we construct the CHG by making one pass over the entire program. In the second step, we gather information about every method and function defined in the program including whether method is defined as virtual or not. This information is stored in a hash table, which is hashed by the name and class of the method. For C functions (non-methods) we assume that they belong to a class, C_{main}. In the third step, the call graph is initialized by creating a node for the *main* function. We maintain a *worklist* of the functions which have been added to the call graph so far. The algorithm proceeds by taking a node (function or a method) out of the *worklist* and retrieving its previously collected information from step 2. At every call-site in the function, we create a node in the call graph if that function has not been previously added to the call graph, This node is also entered in the *worklist*. In case of inherited methods, we traverse up the class-hierarchy graph to find all the proper definitions of the method. If the method was declared as virtual, we traverse down the CHG and find all the subclasses which have a definition of this method. If so, we proceed recursively as above.

In Figure 5, we show the algorithm in detail. In the following subsection, we define some of the terms used in the algorithm.

2.1 Terminology

- **Call graph:** $CG(V, E)$ is a call graph where V is the set of nodes and E is the set of edges.

- **Node:** each node in the call graph is of the form (C_i, m_j) denoting the function $C_i :: m_j()$

- **Edge:** each edge $A \to B$ in CG indicates a call from node A to node B in CG

- **Record:** for a method m defined in class C, the record $R[C, m] \leftarrow \{N, v, L_{fp}, L_{call}\}$, where

    - $N \leftarrow$ name of the method;
    - $v \leftarrow$ virtual flag = 1 if virtual, 0 otherwise
    - $L_{fp} \leftarrow$ list of formal parameters;
    - $L_{call} \leftarrow$ list of call sites;
    - L_{call} contains the list of tuples $< n, t, L_{ap} >$, where
        * $n \leftarrow$ name of the called method or function;
        * $t \leftarrow main$, if it a function(non-method), else, the defined type of the called object; $L_{ap} \leftarrow$ list of actual parameters;

- **Hash table:** Hash table HT stores the records mentioned above hashed by class name and method name

We handle function pointers in our algorithm (although not shown explicitly) as follows. During the information collection phase, we also record if any function pointer is defined and is assigned some function. We also record the actual parameters at function calls and formal parameters during function definitions. In step 3, while adding a node to the worklist, we propagate the information if a function pointer is passed as an actual parameter by binding it to its corresponding formal. While processing a node from the worklist, at every call-site we check if the function call is a function pointer defined earlier in the caller or passed as a parameter to the callee. We update the worklist appropriately and add a correct edge to the correct function.

3 Implementation and Results

We have implemented our algorithm within a restructuring tool called Sage++ [8]. Sage++ is an OO toolkit for building program transformation systems for Fortran 90 and C++. It provides class libraries for restructuring programs. The user is provided with a parser, a structured parse tree, a symbol and type tables to perform analyses at source level. Sage++ parses the whole program but collects only partial information for our information collection phase (step 2) of our algorithm. We had to tweak the Sage++ implementation for generating the CHG in a format as needed by our algorithm. After the information collection phase, we merge the information in the hash table with that of the CHG for a faster look up during the call graph construction phase.

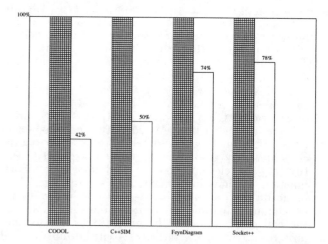

Figure 3: Number of edges (expressed as percentage)

One serious limitation that we have with the Sage++ tool is that it is unable to handle large libraries split across multiple files. The same variable when used in two different files is assigned two different symbol numbers. Currently, we merge the files into one large single file for building the call-graphs.

Table 1: Characteristics of the benchmark programs

Name	Call-sites	Virtual call-sites	Functions	Virtual functions	Description
COOOL	217	1	103	24	mathematical optimization library
C++SIM	61	8	52	14	C++ simulation library
FeynDiagram	55	1	34	3	Library for Feynmann diagrams
SOCKET++	122	1	47	2	C++ library for TCP/IP sockets

The algorithm was run on a suite of benchmark programs comprising of the libraries COOOL, C++SIM, socket++ and FeynDiagram. These OO libraries have been developed at various universities for scientific and technical applications and are publicly available.[1] All these libraries are fairly large (several thousand lines of code) and contain several virtual function calls. In Table 1, we tabulate the program characteristics of the libraries in our benchmark suite. Note that the programs call a subset of the functions defined in the libraries and the numbers in the table indicate the number of call-sites and functions statically called in the benchmark programs.

For each of these libraries we ran our algorithm and constructed the call graphs. We measured the average number of nodes and edges in the call graph across several programs which used these libraries. For comparing our algorithm, we implemented the naive algorithm for construction of call graphs. We also built the call graphs for the same programs using the naive algorithm, i.e. not utilizing the information about class hierarchy and adding all possible edges at the virtual function call-sites. In other words, for every virtual function call we added an edge to all the nodes corresponding to functions with the same name. In the bar charts shown in Figures 3 and 4, we compare the number of nodes and edges in the call graph obtained by using our algorithm and the naive algorithm. The shaded and unshaded bars indicate the number we get using the naive approach and our algorithm respectively. The unshaded part represents the number of nodes or edges expressed as a percantage of the shaded part.

As is obvious in the bar charts that with our algorithm, the number of nodes and edges in the call graphs decrease consistently for every benchmark program. Clearly, the sparser the call graph, the better off we are in conducting other compiler optimizations. Furthermore, the percentage decrease in the number of nodes and edges is not a constant, and it is in part due to different program characteristics, such as:

- *frequency of virtual function calls:* In our experiments, most of the programs had just one virtual function call, except for C++SIM. This explains the improvement in number of edges for C++SIM.

- *the class hierarchy structure:* COOOL and C++SIM have more deeply nested CHG compared to that of socket++ and FeynDiagram. Therefore, every time we eliminate one redundant virtual call, we eliminate a larger subtree (subgraph) of the call graph. Although the idea of level is applicable to trees and not to graphs, in a tree structured call graph, a virtual function occurring near the *main* or root node is more likely to add more redundant edges to the call graph.

- *number of virtual functions with the same name:* Although the programs using COOOL has just one virtual call, there are 24 possible targets for each of these calls. This accounts for the huge reduction in both the number of edges and nodes for the COOOL library benchmarks.

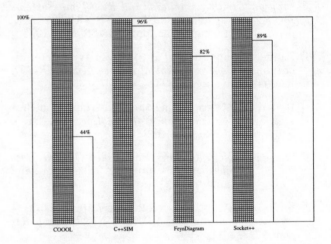

Figure 4: Number of nodes (expressed as percentage)

4   Conclusion

In the context of static flow analyses necessary for optimizing and parallelizing C++ programs, construction of a more precise call graph is very critical. We show that the class hierarchy analysis is an extremely useful analysis in constructing a more precise call graph in the presence of virtual functions. In this paper we have proposed a more precise call graph construction technique which makes use of the class hierarchy analysis. The results we have obtained on the set of benchmark programs are very encouraging. With our precise

---

[1] COOOL: *http://timna.Mines.EDU/cwpcodes/coool/*
C++SIM: *http://marlish.ncl.ac.uk:8080/C++SIM/*
FeynDiagram: *ftp.hepth.cornell.edu/pub/feyndiagram.tar.Z*
Socket++: *ftp.virginia.edu: public_access/socket++-1.6.tar.gz*

algorithm for call graph construction, the percentage reduction in the number of nodes and edges in the call graphs for the benchmark programs we had selected, ranged between 4% to 56% and between 22% to 58%, respectively.

References

[1] Calder, B., Grunwald, D. and Zorn, B., "Quantifying behaviorial differences between C and C++ programs", *Technical Report CU-CS-698, Univ. of Colorado, Boulder*, Jan. 1994.

[2] Cooper, K., and Kennedy, K., "Efficient Computation of Flow Insensitive Interprocedural Summary Information", *Proc. of the SIGPLAN 84 Symp. on Compiler Construction*, Jun. 1984, pp. 247-258.

[3] Dean, J., Grove, F. and Chambers, C., "Optimization of Object-Oriented Programs Using Static Class Hierarchy Analysis", *University of Washington CSE Technical Report 94-12-01*.

[4] Hall, M. and Kennedy, K., "Efficient Call Graph Analysis", *ACM Letters on Programming Lang. and Systems*, Vol. 1, No. 3, Sep. 1992, pp 227-242.

[5] Kumar, S., Agrawal, D. P., Iyer, S. P., "An Improved Type-Inference Algorithm To Expose Parallelism in Object-Oriented Programs", *Third Workshop on Lang., Compilers, and Run-Time Systems for Scalable Computers*, Troy, NY, Kluwer Academic Publ., Chapter 22, pp. 283-286, May 1995.

[6] Pande, H. and Ryder, B., "Static type determination for C++", *Technical Report LCSR-TR-197*, Rutgers Univ., Feb. 1993.

[7] Ryder, B., "Constructing the Call Graph of a Program", *IEEE Trans. on Software Eng.*, Vol. SE-5, No. 3, May 1979, pp. 216-226.

[8] "Sage++ User's Guide", *Unpublished On-line Document*, Department of Computer Science, Indiana Univ., Bloomington, IN.

[9] Srivastava, A., "Unreachable Procedures in Object-oriented Programming", *DEC WRL Research Report 93/4*, Aug., 1993.

[10] Sudholt, M. and Steigner, C., "On Interprocedural Data Flow Analysis for Object Oriented Lang.", *4th Intl Conf. on Compiler Construction*, Paderborn, FRG, Oct., 1992, pp. 156-162.

[11] Wall, D. W., "Limits of Instruction-Level Parallelism", *4th Intl Conf. on Architectural Support for Programming Lang. and Operating Systems*, , Santa Clara, CA, Apr. 1991, pp. 176-188.

[12] Zima, H., and Chapman, B., "Supercompilers for Parallel and Vector Computers", Addison-Wesley Publishing Company, 1991.

Algorithm Call-Graph Construction

Input: C++ program P
Output: Call graph $CG(V, E)$

Step 1: build the class hierarchy graph H

Step 2: Information collection phase

```
foreach class C_i in P do
    foreach method m_j defined in C_i do
        build record R[C_i, m_j]
        foreach call site in m_j do
            build the tuple < n, t, L_ap >;
            insert the tuple to L_call;
        insert R[C_i, m_j] in HT
        enddo
    enddo
enddo

foreach C function (non-method) F_i in P do
    build the record R[C_main, F_i] where v = 0
        foreach call site in m_j do;
            build the tuple < n, t, L_ap >;
            enter the tuple to L_call;
        enddo
    insert R[C_main, F_i] in HT
enddo
```

Step 3: Construction of the call graph

```
create a root node (C_main, main);
initialize worklist by inserting (C_main, main);

while worklist is not empty do
    remove an entry (C_i, m_j) from the worklist;
    retrieve the R[C_i, m_j] from HT;
    retrieve L_call from R[C_i, m_j];
    foreach tuple < m_k, C_l, L_ap > in L_call do
        if m_k is not defined in C_l then
            traverse up H to find the immediate
            predecessor C_l1 which contains a
            definition of m_k;
        else
            C_l1 ← C_l;
        if node (C_l1, m_k) has not been created then
            create the node
            add (C_l1, m_k) to worklist;
        add edge (C_i, m_j) → (C_l1, m_k) to CG;
        if v = 1 in R[C_l1, m_k] then
            traverse down H to find every child C_child
            of C_l such that it has a definition of m_k;
            foreach such C_child do
                if the node (C_child, m_k) has not
                    already been created, create it
                    and add (C_child, m_k) to worklist
                add edge (C_i, m_j) → (C_child, m_k)
                to CG
            enddo
    enddo
enddo
```

Figure 5: Our Call Graph Constructor Algorithm

Automatic Generation of Injective Modular Mappings[*]

Hyuk-Jae Lee

Department of Computer Science
Louisiana Tech University
Ruston, LA 71272

José A.B. Fortes

School of Electrical and Computer Engineering
Purdue University
West Lafayette, IN 47907

Abstract

Many optimizations (of programs with loops) used in parallelizing compilers and systolic array design are based on linear transformations of loop iteration spaces. Additional important optimizations and designs are possible by using recently proposed modular mappings, which are described by linear transformations modulo a constant vector. Previous work on modular mappings focused on conditions that guarantee injectivity of a modular mapping for algorithms with rectangular index sets. This paper generalizes previous work by providing new injectivity conditions that cover the cases when the program index set has arbitrary shape and size, and the target processor array and the mapping moduli are of arbitrary size. A systematic technique to efficiently generate modular mappings is also proposed. The complexity of the proposed generation technique is $O(n^2 n!)$ for a nested loop of depth n with a rectangular index set and a target processor array with as many processors as required. A bounded search scheme is also provided for general cases. Each trial is formulated as an integer linear programming problem with at most $3n$ variables.

1 Introduction

Affine transformations of programs whose execution time is mostly spent in loops have been extensively studied and used for source-to-source program transformations in parallelizing compilers and systolic array design [1]-[4]. Extending the framework of linear algebra, modular transformations, described by linear transformations modulo a constant vector, were recently proposed [5]. Initial work on modular mappings focused on the derivation of injectivity conditions that guarantee that a modular mapping is one-to-one. These conditions assume that algorithms have rectangular index sets and also assume certain constraints on the target processor array. In this pa-

per, injectivity conditions are provided to cover algorithms with arbitrary index sets and rectangular processor arrays of arbitrary size. This paper also investigates an injectivity condition for cases when modular mappings are linear along a subset of the coordinates (i.e., they resemble modular mappings with arbitrarily large moduli). In addition to the derivation of injectivity conditions, this paper addresses the problem of how to systematically generate efficient modular time-space mappings.

The rest of the paper is organized as follows. Section 2 defines modular mappings and briefly reviews previous work on the characterization of injectivity of modular mappings. Section 3 extends injectivity conditions for more general cases. Section 4 studies the problem of generating modular mappings. Section 5 concludes this paper.

2 Modular Time-Space Mapping

Definition 1 A *modular function*, $\mathbf{T}_{\vec{m}} : \mathcal{Z}^n \to \mathcal{Z}^k$, is a mapping of the form: $\mathbf{T}_{\vec{m}}(\vec{j}) = \begin{bmatrix} T_{(1,*)} \cdot \vec{j}_{(mod\ m_1)} \\ T_{(2,*)} \cdot \vec{j}_{(mod\ m_2)} \\ \vdots \\ T_{(k,*)} \cdot \vec{j}_{(mod\ m_k)} \end{bmatrix}$,

where $T_{(i,*)}$ is a row vector.

The matrix $T = \begin{bmatrix} T_{(1,*)} \\ \vdots \\ T_{(k,*)} \end{bmatrix}$ and vector $\vec{m} = (m_1, \cdots, m_k)^T$ are called the *transformation matrix* and *modulus vector*, respectively. ∎

Let $\vec{u}$ and $\vec{v}$ be two vectors with the same number of elements. The notation $\vec{u}_{(mod\ \vec{v})}$ denotes a vector $((u_1)_{(mod\ v_1)}, (u_2)_{(mod\ v_2)}, \cdots, (u_n)_{(mod\ v_n)})$. Therefore the modular function can be described as $\mathbf{T}_{\vec{m}}(\vec{j}) = (T\vec{j})_{(mod\ \vec{m})}$.

To be used as a time-space transformation, a modular function should be injective (one-to-one) when its domain is the index set of an algorithm.

Definition 2 A *modular time-space transformation*,

---

[*] This research was partially funded by the National Science Foundation under grants MIP-9500673 and CDA-9015696.

$\mathbf{T}_{\vec{m}}$, is a modular function that is *injective* when its domain is restricted to the index set $\mathcal{J}$ of an algorithm, i.e., $\mathbf{T}_{\vec{m}} : \mathcal{J} \to \mathcal{Z}^k$ is injective. ∎

This paper considers only the case when $n = k$.

In order for any modular function to be a modular transformation of a given algorithm, T and $\vec{m}$ must be carefully chosen to satisfy Definition 2. This section summarizes previous work on the characterization of injective modular mappings of rectangular index sets.

Definition 3 An index set $\mathcal{J}$ is *rectangular* and denoted $\mathcal{J}_{\vec{b}}$ if $\quad \mathcal{J} = \{\vec{j} \in \mathcal{Z}^n | \vec{0} \leq \vec{j} < \vec{b}\}$.
The vector $\vec{b}$ is called the *boundary vector* of $\mathcal{J}_{\vec{b}}$. ∎

Theorem 1 ([5]) Let $\mathcal{J}_{\vec{b}}$ be a rectangular index set and $\mathbf{T}_{\vec{b}}$ be a modular function of the index set $\mathcal{J}_{\vec{b}}$. Let $\succ$ be an arbitrary total order on the set $\{1, 2, \cdots, n\}$. $\mathbf{T}_{\vec{b}}$ is injective if its transformation matrix T satisfies (1) t_{ii} is relatively prime to b_i, and (2) $t_{ij} = 0$ if $i \succ j$. ∎

In Theorem 1, the modulus vector of the modular function is the same as the boundary vector of the index set, i.e. $\vec{m}$ is equal to $\vec{b}$. This is generalized in [5] to include the case when the modulus vector results from a permutation of the entries of the boundary vector as stated in the following proposition.

Proposition 1 A modular function $\mathbf{T}_{\vec{m}}$ is injective if the rows of a transformation matrix T correspond to a permutation of the rows of a transformation matrix that satisfies conditions in Theorem 1 and this permutation is the same as the permutation of $\vec{b}$ that yields the modulus vector $\vec{m}$. ∎

Other important conditions are derived in [5] and [6], but they are not used for generation of modular mappings in Section 4.

3 Injectivity conditions
3.1 Arbitrary index set and number of processors

Let $|\vec{u}|$ denote $|u_1| + |u_2| + \cdots + |u_n|$ and $\vec{u} * \vec{v}$ denote $(u_1 v_1, u_2 v_2, \cdots, u_n v_n)$. Proposition 2 provides an injectivity condition for an arbitrary index set.

Proposition 2 A modular mapping $\mathbf{T}_{\vec{m}}$ of an algorithm with index set $\mathcal{J}$ is injective if and only if any optimal solution of the integer programming problem*
- minimize $|T\vec{j_1} - T\vec{j_2} - \vec{k} * \vec{m}|$
- subject to $\vec{j_1}, \vec{j_2} \in \hat{\mathcal{J}}, \vec{k} \in \mathcal{Z}^n$,
is such that $\vec{j_1} = \vec{j_2}$. ∎

---
*The objective function with absolute values can easily be converted into linear functions

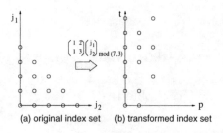

Figure 1: Modular mapping for three processors

The injectivity conditions discussed in Section 2 require the modulus vector to be obtained by permuting the boundary vector of the index set of an algorithm. The modulus vector determines the size of the processor array called *a virtual processor array*. It is often the case that the size of the available target processor array is smaller than that required by a modular mapping and therefore one more mapping from the virtual processor array to the physical target processor array is necessary. The injectivity conditions of Proposition 2 do not have any constraint on $\vec{m}$. Hence, this condition makes it possible to test for injectivity of a modular mapping that maps an index set directly onto the target processor array.

Example 1 Consider an index $\mathcal{J} = \{\vec{j} | j_1, j_2 \geq 0, j_1 + j_2 < 5\}$ (Fig. 1 (a)). Suppose that there are only three available processors. It is impossible for a nontrivial linear mapping to generate a time-space transformation to map all index points into three processors. However, an injective modular mapping with $m_2 = 3$ generates such a time-space transformation because the second element of the modulus vector determines the size of processor array. A modular mapping $\mathbf{T}_{\vec{m}}(\vec{j}) = \begin{pmatrix} t \\ p \end{pmatrix} = (\begin{pmatrix} 1 & 2 \\ 1 & 3 \end{pmatrix} \vec{j})_{(mod\,(7,3))}$ satisfies the injectivity condition of Proposition 2 and the requirement for the size of processor array (i.e., $m_2 = 3$). Injectivity of $\mathbf{T}_{\vec{m}}$ can be verified in Fig. 1 which shows the result of applying $\mathbf{T}_{\vec{m}}$ to the index set. ∎

3.2 Arbitrarily large moduli

This section considers the case when small moduli are necessary (or possible) only for a subset of the coordinates of the index set. For example, a modular mapping $\mathbf{T}(\vec{j}) = \begin{pmatrix} T_{(1,*)}\vec{j} \\ (T_{(2,*)}\vec{j})_{mod\,10} \\ (T_{(3,*)}\vec{j})_{mod\,15} \end{pmatrix}$ has small moduli 10 and 15 for the second and the third coordinates, respectively, but does not include a mod operation in the first coordinate (equivalently, has an arbitrarily large modulus, e.g., larger than the number of points in the index set). Decompose a transformation matrix T into two sub-matrices T^s and T^l where T^s consists of the rows of T with small moduli and T^l consists of the remaining rows of T. For the above example, $T^s = \begin{pmatrix} T_{(2,*)} \\ T_{(3,*)} \end{pmatrix}$ and $T^l = \begin{pmatrix} T_{(1,*)} \end{pmatrix}$. Let $\vec{m}^s$ denote the sub-vector of $\vec{m}$ corresponding to T^s. For the above example, $\vec{m}^s = (m_2, m_3)^T = (10, 15)^T$. Let n_s be the number of elements of $\vec{m}^s$. For this example, $n_s = 2$. The following proposition provides an injectivity condition for this case.

Proposition 3 A modular mapping $\mathbf{T}_{\vec{m}}$ of an algorithm with index set $\mathcal{J}$ is injective if and only if an optimal solution of the integer programming problem,
- minimize $|T^s \vec{j}_1 - T^s \vec{j}_2 - \vec{k}^s * \vec{m}^s|$,
- subject to $\vec{j}_1, \vec{j}_2 \in \hat{\mathcal{J}}, \vec{k}^s \in \mathcal{Z}^{n_s}$, and $T^l(\vec{j}_1 - \vec{j}_2) = \vec{0}$,

is such that $\vec{j}_1 = \vec{j}_2$: ∎

4 Generation of Modular Mappings

This section provides methods to generate injective modular mappings subject to constraints. Consider first the case when $\vec{m} = \vec{b}$. Other cases are discussed later in this section. Consider a directed graph $\mathcal{G}(\mathcal{V}, \mathcal{E})$ generated from T as follows:
- nodes: $\mathcal{V} = \{v_i | v_i \text{ represents the } i^{th} \text{ row of } T\}$,
- edges: $\mathcal{E} = \{(v_i, v_j) | t_{ij} \neq 0, i \neq j\}$.

It is well known in graph theory that a transformation matrix satisfies constraint (2) of Theorem 1 only if the induced graph is acyclic [7].

Proposition 4 Let T be an $n \times n$ matrix. There exists an order $\succ$ such that $t_{ij} = 0$ for $i \succ j$, if and only if the graph G induced from T is acyclic. ∎

A cycle in a directed graph can be detected by Depth-First Search algorithm (see Lemma 23.10 in [8]). The complexity of Depth-First Search is $\Theta(|\mathcal{V}| + |\mathcal{E}|)$ where $|\mathcal{V}|$ and $|\mathcal{E}|$ denote the numbers of nodes and edges, respectively. From $|\mathcal{V}| = n$ and $|\mathcal{E}| \leq n^2$, the complexity becomes $O(n + n^2) = O(n^2)$.

In order to generate a modular mapping that satisfies Theorem 1 from a partially predetermined modular mapping, one does not need to generate and test many possible modular mappings, but needs to generate only one transformation matrix as follows:
- Set all undetermined diagonal entries to one.
- Set all undetermined off-diagonal entries to zero.

The reason for setting all diagonal entries to one is to satisfy the condition (1) in Theorem 1. Off-diagonal entries are set to zero to make the induced graph have minimal edges because any non-zero off-diagonal entry causes an edge in the induced graph. Hence, if the graph contains a cycle, then any other generation of the transformation matrix also induces a cyclic graph.

When $\vec{m} \neq \vec{b}$, the generation of T cannot be based on Theorem 1. Instead, an approach based on Proposition 1 can be used. Suppose that T is given with some undetermined entries and $\vec{m}$ is a permutation of the entries of $\vec{b}$. To check injectivity of $\mathbf{T}_{\vec{m}}$, it is first necessary to find a matrix T' that yields T by permuting its rows in the same way as the permutation of $\vec{b}$ that yields $\vec{m}$. Then, it is checked if T' satisfies Theorem 1 as discussed earlier. This procedure requires $O(n^2)$ time. There are $n!$ possible permutations. Hence, it takes $O(n!n^2)$ time to find a valid optimal modular mapping. In programs of practical interest, the value of n is small enough for this procedure to be executed in a reasonable amount of time.

Example 2 Consider an algorithm with the index set bounded by $\vec{b} = (5, 5, 2)^T$. There exist many constraints on a modular mapping, such as the constraints for preserving dependencies and minimizing communications, and so on. Assume that the following conditions are imposed on a modular mapping:
- $t_{13} = t_{22} = t_{31} = t_{32} = t_{33} = 1$.

The transformation matrix T becomes $\begin{pmatrix} * & * & 1 \\ * & 1 & * \\ 1 & 1 & 1 \end{pmatrix}$. where $*$ denotes the entries to be determined. To check the injectivity condition of Proposition 1, it is necessary to consider 3! modulus vectors by permuting the boundary vector. Consider the following two permutations:

Permutation 1   Permutation 2

The modular mappings with these modulus vectors require (the optimal) two execution time units. Other permutations yield modular mappings resulting in five execution time units. Hence, these two modulus vectors are better choices than any other ones. Consider permutation 1. The matrix T' that yields T by permutation 1 is $\begin{pmatrix} 1 & 1 & 1 \\ * & * & 1 \\ * & 1 & * \end{pmatrix}$. Hence, it is necessary to generate T' that satisfies Theorem 1. By setting diagonal entries to be one and off-diagonal terms to be zero, matrix $\begin{pmatrix} 1 & 1 & 1 \\ 0 & 1 & 1 \\ 0 & 1 & 1 \end{pmatrix}$ is obtained. Fig. 2 (a) shows the graph induced from this matrix. This graph contains a cycle. Thus, T' does not satisfy Theorem 1. Consider permutation 2. The matrix T'' that yields T by permutation 2 is $\begin{pmatrix} 1 & 1 & 1 \\ * & 1 & * \\ * & * & 1 \end{pmatrix}$. By setting undetermined entries, $\begin{pmatrix} 1 & 1 & 1 \\ 0 & 1 & 0 \\ 0 & 0 & 1 \end{pmatrix}$ is obtained. The induced graph shown in Fig. 2 (b) is acyclic. Hence, T'' satisfies Theorem 1. Therefore, an injective modular mapping

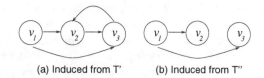

(a) Induced from T'   (b) Induced from T"

Figure 2: Graph induced from matrices T' and T''

$$\mathbf{T}_{\vec{m}}(\vec{j}) = \left(\begin{pmatrix} 1 & 1 & 1 \\ 0 & 1 & 0 \\ 0 & 0 & 1 \end{pmatrix} \vec{j} \right) \bmod (2,5,5) \text{ is generated.} \blacksquare$$

Consider the case when it is necessary to generate a mapping that satisfies the general injectivity conditions in Section 3. The approach used in this section is a bounded search procedure. First, generate the optimal modular mapping without the injectivity condition. Here, 'optimality' of a modular mapping may have many different meanings, such as the minimal execution time, the minimal processor size, or minimal communication overhead. In the next step, the derived modular mapping is checked for injectivity. If it is injective, take the modular mapping as the final solution. Otherwise, generate another modular mapping. Without loss of generality, let "optimal modular mapping" mean "the mapping with the minimal execution time t_{opt}." It is desirable to generate the new modular mapping with the next smallest execution time $t_{opt} + 1$. Thus, in the generation of a new modular mapping, a new condition is added so that the execution time of the new modular mapping can be $t_{opt} + 1$. This modular mapping must be checked again for injectivity. This generation and test step is repeated until a modular mapping satisfies the injectivity condition. At each iteration, one needs to solve the optimization problem of either Proposition 2 or Proposition 3 which has $3n$ or less than $3n$ variables, respectively.

Consider the termination condition of this search procedure. An index set can always be converted into the minimal rectangular index set and then transformed by a modular mapping that satisfies the injectivity conditions of Theorem 1 or Proposition 1. This modular mapping can be used to terminate the search. For example, consider again the case when the optimal modular mapping means the time-minimal mapping. Let $t_{rect,opt}$ be the execution time of the optimal modular mapping for the expanded rectangular index set. Since the image of the modular mapping is a virtual processor array, one more mapping into a physical processor array is necessary. This mapping (into a physical processor array) usually increases the optimal execution time. Let $t'_{rect,opt}$ be the new optimal execution time after mapping into a physical proces-

sor array. Then, $t'_{rect,opt}$ is used for the upper bound of the search procedure. If the modular mapping is not found until the iteration with $t = t'_{rect,opt}$, the iteration is stopped at this point and the generation method is used for the rectangular index set.

5 Conclusions

This paper addresses the problem of systematically generating modular time-space mappings. An $O(n^2 n!)$-time method for generating an injective time-optimal modular mapping is derived when n is the depth of a given nested loop. Although this algorithm is efficient, it can be used only for an algorithm with an rectangular index set, and an arbitrary target processor array. In addition, it may exclude some feasible modular mappings. A method to search all possible feasible modular mappings is also provided. At each trial, it is necessary to solve an integer linear programming problem with at most $3n$ variables. This step repeats until an optimal injective modular mapping is found or the solution becomes worse than that found for a rectangular index set and an arbitrary target processor array.

References

[1] M. Wolfe. *High performance compilers for parallel computing*. Addison-Wesley, 1996.

[2] A. Darte and Y. Robert. Constructive method for scheduling uniform loop nests. *IEEE Trans. Parallel Distributed Syst.*, 5(8), Aug. 1994.

[3] P. Feautrier. Some efficient solutions to the affine scheduling problem part I: One-dimensional time. Tech. Rep. 92.28, IBP/MASI, France, May 1992.

[4] W. Shang and J.A.B. Fortes. Time optimal linear schedules for algorithms with uniform dependencies. *IEEE Trans. Comput.*, C-40:723–742, June 1991.

[5] H.-J. Lee and J.A.B. Fortes. On the injectivity of modular mappings. In *Proc. Int. Conf. Application-Specific Array Processors*, pages 236–247, Aug. 1994.

[6] A. Darte, M. Dion, and Y. Robert. A characterization of one-to-one modular mappings. In *Proc. 7th IEEE Symp. Parallel Distributed Processing*, pages 382–389, Oct. 1995.

[7] F. Buckley and F. Harary. *Distance in graphs*. Addison Wesley, 1990.

[8] T.H. Cormen, C.E. Leiserson, and R.L. Rivest. *Introduction to algorithms*. McGraw Hill, 1989.

Session 7A

Applications

Implementations of a Feature-Based
Visual Tracking Algorithm on Two MIMD Machines

Mark Bernd Kulaczewski

Laboratorium für Informationstechnologie
University of Hannover
D-30173 Hannover, Germany
mbk@mst.uni-hannover.de

Howard Jay Siegel

School of Electrical and Computer Engineering
Purdue University
West Lafayette, IN 47907-1285, USA
hj@purdue.edu

Abstract

As an example of a task that processes complex visual information to generate control signals for a system, an existing feature-based visual tracking algorithm for a static camera was mapped onto two parallel machines representing the MIMD execution model. The algorithm is described and a version suitable for mapping onto parallel machines is developed. Timing results for the implementation on the Intel Paragon and the IBM SP2 are presented, using real image data for all experiments. For each subtask of the algorithm, its performance is measured as a function of data layout. In addition, the impact of the time required to distribute image data across processing elements on the performance is considered. For the subtask of finding the best match of a feature in an image, load balancing approaches dependent on machine characteristics and submachine size are discussed. This type of matching is used in many vision tasks.

1. Introduction

The efficient implementation of image processing tasks has been an area of intensive research in the field of parallel processing. Especially if control information based on image analysis has to be generated under time constraints, single processor systems often prove to be not powerful enough for such applications. An area of computer vision where time constraints play an important part is the field of motion detection and the tracking of moving objects in image sequences. As an example of such an application, a feature-based visual tracking algorithm, originally developed for sequential hardware, was parallelized and mapped onto four different parallel machines [1]. This paper describes aspects

This research was supported in part by the NRaD Naval Laboratory under contract number N66001-96-M-2277, and by Architecture Technology Corporation under contract number 6005.

of implementing this algorithm on two MIMD machines, the IBM SP2 and the Intel Paragon. The functionality of the original algorithm has been demonstrated by tracking pedestrian traffic [2].

The implementation of two subtasks of this algorithm, object detection and feature tracking, on different parallel machines is the focus of this research. The object detection subtask is based on the problem of labeling connected components. The tracking of features is an important general task of all feature-based motion detection algorithms. Different implementations for feature tracking and the impact of data layout on the time required to distribute image data, and, therefore, the achievable image processing rate, is examined.

Section 2 introduces the sequential visual tracking algorithm and presents the developed parallelized version. The implementations on the MIMD IBM SP2 and the Intel Paragon are the subject of Section 3. Section 4 summarizes the results of this paper.

2. The Visual Tracking Algorithms

2.1. Assumptions and Definitions

The sequential algorithm for this application study is based on work presented in [2]. Image sequences to be analyzed are obtained using a static camera. Images analyzed are gray-scale images of size $\underline{C}$ columns by $\underline{R}$ rows. $\underline{I_m}$, $m \geq 0$, denotes the m-th source image of size $C \times R$ obtained from the image source. $\underline{P}$ denotes the set of all pixel coordinates, $P = \{(x,y) : 0 \leq x < C \wedge 0 \leq y < R\}$. $I_m(x,y)$ describes the gray-scale value of the pixel at position $(x,y), (x,y) \in P$. The position $(0,0)$ refers to the pixel in the left upper corner of the image, position $(C-1, R-1)$ identifies the right lower corner pixel. $I_m^{(u,v)}, (u,v) \in P$, denotes a rectangular subimage of I_m with its left upper corner pixel at position (u,v). Let $\underline{G_m}$ be a weighted average of past images $I_j, 0 \leq j \leq m$, defined for all $(x, y) \in P$ as

$$G_m(x, y) = \tag{1}$$
$$\begin{cases} I_0(x, y) & \text{for } m = 0 \\ (1 - a)G_{m-1}(x, y) + aI_m(x, y) & \text{for } m \geq 1, \end{cases}$$

with $0 \leq a < 1$. G_m is called the m-th ground image and incorporates all objects that belong to the background and that are not changing or only slightly changing. The parameter a determines how recent changes affect the ground image. Typical values for a in an environment with almost constant lighting are close to zero.

The m-th binary figure image F_m is defined for all $(x, y) \in P$ as

$$F_m(x, y) = \begin{cases} 1 & \text{if } |G_m(x, y) - I_m(x, y)| > T \\ 0 & \text{otherwise} \end{cases} \tag{2}$$

with T being a threshold value. A typical value for T is ten percent of the maximum gray-scale value. If $F_m(x, y)$ is equal to 1, it is assumed that the pixel at position (x, y) in I_m corresponds to a part of a moving object to be tracked.

If D is a set of points,

$$D = \{(x_1, y_1), (x_2, y_2), \ldots, (x_h, y_h)\},$$

$(x_i, y_i) \in P$, $i = 1, 2, \ldots, h$ then a bounding box B for D is the tuple

$$B(D) = ((\min_i x_i, \min_i y_i), (\max_i x_i, \max_i y_i)).$$

The two elements of the tuple B describe the left upper corner and the right lower corner coordinates of the smallest rectangular box such that every element of D lies within the box or on one of its sides.

For the purpose of this work, a feature or feature window W is defined as a rectangular array of gray-scale values of size W_C columns by W_R rows. The reference point of a feature is the left upper corner with pixel coordinates $(0, 0)$. $W(x, y)$ refers to the gray-scale value of the feature pixel at position (x, y). A feature of an object can be used to track the object.

The measure used in this work to quantify how well a feature matches an image area is the sum-of-the-squared-differences (SSD). The SSD for a feature and a rectangular subimage of I_m with dimensions $W_C \times W_R$ and its left upper corner at position (x, y) is defined as

$$\text{SSD}(I_m, W, x, y) = \tag{3}$$
$$\sum_{i=0}^{W_C - 1} \sum_{j=0}^{W_R - 1} (I_m(x + i, y + j) - W(i, j))^2.$$

An exact match yields an SSD value equal to 0.

To reduce computational complexity, the search for the best match of a given feature is usually restricted to a subimage of I_m. For a given application, there is normally a maximum speed of an object and therefore one can expect a maximum displacement between locations for the best match of a feature in images I_m and I_{m-1}. Let A_R and A_C be the absolute values of the maximum displacements of best feature matches between images I_m and I_{m-1} in the vertical direction and the horizontal direction, respectively. Then the search region A, centered at (x, y), is defined to be the set

$$A(x, y) = \{(u, v) : |u - x| \leq A_C \wedge |v - y| \leq A_R\}.$$

A contains $(2A_C + 1) \times (2A_R + 1)$ positions, allowing positive, negative, and zero displacements in both image dimensions. The actual values of A_R and A_C are determined by the application.

Finding the displacement of a feature window W in I_m, assuming the best match in image I_{m-1} was at position (x, y), is equivalent to solving the minimization problem

$$\begin{aligned} &\text{minimize SSD}(I_m, W, u, v) \\ &\text{subject to } (u, v) \in A(x, y). \end{aligned} \tag{4}$$

The following section describes the structure of the sequential visual tracking algorithm.

2.2. Sequential Visual Tracking

The algorithm starts with the initialization of the ground image G_m, assuming that, at system set-up, no moving objects are present in the image. For each new image I_m, the ground image is updated according to Equation (2). Every p images, where p is application dependent and restricted by available computational resources, the object detection phase is executed. The figure image F_m is calculated by applying a threshold to the difference of G_m and I_m, as defined in Equation (2). The connected components (e.g., an object shape outline) in F_m are computed, and the bounding box for each connected component is determined.

Overlapping bounding boxes are merged recursively into one under the assumption that they belong to the same moving object, and that the separation of the boxes was caused by parts of the object blending into the ground image. The merging stops if the resulting bounding boxes do not overlap. This heuristic results in bounding boxes that describe objects reasonably well if an object's pixels are close enough to a convex set. Because this is a heuristic, it is always possible that in a pathological case two unrelated objects may be incorrectly merged. Bounding boxes associated with connected components below some application specific threshold size are deleted from further analysis, assuming that they are caused by noise in the

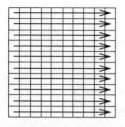 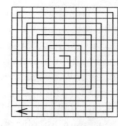

regular row-major pattern   spiral pattern

Fig. 1. Calculation patterns for the SSD measure.

image or moving objects that are irrelevant to the given application.

All remaining bounding boxes correspond to moving objects of interest. In the feature selection phase, a suitable subimage from within an object's bounding box is selected as a feature. In [2], an inherently sequential greedy gradient following selection algorithm is used to determine a feature (i.e., a specific subimage of the given bounding box). This algorithm produces, on average, results sufficiently fast even on a monoprocessor. A presentation of this algorithm is omitted here, because no parallel version for it was implemented.

During the tracking phase, the displacement of the best match for a feature relative to the position of the best match in the previous image is determined by solving the minimization problem of Equation (4). The search region A for a feature is centered at the position of the best match in the previous image. For an exact solution, an exhaustive search over A is performed.

A number of implementation variations for the tracking phase were examined in [2]. In order to reduce computation time for the search for the best match, the calculation of the SSD measure for a given position is provided with the minimum SSD value observed so far. If the running sum of Equation (4) exceeds this value, the calculation for this position is aborted, and the next position is checked. Two different methods to evaluate the double sum are illustrated in Figure 1, the row-major and the spiral pattern. The same patterns can be applied to the order in which positions of the search area A are considered. The best performance was found for a spiral SSD calculation pattern, combined with a spiral search pattern of the search region A. In the following subsection, this algorithm is extended and a version suitable for an implementation on a parallel machine is developed.

2.3. Parallelized Visual Tracking

The segmentation of the figure image, which is based on connected component labeling, is associated with a high computational cost. Because of this, the

sequential algorithm performs this step only every p images. This introduces a delay for the detection of new objects. For the following parallelized version this restriction is dropped. The object detection phase is executed for every image I_m. For every figure image F_m, the whole image is subject to segmentation into connected components. In a full system, objects found with object detection in I_m can be compared with objects tracked from I_{m-1} to I_m to determine if new objects have appeared.

For a working overall system, the feature selection algorithm is invoked only if a new object enters the image sequence or the SSD measure quantifying the quality of the match for a feature exceeds a given value, indicating that this feature should be replaced by a new one. For a typical application, it can be assumed that the feature selection step has to be executed far less frequently than the two other steps. For this work, it is assumed that the feature selection step is performed on a monoprocessor or on one of the processors of the parallel machine. The result of the selection is then made available to all other processors. The focus of this research is on parallel implementations of the detection and the tracking phases.

A pseudocode version of the parallelized visual tracking algorithm is shown in Figure 2. For the presentation, a distributed memory architecture parallel machine with $N=2^n$ PEs (processing elements that are processor and memory pairs) is assumed. The PEs are arranged logically (not necessarily physically) in a mesh with V rows and H PEs per row. PEs are numbered in row-major order from 0 to $N-1$.

For the presentation, image data distribution refers to the process of storing image data into PEs. Data layout describes what data is stored in each PE. Depending on the chosen layout, this can even be the whole source image. Work layout describes how the work is assigned to PEs.

During the image distribution phase, the source image I_m is stored into the PEs of the machine. The exact distribution scheme and data layout scheme is discussed for each implementation separately. For every image, the detection phase and the tracking phase are executed, whereas the feature selection phase is performed only when needed.

The purpose of the object detection phase is to compute the figure image and to determine a set of bounding boxes, with each box corresponding to a moving object in the current image. The algorithm presented is based on a divide-and-conquer approach [3]. Two intuitive ways exist to divide the image into equal subimages. For row striping, each PE works on a subimage of size C columns by R/N consecutive rows. For

```
for all m: DATA DISTRIBUTION PHASE:
            Distribute I_m across PEs
m = 0:      Initialize local subimage of G_0
m ≥ 1:      Calculate local subimage of G_m
            DETECTION PHASE:
            Local Segmentation Step:
            Calculate local subimage of F_m
            Partition local subimage of F_m into
                connected components and calculate
                bounding box for each component
            Merge overlapping local bounding boxes
            Delete bounding boxes below threshold size
                (if not on a subimage edge)
            Extract edge connectivity information
            Combine Step:
            Combine local components based on
                edge information
            If new features needed:
                SELECTION PHASE:
                Determine set of features for each
                    resulting bounding box
            TRACKING PHASE:
            Local Tracking Step:
            Find best match for features on subset
                of search region
            Combine Step:
            Combine local search results to find
                global best match
```

Fig. 2. Pseudocode for the parallelized visual tracking algorithm.

rectangular subimages, and $N = H \cdot V$ PEs, each PE is assigned a subimage of size $C/H \times R/V$.

The chosen work layout for the local segmentation step (row striping or rectangular subimages) determines what part of the source image I_m must be present in each PE (note that each PE may contain all of I_m). In addition to I_m, the object detection phase also uses the ground image G_m and the figure image F_m. For a given work layout for the object detection phase, each PE maintains a subimage of G_m and F_m with the same data layout. For example, for a row striping work layout, each PE maintains the subimage of G_m and F_m obtained by row striping.

For every input image I_m, each PE first determines the connected components of its associated subimage of F_m. This step is implemented using a sequential labeling algorithm within each PE [4]. Each connected component is assigned a unique label and its associated bounding box is computed. Components with overlapping bounding boxes are merged into a new segment. Bounding boxes below some threshold size are deleted if they do not lie on a subimage edge. If a box is on a subimage edge, it might describe a local connected component that is connected to a component in an adjacent subimage, and, therefore, must be considered to

obtain the correct bounding box for the object.

For the subsequent combination of information about subimages, the required connectivity information is derived using the edge pixels of the subimage (pixels on the boundary of a subimage). Every edge pixel with a value of 1 belongs to an area described by exactly one bounding box (within a given subimage). For every edge of a subimage, a list is derived containing the location of contiguous edge pixel segments with value 1 and the associated bounding boxes. Figure 3(a) shows an example of these lists for row striping.

To combine all local results efficiently, recursive doubling is used [5]. For recursive doubling with the result-to-every-PE technique, in each step, $N/2$ distinct pairs of PEs exchange intermediate results and combine these. After $\log_2 N$ steps, all PEs have the final result. For recursive doubling with the result-to-one-PE technique, only one PE has the final result after $\log_2 N$ steps.

In every combine step, the information available on two PEs about adjacent subimages is used to derive the information for the union of these subimages. An example for a combine step is shown in Figure 3. Using the received and the local edge information, the connectivity graph for bounding boxes is constructed. The connected components of this graph are bounding boxes that will be merged into one bounding box. In every combine step, overlapping bounding boxes are merged and isolated boxes below a predefined size are deleted from further analysis if none of their edges lies on a subimage edge. If an edge of a bounding box lies on a subimage edge, this bounding box cannot be deleted because it might be merged with another bounding box in a later combine step. All edge information is expressed in terms of the new computed bounding boxes. Depending on the recursive doubling technique used, the information about the whole image, i.e., all bounding boxes corresponding to objects of interest, is available after $\log_2 N$ steps on exactly one PE or on all PEs.

The goal of a parallelized version of the tracking phase is to minimize the average execution time for this algorithm step. The search area A for the best match of a feature is centered around the location for the best match in the previous image. Reducing the total execution time does not necessarily imply that the search region is divided evenly among available PEs, because data local to each PE determines what part of the search region a PE can work on without additional communication. Involving more PEs may increase inter-PE communication overhead so that it is not worthwhile. It is assumed that every PE has available

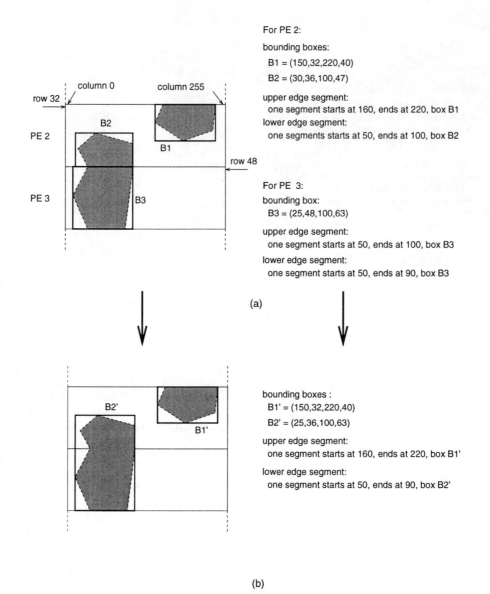

For PE 2:

bounding boxes:
  B1 = (150,32,220,40)
  B2 = (30,36,100,47)

upper edge segment:
  one segment starts at 160, ends at 220, box B1
lower edge segment:
  one segments starts at 50, ends at 100, box B2

For PE 3:

bounding box:
  B3 = (25,48,100,63)

upper edge segment:
  one segment starts at 50, ends at 100, box B3

lower edge segment:
  one segment starts at 50, ends at 90, box B3

(a)

bounding boxes :
  B1' = (150,32,220,40)
  B2' = (25,36,100,63)

upper edge segment:
  one segment starts at 160, ends at 220, box B1'

lower edge segment:
  one segment starts at 50, ends at 90, box B2'

(b)

Fig. 3. Example of combination during object detection with $N = 16$, $R = C = 256$, and row striping, (a) after local segmentation, (b) after combining.

the information about the best match position for each feature in the previous image. Depending on the data layout of I_m, different parallel implementations of the tracking phase are possible.

If the whole image is kept on all PEs, every PE could calculate the quality of the match for any position in the search area without any additional communication. A simple approach to distribute the work across PEs in this case is to divide the search area evenly among PEs, e.g., using row striping. There is a trade-off between the benefit of a distributed load balancing algorithm and an increase in memory usage per PE and the additional time required to distribute

the whole current image to all PEs. This trade–off was examined for the IBM SP2 and the Intel Paragon implementations.

If subimages are chosen as data layout for I_m, an additional number of pixels from adjacent subimages is needed to perform the matching of a feature for all positions corresponding to a subimage. Recall that feature windows are of size $W_C \times W_R$, with their reference point being the left upper corner pixel. For $N = H \cdot V$ PEs arranged logically as a $H \times V$ mesh, and rectangular subimages of size $C/H \times R/V$, an additional $(W_C - 1) \cdot R/V + (W_R - 1) \cdot C/H + (W_R - 1) \cdot (W_C - 1)$ pixels from adjacent subimages are needed. For row

426

striping, an additional $C \cdot (W_R - 1)$ pixels are required.

With subimages on PEs, two general approaches are possible. Without load balancing, each PE calculates the best match for a feature for the subset of the whole search area it can work on using local data only (including the additional overlap data). If load balancing is desired, PEs which need to check many image positions for the quality of a feature match (i.e., a relatively large portion of the search area) assign some of these positions to other PEs. This also involves the sending of image data. The benefit of a load balancing algorithm depends on the size of the workload scheduled and the communication time involved to do so. The impact of a simple balancing algorithm was investigated for the IBM SP2, the Intel Paragon, and the MasPar MP-1.

With or without load balancing, in general, more than one PE may search an area A for a given feature. To find the best feature match for the whole search area, the results of the searches on the subsets have to be combined. Again, a recursive doubling technique is used to combine intermediate results of all best match searches for image I_m.

2.4. Input Data Used

The structure of the parallel algorithm described in the previous section is such that the workload per PE is highly dependent on image content, especially during the tracking phase. Realistic timing data can, therefore, only be obtained with real image data. As in [2], some scenes showing pedestrian traffic were taped and digitized. The color images were converted to eight-bit gray-scale images and the image size reformatted to allow an even distribution of image data across PEs for all submachine sizes used. No additional filtering was performed on images. The feature window size throughout this study is given by $W_C = W_R = 10$. For the image sequences used to obtain timing data, a search region A of size 41×41 positions, i.e., $A_C = A_R = 20$, proved to be sufficient for a reliable tracking operation. All results shown were obtained using input sequences with one moving object and one feature per object to be tracked. The following section describes aspects of the implementation of this algorithm on two different MIMD machines.

3. MIMD Architecture Experiments

3.1. MIMD Machines Used

The IBM SP2 [6] is a distributed memory MIMD architecture. The SP2 sub-system used for these experiments consisted of 16 nodes, each with its own UNIX operating system and 256 Mbytes of main memory. Each node has a communication adapter that connects the node to the interconnection network, allowing overlap of communication and computation. The interconnection network is a multistage interconnection network using the SP2 High-Performance Switch as a building block [7]. The message passing interface used for this study was an implementation of the Message Passing Interface (MPI) [8].

The Intel Paragon is also a distributed memory MIMD architecture [9]. The largest submachine used in this study contains 128 nodes. Each node is equipped with 32 Mbytes of memory and two Intel i860 XP microprocessors. One of these processors, the application processor, executes the application code. The second i860 XP, the message co-processor, is dedicated to message handling only and is not available for the application program. The nodes of an Intel Paragon are connected in a four nearest neighbor mesh, using a message routing system that is independent of the node processors. The Intel Paragon runs a distributed version of the OSF/1 UNIX operating system. The NX communication functions provided the message passing interface for this study.

3.2. Data Layout and Image Distribution

The effect of the work layout scheme (which determines the valid choices for data layout) on the performance of the object detection phase is difficult to predict. The time complexity for the sequential labeling operation on a local subimage is independent of the shape of the subimage. Independent of the work layout, the run time of a combine step depends on image content. Though a worst case time complexity analysis for an artificial image might be possible, the average time needed for the combine step for a typical image sequence with few moving objects is expected to be considerably smaller. A general average time complexity analysis, however, was beyond the scope of this work. It can be shown that row striping results in an implementation with less overhead for the combining computation during the object detection phase [1]. For this reason, row striping was chosen as the work layout for object detection.

For the experiments on the IBM SP2 and Intel Paragon, it is assumed that the new images become available on logical PE 0 at a given rate, i.e., the number of images available from the image source per second. The total time to process an image must therefore take into account the time needed to distribute image data to the respective PEs. Total execution time is defined to be the time needed between the start of image data distribution and the point of time when tracking results for the current image become available. Processing time measures only the time needed for the object detection and tracking phases (including computation and communication times); it does not include the time for the distribution of image data from logical PE 0.

For the IBM SP2 and Intel Paragon implementations, images I_m of size $C = 640$ columns by $R = 512$ rows were used. All results presented were obtained on dedicated machines, and all average times per image are based on measurements with image sequences containing 60 single images. As outlined in the previous section, the data layout impacts the implementation of the tracking phase. Considering the memory available on each PE for both machines, it is possible to keep a complete copy of the current image I_m on every PE, or to store subimages only. Two data layout schemes were implemented. One implementation stores a copy of the current source image into all PEs. The second implementation stores subimages determined by row striping only, following the work layout chosen for the object detection phase. As described in Section 2.3, a PE needs an additional $W_R - 1$ rows of the image for the tracking phase in the case of row striping. To reduce communication overhead, each PE receives this data from logical PE 0 during the image distribution phase (with its own subimage). Thus, PE k, with $0 \leq k \leq N-2$ receives $R/N + W_R - 1$ rows, starting with row $k \cdot R/N$. PE $N-1$ receives R/N rows, starting with row $(N-1) \cdot R/N$.

Different methods to distribute the image data from PE 0 were examined [1]. The fastest implementation was obtained by a recursive doubling scatter method [10]. This method was used exclusively for all results presented.

3.3. Object Detection and Feature Tracking

Because communication and computation can be overlapped in both machines, an exact separate timing of computation and communication across all PEs is not possible. Therefore, as the relevant measure, the sum of the time for detection and tracking phases is determined.

Independent of the total amount of image data kept on each PE, the local segmentation step is performed on the subimage determined by row striping. Local results are combined using recursive doubling with the result-to-every-PE technique.

Three different implementations of the tracking phase were examined, distinguished by different work layout schemes for the search area A. For all methods, partial results of the search were combined using recursive doubling with the result-to-every-PE technique.

For a data layout of whole images on each PE, the $2A_R + 1$ rows of the search region A, numbered 0 to $2A_R$, were assigned to PEs such that PE k performs the matching operation for rows $k + mN, 0 \leq m \leq$

$\lfloor (2A_R+1)/N \rfloor$, and $k+mN \leq 2A_R$. After all matching operations are performed, the local results on each PE are combined to obtain the best match position for a feature for the whole search region.

For subimages on each PE, a balanced and an unbalanced implementation were compared. A PE performs part of the search for unbalanced tracking only if it can cover a part of the search region with its local data. In general, more than one PE is used to search different parts of a given area. The results of the local searches are then combined to determine the global best match position.

The following load balancing algorithm was implemented for balanced tracking. For every feature to be tracked, PE k determines how many rows $\rho(k)$ of the search area A it can cover using local data only. The average tracking workload α is defined as

$$\alpha = \begin{cases} \lfloor (2A_R + 1)/N \rfloor & \text{if } 2A_R + 1 \geq N \\ 1 & \text{otherwise.} \end{cases}$$

A heuristic is used to determine how much of its locally available work a PE assigns to a different PE. Because every PE has the information about data layout and the position of the search area A for a feature, every PE knows the workload of every other PE. The number of average tracking workloads $\delta(k)$ PE k tries to assign to the set of PEs with no work for the current feature is defined as

$$\delta(k) = \begin{cases} 0 & \text{if } \rho(k) < 2\alpha \\ \lfloor (\rho(k) - \alpha)/\alpha \rfloor & \text{otherwise.} \end{cases}$$

Let $\underline{\Psi}$ be the set of $\underline{t}$ PEs with $\delta(k) \neq 0$, i.e.,

$$\Psi = \{\psi_1, \ldots, \psi_t\}, \psi_1 < \psi_2 < \ldots < \psi_t, \text{ with}$$
$$\delta(\psi_i) \neq 0 \text{ for } 1 \leq i \leq t, 0 \leq \psi_i < N.$$

Let $\underline{\Phi}$ be the set of $\underline{s}$ PEs with no work for the feature, i.e.,

$$\Phi = \{\varphi_1, \ldots, \varphi_s\}, \varphi_1 < \varphi_2 < \ldots < \varphi_s, \text{ with}$$
$$\rho(\varphi_i) = 0 \text{ for } 1 \leq i \leq s, 0 \leq \varphi_i < N.$$

Then PE ψ_1 assigns α rows of the search region A to each of the PEs φ_1 through $\varphi_{\delta(\psi_1)}$, PE ψ_2 assigns α rows to each of the PEs $\varphi_{\delta(\psi_1)+1}$ through $\varphi_{\delta(\psi_1)+\delta(\psi_2)}$, etc. This process continues until no work is left to distribute or no PEs are left that can be assigned work. Assigning a workload to a different PE includes sending the required image data, i.e., an image area of $\alpha + W_R - 1$ rows by $2A_C + W_C$ columns, to the respective PE. After PEs performed their assigned work, the local results are combined to determine the best feature match position.

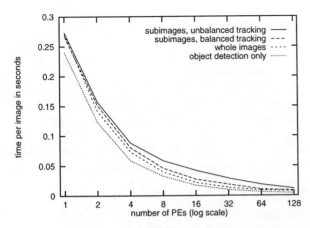

Fig. 4. Average processing times on the Intel Paragon.

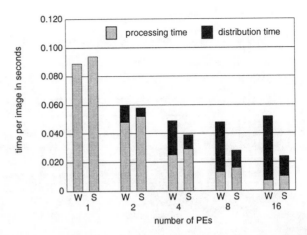

Fig. 5. Total execution times for whole images (W) and subimages (S) on each PE (with load balancing) on the IBM SP2.

This load balancing heuristic does not take into account workloads created by search areas for different features, but rather balances the work one feature at a time. A more sophisticated algorithm could balance the work generated by all features to be tracked as a whole and could consider the relative position of PEs that distribute work and PEs that receive work. A further investigation into different load-balancing approaches was beyond the scope of this work, and is a topic for future research.

3.4. Experimental Results

Figure 4 shows the average processing time for object detection followed by each of the three different implementations of feature tracking for the Intel Paragon. Whole images on each PE is the fastest implementation due to communication free implicit load balancing. Unbalanced tracking with subimages is slower for $N > 2$ than the other implementations, because the processing time is mainly determined by the PE with the highest workload during the tracking phase. The balanced tracking implementation with subimages is slightly slower than the best version due to the additional communication required for balancing, but provides some benefit compared to the unbalanced version for the input data used. To illustrate what fraction of the processing time is spent on object detection, a separate graph that shows the time for local segmentation and combing is included in the figure. The times for object detection were obtained by measuring the time needed for local segmentation and combining if started and ended with a barrier. This ignores possible overlap of the object detection phase and the tracking phase if no barrier after the detection phase is present. A similar performance ratio of the phases was found for the IBM SP2 [1].

The performance of the whole algorithm is determined by the average total execution time, i.e., the average of the sum of distribution and processing time. No overlap of image data distribution and the processing of the current image is assumed. Although such an implementation is possible, the image data distribution would interfere with the other communication steps. This would cause unpredictable timing results.

For the IBM SP2, Figure 5 shows the contribution of processing time and distribution time to the total execution time for different implementations. For whole images on each PE, the distribution time becomes dominant for $N > 4$, whereas, for subimages and balanced tracking, the crossover point lies between eight and 16 PEs. If whole images are distributed to all PEs, the maximum processing rate for the input data used is limited to approximately 20 images per second, achieved for eight PEs. Increasing the number of PEs leads to a lower performance due to the now dominant increase in distribution time. For subimages and balanced tracking, a processing rate of up to 40 images per second for a 16 PE machine is possible.

Similar results were obtained for the Intel Paragon, shown in Figure 6. In the case of whole images on each PE, the time for the data distribution phase becomes dominant for $N > 16$. The maximum processing rate for this data distribution was 25 images per second for 32 PEs. For subimages, the distribution time exceeds processing time for $N > 64$ PEs. A maximum processing rate of approximately 55 images per seconds was observed for a 64 PE submachine.

The parallelized visual tracking algorithm consists of two computation phases with very different properties. The execution time for the local segmentation

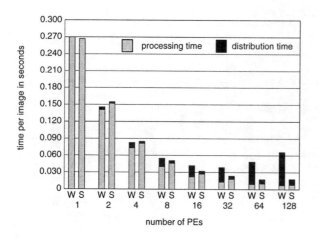

Fig. 6. Total execution times for whole images (W) and subimages (S) on each PE (with load balancing) on the Intel Paragon.

steps of the object detection phase depends primarily on the size of the subimage a PE is assigned. In contrast, the workload of the tracking phase is only determined by image data content. A distributed communication free load balancing of this phase is only possible if every PE has a copy of the whole image. With the assumption that input data is initially available on one PE only, the time to distribute whole images by far exceeds the possible benefit. For the input data used, application of a relatively fast load balancing algorithm allowed reduction of the processing time, while keeping the advantage of distributing only subimages.

Ignoring the time necessary to distribute the image data across PEs, the developed parallelized visual tracking algorithm scales well over a wide range of machine sizes, mainly due to the scalability of the object detection phase, which takes up most of the actual computation time. For both machines, a processing rate of 30 images per second could be achieved with moderate numbers of PEs. This indicates that a symmetric multiprocessor with shared memory, assuming PEs comparable to node processors on IBM SP2, e.g., could also be a platform that can provide the required computational resources for this application.

4. Conclusion

As an example of a computer vision task with real-time constraints a feature-based visual tracking algorithm was mapped onto parallel machines. The algorithm was introduced and a version suitable for mapping onto parallel architectures was developed. This paper presents results for the implementation on two general purpose MIMD architectures. For two subtasks

of the algorithm, object detection and feature tracking, the performance was measured as a function of machine size and data layout, using real image data for experiments. For the subtask feature tracking, different load balancing approaches were examined. Considering the impact of the time for image data distribution on the performance of the whole task it was shown that the best performance on both machines was obtained for some submachine size. The best performance on both machines was obtained if subimages are kept on each PE and a dynamic load-balancing scheme was employed for feature tracking.

References

[1] M. B. Kulaczewski, "Parallel Implementations of a Visual Tracking Algorithm, and Dynamic Partitioning for a Mixed-Mode Programming Language," Master's thesis, School of Electrical and Computer Engineering, Purdue University, Dec. 1996.

[2] C. E. Smith, S. A. Brandt, C. A. Richards, and N. P. Papanikolopoulos, "Visual tracking for intelligent vehicle-highway systems," *IEEE Transactions on Vehicular Technology*, 1997, to appear.

[3] H. M. Alnuweiri and V. K. Prasanna, "Parallel architectures and algorithms for image component labeling," *IEEE Transactions on Pattern Analysis and Machine Intelligence*, Vol. 14, No. 10, Oct. 1993, pp. 1014–1034.

[4] B. K. P. Horn, *Robot Vision*, MIT Press, Cambridge, MA, 1986.

[5] H. J. Siegel, L. Wang, J. J. E. So, and M. Maheswaran, "Data parallel algorithms," in *Parallel and Distributed Computing Handbook*, A. Y. Zomaya, ed., McGraw-Hill, New York, NY, 1996, pp. 466–499.

[6] T. Agerwala, J. L. Martin, J. H. Mirza, D. C. Sadler, D. M. Dias, and M. Snir, "SP2 system architecture," *IBM Systems Journal*, Vol. 34, No. 2, 1995, pp. 152–184.

[7] C. B. Stunkel, D. G. Shea, B. Abali, M. G. Atkins, C. A. Bender, D. G. Grice, P. Hochschild, D. J. Joseph, B. J. Nathanson, R. A. Swetz, R. F. Stucke, M. Tsao, and P. R. Varker, "The SP2 high-performance switch," *IBM Systems Journal*, Vol. 34, No. 2, 1995, pp. 185–204.

[8] M. Snir, S. Otto, S. Huss-Lederman, D. Walker, and J. Dongarra, *MPI: The Complete Reference*, MIT Press, Cambridge, MA, 1995.

[9] G. S. Almasi and A. Gottlieb, *Highly Parallel Computing, Second Edition*, Benjamin/Cummings, Redwood City, CA, 1994.

[10] S. E. Hambrusch, F. Hameed, and A. A. Khokhar, "Communication operations on coarse-grained mesh architectures," *Parallel Computing*, Vol. 21, No. 5, May 1995, pp. 731–751.

Background Compensation and an Active-Camera Motion Tracking Algorithm

Rohit Gupta, Mitchell D. Theys, and Howard Jay Siegel

Parallel Processing Laboratory, School of Electrical and Computer Engineering
Purdue University, West Lafayette, IN 47907-1285, USA

Abstract

Motion tracking using an active camera is a very computationally complex problem. Existing serial algorithms have provided frame rates that are much lower than those desired, mainly because of the lack of computational resources. Parallel computers are well suited to image processing tasks and can provide the computational power that is required for real-time motion tracking algorithms. This paper develops a parallel implementation of a known serial motion tracking algorithm, with the goal of achieving greater than real-time frame rates, and to study the effects of data layout, choice of parallel mode of execution, and machine size on the execution time of this algorithm. A distinguishing feature of this application study is that the portion of each image frame that is relevant changes from one frame to the next based on the camera motion. This impacts the effect of the chosen data layout on the needed inter-processor data transfers and the way in which work is distributed among the processors. Experiments were performed to determine for which image sizes and number of processors which data layout would perform better. The parallel computers used in this study are the MasPar MP-1, Intel Paragon, and PASM. Different modes are examined and it is determined that mixed mode is faster than SIMD or MIMD implementations.

1. Introduction

Motion tracking refers to a method of following a moving object and determining the exact location of the object relative to the observer at any given instant. There are several methods for performing motion tracking. The simplest is to use a static camera. In this approach, the observer (camera) is held stationary and each frame is subtracted from the next frame. In this manner, information about the objects that are moving can be extracted. The simplicity of this algorithm prevents the system from tracking objects once they move outside the field of view of the camera. The advantage of such a tracking system is that high frame rates can be achieved without using special-purpose hardware.

Another method, active motion tracking, involves using a camera mounted on a moving platform. Images from the camera are processed and the camera is then repositioned to keep the target in the center of the field of view. Tracking objects using an active camera

This research was supported in part by NRaD Naval Laboratory under contract number N66001-96-M-2277 and by Architecture Technology Corp. under contract number 6005. Some of the equipment used was supported by the National Science Foundation under grant number CDA-9015696.

necessitates high-speed processing so that fast moving targets can be tracked.

In an attempt to study the effects of data layout, mode of parallelism, and machine size on computation and communication times, parallel implementations of an existing serial motion tracking algorithm were executed on three parallel machines: the PASM prototype [13], the MasPar MP-1 [11], and the Intel Paragon XP/S [1]. A distinguishing feature of this application study is that the portion of each image frame that is relevant changes from one frame to the next based on the camera motion. This impacts the effect of the chosen data layout on the needed inter-processor data transfers and the way in which work is distributed among the processors.

In Section 2, background information, definitions, and related work associated with motion tracking are presented. An overview of the serial algorithm appears in Section 3. Section 4 contains implementation details of the background compensation portion of the tracking algorithm. This computationally intensive section of the overall algorithm was the focus of this study. Edge detection is examined in Section 5 so that the entire algorithm can be analyzed for each machine. In Section 6, results are compared and summarized from the three machines used in this study.

2. Motion Tracking

2.1 Background Information

There are two classifications into which a number of the present methods of motion tracking fall: recognition-based and motion-based [10]. In recognition-based motion tracking, the object being tracked is first recognized and then the position of the object is determined. This allows tracking to be done in three dimensions and also allows the estimation of rotation and translation of the object. A limitation of this method is that it can only be used to track recognizable objects. Furthermore, recognition is a computationally complex task and, hence, the overall speed of the algorithm is reduced compared to motion-based tracking.

Motion-based tracking is a less computationally complex alternative. In motion-based tracking systems, the object being tracked does not need to be recognized. Instead, motion within a frame is detected using a temporal derivative of the images to find areas of motion. If the sampling rate is high, the derivative can be approximated by a simple difference operation between successive frames followed by a thresholding operation. If it is assumed that motion is uniform within discrete objects, then only the edges of objects are important. Tracking only edges, rather than entire objects, decreases the computational burden, if finding the edges of objects is com-

431

putationally simple. To highlight the edges of the moving portion of the frame, the difference image is ANDed with the edge image of the frame. This yields a frame that contains the moving edges (and other noise components) only. The computational complexity required in this approach is lower than the recognition-based approach, and the algorithms contain parallelizable features, e.g., the difference and AND operations. Therefore, a motion based method presented in [10] was selected as a basis for the development of a parallel implementation for this application study.

2.2   Related Work

Parallel implementations of active-camera motion tracking algorithms have been studied. In [17], a system was introduced that incorporated a sensing element (SE) into each PE. The PEs were arranged as a 16-by-16 square mesh SIMD machine with four nearest-neighbor interconnections. The 256-PE mesh was then divided into four quadrants. Each quadrant processes one quarter of the image and determines the location of the object, which was conveyed to the control computer. The camera was then repositioned and the cycle repeats.

The approach is novel in the fact that the PEs receive the image directly from the SEs. In [17] background compensation was not performed, so the algorithm is susceptible to the effects of apparent motion.

Because of the simplicity of the algorithm, very high frame rates (1492 frames per second) were attained. However, the authors acknowledge that the actuators used to move the camera are not capable of such high speeds. It should be noted that the focus of that work was not to study issues of parallel processing.

Another parallel implementation of a motion tracking algorithm was introduced in [9]. There a tracking system is implemented on transputers in a MIMD organization. Three transputer sets were used in parallel. The Host Interface (HI) consists of two transputers that are used to communicate the results and progress of the system. The HI was connected to the two other transputer sets, the Edge Extraction Engine (EEE) and the Tracking Engine (TE). The EEE consisted of up to 16 transputers interconnected in a mesh configuration. The TE was arranged in a tree configuration of up to ten transputers. The master controllers of the three sets of transputers are interconnected using a system bus. All communication between these sets of transputers was performed using this bus.

The important characteristics of the parallel computational model considered there were that the system was a transputer-based MIMD machine utilizing functional parallelism. The issues that were considered were the effect of interconnection topologies, quality of edge detection using Canny and Sobel edge detectors, and load balancing.

The frame rates attained in that research were less than one frame per second when real images were used and about 3.7 frames per second for synthetic images. These rates were much lower than real-time, and also much lower than the desired rates for the work presented here.

In [12], another transputer-based implementation of a tracking algorithm was described. The system consisted of 30 transputers, 24 of which were in the tracking engine. The remaining transputers constitute the image store, the corner store, and the controller. The image store consisted of four transputers, each containing one quarter of the image. The controller was a single transputer that coordinated the operation of the tracking engine. The tracking engine transputers were configured to work independently (e.g., MIMD mode) and it was possible that a single corner of an object may be tracked by multiple transputers. To avoid this situation, the corner store maintains a record of the image plane of each corner and only one transputer is allowed to track a corner within one image plane.

One of the important features of the work was that the search space was reduced so as to increase the speed of processing. The search space was reduced by selecting "regions of interest" that were calculated based on the movement of the object, e.g., the velocity and the direction of the object. The regions of interest were calculated for each corner being tracked and for each frame.

The issues of parallel processing that were relevant in the approach are that the tracking engine transputers are arranged in a MIMD configuration with a controller processor. Load balancing among the transputers was accomplished with the help of the corner store, such that all corners were distributed among the transputers equally. An "optimized" method of distributing the image based on the location of the corners in the image was developed and the execution time of the algorithm was compared to that in the non-optimized method.

The results of the above research have indicated that near-real-time tracking is achievable using this method. A frame rate of 11 frames per second was achieved using 24 transputers in the tracking engine when 64 corners were tracked.

It can be seen from the three approaches described above that none used a standard parallel computer and none performed background compensation. The work presented here includes implementations of the [10] algorithm on commercial parallel machines. This work explores the impact of data allocation strategies, solving complex communication needs, and performing a case study that focuses on the background compensation component. It also examines the entire algorithm while varying the number of PEs, mode choice, and data layout.

3.   Overview of the Study
3.1.   Serial Algorithm for Motion Tracking

In active vision systems, movement of the camera may cause apparent motion of objects in the image. Apparent motion is motion that is perceived by the camera due to its own movement, i.e., if the camera moves past a stationary object, the object's position changes between frames. This will result in the stationary object being present in the difference image because it will not be canceled out in the subtraction of the two consecutive frames. For the difference operation to be applicable in active vision systems, a correspondence between successive frames must be established. Because the background is assumed to be stationary, this process is referred to as background compensation in [10]. In [6], a formula for calculating pixel correspondence based on camera rotations was developed. Using this formula, background compensation is performed. After background compensation, the two images can be compared directly using the simple difference method because the apparent motion of the stationary parts of the image is corrected. An absolute value of the difference between the pixel values is then taken. A block diagram of the complete serial algorithm is presented in Figure 1, where $I(t)$ represents the most recent image frame and $I(t-1)$ represents the previous image frame. In the figure, α, γ, and θ represent the pan angle, tilt angle, and inclination of the camera, respectively.

Because the background compensation algorithm is based on a model that assumes that the rotation of the camera occurs around the center of the lens, and all rotations are not performed this way, there is a small amount of error in the compensated image. Morphological opening is performed to filter the difference image to reduce the effect of these errors.

The next step of the algorithm, edge detection, is performed on the current frame by applying a Sobel 3-by-3 operator. The difference image and the edge image are then ANDed together resulting in an image that contains the edges of the moving object(s) in the current frame only. The relative displacement of the object is then calculated and the angles that the camera must rotate are determined. The camera is then rotated to keep the moving object in the center of the field of view.

The algorithm described in [10] was implemented using a camera mounted on a pan and tilt device controlled by a workstation. A CCD camera provided the frames to a real-time digitizer. The amount of pan/tilt was determined by a potentiometer connected to the platform supporting the camera. The system was shown to be capable of real-time motion detection and could extract moving edges from images when the pan and tilt angles between successive frames were as high as 3°.

Although the serial algorithm is capable of real-time motion tracking, much higher frame rates (100 frames per second or more) and processing of larger images are often required, such as in the case of tracking missiles. Therefore, a parallel implementation of this algorithm was developed with the expectation of obtaining higher frame rates while processing larger images.

The above description of the serial algorithm is summarized from [10]. Several steps of the serial algorithm are not discussed in this paper. The subtraction of the compensated image from the current image, the AND operation, and the thresholding operation are excluded from this paper because they are simple. Parallelizing

the morphological operators is discussed in [16] and is therefore not re-examined here. Thus, this paper focuses on the computationally intensive step of background compensation. Furthermore, it is the background compensation step that is directly affected by the camera motion, which moves some of the previous frame's pixels outside the field of interest, and brings some new pixels (not in the previous frame) into the field of interest. Edge detection is not examined in as much detail here, as many people have already parallelized edge detection algorithms. Edge detection is briefly discussed because it is included in the execution times of the entire algorithm.

3.2. Parallel Algorithm and Computers Used

In the development of the parallel algorithm, several assumptions are made. It is assumed here that the layout of the images in memory is determined before execution and that it remains fixed during the entire process. The inputs to the system are two successive frames, which will be divided equally among the processing elements (PEs), each of which is a processor memory pair, and the camera rotation information, which is known by all the PEs. The output of the system is an image containing the moving edges in the latter frame. Determination of the center of the moving object is not done at this time because different schemes may be used to determine the center, particularly if more than one object is being tracked. Because external I/O varies from one machine installation to another, it is not considered here. This work concentrates on the impact of camera movement on the execution time of parallel implementations of the background compensation step on a commercial SIMD, a commercial MIMD, and an experimental mixed-mode machine.

The Intel Paragon XP/S is a distributed memory commercial MIMD system [1]. The system used for this study has 140 compute nodes, each of which includes a 50 MHz Intel i860 XP microprocessor. The compute nodes have 32 MB of DRAM each, and are arranged in a two-dimensional rectangular mesh with each node connected to its four nearest neighbors. Each node contains another i860 XP processor, called the message co-processor, that is dedicated to handling message-passing operations. The Paragon was programmed using C extended with parallel constructs for communication and synchronization.

The MasPar MP-1 is a distributed memory commercial SIMD system [11]. The system used for this study has 16,384 custom PEs, each of which has a four-bit arithmetic and logic unit (ALU) and 16 KB of memory. The PEs are arranged in a 128-by-128 mesh, with each PE connected to its eight nearest neighbors. Communications are facilitated by a global router multistage network that allows a given PE to establish a path to any other PE in the system. The PEs receive instructions from and are controlled by the Array Control Unit (ACU). MPL was the language used for the programs executing on the MasPar MP-1.

The PASM (partitionable SIMD/MIMD) system is a parallel computer system designed at Purdue University [13]. It is a distributed memory mixed-mode machine that can dynamically switch between SIMD and MIMD modes of parallelism at instruction-level granularity and with generally negligible overhead. PASM can be dynamically reconfigured to form independent or communicating submachines of various sizes. A flexible multistage cube interconnection network allows the connection scheme between the processors to be varied. Therefore, PASM is reconfigurable along three dimensions: partitionability, mode of parallelism, and interprocessor communication. A small-scale proof-of-concept prototype (with 16 PEs in the computational engine) has been built and is being used to study various aspects of parallel processing. Each PE consists of an MC68010 processor and 2 MB of dual-ported DRAM. An extra-stage cube network connects the PEs in the prototype. It can be seen that the hardware used is not competitive in terms of performance with current high-end workstations, however, the studies conducted on PASM can be used to compare the relative performance of an algorithm under different modes of parallelism. PASM is programmed using an explicit language for parallelism called ELP [13].

3.3. Parameters of the Study

The focus of this research is to study the effect of parallel machine characteristics and algorithm mapping on the computation and communication times for a practical application. The results of this study should be applicable to other programs that exhibit similar computation and communication characteristics. Furthermore, insights into the architecture and design of parallel machines can be obtained.

Many studies on the effects of data layout for different application programs have been performed and it has been shown that layout schemes have a significant impact on the computation and communication times of parallel programs. No one data layout is best for all applications.

A goal of this research is to study the effect of two different data layout schemes on the execution time of the motion tracking algorithm. The two data layout schemes considered here are row-striping and rectangular distributions. In row–striping, each PE memory contains a section of an image such that all PEs have the same number of contiguous rows of the image and all the columns. Consider an image of size M-by-M pixels and a parallel computer system having N processors. Each PE then has M/N rows and M columns of each image.

In the rectangular distribution scheme, each PE memory contains a rectangular portion of an image, i.e., for an image with M-by-M pixels in a system of N PEs arranged in an X-by-Y logical mesh, each PE contains M/Y rows and M/X columns of the image. Although these data distribution schemes are not new, what is new is examining how they influence the execution time of the motion tracking algorithm.

An important area of research in parallel computers is to analyze program behavior under different modes of parallelism (i.e., SIMD vs. MIMD). This is a complicated research area because there are very few machines that are capable of executing programs in different modes of parallelism. Examples of such machines are PASM, TRAC [8], OPSILA [2], Triton [4], MeshSP [5], and EXECUBE [7]. Most programs contain segments that are better suited to a particular parallel mode of operation and machines that allow mixed-mode computation can provide the better mode for each segment. Analysis of the execution times can provide insights into how the choice of the mode of computation affects the execution times of parallel programs.

For all test images, random pixel values were generated. This is because the number and type of operations performed in this application, and hence the execution time, are independent of the values of the pixels. Each entry in Tables 1 through 5 is the average of ten trials. Each machine was in single user mode when conducting the experiments. The communication times for the three machines are somewhat unpredictable (even when using the machines exclusively) due to subtleties in the network operating routines (which are not readily accessible to normal users). Images ranged from 128-by-128 pixels to 1024-by-1024 pixels. A selective set of results is presented in the tables.

4. Background Compensation
4.1. Overview

The purpose of background compensation is to remove the apparent motion from the images being analyzed. Because of the assumption that the camera rotates about two axes (horizontal and vertical), Kanatani's formula [6] can be used. In the equations below, α corresponds to the pan angle, γ, to the tilt angle, and θ, to the initial inclination of the camera. The focal length of the camera is denoted by f in the equations. For each pixel location (x_t, y_t) in the latest image, the corresponding pixel (x_{t-1}, y_{t-1}) in the previous image is located. The (x_{t-1}, y_{t-1}) must be calculated for each pixel (x_t, y_t) because not every pixel is displaced by the same distance, in Cartesian coordinates.

$$x_{t-1} = f \frac{x_t + \alpha \sin\theta\, y_t + f\alpha\cos\theta}{-\alpha\cos\theta\, x_t + \gamma y_t + f} \quad (1)$$

$$y_{t-1} = f \frac{-\alpha\sin\theta\, x_t + y_t - f\gamma}{-\alpha\cos\theta\, x_t + \gamma y_t + f} \quad (2)$$

The main focus of this research is to parallelize the background compensation algorithm so that high frame rates are achieved. The effects of data layout choice, machine size, and mode choice were studied so as to achieve the aforementioned goal. The serial algorithm from [10] was parallelized for the three machines used. It should be noted that equations (1) and (2) were derived using the "small angle" assumption, i.e., $\sin\beta = \beta$ for small β (in radians). In the implementation of the parallel algorithm, α and γ were assumed to be 3° each, θ was assumed to be 0°, the focal length was assumed to be 890 and gray scale images were used as inputs (all as was done in [10]).

4.2. Parallel Implementation

Because each pixel has to be mapped from the previous frame to the current frame based on equations (1) and (2), the process of background compensation is computationally complex. For an image of size M-by-M distributed among N PEs, both equations and their inverses need to be evaluated M^2/N times per PE. Using equations (1) and (2), all pixels in the current image can be mapped to those in the previous image, except those pixels in the current image that correspond to sections in the image that have just come into the field of view.

If (x_{t-1}, y_{t-1}) and (x_t, y_t) are in different PEs, (x_{t-1}, y_{t-1}) is sent to the PE containing (x_t, y_t) to perform the difference operation. For a given PE i, the number of pixels transferred and the number of PEs that receive data from PE i is a function of the camera rotation, the focal length of the camera, and the data layout. It is assumed that the focal length of the camera remains constant but the pan and tilt angles can change between frames (within the range of the formula governing the movement of the pixels as discussed above). Therefore, the number of pixels transferred, the number of PEs that will receive data from a given PE, and the identities of the receiving PEs cannot be known *a priori*. To reduce the cost of network operations, pixels are transferred in blocks. This requires only one network setting per block. For MIMD implementations on the Paragon and PASM, the source PE needs to initiate a "send" and the receiving PE (and only receiving PEs) must initiate a "receive" for each block.

Given that the data layout is assumed to be fixed, the number of the PE that contains each (x_{t-1}, y_{t-1}) pixel location can be calculated. Using such a calculation, each PE can determine the destination PE numbers that correspond to all pixels in its own memory. Also, each PE can determine which PEs contain the pixel values it needs (based on the inverses of Equations (1) and (2)). Thus, a list of PEs that will send data to a particular PE i can be constructed. PE i then needs to wait for data only from PEs in this list. Using this method reduces the number of transfers to the minimum possible for the given data layout.

After the pixel mapping calculations (Equations (1) and (2)) and source/destination PE calculations are complete, each PE sends blocks of pixels to the appropriate PEs. The pixel value for a given (x_{t-1}, y_{t-1}) and its location in the destination PE (i.e., corresponding to (x_{t-1}, y_{t-1})) are sent for each pixel in the block. After a PE receives all the blocks it is expecting, it moves the received pixels and any local pixels, (x_{t-1}, y_{t-1}), into their correct position in an intermediate array so a simple subtraction can be performed between (x_t, y_t) and the shifted (x_{t-1}, y_{t-1}).

4.3. Communication Time Analysis

One means to reduce the overall communication time is to analyze the effects of different data layout schemes on the communication time of the algorithm. For a given image size, the number of pixels stored in each PE decreases with increasing numbers of PEs in the system. This means that, in general, the total number (i.e., summed over all PEs) of pixel transfers required will increase as well. It should be noted that the maximum total number of pixels that need to be transferred is the number of pixels in the previous image minus the number of pixels that travel outside the scope of the current image. Therefore, it is expected that the total number of pixels that need to be transferred among the PEs will first increase with the number of PEs in a machine and then level out at a maximum. To confirm this hypothesis, a simulation study was conducted. The total number of pixels that need to be transferred in the rectangular distribution scheme is always less than or equal to the number of pixels transferred in the row-striping method. Another interesting result from the simulation is that in the row-striping method, the total number of pixels transferred is the same for systems containing 32 or more PEs, while in the rectangular distribution scheme it is the same for systems with 512 or more PEs.

The difference between the number of pixels transferred in the the two methods decreases as the number of PEs increases in the system. However, as the number of PEs increases, the number of inter-PE transfers increases. This means that there might be more conflicts in the network and the overall communication time could increase. In addition to this, each transfer incurs network setup costs that add to the communication cost. In Figure 2, a sample communication pattern is presented where M and N, α and β are such that just nearest neighbor communications are needed. Pixels in the image are moved by approximately the same amount under both schemes. In the row-striping case, only one network setting is needed and there are no conflicts. In the rectangular distribution scheme, three network settings are needed per PE and multiple PEs send pixels to one PE, thereby creating conflicts. These extra settings will cause the rectangular distribution to be slower than the row-striping scheme on machines where the overhead to set up the network is large, as in asynchronous communication on the Paragon. Also, more overhead is required to compose the blocks that will be transferred. Thus, there are trade-offs that must be considered for a given M, N and architecture. On the average, row-striping requires more pixels to be transferred per PE until the maximum value is reached for both data layouts. However, the data block construction time, network settings per PE, and number of PEs that send to a given PE (creating conflicts) is worse for rectangular subimages.

4.4. Computation Time Analysis

In both data layout schemes, the number of pixels each PE holds is the same. It is expected that the computation time of the background compensation algorithm will be similar under both layout schemes. To support transferring pixels in blocks, a certain amount of computation to determine source and destination PE numbers, array indexing, etc., is performed by each PE. If a PE maps a previous frame pixel to a point outside the scope of the current frame, the pixel value does not need to be transferred and the computation of the destination PE number and the pixel location in the destination PE are skipped. Such pixels are denoted as rejected. Current frame pixel locations which correspond to points outside the scope of the previous frame are set to zero (i.e., pixels that enter the current frame due to camera movement that are not in the previous frame). Such pixels are denoted as initialized. An illustration shows rejected and initialized pixels in Figure 3.

The distribution of rejected pixels can have a significant impact on the execution time of the background compensation algorithm. This is because if a certain PE has more pixels that will be rejected, it has to perform less computations than other PEs that have fewer rejected pixels. This means that PEs with more rejected pixels will finish computations sooner than PEs with fewer rejected pixels.

Consider the following situation. Let the camera pan by an angle α and tilt by an angle γ, and the corresponding pixel movement in the image be at least r rows and c columns. If the image size has M-by-M pixels and there are N PEs, the maximum number of pixels that any PE will have after determining the rejected pixels is M/N-by-$(M-c)$ in the row-striping scheme. In the rectangular distribution scheme, the maximum number of pixels in any PE is $M/\sqrt{N}$-by-$M/\sqrt{N}$ (because there are PEs with no rejected pixels). Therefore, in the row-striping scheme, the maximum number of pixels that any of the PEs have is cM/N pixels less than the maximum number of pixels in any PE in the rectangular distribution scheme. This is because the rejected pixels are shared among more PEs in the row-striping scheme than in the rectangular distribution scheme, and therefore, the remaining pixels are more uniformly distributed in row-striping. Also, in the rectangular distribution scheme, the maximum number of pixels that any PE processes is more than the maximum in the row-striping case. Therefore, the maximum computation times of the background compensation algorithm under row-striping are expected to be lower. In addition, the more uniform distribution of pixels in row-striping, causes the load to be better balanced across all PEs.

4.5. Parallel Mode Analysis

Certain characteristics of parallel programs make a particular mode (i.e., SIMD, MIMD, or mixed) more suitable than the others. The advantages and disadvantages of executing different program constructs in SIMD and MIMD modes can be found in [14]. For example, interprocessor communication is more efficient in SIMD mode, because the single program synchronization simplifies the needed transfer protocol overhead. As another example, the execution of conditional statements is more efficient in MIMD mode because in SIMD mode the control unit must broadcast all ''then'' and ''else'' instructions to all PEs, and then some PEs are disabled for the ''then'' or ''else'' or both. Mixed mode allows each segment of an algorithm to be executed in the most appropriate mode.

The kernel of the background compensation phase is a doubly-nested loop that goes through all rows and columns of the subimage contained by a PE. The best mode for each part of this kernel is now considered.

The loop control is more efficient in SIMD mode and is expected to decrease the execution time (because the control unit can do it concurrently with PE operations). Due to the multitude of conditional statements in the body of the loop (including deciding if a pixel is rejected and therefore needs no further processing), it is expected to perform better in MIMD mode. The computation time of this kernel is expected to be better under the row-striping data layout scheme, as was discussed in Subsection 4.4. The communication times are expected to be higher in MIMD mode than in SIMD mode, however, for the reasons mentioned above.

Using PASM's mixed-mode computation capability, the parts of the program that are expected to perform better in SIMD mode can be executed in SIMD mode, and those that are expected to perform better in MIMD mode can be executed in MIMD mode. From the above analysis of the algorithm in SIMD and MIMD modes, it follows that the loop control and inter-PE communications of the algorithm should be performed in SIMD mode and the body of the algorithm should be executed in MIMD mode. These mode choices are based on typical parallel programs and are applicable when considering mode choices in general. In this case, these choices are not necessarily optimal. This is because of the nature of the background compensation algorithm.

If this kernel were executed completely in MIMD mode, then if a PE rejects a pixel because it moves outside the image, it can go on to the next pixel. This cannot happen if the loop control is in SIMD mode. By performing the loop control in SIMD mode, the PEs are forced to synchronize at the end of each loop iteration. Thus, no PE can begin to execute the next iteration of the loop (i.e., the next pixel) until all PEs have completed the current iteration. The temporal juxtaposition of loop iterations that occurs if the loop control is in MIMD mode is not possible if the loop control is in SIMD mode. Further details of this phenomenon can be found in [3]. Forcing PEs to synchronize to switch to SIMD mode for inter-PE communications within the body of the loop leads to the same problem. Therefore, mixed mode is not the ideal choice for this phase of the algorithm.

4.6. Results

The algorithm was first implemented on PASM. The algorithm was implemented on four to 16 PEs in SIMD, MIMD, and mixed mode with image sizes of 64-by-64, 128-by-128, and 256-by-256 pixels each. The image sizes used on PASM were smaller than on the other machines because of memory limitations. Potential mixed-mode implementations are to use SIMD for loop control and/or for inter-processor communication. Executing the loop control in SIMD would yield poor performance as discussed in Section 4.5. Executing the inter-processor communications in SIMD has the potential for little improvement relative to computation time, and forcing the synchronizations would yield the same problems as discussed for loop overhead in Section 4.5. Therefore, for the mixed-mode version, the background compensation phase is performed entirely in MIMD mode. (Because other portions of the program are performed in SIMD, the entire program can be thought of as mixed mode.)

To analyze the behavior of the algorithm in an SIMD machine, the algorithm was implemented on the MasPar MP-1. The image sizes used were 256-by-256, 512-by-512, 768-by-768, and 1024-by-1024. The number of PEs used in the study was varied from 16 to 16,384. All of these image sizes could not be used with the chosen numbers of PEs considered because of limiting factors. The first is that in row-striping, the maximum number of PEs that can be used is limited by the dimensions of the image, e.g., a maximum of 256 PEs can be used to process a 256-by-256 pixel image, because in row-striping the minimum number of rows that can be contained by a single PE is one. The other constraint is that each PE has 16 KB of memory, which is not enough to hold the larger subimages when dealing with large images and a small number of PEs. Block transfers were implemented using the global router. Using the global router simplified the calculations needed because determining the number of steps in the relevant directions is not necessary, as would have been required had the X-Net been used.

The algorithm was then implemented on the MIMD Intel Paragon. The algorithm was implemented on four to 128 PEs with image sizes of 256-by-256, 512-by-512, 768-by-768, and 1024-by-1024 pixels. Communication on the Paragon can be overlapped with computation and may result in a significant reduction in the total execution time of the program. However, because the communication is overlapped with computation, it is not easy to calculate the time each PE spends communicating. Therefore, in this study the communication times were not calculated separately.

The communication time of the program is a small portion of the total execution time, so the execution times presented are not decomposed into communication and computation time. The first two columns of Tables 1 through 5 contain a representative selection of the data collected for the background compensation experiments. The difference between the communication times for the two data schemes was low (less than five percent for PASM implementations and less than ten percent for MasPar implementations). This difference will have little influence on the differences between the two schemes' total execution time, so the communication

time alone is not presented. The execution times for all implementations show that the row-striping scheme is the better data layout scheme on all three machines, for the reasons outlined in Sections 4.3 through 4.5.

5. Edge Detection

5.1. Overview

Edges in images are characterized by sharp changes in intensity. Taking a two-dimensional spatial derivative of the image results in high values at points in the image that have large and abrupt changes in intensity. An edge detector that is based on this derivative principle is the Sobel edge detector and is used in this study.

In a parallel implementation of edge detection using a Sobel operator, the image is divided among the PEs. Therefore, to process some of the pixels in a PE, pixels located in other PEs are required. The number of pixels that need to be transferred to each PE is a function of the data layout scheme used, as is explained in the next subsection. The pixels around the edge of the image are initialized to zero, because they do not contain a full 3-by-3 region of pixels. This initialization ensures that the edge detection algorithm is not influenced by pixels that do not get operated on by the full Sobel operator.

Once edge detection is completed, the resulting image is ANDed with the image from background compensation (which was performed prior to edge detection). If a different data layout was used in each portion of the tracking algorithm, the data would have to be redistributed so that the two images could be ANDed (i.e., so each PE would contain corresponding subimages to AND). Therefore, edge detection was investigated to see if row-striping would perform better, and no redistribution would be required, or if the rectangular distribution performed better and the data would have to be redistributed.

5.2. Effect of Data Layout

Consider an image of size M-by-M in a system of N PEs. Assume that $X = Y = \sqrt{N}$, which means that square subimages are used. The following analysis is thoroughly examined in [15] and its application here is summarized for completeness. In the row-striping data layout scheme, each PE contains M/N rows and M columns. Because the Sobel operation is based on a 3-by-3 window, with the center defined as the center pixel, PE i ($0 < i < N-1$) requires the bottom row of pixels from PE $i-1$ and the top row of pixels from PE $i+1$. Therefore, a total of $2M$ pixels need to be transferred. It should be noted that PE 0 only requires a row of pixels from PE 1 and PE $N-1$ only requires a row of pixels from PE $N-2$.

In the square distribution scheme, with the same image and machine sizes as in the row-striping example, each PE contains $M/\sqrt{N}$ rows and columns. In this case, a PE requires pixels from eight neighboring PEs, $M/\sqrt{N}$ pixels are required from each of the four adjacent PEs, and one pixel is required from each of the PEs diagonally adjacent. Therefore, a total of $4M/\sqrt{N} + 4$ pixels need to be transferred. When processing pixels located in rows 0 and $M - 1$, and columns 0 and $M - 1$, transfers that would correspond to pixels outside the image do not need to be performed. For example, for an image of size 256-by-256, in a 16-PE system, row-striping would require 512 pixels to be transferred per PE, while in the square distribution scheme, 260 pixels need to be transferred. Therefore, in the square distribution scheme, less pixels need to be transferred.

A disadvantage of the square distribution scheme is the processing of pixels located on the edge of the image. In edge detection, pixels located in the first and last rows and columns of the image do not need to be processed. This is because a complete 3-by-3 window does not exist around these pixels. In row-striping, PEs 0 and $N - 1$ contain rows 0 and $M - 1$. Pixels in these rows do not need processing. Pixels located in the first and last columns are distributed among all the PEs equally. Therefore, all PEs save on the processing of $2M/N$ pixels. Additionally, PEs 0 and $N - 1$ save on processing $M - 2$ pixels each. The maximum number of pixels that any PE needs to process is $M^2/N - 2M/N$.

In the square distribution scheme, row 0, row $M - 1$, column 0, and column $M - 1$ are not distributed evenly among the PEs. Therefore, PEs that do not possess pixels in any of these locations do not save on any processing of pixels. The maximum number of pixels that are processed by any PE in this scheme is M^2/N.

It is shown that the number of pixels transferred in the square distribution scheme is less than in the row-striping scheme ($4M/\sqrt{N} + 4$ versus $2M$). However, the maximum number of pixels that need to be processed in the row-striping scheme is less ($M^2/N - 2M/N$ versus M^2/N). Let the time to transfer one pixel be τ times the time to process one pixel. Therefore, if $2M/N > \tau \times [2M - (4M/\sqrt{N} + 4)]$, the row-striping method is better, and if $\tau < 2M/N / (2M - (4M/\sqrt{N} + 4))$, then row-striping is better, otherwise, square distribution is better.

The above analysis is based on the assumption that the communication time is directly proportional to the number of pixels transferred. Factors such as transferring all pixels to a particular PE in a block and the number of network operations required will affect the value of τ in the expression derived above. Also, poor synchronization among the PEs can result in higher than expected communication times in MIMD mode. The presence of these variables, can therefore impact the relative performance of using either data layout scheme.

5.3. Results

To accurately study the entire motion-tracking algorithm, image and machine sizes were the same as discussed in the background compensation portion, Section 4.6. The third and fourth column of Tables 1 through 5 are a selection of the results from the experiments.

The communication times for the following implementations were orders of magnitude less than the computation time and are therefore not shown in a graph:

SIMD implementation on PASM, mixed-mode implementation on PASM, MasPar MP-1 implementation, and the Paragon implementation. For the MIMD implementation on PASM the communication time is a significant portion of the total execution time, and as the number of PEs increases from four to 16 the row-striping scheme achieves the lower communication times and the lower computation times. With four PEs, the row-striping scheme and the rectangular distribution require similar numbers of network settings per PE, two and three respectively. With eight or 16 PEs, the row-striping scheme still only needs two settings, where the rectangular distribution now requires five or eight, respectively. This increase in the number of network settings required is why the row-striping scheme is better for more than four PEs on PASM.

A mixed-mode implementation of the edge detection portion of PASM does not suffer the same limitations that the background compensation portion faced (Sections 4.4 and 4.6). Therefore, the mixed-mode implementation performed the portions of the loop body that required multiple conditionals in MIMD, and the rest of the algorithm in SIMD. All PEs send to their nearest neighbors before any communications begin. The difference between any two PEs completing the communication is not large, and so the synchronization of SIMD communications are not detrimental. Also, each PE performs similar numbers of computations with the simpler edge detection process, and so the synchronizations after each loop iteration are not increasing the execution time.

6. Conclusions

The execution times of the entire motion tracking algorithm, minus the time for the morphological opening which was not studied here, are shown in the fifth and sixth column of Tables 1 through 5. These results show that the row-striping data scheme is the better data scheme for this task. (In [16], it was shown that the row-striping layout scheme was better for the morphology tasks on the three machines studied in this paper.) The mixed-mode implementation on PASM showed a small improvement over the MIMD version, which performed much better than the SIMD version, for the reasons discussed earlier. In the mixed-mode version, the edge detection portion of the algorithm used both SIMD and MIMD operations, while the other portions used only MIMD operations. The data show that for the larger machine sizes, frame rates which are greater than real-time, as defined in [10], can be achieved by implementing the algorithm on a commercial parallel machine.

In summary, active camera motion tracking algorithms are computationally complex and achieving high frame rates is not possible with conventional serial computer systems. Parallel computers can provide the computational resources that are necessary to allow high-speed implementations of these algorithms, allow an easy means to revise the algorithm, and support the execution of other useful computations. When serial algorithms are ported to parallel computers, some of the issues that need to be addressed are the data layout schemes available and the parallel modes of operation. In this study, parallel implementations of an existing serial algorithm for performing motion tracking with an active camera were developed for different parallel computers. A detailed analysis of the different components of the algorithm was conducted and execution times were obtained for each component on each of the three parallel machines. A distinguishing feature of this application study is that the portion of each image frame that is relevant changes from one frame to the next based on the camera motion. This impacts the effect of the chosen data layout on the needed inter-PE data transfers and the way in which work is distributed among the PEs.

The implementations of the algorithm proved that high-speed active motion tracking is possible using commercially available parallel computers. The performance of the algorithm is dependent on the data layout scheme used and the image and machine sizes. The degree of effect of different data layout schemes on the execution time of the algorithm is governed by the parallel mode of operation as well. By carefully tuning the application implementation to a particular machine, a significant reduction in overall execution time is obtained, and high frame rates can be achieved.

Acknowledgement: The authors thank Janet M. Siegel and the reviewers for their comments.

References

[1] G.S. Almasi and A. Gottlieb, *Highly Parallel Computing, 2nd Edition,* Benjamin/Cummings, Redwood City, CA, 1994.

[2] M. Auguin and F. Boeri, "The OPSILA computer," in *Parallel Languages and Architectures,* M. Consard, ed., Elsevier Science Publishers, Holland, 1986, pp. 143-153.

[3] T.B. Berg, S.D. Kim, and H.J. Siegel, "Limitations imposed on mixed-mode performance of optimized phases due to temporal juxtaposition," *J. of Parallel and Distributed Computing,* Oct. 1991, pp. 154-169.

[4] C.G. Herter, T.M. Warschko, W.F. Tichy, and M. Philippsen, "Triton/1: A massively-parallel mixed-mode computer designed to support high level languages," *Heterogeneous Computing Workshop (HCW '93),* Apr. 1993, pp. 65-70.

[5] ICE, Inc., *The MeshSP,* Technical Report, Waltham, MA, July 1995.

[6] K. Kanatani, "Camera rotation invariance of image characteristics," *Computer Vision, Graphics and Image Processing,* Vol. 39, No. 3, Sep. 1987, pp. 328-354.

[7] P.M. Kogge, "EXECUBE - A new architecture for scalable MPPs," *1994 Int'l Conf. on Parallel Processing,* Vol. I, Aug. 1994, pp. 77-84.

[8] G.J. Lipovski and M. Malek, *Parallel Computing: Theory and Comparisons,* John Wiley & Sons, New York, NY, 1987.

[9] M. Mirmehdi and T.J. Ellis, "Parallel approach to tracking edge segments in dynamic scenes," *Image and Vision Computing,* Vol. 11, No. 1, Jan. 1993, pp. 35-48.

[10] D. Murray and A. Basu, "Motion tracking with an active camera," *IEEE Trans. on Pattern Analysis and Machine Intelligence,* Vol. 16, No. 5, May 1994, pp. 449-459.

[11] J.R. Nickolls, "The design of the MasPar MP-1: A cost effective massively parallel computer," *IEEE Compcon,* Feb. 1990, pp. 25-28.

[12] J.M. Roberts and D. Charnley, "Parallel attentive visual tracking," *Engineering Applications of Artificial Intelligence,* Vol. 7, No. 2, July 1994, pp. 205-215.

[13] H.J. Siegel, T. Braun, H.G. Dietz, M.B. Kulaczewski, M. Maheswaran, P.H. Pero, J.M. Siegel, J.E. So, M. Tan, M.D. Theys, and L. Wang, "The PASM project: A study of reconfigurable parallel computing," *2nd Int'l Symp. on Parallel Architectures, Algorithms, and Networks (ISPAN '96),* June 1996, pp. 529-536. Invited.

[14] H.J. Siegel, M. Maheswaran, D.W. Watson, J.K. Antonio, and M.J. Atallah, "Mixed-mode system heterogeneous computing," in *Heterogeneous Computing,* M.M. Eshaghian, ed. Artech House, Norwood, MA, 1996, pp. 19-65.

[15] H.J. Siegel, L. Wang, J.E. So, and M. Maheswaran, "Data parallel algorithms," in *Parallel and Distributed Computing Handbook,* A. Y. Zomaya, ed., McGraw-Hill, New York, NY, 1996, pp. 466-499.

[16] M.D. Theys, R.M. Born, M.D. Allemang, and H.J. Siegel, "Morphological image processing on three parallel machines," *The 6th Symp. on the Frontiers of Massively Parallel Computation,* Oct. 1996, pp. 327-334.

[17] Y. Yamada and M. Ishikawa, "High speed target tracking using massively parallel processing vision," *1993 IEEE/RSJ Int'l Conf. on Intelligent Robots and Systems,* July 1993, pp. 267-272.

Figures

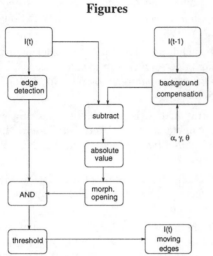

Figure 1: Block diagram of the serial algorithm.

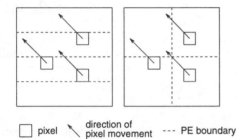

| | pixel | ⬊ direction of pixel movement | --- PE boundary |

Figure 2: Row-striping communication pattern (no conflicts), left. Rectangular distribution communication pattern (two conflicts), right.

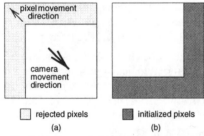

rejected pixels   initialized pixels

(a)   (b)

Figure 3: Location of (a) rejected pixels, and (b) initialized pixels.

Back. Comp.		Edge Detect.		Total Time		Num. PEs
Row	Rect.	Row	Rect.	Row	Rect.	
5.4586	5.7925	0.7459	0.7505	6.5785	6.9180	16
2.7319	2.9243	0.3759	0.3765	3.2948	3.4883	32
1.3684	1.4667	0.1908	0.1895	1.6528	1.7501	64
0.6868	0.7374	0.0983	0.0956	0.8320	0.8800	128
0.3286	0.3722	0.0522	0.0486	0.4042	0.4444	256

Table 1: Execution time in seconds on the MasPar MP-1 with a 256-by-256 pixel image.

Back. Comp.		Edge Detect.		Total Time		Num. PEs
Row	Rect.	Row	Rect.	Row	Rect.	
0.3830	0.3816	0.1138	0.1283	0.5253	0.5735	4
0.2316	0.2213	0.0568	0.0810	0.3100	0.3286	8
0.1292	0.1253	0.0266	0.0534	0.1642	0.1903	16
0.0781	0.0780	0.0158	0.0404	0.0981	0.1249	32
0.0478	0.0490	0.0079	0.0389	0.0580	0.0909	64
0.0368	0.0363	0.0071	0.0408	0.0451	0.0786	128

Table 2: Execution time in seconds on the Intel Paragon with a 256-by-256 pixel image.

Back. Comp.		Edge Detect.		Total Time		Num. PEs
Row	Rect.	Row	Rect.	Row	Rect.	
70.449	75.267	13.483	14.983	93.173	100.55	4
35.636	38.169	6.8576	7.6453	47.146	50.991	8
23.571	25.612	4.3995	5.1235	30.679	32.312	16

Table 3: Execution time in seconds on PASM in SIMD mode with a 128-by-128 pixel image.

Back. Comp.		Edge Detect.		Total Time		Num. PEs
Row	Rect.	Row	Rect.	Row	Rect.	
19.578	22.216	6.1522	8.7144	27.758	35.069	4
10.599	13.089	3.3399	6.3683	14.610	19.782	8
5.3330	6.4096	1.5574	3.9319	7.4050	10.627	16

Table 4: Execution time in seconds on PASM in MIMD mode with a 128-by-128 pixel image.

Back. Comp.		Edge Detect.		Total Time		Num. PEs
Row	Rect.	Row	Rect.	Row	Rect.	
19.317	22.939	4.0464	5.4570	25.913	32.583	4
10.600	13.217	2.1194	2.8109	13.873	18.212	8
5.3358	6.3577	1.1255	1.4760	7.0733	8.8693	16

Table 5: Execution time in seconds on PASM in mixed mode with a 128-by-128 pixel image.

440

Exploiting Task and Data Parallelism in Parallel Hough and Radon Transforms

Dilip Krishnaswamy[†]   Prithviraj Banerjee[‡]

[†] Center for Reliable and High-Performance Computing, University of Illinois, Urbana IL

[‡] Center for Parallel and Distributed Computing, Northwestern University, Evanston, IL

Abstract

Edge detection and shape detection in digital images are very computationally intensive problems. Parallel algorithms can potentially provide significant speedups while preserving the quality of the result obtained. Hough and Radon Transforms are projection-based transforms which are commonly used for edge detection and shape detection respectively. We propose in this paper various new parallel algorithms which exploit both task and data parallelism available in Hough and Radon transforms. algorithms A memory scalable aggressive task parallel algorithm is shown to be the most optimal algorithm in terms of memory scalability and performance on an IBM SP2.

1 Introduction

Edge detection and shape detection in digital images are very computationally intensive problems. Parallel algorithms can potentially provide significant speedups while preserving the quality of the result obtained. Hough [1, 2] and Radon Transforms [3] are projection-based transforms which are commonly used for edge detection and shape detection respectively. Various parallel algorithms [4, 5, 6, 7, 8, 9] have been proposed for these projection-based transforms. However, all research in this area has focussed on exploiting only the data parallelism available in these problems. To date, none of the approaches have explored the task parallelism available in this problem.

Recently, there has been growing interest in simultaneous exploitation of task and data parallelism [10, 11, 12, 13, 14, 15, 16, 17, 18, 19]. The reader is referred to [10, 11] for an introduction to the issue of combining task and data parallelism. We propose in this paper various new parallel algorithms which exploit both task and data parallelism available in Hough and Radon transforms. A detailed presentation is provided for the Hough transform and it is shown that the proposed algorithms can be easily extended to the Radon transform.

2 Hough Transforms

Edge detection is by far the most common approach for detecting meaningful discontinuities in gray level images. An edge is the boundary between two regions with relatively distinct gray-level properties. Consider the problem of detecting lines in a grey scale image with $N \times N$ pixels. An initial preprocessing step is applied to identify the edge pixels associated with the image The edges, which these edge pixels may be a part of, are then obtained by applying the Hough Transform (HT).

This research was supported in part by the Advanced Research Projects Agency under contract DAA-H04-94-G-0273 administered by the Army Research Office.

2.1 Initial Preprocessing To Obtain The Edge Pixels

Let p_{ij} denote the pixel value at x-coordinate i and y-coordinate j in the $N \times N$ image. The image is first skimmed for lines using the method proposed by Davies [20], and a binary image is obtained. In this approach, a differential gradient of the input grey level image is first computed on the pixels using the Sobel masks [20], which provide reasonably accurate estimates of the x and y components of the local intensity gradient G. This results in the first derivative of the gray-level profile of the image. To this, we apply the Laplacian mask [20] to obtain the second derivative, and then follow it up with thresholding, to obtain a bitonal image. The Hough Transform algorithm can now be applied to the binary[0-1] version of this bitonal image to recognize the edges in the original image.

2.2 Algorithm for the Hough Transform (HT)

Let $BinImage(i, j)$ denote the binary (0-1) version of the bitonal $N \times N$ image after thresholding. Let $BinImage(i, j)$ denote the pixel value at x-coordinate i and y-coordinate j. All pixels which have the higher value of 1 in the binary image are considered edge pixels. Let K = the number of edge pixels in the image. In the worst case, $K = O(N^2)$ = the number of points in the image. Let L = the number of significant lines in the image. Usually L is quite small compared to K. For the K points corresponding to the edge pixels in an image, using the Hough Transform [1], we want to find subsets of these points that lie on straight lines. The Hough Transform of a binary image is a set of projections of the image taken from various angles. A straight line in the x-y plane can be characterized by its slope $m = tan\theta$, where θ is the angle the line makes with the x-axis, and the y-intercept d that the line makes with the y-axis. Consider a point (x_i, y_j) and the general equation of a straight line in the slope-intercept form $y_i = mx_i + d$. Infinitely many lines pass through (x_i, y_i) satisfying this equation. Consider now the form of the equation, $d = -mx_i + y_i$ in the md plane (called the parameter space). This yields the equation of a single line for a fixed pair (x_i, y_i). Let the angle θ vary from 0 to $\pi/4$. Hence m varies from 0 to 1. Let us assume that projections are taken in steps of $\delta = \frac{\pi}{4M}$. Let us divide the m axis into M increments, i.e., the Hough Transform is obtained for M projections. Since the angle θ varies from 0 to $\pi/4$, the d axis varies from $-N$ to N. Note that if θ approaches $\pi/2$, the value of d approaches infinity. Hence, we will process angles in the range 0 to $\pi/4$ first and then process the rest of the angles using the algorithm to be discussed by transforming the image. These transformations will be presented in detail later. Let us divide the d axis into D increments. One may typically choose $D = 2N + 1$. For a given value of m and for a given edge pixel (x_i, y_i) we can determine the value of d and round it to the nearest d-intercept value on the d axis. Let us assume an array $TempSum$ of size D. Let us also assume a linked list $EdgeList$. This will eventually contain the edges that have been detected and will be of size $O(L)$. The Hough Transform is obtained using the following algorithm.

The Hough Transform Algorithm:

For each value of m from 0 to 1 in increments of tan(δ)

    Set elements in TempSum array to 0.

    For each edge pixel in BinImage

        Compute $d = -mx_i + y_i$ and round to nearest $d = d_k$

        Increment $TempSum[d_k]$

    For each value of d_j from -N to N in increments of 1

        If ($TempSum[d_j] > lineThreshold$) then

        Add (m, d_j) to the list EdgeList

Hence for M projections of the Hough Transform and with K edge pixels in an $N \times N$ image, the computation cost is $O(MK)$. Let the computation cost be γMK seconds where γ is a constant. Note that we require $O(N^2)$ storage for the image and $O(L)$ storage for the edges in the image. Thus, work related to θ in the range 0 to $\frac{\pi}{4}$ has been accomplished. We shall refer to this work as task T_1. For θ in other ranges, the following simple modifications of the Hough Transform algorithm will suffice.

For θ lying in the range $\frac{\pi}{2}$ to $\frac{\pi}{4}$ (task T_2): Use $BinImage(j, i)$.

For θ lying in the range $\frac{3\pi}{4}$ to $\frac{\pi}{2}$ (task T_3): Use $BinImage(j, N-i)$.

For θ lying in the range $\frac{3\pi}{4}$ to π (task T_4): Use $BinImage(N-i, j)$. Hence the total computation cost is approximately $4\gamma MK$ seconds.

3 Parallel Algorithms for Hough Transforms

We now present new parallel algorithms which exploit both the data parallelism and the task parallelism available in the problem. We initially present a purely data-parallel parallel algorithm (DHT). This is followed by a combined data-parallel and task-parallel parallel algorithm (DTHT). We then show the advantages of exploiting task parallelism to the fullest by using an aggressive task-parallel approach (ATHT). However this algorithm may have limitations in terms of memory scalability, and we therefore present an optimal memory-scalable aggressive task-parallel parallel algorithm (MATHT), which provides the best performance among all the algorithms in general.

3.1 DHT: A Data-Parallel HT

We now present a data parallel coarse grain parallel algorithm for the Hough Transform algorithm presented in the previous section. Let us assume that we have P processors. The data partitioning approach in this algorithm provides the optimum load balancing of the edge pixels across the P processors. In this approach, the image data in the array $BinImage$ is partitioned across the processors. And each processor works on the pixels in its partition. It turns out that it does not matter whether we partition the data in rows or columns or in a two-dimensional grid as the amount of work done in each processor depends only on the number of edge pixels in each processor. One may choose to trivially partition the image data by assigning N/P columns to each processor. Let us call the data-parallel approach with such a trivial partitioning as algorithm DHT0. It is possible that such a partitioning strategy may result in a load imbalance across the processors, if edge pixels are concentrated only in specific regions in the image. Hence one must try to distribute the edge pixels equally among processors. Let us assume that we perform a column-partitioning of the data such that approximately K/P pixels are assigned to each processor, and the column boundaries across the partitions are chosen so that this is the case. This strategy will result in near optimal load balance across

processors. Let us call a data-parallel approach with such a partitioning to be DHT1.

The data parallel algorithm is similar to the sequential version of the algorithm presented earlier, except that now each processor works on the edge pixels in its partition. Hence, for each value of m, an array of local sums is obtained in the array $TempSum$ in each processor. Therefore, a reduction step is necessary with summation to obtain the actual value of the array $TempSum$. This is obtained in $log(P)$ steps, as the partial sums are summed up in a binary tree fashion, such that the result at the end is present in processor 1. The values in the array $TempSum$ are now the same as those obtained in the serial implementation, and the result is available only in processor 1. The salient edges are identified and stored in the linked list $EdgeList$ in processor 1.

Let us assume that α is the startup cost in seconds associated with sending a message and that β is the reciprocal of the bandwidth of the communication network in seconds per word on a distributed memory multicomputer. In the reduction step we have $log(P)$ stages of communication and in each step a partial sum of D words is communicated. Hence, in a single reduction step, the communication cost is approximately $log(P)(\alpha + \beta D)$. Since we have to evaluate M projections, the total communication cost is then $Mlog(P)(\alpha + \beta D)$. By virtue of the load balancing strategy used, each processor works on approximately K/P pixels. Hence the computation cost is approximately $\gamma \frac{MK}{P}$. Hence the execution time is approximately, $\gamma \frac{MK}{P} + Mlog(P)(\alpha + \beta D)$. Since we have to repeat this algorithm for the 4 different ranges of angles, the total execution time then is $4\gamma \frac{MK}{P} + 4Mlog(P)(\alpha + \beta D)$. Note that approximate storage required is $O(L)$ for the edges detected and $O(N^2/P)$ for the image, assuming that approximately N/P columns are assigned to each processor.

3.2 DTHT: Combined Data & Task-Parallel HT

It is obvious from the above discussion that the four tasks T_1, T_2, T_3 and T_4 (associated with the Hough Transform being performed for different ranges of angles) can be executed in any order and independent of each other. In the Data-Parallel approach, given P processors, we assign all P processors to task T_1 initially, followed by assigning the same processors to tasks T_2, T_3 and T_4 in sequence. However, since each of the tasks is of the same granularity in computation and can be run independent of each other, one can assign $P/4$ processors to each of the tasks. Hence we form four groups of processors with each group consisting of $P/4$ processors and execute each of the four tasks concurrently. The computation cost for each of the tasks is then $\gamma \frac{MK}{P/4}$ $=$ $4\gamma \frac{MK}{P}$. Since all tasks execute concurrently, this is indeed the overall computation cost. Since the communication is restricted to just $P/4$ processors, the communication cost is now reduced to $Mlog(\frac{P}{4})(\alpha + \beta D)$. Hence the total execution cost for the completion of all four tasks now becomes $4\gamma \frac{MK}{P} + Mlog(\frac{P}{4})(\alpha + \beta D)$. It is therefore clear that one can considerably reduce the total execution time by employing a combined data and task parallel approach as indicated here. However, this does not come without a price. If the storage for the image is $O(N^2/P)$ in the data parallel approach, it is now approximately $O(N^2/\frac{P}{4}) = O(4N^2/P)$ for the task parallel approach. This is because the entire image has to be stored in each subgroup of $P/4$ processors.

3.3 ATHT: An Aggressive Task-Parallel HT

Let us assume that we have $P = 4Q$ processors. We can assign Q processors for each of the tasks T_1, T_2, T_3 and T_4. From the previous discussion, we can execute the data-parallel parallel algorithm using Q processors on each of the tasks. Instead, we can extend the task parallelism approach even further. We can divide the task T_i into Q tasks, viz. $T_{i1}, T_{i2}, \ldots T_{iQ}$. Consider task T_1 which consists of computing all M projections for θ in the range 0 to $\frac{\pi}{4}$. We can assign task T_{1j} to be the computation of all M/Q projections for θ in the range $\frac{(j-1)\pi}{4Q}$ to $\frac{j\pi}{4Q}$. All Q tasks, viz. $T_{i1}, T_{i2}, \ldots T_{iQ}$ can proceed independent of each other. Thus we have Q tasks in each of the 4 subgroups and hence $4Q = P$ independent tasks running. This eliminates any of the need for communication required between processors as in the data parallel approach. It should therefore take $\gamma(\frac{M}{Q})K = 4\gamma\frac{MK}{4Q} = 4\gamma\frac{MK}{P}$ seconds for execution and would be the fastest among the algorithms presented so far. However, this is certainly not a memory scalable implementation because now each of the P processors requires $O(N^2)$ memory for the image, as each processor now needs to have the entire image in memory. Thus, if memory is not an issue, then aggressive task parallelism is indeed the best approach, as theoretically it can provide near perfect speedups.

3.4 MATHT: A Memory Scalable Aggressive Task-Parallel HT

Let us assume that we have $P = 4Q$ processors. Let us also assume that G words of memory are available in each processor. Let R be the smallest integer greater than or equal to N^2/G. Then, a data parallel approach using R processors or more only will be able to fit in each processor's memory, as it requires $N^2/R \leq G$ words of storage. Hence one must use data parallelism of at least R. Let us now assume that Q is factorizable such that $Q = RS$ where S is an integer. Then, it is clear that one cannot exploit a task parallelism of greater than S in each of 4 subgroups of the P processors. However, one must try to exploit as much of the task parallelism as is available to reduce the communication overheads inherent in a data parallel approach. Thus the ideal solution is to create S tasks in each of the 4 subgroups of processors and employ a data parallelism of R in each of the S tasks. Note that $P = 4RS$ and we now have $4S$ tasks each running on R processors in a data parallel fashion with all $4S$ tasks independent of each other and not requiring communication between them. The total computation cost in this case is then equal to $\gamma\frac{\frac{M}{S}K}{R} = \gamma\frac{MK}{RS} = 4\gamma\frac{MK}{4RS} = 4\gamma\frac{MK}{P}$. The communication cost is given by, $\frac{M}{S}log(R)(\alpha + \beta D)$. Thus the total execution time in this case is given by $4\gamma\frac{MK}{P} + \frac{M}{S}log(R)(\alpha + \beta D)$. For a given parallel system and for a given image size, the value of R is fixed. The above formula for the execution time assumes that P is a multiple value of $4R$. Note that if $P \leq R$, then only a data parallel approach (DHT) is possible. If $R \leq P \leq 4R$, then only the data parallel (DHT) approach and the combined data and task parallel approach (DTHT) are possible. This is indeed a memory scalable algorithm and it also extracts the most of the task parallelism available in the problem at the same time. It also attempts to reduce the communication costs compared to a purely data-parallel approach. We conclude that this is the most optimal approach given memory and processor constraints.

4 Parallel Radon Transforms

A Radon Transform is a general version of the Hough Transform. It is useful for efficient detection of shapes, and for representation and manipulation of image data[3]. The computation of the Radon Transform involves taking projections of a gray level image along various linear contours. This means that one needs to sum up the pixel values along every possible line in the image. Hence while the Hough Transform is applied to a binary image, the Radon Transform is applied to the original gray level image and one has to sum over gray values of all the pixels that may lie on a given line. It is clear that no preprocessing is required for the Radon Transform, since one has to work directly with gray level values. Hence, all the arguments presented for parallel Hough Transforms are equally valid for parallel Radon Transforms. However, all the N^2 pixels in an image need to be considered, and hence in this case, the value of K is simply N^2. Also since, all the pixels are used in this transform, data partitioning is very simple and one can simply allocate N/P columns to each of the P processors and obtain perfect load balance at the same time.

5 Implementation and Results

The parallel algorithms presented in this paper were implemented in C using the MPI communication library [21] on a 16-processor IBM SP2, a distributed memory multicomputer with 64MB of memory on each node. The results are shown for parallel Hough Transforms only. The initial preprocessing step was implemented in a completely data parallel manner and the resulting binary image was redistributed to the processors depending on the partitioning required by a specific algorithm. The overhead of the initial preprocessing and redistribution is very negligible as these operations take a considerably short time compared to the computationally intensive Hough Transform. Results are shown for three image sizes, a 512×512 image, a 1024×1024 image, and a high resolution 4096×4096 image. Since each processor had 64Mbytes of memory, and each word was 4 bytes in length, each processor had exactly $G = 16M$ words of memory space available and hence a $4K \times 4K = 16M$ image could not fit in, as additional memory was required for storage of the lines and other data structures. Hence the 4096×4096 image could not fit into a single processor, but a 512×512 image and a 1024×1024 image could easily fit it. Let us consider the first case of the 512×512 image. Since, this image fits into every processor node, the aggressive task parallel algorithm ATHT provides the best performance. It can be seen that the combined data and task parallel algorithm DTHT had a worser execution time but did have a better execution than the pure data parallel algorithm DHT.

Since the image fit entirely into the node, the memory scalable aggressive task parallel algorithm MTHT had the same result as the algorithm ATHT. Similar results were obtained with the 1024×1024 image. Let us consider the case of the 4096×4096 image. Since, this image did not fit into a single processor node, the aggressive task parallel algorithm ATHT could not be tried out. However, the memory scalable aggressive task parallel algorithm MATHT was used with a data parallelism of 2 and a task parallelism of 8 to get the best performance. Once again as expected, the algorithm DTHT had a worser execution time but did have a better execution time than the pure data parallel algorithm DHT. Speedups could be reported for the various algorithms only for the 512×512 image and the 1024×1024 image, as these could fit into a single

Image Size	Alg DHT0		Alg DHT1		Alg DTHT		Alg AHT		Alg MAHT	
	DP	TP	DP	TP	DP	TP	DP	TP	DP	TP
512 x 512	16	1	16	1	4	4	1	16	1	16
1024 x 1024	16	1	16	1	4	4	1	16	1	16
4096 x 4096	16	1	16	1	4	4	1	16	2	8

Table 1. Data Parallelism (DP) and Task Parallelism (TP) employed in each algorithm (Alg)

Image Size	Serial Time	Alg DHT0		Alg DHT1		Alg DTHT		Alg AHT		Alg MAHT	
		Time	Spd	Time	Spd	Time	Spd	Time	Spd	Time	Spd
512 x 512	1016	129	7.9	102	9.8	86	11.8	74	13.7	74	13.7
1024 x 1024	3754	368	10.2	351	10.7	305	12.3	269	13.9	269	13.9
4096 x 4096	-	10371	-	9642	-	8837	-	-	-	8176	-

Table 2. Execution time in seconds and Speedups (Spd) on 16 processors of the IBM SP-2

processor node. Of the two versions of the parallel algorithm, it can be seen that the partitioning of data with load balancing approach in algorithm DHT1 proved to be consistently better than the blind partitioning approach adopted in algorithm DHT0, for all images.

6 Conclusion

We have proposed data parallel, combined data and task parallel, aggressive task parallel and memory scalable aggressive task parallel algorithms for parallel Hough and Radon Transforms. We conclude that the data parallel approach is most scalable in terms of memory but has the worst performance. The combined data and task parallel approach sacrifices a little on the memory scalability but performs better than the pure data parallel approach. The aggressive task parallel approach provides the best performance if the entire image can fit into the memory of a single processor. The memory scalable aggressive task parallel algorithm is the most optimal algorithm in terms of memory scalability and performance. It is equivalent to the aggressive task parallel approach when the entire image can fit into a single processor. It makes the best utilization of the resources available and always provides the best performance.

References

[1] P. V. C. Hough, "Methods and Means for Recognizing Complex Patterns." U. S. Patent 3,069,654.

[2] R. C. Gonzalez and R. E. Woods. *Digital Image Processing*. Addison-Wesley, 1992.

[3] J. L. C. Sanz, E. B. Hinkle and A. K. Jain. *Radon and Projection Transform-based Computer Vision*. Springer-Verlag, 1988.

[4] A. Rosenfeld, J. Ornelas, and Y. Hung, "Hough Transform algorithms for mesh connected SIMD parallel processors," *Computer Vision Graphics Image Processing* 41, 3(1988), 293-305.

[5] C. Guerra, and S. Hambrusch, "Parallel Algorithms for Line Detection on a Mesh," *Journal of Parallel and Distributed Computing*, 6, 1989, 1-19.

[6] R. E. Cypher, J.L.C. Sanz and L. Snyder, "The Hough Transform has O(N) Complexity on N x N Mesh Connected Computers," *SIAM Journal of Computing*, 19, 5(1990), 805-820.

[7] S. Ranka and S. Sahni. *Hypercube Algorithms With Applications to Image Processing and Pattern Recognition*. Springer-Verlag, 1990.

[8] C. Nagendra, M. Borah, M. Vishwanath, R. M. Owens, and M. J. Irwin, "Edge Detection Using Fine Grained Parallelism in VLSI," *International Conf. on Acoustics, Speech and Signal Processing* 1993.

[9] D. Krishnaswamy, V. Govindan and C. Nagendra, "A Fine Grain Algorithm for the Hough Transform for Mesh Connected Processors," *IEE Hough Transform Colloquium*, London, 1993.

[10] S. Ramaswamy, S. Sapatnekar and P. Banerjee. A Convex Programming Approach for Exploiting Data and Functional Parallelism on Distributed Memory Multicomputers," *Proc. of the 23rd Intl. Conference on Parallel Processing*, Vol II, 116-125, St. Charles, IL, 1994.

[11] J. Subhlok et. al., "Exploiting Task and Data Parallelism on a Multicomputer," *Proc. of the 4th ACM SIGPLAN Symp. on Principles and Practices of Parallel Prog*, pp 13-22, San Diego, CA, 1993.

[12] I. Foster, B. Avalani, A. Choudhary, and M. Xu. A Compilation System That Integrates High Performance Fortran and Fortran M. In *Proceedings of the Scalable High Performance Computing Conference*, pages 293-300, Knoxville, TN, May 1994.

[13] M. Girkar and C. D. Polychronopoulos. Automatic Extraction of Functional Parallelism from Ordinary Programs. *IEEE Transactions on Parallel and Distributed Systems*, 3(2):166-178, Mar. 1992.

[14] P. Banerjee, J. A. Chandy, M. Gupta, E. W. Hodges IV, J. G. Holm, A. Lain, D. J. Palermo, S. Ramaswamy, and E. Su. The PARADIGM Compiler for Distributed-Memory Multicomputers. *IEEE Computer*, 28(10):37-47, Oct. 1995.

[15] S. Ramaswamy, E. W.Hodges, and P. Banerjee. Compiling MATLAB Programs to SCALAPACK: Exploiting Task and Data Parallelism. Proc. of the Intl. Parallel Processing Symposium, 1996

[16] M. Dhagat, R. Bagrodia, and K. M. Chandy. Integrating task and data parallelism in uc. Proc. Int. Conf. Parallel Processing (ICPP-95), pages II-29-II-36, Aug. 1995.

[17] K. P. Belkhale, R. J. Brouwer, and P. Banerjee. Task Scheduling for Exploiting Parallelism and Hierarchy in VLSI CAD Applications. *IEEE Trans. Computer-aided Design Integrated Circuits Systems*, 12(5):557-567, May 1993.

[18] K. McPherson and P. Banerjee. Parallel algorithms for vlsi layout verification. *Journal of Parallel and Distributed Computing*, Vol. 36, no. 2, August 1996, pp. 156-172.

[19] K. McPherson and P. Banerjee. Integrating Task and Data Parallelism in an Irregular Application: A Case Study *Proc. Symp. on Parallel and Distributed Processing*, New Orleans, LA, Oct. 1996, pp. 208-213.

[20] E. R. Davies, "A Skimming Technique for Fast Accurate Edge Detection," Signal Processing, 26, 1(1992), 1-16.

[21] W. Gropp, E. Lusk, and A. Skellum, *Using MPI: Portable Parallel Programming with the Message Passing Interface*. MIT Press, 1994.

Session 7B

Communication and
Synchronization Issues

Communication in Parallel Applications:
Characterization and Sensitivity Analysis[*]

Dale Seed
Anand Sivasubramaniam
Chita R. Das

Department of Computer Science & Engineering
The Pennsylvania State University
University Park, PA 16802.
Phone: (814) 865-1406
{*seed,anand,das*}*@cse.psu.edu*

Abstract

Communication characterization of parallel applications is essential to understand the interplay between architectures and applications in determining the maximum achievable performance. Although a significant amount of research has been conducted on execution-based architectural evaluations, very little effort has gone into capturing the communication behavior of an application mathematically. In this paper, we attempt to characterize the communication behavior of applications by temporal, spatial and volume attributes. We also study the impact of variation in application and architectural parameters on the communication behavior in terms of the three attributes. Our results show that for the chosen suite of applications, the message arrival and spatial distributions can be closely approximated by known statistical distributions and that the temporal as well as spatial distributions of all applications remain unchanged with respect to four parameters considered in this study. These results lead us closer to the belief that it is possible to abstract the communication properties of parallel applications in convenient mathematical forms that have wide applicability.

1 Introduction

Performance evaluation of multiprocessors by analytical modeling and simulation is believed to be grossly over-simplified because of making unrealistic assumptions about the workload. These assumption have been used primarily due to the lack of understanding/characterization of application behavior. The RISC ideology, in the evolution of uniprocessor architectures, has clearly taught us the importance of using realistic workloads (applications) to drive architectural design. It is thus important that we develop realistic workloads by studying application behavior to serve as inputs for multiprocessor design and evaluation.

Of all the overheads in a parallel system, the communication overhead in message traversal across the interconnection network, is usually the most dominant factor in limiting the performance of many parallel applications. This research sets out to characterize the communication behavior of a wide spectrum of parallel applications and to study the sensitivity of these characteristics to variations in application and architectural parameters.

The communication workload generated by a parallel application can be captured by three attributes, namely the temporal, spatial and volume components [19]. Temporal behavior is captured by the message generation rate and the underlying inter-arrival time distribution, spatial behavior is expressed in terms of the message destination distribution or traffic pattern, and volume of communication is specified by the number of messages and the message length distribution. Most multiprocessor performance studies [3] (both analytical models and simulations) have made simplifying assumptions about these three attributes to keep the problem tractable. For example, almost all performance models [1, 8, 25] have used exponential/geometric distribution for the inter-arrival times of messages. Similarly, a uniform traffic pattern and a constant message length have been used to represent spatial distribution and size of messages, respectively. However, these assumptions, the uniform traffic pattern in particular, are believed not to be truly representative of realistic workloads. The credibility of many model-based performance results has thus been questioned frequently.

Understanding these drawbacks, there has been recent interest in actual execution [14, 15, 11, 3] or execution-driven simulation [21, 16, 9, 4, 6, 24, 12] of parallel applications. Parallel applications drawn from NAS [2], Parkbench [13], and SPLASH [20] have been widely used to benchmark parallel machines. Measurement or execution-driven simulation can provide accurate and indepth performance analysis of an architecture for a given set of applications. The main problem with these approaches, however, is that they are expensive. Also, few attempts [5, 23] have been made to characterize the communication properties of applications using these techniques. Specifically, traditional evaluation studies have used only a selected set of applications to examine a candidate architecture. Usually, execution time, speedup, and memory and I/O requests are the performance metrics of interest in these studies [7]. These metrics provide little insight in generalizing the communication properties of applications and expressing them in terms of the above three attributes. On the other hand, if we can express the realistic communication workload in terms of the three attributes, they can be used as communication benchmarks for many divergent studies. A system architect can use the communication information for better architectural design; an algorithm developer can use the communication cost for better algorithm design and analysis; and a system analyst can develop more accurate performance models using realistic workloads.

To abstract the communication behavior in a parallel system, it is essential to know what causes and affects communication. Primarily, communication in a network is induced by two sources. First, is the communication inherent to an algorithm and second is

---

[*] This research is supported in part by NSF grants MIP-9406984, MIP-9634197 and a NSF Career Award MIP-9701475.

the communication generated due to architectural artifacts. The algorithm design and its mapping onto an architecture imposes a certain workload on the underlying network. In addition, architectural features such as the number of processors, network characteristics, type of architecture (shared memory/ message passing), memory consistency model and cache coherence mechanism might affect one or more of the three communication attributes. Further, variations in architectural parameters such as network speed and CPU clock can have a bearing on the application behavior. Any workload characterization study should thus consider all these issues for a complete understanding of application behavior.

A methodology was presented in [5] to abstract the communication properties of a parallel application from actual measurement or execution-driven simulation. The communication traces collected for different applications were analyzed statistically to derive distribution functions for the three communication attributes. It was shown that it is possible to express the message generation and spatial distribution of an application in terms of commonly used distributions. However, the impact of architectural parameters on the communication characteristics was not considered in this study.

The objective of this paper is to analyze the contribution of architectural changes on communication parameters to completely understand the communication workload. Since it is impossible to include all possible aberrations, which would require a full factorial experiment, we confine ourselves to four parameters on a shared memory platform. These are the number of processors, the application problem size, the relative speed of the network to the speed of the CPU, and the memory consistency model (Sequential Consistency and Release Consistency). We also discuss the change in these communication attributes when we move from a shared memory to a message passing setting using a case-study.

The main focus of this research is to answer the following questions:

- Can the changes to the communication behavior induced by architectural parameters be captured by known distribution functions?

- If so, are the original temporal and spatial distributions robust to parametric changes?

- Which communication parameters (temporal, spatial and volume) are affected by changes in the system parameters?

- How sensitive are the communication characteristics to variations in these architectural parameters?

Using an execution-driven simulator called SPASM [21, 22] and a suite of shared memory applications, this study generates and analyzes the communication events in these applications on a 2D-mesh network using wormhole switching and deterministic routing. The network activities are logged and fed to a statistical analysis package called SAS [17] to quantify the distribution functions for the three communication attributes. The applications have been simulated over the range of system parameters under consideration, and the changes in the distribution functions have been studied. The results show that for the chosen suite of five shared memory applications, the message arrival and message destination distributions can be closely approximated by known statistical distributions and that the temporal as well as spatial distributions of all applications remain unchanged with respect to the variations in the four parameters considered. Since this study focuses on shared memory systems where the message lengths are short and fixed by the underlying architecture, the message length

distribution has not been considered. For three of the chosen applications, the inter-arrival times are exponentially distributed while the other two chosen applications have Weibull distributions. Only the means of the arrival rate change as we vary the parameters. These results lead us closer to the belief that it is possible to abstract the communication properties of parallel applications in convenient mathematical forms that have wide applicability.

The rest of the paper is organized as follows. Section 2 outlines our communication characterization methodology. Section 3 discusses the system parameters under consideration and their expected impact on the communication behavior. Section 4 gives details of the simulated architectural platform and parallel applications, and section 5 presents the performance results from our experiments. Finally, section 6 summarizes the contributions from this work and outlines directions for future research.

2   Communication Characterization Methodology

In our earlier work, we have developed a methodology for characterizing the communication behavior of parallel applications. Since the same strategy is employed for the sensitivity analysis of system parameters on the communication behavior, we revisit the methodology in this section.

The traffic characterization methodology captures the communication behavior of parallel applications in terms of the message generation rate, the spatial distribution and the message volume distribution. Specifically, we have focussed on characterizing the behavior on a 2-D mesh topology using wormhole switching and deterministic XY routing. Note that our approach is applicable to any network and we are merely illustrating using a mesh network. The choice of a 2-D mesh also stems from several recent observations [1, 8] stressing the advantages of lower dimensional networks from the physical realization viewpoint.

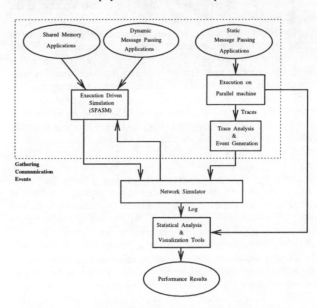

Figure 1: Communication Characterization Methodology

Our workload characterization methodology is outlined in Figure 1. There are three main steps in this approach. The first step is to *gather communication events* from the application. The next step is to take these communication events and *evaluate the performance* on a 2-D mesh network simulator. The final step analyzes the results from the simulation using regression models and statistical techniques to *quantify the temporal, spatial and volume attributes of communication*. The following discussion gives details on each of these three steps.

Step 1: Gathering Communication Events

Our approach uses two strategies to generate communication events (ie. injection of messages into the network) for the network simulator. The first, called the *dynamic strategy*, is employed for applications whose communication behavior can potentially change from one machine to another. Consequently, we cannot afford to pick the communication events from the application execution on an alternate machine and use them to drive the mesh simulator since this would have the same problems as trace-driven simulation [10]. Hence, we resort to an execution-driven simulation of the applications. In an execution-driven simulator, as each communication event is generated, there is also a feedback from the network simulator to the event generator indicating the simulated time for the event (as indicated by the two arrows between the network simulator and the execution-driven simulator in Figure 1). As a result, events are generated and simulated in the correct order.

The other strategy, namely the *static strategy*, is employed for applications whose communication behavior does not change when we move from one machine to another. The order of communication events in the application thus remains the same across hardware platforms. While we could employ the dynamic strategy for these applications as well, we can achieve the same results by exploiting the well-behaved nature of the application using a trace-driven approach. With this approach, we need not pay the high price of simulating the application execution and we can concentrate on the network simulation part. Application execution on a parallel machine would be much faster than simulating the application details.

For the static strategy, we can execute the applications on an available parallel machine and trace the communication events. The traces can then be fed to our 2-D mesh network simulator since the ordering of events provided by the trace would remain the same on all underlying hardware platforms (including our 2-D mesh). But, the time at which a message is injected into our 2-D mesh (time of the event generation) could potentially differ from the time the same message was injected on the alternate machine where the trace was collected. Hence, the timestamp of events in the trace cannot be used in the network simulator directly. However, for the applications that can benefit from the static strategy, the CPU cycles between successive network activities at a node would remain the same across all network platforms, since this is purely a function of the computation in the application which does not vary across network platforms. We can use this information to timestamp the events from the trace to feed into the network simulator (done by the trace analyzer). Incidentally, the traces can be directly fed to our statistical analysis module without passing through the network simulator if we are only interested in obtaining the communication attributes for the execution on the actual parallel machine network (instead of the simulated network). This path is also shown in Figure 1. The reader should note that the static strategy path has not been employed in this study.

Shared memory machines generate a significant amount of induced coherence traffic apart from the inherent communication in the application. Hence the communication behavior can change drastically when we move from one shared memory platform to another. To simplify evaluation of shared memory applications, we have resorted to the dynamic strategy for such cases.

Step 2: Network Performance Evaluation

To characterize the behavior of applications on a specified network, we feed the communication events generated in Step 1 to the corresponding network simulator. A simulation platform gives us the flexibility to study the application behavior over a wide range of system parameters, which is the main motivation behind this study.

The simulation platform that has been chosen for this study is SPASM, a flexible parallel architecture simulator. SPASM can simulate a range of message-passing [22] and shared memory platforms [21]. As with several recent simulators [4, 9, 6], SPASM does not simulate the details of the instruction execution. Instead, it only simulates instructions that may potentially involve network access such as SENDs/RECEIVEs on message passing machines, and LOADs/STOREs on shared memory machines. The rest of the instructions execute at the speed on the native processor. The input to the simulator are applications written in C. The application code is preprocessed to label instructions that need to trap to the simulator, the compiled assembly code is augmented with cycle counting instructions, and the assembled binary is linked with the rest of the simulator modules. For the message passing simulations, the simulated software messaging costs are similar to those experienced on the IBM SP2 (the software overheads amount to $4.63 * 10^{-2}x + 73.42$ microseconds to transfer x bytes of data). For the shared memory simulations, we assume a CC-NUMA architecture employing an invalidation-based cache coherence scheme using a full-map directory. SPASM also allows us to vary the memory consistency model for shared memory platforms.

On both shared memory and message passing platforms, events which involve the network invoke the network simulator with the necessary information (timestamp, source, destination, and message size). The communication events are simulated on our network simulator. Apart from giving detailed execution profiles [21, 22] and average network latencies, the simulator also logs all the network activities which is then fed to our statistical analyzer.

Step 3: Statistical Analysis

To calculate the three communication attributes (inter-arrival time distribution and the corresponding generation rate, spatial distribution, message length distribution), we analyze the log generated by the network simulator. The fields of the log that are of relevance are the time of injection of the message into the network, along with the source, destination and message length information.

We have used the statistical analysis package, SAS [17] for the regression analysis. The package provides a non-linear model with iterative methods for curve-fitting. We have used the multivariate secant method for our study. The procedure takes the input data set and produces an estimate of the parameters and the residual Sums of Squares determined in each iteration. It then fits the non-linear regression models by least squares. The change in the SSE (Sum of Squared Errors) is used as the default convergence criterion, the default value for the change being 10^{-8}. If the convergence criterion is met, the procedure prints the parameter estimates, an asymptotically valid standard error of the estimate, an asymptotic 95% confidence interval for the estimate of the parameter and an asymptotic correlation matrix of the parameters. The predicted values of the dependent variable and the values of the residuals (actual values minus predicted values) can also be obtained.

Modeling Message Generation Behavior: For a given source processor, the log file from the network simulator gives the necessary inputs for inter-arrival times of messages generated by this processor and the number of messages generated for a given destination. The set of data points obtained for the inter-arrival times for each of the processors can be used to obtain the cumulative distribution function (CDF) of the inter-arrival times. This CDF is in turn compared to a known distribution. The data points have been found to be close to each other and hence, we have used known continuous probability distributions for curve fitting. The models used for regression analysis are the equations for CDFs of known distributions like exponential, hypoexponential and Weibull distributions. The best fit has been decided on the basis of the residuals between the actual and predicted values and the width of the 95% confidence interval generated by SAS as a result of the regression analysis.

Modeling Spatial Distribution Behavior: The source, destination tuple from the log files has been used to generate the spatial distribution of messages from a given source processor. We have considered the fraction of total number of messages sent from a given source to each of the destinations. Regression analysis for the spatial distribution function has been done only if the application does not exhibit a uniform distribution. In almost all the cases the distribution was obvious from the histogram of the spatial distribution.

It should be noted that if we analyze an application in detail, it can have different traffic patterns during its execution. It is possible to capture such transient behavior in spatial distribution by collecting message statistics in greater detail. Undoubtedly, the method will be much more cumbersome. In contrast, we have used the overall message count from each processor to every other processor to find the distribution. This gives the average case behavior and should be accurate enough to drive performance models for network simulation.

Modeling Message Length Distribution: For the shared memory applications considered for this study, we have only two fixed size messages (8 bytes for control information and 40 bytes for data information since the cache block size is 32 bytes). Hence, we do not discuss the message length distribution in this paper.

3 System Parameters Under Consideration

As stated in Section 1, we confine ourselves to shared memory systems in this paper. These systems normally tend to rely more on the network performance than their message passing counterparts. However, we briefly discuss the differences we are likely to encounter when we move from shared memory to message passing in [18] using a case study.

The specific parameters that this study focuses on are the number of processors (p), the application problem size (n), the network link bandwidth (b), and the consistency model (c) of the shared memory system. The expected impact of these parameters on the communication behavior of an application is outlined below. On shared memory platforms, message sizes are fixed by the underlying system and on our simulated CC-NUMA machine we have two message sizes, 8 and 40 bytes for control and data transfers. We will confine our discussion to the impact of these parameters on the message generation rate and the spatial distribution.

Number of Processors (p): In an application, the number of computation steps between successive communication steps has a direct correlation to the rate of message injections into the network. As we increase the number of processors employed to solve a given problem size, the computation steps between communication events normally tend to decrease in an application. This effect would increase the message generation rate. However, there is a counteracting effect that can decrease the generation rate when p is increased. If the progress of a CPU is limited by how fast the network can deliver the messages, then the generation rate should decrease (inter-arrival times should increase) when the network latency increases. As we increase p, apart from increasing the

likelihood of traversing more hops in the network, the network contention is also likely to increase. Consequently, the larger latency for message delivery with higher p, would tend to slow down the message generation rate of the CPU. The application characteristics will determine which of these two factors is more dominant in either increasing or decreasing the generation rate.

In terms of the spatial distribution of messages, the impact of p is closely tied to the application characteristics. For applications which employ a static scheduling policy parameterized by p, we do not expect the spatial distribution function to change significantly with p. However, for applications with a very dynamic execution behavior, the spatial distribution can vary with p.

Application Problem Size (n): As with p, the application problem size will have a direct bearing on the computation steps between successive communication events and the average network latency for messages. The relative dominance of these two factors, which in turn depends on an application's characteristics, will influence the changes in inter-arrival times. For the spatial distribution of messages, the same arguments as discussed for the impact of p would apply for n as well.

Incidentally, the reader should note that changes in the application problem size can also help us understand how another architectural parameter, the cache size (which we have not varied explicitly in this paper), can impact the communication characteristics.

Link Bandwidth (b): The bandwidth of a link in the network can be calculated from the flit size and the cycle time it takes to move a flit of a message from one switch to the next. To study the impact of the link bandwidth, we fix the flit size of the network, and vary the network cycle time assuming it takes one network cycle to move a flit from one switch to the next. The link bandwidth (b) is thus inversely proportional to the network cycle time.

As b improves, the average network latency experienced by a message is expected to decrease. Consequently, CPUs that are waiting for a message from another CPU would stall for a shorter time on a faster network before generating the next message. The inter-arrival times of messages into the network is thus expected to decrease for higher b.

Unless an application is extremely sensitive to network bandwidth, we do not expect the spatial distribution of messages to change over practical values of b.

Consistency Model (c): The two memory consistency models that we consider in this study are Sequential Consistency (SC) and Release Consistency (RC). These memory models define the programmer's view of the memory state at different points in the execution. The basic difference between these two models lies in the actions performed when the CPU issues a write. In SC, the CPU is stalled until the write is complete which may involve network actions to invalidate potentially cached copies. Only then is the CPU allowed to proceed. On a RC system, the CPU is not stalled. The write is simply registered in a write buffer, and the CPU is allowed to proceed. Only at a synchronization fence does the CPU stall to ensure that all pending writes in the write buffer are completed. The CPU may however need to stall if the write buffer is full.

Since there are fewer write stalls, we expect the CPU to pump data into the network at a faster rate on a RC system than on a corresponding SC system. The inter-arrival time for message injection into the network is thus likely to decrease for RC. As far as spatial distribution is concerned, we do not expect to see any significant differences between the two consistency models.

4 Experimental Setup

We have used SPASM to simulate a CC-NUMA platform with an invalidation-based protocol and a full-map directory [21, 23]. The parameters for the architectural details used in the simulation are summarized in Table 1. The entire simulation is carried out in terms of CPU cycles. Note that the link bandwidth and write buffer parameters will assume different values when we are studying the impact of these parameters on application behavior.

Cache Access	1 cycle
Memory Access	10 cycles
Message Sizes	8 (control) / 40 (data) bytes
Cache Block Size	32 bytes
Link Bandwidth	1 cycle/byte
Write Buffer	4 entries
Network Interface Buffer	16 entries

Table 1: Simulation Parameters

For this study, we have chosen five shared memory applications (1D-FFT, IS, Cholesky, Maxflow and NBody) with diverse communication characteristics ranging from a well-known regular communication behavior in 1D-FFT to dynamic behavior in applications like Cholesky and Maxflow. A description of these applications is given in [18].

5 Performance Results

The traffic characterization methodology outlined in Section 2 helps us understand the message generation characteristics of each application. The regression analysis performed on the data for the inter-arrival times for message generation allows us to come up with close approximations to the distribution function for the inter-arrival times for all the applications. The known distributions used for regression analysis of the inter-arrival distribution are exponential, with a CDF of $(1 - e^{-x/\theta})$ and Weibull, with a CDF of $(1 - e^{-x/\theta^\beta})$. The means for these distributions are θ and $\theta * \Gamma(1 + 1/\beta)$ respectively. The inter-arrival time and spatial distribution graphs for the five applications are given in Figures 2, 3, 4, 5 and 6 for a 32 processor system. In each of the graphs for the inter-arrival time distribution, the solid line indicates the plot for the actual data points and the dotted line indicates the plot for the fitted distribution. Also, in each of the spatial distribution graphs, the histograms indicate the fraction of the total number of messages sent by a particular processor to each of the other processors indicated on the X-axis. All inter-arrival time graphs as well as spatial distribution graphs have been presented for a representative processor, since the distributions obtained for other processors were identical with only a negligible change in the mean.

In the following discussion, we give a brief description of the tests we have performed, and a summary of the results obtained from the statistical analysis. The reader is referred to [18] for detailed performance results. The results have been organized into four subsections based on the parameter being varied.

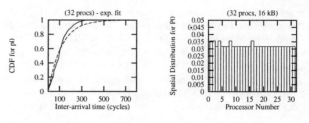

Figure 2: 1D-FFT

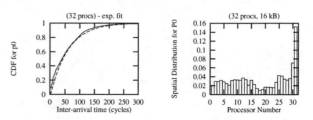

Figure 3: IS

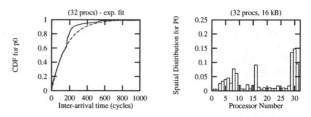

Figure 4: Cholesky

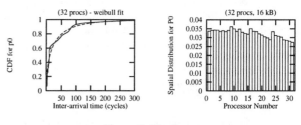

Figure 5: Maxflow

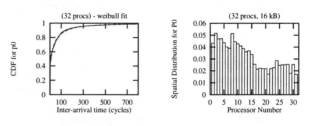

Figure 6: Nbody

5.1 Impact of Varying the Num. of Processors (p)

Increasing p while keeping all other system parameters constant, creates a performance tradeoff that may either result in an increase or decrease in the inter-arrival time of messages. As stated earlier (Section 3), by increasing p, the average network latency for a message is expected to increase while the number of computation steps between successive communication events of a CPU is expected to decrease. These two factors will have contrasting influences on the inter-arrival times of messages into the network. Table 2 shows the fitted distribution functions for the five applications for system sizes of 16 and 32 processors.

In all applications except Maxflow, a higher network latency seems to dominate over any decrease in the number of computation steps between successive communication events of a CPU. This results in an increase in inter-arrival times as p increases. The exception is Maxflow, where the inter-arrival time for processor p0 shows a decrease as shown in Table 2. Since processor p0 serves as the global queue and central distributor of work to all other processors in the Maxflow application (see spatial distribution discussion below), an increase in p results in an increase in the number of accesses to p0. Thus, p0 must satisfy requests more frequently and as a result, its message generation rate increases. However, this decrease in inter-arrival time for Maxflow only appears at p0, while all other nodes experience an increase in inter-arrival time when p increases.

Regardless of whether the inter-arrival time decreases as in Maxflow, or increases as it did for all other applications, our findings show that the same distributions can effectively approximate the CDF as p varies. The only changes necessary, are those made to the distribution means which are shown in Table 2.

	Number of Processors	
Appln.	16	32
1D-FFT	$1 - e^{-x/95.20}$	$1 - e^{-x/117.04}$
IS	$1 - e^{-x/43.32}$	$1 - e^{-x/56.23}$
Cholesky	$1 - e^{-x/140.43}$	$1 - e^{-x/165.21}$
Maxflow	$1 - e^{-x/35.68^{0.78}}$	$1 - e^{-x/22.73^{0.59}}$
Nbody	$1 - e^{-x/23.02^{0.44}}$	$1 - e^{-x/32.48^{0.53}}$

Table 2: Fitted Dist. of Inter-arrival Times Varying p

Due to space constraints, we have shown the spatial distributions for only one system configuration (32 processors) in Figures 2 through 6 and the results for other system sizes are given in [18]. When comparing the spatial distribution plots of each application while varying p, some similarities are observed. Since the 1D-FFT algorithm uses an *all to all* communication regardless of the value of p, a uniform spatial message distribution is expected in all cases and Figure 2 confirms this. In Figure 3, we see that the spatial distribution of IS follows a *favorite processor* pattern. Each logical processor has a favorite processor - the processor with a logical id number equal to one lower than itself modulo the number of processors. For example, in a 32-node system, processor p0 has a favorite processor (p31) which it sends the most messages to. This spatial distribution can be modeled by a bimodal uniform distribution, where for a given processor, a *favorite processor* receives the most messages while other processors in the system receive messages with a uniform distribution. Looking at Figure 4, the dynamic nature of the Cholesky application becomes evident. For Cholesky, the spatial distributions vary for different processors in the system, however, as p varies, the distributions for any single processor seem to follow a similar pattern. For example, the spatial distribution of processor p0 was fitted with a seventh-order polynomial. We are not showing the distributions for other processors due to space limitations. For Maxflow, the

spatial distribution of processor p0 is close to uniform (see Figure 5) while the distribution of all other nodes treat processor p0 as their *favorite processor* since it is the distributor of the workload. Therefore, the distribution of processor p0 can be modeled effectively by a uniform distribution, while all other nodes can be modeled by a bimodal distribution. For Nbody, the spatial distribution for messages seems close to bimodal (see Figure 6) in nature and is independent of p. During execution, processors are assigned to work on different portions of a tree. Probability of communication between processors in a subtree is higher than across subtrees. Since p is not too high, a bimodal distribution results. However, the modality may grow as p and the tree size grow.

5.2 Impact of Varying Problem Size (n)

Simulations of Maxflow, Cholesky, and Nbody for large n require an inordinate amount of time. Consequently, we have restricted ourselves to studying the impact of n to 1D-FFT and IS. To see the effect of varying n on message inter-arrival time and spatial distributions, runs were made with n set to 8K, 16K, 32K and 64K for both applications on a system with 16 processors. Table 3 shows the fitted distributions for the 8K and 64K runs. By comparing the means of the exponential distributions shown in Table 3, we see that as n increases, the average inter-arrival time of messages decreases marginally. The same two factors (computation steps between communication events and the average network latency) encountered with varying p will come into play when we are varying n. For the 1D-FFT and IS applications, communication happens in phases with computation separating these phases. Within a communication phase, n has little influence on increasing the computation steps between successive message generations. However, with larger problems, the injection of messages into the network becomes more skewed resulting in lowering the average network contention experienced by any single message. Consequently, we notice a marginal decrease in inter-arrival times with increasing n. As we predicted earlier, insignificant differences occur in the spatial distribution when n is varied and we have chosen not to show the plots due to space constraints.

	Problem Size	
Appln.	8K	64KK
1D-FFT	$1 - e^{-x/97.34}$	$1 - e^{-x/93.88}$
IS	$1 - e^{-x/44.71}$	$1 - e^{-x/42.54}$

Table 3: Fitted Dist. for Inter-arrival Times (Varying n)

5.3 Impact of Varying Link Bandwidth (b)

	Network Cycle Time in CPU Cycles	
Appln.	0.5	2
1D-FFT	$1 - e^{-x/95.20}$	$1 - e^{-x/242.02}$
IS	$1 - e^{-x/43.32}$	$1 - e^{-x/141.44}$
Cholesky	$1 - e^{-x/140.43}$	$1 - e^{-x/377.58}$
Maxflow	$1 - e^{-x/35.68^{0.78}}$	$1 - e^{-x/122.72^{0.84}}$
Nbody	$1 - e^{-x/23.02^{0.44}}$	$1 - e^{-x/67.53^{0.52}}$

Table 4: Fitted Dist. for Inter-arrival Times (Varying b)

451

By decreasing the network cycle time, b increases. For each application, results for two separate runs are made on a system with 16 processors, varying the value of b for each run. The first run is made on a system with a network cycle equal to half a CPU cycle. In the second run, b was decreased by increasing thea network cycle to 2 CPU cycles. For all applications, the fitted distribution plots closely model the actual data plots and are shown in Table 4. Since the spatial message distributions for the applications did not differ significantly from the results presented in the previous section, we have omitted the graphs due to space constraints. Each figure contains two inter-arrival time plots with network cycle time equal to 0.5 and 2 CPU cycles respectively. Increasing b, reduces the average network latency experienced by a message, and as we mentioned earlier, this results in lower inter-arrival times.

5.4 Impact of Varying Consistency Model (c)

Table 5 shows the fitted inter-arrival time distributions for all the applications for both the Release Consistency (RC) and Sequential Consistency (SC) models. As we expected and stated in Section 3, the spatial distributions are not expected to change when we move from SC to RC which has been confirmed by our experiments. In all applications, the inter-arrival times of messages decrease when using RC. This is mainly due to SC stalling the CPU on a write while the CPU is allowed to continue in RC. Once again, the actual data plots can be modeled by the same distributions as before with slight modifications to the means. For 1D-FFT, IS and Cholesky the exponential distribution with respective means of 88.27, 40.13, 1.55.13 results in the best fit for RC. While the Weibull distribution with means of 32.26 and 20.39 provides the best fits for Maxflow and Nbody, respectively. As the write buffer grows deeper, we expect the message generation rate to increase even more for RC.

	Consistency Model	
Appln.	Release	Sequential
1D-FFT	$1 - e^{-x/88.27}$	$1 - e^{-x/95.20}$
IS	$1 - e^{-x/40.13}$	$1 - e^{-x/43.32}$
Cholesky	$1 - e^{-x/1.55.13}$	$1 - e^{-x/140.43}$
Maxflow	$1 - e^{-x/35.03^{0.84}}$	$1 - e^{-x/35.68^{0.78}}$
Nbody	$1 - e^{-x/21.559^{0.47}}$	$1 - e^{-x/23.02^{0.44}}$

Table 5: Fitted Dist. for Inter-arrival Times (Varying c)

5.5 Summary of Performance Results

As we intuitively predict in Section 3, and as our above results show, the spatial message distributions of the applications in this study do not significantly change with respect to variations in the parameters (p, n, b and c) we consider. Except for Cholesky, which required a seventh order polynomial fit, all other spatial distributions could be easily gleaned from the histograms. We uniformly observe that the message inter-arrival times are susceptible to variations in the above parameters and the distribution functions remain the same while only the means for these functions vary. We also find, that some parameters have a larger influence on message inter-arrival times than others. For instance, decreasing the link bandwidth (increasing the network cycle time) results in substantial increases in the inter-arrival time of messages. For all the applications, message inter-arrival times increase over 100 percent when the network cycle time increases from 0.5 to 2 CPU cycles. Changes of this magnitude are not visible for variations

in the other parameters we test. However, regardless of whether the parameters cause moderate or significant changes in the inter-arrival time, the known distribution functions appear to be robust, and can be used to model the communication characteristics of all the applications in our study. Knowing that the underlying distributions remain the same, we can vary the mean of these distributions to capture the worst and best case scenarios of the workload. These results are encouraging since one can use the mathematical distributions for generating the message arrival and distribution statistics for diverse architectural evaluations.

6 Concluding Remarks

Performance evaluation of multiprocessors via analytical modeling or simulation is often accused of being highly inaccurate due to unrealistic workload assumptions. Specifically, exponential inter-arrival time and uniform message destination distributions, used frequently in many model-based studies, are believed to be grossly over-simplified. A strong belief in the architecture community is that it is probably impossible to quantify the communication behavior of parallel applications mathematically. Actual execution or execution-driven simulations have thus been considered to be the only viable approaches to studying multiprocessor performance. While accuracy and trustworthiness of these evaluation methods are unquestionable, the methods suffer from limited applicability, high cost and inability to evaluate emerging architectures. On the other hand, we are not aware of any research effort to characterize the communication properties of parallel applications in terms of the temporal, spatial and volume attributes. It is possible that interprocessor communication in real applications closely matches some known distribution functions, which can be captured in an analytical or simulation model. Any such knowledge of communication workloads would be widely useful in several research areas apart from making model-based evaluation more accurate,

For confidence in the communication properties expressed by the three attributes (temporal, spatial and volume), it is essential to show that the basic distribution functions are robust to architectural variations. Otherwise, the workload characterization results are of limited use. In this paper, we have attempted to address this issue by analyzing the sensitivity of the communication workload with respect to four parameters, namely, the number of processors, problem size, network bandwidth and memory consistency models. The underlying network for this research is a 2-D mesh that supports wormhole switching and deterministic routing. The execution of five shared memory programs have been simulated on SPASM. From the simulation, the network events have been logged and fed to a statistical package, SAS, to find the message generation rate and spatial distribution using regression analysis.

The results obtained from the regression analysis show that the message inter-arrival and message destination distributions can be closely approximated by known statistical distributions and that the temporal as well as spatial distributions of all applications remain unchanged with respect to the variations in the four parameters considered. 1D-FFT, IS and Cholesky inter-arrival times are exponentially distributed while Maxflow and Nbody have Weibull distribution. Only the means of the arrival times change as we vary the parameters.

Our results make significant pronouncements since they move us closer to the belief that it is possible to abstract the communication properties of parallel applications in convenient mathematical forms that have wide applicability. Although not very exhaustive, we believe that this study will be able to fill in some of the missing links in the study of multiprocessor networks and parallel applications. Also, this study has suggested several interesting directions for future research:

- First, we would like to augment our application suite to include more diverse application domains such as databases. We would like to extend this study to explore the impact of other shared memory parameters such as cache size and cache coherence protocols and verify if the distribution functions remain the same across these parameters also.

- In this paper, we have confined ourselves to shared memory systems. Our ongoing work is investigating how the results would change when we move an application to a message passing system. A problem we are encountering is that there are very few applications currently available that have both a shared memory and a message passing version. The onus is on us to implement one version when the other is available in the public domain.

  It may happen that drastic changes in the underlying architecture, like the ones mentioned above, can change even the distribution function (not just the mean). But it would be nice to find out if we can still make some general statements about how the distribution functions will change.

- Due to cost-effectiveness, Network of Workstations (NOW) are becoming increasingly popular as parallel computing engines. We would like to incorporate such environments into our communication characterization methodology. The results from our study can be used as workloads to evaluate the suitability of emerging network platforms such as ATM and Myrinet for parallel computing. They can also be used to evaluate the capability of the software messaging layers in handling the traffic generated by parallel applications on NOW environments.

References

[1] A. Agarwal. Limits on Interconnection Network Performance. *IEEE Transactions on Parallel and Distributed Systems*, 2(4):398–412, October 1991.

[2] D. Bailey et al. The NAS Parallel Benchmarks. *International Journal of Supercomputer Applications*, 5(3):63–73, 1991.

[3] L. N. Bhuyan and X. Zhang, editors. *Mutliprocessor Performance Measurement and Evaluation*. IEEE Computer Socitey Press, 1994. Tutorial.

[4] E. A. Brewer, C. N. Dellarocas, A. Colbrook, and W. E. Weihl. PROTEUS : A high-performance parallel-architecture simulator. Technical Report MIT-LCS-TR-516, Massachusetts Institute of Technology, Cambridge, MA 02139, September 1991.

[5] S. Chodnekar, V. Srinivasan, A. Vaidya, A. Sivasubramaniam, and C. Das. Towards a communication characterization methodology for parallel applications. In *Proceedings of the Third International Symposium on High Performance Computer Architecture*, pages 310–319, February 1997.

[6] R. G. Covington, S. Madala, V. Mehta, J. R. Jump, and J. B. Sinclair. The Rice parallel processing testbed. In *Proceedings of the ACM SIGMETRICS 1988 Conference on Measurement and Modeling of Computer Systems*, pages 4–11, Santa Fe, NM, May 1988.

[7] R. Cypher, A. Ho, S. Konstantinidou, and P. Messina. Architectural requirements of parallel scientific applications with explicit communication. In *Proceedings of the 20th Annual International Symposium on Computer Architecture*, pages 2–13, May 1993.

[8] W. J. Dally. Performance analysis of k-ary n-cube interconnection networks. *IEEE Transactions on Computer Systems*, 39(6):775–785, June 1990.

[9] H. Davis, S. R. Goldschmidt, and J. L. Hennessy. Multiprocessor Simulation and Tracing Using Tango. In *Proceedings of the 1991 International Conference on Parallel Processing*, pages II 99–107, 1991.

[10] S. R. Goldschmidt and J. L. Hennessy. The accuracy of trace-driven simulations of multiprocessors. In *Proceedings of the ACM SIGMETRICS 1993 Conference on Measurement and Modeling of Computer Systems*, pages 146–157, May 1993.

[11] J.-M. Hsu and P. Banerjee. Performance Measurement and Trace Driven Simulation of Parallel CAD and Numeric Applications on a Hypercube Multicomputer. In *Proc. 17th Annual Intl. Symp. on Computer Architecture*, pages 260–269, 1990.

[12] A. Kumar and L. N. Bhuyan. Evalutaing Virtual Channels for Cache-Coherent Shared-Memory Multiprocessors. In *Proceedings of the ACM 1996 International Conference on Supercomputing*, May 1996.

[13] PARKBENCH Committee. *Public International Benchmarks for Parallel Computers*, February 1994. Report–1, assembled by R. Hockney and M. Berry.

[14] R. Ponnusamy, R. Thakur, A. Choudhary, K. Velamakanni, Z. Bozkus, and G. Fox. Experimental performance evaluation of the CM-5. *Journal of Parallel and Distributed Computing*, 19:192–202, 1993.

[15] U. Ramachandran, G. Shah, S. Ravikumar, and J. Muthukumarasamy. Scalability study of the KSR-1. In *Proceedings of the 1993 International Conference on Parallel Processing*, pages I–237–240, August 1993.

[16] S. K. Reinhardt et al. The Wisconsin Wind Tunnel : Virtual prototyping of parallel computers. In *Proceedings of the ACM SIGMETRICS 1993 Conference on Measurement and Modeling of Computer Systems*, pages 48–60, Santa Clara, CA, May 1993.

[17] SAS Institute Inc., Cary, NC 27512. *SAS/STAT User's Guide*, 1988.

[18] D. Seed, A. Sivasubramaniam, and C. Das. Communication in Parallel Applications: Characterization and Sensitivity Analysis. Technical Report CSE-96-055, Dept. of Computer Science and Engineering, The Pennsylvania State University, November 1996.

[19] J. P. Singh, E. Rothberg, and A. Gupta. Modeling communication in parallel algorithms: A fruitful interaction between theory and systems? In *Proceedings of the Sixth Annual ACM Symposium on Parallel Algorithms and Architectures*, 1994.

[20] J. P. Singh, W-D. Weber, and A. Gupta. SPLASH: Stanford Parallel Applications for Shared-Memory. Technical Report CSL-TR-91-469, Computer Systems Laboratory, Stanford University, 1991.

[21] A. Sivasubramaniam, A. Singla, U. Ramachandran, and H. Venkateswaran. An Approach to Scalability Study of Shared Memory Parallel Systems. In *Proceedings of the ACM SIGMETRICS 1994 Conference on Measurement and Modeling of Computer Systems*, pages 171–180, May 1994.

[22] A. Sivasubramaniam, A. Singla, U. Ramachandran, and H. Venkateswaran. A Simulation-based Scalability Study of Parallel Systems. *Journal of Parallel and Distributed Computing*, 22(3):411–426, September 1994.

[23] A. Sivasubramaniam, A. Singla, U. Ramachandran, and H. Venkateswaran. On characterizing bandwidth requirements of parallel applications. In *Proceedings of the ACM SIGMETRICS 1995 Conference on Measurement and Modeling of Computer Systems*, pages 198–207, May 1995.

[24] J. E. Veenstra and R. J. Fowler. MINT: A Front End for Efficient Simulation of Shared Memory Multiprocessors. In *Proceedings of MASCOTS '94*, pages 201–207, February 1994.

[25] D. L. Willick and D. L. Eager. An analytic model for multistage interconnection networks. In *Proceedings of the ACM SIGMETRICS 1990 Conference on Measurement and Modeling of Computer Systems*, pages 192–202, May 1990.

How Much Does Network Contention Affect Distributed Shared Memory Performance?*

Donglai Dai   and   Dhabaleswar K. Panda

Dept. of Computer and Information Science

The Ohio State University, Columbus, OH 43210-1277

{dai,panda}@cis.ohio-state.edu

Abstract

Most of recent research on distributed shared memory (DSM) systems have focused on either careful design of node controllers or cache coherence protocols. While evaluating these designs, simplified models of networks (constant latency or average latency based on the network size) are typically used. Such models completely ignore network contention. To help network designers to design better networks for DSM systems, in this paper, we focus on two goals: 1) to isolate and quantify the impact of network link contention and network interface contention on the overall performance of DSM applications and 2) to study the impact of critical architectural parameters on these two categories of network contention. We achieve these goals by evaluating a set of SPLASH2 benchmarks on a DSM simulator using three network models. For an 8 × 8 wormhole system, our results show that network contention can degrade performance up to 59.8%. Out of this, up to 7.2% is caused by network interface contention alone. The study indicates that network contention becomes dominant for DSM systems using small caches, wide cache line sizes, low degrees of associativity, high processing node speeds, high memory speeds, low network speeds, or small network link widths.

1 Introduction

Long memory latency has been a lead impediment to achieving the full performance potential of DSM systems. Besides the speed gap between a processor and memory, two dominant factors in such long latency are: 1) overhead of the cache coherence protocol and 2) delays in the underlying communication network. Previous research in DSMs has mostly concentrated on techniques useful for designing better node architectures, protocol controllers, efficient coherence protocols at different levels in the system or applications, etc. Almost all of these evaluations are based on the assumption of a point-to-point communication network with some fixed (constant or a function of the network diameter) latency. Representative examples include various memory consistency models [5], integrated or decoupled protocol controllers [5, 7, 12]. However, it has been reported [10] that network latency is becoming a key architectural bottleneck in designing large scale DSM systems after integrating several of the above techniques.

It is well known that network latency contains two components: minimal latency and contention delays. The former is largely defined by the state of technology in circuit speed and switch design. Contention delays are caused by limited resources related to the network. Current and next generation networks promise to exploit performance aggressively by using different kinds of adaptive routing [11] in addition to higher speed. The essence behind these communication innovations is to reduce network contention. However, several fundamental questions about the potential performance gain by employing advanced network communication mechanisms in DSM systems remain unanswered. In this paper, we take on this challenge and study the problem of quantifying network contention in DSM systems. Specifically, we aim to answer the following questions: 1) how much does network contention affect the performance of DSM systems having more than a dozen processors? 2) how and to what extent does network contention change under different cache organizations, memory systems, processor speeds, network speeds, and link widths?

To address these questions, we first classify the types of potential network contention and point out the shortcomings of existing network models to capture these contention. To fix the these shortcomings, we propose a methodology consisting of three network models to isolate and evaluate the effect of contention occurring at the network interface and within the network respectively. Based on this methodology, we present a comprehensive and in-depth quantitative analysis on network contention using four SPLASH2 [6] benchmark applications. For an 8 × 8 system, the results show that network contention can degrade overall performance of DSM applications by up to 59.8%. Out of this, less than 7.2% is caused by network interface contention, implying that the contention inside the network is a dominant component of the increase in network latency. We also evaluate the effect of network contention when major architectural parameters are varied. It is shown that smaller caches, larger cache lines, lower set associativity, higher processing node speeds, higher memory speeds, lower network speeds and narrower networks can significantly increase the effect of network contention on application performance. These results indicate that

---

*This research is supported in part by NSF Grant MIP-9309627 and NSF Career Award MIP-9502294.

variations of these architectural parameters need to be evaluated together with detailed modeling of network components to derive realistic guidelines for designing new generation DSM systems. This study also suggests that there exists great potential to improve the performance of current and future generation DSM systems by developing techniques for reducing network contention.

The rest of the paper is organized as follows. Section 2 characterizes components of network contention in DSM systems. Section 3 provides a methodology for evaluating network contention. Details of simulation environment are discussed in Section 4. Simulation results and discussions are presented in Section 5. Related work is reviewed in Section 6. Concluding remarks are made in Section 7.

2 Network Contention in DSMs

Let us consider the transmission of a message (request or reply) from one node to another in a CC-NUMA DSM system, as illustrated in Fig. 1(a). Various resources are required for this to succeed. First, space must be available for the message to be constructed in the sending buffer at the sender's network interface. Such space may not be available because of a number of reasons such as: 1) disparity between the processing rates of the node controller and the network interface, 2) link contention between messages in some part of the network. *Sending buffer contention* is said to occur when a message is blocked due to the lack of such space.

Let us consider a wormhole-routed network [11], as used in current generation CC-NUMA DSM systems like SGI Origin. Once a message has been generated, an *injection channel* must be obtained to copy the message flit by flit into the associated router. The message may have to wait when the injection channels are being used by other messages. Such a scenario is referred to as *injection channel contention*.

The entire message moves flit by flit in a pipelined fashion and holds links and the associated buffers in the network. Handshaking flow control signals are used along each link to advance the flits. As the header flit of the message passes through each router along its path, the router must make a routing decision and reserve the corresponding outgoing link for the remaining flits. If the outgoing link is not available, the message will be blocked in the network. This is known as *link contention* (or *virtual channel contention* if multiple virtual channels share a single physical link).

In case multiple virtual channels share a physical link, if more than one virtual channel has flits ready for transfer, the physical link is multiplexed among the channels (*demand-multiplexing*). This effectively reduces the moving rate of each message involved. We refer to this scenario as *physical link contention*.

After the header flit of the message arrives at the destination, a consumption channel in the network interface of the destination node must be obtained to copy the message from the router into the network interface. Again, the message may be blocked when the consumption channels are being used by other messages. This is known as *consumption channel contention*.

Finally, a receiving buffer in the destination's network interface must be obtained to assemble the entire message before it can be delivered to the node controller. If there is no receiving buffer available, the message will again be blocked. This is known as *receiving buffer contention*.

Clearly, the communication time of a message can be significantly affected by any of the above types of contention. However, due to the temporal nature, it is usually very difficult to measure the effect of the network contention on a real DSM machine. Some analytical contention models have been used before. However, the accuracy lost in the analytical models, caused by ignoring the crucial dependency between computation and communication in an application, remains unclear. This leaves simulation as the most plausible approach for quantifying contention.

Due to the complexity of modeling a network, most research in DSMs has ignored network contention partially or entirely. In the WWT [7] and the Typhoon [12] simulators, a constant network latency of 100 processor cycles is assigned for every message independent of the length of the message, the distance traveled, and other traffic in the network. A DSM simulator used in the Stanford FLASH [8] research group models network interfaces. The network latency of every message is calculated based on the length of the message and half of the diameter of the network. None of these DSM simulators has modeled the channel contention or physical link contention. Our results (in Section 5) show that these types of contention inside the network dominate the overall network contention. In next section, we propose some modifications to these network models which can provide us useful information about the types of network contention.

3 Methodology for Modeling Network Contention

The basic idea of our methodology is to construct a series of network models. Each of these simulates the network at an increasing level of detail and is driven by the same DSM node and memory simulator using exactly the same input. Comparing the predicted performance metrics of any two such DSM simulators, the difference tells us the effect of types of contention which are modeled by the more sophisticated simulator. Specifically, we construct a series of three network models as described below. The relations among these models are shown in Fig. 1(b).

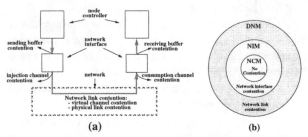

(a)   **(b)**

Figure 1: (a) Various types of network contention in a CC-NUMA system and (b) relations among the network models.

No-Contention Network Model (NCM): This model is an enhancement of the network model used in the original WWT simulator [7]. It assumes: 1) infinite number of sending buffers, 2) infinite number of injection channels, 3) infinite number of consumption channels, 4) infinite number of receiving buffers, and 5) no traffic interference inside the network. These assumptions guarantee that no network contention can ever occur during any communication. Unlike the WWT, in our model each message is delayed by exactly the total time for construction, network propagation, and consumption. The construction time and consumption time vary depending on the length of the message. The network propagation time is a function of both the length and the distance traveled by the message.

Interface Only Network Model (NIM): The NIM model is an enhancement of the network model used in the FLASH project [8]. The NIM model simulates detailed management of the limited number of sending buffers, receiving buffers, injection channels, and consumption channels. The NIM model still assumes no traffic interference inside the network. Such a model captures the types of contention occurring within a network interface. For every message, if there is no contention within a network interface, the message is delayed in this model by exactly the same amount of time as in the NCM model. It is clear that any difference in the predicted performance between this model and the NCM model is caused by contention occurring inside the network interfaces during application execution.

Detailed Network Model (DNM): This model simulates the detailed management of transmission links and intermediate switches, in addition to the network interface. The flow control mechanism used by the network must be modeled as closely as possible. For every message that is not involved in contention inside the network, the message is delayed by exactly the same amount of time as in the NIM model. Such a model captures all types of contention within the network interfaces and every part of the network. It is clear that any difference in the predicted performance between this model and the NCM model is caused by contention occurring in the entire network (including the network interfaces). Any difference in the predicted

performance between this model and the NIM model is caused by contention occurring inside network alone (excluding the network interfaces).

4 Simulation Environment

To apply the above methodology for quantifying the network contention, we have simulated a DSM machine similar to the FLASH [5] but with some important differences described later. In this section, we describe the specific DSM implementation used for collecting the results under different network models. We also outline the *baseline system configuration* and the benchmark applications used.

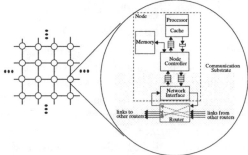

Figure 2: The CC-NUMA architecture simulated.

4.1 The Simulated Architecture

The architecture of the CC-NUMA system we simulated is illustrated in Fig. 2. It has 64 processing nodes. The processor in each node is assumed to be a 200 MHz single-issue microprocessor with a perfect instruction cache and a 128 KB 2-way set associative data cache with a line size of 16 bytes. The cache operates in dual-port mode using write-allocate write-back policies. The instruction latencies, issue rules, and memory interface are modeled based on the DLX design [9]. The memory bus is 8 bytes wide. On a memory block access, the first word of the block is returned in 30 processor cycles (150 ns). The successive words in the block follow in a pipelined fashion. The machine uses a full-mapped, invalidation-based, three-state directory coherence protocol [5]. The node simulator models the internal structures, the queuing and contention at the node controller, main memory, and cache. The queues for network messages contain eight entries each. So does the incoming queue of the processor/cache. All other queues contain a single entry each [4]. Following the assumptions used in [10], the node controller incurs a small fixed occupancy for purely generating/receiving a message. The node controller at the home node of a remote request/response incurs a higher fixed occupancy, because data (in most cases) and directory information must be retrieved and manipulated. In such a case, the memory access is assumed to proceed in parallel with the node controller. The node controller also incurs extra occupancy per invalidation sent. In a scenario where the processor of a node has a load/store miss to a clean block whose home node is the node itself, we assume the memory module can be pipelined with the cache. Thus, the block retrieval, directory manipulation, and cache filling are overlapped. The above architectural features correspond to representative current generation CC-NUMA systems. Table 1 summarizes the system parameters used in our baseline configuration.

Table 1: Default system parameters used in simulation.

Memory Hierarchy Parameters	
Processor frequency	200MHz
Cache access	1 cycle
Cache line size (L)	16 bytes
Cache set associativity	2
Cache size per node	128 Kbytes
Memory word width (W)	8 bytes/cycle
Memory response delay	30 cycles
Cache block fill time	30+L/W cycles
Memory block access time	30+L/W cycles
Node Controller Occupancy	
Directory check	7 cycles
Directory check and update	14 cycles
Each invalidation request	12 cycles
Message forward	3 cycles
Network Interface Parameters	
Outgoing message startup ($T_{outgoing}$)	15 cycles
Incoming message dispatch ($T_{incoming}$)	8 cycles
Control message size	6 bytes
Data message size	22 bytes
Network Parameters	
Network frequency	200MHz
Channel width / Flit size	2 bytes
Link Propagation (T_{link})	1 network cycle
Router switch delay (T_{sw})	1 network cycle
Routing time (T_{rout})	4 network cycles

The major difference between our simulated architecture and the FLASH architecture is as follows: sequential memory consistency, instead of the release memory consistency, is enforced by the coherence protocol. A load/store miss stalls the processor until the first word of data is returned. Therefore, at most one outstanding request can be issued by a processor.

4.2 Implementing Network Models

We assume the nodes in the machine are connected with a pair of virtual networks sharing a physical 2D 8×8 wormhole network [11]. The physical network is assumed to operate at a frequency of 200 MHz. The rest of this section describes the implementation of each network model in detail.

No-Contention Network Model (NCM): The NCM model takes a message from the source node controller and informs the node controller at the destination node that a message has arrived after a time delay equal to the calculated network latency of the message. The network latency of a message is calculated as:

$$latency = T_{outgoing} + (T_{rout} + T_{link}) * distance + (T_{sw} + T_{link}) * length + T_{incoming}$$

where *distance* is the number of hops from the source to the destination, and *length* is the length of the message in flits. $T_{outgoing}$ is the time delay for a message to be constructed by the network interface. T_{rout} is the time needed for a router to make a routing decision based on its knowledge about the network and the requirement of a message contained in the header flit. T_{link} is the time for any flit of a message to propagate over a single physical link. T_{sw} is the time for a non-header flit of a message to pass through a router. The parameters used in our simulation for these network delays are listed in Table 1. In order to guarantee FIFO delivery between a source-destination pair, end-to-end flow control is enforced. It is to be noted that the incoming/outgoing network queues at a network interface are ignored in this model.

Interface Only Network Model (NIM): This model takes into account detailed timing and contention delays associated with structures such as the sending buffers, receiving buffers, injection channels, and consumption channels within the network interface. As discussed in Section 3, for a node to send a message, a space in the sending buffer must be reserved for $T_{outgoing}$ time to construct the message. Once the message is constructed, if there is an injection channel available, it is reserved for $(T_{link} + T_{sw}) * length$ amount of time to pump the entire message into the network. At exactly $(T_{link} + T_{rout}) * distance$ time after the header flit of the message is injected into the network at the network interface of the source node, a consumption channel and a space in the receiving buffer at the network interface of the destination node is reserved for $(T_{link} + T_{sw}) * length$ time. Once the message has been consumed entirely into the receiving buffer, the node controller at the receiving node is informed about its arrival after $T_{incoming}$ amount of time. In case any of the above reservations can not succeed (because of other messages to the network), the message can not move forward and continues to hold the resources it has acquired. Such a network model guarantees the FIFO property of message delivery between each pair of nodes if there is only one injection and one consumption channel at each network interface.

Detailed Network Model (DNM): This model takes into account the internal structures such as data links, channel buffers, signal lines, etc., within and between the routers, in addition to the network interface. It accurately models the mechanisms for wormhole switching [11] such as: distributed routing, book-keeping on channel status, and flit-level asynchronous ready/empty handshaking. In this model, when a message is first injected into the network, the header flit of the message reserves the channels in the routers for the remaining flits of the message, while moving forward along its path from the source to the destination. When the header moves into a router, a delay of T_{rout}

is incurred for the routing decision. If the (desired) outgoing channel (decided by the routing scheme) is available, the header flit reserves that channel and reaches the next router after a time elapse of T_{link}. Each non-header flit of the message can move forward only when its immediate predecessor has already moved as detected using the asynchronous handshaking signals. Every non-header flit incurs a latency of T_{sw} at every router and T_{link} at every link on the path to the message destination. The tail flit of the message releases the previous channel when it leaves each router. When two virtual channels over the same physical link are both transmitting messages, the physical link is demand-multiplexed, resulting in slowdown of both messages. This model guarantees the FIFO property of message delivery between each pair of nodes under the dimension order routing scheme.

4.3 Applications

We used four SPLASH2 [6] benchmark programs presented in Table 2 to drive our simulation environment. These applications were compiled by *dlxcc* using the optimization level equivalent to O2 of *gcc*. We used the default mapping and scheduling policies built into these application codes.

Table 2: Applications and default problem sizes.

Appl.	Comm. Pattern	Problem Size
Barnes	irregular hierarchical	2048 particles, $\theta = 1.0$ 4 time steps
LU	one-to-many regular	256×256 doubles 8×8 blocks
Radix	all-to-all irregular	262144 keys, 512 radix max 524288
Water	neighboring irregular	512 molecules 4 time steps

5 Simulation Results and Discussion

We now present and discuss the results of our simulation study. All results are reported using the total execution time, normalized to the time predicted by the NCM simulator using the baseline configuration for the same application. Each such time is further broken down into four categories: processor computation time (Comput), read stall time (Read), write stall time (Write), and synchronization stall time (Synch). We first evaluate the contention the contention for the baseline system. Next we study the impact of cache organization, memory system, node speed, and network parameters on network contention. In order to isolate their impact, we vary these parameters one at a time with respect to the baseline configuration.

5.1 Network Contention in Baseline System

Figure 3 shows the execution time of each application on the baseline configuration using the NCM, NIM, and DNM model, respectively. As expected, network contention slows down every application. However, the exact effect depends on the application, ranging from 5.3%

(in Water) to 16.8% (in Radix). Radix incurs such high network contention because of the all-to-all irregular communication occurring during its histogram merge phase. It is clear that network contention enlarges the stalling time of each category in every application. The results show that contention within the network interface alone only accounts for a small portion of the total contention, less than 0.84% in our experiments. In other words, contention inside the network is the dominant cause of higher network latency. This observation remains true for all our experiments.

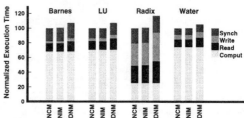

Figure 3: Overall execution time and its breakdown on the baseline system for three different network models.

5.2 Impact of Cache Organization

Let us now examine the impact of alternate cache designs on the network contention. Specifically, we performed experiments by changing the cache size, line size, and set associativity.

Effect of Cache Size per Processing Node: Figure 4 shows the normalized execution times and their breakdowns for the systems with 32KB, 64KB, 128KB, and 256KB cache per node, respectively. Two observations are noteworthy. First, as the cache size increases, the network contention in each application reduces to a constant amount (approximately). This is because when cache is large enough, the largest working set for an application can fit into the cache completely. Our results show that even in such a case the slowdown caused by network contention ranges from 4.8% (in Water) to 16.8% (in Radix). This also shows that our baseline configuration gives us a rather conservative estimate of the network contention[1]. Second, when the cache size decreases, the network contention becomes more significant. The primary reason for this is the extra traffic in the network caused by cache capacity misses. This is true even when the smallest working set of an application still fits in the cache.

Effect of Cache Line Size: Figure 5 shows the execution times for the systems with 128 KB cache per node and cache line size of 16, 32, 64, and 128 bytes, respectively. As the cache line grows larger, the network contention in all application shows the bath-tub behavior, i.e., first de-

---

[1] This is because the baseline configuration assumes a cache size large enough to hold the largest working set of any of the applications we used. This represents a system that generates very little cache-capacity miss traffic and therefore *underestimates* network contention.

creasing to a pollution point and then increasing significantly. The surprising discovery from these results is that the pollution point is relatively small, around 32 or 64 bytes per line, for three out of the four applications. The reason for this is as follows. When the cache line increases, the reply messages which contain data grow longer. The length increase in this type of message causes increase in the time required for transmitting them, thus longer time is spent on the links and routers, causing more network contention. Such an effect not only slows down a message of this type, but also increases the latency of messages of other types.

Similar to a uniprocessor system, longer cache line exploits spatial locality existing in an application at the cost of reducing the benefits of temporal locality. The effect of data pre-fetching because of longer cache line can reduce the number of cache misses. However, the increase in cache line size does not reduce the number of messages by proportion after when the lines size is long enough. In DSM, this leads to an increase in overall volume of network traffic because of unnecessary data pre-fetching results in more network contention and the network latency increases explosively. Such an effect can be observed by examining the difference between the results of NCM and DNM models for Radix: the proportion of the network latency in the overall execution time grows from 19.6% for a 32 byte cache line, to 34.7% for a 64 byte cache line, and to 59.8% for a 128 byte cache line. The reason that Radix shows this effect with smaller cache lines compared to other applications is because the communication to computation ratio is higher in this application.

Effect of Cache Associativity: The execution times of the applications when the cache is organized as direct-mapped, 2-way, and 4-way associative are shown in Fig. 6. When the set associativity is equal to or greater than 2, the proportion of network contention remains almost constant in each application. When the cache is organized as direct-mapped, the proportion of network contention increases in all applications because the cache mapping conflicts increase the network traffic. Our experiments show that a 9.1% (Barnes), 12.4% (LU), 21.1% (Radix), 6.6% (Water) performance degradation occurs for a direct-mapped cache of size 128KB.

In summary, network contention is sensitive to the design choices of cache in a node. This is especially true for cache line size selection. Overall, alternative cache designs other than our baseline configuration tend to increase the impact of network contention in a DSM system.

5.3 Impact of Memory System

We focused on two primary components in designing memory systems for DSM: memory response time and memory bus width.

Effect of Memory Response Time: Memory response time is the time interval from the issue of memory access command to the time when the first word in a memory block is available for use. The experimental results shown in Fig. 7 correspond to three different response times: 20, 30, and 40 processor cycles. As much as 7.4% performance degradation occurs in Barnes, 7.9% in LU, 22.2% in Radix, and 3.1% in Water for a memory response time of 20 processor clock cycles. As the memory responds faster, the network contention increases slightly in all applications because the request and reply messages are generated in a shorter time, resulting in greater traffic congestion in the network.

Effect of Memory Bus Width: Memory bus width dictates the amount of time needed for finishing an access to a memory block after the first word is available. Our experimental results show that as the memory bus becomes wider, the network contention barely changes in each application because of the availability of efficient memory pipelining. Due to lack of space, we are not able to include these results here. Interested readers are requested to refer [4] for more details.

Overall, our study indicates that when the memory module becomes faster in a node, the network contention increases. Between memory response time and memory bus width, the former has a stronger impact on the network contention.

5.4 Effect of Node Speed

In this section, we examine the impact of node speed on the network contention. Our CC-NUMA system is assumed to use an integrated node controller. Therefore, when the node speed increases, all parts in a node (processor, cache, memory, node controller, and network interface) are assumed to become faster proportionately. The results in Fig. 8 show that the network contention increases considerably in most application as the node speed increases. Specifically, the performance degradation because of network contention worsens from 5.3% to 11.3% in Barnes, 5.3% to 7.9% in LU, 16.9% to 22.2% in Radix, and 3.1% to 3.2% in Water, as the node speed increases from 100MHz to 400MHz. The reason for this is, again, that the network is stressed in trying to cope with more traffic generated by the faster processor in a given amount of time.

5.5 Impact of Network Parameters

In this section, we examine the impact of network design (network speed and network link width) on the network contention.

Effect of Network Speed: Not surprisingly, as can be observed from the results shown in Fig. 9, the network contention is significantly worse in a slower network than that in a faster network. Our results show that performance degradation changes from 4.8% to 11.4% in Barnes,

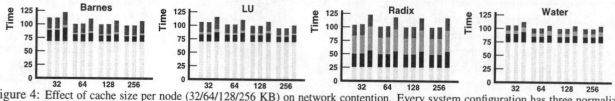

Figure 4: Effect of cache size per node (32/64/128/256 KB) on network contention. Every system configuration has three normalized execution times (from left to right) corresponding to the NCM, NIM, and DNM model, respectively. The breakdown of the execution time is similar to the ones used in Fig. 3.

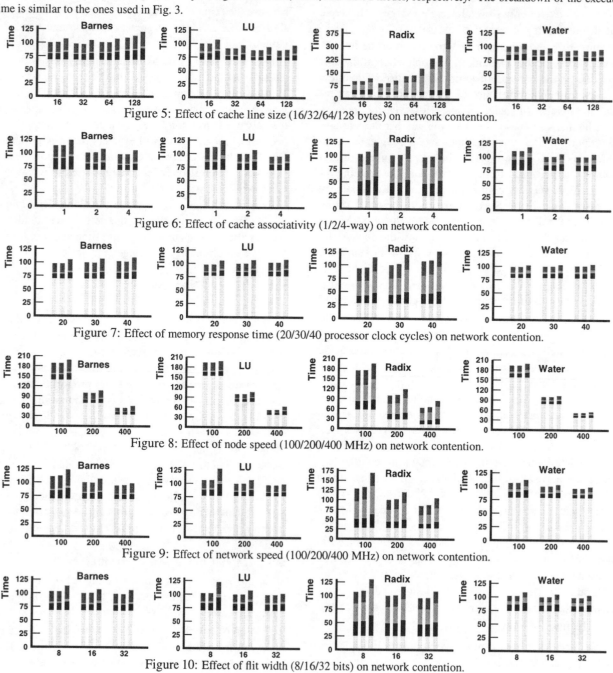

Figure 5: Effect of cache line size (16/32/64/128 bytes) on network contention.

Figure 6: Effect of cache associativity (1/2/4-way) on network contention.

Figure 7: Effect of memory response time (20/30/40 processor clock cycles) on network contention.

Figure 8: Effect of node speed (100/200/400 MHz) on network contention.

Figure 9: Effect of network speed (100/200/400 MHz) on network contention.

Figure 10: Effect of flit width (8/16/32 bits) on network contention.

2.1% to 19.9% in LU, 23.7% to 32.2% in Radix, and 2.7% to 5.6% in Water, as the network speed changes from 400MHz to 100MHz.

Effect of Network Link Width: As expected, from the results shown in Fig. 10, the network contention is significantly worse in a network with narrow links than in a network with wider links. For example, the performance degradation increases from 7.2% to 9.5% in Barnes, 2.8% to 20.1% in LU, 12.9% to 29.0% in Radix, and 4.4% to 6.9% in Water, as the network width reduces from 32 to 8 bits.

In general, a higher bandwidth network does reduce the network contention. However, considering the commonly used narrow links and slower networks in DSM systems, network contention remains an important factor for designing high-performance machines.

6 Related Work

Two most popular network models in DSM research are the constant latency model and the average latency model, as used in the WWT [7] and the FLASH [5, 8] projects. As mentioned before, these models do not provide useful insights into the effect of network contention on DSM system performance. A set of network simulation models for DSM systems have been proposed in [1] to show the tradeoff between accuracy and efficiency of network simulation. However, in this paper, our focus has been to isolate and quantify various types of network contention and study their impact on the overall DSM system performance under a set of design choices. Since network contention remains an important factor in designing DSM systems, in a separate paper, we have proposed a set of useful guidelines for designing better networks for DSM systems [3]. Another research on reducing the invalidation overhead and traffic in DSMs using multidestination message passing mechanism has been presented in [2].

7 Conclusion

In this paper, we have studied the impact of network contention on the performance of four representative applications on a CC-NUMA DSM system. Three network models have been proposed to isolate and evaluate the impact of contention in the network interface, contention in the network alone, and the overall network contention. We have also studied how such contention changes when varying the following architectural parameters: cache size, cache line size, cache set associativity, processing node speed, memory speed, memory bus width, network speed, and network link width.

Our results show that the impact of network contention on overall application performance is significant. Furthermore, the major component of this network contention occurs inside the network alone If network contention is taken into account, application performance can differ by

as much as 60% when compared to the corresponding performance under models that do not take any sort of network contention into account. When compared with models that take only network interface contention into account (and assume contention free transmission within the network), application performance can differ by as much as 50%. These results clearly demonstrate the importance of modeling all types of network contention in general, and contention within the network in particular, while evaluating designs for DSM systems.

Our study also shows that the various architectural parameters can have considerable impact on the effect of network contention on overall application performance. Smaller caches, larger cache lines, lower set associativity, higher processing node speeds, higher memory speeds, lower network speeds and narrower networks can significantly increase this effect of network contention on application performance. These results show that changes in any of these parameters of a DSM system can have a much greater impact on the overall DSM performance if studied in conjunction with methods for reducing the amount of network contention.

Acknowledgment: We want to thank Rajeev Sivaram for providing significant feedback during the preparation of this manuscript.
Additional Information: A number of related papers and technical reports can be obtained from *http://www.cis.ohio-state.edu/~panda/pac.html*.

References

[1] D. C. Burger and D. A. Wood. Accuracy vs. Performance in Parallel Simulation of Interconnection Networks. In *IPPS'95*, April 1995.

[2] D. Dai and D. K. Panda. Reducing Cache Invalidation Overheads in Wormhole DSMs Using Multidestination Message Passing. In *ICPP'96*, pp I:138–145, Chicago, IL, Aug 1996.

[3] D. Dai and D. K. Panda. How Can We Design Better Networks for DSM Systems? In *PCRCW'97*, Atlanta, GA, June 1997.

[4] D. Dai and D. K. Panda. How Much Does Network Contention Affect Distributed Shared Memory Performance? Technical Report OSU-CISRC-2/97-TR14, Feb. 1997.

[5] J. Kuskin et al. The Stanford FLASH Multiprocessor. In *ISCA'94*, pp 302–313, 1994.

[6] S. C. Woo et al. The SPLASH-2 Programs: Characterization and Methodological Considerations. In *ISCA'95*, pp 24–36, 1995.

[7] S. K. Reinhardt et al. The Wisconsin Wind Tunnel: Virtual Prototyping of Parallel Computers. In *Sigmetrics'93*, pp 48–60, May 1993.

[8] M. Heinrich et al. The performance impact of flexibility in the Stanford flash multiprocessor. In *ASPLOS-VI*, San Jose, CA, October 1994.

[9] J. L. Hennessy and D. Patterson. *Computer Architecture: A Quantitative Approach*. Morgan Kaufmann, 1990.

[10] C. Holt, J. P. Singh, and J. Hennessy. Application and Architectural Bottlenecks in Large Scale Distributed Shared Memory Machines. In *ISCA'96*, pp 134–145, May 1996.

[11] L. Ni and P. K. McKinley. A Survey of Wormhole Routing Techniques in Direct Networks. *IEEE Computer*, pp 62–76, Feb. 1993.

[12] S. K. Reinhardt, J. R. Larus, and D. A. Wood. Tempest and Typhoon: User-Level Shared Memory. In *ISCA'94*, pp 325–337, April 1994.

THE IMPLEMENTATION OF LOW LATENCY COMMUNICATION PRIMITIVES IN THE SNOW PROTOTYPE*

Kanad Ghose, Seth Melnick, Tom Gaska[1], Seth Goldberg[2], Arun K. Jayendran[2] and Brian T. Stein

Department of Computer Science

State University of New York Binghamton, NY 13902–6000

ghose@cs.binghamton.edu

Abstract

This paper describes the implementation of a low latency protected message passing facility and a low latency barrier synchronization mechanism for an experimental, tightly–coupled network of workstations called SNOW. SNOW uses multiprocessing SPARC 20s, running Solaris 2.4, as computing nodes, and uses semi–custom network interface cards (NICs) that connect these nodes in a 212 Mbits/sec. unidirectional ring. The NICs include field–programmable gate array logic devices that allow for experimentation with the nature and level of hardware support for tight coupling. The one way protected message passing latency on the SNOW prototype for a 64–byte message is about 9 μsecs., comparable to latencies of low–end to medium range multiprocessors.

Key words: clusters, network of workstations, barrier synchronization, distributed shared memory.

1. INTRODUCTION

The recent years have seen the emergence of tightly–coupled network of stock workstations (NOWs) as cost–effective replacements for small to medium scale multiprocessor systems. The goal of tight coupling in NOWs is to allow the concurrent units to interact with end–to–end message passing latencies and effective bandwidths that are close to what can be realized in the more expensive multiprocessor systems. The virtues of a NOW are well extolled in [Patterson 94]. Despite the emergence of high bandwidth networking technologies, the nature of the conventional network interfaces for workstations and PCs preclude the realization of a low end–to–end latency. The end–to–end latencies realizable with such interfaces routinely exceed several 100s of microseconds, due to the need for invoking operating system services, buffer copying and the heavyweight nature of the protocol layers.

A large body of effort has been thus directed towards the realization of low latency network interfaces. These include enhancements to the network interface card (NIC) and/or switching elements, sometimes including facilities for supporting fast, distributed shared memory [DWB+ 93, IBM 93, HGD+ 94, Kate 94, Hill 95, MAB+ 95], improvements to the software layers [DrPe 93, EWL+ 94, ACPN 95, BDF+ 95, PKC 97] and radical solutions where buffers on the NIC are memory mapped to the address space of the users [MBH 95, GiKa 97].

This paper describes the implementation of a low latency message passing system and a fast barrier synchronization mechanism for a workstation cluster called SNOW (Hardware–supported *S*hared Memory *NOW* or *S*upercomputing *NOW*). The SNOW prototype consists of eight 4–CPU SPARCstation 20s, running Solaris 2.4 and uses a semi–custom network interface card that includes a 212 Mbits/sec. transmitter and receiver, FIFO RAMs, static RAMs, mask programmed and field programmable gate arrays and miscellaneous glue logic. The goal of this project is the construction of a prototype system that allows for experimentation with the nature and degree of hardware support for tight coupling [GhSu 95].

2. REDUCING MESSAGE PASSING LATENCIES

Many of the inefficiencies in traditional implementations of message passing can be traced to functional limitations of the network interface card. In a typical low–end system, these cards are slave devices on the I/O bus, have limited parallelism and a limited amount of on–chip buffer locations, which are not directly addressable by the CPU. The last limitation forces incoming messages to be copied out to the main memory, into a global buffer, before the message header can be examined for authentication checks or packetization. Outgoing messages, similarly, have to go out via a global send buffer in the main memory. In addition to these global buffers, which are in the kernel memory for obvious reasons, private send and receive buffers may exist for each communicating process.

The communication primitives for sending or receiving a message are often implemented as system calls, since OS

. This work supported in part by the NSF through award No. CDA 9700828 and award No. STI–9413854.

1. Also with Lockheed–Martin Federal Systems, Route 17C, Owego, NY 13827
2. Currently with Sun Microsystems, 2550 Garcia Ave., Mountain View, CA 94043

services are needed for authentication checks and copying across address spaces. Notice that the operating system has to be invoked directly (when system calls are made by the applications as they execute the send or receive primitive) or indirectly (through an interrupt):

- Authentication checks and copying from user–space buffers to kernel space buffers (as required by a send or receive primitive) require the intervention of the OS.

- Notifications to the NIC, invoked by a send or receive, also require OS intervention, since the NIC interface is usually not accessible directly by the applications.

- If the NIC is a slave device on the I/O bus, which is often the case, the reception of a message causes the NIC to generate an interrupt, which eventually causes the OS to initiate the DMA of the received message from the NIC buffer to the global receive buffer, on behalf of the NIC.

From the perspective of the software, several things have to be done to cut down on the latency of message passing. First, the number of copying steps that occur when a message is sent or received has to be cut down drastically without compromising protection. Second, OS intervention has to be drastically minimized, again without compromising protection. Examples of techniques that have been devised to meet these goals, used in isolation or in conjunction, include the following:

1. Use of message buffers that are mapped to both the kernel space and the user space. This allows applications to directly access their message buffers without OS intervention and possibly eliminates a copy step. The MMU hardware ensures that the buffers are protected in the appropriate mode at the application level. Several variations are possible.

(i) The buffers are a set of one or more normal main memory pages.

(ii) The buffers are actually locations within the RAM on the NIC, which are mapped to the I/O address space (using hardware within the NIC) and remapped to the memory space of the applications.

(iii) The buffers are actually locations within the RAM on the NIC that are physically wired up to the memory slots using a SIMM extender. This variation requires extensive hardware facilities within the NIC, but allows, unlike variation (ii), buffer locations within the NIC to be written directly from the memory bus.

2. Incorporation of facilities within the NIC to allow received messages to be demultiplexed and multiplexed to/from appropriate buffers after appropriate access checks. This feature eliminates the services needed from the OS for access check and lower level buffer management.

3. Use of device drivers for the NIC that are mapped to the application's address space ("virtualized drivers"), allowing applications to issue commands to the NIC directly. While this approach allows applications to directly issue com-

mands to the NIC, eliminating the OS services that are otherwise required, it may compromise the protection mechanism for message passing and possibly lead to unfair resource sharing.

The approach taken in the SNOW prototype is a combination of all three of these techniques and will now be described.

3. LOW LATENCY MESSAGE PASSING IN SNOW

The key features of the current message passing implementation in SNOW are as follows:

- The message buffers for the virtual channels (VCs) are memory–mapped into the address space of an individual snow process. The buffers are, by default, one page in size but can be multiple pages in length. The MMU protection hardware validates accesses to these buffers.

- Message buffers are pinned down into the main RAM of the workstation to prevent them from being swapped on a routine basis.

- Library functions for setting up, closing and using communication channels are linked to the application processes.

- The library function for a send performs the necessary authentication check and writes the message descriptor to the transmission queue within the NIC in an indirect manner. It deliberately generates an exception that invokes a hand crafted handler to perform these functions. The Solaris first–level interrupt handler was modified to service such interrupts very quickly – the handler simply checks for the interrupt coming from the known physical address within the code for the send routine and, if this test passes, carries out the authentication check based on the information stored in a global VC table. (The Unix pid and the physical address of the interrupt generating instruction are available in TLB registers of the SPARC MMU and accessible through 'hat' functions.)

- The VC table maintained within a NIC is used to demultiplex an incoming message into the appropriate VC buffer. The application routine for a receive does not interact directly with the NIC. The necessary protection for a receive is ensured by the MMU hardware using the mappings established for the receive buffers.

- Buffer management overhead within the send and receive routines are simplified by using fixed–sized packets. Special forms of receive primitives are provided to allow applications to consume messages directly within the receive buffer without the need to copy them into program variables.

We now describe the NIC and user level primitives for low latency communication in SNOW. In particular, we focus on the implementation of the software components.

3.1 The Network Interface Card of SNOW

The network interface card employed in the SNOW prototype is custom–built and includes programmable logic devices to allow the degree and nature of hardware support for tight coupling to be altered. (The bulk of the NIC logic in the first generation of NIC cards was based on field programmable gate array devices. The new NICs for the SNOW prototype employ a mix of mask programmed and field programmable gate arrays.) The NIC uses 266 MBauds transmitter and receiver chips, FIFO RAMS, mask and field programmed gate arrays, 2 MBytes of static RAM and miscellaneous glue logic. The FIFO RAMs are used for flow balance between the transmit/receive logic and the transmitter/receiver. Physically, the NIC is implemented as a SBus card, with a daughtercard.

Within the NIC, several concurrently operating engines implement a number of functions that support high speed message passing, barrier synchronization and page–level coherent distributed shared memory. The SBus interface for the NIC consists of I/O–mapped registers and DMA engines that implement a bus master interface. The transmit engine handles the transmission of locally–sourced messages and implements low level flow control on a per–channel basis. The receive engine has three functions. It implements the reception of messages destined for the node and is also responsible for relaying the incoming message along the ring, if it needs to continue on the next segment of the ring. Additionally, the receive engine is responsible for taking a message that has completed a full circuit of the ring and decrementing the appropriate flow control counter when this happens. The barrier engine is responsible for handling all aspects of barrier synchronization, including the handling of the messages related to barrier synchronization. An independent engine implements the functions that support page level distributed shared memory. The command interpreter engine interprets commands for the NIC issued from the CPU.

The on–board static RAM within the NIC implements additional queues, as well as several tables:

Virtual–channel table: This is a table that stores a pointer to the next free slot for a 64–byte message within the page–sized (4K Bytes) memory buffer for a receive channel. Appropriate routing and higher level flow control information is also maintained within each entry.

Received message queue: This is a raw queue that holds locally destined messages that have not yet been DMAed into the workstation's RAM.

Queue of outgoing message descriptors: The execution of a *send* primitive in the applications eventually results in depositing a message descriptor on this queue. The NIC uses the descriptor to DMA in the actual message from the workstation RAM for transmission.

Barrier table: Entries maintain the 'state' of a given barrier, such as the number of processes at the barrier, whether an interrupt is to be triggered at completion, and the phyiscal memory address of a flag on which local processes spin–wait pending the completion of the barrier.

The software components which interact with the NIC can issue various commands to the NIC, including such functions as: initialization, DMA transfers, reading/writing of internal NIC latches, and other functions for supporting shared memory and barriers. The NIC interface consists of eight 32–bit registers within the SBus address space. The following interface registers are relevant for low latency message passing and barrier synchronization:

- NIC_CMD_REG: a command to be executed by the NIC is written into this register

- NIC_SEND_REG: Descriptors for outgoing messages (a physical address pointer into a message buffer for a virtual channel) is written into this register. The transmit and DMA engines use this descriptor to DMA in the actual message into the NIC and then send it out.

- NIC_ADDR_CNT_REG and WS_ADDR_CNT_REG: These registers contain the information (starting address, word count) needed for software–initiated DMA transfers between the workstation's RAM and the RAM within the NIC. The actual DMA transfers are initiated by writing appropriate commands into the NIC command register. These DMA transfers are used to initialize various tables within the NIC or to read out the contents of various tables and queues within the NIC.

- NIC_LATCH_REG: This register is used by the commands that read and write latches internal to the NIC.

- NIC_STATUS_REG: This register contains the summary status of the NIC.

Additional interface registers are used for implementing the shared memory environment but are not described here. Registers that require mutually–exclusive accesses are protected by software locks.

3.2. Software Components

The primitives used for parallel programming in the SNOW prototype are available in a library as C functions. These library functions are linked to the compiled applications. The basic unit of concurrency is a snow process – which is a standard Unix process that makes use of the message passing and synchronization primitives of the SNOW library. At each node, a daemon process – the snow daemon – is set up to initialize the NIC and subsequently take care of channel setup and extraneous conditions related to message passing. A snow daemon communicates with peer daemons at other nodes using hardwired communication channels that are set up at boot time. As part of the boot time initialization, a pool of page frames are pinned down and a list of these page frames is made available to the snow daemon. These page frames will eventually implement message buffers for the virtual channels between communicating snow processes. Also, at boot time, a set of globally unique virtual channel IDs (global VCids) are pre–assigned to the SNOW daemons at each node. This allows daemons to dispense global VCids to identify communication channels between snow processes as such channels are opened without the need for negotiations among the daemons. The daemon function, on booting, also includes the loading of the executables of the snow communication library into pinned page frames.

3.2.1 Snow processes

Each snow process has an unique software id, hereafter called the sid, formed by concatenating the address of the node where the process runs with a programmer assigned logical id (i.e., sid = node_id.logical id). When a snow process starts up, it makes a call to the SNOW library function:

    int   snow_init(sid)

The snow daemon, invoked as a result of this call, does the following. A set of page frames from the pool of pre–allocated, non–swappable page frames is allocated for use as virtual channel buffers by the calling process. This ensures that each SNOW always has a minimum set of message buffers. These page frames are then mapped into the address space of the calling SNOW process. (A new system call, smap, invoked within snow_init, was added to Solaris for this purpose.) A page containing lock and synchronization variables shared by the snow processes is also mapped to the address space of each snow process.

3.2.2. Buffers and queues

Figure 1 depicts the buffers and queues used in the current SNOW prototype. The message buffers are page–sized, mapped to the application's address space and pinned in workstation's DRAM memory. Each buffer consists of a header, followed by slots for 64–byte messages that are maintained as a FIFO queue, whose pointers are part of the header. Two global queues are also maintained within the memory on the NIC: the NIC_GTQ and the NIC_GRQ, that contain descriptors of messages to be transmitted and 64–byte messages received off the network for local processes, respectively. A message descriptor in NIC_GTQ is a physical address pointer to the actual message in the send buffer for a process, and is used to DMA in the message into the NIC before it is transmitted.

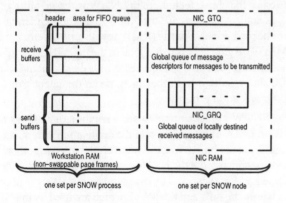

Figure 1. Data Structures Related to Message Passing

3.3. Channel Setup

The application processes (aka snow processes) communicate using unidirectional virtual channels. Each channel thus has two logical end points – the sending process and the receiving process. We describe the setup of virtual channels between snow processes running on different node. Obvious optimizations are used when the end points of a virtual channel are on the same node.

To set up a communication channel from one snow process to another, the process at the sending end executes a snow_open, while the process at the receiving end executes a snow_attach. These functions invoke the services of the snow daemons to set up the channel and are as follows:

    gvcid_t   snow_open(src_sid, dest_sid, &buf)

    gvcid_t   snow_attach(src_sid, dest_sid, &buf)

Both of these functions end up invoking the snow daemons at the respective nodes to perform the channel setup, ultimately returning the global VCids of the channel being set up to the callers and the virtual addresses of the send and receive buffers, respectively, to the callers of snow_open and snow_attach. In serving the snow_open call, the local snow daemon allocates a global VCid (gVCid) for the channel (from its list of pre–allocated VCids) and sends a special setup message to the daemon for the node where the receiving process (named by dest_sid) runs and waits till it receives a response. The daemon at the other end responds only when a snow_attach is performed at that node. A snow_attach performed before the reception of a corresponding setup message by the local daemon returns a failure code; this requires the function call to be retried explicitly, till it can 'bind' with the setup message. When the snow_open and snow_attach calls complete successfully, entries are established for the channel being set up within the global VC tables at the sending and receiving nodes. An entry in these tables, which are indexed by the global VCid, lists the following information: the Unix and snow_pids of the sender and the receiver, the (physical) page frame number for the send or the receive buffer (as the case may be), the virtual address used by the process for the buffer and other miscellaneous information. Corresponding entries are also set up within the VC tables residing on the NICs at either end of the channel. The global VCid returned to the callers of snow_open or snow_attach is specified in subsequent sends, while the buffer address returned in &buf is specified for receives on the opened channel. Library functions are also provided to close VCs.

The global VC table at each node is maintained within the kernel's address space and are inaccessible to the snow processes. When a message is being transmitted, the global VC table information is consulted for authentication checks.

3.4. Sending Messages

A process that has snow_open–ed a virtual channel uses snow_send function to send a 64–byte message (including a

4–byte header), using the following non–blocking primitive:

    status_t   snow_send(gVCid, &msg)

where gVCid refers to the channel being used, and &msg is a pointer to the structure containing the message. A blocking version of this primitive (snow_sendb) is also provided: in this case, the caller is blocked till the actual message is DMAed into the NIC.

The snow_send primitive implements the following steps:

1. A header, containing the specified gVCid is added to the message.

2. The offset of the message in the buffer page is extracted.

3. An interrupt is deliberately generated.

The Solaris interrupt handler is modified to look for this interrupt before it checks for interrupts from other potential sources. The handler performs the following steps to effectively continue the snow_send:

4. A check is performed to see if the interrupt was generated from a know *physical* address within the body of the system supplied trusted library code. If this check passes, the handler proceeds to the next step. (If this check fails, normal interrupt handling resumes.)

5. The physical address of the offending instruction is obtained from it's virtual address available in a TLB register using in–line version of appropriate 'hat' functions. A message descriptor is formed with the physical address.

6. Using the Unix pid of the calling process and the gVCid specified in the call, the global VCid table is used to verify if the caller had opened the channel in the sending mode. If this check passes, the message descriptor formed in Step 5 is written to the NIC_SEND_REG. The handler then returns, allowing the snow_send function itself to return.

The NIC hardware, in response to the writing of the descriptor into the NIC_SEND_REG, copies the message descriptor into its global transmit request queue, NIC_GTQ. Notice that a malicious process can trace the instructions of the send library and directly jump to the instruction that invokes the handler (Step 3) – the authentication check of Step 6 ensures that this process can send a message only on a sending channel that was opened by the process. There is thus no way for a process to use a fake gVCid to send a message on somebody else's channel.

3.5. Receiving messages

The primitives for receiving a message simply allows a process to pick up a message from the receive buffer for the specified channel. Instead of specifying the gVCid of the channel on which the process is attempting to receive on, the starting (virtual) address of the receive buffer for the channel is specified. (Recall that this buffer address was returned by a snow_open). The appropriate protection mechanism in this

case is implemented by the MMU, which ensures that a process can only access the message buffers that belong to it.

A snow process uses the following primitives to receive a message on a specified channel:

    status_t   snow_receive(buf, &msg);
    status_t   snow_breceive(buf, &msg); /* blocking receive */

where &msg is the pointer to structure into which the message has to be copied from the receive buffer (buf) of the specified channel. To avoid this copying where possible, the following primitives are used to implement a zero–copy receive:

    status_t   snow_ncprcv(buf, &slot);
    status_t   snow_bncprcv(buf, &slot); /* blocking receive */

These two primitives generate a pointer to the message (&slot), thereby allowing the message to be consumed in-place. Many concurrent applications can effectively make use of the in–place consumption by accessing the message using its pointer into the received–message queue. An associated primitive:

    status_t   snow_free_slot(buf, slot);

is used to free up the slot once the message has been consumed. Note that these in–place consumptions are possible since message buffers are visible to the applications.

A direct approach for implementing the receive primitives, and one that is used in the implementation of many fast network interfaces, is to allow the NIC to DMA in a received message into the appropriate buffer for a process and then update buffer pointers. A lock (in the main memory) has to be used to allow for atomic updates to the buffer pointers by the NIC and the application. The main drawback of this approach, however, is in the form of extensive additional traffic on the SBus (beyond the DMA of the message) for locking out access to the pointer while it is being updated and the eventual release of the lock. A similar amount of traffic is generated by the applications when they read the receive buffer, leading to an unacceptably high communication latency.

A more fundamental problem that precludes the implementation of the above technique in SNOW is the inability of a SBus device – in this case, the NIC – to *directly* generate an atomic read–modify–write (RMW) cycle on the memory bus (MBUS) to gain access to the lock in the main RAM. Implementing the lock on the NIC card avoids the problem for the NIC, but results in a further increase in the latency of the communication primitives.

The SNOW implementation uses a solution that allows the NIC to DMA–in messages and the application to read messages from the buffer without interfering with each other. It also does not require the NIC to set/release locks in memory. These goals are achieved by using independent sets of pointers within the NIC and the RAM, which are used by the NIC and the application, respectively. Infrequently, the NIC updates its pointers by reading in the pointer maintained within the main RAM by the application. Our implementations simply ensure that the following two conditions for reading messages are met:

(R1) An application should only read buffer slots that contain valid messages that were DMAed in by the NIC.

(R2) The NIC should not overwrite buffer slots that contain valid messages that the application has not yet read.

R1 is met by using a single bit to indicate whether the buffer slot contains a valid message. This valid bit is part of the header for the message, which is written into a buffer slot by the NIC. A receive primitive reads the buffer slots in FIFO order and checks if the item read is valid. A failure indication is returned when the message slot read is marked as invalid. After a valid message has been read out or consumed from a slot, the slot is marked as invalid.

Meeting the second requirement R2 is met by making sure that the pointer used by the NIC for writing incoming messages in FIFO order always "follows" the consumption pointer, *next_msg*, used by the application to locate the next valid message in the buffer. (The *next_msg* pointer is maintained within the header region of a VC buffer.) The NIC maintains a range of slot addresses that it can safely write messages into as two pointers, NIC_NEXT_SLOT and NIC_HI. These pointers are part of the entry for a channel within the VC table kept within the RAM on the NIC. NIC_NEXT_SLOT points to the next available free slot within the buffer, while NIC_HI indicates the extent to which the NIC_NEXT_SLOT pointer can be incremented without intruding into regions where unconsumed messages reside.

When a received message has to be written into a buffer slot pointed to by NIC_NEXT_SLOT, the NIC initiates the DMA as long as the value of NIC_HI, considering wraparound, is ahead of the value of NIC_NEXT_SLOT. After the DMA, NIC_NEXT_SLOT is updated. When an incoming message has to be DMAed and when NIC_NEXT_SLOT equals NIC_HI, the NIC reads in the value of *next_msg* from the main RAM. Two cases now arise:

Case a: (NIC_HI ≠ *next_msg*): In this case, the buffer still has available slots to hold the incoming message. NIC_HI is updated to the value just prior to *next_msg* in circular FIFO order. and the message is DMAed into the buffer slot pointed to by NIC_NEXT_SLOT.

Case b: (NIC_HI = *next_msg*): In this case, there is no space left in the VC buffer, so the NIC generates an interrupt. This interrupt is handled by the SNOW daemon. The daemon copies the incoming message into an overflow buffer (with high and low watermarks) and a special message is sent to the daemon at the sending node to throttle the sender. The incoming messages in the overflow buffer are eventually DMAed into the VC buffer when the receiving process consumes part of the messages already sitting in the VC buffer.

Thus, in the normal course of operations, the NIC can DMA incoming messages into the VC buffer by only consulting pointers maintained locally within the NIC RAM. Occasionally, the NIC has to perform a read of the main RAM to get the most recent value of *next_msg* to update NIC_HI, before DMAing the received message. Finally, the NIC is compelled to generate an interrupt when the receiving VC buffer is full – a situation that should not arise, or at worse, arise only very rarely.

The steps carried out by the snow_receive primitive are now described. (The actions carried out by the other receiving primitives are similar.)

1) The header of the message pointed to by *next_msg* is read out. If the message slot is tagged invalid, snow_send returns an error code.

3) The (valid) message is copied into the user–space message structure using the pointer supplied in the call.

4) The buffer slot from which the message was just copied is marked as invalid.

5) The pointer *next_msg* to the message FIFO is updated.

The implementation of snow_ncprcvs are slightly different.

4. BARRIER SYNCHRONIZATION MECHANISMS

The SNOW prototype provides hardware support within the NIC for implementing fast barrier synchronization. Each barrier used in a parallel application is assigned a global barrier id (gBid), analogous to a global VCid for a virtual channel. The following set of primitives are provided in the SNOW library for barrier synchronization:

```
gbid_t     snow_open_barrier (N, sbid, &flag);
gbid_t     snow_attach_barrier (sbid, &flag);
bstatus_t  snow_report (gBid);
bstatus_t  snow_status_barrier (gBid);
bstatus_t  snow_set_barrier (N, gBid);
```

The function snow_open_barrier sets up a barrier synchronization facility across the nodes and is quite analogous to the snow_open primitive for opening a channel. This function requires a specification of the number of participating processes (N), a programmer assigned barrier id (sbid). The effect of this function is to set up an entry for the barrier in the barrier table within the NIC, as well as a global barrier table, gBT, in the main RAM (the analog of the global VC table), *at each node*. The entry for a barrier in the NIC records the number of processes that remain to report at a barrier – this field is initialized to N. The function, furthermore, sets up and initializes an entry for the barrier in the shared page of synchronization variables at each node for a waiting flag on which local processes spin awaiting the completion of the barrier. The address of this flag is returned in flag. A system–assigned global barrier id (gBid) is returned as the result of the call to snow_open_barrier. The function, snow_attach_barrier is used by a process to attach to a barrier that has been opened.

A process that has opened or attached to a barrier uses the snow_report function to report to the barrier and spins on the local flag associated with the barrier till it clears. The snow_report function invokes the following action. An authentication check similar to that done for a snow_send is performed using the information in the gBT. If this check passes, a special report message is sent out to all nodes (this is a single message going around the ring in our current implementation.) All NICs that receive this message and the NIC in the originating node decrement the count field for the specified barrier in the entry within the NIC's barrier table. If this count falls to zero, implying the completion of the barrier synchronization, the associated flag in the main RAM is cleared, causing all locally waiting processes to continue beyond the barrier.

The snow_status_barrier function is used to read out the status of the barrier, as available from its NIC entry. The snow_set_barrier function is used to reset the barrier – an authentication check is performed to ensure that the barrier is reset by the process that opened it. This function causes the flags and entries within the NIC at all nodes to be reinitialized.

The performance gains with the NIC–assisted barrier synchronizers are significant, compared to naive software implementations (where processes broadcast their reports to each other), as well as efficient software implementations like the Butterfly Barrier.

5. INITIAL PERFORMANCE ESTIMATES

Table I summarizes the best–case latencies for the send and receive primitives individually (for communication between adjacent ring segments in the prototype). The timings for this table are derived from instruction counts for the software components and from the Verilog simulator for the hardware components. The timings are for SPARC–20s, using 50 MHz., 4–way superscalar CPUs and 212 Mbits/sec. transceivers in the NICs. Recall that the message size is fixed at 64 bytes.

The latency of the snow_send primitive is the time between the function invocation and the time when the very first bit is transmitted. The latency of the snow_receive and snow_ncprcv primitives are the times between their invocation and their completion, assuming that the message is in the buffer. Since the overall end–to–end latency depends on the NIC–to–receive–buffer transfer time, a separate entry for this part of the latency is also shown. The wire component refers to the time needed to move the 64–byte message on the physical links between adjacent NICs. The value of the overall latency of a send–receive pair assumes best case timings.

The pass through latency of the NIC is roughly 0.7 μsecs. This leads to a latency of roughly 26.6 μsecs for a send–receive pair across nodes that are 7 hops apart (the worst–case hop–count in our 8–node prototype). Similarly, the best case time for the completion of a barrier report is roughly 16.7

μsecs. (For barriers, only the message header is transferred.) These estimated latencies and the ones shown in Table 1 suggests that the various latency reduction techniques employed in SNOW are quite effective.

OPERATION	COMPONENTS (μ secs.)			TOTAL LATENCY (μ secs.)
	SOFTWARE	SBus	NIC	
send	1.5	0.84	0.56	3.2
wire time	N.A.	N.A.	N.A.	2.2
NIC to receive buffer	N.A.	0.88	2.14	3.02
receive	0.28	N.A.	N.A.	0.28
ncprecv	0.12	N.A.	N.A.	0.12
send–receive pair	1.78	1.72	2.7	9.22

Table I. Latencies for **Protected** Communication

6. RELATED WORK AND CONCLUSIONS

We presented the implementation of protected low–latency message–passing in SNOW. SNOW uses fixed–sized messages, zero–copy and single copy message interfaces, fast authentication checks and an ultra–lightweight system call to reduce message latencies. SNOW uses a hardware programmable NIC to allow for experimentation with the nature and degree of support for tight coupling, including the implementation of distributed, coherent shared memory (which, however, is not described in this paper). The one way latency achieved for protected message passing in an otherwise standard Solaris environment is about 9.22 μsecs., which is comparable to or better than the timings in many low end and middle range multiprocessor. SNOW also incorporates hardware–supported mechanisms for barrier synchronization, and allows a barrier report to complete in about 17 μsecs. for the 8–node (32–CPU) prototype. This time is significantly faster than what would have been realized from an all–software implementation on top of the fast messaging layers.

The SNOW prototype is not unique in its use of a programmable NIC. The programmable Magic chip is used in Stanford's FLASH project [HGD+97] for similar reasons. Many LAN cards used some NOW prototyping efforts, such as the UUNet [vBB+95] and an implementation of the Illinois Fast Messages for Sun SPARCs [PKC 97] incorporate a programmable CPU. The Wisconsin COW [Hill 95] and Sun's research prototype S3.mp uses mask–programmed gate array logic based NICs to implement distributed, shared memory NOWs. The Telegraphos prototype [Kate 94] uses a custom NIC with hardware support for low latency message passing, as well as logic for implementing remote reads and writes. The DEC memory channel mechanism [GiKa 96] uses PCI–based fast NIC logic to implement reflective memory and achieve protected message passing latencies of less than 2 μsecs. IBM's SP/2 cluster uses a custom network interface card and switches to realize one way latencies of roughly 7 μsecs.

The SHRIMP project at Princeton [BDF+ 95] is one of the pioneering efforts for implementing tightly coupled workstations in a message passing framework, using NICs that use communication chips for the early Intel multiprocessors. SHRIMP II implements distributed shared memory in software on top of the fast message–passing hardware. The SNOW prototype differs from the efforts described in [ACPN 95], [IBM 93] and [MBH 95] in its use of hardware support within the network interface for implementing a coherent cache based shared memory environment across the workstation cluster. Further, few of these projects, incorporate a programmable network interface hardware, leaving out the possibility of fine tuning and experimentation. The The ParaStation/ParaPC project [WBT 96] uses a custom, toroidal interconnection and network interface to connect DEC workstations and PCs as a cluster, achieving an impressive 2.5 micro–second latency but only on an unprotected network interface. With protected interfaces, the message latencies are likely to be higher. SNOW, unlike ParaStation/ParaPC also provides hardware support for a distributed shared memory environment.

Several recent efforts have been directed towards the reduction of the message–passing overhead in standard networked environments for TCP/IP. In the Jetstream project [EWL+ 94] developed at HP Bristol, applications can reserve buffer pools on the Afterburner board [DWB+ 93]. Afterburner uses FIFO ports on the network interface, independent transmit, receive engines and a variety of other interesting features. The limitation of the Jetstream effort is that all protocols which can access Afterburner buffers directly must be through kernel services. This inefficiency is overcome in UU–Net [vBB+ 95] and the Illinois FM [PKC 97], where low latency TCP/IP protocols are implemented by letting applications and the NIC share message buffers. Techniques for avoiding buffer copying and buffer management overhead to reduce message–passing and I/O latencies, respectively, have been described in [DrPe 93] and [ThKh 95]. SNOW takes these approaches further and augments the performance with hardware support within the NIC.

The design of the SNOW prototype has gone through some major design changes over the last year. The prototype is expected to be operational by Fall 1997. The implementation of a new NIC design for PCI buses, supporting an external switch, is already in progress to allow PCs to be clustered.

References

[ACPN 95] Anderson, T.E. et al., "A Case for NOW (Network of Workstations)" IEEE Micro, Vol. 15, No. 1, pp. 54–64.

[BDF+ 95] Blumrich, M. A., "Virtual Memory–Mapped Network Interfaces", IEEE Micro, Vol. 15, No. 1, pp. 21–28.

[DWB+ 93] Dalton, C., Watson, G., Banks, D., Calamvokis, C., Edwards, A. and Lumley, J., "Afterburner", IEEE Network Magazine, Vol 7, No. 4., July 1993, pp. 36–43.

[DrPe 93] Druschel, P. and Peterson, L., "Fbufs: A High–Bandwidth Cross–Domain Transfer Facility", in Proc. of the 14th SOSP, December 1993, pp. 189–202.

[EWL+ 94] Edwards, A,. Watson, G., Lumley, J., Banks, D., Calamvokis, C. and Dalton, C, "User–space protocols deliver high performance to applications on a low–cost Gb/s LAN", in Proc. of SIGCOMM–94, Aug 1994, pp. 2–13.

[GhSu 95] Ghose, K. and Subhachandra, C., "SNOW: Hardware Supported Shared Memory Over a Network of Workstations", in Proc. Workshop on Challenges for Parallel Processing, Int'l. Conf. on Parallel Processing, August 1995, pp. 148–154.

[GiKa 97] Gillet, R. and Kaufmann, R., "Using the Memory Channel Network", IEEE Micro, Vol. 17, No. 1, pp. 19–25]. .

[HGD+] Heinlein John J. et al., "Integration of Message Passing and Shared Memory in the Stanford FLASH Multiprocessor", Proc. of the 6th Int'l Conference on Architectural Support for Programming Languages and Operating Systems, Oct. 94.

[Hill 95] Hill, Mark, Web page on the Wisconsin COW, at http://www.cs.wisc.edu/~wwt/cow/html.

[IBM 93] IBM Corporation, SP/2 Product Overview, 1992.

[Kate 94] Katevenis, M., "Telegraphos: High Speed Communication Architecture for Parallel and Distributed Computer Systems", Technical Report Number FORTH–ICS/TR–123, Inst. of Computer Science, Univ. of Crete, 1994.

[ThKh 95] Thadani, M. and Khalidi, Y. A., "An Efficient Zero–Copy I/O Framework for UNIX", Sun Labs draft technical report, January, 1995.

[Mason 94] Mason, Susan A., SBus Handbook, SunSoft Press, 1994.

[MBH 95] Minnich, R. et al., "The Memory–Integrated Network Interface", IEEE Micro, Vol. 15, No. 1, pp. 11–20.

[NAB+ 95] Nowatzyk, A., Abhay, G., Browne, M., Kelly, M., Parkin, E., Radke, B. and Vishin, S., "The S3.mp Scalable Shared Memory Multiprocessor", in Proc. ICPP, Vol. I, 1995.

[Patterson 94] Patterson, David A., (editor & organizer), Record of The First Network of Workstations Workshop, held in conjunction with ASPLOS–VI, 1994

[PKC 97] Pakin, S., Karamcheti, V. and Chien, A., "Fast Messages: Efficient, Portable Communication for Workstation Clusters and MPPs", IEEE Concurrency, Vol. 5, No. 2, pp. 60–73.

[vBB+ 95] vonEicken, T., Basu, A., Buch, V. and Vogels, W., "U-net: A User–Level Network Interface for Parallel and Distributed Computing". in Proc. of 15th Operating System Principles, 1995.

[WBT 96] Warschko, T.M., Blum, J. M. and Tichy, W. F., "The ParaPC/ParaStation Project: Efficient Parallel Processing by Clustering Workstations", Technical Report 13/96, Dept. of Informatics, Karlsruhe University.

Session 7C

Scheduling II - Software

Decisive Path Scheduling: A New List Scheduling Method[*]

Gyung-Leen Park[1], Behrooz Shirazi[1,2], Jeff Marquis[2] , and Hyunseung Choo[1]

[1]University of Texas at Arlington, Dept. of CSE, Arlington, TX 76019, USA
{gpark, shirazi, choo}@cse.uta.edu
[2]Prism Parallel Technologies, Inc., 2000 N. Plano Rd, Richardson, Texas 75082

Abstract

Scheduling parallel tasks, represented as a Directed Acyclic Graph (DAG), on a multiprocessor system has been an important research area in the past decades. One of the critical aspects of a class of scheduling algorithms, called "List Scheduling," is how to decide which task is to be scheduled next. This is achieved by assigning priorities to the nodes or the edges of the input DAG, and thus the task with the highest priority will be scheduled next. This paper proposes a low complexity scheduling algorithm to improve the priority node selection criteria in list scheduling algorithms. The worst case performance of the proposed algorithm is analyzed for general input DAGs. Also, the worst case performance and the optimality conditions are obtained for tree structured input DAGs. The performance comparison study shows that the proposed algorithm outperforms existing scheduling algorithms especially for input DAGs with high communication overheads. The performance improvement over existing algorithms becomes larger as the input DAG becomes more dense and the level of parallelism in the DAG is increased.

1. Introduction

Efficient partitioning and scheduling of parallel programs onto processing elements of parallel and distributed computer systems are difficult and important issues [15-18, 20] in concurrent processing. The process consists of partitioning a parallel program's tasks into clusters and efficiently scheduling those clusters among the processing elements of a parallel machine for execution. Once an application program is partitioned into clusters or tasks, it can be represented by a *DAG* (Directed Acyclic Graph), or a *task graph*, which represents the precedence constraints of the program tasks. The goals of the scheduling process are to efficiently utilize resources and to achieve performance objectives of the application (e.g., to minimize program parallel execution time).

Since it has been shown that the multiprocessor scheduling problem is NP-complete, many researchers have proposed scheduling algorithms based on heuristics. The scheduling algorithms can be classified into two general categories: algorithms that employ task duplication and algorithms that do not employ task duplication. Task duplication algorithms attempt to reduce communication overhead by duplicating tasks that would otherwise require interprocessor communications if the tasks were not duplicated [2, 4, 5, 6, 7, 10, 13, 18]. One of the major problems with task duplication is the issue of data distribution and preserving of data integrity. This paper assumes that the system does not allow task duplication.

Most of the non-duplication scheduling methods can be classified as either a *clustering algorithm* or a *list scheduling algorithm*. The clustering algorithms basically perform the following operations:
1. Initially, each task is considered to be a cluster.
2. An edge between two clusters is selected according to a priority assigned to the edges by the clustering algorithm.
3. The edge is removed (call *edge zeroing*) if it satisfies certain conditions specified by the algorithm. Once an edge is zeroed, the two clusters connected by that edge will be merged into one cluster.

This work has in part been supported by grants from NSF (CDA-9531535 and MIPS-9622593) and state of Texas ATP 003656-087.

472

4. Steps 2 and 3 are repeated until all the edges are examined.
5. The clusters are assigned to the processors in the target system.

The List scheduling algorithms maintain a list of node according to their priorities. A list scheduling algorithm repeatedly carries out the following steps:

1. Tasks ready to be assigned (a task becomes ready for assignment when all of its parents are scheduled) are put onto a priority queue. The priority criteria determines the order in which task are assigned to the processors.
2. Select a "suitable Processing Element (PE)" for assignment. Typically, a suitable PE is one that can execute the task the earliest.
3. Assign the task at the head of the priority queue to this PE.
4. Repeat steps 2 and 3 until the priority queue is exhausted.

Typically, the list scheduling algorithms assume bounded number of processors while clustering algorithms assume an unbounded number of processors. This difference is not significant since these assumptions can be easily removed for each method. A more significant difference between the list scheduling and clustering algorithms is that list scheduling algorithms select *only* a ready node for assignment while clustering algorithms may select *any* node for this purpose.

The critical part in both techniques is the development of a method for assigning priorities to the nodes or the edges of the input DAG. Since a large number of different methods are proposed in the literature, we briefly classify them according to the parameters used for the priority assignment: the node weight, the distance, the critical path, and some combinations of them.

The methods based on the node weight, such as that in HNF (Heavy Node First), assign a higher priority to a node with a larger computation cost [14]. The distance (defined as the sum of computation and communication costs of the nodes on a path) could be either the maximum distance from a root node to the node under consideration (top distance) or the maximum distance from the node being considered to an exit node (bottom distance). For example, HLFET (High Level First with Estimated Time) algorithm assigns a higher priority to a node with a larger bottom distance [1]. A large number of scheduling algorithms use the length of the critical path to assign priorities to the nodes and edges of a DAG. Some examples include Linear Clustering (LC) [9] and Dominant Sequence Clustering (DSC) [21] algorithms. Finally, some algorithms use combinations

of the above parameters to decide the priorities. For example, Critical Path Node-Dominate (CPND) method [11] uses the critical path and the bottom distance for assigning the priorities to the nodes in the input DAG.

This paper proposes a new list scheduling algorithm, *Decisive Path Scheduling (DPS)*, which assigns the priorities to the nodes using the *decisive path* (defined in Section 2). The performance comparison study shows that the proposed algorithm outperforms existing scheduling algorithms especially for input DAGs with high communication overheads. The performance improvement over existing algorithms becomes larger for denser and more parallel DAGs.

The remainder of this paper is organized as follows. Section 2 presents the system model and the problem definition. Section 3 briefly covers the related works. The proposed scheduling algorithm is presented in Section 4. This section also contains the worst case and the optimality analysis of the proposed algorithm. The performance of the proposed algorithm is compared with that of the typical existing algorithms in Section 5. Finally, Section 6 concludes this paper.

2. System model and problem definition

A parallel program is usually represented by a Directed Acyclic Graph (DAG), which is also called a task graph. As defined in [7], a DAG consists of a tuple (V, E, T, C), where V, E, T, and C are the set of task nodes, the set of communication edges, the set of computation costs associated with the task nodes, and the set of communication costs associated with the edges, respectively. $T(V_i)$ is a computation cost for task V_i and $C(V_i, V_j)$ is the communication cost for edge $E(V_i, V_j)$ which connects task V_i and V_j. The edge $E(V_i, V_j)$ represents the precedence constraint between the node V_i and V_j. In other words, task V_j can start the execution only after the output of V_i is available to V_j. When the two tasks, V_i and V_j, are assigned to the same processor, $C(V_i, V_j)$ is assumed to be zero since intra-processor communication cost is negligible compared with the interprocessor communication cost. The weights associated with nodes and edges are obtained by estimation [19].

This paper defines two relations for precedence constraints. The $V_i \Rightarrow V_j$ relation indicates the strong precedence relation between V_i and V_j. That is, V_i is an immediate parent of V_j and V_j is an immediate child of V_i. The terms *iparent* and *ichild* are used to represent immediate parent and immediate child, respectively. The $V_i \rightarrow V_j$ relation indicates the weak precedence relation between V_i and V_j. That is, V_i is a parent of V_j

but not necessarily the immediate one. $V_i \rightarrow V_j$ and $V_j \rightarrow V_k$ imply $V_i \rightarrow V_k$. $V_i \Rightarrow V_j$ and $V_j \Rightarrow V_k$ do not imply $V_i \Rightarrow V_k$, but imply $V_i \rightarrow V_k$. The relation $\rightarrow$ is transitive, and the relation $\Rightarrow$ is not. A node without any parent is called an *entry node* and a node without any child is called an *exit node*.

Graphically, a node is represented as a circle with a dividing line in the middle. The number in the upper portion of the circle represents the node ID number and the number in the lower portion of the circle represents the computation cost for the node. For example, for the sample DAG in Figure 1, the entry node is node number 1 which has a computation cost of 10. In the graph representation of a DAG, the communication cost for each edge is written on the edge itself. For each node, *incoming degree* is the number of input edges and *outgoing degree* is the number of output edges.

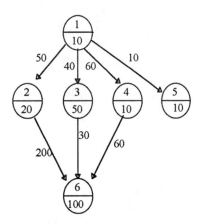

Figure 1. The sample DAG

For example, in Figure 1, the incoming and outgoing degrees for the node V_1 are 0 and 4, respectively. A few terms are defined here for a more clear presentation.

Definition 1: A node is called a *fork node* if its outgoing degree is greater than 1.

Definition 2: A node is called a *join node* if its incoming degree is greater than 1.

Note that the fork node and the join node are not exclusive terms, which means that one node can be both a fork and also a join node; i.e., both of the node's incoming and outgoing degrees are greater than one. Similarly, a node can be neither a fork nor a join node; i.e., both of the node's incoming and outgoing degrees are one. For the sample DAG in Figure 1, V_1 is a fork node while V_6 is a join node. Nodes V_2, V_3, V_4, and V_5 are neither fork nodes nor join nodes.

Definition 3: The *Earliest Start Time, EST(V_i, P_k)*, and *Earliest Completion Time, ECT(V_i, P_k)*, are the times that a task V_i starts and finishes its execution on processor P_k, respectively. When the information on the processor is not necessary, they are denoted just as EST(V_i) and ECT(V_i), respectively.

Definition 4: The critical path is the longest path from an entry node to an exit node in the graph. A *Critical Path Including Communication cost (CPIC)* is the length of the critical path including communication costs in the path while a *Critical Path Excluding Communication cost (CPEC)* is the length of the critical path excluding communication costs in the path. For the sample DAG in Figure 1 as an example, CPIC is $T(V_1)$ + $C(V_1, V_2)$ + $T(V_2)$ + $C(V_2, V_6)$ + $T(V_6)$, which is 380. CPEC is $T(V_1)$ + $T(V_3)$ + $T(V_6)$, which is 160.

Definition 5: The *level* of a node is recursively defined as follows. The level of an entry node, V_1, is one. Let $Lv(V_i)$ be the level of V_i. Then $Lv(V_1) = 1$. $Lv(V_j) = Lv(V_i) + 1$, $V_i \Rightarrow V_j$, for non-join node V_j. $Lv(V_j) = Max(Lv(V_i)) + 1$, $V_i \Rightarrow V_j$, for join node V_j. For example, the level of node V_1, V_2, V_3, V_4, V_5, and V_6 in the sample DAG are 1, 2, 2, 2, 2, and 3, respectively. Even if there was an edge from node V_1 to V_6, the level of V_6 would still be 3 since $Lv(V_6) = Max(Lv(V_i)) + 1$, $V_i \Rightarrow V_6$, for join node V_6. The level of a DAG is the maximum level of the nodes in the DAG.

Definition 6: The *top distance* for any give node is the longest distance from an entry node to that node, excluding the computation cost of the node itself. The *bottom distance* for any given node is the longest distance from that node to an exit node, including the computation cost of the node itself. For example, the top distance of V_6, TD(V_6), is 280 which is $T(V_1)$ + $C(V_1, V_2)$ + $T(V_2)$ + $C(V_2, V_6)$. The bottom distance of V_2, BD(V_2), is 320 which is $T(V_2)$ + $C(V_2, V_6)$ + $T(V_6)$.

Definition 7: The *Decisive Path (DP)* to node V_i is the path which decides the top distance of V_i. For example, the decisive path to V_6, DP(V_6), is the path through V_1, V_2, and V_6 since the path decides the top distance of V_6. The decisive path is defined for every node in the DAG. For example, DP(V_3) is the path through V_1 and V_3. The critical path becomes a special case of the decisive path defined for an exit node.

The multiprocessor scheduling process becomes a mapping of the task nodes in the input DAG to the processors in the target system with the goal of minimizing the execution time of the entire program. This paper assumes a complete graph for the target system; i.e., any processor can communicate with any other processor. The execution time of the entire program after scheduling is called the *parallel time* to be distinguished from the completion time of an individual task node.

3. The related work

As discussed in the introduction, the critical issue in list scheduling and clustering algorithms is the method by which the priorities of the nodes or edges of the input DAG are decided. Since most of the these scheduling algorithms use certain properties of the input DAG for deciding the priorities, we classify the existing scheduling algorithms into four categories according to the properties used: node weights, distances, the critical path, and some combinations of these parameters. This section briefly covers a typical scheduling algorithm in each category. The algorithms are used later for performance comparison against the proposed method.

3.1 Heavy Node First (HNF) algorithm

The HNF algorithm [14] assigns the nodes in a DAG to the processors, level by level. At each level, the scheduler selects the eligible nodes for scheduling in descending order based on computational weight, with the heaviest node (i.e. the node which has the largest computation cost) selected first. The node is selected arbitrarily if multiple nodes at the same level have the same computation cost. The selected node is assigned to a processor which provides the earliest start time to the node.

3.2 High Level First with Estimated Time (HLFET) algorithm

The HLFET algorithm [1] also assigns the nodes in a DAG to the processors, level by level. At each level, the scheduler assigns a higher priority to a node with a larger bottom distance. The node with the highest priority is assigned a processor which provides the earliest start time for the node.

3.3 Linear Clustering (LC) algorithm

The LC algorithm [9] is a traditional critical path based scheduling method. The scheduler identifies the critical path, removes the nodes in the path from the DAG, and assigns them to a linear cluster. The process is repeated until there are no task nodes remaining in the DAG. The clusters are then scheduled onto a processor.

3.4 Dominant Sequence Clustering (DSC) algorithm

The *dominant sequence* is a dynamic version of the critical path. The dominant sequence is the longest path of the task graph for un-scheduled nodes [21]. Initially, the dominant sequence is same as the critical path for the original input DAG. At each step, the scheduler selects one edge in the dominant sequence and zeros it if the edge zeroing reduces the length of the dominant sequence. The scheduler identifies a new dominant sequence since the edge zeroing may change the longest path. The operations are repeatedly carried out until all the edges are examined. DSC tries forward clustering (clustering from the entry node) and backward clustering (clustering from the exit node). Then the clusters providing the shorter parallel time becomes the final clusters.

3.5 Critical Path Node-Dominate (CPND) algorithm

In CPND algorithm, the nodes in the input DAG are classified into three categories: Critical Path Node (CPN), In Branch Node (IBN), and Out Branch Node (OBN). A CPN is the node on the critical path while an IBN is a nodes which is not a CPN but from which there is a path reaching a CPN. An OBN is a node which is neither a CPN nor an IBN. The CPND algorithm tries to schedule the CPNs first. If there are unscheduled IBNs which are parents of a CPN, they are scheduled in the descending order of their bottom distances. OBNs are scheduled after all CPNs and IBNs are scheduled, also in the descending order of their bottom distances. CPND algorithm obtains a schedule using a FAST (Fast Assignment using Search Technique) scheduler [11]. A series of optimizations are then applied to the original schedule to improve the performance of the application. In this paper we use the original, un-optimized CPND schedules since we are interested in investigating the effectiveness of the priority assignment methods. The optimization routines can also be applied to the proposed algorithm later on.

3.6 Comparison

The time complexity and the priority criteria for the aforementioned algorithms are summarized in Table I. The information for the proposed algorithm (DPS) is also included in this table and will be discussed shortly.

Table I. Characteristics of scheduling algorithms

Algorithm	Priority Criteria	Complexity
HNF	Level and Node Weight	$O(V^2)$
HLFET	Level and Bottom Distance	$O(V^2)$
LC	Critical Path	$O(V^3)$
DSC	Dominant Sequence	$O(V^2 log V)$
CPND	Critical Path and Bottom Distance	$O(V^2)$
DPS	Decisive Path	$O(V^2)$

As an illustration, Figure 2 presents the schedule obtained by each algorithm for the sample DAG of Figure 1. In this example, P_i represents processing element i; PT is the Parallel Time of the DAG; and [$EST(V_i, P_k)$, i, $ECT(V_i, P_k)$] represents the earliest starting time and earliest completion time of task i. In this example, the proposed algorithm provides the best parallel time compared to the other algorithms under consideration.

p1: [0, 1, 10] [10, 3, 60] [60, 2, 80][140, 6, 240]
p2: [70, 4, 80]
p3: [20, 5, 30]
       (a) The Schedule by HNF (PT = 240)

p1: [0, 1, 10] [10, 2, 30] [30, 3, 80][140, 6, 240]
p2: [70, 4, 80]
p3: [20, 5, 30]
       (b) The Schedule by HLFET (PT = 240)

p1: [0, 1, 10] [10, 2, 30][140, 6, 240]
p2: [50, 3, 100]
p3: [70, 4, 80]
p4: [20, 5, 30]
       (c) The Schedule by LC (PT = 240)

p1: [0,1,10][10,2,30][50,3,100][100, 4,110][110,6,210]
p2: [20, 5, 30]
       (d) The Schedule by Forward DSC (PT = 210)

p1: [0, 6, 100] [100, 2, 120] [120, 4, 190]
p2: [130, 3, 180] [190, 1, 200]
p3: [0, 5, 10]
       (e) The Schedule by Backward DSC (PT = 200)

p1: [0, 1, 10] [10, 2, 30] [30, 3, 80][140, 6, 240]
p2: [70, 4, 80]
p3: [20, 5, 30]
       (f) The Schedule by CPND (PT = 240)

p1: [0,1,10] [10,2,30] [30,4,40][40, 3, 90][90,6,190]
p2: [20, 5, 30]
       (g) The Schedule by DPS (PT = 190)

Figure 2. Schedules for the sample DAG

4. The proposed algorithm

4.1 Motivation

The basic heuristic behind various multiprocessor scheduling algorithms is that we can reduce the parallel time by first scheduling the task node which will have the most impact on the parallel time. For example, HNF first schedules the heaviest node (the node with the highest computation time), assuming that the heaviest node has more effect on the parallel time than others. The DSC, LC, and CPND algorithms focus on the critical path since it will most likely decide the parallel time of the application. The proposed algorithm, DPS, focuses on the "decisive path" since the length of the decisive path to a node most often determines its starting time. Note that the critical path is a special decisive path defined only for an exit node.

4.2 Algorithm description

A high level description of the proposed algorithm is presented in Figure 3. In step (1), DPS transforms an input DAG to a DAG with only one entry node and only one exit node. The transformation can be done simply by adding a dummy entry node and a dummy exit node with computation costs of zero. The dummy entry node is connected to the actual entry nodes with communication costs of zero. Similarly, the dummy exit node is connected to the actual exit nodes in the same way. Then the transformed input DAG will only have CPNs and IBNs[1]. Step (2) identifies the decisive paths to all the nodes in the transformed input DAG. The decisive path to the dummy exit node becomes the critical path of the DAG.

Step (3) builds the "task_queue" which queues all the DAG nodes, prioritized based on the lengths of their decisive paths. The priorities are decided as follows: DPS puts the CPNs into the task_queue in the ascending order of their top distances (parents first) if there is no IBN for a given CPN. If there are some IBNs reaching a CPN, the IBN belonging to the decisive path of the CPN is selected first among the un-queued IBNs. The same procedure is carried out recursively if an IBN has parents which are not queued yet. After all the parents are queued in the task_queue, the CPN is inserted, as shown in the search_and_put() procedure . Finally, DPS assigns the task_queue tasks (in FIFO order) to the processing elements (PEs). At each step of the

---
[1] Please refer to section 3.5 for the definitions of CPN and IBN.

assignment, the selected PE provides the earliest start time for the task under consideration, taking into account all the communications from the task's parents (i.e., find a suitable PE for assignment). If the completion time of a task is larger than the sum of all the computation costs of the nodes, DPS assigns all the nodes to one processor and exits from the algorithm as shown in steps (7) and (8).

DPS Algorithm
(1) Transform the input DAG so that the DAG has only one entry and only one exit node;
(2) Identify the decisive path to each node;
       /* the decisive path to the exit node becomes
       the critical path, CP */
(3) task_queue = build_task_queue(CP);
(4) for each task, V_i, in the task_queue in a FIFO manner
(5)   find the suitable processor for V_i;
(6)   schedule V_i on the suitable processor;
(7)   if ECT(V_i) ≥ ΣT(V_k), ∀ V_k
(8)   uni_schedule();
(9)   exit(0);

build_task_queue(CP)
/* Let CPN be a set of nodes belonging to CP.
NQ is a set of nodes which are not in the task queue yet.
Initially, NQ contains all the nodes in the input DAG. */
(10) while (NQ ≠ ∅)
(11) for each task V_i, distance[V_i] < distance[V_j], ∀V_j,
     V_i, V_j∈CPN, V_i, V_j∈NQ
(12)   if ∀V_k ∉NQ, V_k ⇒ V_i
(13)   put V_i into the task queue;
(14)   NQ = NQ - {V_i};
(15)   else
(16)   search_and_put(V_i);
(17) return the task queue;

search_and_put(V_i)
(18) for V_d, distance[V_d] + C(V_d, V_i) ≥ distance[V_o] +
    C(V_o, V_i), ∀V_o, V_d⇒V_i, V_o⇒V_i, V_d, V_o∈ NQ
    /* V_d is the iparent of and in the decisive path to V_i */
(19)   search_and_put(V_d);
(20)   put V_d into the task queue;
(21)   NQ = NQ - {V_d};

uni_schedule()
(22) remove the schedule obtained so far;
(23) schedule all the tasks on one processor;

Figure 3. Description of the DPS algorithm

Step (2) takes $O(V^2)$ time for identifying the decisive paths to all the nodes. Step (3) also takes $O(V^2)$ time since it examines all the edges in the input DAG. Step (5) takes $O(V)$ time since |V| processors are enough for this scheduler. Thus, the time complexity of the DPS algorithm becomes $O(V^2)$.

4.3 Analysis of the proposed algorithm

The worst case analysis of the scheduling algorithm is important especially for real-time systems. At first, we will show the worst case performance and the optimality condition of the DPS algorithm for a tree structured input DAG. Then the worst case performance analysis for a general input DAG is presented. The notations used in the proofs are first summarized:

- V_r: is the entry node.
- V_e: is the exit node.
- $V_{k,a}$: is node V_k whose level is a.
- V_p: is an iparent[2] of V_e, which means that V_p is the exit node in the original input DAG before the transformation.
- LDP(V_i): is the length of the decisive path to the task node V_i.
- DPN(V_i): is a set of nodes on the decisive path to the task node V_i.
- FN: is a set of fork nodes.

For a tree structured input DAG, the worst case parallel time obtained by the DPS algorithm is $\max_p\{\Sigma T(V_j) + \Sigma C(V_i, V_j)\}$, $V_i \Rightarrow V_j$, $V_i \in$ FN, V_i, V_j∈DPN(V_p), ∀V_p, $V_p \Rightarrow V_e$. That is, the worst case parallel time is the largest ECT(V_p) which is the sum of computation costs of the nodes on the path to V_p plus the sum of the communication costs from *only* the fork nodes on the path. Theorem 1 proves this assertion by induction. The proof basically says that, for any ichild[2], V_j, of V_i, ECT(V_j) = ECT(V_i)+ T(V_j), if V_i is not a fork node while ECT(V_j) = ECT(V_i) + C(V_i, V_j) + T(V_j) in the worst case if V_i is a fork node with the basis that ECT(V_r) = T(V_r).

Theorem 1: For a tree structured input DAG, the worst case parallel time obtained by DPS, PT(DPS), is $\max_p\{\Sigma T(V_j) + \Sigma C(V_i, V_j)\}$, $V_i \Rightarrow V_j$, $V_i \in$ FN, V_i, V_j∈DPN(V_p), ∀V_p, $V_p \Rightarrow V_e$.
Proof:
The parallel time is the largest ECT(V_p), ∀V_p, $V_p \Rightarrow V_e$, since C(V_p, V_e) = 0 and T(V_e) = 0. We are going to show that ECT(V_p) = $\Sigma T(V_j) + \Sigma C(V_i, V_j)$, $V_i \Rightarrow V_j$, $V_i \in$ FN, V_i, V_j∈DPN(V_p), in the worst case.
1) **Basis:** For the entry node V_r, ECT(V_r) = T(V_r).
2) **Inductive Hypothesis** : for ∀V_j, $V_i \Rightarrow V_j$
2.1) ECT(V_j) = ECT(V_i)+ T(V_j), if V_i ∉ FN.

---

[2] Please refer to section 2 for the definitions of iparent and ichild.

477

2.2) $ECT(V_j) = ECT(V_i) + C(V_i, V_j) + T(V_j)$ in the worst case, if $V_i \in FN$.

3) Inductive Step: Let P_k be the processor where V_i has been scheduled.

3.1) If $V_i \notin FN$, $V_i \Rightarrow V_j$, the suitable PE obtained by step (5) in the algorithm will be P_k since P_k gives the earliest start time $EST(V_j) = ECT(V_i)$. Then $ECT(V_j) = ECT(V_i) + T(V_j)$.

3.2) If $V_i \in FN$, $V_i \Rightarrow V_j$, the suitable PE obtained by step (5) will be P_k if P_k provides a start time for V_j which is earlier than $ECT(V_i) + C(V_i, V_j)$. Otherwise, step (5) will return another processor where $ECT(V_j) = ECT(V_i) + C(V_i, V_j) + T(V_j)$. Thus, it is guaranteed that $ECT(V_j) = ECT(V_i) + C(V_i, V_j) + T(V_j)$ in the worst case. $\square$

Observation: The DPS algorithm generates optimal schedules for tree structured DAGs if the following condition holds: $\sum C(V_i, V_j) \le CPEC - \sum T(V_j)$, $V_i \Rightarrow V_j$, $V_i \in FN$, $V_i, V_j \in DPN(V_p)$, $\forall V_p$, $V_p \Rightarrow V_e$. From theorem 1 we know that the worst case parallel time $PT(DPS) = \max_p\{\sum T(V_j) + \sum C(V_i, V_j)\}$. Thus, if $\max_p\{\sum T(V_j) + \sum C(V_i, V_j)\} \le CPEC$, the schedule is an optimal one. The aforementioned optimality condition then be trivially derived from this inequality.

It is obvious that the parallel time obtained by the DPS scheduler is always less than or equal to the sum of the computation costs of the task nodes in any DAG due to steps (7) and (8) of the algorithm (Figure 3). We will also prove that the parallel time obtained by the proposed algorithm is always less than or equal to the length of the critical path, CPIC, for any input DAG. Note that the parallel time is the same as $ECT(S_e)$, and the CPIC is the same as $LDP(S_e)$. Therefore, proving that the parallel time is always less than or equal to CPIC is equivalent to proving $ECT(S_e) \le LDP(S_e)$.

Theorem 2: For any input DAG, when using the DPS algorithm for scheduling, $ECT(S_e) \le LDP(S_e)$.

Proof by induction:

1) Basis: $ECT(V_{k,2}) \le LDP(V_{k,2})$.

At level one, $ECT(V_r) = LDP(V_r) = T(V_r)$ since V_r is the dummy entry node. Then $ECT(V_{k,2}) = ECT(V_r) + T(V_r)$ if $V_{k,2} \in CPN$. If $V_{k,2} \notin CPN$, the suitable PE is the processor where V_r is scheduled if $EST(V_{k,2}) \le ECT(V_r) + C(V_r, V_{k,2})$. Otherwise $V_{k,2}$ will be scheduled on a different processor where $ECT(V_{k,2}) = ECT(V_r) + C(V_r, V_{k,2}) + T(V_{k,2})$. Therefore, it is guaranteed that $ECT(V_{k,2}) \le ECT(V_r) + C(V_r, V_{k,2}) + T(V_{k,2})$. Thus, $ECT(V_{k,2}) \le LDP(V_{k,2})$ since $LDP(V_{k,2}) = LDP(V_r) + C(V_r, V_{k,2}) + T(V_{k,2})$ for any $V_{k,2}$.

2) Inductive Hypothesis: if $ECT(V_{k,i}) \le LDP(V_{k,i})$ then $ECT(V_{k,i+1}) \le LDP(V_{k,i+1})$

3) Inductive Step:

$V_{k,i+1}$ will be scheduled on the processor where $V_{k,i}$, $V_{k,i} \Rightarrow V_{k,i+1}$, has been scheduled if $EST(V_{k,i+1}) \le ECT(V_{k,i}) + C(V_{k,i}, V_{k,i+1})$. Otherwise $V_{k,i+1}$ will be scheduled on a different processor where $ECT(V_{k,i+1}) = ECT(V_{k,i}) + C(V_{k,i}, V_{k,i+1}) + T(V_{k,i+1})$. So it is guaranteed that $ECT(V_{k,i+1}) \le ECT(V_{k,i}) + C(V_{k,i}, V_{k,i+1}) + T(V_{k,i+1})$. Thus, $ECT(V_{k,i+1}) \le LDP(V_{k,i+1})$ if $ECT(V_{k,i}) \le LDP(V_{k,i})$ since $LDP(V_{k,i+1}) = LDP(V_{k,i}) + C(V_{k,i}, V_{k,i+1}) + T(V_{k,i+1})$.

According to the inductive step, the completion time of any node is shorter than the length of the decisive path to that node, including the exit node. That is, the parallel time is always less than or equal to the CPIC. $\square$

5. Performance comparison

We generated random DAGs to compare the performance of the proposed DPS algorithm with that of the existing scheduling algorithms through a simulation study. We used four parameters the effects of which we were interested to investigate:

1. The number of DAG nodes: DAGs of varying sizes, including DAGs with 20, 40, 60, 80, and 100 were considered.

2. The CCR (Communication to Computation Ratio): CCR is the ratio of average communication cost to the average computation cost. CCR values of 0.1, 0.5, 1.0, 5.0, and 10.0 were considered.

3. The depth or maximum level of the DAG: We were interested to investigate the effect of the degree of parallelism in a DAG on the scheduling algorithms. For a fixed number of nodes, a DAG with a shorter depth (maximum level or level of the dummy exit node) displays more parallelism compared to a DAG with a longer depth. If K is the average number of siblings at a level, and N is the number of DAG nodes, then the average depth of the DAG will be N/K. Thus, for a fixed number of DAG nodes, if the average number of siblings at the same level (K) is small, the DAG represents a tall and lean graph which has a low degree of parallelism. On the other hand, a large value of K generates DAGs with more parallelism among the siblings. In our studies, we ranged the number of siblings (K) from 2 to 10.

4. The average out-degree of a node: The average out-degree of a node controls the density and amount of communication among the nodes. The larger the average out-degree, the denser the DAG is and

more communications are generated. We considered the average out-degrees of 2 to K.

There are 25 combinations of the DAG sizes and the CCR values (5×5). Since there are 9 levels (from 2 to 10) for each combination and each level K has (K -1) cases of outgoing degrees (from 2 to K), there are 45 (1 + 2 + ... + 9) cases for each combination. Since we generated 5 random DAGs for each case, the number of DAGs used for the performance comparison study is 5,625 (25 × 45 × 5). The scheduling algorithms discussed in section 3; i.e., HNF, HLFET, LC, DSC, and CPND, were compared against the DPS algorithm.

For performance comparison, we define a *normalized* performance measure named *Relative Parallel Time (RPT)*, which is the ratio of the parallel time to CPEC. For example, if the parallel time obtained by the DPS is 200 and CPEC is 100, RPT of DPS is 2.0. If LC provides a parallel of 250 for the same DAG, then its RPT is 2.5. A smaller RPT value is indicative of a shorter parallel time. The RPT of any scheduling algorithm can not be lower than one since CPEC is the lower bound for completion time of the DAG.

Figure 4 compares the performance of the scheduling algorithms with respect to the number of DAG nodes. Each case in Figure 4 shows an average RPT value from 1125 runs with varying CCR, K, and average out-degree values. The average values of CCR and K turned out to be 3.3 and 5, respectively. As shown in Figure 4, the number of nodes does not significantly affect the relative performance of scheduling algorithms. In other words, the performance comparison shows similar patterns regardless of N. The pattern shows that for the same set of DAGs, DPS provides a shorter parallel time than the existing algorithms.

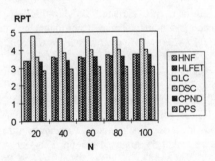

Figure 4. Performance comparison with respect to N (for average CCR = 3.3 and K = 5)

Figure 5 depicts the RPT values for varying CCR values. When CCR is less than one, DSC slightly outperforms the other algorithms. When CCR is one, all the algorithms perform evenly. However, as the CCR value is increased, DPS outperforms the other

algorithms. The performance gap becomes larger as CCR values are increased.

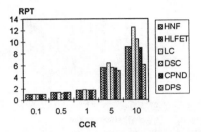

Figure 5. Performance comparison with respect to CCR (for N = 100 and average K=5)

Figure 6 shows the effect of the degree of parallelism in the DAG (represented by K = average number of sibling nodes at each level) on the scheduling algorithms. Recall that for a fixed number of nodes in the DAG, a smaller K value results in a more serial DAG, while a larger K results in a more parallel DAG. In all cases the proposed DPS algorithm outperforms the other scheduling algorithms, however, the performance gap becomes more pronounced for DAGs with a higher degree of parallelism. This is an important result because it shows that the decisive path heuristic does a good job of discriminating the nodes in the difficult case of having many parallel nodes as well as the easy case of having many serial nodes in the input DAG.

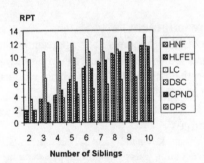

Figure 6. Performance comparison with respect to number of siblings (K) (for N = 100 and CCR = 10)

Finally, Figure 7 depicts the performance results when the amount of communication, represented by the average out-degree of the nodes, in the DAG is varied. It seems the studied scheduling algorithms are not sensitive to the degree of communication (or dependency) in the DAG. The relative performances remain fixed for varying average node out-degrees. However, in almost all cases, DPS outperforms the other algorithms.

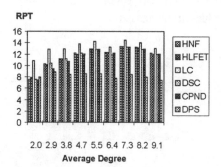

RPT

2.0 2.9 3.8 4.7 5.5 6.4 7.3 8.2 9.1
Average Degree

Figure 7. Performance comparison with respect to average out-degree of a node (for N = 100, CCR = 10, and K = 10)

6. Conclusion

One of the critical issues in a list scheduling algorithm is the development of a method for assignment of priorities to the nodes or edges of an input DAG. In this paper we proposed a novel method, called decisive path scheduling, for determining node priorities in a list scheduling algorithm. Through an extensive performance study, it is shown that the proposed algorithm outperforms many of the existing list scheduling , as well as clustering, algorithms. The paper also establishes an optimality condition for tree structured DAGs and provides a worst-case analysis of the proposed algorithm.

Acknowledgment

We would like to express our appreciation to Dr. Tao Yang and his research group for providing the source code for the DSC schedulers which was used in our performance comparison study.

References

[1] T. L. Adam, K. Chandy, and J. Dickson, "A Comparison of List Scheduling for Parallel Processing System," *Communication of the ACM*, vol. 17, no. 12, Dec. 1974, pp. 685-690.

[2] I. Ahmad and Y. K. Kwok, "A New Approach to Scheduling Parallel Program Using Task Duplication," *Proc. of Int'l Conf. on Parallel Processing*, vol. II, Aug. 1994, pp. 47-51.

[3] F. D. Anger, J. J. Hwang, and Y. C. Chow, "Scheduling with Sufficiently Loosely Coupled Processors," *Journal of Parallel and Distributed Computing*, vol. 9, 1990, pp. 87-92.

[4] H. Chen, B. Shirazi, and J. Marquis, "Performance Evaluation of A Novel Scheduling Method: Linear Clustering with Task Duplication," *Proc. of Int'l Conf. on Parallel and Distributed Systems*, Dec. 1993, pp. 270-275.

[5] Y. C. Chung and S. Ranka, "Application and Performance Analysis of a Compile-Time Optimization Approach for List Scheduling Algorithms on Distributed-Memory Multiprocessors," *Proc. of Supercomputing'92*, Nov. 1992, pp. 512-521.

[6] J. Y. Colin and P. Chretienne, "C.P.M. Scheduling with Small Communication Delays and Task Duplication," *Operations Research*, 1991, pp. 680-684.

[7] S. Darbha and D. P. Agrawal, "SDBS: A task duplication based optimal scheduling algorithm," *Proc. of Scalable High Performance Computing Conf.*, May 1994, pp. 756-763.

[8] H. El-Rewini, T. G. Lewis, and H. H. Ali, "Task Scheduling in Parallel and Distributed Systems," Prentice Hall 1994, pp.85.

[9] Kim, S. J., and Browne, J. C., "A general approach to mapping of parallel computation upon multiprocessor architectures," *Proc. of Int'l Conf. on Parallel Processing*, vol. III, 1988, pp. 1-8.

[10] B. Kruatrachue and T. G. Lewis, "Grain Size Determination for parallel processing," *IEEE Software*, Jan. 1988, pp. 23-32

[11] Y.-K. Kwok, I. Ahmad, and J. Gu, "FAST: A Low-Complexity Algorithm for Efficient Scheduling of DAGs on Parallel Processors," *Proc. of Int'l Conf. on Parallel Processing*, vol. II, 1996, pp. 150-157.

[12] C. H. Papadimitriou and M. Yannakakis, "Towards an architecture-independent analysis of parallel algorithms," *ACM Proc. of Symp. on Theory of Computing (STOC)*, 1988, pp. 510-513.

[13] G. Park, B. Shirazi, and J. Marquis, "DFRN: A New Approach on Duplication Based Scheduling for Distributed Multiprocessor Systems," To be appear in *Int'l Parallel Processing Symp.* 1997.

[14] B. Shirazi, M. Wang, and G. Pathak, "Analysis and Evaluation of Heuristic Methods for Static Task Scheduling," *Journal of Parallel and Distributed Computing*, vol. 10, No. 3, 1990, pp. 222 -232.

[15] B. Shirazi, A.R. Hurson, "Scheduling and Load Balancing: Guest Editors' Introduction," *Journal of Parallel and Distributed Computing*, Dec. 1992, pp. 271-275.

[16] B. Shirazi, A.R. Hurson, "A Mini-track on Scheduling and Load Balancing: Track Coordinator's Introduction," *Hawaii Int'l Conf. on System Sciences (HICSS-26)*, January 1993, pp. 484-486.

[17] B. Shirazi, A.R. Hurson, K. Kavi, "Scheduling & Load Balancing," *IEEE Press*, 1995.

[18] B. Shirazi, H.-B. Chen, and J. Marquis, "Comparative Study of Task Duplication Static Scheduling versus Clustering and Non-Clustering Techniques," *Concurrency:Practice and Experience*, vol. 7(5), August 1995, pp. 371-389.

[19] M. Y. Wu and D. D. Gajski, "Hypertool: A Programming Aid for Message-Passing Systems," *IEEE Trans. on Parallel and Distributed Systems*, vol. 1, no. 3, Jul. 1990, pp. 330-340.

[20] M.Y. Wu, A dedicated track on "Program Partitioning and Scheduling in Parallel and Distributed Systems," in the *Hawaii Int'l Conference on Systems Sciences*, January 1994.

[21] T. Yang and A. Gerasoulis, "DSC: Scheduling Parallel tasks on an Unbounded Number of Processors," *IEEE Trans. On Parallel and Distributed Systems*, vol. 5, no. 9, pp. 951-967, Sep. 1994.

Modeling The Impact of Run-Time Uncertainty on Optimal Computation Scheduling Using Feedback

R.D. Dietz, T.L. Casavant, T.E. Scheetz, T.A. Braun, M.S. Andersland
sedia@eng.uiowa.edu

Parallel Processing Laboratory
Electrical and Computer Engineering Department
The University of Iowa
Iowa City, Iowa 52242

Abstract

Increasingly, feedback *of measured run-time information is being used in the optimization of computation execution. This paper introduces a model relating the static view of a computation to its run-time variance that is useful in this context. A notion of* uncertainty *is then used to provide bounds on key scheduling parameters of the run-time computation. To illustrate the relationship between fidelity in measured information and minimum schedulable grain size, we apply the bounds to three existing parallel architectures for the case of run-time variance caused by monitoring intrusion. We also outline a hybrid static-dynamic scheduling paradigm—SEDIA—that uses the model of uncertainty to optimize computation for execution in the presence of run-time variance from sources other than monitoring intrusion.*

1 Introduction

There are many parallel-specific optimization techniques that *assume* the availability of static run-time information. Static scheduling heuristics, for example, rely on *known* task durations and communication latencies. In the past, such information has been extracted/predicted from source code as needed [9]. To more accurately plan for *run-time variance* in computation execution, optimization methods are increasingly utilizing *measured* run-time information. For example, there have been several investigations into the use of profile information with compiler optimizations for sequential machines [3, 10, 15, 16]. Measured run-time information can only be useful in these contexts if the computation model is valid. The validity of static run-time information is even more difficult to ensure in a parallel and distributed setting. To characterize this difficulty, we will model the impact of run-time uncertainty regarding key scheduling parameters on the performance of scheduling optimizations in this paper.

It is probable that the best solutions in parallel computation optimization are neither static nor dynamic in nature, but rather of some hybrid form. Usually these solutions are only obtained after a large amount of "hand tuning". Present investigations may lead to advances in the automation of such optimizations. These investigations are focusing on the use of run-time variance knowledge in the optimization process [7, 14]. They have not studied the enhancement of dynamic mechanisms because of the lack of a model relating variance to <u>both</u> the static and dynamic aspects of scheduling.

In this paper we show how an uncertainty model we have developed can bridge the gap between static and dynamic scheduling by illustrating its application to the static and dynamic scheduling of tasks. For simplicity, but without loss of generality, the model presented is developed in the constrained context of monitoring intrusion. This context allows the model to build upon our past research and modeling experience in the areas of trace recovery [1] and uncertainty [17], while encompassing the more general causes of run-time variance. To illustrate how the model may be used as the foundation for improving parallel computation schedule optimization, we will also briefly outline a two part scheduling paradigm known as SE-DIA (**S**tatic **E**xploration/**D**ynamic **I**nstantiation and **A**ctivation).

2 Background

In the literature, the term "task" is sometimes used interchangeably with "grain", "thread", "process", etc. In this paper, a computation *grain* is assumed to be the most atomic sequentially-executing portion of work in the computation. A *task* is considered to be a sequence of such grains; hence, a task has a "grain-size".

We formally define the computation itself using the well-known *task precedence graph* (TPG) model. This model views a computation as a directed acyclic graph (DAG) defined by the tuple $\Phi = (V, E, C, T)$. Here V is a set of vertices representing the computation's tasks, E is the set of edges representing dependency between the tasks (i.e., communication activity), C is the set of communication latencies corresponding to the edges, and T is the set of task durations corresponding to the vertices. It is assumed that the same units of measurement are used for members of C and T. Computation executions are described by their (static) *execution schedule*, denoted

481

as $\Sigma = (O_0, O_1, \ldots, O_{n-1})$. Here, n is the number of processing elements (PEs) in the architecture and each O_i, $0 \leq i < n$, is a clustering of tasks assigned to the ith PE.

To make quantitative comparisons between a computation's execution schedules, we use the *parallel execution time*, denoted $T_P(\Sigma, \Phi)$. This function corresponds to the total execution time required to complete a computation using a specified execution schedule. Many scheduling algorithms use this metric to make scheduling decisions, statically determining its value from a critical path analysis. For computation run-time, this function equates to the time difference between the start of the first task and the end of the last task in a computation.

Using run-time information for optimization implies the use of *feedback* since information must be gathered from computation execution <u>before</u> it can be used for computation optimization. There exist several types of computation information that may be measured at run-time. These can be distinguished as *samples*, *profiles*, or *traces*. <u>Samples</u> correspond to information gathered at predefined intervals; for example, information gathered via a timed interrupt routine on each PE. <u>Profiles</u> are simple statistics gathered about the computation, such as the number of times a function is executed or a branch is taken. Such information is typically derived from "counters" inserted in the portion of the computation under study. Finally, <u>traces</u> consist of ordered sequences of *events* in a computation. At a bare minimum, each such event would consist of a unique identifier and time-stamp recorded via monitoring code inserted in the computation source code. Trace information is naturally applicable to parallel scheduling because scheduling presupposes computation measurements involving time; namely, task weights and communication delays in a TPG. Also, since profiles may be derived from traces (via post-processing of event identifiers), the use of traces does not preclude the growing number of profile-based compiler optimization studies [3, 10, 15, 16].

The collection of traces in a software-intensive manner causes intrusion and uncertainty which diminishes the fidelity of the run-time information being gathered. Our research into **trace recovery** [1], however, has shown that such intrusion may not only be modeled in parallel systems, but largely compensated for via post-processing. In generalizing the trace recovery process to fit existing parallel architectures, we found that a critical aspect of our modeling was the *uncertainty* inherent in these architectures and programs [17]. The presence of this uncertainty implies that the actual intrusion from software probing must be bounded between a minimal monitor statement intrusion, ΔM, and additive worst-case term, δM_{MAX}. Another contribution can be attributed to the lack of clock precision in parallel systems, quantified by the term $ClkP$. This term describes the number of CPU clock cycles that make up 1 cycle of the clock used by the time-stamp mechanism. Table 1 shows measured/calculated values for ΔM, δM_{MAX}, and $ClkP$

Architecture	ΔM	δM_{MAX}	$ClkP$
N-Cube	7 cycles	17 cycles	1 cycle
Paragon	29 cycles	31 cycles	5 cycles
KSR	8 cycles	56 cycles	8 cycles

Table 1: Example Uncertainty Parameters

on some existing parallel systems.

We now restate the bound on the uncertainty of the ith trace event time, δ_i, (developed in [17]) as

$$\delta_i \leq \delta M_{MAX} \cdot n_i + 2 \cdot ClkP . \qquad (1)$$

Here, n_i denotes the number of previously recovered trace events (hence, it is an artifact of trace recovery). The uncertainty bounds determined by this equation may be added as a new field in the recovered trace (as recovery proceeds) alongside the event identifiers and time-stamps.

3 Uncertainty & Scheduling

We now formally define *information uncertainty* and discuss its relation to scheduling optimality. This analysis is a generalization of previous work by Gerasoulis, Jiao, and Yang [7], whose intent was to justify the use of estimated computation information for scheduling in their PYRROS tool.

To model information uncertainty, we first introduce two TPGs: $\Phi^a = (V, E, C^a, T^a)$, with $c_{i,j}^a \in C^a$ and $t_i^a \in T^a$; and $\Phi^m = (V, E, C^m, T^m)$, with $c_{i,j}^m \in C^m$ and $t_i^m \in T^m$. Φ^a models the *actual* computation—i.e., the exact DAG for the computation if it could be measured without intrusion at runtime. Φ^m is the *measured* view of this computation—i.e., the software-measured information that may be used to optimize the execution of Φ^a. As implied by the superscripts, the result of measurement intrusion appears in the edge and vertex weights, $c_{i,j}$ and t_i. It has no impact on the structure of the TPG (i.e., V and E).

Any difference between Φ^a and Φ^m due to uncertainty-induced intrusion may be formally captured by the following bounds:

$$(1 - \varepsilon^{m-}) \cdot t_i^a \leq t_i^m \leq (1 + \varepsilon^{m+}) \cdot t_i^a \qquad (2)$$

$$(1 - \varepsilon^{m-}) \cdot c_{i,j}^a \leq c_{i,j}^m \leq (1 + \varepsilon^{m+}) \cdot c_{i,j}^a . \qquad (3)$$

Here, ε^{m-} and ε^{m+} are termed the (lower and upper) *uncertainty margins* of the TPG measurement technique. These margins propagate to the parallel time function (through a critical path analysis), implying

$$(1 - \varepsilon^{m-}) \cdot T_p(\Sigma, \Phi^a) \leq T_p(\Sigma, \Phi^m) \leq (1 + \varepsilon^{m+}) \cdot T_p(\Sigma, \Phi^a) . \qquad (4)$$

Intuitively, this equation says that a schedule's measured/estimated execution time is bounded within fixed uncertainty margins of the actual execution time of the same schedule.

To see the effect of such uncertainty margins on scheduling, we first define three schedules: Σ_h^m, Σ_{opt}^m, and Σ_{opt}^a. Σ_h^m corresponds to the schedule created by a scheduling heuristic whose knowledge of the computation is based on measurement, Φ^m. Σ_{opt}^m corresponds to the optimal schedule for this measured computation TPG. Finally, Σ_{opt}^a represents the (ideal) schedule that would actually be optimal at run-time (with respect to Φ^a). Obtaining this last schedule is the primary goal in scheduling research of relevance here. While it may not be readily attainable, it provides an important performance bound for analysis.

As with uncertainty, a scheduling heuristics performance can be bounded using the equation

$$T_p(\Sigma_h, \Phi) \leq (1 + \varepsilon^h) \cdot T_p(\Sigma_{opt}, \Phi) . \quad (5)$$

Here, ε^h is an upper bound on a scheduling heuristic's possible deviation from an optimal scheduling solution. The single-sided nature of this bound reflects the fact that a scheduling heuristic can never create a schedule that performs better than the optimal schedule.

Using equations (4) and (5), one can compare the performance of a schedule created heuristically from run-time information with known uncertainty (Σ_h^m) to that of the optimal run-time schedule (Σ_{opt}^a). The following theorem formalizes this limit on the ability to assess performance due to both information uncertainty and the use of scheduling heuristics.

Theorem 1
$$T_p(\Sigma_h^m, \Phi^a) \leq \left(\frac{1+\varepsilon^{m+}}{1-\varepsilon^{m-}} \right) \cdot (1 + \varepsilon^h) \cdot T_p(\Sigma_{opt}^a, \Phi^a)$$

Proof: This theorem can be proved by direct manipulation of the defined bounds. From (4), it is apparent that

$$T_p(\Sigma_h^m, \Phi^a) \leq \left(\frac{1}{1-\varepsilon^{m-}} \right) \cdot T_p(\Sigma_h^m, \Phi^m) . \quad (6)$$

From (5), we know that

$$T_p(\Sigma_h^m, \Phi^m) \leq (1 + \varepsilon^h) \cdot T_p(\Sigma_{opt}^m, \Phi^m) . \quad (7)$$

Substituting the right-hand side of (7) into the right-hand side (6), we obtain

$$T_p(\Sigma_h^m, \Phi^a) \leq \left(\frac{1}{1-\varepsilon^{m-}} \right) \cdot ((1+\varepsilon^h) \cdot T_p(\Sigma_{opt}^m, \Phi^m)) . \quad (8)$$

By definition, we know that

$$T_p(\Sigma_{opt}^m, \Phi^m) \leq T_p(\Sigma_{opt}^a, \Phi^m) . \quad (9)$$

Again using substitution, this time into the right-hand side of (8), we have

$$T_p(\Sigma_h^m, \Phi^a) \leq \left(\frac{1}{1-\varepsilon^{m-}} \right) \cdot (1+\varepsilon^h) \cdot (T_p(\Sigma_{opt}^a, \Phi^m)) . \quad (10)$$

From (4), we know that

$$T_p(\Sigma_{opt}^a, \Phi^m) \leq (1 + \varepsilon^{m+}) \cdot T_p(\Sigma_{opt}^a, \Phi^a) . \quad (11)$$

A final substitution of the right-hand side of (11) in the right-hand side of (10) yields

$$T_p(\Sigma_h^m, \Phi^a) \leq \left(\frac{1}{1-\varepsilon^{m-}} \right) \cdot ((1 + \varepsilon^{m+}) \cdot T_p(\Sigma_{opt}^a, \Phi^a)) ,$$

which is easily rearranged as

$$T_p(\Sigma_h^m, \Phi^a) \leq \left(\frac{1+\varepsilon^{m+}}{1-\varepsilon^{m-}} \right) \cdot (1 + \varepsilon^h) \cdot T_p(\Sigma_{opt}^a, \Phi^a)$$

to complete the proof. □

4 Modeling Uncertainty

As demonstrated in the previous section, to analyze the effects of uncertainty in run-time information on schedule fidelity we need to determine three bounding (error) margins: ε^h, ε^{m-}, and ε^{m+}. ε^h, the error associated with heuristic scheduling, may be determined in at least two ways. First, as with other NP-complete problems, conservative values may be derived theoretically. It has been documented, for instance, that a number of parallel scheduling heuristics provide schedules provably within a factor of 2 of optimal [6], implying $\varepsilon^h = 1$. Alternately, values may be obtained from empirical data. For example, El-Rewini and Lewis state that the *highest level first* (HLF) heuristic provides schedules within 5% of the optimum in 90% of random cases [4], implying that $\varepsilon^h = 0.05$ for this heuristic. Unfortunately, the problems associated with run-time information measurement in parallel systems have not received as much attention as parallel scheduling, making ε^{m-} and ε^{m+} less quantifiable than ε^h. For this reason, we next outline how values for these uncertainty bounds (both with and without the application of trace recovery) can be derived.

4.1 Fundamental Modeling

To quantify ε^{m-} and ε^{m+}, we must first assume that each trace event consists of three components: an event identifier, i; a measured time-stamp, ts_i^m; and the uncertainty term, δ_i. This uncertainty term is assumed to equate to either the (maximum) bound in equation (1) or the (maximum) variance found in existing trace data. Given this information, we know that the intrusion associated with trace event i is within δ_i time units of the minimal time-stamp intrusion, ΔM, as shown in Figure 1(a). Here, the total

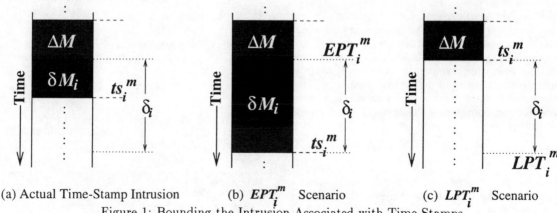

(a) Actual Time-Stamp Intrusion   (b) EPT_i^m Scenario   (c) LPT_i^m Scenario

Figure 1: Bounding the Intrusion Associated with Time-Stamps

intrusion due to software monitoring is $\Delta M + \delta M_i$, where $0 \leq \delta M_i \leq \delta_i$.

To find worst-case bounds on the intrusion associated with a given time-stamp, ts_i^m, we must determine the *earliest possible time* and *latest possible time* that this time-stamp could have occurred, denoted EPT_i^m and LPT_i^m, respectively. As shown in Figure 1(b), to calculate EPT_i^m we assume that the time-stamp incurred the full amount of the uncertainty-induced intrusion (i.e., $\delta M_i = \delta_i$); hence, for any time-stamp

$$EPT_i^m = ts_i^m - \delta_i . \qquad (12)$$

Similarly, as shown in Figure 1(c), LPT_i^m corresponds to the least amount of the uncertainty-induced intrusion (i.e., $\delta M_i = 0$); hence, for any time-stamp

$$LPT_i^m = ts_i^m + \delta_i . \qquad (13)$$

To allow a comparison of a trace-measured TPG to its corresponding actual TPG, we now relate the actual run-time time-stamps to the trace event time-stamps. This is accomplished by defining bounds for the actual time-stamps, EPT_i^a and LPT_i^a, in terms of (12) and (13), allowing us to bound the actual time-stamp value as

$$EPT_i^a \leq ts_i^a \leq LPT_i^a . \qquad (14)$$

Such bounds can be defined independent of the application of trace recovery.

If the time-stamps in the trace <u>are not</u> trace recovered, the effects of the (accumulating) known intrusion, ΔM, must be considered. For the ith trace event, this implies $EPT_i^a = EPT_i^m - n_i \cdot \Delta M$ and $LPT_i^a = LPT_i^m - n_i \cdot \Delta M$; which expand to

$$EPT_i^a = ts_i^m - \delta_i - n_i \cdot \Delta M \qquad (15)$$

and

$$LPT_i^a = ts_i^m + \delta_i - n_i \cdot \Delta M . \qquad (16)$$

In these equations, n_i is the number of trace events contributing to the accumulation of intrusion for the ith event—a number which would be computed during trace recovery. If the time-stamps in the trace <u>are</u> trace recovered, the effects of the ΔM terms have already been removed from the time-stamps, therefore $EPT_i^a = EPT_i^m$ and $LPT_i^a = LPT_i^m$, or equivalently,

$$EPT_i^a = ts_i^m - \delta_i \qquad (17)$$

and

$$LPT_i^a = ts_i^m + \delta_i . \qquad (18)$$

This follows from intuition, since these are exactly (15) and (16) with $\Delta M = 0$.

4.2 TPG Measurement Concepts

Having modeled the effects of uncertainty on individual time-stamps in a run-time trace, we can extend the model to capture the behavior of a complete computation containing multiple monitoring points and multiple occurrences of individual monitors. The following lemma characterizes the *monitoring coverage* necessary for complete TPG measurement using traces.

Lemma 1 *Complete measurement of a computation's TPG, $\Phi^a = (V, E, C, T)$, requires at least $2 \cdot |V|$ monitoring points.*

Proof: Assuming that Φ^a is composed of atomic tasks, we need not worry about taking measurements

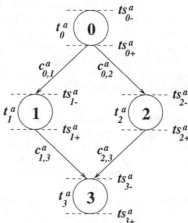

Figure 2: Computation TPG Measurement via Traces

within tasks, only around them. (The grain packing work of Kruatrachue and Lewis [11] indicates that the smallest atomic grains possible should be measured to achieve optimal execution.) As shown in Figure 2, this implies that $2 \cdot |V|$ monitoring points are required to measure the computation task durations. The use of atomic tasks further implies that the dependency between tasks in the TPG only appears at task edges. For this reason, the same $2 \cdot |V|$ monitoring points used for task measurement may be used to measure communication latencies. Note, the existence of "join" points in the TPG implies message synchronization at the join's monitoring time-stamp (ts_{3-}^a in Figure 2, for example). Potentially, the largest communication latency at such points may mask shorter communication latencies. This masking can be avoided by aggregating measurements from several individual computation executions. Using the fact that communication costs are 0 for tasks assigned to the same PE, the placement of the tasks involved in join points can be varied over multiple traces so that each communication's pair of time-stamps are correct in at least one trace. It is for this reason that $2 \cdot |V|$ monitoring points is a minimum. $\square$

By denoting the time-stamp associated with the <u>prior</u> monitoring event for the ith task as ts_{i-} and the time-stamp of the <u>later</u> monitoring event as ts_{i+}, the task duration, t_i, can be calculated as

$$t_i = (ts_{i+} - ts_{i-}) . \qquad (19)$$

Similarly, the communication latency from the ith task to the jth task, $c_{i,j}$, can be calculated as

$$c_{i,j} = (ts_{j-} - ts_{i+}) . \qquad (20)$$

Note, since multiple traces worth of data are required for join portions in a TPG, we assume that ts_{j-} and ts_{i+} in the above equation are from the same (correct) trace. Using these definitions and EPT_i^a / LPT_i^a, the actual task durations and communication latencies can be bounded as

$$(EPT_{i+}^a - LPT_{i-}^a) \leq t_i^a \leq (LPT_{i+}^a - EPT_{i-}^a) \qquad (21)$$

and

$$(EPT_{j-}^a - LPT_{i+}^a) \leq c_{i,j}^a \leq (LPT_{j-}^a - EPT_{i+}^a) . \qquad (22)$$

For the <u>unrecovered</u> measured time-stamps, substitution of (15) and (16) into (21) and (22) yields

$$(ts^m_{i+} - \delta_{i+} - n_{i+} \cdot \Delta M) - (ts^m_{i-} + \delta_{i-} - n_{i-} \cdot \Delta M)$$
$$\leq t^a_i \leq (ts^m_{i+} + \delta_{i+} - n_{i+} \cdot \Delta M) - (ts^m_{i-} - \delta_{i-} - n_{i-} \cdot \Delta M)$$

and

$$(ts^m_{j-} - \delta_{j-} - n_{j-} \cdot \Delta M) - (ts^m_{i+} + \delta_{i+} - n_{i+} \cdot \Delta M)$$
$$\leq c^a_{i,j} \leq (ts^m_{j-} + \delta_{j-} - n_{j-} \cdot \Delta M) - (ts^m_{i+} - \delta_{i+} - n_{i+} \cdot \Delta M) .$$

Since the monitoring statements used to measure a task duration must execute in sequence, we know $n_{i+} - n_{i-} = 1$. Unfortunately, we have no similar guarantee for the monitoring statements used to measure communication latencies. Applying (19) and (20) and simplifying, we find that the two previous equations can be rewritten as

$$t^m_i - (\delta_{i-} + \delta_{i+} + \Delta M) \leq t^a_i \leq t^m_i + (\delta_{i-} + \delta_{i+} - \Delta M) \quad (23)$$

and

$$c^m_{i,j} - (\delta_{i+} + \delta_{j-} + (n_{j-} - n_{i+}) \cdot \Delta M)$$
$$\leq c^a_{i,j} \leq c^m_{i,j} + (\delta_{i+} + \delta_{j-} - (n_{j-} - n_{i+}) \cdot \Delta M) . \quad (24)$$

A similar analysis for <u>recovered</u> time-stamps ((17) and (18)) yields

$$t^m_i - (\delta_{i-} + \delta_{i+}) \leq t^a_i \leq t^m_i + (\delta_{i-} + \delta_{i+}) \quad (25)$$

and

$$c^m_{i,j} - (\delta_{i+} + \delta_{j-}) \leq c^a_{i,j} \leq c^m_{i,j} + (\delta_{i+} + \delta_{j-}) . \quad (26)$$

4.3 Worst-Case Analysis

Equations (23)–(26) describe how uncertainty propagates through time-stamp mechanisms to TPG measurements. We can use this model to derive values for the uncertainty margins, ε^{m-} and ε^{m+}. To do this, the above equations must be rearranged in the form of (2) and (3). This process will now be illustrated for <u>unrecovered</u> traces ((23) and (24)).

The first step is to change the additive bounds in (23) and (24) into multiplicative bounds like those in (2) and (3). This is accomplished by "dividing out" the measured values, t^m_i and $c^m_{i,j}$, to obtain

$$t^m_i \cdot \left(1 - \frac{\delta_{i-} + \delta_{i+} + \Delta M}{t^m_i}\right) \leq t^a_i \leq t^m_i \cdot \left(1 + \frac{\delta_{i-} + \delta_{i+} - \Delta M}{t^m_i}\right)$$

and

$$c^m_{i,j} \cdot \left(1 - \frac{\delta_{i+} + \delta_{j-} + (n_{j-} - n_{i+}) \cdot \Delta M}{c^m_{i,j}}\right)$$
$$\leq c^a_{i,j} \leq c^m_{i,j} \cdot \left(1 + \frac{\delta_{i+} + \delta_{j-} - (n_{j-} - n_{i+}) \cdot \Delta M}{c^m_{i,j}}\right) .$$

The dependence on individual TPG values in the fractional portion of these equations can be removed using the maximum numerator and minimum denominator values. For the denominators, this simply implies using the minimum of the appropriate TPG measurements—i.e., $\min_{0 \leq i,j < |V|}\{c^m_{i,j}\}$ or $\min_{0 \leq i < |V|}\{t^m_i\}$. When trace recovery is performed, specific values of δ_{i-}, δ_{i+}, n_{j-}, and n_{i+} can be enumerated and the maximums of the above bounds can be found by simple comparison. When trace recovery is not performed, we must examine the worst-case extremes for these values to determine the maximum bounds.

To do this, we first expand the δ terms in the following four (numerator) maximums:

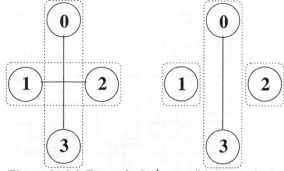

Figure 3: (a) Example Φ^{-1} (b) Example Φ^*

$$\max_{0 \leq i < |V|}\{\delta_{i-} + \delta_{i+} + \Delta M\} ,$$

$$\max_{0 \leq i < |V|}\{\delta_{i-} + \delta_{i+} - \Delta M\} ,$$

$$\max_{0 \leq i,j < |V|}\{\delta_{i+} + \delta_{j-} + (n_{j-} - n_{i+}) \cdot \Delta M\} ,$$

and

$$\max_{0 \leq i,j < |V|}\{\delta_{i+} + \delta_{j-} - (n_{j-} - n_{i+}) \cdot \Delta M\} .$$

Applying the uncertainty definition of (1) and simplifying terms, these become

$$\max_{0 \leq i < |V|}\{(n_{i-} + n_{i+}) \cdot \delta M_{MAX} + 4 \cdot ClkP + \Delta M\} ,$$

$$\max_{0 \leq i < |V|}\{(n_{i-} + n_{i+}) \cdot \delta M_{MAX} + 4 \cdot ClkP - \Delta M\} ,$$

$$\max_{0 \leq i,j < |V|}\{(n_{i+} + n_{j-}) \cdot \delta M_{MAX} + 4 \cdot ClkP + (n_{j-} - n_{i+}) \cdot \Delta M\} ,$$

and

$$\max_{0 \leq i,j < |V|}\{(n_{i+} + n_{j-}) \cdot \delta M_{MAX} + 4 \cdot ClkP - (n_{j-} - n_{i+}) \cdot \Delta M\} ,$$

which are upper bounded by

$$\left(\max_{0 \leq i < |V|}\{n_{i-}\} + \max_{0 \leq i < |V|}\{n_{i+}\}\right) \cdot \delta M_{MAX} + 4 \cdot ClkP + \Delta M ,$$

$$\left(\max_{0 \leq i < |V|}\{n_{i-}\} + \max_{0 \leq i < |V|}\{n_{i+}\}\right) \cdot \delta M_{MAX} + 5 \cdot ClkP - \Delta M ,$$

$$\left(\max_{0 \leq i < |V|}\{n_{i+}\} + \max_{0 \leq j < |V|}\{n_{j-}\}\right) \cdot \delta M_{MAX}$$
$$+ 4 \cdot ClkP + \left(\max_{0 \leq j < |V|}\{n_{j-}\} - \min_{0 \leq i < |V|}\{n_{i+}\}\right) \cdot \Delta M ,$$

and

$$\left(\max_{0 \leq i < |V|}\{n_{i+}\} + \max_{0 \leq j < |V|}\{n_{j-}\}\right) \cdot \delta M_{MAX}$$
$$+ 4 \cdot ClkP - \left(\min_{0 \leq j < |V|}\{n_{j-}\} - \max_{0 \leq i < |V|}\{n_{i+}\}\right) \cdot \Delta M .$$

We then determine what values of n_{i-}, n_{i+}, and n_{j-} will complete the worst-case nature of this bound. The following may be derived from Lemma 1:

$$\max_{0 \leq i < |V|}\{n_{i+}\} = 2 \cdot |V|$$

$$\max_{0 \leq i < |V|}\{n_{i-}\} = \max_{0 \leq j < |V|}\{n_{j-}\} = 2 \cdot |V| - 1$$

$$\min_{0 \leq i < |V|}\{n_{i+}\} = 2$$

$$\min_{0 \leq i < |V|}\{n_{i-}\} = \min_{0 \leq j < |V|}\{n_{j-}\} = 1$$

To tighten these upper bounds, we must determine the minimum number of PEs, N^{PE}_{MIN}, needed to com-

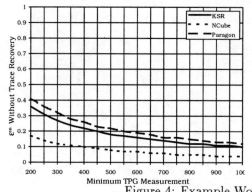

Figure 4: Example Worst Case ε^{m-} and ε^{m+} (without TR)

pletely measure a computation's TPG. This is the number of PEs over which we must "spread" the computation in a worst-case manner to force exposure of all of the communication [2].

Lemma 2 N_{MIN}^{PE} *is lower bounded by the number of strongly connected components (SCCs) in the transformed TPG, Φ^*. Here, $\Phi^* = \Phi^{-1} - \{c_{i,j}\}$, where for all $t_i \in V$ and $t_j \in V$ there exists a $t_k \in V$ such that $c_{k,i} \in E$ and $c_{k,j} \in E$.*

Proof: Exposing all communication implies assuring that the sender and receiver of each communication exist on different PEs. (Note, this does not preclude the possibility of aggregating multiple traces as motivated in the proof of Lemma 1.) We know this number must at a minimum reflect putting pairs of dependent tasks on separate PEs. Algorithmically, this number of PEs is equal to the number of SCCs in Φ^{-1}, the inverse of the TPG. An example of this for the TPG in Figure 2 is shown in Figure 3(a), where the SCCs are highlighted in dotted lines. This number is not an accurate lower bound on the minimum number of PEs needed, because it does not reflect the placement requirements for independent children of the same task (i.e., "forks" in the TPG, such as t_0 in the example graph). Such tasks cannot execute on the same PE because need for consecutive execution of the children would prohibit arbitrary communication with the parent. For this reason we define a new graph, Φ^*, which consists of Φ^{-1} with edges removed for those task pairs having common parents in Φ, expressed mathematically as $\Phi^* = \Phi^{-1} - \{c_{i,j}\}_{\forall\{t_i,t_a\}\in V, \exists t_k \in V \ni: \{c_{k,i}, c_{k,j}\}\in E}$. Figure 3(b) shows an example of this graph, again with SCCs highlighted in dotted lines. $\square$

From Lemma 2, we determine that no more than $|V| - (N_{MIN}^{PE} - 1)$ tasks may be on any one PE, since each of the required N_{MIN}^{PE} PEs must have at least one task assigned to them. Thus, the previous maximum bounds become:

$$\max_{0 \leq i < |V|}\{n_{i+}\} = 2 \cdot (|V| - (N_{MIN}^{PE} - 1))$$
$$= 2 \cdot |V| - 2 \cdot N_{MIN}^{PE} + 2$$

and

$$\max_{0 \leq i < |V|}\{n_{i-}\} = \max_{0 \leq j < |V|}\{n_{j-}\}$$
$$= 2 \cdot (|V| - (N_{MIN}^{PE} - 1)) - 1$$
$$= 2 \cdot |V| - 2 \cdot N_{MIN}^{PE} + 1$$

Substituting these values into the four numerator equations above and simplifying, we obtain

$$(4 \cdot |V| - 4 \cdot N_{MIN}^{PE} + 3) \cdot \delta M_{MAX} + 4 \cdot ClkP + \Delta M ,$$
$$(4 \cdot |V| - 4 \cdot N_{MIN}^{PE} + 3) \cdot \delta M_{MAX} + 4 \cdot ClkP - \Delta M ,$$
$$(4 \cdot |V| - 4 \cdot N_{MIN}^{PE} + 3) \cdot \delta M_{MAX} + 4 \cdot ClkP$$
$$+ (2 \cdot |V| - 2 \cdot N_{MIN}^{PE} - 1) \cdot \Delta M ,$$

and

$$(4 \cdot |V| - 4 \cdot N_{MIN}^{PE} + 3) \cdot \delta M_{MAX} + 4 \cdot ClkP$$
$$+ (2 \cdot |V| - 2 \cdot N_{MIN}^{PE} + 1) \cdot \Delta M .$$

The final phase of determining worst-case ε^{m-} and ε^{m+} is to rearrange the form of the above equations into that assumed by the uncertainty margins in equations 2 and 3. Currently, the above equations are in the form

$$(measured\ value) \cdot \left(1 - \frac{X_1}{Y_1}\right)$$
$$\leq (actual\ value) \leq (measured\ value) \cdot \left(1 + \frac{X_2}{Y_2}\right).$$

The form of the uncertainty margins, however, is

$$(actual\ value) \cdot \left(1 - \varepsilon^{m-}\right)$$
$$\leq (measured\ value) \leq (actual\ value) \cdot \left(1 + \varepsilon^{m+}\right).$$

To transform the previous equation form into this latter form, we first rearrange the bounds so that the measured value is in the middle, yielding the form

$$(actual\ value) \cdot \left(\frac{1}{1 + X_2/Y_2}\right)$$
$$\leq (measured\ value) \leq (actual\ value) \cdot \left(\frac{1}{1 - X_1/Y_1}\right).$$

Simple algebra then yields:

$$\varepsilon^{m-} = X_2/(Y_2 + X_2) \tag{27}$$

and

$$\varepsilon^{m+} = X_1/(Y_1 - X_1) \tag{28}$$

Combining these definitions with the preceding analysis, for <u>unrecovered</u> traces we find that

$$X_1 = (4 \cdot |V| - 4 \cdot N_{MIN}^{PE} + 3)\delta M_{MAX} + 4 \cdot ClkP + \Delta M ,$$
$$X_2 = (4 \cdot |V| - 4 \cdot N_{MIN}^{PE} + 3)\delta M_{MAX} + 4 \cdot ClkP - \Delta M ,$$

and $Y_1 = Y_2 = \min_{0 \leq i < |V|}\{t_i^m\}$ for task durations, and

$$X_1 = (4 \cdot |V| - 4 \cdot N_{MIN}^{PE} + 3) \cdot \delta M_{MAX}$$
$$+ 4 \cdot ClkP + (2 \cdot |V| - 2 \cdot N_{MIN}^{PE} - 1) \cdot \Delta M ,$$

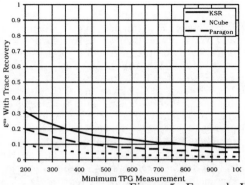
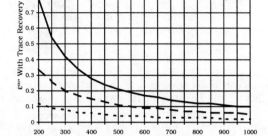

Figure 5: Example Worst Case ε^{m-} and ε^{m+} (with TR)

$$X_2 = (4 \cdot |V| - 4 \cdot N_{MIN}^{PE} + 3) \cdot \delta M_{MAX}$$

$$+ 4 \cdot ClkP + (2 \cdot |V| - 2 \cdot N_{MIN}^{PE} + 1) \cdot \Delta M \ ,$$

and $Y_1 = Y_2 = \min_{0 \leq i,j < |V|} \{c_{i,j}^m\}$ for communication latencies. Figure 4 shows plots of worst-case ε^{m-} and ε^{m+} values versus a range of communication latency minimum values for the application (whose TPG is shown in Figure 2) and the three architectures parameterized in Table 1.

Similar equations for <u>recovered</u> traces can be found by setting $\Delta M = 0$ in X_1 and X_2, yielding

$$X_1 = X_2 = (4 \cdot |V| - 4 \cdot N_{MIN}^{PE} + 3) \cdot \delta M_{MAX} + 4 \cdot ClkP \ .$$

Y_1 and Y_2 are the same as in the unrecovered case. Figure 5 shows plots of these worst-case values for the same architectures and range of minimum computation values as in Figure 4.

The plots in Figure 4 and 5 illustrate the relationship between uncertainty and grain size; namely, as smaller computation measurements are made, uncertainty about these measurements increases. This is an important relationship, because existing research [11, 13] has shown that the ability to optimize the execution of a parallel computation relies on the ability to finely dissect the computation into small, atomic grains. From these figures, it is obvious that the effects of uncertainty should be considered when determining a lower limit on the size of these grains. For example, it appears that the KSR would require a much larger communication grain-size than either the N-Cube or Paragon to achieve comparably low uncertainty perturbations. This is likely an artifact of the uncertainty overhead inherent in the KSR's virtual shared memory programming paradigm and architectural support.

5 Hybrid Static/Dynamic Scheduling (SEDIA)

Monitoring intrusion may be viewed as <u>one</u> contributor of many to the uncertainty margins (ε^{m-} and ε^{m+}) in equations (2) and (3), and Theorem 1. In reality, these uncertainty margins also model the broader notion of *run-time variance* in the computation. Causes of such variation could include: input dependence, operating system interactions, loosely coupled system components, etc. Applying the theoretical results of Section 3, we have formally related the sensitivity of scheduling optimizations to such run-time variations. Using this model, we are developing methods to improve the optimization of computation execution in the presence of run-time variation. The following discussion gives a flavor of the ways in which the model may be applied.

Dynamic scheduling mechanisms are traditionally restricted to simple, generic scheduling decisions (as opposed to more complex static scheduling heuristics) since these decisions must be based on run-time measurements of unknown correlation with the static structure of the computation. To address this aspect of dynamic scheduling, Theorem 1 provides a critical link between variation in a computation's run-time structure and the implications of this variance on execution optimality. Specifically, a relatively small number of static schedules for computation DAGs whose components fall within the bounds defined by (2) and (3) could be statically enumerated. If these static schedules vary widely, a dynamic executable could be built that represents a merger of the likely static schedules and incorporates the dynamic mechanisms needed to switch to the most appropriate (i.e., most optimal) schedule "on the fly".

For such dynamic mechanisms to be successful in efficiently selecting and executing multiple schedules, the mechanism's use of run-time resources must be kept extremely simple and the set of candidate schedules must be minimized. Static analysis helps achieve this desire by allowing most aspects of these decisions to be made prior to execution; namely, the identification of *switch points/key parameters* in the computation DAG that need to be measured, and the *threshold values* to be used. The first of these refers to the locations within the executing computation where the dynamic scheduling mechanisms may decide that a different schedule should be executed. These locations and the computation measurements needed for decision making can be determined through a sensitivity analysis. Since differences in the statically enumerated schedules are related to differences in the computation DAG (falling within the uncertainty/variance bounds of Section 3), this sensitivity analysis amounts to tracking which DAG values stay the same and which values change between all the different enumerated schedules. The other advantage of these dynamic mechanisms is statically determined threshold values. These define target values for comparison with key parameters at the switching points. These values can be determined in a manner similar to the sensitivity analysis described above—by observing the differences in the computation DAG values corresponding to different enumerated schedules, threshold values that identify different schedules and/or imply no change—a hysteresis zone may be calculated. This hysteresis is important to prevent thrashing.

A more straightforward (but less robust) use of the model in the previous sections involves strictly static scheduling. If monitoring intrusion is the major contributor to run-time variance in computation execution, static scheduling will likely benefit from performing trace recovery [1]. Candidates for this type of benefit include real-time systems and parallel embedded designs, where the technology or cost margins may preclude the use of hardware monitoring.

Others have also proposed uses for run-time variance knowledge in the parallel optimization realm. Pande and Psarris, for example, presented a methodology for porting an existing schedule between machines that differ in computation latency [14]. Their results show that schedules for similar architectures can be regenerated from existing schedules using knowledge of variance in communication latency. Gerasoulis, Jiao, and Yang have also studied the relationship of run-time variance to scheduling for the PYRROS environment [7]. In their research, they used a PYRROS-specific variance analysis to justify the applicability of using estimated values for static scheduling.

6 Conclusions

This paper motivated and presented a model for capturing information fidelity in computation measurement. First, a theoretical analysis relating computation measurement uncertainty and parallel scheduling was presented, indicating how uncertainty perturbs the optimality of scheduling heuristics. Our existing modeling of trace time-stamp intrusion and uncertainty was then extended to encompass computation measurements. This modeling illustrated how uncertainty information can be parameterized for existing architectures and applications. Parameterization data for three existing architectures was then used to plot the resulting worst-case uncertainty equations, illustrating the tradeoff between uncertainty in computation measurements and measurement granularity. Finally, an overview of how to apply the model described in this paper to computation optimization was presented. We are actively exploring an implementation of this optimization methodology in form of a parallel scheduling paradigm known as SEDIA (Static Exploration/Dynamic Instantiation and Activation).

References

[1] M.S. Andersland and T.L. Casavant, "Recovering uncorrupted event traces from corrupted event traces in parallel/distributed systems," *20th Int. Conf. on Par. Processing*, St. Charles, IL, Aug. 1991, pp. II:108-116.

[2] M.S. Andersland, T.L. Casavant, T.A. Braun, R.D. Dietz, and T.E. Scheetz, "Using accurate trace feedback for monitoring and performance tuning of parallel computing systems," TR-ECE-95-706, July 1995. *http://www.eng.uiowa.edu/~trace/documents/ tech_reports/tr_arpa_prop95.ps.Z*

[3] P.P. Chang, S.A. Mahlke, W.Y. Chen, N.J. Warter, and W.W. Hwu, "IMPACT: An Architectural Framework for Multiple-Instruction Issue Processors," in *Proc. of the 18th Annual Int. Symp. on Computer Architecture*, May 1991, pp.266-275.

[4] H. El-Rewini, T.G. Lewis, and H.H. Ali, *Task Scheduling In Parallel And Distributed Systems*, Prentice-Hall, Inc., New Jersey, ISBN 0-13-099235-6, 1994.

[5] Joseph A. Fisher, "Trace Scheduling: A Technique for Global Microcode Compaction," *IEEE Trans. on Computers*, Vol. 30, No. 7, July 1981, pp.478-490.

[6] R.L. Graham, "Bounds on Multiprocessing Timing Anomalies," in *Siam J. of Appl. Math.*, Vol. 17, No. 2, March 1969, pp.416-429.

[7] A. Gerasoulis, J. Jiao, and T. Yang, "Experience with Graph Scheduling for Mapping Irregular Scientific Computation," in *Proc. of the 1st IPPS Workshop on Solving Irreg. Problems on Dist. Memory Machines*, Santa Barbara, CA, April 1995, pp.1-8.

[8] S.L. Graham, P.B. Kessler, and M.K. McKusick, "gprof: a Call Graph Execution Profiler," *Proc. of the SIGPLAN '82 Symp. on Compiler Constr.*, ACM SIGPLAN Notices, Vol. 17, No. 6, June 1982, pp.120-126.

[9] M. Gupta and P. Banerjee, "Compile-Time Estimation Of Communication Costs On Multicomputers," *Int. Par. Processing Symp.*, March 1992.

[10] U. Holzle, "Adaptive Optimization for SELF: Reconciling High Performance with Exploratory Programming," Ph.D. Dissertation, Aug. 1994.

[11] B. Kruatrachue and T. Lewis, "Grain Size Determination For Parallel Processing," *IEEE Software*, Jan. 1988, pp.23-31.

[12] L. Lamport, "Time, Clocks, and the Ordering of Events in a Distributed System," *Comm. of the ACM*, Vol. 21, July 1978, pp.558-564.

[13] C. McCreary and H. Gill, "Automatic Determination of Grain Size for Efficient Parallel Processing," *Comm. of the ACM*, Vol. 32, No. 9, Sept. 1989, pp.1073-1078.

[14] S. Pande and K. Psarris, "Program Repartitioning on Varying Communication Cost Parallel Architectures," *J. of Par. and Dist. Comput.*, March 1996, pp.205-213.

[15] K. Pettis and R.C. Hansen, "Profile Guided Code Positioning," in *Proc. of the ACM SIGPLAN '90 Conf. on Prog. Lang. Design and Impl.*, White Plains, New York, June 20-22, 1990, pp.16-27.

[16] A.D. Samples, "Profile-Driven Compilation," Ph.D. Dissertation, University of Berkeley, April 1991. *http:// www.cse.ucsc.edu/~brucem/samples.html*

[17] T.E. Scheetz, T.A. Braun, T.L. Casavant, J.A. Gannon, M.S. Andersland, and R.D. Dietz, "Effectiveness of Software Trace Recovery Techniques for Current Parallel Architectures," *Int. Conf. on High Perf. Comput.*, New Delhi, India, Dec. 27-30, 1995. *http:// www.eng.uiowa.edu/~trace/documents/conference/ hipc95.ps*

[18] M.L. Simmons, A.H. Hayes, J.S. Brown, and D.A. Reed, *Debugging and Performance Tuning for Parallel Computing Systems*, IEEE Computer Society Press, 1996.

Trace-driven Analysis of Migration-based Gang Scheduling Policies for Parallel Computers[*]

Sanjeev K. Setia
Computer Science Department
George Mason University
Fairfax, VA 22030

Abstract

Gang scheduling is a job scheduling policy for parallel computers that combines elements of space-sharing and time-sharing. In this paper, we analyze the performance of gang scheduling policies that allow the remapping of an executing job to a new set of processors. Most previously proposed gang-scheduling policies do not allow such job remapping under the assumption that it is prohibitively expensive. Through a detailed trace-driven simulation, we analyze the tradeoff between the benefits and overheads of such job relocation. Our results show that gang-scheduling policies that support such job relocation offer significant performance gains over policies that do not use remapping.

1 Introduction

The topic of job scheduling strategies for parallel computers has received considerable attention in recent years [4]. In particular, gang scheduling, a policy that combines elements of space-sharing and time-sharing, has been shown to provide good performance [2, 3].

Several variants of gang scheduling for distributed memory parallel systems, notably Distributed Hierarchical Control (DHC) [2, 3], have been proposed and analyzed in the literature. Under most of these policies, a one-to-one mapping is established between the processes of a job and a set of processors when the job is first scheduled for execution and this mapping is maintained for the duration of the job's execution. The underlying assumption is that remapping a job to a new set of processors once it has started executing is prohibitively expensive.

One of the problems that can occur under such policies is that processing power is wasted in situations where the number of idle processors in the system is not sufficient for any of the queued jobs to execute. Much of the previous work on gang-scheduling has focussed on the issue of mapping jobs to processors with the goal of minimizing such wasted processing power.

In this paper, we examine the performance of migration-based gang scheduling policies that allow the remapping of an executing job to a new set of processors. The ability to remap jobs makes wasted processing power less of a problem for these policies. However, on distributed memory multicomputers, the overhead of remapping a job to a new set of processors can be quite substantial, especially if the job has a large data set.

The main subject of this paper is this tradeoff between the benefits of remapping an executing job to a new set of processors and the costs entailed by such remapping. We analyze the performance of migration-based policies via a detailed trace-driven simulation. The traces used in the simulation are job accounting traces recorded over several months for the batch workload executing on the 512-node IBM SP2 at the Cornell Theory Center. Unlike previous studies that have considered migration-based policies [7, 1], our simulation models take into account the overhead incurred while remapping a job to a new set of processors.

The main contribution of this paper is that we show that the benefits of remapping a job during its execution outweigh the costs of the migration entailed by the remapping. Furthermore, we analyse several issues that arise in the design of migration-based gang scheduling policies such as the manner in which quanta are allocated to jobs, and the use of job priorities for improved performance.

2 The Parallel Environment

The hardware environment considered in this study is a distributed-memory parallel computer such as the IBM SP2, the Intel Paragon, or the Cray T3D. We assume that the system is balanced with respect to I/O. Specifically, we assume that the system has adequate I/O bandwidth for swapping jobs out of memory to disk and loading jobs into memory from disk, and that this bandwidth scales with the size of the system. Further, we assume that a job can only execute if its entire address space is resident in memory, i.e., we assume that applications do not use demand paging.

The workload considered for this study consists of batch

---

[*] This work was partially supported by NSF grant CCR-9409697

489

jobs that are typically submitted to a supercomputer via a system such as the Network Queuing System (NQS) or IBM's LoadLeveler. The execution times of these batch jobs varies widely, ranging from a few seconds to several hours. The goals of the scheduling policies considered in this study are to reduce the job turn-around time for the individual user, and to increase the overall system throughput for the system manager. These policies do not address the issue of supporting interactive application, e.g., editors, email, etc. on the same nodes executing batch jobs.

3 Scheduling Policies

Matrix-based Gang Scheduling These policies are based on Ousterhout's matrix algorithm [6], and do not permit migration of executing jobs to a new set of processors. In the matrix algorithm, scheduling space is viewed as a matrix, with rows representing scheduling time slots (quanta), and columns representing processors. Incoming parallel jobs are mapped to a set of processors within a slot in this matrix according to a packing algorithm with the goal of minimizing fragmentation. Once a job is mapped on to a certain set of processors it executes on that set until it finishes. All the jobs in a time slot are dispatched at the same time at the beginning of a quantum and preempted at the end of the quantum. If the set of processors being used by a job is free in a slot(s) other than its assigned slot, then that job is also scheduled in these slots, thereby increasing the utilization of the system. Similarly, if a job terminates before the time quantum has expired, then jobs in other slots which can run on the processors freed by the departing job, are dispatched on those processors. Finally, if the sets of processors in use in two different slots do not intersect, then these slots are merged into a single slot.

Distributed Hierarchical Control (DHC) Feitelson [3] described this algorithm for packing jobs into the scheduling matrix. We refer the reader to [3] for a more detailed description of this policy. For the purposes of this paper, it suffices to note that this policy was shown to have superior performance to other packing schemes.

Migration-based Gang Scheduling The policies in this category are gang scheduling policies in the sense that each job is executed on its allocated processors for a quantum by dispatching and preempting all its processes at the same time. However, unlike the matrix-based policies, there is no concept of jobs being allocated to a fixed "slot" in a two-dimensional scheduling space.

Under these policies, the system scheduler maintains a queue consisting of jobs submitted to the system. The order in which jobs are selected from the system queue is based on a negative-feedback priority scheme similar to that commonly used in uniprocessors. Each job has an associated priority which is inversely proportional to the service demand (product of the processing time and number of processors allocated to the job) accumulated so far by the job.

If there are idle processors in the system, the scheduler examines the job queue and selects the job with the highest priority that can be scheduled on the available processors. It repeats this step until there are no waiting jobs or the remaining number of idle processors is insufficient for any waiting tasks. When a job completes its time quantum, it is preempted, its priority is updated, and it rejoins the system queue.

The next time the job receives a time quantum it could potentially execute on a different set of processors from the set used in the previous quantum. This implies that the state of a job, i.e., any memory or disk context established by a job during a time quantum may need to be migrated the next time it is dispatched. If the job is still in memory, then the contents of its address space are migrated to the new set of processors allocated to the job. If the job has been swapped out of memory, then it is loaded from disk into the memories of the new set of processors. Since this entails overhead, the system scheduler should attempt to reallocate the same processors to a job that it previously ran on, if possible. Periodically, the scheduler recalculates the priorities of all the processes in the system (e.g., by dividing them by 2) so that jobs are not penalized forever for past processor usage.

We consider two migration-based policies that differ in the manner in which time quanta are allocated to jobs. *Feedback with Global Quantum Allocation (FB-GQA)* This policy is similar to the matrix-based policies described above in that a set of jobs selected for execution are dispatched simultaneously at the beginning of a quantum and preempted simultaneously at the end of a quantum. Thus, this policy involves a system-wide context switch with each job allocated a quantum of the same length.

Jobs are selected for execution during a quantum using the procedure described above. If a job completes before the quantum expires, the freed processors are allocated to the waiting jobs in a similar manner. At the end of a quantum, all the jobs executing in the system are preempted, and the scheduling procedure repeats.

We note that under this policy the length of a time quantum has to be large enough to amortize the cost of any migration that occurs when the jobs are dispatched. This cost is directly proportional to a job's memory and disk requirements, Since each job is allocated the same quantum, the length of this quantum must be selected taking into account the largest migration and swapping costs of the dispatched jobs.

Feedback with Individual Quantum Allocation (FB-IQA) Under this policy, each job is allocated a time quantum that is directly proportional to the cost of loading it into memory. More specifically, the time quantum allocated to a job is equal to $\max(Q, af \times loading\_cost)$, where Q is the default system quantum length, af is an amortization factor, and $loading\_cost$ is the measured time for loading the job into memory. Since $loading\_cost$ will differ from job to job and will vary from quantum to quantum, this implies that each job is allocated a different time quantum. This also implies that there is no system-wide context switch at the end of a quantum; instead each job is preempted individually when its quantum expires.

Jobs are selected for execution using the procedure described above. However, under FB-IQA, there exists the possibility of starvation for jobs requesting a large number of processors under high load conditions. To prevent starvation, we associate a timer with a job once it reaches the head of the system queue. If this timer expires and the job is still in the queue, it implies that the job is being repeatedly passed over by the scheduler. Any processors freed after this timer has expired are marked as reserved for the starving job. However, a long period can elapse before enough processors can be reserved for the waiting job. Hence, the reserved processors are not held idle; instead they are allocated to any dispatchable jobs in the queue. When the sum of the number of reserved processors and free processors becomes equal to or larger than the number of processors requested by the starving job, the scheduler preempts the jobs executing on the reserved processors and dispatches the starving job.

4 Simulation Model Description

Workload Model Our simulation study is driven by job accounting traces collected from the 512 node IBM SP2 at the Cornell Theory Center. Specifically, we use traces for jobs that arrived during the time period of September 17 to October 23, 1995, and completed successfully. We refer the reader to [5, 8] for a detailed description of this workload.

An important workload characteristic for the purposes of this study is the memory demand of a job. Unfortunately, the workload traces described above do not contain any information about the memory usage of jobs. In our simulation, we make the pessimistic assumptions that small jobs have a memory demand that is uniformly distributed between 0 and 32 Mbytes per node, and that large jobs have a memory demand that is uniformly distributed between 0 and 128 Mbytes per node.

System Model The overhead for swapping and migration of jobs is a key factor in the tradeoff between matrix- and migration-based policies. In addition to factors such as the I/O bandwidth available in the system, this overhead will depend in a complex way on the interaction between the memory management policy and the job scheduling policy. For example, the memory manager could decide not to swap a certain job out of memory if it knew that the job would be dispatched by the scheduler in the near future. In our study, we do not consider this interaction. Instead we use two different cost models for swapping and migration overhead that correspond to two extreme cases. Our reasoning is that the overhead incurred for swapping and migration under any memory management policy will lie in between these two extremes.

Under the first model, which we refer to as the *Never Swap* model, we assume that a job is never swapped out of memory during its execution. This corresponds to a situation where there is infinite memory per node (or a situation where the memory available on each node is much larger than the memory requirements of jobs). While there is no cost for swapping or loading a job into memory under this model, we do assess a cost for remapping a job. This cost has two components – a fixed component (F) and a component that depends on the amount of data migrated per node and the available node-to-node communication bandwidth.

Under the second model, which we refer to as the *Always Swap* model, we assume that a job is swapped out to disk after each quantum. Thus, under this model, a job has to pay the overhead of being swapped in and out of memory for each quantum it receives. We assume that the system has a constant I/O bandwidth per node. We assume that the cost of loading a job into the memory of the same processors it executed on during its previous quantum is equal to the cost of swapping a job out of memory. In the case of migration-based policies, depending on how swapping is supported by a specific system, there may be an additional cost for migration. We model such situations in our simulation by assessing a greater cost for loading a job into memory when it is migrated. Remapping a job is assumed have an additional cost equal to the product of the swapping cost and a system-dependent constant called *migration cost factor (mcf)*.

Methodology The performance of the policies described in Section 3 was analyzed via simulation. The primary metrics used to compare the performance of the policies are the average response time and the average normalized response time, where the normalized response time is defined as the ratio of a job's response time and its service time. The average response time is used to gauge the performance of a policy from the system point of view, whereas the normalized response time reflects the performance of a policy from the user point of view.

5 Summary of Results

We now summarize the main results of our performance study. The reader is referred to [8] for a more detailed

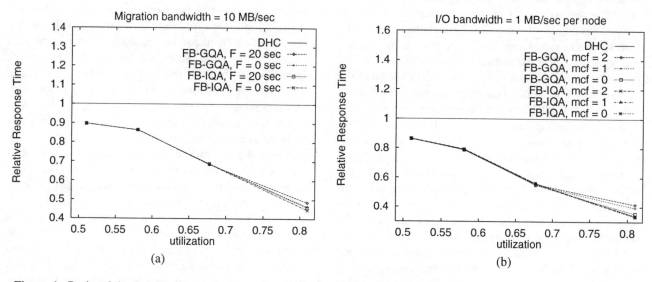

Figure 1: Ratio of the average response time of various migration-based policies to that of DHC as a function of system utilization under the (a) *Never Swap* overhead model (b) *Always Swap* overhead model.

discussion.

1. The performance of the DHC and FB-GQA policies is quite sensitive to the global quantum length. The quantum length has to be selected so that it is large enough to amortize the swapping and migration overheads experienced by jobs in the workload, but small enough so that the normalized response times of small jobs are not adversely affected. The FB-IQA policy, on the other hand, has the desirable property that its performance is relatively insensitive to the default quantum length.

2. The migration-based policies, FB-IQA and FB-GQA, can outperform DHC by a significant margin for both the *never swap* and *always swap* overhead models (see Figure 1). Since the two models represent extreme cases for swapping and migration overheads, we conclude that this result will also be true under realistic memory management policies.

3. The FB-IQA policy has slightly better performance than FB-GQA. Since it also has the desirable property that its performance is relatively insensitive to the default quantum length, it is preferable to FB-GQA.

4. The main reason for the superior performance of the migration-based policies (for the workload considered in this study) is that these policies can use feedback-based priority schemes to give competing jobs an equal share of the available processing capacity, and to give higher priority to newly arrived jobs.

Acknowledgements

We would like to thank Steve Hotovy for making the workload trace from the Cornell Theory Center available to us.

References

[1] S.-H. Chiang and M. K. Vernon. Dynamic vs. Static Quantum-Based Parallel Processor Allocation. In *IPPS Job Scheduling Workshop*, April 1996.

[2] D. Feitelson. A survey of scheduling in multiprogrammed parallel systems. Technical Report RC 19790, IBM Research Division, October 1994.

[3] D. Feitelson. Packing Schemes for Gang Scheduling. In *IPPS Job Scheduling Workshop*, April 1996.

[4] D. Feitelson and L. Rudolph, editors. *Job Scheduling Strategies for Parallel Processing*, volume 949 of *Lecture Notes in Computer Science*. Springer Verlag, 1995.

[5] S. Hotovy, D. Schneider, and T. O'Donnel. Analysis of the Early Workload on the Cornell Theory Center SP2. Technical report, Cornell Theory Center, 1995.

[6] J. K. Ousterhout. Scheduling Techniques for Concurrent Systems. In *Proc. of the Third Intl. Conf. on Distributed Computing Systems*, pages 22 – 30, October 1982.

[7] E. W. Parsons and K. C. Sevcik. Multiprocessor Scheduling for High-Variability Service Time Distributions. In *IPPS Job Scheduling Workshop*, pages 76–88, April 1995.

[8] S. Setia. Trace-driven Analysis of Migration-based Gang Scheduling Policies for Parallel Computers. Technical Report TR97-03, Computer Science Dept., George Mason Univ., 1997.

A Global Computing Environment for Networked Resources*

Haluk Topcuoglu   and   Salim Hariri
Department of Electrical Engineering and Computer Science
Syracuse University, Syracuse, NY 13244-4100.

Abstract

Current advances in high-speed networks and WWW technologies have made network computing a cost-effective, high-performance computing alternative. New software tools are being developed to utilize efficiently the network computing environment. Our project, called Virtual Distributed Computing Environment (VDCE), is a high-performance computing environment that allows users to write and evaluate networked applications for different hardware and software configurations using a web interface. In this paper we present the software architecture of VDCE by emphasizing application development and specification, scheduling, and execution/runtime aspects.

1 Introduction

The new trends in networking protocols (including ATM and Fast Ethernet) and emerging WWW technologies have enabled the development of a cost-effective, high-performance, distributed computing environment, *network-based computing*. The target of current research on software tools and problem solving environments is to exploit fully the underlying network-based computing framework. We are developing a network-based computing environment called Virtual Distributed Computing Environment (VDCE). VDCE is composed of distributed sites, each of which has one or more VDCE Servers. At each site the VDCE Server runs the server software, called *site manager*, which handles the inter-site communications and bridges the VDCE modules to the site databases. The main goal of the VDCE project is to develop an easy-to-use, integrated software development environment that provides software tools and middleware software to handle all the issues related to developing parallel and distributed applications, scheduling tasks onto the best available resources, and managing the Quality of Service (QoS) requirements.

In this paper we present the VDCE-based application development, which can be divided into a pipeline

of three phases: application design and specification, scheduling, and execution/runtime. VDCE provides a web-based graphical user interface, the Application Editor, that helps users to design and build parallel and distributed applications. The VDCE Application Scheduler component is a distributed runtime scheduler that uses performance prediction of individual tasks of an application to achieve efficient resource allocations. The third component, the VDCE Runtime System, is responsible for monitoring the networked resources, setting up the execution environment of a given application, monitoring the task executions on the assigned resources, and providing communication and synchronization services for intertask communications.

The rest of the paper is organized as follows. In Section 2 we present the application design and specifications issues. The Application Scheduler is explained in Section 3. We present the VDCE Runtime System in Section 4. Concluding remarks and future work are given in Section 5.

2 Application Design and Development

The Application Editor component of VDCE is a web-based, graphical user interface for developing parallel and distributed applications. The end-user establishes a URL connection to the VDCE Server software within the site (*Site Manager*), which runs on a VDCE Server. After user authentication, the Application Editor is loaded into the user's local web browser so that the user can develop his/her application.

The Application Editor provides menu-driven task libraries that are grouped in terms of their functionality, such as the matrix algebra library, C^3I (command and control applications) library, etc. A selected task is represented as a clickable and draggable graphical icon in the active editor area. Each such icon includes the task name and a set of markers for logical ports. The process of building an application with the Application Editor can be divided into two steps: building the application flow graph (AFG), and specifying the

*This research is supported by Rome Laboratory contract number F30602-95-C-0104.

493

task properties of the application.

After the application flow graph is generated, the next step in the application development process is to specify the properties of each task. A double click on any task icon generates a popup panel that allows the user to specify (optional) preferences such as computational mode (sequential or parallel), input/output files, machine type, and the number of processors to be used in a parallel implementation of a given task. If an input of a task is supplied by its parent tasks, the file entry is marked as *dataflow*. Figure 1 shows the application flow graph of the Linear Equation Solver and the contents of the task properties window for LU_Decomposition and Matrix_Multiplication tasks.

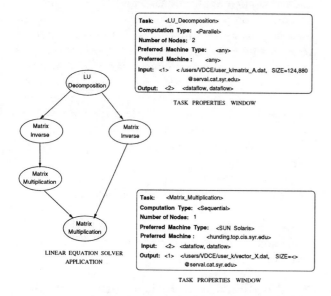

Figure 1. Application Flow Graph of Linear Equation Solver

3 Application Scheduling

The main function of the Application Scheduler module in VDCE is to interpret the application flow graph and to assign the most suitable available resources for running the application tasks in order to minimize the schedule length (total execution time) in a transparent manner. Our scheduling heuristic is based on *list scheduling* [2, 3, 4]. In list scheduling, each node (task) of the graph is assigned a priority before the scheduling process. The VDCE scheduling heuristic uses the level [4] of each node to determine its priority. The node (task) with a higher level value will have a higher priority for scheduling. The level of a node in the graph is computed as the largest sum of computation costs along the path from the node to an

1. Receive application flow graph from Application Editor.
2. Select k nearest VDCE neighbor sites,
   $S_{remote} = \{S_1, S_2, \ldots, S_k\}$, for local site S_{local}.
3. Multicast application flow graph to each S_i in S_{remote}.
4. Call $Host\_Selection\_Algorithm$ (local and remote sites).
5. Receive the outputs of $Host\_Selection\ Algorithm$, from each S_i in S_{remote}.
6. Initialize $ready\_tasks = \{task_i | task_i$ is an entry_node$\}$.
7. For each $task_i$ in $ready\_tasks$ set:
   If the $task_i$ is an entry task or $task_i$ does not require input
      •Assign $task_i$ to S_j, which minimizes $Predict(task_i, R_j)$.
   Else
      •Determine the site(s), S_{parent}, which is assigned for one or more of the parent nodes of $task_i$.
      •For each site S_j in S_{remote} evaluate:
      $$Time_{total}(task_i, S_j) = transfer\_time(S_{parent}, S_j)$$
      $$\times file\_size + Predict(task_i, R_j)$$
      •Assign $task_i$ to S_j, which min. $Time_{total}(task_i, S_j)$.
   Store resource allocation information for $task_i$.
   Update the $ready\_tasks$ set by removing $task_i$, and adding children nodes of $task_i$.

Figure 2. Site Scheduler Algorithm

exit node. For the computation cost, the task (node) execution time on the base processor, which is already measured and stored in the *task-performance database* at site repository, is used. In VDCE the level of each node of an application flow graph is determined before the execution of the scheduling algorithm. VDCE provides distributed scheduling in a wide-area system in which each site consists of its own Application Scheduler running on the VDCE server. After the best schedule of the whole application is determined by the local site and a set of nearest remote sites, the resource allocation table is generated and transferred to the Site Manager running on the VDCE server. Application tasks are scheduled within a site (or within the nearest-neighbor sites) to decrease inter-task communication time. The Application Scheduler, which is based on [1, 5], has two built-in algorithms: *site scheduler algorithm* and *host selection algorithm*, as shown in Figure 2 and Figure 3, respectively. When the Application Scheduler receives the execution request of an application, it runs the site scheduler algorithm. A subset of remote sites is selected and the AFG is multicast to these sites, at which the Application Schedulers will run the host selection algorithm. The built-in host selection algorithm at each remote site determines the best available machine within the site for each task, which minimizes the predicted execution time. Then each site sends the mapping information of each task,

1. Retrieve task-specific parameters of AFG tasks from *task-performance database*.

2. Retrieve resource-specific parameters of a set of resources, $R_{set} = \{R_1, R_2, \ldots, R_m\}$, from *resource-perf. database*.

3. Set $task\_queue = \{task_i | task_i \text{ in AFG}\}$.

4. For each $task_i$ in task_queue

   • Evaluate the performance prediction time of $task_i$, $Predict(task_i, R_i)$, for all R_i in R_{set}.

   • Assign $task_i$ to R_j, which minimizes the performance prediction time, $Predict(task_i, R_j)$.

Figure 3. Host Selection Algorithm

i.e., machine name and predicted execution time, to the local site. For the entry tasks that have no parents, or the tasks that do not require any input file for execution, the site scheduler algorithm selects the site (the resource within the site) that minimizes the prediction time for the task. For other cases the local-site scheduler algorithm selects the best site, based on the summation of predicted execution time and transfer time of the task input files. The site at which a parent task is scheduled is determined to evaluate the transfer time. The inter-task transfer time is based on the network transfer time between a site and the parent's site, and the size of the transfer. The input size of the application can be used for the transfer size parameter. For parallel tasks, the host selection algorithm is updated to select the number of machines required within the site. The core of the given built-in scheduling algorithms is the performance prediction [6] phase, which is provided by separate function evaluations of each task on each resource.

Each site has a site repository for storing user-accounts information, task and resource parameters that are used by the scheduler. A *user-accounts database* is used to handle user authentication. In user-accounts database, each VDCE user account is represented by a 5-tuple: user name, password, user ID, priority, and access domain type. A *resource performance database* provides resource (machine and network) attributes or parameters such as host name, IP address, architecture type, OS type, total memory size of the machine, recent workload measurements, and available memory size. A *task performance database* provides performance characteristics for each task in the system and is used to predict the performance of a task on a given resource. Each task implementation is specified by several parameters such as computation size, communication size, required memory size, etc. A *task constraints database* is used to store the location information of each task (i.e., the

absolute path of the task executable) for each host.

4 Application Execution and Runtime Support

The VDCE Runtime System separates control and data functions by allocating them to the Control Manager and Data Manager, respectively. The Control Manager measures the loads on the resources (hosts and networks) periodically and monitors the resources for possible failures. The Data Manager provides low-latency and high-speed communication and synchronization services for inter-task communications.

4.1 Control Manager

Functionally, the Control Manager services are grouped into two modules: the *Resource Controller*, and the *Application Controller*.

Resource Controller The Resource Controller within a site contains three different processes: a Site Manager, a Group Manager for each group leader machine, and a Monitor daemon for each VDCE resource. In what follows we summarize the functions of the Resource Controller components shown in Figure 4.

The *Monitor* daemon periodically measures the up-to-date resource parameters, i.e., CPU load and memory availability and sends the values to the Group Manager. The Group Manager sends to the Site Manager only the workloads of the resources that have changed considerably from the previous measurement [7].

Another function of the Group Manager is to periodically check all hosts in the group by sending echo packets to hosts and waiting for their responses. When a failure of a host is detected, the Group Manager passes this information to the Site Manager. The host is then marked as "down" at the site's resource-performance database.

The Site Manager component of the Resource Controller periodically updates the resource-performance database at the site repository with the monitoring information (i.e, the workload measurement and failure detection information of the resources), and it updates the task-performance database with the execution time after, an application execution is completed.

Another function of the Site Manager is to multicast the resource allocation table to the Group Managers that will be involved in the execution. Each Group Manager sends an execution request message and the related portion of the resource allocation information to the Application Controller of the related machines. Additionally, the inter-site coordination

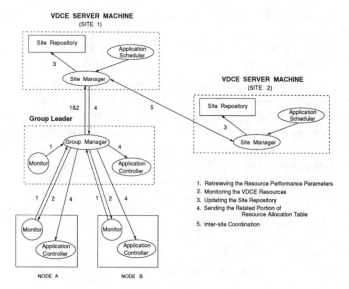

Figure 4. Interactions Among the Resource Controller Components

and message transfer (for scheduling and monitoring purposes) are handled by Site Managers.

Application Controller The Application Controller sets up the execution environment and manages the services provided by interacting with the Data Manager. After the Application Controller receives an execution request message from the Group Manager, it activates the Data Manager. The Data Managers on the assigned machines set up the application execution environment by starting the task executions and creating point-to-point communication channels for inter-task data transfer. When all the required acknowledgments are received an execution startup signal is sent to start the application execution.

The Application Controller monitors the application execution on the assigned machines. If the current load on any of these machines is more than a predefined threshold value, the Application Controller terminates the task execution on the machine and sends a task rescheduling request to the Group Manager.

4.2 Data Manager

The VDCE Data Manager is a socket-based, point-to-point communication system for inter-task communications. The Data Manager activates the communication proxy and sends the resource allocation information, including the socket number, IP address for target machine, etc., that will be used for communication channel setup. After the setup is completed successfully, the communication proxy sends an acknowl-

edgment to the Application Controller. The execution startup signal is sent to start the task executions, as explained in the previous section.

The VDCE Runtime System provides several user-requested services such as I/O service, console service, and visualization service. A user can request these services while developing his/her application with the Application Editor. I/O Service provides either file I/O or URL I/O for the inputs of the application tasks. The user can suspend and restart the application execution with the console service. The VDCE visualization service provides application performance and workload visualizations.

5 Conclusion

We have presented the design of the Virtual Distributed Computing Environment (VDCE) for networked resources. We have successfully implemented a proof-of-concept prototype on campus-wide resources that supports the application design, scheduling, and runtime aspects. We are improving the current implementation of the VDCE so that it can support accesses to several geographically distributed sites. We are also implementing a distributed shared memory model that will allow VDCE users to describe their applications using a shared memory paradigm.

References

[1] F. Berman, R. Wolski, S. Figueira, J. Schopf, and G. Shao, "Application-Level Scheduling on Distributed Heterogeneous Networks," *Proceedings of Supercomputing 96*, November 1996.

[2] T.L. Adam, K. Chandy, and J. Dickson, "A Comparison of List Scheduling for Parallel Processing Systems," *Communications of ACM*, Vol 17, no. 12, pp. 685–690, Dec 1974.

[3] H. El-Rewini, H. Ali, T. Lewis, "Task Scheduling in multiprocessing systems," *IEEE Computer*, December 1995.

[4] Y. Kwok, I. Ahmad, "Dynamic Critical-Path Scheduling: An Effective Technique for Allocating Task Graphs to Multiprocessors," *IEEE Transactions on Parallel and Distributed Systems*, Vol. 7, pp. 506–521, 1996.

[5] J. Weissman, A. Grimshaw, "A Federated Model for Scheduling in Wide-Area-Systems," *Proceedings of HPDC5*, pp. 542–550, 1996.

[6] Y. Yan and X. Zhang, "An Efficient and Practical Performance Prediction Model for Parallel Computing on Non-dedicated Heterogeneous NOW," To appear in *Journal of Parallel and Distributed Computing*.

[7] H. Casanova, J. Dongarra, "Netsolve: A Network Server for Solving Computational Science Problems," *Supercomputing 96*, November 1996.

Panel 4:

COTS Parallel Processing: Are We There Yet?

Moderator and Organizer

Hank Dietz
Purdue University

Addendum

Real-time Multicast in Wireless Communication

Sandeepan Sanyal   Laila Nahar   Sourav Bhattacharya*
Department of Computer Science & Engineering
Arizona State University
Tempe, AZ 85287-5406
{suman, laila.rahman, sourav}@asu.edu

Abstract

This paper presents the reconfiguration of multicast tree at the instance of node migration in cellular wireless networks. We consider a novel, and highly practical, formulation of the real-time multicast problem. Unlike the traditional notion of source to leaf node message transmission time being the measure for real-time, we consider the multicast tree re-construction time (in the event of a node migration) as the measure for real-time constraints. The overall goal is to minimize both the delays - i) delay of re-constructing the multicast tree and ii) source to destination transmission delay. In this paper we introduce and provide solutions for the first objective, while the current research in real-time multicast tree considers the latter objective only. We propose three heuristics to solve the real-time multicast tree re-construction problem and present analysis and simulation results for different factors that contribute differently to the reconstruction delay.

Key Words: Cellular Network, Hypercube, Real-Time Multicast.

1 Introduction

Wireless communication has become an emerging technology for today's computer and communication industries. The goal is to allow the user (high performance portable computers, data terminals and devices) to access to the capabilities of the global network at any time without regard to location or mobility.

---

*Also, affiliated to the Honeywell Technology Center, Phoenix, Arizona.

1.1 Real-time Multicast

Multicast communication is the delivery of a message from a source to an arbitrary number of destination nodes. Multicast in real-time environment is an important issue. Current research in real-time multicast concentrate on the worst case source to destination node message transmission time. Optimization goals had been used in multicast algorithms to determine what constitutes a good tree. As stated, one such goal is providing minimum delay along the tree, which is important for multimedia applications such as real-time video conferencing. Another optimization goal is making use of the network resources as efficiently as possible. Dijkstra's shortest path algorithm [6] has been used to generate the shortest paths from the source to destination nodes; this provides the solution for delay optimization. Multicast algorithm that perform cost optimization have been based on computing the minimum Steiner tree which is a NP-complete problem [8].

In this paper we consider a dual formation of the real-time multicast problem, namely, the time required to reconfigure the multicast tree when a node changes its physical location in a cellular network. Node migration is very common and frequent event in wireless network. A node migration may temporarily break the multicast tree, in which case the reconstruction problem (and, associated delay) becomes an important issue - as addressed in this paper.

1.2 Contribution

In this paper, we define a new metric for real-time multicast - delay of reconstruction at the instance of node migration. Figure 2 illustrates the idea of node migration. Our goal is to rebuild the multicast tree dynamically, i.e., the tree is to be reconfigured within least amount time delay. We propose three approaches as follows:

500

- Request-Reply-Rejection (RRR): When a node migrates, orphan nodes request other nodes to be their parent; requested node either accepts or rejects the request depending on real-time constraints and the broken multicast tree is reconfigured eventually.

- Look-ahead Alternate Parent (LAP): Each node holds a local parent table containing a number of alternate parent-ids; the node can be attached immediately to any of the alternate parents, when it becomes orphan.

- Look-ahead Alternate Edge (LAE): This approach adds a number of extra links for each link in the multicast tree; in case of node migration, a torn link can be replaced instantaneously by one of the extra links.

2   Problem Formulation

We consider the multicast reconfiguration problem on cellular network. For ease of multicast operation, rapid maintainability and other well known advantages of logical/symmetric topologies, we assume a mesh of hypercube topology interconnection among the migrating nodes (although, our research is complimentary to the specific topology selection). Nodes within each cell are connected using a hypercube, while across the cells a mesh topology is adopted. The multicast tree is embedded onto this mesh of hypercube topology. Our focus is not how to generate a good multicast tree, and we adopt any well-known multicast tree generation heuristic. Figure 1 shows a multicast tree constructed on top of the hypercube, where S is the source node; D_1, D_2, ...D_n are n destination nodes. Destination nodes may be spread across different cells. Multicast tree includes both internal or forwarding nodes.

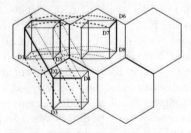

Figure 1: Multicast embedded on hypercube, S = source, $D_1...D_8$ are destination nodes.

A node, migrating from cell i to cell j creates an empty node position in cell i, while occupies a (pre-

viously empty) node position in cell j. If d_k is a member of the multicast tree, then the multicast tree might have got disconnected due to the migration of d_k. Migration of a node, belonging to the multicast tree, can lead to any of the three situations:

1. a leaf node of the multicast tree migrates, i.e., d_k is a leaf node

2. an internal forwarding node migrates, i.e., d_k is an internal node of the multicast tree but not a destination

3. an internal destination node migrates, i.e., d_k is both an internal and destination node of the multicast tree

In each case, the multicast tree temporarily gets disconnected (Figure 2). When the forwarding destination node D11 moves to an adjacent cell, D6 and D9 becomes orphan. A rapid reconstruction of the migrated node to the hypercube topology is first needed, and then a rapid reconfiguration of the multicast tree is required. The time delay of the multicast tree reconstruction is our problem focus, while maintaining the height balance and node degree of the tree.

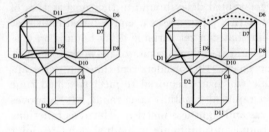

Figure 2: Node D11 migrates a)before move b)after move

During the multicast tree re-construction phase, a number of design issues arise, e.g., minimization of the worst case delay from the source to leaf node (which is the focus of existing research), traffic optimization in the multicast tree (which is addressed in the Steiner tree problem domain), minimization of the time for reconstruction of broken multicast tree (which is the focus of our proposed research), height balance property of the multicast tree, the fan out of each node and so on. This paper focuses primarily on multicast tree re-construction delay, while keeping height-balance and node degree in design objectives.

Applicability of Previous Research

A number of related, but orthogonal, research issues require clarification. Dijkstra's shortest path algorithm [6] and Steiner tree generation problem [8, 7] employed for delay optimization and cost optimization constraints in real-time multicast can produce traffic and tree height economized/minimized real-time multicast tree. However, they do not consider multicast tree re-construction. Some heuristics for the Steiner tree problem have been developed that take polynomial time and produce near optimum results [9]. In [13] KMB algorithm, a network is abstracted to a complete graph consisting of edges that represent the shortest paths among source node and destination nodes. These research results do not provide any means for minimizing the re-construction delay. [8] examines the dynamic update of the tree if destination nodes join or leave the tree occasionally. The dynamic algorithms proposed for *multipoint problem* satisfy bandwidth constraints based on minimum spanning tree algorithms for Steiner tree problem. [10] discusses optimization on both traffic cost and delay, however, they assume that cost and delay functions are identical. [11] proposes two heuristics (which we call the KPP algorithm) that address delay-bounded Steiner trees; the KPP algorithm extends the KMB algorithm by taking into account an integer-valued delay bound in the construction of shortest paths. [2] proposes a source-based multicast algorithm that can set variable delay bounds on destinations and handles variants of network cost optimization goals. [12] considers real-time multicast applications which are required to meet specified time and geographical (spatial) constraints. It improves steadiness and tightness metrics, defined as functions of maximum and minimum individual point-to-point delay. However, to our knowledge no previous research has considered the issue of minimizing the multicast tree re-construction delay.

3 Proposed Approaches

The three heuristic solutions are described in the following, along with their pseudocodes.

3.1 Basics of hypercube multicast

Hypercube structure has been the subject of extensive research [14, 15, 16]. Topological properties of the hypercube, e.g., regularity, symmetry, extensibility, small diameter, and the embeddability of many other topologies (such as ring, mesh, and tree) have been discovered. Heuristic multicast algorithms for hypercubes are proposed in [17, 18, 19].

Since our choice of logical topology includes the hypercube, some well-known properties of hypercube are repeated as background information. An n-dimensional hypercube, or n-cube consists of $N = 2^n$ nodes. In the n-cube graph, $Q_n(V, E)$, for a vertex $v \in V(Q_n)$, $a(v)$ will represent the n-bit binary address of v; $|a(v)|$ denote the number of 1's in binary number $a(v)$. Then, $e = (u, v) \in E(Q_n)$ if and only if $|a(v) \oplus a(u)| = 1$. This implies that $deg_{Q_n}(u) = n$ for every node $u \in V(Q_n)$. Furthermore, if $a(v) \oplus a(u) = 2^i$, edge e is said to be at dimension i. Any particular node in the n-cube, with an n-bit address as $b_{n-1}b_{n-2}...b_1b_0$, has n Gray-adjacent neighbors. The *distance* (the length of a shortest path, in number of links) between two nodes is equal to the *Hamming distance* of their binary addresses.

3.2 Request-Reply-Rejection (RRR)

The first solution approach, named as "Reply-Request-Rejection" is designed to operate at runtime, i.e., to be invoked at a time the multicast tree gets fragmented (due to node migration) and requires to be connected or re-constructed. However, in principle it can also be used in background computation to augment the LAP and LAE approaches proposed subsequently. We assume that the initial multicast tree is height balanced since the current multicast tree generation algorithms or heuristics may achieve this. The assumption[1] has been taken to economize the worst case message propagation delay from the source node to the destination node. The goal is to reconfigure a suddenly broken multicast tree in a way such that the newly constructed multicast tree remains height balanced. Figure 3 illustrates a scenario of orphan nodes. Figure 4 illustrates the pseudocodes for RRR approach.

An orphan node at d th level can request any node from $d-2$-nd to d-th level, to be its parent node in order to keep the resultant tree height-balanced. Also, the requested node must be hypercube adjacent to the requesting one. For a d-cube with mesh topology on top, one node may have $d+6$ adjacent nodes. So, the time complexity of request-reply-rejection is $O(d)$ times the complexity of a single parent node seek. Since, individual parent node ids are computed by Gray-adjacencies, each parent seek operation takes $O(1)$ time, resulting in a total of $O(d)$ time complexity of RRR. During idle time, an orphan node

---

[1]Note that the height balanced property ensures that no destination node in the multicast tree has unduly long path length delay compared to the other destination nodes.

connected to a parent may continue finding a more optimal parent; and consequently update the multi-cast tree. The approach of RRR can be extended to background computation also.

Figure 3: a) Node d_k migrates b) $d1$ and $d2$ become orphan

---

Input: $G(V, E)=$ graph with underlying topology spanning over all the cells; $s=$ source node, $D=$ set of destination nodes, $C=$ set of cells, $I=$ set of intermediate nodes, $P_m=$ probability of migration $(0.0-0.1)$, $L_f=$ load factor $(0.0 - 0.1)$.
Output: (Max, and avg) reconfiguration time
Procedure request-reply-reject
$\forall n \in V$ do   /* n = migrating node id */
   if $(n \in D \cup I) \cap n \in$ {orphan node}
      seek_parent(n);   continue;
   if need_transmit_data **then**
      transmit_data();

Procedure seek_parent(n)
$l \leftarrow$ cur_level(n);
$\forall x \in$ {hypercube adjacent} $\land$ in_tree (x) do
   if not$(l - 2 <=$ cur_level$(x) <= l)$ continue;
   if succ_cont$(x) =$ succ_limit continue;
   if balance(n,x)=FALSE continue;
   parent(n) $\leftarrow$ x;
   adjust parameter with parent;
   orphan(n) $\leftarrow$ TRUE;   return TRUE; endfor;
return FALSE;

Figure 4: Pseudo-code algorithm for RRR

3.3 Look-ahead Alternate Parent (LAP) and Look-ahead Alternate Edge (LAE)

These two approaches are based upon precomputed alternate multicast tree reconstruction techniques.
LAP: Each node has a local parent table containing current parent-id and a number of alternate parents-ids computed in background. When a node moves from one cell to another, it's direct children become orphans, which need to be reconnected. Orphan nodes select next alternate parent as current parent from the alternate parent table instantaneously. This immediate parent selection reduces the time to connect orphan nodes, consequently reducing delay of reconfiguring multicast tree. Since the alternate parents are computed in advance, the approach has been considered a look-ahead one. The pseudo-code algorithm for LAP has been illustrated in Figure 5.

Input: $G(V, E)=$ graph with underlying topology spanning over all cells, $s=$ source node, $D=$ set of destination nodes, $C=$ set of cells, $I=$ set of intermediate nodes, $P_m=$ probability of migration $(0.0-0.1)$, $L_f=$ load factor $(0.0 - 0.1)$
Output: (max, and avg) reconfiguration time
Procedure LAP/* invoked at a node migration */
$\forall n \in V$ do   /* n is the migrating node */
   if $(n \in D \cup I) \land n \in$ {orphan nodes}
      if table_empty
         seek_parent(n);   continue;
      else   *instantaneous_connection(n)*;
   if need_transmit_data
      transmit_data();   continue;
   background_compute(n);
Procedure instantaneous_connection(n)
   parent(n) $\leftarrow$ $x|x \in$ {alternate_parent(n)};
   adjust parameter with parent;
   adjust alternate-parent table;
   orphan(n) $\leftarrow$ FALSE;
   return TRUE;
Procedure seek_parent(n)
$\forall x \in$ {hypercube adjacent}-{alternate_ parent(x)} do
   if allow_parent(x,n);
      parent(n) $\leftarrow$ x;
      adjust parameter with parent;
      orphan(n) $\leftarrow$ FALSE;
      return TRUE;
return FALSE;
Procedure background_compute (n)
if $|$ {alternate_parent(n)}$|=$parent_limit
   return;
$\forall x \in$ {hypercube_adjacent}-{alternate parent entry}
   if allow_parent(x, n)
   {alternate_parent(n)}$\leftarrow$ {alternate_parent(n)} $\cup$ {x};
return;

Figure 5: Pseudo-code algorithm for LAP

LAE: Look-ahead alternate edge is a generalization of look-ahead alternate parent, where the multicast tree connecting intra-cell and inter-cell nodes are added with few extra links. When the number of extra link is 1 ($k = 1$), this approach becomes identical to LAP. By definition, a multicast tree does not contain a cycle, however, sacrifices in link fault vulnerability. As a result, when a node migrates, a tree re-construction becomes immediately necessary. The idea in LAE is to add a few (k, a design parameter) extra links to the multicast tree, making it not a perfect tree, but more link fault-tolerant.

Following is the sequence of events that will happen for the LAE:

- time 0: The multicast tree is in operation. Links e_1 through e_N are part of the core multicast tree, connecting the source and destination nodes. An added set of links $e_{N+1} \cdots e_{N+K}$ are joined to the multicast tree, but they do not carry any message.

- time $0 + \Delta t$: A node, V_j, migrates from one cell to another breaking the multicast tree. Few of the links in the link set $e_1 \cdots e_N$ are destroyed. Apparently, there is a need to re-construct the new multicast tree. In this case, the need for re-constructing the tree may not be needed. The extra K links can make sure that the tree still remains connected. So, we simply re-route some of the messages, so that original traffic flow is still retained.

- time $0+ \Delta t$ + few additional instants: Now, since we have consumed some of the redundant K links, carry out a computation in the background; i.e., without affecting the main multicast operation - to design few more extra links. These extra links will be used next time when a node migration takes place.

All modules for LAP can be used suitably for LAE. LAE can be considered as multihop look-ahead alternate parent approach. The pseudo-code algorithm for LAE has been illustrated in Figure 6.

4 Analysis

This section discusses the issues of network management and derives a number of analytical results related to the proposed heuristics. Probability analyses of LAP and LAP approaches and the optimization objectives are also given in this section.

Procedure LAE
$\forall n \in V$ do
    if $n \in D \cup I \wedge n \in$ {orphan nodes}
        if table_empty
            seek_edge(n);   continue;
        else   *instantaneous_connection(n)*;
    if need_transmit_data
        transmit_data();   continue;
    background_compute(n);
Procedure instantaneous_connection(n)
$x \leftarrow n$;
$\exists! S | S \in$ {alternate_edge(n)} do
    while $S <> \phi$ do
        $y \leftarrow a | a \in S$;   parent(x) $\leftarrow$ y;
        adjust with parent;
        orphan(x) $\leftarrow$ FALSE;
        $S \leftarrow S$ - {y}; $x \leftarrow y$;
    adjust alternate edge table;
    return TRUE;
Procedure background_compute(n)
if |{alternate_edge(n)}|=edge_limit;
    return;
$x \leftarrow n$; $S \leftarrow \phi$;
$\forall y | y \in S \wedge$ {hypercube_adjacent(x) do;
    if allow_link(x,y) $S \leftarrow \cup$ {y};
if $S <> \phi$
    {alternate_edge(n)}$\leftarrow${alternate_edge(n)}$\cup$ {S};
return;

Figure 6: Pseudo-code algorithm for LAE

4.1 Definition of Node-id, Cell-id and Hypercube Neighbor

Proposition: For hexagonal repetitive cell structure, let the intra-cell topology be a (d-6)-cube and the inter-cell topology be a hexagonal mesh. Each node in this topology will have an outdegree = d.

Gray-coding of each node: Figure 7 defines the cell-id ($L1$) and the node-id ($L2$).

Figure 7: Definition of node-id

1. All nodes within any particular cell have identical value of $L1$, i.e., the cell-id.

2. $L2$ represent the $(d-6)$-bit id of the node in the $(d-6)$-cube contained within the particular cell.

Cell-id is defined as follows. Each cell has a row id and a column id. Each cell in a row has the same row number; cells in the left diagonals have the same column number. Selection of left diagonal as column id is arbitrary; selection of right diagonals would have given the same effect.

Lemma: $L1 = \lceil (log_2(\text{maxrow})) \rceil + \lceil (log_2(\text{maxcol})) \rceil$ and $L2 = d - 6$, where maxrow = maximum number of rows, maxcol = maximum number of columns and $d-6=$ number of bits needed to represent the nodes within a cell for $d-6$ dimensional hypercube.

Theorem 1: *Two nodes are adjacent under the underlying hierarchy of hypercube topology iff any of the following properties hold*:

1. Two nodes have same cellid (i.e., nodes are in the same cell) and node id is gray-adjacent.

2. Two nodes have same nodeid and any of the followings holds:

    (a) $row_i = row_j$, $col_i = col_j \pm 1$

    (b) $row_i = row_j \pm 1$, $col_i = col_j$

    (c) $row_i = row_j + 1$, $col_i = col_j - 1$

    (d) $row_i = row_j - 1$, $col_i = col_j + 1$. Condition (c) and (d) will change subsequently if right diagonal is the column-id.

Height balance constraint in RRR approach:
Lemma: To retain the height balance property, an orphan node previously at d-th level can request nodes at $d-2$ th to d th level as its parent.

4.2 Probability Analysis of LAP

Let p denote the probability of node migration from one cell into another. Assume p to be independent for different nodes. We estimate the following three parameters: probability of maintaining reliable connection (R_{LAP}), average update cost (C_{LAP}), and average space requirement (S_{LAP}). If each update requires average cost, C, then

$$C_{LAP} = [1 - (1-p)^n] \times C(pernode) \qquad (1)$$

For a node, if each alternate parent entry requires α space, then the total space

$$S_{LAP} = n \times \alpha(pernode) \qquad (2)$$

Probability of maintaining reliable connection means the probability of any way instantaneous connection is possible. Therefore,

$$R_{LAP} = 1 - p^n \qquad (3)$$

Let the maximum time to connect a node instantaneously with alternate parent $=\delta t$. If maximum data rate is K_{LAP} bps, then temporary buffer space required, $TS_{LAP} = K_{LAP} \times \delta t$ bits. In other words, if a node has TS_{LAP} bits buffer space for data then for K_{LAP} bps maximum data transmission rate the maximum duration a node can be orphan is δt. Beyond that, there will be a loss of data.

Optimization Objectives: The three parameters S_{LAP}, C_{LAP} and R_{LAP} are functions of p and n. For a particular value of p as n increases, each one of the three parameter increases. But our goal is to minimize S_{LAP} and C_{LAP} while keeping R_{LAP} as high as possible. Let, our optimization metric be M_{LAP}. Now, $M_{LAP} \alpha R_{LAP}$, $M_{LAP} \alpha \frac{1}{S_{LAP}}$, $M_{LAP} \alpha \frac{1}{C_{LAP}}$,

or, together

$$M_{LAP} \alpha \frac{R_{LAP}}{S_{LAP}} \times C_{LAP}$$

or,

$$M_{LAP} = K_{LAP} \times \frac{R_{LAP}}{S_{LAP}} \times C_{LAP}$$

hence,

$$M_{LAP} = K_{LAP} \times \frac{1-p^n}{n\alpha[1-(1-p)^n]C} \qquad (4)$$

For simplification, let $K_{LAP} = 1$, $\alpha = 1$ and $C = 1$. Then the equation becomes

$$M_{LAP} = \frac{1-p^n}{n[1-(1-p)^n]} \qquad (5)$$

We can construct a plot for optimization metric, M_{LAP}, using the above equation for different values of p and n. As p and n increase, both the numerator and denominator increase proportionately for fixed values of K_{LAP}, α and C. Our purpose is to maximize M_{LAP}. From Figure 8, it can be seen for increasing values of p and n, M_{LAP} reduces. This result is for a particular case when all constants are 1, while for non-unit constants the result will scale accordingly.

5 Performance Measures

5.1 Simulation Environment

Simulation results are shown for the look-ahead alternate parent (LAP) approach. A 64-cell cellular

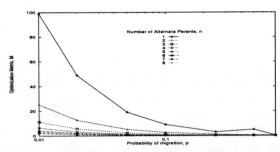

Figure 8: Optimization metric for LAP

network is considered with each cell having a 3-cube. Each node has 3 hypercube-neighbors, and 6 other neighbors from 6 adjacent cell hypercubes. We start each simulation with an initial multicast tree structure. Subsequently, during node migration different parts of the multicast tree are broken, and the reconstruction process is done employing our proposed algorithm for LAP.

5.2 Input/Output Parameters

We have considered four input parameters: probability of migration, load factor, child limit and parent limit. Ten output metrics are used for performance measure (only few are shown in the plots due to lack of space): occurrence of data interruption due to node migration, occurrence of 'no-data' interruption due to node migration, number of successful 'seek to connect' (i.e., number of times an orphan is successfully connected), number of failures in 'seek to connect', number of data transmission during instantaneous connection, number of successful data transmission, number of quanta in background computation, number of idle quanta, worst-case reconstruction delay and average reconstruction delay.

5.3 Simulation plots and discussion

Simulation is continued until steady-state is reached. During steady-state, the multicast tree consists of some orphan nodes; alternate parent table of some other nodes are also partially filled up. The program is run for 500 time units and parameters are measured in "node-time quanta".

Figure 5.3 shows *probability of migration* vs. *number of quanta in background computation*. A constant amount of background computation is done at zero *probability of migration*. At the instant when each node has already filled up its alternate parent table or

there are no node that can be chosen as an alternate parent, nodes will not spend time in background computation. As *probability of migration* increases, updation of alternate parent table will be increased. But again, beyond a certain point all quanta will be spent in migration. As load factor increases, background computation decreases. This implies the tradeoff between background and foreground approach.

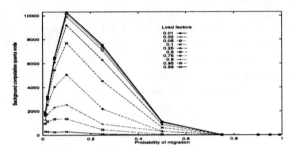

Figure 9: Probability of migration vs. Background computation quanta node

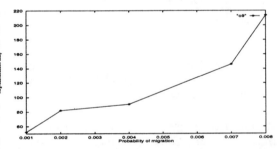

Figure 10: Probability of migration vs. Average reconstruction delay

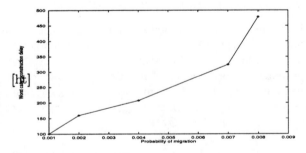

Figure 11: Probability of migration vs. Worst-case reconstruction delay

Figures 10 and 11 show the plots of *probability of migration* vs. *average and worst-case reconfiguration delay*. For the simplicity in simulation, we have considered a 3-dimensional hypercube, where number of empty slot is few; however, dimension 4 and higher are better for realistic scenarios. Average reconfiguration delay and worst-case reconfiguration delay rise rapidly with probability of node migration. In both cases, the delay exceeds the limit after certain point of probability of migration. If we increase dimension of the hypercube, this point will shift rightward.

6 Conclusion

We have considered the real-time multicast tree problem for wireless network with frequent node migration. The dual formulation of real-time multicast problem has been proposed. We have given emphasis on the practical importance of the issue of multicast re-construction time (in the event of a node migration) and proposed three solution heuristics. We have discussed their performance issues and derived the optimization objectives. Our simulator measures different performance metrics as a function of different system configurations when a node migration occurs. The simulation results provide us with performance results which very closely resemble our analytical findings. Our ongoing research is currently being extended into an implementation phase on a testbed which includes wireless PCs, ATM-interconnected workstations and high-speed Myrinet switches.

References

[1] Zhang L., Deering S., Estrin D., Shenker S., and Zappala D., "RSVP: A New Resource ReSerVation Protocol", *IEEE Networks*, 8-17, September 1993.

[2] Qing Z., Parsa M. and Garcia-Luna-Aceves J.J., "A Source-Based Algorithm for Delay-Constrained Minimum-Cost Multicasting", *Proc. of INFOCOM 1995.*

[3] Varma A., and Bauer F., "Distributed Algorithms for Multicast Path Setup in Data Networks", Technical Report, UCSC-CRL-95-10, Aug. 1995.

[4] Kompella V.P., Pasquale J.C., and Polyzos G.C., "Two Distributed Algorithms for the Constrained Steiner", Technical Report CSL-1005-92, Computer Systems Laboratory, University of San Diego, Oct. 1992.

[5] Scott Corson M., and Ephremides A., "A Distributed Routing Algorithm for Mobile Wireless Networks", *Wireless Networks*, 1:61-81, 1995.

[6] Dijkstra E., "A Note on Two Problems in Connection with Graphs", *Numerische Mathematik*, 1:269-271, 1959.

[7] Hakimi S., "Steiner's Problem in Graphs and its Implication", *Networks*, vol. 1, pp. 113-133, 1971.

[8] Waxman B., "Delay-Bounded Steiner Tree Algorithm for Performance-Driven Layout", *Journal on Selected Areas in Communication*, 6:1617-1622, Dec 1988.

[9] Takahashi H., and Matsuyama A., "An Approximate Solution for the Steiner Problem in Graphs", *Mathematica Japonica*, 6:573-577, 1990.

[10] Bharat-Kumar K. and Jaffe J., "Routing to Multiple Destination in computer Networks", *IEEE Trans. on Communications*, COM-31:343-351, 1983.

[11] Kompella V.P., Pasquale J.C., and Polyzos G.C., "Multicast Routing for Multimedia Communication", *IEEE/ACM Transactions on Networking*, 1(3):286-292, 1993.

[12] Max R.Pokam, and Michel G., "Guaranteeing Spatial Coherence in Real-time Multicasting", *International Symposium on Information Theory*, 41, May 1995.

[13] Kou L., Markowsky G., and Berman L., "A Fast Algorithm for Steiner Trees", *Acta Informatica*, 15:141-145, 1981.

[14] Lee T.C., and Hayes J.P., "Fault Tolerant Communication Scheme for Hypercube Computers", *IEEE Trans. Comput.*, 41, 10, oct. 1992, 1242-1256.

[15] Saad Y., and Schultz M., "Data Communication in Hypercubes", *Res. Rep.*, YALEU/DCS/RR-428, Dept. Comput. Sci., Yale Univ., 1985.

[16] Sullivan H., and Bashkow T., "A Large Scale, Homogeneous, Fully Distributed Parallel Machine", *Proc. 4th Symp. on Computer Architecture*, 1977, pp. 105-117.

[17] Bhattacharya S., Albert C. Liang, and Tsai W., "Fault-Tolerant Multicasting on Hypercubes", *Journal of Parallel and Distributed Computing*, 23:418-428, 1994.

[18] Lan Youran, Esfahanian A., Lionel M.N., "Multicast in Hypercube Multiprocessors", *Journal of Parallel and Distributed Computing*, 8:30-41, 1990.

[19] Lin X., Ni L.M., "Multicast Communication in Multicomputer Networks", *Proceedings of 1990 Intl Conf. on Parallel Processing*, Aug. 13-17. 1990, pp III 114-118.

[20] Takeshi Hattori, "Personal Communications System and Wireless Technology", *NTT Review*, Vol.7 No.3:56-65, May 1995.

[21] Albert Y.H.Zomaya, Editor, "Parallel and Distributed Computing Handbook", McGraw Hills, 1996.

[22] Chen Kwang-Cheng, "Medium Access Control of Wireless LANs for Mobile Computing", *IEEE Network*, September/October 1994, pp 50-63.

[23] Nahar L.K, Bhattacharya S, "Dynamic Network Management for Firmware Controlled Network Topology", *Proceedings of the COMPSAC, 1996, Seoul, Korea*, Aug 1996 (to appear), pp 398-399.

Author Index